Florence A. Grove

We can not escape history. . . . The fiery trial through which we pass will light us down, in honor or dishonor to the latest generation. . . . The world knows we do know how to save it. We, even we here, hold the power and bear the responsibility. In giving freedom to the slave we assure freedom to the free. . . . We shall nobly save or meanly lose the last, best hope of earth.

—Abraham Lincoln, *Message to Congress,*
1 December 1862

THE STREAM OF

American Book Company

American History

VOLUME ONE

LELAND D. BALDWIN

University of Pittsburgh

NEW YORK CINCINNATI CHICAGO BOSTON ATLANTA DALLAS SAN FRANCISCO

To Ruth,
who has been my companion voyager on
The Stream of American History

PREFACE

THIS book is in large part an examination of American dilemmas and of how they have been met or evaded. It originated in the profoundly rooted belief that only truth can set men free. While I certainly cannot claim to have proved anything which reaches the dignity of a historical law, there nevertheless have arisen a number of attitudes and approaches about which the reader is entitled to know.

(1) I believe that the historian has a cultural and moral duty. Historians have long been plagued by the guilty feeling that their presentation of history is influenced as much by their personal and cultural views as by facts. And yet "we cannot sacrifice the demand for scientific certainty without injury to the conscience of our civilization." So says the Dutch historian Johan Huizinga* as he addresses himself to the problem of defining history. His definition in the end is this: *"History is the intellectual form in which a civilization renders account to itself of its past."* History, to telescope his explanation, is broader than the organized facts and at the same time more precise, inasmuch as it seeks to find their essential meaning—the truth behind them. If history is called an intellectual form, the destructive split between historical research (the facts) and the cultural bias of historical writing is thus removed. Every culture creates this form anew in accord with the critical requirements of its conscience.

History is far more than facts; it is an insight into the processes of human life. *Truth* is not the sum of the facts, for they can be and are marshaled to prove any point of view. That the adult is sometimes surprised when he learns this reality seems to me a striking proof of John Dewey's observation that the schools tend to create a fictitiously idealistic picture of our society. But, asks the neutral, how can we be sure of the eternal verity of the supposed truth even after careful analysis (whether

* "A Definition of the Concept of History," in Raymond Klibansky and H. J. Paton, eds., *Philosophy and History* (1936), 8–9. An opposing view is set forth by H. Butterfield in *The Whig Interpretation of History* (1951).

or not scientific) of the facts and their meanings? The answer is that we can't, but if we wish to survive we must accept it as the basis for action in this generation. To deny that knowledge of history should be one of the determinants which shape our course of action is to turn the writing of history into something which is not even an art, for it is sterile—and art is fructifying. It is to accept the philosophy of acquiescence, which is the hallmark of defeat and from which even the Orient is turning.

(2) I believe in democracy. Traced to its sources all human action stems from the acceptance of certain axiomatic values by acts of faith. In that sense I cannot be neutral, for I have accepted the democratic way with its inherent values of human dignity and high moral aspirations. I believe, however, that a candid study of the facts of history will strengthen the conviction that democratic values are true values; I am a propagandist for democracy because I believe in the propaganda of truth.

Enemies of democracy and even some naïve idealists assert that the "American way" is one of intolerance, race prejudice, and legal and economic oppression. Nothing could be more wrong. American history is concerned with those problems not because they are more common here than in other nations but because the American as a man of conscience has refused to become reconciled to them and give up the fight against them. With Boyd Bode I believe that we can afford to tell the truth because democracy is more concerned with the citizen's growth than with his conformity, and because we believe in the innate sense of the common man and that *truth* will prevail if it is given a decent chance to be heard.

(3) I believe in the unity of history. History is dynamic, a stream which presents primarily the conflict between freedom and slavery. Into this there enters, now in one way, now in another, the conflict between the local and the universal, between nationalism and internationalism, and between free international co-operation and enforced co-operation. Thus the history of the United States is an integral and necessary part of the world pattern and must be treated as such.

While I believe that history shows unity and pattern, and I believe that the outcome will be good, I can sympathize with the claims of those who deny these ideas. I cannot apportion good to Jefferson and evil to Hamilton, for the total triumph of either could have been disastrous. In any case, however one-sided our sympathies may be, we cannot afford to confuse constructive conservatives like Hamilton and Rockefeller with statist wreckers like Hitler and Stalin. What the future will say of the contestants in our day is beyond my ken—I must view them in the light of my conscience, else I am a traitor to the process of history.

I say this despite the fact that I cannot prove that history shows that there has been progress in the usually accepted sense of that disputed word. Indeed, any logical pattern that I devise may be ripped to pieces by tomorrow morning's newspaper. But I believe that there is a discernible process at work, even though we may not always be sure of its logic.

Kierkegaard nailed down the smug certainty of his age when he said: "Take away the paradox from the thinker and you have the professor." *Mea culpa!* I have sinned along with others of my craft. What I offer therefore is a balance of Yes and No, an equilibration of uncertainties. I am concerned with the contradictions and conflicts in the historical process as steps to what came next—often further contradictions and conflicts, but on another and, I believe, higher plane.

Herein lies the hope and comfort of man so far as the secular world can take him. The act of equilibrating uncertainties gives us moments of tranquil faith almost mystical in their poignancy. The act of combating the demonic forces which strive for mastery both within us and in the social order around us breeds self-reliance. Here is neither Hegel nor Marx, nor is it altogether Kierkegaard, for there is no room for pessimism; we may never arrive at our goal but we have the infinitely greater pleasure of a journey in which new vistas of truth are continually unfolding. Here is the prospect of American maturity, the promise of a splendid new world of understanding and justice.

This presentation is the result of years of study and reflection on the meaning of history, some of the steps in which appeared from time to time in print. I have drawn largely on those publications in so far as they apply to American history and its world setting. I must also apologize if I have engaged in unconscious plagiarism. I have the feeling that I have drawn from the historian's stock in trade striking phrases and ideas which might with enormous labor be traced to specific inventors. I hope that if such inventors recognize their handiwork they will consider my borrowing a compliment rather than a deliberate theft.

I am under no illusion that an adequate view of American history can be presented so simply that it can be understood without pauses to reflect and without frequent review of what has gone before. This book deliberately seeks to furnish something which the reader must stretch his mental powers to grasp, but which can be reached if he is willing to put forth the effort. I am well aware that many instructors will prefer a plain, factual "handbook" as a text. Still, American history is far too extensive to be covered adequately in class lectures and discussions, and it may be that they will find it of value to assign as readings those phases which they do not have time to cover in class.

I cannot close without expressing my thanks for the stimulus offered by my students and the help and encouragement given by my colleagues at the University of Pittsburgh. Especially helpful was Professor Asher Isaacs, who carefully conned the entire manuscript from the standpoint of

an economist; he is not, of course, responsible for all of the views which
I retained. I wish also to acknowledge my indebtedness to Professor Allan
Nevins of Columbia University, who was instrumental in helping me to
avoid a number of pitfalls. Mr. Richard R. Smith has most kindly assisted me throughout the task with counsel which could have been given
only by one with a long experience in textbook publishing. Lorene Byers
rendered valuable aid in research and checking. Lastly I must mention
my wife's patient assistance through the long years spent in research and
writing.

CONTENTS

Part I **THE GENESIS OF THE NATION: TO 1787**

I WESTERN CIVILIZATION AND AMERICA   5
     1 The Course of Western Civilization
     2 Geographical Influences in American History
     3 Nature's Children

II THE CONFLICT FOR THE NEW WORLD   48
     1 *Mundus Novus*
     2 The Struggle for the Caribbean
     3 In Quest of the Northwest Passage

III THE ENGLISH ROOTS   81
     1 The Rise of England's Law and Institutions
     2 The Completion of the English Process
     3 Democracy: Its Meaning and Its Method

IV TRANSPLANTING ENGLAND TO AMERICA   106
     1 The Founding of the Southern Colonies
     2 The Settlement of New England
     3 The Settlement of the Middle Colonies

V THE SETTLER AND HIS PROBLEMS   145
     1 Why He Came and What He Found
     2 Social and Religious Ferment
     3 The Racial Complex
     4 The Old West

VI COLONIAL GROWING PAINS   173
     1 England's Halfhearted Mercantilism
     2 The Democratic Struggle

    3   The Battle for North America
    4   The Causes of the American Revolution

vii THE ROAD TO REVOLUTION   209
    1   Western Lands and the Revolution
    2   The Era of Genteel Protest
    3   The Radicals Take Over
    4   The Road to Independence

viii THE WINNING OF INDEPENDENCE   239
    1   The Nature of the War
    2   Military and Diplomatic Conflict
    3   The Social Revolution

Part II THE RISE OF NATIONALISM: 1787–1840

ix THE FORMATION OF THE FEDERATION   285
    1   The Confederation Period
    2   The Second Constitution
    3   Hamilton the Force

x THE BATTLE FOR THE DEMOCRATIC PROCESS   315
    1   Jefferson the Counterforce
    2   The Rising Conflict
    3   The Federalist Journey Toward Limbo

xi THE ORDEAL OF THOMAS JEFFERSON   348
    1   Jefferson the Force
    2   Measures Short of War
    3   Hamilton and Jefferson in the Stream of American History

xii THE RISE OF TRANS-APPALACHIA   372
    1   The Old Northwest
    2   The Old Southwest
    3   The Pattern of Western Settlement

xiii THE WAR OF 1812   401
    1   The Causes of the War of 1812
    2   The War of 1812 in the North
    3   The Jackson Legend

xiv THE JACKSONIAN ERA   429
    1   New Men and New Measures
    2   Democracy and Sectionalism
    3   The Reign of Old Hickory

4 Jacksonian Democracy in the Stream of American History

xv AMERICAN NATIONALISM ABROAD   470
  1 The Rise of the Latin-American Nations
  2 The North Atlantic Triangle
  3 The Spread of American Commerce

xvi THE INDIAN SIDE OF THE FRONTIER   503
  1 The Indians' View of the White Advance
  2 The Passing of the Woods Indian
  3 The Fur Traders' Frontier
  4 The Permanent Indian Frontier Policy

xvii THE WHITE SIDE OF THE FRONTIER   530
  1 The Significance of the West
  2 Life in the West
  3 The Land

xviii THE MATERIAL SCENE   556
  1 The Rise of American Technology
  2 The Revolution in Transportation
  3 Capital and Labor
  4 The Agricultural Scene

xix MOLDING THE AMERICAN MIND   587
  1 The Aristocratic Ascendance
  2 The Roots of Change
  3 The Immigrant Tide

xx THE TRANSCENDENTAL PROTEST   612
  1 The Age of Reform
  2 American Utopianism
  3 The Emergence of American Character

Part III THE SECTIONAL CONFLICT: 1820–1877

xxi BACKGROUND FOR CONFLICT   643
  1 The Cotton Kingdom
  2 Machine Tools and Corn Belt
  3 The Antislavery Impulse
  4 The South as a Conscious Minority

xxii MANIFEST DESTINY   683
  1 The Psychology of Agrarian Imperialism
  2 The Borderlands

3 The Approach to War
4 The Mexican War

XXIII THE PREPARATION OF THE SOUTHERN MIND   717

1 The Compromise of 1850
2 The Southern Struggle Over Compromise

XXIV THE PREPARATION OF THE NORTHERN MIND   741

1 The Northern Struggle Over Compromise
2 Douglas and Nebraska
3 The Republicans and Kansas
4 The Emergence of Lincoln

XXV THE HOUSE DIVIDING   774

1 The Presidential Campaign of 1860
2 The Failure of Compromise
3 The Strategic Border States
4 The Crystallization of Sectional Attitudes

XXVI BEHIND THE ARMIES   813

1 The Civilian Battle
2 The American Question Abroad
3 The Sinews of War

XXVII THE CIVIL WAR: AMERICAN ILIAD   846

1 The Strategy of the Civil War
2 Triumph in the West
3 Stalemate in the East
4 The Decisive Year

XXVIII THE TRAGEDY OF RECONSTRUCTION   891

1 Presidential Reconstruction
2 Congressional Reconstruction
3 The South During Reconstruction
4 The Civil War and Reconstruction in the Stream
   of American History

GENERAL BIBLIOGRAPHY   935

INDEX OF AUTHORS IN BIBLIOGRAPHICAL NOTES   938

INDEX OF SUBJECTS   945

MAPS

Evolution of Geographical Perspective	11
Medieval Trade Routes	13
The World	15
Relief Map of the United States	26
Average·Length of Frostless Season	27
Average Annual Rainfall	28
Agricultural Regions of the United States	31
Petroleum Fields, Iron-Ore Producing Localities, Potential Water Power, Coal Fields	33
Principal Indian Nations and Linguistic Stocks	42
Western Europe as Connected with American History	49
The Voyages of Columbus	52
Voyages of Discovery	54
Spanish and Portuguese Empires in America	61
The Spanish Caribbean Empire	68
Wars of the Iroquois (Five Nations) for Empire	76
Claims under Early English Charters	108
Chesapeake Region in the 1670's	116
South Carolina and Georgia	119
Northern and Middle Colonies Around 1650	128
New England and New York About 1700	134
Boundary Claims of Northeastern Colonies	137
Grants to Duke of York, 1664, 1682	139
The Thirteen Colonies on the Eve of the Revolution	149
Expansion of Settlement	167
French Thrusts Against the English and Spanish Late in the 17th Century	189
The Great French and Indian War on the Ohio	195
The Great French and Indian War in the North	197
The Expulsion of France from North America	198

The West on the Eve of the Revolution 214
Concord and Lexington, 18–19 April 1775 229
The Siege of Boston 231
The War in Canada and Northern New York 233
Principal Thrusts of the Revolution 252
Campaigns Around New York City 255
Scene of Washington's Campaigns in the Middle States 257
Main British Movements in the South, 1780, 1781 262
The Yorktown Campaign, Sept.–Oct. 1781 264
Siege of Yorktown 264
North America, 1783 268
Land Cessions of the States 272
Distribution of Votes in Ratification of the Constitution 296
The Barbary States 352
The Survey of the Public Domain 373
Ohio Settlement and Indian Wars 375
The Old Southwest, 1783–1813 382
The Louisiana Purchase, 1803 388
Principal Highways and Waterways to
     Trans-Appalachia About 1835 392
Westward Movement 394
Vote in House of Representatives on Declaration of War,
     12 June 1812 405
Election of 1812 405
War of 1812, Region of the Great Lakes 411
Niagara Frontier 411
Battle of Lake Champlain 411
War of 1812 422
Battle of New Orleans 422
Campaign of 1814 on Chesapeake Bay 422
The March of Manhood Suffrage, 1800, 1830, and 1860 443
House Vote on the Tariff of 1816 448
House Vote on the Tariff of 1828 448
Gerrymandering in Alabama, 1910 451
Latin America About 1823 472
Scene of the Fisheries Disputes, 1783 480
Maine Boundary Controversy 486
Indian Cessions East of the Plains 510
The Fur Traders' Frontier 515
Removal of the Five Civilized Nations from the
     South to Indian Territory 523
Ratio Between Time and Distance of Travel
     from New York, 1800, 1830, 1860 566

The Peak of the Canal Era   569
Growth of Railroads to 1860   572
Growth in Density of Population, 1790, 1820, and 1850   606–607
Growth of Public Education   614
Sections About 1860   645
The Missouri Compromise of 1820   666
Northern Mexico in Colonial Times   690
Revolutionary Texas, 1836   695
Principal Land Grants in Texas   695
Scenes of the War with Mexico, 1846–1848   708
Campaigns in the Valley of Mexico   708
Territorial Growth of the United States to 1853   714
Highlights of the Slavery Controversy in the 1850's   725
Caribbean Clash   738
Kansas Border Troubles   756
Election of 1860 by States and Counties   781
Scene of the Civil War   792, 793
The Western Virginia Front, 1861   800
Strategy of the Civil War   848
Vicinity of Chattanooga   858
McClellan's Peninsular Campaign   863
Virginia, Maryland, and Pennsylvania, 1861–1865   864
Battle of Gettysburg   875
Chattanooga to Atlanta   882
Southern Reconstruction   905

PART I

A CREDO FOR DEMOCRACY

I. Definition

I believe that democracy is a positive political process for working toward liberty, equality, and fraternity, and that, though it bears in itself the means of improvement, it can never lay claim to perfection without destroying its essential nature.

II. Purpose

I believe that democracy seeks to preserve and to reconcile the rival sovereignties and moral values of the individual on the one hand and of society on the other, as positive aids toward a higher moral order.

III. Method

I believe that democracy operates by seeking successive compromises in order to maintain a balance among constantly changing alliances of social interests; and that these compromises are expressed in laws which are supreme and can be changed only by the will of the people.

IV. Rights

I believe that democracy ensures the supremacy of law by guaranteeing to the people certain civil liberties which in substance are not subject to compromise; that among these are freedom of speech, press, religion, and assembly; the right to a day in court; and the right to change their government or its policies by the exercise of the franchise in order to promote the public welfare.

V. Duties

I believe that democracy depends upon the balance wheels of self-restraint and moral courage. Self-restraint teaches the people when to forego their own desires and opinions; it is the basis of social order. Moral courage demands that the people stand up for what they believe is right, whatever the consequences; it is the means by which society advances. These balance wheels cannot function unless the people are taught to know their daily rights and duties and to exercise them faithfully and intelligently; to recognize and prevent the undermining of civil liberties even at the sacrifice of consistency during a crisis; and to return to tolerance and compromise when the crisis is past.

—Leland D. Baldwin, *Best Hope of Earth: A Grammar of Democracy* (1948), 11–12.

THE GENESIS

OF THE NATION

to 1787

ONE OF THE MOST MAGNIFICENT AND YET LEAST PUBLICIZED wonders of the modern world can be seen on any clear night by the traveler on a plane flying between Boston and Washington. For a distance of four hundred air miles the observer is never out of sight of the myriad, multi-colored lights of a metropolitan center. The impression left on the mind is that of one solid urban conglomerate—an impression not far from right, as one will see if he tries to breast the highway traffic the next day. It is this urban conglomerate, centered on New York City, which has become the financial and to a considerable extent the commercial, indus-trial, cultural, and political heart of the world.

And yet less than four hundred years ago there was nothing in this region but forests and the cornfields of the sparsely scattered Indian na-tions. The purpose of this book is to tell how the wilderness of North America gave way to civilization and to place that process in its proper position in the pattern of world history. This means that we must analyze our original heritage and the borrowings we have made since, examine the way in which they have reacted on our natural environment to produce a new phase of Western Civilization with its democratic and technological aspects, and see how we have shared in making and solving world problems —in the rubbing and grinding of civilizations and cultures which have made the present and will make the future.

This means, then, that we shall see that the United States has not evolved in isolation. As colonies or nation we have participated in every world war from the seventeenth century onward. We have been affected by every important European philosophical, economic, technological, and educational movement. We were formed in the social and economic image of Europe, and it has required centuries of struggle and the strong pressure of geographic environment to alter that image. At no time have we ceased to share actively in the evolution of the vital movements which have made the modern world and led to the gradual consolidation of political and cultural units, reducing them from many thousands to a few score. The political effect of this consolidating process has been the welding of states and tribes into nations. Apparently the nation is not the destined goal, for the urge toward unification has brought about the movement called internationalism. It is still too early to say whether the next stage of development will be the creation of a world state or of a few superstates each composed of a group of nations.

We will try first to explain what Western Civilization was and what happened when its traders, conquistadors, and settlers struck the shores of the New World. We will show the conflicts between the Europeans and the natives, the parallel conflict between the various European nations, and the division of the Americas among the different European cultures. At that last point the patterns of New World cultures were set, and within another lifetime new nations had sprung up from Canada to the Strait of Magellan.

Chapter I

WESTERN CIVILIZATION
AND AMERICA

1   The Course of Western Civilization

IN FIVE centuries the people of Europe have literally changed the face of the earth. Their dynamism is amazing. Alone among civilizations they have developed the scientific method, harnessed the secret energies of Nature to their machines, alleviated pain, stamped out dis- **Dynamism** eases, assuaged human misery, instructed the masses, con- **of Euro-** quered and settled whole continents, forced their yoke on **pean peo-** ancient and perhaps superior cultures, and, greatest of all, **ples** opened to the once-despised common herd the right not only to participate in its own government but to share in a life whose richness surpasses that once known to kings.

These are the unique accomplishments of Western Civilization, and its accomplishments are its characteristics and its definition.

The dynamism of the European peoples has been inherited by America, and indeed America has given to Western Civilization some of the characteristics which distinguish it most sharply from Asia. Here are some of the ways in which we shall see America influence Western **Specific** Civilization: **American** **influences**

1) Its gold and silver paid for the rise of the Spanish Empire and precipitated the early stages of the modern struggle between autocracy and developing democracy.

2) Its resources promoted the rise and helped cause the fall of the first British Empire.

3) It furnished an escape for the surplus and discontented population of Europe.

4) It furnished the atmosphere of freedom which fosters democracy and gave the first body blow to special privileges in government and society.

5) It applied scientific technology to its enormous natural resources and developed the modern mass-production methods which demonstrate the possibility of a high living standard for the masses.

6) It twice interfered decisively in world wars.

Each civilization possesses certain outstanding characteristics which distinguish it from others. When we examine the warp of Western Civilization, we find three conspicuous threads running through it: (1) the

Main threads of Western Civilization
struggle between evolving democracy and the idea of authoritarian control; (2) the growth of science and technology and their application in conquering Nature and using its resources in industry and commerce; and (3) the evolution of geographical perspective.

Historical action arises from influences as complex as the mind of man, his society, and the natural world in which he lives. If there is any permanent factor in history, it must be sought in human psychology and studied

The individual and society
in connection with the way in which man reacts in his physical and social environment. Each man has an urge to get his own way, but he knows that to survive he must live in society and that society cannot exist unless individuals give up some of their independence. The amount of independence that must be surrendered immediately becomes a subject of conflict. Each person sets up a standard of justice (or good, or perfection) that coincides with the amount of independence he is willing to surrender. This personal standard of justice is controlled and changed from time to time by the struggle between his naked desires and his conscience, his conscience being his understanding of what God or society would have him do.

Out of this struggle for justice arises morality; man is by nature a moralist because he is always choosing between selfishness and society. When he has chosen, he seeks to convince his conscience that his standard

Man is moral
of justice is right; he builds into his moral structure any course he favors, even if it only concerns taking the biggest piece of pie from a plate. And he is, in addition, consciously or unconsciously striving to force his standard on others—on society. His basic reaction to an idea is to ask about its morality: is it right or wrong, just or unjust to his concept of what the social order should be? This struggle between the individual and society is paralleled by a similar struggle between each nation and the community of nations.

It is obvious that without some influence to control and guide this interaction between the individual and his fellows, no society could be stabilized. It is law that provides the stabilizing influence. Law arises

Compromise versus force
when one segment of society or when the various segments can agree on a compromise. Basically these are the only two ways in which society can be organized: by a triumph of

part of the wills, or by a compromise of wills. Thus, any existing society is an expression of justice (or good) as understood by the nation or the social caste in control.

The first method, of force, is characteristic of societies governed by an élite class, as the nobles of Europe in the past and the bureaucracy of Soviet Russia today. The aim of this method is to set up a "perfect" structure of state and society and jam humanity into it. The second method, of compromise, has been and is practiced chiefly by the peoples of the democratic nations. They insist that any attempt to force a rigid system on society will cause the triumph not of good but of evil. Their reason is simple: times change. The good law of today becomes the strait jacket of tomorrow. Compromise, they hold, is a gradual approach to good by realistic steps. Therefore they do not set up a structure; instead, they develop a process—democracy—that will enable society gradually to adapt itself to changing times. Democracy sets up a goal which it quite frankly admits it can approach but never reach: it is self-realization of the individual in a society which protects him by giving him a share in its day-to-day evolution. In English-speaking countries we believe that the first duty of men is to get along together by persuasion and compromise; we tend to define civilization not primarily as an advanced stage of culture but as the substitution of persuasion for force.

Throughout history the fates of democracy and science have been inextricably interwoven. The reason is plain: to remain in the position of power, an élite class must command the unquestioning faith and obedience of the masses. But science probes into current beliefs and **Democracy and science** attitudes and raises questions and doubts as to their validity and worth. Sooner or later it must begin to undermine the "perfect" structure. To save itself the élite class must crush science. Science, then, finds its only protection in the open minds of a democratic society, which actually encourages change. On the other hand, democracy depends for its existence upon popular enlightenment; and in a complex society this is possible only by the technical processes that give us paper, printing, easy transmission of news, and the time that the machine frees to us for education in childhood days and adult evenings.

Popular enlightenment has a never-ending task, for it must frequently try to alter or combat established ideas—the mythus. The mythus is the body of beliefs (true or false) which by its emotional appeal produces a spirit of loyalty to the leader or the ideal. It is the encrusta- **The mythus** tion of wishful thinking and self-complimentary explanations that forms about human actions and institutions to explain their origin, nature, and development, to "mobilize men for action."

Usually the mythus is interlaced with facts and so has a convincing air of authenticity. It may be a subtle or misleading explanation of destructive doctrines, as Nazism or Sovietism. Or it may furnish a positive urge to social and spiritual betterment; this is the way in which most people interpret the body of Christian doctrine and practice. Between the extremes lies the democratic mythus: democracy's aspirations are high, but the mythus makes such optimistic interpretations of democratic practices that it is possible to ignore the numerous exceptions that breed injustice. It would be far better to acknowledge the sordid facts of social ills and try to cure them.

Democracy's compromise of interests may reduce injustice but cannot automatically banish it. All that democracy can do is give justice and morality a fighting chance; we must do the fighting. But whatever choice **Democ-** between alternatives we make, hardship on individuals or **racy no** interests may result. Failure to build a flood-control dam **cure-all** may save money for the taxpayers but ruin the people of a river valley. We may even bring on disaster by a well-meant but impractical attempt to remedy a social ill. There is no way to escape the penalties of human existence.

In the interaction of the conflicting forces of the human spirit and of society is found the practical method by which we have advanced. History is full of selfishness, injustice, oppression, and other evils; but it is also full of love, mercy, justice, and high moral principles. Democracy has developed as an instrument for the control of this conflict between principles and practices. A realization of this fact is the basis for a balanced and temperate view of events, whether good or evil.

American education tends to implant the idea that all our institutions are perfect. To assume this is only to invite cynicism and the rejection of personal responsibility when later we learn that there have been imper- **Under-** fection and sometimes downright injustice in the application **standing** of our systems and policies. The learning of "facts" is not **the conflict** enough; understanding of this historical conflict, of the age-old conflict between principles and practices, is essential. As Mildred McAfee Horton expresses it, our young men and women "believe in democracy enough to die for it, but they don't always recognize it when they see it, or distinguish it from its enemies when it is attacked."

Five hundred years ago, though Western Civilization was different in kind and degree from the civilizations of China and India, the latter two doubtless had the advantages. The Orient had known for thousands of **Oriental** years heights of art and luxury whose satisfactions perhaps **civilization** we do not know yet in spite of our gadgets. Moreover, it had reached a fairly satisfactory state of balance with Nature, which perhaps could have continued indefinitely. This balance was maintained at vast expense of human misery at the bottom of the social scale, but even the peasant knew how to live and die graciously and could find in philosophy the consolations which society refused him. Still, the fact remains that the Orient failed to conquer Nature and provide its people with an abundant life. As Hu Shih, the Chinese statesman and philosopher, has pointed out, the Orient has a truly materialistic civilization because it is limited by matter and is incapable of transcending it.

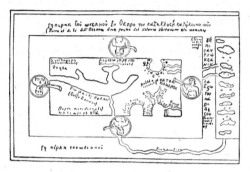

Map of the world according to Cosmas, sixth-century traveler and monk, in his *Topographia Christiana*

Its contentment with little and its fatalistic resignation are more materialistic than its actual hovels and images of the gods. Only the civilization which uses its full ingenuity to overcome and utilize the material in service to mankind is—or can be—highly idealistic and spiritual. That is, if it can utilize the material without worshiping it.

Western Civilization might have run the same course as the Orient had it not been that down through the ages there had been added special ingredients that were to set it on the track of a more successful conquest of Nature than had ever before been seen. Freedom, democracy, and science made starts in the Mediterranean cultures, but **Western** in each case the rise of a privileged ruling class defeated **departures** them. Science languished or was crushed; slavery brought contempt for manual labor with the result that men were ashamed to perform practical experiments. Nevertheless, we have inherited much from all these societies. Greece passed on her great discovery that our desire to know the truth can never be satisfied until we are willing to submit our findings to the test of reason. Rome's most enduring bequest was a code of laws that today holds sway over most of the Western nations except those that speak English, and it has vitally influenced them also. The Roman Empire tried to seek the truce with Nature that China and India had sought. But it was so complex and far-flung that it could not solve the problems it had to solve to create a static society. It really fell of its own weight.

Christianity owed much to Hebrew monotheism and divine revelation; also it had elements of fatalism. But Greek philosophy and barbarian

vigor refused to let Christianity lie quiescent. The Middle Ages wrought a
mighty change. The Mediterranean world was inhabited by

**Mission of
the Church**

debased slaves, starveling peasants, commoners on the dole,
northern barbarians whom the lordly Romans regarded as
incapable of becoming civilized. The Church took over the civilizing
mission of Rome, fastened the yoke of discipline on the hot-blooded barbarians, and taught the dignity and necessity of labor to a society that
had despised the laborer. Discipline and labor are two of the most important ingredients in an industrial society; they are two of the many gifts
of the Church to the modern world.

Moreover, the Church emphasized Christian salvation as an individual
matter, each man responsible for his own fate. This was the bridge between ancient statism and modern individualism. The idea that the individual exists for the benefit of the state began to yield to the democratic
idea that the state exists for the individual *and* society.

The existence of this bridge was not evident until late in the Middle
Ages. At its best, medieval society attained a well-rounded perfection, a
unity that has never been equaled before or since. Everything fitted neatly

**Medieval
unity**

into a divine plan. There were three classes of society: the
nobles, who ruled and fought; the clergy, who were the moral
and intellectual guardians; and the workers, who furnished
material support. The business of men on earth was to prepare for the enjoyment of eternal life. The pope was regarded as the final earthly authority on matters of faith and morals, but he also usually claimed a veto
over the actions of kings. This veto was the subject of bitter dispute for
centuries.

As cities began to grow up at trade-route intersections in Italy and in
the northern wilderness, trade and manufacturing increased; the wealth
that began to flow to the burghers in the cities made them economic

**Rise of
the cities**

powers. These burghers saw that the wide peace necessary
to commerce was better promoted by a king than by warring
feudal lords, so they backed the king in his efforts to unify
the realm. Old social divisions broke down. The burghers got the ear of the
king in matters of government. Feudal conglomerates were slowly welded
into nations; kings declared their independence of the pope, asserting that
their "divine right" to rule was given them directly by God.

The evolution away from medieval attitudes and loyalties was further
influenced by the rediscovery of ancient Greek knowledge. Men were fascinated by the Greeks' intellectual curiosity and sublime self-confidence.

**Renas-
cence**

Then the Renascence crossed the Alps, and Martin Luther
showed the kings of northwest Europe how to break away
entirely from the Catholic Church. The magnificent medieval
structure toppled. The ideal of the nation-state grew up. Religious faith

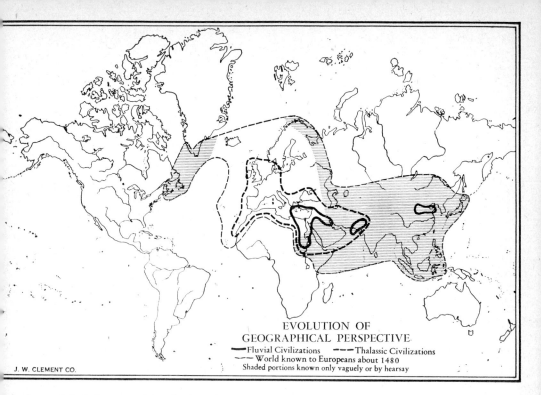

EVOLUTION OF
GEOGRAPHICAL PERSPECTIVE
———Fluvial Civilizations ————Thalassic Civilizations
————World known to Europeans about 1480
Shaded portions known only vaguely or by hearsay

J. W. CLEMENT CO.

was labeled superstition by a science that began to hold all knowledge up to the test of reason and experiment. Men now lived in the present; even their wars were fought for commercial and territorial advantage or for civil freedom, no longer for faith.

All Europe was caught up in the mighty tide. Even those nations least inclined to break away from the Catholic Church—Portugal and Spain—felt the deliciously dangerous quickening of the spirit of the times. They became the leading contenders for the overseas prizes that a generation of great navigators had suddenly revealed to the awakened eyes of Europe.

Until the fifteenth century Europe knew little of the world south or east of the Mediterranean. The northern Italian cities of Venice and Genoa provided the junctions between the maze of trade routes through the northern wilderness and the long sea and caravan routes **Knowl-** that led out of the mysterious Orient down to the seaports **edge of** of the Levant. Europeans were far from clear as to the rela- **Asia** tive geographical positions of Asian lands and islands. It was known that there was a sea passage from India to Cathay (China), but there was a tendency to lump together the whole Orient—"The Indies."

Few had visited Asia. In an age that reveled in the occult and miraculous, their tales were a little fuzzy along the line between what they had seen and what they had heard. There were, they said, Cyclopes, with one eye in their foreheads; a horse called the unicorn because it bore a single horn in its forehead; and upas trees which rained death on all who passed

11

beneath. They mentioned, too, the splendid Christian kingdom of Prester John, somewhere in the fastnesses of Africa or Asia.

However tall the tales, one thing was certain. From the Orient there had issued since earliest antiquity a stream of the only luxury goods Europeans had ever known: silks and brocades for the nobility, jewels for sacred altars, pearls for my lady's ears and perfumes for her hair; dye-stuffs for Western linens and woolens, rugs for bourgeois homes, and spices for sour wines and half-spoiled meats. The goods that Europe sent to the East in exchange—coarse textiles, wine, lead, antimony, and mercury—were welcomed, but they were insufficient to pay for the luxury goods. The difference was made up by gold and silver. For centuries European treasure had been drained off into the East. Somewhere in that mysterious realm, it was evident, lay untold wealth ready to the itching hands of whatever Christian adventurers could get to it.

That was the problem: how to get to it. The route to the East was closed not only by the Italian monopoly but by the landlocked nature of the Mediterranean. A vague tradition suggested that there was a water route around Africa. There were those who dared to fly in
Fear of the Atlantic
the face of common sense as understood by the man in the street and propose a voyage westward to the Indies, on the assumption (believed by learned men for two thousand years) that the earth was shaped like a ball. Now the dream of a westward passage to the Indies was not new, for Eratosthenes had suggested it as early as the third century before Christ, and Aristotle, Strabo, and Seneca had all played with the idea. In 1267 Roger Bacon, that tragic Franciscan scientist born out of time, had collected citations from ancient writers to prove that Spain and Asia were not far apart. These were published in 1410 in a curious hodge-podge called *Imago Mundi,* and manuscript copies soon became common.

The learned might desire to have their theories tested, but the common sailors in the reeking little ports of Western Europe would have no part of it, for where there is no knowledge superstition and fear rush in to fill the void. If one sailed west into the Green Sea of Darkness, his craft might be held fast in the great seaweed beds of the Sargasso Sea; the great fish with a sucker in his head would hold it motionless until all on board starved, or the giant squid would encircle the ship in its relentless tentacles and pull it down to destruction. Even if the voyager escaped these terrors, he would come inevitably to the end of the world, and the irresistible current would pull him over the edge.

Terrors aside, responsible sea captains stuck at the practicability of reaching the Indies with the ships and navigating instruments then available. They had only small, tublike caravels with top-heavy poops and clumsy lateen sails. They had little idea of distances and only the rough-

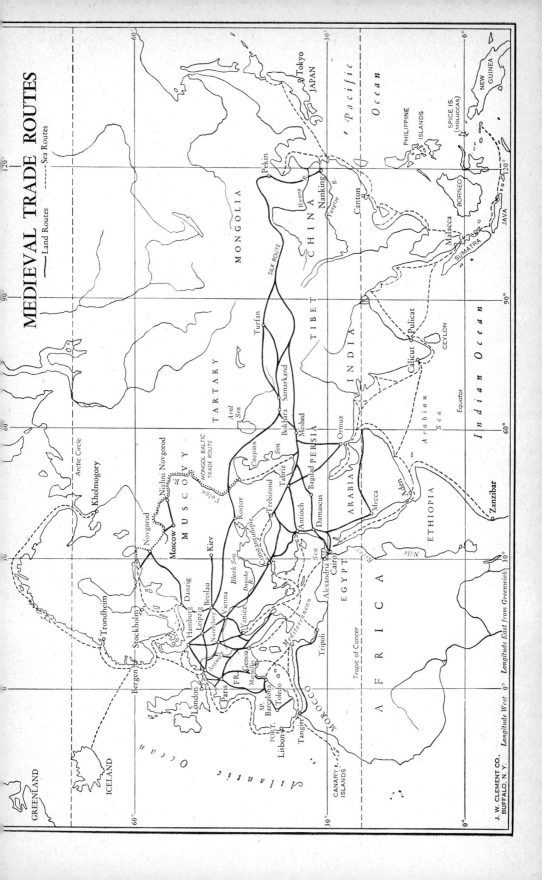

est methods of reckoning position. Sailors religiously hugged the shore or dashed fearfully from cape to cape. Most of the Atlantic islands were discovered by ships blown out of their courses.

When the Portuguese and Spanish voyagers of the late fifteenth century demonstrated the global nature of the earth, geographers were confronted by the problem of how to portray a map of the globe on a piece of flat paper. Mercator, a Flemish mathematician, geographer, and cartographer, solved the difficulty by expanding the northern and southern polar regions out of all proportions, so that the world looked like a cylinder slit and spread out flat. One result is that Greenland seems to be larger than South America! The old view of

Effect of Mercator

"The Sea of Darkness," from the *Historia* of Olaus Magnus (1490–1568)

the world as composed chiefly of land with a central Mediterranean Sea now gave way to the view that Europe, Asia, and Africa formed an island in a vast global ocean. Popular grasp of the new concept lagged, for one reason, because Mercator's projection concealed the fact that the land masses of the northern hemisphere were really grouped around a central core (the Arctic Sea) and were closer to each other than the necessary round-about routes of travel would seem to indicate.

Nevertheless, the discovery of the unitary nature of the ocean revolutionized the political and economic patterns of the globe. Navies had played some part in the power politics of the ancient Mediterranean World, but armies had taken their place in the contests of Western Europe during the Middle Ages. Now, with some of the goals of national strife transferred to America and the Orient, sea power came back. Spain, Holland, and France each had their turn at ascendance on the ocean, and later the term *Pax Britannica* indicated the more or less general world peace enforced by the British navy. The digging of the Suez and Panama canals, by connecting oceans hitherto distant from

Role of sea power

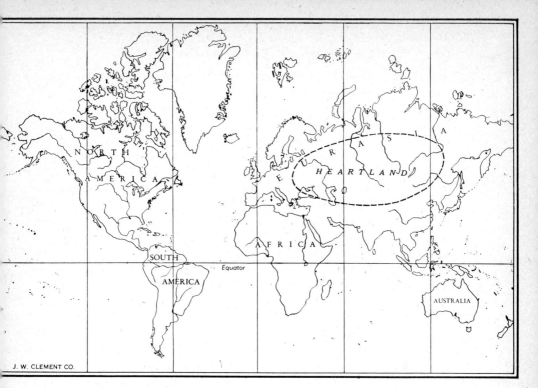

THE WORLD according to Mercator (above) and seen as a globe (below)

LAND HEMISPHERE

WATER HEMISPHERE

each other in terms of sailing time, made sea power an obsession of diplomats and military strategists.

Modern European expansion has been far more than an expansion of European colonists, goods, and ideas. Just as Greek culture merged with what it found in the ancient Near East to form Hellenistic culture, so **Non-Euro-** European culture has merged with what it has found all over **pean con-** the globe to form Western Civilization. It may well be **tributions** doubted if Europe could have changed successfully from an agrarian and napkin economy (petty saving without productive investment) to an industrial and venturesome capitalist economy if it had not been for the products of the rest of the world. Note how important are the non-European contributions to early modern commercial and industrial development: cotton, raw silk, tobacco, chocolate, tea, coffee, spices, sugar, dyestuffs, copra, ship stores and timbers, furs and skins, drugs such as quinine, precious metals, and presently some other metals in quantities not easily obtainable in Europe. European agriculture gained notably by maize, the tomato, and the potato; and important new industries were founded upon the manufacture of cotton, silk, carpets, and china, to mention only a few. The proportion of manufactured goods that was exported rose rapidly along with the rise in imports; by 1800 England owed its prosperity largely to non-European trade, and that also was no mean factor in the economy of other Western European states.

The importance of overseas products and markets to European economy led immediately to an international struggle for their control, with the result that the old pattern of political power in Europe was shattered forever. The change did not stop there. Expansion of Euro- **Expansion** pean peoples to new continents and of European technologies **of Europe** to old civilizations was in the twentieth century to snatch from Europe's hands the control of its own destinies. For better or worse, Western Civilization in one form or another had become world-wide.

What were the specific impulses which led to these vital changes? Some of them, of course, were purely psychological, such as the spirits of curiosity and adventure, the desire to expand the bounds of knowledge, **Impulses** and the patriotic desire to advance the power and glory of **behind ex-** one's nation. Add to this the resentment over political, eco- **pansion** nomic, and religious oppression which did so much to build up the English colonies in North America. The economic impulse to gain wealth by getting gold, raw materials, or markets was, in the earlier period at least, accompanied by the missionary impulse. Portuguese, Spanish, and French adventurers were partly activated by a sincere desire to save souls, and conversion to Christianity became a powerful support to cultural intermingling and political and economic imperialism. Protestant nations were to learn the knack in the nineteenth century.

The seventeenth century brought changes in a flood to Europe. For the first time science came completely into its own. Time after time the promise of a technology like that of modern times had been vetoed by the growth of social castes and special privilege. Now the stars were propitious. The growth of cities brought together the instruments of secular learning and the tools of the manufac- turer and stimulated the rise of science. Self-government was broadened in the cities to obtain the allegiance of the higher artisans, and presently there began to appear something like a free society.

Elements of the modern age

Out of all this developed the idea of progress, suggested first by the French. Men asserted that they could build one step on another and thus become better and better. The usual aim was human happiness. It is not necessarily cynical to observe that we may have mistaken *change* for *progress;* but, however that may be, the idea of progress has been so generally believed by thinkers that it constitutes the central psychological difference between ancient and modern times.

Idea of progress

The new national states that sprang up in the later Middle Ages found that size, population, and resources were decisive in power politics; and in consequence the movement toward nationalism was strengthened. When the great navigators showed Europe the rich world beyond the seas there began a bitter clash among the powers of Western Europe for commercial and colonial supremacy. It was the first phase of imperialism, that is, political and/or economic rule of other areas or nations. Nationalism became more than a healthful diversity; at times it became an obsession.

Rise of nationalism

Still, ever since the fall of Rome, the idea of unification has appealed to Europe, but her nations will accept only a unification that will preserve their precious diversities. Thus far Europe's political capacities have proved unequal to the task, though repeated attempts have been made to turn her states into a system of satellites revolving around a central sun. These attempts centered in the Holy Roman Empire of Charles v, the Spain of Philip ii, the France of Louis xiv and Napoleon, and the Germany of Wilhelm ii and Hitler. Though these attempts invariably involved complex economic rivalries, their significance to the future lay in the struggle between absolutism and democracy. The fate of both hung upon a rivalry between land and sea. Over a period of four centuries the sea conquered, and from 1815 to 1914 there reigned the *Pax Britannica*, the longest era of comparative peace since the rupture of the *Pax Romana*.

Problems of unification

During the long struggle it was the people of Great Britain who constituted the core of resistance to the unification of Europe by force. Britain's weapons are well known: first, the fleet, which kept all but un-

Britain's weapons disputed control of the paths of maritime commerce. Second, the balance of power—the method of balancing any strong state or states with a combination just as strong: the equilibrium made it unprofitable for either side to attack. This technique has been used widely in Europe; England simply used it most successfully. The world has not yet proved that any other method will any more surely prevent wars.

England's third weapon lay in the fact that she usually favored the small nations and in general was trusted by them. England was the only great power which expressed in its laws and institutions the general human **England the hope of democracy** desire for freedom. Democracy was evolving there and most of the time was under severe handicaps elsewhere in Europe. If England went under, democracy would go with her, and the cause of human freedom would be crushed under the heel of whatever police state dominated the continent. Therein lay the significance to us of England's long struggle to prevent unification of the continent. It has been fortunate for the cause of democracy that Britain's commercial interests and those of the rising common man have usually coincided. England, while thoroughly egotistic, is the only power which over a long period was able to call forth in other peoples that aspiration for freedom which transcends national boundaries. The effect has been tremendous. Only in our generation has another power, the Soviet Union, been able to match this dynamic appeal by a crusade for economic "freedom" as opposed to political freedom.

It is true that for a few brief years the French Revolutionists roused the spirit of liberty in the European nations. But French methods were extreme: they burned down the house because the roof leaked and lived in the rain until a new house was built. Napoleon rebuilt the **France and liberty** house—reorganized France—but on a basis of absolutism. Since then France has never quite blotted out the shadow of the dictator. The French example is a warning against sudden, sweeping changes. Gradual and moderate changes are more likely to be permanent; they avoid the chaos that accompanies revolutions and in the long run usually do just as much good.

The chief fruit of the French Revolution was the tragic acceleration of the growth of nationalism with all its bitter rivalries. Under the pretense of promoting unity and efficiency in the struggle for national survival, the **Ascendance of nationalism** continental monarchs subtly and successfully prevented the rise of all but the mere forms of liberty. Particularly in the great states of Germany, Austria-Hungary, and Russia the tremendous power of the Industrial Revolution was chained to the chariot wheels of the national states and utilized less to raise the standard of living than to increase military power. The small nations of

Scandinavia, and Holland, Belgium, and Switzerland developed a high degree of democracy and a good standard of living, partly because they took little share in the international rivalries of the continent and devoted themselves to hard and intelligent work.

The role of England was no less decisive in the development of modern science than in the preservation of freedom. Hitherto men had sought truth by the study of the Bible and Aristotle. Sir Francis Bacon proclaimed a new basis: "It is by instruments and helps that the work is done." Let men experiment and observe, let them lay fact beside fact, and presently the truth would spring out writ large in Nature's own words. "The true and lawful goal of the sciences is none other than this: that human life be endowed with new discoveries and powers." Here was an expression of the utilitarian idea that forms the foundation of so much of our modern way of life. It is true that scientific method has gone beyond Bacon's inductive method and that today hypothesis is its chief instrument. It is true, too, that other men had conducted experiments and that in Bacon's own time Galileo and Descartes were also concerned. Yet it was Bacon who did much to define the method and whose spirit has so permeated modern science that he can be named its father.

Baconian scientific method

In the modern world scientific enterprise is closely allied with economic success; so it was natural that England should become the founder of the Industrial Revolution and the leader in each economic development thereafter. This fact brings up capitalism, which, simply defined, means production for profit. Often it is called private enterprise or, very simply, the profit-and-loss system. It promotes the accumulation of savings which can be converted into machines or used in commerce; it fosters the growth of a class of men who have nothing to sell but their labor and gathers them into a factory (or mine, lumber camp, restaurant, or even a farm) equipped with machinery where that labor can be utilized and remunerated with wages; it makes plans for the future and takes risks on those plans; it must operate with the goodwill of the state in order to protect its property and its interests; and historically it has depended upon a constantly widening market, whether found in new countries or created at home by the wages it pays to labor.

Capitalism

Let us note here one accompaniment of capitalism which will become clearer as we go on. Western Christendom was split into two wings, Protestant and Roman Catholic, but theology was the least of their differences. Protestantism was embraced by the rising capitalistic nations, such as England, Holland, and northern Germany, and it was strong among the manufacturing classes even in the nations that remained Catholic. The Huguenots of France are an illustration of this last.

Calvinism and capitalism

John Calvin of Geneva was the "reformer" whose interpretation of

Protestantism best suited developing capitalism. He stressed individual responsibility, thrift, savings, hard work, sobriety—all necessary if the poor nations of Europe were to participate in capitalism. The basis of Calvinism was conduct; this led too often to material standards that honored wealth and power. And yet in a curiously contradictory way Protestantism was spiritual because it preached social responsibility and disdained worldly goods; it prayed oftener for spiritual blessings than for rain on its wheat fields. This cleaving to contradictory standards has often been called hypocritical. Perhaps it was, but it got results.* At any rate, Protestantism was the hammer and anvil on which the new scientific order was formed. It accompanied the rise of science, the conquest of material things, mass production, and the high standard of living.

Of course, there were many gradations of opinion among both Catholics and Protestants: many Protestants did not adopt the harshness of Calvinism; on the other hand, there were many Catholics who practiced the precepts of Calvin's Puritans even though they rejected the theology. On the whole, however, Catholicism remained the more spiritually aspiring of the two. It preserved the gentler virtues of reverence, faith, love for beauty, and the struggle for perfection.

Modern capitalism originated in Italy, and with it came the development of many of the credit, exchange, and banking techniques which we still use. At first it was less concerned with manufactures than with commercial risks, the transportation and sale of goods. The first **Mercantilism** modern capitalists were therefore merchants, and the current economic doctrine came to be known as mercantilism. The doctrine also had a political tinge. Ordinary business was transacted in hard cash, and people and statesmen alike thought of this cash in terms of its intrinsic value as gold and silver. The substitution of the wages system for the old payment in kind, the growth of commerce, and the rising scale of governmental undertakings in administration and warfare resulted in a scramble for gold. Thus it was easy to assume that the amount of precious metals that a nation held was the most important measure of its power, and since kings aimed at power they fostered manufactures (at the expense of agriculture) because thus the stock of bullion was increased.

States extended their control over trade and industry and endeavored to set up what we today would call a planned economy. Monopolies over the sale of such articles as salt and ale were granted in exchange for round contributions to the treasury; or a king might grant to certain favorites (to the exclusion of his other subjects) the right to trade in a certain part

* Best treatment of this topic is Richard H. Tawney, *Religion and the Rise of Capitalism* (1926. Also Pelican ed., 1947).

of the world, such as Russia, Turkey, or the East Indies. The monopoly system was to play a large share in the planting of the English colonies in America.

Europe's rising discontent with mercantilism's advocacy of governmental controls and monopolies led in the 1750's to the emergence of a French school called the Physiocrats, who founded a new science: economics. Basing their ideas on the work of the English phi- **Physiocrats** losopher John Locke, they held that there was a natural law **and cap-** not only in morals and politics but also in economics. Their **italism** endeavor was to discover this law, and they believed that they had found it in the principle of individual freedom. In order to implement it, all that was necessary was to leave individuals to themselves, for they would normally act in accordance with this law. Let the government, therefore, stand aloof from economic activities and interfere only as a benevolent policeman to protect life, liberty, and property. *"Laissez faire et laissez passer, le monde va de lui-même."* Let goods be made freely, let them (and people) pass freely through frontiers; the world goes on of itself.

But there was another aspect of the Physiocrats' economics. Agriculture and the extractive industries, they maintained, were the only wealth of a nation, for everything else depended upon them. All taxes, wherever along the line they might be collected, were passed back to **Physiocrats** the farmer; therefore why not do away with the tangle of **and agrar-** taxation and lay a *single tax* on the cultivator's surplus? The **ianism** chief Physiocrats belonged to the landowning class and were concerned with protecting themselves from the stifling mass of mercantilistic regulations. They were to furnish some convenient arguments to the agrarians of the new American nation.

The growing British opinion that the government should not interfere with private trade or manufacture was set forth in 1776 in *The Wealth of Nations* by Adam Smith, a Scot. His book wielded enormous and longlasting influence and became the bible of the so-called eco- **Industrial** nomic liberals. In the end English manufactures displaced **capitalism** merchants and agriculturists, and industrial capitalism took control of government policy. Laissez faire prevailed, the state hesitated to interfere with private enterprise except to defend legally the rights of property, and Adam Smith's "law" of supply and demand was presumed to be a fairly adequate regulatory device. As it was, shrewd entrepreneurs found it possible by fair means or foul to amalgamate other factories with theirs and thus build up monopolies or near-monopolies.

By the end of the nineteenth century, however, industrial entrepreneurs in both America and Europe had pretty nearly lost control of their factories, and bankers had taken over and instituted finance capitalism. Also,

Finance capitalism by this time surplus capital had moved to the outer part of the world to develop new markets and sources of raw materials, and to be invested in public utilities or perhaps in factories where labor was cheaper and more docile than at home. This movement caused or at least accompanied the imperialism of the late nineteenth century, when states began a new race for colonies in order to advance the interests of their finance capitalists.

In Germany the state bound capital to its interests. Almost from the first a form of state capitalism existed there, at least as far as control was concerned. The national rivalries which began before World War I and **State capitalism** were accelerated by the jealousies which followed led capital in other countries to demand government protection in various forms, including high tariff walls. It was the entry of the camel's head into the tent. The depression of the 1930's brought in the rest of the beast, for governments could not afford to allow hardships to threaten social stability, even if they had to take over the roles of the financiers by acquiring control of shaky enterprises and by competing with those which would not conform to the new pattern. Though this state capitalism has not yet extinguished private enterprise (except in Russia and some of her dependents), it is widespread and may lead to socialism.

The distinction between capitalism and socialism is double. First, capitalism is private enterprise, and socialism is state ownership and management of the means of production. The second distinction lies in the theory **Capitalism, socialism, statism** of income: capitalism says "from each according to his ability, to each according to his *production*"; socialism teaches "from each according to his ability, to each according to his *need*." Either economic system can be politically democratic or totalitarian: democratic capitalism is commonly called capitalism; nondemocratic capitalism is fascism; democratic socialism is commonly what is meant by the plain term socialism; and nondemocratic socialism is communism and is marked by the control of consumption as well as production. As a matter of fact, both totalitarian capitalism and totalitarian socialism when put into practice exalt the authority of the state, that is, the gang in control of the state, whether Hitler's Nazis or Stalin's *Politburo*. Capitalism as private enterprise and socialism as support according to need both disappear. What is left is often called state capitalism or state socialism, according to one's prejudices. Actually it is something much stronger— statism. Politics and economics are merged in the total state, and individual freedom disappears. This is the stark menace which confronts this generation.

We noted that in modern times diplomats and strategists have regarded control of the sea as the prime essential of empire. After World War I this view of the bases of power was challenged by Halford Mackinder, who asserted that the empire which ruled the "Heartland" interior of Eurasia would rule the world because it could not **The Heartland** be assailed by navies. This thinking lay at the root of Hitler's "geopolitical" strategy by which he sought to seize the Heartland, and it may also give the Soviet Union confidence in its destiny to dominate the world. The present century may well see a conflict between the land-based armies of the Heartland and the land-sea-air team of the maritime democracies.

This situation points up the vital role played by technological changes in the evolution of geographical perspective. The most obvious factor is transportation. In the fifteenth century the development of the carrack with its heavy spread of sails and its great carrying capacity was important in widening the European horizon to encom- **Role of technology** pass the globe. Further refinements in shipbuilding had a profound effect on the nature of sea power and commerce, and the coming of the steamship shortened travel time and emphasized the importance of coaling bases. The airplane has enabled man for the first time to travel by the shortest routes, all but regardless of natural barriers. Scarcely less important are weaving and chimneys, which by making possible clothing and artificial heat have enabled high cultures to develop in colder climates than formerly. Perhaps in time medicine and air-conditioning will play a similar role in the tropics.

The airplane, by demonstrating the unity of the ocean of air, has probably closed our view of geography until artillery is emplaced on the moon. By enabling us to see all the continents as grouped around a central sea it has struck a fatal blow to the fallacies nursed by Mercator's projection. By showing that New York, Chicago, and Seattle **A closed world** are roughly equidistant from Moscow it has destroyed for all but a few hardy souls the illusion of American isolation. The utilization in warfare of the direct airways offered by the Arctic is certain; in peace it can be delayed or limited only by national suspicions or lack of pay loads.

It is very likely that the peacetime Mediterranean of the future will be the North Atlantic. Perhaps, though this is by no means yet certain, air power has placed North America in a strategic position, which in the air age (barring an atomic or bacterial upset) may be as advantageous as that of Britain was in the age of sea power. It must be borne in mind that atomic energy cannot suddenly solve the problem of transportation in economics and warfare. Roads, railroads, ships, and planes will continue to be important even though powered by fissioned atoms, and the routes they travel will also be important. The closing of the geographic scene means that no nation can expand into empty spaces or into those politically unoccupied but must get along with what it has or take from someone else. Disruption in any of the great population centers affects us all because in our complex civilization we all live in glass houses, and the airplane and the rocket have brought us no more than a stone's throw apart.

In this century the United States and the Soviet Union are the heirs of the two great conflicting forces of history: democracy and totalitarianism. For almost five thousand years totalitarianism or its kindred doctrines **Demo-** of aristocracy and special privilege ruled Western Civiliza-**cratic pros-** tion, except for a brief time in Greece. Today the machine **pects** makes it possible not only to do away with human drudgery but also to cast aside the psychological heritage of a slave-based society: contempt for manual labor, dictation over men's lives, and calling a segment of society inferior in race or ability as an excuse for exploiting it. For the first time we have the technical resources which make democracy possible in a complex society: the paper, the printing presses, the communication facilities, and the leisure for education. Democracy and science are working together, and if they win they must win as a team. On that union depends the issue of whether the common man shall walk in freedom and individual dignity or bow his neck to the yoke of slavery.

2   Geographical Influences in American History

The battle between Nature and Western man has had no more vivid illustration than in North America. The opening of the continent began just at the moment when European techniques had reached the stage where **The lure of** they could wage successful warfare against Nature and had **America** already raped Europe's superficial resources in the preliminary skirmishes of the battle for the world. The demand for furs and timber was urgent, and it was not long until there was an even greater cry from an expanding population for food, minerals, and tropical luxuries.

Europeans, reared in an economy of scarcity, were dazed by the natural riches of the New World. Even the most unimaginative travelers became lyrical over the enormous expanse of the new continent, and there was a pardonable element of exaggeration in the tales they told. The fish off Newfoundland gathered in such shoals that ships could hardly make way through them; wild strawberries reddened the fields in early summer; clouds of pigeons darkened the sun and when they lighted bore down the stoutest trees; buffaloes covered the plains as far as the eye could reach; and trees were so tall that it took two men and a boy to see to the top. Here the men of straitened little Europe could find the elbowroom they craved, the freedom from feudal restraint, and the natural resources to give them a life so abundant that the like existed only in fairy tales. The "barbaric yawp" of Walt Whitman was only a faint and cultured echo of the exuberant whoops with which the pioneers fell upon the New World paradise.

North America and Eurasia lie with their northern shores staring icily at each other across the pack of the Arctic Sea. In the east it is scarcely one thousand miles from Norway to Greenland; the two continents are within sight of each other at Bering Strait, and people have been known to cross on the ice. North America is shaped roughly like the shield one sees on the arms of the United **North America** States and is located almost altogether in the North Temperate Zone, except that the crown is in the Arctic and the spike at the bottom trails southeasterly through the Torrid Zone to join South America a few hundred miles above the equator. The body of the continent is a little less than 3000 miles square, but the extremities on the Arctic Sea and the Gulf of Panama are about 5000 miles apart. The continental United States occupies about one third of North America, is roughly 2500 miles wide at the midriff and half as much from the Gulf of Mexico to the Canadian border; it has 3,022,387 square miles and about 1,900,000,000 land acres; Alaska adds 586,400 square miles, which make the total more than 3,608,-000. Canada has 3,851,000 square miles. It is a curious fact that most of South America lies farther east than does North America, and that a line drawn directly south from Boston would cross the Andes and strike the Pacific Ocean off the coast of Chile. A line drawn eastward from Key West would run through the Sahara, the teeming valleys of the Nile, the Indus, and the Ganges, and on through China to Formosa and the lesser islands of the Hawaiian chain.

In the days of sailing ships, winds and currents were vital factors in navigation. In the oceans north of the equator, currents run clockwise around the ocean; and during much of the year winds in the north blow east and in the south blow west. Ships from Europe thus swung down the coast of Africa before turning west, and ships from the Caribbean and the Gulf of Mexico found it **Winds of the North Atlantic** useful on their way to Europe to sail through the Florida Strait and up the North American coast. The wind in the extreme North Atlantic, however, blows west in the spring and autumn; so it was possible for ships to go directly to North America at those times of year and to return before the westerly winds of summer or winter.

The continental shelf is a submerged plain along the coast which is very broad from New England to Newfoundland and is known as the "Banks." In the shallow waters of the Banks, particularly off Newfoundland, great shoals of fish, especially cod, are attracted by the cold water of the Labrador Current and by the organic mat- **The Banks** ter brought down by the St. Lawrence and other streams. Here, then, is

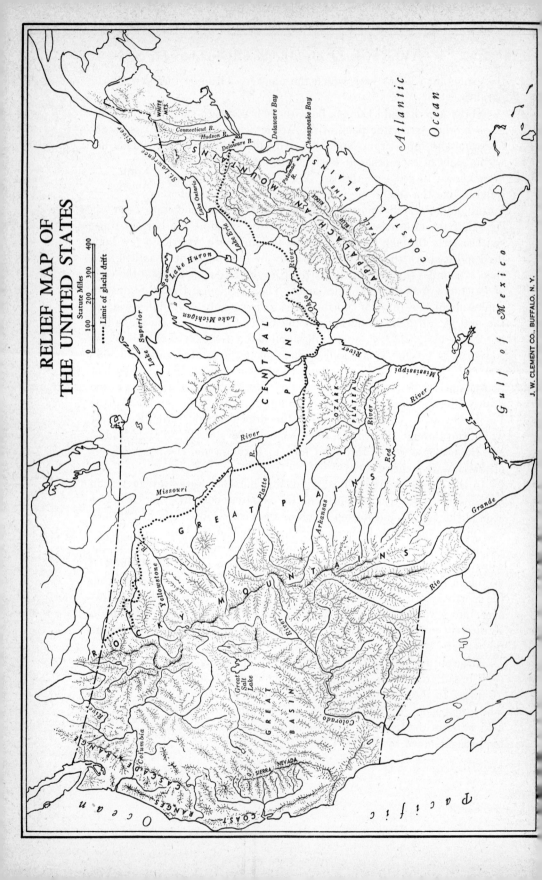

RELIEF MAP OF
THE UNITED STATES

Statute Miles
0 100 200 300 400

····· Limit of glacial drift

Atlantic Ocean

Gulf of Mexico

Pacific Ocean

J. W. CLEMENT CO., BUFFALO, N.Y.

APPALACHIAN MOUNTAINS

COASTAL PLAINS

WHITE MTS.

Connecticut R.
Hudson R.
Delaware R.
Delaware Bay
Chesapeake Bay
Potomac R.

St. Lawrence River

Lake Ontario
Lake Erie
Lake Huron
Lake Michigan
Lake Superior

Soo Canal

CENTRAL PLAINS

Ohio River

Mississippi River

OZARK PLATEAU

GREAT PLAINS

Missouri River
Platte R.
Yellowstone R.
Arkansas River
Red River
Rio Grande

ROCKY MOUNTAINS

GREAT BASIN

Great Salt Lake

Colorado River
Columbia River

CASCADE RANGE
COAST RANGES
SIERRA NEVADA

FALL LINE

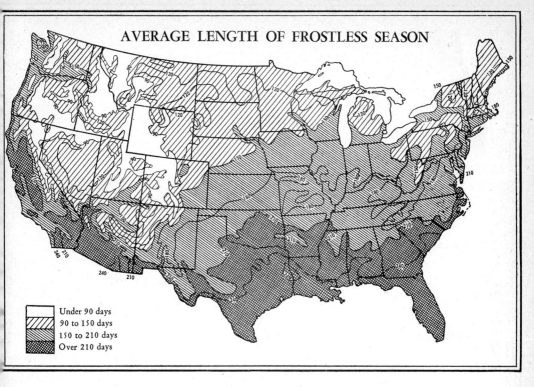

AVERAGE LENGTH OF FROSTLESS SEASON

Under 90 days
90 to 150 days
150 to 210 days
Over 210 days

one of the richest fishing grounds in the world, one which European fisher-men may have visited long before 1492. The right to fish on the Banks or to land on the adjacent shore has been a frequent source of diplomatic friction between nations and has contributed its share to causing wars. Not far behind in importance are the banks and rivers of the Pacific coast from California on up to Alaska, which have long been important for their salmon catch and are rapidly forging to the front with commercial catches of halibut, herring, and other species.

The western third of North America is covered by an immense cor-dillera system which extends from Alaska into the tropics, but which boasts no peak more than slightly over twenty thousand feet high. In the east there is a relatively narrow coastal plain backed by the old, eroded Appalachian system. Between the two mountain systems lies a great plain, once the bottom of the ocean, **Surface and climate** which extends from the Gulf of Mexico to the Arctic Sea, and it is possible to travel from one to the other without reaching an altitude of two thou-sand feet. A "continental" climate results whenever a body of land is large enough to have an interior protected from the moderating influence of the sea and which consequently reacts to seasonal changes. The great interior valley of North America is open to the tropics on the south and to the Arctic on the north; so its superheated southern winds bake the wheat fields of Canada in the summer, and its frigid winter winds make Texas blizzards famous. The Pacific coast is protected from extremes of tempera-

27

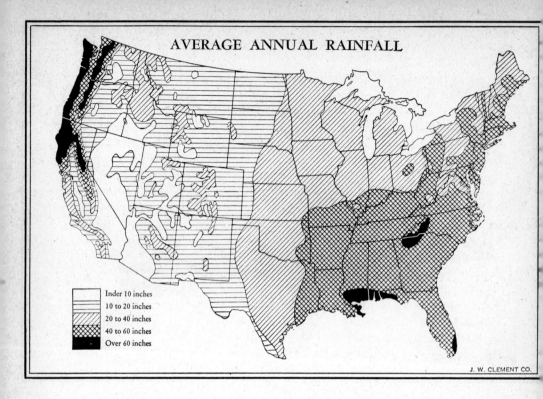

AVERAGE ANNUAL RAINFALL

Inder 10 inches
10 to 20 inches
20 to 40 inches
40 to 60 inches
Over 60 inches

J. W. CLEMENT CO.

ture by the Cascades and Sierras, and with the aid of the Japan Current it consequently has the most delightful climate on the continent. On the east the Appalachians are too low to protect the Atlantic coast, so at least in the north it is also given to extremes. The North American winter, however, is seldom crippling except in the extreme north, and railroads and highways are usually open to traffic during the entire year.

One of the most remarkable climatic features of North America is that the eastern half (from about the 100th meridian) receives two thirds of the continent's rain and constitutes, next to Europe, the largest area of **Rainfall** beneficently watered land anywhere in the Temperate Zones. Droughts and floods are both unknown (or would be if Nature had its way) except as local phenomena. American rainfall is more violent than that of Europe, and the result is that our soil is more likely to leach and erode than is the heavy soil of Europe under its more gentle rainfall. However, rainfall and fertile soil make this one of the most reliable crop lands in the world and consequently the world's largest and most consistent food producer. The grain production of the United States and Canada runs to about seven billions of bushels—probably about one third of the world's total—though the two countries hold only about seven per cent of the population of the globe.

The river systems of North America have been a curse and a blessing. For thousands of years they have been carrying the soil to the sea, as the

28

nature of the lower Mississippi proves, but the white man's "mining" of forests and soil has accelerated the process. On the other hand, the rivers have always been important transportation **Rivers** links. The Mississippi system and the Great Lakes–St. Lawrence system interlace at numerous places on the headwaters, and so with the aid of short portages opened the interior of the continent to canoe transportation from Canada. The two systems thus virtually formed a unit, as the French soon learned, and the imperial conflict for control of the interior of North America was vitally affected by the fact. Later on the rivers were useful for carrying flatboats downstream, and in the canal era the portages were traversed by canals. The steamboat, however, for the first time took full advantage of the transportation possibilities of the rivers, and this utilization has persisted to a certain extent even into the day of the railroad.

The nature of the Atlantic coast was of vital significance in the successful planting of the English colonies. In the first place numerous rivers were navigable by the ships of that day to a ledge of rock marked by waterfalls and known as the Fall Line. In New England the Fall Line is near the coast, except on the Connecticut River, **The Atlan-** but from the Hudson on south it varies up to about one hun- **tic coast** dred fifty miles from the coast. Not only was the coastal plain in the south fertile and easily accessible, but the climate was mild enough to encourage the growth of such staples as tobacco, rice, and indigo, and so brought about the growth of great plantations and slavery. Between the Fall Line and the Appalachians lie the foothills known as the Piedmont, also suitable in places for great plantations but more encouraging to general farming. Within the mountain folds there are numerous arable valleys with an altitude sufficient to give them a climate comparable to that of Pennsylvania and suitable for grain crops. One of the valleys, the Great Valley, known part of the way as the Shenandoah, reaches from the Hudson River to Georgia with only minor interruptions and through most of its course is composed of a rich brown loam. Such a valley not only was useful as a granary but afforded an easily traveled road between north and south.

The Appalachian Mountains compose an old and eroded system; they were formidable not so much for their height as for their ruggedness and luxuriant forestation. The interior of the continent was easily accessible to the English colonists only around the southern end of the **The Appa-** system or by way of the upper Hudson, which afforded **lachian** water-level routes by way of the Mohawk River or the Lake **barrier** Champlain chain. Other trails existed across the mountain passes, but they were difficult to traverse. The importance of the Appalachians was threefold: they prevented overexpansion of the English settlements; they protected the rear of the settlements against invasion, at least in a limited measure; and, by confining the settlers to a coastal region easily controlled by Great Britain, they promoted the union of the colonies in the Revolution.

The richest part of the United States, that just south of the Great Lakes, is the gift of Canada. A succession of great glaciers scraped the eastern two thirds of Canada down to the primitive rock and carried the soil southward. The denuded area (the Laurentian Shield) **Canada** can never be exploited agriculturally, but it has great wealth in timber, water power, and minerals. The Maritime Provinces and a strip along the St. Lawrence yield grudging obedience to the plow, and the between-the-lakes section of Ontario is rich. These areas are not, as so many Americans think, part of the frozen north but have a climate milder than some parts of the United States south of them. The most valuable agricultural area of Canada is the semiarid wheat and cattle belt east of the Rockies in the southern parts of Alberta, Saskatchewan, and Manitoba. Fish and furs have always been important to Canada, but lumber, paper pulp, and metals are becoming more significant every year.

The territory north of the Ohio and Missouri rivers, as noted above, owes its fertility to the smoothing and mixing action of the glaciers and to their deposits of lime, iron, nitrates, and phosphates. This area, except on the western prairies, was notable for its deciduous forests **The North** and its great mineral deposits, and it is a noticeable fact that American population, agriculture, and industry are best developed there. Particularly blessed is the corn belt, which extends across the glaciated soil from Ohio to Nebraska. The corn belt attracted eastern farmers as soon as it was opened, for their lands were not only worn out but naturally poorer; the only area that could compete was the Great Valley. Glaciated soil is almost inexhaustible by cultivation, but it can be lost through erosion. In many areas it is very stony. This is particularly true in New England, where the soil is sometimes rich but where in colonial days a farmer had to spend from one to two months grubbing each acre of stones before he could plant. Even at that, each winter forced a new "crop" of stones to the surface, and these had to be removed by additional weeks of labor. The inevitable result was to discourage agriculture and turn enterprise toward the forest and the sea.

South of the glaciated regions lies a borderland that includes the southern part of the Appalachians and much of Kentucky, Tennessee, Arkansas, and Missouri. These areas include pockets of soil rich with bone- and flesh-building minerals; the areas around Nash- **The Border States** ville and Lexington, for instance, are famous for their horses. Other areas bear a climatic relationship to the Gulf Plain, and these have been strong enough to give the borderland a marked southern character. The same influence is strong in North Carolina, Virginia, and Maryland, where climate and soil suited the area to tobacco planta-

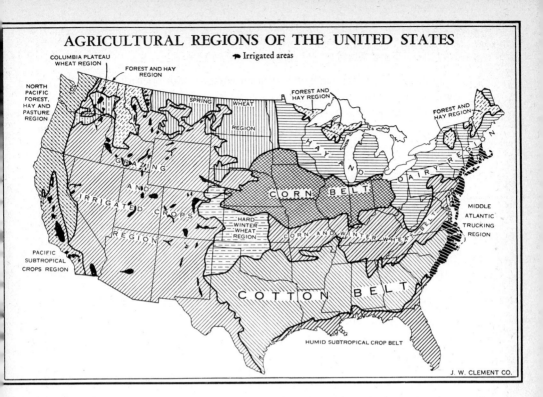

AGRICULTURAL REGIONS OF THE UNITED STATES

tions and to slavery. It was this fact that first encouraged the introduction of Negro slaves and gave us one of the two or three most fateful and unsolvable problems in our history.

The real South—often called the Deep South—includes the Gulf and southern Atlantic coastal plains and is historically marked by cotton culture. The reasons for this concentration on cotton lie in the mild climate with its long growing season and in the summer rains, for to **The South** cotton culture they are more important than the kind of soil. Southern soil, which is usually red or yellow, is rich enough, though lighter than that of the North except for the black belt of Alabama and the black waxy of Texas. The trees of the South are predominately coniferous, and in the Border States they blend into the deciduous forests of the North. Slavery was actually passing in the tobacco-planting areas when the invention of the cotton gin and the leap in the demand for cotton gave it renewed life. Slavery was profitable (at first) because cotton culture kept the workers busy so much of the year; even during the short winters they could be used to clear new land. But the very suitability of the South for cotton proved its undoing. The area has up to sixty inches of rainfall, about double that of the North; and since the ground gets no winter rest from the beating rain, the water soaks in and leaches away the chemicals and erodes the soil. The life of the soil of the South, therefore, has been limited, and this fact has had tremendous influence on American political, social, and economic history.

31

West of the 96th meridian the colonists found open plains taking the place of the forest. Indeed, grassy prairies thrust eastward between the river bottoms, chiefly through Iowa and Missouri into Illinois. The Ameri-can pioneer developed distinct techniques of exploitation as he made his way westward through one of the most bounti-fully wooded and watered areas in the world, and the open plains where trees were scarce and rainfall scanty taxed his ingenuity and were to have a profound effect in delaying the conquest of the West. In-deed, the call of the fertile Oregon valleys and of gold in the Rocky Moun-tain highlands was heeded first, and the pioneers actually closed in on the Great Plains from both east and west. The eastern plains have a broad strip of black prairie soil stretching from central Texas to northern Minnesota, with a wedge eastward through Illinois; the black so-called chernozem soil farther west, which is even richer, though less well wa-tered; and the chestnut soils just east of the Rockies. These various soils would seem to owe their properties to the types of grass they once sup-ported and to the amount of rainfall. The grass got shorter and the rain-fall scanter as one moved west.

The Great Plains

The fourth great area of the United States, the Pacific Slope, is a jumble of mountains and arid plateaus and basins, with a strip of well-watered mountains and valleys along the coast from San Francisco north-ward. In a state of nature the Rocky Mountain region is best suited to grazing, but even that has to be carefully super-vised lest overgrazing result. The mountains in the north are wooded and moist, and their drainage is being utilized in irrigation proj-ects, for the soil even of the supposed deserts is often unusually rich. The water problem does more than anything else to bind the Pacific Slope into a conscious whole. Nevertheless, the area is rich in timber and minerals, and the water problem can be solved.

The Pacific Slope

The mineral resources of the United States are unsurpassed so far as is yet known by any country except possibly the Soviet Union; even this exception is doubtful if the comparison is extended to North America and Asia. The enormous beds of bituminous coal found in the Appalachians comprise perhaps one half of the world total. Iron ore is found in many places in the East, particularly in Pennsylvania, in Michigan and Minnesota, and is being disclosed at many other places throughout the continent. Petroleum has been found chiefly in Pennsylvania, Oklahoma, Texas, and California, and other pools are known; the rate of consumption, however, may soon make us petroleum-poor. Copper is found in numerous places, chiefly Michigan, Utah, Mon-tana, and Arizona. Gold and silver occur throughout the Rocky Mountain highlands. Bauxite deposits are found in Arkansas, but of course alumi-num is present everywhere in clay and can be extracted in commercial

Mineral and power resources

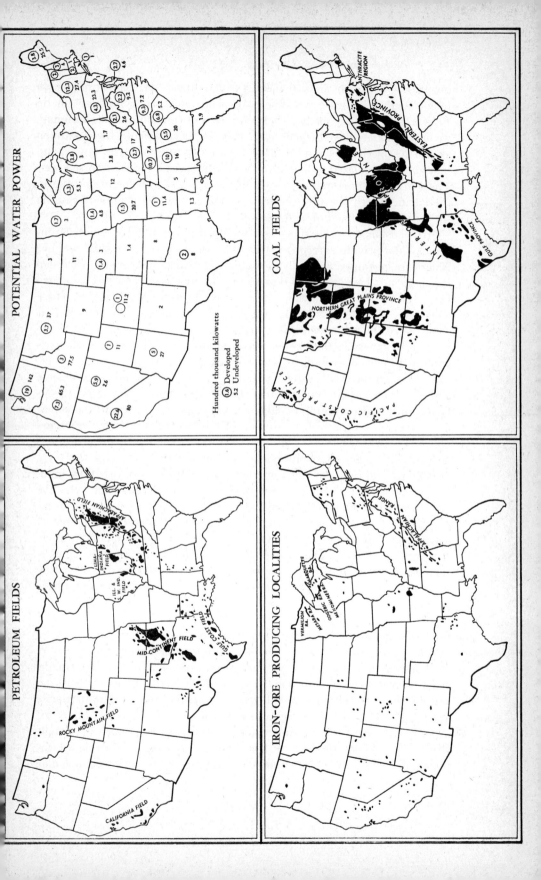

POTENTIAL WATER POWER

Hundred thousand kilowatts
- ⑯ Developed
- 5.2 Undeveloped

PETROLEUM FIELDS

APPALACHIAN FIELD
LIMA-INDIANA FIELD
ILL. & W. IND. FIELD
MID-CONTINENT FIELD
GULF COAST FIELD
ROCKY MOUNTAIN FIELD
CALIFORNIA FIELD

COAL FIELDS

ANTHRACITE REGION
EASTERN PROVINCE
INTERIOR PROVINCE
GULF PROVINCE
NORTHERN GREAT PLAINS PROVINCE
PACIFIC COAST PROVINCE

IRON-ORE PRODUCING LOCALITIES

VERMILION RA.
MESABI RA.
MARQUETTE RA.
GOGEBIC RA.
MENOMINEE RA.
APPALACHIAN RANGE

quantities; titanium, another metal extracted from clay, is of prospective importance. For nickel we have to depend on Canada, and for tin on Bolivia. Of the rarer metals, such as tungsten, vanadium, and chromium, we unfortunately have little or none. However, a continent as well watered as North America is bound to have a large potential of water power, and indeed it is calculated to have close to one hundred billions of horsepower. The coal of the East may be a rival of water power for generations, but in the Pacific Northwest the scarcity of both coal and oil is already causing the rapid development of water power.

It is customary to attribute our wealth to the stimuli of American ingenuity and private enterprise. This is a sound view, as we shall see, but American ingenuity and private enterprise would never have exceeded those of half a dozen other nations had it not been for two **Origin of U.S. wealth** advantages which it is too often the custom to ignore. These were 1) the existence of a rich continent with cream that could be readily skimmed off by the techniques of the time, and 2) the relative weakness in the United States of Federal and state governments and the absence of certain restrictive European institutions, such as mercantilism and the guild system, which strait-jacketed European commerce and manufactures. In other words, the relative lack of privileged classes (either of politics, capital, or labor) in the new continent and the superabundance of natural resources operated together to build up a social and political system which not only promoted the skimming of the cream but measured it out for a large proportion of the people.

The natural riches of the North American continent have vitally influenced American psychology. The first and most obvious effect was the growth of what Stuart Chase calls the concept of infinity. Until the verge **Concept of infinite resources** of our own century Americans were literally incapable of grasping the idea that there is any limit to our natural resources. They saw no more reason to save timber or minerals than would a gardener beside a waterfall see reason to be sparing of water. A man as cautious and observant as Jefferson thought that it would take the population sweep six centuries to reach the Pacific. Mineral and timber wealth was regarded as literally inexhaustible. The challenge to Europe's prodigal sons was irresistible. They were possessed of a furious yearning to conquer and strip Nature, to reduce it to order and usefulness.

The conquest was not easy. This generation, as it drives through the smooth green fields (say of Ohio), has no idea of the incredible toil that was necessary to fell the forest, log or burn off the trees, and to battle for **American nationalism** decades with stumps, second growth, roots, stones, and briars. We see the drama of the Cotton Kingdom which in a single generation swept from the sea islands of Georgia to the plains of Texas, or of the lumberjacks who began life in Maine and died among the Douglas firs of Puget Sound. The drama conceals the fact that failures were more numerous than successes, that fortunes gained from cotton disappeared with the leaching of the soil and the dislocations of civil war, and that fortunes skimmed off the land by lumbering disappeared into the land in fake gold mines or wildcat oil wells. These are words of warning lest we paint too rosy a picture of the conquest of the continent; yet the fact remains that fortunes were made, and they were long-lived enough to give to the generalty of Americans the hope that they could found economic dynasties, however little they had in hand at the beginning. The medieval European dreamer retired to a monastery to nurse his frustrations; he was touted by future generations as a great idealist. The American dreamer became a builder, because it was possible for him to build; his reward has been to be called a crass materialist.

One of the most curious of American phenomena is the contradiction between our ideal of thrift and our practice of waste. Actually nothing could be more natural. The ideal of thrift is hereditary, not only because Europeans lived in an economy of scarcity and had to save, **Thrift and** but because it entered into the religious teachings of Chris- **the con-** tianity, particularly Calvinism. Even more important, per- **cept of in-** haps, is the fact that developing capitalism found savings **finity** essential for the purchase of machinery, raw materials, and transportation equipment, and so glorified thrift as the road to wealth and the respect of the community. In America, however, the concept of thrift and the concept of infinite resources have been at war. Those who favored thrift found themselves undersold by those in haste to be rich. The lumberman who threw away the waste and cut down more trees underbid the lumberman who thriftily utilized the less profitable waste. The miner who skimmed off the high-grade ore undersold the one who sought to utilize the lower grades. The oil man who wished to pump slowly found that rivals sank wells near his boundaries and drained off his oil. Regulation of such wasteful methods would have seemed wise, but our Federal and state governments had been deliberately molded to prevent them from interfering with private business. The concept of infinity won. Thrift was found only in activities where cash had to be paid out for materials, and even there its hold was tenuous. Its safest retreat was found in children's copybooks.

Americans think of themselves as liberal and forward-looking. This concept is ordinarily true in the material aspects of our life, but it does not contradict the fundamental conservatism of our society. We change our machines and our style of dress more easily than our **American** mental and moral and social outlook. It is significant that **conserva-** no liberal political party has ever been able to assume power **tism** and remain liberal; our basic political rivalries have not been between conservatives and true liberals, but between conservatives and ultraconservatives. Our ancestors sensibly asked themselves why they should plump for great changes when moderate changes in the distribution of our great natural wealth would solve their problems. They preferred to use the word liberal in a nonpolitical sense as denoting tolerance, generosity, public spirit, and most of all unbounded faith in the future of America and a willingness to gamble largely on that faith. Such liberalism was justified.

Conservatism had other legitimate origins. The Calvinist point of view dominated the colonists, whatever their theology. With a continent begging to be raped they could scarcely avoid regarding themselves as chosen **Calvinistic** of God, and they desired only to be let alone to exercise the **conserva-** individual responsibility which Calvin had made the basis of **tism** his system. Calvinist standards of success could apply only to a limited few in the bitter European economic struggle, but America's riches made possible their attainment by more people. John Calvin and not Adam Smith deserves to be canonized as the patron saint of American chambers of commerce and businessmen's clubs. He it was who saw a divine order in private enterprise and individual responsibility; and if he gave the state more power than we wish, it was only in order to enforce the ascendance of those who had proved themselves worthy. The eminent Episcopal jurist John Marshall had similar ideas—and so did Quaker Herbert Hoover and Catholic Al Smith.

Our conservatism was strengthened in yet another way by our natural conditions. The isolation and insecurity of the first settlers bred within them a fierce desire to hold on to the habits and beliefs of the homeland, **Conserva-** altered only by the particular theologies or ambitions which **tism be-** had brought them to America. They clung to the moral and **cause of** emotional content of their heritage long after material con- **isolation** ditions had outmoded them, by setting up a tight little society, based upon state churches and a landed and merchant aristocracy, which attempted to enforce religious dogmas and social distinctions. They were Englishmen, and, like the proverbial Englishman on safari who dresses for dinner, they were determined to preserve the old ways. It is amazing how well they succeeded, in spirit if not in detail. Since their leaders were not noblemen but merchants and gentry, it was natural that their aristocracy was made up of merchants and gentry, but that was as far as they went willingly. The battle was joined from the beginning over the degree of change that was necessary and advisable. The defeated in any generation found it possible to move on west to new scenes where perhaps they in turn could become the successful and relatively privileged ultraconservatives.

This desperate clinging for comfort to the old ways in the midst of new conditions has accentuated the natural tendency to hold to a body of theory which is obviously contradicted by practice. On the frontier, where life was so radically different that it dissolved the social pat- **Split be-** tern into new and more democratic forms, people desperately **tween the-** sought an anchor in the religious dogmas and emotions and **ory and** the antiscientific prejudices which they had brought with **practice** them. The split between ideas and realities led to astounding illogicalities, directly traceable to wishful thinking. When morality loses vital connection with facts, there is a tendency to offer legality as a substitute. Legality becomes a matter of technical adherence to laws, while at the same time it shrewdly defies their spirit. Injustice can then be rationalized on the ground that no law is being violated.

The history of our ancestors' relations with the Indians is a case in point. The notorious Walking Purchase made in 1737 by the Penn heirs is a brilliant example. A treaty with the Delaware Indians provided that they would sell as much land as lay between the Delaware River **Rationaliz-** and a parallel line at a distance of about six miles and as **ing the In-** long as a man could walk in a day and a half. The Penns **dian prob-** proceeded to besmirch the record of their Quaker father: the **lem** route to be walked was surveyed in advance; the fastest walkers in the province were hired and succeeded in covering twice the normal distance; lastly, the fourth side of the purchase was not drawn along the shortest line to the nearest point on the Delaware but in a totally unexpected direction to a much farther point. The result was that instead of two hundred square miles the Penns took over twelve hundred, and an entire tribe of the Delaware Nation lost its home. But it was all perfectly legal.

The split between the ideal of Christianity and the reality of Indian conflict led to some colossal rationalizations. Once the whites had gained a foothold, they refused hospitality to the Indians, killed off the game, seized their land and goods, and subjected them to insult, enslavement, or slaughter. It is curious to note our ancestors' innocent astonishment and injured resentment when the Indians retaliated. Europeans regarded their status as Christians as giving them legal and moral rights to possession of heathen lands and heathen bodies, though it carried with it the corresponding duty to bring Christian enlightenment to the savages. It was typical of Anglo-Saxon legalism that English settlers (unlike those of Spain and France) were careful to purchase Indian lands. Some may have sought thus to be relieved of legal and moral responsibility for the occupants, but not all. Many New England magistrates sought to preserve the lands of such Indians as adopted Christianity and agriculture, a policy which had some resemblance to Spanish and French practice. English settlers, however, rather generally opposed assimilation of the Indians.

It may be suggested that our national wealth has frequently led us to evade our problems rather than to endeavor earnestly to solve them. We

have become the apostles of waste and superficiality because these have at
Paradox of times actually been practical, workable national programs.
waste and The consequent drain on our natural resources is viewed
democracy with alarm by an increasing number of observers. Of course,
it is easy to point to denuded and eroding hills, lowered water tables,
streams and coasts filthy with sewage and industrial waste, resources
skimmed off by reckless competition or blown up in warfare, and to the
fact that about one third of our population gets along on less than what is
usually assumed to be a decent living standard.

But what is the significance of all this? Paradoxically, it means that
for the first time in history democracy has a fighting chance to win in the
age-old battle with totalitarianism. The riches of North America bred a
society in which abundance took the place of scarcity; for the first time
privilege could not snatch all the economic power for itself and tread down
the common man. Democracy came into its own, and with it came the
atmosphere of freedom which science and technology need in order to
grow. Not only was this true in the United States, but the riches of America
operated to extend much of the same atmosphere of freedom to the remainder of Western Civilization and gave to England, the champion of
democracy, the strength to survive. Out of the blood and oppression of the
Anglo-American sweep to the Pacific and out of the rape of this splendid
continent has come the opportunity that we hold in our hands today. One
can only stand in awe before the mysterious processes of history. It is more
than mysterious—it is mystical.

3   Nature's Children

The North American Indian looked upon Nature not as an enemy to
be conquered and exploited but as a fostering mother whose laws were
to be obeyed and whose chastisements were to be borne patiently. Men
The Indian and animals alike were Nature's children; and even when
and Na- the Indian ate the animals, he was often obliged by custom
ture to preserve the bones from dishonor. His debt to animals
was never far from his mind. He traveled on trails which buffaloes had
beaten with unerring instinct by the most feasible routes across the Appalachians; he planted his corn in the "beaver meadows" formed by alluvial
deposits upstream from beaver dams; on the plains he found that the bison
was the center of life: food, clothing, shelter, and weapons. The Indian ate
bountifully when Nature provided a feast; otherwise he lived on short
commons or actually starved to death. He had little concept of how to
force Nature's hand; probably the farthest he went was to place a fish in
a hill of corn for fertilizer, or to burn away the trees in order to encourage
the grass and attract game. It was a way of life which doubtless could
have gone on indefinitely.

The Indian would seem to have emigrated from Asia across Bering Strait or along the Aleutian chain uncounted thousands of years ago. Something less than three thousand years ago there grew up the brilliant Mayan civilization of Central America, which spread to other nations and which the Spaniards found in decadent form among the Aztecs of the Valley of Mexico. On the coast of **Civilizations** Peru there existed concurrently with the Mayas a series of pre-Incan civilizations, which also the Spaniards found in decadent form among the Incas of the Andes. There was interchange between Mexico and Peru across a bridge of scarcely less brilliant cultures, which in some cases found

An early representation of natives of the New World, probably issued in Augsburg around 1500

separate existence as Spanish provinces and as modern nations. Advanced as these cultures were, they did not possess the wheel, the arch, and the ship; they had no draft animals, and among metals worked only copper, gold, silver, and occasionally platinum and the alloy bronze. Nevertheless they became exploiters of Nature, and the results of their ruthlessness can be seen today in the denuded and eroding hills of Mexico and Peru, and in other parts reclaimed by the jungle. Their cities returned to the desert or jungle, their delicate gold and silver ornaments were melted down into bullion, and their arts, customs, and religions survive only in decadent forms and are subject to an alien culture.

Yet, curiously enough in the eyes of the lordly white man, these peoples were among the greatest benefactors of modern civilization. The American Indian gave to the world about thirty important products which

Agriculture today yield about five sevenths of the world's agricultural wealth. Among these are corn, white and sweet potatoes, tobacco, tomatoes, peanuts, pineapples, cacao (chocolate), several valuable varieties of beans and squash, and the most useful varieties of cotton plants and rubber trees. It is worthy of note that most American products were raised in hills, not sown broadcast as were European grain crops. The American Indian had neither the plow nor a draft animal to pull it; so he was forced to specialize in crops which could be planted in a hole dug among the trees or the grass by a hoe, spade, or digging stick. As the dirt was mounded about the plant, the beating American rains could get in their eroding work.

Indian corn has become a staple crop in Africa and India but has never flourished far north of the Mediterranean because the climate does not afford the hot nights which corn requires for growth. It is known abroad

Indian corn by a variety of names: maize, mealies, Syrian durra, Turkish wheat, Egyptian corn, and Spanish corn. Corn is an artificial development so highly domesticated that it will not grow wild. Presumably it came originally from a grass which grew a seed in a pod, but botanists differ as to whether it was developed in the Mayan or Incan areas, and the wild ancestor has not yet been located with certainty. At any rate, the Indians carried corn to a state of development remarkable for its variety—flint corn, dent, meal, sweet corn, and popcorn; ears ranging from thumb size to three feet in length; grains smaller than wheat to those an inch in diameter; stalks knee-high and those triple the height of a man; growing seasons that require anywhere from two to eleven months to mature; and grains that are white, black, yellow, red, blue, pink, brown, or parti-colored in spots, bands, and stripes. The white botanist, in fact, has been able to make no fundamental improvement in corn culture until the very recent development of hybrid strains. Corn is useful not only directly as human food but as a source of oil, sugar, starch, and alcohol, and particularly as an unexcelled fattener for swine and beef cattle.

The spread of corn culture is one of the fundamental factors in the development of New World societies, for where it appeared it had a tendency to tie down the wandering savage tribes and gradually raise them to

Spread of corn culture the stage of barbarism. Corn was raised almost everywhere in South America except in the moist Amazon lowlands (where manioc took its place) and on the pampas of the Argentine. Corn was probably introduced into the eastern United States by immigrants from Mexico, probably ancestors of the mysterious Mound

Builders, who lived chiefly in the region between the Great Lakes and the Ohio. Their influence on the savage aborigines was marked even though the civilizers ceased separate existence by the time of the coming of the white man, except for the sun-worshiping Natchez, who were massacred or scattered by the French in a series of wars after 1716. Another bequest of Mexico was the institution of the sacred fire, found among many of the maize growers and vaguely connected with sun worship.

It is worth while to repeat in connection with the Indians of the United States (particularly those of the East) that they distinctly were not savages but barbarians. They possessed rich and flexible languages (about three hundred of them) capable of indefinite expansion with **Indians of** cultural growth; they were not nomadic but possessed fairly **the United** well-defined national boundaries; and they kept elabo- **States** rate public records by memorization aided by designs in wampum. Anatomically the Indians differed as markedly among themselves as do white men. In general, however, they were broad-faced, copper-skinned, and had straight black hair and brown eyes. Their number in 1492 will never be known, but the best guess is that north of Mexico it was somewhat less than one million.

North American Indians are divided into linguistic stocks too numerous to be recited here in detail. Only four will be mentioned. Most advanced culturally were the Muskhogee of the Gulf States. These were the so-called Civilized Nations, and they included the **Four great** Creeks (with the Creek offshoot, the Seminole), the Choc- **Indian** taw, and the Chickasaw. They adopted European grains, **families** fruits, and stock with alacrity and by 1800 were probably as high in the scale of civilization as many of the whites who supplanted them.

In the lower Appalachians were the Cherokee, usually counted among the Civilized Nations but actually a detached nation of Iroquoian stock. The Iroquoian nations completely surrounded Lakes Erie and Ontario and occupied most of the present states of New York and Pennsylvania. Siouan nations, particularly the Catawba, were wedged in between the Muskhogee and the northern Iroquois and stretched west of the Mississippi from the Arkansas River northward; they appear in history as the Osage, the Iowa, the Winnebago, the Mandan, the Crows, and of course the Sioux. All around the northern Iroquois and considerably mixed with other elements were the Algonquins. They included all of the New England nations, and in addition the historic Delawares, Shawnee, Illini, Miami, Fox, Ottawa, Chippewa (or Ojibway), Blackfeet, and Cheyenne. What follows is chiefly descriptive of the Eastern, or Woods, Indians.

The term tribe as it is used in connection with the political organization of the Indians might better be replaced by nation. That is, each linguistic group was composed of nations just as truly as we have English-

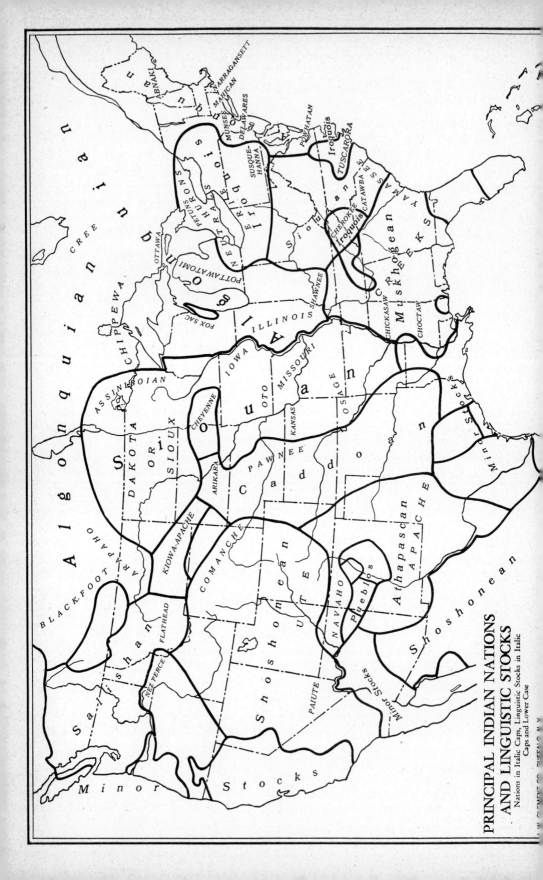

PRINCIPAL INDIAN NATIONS
AND LINGUISTIC STOCKS

Nations in Italic Caps, Linguistic Stocks in Italic
Caps and Lower Case

speaking nations. It was common, especially among the **Organization** Muskhogee and Iroquois, for the nations to form confederacies (such as the Creek, Choctaw, Chickasaw, Huron, and Five Nations), but these never included all the nations of the same linguistic stock and were often at enmity with their kin. Below the nation

was usually the phratry, a social and ceremonial division usually without civil functions. Below the phratry was the clan, or totem, the basic social and political unit, intermediate between the individual and the nation. The members of the clans ordinarily regarded themselves as having a common descent from an ancestor whose creator or patron spirit was a certain animal-like being; descent, however, was through the mother, for the father was always a member of another totem.

A Sioux totem

The government of the Indian clans was by councils, usually attended by both men and women. Sachems were the civil governors and judges of the clans and represented the clans in the national councils, of which women were not members; chiefs were the military leaders. Both sachems and chiefs were elected and were chosen for personal qualities, though descent from illustrious an- **Government** cestors was an advantage to an aspirant. Practically all official meetings were accompanied by ritual dances. Democracy was carried so far that any member of the nation could dissociate himself from the general decision and go his own way. White men did not understand the Indian political system and so interpreted it in Western European terms. Thus Powhatan became an emperor, and his daughter Pocahontas a princess. An amusing illustration of white misunderstanding is found in the fact that James I censured John Rolfe for marrying into a royal family without his consent and left Rolfe in the gallery with the commoners while Pocahontas was introduced to court society. Even when the whites came to understand the true functions of chiefs and sachems, they deliberately picked out certain complaisant individuals to represent the Indians and bribed and flattered them in order to be able to manage them and thus give a color of legality to their swindles. In this way chiefs came to exercise personal power which was quite undreamed of before the coming of the whites.

Land did not belong permanently to the individual but to the clan; indeed, the Indian proved to be incapable of understanding the European institution of individual ownership of land. National or totem areas were more or less defined, and the holders hunted and cultivated within them. Village holdings were ordinarily cultivated **Land** in common, and crops were divided by customary rules. **tenure**

When the soil and firewood were exhausted, the villagers moved. Families or groups of relatives sometimes took up garden plots at some distance from village social centers; the occupants claimed the land, but the claim lapsed when they moved. The closest thing to soil ownership was found in arid regions, where generation after generation tilled the same fields.

The Indian was an animist; that is, he believed in magic powers which dwelt in or were protectors of animals, objects, or men. It is said that only occasionally, and then probably after contact with whites, did he ap-

Religion proach the concept of a Great Spirit. Spirits did not possess moral qualities; but because they could be benevolent or vindictive, he sought to retain their goodwill by prayers, incantations, dances, sacrifices, ordeals, or by observing taboos on certain foods and actions. Life after death was not concerned

A Huron totem

with reward and punishment but was vaguely conceived as passed in a happy hunting ground in company with the culture-hero who had founded the nation or taught it various skills. Religious rituals were in charge of priests, but almost as important and sometimes identical were the shamans (medicine men), who claimed to have power over the spirits and ability to foresee and influence events. Since illness was caused by spirits, the shamans also doubled as doctors; the methods of cure varied from outright hocus-pocus to a sound pharmacopeia of herbal remedies. An integral part of Indian life was the mystic lodge or fraternity, which sometimes adopted complicated rituals often built about the sacred calumet pipe. The decoration and manner of smoking of the calumet pipe also played a large part in the preliminaries of war and peace.

The economy of the Indian of the eastern United States was mixed. He was a hunter and fisherman, but the necessity of tending the fields forced him to live a settled life in one locality, varied only by fall or

Indian economy winter hunts and by removes to new garden and hunting areas. Until the white man arrived his tools and weapons were of wood, stone, and bone, occasionally of copper; the only domesticated animal was the dog; he traveled on foot or in a canoe made of bark or hollowed out of a log. Pottery making was widely practiced, but the products were inferior. Other utensils were made of gourds, basketry, or hollowed-out wood. Clothing was made from deerskin, furs, and woven hair, vegetable fiber, or bast. Fleas were such a plague as sometimes to force the removal of villages. Soap and cleaning fluid were unknown, but then soap was none too plentiful even in Europe, nor was its use favored even in élite circles. The division of labor between the sexes was not unfair: women performed household and agricultural duties; the men made tools, utensils, weapons, aided in erecting houses and sometimes in making clothing, undertook the arduous duties of hunting and fighting, and memorized an astonishing bulk of public records and rituals. Dwellings varied with season, custom, and materials available. Common types were made of logs or poles covered with either a gable or a barrel-vaulted roof and overlaid with bark. Common among the Algonquins was the wigwam, a domelike structure of saplings covered with bark, mats, or wattle. The nations of the Great Plains lived in conical tepees of hide, or in dome-shaped huts covered with grass, hides, or earth. It was common for villages to be surrounded by log palisades.

Trade between nations was of course common in the more obvious articles of cornmeal, salt, tobacco, skins, furs, rugs, and mats. Certain nations were able to make a good thing of their control of copper workings or beds of superior flint, obsidian, or bright-colored clays useful as paints. Skills such as those involved in mak- **Trade and** ing wampum beads from sea shells or drilling and finishing **wampum** calumet pipes were well paid. Other articles of trade were ornaments of alluvial gold, medicinal roots and herbs, and oil of nuts or sunflower seeds. The commonly accepted medium of exchange was wampum beads, valued according to their color and finish; the natural colors were white and a dark blue, but sometimes the beads were dyed red. They were universally used for adornment and badges of rank, and in the form of strings and belts they were a necessary ceremonial accompaniment of international councils; the strings of red beads were used in declaring war, the white beads in negotiating peace, and the dark beads in expressing sorrow. The national treasuries consisted of wampum and at the same time composed to the initiated a sort of national archives.

Before the coming of the white man Indian warfare amounted to little more than a hazardous sport except, of course, when great folk movements or scarcity of game gave it a serious aspect. A stone-age battle was ordinarily a short exercise in which bands of painted enemies fought for a while, then withdrew with a few prisoners; **Warfare** perhaps even more often warfare consisted of a night raid on a rival village. Indians regarded it as foolish to fight unless the odds were stacked in their favor. Reverses or bad omens quickly discouraged them, and individualism was so ingrained that such warriors as chose were perfectly entitled to go home. In all the annals of Indian warfare there are records of only a few protracted sieges of fortified places.

Prisoners were usually adopted, but occasionally they were tortured or burned in a ceremony that was semireligious in nature. The brave who stood torture stoutly might have his heart eaten in the belief that it

Prisoners and trophies would give the eater courage, but cannibalism was not a common practice. It would seem that at one time heads were taken as trophies, but by 1400 this practice had degenerated into scalping. The process was painful and disruptive of the victim's beauty but not necessarily fatal; legend says that one time in the West there existed a Society of Indian Scalpees. When the white man appeared, scalping was apparently practiced only in the Appalachian region; the spread of the custom is said to have been due to the scalp bounties offered by white governors. Before being horrified at Indian tortures it is salutary to remember that at the time torture and burning at the stake were common in Europe—not necessarily for prisoners of war but for one's fellow citizens with whom one disagreed—and that the Indians' resources in the technology of torture paled beside those available to the more ingenious European "questioner."

The wars caused by trade rivalries introduced and promoted by whites were fought with a cruelty and bitterness that probably did not exist before. Widespread burning, scalping, and killing became the order of Indian **White effect on warfare** warfare, but in this the Indians only did as the white men. It is worth noting that there are numerous accounts of white captivities and escapes, but only a handful of Indians who were captives escaped; the reason is that after the whites found that Indians made poor slaves, they simply slaughtered their captives.

The character of the Indian was originally quite different from that portrayed by the white encroachers. To members of his own nation he was honest, truthful, kind to children and old people, hospitable to a fault, **Character** and tolerant of others' opinions. He knew how to relax, but he also could undergo tremendous hardship and fatigue. Though naturally nervous, excitable, and talkative, etiquette bade silence and dignity on ceremonial occasions; anyhow, who would wear his heart on his sleeve in the presence of the race which hated and despised him and sought to rob him of everything he had? The same man might howl dolefully over a bruised thumb but bear torture and fire without flinching or groaning.

The great weaknesses of the Indian, as with any barbarian, were his cupidity and his vengefulness; they lessened his self-control and good sense, divided nations and confederacies, set nation against nation, and made the Indian the easy victim of the plots which the white man wove to spread dissension. Add to these, however, the shortsightedness common to peoples who depend on Nature's bounty. The picture of the Indian that has come down to us was drawn after the Indian virtues had been undermined by the alcohol, diseases, and oppression of the whites. It is true that by the *best* white standards Indians were dirty, uncouth, thievish, treacherous, lazy, and drunken, but the men who accused them were often no better and, moreover, did their best to promote viciousness among the Indians for reasons of their own. In commenting on the Greek story of Œdipus, Gilbert Murray has this to say: "Unnatural affection, child-murder, father-murder, incest, a great deal of hereditary cursing, a doubtful fratricide and a violation of the sanctity of dead bodies—when one reads such a list of charges brought against any tribe or people, either in ancient or in modern times, one can hardly help concluding that somebody wanted to annex their land."

BIBLIOGRAPHICAL NOTE

Geographical Influences in American History

The geographic aspects of the continent are best presented in J. R. Smith and M. O. Phillips, *North America* (3rd ed., 1942). History and geography are linked by Ralph H. Brown, *Historical Geography of the U.S.* (1948); and Ellen C. Semple and Clarence F. Jones, *American History and Its Geographic Conditions* (1933).

Nature's Children

The last quotation appears in James T. Adams, *Founding of New England* (1921), 14–15. Paul Radin, *The Story of the American Indian* (1927) analyzes culture patterns of both the Americas and traces their spread. For the Indian background see Clark Wissler, *The American Indian* (3rd ed., 1938); and Livingston Farrand, *Basis of American History* (1904). Most of the original accounts of Indian customs have long been out of print, but see the old but useful Frederick W. Hodge, *Handbook of American Indians* (2 v., 1907–10); John Heckewelder, *Indian Nations* (1876); David Zeisberger, "Northern American Indians" in *Ohio Archaeological and Historical Quarterly,* 19:1–173 (January and April 1910); Henry R. Schoolcraft, *The Indian Tribes* (6 v., 1851–57); Lewis H. Morgan, *League of the Iroquois* (1851, new ed., 1904); and Edna Kenton, *The Indians of North America* (2 v., 1927), a condensation of R. G. Thwaites's monumental *Jesuit Relations*. A diffuse but very useful summary of race relations appears in William C. Macleod, *The American Indian Frontier* (1928).

Chapter II

THE CONFLICT
FOR THE NEW WORLD

1 *Mundus Novus*

IT WAS no accident that Portugal and Spain were the first European nations to embark on overseas imperialism. Their long wars with the Moslem invaders of the Hispanic Peninsula early forced them to build up
Portugal's   fleets for protection against their seafaring enemies, and it
African   was easy to pass to a brisk trade in wine, olive oil, cork, and
ventures   hides. In 1341 Italian navigators in the service of Portugal
visited the Canaries, and the Madeiras and the Azores were discovered or rediscovered within the next century. Such expeditions had by 1415 inspired Portugal's Prince Henry the Navigator to begin sending out an annual succession of ships to explore the African coast and trade. Henry now established himself at Cape St. Vincent and set up a school of navigation staffed by the best technical brains that Europe afforded. The result was seen in the next century, when Portuguese navigators were acknowledged to be the best in the world.

Though Henry's African ventures resulted in an important trade in ivory, gold, and Negro slaves, his primary objective was to find a new route to the East. He may have planned to cut Portugal into the Italian spice trade, but it is more certain that in true medieval fashion he hoped to find the Christian kingdom of Prester John (perhaps Abyssinia) and join forces in a crusade to expel the Moslems from the Holy Land. By the time of Henry's death in 1460 his ships had crept down the African coast beyond the Cape Verde Islands to the Guinea coast. Finally, probably in 1488, Bartholomew Dias passed the Cape of Good Hope and found that the coast of Africa definitely trended northward. The route to India was now clear.

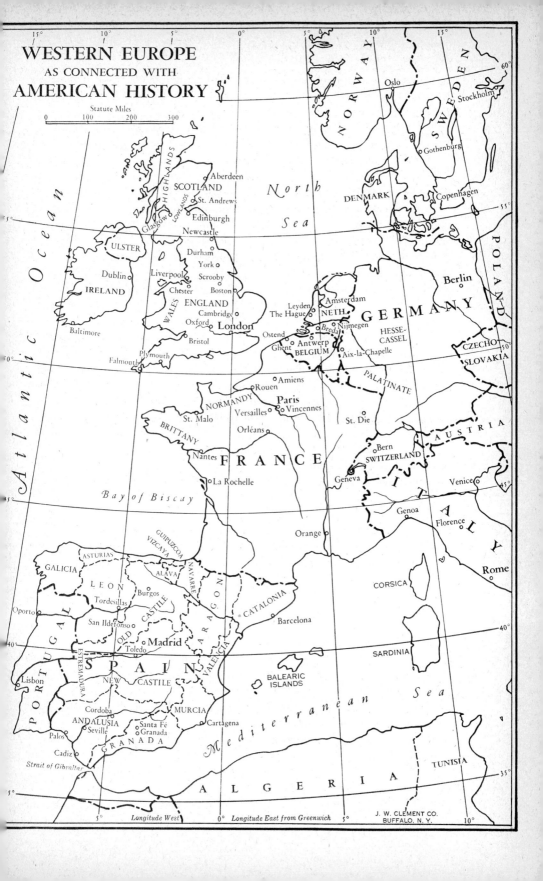

WESTERN EUROPE
AS CONNECTED WITH
AMERICAN HISTORY

Statute Miles
0   100   200   300

Atlantic Ocean

HIGHLANDS
SCOTLAND
Aberdeen
St. Andrews
LOWLANDS
Glasgow
Edinburgh
Newcastle

ULSTER
Durham
York
Dublin
Liverpool
Scrooby
Chester
Boston
IRELAND
WALES
ENGLAND
Cambridge
Baltimore
Oxford
London
Bristol
Plymouth
Falmouth

North Sea

NORWAY
Oslo
SWEDEN
Stockholm
Gothenburg
DENMARK
Copenhagen
POLAND

Leyden
Amsterdam
The Hague
NETH.
Breda
Nijmegen
Ostend
Antwerp
Ghent
BELGIUM
Aix-la-Chapelle

Berlin
GERMANY
HESSE-CASSEL
CZECHO-SLOVAKIA
PALATINATE

Amiens
Rouen
NORMANDY
Paris
St. Malo
Versailles
Vincennes
Orléans
St. Die
BRITTANY
FRANCE
AUSTRIA
Nantes
Bern
SWITZERLAND
La Rochelle
Geneva
Venice

Bay of Biscay

Orange
Genoa
Florence
ITALY
Rome

GUIPUZCOA
VIZCAYA
ASTURIAS
GALICIA
NAVARRE
ALAVA
LEON
ARAGON
Burgos
CASTILE
Tordesillas
CATALONIA
Barcelona
Oporto
PORTUGAL
San Ildefonso
OLD
Madrid
Toledo
NEW
CASTILE
Lisbon
ESTREMADURA
VALENCIA
SPAIN
CORSICA
SARDINIA

BALEARIC ISLANDS

Cordoba
MURCIA
ANDALUSIA
Santa Fé
Seville
Granada
Cartagena
GRANADA
Palos
Cadiz
Strait of Gibraltar

Mediterranean Sea

ALGERIA
TUNISIA

Longitude West   0°   Longitude East from Greenwich

J. W. CLEMENT CO.
BUFFALO, N. Y.

Among the galaxy of navigators at the Portuguese court, or at least in Lisbon, was the Genoese Cristoforo Colombo, or Christopher Columbus. Born probably about 1446, he had spent years in Genoese and Portuguese

Christopher Columbus (1446?–1506)

ships and had traveled south to Guinea and probably as far north as Iceland. It is likely that the circumstances of Columbus's life and voyages will always be a subject of dispute. The version usually accepted is that Columbus early formed the ambition to discover the Indies by sailing west, and he may have been encouraged in this desire not only by scientific opinion and tales of shadowy western islands but by more circumstantial knowledge. Although he seems from the first to have regarded himself as a man of destiny, Columbus was one of the most obscure among the navigators who swarmed in Lisbon, and possibly not notably proficient in comparison to the men who had gone to Henry the Navigator's school. When he finally obtained a chance to lay his plan before King John II, it appears that he may have ruined whatever chance he had by what were regarded as exorbitant demands for profit and power over the lands he might discover.

About 1484 Columbus appeared in Spain, where he was to win immortality as Cristóbal Colón. Though it was not immediately apparent, he had arrived in an auspicious era. The Spanish kingdoms after centuries of

Columbus obtains Spanish support

conflict with the Moors were at last united in Aragon and Castile; and their monarchs, Ferdinand and Isabella, had provided for the union of these two crowns in their descendants. Now they were engaged in the conquest of Granada, the last Moorish foothold in Spain. The two rulers gave Columbus a little cautious encouragement, and for years he waited, living from hand to mouth and turning prematurely old. At last in 1492 Granada fell. Isabella listened to the importunate Genoese again and agreed to support his voyage of discovery. At the last moment the intemperate Columbus almost spoiled his chances: he demanded to be made a knight, don, admiral of Castile, viceroy of any lands he might discover, and owner of one tenth of their wealth. Isabella turned him down, then changed her mind.

That August Columbus left Palos with three tiny caravels, the *Niña*, *Pinta,* and *Santa María,* and headed for the Canaries, in the belief that they lay about twenty-five hundred miles due east of the Indies. The full

Discovery of America

and true story of the voyage will never be known, for only extracts of Columbus's journal have survived. There was danger of mutiny, but the admiral faced it down and pointed to increasing signs of land. The night of the very next day Columbus himself saw a light like a "wax candle rising and falling"; and the next morning, 12 October 1492, a landing was made on an island of the Bahamas which Columbus named San Salvador. Probably it was the island now called Watling.

Columbus envisioned an earth about one fourth smaller in circumference and with the Americas completely lacking. He supposed that he had, by sailing west, bumped into the screen of islands off the coast of Asia; and he died in the belief that with a little better luck he **America** could have found the Strait of Malacca and sailed into the **supposed to** Indian Ocean. Even when he later discovered South Amer- **be the** ica he believed it to be about where Australia actually is. But **Indies** for the moment he was completely happy. As he "discovered" along the coasts of Cuba and Santo Domingo (long known as Española), the report

A woodcut from Columbus's *La Lettera dell'isole,* published in 1493, shows Ferdinand on the European shore and Columbus landing on the New World shore of the ocean

he wrote for Ferdinand and Isabella foreshadowed the threefold nature of Spanish exploitation: conversion, gold, and slavery; for he found a swarming population of merry, dark-skinned innocents, whom he naturally called Indians and whom he wrote down as suitable for conversion to the Christian faith and for use as slaves on the plantations and in the gold mines which he felt sure would soon come into existence. On Christmas Day the largest vessel, the *Santa María,* ran aground on the north shore of Santo

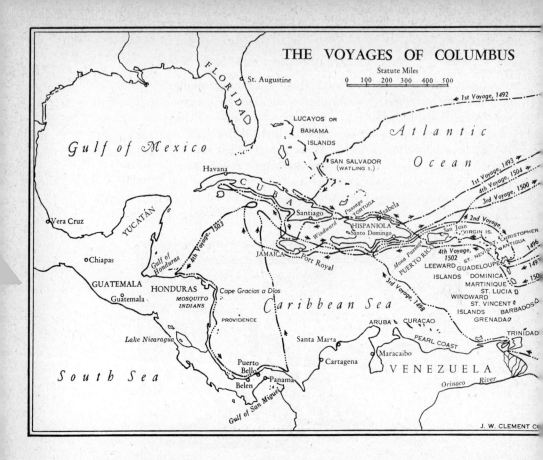

THE VOYAGES OF COLUMBUS

Domingo; at this point Columbus built a fort and left forty men as colonists, then departed for Spain.

His reception was all that could have been asked. The wonders of the Indies lost nothing in the telling, and enthusiastic adventurers flocked to join the second expedition, which left in September 1493. After a lei-

Beginning of Spanish settlement

surely cruise along the Lesser Antilles Columbus arrived at the site of his colony, only to discover that the men had been massacred as the result of their rapacity. The city of Isabela was founded farther east along the same coast, and immediate search for gold was begun. Famine and sickness soon appeared, and Spanish extortion led to "rebellion" among the Indians. Columbus fluctuated between extremes of lenience and brutality and proved utterly incapable of governing the hardheaded, individualistic Spaniards. In 1496 he returned to Spain to defend his actions, abased himself before the king and queen in the humble garb of a Franciscan friar, and was triumphantly reinstated in the royal favor.

His third voyage, in 1498, led him to the mouth of the Orinoco, flowing from the depths of a great continent. Meanwhile Columbus's brother, Bartholomew, had moved the colonial capital to the south coast of Hispaniola to a new city which he named Santo Domingo, to be near the gold mines which had at last been discovered. They proved to be a disappointment, and this added to the colonists' resentment at the Columbus brothers' caprice and oppression. In the end a new governor came out from Spain, and Christopher was shipped home in chains. He was stripped of his power to govern, but not of his share of profits, and was allowed to go on a fourth voyage. In 1502 he sailed along the coast of Central America, which another voyager, Bastidas, had visited a year before. He died in 1506 of disease, premature senility, and a broken heart.

Later voyages

Up to that time the importance of Columbus's discovery was not evident, and his islands were called "false and deceitful countries, the ruination and sepulcher of Spanish gentlemen." The disappointment was all the greater to Spain because in 1499 Vasco da Gama returned from a voyage to India which gave promise of diverting the spice trade from the Italian cities to Lisbon. In view of the weakness of Portugal it is all the more remarkable that a succession of great captains in a single decade actually subjugated the coasts around the Indian Ocean from East Africa to the Strait of Malacca; they then proceeded through the strait to the authentic Spice Islands, to China, and by 1542 to Japan. The exploits of this handful of men pitted against the armies and navies of an old and powerful civilization make the conquests of Cortes and Pizarro seem paltry. The élan of the Portuguese, served as it was by better artillery and better ships than the Orientals possessed, imposed a commercial sway which was not shaken for a hundred years.

Portugal in the Orient

Upon Columbus's return from his first voyage the Portuguese court, with some measure of plausibility, prepared an expedition to seize the new islands as a part of the Azores. Ferdinand in alarm secretly besought Pope Alexander VI for a bull awarding the discoveries of Columbus to Spain. Alexander, a Spaniard, complied readily, but Portugal's threats eventually forced Ferdinand to agree to set the division line at a point 370 leagues west of the Cape Verde Islands; this was by the Treaty of Tordesillas, 7 June 1494. The length of the league used was not specified, nor was the particular island from which the distance was to be calculated.

Demarcation Line

That Brazil was known to John II during these negotiations is believed implicitly in Portugal and Brazil. There is nothing inherently improbable in the theory. All maritime countries strove to keep their secrets. Logs, reports, and navigating instructions were rigorously impounded, charts were guarded zealously, and many historical accounts were truncated or destroyed. The inevitable result was that the maritime service of each nation strove to entice pilots and captains from the service of its rivals and often paid them handsome

"Secret" voyages

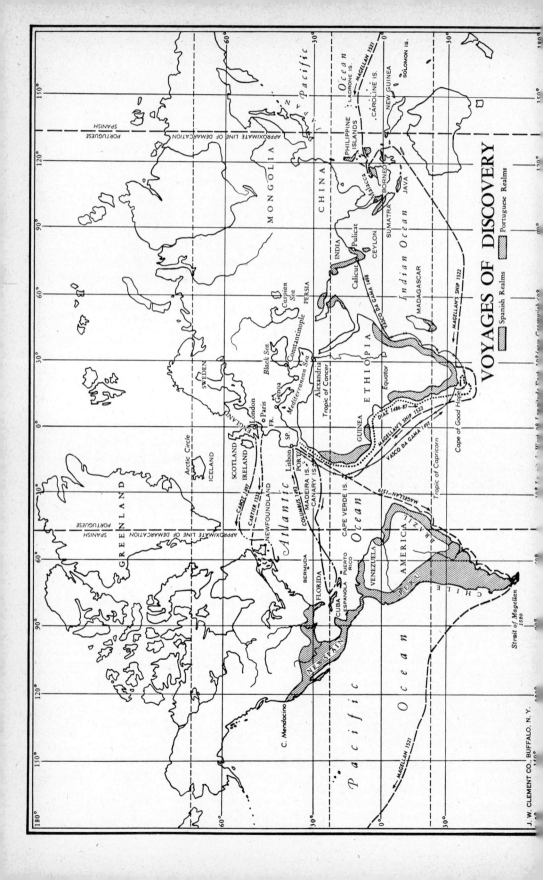

VOYAGES OF DISCOVERY

Spanish Realms

Portuguese Realms

salaries, not so much for their skill as for a chance to pick their brains.

Even at best, maps were far from accurate, for astronomical instruments and geographical measurements were faulty. The compass and the astrolabe (later the quadrant) were the chief navigational reliances until 1730. It was possible to arrive at the latitude with fair ac- **Difficulties** curacy, but the longitude was based on the roughest kind **of naviga-** of calculations of the sailing rate. The result was that **tion** with variations in winds and currents navigators were sometimes off as much as two thousand miles in crossing the Pacific. It was not until the 1730's that the chronometer made it possible to calculate the longitude, and at the same time the sextant improved the calculations of latitudes.

Spanish ignorance of the geography of the East was profound, for the Portuguese were quite successful in concealing all but the broad facts of their discoveries. Thus, for a generation Spanish conquistadors toiled through swamp and forest seeking the golden cities of Marco **Slow prog-** Polo; near the crest of every new mountain they hastened **ress of dis-** their steps, eager to be first to catch sight of the great city **covery** of Quinsay or of the Yellow River. The masters of caravels who passed beyond the last familiar cape scanned the waters hopefully for the spicy Moluccas or at least for the junks of the China coast. Knowledge was gained slowly and painfully. Explorers were down uncomfortably close to the water and had no telescopes. With their vision limited to a few miles, they easily confused islands and peninsulas and because of their crude instruments never knew their precise latitude and longitude. They could not sail boldly along the coast until they found what they wanted, for freakish winds and treacherous currents might easily have driven their frail ships aground. Moreover, their chief object of search was gold, and this necessitated slow investigation and oftentimes hard fighting with the Indians. In addition to this the ships of the sixteenth century were too cramped to carry many supplies and had frequently to return to base; long voyages were almost invariably hampered by foul water and spoiled food, and usually by scurvy and eventually semistarvation.

A conventional map of the fifteenth century

Nevertheless, to judge by surviving maps and records of voyages, enthusiastic navigators, chiefly Portuguese and Spanish, had ranged so widely along the Atlantic coasts from Labrador to the Rio de la Plata that

Age of the conquistadors the eastern outlines of both North and South America were known before the death of Columbus in 1506. The more complicated central portion was explored more slowly. Balboa's discovery in 1513 that a "South Sea" lay beyond the isthmus of Darién was of unique importance. Spanish ships were soon nosing into the bays along the west coast, though Pizarro's conquest of Peru did not begin until 1531 and that of Chile even later. Conquistadors moving across the Andes met others advancing up the Rio de la Plata and the Paraná and conquered the pampas of Argentina. Colombia with its heaps of golden ornaments fell to Quesada in 1536.

Meanwhile in Mexico Cortes had in 1519 begun the conquest of the first great Spanish treasure, and his captains and successors roamed the jungles of Central America and the northern plains in search of more magic cities to conquer. Ponce de León sought the "Fountain of Youth" in Florida as early as 1513 but failed to find it or to plant a colony. In 1526 Ayllón started a settlement in South Carolina but died after two years, and the survivors gave up. Hernando de Soto led a magnificent expedition to Florida which between 1539 and 1543 wandered as far north as Missouri; in the end he was buried in the Mississippi, which he had discovered, and a miserable remnant of his men reached Mexico. In 1540 Coronado discovered the Zuñi pueblos and wandered across the plains as far as Kansas. It was apparent that no more golden cities lay in the North.

Meanwhile the picture of the world was changed by a dramatic voyage. The skilled Portuguese cosmographers began to suspect that Portuguese and Spaniards were exploiting entirely different areas of the globe and

Magellan's voyage suggested that Balboa's South Sea was not one of the island-girt seas off the coast of Asia but an ocean which lay between the Indies of Columbus and the Indies of Portugal. A Portuguese navigator named Ferdinand Magellan, or Fernão da Magalhães, who had served in the East Indies, became convinced that there was a water route *westward* to the Indies. Magellan proposed to prove his contention by passing through the strait which rumor said lay south of Brazil and sailing across the new ocean to the Moluccas. When Portugal rejected his plan, he moved to Spain and convinced Charles v that the line drawn at the Treaty of Tordesillas when extended to the Orient would give him possession of China and the Moluccas. This reasoning was an error, though by a compromise Spain did eventually get the Philippine Islands. Magellan began his historic voyage in 1519 with the sole purpose of reaching the Moluccas, and it was only after his death in the Philippines that one of his captains decided to return to Spain by sailing on around the earth. At any rate, Magellan deserves the credit for proving at last that Columbus had not discovered Asia, but a new continent. The finishing touch, however, was not laid until 1728, when Bering proved that a strait lay between Asia and America.

The discovery of America seems to have made little impression on the European public until the sixteenth century was almost half gone. Indeed, most contemporary chroniclers failed to mention the discovery, though a letter of Columbus had appeared in print in 1493 and had been turned into rhyme and was being sung in the **The New** streets of Florence. Learned men, however, were interested. **World** Peter Martyr, an Italo-Spanish diplomat and bureaucrat who was to become prominent in the government of Spanish America, hailed Columbus in 1493 as the discoverer of *Mundus Novus,* "a new world." Columbus himself was convinced at the mouth of the Orinoco that he had discovered a veritable New World not connected with Asia. This continent, however, by a peculiar circumstance was not fated to bear his name.

A Florentine navigator and ship chandler named Amerigo Vespucci appeared in Spain about 1490 on business for the Medici, the great banking family which ruled Florence. Successively in the service of Spain and Portugal, Vespucci made several voyages to the new lands. **Amerigo** The surviving accounts which he wrote were letters to per- **Vespucci** sonal friends and were, it would seem, incomplete, mangled, **(1451–** or filled with lies—critics still differ. At any rate he seems to **1512)** have claimed to have accompanied a Spanish expedition which touched on the Orinoco coast in 1497, the year before Columbus appeared there. Vespucci also claimed to have accompanied a Portuguese expedition to Brazil in 1501, and he spoke of the regions he found "which may be called a new world since among our ancestors there was no knowledge of them."

In the year 1507 a printed copy of the French edition of a Vespucci letter which told the story of his "four voyages" fell into the hands of a little group of scholars in the College of Saint-Dié in Lorraine. They translated it into Latin and together with an introduction **America** issued it as a pamphlet. The introduction was the work of a **named for** young geographer of twenty-three, Martin Waldseemüller, **Amerigo** who proposed that since Amerigo (Americus in Latin) had discovered a fourth part of the world—after Europe, Asia, and Africa—it should be named America for him. At the same time Waldseemüller issued a map of the world on which he placed the word *America* behind the Brazilian coast.

The name America had scarcely begun to win acceptance when there began to be complaints not only that Amerigo Vespucci did not deserve this commemoration but that he had deliberately sought it. The accusations have been almost universally accepted, and the consensus seems to be that Vespucci was a rascal who stole another man's laurels. However, the name was first given to Brazil only, and he may never have known of the action. The name was extended northward (apparently first in Mercator's map of 1541) only after Vespucci's death, and the terms North America and South America were not accepted until the seventeenth century.

The Age of the Conquistadors lasted less than a single lifetime from the discovery. By 1550 the conquistadors had laid at the feet of their sovereigns a vast continent and had placed on it from Mexico to Pata-

Passing of the conquistadors

gonia a stamp that will never be erased. It was as though the English in the half-century after Jamestown had explored the entire North American continent, founded all its great cities, and opened all its gold and silver mines. The conquistadors were men with special aptitudes—heroic, inured to hardship, rash but indomitable, and often with a winning naïvety and manly sentimentality.

If the conquistadors ever had dreams of setting up independent empires, those dreams came to nothing. No important leader failed to be supplanted by a royal administrator, tried in service, dry in personality, expert in detecting any menace to the royal prerogatives, and usually old in years. Thereafter the penetration of the New World was an authoritarian enterprise checked by the king as carefully as distance permitted. The cruelties of the conquistadors did not survive into the later period, though in English-speaking countries the "Black Legend" has embalmed the slander that the Spanish imperial pattern was fraught with brutality and oppression. Actually the cruelties, even of the conquistadors, were no different in kind from those of the adventurers of other nations.

To understand the pattern of Spanish empire, it is necessary to understand the Spain of that day. Centuries of conflict with the Moors had made crusaders of the Spaniards, with all the intolerance that went with

Spanish character

that term, and yet with a sense of a divine mission and a piety and love for souls that modern men find hard to comprehend. In a real sense all Spaniards were soldiers and so preferred fighting to working, a tremendous handicap in building up an old economy or in developing a new one; and, like soldiers, they were continually trying to "rank." But even more outstanding was their egotism, that tremendous individualism which makes the vaunted individualism of the English look like communistic co-operation. It was not democracy, for it had no element of compromise in it. Only the hand of the king could keep Spain from being torn by faction; he ruled thought, purpose, and action, excluding any philosophy that might undermine this unity and seeking out by the Inquisition any whisper of dissent.

The result was that Spain was a poor land but teemed with pride; grandees and hidalgos might regard themselves as privileged, but it was a saying that below the king all men were equal. Certainly a swineherd did not hesitate to command the hidalgos whom he led to the conquest of Peru. Tradition was preferred to reason; agriculture languished, and manufactures were soon to be blighted by the expulsion of the artisan classes, the Moors and Jews, whose crime was that they were *different*. The Spaniards were creative, had initiative, and were capable of tremendous bursts of energy, but they lacked the discipline of steady habits. At the same time long mingling with the Moors had bred an almost Oriental ceremonialism, which survives today in the punctilio that dignifies and, at the same time, straitens and hampers Hispanic American life.

For almost three centuries the Spanish Empire in America was a world to itself, cut off (by law at least) from any contact with the rest of the world save Spain and its other colonies. It developed a culture of its own that was certainly not native and yet not altogether **Spanish im-** Hispanic. So huge and diverse was this empire that there **perial poli-** grew up a score of provinces, each with a separate germ **cies** that was some day to develop into national consciousness. All were subject to the king's Council of the Indies, which handled trade through the India House.

There were three guiding policies in the government of the empire. (1) All power centered in the provincial viceroy or captain-general, usually a nobleman from Old Spain; Hispanic American Creoles (native-born whites) were permitted self-government only in their cities, and even there they were strictly supervised. (2) Mercantilism was intended to be the economic standard of the empire; it was the function of the colonies to furnish precious metals and tropical products to the mother country and to buy manufactured goods imported only through Spain. (3) Since Spain itself could not expect to people such a vast territory, it deliberately sought to Hispaniolize the natives and to mix as much Spanish blood as possible into a new race amalgam. The empire thus quickly became the home of complex mixtures of white, Indian, and Negro blood. Negroes were introduced when it was found that most Indians were not adapted to the grueling labor of plantations and mines.

The instruments of Hispaniolization were the Spanish planters and the missionaries. The planters were granted lands and Indians to work them but in exchange were to protect, educate, and Christianize their charges. Missionization was regarded as cheaper than conquest and **Spreading** was so important as a defense measure that it was charged **Spanish** to the war fund. When the wild tribes beyond the frontiers **culture** threatened trouble or were penetrated by non-Spanish traders, missionaries were sent in to Christianize the natives and to introduce them to Spanish culture, thus erecting a barrier against foreigners. South America was sowed with such mission areas. Both Florida and Texas owed their missions to the threat of French encroachment; and California was not entered until about 1769, when the Viceroy of New Spain (Mexico) saw the paw of the Russian bear reaching down the coast from Alaska.

The larger story of Hispanic America was one of civilization. Spaniards boasted that wherever Spain established its power it set up a school. The teachers were monks and priests, and naturally they taught the views of the Church. The University of Mexico and the University of San Marcos (in Lima) were founded in 1551; and in time others were established, not simply to train monks but to turn out mining engineers, metallurgists, lawyers, and physicians. A printing press was operating in Mexico as early as 1539, though it and later presses were strictly limited and censored so that they produced chiefly textbooks and religious tracts. The Indians were apt pupils in the handicrafts and soon went on into trades, the arts, or religious callings.

Despite its real accomplishments, Spanish American culture was hampered by conservative habits which ossified government. The wonder is that the liberal ideas of the eighteenth century made their way into the **Defects of Spanish rule** Spanish colonies at all. Yet Spain probably gave more culturally to her colonies than England gave to hers. At least she gave all she had. As the poet Núñez de Arce puts it: "Spain oppressed you but do not blame her, for when was barbarous conquest just and human? She gave you her blood, her noble language, her laws, and her God. To you she gave all except liberty—and how could she give you that which she did not herself possess?"

The form of the Spanish Empire was set by the Hapsburg kings, of whom Charles, grandson of Ferdinand and Isabella, became the Emperor Charles v and ruler over the largest European area since Charlemagne. **Zenith of the Spanish Empire** The empire was too large for one man to govern, and Charles divided it in 1555 between his brother and his son. The latter, Philip ii, ruled Spain and the Low Countries, and in 1580 actually added Portugal and its eastern commercial empire and Brazil to the Spanish dominions, where they remained until Portugal broke away in 1640. The Spanish Empire, which had begun in 1492, entered its decline under Philip, despite his conquest of Portugal. The empire essentially owed its inception to royal marriages and to American gold; it never built up a firm industrial foundation. In the long run American treasure may have been a curse to Spain. The wars on which Charles and Philip embarked for faith and empire were too vast for even the wealth of the New World.

Spain's industrial decline had begun to inflate prices after the expulsion of the Moors and Jews, but now the influx of treasure aided existing tendencies in working a price revolution in Europe which in the sixteenth **Decline of Spain** century quadrupled prices. European workers were hard hit by the inevitable lag in wages, and this hardship led to emigration. To add to the confusion, the flow of specie was accelerated to the hoards of India and China in exchange for luxuries. Spain's

LOUISIANA

VICEROYALTY OF NEW SPAIN

FLORIDA
CAPTAINCY
GENERAL
OF CUBA   CUBA

CAPTAINCY
GENERAL
OF GUATEMALA

A t l a n t i c

O c e a n

Spain

Portugal

Approximate location of Demarcation Line of 1494

CAPTAINCY
GENERAL OF
VENEZUELA

VICEROYALTY OF
NEW GRANADA

GUIANA

Equator

PRESIDENCY
OF QUITO

Amazon   River   Belém (Pará)

Olinda
Recife (Pernambuco)
Alagóas

B R A Z I L

MATTO
GROSSO

São Salvador
(Bahia)

P a c i f i c

VICEROYALTY OF PERU

PRESIDENCY
OF CHARCAS

MINAS
GEREAS

Paraguay R.

Paraná R.

São Paulo

Rio de Janeiro
Santos

O c e a n

Asunción

Jesuit Missions

Santa Catarina

Paraná R.

Uruguay R.

RIO GRANDE
DO SUL

CAPTAINCY GENERAL OF CHILE

VICEROYALTY OF BUENOS AIRES

Colonias

Buenos Aires   Montevideo

SPANISH AND
PORTUGUESE EMPIRES
IN AMERICA

. W. CLEMENT CO., BUFFALO, N. Y.

wars lost both Spanish treasure and Spanish blood, and her mistaken economic policies also resulted in a decline of her agriculture and manufactures and a further decline in population. Cattle raising took the place of farming in Spain, and foreign goods (paid for in gold and silver) took the place of domestic manufactures. By 1600 the trade of Spain was tacitly under foreign control, and five sixths of the goods exported to America had been brought to Spain from foreign shops in foreign bottoms.

The Spanish monarchs, possessing an empire that was decaying economically, sought frantically for a means of arresting the dry rot, but failed. An incredible confusion caused by eccentric, though well-meant, regulations hampered trade. Taxes were high; but even at **Economic confusion** that, governmental expenditures in the colonies sometimes had to be drawn from other sources of royal income. The real burden was not in taxation but in the lack of economic opportunity. The American empire was rich. The Caribbean area had for sale limitless quantities of plantation products, yet was begging not only for manufactures but for such simple items as salt fish and barrel staves. The Rio de la Plata offered millions of hides and was willing to take smuggled goods in exchange for silver brought from Bolivia and diamonds from Brazil. It was only natural that traders of other nations should rush in to fill the vacuum left by the Spanish royal policies.

There is a striking contrast between the colonial history of the Spanish possessions and that of Brazil. The latter had no clear-cut age of the conquistadors and no long period of doldrums, for the conquest of her forests and swamps was the unremitting labor of centuries. Her history is one of clash and confusion: cannibals ply their ghostly **Brazil's turbulent history** business with religious fervor; slave hunters fall like the wrath of God upon the Indian villages of the interior; Negro slaves die like flies in the sugar mills; the gold and diamond fields echo with the clamor of riotous pioneers; dashing French Huguenots and canny Dutch invaders are hurled back in a remarkable wave of nationalistic enthusiasm. In fact, there was no long interval in which the germ of national consciousness slumbered undisturbed in the seed; the settlements were scarcely out of sight of the coast before they were so avowedly Brazilian that Portugal's control of its overgrown colony was often more apparent than real.

The Brazil which grew up through three centuries of colonial adventure was Hispanic in its fierce individualism and its lofty disdain for manual labor. And yet it was different. The Portuguese settlers had lacked the rigidity of the Spanish, were less the crusaders, and **Brazilian character and racial mixture** more the compromisers. This character did not bring democracy, but it did bring more individual freedom despite the king's valiant attempt to ape the Spanish imperial ways. The blood of the Negro entered into Brazilians, particularly in the north, and diluted racial prejudice, softened the lineaments of the conquerors, and made the Brazilian gayer and perhaps more affected than either the Portuguese or the Indian. Other nations of America have combined Hispanic, Indian, and Negro stock, but none of them has produced so successful a racial and cultural alloy.

2   The Struggle for the Caribbean

For three centuries (1500–1800) like a splendid, slow-moving mastiff surrounded by snapping mongrels, Spain fought a losing battle with her neighbors—England, France, and Holland. Here for the first time since the Roman wars against Carthage the vital influence of sea power upon history became apparent to nations that for a thousand years had remained comparatively independent of sea-borne commerce. Spain and her enemies fought over three fundamental differences. First was Spain's insistence that the western ocean was a *mare clausum*—a sea closed to the ships, merchants, and colonists of other nations. Second was her claim that discovery was the basis for the ownership of new lands; others held that effective occupation was the test of ownership.

Bases of contention

Finally the Spanish opposed the axiom of "no peace below the line," referring to a line drawn in part along the Tropic of Cancer. The other maritime powers sought to transfer to the Indies, East and West, the status that had prevailed in Europe when every seaman was half a pirate. Kings might haggle peaceably and popes might decree, but in the southern and eastern seas the wars went on. Thus it was possible for England and Holland to be at peace or even in alliance in Europe, while in India their great trading companies were fighting one of the decisive wars of history. This convention became a convenient means of jockeying for power, for it enabled the left hand to rob while the right hand took no part in the crime.

Spain's America held a double inducement: plunder and trade. At first the plunder motive was strongest, but by 1700 trade had become the chief objective. Before the death of Columbus certain curious gentlemen of French, Portuguese, and English origin had turned the prows of their ships westward in order to look at the new lands. In 1523 a French fleet from Dieppe cut out two Mexican ships near the Azores and captured in them part of the riches of Montezuma. When some of the plunder was presented to the French King Francis i, the Emperor Charles v protested and reminded him that the pope had divided the non-Christian world between Spain and Portugal. Francis was amused. "Show me," said he, "Father Adam's testament by which he divided the world between my brothers of Spain and Portugal."

Beginning of French plundering

Evidently the king of Spain was unable to produce the will, for French mariners were soon cutting off Spain's wealth at its Caribbean sources. By the nature of wind and current, ships bound from the Caribbean to Spain had to pass through the Florida Strait, and here the French corsairs picked them off. French squadrons, manned principally by Huguenots, sacked and devastated the open towns of the Antilles and the Spanish Main. Eventually the great forts which one sees in the Caribbean were built, and a convoy system was set up. In 1564 Admiral Coligny, the Huguenot statesman, sought to clinch French control of the Florida Strait by planting Ft. Caroline on the St. Johns River. A Spanish force under Pedro Menéndez de Avilés promptly founded a rival base at St. Augustine (1565), and a little later by a series of tricks succeeded in massacring the French settlers. Later the Spanish extended forts and Jesuit missions as far north as the Chesapeake Bay region, which they called Axacan, but were finally forced by starvation and Indian hostility to withdraw to Florida and the sea islands. The opening of civil wars in France discouraged further French activities in America.

During these years England's policy toward Spain was friendly, partly because of her ancient enmity toward France, partly because English woolens found a market in the Hapsburg dominions. The split grew from **England and Spain break** the time of Henry VIII's break with Rome and his divorce from his Spanish wife. Gradually relations deteriorated, as the commercial interests of Spain and England clashed, until finally Charles V felt compelled to prohibit trade with England and to seize English merchants in Spain. Thereupon English privateers sailed for the Spanish imperial sea lanes. When Elizabeth ascended the throne (1558) of a well-nigh ruined nation, she attempted to temporize while she rebuilt England's manufactures and trade. During her reign English merchants began trading with Russia, Turkey, and finally in 1600 formed the East India Company, which was one day to rule India. In 1567 an English fleet under command of John Hawkins of Plymouth was crippled by a storm and sought refuge in San Juan de Ulúa, near Vera Cruz; there it was caught by a Spanish fleet, and only a handful of men in two small ships escaped, one commanded by Hawkins and the other by his nephew, Francis Drake. Elizabeth now utilized Hawkins in preparing the navy for the coming showdown. Henceforth England was to depend on the skill of her sailors, the accuracy of her gun pointers, and the seaworthiness and maneuverability of her ships.

Meanwhile Drake stepped into Hawkins's seagoing shoes and found them a perfect fit. In alliance with French Huguenot privateers and Dutch Sea Beggars in rebellion against Spain, English seamen swept Spanish **Drake and the war with Spain** trade from the narrow seas and tumbled its wealth into English ports. When political expediency forced Elizabeth to patch up a peace with Spain, the Sea Beggars returned to Holland to begin their great struggle for Dutch independence, and Drake departed on a series of depredations against the Spaniards which eventually led him around the world. By now English pirates had succeeded French corsairs as the scourge of the Indies. Santo Domingo and St. Augustine were plundered and burned, and Cartagena held for ransom.

· Their ventures, in which Elizabeth secretly shared, were shrewdly calculated to weaken King Philip's power and strengthen England's political and financial position. The war that inevitably followed was caused by religious, political, and commercial rivalries as well as by resentment at English depredations in the Caribbean. The defeat in 1588 of the "Invincible Armada" marked the beginning of the decline of Spanish power, though of course this was not immediately apparent. When in 1603 James Stuart of Scotland came to the English throne he quickly ended hostilities, asserting that wars were private matters between rival princes. He pointed out that he had never been at war against Spain, so how could England be, now that he was its king?

During the first half of the seventeenth century, while England and France were busy with internal problems, it was Holland's turn to become the scourge of the Indies. As subjects of Charles v the Netherlanders, under convenient legal fictions, had engaged to a certain **Dutch com-** extent in commerce with the West Indies, and now that they **mercial** were free they did not propose to give it up. Dutch manu- **supremacy** factures were both good and cheap, and Dutch traders were anxious to meet the needs and preferences of their customers. Now they developed a triangular trade based on trade goods, Negro slaves, and plantation products. Before long Holland had a strangle hold on the great trade in plantation products, which Spain persistently regarded as illegal. Holland, with her natural rivals preoccupied at home, became enormously prosperous and powerful. It is said that as much as ten per cent of her three million inhabitants were always at sea. The Dutch made important changes in the build and rig of their ships, which made them the best afloat, and sought to solve the problem of scurvy by seizing and settling convenient way stations where fruits and vegetables could be grown for the use of passing ships.

Dutch naval activity easily dominated the scene between 1621 and 1640. Her far-flung navies were found in every sea, and her admirals, soldiers, and traders seemed about to conquer the world. The footholds she had already gained were consolidated. Portugal was tum- **The Dutch** bled from her pre-eminence in the East, and the Dutch took **Empire** over her trade empire from the Cape of Good Hope to Japan. The slave barracoons of West Africa fell into their hands and with them the lucrative slave trade to Brazil and the Caribbean. Along with these prizes went the trade of Spanish America, the interim ownership of the sugar plantations of the "bulge" of Brazil, and one of the richest fur-trading areas of North America. The West Indies lay naked and cowering beneath the lash of the new master, who had once been their mother's slave. Fleet after fleet ran before the trades and around the Caribbean, ravishing the rich colonial cities as they went. It was a brave dream that these taciturn realists from the salt marshes of the North Sea tried to make come true, but in the end the empire vanished except for the East Indies and a few colonies in the Caribbean area. Holland simply did not have the population to hold it together and win the wars which inevitably occurred. Even more fatal was her mistake in failing to lay an agricultural base for her empire. As a result, when Cromwell in a sharp war seized a part of Holland's carrying trade, she was forced to swallow the bitter dose. Her own colonies were not a sufficient plantation base, and she began her long decline.

During the settlement of the islands of the Lesser Antilles, chiefly after 1625, there arrived perhaps as many as a hundred thousand masterless men drawn from a dozen European nations. Thousands died in battle **Settlement** with Carib cannibals, or of drink and yellow fever, but they **of Lesser** succeeded in clearing thousands of little plantations. The **Antilles** overproduction of tobacco was so great that the bottom fell out of the market in 1639. Thereupon the Dutch, who controlled the carrying trade, suggested sugar. This was more grueling work than growing tobacco, and either white men could not stand the long hours in the sun or their labor was too expensive. At any rate, the Dutch obligingly brought in Negro slaves on credit. This action changed the picture completely: the small plantations were consolidated into large ones. The only economical labor was that of slaves, black or white, and their conditions were so brutal that transportation to the plantations of Barbados became the worst punishment that an English court could mete out to criminal or rebel.

White men, whether free or indentured, were now a drug on the labor market. Thousands of human derelicts of all nations wandered in tiny canoes and worm-eaten old ships from island to island in desperate search **The bucca-** of some means of gaining a living. The struggle among them **neers** was as obscure, conscienceless, and destructive as conflicts between rival species of ants. We hear vaguely of international alliances, shipwrecks, epidemics, and massacres. Those who survived gradually took up the role of pirates and lived by plundering the Spanish. A generation or so before this the Spanish had abandoned the mountains of western Santo Domingo, the part now known as Haiti, and here there had gathered groups of white castaways and fugitives from justice who lived by hunting wild cattle. Presently the stream of derelicts from the Lesser Antilles came in contact with the lawless population of Haiti, and the two factions joined and formed the famous buccaneers. This is not the place to tell of their "romantic" exploits—someone has said that romance is crime in the past tense—but by 1660 they had become in their turn the scourge of the Indies. No matter what wars were in progress in Europe, they knew no enemy save Spain.

During the latter half of the seventeenth century there was a gradual development of antipathy between France and England and a rapprochement between England and Spain. The buccaneers flourished during this period because either England or France needed them as cat's-paws against Spain. The two chief buccaneer bases and markets were at Port Royal in the English colony of Jamaica and on the French island of Tortuga, just off Haiti. **The buccaneers and European diplomacy** The increasing regularization of trade with Spain in the Caribbean meant that powerful European commercial interests demanded the blotting-out of the buccaneers. The official understanding between England and Spain finally made such progress that in 1671 the former closed the buccaneer base at Port Royal; the buccaneers only shifted to Tortuga. The ambition of Louis xiv to seize Spain's plantations and Holland's remaining carrying trade led to a war in which Holland's land power was menaced and her carrying trade drastically reduced; in the end she was saved only because her stadholder ascended the English throne.

France had made such steady progress toward Caribbean supremacy that English hostility was ensured; moreover, the throne of Spain was about to fall vacant, and Louis xiv aspired to have it occupied by one of his own descendants. Both considerations led him to order the blotting-out of the buccaneer menace to Spain. The doctrine of "no peace below the line" was abrogated. The buccaneers lost their half-legal character and became out-and-out pirates, though for another generation they found bases and markets for their plunder in the English colonies on the North American mainland. By now the mixed populations of the Spanish islands had learned the secrets of piracy, and soon the shipping lanes of the Caribbean swarmed with pirate craft which were to afflict legitimate commerce until after 1800.

Long before this, Spanish commercial restrictions had become a hollow shell. One of the most lucrative commercial prizes was the *asiento,* or contract for supplying slaves to Spanish America. With the decline of Holland the West African slave coast was taken over piecemeal by European rivals, and these nations muscled in with a contraband slave trade. England took over the *asiento* in 1713 as **Decline of Spain** a result of her victory in the War of the Spanish Succession and kept it until about 1750. Spain, though she gagged and temporized, was forced by her defeats to deny most of what she had fought for all through her imperial course. The realm that the valor of the conquistadors and the hard realism of the Hapsburgs had created could sink no lower. But still her

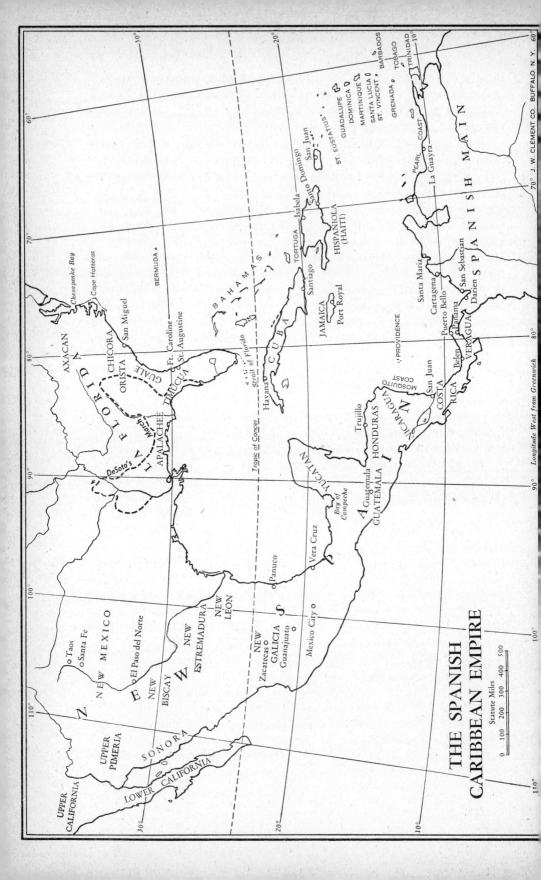

THE SPANISH
CARIBBEAN EMPIRE

Statute Miles

0   100   200   300   400   500

hidalgos with their magnificent gift for self-delusion held as an article of faith that their empire was a second Rome, destined through the favor of God to be an eternal arbiter in the affairs of mankind. Each of their monarchs, even the life-long senile Philip the Bewitched, they saw as the most puissant and magnanimous prince in Christendom. In the cool of the evening as they sat over their wine they congratulated each other upon their good fortune in having a king so clement as to grant such easy terms to his enemies.

3 In Quest of the Northwest Passage

It is not likely that we will ever know the full story of the European discovery of northeastern North America. The Norse settlers of Iceland made their way to the west coast of Greenland late in the tenth century and founded a colony which hung on for several hundred years. About the year 986 a ship was storm-driven to the southwest and sighted a low coast line, but it was not until **Norse voyages to America** about 1000 that Leif the Lucky followed up the discovery and landed on a coast where grapes grew; one linguist would have it that the word used referred not to grapes but to cranberries. Several attempts were made to settle this "Wineland the Good," but the natives proved too strong for the immigrants, who returned to Greenland; however, trading and timber-cutting expeditions were frequent for several generations. The story of the chief adventurers was passed on in the form of sagas, which, however, were not written down until the fourteenth century. Attempts have been made to prove that the Norse settlements were in New England, perhaps as far south as Narragansett Bay, but it is more likely that they were somewhere near the St. Lawrence.

Out of the vague shadows of the Middle Ages there have come other references to western voyages. Irishmen set sail for St. Brendan's Isle (possibly Iceland, for the Norsemen found some Irishmen there), and a Welsh prince named Madoc disappeared toward a western land with shiploads of emigrants. The fishing folk of western France claim that the cod upon which their ancestors **Other early voyages** depended disappeared in the fourteenth century but were soon located upon the Newfoundland Banks; thereafter the French made annual voyages to the new fishing grounds. However that may be, it is certain that Cape Breton had received its name not long after 1500 from the number of Breton fishermen who resorted there. Basques, the whalers of Europe, may have sought their prey in North American waters at an early date. At any rate, during the fifteenth century various voyagers returned from the west with tales which may have indicated that they had been in America. Certainly the seaports of Western Europe were rife with rumors of lands beyond the Atlantic.

The first authentic voyage to the north was that of the Italian John Cabot, who in 1497 under the patronage of Henry VII sailed from Bristol in the tiny *Matthew* with a crew of eighteen men. His landfall has been variously identified with Labrador, Cape Breton Island, and Newfoundland; at any rate, the term "new found land" was soon attached to the island most frequented by English fishermen. Cabot was convinced that he had discovered "the territory of the Grand

John Cabot

Portions of inscriptions on Dighton Rock, near the town of Berkeley, Massachusetts. Once considered a runic memorial, it is now believed to be the work of Indians of historic times.

Cham"; and, since he had made a lucrative bargain with Henry, he made himself very popular by passing out spice islands and bishoprics. A jealous Venetian wrote that "honors are heaped upon Cabot, he is called Grand Admiral, he is dressed in silk, and the English run after him like madmen." With this rout of madmen plucking at his silken doublet, Cabot disappears from history, for if he returned from a voyage begun in 1498 no reliable account has survived. His first voyage, however, was the basis for England's later claim to North America.

The sixteenth century saw no permanent settlements north of Florida, but fish-drying camps and fur-trading posts abounded. There was a sound economic basis for the fishing business in that nearly half the days on the Catholic calendar were fast days on which one might eat fish, but no flesh; and then the kings of Western Europe soon saw that by encouraging fisheries they would also encourage the training of mariners and the building of ships. An Elizabethan sailor wrote that one might know when he was over the Newfoundland Banks

Fishermen

by the "incredible multitude of sea foule" hovering over the water to pick up the offal left by codfishermen. Basque whalers also drove a profitable trade, for whalebone was useful in making corsets for court dandies and fine ladies, and whale oil was used in soap and as an illuminant.

When the fishermen went on shore to salt their catches, they came into contact with the Indians, who, fighting a battle for life against subarctic cold with weapons of stone and bone, were struck by the enormous superiority of iron weapons and utensils. To obtain knives, axes, needles, and kettles the Indians eagerly bartered their furs. **The fur trade** Doubtless many a fisherman sailed off with a king's ransom in furs, chuckling at the way he had overreached the simple savage; the Indian, crouching before his wigwam and skinning his game with his new knife, no doubt grunted in amazement that the Great Spirit had made fools so great as to trade such tools for a few paltry furs.

The American fur trade began in the nick of time, for European fur animals were just about trapped out. The demand for furs arose not simply from a need for protection against the cold but also from the custom which obliged noble or burgher to demonstrate his wealth by **European demand for furs** wearing fur. Even a shred of fur was better than none at all and entitled the wearer to at least a shred of respectability. Beaver fur was especially in demand for felt hats. These hats could be remade no less than three times and would perhaps pass successively from the head of a French guardsman to a Spanish merchant, a Brazilian planter, and finally end a long and useful career on the oily pate of a West African chief. Indeed, fur hats became a necessary article of social ostentation; even handy badges of religion and politics. A tall crowned hat was useful to lengthen the face to indicate staid social and religious preferences, while a lower crown with a rakish feather indicated a merry secular outlook on life. The hat, moreover, was a necessary article to doff if one went to court or into society, and even more necessary to keep on if one's principles were opposed to acknowledging social superiors—and the more magnificent the hat, the more pointed was the political opinion thus expressed.

Fishermen and fur traders were loath to disclose their favorite haunts and greatly resented it when English and French monarchs gave to favored nobles monopolies over stretches of coast. Nevertheless, official explorers gradually ferreted out their secrets. The explorers' **Renewed interest in the Northwest Passage** main quest was for a Northwest Passage around North America by which they might cut into the Portuguese monopoly of the spice trade. The brothers Corterreal, sailing under Portuguese license, probably made several voyages around 1500. They kidnaped a cargo of slaves from a shore which they called *Laboratoris Terris*, a name which may have been corrupted to

Labrador. A Spanish voyager, Gómez, seems in 1524 to have touched a part of the coast perhaps as far north as Nova Scotia in a search for the Northwest Passage.

More important than these voyages was that of a Florentine named Verrazano, who sailed in 1524 under the patronage of Francis I. He made a careful exploration of the coast, possibly from South Carolina to New-foundland. He probably gave to the area the name New **Verrazano** Gallia, which later appeared as New France. One peculiar **and Cartier** result of Verrazano's explorations was his claim that a west-ern body of water approached close to the Carolina coast; perhaps he mistook the nature of a Carolina sound or of Chesapeake Bay. At any rate, the error gave rise to a persistent opinion that the "South Sea" lay not far back of the Atlantic coast; hence the terms of the English colonial charters which gave strips of land running from "sea to sea." In 1534 Jacques Cartier of St. Malo in Brittany began a series of voyages to the St. Lawrence, apparently in search of Verrazano's sea. He named the heights of Quebec and Montreal, but his progress toward China was stopped by the rapids which were later derisively named Lachine (China) Rapids. A settlement which was attempted in 1541 was a dismal failure. French troubles with Huguenots and Spaniards forbade any further set-tlements until the next century.

The most indefatigable seekers for the Northwest Passage were Eng-lishmen, though occasionally they were backed financially by Dutchmen or Danes. John Cabot's voyages seem to have been followed up by his son Sebastian, who claimed to have explored in 1509 an area **English** that might have been Hudson Bay. During Elizabeth's reign **voyagers** London's Muscovy Company held the monopoly of Eng-land's northern trade, but its interest was in the discovery of a Northeast Passage to Russia or even to China. By the intercession of the queen Sir Humphrey Gilbert managed to break the Muscovy Company's privileges and to initiate a series of northwest voyages by Martin Frobisher in the 1570's. Gilbert attempted to found on Newfoundland a colony which could serve as a base for these explorations, and it was on his return in 1583 that he was lost at sea. Nevertheless, the search was continued during that decade by John Davis, and later by others. By 1610 Henry Hudson, profiting by the work of his predecessors, was able to enter and partly explore Hudson Bay before his crew, angered by his stubborn refusal to head for home, cast him adrift and returned to England. Though a long train of explorers followed in Hudson's wake, they were searching for a passage which was not to be successfully traversed until the famous voyage of Roald Amundsen in 1903–1906.

Late in the sixteenth century the governments of France, England, and Holland began serious attempts to take the fur trade of North

America away from individual adventurers and to place the monopoly, together with rights of settlement, in the hands of chosen individuals or corporations. These attempts were in accord with mercantilism, which endeavored to promote state control and a planned economy. Here we will turn to Canada **Samuel de Champlain in New France** and leave the details of English settlement to a later chapter. Though a succession of French fur companies began operating under royal grants on the St. Lawrence about 1584, it was not until Samuel de Champlain took over the management of one of them in 1608 that any degree of prosperity was attained. Settlements were made at Mount Desert, now in Maine; at Port Royal, in Acadia; and trading posts were established at Quebec and Montreal. Though in 1613 Samuel Argall of Virginia raised a fleet of ten ships among the English vessels that were trading along the coast and destroyed the first two settlements, Champlain persisted. He went himself into the wilderness to explore, not only to further the fur trade but presently to seek clues of the route to China. Also he brought into the northern wilderness the same religious zeal which possessed the Spaniards, and he sent missionaries to live among the Indians and convert them.

In 1627 New France was placed under control of a new fur monopoly, the Company of New France, which got off to a bad start when an English fleet seized Quebec. Though French power was re-established three years later by the coming of peace, the colony's growth was slow. **Company of New France** These were nevertheless formative years. Feudal tenure of land (seigniory) was introduced. Huguenots were forbidden to immigrate, and the Catholic Church built up a power which permeates the daily life of the French Canadian to this day. This was, however, the period of the great Iroquois wars which threatened to blot New France out of existence, so the decision in 1663 of Louis xiv to displace the inefficient Company of New France and take the rule into his own hands may have been the colony's salvation.

The king acted energetically. Settlers and supplies poured into the languishing colony. Agriculture and local handicrafts were stimulated. Troops arrived to turn the tables on the Iroquois. Fur traders were ordered to be more active—and at the same time were handicapped **Royal government in New France** by inconsistent regulations. Indeed, New France soon learned by experience both the vices and the virtues of government regimentation. The result was that while new times were better than the old, Canadians in the lower country lost their initiative and either languidly obeyed the royal decrees or found a way around them while they waited for the king to forget or change his mind. Nothing could be undertaken without a royal finger being first thrust into the pie. In order to increase the population, shiploads of women were sent from France and bachelors were ordered to marry. The measure was highly successful: by 1760 the white population of Canada had reached sixty-five thousand. But at the same time the population of New England alone was four hundred seventy-three thousand, a fact which may prove the superiority of free enterprise as a matrimonial as well as an economic stimulus.

One of the most important of Champlain's moves had been to send young white men to live among the Indians and learn their languages and customs. These men became known as *coureurs de bois,* or woodrangers.

Coureurs de bois When the king took over New France, he ordered the Indians to come to the settlements with their furs to trade and forbade Frenchmen to go into the woods. Before long the woodrangers, with the connivance of corrupt officials, waylaid the Indian fur brigades on the upper waters and bought their winter's fur catch for enough brandy to provide a short spree. When royal officials tried to stop this practice, the answer was that if the Indians did not get French brandy they would get English rum and English heretical doctrines with it. As a matter of fact, English rum and trade goods were cheap, and more and more Indians formed the habit of going to English posts. Presently French traders went there also to buy their supplies and found a ready welcome. Numbers of Frenchmen, at one time an estimated eight hundred out of a population of ten thousand, slipped out from under the royal thumb on the St. Lawrence and gathered in roaring brigades at strategic centers like Detroit, elected leaders, built forts and warehouses, and then scattered in small groups to roam the wilderness and trade.

It was not until after 1700 that Church and government between them succeeded in arresting the movement from the St. Lawrence. But the Frenchman of the frontier had already become a child of the woods in a

Canadians roam over North America sense that few Englishmen ever did; and his half-breed sons, when they visited Montreal, were as out of place as they would have been in Paris. Paddling in their canoes, portaging laboriously around the rapids, braving the cold of subarctic winters, starving, racked by fever and fatigue, these indomitable *coureurs de bois* ranged from Baffin Bay to Texas, opening a continent to white commerce and placing an indelible stamp upon the nations which sprang up after them. Some founded dynasties among the Indian tribes; some, known as *voyageurs,* ranged on the plains to Spanish Santa Fe and eventually as far as the Pacific coast; others squatted in rude agricultural clearings from the Appalachians westward to Missouri and were eventually absorbed in the American settlements. Quite often they were more closely identified with the Indians than with the French and during the wars of the eighteenth century took service indifferently as guides or hunters with the English, French, or Americans.

One of the most significant of Champlain's discoveries was that the St. Lawrence flows from the southwest on a course roughly parallel with the Atlantic, usually at a distance of about three hundred miles. However, between Quebec and the chain of Great Lakes from which the river flows there lay a series of strong Indian confederacies composed of Iroquois nations who, in effect, were a racial island surrounded by hostile Alonquins. The strongest Iroquois confederacy was that of the Hurons, north of Lake Ontario. Even before the arrival of the French they had built up a remarkable trade empire. Huronia was in effect a military, manufacturing, and commercial nation which held the surrounding "backward nations" in economic serfdom and drew from them the corn, tobacco, hemp, fish, and furs on which its domination rested. The result was a delicately balanced economy which eventually proved disastrous. When the French appeared, the Hurons saw the advantage of acting as middlemen for European goods and set themselves successfully to the task of preventing the French and the tribes of the interior from coming into direct contact. Iron and textiles were working a profound economic change, even in tribes which had never seen a white man, and the Hurons profited enormously.

Huronia

In 1609 on an expedition to the lake which now bears his name Champlain had delighted his Algonquin allies by firing on an Iroquois war party and routing them. It was the opening gun in a fateful conflict, for the war party came from the Indian confederacy which was to thwart French ambitions in New France. The Five Nations (later Six) inhabited upper New York State and extended across the upper St. Lawrence; they were, from west to east, the Seneca, the Cayuga, the Onondaga, the Oneida, and the Mohawk. Technically the confederacy was known as the "Five Nations," but the name *Iroquois* in its political sense has quite generally been confined to it. The location of the Iroquois was decisive. The only water-level passage across the Appalachian highlands between Maine and Virginia was the Hudson River–Lake Champlain route through the Iroquois hunting grounds, the path whose possession meant victory or defeat in our colonial and early national wars. The Iroquois thus controlled the best trade route between the coast and the Great Lakes and could send their war parties at will down the St. Lawrence, down the Delaware, the Susquehanna and the Ohio, or into the vast network of waters between the Mississippi and the Great Lakes.

The Five Nations

The Five Nations readily grasped the advantage of possessing the white man's weapons and succeeded in persuading the Albany Dutch traders, and after them the English, to sell firearms only to them. The monopoly was won in the nick of time, for the beavers had been hunted out of upper New York and the Iroquois were confronted by the choice of sinking into obscurity or building up a trade empire. Economic necessity quickly forced them to weld

Iroquois strategy of terror

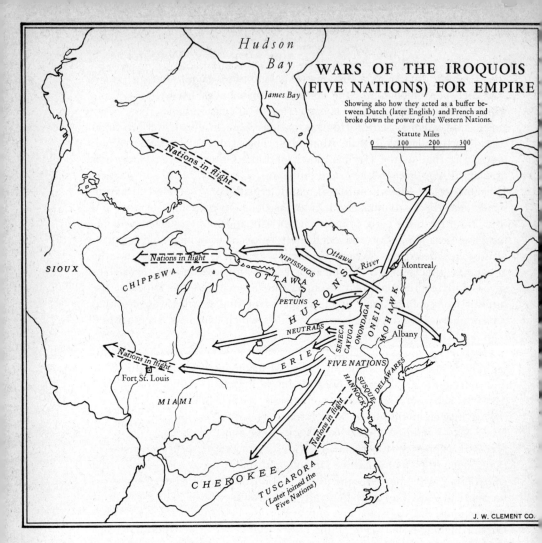

WARS OF THE IROQUOIS (FIVE NATIONS) FOR EMPIRE

Showing also how they acted as a buffer between Dutch (later English) and French and broke down the power of the Western Nations.

Statute Miles
0   100   200   300

J. W. CLEMENT CO.

their loose confederation into a closer union in preparation for a war for empire. Their diplomatic weapon was the old one, "divide and conquer," and they proved themselves masters of the strategy of terror. While they struck down one victim, their emissaries were in the villages of the next speaking soothingly of the wonders of the "Great Peace"—the Iroquois euphemism for the new world order. But their ferocious joy in slaughter gave their claims the lie.

Their first aggressive move was to rob the Huron traders carrying furs down the Ottawa River to Montreal, but the Hurons countered by forging a steel ring of foes around the Five Nations and even succeeded by fifth-column tactics in winning away the weaker nations of the **Conquest of Huronia** confederacy. The French came to the rescue of their Huron customers but were not in a position to do much and were in their turn grievously harassed. The Seneca and Mohawk, the largest of

76

the Five Nations and the ones most in favor of war, determined upon a crushing blow such as had no precedent in Indian annals. It was a forest blitzkrieg. Early in 1649, while the snow was still on the ground, they made a supreme attack on Huronia. Town after town fell amid blood and fire. The survivors fled to the forest, and that winter famine and smallpox carried them away by thousands, for their ill-balanced economy told against them.

This tremendous victory reduced the other nations to a state of paralysis and destroyed all chances of co-operation. One after another they fell, each fighting desperately in its turn, but quite alone. Town after town was captured by the fierce Iroquois warriors, who up-ended their **The Iro-** canoes as scaling ladders and poured over the defending **quois trade** palisades. To Labrador and Hudson Bay in the North, to **empire** the Gulf plains in the South, and to the prairies of Illinois in the West, the Iroquois carried the terror of their muskets. Even Montreal survived only by "a continuous miracle." Over the entire eastern half of the North

A totem of the Five Nations

American continent there was a profound disruption of the old balance of power. Part of the remaining Hurons fled westward to the vast pulpwood plains and often conquered the more primitive nations by their superior weapons and drove them pell-mell against their neighbors. The newcomers, fugitives though they were, were envied and feared for their possession of iron. Closer home, the upper Ohio Valley was denuded of inhabitants and kept as an Iroquois game preserve. The price of empire, however, had been terrible. Probably they had never had more than three thousand warriors (less than Huronia), and in 1660, says Parkman, the inspired chronicler of these wars, there were only twelve hundred left of true Five Nations stock; already they had been forced to adoption as a means of recruiting their strength. Nor was their dominion ever completely successful. Only part of the furs of the great Northwest came to Albany; the rest still found their way by devious routes to Montreal.

The royal assumption of control in Canada marked the beginning of the slow decline of the Iroquois empire. An army of twelve hundred Frenchmen devastated the Mohawk Valley in 1666, and the next spring the Iroquois sued for peace. In the long run the suicidal wars of conquest in which the Iroquois had wasted their strength served only the purposes of the whites. The destruction of Huronia opened the way to the West for the French, for the Iroquois could not patrol all the forest waterways. On the other hand, the Iroquois depended on English goods and firearms and so could not permit the French to consolidate a trade monopoly by descending the Hudson and blotting out the weak Dutch and English colonies. The Dutch and English colonial governments usually got the point and did all they could to encourage the Iroquois incursions against New France. When the Iroquois sought to play the French and English against each other, both egged them on to distant wars which would weaken them further, for each feared that the Iroquois might by a supreme effort drive them out of their foothold. The Iroquois were perfectly conscious of the dangers of their situation, and one of their great fears was that the French and English would unite to blot them out.

Iroquois wars serve white purposes

The Iroquois were their own worst enemies. In spite of their tremendous dynamism they possessed all of the barbarian's susceptibility to flattery and bribery and too much of his partiality for the short-term advantage. Their confederacy failed to articulate. When the chiefs sought to build up their trade empire by diplomacy, the arrogant young men wantonly tore down the structure. French missionaries made an entrance and enticed about a fifth of the Iroquois families to settle peaceably in Canada, probably not a difficult task for there were plenty of warriors who opposed the confederacy's mad career of conquest. Alcohol spread its insidious net over the upland villages and gnawed at the vitals of national power, and the pestilences which had frequently been allies of the Iroquois now struck in their midst. Though the Iroquois tried to walk with all the old pride and arrogance, their empire was an empire only of terror, not of carefully organized and dominated trade. They were bound to the chariot of the white man with invisible but unbreakable chains.

Decline of the Iroquois

BIBLIOGRAPHICAL NOTE

Mundus Novus

PORTUGUESE VOYAGES: See Charles R. Beazley, *Prince Henry the Navigator* (1895); Edgar Prestage, *The Portuguese Pioneers* (1933); and Samuel E. Morison, *Portuguese Voyages to America in the Fifteenth Century* (1940).

COLUMBUS: There are numerous biographies of Columbus, but the most recent is Samuel E. Morison, *Admiral of the Ocean Sea* (1942). Salvador de Madariaga, *Christopher Columbus* (1940) is an interesting venture into the psychology of the great discoverer. If Morison and De Madariaga ever meet, it will be at dawn over coffee and pistols. See also George E. Nunn, *Geographical Conceptions of Columbus* (1924); and Lionel C. Jane, ed., *Select Documents Illustrating the Four Voyages of Columbus* (2 v., 1930–33).

SPANISH EMPIRE: Among the numerous accounts the most complete is Roger B. Merriman, *The Rise of the Spanish Empire in the Old World and the New* (4 v., 1918–34). Later and briefer are Clarence H. Haring, *The Spanish Empire in America* (1947); and Salvador de Madariaga, *Rise of the Spanish American Empire* (1947). Edward D. Salmon, *Imperial Spain* (1931) offers an excellent portrayal of background. Best one-volume treatment of exploration and conquest is Frederick A. Kirkpatrick, *The Spanish Conquistadores* (1934).

BRAZIL: The number of treatments of Brazil in the English language is growing amazingly. Among others see Gilberto Freyre, *The Masters and the Slaves: A Study in the Development of Brazilian Civilization* (1946) and *Brazil: An Interpretation* (1945).

The Struggle for the Caribbean

GENERAL TREATMENTS: See Arthur P. Newton, *The European Nations in the West Indies, 1493–1688* (1933); and Philip A. Means, *The Spanish Main, Focus of Envy* (1935).

BUCCANEERS: It is a rare year when the exploits of the buccaneers do not receive new treatment. Among the best are Ernest A. Cruikshank, *The Life of Sir Henry Morgan* (1935); Clarence H. Haring, *The Buccaneers in the West Indies* (1910); and John Masefield, *On the Spanish Main* (1906). Those who wish to dip into the quaintly bloody sources should read Alexandre Exquemelin, *Buccaneers of America* (many ed.). The survival of piracy is treated in John F. Jameson, ed., *Privateering and Piracy in the Colonial Period* (1923).

ENGLAND: See James A. Williamson, *Sir John Hawkins* (1927) and *The Age of Drake* (1938); and Julian S. Corbett, *Drake and the Tudor Navy* (1912) for the most satisfactory treatments of Elizabethan sailors. English aspects of commerce are treated in George Edmundson, *Anglo-Dutch Rivalry during the First Half of the Seventeenth Century* (1931).

FRANCE: For the French settlements in Florida and Canada see Francis Parkman, *Pioneers of France in the New World* (1865). On French commerce see Stewart L. Mims, *Colbert's West India Policy* (1912).

In Quest of the Northwest Passage

NORSE VOYAGES: See Geoffrey M. Gathorne-Hardy, *Norse Discoverers of America, the Wineland Sagas* (1921); and J. E. Olson and E. G. Bourne, eds., *The Northmen, Columbus and Cabot* (1906).

NORTHERN EXPLORATION: See John B. Brebner, *Explorers of North America, 1492–1806* (1933); and Nellis M. Crouse, *In Quest of the Western Ocean* (1928). Biographies include those of Gilbert by Donald B. Chidsey, William G. Gosling, and David B. Quinn; *Henry Hudson* (1928) by Llewelyn Powys; and *Champlain* (1948) by Morris Bishop. Contemporary accounts are in Henry S. Burrage, ed., *Early English and French Voyages* (1906).

FUR TRADE: For its significance see Harold A. Innis, *The Fur Trade in Canada* (1930); Sydney Greenbie, *Frontiers and the Fur Trade* (1929); and Clarence A. Vandiveer, *The Fur-Trade and Early Western Exploration* (1929). See also Henry P. Biggar, *The Early Trading Companies of New France* (1901).

NEW FRANCE: Francis Parkman's multi-volumed classic on the struggles for North America will be referred to frequently. The abridgement by John Tebbel under the name *The Battle for North America* (1948) enhances rather than detracts from the value of Parkman's work. George M. Wrong, *The Rise and Fall of New France* (2 v., 1928) draws on new material unavailable to Parkman. Attention should be given to the *Chronicles of Canada* series.

IROQUOIS: For a brief but fascinating account of the heyday of the Iroquois see George T. Hunt, *The Wars of the Iroquois* (1940). The Iroquois also appear in most of Parkman's works.

Chapter III

THE ENGLISH ROOTS

1 *The Rise of England's Law and Institutions*

IN THE fifteenth century England was a little nation of perhaps two and a half million people on part of an unimportant island on the fringe of the known world. Then suddenly it cut loose spiritually from the continent, and at the same time the discovery of the New World made **England's** it apparent that England lay at the center rather than the **rise to** periphery of the world. No other people since the days of **greatness** the Roman Republic have shown such vigor and enterprise. The coal in the English ground became the foundation of unprecedented industries, and the oaks of the English forests were hewn into mighty fleets whose mission it was to protect and extend the empire built on those industries. Yet the success of England depended less on industry and naval might than on the fact that, despite all her faults, she rode upon the wave of the future. And she rode this wave because the inscrutable processes of evolution had bred in the English people the early stages of the way of life that we know as democracy.

Laws and institutions are created by the circumstances and the psychology of a people, so we must look into the background and the mind of the Englishman. The first fact to be noted is that England is an island. The Englishman never loses his consciousness of being an **The Eng-** islander, for at no point is he more than about seventy miles **lishman** from tidewater. He and his fellow islanders have a sense of **and his is-** being shipmates voyaging together into the sun of destiny. **land** Out of this physical and psychological insularity arises the fact that the Englishman can be and is selective in what he accepts from the outside world. Second, the English weather and the English landscape possess few sharp contrasts. Someone has said that the English have no climate: they have only samples of weather. These samples may consist of rain, sun, and fog, but they rarely go to extremes. Nor does the topography go to extremes, for there are in England proper no startling mountains to impel frightened men to magic. It is a land for the husbandman, made intensely green by the abundant moisture, fertile under the plow, and with the light of the sun blended and subdued by clouds or mists. Here, says Santayana, the conflict between light and darkness ends in compromise.

It is often said that the United States is not an Anglo-Saxon country. That is quite true; neither is England. For centuries the island was overrun by conquerors with characters already formed: the imaginative, style-conscious, and charmingly impulsive Celt; the brooding, **Racial elements** individualistic Saxon, whose caution bred tolerance and hesitancy to the extent of sluggishness; the Dane, half merchant and half pirate, a master realist, shrewd, practical, concise. There was the parvenu Norman, intellectually subtle but bound to earth by an unparalleled administrative genius; a worshiper of good form in law, religion, and the arts; who never moved without legal excuses, sound if possible, but at least plausible. To the Englishman who was being formed the Celt furnished the soul, the Saxon the body, and the Dane the mind; the Norman, ably assisted by the medieval Church, breathed into him the life of discipline, order, and good form. There have been others; for centuries there has been a steady stream of immigration into England. The name Anglo-Saxon, then, might well be dropped and the term "English speaking" substituted. That may mean little beyond rather definite common attitudes toward individual rights and responsibilities, but then Anglo-Saxon should not be wrested to mean any more.

The Englishman has been a persistent peasant, with a peasant's consciousness of the vagaries of Nature and suspicions of newfangled methods. Like the peasant he has held himself free of preconceived programs in **Peasant characteristics** order to be able to meet the unexpected. In other words, he is first of all a man of action. The thinker is apt to turn up with a plan, so away with the thinker and in with makeshifts—"muddling through." Naturally a lazy, shortsighted, and uninspired leader thus sometimes is preferred to a brilliant one. Out of this distrust of thought there sometimes arise a stagnation of the intellect, an indifference to learning, and a calm acceptance of inconsistency. Judgment becomes utilitarian, and policies are weighed by their results. There is no such thing as a universal, no perfect scheme of things. This background explains the English practices and characteristics we all know: understatement, muddling through, compromise, tolerance, and reverence for the old and well-tried.

But this is only half the story, for the Englishman is more dualistic than most of humanity. Action forces a comparison and choice of modes of action, and out of this conflict arises conscience—the individual's view of what society would have him do. The peasant Englishman tried to follow Nature, which judged by the results (reality) ; Christianity judged by the means (morality) and put others above self in a completely idealistic sense. The dilemma has always puzzled the world. We call the Golden Rule our ideal, but any attempt to force it on others may result in oppression and intolerance and destroy its idealism. The Englishman therefore seeks the practical ground between right and wrong and finds hypocrisy, the way station on the road from vice to virtue. He has not lost his sense of right ; he has only compromised with it and sentenced himself to a life of attempting to convince himself that his actions and his conscience agree. Henceforth he becomes absorbed in the conflict of good and evil: ethics. Nevertheless, his standards are moral, even if he does not live up to them ; and his heroes must be endowed with moral grandeur, real or legendary. Robin Hood must rob only to help the poor.

Dualism

Upon the balance between sordid facts and idealistic aspirations the Englishman has based his laws and his institutions. What exists is right ; and if any interest or person perceives that facts have changed, it is his responsibility to bring the condition to public attention— otherwise nothing will be altered. Changes thus come by conflict between force and a rising counterforce. Democracy operates only to the extent that we take a personal interest in making it work. English law is (like our own Bill of Rights) devoted to the protection of the privileges of the citizen. Duties and responsibilities are not legal, but social and moral. In a way this is only realistic: what law can prevent the coal miner from striking if he chooses? The social or moral sense is essentially the only restraint that free men can afford to acknowledge.

Pragmatic basis of laws and institutions

To the medieval Englishman the word liberty meant franchise or privilege, and hence its invariable pluralization. The liberties of the wood-cutter, the abbey, the town, or the baron were the privileges that had been granted to them as individuals, institutions, or classes, or what was even better, had come down to them out of the past. They were in effect the constitution, written or traditional, of the individual or institution. The medieval Englishman's concept of liberties was quite unconnected with such idealistic universals as the Natural Rights of mankind. Each individual struggled for concrete liberties, liberties not drawn from inspired essayists but which he could count off on his thick Saxon fingers. Note the twenty-seven liberties which Thomas Jefferson ticked off in the Declaration of Independence as having been denied by King George. The historical sense of medieval men was very weak, so they frequently based their claims on misinterpretations

Concrete liberties

of charters such as the *Magna Charta* (1215), which in fact was chiefly an attempt by the barons to limit the royal power in their own favor. Oppression was a violation of the concrete liberties of the subject, and revolution was looked upon not as change but as restoration of the good old ways. The attitude did not wholly die out. The American Revolutionists saw themselves as fighting to *restore* "the rights of Englishmen," and the Confederate States fought to restore the original meaning of the Constitution of the United States.

Now your liberties and mine have a habit of clashing. Hence the common law. Here we see a curious illustration of the Englishman's opposition to change even when he was taking full advantage of it. New things arose constantly, but they had to be identified as something old, or at least concealed in its clothes. The purpose of the common law was to preserve the liberties of the individual against other individuals and even to a reasonable extent against society itself. The common law was superior to all men, even the king. "The King," said Bracton, "is under God and the Law." Whether or not this idea had always been true, medieval kings very early accepted it. As times changed there arose new problems not covered by the common law. Even by the year 1300 the practice of law had become a professional mystery, the peculiar preserve of the "sergeant-at-law." Royal judges were drawn from the ranks of the lawyers, and whenever a new problem arose they settled it as nearly as they could in the spirit of the law. That decision then furnished a precedent that was followed when the same problem arose. The common law thus became a living organism which grew from generation to generation by cellular multiplication. The law was complicated, but it was indestructible.

The common law

Out of this tangle there arose, however, certain clearly defined rules to protect the individual. Warrants were necessary for arrests or for search and seizure; freedom of speech was developing; only juries could convict for important crimes, and increasingly strict rules governed procedure and evidence; even in religion Christendom probably had no freer country than England.

Civil liberties

By 1300 Parliament had begun to take on recognizable shape. The body was regarded fundamentally as a court, so its enactments were in a sense judicial precedents. At first Parliament was composed of all nobles, clergy, and judges summoned to attendance by the king, plus representatives of county gentry and the well-to-do townsmen. Gradually this "Great Council" split into two houses: Lords and Commons. The Commons, which was one day to rule a quarter of the earth, entered history literally on its knees. Old pictures show the king on his throne, with his councilors seated before him on woolsacks and the lords spiritual and temporal at each side. At the end of the hall and out-

Parliament

side a wooden bar knelt the Commons. They could be heard only through their presiding officer, the "Speaker."

Parliament was not, however, the subservient creature of the king. While outwardly respectful it learned to take shrewd advantage of the king's need for money, levying on him what has aptly been **Growing power of Parliament** termed "constitutional blackmail." The English people had a stubborn dislike for taxes not laid by their representatives and always insisted that "grievances be redressed" (reforms made) before taxes were approved. The Commons thus strengthened their right to initiate taxes and money appropriations; they specified the manner in which money should be spent; they sometimes managed to force the king to abandon the slick and "unconstitutional" methods by which he supplemented his income. Perhaps some of this boldness rose from the growing conflict between king and great nobles: really two great alliances of nobles which each strove to put its own man on the throne and control elections by force or fraud and thus pack the Commons. One worthy result was that Parliament established its right to elect or depose the king.

Eventually the struggle degenerated into a civil conflict known as the Wars of the Roses (1455–1485), from

An Act Declaring and Conftituting the People of *England* to be a Commonwealth and Free-State.

BE it Declared and Enacted by this prefent Parliament, and by the authority of the fame, That the People of England, and of all the Dominions and Territories thereunto belonging, are and fhall be, and are hereby Conftituted, Made, Eftablifhed and Confirmed, to be a Common-wealth and Free-State: And fhall from henceforth be Governed as a Commonwealth and Free-State, by the Supreme Authority of this Nation, The Reprefentatives of the People in Parliament, and by fuch as they fhall appoint and conftitute as Officers and Minifters under them for the good of the People, and that without any King or Houfe of Lords.

Die Sabbathi, 19 *Maii,* 1649.

ORdered by the Commons affembled in Parliament, That this Act be forthwith Printed and Publifhed.

Hen Scobell, Cleric. Parliamenti.

London, Printed for *Edward Husband,* Printer to the Honorable Houfe of Commons, and are to be fold at his Shop in Fleetftreet, at the Sign of the Golden-Dragon, near the Inner-Temple, *May* 31. 1649.

An act passed by the House of Commons and printed in May 1649, declaring the "rights of Englishmen"

which emerged the gifted royal House of Tudor. The Tudors reigned with a semblance of despotism, but their policy succeeded because they shrewdly anticipated and expressed the will of the nation. They froze out the survivors of the old nobility or made them royal lackeys; with their left hands they encroached subtly on the popular **Mission of the Tudors** liberties, but with their right hands they ostentatiously promoted trade, scratched the ears of the sergeants-at-law, and fed the national ego. The program pared away the conflicting edges of inconsistent liberties, developed a sense of common interest among Englishmen, and cleared the way for a truly national policy. The alacrity with which

Parliament consented to sever the ties with the Roman Catholic Church was indicative of a will which, if it was not unanimous, was at least effectively national.

When in 1558 Elizabeth ascended the throne, foreign events had forced the English Church more and more to the Protestant side. Elizabeth with calculating shrewdness set out to create a party of the center which should be neither Catholic nor too enthusiastically Protestant. The **Elizabeth's religious and political problems** Anglican Church was organized on aristocratic lines, but its doctrines were purposely defined with such vagueness that they provided a mesh through which any "reasonable" conscience could squeeze. Foreign opposition played an important part in rallying about her the majority of a stubbornly patriotic people. For thirty years she played contentious nations and factions against each other, used her doughty and willing "sea-dogges" as secret weapons against a threatening Spain, and aided the fighting Dutch in thwarting France and Spain in their ambitions to hold or acquire the Low Countries. Elizabeth was in many ways a mean-spirited sovereign and a diplomatic double-crosser, but she was patriotic—and successful. By 1588, when Spanish King Philip II sent his arrogant "Invincible Armada" against the heretic queen, England had had time to grow strong. With the help of the Dutch and the god of storms the great fleet was defeated and scattered.

Elizabeth's economic problems were no less complicated. She sought to build up the navy, promoted fisheries in order to train sailors, and incorporated trading companies to encourage manufacture and foreign trade. **Extremes of wealth and poverty** Serfdom and villeinage had long since disappeared in England, but with their freedom the agricultural workers by payment of money rent had destroyed their right to remain on the soil they tilled. Under the Tudors the growth of woolen manufactures led to "enclosures," that is, to the ejection of many renters from their farms and the enclosure of the land as sheep pastures. Except for a few men retained as shepherds, these particular agricultural laborers were turned out to shift for themselves, and those who could not get work in industry were condemned to vagrancy and crime. Thus, we have in sixteenth-century England a parallel growth of prosperity and poverty, a spectacle which has too often accompanied the great ages of history. In this case it meant that there was being built up a surplus population which was ready and anxious to go to America.

2   The Completion of the English Process

When in 1603 James Stuart became King of England as James I, he was gratified to exchange the halter of Scotia's long-faced moral dictators for the divinity which hedged English kings as the result of a century of Tudor rule. As a matter of fact Stuart rule was milder than that of the Tudors, but the Stuarts were not ruling over the same people as had their predecessors. The nobility and the **English political parties** middle class of bourgeois—the common people scarcely counted yet— were each richer, stronger, and more united, and therefore harder to manage. It was only by heroic restraint in asking Parliament for special money grants to run the government that James I and then his son Charles I managed to avoid disaster. Not satisfied with what the Tudors called the "royal prerogative," they sought to enforce their "divine right."

In those days the line between religion and politics was so thin as to be invisible; that is, it was just as much treason to deny the king's religious authority as to deny his civil authority. James and Charles sought to force everyone to conform to the established Church of England and harried Nonconformists unmercifully; Archbishop Laud of Canterbury was Charles's chief instrument in this activity. The result of the religious and civil oppressions of the Stuarts was that party lines were gradually drawn. There were three: the king's party, which upheld divine right; that of the great nobles, which wished to make a puppet of the king; and that of the gentry and the wealthy bourgeois (the middle class of that day), who did not propose to let either of the other parties interfere with their liberties or with what was much the same thing, business.

It was with the last party that the Puritans found their niche. The Puritans were those overly enthusiastic Protestants who desired to "purify" the Church of England of "Romish" practices. Despite Archbishop Laud's vigorous efforts to stamp them out, they now almost controlled the eastern counties of the kingdom and included in their ranks or among their sympathizers a ma- **Puritan ambivalence** jority of the wealthy merchants and manufacturers of the cities. Such Puritans as John Milton sought to preserve the traditional medieval unity and at the same time be hospitable to the new classical learning of the Renascence and to dawning science. And yet orthodox Christianity and the new learning were enemies, for the first claimed to have by divine revelation a monopoly on truth and virtue while the latter submitted truth to the practical test of reason. In the light of that day only the hypocrite could have both. The Puritans, most of them, hesitated, then straddled. They proposed to use the new learning as an instrument in expounding the Scriptures, for truth and reason must agree, but they wished to keep the unlearned from simplifying doctrine and going off on erroneous tangents.

The "Low Church" Puritan found in the Bible the complete guide for life and eternity, the mentor of morals and manners, the form of Church

organization and ritual, and even a political constitution. He appealed
Puritan and from the tyranny of king and Church to the tyranny of a
Anglican Book. He espoused John Calvin's doctrine of predestination:
theologies that for its sins God had doomed the entire human race to
damnation but, for reasons best known to Himself, had decided to lift
certain individuals to salvation. The ones elected to be saved had done

Profane Liberty   *Envious Hipocresie*   *Iesuitecall Pollicie*

Three Grand Enimies to Church and State

An English broadside of the seventeenth century

nothing to deserve it; they were merely resoundingly fortunate. On the
other hand, the "High Church" Anglican believed that the Bible only laid
down general principles and that man was entitled to use his reason in
working out details—or at least the Archbishop of Canterbury could use
his reason for them. Men were not doomed to damnation, but each one had
the power of choosing salvation.

Centuries before this an English bishop had proclaimed that "Manners
makyth man." The proof was seen now, for beyond the problem of predestination the two parties had little that was theological to quarrel about.
"Manners Both laid stress on conduct. The Anglicans, though they fa-
makyth vored separation from Rome, approved Roman vestments
man" and ritual; they loved gaiety and spontaneity, music, dancing, and rich dress, and admired beauty whether in the moods of Nature
or the stained glass of churches. With each of these most Puritans took
issue, consciously cultivating sobriety of dress and conduct and strictly
avoiding sentiment and emotions.

Calvinism itself, like English customs, was both democratic and aristocratic. No priest had a right to mediate between God and man, hence the
democratic form of the Presbyterian wing by which the laity controlled

the Church and often formed a sounding board for popular discontent. Even more democratic were the Separatists, who wanted to leave the Church of England and let each local congregation govern itself; hence the name Independents and Congregationalists. On the opposite extreme the elect **Puritan seeds of democracy and aristocracy** could scarcely avoid forming an aristocracy among themselves, for they would be saved and the damned would not. They had, moreover, a deep distrust of human nature, and it was the duty of the clergy and gentry to restrain their less well-instructed brethren. That was a duty for which they were responsible to God, so how could they be responsible to men?

It was simple for the Puritan to arrive at the conclusion that he was one of the elect. (1) He was good, he was pious, he was holy in life and conversation. God enjoined the dignity and the necessity of labor, so he lived soberly and worked long hours. (2) God prospers the righteous, so the Puritan not only desired to be rich for the sake of riches themselves, but because wealth would prove that he was righteous. Unfortunately this desire sometimes **Self-righteousness and benevolence** led to sharp practice—strictly legal, of course, even if legislation had to be discreetly influenced. One may call these attitudes hypocritical and self-righteous, but they were none the less valuable incentives in building up the industrial and commercial supremacy of England. They were to survive as habits long after Calvinist theology had passed away. (3) On the other hand, the man to whom God entrusted wealth regarded himself as merely a steward; his duty was to administer it for the glory of God and the good of society. He preached sobriety, industry, and thrift and felt such responsibility for those under him that he sometimes cut their wages to the point where they had no other choice than sobriety, industry, and thrift. However, the Calvinist's sense of stewardship made him interested in social uplift and in civil and economic reforms. In time this was to swell into a great "benevolent movement" which was to exercise a tremendous effect on modern world history.

It was a system that could not be beaten. It had the toughness of realism but the advantages of idealism. No spirit of Christian meekness made the Calvinist suffer the buffets of the wicked a moment longer than it took to collect his might against them. He was a radical but not a destroyer, a revolutionary but not an enemy of **Utility of Puritanism** government. His feet were always on the ground, and his head was above the clouds communing with heaven. John Cotton of Boston proclaimed a brace of Christian virtues: "Diligence in worldly business, yet deadness to the world." It might have been for our benefit that he added these words: "Such a mystery as none can read, but they that know it."

James had clashed with the common-law concept that the king was under the law, but the first showdown came in 1628 when Charles I, who badly needed money to carry on the government, was forced to agree to **Gradual** the *Petition of Right*. Though he thus promised not to make **approach to** illegal arrests nor to levy illegal taxes, Charles soon reneged **civil war** and ruled without Parliament by resurrecting methods of raising taxes once approved but at the time obsolete. Eventually he was faced with rebellions in Scotland and Ireland; but when he called Parliament, it refused to vote money until grievances were redressed. This was the famous Long Parliament, which lasted for twenty years. Charles was in a panic, and early in 1642 he attempted to crush the opposition in Commons by arresting its leaders. But the birds had flown. The alternative was war.

At first the great nobles led the war against the king, but it soon became evident that they were halfhearted and wished for an accommodation with the king which would put him under their control and freeze out **Cavaliers** the middle class. At this juncture Oliver Cromwell came to **and Round-** the fore with his brigade of Ironsides raised in the eastern **heads** counties among "honest sober Christians" who "made some conscience of what they did." The result was to stiffen the Parliamentary army and put it under the control of Cromwell and the Puritans. The great nobles either retired to their estates or went over to the king. The war was now a straight issue between Cavaliers and Roundheads, as the two sides were called. In the end Charles was captured, tried for treason and convicted, and executed in 1649. The law had vindicated its supremacy over the king.

Though the Puritan victory did not bring democracy, it did encourage politico-religious sects which sought the elevation of the common man; the aristocratic accusation was that they sought to pull the wealthy down, **"The poor-** and so they were called Levellers. In the officers' council of **est he"** Cromwell's New Model Army the common man for the first time found a voice, for these men were composed not only of gentlemen but of clerks, stable boys, and pot-wallopers risen from the ranks by ability and force of character. Colonel Rainsborough spoke for them when he exclaimed that "the poorest he that is in England hath a life to live as the greatest he" and that therefore every man should partake in the choice of "those who are to make the laws for him to live under." When it was objected that this was unwise because it would endanger the concrete liberties of Englishmen, such as the holding of property, Rainsborough stuck to his guns. "If this is true," he exclaimed, "then I would fain know what the soldier hath fought for all this while? He hath fought to enslave himself, to give power to men of riches, men of estates, to make him a perpetual slave."

After the death of Cromwell, the revulsion from Puritan rigidity brought another Stuart, Charles II, to the throne in 1660. The Puritans were now ridiculed as hypocrites

> That with more care keep holy-day
> The wrong, than others the right way:
> Compound for sins they are inclined to
> By damning those they have no mind to,
> Still so perverse and opposite
> As though they worshipped God for spite.

The accusations were just. But critics are too apt to forget Milton, sitting with his sightless eyes fixed on the pageant of *Paradise Lost* while sublime verse falls from his lips; Bunyan, confined to his cell, yet free to traverse the long road of the *Pilgrim's Progress;* George Fox, founder of the Society of Friends, suffering with joy for his Master's sake; and William Penn, shrewdly outbargaining an indolent monarch for a New World forest where men might worship in freedom and incidentally fill the Penn coffers with quitrents. The Puritans had lost their chance to dominate the country politically, but they held on effectively to economic control.

The civil war had given England one of the severest lessons in its history. It renewed the English horror of civil war and standing armies; it inculcated a new respect for gradualism as an instrument of change; it bred a new sense of discipline, the bequest of rigorous Puritan training, and convinced the nation that it must act as a unit. Strongest of all, perhaps, was a healthy distrust of **Results of the English Civil War** "popular" government which kept the nation from advancing faster along the road to democracy than the preparation of the people warranted.

Charles II aimed at absolutism, but such progress as he made was destroyed by his brother and successor, James II, who moved too fast toward his objective of restoring divine right and Catholicism. The Whig and some Tory lords united in offering the throne to Mary, **Glorious Revolution, 1688** James's Protestant daughter, and her husband, William of Orange. The throne had become something of a hot seat, and William accepted it only because as stadholder of Holland he was the Protestant champion of Europe against the overwhelming might of Louis XIV, and he needed England's help. William readily paid for English support by assent to the *Bill of Rights,* the third great document (after *Magna Charta* and the *Petition of Right*) in the English constitution. By it the king as executive of the realm was forbidden among other things to suspend the laws, to levy taxes, or to require excessive bail, lay excessive fines, or impose cruel or unusual punishments; and the freedom of members of Parliament from royal interference or arrest was confirmed.

This so-called Glorious Revolution of 1688 was chiefly the work of a group of powerful Whig nobles, and it fastened the shackles of a Whig oligarchy on England. The significant thing was that Parliament (really

Supremacy of Parliament the House of Commons), not the oligarchy as such, had assumed control over English purse strings and policies. This was made clearer in the next century, when a committee of Parliament known as the Cabinet began to take over the executive functions of the king. For centuries kings and nobility had striven to control the Commons by packing; but packed they ever so well, the old spirit of truculent independence flared forth in every generation. As long as the Commons continued to be drawn from any large section of the nation it was impossible for one party to control it. A sufficiently aroused people could always make itself heard through this hereditary trumpet of popular liberties. The final decision was made in 1688. Once and for all the power of the people as expressed in Parliament superseded that of the king.

The essential characteristics of English law and politics were now complete. It was, however, the molding of a process, of methods and attitudes, rather than of a clear-cut goal or even of a program. There were

Completion of the English process still a host of political and social details to be worked out, but the process was set. Religious toleration was to make its entry; the House of Commons was to triumph over the Lords; the king was to lose his executive functions; and the middle class was now in a position where it could eventually take over. Parliament was to be the instrument of change. Thereafter amendments were to be the results of slow pressure upon Parliament, pressure exerted by public opinion and formed by merchants, journalists, economists, philanthropists, and the rising voice of the laboring man as he shouldered his way to the front and demanded that he be given a share in the good things of life.

There was yet one more factor to be added, a purely theoretical one, but one which nevertheless was to affect the world profoundly. Rebellion against kings had long been regarded as a sin against God, but Puritan

Locke and Natural Rights apologists excused it by asserting that among God's natural laws for the universe was the right of men to govern themselves. It was thus a duty to resist tyranny.

John Locke now came forward with his *Two Treatises on Government* (1690) to systematize and expand the idea. All liberties, said he, had originally been vested in men as *Natural Rights* born in them because they were human beings. Conflict between these rights, however, had led to the setting-up of a government by a *social compact* (or *contract*) among the people which was intended to reconcile and protect those Natural Rights. The king was merely the agent of the people, appointed to administer the laws by a supplementary *political compact* between people and king. Thus, men are not antisocial creatures to be kept in order by the stern hand of a king but are rational beings who preserve good order by the checks of common sense and the balancing of powers between executive and legislature. Englishmen had rebelled against a king who had attempted to upset this balance.

Locke continued. The business of government is not to regulate every move of the individual but to preserve order and protect private property. The protection of property, in fact, is the tie which binds sensible men together in the common interest and forestalls useless revolutions. With an agreement on property as the center of life, it will be possible to permit majority rule, religious tolerance, and freedom of thought and speech. Government must be by laws which act on all alike; such laws are based upon the public good and can be passed only by the legislature; and taxes can be levied only by the consent of the people through their legislators.

Protection of property

The doctrine of Natural Rights was a fateful one for Englishmen. Hitherto they had fought for limited and concrete liberties, one or two at a time, without deep thought of any goal. Now they were told that a whole galaxy of liberties was theirs by natural right; all they needed to do was to ensure good order by protecting private property. Vested interests, obviously including the great nobles and the Puritan merchants and industrialists, saw the point at once. It was their moral *duty* to ensure good order by upholding Natural Rights, among which the central one just happened to be the amassing and holding of property. Lawyers leaped at the chance to proclaim that the common law was the perfect and completed expression of the eternal principles of Natural Rights. For a hundred years the common law almost ceased to evolve, except that it carefully trained around property a thorny hedge warranted to be proof against the attacks of a hungry populace.

Natural Rights displace concrete liberties

Such confidence did the vested interests have in their hedge that they believed it impenetrable to political attack, and so they yielded step by step to the popular demand for the extension of the franchise until at last manhood suffrage was the rule throughout the English-speaking world. Their confidence was misplaced. Political democracy breached the hedge of property rights in the democratic nations by seizing one concrete liberty after another—the right to strike, accident compensation, minimum-wage laws, social security, laws against labor injunctions, graduated income taxes, and others too numerous to mention. But it was an uphill fight. Locke had not balanced Natural Rights with natural responsibilities, and the right to amass property led inevitably to a clash between the economic power of the few and the liberties of the many. Finally society came to see that it was possible

Political democracy

to let the individualistic basis of law prevail to the point where the predatory individual could legally injure society itself; the result was an effective demand for the modification of the individualistic basis of law and the recognition of the interests of society.

As a matter of history, Natural Rights have been used chiefly as an excuse for some action whose legality is troublesome to defend or doubtful. When it has come to an actual defense of their rights, the English **Value of** have used their traditional method of evolution by conflict **Natural** between the new and the old and the seizure of concrete **Rights** liberties. Natural Rights passed long ago as a philosophically tenable doctrine, but English-speaking people still cling to them as a rather vague goal, a sort of expression of desire. At that they have their uses, because in theory they bring us closer to the goal of respect for human dignity. A race wedded only to concrete liberties will have difficulty in acknowledging the right to respect of anyone who has not yet "earned" it, the Negro, for example; but if it believes in Natural Rights, such acknowledgement is a powerful psychological reinforcement to the Negro's own struggle to attain equality.

3 Democracy: Its Meaning and Its Method

Democracy is probably the most dynamic force that has ever struck the modern world. Certainly with its twin, the Industrial Revolution, it has knocked down so many of the Humpty-Dumptys of tradition that the **Dynamic** world will never be the same again. Democracy was not, of **democracy** course, developed solely by England nor even by the English-speaking peoples. There were forms of democracy rising in the Middle Ages in most of the countries of Western Europe, but it may be doubted if they would have survived, or at least triumphed, without the example and the encouragement (often unconscious) of England. The mechanics of the democratic process can be best observed in the English-speaking countries. Let us turn now to an exposition of those mechanics as we know them today so that we may watch their evolution throughout our history.

Democracy is a positive political process for putting the evolving will of the people into effect in order to advance toward liberty, equality, and fraternity. It bears in itself the means of improvement, but it is a process **Definition** and not a structure and therefore can never lay claim to **and pur-** perfection without destroying its essential nature. Democ- **pose** racy seeks to preserve and reconcile the rival sovereignties and moral values of the individual and of society and to use them as positive aids in developing a higher social and moral order. It means the federation of individuals to form society, not their complete surrender to society.

The first characteristic of the method of democracy is this: *government* of the people, by the people, and for the people. In the modern states this means in a practical sense that the people wield not immediate power but, through their representatives, *ultimate* power. It is, however, their duty to exert continual pressure in the direction of their desires. Such popular pressure is usually **Popular pressure** readily discernible, and it is notable that lobbyists of special interests are most successful when the pressure they exert is in harmony with the trend of the times. The very populousness of the modern state and the complexity of its problems signify that the chief result of an election is to register approval or disapproval of the trend the government has taken. Unfortunately no fool-proof way has yet been found by which party members can choose good candidates. The primary has been rather a disappointment and often an aid to deliberate abuse because it lends itself to machine control and to the exclusion of selected groups, such as Negroes, from political rights.

The will of the people is determined and put into effect by *a changing balance of social conflict,* that is, by a never-ending regrouping of social forces in temporary alliances to promote their own interests. The majority force no sooner takes office than a counterforce begins to **Changing balance of social conflict** form to combat it. This counterforce operates by certain rules and restraints (whence it is known in England as "His Majesty's loyal opposition"), but it takes shrewd advantage of its opponents' mistakes and in the end always becomes in its own turn the force in control. Then the process is repeated as a new alignment of counterforces molds itself in conformity to new trends and strives to overturn the force intrenched in office.

Democracy, and only democracy, frankly seeks guidance in this interplay of social interests and is willing to change its program as the political, economic, and social balances shift. "Good" to the democrat lies in the *method* to be used for improvement. Now regardless of our desire to be honest and accurate, our different backgrounds, interests, and attainments lead us to hold different views of the same problem and to favor different solutions. So one group or another of us is always viewing with alarm whatever solution is proposed and prophesying the downfall of the American way if it is put into effect. Totalitarians, on the other hand, seek to strangle social conflict by setting up a single complete and "perfect" structure which forbids free expression of desires and to which they insist that society must conform. As Sgt. Alvin C. York, the outstanding American hero of World War I, said: "In a free country there's a heap more complaint than suffering. In a dictatorship there's a heap of suffering and no complaint."

But how does democracy insure that its social conflict does not result in the triumph of might over right? There is no insurance save in the

eternal vigilance of the people. Said Jefferson: "I know no safe depository
Democracy of the ultimate powers of society but the people themselves;
must be and if we think them not enlightened enough to exercise
evolution- their control with a wholesome discretion, the remedy is not
ary to take it from them, but to inform their discretion by education." We set up certain methods which are intended to provide insurance, but they are valueless unless we make ourselves responsible for their
use. The exercise of democracy is like walking: a continually arrested
falling forward. If one does not put out his foot to catch himself, he will
fall; just so, if we in a democracy do not continually readjust our social
balance, we pass over to totalitarianism. Constitutions and laws, be they
ever so perfect, are no guarantee in themselves. Indeed, the good law of
today may become the strait jacket of tomorrow, for times change and
institutions must change with them or human liberty is lost. There is no
automatic fool-proof way to guarantee liberty.

The basic controls of democracy lie in the individual's self-restraint
and courage, often without hope of heaven or fear of hell. Both are moral
qualities; and whether or not they are regarded as innate, they can be
Controls developed and strengthened by precept and example. Self-
lie in the restraint is the monitor that tells us when to forego our own
individual desires and opinions and yield to the general will: it is the
basis of social order. Courage is the quality that enables us on occasion
to stand up against the general will for what we believe is necessary because it is just: it is the means by which society advances. No law of
church or state can take from us our right to object, if we are willing to
take the consequences. Self-restraint is good, but it is the lesser virtue
because it can become the acquiescent tool of tyranny. Courage can on
occasion become the spearhead of tyranny, but its active nature makes it
even more the vitally necessary spearhead of liberty. There always will
be men and women with the courage to stand up for what they believe is
right, whatever the consequences. "The tree of liberty," said Jefferson,
"must be refreshed from time to time with the blood of patriots and
tyrants."

Thus successful democracy (like walking) demands a superb sense of
balance and restraint. The purpose of education in a democracy is to teach
this balance and restraint—a "sense of the limits of power." There ap-
The demo- pears to be danger that as political democracy increases the
cratic effectiveness of democratic government will decrease. This
"paradox" danger is only apparent, not real. There is no paradox here,
for the democratic process has never envisaged the admission of new
voters to a share in the government until they are prepared. Social classes
have been undergoing the educative process that we daily see illustrated
in the growth of a child into a responsible voter. It is true that without

this educative process democracy will break down; that is why it is absolutely essential for us to educate both the child and the adult in and out of school.

Democracy calls for training in the ideals of the aristocrat. In its best sense the word aristocracy means the ascendance of intellect, character, and judgment—and that is exactly what Jefferson sought. Surely no fair-minded democrat would object to deferring to such aristocratic leaders. "There will be a social order," says T. V. **Democratic aristocracy** Smith, "in which every man lives richly his own life, leads where his knowledge justifies, and follows where his ignorance compels." In order to be ideally successful a democracy would have to be made up of aristocrats in the best sense.

There most of us stick, for we are convinced that most men have low instincts, in spite of the fact that it has not been proved that the masses cannot be educated up to aristocratic standards. American education has striven to promote democracy, and in a less complex age it had some success. Lately, however, it has begun to lag in its approach to the aristocratic standard, not because of any fault in the educators, but because we the people have wanted it to lag. We refuse to make the career of teaching attractive to the best talent, we fear to launch out on ambitious and progressive educational programs, and we even refuse to finance the schooling of the new generation on a scale proportionate to that of the old.

We have good sound reasons. Who, runs the familiar refrain, will collect the garbage if everyone is educated? The answer lies not in a permanent slave class, but in rewards. If no automatic system of disposal can be found, many of us would collect garbage for three months if during the rest of the year we could live graciously after our own ideals with books or sports or travel. The chains of a materialistic civilization have to a considerable extent given us false and selfish standards and kept us from boldly launching out to build the aristocratic society, which in the end is the only possible foundation for a true democracy.

The historian Rostovtzeff finds the cause of the decay of ancient civilization in "the gradual absorption of the educated classes by the masses and the consequent simplification of all the functions of political, social, economic, and intellectual life, which we call the barbari- **Failure to** zation of the ancient world." Granting that this is true, sal- **educate** vation would have lain not in the compartmentation of **brings de-** classes but in the education of the masses. A society cannot **cay** stand still, for a living organism which has stopped growing has paved the way for death. Perhaps universal education was impossible in the ancient world, but we have no excuse for saying that today except for our own fear and selfishness. Our failure to educate successfully will mean the swallowing-up of civilization by the ignorant masses as inevitably as in ancient Rome.

Successful democracy demands that not only must we know the point at which to compromise, but we must know when not to compromise. An opponent of liberty has expressed the democratic dilemma succinctly: "I demand liberty in the name of your principles: I refuse it
Limit of tolerance to you in the name of mine." Here is a pitfall, open and unconcealed, but one around which the narrowness of the democratic path does not permit a detour. The enemies of liberty are experts in hiding behind our civil liberties while they undermine the foundations of democracy, which are those very civil liberties. These enemies, however, will be a problem in our country only to the extent to which we fail to implement democracy; it is in a way an indispensable barometer of how well or how ill democracy is performing its functions. "I think," wrote Justice Holmes in his famous dissent in the case of *Abrams v. United States,* "that we should be eternally vigilant against the attempts to check the expression of opinions that we loathe and believe to be fraught with death, unless they so imminently threaten immediate interference with the lawful and pressing purposes of the law that immediate check is required to save the country."

There will come a time when outside events, usually combined with our own shortsightedness, will demand that we lay aside our tolerance and fight. Lincoln was confronted by the dilemma of setting aside Constitu-
Practical dangers of tolerance tional guarantees or of observing the letter of the law and handicapping the war to save the Union. His decision was that he would not allow the Constitution to prevent the preservation of the democracy which it had been established to preserve. The danger that democratic tolerance will promote its own death was clearly illustrated when Kerensky, by allowing complete freedom to the Bolsheviks in 1917, paved the way for the overthrow by Lenin of Russia's liberal republic; a similar toleration of Hitler in the 1920's led to the insitution of the Nazi régime in 1933 and the death of German democracy.

It is this kind of sordid fact that lies behind the democratic diplomatic policies which to the idealist seem inconsistent with the principles of democracy. Wendell Willkie expressed a cold fact when he said that only
Democratic realism the productive are strong, and only the strong are free. Coach Leahy of Notre Dame said it another way: prayers work best when the players are big. We must learn that such order as nature has is dog eat dog. We need might that right may survive. But we must have so sound a sense of values that when the victory is won we will go back to the method of tolerance and compromise. Without right our might is no different from that of the brute.

This view of the mechanics of democracy would not be clear unless it pointed out that there are minor differences of method among the democratic nations. The essential point is not whether the constitution is written or unwritten, whether the laws are declared in the name of a king or a president, or whether elections are held at stated intervals or whenever the executive loses the **The test of democracy** confidence of the majority of the legislature. The essential test is whether or not the people can and do toss out the executive and the lawmakers and put in others more nearly to their liking.

The ideal way of advancement is not to tear up the social tree and replant it, but to stir up the earth around the roots and let in the air and moisture. Admittedly there are times when a social system has become so solidified that gradual change is all but impossible. **Democracy** How then can democracy get its start in a nation which has **comes by** never known it? It may make headway secretly among seri- **struggle** ous thinkers. It may be preached openly in a state still ostensibly autocratic but too decadent and inefficient to enforce restrictive laws. It may even be instituted occasionally by a monarch or dictator with the best interests of his people at heart. The commonest method, however, is by revolution—and seldom a single revolution, for the autocratic elements are usually strong enough to keep the political pendulum swinging for generations. This condition is especially observable in Hispanic America. The winning of democracy takes a long struggle. On the palace of the Viceroy of India there was inscribed this motto: "Liberty will not descend to a people; a people must raise themselves to liberty." Democracy cannot succeed until a people agree to it and write its precepts in their hearts, and that takes generations. Heine observed that the Frenchman loved freedom as his mistress, the Englishman as his wife, and the German as his grandmother. It was a more bitterly tragic German than Heine who wrote: "The flag of the democratic Republic was never raised in our hearts."

Democracy is the political expression to the highest degree of human judgment, balance, restraint, and courage. It is not being, but becoming; it can be lost, but never fully won. It is eternal conflict because each generation will have problems which have never been faced **Democracy** before, and which must be met with skill and courage; **is in con-** everything depends on their solution, for democracy once **tinual dan-** lost can be regained only with blood and toil. It is no **ger** wonder, as Jefferson said, that "timid men prefer the calm of despotism to the boisterous sea of liberty." "All life is an experiment," said Justice Holmes. "Every year, if not every day, we have to wager our salvation upon some prophecy based upon imperfect knowledge." There are no sure guides; each generation must depend upon itself. Even if democracy disappears, humanity will begin the long struggle back, for the yearning for liberty is fundamental in human nature.

Democracy does have certain rules which govern its procedures. In the first place it is a *government by law,* not by the whims of rulers. The basic issue between any two forms of government is over the right to make the law and to control its administration. Only at **Supremacy** this point is the form of government important, for if the **of the law** constitution and its application do not put these powers into the hands of the people that government is not a democracy. In a democracy the law is supreme, even over the highest executive power.

In order to protect individual liberty under law the people reserve to themselves certain *civil liberties:** freedom of speech, press, religion, and assembly; the right to a "day in court" to protect themselves against executive tyranny or misapplication of the laws; and the **Civil liber-** right to change their executive or their legislative repre- **ties** sentatives when new problems or a shifting balance of opinion demands new policies. Civil liberties may change their form (as when a panel of judges replaces a jury); but these changes must be made with the full knowledge and consent of the people, and the substance of the guarantees of liberty must not be altered. Without these civil liberties there can be no change willed by the people because without them the people cannot develop or express a desire for change. The right to investigate, decide, and recommend is fundamental, even to a minority so small it can never hope to gain office.

The second rule of democracy is that *both sides must be willing to compromise.* The only thing which we can consider inevitable is a change of circumstances. In order to survive we must be prepared to adapt our- **Necessity** selves to change, and the means we use to become adapted **of compro-** with the least social strain are civil liberties. Therefore no **mise** subject of conflict is exempt from compromise *except the exercise of civil liberties,* for it is by breaking down civil liberties that totalitarianism makes its insidious entry. Of course, this is a hard rule to obey, but no people can implement democracy until they are willing to agree to accept it. It means that a sincere effort is made to distinguish between moral principles on the one hand and opinions, prejudices, and self-destructive stubbornness on the other. Enforced religion, prescribed modes of dress, censorship of news, race prejudices, prohibition, all lose or will lose their standing as principles. Thus, with principles reduced to a minimum (and ideally including only the support of civil

* Technically *civil liberties* are exemptions from arbitrary governmental interference with person, opinion, or property; *civil rights* are those such as the right to be free from slavery, to sue, give evidence, and to hold property; and *political rights* imply participation in the management of the government.

liberties), the democrat finds that he can agree with his fellows on most issues and that subjects of conflict can usually be compromised.

The method of compromise means that laws and rights are evolutionary, not static. *Democracy is a process, not a set form.* It is in a way a continuous revolution. The force now entrenched in the government finds itself confronted by a counterforce which arises from new conditions and new alliances. Their clash results in compromise, or perhaps the intrenched force steps down and the counterforce rises to supplant it. But once a force yields on an issue, that issue is ordinarily settled; the pivot of social balance moves onward. The fact that the names of political parties in a democracy go unchanged, perhaps for generations, is deceptive; each party may keep a fundamental *attitude* (as liberal or conservative), but its practical program usually accepts accomplished facts and goes on from there.

Democracy a process, not a set form

A third rule of democracy is that it *never lays claim to perfection.* To do so would make it no better than other political theories which refuse to recognize change because they regard themselves as already perfect. The democrat instinctively distrusts a clear-cut victory for one side, for he insists on the rule of live and let live; and in order for the defeated party to live, it must maintain a reasonable degree of strength. Many sincere zealots distrust democracy because it does not bring complete political, social, and economic justice immediately, and they jeer about the democrats' promise of "pie in the sky." The informed democrat need not be alarmed by the zealots' demand for perfection. They fail to see that the good law of today is the strait jacket of tomorrow, simply because times change. Since the basis of democracy is a changing balance of social conflict, an individual or an interest will get what it has inherited or what it earns by its own efforts. It takes no mental giant to find areas of despotism in any existing democracy, but there has never been another civilized society where progress advances more smoothly and steadily and where the individual has a greater effect upon its course.

Democracy will never be perfected

Christian perfectionists are undoubtedly right: we will never have a perfect society or government until the human heart becomes perfect. Even that would not guarantee an end to struggles over differences of opinion, nor would it guarantee Mother Nature's co-operation in making everything smooth and easy. Democracy is not, never has been, and never will be perfect, but it bears within it the means of approaching perfection. *Freedom is and always has been relative.* Some men have attained some liberty at some times and in some places, and we believe that through the generations more men are attaining more liberty at more times and in more places. For

Freedom is relative

that reason we must judge not by the perfect standard but by whether the means of improvement are present and whether they have been and are being used. The history of democracy is not lily-white; indeed, it has often been gray—a dirty gray—but by its union of might and right it has steadily advanced the cause of the common man.

The division of political opinion between left and right had its origin during the French Revolution, when in the Legislative Assembly the members who favored greatest changes were seated on the left of the **Divisions** presiding officer and those who desired fewest changes were **of political** seated on the right. Today few people can judge accurately **opinion** the divisions of political opinions. No matter how moderate one of them might be, its name can become a term of scorn or opprobrium. Thus, democratic socialism is persistently confused with communism, from which it is as different as night from day; New Deal is frequently used to indicate socialism and/or communism; and communists flatly call the democratic nations fascistic. Nevertheless, the divisions of political opinion can be and should be distinguished carefully. These are the four major groups:

1) *Reactionary:* desires to return to the past; must be used only in connection with those who are opponents of liberty. Here belongs the absolute monarchist, who would have the state controlled for the benefit of a "noble" class, and the nondemocratic capitalist (fascist), who would have the state controlled by the owners of capital; the latter claims to be a counterrevolutionist, which really means a revolutionist against revolution. His object is to erect the "perfect" state and to stifle all social conflict.

2) *Conservative:* desires to keep things pretty much as they are; approves past changes, but at any move toward further change insists in alarm that our way of life is at stake and he will never agree to it. But he does in the long run, meanwhile swearing that it is the last change he will accept. He is a necessary curb on the liberal (whose reforms are often hasty and half-formulated), and he is at his best in fighting ill-considered action and in consolidating the gains the liberals have made.

3) *Liberal:* desires gradual change by means of force and counterforce. He may want little or great change. Democratic socialists belong in this group because they wish to change gradually as public opinion is educated: that is, they desire the state to control the means of production but would approach it only as the people are convinced. The liberal's function is to prevent the conservative from freezing the social structure in a dogmatic pattern and thus arresting progress.

4) *Radical:* desires to tear everything up by the roots and plant anew after whatever pattern he believes is perfect. Historically the term was applied to democratic revolutionists, but today it is pretty well con-

fined to revolutionary or nondemocratic socialists (communists) and the revolutionary socialist wing of the Nazis. The radical's present object is to erect the "perfect" state and to stifle all social conflict. In a very real sense, however, Stalin's policies can be called counterrevolutionary, for the Soviet has been liquidating Marxist communism.

For generations these opinions were spoken of as extending from the reactionaries on the extreme right in a straight line to the radicals on the extreme left. It rarely occurred to anyone that there could be any resemblance between the two extremes. Since World War I, however, the resemblance has become marked—note how marked when we set up these four political opinions on the face of a clock. The method may not be strictly accurate for the divisions of opinions within the quadrants (they differ with time and country), but it will not lead the observer far astray.

The most interesting fact clarified by the clock face is the juxtaposi-

DEMOCRATIC HEMICIRCLE

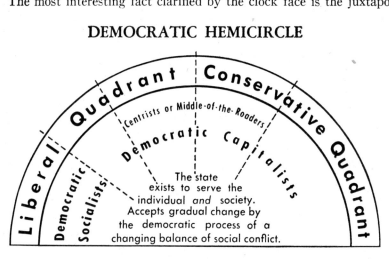

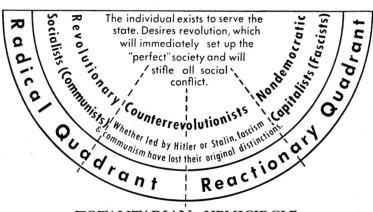

TOTALITARIAN HEMICIRCLE

tion of extreme right and extreme left. Their basic principles are so similar as to be almost interchangeable. That is why a certain New York

Affinity between extreme right and left

Congressman could lead a communist mob in the afternoon, then put on his tuxedo and deliver an inspiring address to a fascist banquet in the evening. That is why Mussolini could begin his career as a revolutionary socialist and transfer to fascism without passing through the democratic quadrants. That is why Hitler was able to weld together the Nazi Party from fascist and communist elements. That is why Russia in her occupied zones can safely entrust high administrative and political offices to former fascists.

The reason for this easy transfer can be made even clearer. In the beginning a communist was a nondemocratic socialist, and a fascist was a nondemocratic capitalist. Each theory is based on dominance by a class, and once the radicals had liquidated the middle class, or the reactionaries had drugged the working class, the basis could not easily be shifted—theoretically it is impossible. Actually, when each party came into power, the leaders seized absolute control of industry, and the distinction between socialism and capitalism lost its meaning *except for purely propaganda purposes:* their nondemocratic (or totalitarian) nature was retained in both cases. So far as the effective leaders of Germany and Russia were concerned, the struggle between them in World War II was strictly for power; whichever won could have absorbed the other without digestive pains. All that would have been needed was a few lessons devoted to party clichés and a reversal in loyalty between brown and red.

In order to understand this process, it must be recalled that in practice the totalitarian state throttles both private capitalism and socialism. The struggle today is between democracy and totalitarian soviet im-

Soviet imperialism is not communistic

perialism. The communism of Marx may have had some title to be called socialism, for not only did it promote government ownership of the means of production but it upheld the socialistic tenet "from each according to his ability, to each according to his *need*." Under Stalin, Russia gave up the socialistic aspects of communism when it put into its constitution the proviso "from each according to his ability, to each according to his *production*." This, to be exact, is more like state capitalism than communism, but we should not take terms too seriously here. Soviet use of the word communism is inaccurate and is retained only for its psychological value and because soviet imperialists can thereby hoodwink sincere though unbalanced individuals of other lands (fellow travelers as well as communists) into serving as a fifth column for Russia's nationalistic program. Marxist communism is almost dead in Russia, except as gabbled precepts, and the real communists are found outside the iron curtain. They will be the first ones liquidated if Soviet Russia ever gains control, unless they renounce the *practice* of their ideology and plump for statism.

The fact that political parties in a democracy are made up of temporary alliances renders it perfectly possible and indeed common for individuals or parties to occupy different quadrants in different times and places or on different issues. Thus, the Democratic Party of the 1930's covered both the liberal and the conservative quadrant though its weight was on the left; at the same time the Republican Party covered almost as wide a range (even including a few socialists), but its weight was on the right. Mere party names mean nothing; we must study the opinions of their members to know where to place them. It is noteworthy also that individuals have a tendency to retain the opinions formed in early maturity. Thus, it is possible for a liberal young man to become a conservative (or almost reactionary) old man without having changed his opinions: successive triumphs by new alliances of liberal interests push the dividing line farther to the left in each generation; so when our liberal young man becomes ossified with age, he finds that the dividing line has passed him and left him stranded on the conservative side.

[margin note: Party names mean little]

While it is true that the pivot of social conflict in the democratic hemicircle moves to the left (brings the common man to the fore more and more), it must be understood that the *method* used remains democratic. This point is made clearer if we picture new issues and causes (possibly first proposed by revolutionists) as coming into the liberal quadrant for adjudication by the democratic process, then passing clockwise over the dividing line into the limbo of conservative lost causes. The issue of social security had this history; socialized medicine is being subjected to the process. On each issue the indicator fluctuates for a while between the two points of view, then comes to rest at some reasonable point between; thereafter it is usually accepted as settled, and such changes as occur will be administrative.

BIBLIOGRAPHICAL NOTE

The Completion of the English Process

For the English and European economic and political background see Edward P. Cheyney, *European Background of American History, 1300–1600* (1904). The above view of English origins of the democratic process is from Leland D. Baldwin, *God's Englishman: The Evolution of the Anglo-Saxon Spirit* (1944).

Democracy: Its Meaning and Its Method

This section is reprinted almost verbatim from Leland D. Baldwin, *Best Hope of Earth: A Grammar of Democracy* (1948).

Chapter IV

TRANSPLANTING ENGLAND
TO AMERICA

1 *The Founding of the Southern Colonies*

WHILE the world was going mad over the golden will-o'-the-wisp that lay at the bottom of mercantilism and that lured so many gallant hidalgos to their deaths, a little group of men in London was working to undermine the reign of gold and substitute the reign of **Sir Walter** commerce. The leader of this group was that pearl-en-**Raleigh** crusted mirror of fashion, Sir Walter Raleigh, whose contradictions of character made him the typical man of the English Renascence. After a day spent in dancing obsequious attendance upon Queen Elizabeth and intriguing in corners for the overthrow of the current favorite, he would retire to his study in the turret of his house in the Strand and there pass most of the night with the classics or the poetic muse. Raleigh had proved his courage in the wars, his arrogance and his subtlety in the scramble at court for royal favor and for confiscated lands; now he was to show his vision, his perseverance, and his patriotism in another field.

Raleigh received his inspiration from his half-brother, Sir Humphrey Gilbert, who died on his quest for the Northwest Passage to the Pacific. Raleigh succeeded to Gilbert's patent and added to Gilbert's dream one **Opposition** of his own. He saw that the central idea of mecantilism **to mercan-** was unsound and that gold was only an instrument of com-**tilism** merce. As one of his friends wrote: "That is the richest land that feeds the most men." Moreover, "he that rules the sea, rules the commerce of the world and to him that rules the commerce of the world belongs the treasure of the world and indeed the world itself."

This rule he hoped to gain for England by adding her surplus population and her surplus cash to the vast strategic and natural resources of America. He proposed to increase England's wealth by planting an "English nation" in North America which should be an outlet for the "sturdy vagabonds" that swarmed in the hedgerows of once merry England and a market for the goods that England's manufacturers were itching to make.

In 1584 Raleigh sent out an expedition which explored the North Carolina coast, and when the report was presented to the "Virgin Queen," she, in a moment of self-gratulation, named the land Virginia. Other expeditions followed, but a full-dress attempt in 1587 to plant on Roanoke Island a colony of one hundred fifty men, women, and children only resulted in the dis- **Raleigh fails as a colonizer** appearance of the colonists. The mystery has never been certainly solved, though there are indications that they were massacred by the Indians. Raleigh spent on his Virginia ventures the sum of £40,000, a truly enormous amount for that day. Eventually he could stand the drain no longer, and to recoup his fortune he sold a part of his rights in Virginia and turned toward the reputed wealth of Manoa in the backlands of Guiana and the disgrace which brought him at last to the executioner's block. But he never lost his faith in Virginia. "I shall yet live to see it an English nation," he wrote. He did, and the realization that he had planted the seeds of England's greatness overseas must have warmed his heart while he pored over his books in the bleak prison of the Tower of London.

Raleigh failed partly because England was occupied with the war against Spain; it was therefore natural that upon the conclusion of peace, new plans for colonization were made. Raleigh's experience showed that such an undertaking would require the resources of more than one man. The joint stock form of enterprise already **Joint stock companies** in use by companies of merchants trading to the East Indies, Muscovy (Russia), and the Levant offered a method of providing capital. Successful colonies must rest on agriculture, but here plans were made for settlements devoted to trade, fishing, and lumbering and fed chiefly by "supply" fleets from England.

Presently a group of merchants and investors from London and another from Plymouth, Bristol, and other western English cities applied for royal charters. King James issued (1606) a single charter to them as the Virginia Company and provided that it should be gov- **London and Plymouth companies** erned by a Council of Virginia sitting in London and appointed by him. The two groups, however, were each permitted their own area: the London Company was to take the coast of what is now North Carolina and Virginia, and the Plymouth

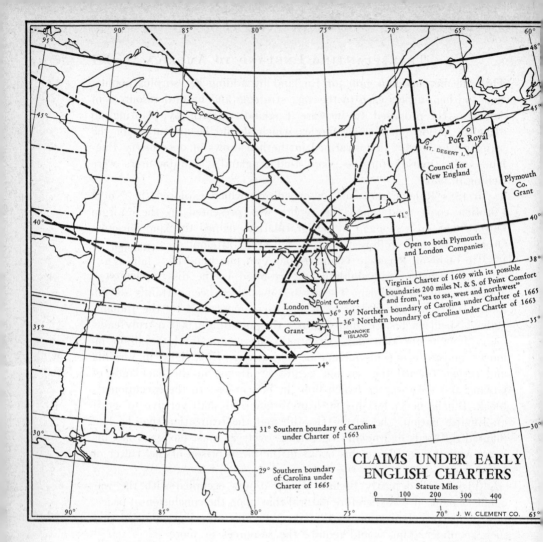

CLAIMS UNDER EARLY
ENGLISH CHARTERS

Statute Miles
0   100   200   300   400

Company what is now New England; the coast between was open to either. Though the settlers were not self-governing, they were to enjoy much the same civil rights as Englishmen at home. Economic power was held strictly by the companies, and settlers were to labor for the companies and receive their support from the general fund. The principal leader of the London Company was Sir Thomas Smith, the richest merchant of his day, who had been a backer of several of the great chartered companies and was founder and first governor of the East India Company. Associated with him in the Virginia venture were the Puritan Sir Edwin Sandys and the Earl of Southampton, the patron of Shakespeare.

The charter was modified in 1609, when the two companies were separated and the London wing became the Virginia Company of London. The Plymouth wing devoted itself to fishing and trading until 1620, when it was metamorphosed by a royal patent into the **Virginia Company of London** Council for New England. The Virginia Company of London now had both political and economic control, and an amended charter of 1612 did not change this basic fact. The way was left open for common settlers to become land owners. Its boundaries were set as extending two hundred miles north and south of Cape Comfort "up into the land, throughout from sea to sea, west and northwest." If the northern boundary extended northwest, as Virginia claimed, she would have had most of the North American continent.

The London Company's expedition of one hundred four settlers in three ships under the command of Christopher Newport sailed into Chesapeake Bay 26 April 1607 and a few days later landed on a low peninsula on the north shore of the James River. There, not far from the site of the ill-fated Spanish mission of 1570, was begun the erection of a fort and of a village which was named Jamestown. **Founding of Jamestown, 1607** Newport sailed away to begin a career of shuttling across the Atlantic in the service of the London Company. Most of the colonists were aristocrats who would not stain their hands with toil and preferred to look for gold. To make matters worse, quarrels broke out; and even the ravages of malaria, which took all but about forty of the colonists, did not stop them.

OFFERING MOST
Excellent fruites by Planting in
VIRGINIA.

Exciting all fuch as be well affected
to further the fame.

LONDON
Printed for SAMVEL MACHAM, and are to befold at
his Shop In Pauls Church-yard, at the
Signe of the Bul-head.
1 6 0 9.

Title page of an advertising brochure which attempted to lure colonists to Jamestown

Newport brought new colonists and new supplies twice in 1608, but Jamestown survived the next winter only by the vigor of John Smith, a veteran of the Turkish wars and a member of the council, who gained such ascendance that he even put the gentry to work. On **Captain John Smith (1580–1631)** one occasion he was captured by Indians, and it has been claimed that his life was spared only by the intercession of Pocahontas, the daughter of the chief of the Powhatan Confederacy. At any rate, Smith stood very high with the Indians and was able by blandishments and loaded muskets to get enough corn from them to keep the colony alive. In the summer of 1609 a fleet with about four hundred additional colonists arrived. The colony now had about five hundred people, but when Smith was injured in an explosion and left for England it fell into anarchy, and white arrogance promoted Indian trouble. The winter of 1609–10 was "The Starving Time," when all but about sixty perished. In the spring the survivors started back to England but before they reached Chesapeake Bay they learned that a new governor,

Lord Delaware, was approaching with three ships and settlers. Virginia was saved.

During the next few years the colony was firmly planted. Farmers and craftsmen were brought in. A line of wholesomely severe governors preserved order and withstood the Indians. The system of common crops **Economic** and storehouses was done away with, and each colonist re- **and politi-** ceived his own tract of land. Nevertheless, Virginia had a **cal growth** bad name in England and investors hesitated to sink more money in the venture. About 1612 John Rolfe, the same who later married Pocahontas, began experimenting with the cultivation and curing of

Some exploits of the intrepid Captain John Smith, according to his *Generall History of Virginia, New-England, and the Summer Isles* (1624)

tobacco, and it soon became evident that here was the colony's economic anchor. Tobacco culture boomed, and the Crown helped by giving Virginia the monopoly in the English dominions and raising the tariff on Spanish and Portuguese tobacco; all Virginia tobacco, however, had to be shipped to England. Sir Thomas Smith as "treasurer" had been in effect dictator of the Virginia Company and had worked loyally to establish the colony firmly; now the growing democracy of England was reflected in the demand of the stockholders for a greater voice, and their leader, Sir Edwin Sandys, procured the charter of 1612 with its "democratical" leanings. Presently dissensions rent the company over the control of the tobacco monopoly, fisheries, fur trade, and the ownership of land grants in Virginia and the Bermudas. The company, however, sought to meet the colonists' discontent with their government by setting up in 1619 a representative assembly called the House of Burgesses.

It marked the abandonment of dictation by the company and the introduction of the English common law.

The Virginia Company now began to promote a higher quality of immigration, to build churches, inns, and schools, and to try its hand at manufactures. The latter endeavor, however, was hampered by the popularity of tobacco. Financial stringency led to a renewal of **Fall of the** dissension, and both colonists and English investors could **Virginia** point to confusion and ineptitude in the administration of **Company** Virginia. This was used as an argument against the democratic party both in the company and in Parliament. To cap confusion by disaster

the Indians rose in 1622 and massacred 347 persons and destroyed much property before they could be subdued. A royal inquiry ensued in 1623. It revealed that 5500 people had gone to Virginia, 300 had returned to England, 4000 had died, and only 1200 remained. The "democratical" government of the Virginia Company was a failure and had been signalized by dissension, waste, corruption, and unsound investments. The Crown entered suit for the voidance of the charter, and in 1624 the company lost its powers and Virginia became a royal colony.

Sir William Berkeley, who was to serve as governor for most of a generation, arrived in 1642 and quickly became popular because of his liberal economic policies and his vigorous

POWHATAN
Held this state & fashion when Capt. Smith was delivered to him prisoner 1607

Powhatan, as Captain John Smith described him

support of the provincial militia in putting down an Indian **Governor** rising in 1644. Virginia had its popular party during the **William** English Civil War, led among others by William Claiborne **Berkeley** and including a large number of Puritans who resided **(1608–** chiefly on the "Southside" of the James. Berkeley, heart and **77)** soul a cavalier, gave his support to the king and harried the popular party so vigorously that a thousand Puritans emigrated to Maryland. Berkeley welcomed refugee royalists to Virginia, though it is certain that there were not as many nobles among these cavaliers as modern genealogists like to think. Berkeley was deposed in 1652 by a Cromwellian commission which included the ubiquitous Claiborne, but he assumed power again in

1660 after the restoration of Charles II. In general, Virginia had approved of Berkeley's royalism; it received its reward when Charles II elevated it to the rank of a "dominion" by quartering its seal on his arms along with those of England, Scotland, and Ireland.

During the Civil War in England the Dutch had carried on a brisk trade which brought a considerable measure of prosperity to Virginia. Cromwell's attempt to break the Dutch carrying trade brought the to-

Rise of large plantations

bacco monopoly under English control. Charles II restricted trade rigidly and thereby fostered the social and economic revolution which was under way. By now there were around forty thousand inhabitants, most of them of English stock. Early Virginia had been a land of small farms, but now it was becoming one of great plantations chiefly because it was hitched to a one-crop economy, tobacco. This condition was not simply because the English government and English merchants insisted upon it, though the first did impose enormous revenues and the latter collected inflated commissions.

Tobacco "making" was a year-round occupation, for it not only kept the planter busy in the growing season but enabled him to put his slaves or servants to clearing new land during the winter. Three to eight years of straight tobacco planting were enough to ruin a farm as far as the agricultural techniques of the time were concerned. But tobacco was easily raised by unskilled labor, it kept well, and was in fact the only Virginia agricultural product in considerable demand. Land was cheap, and labor was dear; so the inevitable result was that the settlers robbed the soil with tobacco, grew a few poor crops of corn or wheat, then left the fields to erode or lie fallow while they concentrated on new land.

Concentration upon tobacco resulted in an overproduction which sadly depressed prices. The settler on a small and worn-out farm could not make a living, and so he sold his land and moved farther west or away from the rivers. Land was thus concentrated in the hands of great planters, who could afford to rotate crops or let land lie fallow while they exploited their newly cleared and productive fields. In any case the rivers, which were the highways of the colony, were now accessible to small farmers only by grace of the great riparian planters. The latter did not hesitate to squeeze every advantage out of the situation.

The use of the rivers as highways blocked whatever chance there may have been for the growth of towns with their professional and artisan classes. The introduction of Negro slavery in 1619, though it was slow of growth, added to the social and economic distinctions which were developing. Berkeley himself owned a large plantation and so was by nature and position sympathetic with the developing aristocracy. He was in particular an enemy of schools. "I thank God," he said, "there are no free schools nor printing, and I hope we shall not have any these hundred years, for learning has brought disobedience and heresy and sects into the world and printing has [*spread them*] and libels against the best government. God keep us from both."

This growing aristocracy was by no means composed entirely of "cavalier blood." Yeomen farmers could and did join it by ability, lucky marriages, or crooked land deals. The new caste was thus cemented less by blood and background than by common interests. The governor permitted embezzlements of tax tobacco and the collection of exorbitant customs duties, and he made huge **Planter aristocracy** land grants to favorites. Berkeley did not disdain to take his share and meanwhile shamelessly kept his control of the House of Burgesses by bribery with land, privileges, and a high per-diem payment of tobacco to the members for their maintenance during sessions. Control was further solidified by laws of primogeniture and entail, which passed lands intact to the eldest son, and by strict limitation of the suffrage to the well-to-do. The parish vestry, which controlled the moral and religious life of each community, and the county court, which controlled its civil life, soon became closed corporations, that is, self-perpetuating. Meanwhile the tobacco trade had fallen into the control of London merchants who bought tobacco cheap and sold goods dear; sometimes the tobacco price went down to a halfpenny a pound. The "law" of supply and demand was not permitted to work, and prices remained low even in bad crop years. Those years also had poor food crops, so that suffering among the poor was widespread.

An explosion was inevitable, but it came from an unexpected quarter. Displaced farmers had to live, and they naturally went west. There they were joined each year by about fifteen hundred redemptioners who had completed their terms of service (in payment for ocean passage) and now took up their fifty-acres headright on the frontier. Virginia had sought to guard its frontier along **Berkeley and Indian troubles** the Fall Line by giving lands to "societies" of "warlike Christian men," on condition that they erect "palisadoes" for defense. In these palisades one can find the genesis of the later "stations" of Kentucky. Conflict came late in 1675 when a party of militia out along the Potomac to avenge an Indian murder attacked the wrong Indians, a band which was fleeing southward from the Iroquois. The flame soon involved both Virginia and Maryland, and Indian war parties were appearing far within the line of settlements. To the amazement of Virginia, Berkeley refused to allow the militia to march against the Indian towns lest they also attack the "friendly" Indians—as they probably would have—and most men were convinced that it was because of his investment in the fur trade. The suffering frontiersmen refused to wait any longer, and early in 1676 the "commoners" on the upper James, largely Southside Puritans,

Cartouche of a map, dated before 1700, from an atlas
of maps collected and bound in Holland, 1763

embodied themselves under Nathaniel Bacon (1647–1676), a young member of the governor's council. In defiance of Berkeley's prohibition they marched out and severely defeated the Indians. This action did not, however, put a stop to the raids.

Berkeley prepared to seize the "rebel" upon his return, but the country threatened to march to Bacon's rescue and aid him in enforcing reform. The governor was alarmed and to placate the populace dismissed

Bacon's Laws

his corrupt House of Burgesses, which had held office for fifteen years, and called for a new election. Bacon emerged from the wilderness and was elected to the new house, but when he went to Jamestown he was arrested and forced to make a public apology before he was released. When it became evident that Berkeley still opposed action against the Indians despite the continuous raids, Bacon entered Jamestown at the head of five hundred men and demanded a commission to lead a force against the Indians. The governor yielded reluctantly. Bacon then took the opportunity to force through the Burgesses the acts known as "Bacon's Laws." Manhood suffrage was reinstituted, legal fees were limited, popular representatives were to lay county taxes, parish vestrymen were to be chosen by election, terms of public office were limited, and the governor's councilors were no longer exempt from taxation. Not another country in the world could boast such democratic laws. Berkeley was forced to sign them, but, as might have been expected, the king disallowed them.

As soon as Bacon was out of sight Berkeley began to raise an army among the great planters and begged troops from England. Bacon held no illusions that planters and people were reconcilable, nor did he doubt on which side the king would be. Maryland and North Carolina were suffering from the same economic troubles **Bacon's Rebellion** as Virginia, and Bacon now began to plan a union among the three to fight for independence, probably with the aid of France or Holland. There actually was an abortive revolt in Maryland, but the North Carolinians did not rise for another year. When Berkeley fled to the eastern shore of the bay, Bacon marched against the Indians again and defeated them. Berkeley now returned and seized Jamestown, but Bacon forced him out and burned the town lest it be of further use to the governor. A month later, October 1676, Bacon died of fever. The rebellion did not collapse at once, but it did break up when troops began to arrive from England. Though Charles ii had issued a pardon to all rebels save Bacon and had recalled the governor, Berkeley refused to leave until he had taken his revenge by hanging a score of rebels and plundering the property of anyone who had not stood with him. The king was outraged, and Berkeley felt the fact so keenly that he died of a broken heart soon after arriving in England.

The failure of Bacon's Rebellion was of deep significance for Virginia. The small farmers on tidewater sank to the status of poor whites or moved west to the Piedmont. Even though tobacco prices remained low, the conservatism of the planter class was so deep that **Significance of Bacon's Rebellion** a later governor sheared the Burgesses of their judicial functions and forced them to impose a permanent tax on tobacco for the regular support of the governor and other Crown officials. Virginia thus lost its most powerful weapon of defense. With the executive and the judiciary under control of the Crown, Virginia became the most perfectly disciplined of the Thirteen Colonies and an example for the others to shun. Nevertheless, democracy was not dead; it had only retired to the Piedmont with Bacon's retreating troopers. The time was to come when a man from the Piedmont was to lead Virginia in a greater and more successful rebellion and write a Declaration of Independence for a new nation.

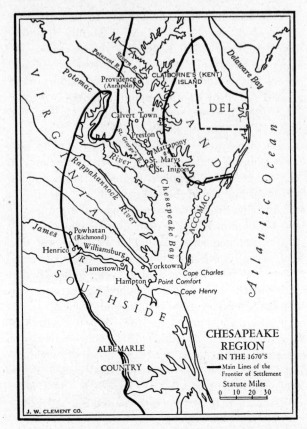

CHESAPEAKE REGION IN THE 1670'S

The first successful proprietary colony was Maryland. George Calvert (1580?–1632), first Baron of Baltimore in the Irish peerage, had been active in the Virginia Company and the Council for New England, and in

Maryland granted to Calvert

1623 he failed in an attempt to found a colony on the Avalon Peninsula in Newfoundland. In 1625 he became a Catholic and added to his economic objectives the desire to found in America a refuge for English and Irish Catholics. Charles I, who had leanings toward Catholicism, obliged him with a gift of land: the slice of Virginia lying between the Potomac and the fortieth parallel, and including also the eastern shore of the Chesapeake in the same latitude. Baltimore was to exercise civil and criminal jurisdiction, "with the advice, assent, and approbation of the freemen of the province." However, the charter expressly gave him the same rights as those exercised by the Bishop of Durham in the County Palatine of Durham in England; and, since these rights were absolute, the Baltimores asserted that only they could initiate legislation and that the assembly was merely a debating society with no practical jurisdiction. The fact was that the Baltimores were moderate men who aspired to temper their despotism with benevolence, but their colonists showed their Englishness from the first by a stubborn campaign to make the assembly the real governing power.

George Calvert died before his charter received the final seal of approval, and his son Cecilius inherited. Cecilius made his brother Leonard leader of the first colony, which in 1634 settled at St. Marys just north of the mouth of the Potomac. The Calverts profited by the **Settlement** experiences of Virginia and established sound agricultural **of Mary-** and Indian policies. Plantations grew up on the coast, **land** chiefly cultivating tobacco, but the annual quitrents payable in perpetuity to the proprietor discouraged immigration.

The colony had never been intended solely for Catholics, and followers of all Christian creeds had been welcomed and protected; indeed, the majority of the settlers of St. Marys were Protestants. Because of the conflicts in England and the colonies, the policies of the Calverts had to be delicately balanced between Catholics and Protestants and between king and Parliament, but there is no reason to doubt the Calverts' sincere belief in religious tolerance. Unfortunately the settlers were not as liberal. Baltimore had just managed to save his palatinate from a Jesuit attempt at control when his governor was met by a rebellion of the Puritans who had left Virginia and settled near Annapolis. Maryland had been cut from Virginian territory, and Virginia nursed an ambition to recover it. William Claiborne, the Virginia trader, thus managed for years to carry on a "war" with unofficial Virginian support. In 1644 Claiborne drove the governor out of the colony. Calvert fled to the protection of Governor Berkeley, who presently sent another Virginia army to restore him.

Lord Baltimore now shrewdly strengthened his position by sending out a Protestant governor and at the same time protected his Catholic followers by having the assembly accept the Toleration Act of 1649. This protected persons "professing to believe in Jesus **Toleration** Christ," while threatening non-Christians with death. Clai- **Act** borne, momentarily ascendant in Virginia, led another Virginia army to Maryland and established a Puritan régime which did away with toleration. However, Lord Baltimore's political lines had been well laid, and in 1657 Cromwell ordered the restoration of his government and of toleration. Thereafter Virginia ceased to interfere in Maryland.

The history of the Carolinas showed proprietorship at its worst. The Carolina Grant was made in 1663 and 1665 by Charles II to a group of eight nobles headed by Shaftesbury, Albemarle, and Clarendon, and it

Carolina Grant

included everything between the present southern boundary of Virginia (a second steal from that province) southward to 29°, well below St. Augustine. The philosopher John Locke drew up an elaborate plan, called "The Fundamental Constitutions of Carolina," which provided for a hierarchy based on slavery and serfdom and running up to a nobility equipped with outlandish titles. Fortunately the plan was recognized as unworkable, though it did in some degree influence the growth of a landed aristocracy in South Carolina. It soon became evident that the proprietors were interested only in quitrents and proposed to make no contributions to the development or protection of the colony. By 1690 the proprietors had recognized the separateness of the two settled extremes of their colony and were sending out a governor to each.

Seal of the proprietors of the Carolinas

Most of the proprietors had in fact become disgusted with the situation and sold their shares.

North Carolina, known as Albemarle until about 1690, was occupied as early as 1654 by an overflow of population from Virginia which settled on Albemarle Sound. As Virginia's troubles multiplied, settlers

The Carolinas

continued to move in—mostly poor men who raised tobacco, grain, and hogs and traded indifferently with merchantmen and pirates. From the first the proprietors had little success in collecting their quitrents from this rather turbulent democracy, and finally in 1729 North Carolina became a royal colony. South Carolina had a quite different history. Charleston was settled in 1670 and immediately began to flourish because of the Indian trade, which engaged the attention of many energetic traders and investors. Presently the early settlers along with a considerable complement of newcomers, including many Huguenots, turned their attention to agriculture. Rice became the staple crop about 1693, and the plantations engaged in its culture absorbed thousands of Indian and Negro slaves. Indigo was grown from the first but did not become important until after 1744. The proprietors considered South Carolina well worth holding, but their failure to send help during the Yamassee Indian War led to a rebellion in 1716. A request to the king to make it a royal province was promptly granted. The proprietors sold their rights in the land to the Crown in 1729, except that Carteret kept a strip across northern North Carolina.

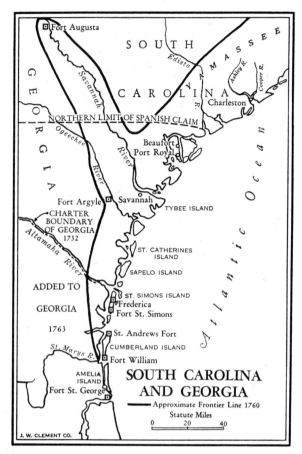

The map shows the following labels:

Fort Augusta · SOUTH · G E O R G I A · Savannah R. · Edisto · TENNESSEE · Ashley R. · Cooper R. · CAROLINA · Charleston · NORTHERN LIMIT OF SPANISH CLAIM · Ogeechee R. · Beaufort · Port Royal · River · Fort Argyle · Savannah · TYBEE ISLAND · CHARTER BOUNDARY OF GEORGIA 1732 · Altamaha River · ST. CATHERINES ISLAND · SAPELO ISLAND · ADDED TO · GEORGIA · 1763 · ST. SIMONS ISLAND · Frederica · Fort St. Simons · St. Andrews Fort · St. Marys R. · CUMBERLAND ISLAND · Fort William · AMELIA ISLAND · Fort St. George · Atlantic Ocean · SOUTH CAROLINA AND GEORGIA · Approximate Frontier Line 1760 · Statute Miles · 0 20 40 · J. W. CLEMENT CO.

Though Georgia was founded a lifetime after the Carolinas, its place as a southern colony makes treatment at this point logical. The remarkable economic expansion which affected mother country and colonies alike after the Treaty of Utrecht led to troubles with Spain which seemed to forecast war. Under the circumstances it **Georgia** was considered wise to found a military colony below the Savannah River as a buffer between South Carolina and Florida. At this time a group of philanthropic gentlemen had managed to push through some prison reforms in England with the result that thousands of poor debtors had been released from prison. The proposed military colony seemed the place to put them in, and so in 1732 the Crown granted to the philanthropic gentlemen as trustees a charter to settle and govern for twenty-one years the land between the Savannah and Altamaha rivers on west to the South Sea. Note that the Crown was now less generous than it had been under the Stuarts and limited the governmental powers of the trustees and the duration of their charter. Land grants were limited to five hundred acres; there were to be no slavery and no hard liquor; and the trustees were not to own land in the colony. The project was so popular that contributions poured in plentifully; the settlers actually did not have to pay taxes until after the expiration of the trusteeship!

Seal of the Georgia trustees

General James Oglethorpe (1696–1785) was appointed "agent" (the trustees governed from England) and in 1733 surveyed and settled Savannah. German, Scottish, and English immigrants came, but for some reason few debtors. Oglethorpe was a wise administrator but was very busy warding English and Spanish enemies off the colony. The people soon came to resent the authoritative hand of the trustees and demanded self-rule, even if they had to pay taxes. The original intent to raise wine and silk proved impractical, and the settlers demanded the right to hold large plantations, own slaves, and drink hard liquor. The trustees gradually yielded; and in 1752, when Georgia became a royal colony, it had become economically very like South Carolina. It never flourished greatly during the colonial period, however, and in 1775 had possibly thirty thousand inhabitants, of whom a few more than half were whites.

The form of local government which developed in the South was the natural outcome of its physical and economic conditions. A broad, flat land of magnificent distances, it was sparsely populated; the great **Southern** planters were the political and economic rulers, at least on **local gov-** the coast. Most of the inhabitants had not come as congre-**ernment** gations nor even as families (as in New England), nor was it usually necessary for them to crowd together for protection against the Indians. The English county therefore was easily adaptable to southern conditions. A county court, ordinarily of eight justices, performed all the functions of local government: made the ordinances, enforced them, and handled judicial matters. There were in addition a sheriff and a county lieutenant who commanded the militia. Justices were technically appointed by the governor, but, since he always accepted the recommendation of the court, it was in effect a closed corporation with the control carefully kept in the hands of the aristocracy. The Church of England was officially established. Its parishes were both civil and ecclesiastical units, convenient areas for assessment of church tithes and poor rates and for care of roads. The parish vestry controlled these functions; the vestrymen were at first elected by the people, but presently the vestry also became self-perpetuating.

2 The Settlement of New England

New England, the demesne of the Virginia Company of Plymouth, saw only one serious attempt at settlement, when in 1607–08 the "Popham Colony" existed for a winter near the mouth of the Kennebec. Thereafter the company contented itself with trading voyages; it was on one of these that John Smith gave to the coast the name by which it is still known. Possibly fishermen and traders had passed several seasons in residence on the mainland; but when in 1620 the Plymouth Company was rechartered as the Council for New England, the first permanent colony was yet to be planted on its territory. The council, in fact, made no determined attempts to improve its opportunities but after parceling out its holdings to groups of would-be settlers and individual proprietors quietly passed out of existence in 1635. Its lavish grants had been made with little regard to geographic realities; so it left to its successors a considerable heritage of boundary controversies.

Council for New England

Early in the reign of James i the members of a Separatist congregation from Scrooby in eastern England fled to Leyden under the leadership of their pastor and were joined by others of like persuasion. They preferred, however, to live in an English land. In 1620 the London Company gave these Pilgrims, so called because of their wanderings, a grant in Virginia. To outfit them seventy London merchants bought shares to the value of £7000 in the profits of the venture. The agreement was that the settlers would labor for seven years for their maintenance, at the end of which time all profits, goods, and real estate were to be divided between backers and settlers. Only part of the Leyden congregation could leave; and when the *Mayflower* sailed from Plymouth in September 1620, the majority of her one hundred and two passengers were from England, and some of them were not even Puritans. They arrived off Cape Cod in November, probably by whim of the weather; at any rate, they decided to settle there. The place was outside the jurisdiction of any government, so in order to forfend disorder the men in the company signed the "Mayflower Compact," by which they agreed to form a government and abide by its laws. A boat party then explored the bay and decided upon a harbor which was named Plymouth. Late in December the Pilgrims landed. "It hath generally been observed," wrote a Puritan commentator in 1670, "that when the English come to settle a divine hand makes way for them by removing or cutting off the Indians either by wars one with the other or by some

The Pilgrims

raging mortal disease." Smallpox had recently carried off half the local Indian population, and the survivors gave white men a wide berth; indeed, there was no serious Indian problem for the Plymouth Colony for a generation.

The winter was severe, food was short, and disease struck the little company sheltered in its wattle-and-daub huts; more than half of them died. However, in the spring an Indian ventured into the village, and **Plymouth plantation** since he was well treated he and his friends began to educate the Pilgrims in the ways of the wilderness. The abandoned fields of the Indians were planted in corn, trade was opened in furs and buckskin, panel wood was cut for shipment to England, and sassafras was dug for use in English pharmacopeias. The Pil-

The first seal of Plymouth Colony

grims were sober, industrious, and ready to work hard in field and forest —all assets hitherto rare in American colonization. A profitable fur trade was built up. New settlers arrived each year, new towns were settled, and the colony made modest headway (though it never actually prospered) under the guidance of Governor William Bradford. A land grant was obtained in 1621 from the Council for New England by the merchant backers of the colony, but since there was no political charter the laws passed under the Mayflower Compact served as the basis of government until 1691. Long before this Plymouth had repaid its backers and bought up the title to the land.

During the decade of the 1620's perhaps a dozen fishing and fur-trading settlements were established along the New England coast, and a few managed to hang on. In 1628 six English Puritans led by John **Massachusetts Bay Company** Endicott obtained from the council the grant of all the land between the Merrimac River on the north and the Charles on the south, and extending westward to the South Seas. The organization was in 1629 confirmed in its grant by Charles I, given civil jurisdiction, and named the Massachusetts Bay Company. Though its incorporators were Puritans, it was as yet intended to be the usual type of trading and colonizing company. Meanwhile in 1628 John Endicott led a group of forty to Cape Ann and near there founded Salem on a site already occupied by the remnants of one of the trading settlements. Salem was to become one of the great seaports of early America.

At this time the quarrel between king and Parliament was at an acute stage, and a large element among the Puritans began to look toward America as a refuge not only from the king's political and religious persecution but as a fertile field for the planting of a theocratic state. A group of leading Puritans now approached the company and proposed that it transform itself from a trading venture into a religious commonwealth which would admit to membership only sound Puritans. To avoid royal interference the stockholders were to pack up their charter and move to New England. After some debate the proposition was accepted, and a London lawyer named John Winthrop (1588–1649) was elected governor.

This arrangement led to one phase of the Great Migration, the movement during which sixty thousand or more persons left England, chiefly for the Caribbean islands, Virginia, and New England. The impulsion was of mixed origin, but economic unrest was doubtless **The Great** dominant in most cases, for both agriculture and cloth **Migration,** making were in a period of depression. Knowledge of colo- **1620–1640** nizing methods had been so far advanced that men now felt they had some chance of betterment in the New World. Fear of civil and international strife must also have played its part. Religious motives ranked high among those who went to New England, for Archbishop Laud was harrying Nonconformists out of the kingdom so successfully that he has wryly been called "the father of New England." God, said a Puritan pastor, sifted a whole nation that He might send choice grain into the wilderness; the New Englander has never quite lost the thrill of that accolade. It is supposed that about twelve thousand went to Virginia, Maryland, and the Bermudas, and eighteen thousand to New England. The latter received an influx from the strongly Puritan eastern counties of England, where Cromwell later raised his Ironsides, and as a result Yorkshire and East Anglian customs and dialects have had a marked influence on the northern part of the United States. The Great Migration ceased abruptly with the beginning of the English Civil War; thereafter New England's truly remarkable growth was largely due to natural increase.

Winthrop arrived in New England in 1630 with one thousand colonists and established Boston as the capital of the commonwealth, while seven other towns were laid out in the vicinity to provide room for later comers. The straggling fur posts of the ungodly were swal- **Settlement** lowed up and their wassailing and wenching denizens **of Massa-** shown the way back to England. Rival claimants of grants **chusetts** by the Council for New England were coldly disregarded. **Bay** In the end this disregard, together with the outspoken Puritanism of the colony, led the Crown to demand that the charter be returned to England. When the colony evaded the issue, a judgment was obtained against the company; but the Atlantic Ocean was an effective barrier to its service, and presently the English Civil War intervened. In granting their charter, the Bay colonists asserted (though on unsound legal grounds), the king had yielded all right to interfere with them; just to keep the record straight they also refused to obey Cromwell's Parliament. Even when Charles II was restored they still forbore to issue writs in the king's name. Distance from England was their protection, and procrastination was the weapon they always used while they waited for the political wind to shift. The result was that for half a century Massachusetts was in reality an independent republic. John Endicott, captain of the Salem trainband (militia company), symbolized this one day on parade when he cut from the English flag the cross of St. George because it was a relic of popery.

Seal of the Massachusetts Bay Company

Massachusetts Bay Colony, it may as well be said at once, was not intended to be politically democratic nor religiously tolerant. It was settled of Puritans, by Puritans, and for Puritans; any others who came in were welcomed if they were sober and industrious and did not criticize the régime, but they remained on sufferance and did not share in the government. It was intended to be a City of God, the first of a long line of American utopias. Massachusetts was an experiment in government by the righteous and was intended to be a theocracy, that is, a government by God, with its principles drawn from the divinely inspired precepts of the Bible as interpreted by the learned Calvinist clergy of the colony. Government and society were permeated by a strong distrust of human nature. "Democratie" was feared and hated as an invention of the devil, intended to enable the ignorant and emotional rabble to get the bit of government into their own teeth and thus promote licentiousness and economic chaos and expedite their progress on the road to hell.

Puritan theocracy

Winthrop was a man of integrity, wisdom, and dignity, and the rapid progress of the colony was in large part due to his guidance. Nevertheless, he was so swayed by the clergy that his naturally gentle disposition was swallowed up in a zealous determination to brook no interference with his City of God. "Whatsoever sentence the magistrate gives," was his dictum, "the judgment is the Lord's." The execution of New England Quakers and witches has probably been stressed too much, for it was only a pale reflection of what England and Europe were doing. Nevertheless, the Puritans believed in persecution. "It is wicked for falsehood to persecute truth," they asserted, "but it is the sacred duty of truth to persecute falsehood."

The Massachusetts charter provided that government should be in the hands of a governor, eighteen assistants, and a quarterly General Court composed of all the stockholders (including governor and assistants). Admission to the company as stockholders, or "free- **Govern-** men," was open only to male members of the Puritan con- **ment of** gregations, and among them only to those whose godliness, **Massachu-** industry, and economic soundness met the test of a search- **setts** ing clerical examination. At first there were only twelve freemen in the colony, and of course all held official positions. Presently over a hundred men demanded admission as freemen; Winthrop consented reluctantly, asserting that *all* authority lay in the hands of the governor and assistants and that the only function of the freemen was to elect assistants whenever a vacancy occurred. Winthrop and the assistants undertook to make laws, execute and judge them, and lay taxes.

The citizens of the towns were Englishmen, and they did not propose to suffer the dictatorship of either a Charles I or a Winthrop. Watertown on the far western frontier—six or eight miles from Boston—refused to pay a tax on the ground that it had not consented to the levy. Winthrop huffed and puffed and blew them down. By this time the other towns were aroused and insisted that each town should have the right to send two deputies to the General Court to act with the assistants in levying taxes. In 1634 the deputies demanded and obtained a sight of the charter. The cat was now out of the bag. The lawmaking power legally lay with the freemen. Winthrop was forced to agree that the two deputies from each town to the General Court should make the laws, and that all the freemen together should elect both governor and assistants annually. Winthrop lost the governorship, and the deputies took some revenges; respect for clergy and gentry was so general, however, that Winthrop was able to return to power two years later. Presently deputies and assistants began to sit apart, and a bicameral legislature was thus instituted. Winthrop never became reconciled to this intrusion of "democratie" and died in the conviction that Massachusetts was on the road to hell.

Its damnation, however, was greatly delayed by shrewd tactics on the part of the theocrats. The synod of clergymen usually managed to sit at the same time as the General Court, and their advice was often sought, since in a theocratic commonwealth points of social and economic legislation often turned upon interpretation of **Triumph of** Scripture. The Puritans of Massachusetts had not been **theocracy** Separatists (as had the Pilgrims) but had hoped to remain in the Church of England and work for its purification. Now they began to draw apart in spirit if not in name. It was evident that Massachusetts Bay by its qualifications for the vote and its laying of a general tax for the support of the pastors had founded a state church, though it was Congregational rather than Episcopal. Though presumably neither state nor Church dominated the other, they marched closely together to preserve the purity of congregations and government and to fight the insidious progress of democracy.

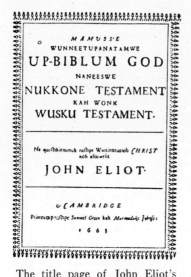

The title page of John Eliot's translation of the Bible into an Indian tongue

At first legal judgment had been at least theoretically based on the Bible, though doubtless the English common law was used oftener as more practical. As time passed the Bible lost ground and the common law gained, but the harshness of the Old Testament was evident for generations in New England jurisprudence. Meanwhile, however, the theocracy had a half-century of ascendance. General Court and ministerial synod were often at variance, but in 1651 the Cambridge Platform was accepted. This was aimed at preventing individual churches from breaking away from the State Church, and it provided that the courts must punish religious offenses and enforce rules made by the clergy to govern the dress and recreational and other activities of their congregations.

The triumph of theocracy over democracy was promoted by a series of crises which convinced the moderates that they must join with the conservatives to prevent the congregations from breaking up the commonwealth; such a result would have been fatal in view of the **Roger Williams (1604?– 83)** hostility of Archbishop Laud and the Indians and the threats by Dutch and French. Roger Williams, minister at Salem and Indian trader on Narragansett Bay, had been one of the most distinguished Puritans to come to New England. As a convinced Separatist he opposed the growing power of the theocracy and demanded separation of state and Church; as a liberal he advocated absolute religious liberty. As a friend of the Indians he indirectly denied the right of the king to give away Indian lands. Then, to make matters worse, he opposed the right of the state to force nonchurch members to take the oath of allegiance and to attend services and pay taxes for the support of the Church.

Williams was now brought to trial by the theocracy and sentenced to exile, but since it was winter his banishment was stayed until spring.

However, he refused to cease his activities, and the magistrates resolved to arrest him. Warned secretly by John Winthrop, Williams fled in January 1636 to his friends the Narragansett Indians. Others soon joined him, and presently on land purchased from the Indians they founded Providence Plantation, the nucleus of Rhode Island. Government was based upon a social compact strictly limited to civil affairs. Williams continued his fur trade and added commerce with England and New Amsterdam; before his death he was to become one of the richest men in New England.

Foundation of Rhode Island

A couple of years later, in 1638, the brilliant but slightly fey Mrs. Anne Hutchinson appeared in Boston and threw the colony into a turmoil over certain theological considerations which seemed important to the Calvinists of that day. Soon her teachings entered politics to the extent that a Boston trainband almost refused to march against the Indians with a chaplain who had opposed her. One can sympathize even with the theocratic martinets of the province when they packed Mrs. Hutchinson off to Rhode Island. When she and her family were massacred by Indians, the theocracy naturally considered it a righteous judgment.

Anne Hutchinson (1590?– 1643)

Other malcontents followed the exiles in rapid succession, until it justly earned the name of the province of the "otherwise-minded," a long and uncompromising thorn in the side of a godly New England. Roger Williams's ascendance was such that he managed to enforce complete religious tolerance, even for atheists, but the Rhode Islanders did not by any means avoid healthful squabbles. Most of them, in fact, are not to be confused with the rigidly formal Calvinists of the other New England colonies. They were pietists: that is, they sought to substitute the devotional and personal side of Christian experience for the cold intellectualism of the Puritans. Each of the Rhode Island settlements would have preferred to go its own way, but finally their fear of the Indians and of their more powerful neighbors resulted in their union. Their common hatred of authoritarianism made them the most democratic of the English colonies. Religious tests were outlawed, but the franchise was extended only to landowners.

Growth of Rhode Island

In England the Long Parliament in 1644 passed an act which set up the "Incorporation of Providence Plantations" and gave Rhode Islanders the right to hold land and carry on civil government. Rhode Island was especially anathema to Massachusetts, which unsuccessfully tried to get the Long Parliament to rescind its act of incorporation. A royal charter granted in 1663 remained in effect until 1842. It is interesting to note, however, that Roman Catholics and Jews were disfranchised in later years.

A more orderly migration from Massachusetts was that which began in 1635 to the valley of the Connecticut River. The nucleus of the move-

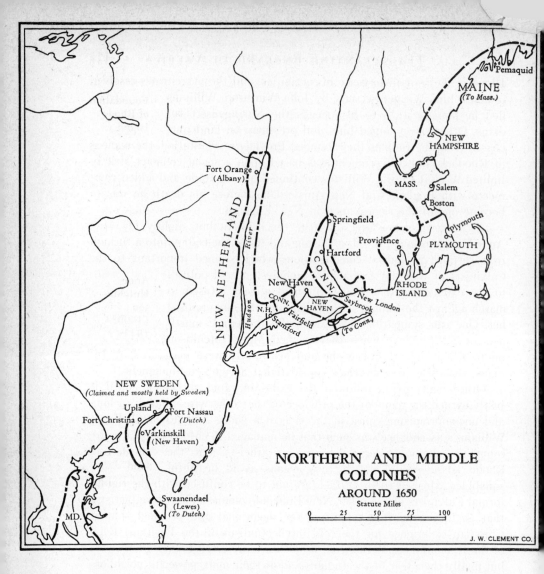

NORTHERN AND MIDDLE COLONIES
AROUND 1650
Statute Miles
0   25   50   75   100

J. W. CLEMENT CO.

ment was composed of several congregations who yearned toward the
fat lowlands of the Connecticut, and who also objected to
theocratic centralization in Massachusetts. Their leader
was the Rev. Thomas Hooker, a man of low birth but high
determination. "He was a person," said one of his opponents, "who,
while doing his Master's work, would put a king in his pocket." Hooker
and his followers were probably allowed to emigrate to Connecticut because the Dutch were creeping up on the flank of Massachusetts and
had established trading forts on the sites of Hartford and Wethersfield.
Allied with Hooker were other settlers at the mouth of the river. Here
one of the numerous cessions of the Council for New England had fallen
into the hands of a group of Puritan noblemen led by Lord Saye and

**Connecti-
cut**

128

Sele and by Lord Brooke. In 1635 John Winthrop, Jr. built Saybrook to maintain the group's authority over the valley. The English settlers avoided a clash but by hook and crook managed to squeeze out the Dutch.

In 1639 the General Court of the Connecticut Valley towns drew up the Fundamental Orders of Connecticut, which provided a frame of government. In form the government was much like that of Massachusetts, but admission to the franchise was by vote of the **Character** householders of the town. Theoretically there was no re- **of Con-** ligious qualification; but since the body of citizens was **necticut** Puritan, the candidate doubtless had to be of godly persuasion. In 1662 Connecticut received a royal charter which made it a corporate colony with boundaries almost the same as the modern state. The charter remained in use until 1818. To the very end of the colonial period Connecticut remained slow, peaceful, shrewd, and cautiously conservative, "the land of steady habits," the essence of Yankee character. The province was rather cut off from the world and, indeed, embodied something of that Puritan concept of the City of God which the king had destroyed in Massachusetts. Yet in its original form it was politically advanced, for it based its government and its laws on the consent of a rather freely chosen electorate and upon a liberal view of the public good.

Meanwhile farther west on Long Island Sound other dissidents had established another utopian colony at New Haven. Their complaint, however, was that Massachusetts was not theocratic enough. New Haven itself was settled in 1638, and it set up a government which **New Haven** was based frankly on the Bible and which rejected juries because they were not included in the Mosaic Law. New Haven had been established by men who had no legal right to the land, not even a scrap of paper from the Council for New England, but who expected to build up a commercial empire. Scattered towns which sprang up on both sides of Long Island Sound were annexed, until in 1643 the colony had to establish a representative government on the usual New England pattern; it was, however, still a "Bible commonwealth" in its laws and its intent. This confederation actually had one member on Delaware Bay, at Varkinskill on the Jersey shore. By the charter of 1662 Connecticut and New Haven were joined, and the latter lost its imperial members on Long Island and Delaware Bay.

Massachusetts dissenters, along with scattered fur traders and fishermen, were responsible for the settlement of New Hampshire and Maine. The Council for New England had left the ownership of the area in dispute, but finally in 1635 New Hampshire was confirmed **Maine and** to John Mason and Maine to Sir Ferdinando Gorges. Both **New** men had been active in trade and colonization since 1606, **Hampshire** but their ventures were almost uniformly failures. Mason died immediately after the confirmation of his grant, and Massachusetts took over New Hampshire; Maine also fell to the Bay Colony in the 1650's. On this wild northern coast Massachusetts seems to have relaxed its theocratic restrictions.

The universal local administrative unit of New England was the town; counties were eventually established, but they were little more than judicial districts. To the town belonged the administration of roads

The New England town

and schools and the management of all other local business. These matters were disposed of in town meetings, which anyone might attend but at which only the freemen might vote. Here also was elected the board of selectmen who managed town

Seal of the Dominion of New England

business between meetings. The town meetings were by their very nature breeders of democracy, and even the theocracy never quite succeeded in taming them. New towns were established by permission of the General Court, usually on application of a body of freemen who wished to "swarm" to a certain location.

Towns were laid out about a central common, with a place for church, parsonage, and school; each resident family received a home lot on which to build a house, an out-lot for cultivation, and a right to share in the common woods and pasture lands. Though the town was in part derived from English precedent, it was suited to New England. It afforded protection from the Indians and easy access to church and school during the severe winters; and, moreover, fertile spots were scarce and had to be fairly distributed. Frontier towns were expected to act as buffers between the Indians and the old towns, and it was illegal for settlers to abandon their lands. On the other hand, the older settlements were required to provide armed patrols in time of danger and men to watch and work in the harvest fields with the frontiersmen.

New England's rigorous climate, broken terrain, and rocky soil forbade a reliance on staple crops and slavery and confined farming for the most part to small tracts laboriously cultivated by the owners. Thus, the colonists were early driven to nonagricultural enterprise. The fur trade was important in the South until the 1670's, after which it retreated to the North. The abundance of timber led to the rise of shipbuilding, an activity carried on so successfully from the very first that the shipyards of England and Europe were soon being regularly undercut in price. By 1676 Massachusetts had seven hundred thirty trading vessels. In other lumber products, also, New England challenged the traditional supremacy of the Baltic.

New England manufacture and commerce

DIEV · ET · MON · DROIT

¶ By the King.

❧ A Proclamation forbidding the diſorderly
Trading with the Saluages in New England in America, eſpecially the furniſhing of the Natiues in
thoſe and other parts of America by the Engliſh with
Weapons, and Habiliments of Warre.

Heading of a royal proclamation which set
down regulations for trading with the Indians
in New England

Panels of "English oak" from New England fitted out England's fine old manors. Barrel staves, hoops, and headings were exported to hold the tobacco of Virginia, the molasses of the West Indies, and the wine of Europe. New England became a regular source of planks, clapboards, shingles, tan bark, potash, spars, masts, and other ship stores.

Codfishing was engaged in from the first. By 1675, it is said, four thousand men and six hundred sixty-five boats were engaged in the business, and there were thumping big exports of salt fish to the Catholic countries of Europe and America. Soon afterwards New Englanders were pursuing whales, and when prey became scarce in adjacent waters they moved on to the polar regions. Iron smelting began in Massachusetts, probably in 1644, and eventually spread to the surrounding colonies; iron was not only in demand for domestic use but necessary in shipbuilding. The manufacture of rum from molasses provided a cheap and potent liquor for the Indian trade. Trade was indeed the lifeblood of New England, the only means by which it could obtain the goods to give it a European standard of living. Out of it grew the shipping towns of Salem, Boston, Newport, New Haven, and a score of others, whose skippers nosed into every Atlantic port and traded with Italian silk merchants, French wine merchants, Acadian trappers, Caribbean pirates, and Creole planters, without asking embarrassing questions about the origin or customs status of the goods they desired.

A sharp war in 1636–37 against the Pequot Indians of the Connecticut Valley was ended only when two fortified towns were burned out and close to a thousand Indians killed. The four colonies of Massachusetts, **New England Confederation, 1643–84** Plymouth, Connecticut, and New Haven now joined for mutual protection in the New England Confederation. The mere fact that a league was formed was a tacit assertion of independence from England. It was intended not only for defense against the Indians but also to maintain its members' independence from France and Holland. It was characteristic of Puritan self-righteousness that another motive was to find a way to divide Rhode Island among her three next-door neighbors; thus, though Rhode Island asked to join, she was told that she was too schismatic and tumultuous. The members had an equal vote, but Massachusetts with superior wealth and perhaps two thirds of the population excited the jealousy of the others and on occasion vetoed the majority decision by simple refusal to accede. However, the confederation had some successes in the field of foreign relations. A trade agreement was signed in 1644 with French Acadia, and in 1650 a boundary was negotiated between New Haven Colony and New Netherland. The union of Connecticut and New Haven in 1662 weakened the confederation to the extent that it did not articulate well, but meetings were held until 1684.

The old strength of the confederation was sorely missed when King Philip's War suddenly broke out in 1675. This was an attempt on the part of the Wampanoag under Philip, followed by the Narragansett and **King Philip's War** the other remaining New England Indians, to wipe out the colonies. They might have succeeded if they could have laid aside their ancient antipathies. The war arose from a variety of causes, among them the confederation's continual interference in the quarrels of the red men and the perpetual legal harassments by covetous settlers in an attempt to gain possession of Indian lands. At first the colonial forces were defeated and white towns destroyed. It was almost a year before the tide turned. Philip's death in battle in August 1676 ended the southern phase of the war, but with French arms it was continued in Maine and New Hampshire until 1678. Summary statistics are at best informed guesses. New England may have had about fifty thousand white inhabitants, of whom at least a thousand (and probably many more) perished. One authority would have it that of ninety towns fifty-two were attacked and twelve were destroyed. The war cost the colonies the staggering sum of £100,000. It was a generation before the frontier line once again reached the stage from which the war had caused it to retreat. On the other hand, the Indians in southern New England, probable about ten thousand in number (of whom certainly no more than a third were warriors), were all but completely wiped out by war, disease, and slavery.

While New England lay prostrate from the war, Charles II seized the opportunity to bring Massachusetts to book for a series of highhanded actions. It had annexed Maine and New Hampshire, coined money in its own name, flouted the Navigation Acts, and refused politi- **Charles II** cal rights to Episcopalians as well as forbidden them to **and Massa-** worship publicly according to Church of England forms. **chusetts** Massachusetts had to yield when in 1679 New Hampshire was made into a royal colony, but in everything else it managed to temporize. The king's patience gradually evaporated, and in 1684 he had the Massachusetts charter annulled by a decree in chancery. This action was all the easier because at the same time he was moving against the charters of the English cities and displacing their magistrates.

When Charles died, his brother, James II, swept together the New England colonies as the Dominion of New England and late in 1686 sent over Sir Edmund Andros as governor. In 1688 New York and New Jersey were added to his realm. Andros was perhaps not unduly **Dominion** harsh; in fact, he governed with the advice of an appointive **of New** council of New Englanders. However, the régime threat- **England** ened the validity of land titles, sought to lay quitrents, imposed arbitrary taxes, and limited the holding of town meetings. The displaced ruling caste naturally sought to blow Andros's every act up into a semblance of tyranny, and the fuse was laid for revolt. The opportunity came when in March 1689 word arrived in Boston of the Glorious Revolution in England and of William's order to all displaced magistrates to resume their duties. At this the people—ably led, of course—rose and imprisoned Andros and restored the last governor under the old charter.

But the old order could not be restored, for a large part of the people were determined that the theocracy should not be permitted to resume control, and even William and Mary were opposed to approving a régime

NEW ENGLAND AND
NEW YORK ABOUT 1700

Statute Miles

0   10   20   30   40   50

J. W. CLEMENT CO., BUFFALO N. Y.

Massachusetts a royal colony

that was in fact independent of the laws and sovereignty of the mother country. In the end Massachusetts received (1691) a new charter. It became a royal colony with a governor appointed by the king, an assembly elected by property holders (rather than church members), and a council nominated by the assembly but subject to the governor's approval. Laws were subject to review by the king. Maine was retained, but New Hampshire resumed its status as a royal colony. Freedom of worship was instituted, and religious tests were abolished for voters. It was the end of the theocracy, at least in theory, but the influence of the clergy remained strong for generations.

3   The Settlement of the Middle Colonies

The Dutch were not primarily interested in settlements, but the strong manufacturing and commercial concerns of the nation sought outlets in trade with the Indians along the North American coast. In 1609 the Englishman Henry Hudson in the service of the Dutch East India Company sailed the ship *Half-Moon* into New York Harbor and passed the bottle among the Delaware Indians on an island which has thenceforth been known by the appropriate Indian name of Manhattan, "the-island-where-we-all-got-drunk," **Dutch settle New Netherland** according to a missionary to the Delawares.

The name New Netherland was given to the country, and by 1614 trading posts appeared on Governor's Island and at Albany. The region passed in 1621 to the West India Company. A series of forts and settlements now sprang up: Fort Orange at Albany, Fort Nassau on the Delaware, Fort Good Hope on the Connecticut. New Amsterdam was founded on Manhattan Island, which was purchased from the Delaware Indians by Director-general Peter Minuit for forty dollars' worth of trade goods in 1626.

Seal of New Netherland

The West India Company considered the furs and wheat of New Netherland secondary to the sugar of Brazil and the plunder of Spanish Caribbean fleets and cities and so gave the new enterprise little but orders. Government and economic enterprise in the colony were so strictly reserved to the company that immigration was slow; twenty years after the settlement the total popu- **Slow progress** lation of New Amsterdam was only about four hundred; and, at that, eighteen languages were spoken. Even at the end of Dutch rule (1664) the entire region possessed only about eight thousand inhabitants, of whom possibly no more than a scant majority was Dutch. The paucity of Dutch settlers is hard to explain, for the poverty of the Dutch masses was notorious. It may be that prospective settlers were scared away by the tyrannical and warlike policies which we will soon describe.

An attempt was made to stimulate immigration by granting huge tracts of land along the rivers to wealthy "patroons" who would bring in settlers as tenants and be permitted to reign over them as petty monarchs. This attempt to introduce feudal land tenure failed for several reasons, and of the original patroons only the Van Rensselaers were successful in retaining their holdings near Albany. This family became so powerful that it flouted the authority of the company and engaged in open trade with the Indians.

The political administration of the colony was as unfortunate as its economic life. Holland was frankly governed by an oligarchy of aristocrats and merchants who, next to the twin evils of Spanish rule and bad

Oppression and Indian war investments, hated democracy. The aim of the company was to preserve an autocratic "ship's company" model of government, but the stubborn settlers (reinforced by refugee New Englanders on Long Island) forced from the directors-general grudging and oft-retracted compromises by which they accepted advisers from the towns. The company's policy of demanding that their directors produce dividends without compensating investments forced the levying of burdensome taxes, which were even extended to the Delaware Indians.

Director-general William Kieft is remembered for his graft and Indian wars. The Delawares not only were subjected to tribute by the Dutch and the Iroquois but were being driven from their hunting grounds by Dutch farmers. One trouble led to another until in 1643 a band of Delawares fled from Dutch-armed Iroquois and sought refuge in the Dutch settlements. Kieft sadistically fell upon them, and his soldiers paraded eighty gory heads on pikes through the streets of New Amsterdam. A bitter war followed, which was not ended until the next year when a New England mercenary took the Delaware main "castle" near Stamford and slaughtered seven hundred warriors. New Netherland had paid for the selfishness of company and governor with the death of about two thousand settlers.

The story of New Sweden was a brief and curious interlude in the history of New Netherland. Sweden, at the time one of the great powers of Europe, had trade ambitions like its neighbors. Accordingly it also **New Sweden** chartered the New Sweden Company, and in 1638 a small number of Swedes under command of Peter Minuit, now in Swedish service, sailed up the Delaware and built Fort Christina on the site of Wilmington. Within a few years about four hundred Swedes were established from the Schuylkill River southward under the absolute but able governorship of four-hundred-pound Johan Printz. Since Sweden and Holland were allied at the time, the Dutch allowed the Swedes to remain. Printz, however, undertook to drive both Dutch and New England settlers from the Delaware in order to pre-empt the fur trade. The result was that in 1655 peg-legged Director-general Peter Stuyvesant of New Netherland sailed up the river with an overwhelming force and annexed New Sweden.

New Netherland itself was living on borrowed time, for English settlements were pressing in on the east and the south. The company's policies now came home to roost, for its plunder had gone into dividends, and a **English seize New Netherland** series of disasters left it without energy or resources to defend its possessions. During the English Civil War, New Amsterdam had been the base of a flourishing trade with the English colonies in Dutch manufactures. This trade was actively resented by English merchants, and during the First Anglo-Dutch War

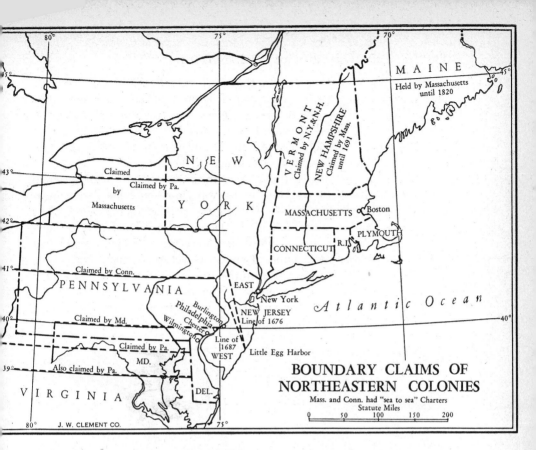

BOUNDARY CLAIMS OF NORTHEASTERN COLONIES

Mass. and Conn. had "sea to sea" Charters
Statute Miles
0   50   100   150   200

Cromwell sent a fleet to seize the city; it was saved only by the premature end of the war. During the next decade the Dutch continued to control a share of English colonial trade; when it became evident that the Second Anglo-Dutch War was in the offing, Charles II made a gift of this "nest of interlopers" to his brother James, then Duke of York. An English fleet under Richard Nichols took New Netherland in 1664 and gave the name New York to the colony and its chief town. Thenceforth, except for sixteen months in 1673–74 during the Third Anglo-Dutch War, the area was English.

English rule was welcomed even by many of the Dutch settlers. Nichols proclaimed the "Duke's Laws," which gave the people control over their local government and continued the religious freedom and land titles which they had enjoyed under the Dutch. James granted large estates on the Hudson to prosperous merchants and fur traders, and these became the founders of **The "Duke's Laws"** an Anglo-Dutch landed aristocracy (often confused with the patroons) whose hold on the Hudson Valley was not shaken loose until after 1846. In order to facilitate the collection of tariffs the duke confined exports and imports to the city of New York, a measure much favored by the merchant aristocracy because it gave them a trade monopoly which enabled them to control prices for their own benefit. These arrangements bore hard on the small farmers and fishermen of Long Island, whose natural trade ties were with Boston. The result was a growing demand for a popularly elected legislature which should control trade and taxation. For almost two decades the Long Islanders were forced to resort to smuggling and at times outright defiance of the law.

The clamor was so great that in 1683 the Duke of York finally granted an assembly. Before it was well under way James became king and at once revoked his concessions, restored the aristocracy to power, and added New York to the Dominion of New England. Governor Andros, whose hands were full in New England, put New York under Deputy Governor Francis Nicholson. When word of the Glorious Revolution reached New York, the democratic "rabble" rose (1689) under a German merchant named Jacob Leisler and ousted Nicholson and the magnates from control. For almost two years Leisler and a democratic council controlled the lower part of

Leisler's rebellion

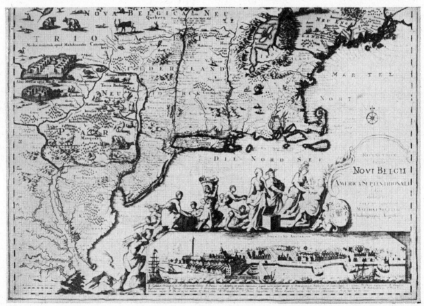

The New York Historical Society

A map of New Netherland, dated around 1700 and printed in Holland

the province and ruled with moderation. They surrendered peaceably to the new governor sent out by William III in 1691. The aristocrats, however, found an ally in the new governor, and Leisler and his son-in-law were convicted on a trumped-up charge of treason and hanged. The new régime resumed the old policy of granting estates of up to half a million

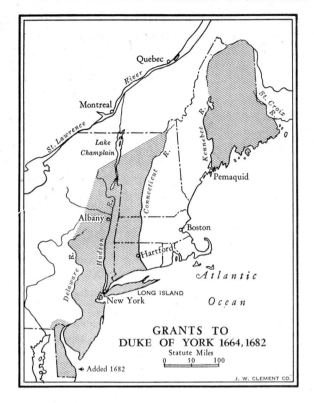

GRANTS TO
DUKE OF YORK 1664, 1682
Statute Miles
0   50   100
◄ Added 1682

J. W. CLEMENT CO.

acres to aristocratic favorites. Nevertheless, the elected assembly was restored, and the farmers made slow headway against the merchant aristocracy's control of trade.

The Duke of York's original grant comprised all the region between the Delaware and Connecticut rivers, and he added the west bank of the Delaware by right of conquest. The duke, however, did not value his new province highly; he allowed the eastern section to pass into the hands of Connecticut, Delaware was deeded to William **New Jersey** Penn, and two favorites named John Berkeley and George Carteret were given the tract between the Delaware and the Hudson which was now named New Jersey for Carteret's island home in the English Channel. In 1676 the tract was divided into East and West New Jersey, but by 1680 both sections had fallen into the hands of two groups of proprietors, both made up chiefly of Quakers. West New Jersey had been granted by its proprietors in 1677 a remarkably liberal charter, probably drawn up by William Penn. The two Jerseys were reunited in 1692; and in 1702 New Jersey became a royal colony.

No other of the Thirteen Colonies was so decisively influenced in its development by one man as was Pennsylvania by William Penn. Born in 1644, William Penn was the son of Admiral Sir William Penn, who served **William** Cromwell and king in turn and was one of the many to **Penn** whom the impecunious Charles II owed money. Young Penn **(1644–** received a "worldly" education abroad but about 1668 defi-**1718)** nitely cast his lot with the Quakers. He was handsome, eloquent, and possessed of such tact and gentle goodness that he was able to be at home both in the king's court and in a Quaker meeting. He may have forsworn the vanities of the world (and, indeed, on several occasions suffered imprisonment for his convictions), but he had not forsworn his business acumen and soon began to exhibit the shrewdness which has enabled so many Quakers to forecast and profit by the winds of commerce and politics.

In 1670 Penn inherited his father's considerable estates and social prestige. He dreamed of using them not simply for the benefit of his persecuted fellow Quakers but to carry out a "Holy Experiment," the **Penn ac-** foundation of a utopian asylum where men could both gov-**quires Penn-** ern themselves and worship as they pleased, free from inter-**sylvania** ference by a world devoted to political and religious oppression. Charles II, who favored religious tolerance because he wanted Catholics tolerated, promoted Penn's plans. An early flyer in New Jersey real estate convinced Penn that there was value in colonial ventures both to mankind and to the Penn purse, and he persuaded Charles to let him have a segment of wilderness in lieu of the bad debt of £16,000 which Penn had inherited from his father. The king consented and deeded to him a vast province east of the Delaware, to which he gave the name of Pennsylvania (Penn's Woods) in honor of the admiral. The charter of Pennsylvania was granted in 1681. The boundaries, though as carefully stated as the knowledge of the time permitted, were in dispute at one point or another until after the Revolution. The "three lower counties" of Delaware were deeded to Penn in 1682 by the Duke of York and formed a part of Pennsylvania until 1703, when they were given a separate assembly though they had the same governor. The separation was logical, for the two provinces differed racially and religiously.

Pennsylvania, by the terms of the royal grant, was held in feudal tenure with an annual payment of two beaver skins. The king had learned caution in deeding away political and economic rights to this last but **Govern-** one of the Thirteen Colonies. It was provided that its laws **ment of** must be consistent with those of England and subject to **Pennsyl-** review by English courts; Parliament could levy taxes and **vania** customs duties; and the proprietor agreed to enforce the Navigation Acts. Penn entered with zeal upon the execution of his "Holy Experiment." Though himself an aristocrat and a courtier, his religion and his natural bent combined to make him a democrat, and he drew up a Frame of Government which gave the franchise to landowners and taxpayers and set up an elective legislature of two houses. Civil liberties were protected, treason and murder were the only capital offenses (in a day when England had over two hundred), and freedom of worship was extended to all who believed in God. The plan was eventually modified to provide for a governor and a unicameral assembly.

As might have been expected, an antiproprietary party developed and from 1692 to 1694 succeeded in having the charter suspended on the ground that Penn was a Stuart sympathizer. In the long run Penn's plan provided more liberties than the controlling conservative party in the colony would allow to the people. The principal quarrel between Penn's heirs and the assembly, however, was over the taxation of the Penn estates and of "unseated" lands still in possession of the proprietors. The problem was not settled until in 1779 Pennsylvania bought most of the lands remaining to the Penns.

As soon as his charter was granted Penn sent over a relative to take possession of the provinces and commissioners who laid out the capital city of Philadelphia (*brotherly love*) in the gridiron pattern which has become so familiar in this country. Penn himself followed in 1682 and signed a treaty of amity with the Delawares. It was not until Penn's own descendants began to abuse their trust that the Indians turned against the province. Penn had intended to reside permanently in Pennsylvania, but in less than two years he had to return to England to defend his claims against Lord Baltimore. The dispute dragged on until the laying-out of the present boundary by the surveyors Charles Mason and Jeremiah Dixon in 1763–67.

Settlement of Pennsylvania

Though political and religious disturbances kept him away from his province except for one other two-year visit at the turn of the century, Penn sought diligently for colonists. English, Welsh, and Irish Quakers settled in and around Philadelphia and made up the backbone of the city and province. Non-Quakers, however, were welcomed. There was a great immigration first of Germans and later of Scotch-Irish. The success of Pennsylvania was certain from the first because of the destruction of the Indian nations by the Iroquois and the Dutch, because of the pioneering work done by earlier settlers, because of the supplies readily available in the older colonies, and because of the region's adaptability to agriculture and commerce. By the time that Penn died in 1718 his province had a population of about fifty thousand and was probably outranked only by Massachusetts and Virginia; Philadelphia, with about nine thousand people, was the largest city in the colonies next to Boston.

The Middle Colonies were in climate and terrain a compromise between New England and the South. The areas first settled were fertile

and fairly well drained, and they became such prosperous farming com-
Character munities that the Middle Colonies soon became known as
of the Mid- the "bread" colonies; their exports not only of grain but of
dle Colonies beef and pork might better have given them the name of
"bread and meat" colonies. Their food exports gave the ports of New
York and Philadelphia a firm economic basis, and furs, lumber products,
shipbuilding, and miscellaneous manufactures strengthened it. The Middle Colonies were not only a compromise between the commercial interests of New England and the agricultural interests of the South but
also a social and political compromise. They had neither great plantations
nor the New England type of villages but (outside of certain manorial
estates) farms small enough to be operated by the owner with the help
of his family or one or two indentured servants. The functions of local
government were divided between counties and townships, and this compromise was to stretch westward across the continent between a southern
belt of counties and a northern belt of townships modeled on those of
New England.

BIBLIOGRAPHICAL NOTE

The Founding of the Southern Colonies

GENERAL: Throughout the colonial era one must bear in mind the following
for all regions. Charles M. Andrews, *The Colonial Period of American History* (4 v., 1934–48), decidedly Tory in outlook but most valuable of the
summaries of the colonial period. Herbert L. Osgood, *American Colonies in
the Seventeenth Century* (3 v., 1904–07) and *American Colonies in the
Eighteenth Century* (4 v., 1924–25) are concerned chiefly with legal, institutional, and administrative problems. For political aspects turn to John A.
Doyle, *English Colonies in America* (5 v., 1882–1907). On the commercial
aspects of the British Empire see George L. Beer's summary *Commercial
Policy of England Toward the American Colonies* (1893) and his more de-
tailed *Old Colonial System, 1660–1754* (2 v., 1912) and *British Colonial
Policy, 1754–1765* (1907). Over-all treatment of the problems of empire is
Lawrence H. Gipson, *The British Empire Before the American Revolution*
(5 v., 1936–1942). Thomas J. Wertenbaker offers a three-volume survey:
The Founding of American Civilization: The Middle Colonies (1938), *The
Old South* (1942), and *The Puritan Oligarchy* (1947). Good one-volume
surveys are offered by Curtis P. Nettels and Max Savelle.

BACKGROUND OF COLONIZATION: This may be followed in the biographies of
Raleigh by Irwin Anthony, Donald B. Chidsey, and Milton Waldman (the
last is standard); and in William R. Scott, *Constitution and Finance of Joint-
Stock Companies* (3 v., 1912); David Hannay, *The Great Chartered Companies* (1926); and Edward K. Chatterton, *English Seamen and the
Colonization of America* (1930). *Richard Hakluyt and the English Voyages*
(1928) by George B. Parks deals with an associate of Raleigh who was an
indefatigable collector of seaman's accounts. The Hakluyt collections appear

in numerous volumes under the imprint of the Hakluyt Society, together with a re-issue of *Purchas His Pilgrimes*, a similar undertaking. H. S. Burrage, ed., *Early English and French Voyages* (1906) offers selections from Hakluyt.

VIRGINIA: Philip A. Bruce has blanketed Virginia in the seventeenth century with his *Social Life* (1907), *Economic History* (2 v., 1896), and *Institutional History* (2 v., 1918) and has collected the biographies of her great men in *The Virginia Plutarch* (2 v., 1929). Thomas J. Wertenbaker has added *Patrician and Plebeian in Virginia* (1910), *The Planters of Colonial Virginia* (1922), *Virginia Under the Stuarts* (1914), and *Torchbearer of the Revolution* (1940), the story of Bacon's Rebellion. Other useful books are Wesley F. Craven, *Dissolution of the Virginia Company* (1932); Louis B. Wright, *The First Gentlemen of Virginia* (1940); and Charles M. MacInnes, *The Early English Tobacco Trade* (1926). For the whiskeradoed Captain Smith see Edward K. Chatterton, *Captain John Smith* (1927); and John G. Fletcher, *John Smith—also Pocahontas* (1928).

MARYLAND: See William H. Browne, *George and Cecilius Calvert* (1890); Newton D. Mereness, *Maryland as a Proprietary Province* (1901); Bernard C. Steiner, *Beginnings of Maryland* (1903); and C. C. Hall, ed., *Narratives of Early Maryland* (1910).

CAROLINAS: See Charles L. Raper, *North Carolina, a Royal Province* (1901); William R. Smith, *South Carolina as a Royal Province* (1903); Shirley C. Hughson, *Carolina Pirates and Colonial Commerce* (1894); A. S. Salley, ed., *Narratives of Early Carolina* (1911) and *Introduction of Rice Culture into South Carolina* (1919); and Harriott H. R. Ravenal, *Eliza Pinckney* (1896), who introduced indigo culture.

GEORGIA: See James R. McCain, *Georgia as a Proprietary Province* (1917); and Amos A. Ettinger, *James Edward Oglethorpe, Imperial Idealist* (1936).

The Settlement of New England

GENERAL: Excellent over-all account is James T. Adams, *Founding of New England* (1921). For explorers before the *Mayflower* see Henry F. Howe, *Prologue to New England* (1943); and Charles K. Bolton, *The Real Founders of New England* (1929).

PLYMOUTH: George F. Willison, *Saints and Strangers* (1945) is the most up-to-date account of the Pilgrims. While preserving the flavor of the times, it delightfully debunks later ideas in a manner usually to the Pilgrims' advantage. See also William T. Davis, ed., *Bradford's History of Plymouth Plantation* (1908). Daniel Plooij, *The Pilgrim Fathers from a Dutch Point of View* (1932) is good medicine.

MASSACHUSETTS BAY: See Samuel E. Morison, *Builders of the Bay Colony* (1930); and for the business angle Frances Rose-Troup, *The Massachusetts-Bay Company and Its Predecessors* (1930). On Winthrop see Robert C. Winthrop, *Life and Letters of John Winthrop* (2 v., 1864–67); if that is not Winthrop enough, read Winthrop's own account of his tribulations in J. K. Hosmer, ed., *Winthrop's Journal "History of New England, 1630–1649"* (1908).

OTHER COLONIES: See Charles M. Andrews, *The Beginnings of Connecticut* (1934) and *The Rise and Fall of the New Haven Colony* (1936); Dorothy Deming, *Settlement of the Connecticut Towns* (1933); Isabel M. Calder, *The New Haven Colony* (1934); James P. Baxter, *Sir Ferdinando Gorges and His Province of Maine* (3 v., 1890); Charles W. Tuttle, *Life of Captain John Mason* (1887); William H. Fry, *New Hampshire as a Royal Province* (1908); Warren S. Archibald, *Thomas Hooker* (1933); Winifred K. Rugg, *Unafraid: A Life of Anne Hutchinson* (1930); Samuel H. Brokunier, *The Irrepressible Democrat, Roger Williams* (1940).

ECONOMIC: See Ralph D. Paine, *Ships and Sailors of Old Salem* (1912); and James D. Phillips, *Salem in the Seventeenth Century* (1933). William B. Weeden, *Economic and Social History of New England, 1620–1789* (2 v., 1890) is old but still good.

THEOLOGY AND INTELLECT: These have been run through the colander numerous times. See Samuel E. Morison, *The Puritan Pronaos* (1936); Herbert W. Schneider, *The Puritan Mind* (1930); Perry Miller, *The New England Mind* (1939), and with Thomas H. Johnson, eds., *The Puritans* (1938), a collection of Puritan writings with an excellent introduction.

INDIAN WARS: See Howard Bradstreet, *The Story of the War with the Pequots Re-told* (1933); and George W. Ellis and John E. Morris, *King Philip's War* (1906). One of the most famous narratives of Indian captivity rose from the latter war: Mary W. Rowlandson, *Narrative of the Captivity and Restoration of Mrs. Mary Rowlandson* (many editions).

TUMULTS AND "INTESTIN BROYLS": The rebellious character of New England is best followed in James T. Adams, *The Founding of New England* (1921) and *Revolutionary New England, 1691–1776* (1923). See also Viola F. Barnes, *The Dominion of New England* (1923); John F. Sly, *Town Government in Massachusetts* (1930); and C. M. Andrews, ed., *Narratives of the Insurrections, 1675–1690* (1915).

The Settlement of the Middle Colonies

NEW YORK: For its history from the beginning, bear in mind Alexander C. Flick, ed., *History of the State of New York* (10 v., 1933–37). Also of note for early history are John F. Jameson, *William Usselinx, Founder of the Dutch and Swedish West India Companies* (1887); Ellis L. Raesly, *Portrait of New Netherland* (1945); Bayard Tuckerman, *Peter Stuyvesant* (1893); and Samuel G. Nissenson, *The Patroon's Domain* (1937).

NEW JERSEY: See Edwin P. Tanner, *The Province of New Jersey, 1664–1738* (1908); and Edgar J. Fisher, *New Jersey as a Royal Province* (1911). Standard work is Amandus Johnson, *The Swedish Settlements on the Delaware* (2 v., 1911).

PENNSYLVANIA: See William R. Shepherd, *History of Proprietary Government in Pennsylvania* (1898); and S. G. Fisher, *Pennsylvania: Colony and Commonwealth* (1897). Just as useful for most readers will be books on the Penns, notably Mabel R. Brailsford, *The Making of William Penn* (1930); Bonamy Dobrée, *William Penn, Quaker and Pioneer* (1932); and Arthur Pound, *The Penns of Pennsylvania and England* (1932).

Chapter V

THE SETTLER

AND HIS PROBLEMS

1   *Why He Came and What He Found*

THE average settler was drawn to America by a somewhat different view of its attractions from that of companies and proprietors. Probably first was a yearning for land, in the belief that the possession of land would solve the terrible economic and social problems which weighed upon the common man. Second we may rank the **Why set-** desire for religious and political independence, for the two **tlers came** were closely joined in the thinking of the seventeenth century. Even where colonists imposed their system of beliefs on those who followed, it was because they feared to lose the very liberties they had left England to find. Third came the flight from service in the mass armies which were growing up in the European states and from the repeated ravages of war; this applied particularly to emigrants from the Rhine Valley. Of course, the search for adventure or speculative wealth must have played its part even among the common people, and there may also have been a desperate feeling that any new life would be better than the old one. One thing is certain: by far the most of those who came were volunteers, even though they sold their services for a term of years to pay their passages. There was a quality of enterprise and daring about them which was probably lacking in those who did not come. Nevertheless, we should not sneer at those who remained behind: they stayed to solve the problems from which our ancestors fled.

The majority of settlers doubtless paid their own passage or were assisted by the companies, but there were numbers who were not so fortunate. These became indentured servants and slaves. The former class

Redemptioners

was made up of white persons who were bound to labor for a term of years. Poor people who voluntarily signed indenture papers were known as free-willers or redemptioners; their agreement permitted ship captains to sell their services for a period of years, usually three to five, for a sum of money which would pay their passage. Such redemptioners were not always unskilled laborers, for artisans, clerks, and schoolmasters sometimes availed themselves of the opportunity and when they had served their time took up land or followed their occupations for their own profit.

Convicts formed another class of indentured servants, for their punishment was often commuted to or set as transportation to the colonies, there to have their labor sold to reimburse the law and the ship captains

Convicts

for their trouble and expense. Because of the brutal criminal code, which set extreme penalties for light offenses, many so-called criminals were really no more than farm lads caught poaching hares or waifs caught stealing bread; but there can be no doubt that the proportion of hardened criminals was high enough to insure the nucleus of an American criminal brotherhood and to occasion vigorous protests to the transporting authorities on the part of colonial governments.

The insatiable demand for labor led to the importation of a third class of indentured servants. These were boys and girls, vagrants, or poor people without influence who were enticed away or actually kidnaped by

Kidnapees

men known as "spirits," because they spirited away their victims and sold them to ships' captains. During the seventeenth century the English government looked with favor upon the draining away of the poorer part of the population, so it was not until growth of industry in England increased the demand for labor that a serious effort was made to stop kidnaping.

It is possible that about a third of the immigrants into the Thirteen Colonies entered as indentured servants. They were protected by a legal code in each colony; but as the standards of the time were not humane,

Condition of indentured servants

their years of servitude were not happy. There was, however, time to become acclimated and to learn American methods, and when their term was over they were given "freedom dues" consisting of a small sum of money or of clothing, tools, and livestock. They could then work where they pleased, rent or purchase land, or in Pennsylvania and the South receive fifty acres of land as part of the freedom dues. No social stigma followed them, and those with initiative and ability rose rapidly in the economic scale.

The voyage across the Atlantic was a chapter of horrors for all alike, whether they paid their own passage or came as servants. Tiny wooden ships were packed with hundreds of passengers, each one entitled only

to as much space between decks as he could lie upon. Water
was scant and stinking, food spoiled or unpalatable, sea-   **The**
sickness continuous, and it was nothing unusual for epi-   **voyage**
demics to carry off a third of the passengers during the voyage, which
might last anywhere from one to six months. Infants rarely survived the
passage. Boredom promoted drunkenness and quarrels. Captains and
crews sometimes robbed the dead, bullied and mulcted the living, and at
the end of the voyage forced their passengers to surrender their valuables
and sign new and outrageous indentures before they were permitted to
set foot on the blessed land.

Indentured servants were often spoken of as slaves, with justice, for
during their terms they were little if any better off. The first Negroes
brought to Virginia, in 1619, were technically indentured servants, but in
1661 slavery was recognized legally. The displacement of
small farms by great plantations gradually increased the   **Negro**
demand for Negro slaves in the South, especially after it   **slavery**
became evident that Indians did not make tractable nor long-lived labor.
The Negro worked fairly well at unskilled occupations if he was super-
vised, he was cheerful and tractable, learned the English language and
American customs readily, and bred rapidly and lived long. In the North
slavery was introduced by 1636, but the institution was not well suited
either to commerce or to farming, and so at the time of the Revolution
was on the way out north of Mason and Dixon's Line. The Dutch supplied the first Negro slaves, chiefly from West Indian sources, but after
1672 English ships joined the trade. Negroes did not enter rapidly, however, and there were only about six thousand in the colonies in 1700.

The possession of land had for thousands of years been the European's
Open Sesame to independence, wealth, power, and prestige. It is true that
the power of land was beginning to bow before that of commerce, but
the average man sensed that fact only dimly if at all and   **Signifi-**
found America's chief attraction in its cheap land. Here   **cance of**
were millions of acres of fat land waiting to be exploited   **cheap land**
either by the plow or by the speculator. A history of the United States
could easily be written in terms of the history of real estate, and it would
illuminate nearly every problem that has confronted us. The proprietors
were, of course, land speculators on a grand scale. Their concern was to
attract settlers who would buy land, and they were even willing to give
away fifty acres as a "head right" to redemptioners in order to people the
country and raise the value of the remaining land. Land thus became the
basis of American enterprise; and, because there was land enough for
all, it was natural that private enterprise should enter into the warp and
woof of the economic cloth the settlers were weaving. Moreover, because
most of the families in the typical farming community (not in the cities

or in the tidewater-plantation areas) were about equal economically, there was a powerful impetus toward social and political equality.

The land rights of proprietors were not always quenched when their political rights passed to the Crown. Great "unseated" estates acquired as speculations existed in almost every colony, either granted by the original proprietors or by complaisant royal governors.

Quitrents When these estates were parceled out, however, the sellers retained the right to collect perpetually a small annual fee called a quitrent; this right was legally inextinguishable, and even when the Crown acquired a proprietor's land rights, as in Virginia and the Carolinas, it collected the quitrent. The institution of the quitrent began in England after the Black Death, when a money economy began to rise and the annual labor and produce owed to the lord of the manor was commuted to an annual cash payment. To the Thirteen Colonies the custom was a constant source of friction from New York southward—but not in New England, for there the quitrent system was never enforced and fell into disuse. Boundary disputes between proprietors naturally made farmers in the disputed areas uncertain of their titles and caused them to band together for protection and refuse to pay either proprietor. Under a determined proprietor or agent failure to pay quitrents could and did result in loss of the land, and this threat was a fruitful source of many of the rebellious movements of the colonial period. Just as bad in the Crown colonies was the fact that quitrents gave the royal governors an independent revenue and thus reduced the hold of the assemblies over the provincial purse strings.

By 1688 the transfer of culture from England to America was well under way. The cities had become the entrepôts both of progress and of reaction with their schools, printing presses, and developing leisured aristocracy. Education flourished best in New England with

Education its dame schools, the ministers' Latin classes, and with a boys' finishing school called Harvard College, founded at Cambridge in 1636. It is worth noting that since the early New England leaders were largely from the eastern English counties they had been educated at Cambridge University; so that institution's intellectual influence ran strong in America. The children of southern planters were probably educated by redemptioner schoolmasters, and after 1693 could go on to the College of William and Mary in Williamsburg, Virginia.

Religious toleration was more a necessity than a conscious virtue, for there were too many sects to be combated successfully; and, moreover, real-estate speculators would not drive away a prospective sucker just because he believed in baptism by immersion rather than by

Religious tolerance sprinkling. Consequently, though state churches were established in nine of the colonies, there were only occasional flurries of persecution in the seventeenth century, and they died out in

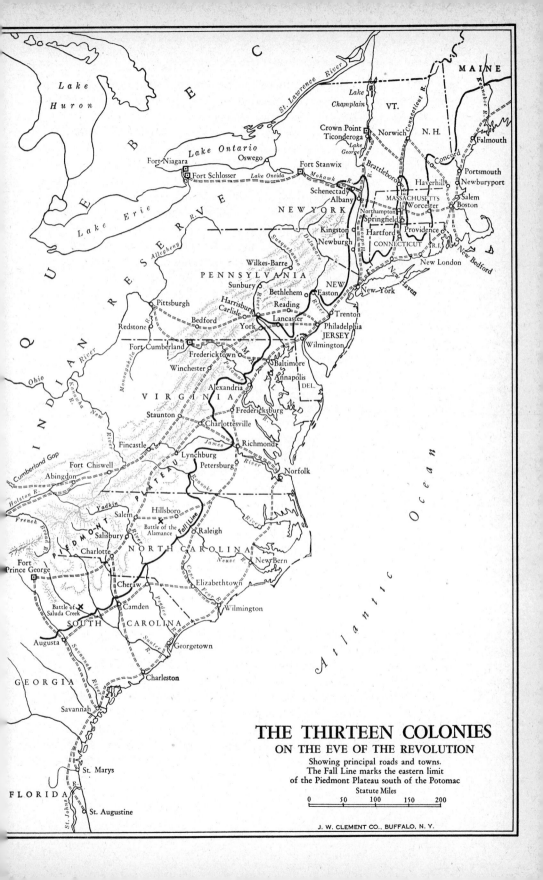

THE THIRTEEN COLONIES
ON THE EVE OF THE REVOLUTION
Showing principal roads and towns.
The Fall Line marks the eastern limit
of the Piedmont Plateau south of the Potomac

Statute Miles

| 0 | 50 | 100 | 150 | 200 |

J. W. CLEMENT CO., BUFFALO, N. Y.

the next century. However, Protestants retained considerable distrust of Catholics, and conservative Episcopalians and Congregationalists looked askance at the more "enthusiastic" evangelical sects.

It is true that crudeness and even savagery still sat upon the land. Disease, crop failures, extreme cold and extreme heat, and perils from the Indians were the hazards of life in the New World; but not all of **Changed** them were new to the settler from the Old World. Hardest **mode** to bear for men and women from the villages of Europe **of life** was the solitude of the isolated clearing; the time was yet distant when the pioneer would revel so much in solitude that he would move on when he could see the smoke of a neighbor's fire in the distance. The extremes of temperature, the starving times which lowered vitality, the monotony and the distance from home, but most of all the dark forest from which hostile eyes watched the progress of the settlements—all combined to make life in the New World a frightening experience. Frayed nerves, quarrelsome moods, and stark insanity resulted, and these lay at the bottom of many an antisocial act and mysterious incident.

Agricultural methods were often slack and unnecessarily wasteful of soil chemicals. The English lived in huts of bark, sod, or wattle-and-daub until they could build their hereditary houses of clapboards and thatch; the Dutch used stone and brick; and the Spanish used stone, adobe, or planks. It was apparently the Swedes who introduced the log house, for such structures had been common in Sweden for centuries, though it is possible that logs had been used for fortifications by the English settlers. The name log cabin has become generic, but technically it is a rude structure built of round logs; the log house is built of well-fitted squared logs.

The success of the Thirteen Colonies was assured by 1688, when the Glorious Revolution drove the Stuarts from the English throne. A narrow but continuous line of English settlements stretched a thousand miles **The colo-** from Maine to Charleston and reached inland to the Fall **nies in** Line. The Dutch and Swedes had lost their political foot- **1688** holds; the Indians on the east of the Appalachian Mountains had been crushed except in the extreme South, and the Iroquois had been used as a buffer against the French and the other Indian nations and in the process had assured their own strangulation. All but a few of our great coastal cities had been founded, and all of the present coastal states except Georgia had taken form and were building up their political, social, and economic consciousness. The ascendance of the English language, of English institutions, and of Protestantism was assured. At the moment the overwhelming majority of the population was also English, but the minority of Irish, Dutch, German, and other elements was destined to increase in proportion and to exercise a profound influence on the future nation. The population, which was about two hundred fifty thousand at this time, was to double every twenty-five years during the next century, partly by immigration but chiefly by natural increase, until on the eve of the Revolution (1775) it had reached approximately two and three quarter millions.

2   Social and Religious Ferment

A view of the Thirteen Colonies during the half-century or so before the Revolution would be prophetic of the social and economic complexities which were to characterize the later nation. Overwhelmingly English in composition, the colonies in the seventeenth century had been so far as local conditions permitted carbon copies of such aspects of English life as their founders chose to emphasize. Even before 1700 the picture began to alter rapidly. The Puritanism of New England was watered down by the royal defeat of the theocracy and the entry of new elements which insisted on separating politics from religion. The religious and racial diversity of the Middle Colonies was increased by the entry of Quakers, German sectarians, and Scotch-Irish Presbyterians, and the fur trade gave way to farms. From the Chesapeake southward the defeat of the small farmers in Bacon's Rebellion and like movements in other colonies turned the Tidewater over to the great planters and brought in floods of Negro slaves.

Changes after 1700

A growing social cleavage was one of the most evident changes brought by the new century. From the first there had been men who were entitled to add the coveted "gentleman" when they signed their names, and presently they were joined by rising families who had made money and who succeeded in playing down their humble origin. The new aristocracy had jelled by the end of the first quarter of the century. In the North it was mercantile, speculative, and official; and in the South planting, speculative, and official. In both sections it was dominantly Church of England, though there were many exceptions. The northern sector was more staid and possibly more progressive than the sports-loving gentry of the South, but both took their church duties less seriously than their social duties, placed manners above morals, aped English fashions and tastes, and treated their "inferiors" courteously but firmly. Leisure and independent fortunes were their universal earmarks, and without these no one could hope to be counted among them. Manual labor and economic dependence were the marks of Cain. On the other hand, they were usually fairly well educated and interested in cultural activities; and they promoted civic progress where it did not touch their pocketbook nerves too closely. Certainly they agreed that they were born to lead if not actually

The colonial aristocracy

to rule, and they assumed control of public affairs as a matter of course and probably with a conscious sense of *noblesse oblige*.

Clergymen, lawyers, and medicos who did not have personal fortunes were a distinct cut below the aristocracy, though they might be admitted to frequent social contacts. These, together with merchants who

The middle class

waited in person upon their customers, minor officials, contractors, and ship captains were not in the charmed circle, but the fact that they could vote in a day when the suffrage was rigidly limited to property holders gave them standing as useful tools. The common people of the cities were the "honest mechanics"—"honest," that is, if they knew and kept their places. The riffraff of wharf and gutter were, of course, beneath notice. It was the middle class, however, which was to lead the cohorts of revolution and reap its reward by becoming in turn a new merchant and industrial aristocracy after exiling those members of the old aristocracy who had had the bad judgment to fight for the king.

The next social class was that of the small farmers. Those near the cities tended to form a more or less conservative element, perhaps partly because they were themselves more than ordinarily prosperous, or because

The small farmer

they rented their land from aristocratic squires or were in some way dependent upon them. The limitation of the suffrage was a distinct encouragement to conservatism. Toward the interior of the country society was cruder, and political complexions and sympathies were more democratic. Farmers worked hard for a living, got their goods to market with difficulty, seldom saw more than enough cash to pay their taxes and quitrents, and were often worried about the danger of losing their farms to mortgagors or to a rival proprietary who might get a Crown judgment against the one who had granted their title. A broad belt of such small farmers ran from Maine to South Carolina (except in upper New York, where the Iroquois still lived) between the Fall Line and the mountains, and in general they had more in common than did the aristocrats, who after all were commercial in the North and planting in the South.

Cities were, of course, the center of economic and intellectual life, the entrepôts of European ideas, culture, and goods, and the foci from which intellectual and economic power radiated. Boston (with about

Colonial cities

thirty thousand inhabitants in 1775) was the intellectual capital of the colonies and retained its position until the Civil War. Penn's "greene country towne" of Philadelphia was larger (about thirty-five thousand in the immediate vicinity in 1777) and much more progressive in civic undertakings, with its paved and lighted streets, its pioneer public library, its clean city hospital, and workhouse prisons. Philadelphia flourished because of its extensive and fertile back country and progressed because of its public-spirited citizens. New York (about twenty thousand in 1775) was handicapped by the Iroquois occupancy of its back country and perhaps also by the monopolistic economic measures of its aristocracy. Baltimore (six thousand people in 1775) was the only large town on Chesapeake Bay, though Annapolis, Alexandria, Norfolk, and Williamsburg managed to grow a little. The most sophisticated city in the colonies was Charleston (about fifteen thousand in 1775), with its "season" during which the carriages of wealthy rice and indigo planters crowded its streets. Its theater and ballrooms were the resorts of a gay and cultured society. The buzzards, however, were Charleston's scavengers—perhaps at that an improvement over other cities, where garbage disposal and sanitary arrangements were notoriously neglected. The inevitable result in all cities was frequent epidemics.

Geography and climate had conspired to deprive the South of any important urban society between Baltimore and Charleston. The climate and the fertile tidewater plain promoted the growth of great plantations and the increase of slavery. The many navigable rivers made towns unnecessary because ships from England were **Plantation life** able to anchor opposite the planters' houses to deliver their goods and take on tobacco and other plantation products. The planter thus lived in state in the midst of his acres, luxuriously clothed and furnitured by London, visiting his lordly neighbors, hunting to hounds, and attending horse races, militia musters, court sessions, and sometimes church. He had his joys in life but was not free from care, for he had to look after the management of his property and devote considerable attention to public business. His London factor gave him a low price for his tobacco and charged royally for the civilized goods he sent out; so the planter was chronically in debt and plunging deeper, partly because he never knew what his tobacco would sell for and therefore could not order supplies accordingly. The situation was a fertile cause of the irritation which promoted revolution.

At least in earlier generations the southern planter was interested in law, the classics, and in English and French literature. This interest was not an affectation but was intended to teach good manners and gentlemanly restraint and to make him a better civic leader and governor of his slaves. Unfortunately the influx of uneducated landholders into the planting class watered down the old standards, and the result was sometimes less efficient government and an increase of arrogance toward inferiors and of brutality toward slaves. It is, however, only necessary to point to such leaders as Jefferson, Madison, and Mason to realize that the old standards persisted at least in some quarters.

Colonial intellectual life was rather limited by circumstances and for the most part reflected the utilitarian standards of a new and unstabilized society. There were philosophers, astronomers, geographers, botanists, and medicos in the colonies who were recognized abroad, but their number was not large. Benjamin Franklin was one of the few American pure scientists who lived before our own century, and his contributions to electrical and physical research were invaluable. John Winthrop IV, a Harvard professor, shocked the orthodox by showing that earthquakes and comets were natural phenomena, and not vehicles of the wrath of God. Literature was largely trivial in artistic value and practical in nature: almanacs containing weather forecasts and sage advice, sermons bearing comfort and warning, deliciously chilling accounts of Indian captivities, and poems replete with lugubrious moral lessons. The first long-lived newspaper was the *Boston News-Letter* (1704), but others quickly followed. Editors clipped their news from papers from other cities, or printed excerpts from letters handed to them by private correspondents. One peculiarity was that they laid little stress on local news, for of course everybody already knew it. The financial support of newspapers was always precarious, and the publisher had to eke out a living by job printing and selling books and stationery.

Intellectual life

Before the Revolution the oustanding native American was undoubtedly Benjamin Franklin. Born in Boston and brought up to the printing trade, he went to Philadelphia in 1723 and eventually became its leading citizen. There he published the *Pennsylvania Gazette, Poor Richard's Almanack,* and a long stream of important books and pamphlets, and became prominent as a civic leader and a manager of the antiproprietary party. He was a shrewd businessman and set up printing partners at advantageous places throughout British America to such profit that he retired from business at the age of forty-two. He then devoted himself to physical research, chiefly in electricity, and the management of the royal post office in America, and was active in intercolonial affairs. He was chief founder of the oldest learned society in the United States, the American Philosophical Society (1743), and of the college which was presently to become the University of Pennsylvania.

Benjamin Franklin (1706–90)

In 1757 he went to England as agent for Pennsylvania and remained there almost constantly until the Revolution. His work as a scientist had already made him prominent, and his added activity in London as a lobbyist and political pamphleteer made him in the eyes of England's public the typical American: shrewd, humorous, and common-sensical. His battle to preserve American rights within the British Empire was lost, and he returned home in time to sign the Declaration of Independence. Later his immense prestige in France made him the key American

representative there. After the Revolution he was a member of the Constitutional Convention of 1787 and thrice president of Pennsylvania.
Franklin's writings were lively and witty in a day when colonial literature was notoriously dry, and his *Autobiography* is usually accepted as
the first distinguished contribution to American literature. Perhaps even
more important, his insatiable curiosity led him to speculate in many

A CONFERENCE between the D---L and Doctor D-E.
Together with the Doctor's Epitaph on himself.

Historical Society of Pennsylvania

A cartoon of 1764 directed against Benjamin Franklin ("Dr. Dove") for his alleged
devilish and Machiavellian double-dealings

fields, and for a century or more his theories furnished research leads for
a number of crafts and professions, including shipbuilding, meteorology,
and physics.

One of the most significant changes being wrought in American life
was in religion. The evolution was most notable in the North, where
from the first religion had been most influential. With increasing wealth
New England's Puritanism was greatly weakened, and its
decline was hastened by the royal assumption of control in **Growth of**
Massachusetts. The change was hastened also by popular **secularism**
revulsion against the witchcraft hysteria which swept Massachusetts in
1692. Hallucinations and private enmities combined to bring accusations

against hundreds of innocent people, and nineteen persons—and two dogs—were hanged (none was burned), before courts and public suddenly recovered sanity. By 1700 secular interests had begun slowly to displace religious interests, and the change, though most marked in New England because of the contrast, was clearly discernible in all of the colonies.

The result was a curious divergence in religious approaches. None of them wholeheartedly accepted Calvinist theology, but each of them retained some of its psychology. All, however, were American adaptations of current European trends. The first was "intellectual" in its sympathies; it followed the new scientific view of the universe as proclaimed by Copernicus and Newton and rejected the stern and highhanded deity of Calvin. Belief in predestination was weakened, and faith in freedom of the will strengthened. This was, of course, the American phase of the so-called Enlightenment. Men now, like the Greeks, sought truth in the things about them rather than in revelation and found no proof of the existence of sin and immortality. The universe was looked upon as the creation of an impersonal deity who set up laws to govern it, then took no more interest in it. This new view of God was known as deism, and after the middle of the eighteenth century it found expression in American periodicals and acceptance among great numbers of the educated class, including many of the men who were to become Founding Fathers of the new nation. The part of the Enlightenment which sank deepest into the masses was the belief in progress. This was not a philosophical acceptance but a practical one, drawn from the fact that the wilderness was giving way to civilization.

The Enlightenment

On the other extreme were the "enthusiasts." They laid emphasis upon emotional religion and found a ready response among the uneducated masses (especially on the frontiers) who could not appreciate the new importance of science and intellect. This movement was parallel to the evangelical movement on the European continent and to the Wesleyan revival in England; in fact George Whitefield, the English revivalist, toured the colonies and preached an active personal experience of salvation from sin. The greatest revivalist, however, was Jonathan Edwards (1703–1758) of Massachusetts. Edwards was probably the most brilliant of colonial theologians and philosophers, but he opposed the intellectualist trend in religion. A strong Calvinist, austere, saintly, mystical, and remorselessly logical, he strengthened Calvinist theology by yielding a little here and there and by abandoning its formalism for evangelicalism. He preached a vengeful God bent on sending sinful men to eternal torment, Whose wrath could be escaped only by individual repentance and conversion. These were emotional and individual terms which the masses could un-

**Evangelicalism:
The Great
Awakening**

derstand, and the result was the Great Awakening, which during the generation after 1734 swept southward from Massachusetts and surged on to the frontier.

The upper classes regarded the moral precepts and the terrors of religion as necessary to keep the masses in order. Even a natural optimist and deist like Franklin could say that "talking against religion is unchaining a tiger; the beast let loose may worry his liberator." As a result the gentry in general clung to the old forms, fought for the right of the Church to associate itself **Decadent theocracy** in political control, and even upheld much of the old theology even though they might not believe it themselves. The decaying theocracy of New England, led by Increase and Cotton Mather, sought to preserve its control by replacing the loose congregational system of church organization by a more tightly knit presbyterianism. They failed to arrest the decline of their control, though they probably slowed it down, especially in Massachusetts and Connecticut.

Their greatest opponent, the Reverend John Wise of Ipswich, wrote two notable pamphlets which ably defended democratic control by congregations on the ground of Natural Rights. "The end of all good Government," he wrote, "is to Cultivate Humanity, and **John Wise** Promote the happiness of all, and the good of every Man **(1652–** in his Rights, his Life, Liberty, Estate, Honour, etc. with- **1725) and** out injury or abuse done to any." It was a significant argu- **democracy** ment, for in defending democracy's superiority in church government he also proved its superiority in political government. Wise had a demonstrable effect on the ideas of Samuel Adams, one of the most democratic and influential of the Revolutionists.

Out of this religious ferment there arose factors of immense significance to the future of the United States. Minor religious differences led to a multiplication of sects and made control by state churches more hopeless than ever. Toleration was made necessary by di- **Results of** versity and was also promoted by the growing power of **religious** secularism. The decline of social uniformity forced relaxa- **ferment** tion of the so-called Blue Laws which regulated manners and morals. The revivalists' emphasis on individual responsibility for repentance and conversion was in line with growing democratic feeling, and so was the break-up of control by the state churches. The stimulation of religious activity also stimulated the interest of the denominations in higher education. The feeling of Christian brotherhood awakened by the revivals was a powerful humanitarian influence. There were also curiously contradictory psychological results of the religious ferment. Emotionalism (almost to the extent of a neurosis) entered into American life and was doubtless strengthened by Celtic influence. On the other hand, there were planted the seeds of respect for intellect and education. Individualism and social pressures grew side by side and later made possible the simultaneous flowering of "rugged individualism" and prohibition of alcohol.

These contradictions came in part from the contradictions of Calvinism but perhaps even more from the contradictions of human nature in a land where human nature attained unprecedented expression. Even **Shift to** while political democracy was maturing, its great enemy, **economic** concentrated and privileged economic power, was also ma- **controls** turing. Calvinism had followed historical precedent by setting up control of society by church and state, that is, ministry and gentry. When Calvinism and ministry decayed, the gentry retained the concept of leadership and responsibility (regardless of their church affiliation) and now came to exercise control through economic power. The shift in approach was significant, for it foreshadowed one of the most powerful conservative influences in later American development.

The growth of secularism was reflected in education. Harvard was bitterly accused by the orthodox of harboring intellectualism, and Yale was set up in 1701 as a refuge for spirituality. A generation later it also **Education** had succumbed, and Princeton (1746) was founded as a substitute by the Presbyterians under the presidency of Jonathan Edwards. Elementary education everywhere preserved fundamentally a religious and moralistic cast, but in New England it was a state function which was carried on at public expense and gradually took on the secular tinge of society. It is worth noting that Massachusetts was the first English-speaking government to make elementary education the business of the state, and it utilized the first American textbook, *The New England Primer* (about 1690). In the Middle Colonies education was left chiefly to the sects, and in the South to the parish rectors or to individual parents. Academies, intended to prepare boys for college, appeared in all sections near the coast by the middle of the eighteenth century. They preserved a core of Greek and Latin but yielded to the demand for the more utilitarian sciences, mathematics, and modern languages. A medical college was founded in Philadelphia by Benjamin Rush in 1765, but most medical education was still by apprenticeship.

Beyond the simplest rudiments formal education was available only to the fortunate few. That did not mean that the masses were necessarily cloddish, for information was ready to be seized by those who were interested. Sermons were heavy with theological and politi- **Popular** cal matter. The Bible and books of sermons and devotional **education** reading were common, and sometimes the works of English poets and political writers were found even in the homes of the humble. Newspapers and magazines were few, but they were literally read to pieces. These, together with almanacs, were crammed with homely wisdom, encyclopedic information, and literary quotations; gradually they undermined superstition and inculcated the rudiments of science. Libraries existed, but they were owned by individuals, associations, and colleges, so were not ordinarily open to the public. Music was little more than ballads imported from England, except in the cities, and even there it was usually tinkling and sentimental.

Many commentators have exaggerated the influence of French political thought upon the Thirteen Colonies, partly because the intellectual renascence known as the Enlightenment was ascendant in France in the generation prior to the Revolution. As a matter of fact, the **No great** Englishmen Locke and Newton were two of the most vital **French** influences in the inception of the French phase of the En- **influence** lightenment, though indeed Voltaire and Rousseau must have influenced English thought in turn. Montesquieu (died 1755) is the only discoverable Frenchman who was widely read and commented upon in the colonies, and that probably because his emphasis upon the molding effect of environment was so plainly proved in America. Incidentally, the Italian reformer Beccaria was also known, but chiefly through the English lawyer Blackstone. Even the French Physiocrats, with their emphasis on agriculture as the basis of all wealth, had nothing to offer the agricultural Americans but a systematic "scientific" explanation of the American economic scene. Indeed, the flow in the pre-Revolutionary era was the other way, and Rousseau drew his "noble savage" at least in part from America. The French Alliance of 1778, however, and especially the French Revolution were to make Americans much better acquainted with French thought.

One cannot, however, ignore the fact that Frenchmen were comparatively common in the colonies during the pre-Revolutionary era and that French books were read by some educated Americans. The French student Fäy estimates that one fourth of the books imported **French** into New York from 1770 to 1774 were in French. As early **manners** as 1761 John Adams rated France superior to England. French manners were certainly popular with the upper classes, and French fencing masters and dancing masters found ready employment. But it was difficult for the average American to forget the hatred engendered by the French wars, to slough off the contempt for the "frog eaters" or to regard French manners as manly, to separate French political tyranny from French thought, or to see anything good in French Catholicism. An amusing instance of American simplicity was shown when a Boston merchant in 1778 entertained some French naval officers at dinner and to do them honor served a whole green frog in each plate of soup!

3 *The Racial Complex*

The national and racial composition of the population of all the colonies underwent a profound change during the eighteenth century. The Swedes of the Delaware seem to have had little influence beyond their introduction of log architecture. The Dutch, also, after their heyday were readily assimilated and today are remembered chiefly by a faint historical and architectural aroma, by the popularity of Santa Claus, and by a succession of "vans" in New York's social register. French Huguenots came to all the colonies after Louis xiv revoked the Edict of Nantes, which had protected Calvinism in France. They brought with them a great variety of manufacturing and mercantile skills, an aura of much-needed culture, and an undying hatred of France. Most of them were absorbed readily, but several Huguenot congregations maintained a separate existence for generations. Huguenot emigrés were among the ancestors of such early worthies as Paul Revere, John Sevier, John Jay, Alexander Hamilton, Gouverneur Morris, George Washington, and the Laurens family. Fewer in number were Spanish and Portuguese Jews, but from the very first they were prominent in the mercantile pursuits and in the benevolences for which Jews are noted. They were not numerous enough to rouse more than a modicum of jealousy. Their principal center was Newport.

Miscellaneous immigration

German immigrants appeared in all the colonies, but most of them came to Pennsylvania—Quakers' Valley, to them. As early as 1683 the Reverend Daniel Pastorius settled with a German congregation in Germantown, now a part of Philadelphia. Penn was alive to the possibility of developing his province with German settlers and sowed Switzerland and the Rhineland with the most glowing promotion literature Europe had yet seen. His efforts were abetted by independent and unscrupulous agents called "Newlanders," who described the American paradise in ecstatic terms. The Germans in their Rhineland home were crowded, overtaxed, in the path of ravaging armies, and persecuted for their religion. Under the blandishments of Penn and the Newlanders they left Germany, sometimes fleeing from their lords secretly, and for two generations poured into America. By 1760 there was a broad belt with about one hundred thousand "Pennsylvania Dutch" between Philadelphia and the Susquehanna River. They gave a permanent color to the region, and some of their descendants still speak a German patois, especially in the communities founded by pietist sects like Dunkards and Mennonites. The Lutherans were readier to mix with their British and Irish neighbors. It is a curious note that many of the German mercenaries brought over by the British during the Revolu-

German immigration

tion were left here at the close of the war, and many of them settled in the Pennsylvania Dutch counties.

Germans contributed one of the most valuable elements in the American heritage. Unlike modern Germans they sought no short cut to affluence but relied on thrift, patience, industry, and big families. They were the only immigrants who we can say with certainty possessed the peasant's mystical love for the soil. German farmers were renowned for their thoroughness and intelligent application of scientific methods. Their manual dexterity and mechanical inventiveness, together with their agricultural methods, made the Pennsylvania-German counties the most prosperous and progressive region in the English colonies. Germans not only engaged in type founding, paper making, and glass making but were the finest wood and iron workers in the colonies; and their Conestoga wagons and "Kentucky" rifles led the westward movement. Their folk arts have survived not only in museums but as a part of the American tradition. Music was greatly loved among them, and their town of Bethlehem was a center for the greatest of European music at a time when most Americans were still singing psalms and ballads through their noses.

The German flood was still running strong when about 1718 Ulster Irishmen began to enter in large numbers through Philadelphia, Baltimore, and Charleston. This element, often known as the Scotch-Irish, was descended from Lowland Scots and English who had been settled in Ulster by James I in an abortive attempt to drive out or exterminate the Irish and repeople the island with Protestants. The Scotch-Irish were rugged people, Presbyterian in religion. They were devoted to flax culture, sheep raising, and whisky, and they held their ground against English landlords and Catholic Irish and built up a prosperous farming and household-manufactures community. Before 1700, however, the English Parliament began to restrict their woolen and linen industries, then presently denied them a share in government and taxed them to support the Episcopal establishment. An attempt of the landlords to raise the rents was the last straw, and the Scotch-Irish in great numbers began to sell out their farm improvements and go to America. The Penns pushed them out beyond the German settlements to the Susquehanna frontier. It is likely that all together about two hundred thousand Scotch-Irishmen arrived in America before the Revolution. They settled in every colony, but most of them went first to Pennsylvania or the Carolinas.

Ulster had been a frontier between Protestantism and Catholicism, subject like the new home to massacre and countermassacre; so the Scotch-Irish had developed frontier characteristics before they emigrated.

Scotch-Irish character

Contentious, boisterous, individualistic, restless, mentally rigid, impatient of restraint—and courageous and hardy—they were ideal pioneers. Essentially unimaginative and unaesthetic, yet always dreaming of better land farther on, they only scratched the soil, then moved on to the next valley and left to a German plodder the patient reclamation of the soil. In them the democracy inherent in one side of Calvinism found complete expression; the Presbyterian kirk was as important a school for self-government as the provincial assemblies. It was a rough-and-ready school for men who believed in self-reliance and direct action. It is no wonder that the Revolution was sometimes known as the Presbyterian Rebellion.

There was no readily distinguishable movement of Celtic Irish as there was of Germans and Scotch-Irish, yet there can be no doubt that they began to arrive even earlier and in even greater numbers. Scattered through every colony as redemptioners, many of them apparently lost their Catholicism and merged with their neighbors. On the frontier they formed an important element in the amalgam that was forming, and probably they did much to alter the English temperament. The Celtic Irishman has contributed a romantic dash and color to American political and military life. His companionableness and blarney, his large warm heart, his human sympathies, and his willingness to give kindly personal services at the expense of what he considers irrelevant rules have given him a niche as a straw boss and politician. His lovableness has been transmuted into American friendliness, and his hyperbole has reappeared as giantism in American story and American ideals. Not English patter, but the crackle of Irish humor has been adapted by the American; though along with it has also come Scots dryness and the English sense of incongruity. On the other side, Celtic slipperiness has helped to give us the too common idea that any action is justifiable if one can get away with it. Lastly, the Celt has heightened a certain volatility which makes us too often subject to national surges of hysteria and to the slogans and nostrums of quack statesmen.

Irish character

The Scots came to America as families or small congregations and settled in every colony. The greatest single recorded migration was chiefly to North Carolina after the Young Pretender's defeat at Culloden in 1746. The poverty of Scotland had long been a barrier against the snares of luxury and political absolutism. The knightly tradition with its earmarks of lavishness and gentility never put down roots. Poverty made the Scot closefisted in spending for useless show, but in business matters he exhibited a persistence, carefulness, and cautious daring that made him the world's outstanding merchant. The Scots are the true shopkeepers, not the Eng-

Scottish immigration and influence

lish. Nowhere is there more reverence for the things of the mind than there is in Scotland; this has led to a certain mental rigidity and disputatiousness which exalts logic. The Scots in America were prominent as merchants, ministers, lawyers, and schoolmasters. Their influence on the formation of American character was profound, in that it helped to alter the English tradition by giving the American a certain respect for logic and universal education—indeed, the Scottish universities were more the Meccas of American colonial youth than were Oxford and Cambridge —and the lawyers that Scotland sent to America were the logicians of the Revolution. The peculiar homespun brand of American democracy is as much the child of Scotland as of the frontier. Robert Burns examined fine clothes and fare, noble blood and high degree, and announced: "The rank is but the guinea's stamp; the man's the gold for a' that." This is the inherited belief of the average American.

Fully as important as any of the foregoing immigrant elements was the Negro, the only one who came perforce. The races of Africa are as diverse as those of Europe with just as profound differences in physique, culture, and psychology. However, it is impossible to assess their separate influences in the American scene. It would **Negro immigration** seem that most of the slaves were brought from the region between the Gambia and Niger rivers, and slavers classified the tribes to which they belonged by their desirable or undesirable characteristics. The demand for slaves led to vast wars of conquest in the interior of Africa, and from these a constant stream of slaves poured down to the barracoons (slave pens) on the coast. It will never be known how many Negroes were imported into the Thirteen Colonies, but the slave population in 1775 was probably five hundred thousand.

Bristol was the chief English port engaged in the slave traffic, and it carried on the notorious Triangular Trade: to the barracoons on the Guinea Coast of Africa with trade goods to exchange for slaves, thence with the slaves across to the West Indies or the North **Triangular trade** American continent, and thence with plantation products to England. New England, New York, and Philadelphia entered the Triangular Trade before 1700; their routes and commercial dealings were various and complex, but their emphasis was usually on exchanging slaves for molasses and for money in the West Indies. The molasses was taken home and made into rum, and the rum was used as the chief article of barter for slaves in Guinea. The Middle Passage, from Africa to America, was notorious for its horrors both from confinement of the shackled slaves between three-foot decks and from disease. It would seem that the English slavers treated their cargoes better than did the New Englanders.

From the first, sentiment existed against slavery, but it was usually stifled by economic arguments. The original claim that Negroes had to be imported because white men could not stand the hard labor in the sun has long since been exploded. Slavery was introduced because it furnished quickly and with comparative cheapness a large and relatively docile labor force which had no concept of civil rights, did not look forward to freedom, and did not expect even the low standard of living of European village life. The contribution of the Negro in the form of labor to the economic enrichment of America is seldom realized by whites and has never (even since emancipation) been rewarded by more than a bare subsistence.

In his native habitat the Negro was probably in about the same stage of development as the northern Europeans were when they first came into contact with the Roman Empire. The Negro was not civilized in the sense of being disciplined and self-restrained; perhaps this **Negro culture** is just another way of saying he lacked the same inhibitions as Europeans. He was improvident and volatile in his emotions, given to rapid and often extreme changes of mood. The Negro in Africa was courageous in war, but like barbarians of any color he showed it in undisciplined bursts, rarely in the sustained effort that brings victory over great odds. It was of course inevitable that long inferiority as a slave and social helot in America should sometimes result in that irresponsibility toward military duty which is often labeled cowardice.

As yet the inculcation of basic disciplines and inhibitions has met with success only in certain aspects; perhaps that is because the white man has always feared that complete re-education will have to bring an admission of equal status. At any rate, Negroes absorbed **The Negro in America** rapidly the superficial aspects of American culture both because the race is readily adaptable and because members of the various Negro tribes were separated and had to learn English in order to communicate with each other. Though generally indolent and untrustworthy when set a separate task, the slave worked well and sometimes efficiently under supervision.

Christianity was readily adopted (and sometimes mixed with heathen practices) because it is a religion of comfort for the lowly and oppressed, a fact that is often forgotten today. A few Negroes learned to read, and a few attained some distinction as writers, notably the poetess Phyllis Wheatley. In their native Africa and in the plantation days Negroes were apt and skillful artisans; and there seems no reason but lack of background and opportunity why they should not be again. Some of the Negro cultures were relatively high, but the only important vestiges that remain in the United States are found in folklore and music. These, however, have become part and parcel of American life and give it a mood, color, and dramatic value quite foreign to the Western European.

The increase in the proportion of Negro slaves to whites in the southern colonies caused fear of slave insurrections. The danger was especially great in South Carolina, where in 1773 there were said to have been 110,-000 Negroes to 65,000 whites. Insurrections occurred, too, and were stamped out brutally, though after several experiences codes were enacted to forbid the routine cruelty which **Drawbacks to slavery** led to revolt. The increase in Negro population in the southern colonies and the decrease in plantation profits led several provinces to prohibit the importation of slaves; these laws were disallowed by the Crown because of the value of the trade to British merchants and were fruitful causes of colonial protests.

4   The Old West

The words *frontier* and *West* have been used so loosely that they have lost preciseness and, indeed, have come to be synonyms. We shall in future distinguish between them for clarity and convenience. The frontier was the advancing line—actually a broad, serrated belt or **The frontier** border—of contact between the wilderness and the fore- **and the** runners of civilization. It was an area of open spaces and **West** conflict, the domain in which the Indian contested for control with traders, trappers, cattlemen, miners, pioneer hunter-farmers, and the Seventh Cavalry. The West was the sparsely settled, definitely agricultural, and politically vociferous area behind that frontier, sometimes still menaced by Indians. Its interests differed from those of the old settled areas; and when the two became enough alike to be able to support much the same program for much the same reasons, the West had ceased separate existence.

The settlement of new lands in the area east of the Great Plains usually followed a rather well-defined pattern. The frontier stage of penetration was by the fur trade, ordinarily engaged in by rough characters who had much in common with the Indian way of life; in fact, in later days they often were part Indian in **Stages of** blood. Their mission was to learn about the country and its **settlement** possibilities, and to introduce alcohol and the diseases of civilization which would make white conquest easier. The second stage—which, however, did not always appear in the North—was the cattleman's frontier. Well before 1700 the Virginia back country had been overrun with great herds of wild cattle and horses which fed on the luxuriant pea vines native to that region. "Cowboys" found it profitable to organize hunts and to drive the animals into "cowpens," where they could be branded. The third stage was that of the agricultural settler. It usually began before the traders or cattlemen passed on, for the first agriculturist was a squatter who mixed his activities. He lived in a rough cabin, girdled trees to kill them and let in the light on his corn patch, and then when neighbors pressed in sold his "improvements" and moved on where the hunting or forage was better. The permanent settler followed close upon the heels of the squatter. Last came the growth of industries which endeavored to meet the local need for manufactured products. When the industrial interests became so prominent that they tried to legislate wages and boost the price of land, the area had joined the East, and it was time for a new swarming. All of this would happen in the space, perhaps, of a generation.

The Piedmont area between the Fall Line and the mountains and the nearer valleys among the mountains are known as the Old West. The New England back country was a part of the Old West because there **The Old** were a striking social and economic likeness and political **West** fellow feeling from one end to another of the westward belt. There can be no doubt that the Old West was the preparation ground for many of the economic and social techniques and for much of the psychological state of mind which the pioneers took with them as they burst the mountain barrier and began their sweep to the Pacific. For that reason it deserves some description at this juncture.

New England lived chiefly by the produce of small farms, forest, and sea. The small farms were able to grow little more food than was necessary to maintain the teeming families of their proprietors. The main ex-**Back coun-** ports were horses, apples, and home manufactures, the most **try New** important of which were the young men and women who **England** even before 1700 were settling in the other colonies as far south as Carolina, and who were destined to spread across the northern part of the country as far as the Pacific. The New England towns had originally been founded on provincial grants of land to congregations, but by 1725 this practice had shifted to grants to speculators. The result was to deepen the growing gulf between creditors and debtors and between coast and interior. The embittered surplus population either left New England or retreated northward, far up the river valleys to the upper reaches of Maine, New Hampshire, and Vermont. The settlers of Vermont occupied disputed territory, but they saw no reason for acknowledging allegiance to any coastal government, and so they set up a sort of autonomous republic which played off New York and New Hampshire against each other and later the British against the Continental Congress. Here dwelt a tight-lipped, self-sufficient pioneer society which was to stand for two centuries against scalp-lifters, rocky soil, rugged winters, and mechanization, and has only fallen in our own day before the radio and the summer boarder.

The Old West from Pennsylvania southward was even in colonial days more of a unit than the coast. The Great Valley ran almost un-

EXPANSION OF SETTLEMENT

SHOWING APPROXIMATE FRONTIERS

——— About 1700 ▬▬▬ About 1760 ----About 1780

Principal French settlements about 1780 (incl. La. & Fla.)

Spanish settlements

Statute Miles

0   100   200   300

J. W. CLEMENT CO., BUFFALO, N. Y.

broken from the Hudson River to Georgia and furnished a highway along which the pioneers moved at will, and from which the waters of the valley flowed eastward to the Piedmont or westward to the Mississippi. As early as 1732 Germans moved southward along the valley from Pennsylvania, and very soon Scotch-Irishmen entered from both Pennsylvania and the Carolinas. The Appalachians and the hostility of the Indians delayed the westward movement for a generation, but the result was only to make the sweep more irresistible when it began.

Unity of the Old West

There was a unity based upon like conditions of life and upon like

167

problems—problems which were to follow the frontier west to the Pacific. First, of course, was the danger from Indians, whose way of life was menaced by the forest-destroying whites. Next was the perennial problem of how to get legal possession of land quickly, cheaply, and in generous quantities. Then came the problem of transportation, for the pioneer's furs, flour, ginseng, and lumber products were too heavy to be carried far over mud roads, even when no mountains intervened. This led to chronic indebtedness, for exports were never sufficient to pay taxes and quitrents and leave enough over to buy tools, gunpowder, salt, and the few other imported necessities. A corollary was that there was no surplus to devote to the support of schoolmasters and clergymen, and the West inevitably in its second generation slipped a notch down the cultural scale below the men who had founded it. The West was therefore of necessity all but self-sustaining. The only cure lay in self-government, which would enable it to legislate taxes, land policies, and improvements in transportation, but this the East stoutly refused to consider until after independence.

The Old West was the meeting place of the nations, and its mountain valleys were the mixing bowls of the new nation. The Scotch-Irish took to the new environment with an aptness that made them its most prominent (at least its noisiest) element, thus giving posterity **Homo occidens** the idea that they monopolized the West. Such was far from the case. The restless, the adventurous, and the needy of every race were there helping to mold the characteristics of the West. The traveler in the hinterland saw what he chose to see. The aristocrat called it a "lubberland," and even the best-disposed admitted that dirt and laziness existed among the froth of outcasts who were thrust continually ahead of the settlements or who were left like islands in pockets of poor soil. But, as one observer recorded, the European who went West felt a "sort of resurrection . . . he now feels himself a man, because he is treated as such."

The Western European, long since removed from ancestral forests and lapped in the security of town and castle, was now breeding the pioneer once more. This was a free society and, like all free societies, was democratic. The pioneers were, like their surroundings, insensitive, uncouth, and at times semibarbarous, but taste and refinement were not proper weapons to conquer savage and wilderness. The man of the Old West gloried in his freedom from restraint and bitterly fought any attempt to subject him to regulations. He was subject to sudden gusts of passion, like his distant ancestor in the German forests, and his religion was compounded of simple and primitive emotions. The pioneer had no regrets for the civilization of Europe or even of the Tidewater except as he hoped to make his chosen region prosper; he was no longer English, Scotch-Irish, or German, nor even Pennsylvanian or Virginian, but that new man, an American. He lived in a log house, he ate of plentiful but plain fare, he bred large families, he went to church or not as he pleased, and he considered a man worthy or unworthy for his own sake and not for his father's title or wealth. Education was all right, especially for the ministry, but common sense and a knack with rifle and ax were more useful.

He looked about him at the vast wilderness owned by Indians and proprietors and held that "it was against the laws of God and Nature that so much land should lie idle while so many Christians wanted it to work on and to raise their bread." This was simply an eighteenth-century way of saying, "The earth belongs to him that gives it value"—to the cultivator, not the hunter, the speculator, or even the cattleman. He therefore hated the Indians because they in their dependence on game sought to stop the whites from leveling the forests and killing off or driving out the game. He hated the speculator (even though he might be a fellow Westerner) who got hold of vast tracts of land and held them unoccupied for a rise in value, or who sought to make the land a source of permanent income in the form of quitrents. This attitude toward "engrossers" of land was fundamental and permanent and was used by the pioneers to justify all sorts of violence.

The pioneer and the land

The man of the Old West was not a sensitive creature, and he found it perfectly possible to keep a clear conscience while he defied proprietors and quitrents, squatted wherever he found a fertile valley, and massacred the Indians who protested at his highhandedness. His Calvinism lay broad and deep and made him look upon God as a business partner and a tribal deity who regarded with favor self-reliance and direct action. There is a story of a Western preacher—a Scotch-Irishman—who during the Revolution opened a recruiting meeting with this remarkable prayer: "Lord God, if Thou art unwilling by divine grace to assist us, *do stand aside and let us fight it out!*"

BIBLIOGRAPHICAL NOTE

Why He Came and What He Found

ECONOMIC LIFE: See Beverley W. Bond, *The Quit-Rent System in the American Colonies* (1919); Abbott E. Smith, *Colonists in Bondage: White Servitude and Convict Labor in the American Colonies* (1947); Lyman Carrier, *The Beginnings of Agriculture in America* (1923); Harold Shurtleff, *The Log Cabin Myth* (1939); and Edgar A. J. Johnson, *American Economic Thought in the Seventeenth Century* (1932).

COLONIAL SOCIETY: See the appropriate volumes in *A History of American Life* and *The Pageant of America;* Arthur W. Calhoun, *Social History of the American Family* (3 v., 1917); Seymour Dunbar, *History of Travel in America* (4 v., 1915); Sydney G. Fisher, *Men, Women, and Manners in Colonial Times* (2 v., 1898). See also Richardson L. Wright, *Hawkers and Walkers in Early America* (1927); and the numerous readable volumes by Alice Morse Earle.

Social and Religious Ferment

COLONIAL CITIES: The literature is replete with interest and significance. Most valuable is Carl Bridenbaugh, *Cities in the Wilderness* (1938). See also Carl and Jessica Bridenbaugh, *Rebels and Gentlemen: Philadelphia in the Age of Franklin* (1942); Esther Forbes, *Paul Revere and the World He Lived In* (1942); Gertrude S. Kimball, *Providence in Colonial Times* (1912); James D. Phillips, *Salem in the Seventeenth Century* (1933); Harriott H. R. Ravenel, *Charleston, the Place and the People* (1906); John T. Scharf, *Chronicles of Baltimore* (1874); and Thomas J. Wertenbaker, *Norfolk* (1931). On Boston see Nathan H. Chamberlain, *Samuel Sewall and the World He Lived In* (1897); acquaintance should be made with the *Diary of Samuel Sewall, 1674–1729* (1927).

BENJAMIN FRANKLIN: The shrewd Philadelphia printer and politician who became America's first citizen of the world has been often portrayed. The latest full-length biography is by Carl Van Doren (1938). James Parton's two volumes (1864) are still among the most readable. Paul L. Ford, *The Many-Sided Franklin* (1899) gives a balanced portrayal of his many interests. Of the many editions of Franklin's writings the Albert H. Smyth edition (10 v., 1905–07) is usually preferred.

SOUTHERN PLANTERS: For their life in the eighteenth century see particularly Ulrich B. Phillips, *Life and Labor in the Old South* (1929). Interesting contemporary accounts are *Secret Diary of William Byrd of Westover, 1709–1712* (1941); and Philip Vickers Fithian, *Journal and Letters, 1773–1774* (1943).

INTELLECTUAL HISTORY: Some hardy souls have cast doubt on the existence of such a thing as the history of American thought, but hardier ones have been found to launch into its exposition. Among these are Merle Curti, *Growth of American Thought* (1943); and Max Savelle, *Seeds of Liberty: The Genesis of the American Mind* (1948). Vernon L. Parrington, *Main Currents in American Thought* (1927–30. Vol. 1, *The Colonial Mind;* Vol. 2, *The Romantic Revolution;* and Vol. 3, *The Beginnings of Critical Realism*), was the pioneer in the field and, despite being supplanted in parts, is a *must* for the serious reader. See also Michael Kraus, *Intercolonial Aspects of American Culture* (1928) and *The Atlantic Civilization* (1949); and Leonard W. Labaree, *Conservatism in Early American History* (1948). Useful biographies are Ralph and Louise Boas, *Cotton Mather: Keeper of the Puri-*

tan Conscience (1928); Henry B. Parkes, *Jonathan Edwards* (1930); and Perry Miller, *Jonathan Edwards* (1949). For the witchcraft frenzy see George L. Kittredge, *Witchcraft in Old and New England* (1929).

The Racial Complex

GENERAL: See Marcus L. Hansen, *The Atlantic Migration, 1607–1860* (1945) and *The Immigrant in American History* (1940); George M. Stephenson, *History of American Immigration, 1820–1924* (1926); and Carl Wittke, *We Who Built America* (1939). The reception of the immigrant in colonial times is treated in E. Emberson Proper, *Colonial Immigration Laws* (1900); and an attempt is made to sort out national origins in Howard F. Barker, "Report of a Committee on Linguistic and National Stocks," in American Historical Association, *Annual Report,* 1931, Vol. 1, pp. 103–441.

FRENCH: Charles W. Baird, *History of the Huguenot Emigration to America* (2 v., 1885); Arthur H. Hirsh, *Huguenots of Colonial South Carolina* (1928); Lucien J. Fosdick, *The French Blood in America* (1906).

JEWS: Leo M. Friedman, *Early American Jews* (1934).

GERMANS: Albert B. Faust, *The German Element in the U.S.* (2 v., 1909, 1927); Lucy F. Bittinger, *The Germans in Colonial Times* (1900).

SCOTCH-IRISH: Charles K. Bolton, *Scotch-Irish Pioneers in Ulster and America* (1910); Wayland F. Dunaway, *The Scotch-Irish of Colonial Pennsylvania* (1944); Henry J. Ford, *Scotch-Irish in America* (1915); Maude Glasgow, *The Scotch-Irish in Northern Ireland and in the American Colonies* (1936); and Charles A. Hanna, *The Scotch-Irish* (2 v., 1902).

SCOTS: John P. MacLean, *Scotch Highlanders in America* (1900).

IRISH: Attempts to segregate Irish blood and contributions in the colonial period always result in sweeping and unjustified claims or in confusion. Irish writers have tried to break down the distinction between Irish and Scotch-Irish, but there is no doubt that it was recognized and that the latter term was used in colonial times; unfortunately the word Irish was used even more to indicate either or both elements. Louis Adamic rejects the distinction in his *Nation of Nations* (1945); and this rejection, along with grievous imbalances in the assessment of the significance of obscure national elements, destroys the reliability of the work.

NEGROES: Ulrich B. Phillips, *American Negro Slavery* (1918) is standard on its subject. A recent work is John H. Franklin, *From Slavery to Freedom* (1947); it has an extremely valuable bibliography. See also Elizabeth Donnan, ed., *Documents Illustrative of the History of the Slave Trade to America* (4 v., 1930–35).

The Old West

OLD WEST: For a sympathetic view see J. Hector St. John de Crèvecœur, *Letters from an American Farmer* (Everyman ed. 1926), especially Letter III, "What Is an American?" Fully as interesting and quite in contrast is William

Byrd's *Secret History of the Line* (1929), an account of the surveying of the boundary between Virginia and North Carolina through the back-country "lubberland." Other contemporary narratives are John Bartram, *Travels* (1791); Andrew Burnaby, *Travels* (1775, reprinted 1904); Pehr Kalm. *Travels* (1772); and Gottlieb Mittelberger, *Journey to Pennsylvania in 1750 and Return to Germany in 1754* (1898). See also Newton D. Mereness, ed., *Travels in the American Colonies* (1916).

NEW ENGLAND'S WEST: See Roy K. Akagi, *Town Proprietors of the New England Colonies* (1924); Melville Egleston, *Land System of the New England Colonies* (1886); and Lois K. M. Rosenberry, *Expansion of New England* (1909).

Chapter VI

COLONIAL GROWING PAINS

1 *England's Halfhearted Mercantilism*

THE colonies of England were planted later than those of most of the other nations, but they were first to reach economic and political maturity. The reasons lay primarily in the nature of the English people and in their laws and institutions. Most important was the fact that mercantilism was never practiced more than halfheartedly by England; so it was possible for the colonies to attract swarms of immigrants, to build up their manu- **Why the colonies matured early** factures and commerce, and to exercise all but complete self-government. The colonists were self-governing because they were Englishmen and as such expected to manage their own affairs. Distance promoted self-reliance, and troubles in England itself promoted a salutary neglect of the colonies, but the royal charters were liberal from the first and generally remained so. Immigrants were usually workers; few nobles came over and fewer remained. Liberal land policies promoted widespread prosperity, forced town employers to raise the wages of their workmen in order to keep them, and ensured a society that was relatively classless because there was an approximately equal opportunity for all.

It seems likely that the popular imagination has overrated the role of religious freedom as a reason for planting the colonies; on the other hand, it certainly had some share in attracting immigrants. British sea power protected the colonies from foreign conquest in one direction, while toward the land the rugged diplomacy of fur traders and royal governors weakened the Indians, the French, and the Spanish. Finally, though it was not generally recognized in that day, the Thirteen Colonies were highly favored by geographical position, climate, and soil. Their location between the Caribbean and Europe gave them a strategic commercial position; their climate was an invigorating aid to enterprise; and their agricultural staples and forest products afforded a firmer basis for economic strength and the growth of a transplanted European population than did the sugar, the cacao, and the silver mines of the tropics.

All of the Thirteen Colonies were founded as a result of private enterprise. Indeed, the British Empire has been chiefly the creation of individuals and trading companies, and only with the greatest reluctance

Types of government has the government stepped in to remedy neglect and exploitation—usually in response to an aroused public opinion. The gradual change-over from proprietary and corporate (sometimes called company or charter) colonies to royal colonies was therefore in keeping with imperial evolution and was hastened in many cases by the colonists' hope that royal governors would be more lenient (they said impartial) than the governors sent out by proprietors or companies. The British government also desired the change because it could then act directly through its governors rather than through elected or proprietary governors. In 1775 Pennsylvania, Delaware, and Maryland were the only surviving proprietorships. Connecticut and Rhode Island were the only charter colonies, though in both cases the charters were held by the people and not by a British company.

The official point of view of the English government from first to last was mercantilist; that is, the colonies existed for the benefit of the mother country. It was the purpose of a long series of Navigation Acts to inte-

Mercantilism a planned economy grate the Thirteen Colonies (and all other English possessions) into a planned economy contained within a self-sufficient empire. It was the belief of that day that trade was a sort of warfare, and that the victor in a transaction was the party that came away with the most gold or silver. Navigation laws for the control of commerce had existed from medieval times, and it was natural that they should be extended to the colonies. Cromwell made the first significant attempt to set up an exclusive system by the acts of 1649 and 1651. These led to the First Anglo-Dutch War, by which the Dutch strangle hold on world commerce was perceptibly loosened. After the accession of Charles II additional acts promoted two other Anglo-Dutch wars.

The final Navigation Act of 1696 integrated and tightened the system. The purpose of the acts was to confine trade within the Empire to Empire ships; foreign ships could touch only at the ports of Great

Navigation and Trade Acts Britain and Ireland, and even then they could deliver only goods produced in their own countries. Tobacco, rice, naval stores and timbers, beaver skins, sugar, dyes, and other enumerated articles produced in the colonies had to be landed in England (not Scotland or Ireland) before they could be sent on to foreign purchasers; European goods (with minor exceptions) had to pass through England likewise. A succession of supplementary regulations known as the Trade Acts undertook to carry out the economic planning envisioned by mercantilism, by setting up an elaborate system of controls, bounties, and rebates.

The administration of the Navigation Acts from 1696 was in the hands of a committee composed of "experts" and Cabinet officials called the Board of Trade and Plantations. It was the precursor of the modern Colonial Office and worked closely with the Cabinet official **Board of** known as the Secretary of State for the Southern Depart- **Trade and** ment, the precursor of the modern Colonial Secretary. The **Plantations** board included in its duties an examination of all laws passed by the colonial assemblies and on occasion disallowed them by use of the royal veto. The Navigation and Trade Acts were enforced by admiralty courts which were based on Roman law and so did not need to refer their cases to the decisions of juries, which were likely to be in sympathy with violators of the acts. The active members of the board were usually from the great merchant families, and few of them had ever been in the colonies. This situation led inevitably to uninformed and arbitrary decisions intended to promote the narrowest views of mercantilism. In addition, British governmental organization was never more confused and contradictory than in the eighteenth century. Too many departments and officials had their fingers in the colonial pie, so that the administration was at one and the same time confused, contradictory, lax, and arbitrary. It was not until 1768 that a Secretary of State for the Colonies was appointed, and at that his powers were not clear.

These restrictions sound worse than they actually were. Tobacco was the only vitally important product affected in the Thirteen Colonies, and in return for the handicap the colonists enjoyed a virtual monopoly of its sale in the Empire. Their principal products, such as **Effect on** most furs, lumber, fish, grain, and meat, were not affected. **the colonies** Of course, English merchants had promoted the Navigation Acts, and they expected to profit by them, but there was no intention to shut the colonies out. It was expected that colonial trade, also, would boom as a result—and it did. It is true that some of the Trade Acts bore hard on colonial manufactures of iron, hats, and wool products, but on the other hand bounties were granted to encourage the production of naval stores, hemp, and lumber. By and large the colonies were no exceptions to the economic thinking of the day. They were highly mercantilistic in their attitudes toward foreign countries, toward each other, and toward the mother country in so far as their own trading and manufacturing interests were involved. However, the advantages offered by imperial bounties and monopolies were so great that most colonists were highly in favor of the Navigation Acts until they were used as a means of taxation and imperial interference in local affairs. It is interesting to note that the limitations on enumerated products fell hardest on the West Indian colonies, which remained loyal; the greatest share of bounty payments went to the mainland colonies, which revolted.

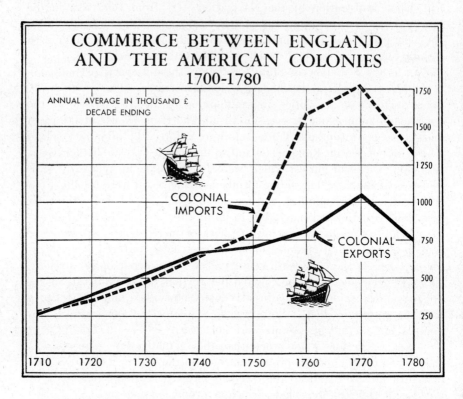

COMMERCE BETWEEN ENGLAND AND THE AMERICAN COLONIES
1700-1780

ANNUAL AVERAGE IN THOUSAND £ DECADE ENDING

COLONIAL IMPORTS

COLONIAL EXPORTS

1750
1500
1250
1000
750
500
250

1710 1720 1730 1740 1750 1760 1770 1780

The colonial trade was of immense value to England. From the American colonies as a whole during the first third of the eighteenth century England imported products considerably in excess of what she sold them, but her profitable export to the European continent of such staples as sugar and tobacco far more than made up the difference. But this was not the whole picture. The northern commercial colonies sold to the mother country less than half as much as they took, and the southern plantation colonies were steadily falling behind. The sugar islands had a favorable balance of not less than two to one, but this balance was spent in England by the absentee planters, known in Parliament as the "West Indian lobby." By the eve of the Revolution, though the continental colonies' trade with England had increased fourfold, the adverse balance had increased eightfold.

Value of colonial trade

Throughout this period the planters of the South were falling deeper into debt, and the sight of their rice, indigo, and tobacco being resold at an enormous profit by English merchants only increased the irritation which finally led the southern aristocracy to revolution. The commercial colonies, however, had a remedy. They carried on a complex interchange of goods not only within the Thirteen Colonies but wherever there was a profit to be made, and they were not above illicit traffic. The Triangular Trade was one of their most profitable ventures, and this depended largely upon great quantities of cheap rum. Rum was also the tipple of the poor throughout the Thirteen Colonies, was the basis of the Indian trade, and found a ready market in England and the colder countries of Europe.

Significance of the molasses trade

Rum was made from molasses, and to obtain this the shippers sent great quantities of barrel staves, fish, salt meat, flour, and other products to the West Indies (which would have starved without them) and took in exchange molasses and silver dollars. Sometimes they demanded cash of English West Indian purchasers, then sailed off to a French island and bought molasses at half the price asked by English planters. This price reduction was possible because the soil of the English islands was so exhausted by long and wasteful use that they could not compete with the fresh soil of the French islands, where the sugar industry was comparatively young. The West Indian planters'

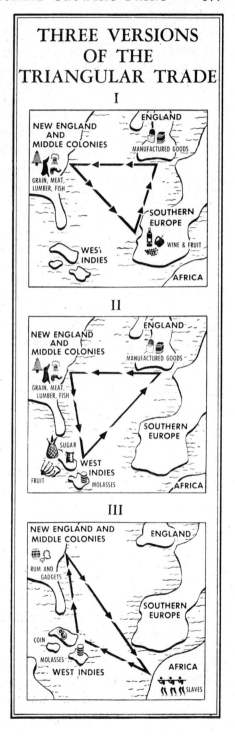

THREE VERSIONS OF THE TRIANGULAR TRADE

lobby resented this situation and demanded and got the Molasses Act of 1733, which laid a prohibitive duty on rum or molasses bought in foreign islands. This was a dog-in-the-manger tactic, for the mainland colonies were developing faster than the English sugar islands and the latter could not absorb all the surplus of the commercial colonies, they could not fill the demand for molasses, and they could not furnish the needed hard cash.

It was a dangerous situation. If the Molasses Act was obeyed, it would mean not only that the commercial colonies could not obtain the specie to pay their debts to England but that British trade would be dealt a staggering blow. Obviously the act became a dead **Colonial** letter the day it was passed. The vast extent and irregular **smuggling** contour of the Atlantic Coast and the paid complaisance of customs officials combined to encourage smuggling. Probably there was also considerable smuggling of European goods. It seemed silly to deliver a cargo of salt fish and flour in the Mediterranean, then to carry the exchange cargo of wine, silks, furniture, and paper to England, pay a duty, land it, and take on a similar cargo or the same for transportation to America. Still, except for molasses, it is not likely that there was an unreasonable proportion of goods smuggled into the Thirteen Colonies. Nevertheless, there was enough to form a vested interest composed of merchants and undersalaried customs officials who found it to their advantage to oppose the lowering of duties.

Whatever else may be said about them, it is evident that the Thirteen Colonies were expanding enormously. From about two hundred thousand in 1688 their population grew to around two and three quarter **Colonial** million in 1775; at the latter date the British Isles had only **economic** about ten million people. The economic expansion was even **expansion** more remarkable, as can be seen in the rising standard of living and the growth of commerce. Merchants and agriculturists alike were able to plow their profits back into their businesses, a fact which may account in considerable part for the colonies' excessive imports of manufactured goods from England. This phenomenon, of course, is familiar in any new and growing country, for it must in part expand its own facilities on capital goods borrowed from older regions. On the other hand, colonial debts drained so much specie from the country that internal business was handicapped for lack of the currency so necessary in an expanding economy. Attempts were made to fill the need by issuing paper money, but this only brought inflation. The Crown endeavored to put a stop to the practice by disallowing bills intended to create currency. Such vetoes were generally favored by the creditor merchants of the seaboard, but there was a swelling chorus of protest from the debtor classes, who wished to pay their mortgages and quitrents with cheap paper money. The result was the growth of hard feeling between creditor and debtor sections, usually the coast and the interior respectively, and the planting of enmities which were to bear bitter fruit in later years.

Probably ninety-five per cent of the people in 1775 were engaged in agriculture, yet most of these were concerned with spare-time manu-factures, the women with linen and woolen textiles, and the men with tanning and utilizing leather, making potash, twisting ropes, **Colonial** and lumbering and hauling. There was some copper smelt- **manufac-** ing in Connecticut and New York, and iron smelting in **tures** every colony except Georgia; Parliament prohibited the manufacture in America of articles of iron and a few things like hats, but the ban was little heeded. A few small glass factories made window glass and trade beads. Paper manufacture and printing did very well. Quarrying and brick and tile manufacture were, of course, among the earliest activities. Rum manufacture flourished in spite of the Molasses Act. Shipbuilding and manufacture of ship stores were basic industries along the coast as far south as Norfolk, but were most important in New England. Ships could be built for as little as half what they cost in Europe, and because shipping was so important to the Empire the Board of Trade refused to limit it. It is said that by 1760 one third of the shipping under the British flag had been built in America. Fishing and whaling followed naturally on shipbuilding.

This expansion, truly amazing for that century, was possible because no serious attempt was made to enforce mercantilism until 1764—and then came the Revolution. The Molasses Act of 1733 failed of its pur-pose because Robert Walpole, the minister then in power, believed in letting sleeping dogs lie. His ascendancy (1721– **Salutary** 42) has often been called a period of "salutary neglect for **neglect** the colonies." In spite of Navigation Acts and a nosy Board of Trade and Plantations, the phrase might well be extended to cover the entire length of colonial history up to 1764. England, busy with internal strife and foreign wars or checked by unconventional statesmen who distrusted mercantilism, let the colonies go pretty much their own way. As a re-sult they became strong enough to assert their rights when it became evident that a too consistent mercantilism would drag colonies and mother country down in common ruin.

It is obvious to us, as we look back, that the British Empire was drifting toward a crisis and that the more strictly mercantilism was en-forced, the sooner the crisis would come. It is probable that during the eighteenth century British mercantilism failed to crash **Growing** because of the Americans' free trade with the French and **imperial** Spanish West Indies. As a result of the wars of that century **economic** England added Canada and some additional sugar islands, **crisis** but Canada's temperate-zone products were more than the Empire could absorb and only disturbed the economic balance further. Probably in the end the economic strength of the Empire was saved by two things: India's trade and hoarded treasure, and the sudden overwhelming manufacturing supremacy brought by the Industrial Revolution. An independent United States actually seems to have been an asset to British trade.

2 *The Democratic Struggle*

The political history of the colonial period can be compared to the struggle among three wrestlers in one ring; there can be nothing but mutual exhaustion unless two of them unite to toss the third out of the **Three con-** ring, and then go on to settle the issue between them. Just **tending** so the king, the coast, and the interior wrestled with each **forces** other at an increasing tempo for a century until, in the Revolution, coast and interior united to toss the king out of the country. Since then the American political story has been chiefly concerned with the struggle between the two victors or their heirs and assignees. The story of the colonial struggle is long and involved and well worth more attention than the bare outline we can present here. There were many alarums and excursions, and curious alliances were formed and broken. In general, coast and interior allied to oppose the royal power, and coast and king united against the interior. Somehow king and interior only occasionally found anything in common.

The governors of the colonies were intended to be the viceroys of the king (in reality, of Parliament). This condition was true even where a proprietor stood between king and governor, and also in the corporate colonies where the governors were elected by the people **Powers of** but were nevertheless obliged to enforce the Navigation **governors** Acts and to carry out instructions of the Board of Trade. But this was not all. In addition to representing the king, the governor was also head of the executive, legislative, and judicial branches of the provincial government. He appointed the numerous members of the hierarchy of executive and judicial officials from justices of the peace, sheriffs, and militia officers on up to judges. He usually appointed or at least nominated the members of his executive council, which, in every province but Pennsylvania (where there was a unicameral legislature), served as the upper house of the legislature and in some colonies as supreme court. Governors were obviously in an impossible situation, for no man can serve two masters. Though some of the governors were native-born, most were Englishmen. There were men of tact and ability among the executives, but the majority had little ability, prestige, or personal fortune; most of them were mere "placemen" sent out as a favor to a courtier who wished to provide for an impecunious friend.

Many were lieutenant-governors serving in place of an aristocratic governor who preferred to stay in London. Some regarded their appointment as the chance of a lifetime and made such indecent haste to fill their

Inside cover of Benjamin Franklin's *Plain Truth* (1747). Hercules, sitting on a cloud with club in hand, gazes down on a wagoner who, kneeling, is praying for divine aid in rescuing his horses and heavy wagon, mired in the mud. "Heaven helps only those who help themselves" is the adage. This engraving is believed to be the first American attempt to depict a political situation.

purses (by selling offices, land grants, etc.) that the colonial assemblies naturally learned to be suspicious of governors.

A century-long battle was carried on between governors and assemblies as the latter fought step by step for the same liberties that Parliament had wrung from the reluctant Stuarts. The governor's power of appointment was limited in various ways, in later years by appointing legislative commissioners to command provincial armies or carry out other functions and report back to the assembly. Dissatisfaction with the governor as the link between king and colony was so intense that the colonies demanded and obtained the right to send official agents to London to look after their interests. It was as agent for several of the colonies that Benjamin Franklin made his political reputation. Legally only the governor could summon the assembly, and he could prorogue it at will; over stiff opposition some colonial assemblies provided that they would meet at least once every three years. They won freedom from prosecution for utterances in the

Colonial struggle for rights

assembly, the right to judge the qualifications of their own members, and the right to initiate tax and appropriation bills and to appoint tax collectors. The Board of Trade sent frequent and meticulous instructions to the governors, and those who lost major engagements were quickly recalled and perhaps also forfeited their bonds. Out of 8563 laws submitted to the Board of Trade, 469 were disallowed.

In all of these struggles the assemblies held one important trump over the governors—their control of the purse strings gave them the right to vote salaries: the good little governor would find himself amply rewarded; the bad one would find his salary cut or withheld altogether. The weapon was particularly potent against impecunious placemen. Three colonies were exceptions. Georgia's governor was paid by the king, and North Carolina's by quitrents which were not always collectible. Virginia had made the mistake of voting the governor the right to collect a perpetual tax on tobacco, and this placed him beyond the control of the House of Burgesses.

The battle over control of the courts was particularly bitter. The assemblies claimed that, like the British Parliament, they had the right to protect judges from summary dismissal by the executive; but governors and the Board of Trade refused to yield, and the

Control of courts right was never established, though the assembly could be mean and withhold the successor's salary. The governors' right to establish special courts to try special cases resulted in the famous Zenger trial in New York in 1735. John Peter Zenger in his *New-York Weekly Journal* had published articles prepared by the governor's political enemies and critical of the governor's course in setting up a special court to try a salary dispute. Zenger was tried for libel before judges who attempted to confine the jury to its traditional role of deciding the fact of whether he had published the articles. He was defended by Andrew Hamilton, an eminent Philadelphia lawyer, who appealed with success to the jury to declare Zenger not guilty on the ground that what he had published was true and therefore not libel.

The decision was of importance in the development of freedom of the press, for it furnished a precedent that a newspaper could publish the truth. However, in the end the colonial governors were shorn of most of their judicial powers. The King's Privy Council was the supreme court of the Empire, and American cases could be appealed to it. As a matter of fact they seldom were, for the reason that if the appellant lost he had to pay all expenses and damages, and at a distance of three thousand miles from home that was not a risk worth running.

Out of the colonial political melée several facts and trends became clear. Two rival ideas of the structure of the Empire were growing up. The British regarded the Empire as an aggregation of states under the

Parliament of the United Kingdom, with power flowing outward but none inward, except that Parliament was elected by the United Kingdom. The colonies were legally **Structure of the Empire** analogous to cities which, like the colonies, had been chartered by the king but were now subject to Parliament.

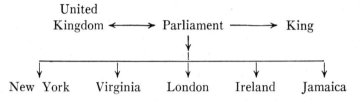

The American interpretation was that the Empire was made up of equal states, each under its own parliament, with the king as the co-ordinator and the Parliament of the United Kingdom legislating for him in matters that were distinctly of common imperial interest.

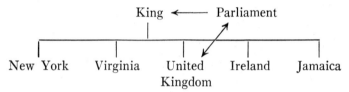

Basically Americans rejected the idea that Parliament's laws, even if passed on through the king, could bind them: they would be accepted only by enlightened common consent. This was exactly the basis of the British Commonwealth of Nations in the first part of the present century. The tragedy is that in the eighteenth century British statesmen could not conceive of sentiment as being a tie that binds tighter than laws.

The governors' claim of tremendous powers was indicative of Parliament's determination to rule America in the same way as the Stuarts had tried to rule England. It was agreed that Americans were entitled to the rights of Englishmen (civil liberties), but they exercised self-government only by grace of king and Parliament, with no more sovereign power than that allowed to an English municipality. It was an article of faith that colonials were inferior simply because they were colonials. The English process, as far as it was understood, was regarded (at least by English gentlemen) as the private property of English gentlemen.

English electoral districts had long since ceased to be apportioned by population but remained almost exactly as they had been in the time of Elizabeth. The voters of so-called rotten boroughs disposed of the elec-

Theories of represen- tation tion to the highest bidder; owners of vacant fields (pocket boroughs) where once flourishing towns had stood were still entitled to send two representatives to Parliament. On the other hand, great cities in the industrial Midlands were unrepresented. The system, however, was advantageous to the aristocracy because it gave them control of Parliament, and so they defended the doctrine of virtual representation: it did not matter, said they, where a member of Parliament lived or what sort of district he represented, he was still the virtual representative of the citizens of an area where a vote was never cast. Americans, especially those in the West, rejected the doctrine out of hand. It was evident to the Piedmont farmers that Tidewater planters did not support their interests in the assembly, and they insisted that an area was not represented unless it sent one of its own residents to the assembly.

This reasoning led naturally into the political struggle between coast and interior—or between the Gentleman's Party and the Country Party. When coast and interior united against the Court Party (or Governor's, **Coast versus interior** or Proprietary), they were known as the Colony Party. All electoral districts had been on the coast at first, and as these grew in wealth and conservatism it was easy for the Gentleman's Party to control the assemblies. As the interior grew in population it presented its needs. The Gentleman's Party almost invariably received these petitions coldly, for its members were profiting by collecting taxes from the interior but refusing to furnish services. Next there was a demand for a redistricting (usually the erection of new counties) to give the interior its fair share of representatives in the assembly.

Sometimes the Gentleman's Party made concessions, but it rarely permitted control to slip away from its strongholds. Thus in Virginia, where counties were equally represented, the new western counties were much larger in area and population than the older counties, but since they were fewer in number they could not outvote Tidewater. The reasons the Gentleman's Party gave in the various provinces for such discrimination seemed good to it: the West was always draining away the coast population and thus raising workmen's wages, and anyhow the West was always trying to overturn the old established ways which God had ordained for the convenience of the Gentleman's Party and the better guidance of the ignorant horde. The cure was simple: limit sales of western lands and prevent a redress of grievances. In that way fewer people would leave the coast, wages would be low, and God's will would be done on earth as in Heaven.

The struggle between coast and interior found its most dramatic crisis in the Carolinas. The interiors of these provinces had received a mixed population which suffered from the numerous political and economic ills incident to the frontier. Worst of these were the high prices demanded by coastal land speculators and the extortionate legal fees charged by the local official class, which acted hand in glove with the speculators. Outbreaks began in North Carolina in 1765 and led eventually to an association, the Regulators, intended to hold down legal fees and land prices. Presently it undertook to break up court sessions which tried to confiscate farms on which mortgages and fees were unpaid. A period of turbulence followed. In 1769 the Regulators actually got a majority in the assembly, but Governor Tryon dissolved it and saved the Gentleman's Party. The Regulators in despair resorted to violence, but Tryon at the head of the Tidewater gentry defeated them at the Alamance River in 1771 and suppressed the reform movement. Some of the defeated elements moved to the mountains and settled on the westward-flowing waters of the Watauga River.

The Regulators

There was a parallel Regulator movement in South Carolina, where well over half of the white population lived in the interior but had no representation in the assembly and had to go to court in Charleston and have their cases tried before Tidewater juries. When the assembly failed to grant reforms, disorder followed and was suppressed only after a series of skirmishes which ended in a Regulator defeat at Saluda Creek in 1769. The result was that during the Revolution many of the discontented people of the interior plumped for King George when the Tidewater gentry took the side of Congress. Curiously enough, among these Loyalists were many of the Scottish clansmen who had fled to the Carolinas after their defeat in the Scottish rising of 1745 in favor of the Young Pretender.

The assertion sometimes made that democracy did not exist in the Thirteen Colonies results from a failure to understand that democracy is a process, not a completed structure of popular government. As a process democracy was very much alive during the entire colonial period, both as (1) a movement among the common people to widen their political and economic rights, and as (2) an effort by the colonies to make good their rights within the Empire. The "compact" as an agreement among the people as the basis of government was well understood, and it found expression in the Mayflower Compact, the Fundamental Orders of Connecticut, and the Watauga Association, to mention only a few which preceded the great example of the Constitution of 1787. The people felt that the compact should be expressed in writing as their colonial constitutions (charters) were, in order to minimize uncertainty. It was this compact as concretely expressed in the charters and in the rights of Englishmen that was the goal of the colonial political struggle. Without the strength and

Democracy existed in the colonies

experience gained in this struggle the colonists could never have succeeded in the War for Independence and the formation of the Union.

It is notable that though the democratic process was perfected in England, the Thirteen Colonies soon passed the mother country in the application. The reason sprang primarily from the wide spread of land **Land the** ownership and the early adoption of land ownership as the **basis of** chief qualification for the franchise. This was in line with **democracy** the practice in England, but there the possession of land was limited to the few and only extremists like the Levellers dreamed of manhood suffrage. In America, however, the feudal tenure and transfer of land were unnecessary and, indeed, impossible. The common man suddenly found himself in the possession of political power and with sufficient land to make him all but economically independent. The attempts of the Tidewater gentry to concentrate wealth and power in their own hands he naturally and rightly regarded as an attempt to thrust him back into the pit from whence he had been digged, and so he fought with all his energies to preserve and extend his political and economic rights.

It is quite true that the mechanics of elections lacked our modern refinements. The franchise for participation in the election of provincial legislators was based upon land ownership or upon large personal prop- **How** erty or salary and was usually confined to men. In New **democracy** England nominations were often made in a sort of pre- **developed** liminary election, and at the regular election men could vote in person or by proxy. Little is known about the method of nomination elsewhere, but it seems likely that candidates were nominated and seconded on the spot, then voted upon. In the South elections were often by a show of hands; the ballot was used in the North, though it was not often secret. Gradually nominations were taken over by party meetings or conventions, of course carefully controlled by the aristocracy but containing the method and machinery which could be and eventually were taken over by the people. Candidates declared their principles in broadsides or in letters published in newspapers. Eventually voting was by voice before registrars or by nonsecret ballots. The aristocracy still "set up" their candidates, but now they toadied to the voters—at least on election days.

The battle of the coastal aristocracy against the governors was an essential step in the evolution of democracy. They represented themselves as promoting the welfare of the whole community (to get the votes of the lesser fry) and based their arguments on Natural Rights. Commoners thus came to accept and defend political equality, and even the unfranchised classes (*possibly* ninety per cent of the white population) showed their vocal and muscular power in public affairs and gave the party they favored a radical tinge. The aristocrats had thus undermined their own control even while they were winning it from the governors. Once the common man's awe of them passed, the democratic movement would begin its irresistible march. "The mob," wrote Gouverneur Morris in 1774, "begins to think and reason. Poor reptiles! It is with them a vernal morning; they are struggling to cast off their winter's slough, they bask in the sunshine, and ere noon they will bite."

The American people emerged from the colonial period with the tenets of democracy burned into their hearts far more deeply than they were burned into English hearts.

(1) They understood the reality of the democratic process and the method of advance by persistent struggle **Democratic tenets set** and temporary compromise. The changing balance of social forces as expressed in the political war of maneuver was accepted as the natural and inevitable means of progress.

(2) They understood the necessity of the basic civil liberties, of popular control of legislative power, and the usefulness of the legislature's check upon executive and judiciary. It was generations before they lost their fear of a strong executive and an independent judiciary.

(3) They had a deeply ingrained fear of the union of Church and state. Though the union existed in nine of the Thirteen Colonies, it had been shorn of aggressive power and was to be wiped out by 1838.

(4) They understood the economic basis of democracy and realized that democracy could not exist in the face of ungoverned economic concentration. This was the crux of the democratic battle during the colonial period, and it has remained the crux down to our own day. The main battle has never yet been against property as property, but against the abuse or potential abuse of the power which property gives.

3   The Battle for North America

The seeds of the eventual quarrel between mother country and colonies did not all come out of packages labeled economic or political. Indeed, the Thirteen Colonies regarded themselves as adults, and there was a long history of common efforts with the mother coun- **Wars** try, younger-son resentments, and family quarrels. **between**

In order to lay a further background let us take up the **France and** series of wars which culminated in the expulsion of France **England** from North America. Up to 1689 the English had technically been at peace with France save for a few years of halfhearted combat and in the colonies had been content to let the Iroquois pull their chestnuts out of the fire. However, the accession of the Dutch stadholder to the English throne as William III led to the initiation of a long series of wars, which were to last until 1815. These wars sprang from complex causes. In Europe they involved the balance of power with its problems of royal successions and ownership of provinces. In the Caribbean, Africa, and India they variously concerned trade in slaves and manufactured goods, and the control of plantation areas, especially sugar islands.

In North America overtrapping had led to a glut of furs which was depressing prices to the verge of ruin, and at first England and France fought for a fur monopoly which would enable the winner to raise prices to profitable levels. Later on the English were more concerned with clinching their title to the rich agricultural lands of the Ohio Valley. A brief table of the wars is appended for convenience.

Date	European Name	American Name	Peace Treaty	Principal Contestants	Some American Issues
1689–97	War of the English Succession	King William's War	Ryswick	England, Spain, Holland v. France	———
1701–13	War of the Spanish Succession	Queen Anne's War	Utrecht	England, Holland, Austria v. France, Spain	Control of Nova Scotia, Hudson Bay
1740–48	War of the Austrian Succession	King George's War	Aix-la-Chapelle	England, Holland, Austria, v. France, Spain, Prussia	Capture of Louisbourg
1756–63	Seven Years' War	Great French and Indian War	First Paris	England, Prussia v. France, Austria, Russia, Spain	Control of Ohio Valley, Canada, and Florida. Louisiana deeded to Spain
1775–83	War for American Independence	American Revolution	Second Paris	England v. U.S., France, Holland, Spain	American independence and territorial concessions. Florida returned to Spain
1792–1815	Wars of the French Revolution and Napoleon	[War of 1812 a minor accompaniment]	Congress of Vienna	France v. Europe	Louisiana sold to U.S.

A few years after the close of the war with the Iroquois, New France received as governor a remarkable man, Comte de Frontenac. In 1673 the trader Louis Joliet, accompanied by Father Jacques Marquette, had

Frontenac and La Salle floated down the Mississippi as far as the Arkansas, thus demonstrating that the great river flows into the Gulf of Mexico rather than the Pacific. Since he was unable to break through the Iroquois barrier, Frontenac resolved to fight English

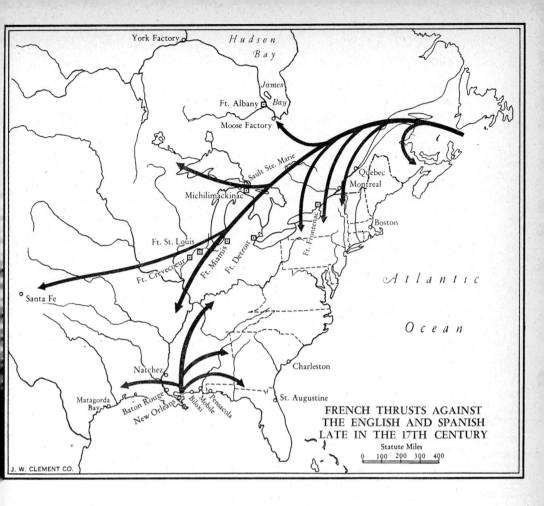

FRENCH THRUSTS AGAINST
THE ENGLISH AND SPANISH
LATE IN THE 17TH CENTURY

Statute Miles

0   100   200   300   400

J. W. CLEMENT CO.

trade by draining the furs of the interior down the Mississippi. His
strategy was simple: encircle the English on the interior, choke off their
fur trade, and confine them to the coast. His principal tool in this attempt was Robert Cavelier de la Salle, who embarked upon a remarkable series of exploring and trading ventures.

La Salle's very success was against him. The *coureurs de bois* resented the extension of royal power and wished to be free to deal in
cheap English goods; the Jesuits, who were expected to sow obedience
to France along with the Christian faith, developed an   **La Salle's**
ambition to erect a mission empire on the Great Lakes,   **imperial**
and to do this they would have to exclude both traders   **ventures**
and meddlesome officials like La Salle. The result was that traders and
missionaries stirred up the Iroquois against him. When in 1679 he appeared in northern Illinois and won over the Illinois Indians, it was a
signal for the Iroquois to fall upon the Illinois like a bolt of lightning
as punishment for their trade defection. Undismayed, La Salle finished

Joliet's and Marquette's work by descending the Mississippi to its mouth and there taking possession (1682) of its great basin in the name of France, and naming the area Louisiana in honor of the king. A few years later La Salle returned from France with settlers, intending to plant a colony at the mouth of the Mississippi, but he overshot the mark and landed on the coast of Texas. He set out in search of the river, but he never found it; he was murdered by his own men, and the settlers scattered among the Indian tribes or made their way to Illinois.

La Salle's appearance in the south was the beginning of French inter- ference in a trade struggle which was being waged between the Spanish of La Florida and the English of South Carolina. Spain's power had been **Spanish in** secured by Franciscan missions in Guale, or "Wallie" as **La Florida** the English called it, on the Georgia coast and other mis- sions on the Gulf Coast. These introduced the Muskhogean nations (the Creek, Choctaw, and Chickasaw) to European civilization. Cattle and horses were introduced, agricultural methods were improved, and Spanish traders were permitted to carry a minimum of ironware to the Indians.

This careful balance as established by the Spanish government and missions was upset immediately after the foundation of Charleston in 1670. English traders traversed the woodland paths and brought with them a flood of trade goods which wrought a revolution in **Carolina** the economy of the Gulf Plain. In exchange for their goods **trade** the newcomers took deerskins for export to Europe and slaves to labor in the Carolinas, New England, or the Caribbean islands. To obtain slaves the traders kept the nations of the interior in constant warfare against each other and caused the death of several aborigines for every one brought into captivity. The net result was that Charleston be- came the entrepôt of the richest Indian trade in North America south of Albany. This was not the work of uncouth frontiersmen, for Carolina policy was the deliberate creation of the official class, who sought not only to line their pockets but to build a British empire. They saw, long before the English court and Cabinet, that a struggle was developing for North America, and they successfully sought to bind the Muskhogee to the English economic sphere to use as allies against Spanish and French.

The first serious French intervention began in 1699, when a Cana- dian named d'Iberville founded Biloxi and set himself to wean the Mus- khogee away from the English. The capital was moved in 1718 to New **French** Orleans, a high spot in the marshes above the mouth of the **settle** Mississippi. The colony prospered modestly, but New **Louisiana** France and Louisiana co-operated poorly and Illinois soon passed into the southern sphere of influence. The Mississippi became the channel of a considerable traffic in furs, hides, and French manufactures. These were carried in plank or dugout bateaux which were rowed, sailed, or hauled at the end of a rope by sheer brute force against the river's swift current. Presently the French extended their trade into Texas. The Spanish government countered in its usual manner by setting up missions among the Indians; but, though Spain preserved its political power, French trade expanded across the plains as far as Santa Fe. The famous "Mississippi Bubble" of 1720 was based on prospects of trade in Louisiana. John Law, a Scottish banker in France, organized a company to develop Louisiana and confidently predicted fortunes for

A caricature of 1720 after the "Mississippi Bubble" burst

all stockholders. The stocks boomed, and Paris went into a frenzy of buying and selling. In the end, of course, the whole thing proved to have been a speculative venture.

During King William's and Queen Anne's wars the French policy of encirclement was fairly successful. In the north the English were kept off balance by raids against the frontier towns, though in the end they succeeded in seizing and retaining Nova Scotia (Acadia). In the south the Carolinians ravaged the Spanish missions of La Florida, but in April 1715 the Indians in the English sphere of influence revolted. This so-called Yamassee War raged all summer until troops from North Carolina and Virginia enabled the besieged South Carolinians to get the situation in hand.

Results of early wars

Far to the north at Hudson Bay the English actually succeeded in outflanking the French attempt at encirclement. In this region, called Prince Rupert's Land, the English Hudson's Bay Company warred with the French for control. The balances teetered for years between the opposing forces, ships clashing amidst the ice floes, and defeated traders —usually Englishmen—being turned out into the wilderness to perish. The Treaty of Utrecht (1713), by one of those curious *non sequiturs* which made colonial conquests mere pawns in the diplomatic game, took Prince Rupert's Land from the Canadian conquerors and gave it into the undisputed possession of the Hudson's Bay Company. Thenceforth the company began its climb to the position of feudal dominance which it occupied on the roof of the world for the next two centuries.

The Treaty of Utrecht established in America a balance of power which was supported by a careful distribution of colonies and an agreement by France and Spain that their colonies would never be merged.

The American balance of power It was not long, however, before the tremendous growth of the economic power of the British Empire everywhere and of the Twelve Colonies in particular began to threaten the balance. England and the colonies further disturbed the balance by various illegal trading activities and territorial extensions in the Caribbean and by the foundation of Georgia in 1733, a deliberately planned military buffer between South Carolina and Spanish Florida. Aggression was so open and imperialist sentiment so widespread that the renewal of war was inevitable.

New England had participated without much success in the earlier wars, chiefly in the form of abortive expeditions against the French Maritime Provinces. King George's War was preceded by a colonial war **King George's War** against Spain, known as the War of Jenkins' Ear, into which the colonies entered more wholeheartedly than ever before. A rash of recruiting broke out with many speeches in the provincial assemblies and much beating of drums and consumption of rum. About four thousand men, chiefly from the North, accompanied the disastrous expedition against Cartagena and Havana, and most of them perished of fever. Georgia, under the leadership of its founder, General James Oglethorpe, welcomed the conflict and in 1740 invaded Florida and laid fruitless siege to St. Augustine. King George's War saw one very successful colonial venture. Louisbourg on Cape Breton Island was the Gibraltar which guarded the St. Lawrence for France and was regarded as impregnable. When in 1745 the New England colonies proposed its capture, cautious souls were aghast, and Ben Franklin remarked that some people "seem to think that forts are as easy taken as snuff." But the comic-opera expedition of bumpkins and codfishermen, led by a battery of Puritan parsons and a country merchant named William Pepperell, and armed with a written "receipt for taking Louisbourg," actually took it in an alcoholic jollification which a caustic observer likened to a Harvard commencement. In the stalemate peace of Aix-la-Chapelle in

1748 Louisbourg was turned back to the French, much to the resentment of New England; but to balance it the British government founded a military colony at Halifax in Nova Scotia.

As the final stage of the Anglo-French struggle approached, it became evident that the odds were on the side of the English. The Thirteen Colonies possessed a total of about one and a half million people in 1755; New France had only sixty-five thousand Europeans. The **French and** English colonies were more than self-sufficient agriculturally **English** and had made a good beginning in manufactures; the **colonies** French barely raised a subsistence and were completely de- **compared** pendent on France for goods. The English had a compact inner line of about a thousand miles to defend and a dense population which could afford a defense in depth; New France and Louisiana (the latter with about five thousand inhabitants) had a long crescent-shaped outer line of about two thousand miles from Quebec to New Orleans and were traversed only by waterways and forest trails. The English were self-governing, and the French were absolutely subject to au-thority, but in this case the advantages were reversed. The Thirteen Colonies were jealous of each other, factious within, and anxious to avoid expense and responsibility by casting the bur-den of defense on the Crown while they stuffed themselves with war profits. The French officials were often intriguing, corrupt, and inefficient, but the people were hardy, woods-wise, and generally obedient, and there was unity of command. Moreover, they were commanded during most of the war by the Marquis de Montcalm, a military and diplomatic genius who wielded his power with skill and courage, like the thrust of a French rapier against the clumsy English broadsword.

New York Public Library

An exhortation which first appeared in *The Pennsylvania Gazette,* 1754, urging the colonists to form a union against the French and Indians. It was revived in 1765 against the Stamp Act and, again, during the Revolution.

The half dozen years between the wars were no more than an uneasy armistice. The American pioneers were now crowded against the Appa-lachian Mountains and demanding access to the fertile valleys across the mountains. With the decline of the Iroquois the Delawares **Clash over** and Shawnee, forced out of the East by white pressure, oc- **the Ohio** cupied the upper Ohio and were followed by Pennsylvania **Valley** traders. The old French route between Louisiana and Canada had been by way of the Fox and Wisconsin rivers, which led from Lake Michigan to the upper Mississippi. Now a bitter war with the Fox Indians forced the French to open routes from Lake Erie to the Ohio tributaries which brought them within the area claimed by the Pennsylvania traders.

Preliminary hostilities led to French seizure of the portages from Lake Erie to the upper Allegheny, then considered part of the Ohio, and the erection of a line of forts. At the same time Virginia fur traders appeared as the vanguard of the Ohio Company of Virginia, which planned to settle thousands of immigrants in the area. In 1754 the French seized the "forks of the Ohio" (now Pittsburgh), just after a handful of Virginians had arrived to fortify it, and erected their key stronghold, Fort Duquesne, named for the governor of Canada. Meanwhile three hundred Virginians under young Colonel George Washington hewed a road across the mountains but were besieged by the French in Fort Necessity at the Great Meadows and, upon surrender (4 July 1754), were sent ignobly back to Virginia.

Both the British and the French government were reluctant to fight, and the British actually offered to accept the crest of the Appalachians as a western boundary if the French would make concessions on the Bay of Fundy. But the French refused, and the British now **British plan of 1755** planned an ambitious series of thrusts against the long line of French communications. Elongated Canada was a great serpent which lay north and west of the English colonies, and the throat into which sustenance must enter was the St. Lawrence. To the simple nonmilitary mind it would seem that if Louisbourg and Quebec were taken the serpent must soon starve to death, and England would have a quick and cheap victory. But the eighteenth century thought in more magnificent terms; it was more worthy of a great nation to hack the serpent to pieces, as Saint George presumably had done with the dragon. Also, there would be more glory for more generals, not to mention more graft on army stores.

The first series of thrusts in 1755 were uniformly unsuccessful; and the southernmost, against Ft. Duquesne by an imported British army under General Edward Braddock, was disastrous. The French, despairing of holding the fort, laid a desperate ambush and to their **British defeats** astonishment killed and wounded about two thirds of the British advance force of twelve hundred; Braddock was among the slain.* Washington redeemed his defeat of 1754 by covering the retreat with Virginia troops. The result was that the Indian nations (except the Iroquois), who had been waiting on the sidelines, now joined the French and fell like thunderbolts on the English settlements in the Great Valley. Their hearts were in their work, for of the whites the American pioneers were the greatest menace to the Indian way of life and

---

* For new light on old ideas of Braddock's "stupidity" see Stanley M. Pargellis, "Braddock's Defeat," in *American Historical Review,* 41:253–69 (January 1936).

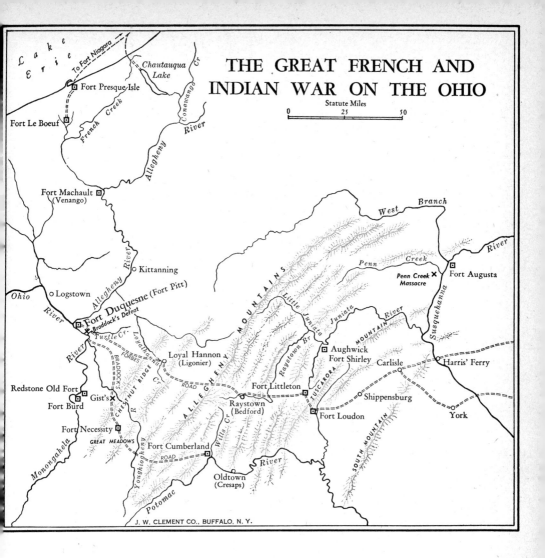

THE GREAT FRENCH AND
INDIAN WAR ON THE OHIO

Statute Miles

J. W. CLEMENT CO., BUFFALO, N. Y.

the fur-trading French were the least. Here, once more, Washington added to his growing reputation by his activities in defense of the frontier. War began in Europe in 1756 after England had consolidated an alliance with Frederick II (the Great) of Prussia, and France had allied with Austria, Spain, and Russia. In 1756 Montcalm was on the offensive, and that year and the next he won outstanding successes in spite of the lack of weight behind the French punches. British armies were being defeated everywhere, not only in America but in India, and Frederick of Prussia also learned the meaning of defeat.

One of the chief objectives of British policy was to retain the loyalty of the Iroquois in this crisis, a difficult task, for they were being courted by the French. Moreover, New Yorkers had allowed their defenses to go

Sir William Johnson (1715–74) to ruin and to make matters worse had reneged on presents and cheated in land deals. All that saved the alliance was a young Irishman, Sir William Johnson, who was for thirty years the dominant figure on the frontier and from 1755 the king's agent for Indian affairs in the North. He had come to the Mohawk Valley as a land agent and had prospered so mightily in trade and land speculation that when the Mohawk took him into the nation they named him Chief Big Business. He was a big man with the gift of blarney, equally at home in a dance around the war pole or around a New York ballroom. He lived in a great manor house with his own fiddler, harper, and dwarf jester, with many feudal retainers, mistresses, and various-hued progeny. Fellow Mohawk, come to eat of his roasted ox, crowded his halls. He had a way with Indians such as had not been seen since Frontenac. He carried the Mohawk in his waistcoat pocket and with them the Iroquois. It was well for England that he did.

William Pitt reverses the tide In 1757 William Pitt the Elder, the great British war minister, took charge and reversed the tide. "I am sure that I can save this country," he announced with supreme egotism, "and that nobody else can." What is more, he did. Bungling and ineptitude were replaced by efficiency and promptness. Incompetent generals and admirals were replaced, and supplies were poured into America to equip new colonial levies. Almost as important was the tactical revolution which Pitt may not have initiated but which he did not discourage. American leaders like Washington and Robert Rogers (of Rogers' Rangers) had based their tactics on intelligent adaptation of Indian skirmishing methods. Now British commanders successfully copied these tactics and drilled light-armed infantrymen in open-order warfare. Prominent in this flouting of ponderous European military traditions were Lord George Howe and Colonel Henry Bouquet, a Swiss mercenary. To Bouquet in particular, with his Royal American Regiment, raised among the Germans of Pennsylvania, goes the credit for the development of the principles which were in time to revolutionize modern warfare. The magniloquent plan of 1755 was revived and carried to success. Louisbourg and Fort Duquesne were taken in 1758. The latter fell to General John Forbes, who had cut a road across the Pennsylvania mountains. The "forks of the Ohio" was renamed Pittsburgh in honor of Pitt, and the erection of Fort Pitt was begun. Forbes's victory meant the fall of French power in the Ohio Valley, and Bradstreet's seizure of Fort Frontenac at the foot of Lake Ontario cut off the Great Lakes from the St. Lawrence.

The year 1759—known as "the wonderful year"—saw a remarkable series of victories. French fleets were defeated or bottled up; India was saved by Robert Clive in a remarkable campaign which resulted in con-

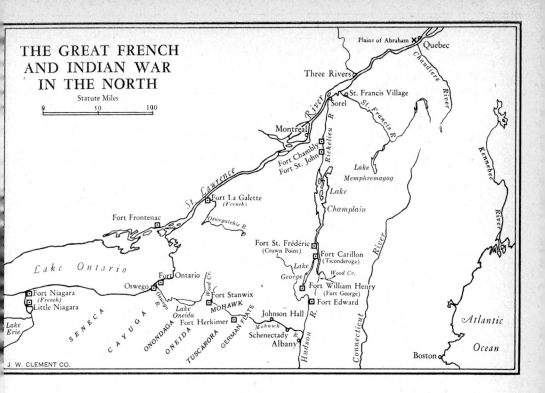

THE GREAT FRENCH
AND INDIAN WAR
IN THE NORTH

Statute Miles

0   50   100

J. W. CLEMENT CO.

fining the French to a few small ports; additional West In-   **1759, "the**
dian sugar islands fell to the British fleets; and England's   **wonderful**
allies in Germany were resoundingly victorious. General   **year"**
James Wolfe appeared before Quebec in June and began a siege. The
summer was drawing to a close when Wolfe sent forty-five hundred troops
in a night climb up a steep bluff to the Plains of Abraham, and on 13
September won a decisive victory. Both Wolfe and Montcalm fell in the
battle. It was the end of France in America, though Montreal did not fall
until the next year.

Peace might have come in 1761, for France was exhausted; but her
ally Austria refused, and, moreover, Pitt insisted that the power of
France must be utterly destroyed. French and Spanish Bourbons now
secretly signed the Family Compact for common action   **Treaty of**
against England. Pitt suspected the situation and desired to   **Paris, 1763**
declare war against Spain at once, but the new king,
George III, was desirous of peace and forced him to resign. The sacrifice
of Pitt perhaps only hastened the entry of Spain. Nevertheless, to the
chagrin of the Bourbons the war machine which Pitt had built up quickly
seized Florida, Cuba, and the Philippines. By the Treaty of Paris, 1763
France lost everything but a number of scattered islands and ports, and
England became dominant in North America, Africa, and India. The
cession of Canada by France and Florida by Spain gave England all of

197

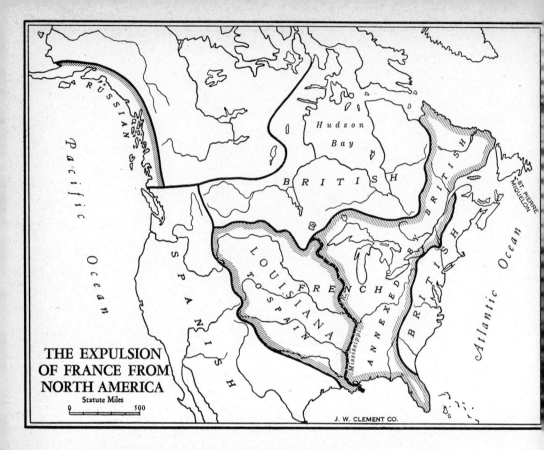

THE EXPULSION
OF FRANCE FROM
NORTH AMERICA

Statute Miles

0   500

J. W. CLEMENT CO.

North America east of the Mississippi except the area around New Orleans. Louisiana was deeded to Spain, partly as recompense for the loss of Florida, partly because it was unprofitable and administratively a nuisance. All France had to show in America for over two centuries of effort was two tiny islands off Newfoundland for drying fish, a handful of sugar islands, and Cayenne in Guiana.

The record of the Seven Years' War would not be complete without recounting the considerable contributions made by the Thirteen Colonies and also the disgraceful way in which they gave vent to their curious

Colonial opposition to war   welter of antagonisms. The conservative isolationists of the coast feared the political, economic, and social effects of western settlement and, upon the outbreak of war, joined with the timid and the stingy to block the prosecution of a war whose success could only lead to expansion. Moreover, the separatist habits of a century were hard to overcome. Those colonies which had no frontiers to be raided or western lands with which to speculate saw little reason for aiding those which had. Every possible excuse was used by the colonies to refuse or delay or renege in supporting the war. Almost everywhere the

Colony Party regarded the crisis as a golden opportunity to wring concessions from governors. Pitt demanded quotas of men, money, and supplies (two fifths of the expenditure was repaid), but the response was usually slow even where it was not grudging.

Necessity and inclination united to make the colonies insist that they could support the war only by issuing legal-tender paper, a policy before which the despairing Board of Trade had to bow. Of course inflation followed with its usual train of hoarding, profiteering, **Trading** shortages, and bitterness between debtors and creditors. **with the** Northern shippers refused to give up their profitable trade **enemy** with Canada and the French West Indies and found various subterfuges under which to continue it. Indeed, the drain of provisions was so great that British commissaries found it difficult to keep the armies fed. The navy and the customs service united to stop this treasonable trade with the enemy; and customs officials introduced writs of assistance, sometimes called general warrants, which did not, like special warrants, name the place to be searched or the goods for which search was to be made. Colonial resentment ran so high that opposition took the color of a noble and patriotic crusade, and the king's officers to their surprise found themselves taking in popular opinion the place of the French as the enemies of liberty.

It is evident that the weakness of the colonies lay in their disunion. At the Albany Congress in 1754 the representatives of seven colonies sought to remedy this by recommending a Plan of Union proposed by Benjamin Franklin. There would have been a president- **Albany** general appointed by the Crown and a grand council made **Plan** up of representatives apportioned according to financial **of Union** contributions and elected by the various assemblies. Together they would have the power to lay taxes, make war, conduct Indian affairs and foreign trade, and govern western settlements. Laws would be subject to approval by the king. Unfortunately both colonies and Crown opposed the plan. The colonies rejected it because they would have had to surrender some of their precious autonomy to the Union government and some to the Crown. The London bureaucrats criticized it because of its squinting toward democracy and called it the opening wedge for American independence. In the end it was quietly allowed to gather dust. Nevertheless, it proved that at last there were in the colonies men who realized the virtue of union. Franklin, like Pitt, seems to have been enchanted by the vision of an Anglo-American empire which would bestride the world, a new Rome to act as the mentor and lawgiver to mankind.

Despite some of their shady actions, it is nevertheless true that the colonies furnished the bulk of troops and supplies used in the campaigns fought on their own soil, though New York, Connecticut, and Massachu-

Colonial military participation
setts raised seven tenths of the total number of troops. On the whole the colonials fought bravely, and their leaders gained experience which was to be invaluable during the Revolution. The loyalty and effectiveness of colonial troops would have been improved by a more reasonable regard by the British for colonial feelings. As it was, any colonel's commission granted by the king was superior to the highest colonial commission. The raw American levies, though characterized by a British general as "the scum of the worst people," did not resemble the broken-spirited cattle which composed the ranks of the British regular army and refused to be treated like them. Officers and men alike resented the arrogance and brutality of the king's officers, and this mismanagement and abuse did much to plant the seeds of the Anglophobia of which the Revolution was only the first of many harvests.

4   The Causes of the American Revolution

The American Revolution was caused by the British decision to enforce mercantilism. Like all oversimplifications, the statement requires explanation. Let us begin with the British reasons for the decision. First,
End of salutary neglect
and most important, was the enormous debt of about £140,-000,000 which saddled the mother country as a result of the French wars. While the financial support of Great Britain's government depended to a considerable extent upon customs and excise duties, the burden nevertheless fell upon the country landlords in the form of a land tax. Their spokesmen in Parliament did not ask help with the debt even though it had been partly incurred in American defense, but they did feel that the overgrown American colonies should help to pay current expenses of their own administration. Second, British manufacturers (not primarily the merchants) viewed with alarm the rising fabricating industries of America and pointed out that English prosperity would decline as America gained; they were wrong, of course, but their argument was consistent with mercantilism. Third, the West Indian sugar planters' lobby was determined to put an end to the mainland's trade with the French and Spanish sugar islands.

Fourth was the resolve of George III to "be king." George was neither a villain nor a man of great conscience but simply a country gentleman of unimpeachable family life and private morals whom fate miscast as a
George III
king. He came to the throne in 1760 at the age of twenty-two, the first English-born monarch of the House of Hanover. He regretted the ascendance of Parliament over the kingly power and resolved to devote his life to the building up of his "prerogative," by which he meant the right of the king to dictate how Parliament should

handle legislative and executive matters. In order to gain his ends it was necessary to build up the remnants of the old Tory Party in Parliament into a powerful party of the "king's friends," strong enough to overthrow the great Whig families who had dominated British government since 1688. This the king proceeded to do by dispensing bribes in the form of sinecure jobs and lucrative contracts and by sedulous use of royal social favors. George was a shrewd operator, and he worked so quietly that it was not generally known that he was acting as puppeteer, and in fact the Thirteen Colonies supposed that the revival of mercantilism was the work of Parliament—which of course it was, in great part. Nevertheless, George was striving consciously to fulfill his ideal of the "patriot king" and to bind the Empire into an efficient, well-articulated, and centrally controlled unit.

The end of salutary neglect was such a challenge to American interests and evolutionary tendencies that it was bound to affect nearly every aspect of colonial life from Newfoundland to Guiana. Those on the fringes, however, were dependent upon British favors and protection, and only the Thirteen Colonies were mature **American reactions** enough and strong enough to rebel. Britain had opened the way when she removed the French menace from the colonial flank; on the other hand, the removal of this menace meant that Britain no longer needed to make concessions to the colonies to get their aid against the French and so now for the first time felt free to enforce mercantilism. Each analyst of the causes of the American Revolution has his own way of handling the colonial reaction to the challenge of British policies, and doubtless one is as good as another. Here we shall take them up in three categories: economic, political, and psychological.

The British action in reviving mercantilism was a direct threat to American prosperity. The Seven Years' War had been fought to free the way for expansion, by which Americans meant commercial expansion into the Caribbean and expansion of trade and settlements into the Mississippi Valley. Indeed, the American debt struc- **Threat to prosperity** ture, as we have seen, was such that it could be handled only by such economic expansion as would provide the profits with which to pay British merchants and investors. During the decade after the Peace of Paris it became apparent that Great Britain envisioned the role of economic expansion as chiefly reserved to its own investors, merchants, and manufacturers, and the colonists found their expansion blocked on several fronts.

The rising manufacture of iron products, textiles, and other goods was limited or forbidden. The restrictions on trade with foreign nations and colonies were enforced, and smuggling was repressed. Tobacco plant-ers, whose lands were worn out and who were mortgaged lock, stock, and barrel to British merchants, were relentlessly blocked when they sought to turn to food products and home manufactures. Westward expansion was discouraged lest it carry settlers away from easily controlled areas, and such land sales as were permitted were to be under the ægis of new colonies which would be strictly subservient to royal authority. The western fur trade was placed under the supervision of the governor of Quebec, who naturally desired to maintain the transmontane area as a great game preserve in which the Indian nations might trap for the benefit of British investors.

Hard money was drawn off in servicing debts owed to British merchants, and it was made more difficult to trade with the French and Spanish sugar islands, the old sources of gold and silver. The importation of British coins was prohibited, and so was the coining of Spanish bullion. The only substitute that could be used in carrying on business was paper money; and the British government ordered the retirement of old issues and forbade the printing of new issues. Last, a British army was quartered in the colonies, ostensibly for defense against the Indians—in Boston and New York City! There was a presumption that it was intended to enforce the legal and economic decrees of the British Parliament. At any rate, a part of the expense of its maintenance and a great deal of the bother of providing for it were saddled upon the colonies.

These measures affected not only merchants, planters, and land speculators. Farmers received low prices for their produce and paid high prices for merchandise; when they fell behind financially their mortgages were foreclosed, and they found it difficult to get new land farther west. Town workers also were caught in the spiral of inflation. True, it was not just to blame Great Britain alone for this, but they saw that the colonial magnates who were their economic and political oppressors were backed by British policies; so it was natural to blame the British. These economic measures, of course, could have been obeyed, but obedience would not only have resulted in a cessation of growth economically and territorially but would doubtless have brought widespread bankruptcy and a drastic cut in the standard of living. It was against human nature to obey.

The British action in reviving mercantilism was a direct threat to evolving American democracy. It would be a mistake to interpret the general American view of the Revolution as carried on in support of **Threat to** abstract principles of liberty and justice. On the contrary, **evolving** Americans sincerely regarded the rights of Englishmen as **democracy** constituting a concrete basis for a way of life and as having been in actual practice in the colonies. Now this way of life was in danger of being lost through Parliamentary action. They had a clear concept of civil liberties and of the English process (far clearer than did the English masses) and believed that they were menaced by the royal use of general warrants and by the trial of cases in admiralty courts, which sat without juries. They resented the English doctrine of "virtual representation" and insisted that representatives must be residents of the communities they represented; anything else was taxation without representation. They regarded the Empire as a body of equal and self-governing states under a common figurehead monarch and accused Parliament of changing its nature when it attempted to assert legislative (and in effect executive) authority over provinces which had their own legislatures.

It is true that Americans differed in details over the tenets by which they wished to be governed and agreed only that they wished self-government. Only a few aristocrats and job holders took exception to that, and the ideal was supported even by most of those **Doubtful** who later became Tories. It is human nature to seek to **legal basis** support a desired course of action by a hog-tight, bull-proof, **of Ameri-** and horse-high legal fence. The first resort was to the colo- **can claims** nial charters, but this ground had to be abandoned, for many of the charters gave the king the power of veto over colonial legislation and subjected the colonies to trade regulation. The second resort was to English precedents, the so-called "rights" of Englishmen. They soon discovered to their dismay that American evolution was moving toward somewhat different forms and goals. English representatives did not necessarily reside in the districts they represented; general warrants were legal; the English legal analogy to the colonial charters was the city corporation charters, which gave no power independent of Parliament. From the time of Cromwell, Parliament had actually legislated for the colonies. In other words, in these and other instances the American contentions were not indisputably sound *legally,* however *just* they may have been.

The Americans never abandoned their contention that Parliament's interpretation of the constitution was a menace to liberty, but they did seek a third trench which would be more widely understood and accepted. They found it in John Locke's doctrine of Natural Rights, **Natural** which had come to be the basis of the French Enlighten- **Rights a** ment and which was thoroughly approved by most of the **third trench** European intelligentsia. It will be remembered that Locke saw the Natural Right to hold property as the main balance wheel of society. Presto! Parliament was endeavoring to confiscate American property, so by analogy to Locke's own defense of the Revolution of 1688 the Americans had a right to insist that their government must obey the will of the governed (American property holders) and if it did not they had a right to change it. Of course there were problems: back-country men like Jefferson questioned the holding of property as a Natural Right, especially when it was held in great quantities; then there was the embarrassing fact that many of the Tories were great property holders. In the end the Revolutionists interpreted Natural Rights each in his own manner and left practical definitions for a later time. The beauty of Natural Rights as a defense was that nearly everyone acknowledged them even though they were incapable of legal and historical proof. It is both sound and popular to champion right and attack evil.

A significant phase of the democratic protest was the opposition to any attempt to strengthen the Church of England in the colonies. The Society for the Propagation of the Gospel in Foreign Parts, which supported
Opposition to an Anglican episcopate missionaries in the colonies, pointed out that the Church of England was being outdistanced by dissenting sects not only because Episcopal clergymen had to go to England for ordination but because the Church had no central control in America. They therefore urged the appointment of an Anglican bishop for America. American democrats rabidly opposed the establishment of a colonial bishopric, and (perhaps consciously) exaggerated its dangers. New England's Congregational clergy had never seen much difference between Anglicans and Roman Catholics and now professed to see in growing English tolerance the prospect of a return of the Church of England to the Roman fold. The middle colonies and the backlands of the southern colonies were a welter of sects, all bitterly opposed to the Church of England, which they saw as the instrument of a political and social aristocracy.

As a matter of fact, there was little danger of the appointment of a bishop. Even southern Anglicans opposed it because it would have destroyed the parish vestry's control of the clergy. The British government opposed it because it would have raised America to an equality in ecclesiastical matters and would have set back the program of centralizing control of the Empire in London. Doubtless intelligent Americans knew all this, but the issue had such an emotional appeal to the masses that it was a valuable anti-British weapon. The revolutionary movement was therefore given a decided (though specious) religious coloration.

In assessing the reasons for American revolt it is well to avoid overemphasis on economics or politics or religion. It has been held that revolutions do not arise out of the desperation of misery but out of a vision
Revolution rises out of feasibility of something better. British economic pressure was unwise and oppressive, but the Thirteen Colonies were even at the worst treated far more liberally than were the colonies of any other power in that century. Had George III realized his wildest dreams of imperial centralization, the Thirteen Colonies would still have been the freest on earth. No, the American Revolution did not arise from

the desperation of misery, whatever the protests made by our shrewd and highly articulate ancestors. It arose from the belief that conditions could and should be better and that self-government was the only guarantee of this betterment. "The Revolution," says Van Tyne, "was one of the glories of British history. . . . The colonies of no other nation in that age had progressed so far in the attainment and enjoyment of political liberty as to have 'snuffed' the taint of tyranny in those acts of the British Government which precipitated the struggle." Well did he conclude with the words: "The freest of peoples were the first to rebel."

Possibly, and here opinions will clash, the Revolution was bred more in the psychology of the people than in their economic and political condition. There was considerable basis to the British plaints that the Americans were selfish, ungrateful, and obstreperous; on the other hand, the British laid themselves open to some of **Psychological reasons** the same charges. There was American resentment at British sneers and patronization, at the opinion that an American was inferior simply because he was a colonial. There was resentment that the best governmental positions in the colonies went to English placemen. There was resentment that holders of the king's commission outranked colonial officers and at the open contempt with which British officers regarded American officers and soldiers. There was continually growing resentment that British investors, merchants, and manufacturers expected to pluck the American economy at will, demanding perquisites and privileges that were not so much impossible as insulting. Americans were relatively classless and very proud and self-reliant. They saw no reason for continuing to give down milk at the British behest, especially since they could put a stop to it. They were big enough to rebel, and they did.

On the morning of the Battle of Lexington Levi Preston ran sixteen miles to get into the fight. Seventy years later he was asked his opinion of the oppressions that had led to the war.

"Oppressions?" exclaimed the old man. "What were they? I didn't feel any. The Stamp Act? I never saw one of the stamps. The tea tax? I never drank the stuff."

"Well," said the interlocutor, "I suppose you had been reading Sidney or Locke about the eternal principles of liberty?"

"Never heard of them. We read only the Bible, the catechism, Watts' hymns, and the almanac."

"Then what did you mean by going into that fight?"

"Young man," was his answer, "what we meant in going for those redcoats was this—we always had governed ourselves, and we always meant to. They didn't mean we should!"

BIBLIOGRAPHICAL NOTE

England's Halfhearted Mercantilism

BRITISH COMMERCIAL POLICY: Regulation of American trade can be followed in Lawrence A. Harper, *The English Navigation Laws* (1939). The Board of Trade and Plantations is examined in monographs by Charles M. Andrews, Arthur H. Basye, Ralph P. Bieber, and M. Marion Spector. George R. S. Taylor, *Robert Walpole and His Age* (1931) is general and useful. On the commercial aspects of the British Empire see George L. Beer's summary *Commercial Policy of England Toward the American Colonies* (1893), and his more detailed *Old Colonial System, 1660–1754* (2 v., 1912) and *British Colonial Policy, 1754–1765* (1907). Over-all treatment of the problems of empire is Lawrence H. Gipson, *The British Empire Before the American Revolution* (5 v., 1936–42).

AMERICAN BUSINESS: See Robert A. East, *Business Enterprise in the American Revolutionary Era* (1938). For the North see Virginia D. Harrington, *The New York Merchant on the Eve of the Revolution* (1935); and for the South, Leila Sellers, *Charleston Business on the Eve of the American Revolution* (1934). More colorful are Charles W. Taussig, *Rum, Romance and Rebellion* (1928); and William S. McClellan, *Smuggling in the American Colonies at the Outbreak of the Revolution* (1912). Of corollary interest is Frank W. Pitman, *Development of the British West Indies, 1700–1763* (1917); for the eventual fate of the British sugar islands see Lowell J. Ragatz, *The Fall of the Planter Class in the British Caribbean, 1763–1833* (1928).

MANUFACTURES: Follow in Victor S. Clark, *History of Manufactures in the U.S., 1607–1860* (3 v., 1916); Arthur C. Bining, *British Regulation of the Colonial Iron Industry* (1933); Robert G. Albion, *Forests and Sea Power* (1926); and Rolla M. Tryon, *Household Manufactures in the U.S., 1640–1860* (1917).

CURRENCY: See Charles J. Bullock, *Essays on the Monetary History of the United States* (1900); Andrew M. Davis, *Currency and Banking in the Province of Massachusetts Bay* (1901); Curtis P. Nettels, *Money Supply of the American Colonies Before 1720* (1934).

The Democratic Struggle

GOVERNMENT: See Oliver M. Dickerson, *American Colonial Government, 1696–1765* (1912); Evarts B. Greene, *The Provincial Governor* (1898); Leonard W. Labaree, *Royal Government in America* (1930); Mary P. Clarke, "Parliamentary Privileges in the American Colonies," in *Essays in Colonial History Presented to C. M. Andrews by His Students* (1931); Elmer B. Russell, *Review of American Colonial Legislation by the King in Council* (1915); and George A. Washburne, *Imperial Control of the Administration of Justice in the Thirteen American Colonies, 1684–1776* (1923). On one colony see Donald L. Kemmerer, *Path to Freedom: The Struggle for Self-Government in Colonial New Jersey* (1940).

COLONIAL AGENTS: See James J. Burns, *The Colonial Agents of New England*

(1935); Winfred T. Root, *Relations of Pennsylvania with the British Government* (1912).

FRANCHISE: See Cortlandt F. Bishop, *History of Elections in the American Colonies* (1893); and Albert E. McKinley, *The Suffrage Franchise in the Thirteen English Colonies in America* (1905).

The Battle for North America

EARLY PHASES: On the north see Francis Parkman, *Count Frontenac, La Salle,* and *A Half Century of Conflict.* On the south see Verner W. Crane, *The Southern Frontier, 1670–1732* (1929); William E. Dunn, *Spanish and French Rivalry in the Gulf Region of the United States, 1678–1702* (1917); Herbert E. Bolton and Mary Ross, *The Debatable Land* (1925); and John T. Lanning, *Spanish Missions of Georgia* (1935) and *Diplomatic History of Georgia* (1936). See also Almon W. Lauber, *Indian Slavery in Colonial Times* (1913).

SEVEN YEARS' WAR: See Parkman, *Montcalm and Wolfe* (1884); and Julian S. Corbett, *England in the Seven Years' War* (2 v., 1907). Washington's part may be traced in Douglas S. Freeman, *George Washington* (2 v., 1948). The initial period of defeat is handled by Stanley M. Pargellis, *Lord Loudoun in North America* (1933); and the period of victory by John C. Long, *Mr. Pitt and America's Birthright* (1940) and *Lord Jeffrey Amherst, A Soldier of the King* (1933).

COLONIAL ATTITUDES: Follow in William L. Grant, *Colonial Policy of Chatham* (1911); Kate Hotblack, *Chatham's Colonial Policy* (1917); Eugene I. McCormac, *Colonial Opposition to Imperial Authority During the French and Indian War* (1911); and Richard Pares, *War and Trade in the West Indies, 1739–1763* (1936).

The Causes of the American Revolution

All histories of the Revolution are concerned with the causes, but their theses are not always evident. Earlier British and American historians differed absolutely, but during the last generation the "revisionists" have approached each other on a less nationalistic meeting ground. The impetus to this "revisionism" came from Moses Coit Tyler, who first treated the literary battle which preceded and accompanied the Revolution in his *Literary History of the American Revolution, 1763–1783* (2 v., 1897). Tyler concentrated on the ideas and spiritual moods of the contestants, and in so doing was the first to lift the argument from an oversimplified view of good versus evil to the view that it was a controversy in which both sides were sincere and patriotic, however much they differed in policies and points of view. Since then historians have been concerned with reflecting the actual principles of the contestants rather than in tarring one side with the blame.

GENERAL: Claude H. Van Tyne's *Causes of the War of Independence* (1922) is the classic statement of revisionist doctrine. Hugh E. Egerton's *Causes and Character of the American Revolution* (1923) is an English presentation of generally similar conclusions. Most recent and satisfactory is John C. Miller,

Origins of the American Revolution (1943); it must be supplemented by Thomas B. Abernethy, *Western Lands and the American Revolution* (1937).

THEORETICAL AND LEGAL: Charles H. McIlwain, *The American Revolution: A Constitutional Interpretation* (1923) deals with constitutional precedents; and Randolph G. Adams, *Political Ideas of the American Revolution* (1922) is concerned with reconciling imperial and colonial points of view. A more recent study is Charles F. Mullett, *Fundamental Law and the American Revolution, 1760–1776* (1933). Briefer is the analysis in Charles E. Merriam, *History of American Political Theories* (1920).

RELIGIOUS: Use Arthur L. Cross, *The Anglican Episcopate and the American Colonies* (1902); and Alice M. Baldwin, *The New England Clergy and the American Revolution* (1928).

ECONOMIC: Arthur M. Schlesinger, Sr., *Colonial Merchants and the American Revolution, 1763–1776* (1918) is essential.

Chapter VII

THE ROAD TO REVOLUTION

1 *Western Lands and the Revolution*

OUR examination of the reasons for the early maturing of the Thirteen Colonies makes it abundantly evident to us—with our excellent hindsight—that they were getting too big to spank. Their tremendous expansion offered Britain an opportunity to wield the strength **Britain's** of a continent greater than Europe, with a population and **lost oppor-** an economy that would have made the Empire unassailable **tunity** —and at the mere expense of a little more tolerance and family understanding. But that was not the spirit of the century. Most of those Englishmen who studied the matter were convinced that it was not more tolerance that was needed, but less. The crisis, they said, came because the king's ministers let the reins of colonial government lie too loosely. Only a few prophets rose to draw back the curtain of the future and disclose to these willful merchants and country gentlemen what they were casting away, and they were reviled for their pains as Cassandras and traitors. Perhaps only thus was it possible for the day to come when the prodigal son would return clothed in a gold watch, patent-leather shoes, and a hundred-dollar suit, and with enough money in his wallet to lift the parental mortgage, if he chose.

Before the outbreak of rebellion there were three great regions of protest: the mercantile northern coast, the planting South of the Tidewater, and the land-grabbing, Indian-hating Old West. It is true that the chain of events which led to revolution actually occurred **Importance** on the northern coast, principally in Massachusetts, and **of land** that without these events revolution might never have **hunger** come. On the other hand, the debt-ridden condition of the southern planters and their attempts to recoup their fortunes in western lands, together with the insatiable land hunger of the pioneer of the Old West, were factors which made both ready to support revolution when it began. For that reason the story of western lands between 1763 and 1775 deserves attention.

It will be recalled that even as early as Bacon's Rebellion (1676) the tobacco colonies had been able to make a living only by robbing the soil. The growth of plantations in the Tidewater gave a specious appearance of prosperity to the great landholders, but in fact the price of tobacco never recovered in proportion to its cost of production. Consequently the planters fell into debt to their London factors, who mercilessly depressed the price of tobacco even while they multiplied the price of manufactured goods. The planters' wealth had been taken from the surplus riches of the soil, and now that the soil was depleted many of them actually faced poverty. Even after the price of tobacco rose a little there was a conviction that tobacco would have to give way to wheat as Virginia's chief crop. But old habits and the large investments in slaves stood in the way. When the House of Burgesses sought to pass laws to limit tobacco export and to limit or stop the importation of Negroes, the Crown vetoed them. Royal officials did not wish to see the tobacco revenues reduced; the merchants feared that reduction in the tobacco output would raise prices and endanger their control of the market; and London and Bristol did not propose to lose their lucrative profits from the slave trade. British interests had the planters over a barrel and did not propose to let them up.

Exhaustion of Tidewater soil

The Tidewater aristocracy still controlled the House of Burgesses, but it was evident that power would soon pass to the Piedmont. The Old West was losing its frontier character with the growth of its prosperity and sense of responsibility. The Piedmont, however, had fewer great plantations and more independent farmers. Its tobacco was packed in great hogsheads which were "rolled" (that is, drawn by slaves or horses) like thick wheels thirty or forty miles to navigable water. The transportation of wheat was a greater problem, and thousands of farmers were content to grow their food, make their own clothing and whisky, mold their bullets of back-country lead, forge their tools of back-country iron, and depend upon England for little besides gunpowder. Life in the Piedmont had its advantages, but its agricultural methods were no less wasteful than those in the Tidewater, and it was to be only a matter of a generation before it was overtaken by the same blight of acid soil and water erosion. Even as it was, the Piedmont could not absorb all comers. As early as the 1730's the pressure of population was bursting the Blue Ridge barrier, and people were pouring into the Great Valley. By 1760 the best lands there had been taken up, and thousands of families were ready to cross the mountains as soon as the Indian claims were cleared away.

Rise of the Piedmont

We saw how the West looked upon the Seven Years' War as a battle for more farm land. Even before the war the traders beyond the frontier had bargained with the Indians for choice bottom lands for themselves or acted as agents for eastern speculators. By 1750 a score of would-be land companies were active in seeking grants to western lands. Land speculation was an all but universal preoccupation, and there was scarcely a prominent merchant or trader, planter or frontier leader who did not engage in it. Virginia interpreted its charter as granting it all the land from a point two hundred miles north of Old Point Comfort "west and northwest" to the Pacific Ocean; in other words, it claimed most of the interior. The Ohio Company of Virginia, composed of representatives of such prominent families as the Lees and the Washingtons, obtained a Crown grant on the upper Ohio in 1748; and, as we have seen, its attempt to settle what is now southwestern Pennsylvania was a factor in beginning the Seven Years' War with France. Immediately after the Ohio Company received its grant the dominant Tidewater political faction, led by Dr. Thomas Walker, organized the Loyal Land Company and obtained a Virginia grant to a huge area farther down the Ohio; connected with this enterprise were such prominent frontier names as Jefferson, Lewis, and Henry.

Penetration of the West

The expulsion of the French from the continent was a calamity to the Indians, for it put an end to the diplomatic balance between French and British, which was the Indians' only hope of salvation. The British commanders and diplomats who took possession of the West assured the Indians that they had not come to settle and showered them with gifts of food and trade goods. Then gradually the gifts stopped; a parsimonious government had turned the spigot. American traders appeared once more and resumed their old cheating practices. British forts rose at strategic points. Indians who carried their furs to Fort Pitt reported that the axes of the farmers were ringing in the bottom lands of the Monongahela, where was rising the first permanent English-speaking trans-Appalachian settlement. Conditions were ripe for trouble, and the Canadians stirred up the Indians' hope of relief by spreading the word that the French were coming back.

Pontiac's War, 1763–66

Early in 1763 the great Ottawa leader, Pontiac, found it possible to draw the nations together in desperate resistance. The blow fell in May 1763. Detroit and Pitt were the only important forts left standing in the West, and they were stubbornly besieged; the garrisons of most of the rest and the settlers around them (except Canadians) were massacred. British relief expeditions set out promptly, though as usual even the colonies most affected were reluctant to vote aid. The Swiss mercenary, Colonel Henry Bouquet, defeated the Delawares and Shawnee at Bushy Run east of Pittsburgh, and in 1764 went on to the Ohio wilderness and imposed peace. The Seneca had already been persuaded to withdraw, and now the Lakes Indians gave up.

Hitherto the West had been left pretty much to the individual colonies, and the result had been contention, confusion, corruption, and exploitation of the Indians. In 1755 some improvement had been made by

Indian relations

making Sir William Johnson Superintendent of Indian Affairs in the North and Edmund Atkin (followed by John Stuart) in the South. The devastation of Pontiac's War and the reluctance of the colonies to provide for their own defense now convinced the British government that it must assume the responsibility for the administration and defense of the West. The formation of a desirable policy, however, was not easy. British manufacturers contended that the West should be preserved for the Indians and the fur trade, lest white settlers there, cut off by geography from sufficient British goods, develop their own manufactures. Merchants and investors, who dominated the British Cabinet, pointed out that if the white farmers did not obtain new lands they would be certain to turn to manufactures.

Pontiac's War precipitated a temporary decision that settlement would not be permitted west of the watershed of the Appalachians. This proclamation was made in such haste that it did not provide a civil gov-

Proclamation Line of 1763

ernment for the French settlements on the Wabash and the Mississippi. The Indian trade, however, was intended to be regulated firmly, and all traders were to be licensed and bonded. Johnson and Stuart, as Crown agents in charge of the Indian trade, had a task that was well-nigh impossible, but they did succeed in cutting down the worst of the exploitation. The Proclamation Line was chiefly the work of Lord Shelburne, former President of the Board of Trade and one of the most consistent British friends of America during the troublous years from 1763 to 1783. Soon afterward Shelburne became Secretary of State for the Southern Department and as such tried to clear the way for American settlement in the West.

Americans were not disposed, however, to acknowledge Shelburne as a friend. The new policy was a dismal failure. The end of Pontiac's War brought a stampede of the farmers pent up east of the mountains to settle

Pressure of settlers

on the new lands. They were long, lean men schooled in the wars of the Old West, men who traveled with pigtail twist in their cheeks, watchfulness in their eyes, and six-foot rifles in their hands. Sometimes they settled by single families in isolated clearings; sometimes there came whole settlements at a time and struck the ancient forests with the devastating effect of a cyclone. But however they came, it was to build homes for themselves and their children. Governments may have been fighting over such trifles as prestige and the fur trade, but the Anglo-American pioneer knew very well that he had withstood savage attacks and borne long vigils in besieged blockhouses only in order to secure freedom and elbowroom.

In addition, the old land companies had been revived, and traders who had been despoiled by the Indians were demanding compensation in western acres. Washington was at the head of a lobby of veterans which was trying to get the Virginia government to honor its promise of a soldiers' bonus in the form of land; prospects of success seemed so dim that many of the soldiers sold their **Pressure of speculators** certificates for ready cash, and these eventually became the basis of most of Washington's vast western land holdings. Men such as Washington, Franklin, Johnson, and Patrick Henry were active among the suppliants who besieged the British ministry for confirmation of land grants, pulled wires in legislative assemblies, or plied the Indians with rum and blandishments to persuade them to sell. Possession of salt licks and lead mines was as eagerly disputed as were coal, oil, mineral, and timber lands a century later.

The inevitable result of colonial pressure was the abandonment of the Proclamation Line and the setting of a new one which, such is human optimism, was intended to be permanent. At Fort Stanwix in 1768 the Iroquois (who claimed suzerainty over the Shawnee and Delawares) sold to the Crown and to the Penns the land east **Indian land cessions** of the Allegheny and Ohio rivers; this not only included the Shawnee and Delaware hunting grounds but also part of that claimed by the Cherokee, ancient enemies of the Iroquois. In 1760 the Cherokee, incensed by the murder of hostages, had risen along the Carolina border and been subdued only after a sharp conflict in which their towns were devastated. They did not now feel able to withstand white encroachments, and so in 1768 at the Treaty of Hard Labor they surrendered the area from the Kanawha Valley eastward. Virginia naturally claimed much of the surrendered territory and by supplementary agreements with the Cherokee, who were quite willing to sell Iroquois land, took over everything east of the Kentucky River. This action again was hard on the Shawnee and Delawares.

At any rate, the total effect was to weaken the royal agents' control of Indian relations. Moreover, the program set up in the Proclamation of 1763 was too expensive, and therefore control of the Indian trade (but not of land sales) was handed back to the colonies, which **Provinces control Indian trade** let the traders resume their old exploitation. Individual land speculators got the Indians drunk and bought up great tracts of bottom land. Predatory long hunters like Daniel Boone invaded the Indians' game preserves, especially in Kentucky, and slaughtered the

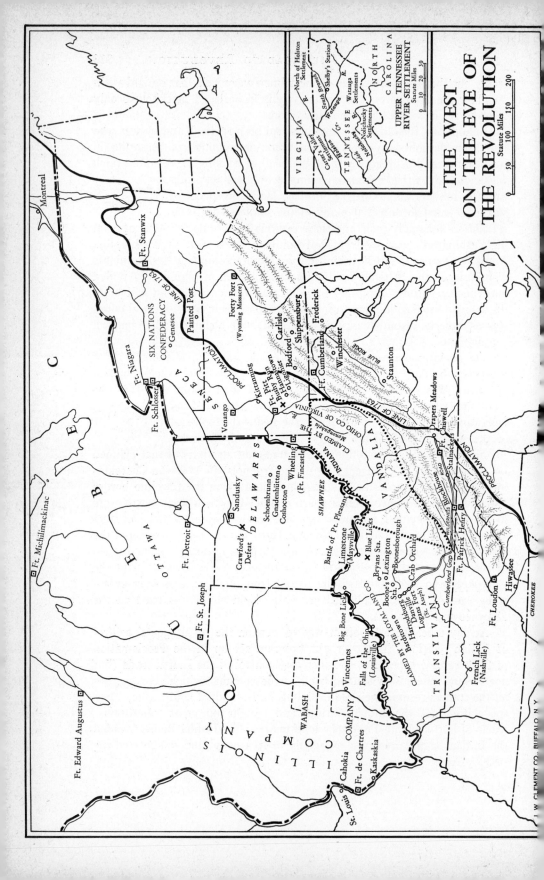

THE WEST
ON THE EVE OF
THE REVOLUTION

Statute Miles
0   50   100   150   200

UPPER TENNESSEE
RIVER SETTLEMENT
Statute Miles
0   10   20   30

deer and buffaloes in thousands for their skins. The Indians plundered the hunters and ordered them out, but the only result was irritation on both sides. Two ways of life were at odds, and conflict was inevitable.

One of the most inveterate of land speculators was Benjamin Franklin, but since Pennsylvania's wild lands belonged to the Penns he had to look abroad for his acres. Thus he was interested in New York and Nova Scotia lands and in various projects in the western area claimed by Virginia. He looked with alarm upon Virginia's **Indiana Company** westward expansion, and it is possible that his Albany Plan of Union, which proposed the administration of the West by the United Provinces, was not only patriotic statesmanship but a scheme to block Virginia's imperialism. Franklin and Sir William Johnson were members of a group of capitalists known as the Indiana Company, which had bought up the claims of certain "suffering traders" who had been despoiled by the Indians. Johnson cajoled and intimidated the Indians into reimbursing the loss with a cession in West Virginia which overlay the Ohio Company's claims. The politically dominant Loyal Company, delighted at this bilking of the Ohio Company, obtained Virginia's seal of approval.

The Indiana Company now sent a certain Samuel Wharton to London to look after its interests. Wharton was a smooth and unscrupulous operator, which was probably why he was chosen, and he nursed the company's few hundred thousand acres into a truly grandiose project. British politicians were taken into partnership, and **Vandalia Company** the growing opposition of the Loyal Company was countered by absorbing the Ohio Company and Washington's group of veterans with their land-bonus certificates. The name was changed to the Grand Ohio Company (sometimes called Walpole from its leading British member), and it planned a huge new proprietary colony in Kentucky and West Virginia to be called Vandalia; hence the common name of Vandalia Company. Its tentacles reached so deeply into British politics and finance that it actually forced the resignation of a Colonial Secretary who opposed it. In 1773 the Crown had ordered the final papers to be drawn up, but the defeated British politicians and the Loyal Company managed to delay the final steps, and Vandalia was eventually eclipsed in the scramble that began with the opening of the Revolution.

In the end the Loyal Company won because it was on the scene and knew the value of actual possession. Lord Dunmore, Governor of Virginia from 1771, became an enthusiastic partner in the company, backed its western surveys, and found a loophole in the Vandalia **Virginia occupies the West** armor by which he could grant the land bonuses claimed by provincial soldiers. Washington and other holders of land certificates saw on which side their bonuses were buttered and went along.

The Loyal Company was chiefly interested in Kentucky and in 1774 proceeded to make surveys and to begin a settlement at Harrodsburg. Southwestern Pennsylvania was claimed for Virginia by Dunmore, seized by a *coup d'état,* and occupied by Virginia until the close of the Revolution. In 1774 the Shawnee rose against Virginia because of her land seizures and a series of cold-blooded murders by settlers, but Andrew Lewis defeated them in a sharp battle at Point Pleasant at the mouth of the Kanawha. This victory, the only important battle in what is known as Dunmore's War, meant a *de facto* occupation of the Ohio Valley by Virginia, no matter what papers might be drawn up by the lawyers of the Crown.

Meanwhile some Virginians who had been living near the source of the Holston River moved southward to the Watauga River in 1769, in what proved to be a part of North Carolina on both sides of the present North Carolina–Tennessee boundary. There they were **Watauga** joined by fugitive Regulators, and in 1772 they set up by **settlements** compact the Watauga Association, which imposed a simple form of government and operated for their protection against outlaws. The Watauga settlements grew and spread through the mountains and took a decisive part in the frontier wars and the Revolution. Its leaders were a dour Scotsman, James Robertson, and John Sevier, a more polished and debonair backwoodsman of French and English descent.

In 1774 a prominent North Carolina judge named Richard Henderson formed the Transylvania Company to buy up and settle Kentucky. The Cherokee claim was purchased at the Treaty of Sycamore Shoals in **Transyl-** 1775, and a plan of government was drawn up that would **vania** have been as restrictive as the charter of Maryland. Henderson and his associates had suffered at the hands of the Regulators and proposed that there would be no such nonsense in Transylvania. Early that year Daniel Boone marked out the Wilderness Road through Cumberland Gap, at the extreme southwestern corner of Virginia, and soon afterward built Boonesborough and brought in three hundred settlers. The new settlement was opposed by Virginia, which had fought a war to "clear" the same land, and after the Revolution began it was organized by Virginia as Kentucky County.

One can well imagine what confusion there was in individual land titles as a result of the welter of claims. The problem was one of the bitterest that confronted the West. The pre-Revolutionary history of the **Quebec** crossing of the mountains, however, offered yet one more **Act, 1774** complication. In 1774 the Quebec Act provided that French-Canadians should live under French civil law (which did not provide for juries), that the Roman Catholic Church should be recognized, and that the province should be extended to include all the territory north of the Ohio and east of the Mississippi. The law was a wise recognition of the rights of Canadians, but it was regarded by the Thirteen Colonies as an opening wedge for the abolition of jury trial and the strengthening of the Anglican Church as an instrument of royal control. But worst of all it assumed royal possession of the West, abrogated Virginia's land claims, hampered the Virginia and Pennsylvania fur trade by placing it under the governor of Quebec (who, of course, favored the Montreal traders), and blasted the hopes of the speculators who were already casting their eyes on the fat lands of Ohio. The Quebec Act was therefore an important factor, though not intended to be oppressive, in promoting revolution.

2 The Era of Genteel Protest

It now remains to follow the main course of events which led to the outbreak of revolution and the declaration of independence. When George Grenville, brother-in-law of Pitt but a willing tool of George III, became prime minister in 1763, he was confronted by tremendous financial and administrative problems. His solutions may not have been wise, but they were vigorous. We **Grenville's Sugar Act, 1764** have already noted the Proclamation Line of 1763. In addition, Grenville proposed four acts affecting the colonies. The first, the Revenue Act of 1764, usually known as the Sugar Act, was intended for the raising of revenue for the support of the army, for the regulation of colonial trade, and for the encouragement of British trade. Its provisions were too numerous to analyze here. In general they laid a high duty on such foreign goods as sugar, wines, and silks imported directly into the colonies and a lower one on those which passed through England; the purpose, of course, was to give English merchants an advantage. The duty on molasses was reduced from a sixpence which was rarely collected to a threepence which was plainly intended to be collected. An already narrow margin of profit on rum was in danger of disappearing. It should be noted, however, that two years later this duty was reduced to one penny a gallon, payable alike on British and foreign molasses.

The scarcity of coin in the colonies had led Massachusetts to establish a land bank which loaned bills of credit to farmers on the security of their farms. This was suppressed by Parliament in 1741, and in 1751 Parliament went on to forbid all of the New England governments to issue legal-tender bills of credit. Now, by the Currency Act **Currency Act, 1764** of 1764, Parliament extended the provisions of 1751 to all the colonies. The effect was promptly to align the paper-money provinces of the South with the molasses smugglers of the North.

The mills of the Parliamentary gods continued to grind. Grenville did

The BOSTONIAN'S Paying the EXCISE-MAN, or TARRING & FEATHERING

A British thrust at Boston's treatment of tax collectors, London, 1774

not expect to raise in the colonies more than about £100,000 of the £350,000 that the American military establishment would cost. Even that much would not have been produced by the Sugar Act; so he proposed to raise additional funds by providing that all legal documents, bills of lading, pamphlets, newspapers, advertisements, almanacs, calendars, playing cards, and dice must bear revenue stamps ranging from twopence to six pounds. Colonial opposition was immediate and intense. Grenville called in the colonial agents and asked them to propose a substitute or to agree that the colonies would appropriate the necessary money outright. His efforts were fruitless; and in 1765, while Pitt was ill with gout, he pushed through the famous Stamp Act. Thus for the first time Parliament undertook to levy on the colonies an internal revenue tax. To make it worse, cases arising under the act were to be tried in admiralty courts, which sat without juries.

Stamp Act, 1765

Even before the news of the Stamp Act reached America, Parliament passed the Quartering Act to provide for a military establishment in America. This act forced the colonies in which the troops were stationed to provide at least part of the expense of quarters and provisions. General Thomas Gage, commander in chief in America, selected New York as his headquarters. The **Quartering Act, 1765**
province resented the burden and refused to obey the act in full; as a result there was a three-years struggle in which the colony was at last forced to yield.

The passage of these four acts, as might have been foreseen, led to a crisis. The fact that Parliament had also placed bounties on a number of products was no solace. The new tax collections went directly into the government treasury, and though it was true that the money
was to be used to maintain the army in America, yet it was **The Stamp Act crisis**
pointed out that it would be spent in England for English
goods. The Stamp Act provided the rallying point for colonial resistance. Though it might only occasionally affect a large part of the people, espe-cially in the West, its imposition of an internal revenue tax was a clear-cut proof to legalists of Parliament's flouting of constitutional safe-guards. Even the American agents in London were surprised by the public reception of the Stamp Act, and Benjamin Franklin, who had sought a position as collector for one of his friends, barely managed to save his political bacon. The news of the act was met with the tolling of bells, days of mourning, and resolutions of protest. Rioters hanged the stamp collectors in effigy and sacked the house of Massachusetts's Governor Thomas Hutchinson, a colonist born. Merchants banded together in non-importation associations and agreed to order no English goods. Sons of Liberty associations sprang up to enforce the boycott and to club down opposition. Patrick Henry pushed through the House of Burgesses the "Virginia Resolves," which threw down the gauntlet to illegal taxation, and other provinces followed suit. At the call of Massachusetts the Stamp Act Congress met in New York in October, and representatives of nine colonies joined in a dignified protest and statement of the American point of view.

Within a year of the passage of the Stamp Act British exports to America fell off one third. British merchants, shippers, and manufac-turers felt the blow keenly and added their protests to that of the Stamp
Act Congress. Grenville had passed out of office, and his **Repeal of the Stamp Act, 1766**
successor, bedeviled by the shopkeepers of England and
with the thunder of the Great Commoner ringing in his
ears ("The Americans are the sons, not the bastards of England . . . I rejoice that America has resisted"), yielded and led the movement for repeal of the act. Grenville's fall, be it noted, had nothing to do with the American problem but followed a tiff with the king; in fact, British

ministries until 1782 never were made up with an eye to American relations but rather to domestic and European issues and personal rivalries. The transports of joy with which the Thirteen Colonies greeted the repeal wafted away the high resolves and the organs of protest almost as though they had never existed. The news was alloyed only slightly by the Declaratory Act (1766), which asserted that Parliament had the right to legislate for the colonies "in all cases whatsoever."

William Pitt (now the Earl of Chatham) was head of the British Cabinet in 1767; but, since he was half-insane with the gout, the real responsibility fell on a flibbertygibbet statesman revealingly called **Townshend** "Champagne Charlie" Townshend, who was Chancellor of **Duty Acts,** the Exchequer. The gentry took the opportunity to force a **1767** reduction in the land tax, and Townshend now proposed to make up the difference from the American pocketbook—thereby establishing his claim to be the father of American independence.

Taking advantage of the distinction the Americans had drawn between internal and external taxes, he put through a series of acts laying import duties at American ports on paint, paper, lead, glass, and tea shipped from England. The use of writs of assistance (general warrants) was authorized, and admiralty courts were established at Halifax, Boston, Philadelphia, and Charleston. Essentially these were to perform the functions of federal courts, since the only other royal courts in America could be hamstrung by provincial legislatures. However, it is hard to avoid the conclusion that they were set up because they could sit without juries drawn from a population which was set on thwarting the laws. In addition to the foregoing provisions, a board of customs commissioners was established in America. Up to this time the American customs had yielded about £2000 a year at a cost of £9000; thereafter they yielded £30,000 at a cost of £13,000.

But these were not the worst features of the acts. Even more menacing were the subtle implications. Since the Americans would not accept an internal revenue tax, it was proposed to levy external tariffs (which, **Purpose of** to be consistent, they must accept) and to see to it that the **Townshend** tariffs were collected. The support of the army now took **Acts** second place to the principle of imperial control. The money raised by the acts was earmarked for an American civil list composed of the royal governors, judges, and other officials who had hitherto been dependent on the provincial assemblies for their salaries. Thus would the Crown snatch from the colonies their old control of the purse strings, which had been their chief weapon in the battle for provincial autonomy.

Townshend died in September 1767, but the evil that he did lived after him. The second wave of colonial protest was now well under way. Rioting broke out in Boston when John Hancock's sloop *Liberty* was seized; troops were sent to the city, and the provincial assembly was dissolved. Virginia again led in legislative protest, and the House of Burgesses passed the Resolves of 1769, which were written by George Mason and introduced by George Washington. Once more the merchants and planters came forward with their nonimportation agreements and, as before, were backed

Protest against Townshend Acts

The Boston Massacre, from an engraving by Paul Revere

by public sentiment and clubs of bully boys. As in 1766, British merchants were terrified, and at their demand the Townshend duties were repealed (1770) except for a threepence tax on tea, kept to preserve the principle.

Boston had become a town virtually in a state of siege, except that it was the troops who were terrorized and subjected to petty persecution by the Bostonians. In March a crowd of rowdies, knowing very well that the British troops had strict orders not to fire on the populace, pelted and insulted a patrol and mocked it with commands of "Fire!" In the confusion the patrol did fire, and four or five of the mob were killed. A young lawyer named John Adams risked his career to defend the soldiers in court, and they

Boston Massacre, 5 March 1770

got off with only technical punishment. Just the same, the troops were withdrawn to an island in the harbor. The whole affair lent itself to deliberately false interpretation by the American extremists.

The Townshend Acts episode finally brought home to American legal theorists the fact that American rights could be jeopardized just as much by external as by internal taxation. An important aid in driving this home was John Dickinson's *Letters of a Pennsylvania* **Dickinson's** *Farmer*. He acknowledged the function of Parliament as the **Letters** co-ordinator of the Empire and yielded its right to "regulate" commerce by tariffs, but not to tax it for revenue. Dickinson, a citizen alternately of Pennsylvania and Delaware, was a conservative who adopted the method of revolution with the greatest reluctance. Though he voted against the Declaration of Independence, he was one of the two members of Congress at that time who actually took up arms in its defense. Later on he was influential in drawing up the Articles of Confederation and the Constitution. In contrast to Dickinson was the equally statesmanlike Joseph Galloway of Pennsylvania, who labored to protect American rights by the adoption of an imperial written constitution. When the war began he became a Loyalist and went into exile.

No less significant in the long view was George Mason of Gunston Hall, a neighbor of George Washington. Though he all his life professed distaste for public business and preferred to regard himself as a private **George** gentleman, Mason's thinking exercised a profound effect **Mason** upon two generations of Virginians. He was the author of **(1725–92)** several of the resolutions with which Virginia met the encroachments of the Crown, and these resolutions afforded a ground of departure for the debates in the Continental Congresses. The famous Virginia Declaration of Rights was his work, and he went on to write the Constitution of Virginia. The effect of both upon Jefferson's Declaration of Independence and upon the French Declaration of the Rights of Man has been frequently pointed out. Though Mason was a member of the Constitutional Convention of 1787, he opposed the Constitution, partly because it quietly accepted slavery. Nevertheless, it was his agitation that was largely responsible for the Bill of Rights amendments to the Federal Constitution.

3   *The Radicals Take Over*

It is readily apparent that the British colonial policy of the 1760's was characterized less by a clear and decisive program than by typically British "muddling through." One good reason for this was the battle for **King's pre-** power that was being fought between the corrupt Whig **rogative** oligarchy and the equally corrupt Tory party which the **victorious** king was constructing. In the 1760's the king's power was great enough to enable him to hamstring Whig policy, but it was not until 1770 that he was able, through his favorite, Frederick North, Baron North, usually known as Lord North, to obtain the complete control of the House of Commons which he exercised until 1782.

The king's success was due to the bankruptcy of Whig talent as well as to corruption. Townshend's dismal failure should have been a warning, but at this stage George III was incapable of envisioning failure in his grand enterprise of which the nub, it was now evident, was the conquest by force or bamboozlement of the Thirteen Colonies. North was a charming, tactful, and able gentleman who under different circumstances might have made a name for himself as a leader. It is certain that he undertook a policy of coercion reluctantly and against his better judgment; but he deliberately chose the part of king's tout rather than that of a free moral and political agent.

George did not move with undue haste. The next three years were the lull before the third and last great storm, and during the period colonial imports from Britain actually tripled. The first two great waves of protest had been chiefly directed by the conservative merchant class of the northern coast. Of course, nonimportation had hurt the business of the merchants, and it was sometimes necessary for the organizations to punish wavering members by sicking the strong-arm boys on them. On the other hand, few merchants had hesitated to take advantage of the scarcity of goods by charging outrageous prices, and this fact naturally bred popular resentment and in some cases direct action. Confronted by this monster of their own creation, the merchants gladly ceased resistance upon the repeal of the bulk of the Townshend duties, even though much public sentiment opposed yielding. Thereafter a strong faction of the merchants chose submission to royal "tyranny" in preference to "mob rule" and left their southern planter allies in the lurch. It was the beginning of the split between radicals and conservatives, the two elements which were to develop into the Whigs (Patriots, Rebels) and Tories (Loyalists) of the Revolution. These radicals were not radical in the present-day totalitarian sense, but they did seek to obtain independence by intimidation, violence, and revolution.

The radical leaders who now took control in the North were not as a rule drawn from the social and propertied élite. Their methods they had learned from the merchants' associations, but they found their support in the working-class "mob" and to an increasing extent in bands of night riders among back-country men. The Sons of Liberty clubs once more became prominent. Among the Delaware Indian chiefs who had danced in council with William Penn was one named Tammany, who bore the same name as the Delaware culture hero. During succeeding generations the name had gradually ac-

Split in opposition to British policy

Saint Tammany

quired a legendary halo. The Sons of Liberty now borrowed St. Tammany as patron, and 12 May, his name-day, was widely celebrated with mock-serious Indian rituals. During the Revolution St. Tammany became the "patron saint" first of the Pennsylvania Line, then of the whole army. The name still survives by legitimate descent in New York's Tammany Hall.

Samuel Adams of Massachusetts was the most persistent of the northern gadflies, and so great were his organizing powers and so far-flung were his propaganda activities that the opinion has been expressed **Samuel** that without him there would never have been an American **Adams** Revolution. It *may* be somewhere near the truth to say that **(1722–** without Sam Adams and George III there would not have **1803)** been an American Revolution. Adams was a Harvard man, a failure in business who found refuge in politics, and who during the days of his greatest activity was actually living on charity. His father's fortune had been sadly depleted by the Parliamentary destruction of the Massachussets land bank in 1741. Young Adams neither forgave nor forgot, and this attitude probably sharpened a naturally contentious and intriguing bent. He later acknowledged that by 1768 he had set his heart on independence from Great Britain.

Adams and his friends sought to keep discontent alive by promoting committees which would stir things up in New England's town meetings. At first Adams's style was cramped by the moderation of the brilliant **Leaders of** lawyer James Otis, but in 1769 Otis was removed from **protest in** politics by a crack on the head by a royal official in a tavern **Massachu-** brawl. More favorable to direct action was John Hancock, a **setts** rich merchant smuggler, but such a combination of vanity and mediocrity that Adams once called him an empty barrel. Nevertheless, he carried weight with the people and during and after the Revolution was the political boss of the state. Only less prominent was Joseph Warren, a physician who was to enter the army and fall at Bunker Hill. John Adams, a rising young lawyer and distant cousin of Samuel, was the ablest constitutionalist in the colony and, though he excused revolution, did not favor Sam Adams's use of the mob.

The crusade for direct action made discouragingly slow progress until June 1772, when the revenue cutter *Gaspee* ran aground near Providence and was plundered and burned by the local smugglers who resented its **Adams** "piratical" campaign against them. Official inquiry drew an **makes** absolute blank. Soon afterward the Crown actually set up **headway** in Massachusetts at its own expense the civil list which had long been threatened. These events were meat for Adams's ax, and he was able to blanket New England with Committees of Correspondence, whose function was to exchange information (and misinformation) for each other's stimulation and encouragement. It was the yeoman work performed by these committees that made New England the powder maga-zine of rebellion. The expansion of the committees to other provinces was not long delayed.

Adams's work was aided by his publication of some letters of the native-born but Tory Governor Thomas Hutchinson of Massachusetts and of Andrew Oliver, the lieutenant-governor, letters which were care-fully "edited" to make clear that certain expressions were **Hutchinson** interpreted as attacks on American liberties. These letters **and Oliver** had been obtained in England by Franklin (he never dis- **letters** closed how), and the furor led to his arraignment before a committee of the Privy Council in a public spectacle at the Cockpit Tavern. Franklin may have committed an unethical act (though it was common enough in that day, and Franklin's own letters were opened regularly by the min-istry), but it was bad politics to force the foxy old pamphleteer and politician to undergo public ridicule. It was about this time that Franklin received proof that George III was actually pulling the strings of the min-istry, and this probably did as much as the Cockpit episode to cause his dream of a great Anglo-American empire to fade.

Events were now rushing toward a crisis. The venerable Honourable East India Company had brought millions into England by its plunder and exploitation of the Orient, but its members had milked off the gold and left the company in danger of bankruptcy. Failure **Crisis of the** would have canceled the considerable annual income which **East India** the government received from it and would have endangered **Company** England's strangle hold on India. The logical way out was for the govern-ment to take over all but the purely trade functions of the company, but the stockholders knew that would end their era of easy plunder. They found refuge in politics; Crown control of India, they warned dolefully, would mean Crown supremacy over "the liberties of the people"—by which phrase, of course, they meant privileged private enterprise. The Americans, whose colonies were governed by charters originally of an ilk with the company, also professed alarm and rallied to its support.

Lord North, with unanswerable logic, proposed that the Americans should save the company. The company had lost one of its larger markets when the Americans turned to smuggled Dutch tea; North now arranged (Tea Act, 1773) for the company to sell its great tea sur- **Tea Act,** plus in America at a price so absurdly low that even after **1773** the threepence tax was paid it would undersell the Dutch. The plan was for the company to sell the tea directly to American mer-chants without benefiting English middlemen. An easy corollary, North asserted, was that he would thus also show the hollowness of the colonists' pretended scruples against Parliamentary taxation. Let the price be cheap enough, and they would buy.

In the light of what happened it is interesting to note that Boston had been sewed up so tightly by revenuers that it was no longer a nest of smugglers. It was Providence, New York, and Philadelphia which had

Reception of the tea

now built up a vested interest in smuggling and which put up the first yelps about cheap tea interfering with liberty.

Indeed, there was danger of monopoly, for the tea was consigned to specified merchants who would thus control the entire legal supply; it was easy to conclude that the Crown would go on to award such monopolies in other articles, and in the end corporations would control America, and behind them pulling the strings would be Parliament. American merchants now had to decide whether they more feared Parliament's commercial restrictions or the "mob," and they divided accordingly.

Tea was the logical point of attack, for at this time it was the great American tipple, and patriots feared that the temptations would be irresistible. The propaganda hounds were unleashed. Not only was tea represented as a threat to American liberties, but physicians chimed in to declare that it was rusting away American teeth and innards and reducing the population to a truly pitiable physical condition. Boston (Dec. 1773) joined the campaign for coffee and American liberties, when a crowd of men·disguised as Indians—and probably led by Samuel Adams and John Hancock—boarded a tea ship and dumped the "cursed weed" into the harbor. Success met the patriots: the consignees resigned in terror, and some royal governors tactfully yielded to public demand and refused to let the tea land. All up and down the coast cargoes were tossed overboard or burned—in Annapolis with the ship.

Boston had been busily giving itself a bad name ever since the days of the Stuarts, and it was only natural that it should be selected as the chief object of British resentment. In April 1774 Lord North was armed

Intolerable Acts, 1774

with the so-called Intolerable Acts, which bore chiefly against the Bay Colony. (1) The Port of Boston was closed, except to firewood and provisions, until the loss of the tea was made good. (2) British officials accused of offenses committed in the line of duty might be tried in other colonies or in England. (3) A quartering act gave British commanders considerable discretionary power. (4) The charter of Massachusetts was amended to strengthen royal control; the town meetings, "hotbeds" of democracy, were limited to one session a year; and General Gage was made governor of the colony. (5) Not strictly one of the Intolerable Acts but passed about the same time and classed with them in the American mind was the Quebec Act.

The menaces of the French and Indians had failed to force the jealous colonies to agree, but the stubborn young king succeeded without trying. There was a flood of protest in the colonial press, and town meetings and

legislative assemblies poured forth resolutions of sympathy   First Conti-
with Boston and followed them by donations of food. In   nental
Williamsburg the Virginia House of Burgesses on the mo-   Congress
tion of Thomas Jefferson appointed a day of fasting and prayer. When it
was dissolved by the governor, a rump met in the Raleigh Tavern and
called for a continental congress. This First Continental Congress met in
Carpenter's Hall in Philadelphia in September 1774. Among its members
were such radicals as Samuel Adams and John Adams of Boston, and
Patrick Henry and Richard Henry Lee of Virginia; but opposite them
were many moderates and conservatives, who feared democracy as mob
rule. Neither party knew that the king was directly involved in the Intolerable Acts but supposed them to be the work of Parliament.

To the amazement of the conservatives, the roaring New England
radicals sat back meekly and let the gentlemanly Virginia and Carolina
planter-radicals carry the ball. The conservatives, led by Joseph Galloway of Philadelphia, fought in vain against them. In the end the radicals
had the advantage and carried a call upon the king for redress in the
form of a petition to the Throne and a dignified "Declaration of Rights."
The protest was made more pointed by adopting "The Continental Association," an agreement not to import from or export to Great Britain
or the West Indies. As a result a number of the right-wing faction, including Galloway, went over to the Loyalist side. The last act of the
Congress was to call a second meeting for May 1775.

The acts of the Congress led to a sharp but unequal division of British
opinion. The landed gentry, anxious to hamper American competition in
foodstuffs and conscious that the land tax would go up if the colonies
won their fight with Parliament, urged force—and got the
higher taxes anyhow. The merchants, with their American   British pub-
trade reduced to a shadow, urged appeasement at first, but   lic opinion
they were soon convinced that the government must act firmly to retain
the American market. They could afford to take a strong stand because
a brisk demand in other markets was for the moment giving them all
the orders they could fill. The masses had never had any clear concept
of the way in which the king was hamstringing the democratic process,
and now they came out vigorously for a firm policy against America. The
king, always popular, had never been so high in public favor.

English liberal clubs which had for years been fighting a brisk and
dramatic battle to preserve British civil liberties championed the American cause because the Americans were fighting for the liberty of Englishmen as well as their own. Their leaders were Isaac Barré;
the magnetic, self-seeking rascal John Wilkes; and Edmund   Liberal
Burke, the Irish orator. It was Burke who in March 1775   opinion
delivered his magnificent speech "On Conciliation with America," crying

out to Parliament not to break American strength because in so doing it was British strength that would be broken. It was natural that after hostilities began most of the merchants and liberals should either back the war or oppose it only with caution, though there were some who consistently advocated peace, even at the price of separation. Meanwhile the Whigs gleefully seized the juicy opportunity to make political capital. They pointed out to the shortsighted merchants that "A Shop-keeper will never get the more Custom by beating his Customers, and what is true of a Shop-keeper is true of a *Shop-keeping* Nation."

In the midst of the crisis (January 1775) the gout-ridden Chatham roused himself and, leaning on the arm of Benjamin Franklin, returned to the House of Lords to lead the hopeless battle for conciliation. "What

Chatham and American liberty

I demand for America," he cried, "is not pardon, not indulgence, but justice. . . . We shall be forced ultimately to retract; let us retract while we can, not when we must. . . . If the ministers thus persevere in misadvising the king . . . they will make the crown not worth his wearing. I will not say that the king is betrayed, but I will pronounce that the kingdom is undone." While Pitt drew the line at any American attempt to thwart the Navigation Acts or the sovereignty of Parliament as cornerstones of empire, he bitterly opposed their use as weapons of enslavement. Probably at the suggestion of Franklin, he sought to have Parliament recognize America's status as a dominion. Even after the Declaration of Independence he was convinced that what the Americans wanted was not independence but liberty, and in 1777 he advocated negotiation. Said he: "We have tried for unconditional submission; try what can be gained by unconditional redress." It was not until the rebel colonies entered into an alliance with France, the national enemy, that he set his face against them and fell prostrate on the floor of the House of Lords while proclaiming the sovereignty of Parliament; he died a few weeks later.

Lord North interpreted the action of Congress as a challenge and proceeded to blockade commerce from nine of the Thirteen Colonies, though at the same time he offered to refrain from taxation if the colo-

Whig sentiment strengthened

nies would guarantee to support the army and the civil list. He might better have saved his ink, for the colonists were rapidly passing beyond the reach of compromise, however reasonable, let alone an offer as specious as this. Effective control of the colonies was in the hands of the Committees of Correspondence, now reorganized as Committees of Safety, and the Liberty Boys organized patriotic rallies, plundered the homes of Tories and tarred and feathered the owners, and kept the lukewarm and the fearful in line. The merchant element (except for the fire-eaters like Hancock) were under suspicion and subject to continual check.

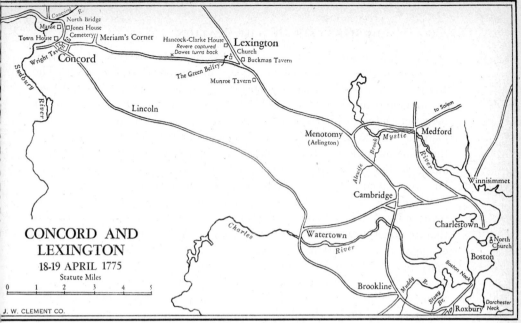

Adapted from *Atlas of American History*, edited by James Truslow Adams and R. V. Coleman; copyright 1943 by Charles Scribner's Sons; used by permission of the publishers.

During the winter of 1774–75 the Whigs fought a desperate battle against the conservatives in a number of the colonies. Indeed, Virginia and Massachusetts were the only two large colonies about which there was no doubt. The aristocrats of New York plumped for peace and order and retained their strangle hold on the colony until it was literally pried loose by mobs under Isaac **Crucial winter of 1774–75** Sears and Alexander McDougall. Pennsylvania's Quakers and Episcopalians were almost as obdurate, and it was not until the Presbyterian counties were heard from that the issue was settled. By spring it was evident that the decision everywhere was in favor of the radicals. During the winter provincial congresses began to take over civil administration; the king's writ reached no farther than the range of the British muskets. War was now indubitably ahead, and committees and provincial congresses began to gather and store arms and munitions and to organize and train provincial militia volunteers. Certain of the Massachusetts militia units were called minutemen because they were ready for any emergency "at a minute's warning."

With so much static in the air it was inevitable that gunpowder somewhere should be ignited. On the night of 18 April 1775 Governor Gage, who mustered less than four thousand effectives in Boston, sent seven hundred troops to seize a powder magazine at Concord. Two Bostonians, a tanner named William Dawes and a silversmith named Paul Revere, were sent off by the Boston Whig Committee to warn the minutemen along the **Lexington and Concord, 19 April 1775**

229

eighteen-mile route to Concord. The next morning the redcoats encountered about fifty minutemen drawn up on the green at Lexington. The British commander's order to disperse was followed by a shot and then a volley, and the minutemen fled with a loss of eight killed. It has never been determined which side fired the initial shot. A stout resistance was made at Concord, and the British began their return to Boston with their mission only partly accomplished. Minutemen and militia swarmed along the line of march, firing from behind fences and trees, and the regulars were saved from rout only by a relief column from Boston.

Casualties were not important, for only forty-nine Americans and seventy-three British had been killed; the significance of the day was that it precipitated military action and the Americans proved to them-

Signifi-cance and results selves that they could defeat the British. That night the provincials closed in and began the siege of Boston, which was to last for eleven months. And that night or very soon afterward Sam Adams set himself to the concoction of atrocity stories which were to be invaluable in swinging the doubtful to the Whig side and were to be the pabulum of the first generations of the infant nation. Somewhat later the British also began to invent yarns of how the minutemen took the scalps and gouged out the eyes of the dead and wounded. The time was to come when there would be enough atrocities on both sides to keep the editors busy without the necessity of inventing them.

4 *The Road to Independence*

The Second Continental Congress met in Philadelphia, 10 May 1775, and accepted the fact of war. It was essentially a diplomatic conference and had no legal or national status or guiding body of constitutional

Second Continental Congress practices. However, it assumed that its members were fully empowered to act and therefore took over the administration of national functions, including diplomacy and the prosecution of the war. New England had been so prominent thus far that its envoys were willing to recognize the South and attach it to the common cause by voting for George Washington of Virginia as commander in chief of the troops besieging Boston. He assumed command on 2 July.

Meanwhile events moved on in Massachusetts. The commander of the besieging New England militia, Artemas Ward, took some weeks to organize. Suddenly on the night of 16 June he forced the British hand

Bunker Hill, 17 June 1775 by sending three thousand men to seize and fortify Bunker Hill (by mistake they fortified Breed's Hill) on the Charlestown peninsula looking across at Boston from the north. Thus dominated, the British had no choice but to attack. The American

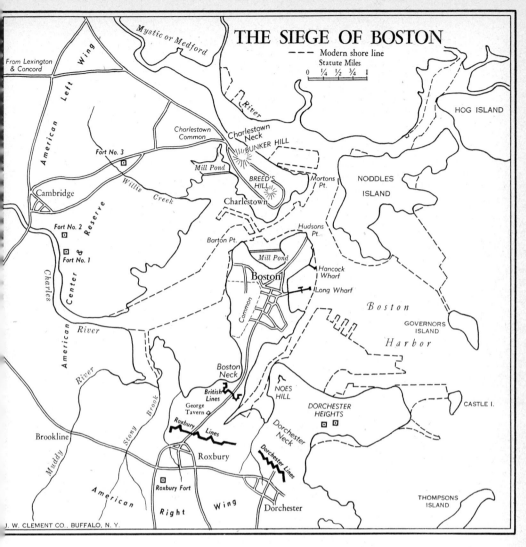

THE SIEGE OF BOSTON

- - - Modern shore line
Statute Miles
0   ¼   ½   ¾   1

From Lexington
& Concord

Mystic or Medford

American Left Wing

HOG ISLAND

Charlestown
Common

Charlestown
Neck

BUNKER HILL

Fort No. 3

Mill Pond

BREED'S
HILL

Mortons
Pt.

NODDLES

ISLAND

Cambridge

Willis Creek

Reserve

American Center

Charlestown

Barton Pt.

Hudsons
Pt.

Fort No. 2

Mill Pond

Hancock
Wharf

Boston

Charles

Fort No. 1

Long Wharf

River

Boston

American

River

GOVERNORS
ISLAND

Harbor

Boston
Neck

British
Lines

NOES
HILL

CASTLE I.

George
Tavern

Roxbury
Lines

DORCHESTER
HEIGHTS

Brookline

Muddy

Stony

Brook

Dorchester
Neck

Roxbury

Dorchester Lines

Roxbury Fort

American Right Wing

Dorchester

THOMPSONS
ISLAND

J. W. CLEMENT CO., BUFFALO, N. Y.

fortifications probably could have been outflanked simply by occupying
Charlestown Neck with troops, but in eighteenth-century style General
William Howe, who was in charge of the assault, chose the dramatic way.
Doubtless it was also considered that a good trouncing by a stand-up
charge would have a wholesome effect on the Rebels. Two thousand
regulars landed on the beach and charged up the hill, only to be repulsed
with great slaughter. The third British charge succeeded, chiefly because
the Americans had run out of powder and had to abandon their positions.

The British loss in killed and wounded of 1054 (against 441 for the
Americans) was over half of the force engaged. With only 40,000 effectives
in the entire imperial army, the British could not have afforded many more
such victories. Naturally the Americans regarded it as a
moral victory, and it has ever since helped to build up a

Results

231

rather too typical American contempt for careful military preparations. At any rate, Bunker Hill was decisive in two ways: Americans were inflated by their success and less than ever inclined to yield; on the other hand, wounded British pride now could be assuaged only by American blood.

While the siege of Boston dragged on, military history was being made in both the North and the South. In May Benedict Arnold with a Connecticut column and Ethan Allen with some Vermonters ("Green Mountain Boys") joined in a surprise attack on the British stronghold at Ticonderoga and to everyone's surprise took it together with stores of cannon and ammunition. Hastily outfitted ships cruised along the coast and seized British store ships. Part of the British plan was to cripple American seaports in order to prevent aid to Boston. Thus it was that in October a small fleet seized Falmouth (or Portland, Maine) and after driving out the inhabitants burned it to the ground.

Military events in the North

It was evident to amateur strategists that the issue of independence might depend on whether the water-level route through the Hudson River and Lake Champlain could be denied to the British. The obvious way to block it was to close the St. Lawrence by winning the support of the French-Canadians. Already the First Continental Congress had seen this possibility and tried to counter the colonists' former insults to the French as papists and scalpers by eating a banquet of crow garnished by flattering speeches. In the autumn of 1775 Congress cast the dice. Two meagerly outfitted columns invaded Canada; one, led by General Richard Montgomery, moved by way of Lake Champlain and took Montreal; the other, led by General Arnold, went by way of the Kennebec wilderness. On 31 December the famished and decimated columns tried unsuccessfully to storm Quebec; Montgomery was killed in the attack. Arnold began a siege, but the French refused to come to his help: generations of distrust and the intemperate American clamor against the Quebec Act now bore bitter fruit. In the spring Arnold retreated to Lake Champlain, where he built a little fleet with which he fought a heroic and successful campaign to delay Sir Guy Carleton, the Governor of Canada, in entering New York by the back door.

Repulse from Canada

In March Washington was ready to carry the siege of Boston to a crisis and seized and fortified Dorchester Heights south of the city, a strategic point which the bemused British commander (now Sir William Howe) had unaccountably neglected. As a result Howe hastily evacuated the city and, taking as many as possible of the Boston Tories with him, sailed off to Halifax.

Siege of Boston ended

When the coastal gentry of the Carolinas declared for Congress, the natural reaction of the old Regulators in the interior was to take the

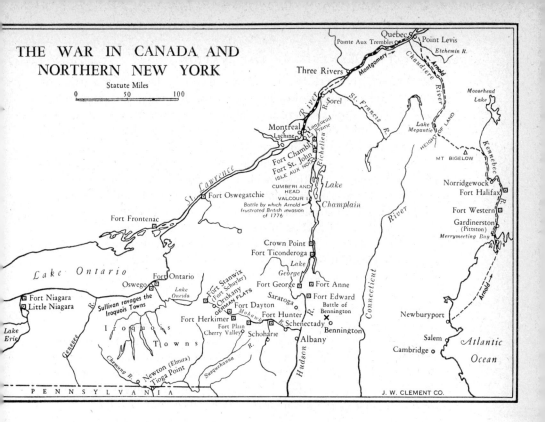

THE WAR IN CANADA AND
NORTHERN NEW YORK

Statute Miles

king's side. In February 1776 a body of Regulators and of Highland veterans of Bonnie Prince Charlie's rising in 1745 started **Military** for the coast to co-operate with a British fleet. Unfortu- **events in** nately for them, a Whig force intercepted and scattered **the South** them at Moore's Creek Bridge. The fleet was delayed, and when in June it laid siege to Charleston it was repulsed. There now began a bitter partisan warfare between the two factions in the Carolinas, and it did not cease (whatever the fortunes of the official armies) until the close of the war. In Virginia Rebel sentiment was more unanimous, and Lord Dunmore was forced to take refuge on a warship; he sought a rather irresponsible revenge by burning down part of the little city of Norfolk on New Year's Day.

The radical members of Congress had been ready for independence from the opening day, but the moderates and apparently the body of public opinion were not ready. The radicals, as Sam Adams expressed it, decided to "wait till the fruit is ripe before we gather it." **Trend to-** Unlike most fruit, that of independence ripened during the **ward inde-** winter. The military events just recounted helped to bring **pendence** the flush of maturity to its cheek, and this was not delayed for any want of editing of the news bulletins. Still, something was wrong. The radicals cannily said nothing about independence; and, though the Tories correctly warned of where the trend was leading, the fact was that the Revolution was slowing down. Even as staunch a patriot as John Adams wondered if the radicals were not going too fast when one day a neighbor accosted him. "Oh! Mr. Adams," said the man, "what great things you have done for us! There are no courts of justice now in this province, and I hope there never will be another." The keystone province, Pennsylvania, lagged farthest behind in spite of the radicalism of the Scotch-Irish. The Germans regarded both their English and their Scotch-Irish neighbors with suspicion and were inclined to back up the Quakers, who were both Tories and pacifists.

Colonial moderates led by John Dickinson of Pennsylvania, who still hoped for reconciliation, received a respectful hearing simply because the radicals feared to lead and were trusting to time. The chief reason for the radicals' indecision was that in the past they had built up a popular ideal of George III as a monarch who loved justice and liberty but was being thwarted in his good intentions by ministerial ogres. It had been the custom to speak of the British regulars as "ministerial troops" and some even referred to the provincial militia as "the king's troops." Though the radical leaders now knew that the ministers were nothing more than the king's marionettes, their problem was how to erase the popular portrait which they themselves had painted.

Benjamin Franklin came forward with the answer. In 1774 he had met in England an exciseman named Thomas Paine, who had been dismissed from the service for daring to organize his fellows to demand a

Thomas Paine (1737– 1809)

raise in pay. Now Paine had considerable ability as a scribbler, so when he appeared in Philadelphia with Franklin's recommendation he found employment as a journalist. It was therefore natural that Franklin should call upon his protégé for help. The result was the pamphlet *Common Sense*, published in January 1776, which there can be no reasonable doubt struck the spark that lit the fire of independence. Paine served out the war as soldier, diplomat, and pamphleteer; his little periodical *The Crisis*, it was said, was as useful to the Revolution as the sword of Washington. After the war he returned to Europe. In France during the French Revolution he wrote the *Rights of Man* in its defense and was a member of the Convention. While in prison during the Jacobin régime he wrote his confession as a deist, *The Age of Reason*, and this work, deliberately misrepresented by the pious nineteenth century as the work of an atheist, led to the invention of many scurrilities against him and served as an excuse for snatching away his laurels.

But it was in *Common Sense* that Paine lived his moment of glory and generous vengeance. In terse, breathless sentences which still have the power to stir, he tore from the eyes of the colonists the veil of inde-

cision which was already slowing down the revolutionary
effect. The country, Paine thundered, was "fighting, she
scarcely knew for what, and which, if she could have obtained, would have done her no good." With remorseless logic he attacked
the institution of kingship, then went on to expose George III as puppeteer
to a dummy ministry. Why lock the door against absolute monarchy, he
asked, then give to this Pharaoh of England the key in the shape of a
control of places and pensions? It was time to end the anomaly of "legislation without law; wisdom without a plan; a constitution without a
name; and, what is strangely astonishing, perfect independence contend-
ing for dependence." It was time to end doubts and suspicions by tying
the colonies together with the bond of independence.

Common Sense

> Now is the seed-time of continental union. . . . Everything that is
> right or reasonable pleads for separation. The blood of the slain, the
> weeping voice of nature cries, IT IS TIME TO PART. . . . O! ye that love
> mankind! Ye that dare oppose not only the tyranny but the tyrant, stand
> forth! Every spot of the old world is overrun with oppression. Freedom
> hath been hunted round the globe. . . . Receive the fugitive, and prepare
> in time an asylum for mankind.

The effect of *Common Sense* on the American public was like an
electric shock. Undoubtedly the spirit of independence was already there:
it needed only the shock to bring it to life. It is said that one hundred
twenty thousand copies of *Common Sense* were sold in the
first three months, and half a million altogether. If correct,
that would have been probably one for each family in the
country. Hitherto Americans had regarded it as their mission to preserve
the liberties of both England and America or see them buried in a
"common grave." Now they saw America as the last refuge of liberty in
a world devoted to tyranny, and the vision gave them strength and purpose. The psychological jam was broken, and the radicals rushed the
word "independence" boldly into print and added free trade, westward
expansion, and isolation from Europe's quarrels. America, they said, was
destined to be the ark "in which all the liberty and true religion of the
world are to be deposited." It was the birth of the American mission.

The American mission

Meanwhile events marched. Word came that the king was sending
peace commissioners, but the effect was canceled by further word that
he was also sending German mercenaries. The British navy blockaded the
coast, prohibited American trade with the world, seized
American ships, and closed the fisheries. Truly it appeared
that Britain was closing every exit but the one labeled
"independence." Congress acknowledged the situation by
advising the provinces to set up governments with authority derived not
from the king but from the people, on the ground that it was "necessary

Growing demand for independ- ence

that the exercises of every kind of authority under the said crown should be totally suppressed." A grass-roots movement for independence began to appear in local conventions and provincial congresses, particularly in New England and the South.

Then on 7 June 1776 Richard Henry Lee, as directed by the Virginia Convention, introduced into Congress a resolution that "these United Colonies are, and of right ought to be, free and independent States," and **Declaration of Independence** calling for a plan of confederation and a search for foreign alliances. The consideration was postponed to give the Middle Colonies a chance to get instructions: in Pennsylvania they were obtained only when the radicals ousted the legal assembly and held a provincial conference. On 2 July Congress voted, and every state sustained Lee's resolution except New York, which did not come over until the 15th. On the 4th a formal declaration prepared by Thomas Jefferson was adopted, though the engrossed copy was not signed until 2 August. The signing was a solemn occasion, of course, and John Hancock, who signed first as president of Congress, is said to have delivered a little admonition to the effect that after this step they must all hang together. "Yes," rejoined Franklin, who was never at a loss for a quip, "we must indeed all hang together, or most assuredly we must all hang separately." .

The thoroughness of Paine's preparation is shown by the fact that the burden of American protest up to this time had been directed against Parliament, but the Declaration was directed against George III. There was also the necessity to exhibit at least a superficial consistency. Americans had insisted that the Empire was composed of equal states joined by a common sovereign, so how could they declare independence to escape from the control of Parliament when that control had never been acknowledged? So now the Declaration renounced allegiance to George on the ground that he had used Parliament as a cat's-paw in a campaign to wield tyrannical power.

Jefferson later spoke of the Declaration of Independence as intended to be an expression of the American mind. It was certainly that in the cautious legalism with which it sought to justify its conduct out of a "decent respect to the opinions of mankind." Not only did it exhibit the hereditary English partiality to concrete liberties by ticking off under twenty-seven heads the "repeated injuries and usurpations" of George III which had led to rebellion and independence, but it also buttressed its case by appealing to John Locke's doctrine of Natural Rights and sometimes using his phraseology. Modern science may have laid the ax to the adored concept of Natural Rights, but it can never destroy the emotion that surges up in the human heart to meet these noble words:

We hold these truths to be self-evident, that all men are created equal, that they are endowed by their Creator with certain unalienable Rights, that among these are Life, Liberty and the pursuit of Happiness. That to secure these rights, Governments are instituted among Men, deriving their just powers from the consent of the governed. That whenever any Form of Government becomes destructive of these ends, it is the Right of the People to alter or to abolish it, and to institute new Government, laying its foundation on such principles and organizing its powers in such form, as to them shall seem most likely to effect their Safety and Happiness.

BIBLIOGRAPHICAL NOTE

Western Lands and the Revolution

LAND COMPANIES: The classical account of the western origins of the Revolution is Thomas P. Abernethy, *Western Lands and the American Revolution* (1937), which covers the subject from around 1740 to 1789; it contains an exhaustive bibliography. See also Lawrence H. Gipson, *The British Empire Before the American Revolution* (v. 4, 1939). On land companies, in addition to the above, see Shaw Livermore, *Early American Land Companies* (1939); Clarence W. Alvord, *The Mississippi Valley in British Politics* (2 v., 1917); Charles H. Ambler, *George Washington and the West* (1936); and George E. Lewis, *The Indiana Company, 1763–1798* (1941). Among other contributions to background is Avery O. Craven, *Soil Exhaustion as a Factor in the Agricultural History of Virginia and Maryland, 1606–1860* (1926), which examines agrarian discontent in those states.

INDIAN RELATIONS: See John R. Alden, *John Stuart and the Southern Colonial Frontier, 1754–1775* (1944); Francis Parkman, *The Conspiracy of Pontiac* (1870) is still great reading, but Howard H. Peckham, *Pontiac and the Indian Uprising* (1947) presents new material.

WESTERN COLONIES: See William S. Lester, *The Transylvania Colony* (1935); Thomas E. Matthews, *General James Robertson* (1934); and Carl S. Driver, *John Sevier* (1932).

The Radicals Take Over

BRITISH BACKGROUND: See Lewis B. Namier, *England in the Age of the American Revolution* (1930) and *Structure of Politics at the Accession of George III* (1929); Dora M. Clark, *British Opinion and the American Revolution* (1930); and Fred J. Hinkhouse, *Preliminaries of the American Revolution as Seen in the English Press, 1763–1775* (1926). For the king see Frank A. Mumby, *George III and the American Revolution* (1923); and Manfred S. Guttmacher, *America's Last King: An Interpretation of the Madness of George III* (1941). John C. Long, *Mr. Pitt and America's Birthright* (1940) is again useful.

AMERICAN BACKGROUND: Portrayed in such books as Philip Davidson, *Propaganda and the American Revolution, 1763–1783* (1941); Carl Becker, *History of Political Parties in the Province of New York, 1760–1776* (1909); John R. Alden, *General Gage in America* (1948); and Allen French, *General Gage's Informers* (1932) and *The Day of Concord and Lexington* (1925).

BIOGRAPHIES: Among many see John C. Miller, *Sam Adams* (1936); Herbert S. Allan, *John Hancock* (1948); Kate Mason Rowland, *George Mason* (2 v., 1892); and Helen D. Hill, *George Mason, Constitutionalist* (1938). Dickinson and Galloway are treated in Charles H. Lincoln, *The Revolutionary Movement in Pennsylvania, 1760–76* (1901). Then there is Edwin P. Kilroe, *Saint Tammany and the Origin of the Society of Tammany* (1913).

The Road to Independence

EARLY MILITARY EVENTS: Allen French, *The First Year of the American Revolution* (1934) deals exhaustively with the events of 1775–76. Relations with Canada are treated in Justin H. Smith, *Our Struggle for the Fourteenth Colony* (1907); and in George M. Wrong, *Canada and the American Revolution* (1935). On Arnold see the biographies by I. N. Arnold (1880) and Charles C. Sellers (1930).

DECLARATION OF INDEPENDENCE: See Carl L. Becker, *The Declaration of Independence: A Study in the History of Political Ideas* (1922); and Julian P. Boyd, *The Declaration of Independence: The Evolution of the Text* (1945). The two best biographies of Paine are by Moncure D. Conway (2 v., 1892) and Mary A. Best, but there is room for a better. Richard Henry Lee is treated in Burton J. Hendrick, *The Lees of Virginia* (1935). Catherine Drinker Bowen, *John Adams and the American Revolution* (1950) is essential for politics and diplomacy.

Chapter VIII

THE WINNING OF INDEPENDENCE

1 *The Nature of the War*

THE American Revolution was far more than a war. Fully as important were the political and social battles being fought in the states, which in their outcome vitally affected the nature and the course of the war. In retrospect the Revolution falls into three phases. The first one (which we have already viewed) covers the fifteen months after the battle at Lexington, during which the **Character of the Revolution** hope of reconciliation with the mother country faded as the radicals outmaneuvered the moderates, took control of the states, and carried a resolution for independence. The second phase was the period of military decision and of radical ascendance; as Allan Nevins says, only the fact of the existence of thirteen states conserved the political and institutional experience of the colonial period and prevented the Revolution from overshooting the mark and going to the extremes of the French and Russian revolutions. The third phase was the swing back to relative conservatism, which came in the latter 1780's and brought with it the Second Constitution of the United States, under which we still live.

Incompetence, overconfidence, and lost opportunities are to a surprising degree the stuffs of which history is made. That this should be true in the American Revolution is not surprising. The generals and statesmen of the new Union were men with little or no training, **The nature of the struggle** leading armies without history or tradition, steering a government that was not a government, and leading a people whose local rivalries were often more powerful than their national patriotism. The British were little better. They had the training, the traditions, and the government; but they were weakened by wars, debt, and corruption, divided by jealousies, and a prey to political and economic charlatans. An arrogant caste system and a cynical program of bankrupting the public welfare had united to create doldrums in which the ship of state lay helpless while officers rioted in the cabin and the crew lounged sullen and indifferent about the deck.

The popular view of the Revolution has come to be that it was a dignified and high-souled crusade in which rich and poor unanimously laid aside contention and self-seeking and pulled together for the com-**The human record** mon good. Quite the contrary. The wonder is that independence was ever won. The careful reader cannot avoid being shocked by the way in which jealousy, intrigue, profiteering, cowardice, and treason all plagued the Revolutionary effort, not to mention incompetence, procrastination, and differences of opinion which were no less bitter even when they were honest. Of course there were many high-souled, self-sacrificing men, of whom Washington was an example, in high position who worked quietly, intelligently, and patiently against desperate odds, and who triumphed partly because they were aided by resounding luck. Even more numerous in the Revolutionary ranks were men like us, who did what they had to do (which on occasion turned out to be heroic); never volunteered for extra duty; griped at shortages, inflation, long marches, and brass hats; passed the buck when possible; kept their heads down when the bullets were flying; and survived to agitate for a bonus. It was a record neither of angels nor of devils, but of very human men and women who did not always know what they wanted. Let us accept it as such.

The Revolution was a continual puzzle to the soldiers and diplomats of the time. By all the rules the Americans should have lost, but they refused to heed any attempts to disqualify them. Green young officers **American open-order tactics** diligently studied their manuals by bivouac fires; but since their men served only briefly and they did not possess the equipment for building up a regular army, they had to substitute intelligence for book rules. Like the Indians they persisted in hiding behind trees and fences while they loaded and fired; and, if they were too hard pressed, they frankly ran instead of remaining to receive enemy bayonets in their guts. American rifles could hit a sizable target at four hundred yards, while British muskets, though they fired perhaps four times as fast, scarcely could hit the same target at seventy-five. Nevertheless, since musket fire was delivered in volleys, the record of hits was fairly high. On the whole the musket was preferred by both sides for regular military formations, and the rifle was utilized by skirmishers. In time the lessons of the Revolution percolated military skulls and radically altered European tactics by the introduction of open-order combat.

The wild Americans broke the rules in other ways. The careful parade-ground battle tactics of Europe had been developed to substitute etiquette for the horrible bloodshed of the religious wars of earlier centuries; with these had come the rule that war was a test of strength, not of right and wrong, for it was evident that wars fought for principles could end only with complete collapse. War, moreover, was the business of professionals, and laymen were excluded. Now the Americans, both Patriots and Loyalists, with the complete lack of comprehension that was to be expected in such a wilderness, tossed civilized rules aside and returned to the savage sixteenth century. They flouted humane professional standards and fought to kill. They ignored the line between professionals and civilians; they hanged civilians on the opposite side and plundered civilians on both sides. Civilians, in fact, took pot shots at the regulars and gathered in guerrilla bands to fight and plunder. Prisoners of war were sometimes slaughtered or abused, and conventions regarding prisoners were broken. Worst of all, they resurrected the horrors of ideological warfare. War was no longer a game, but was fought to win; that was one reason why the rules had been tossed overboard. One suspects that there was something wrong with the official estimate that only four thousand American soldiers were killed in the war. **Revival of ideological warfare**

Though the United States at the beginning of the war had something under three million people, it was never able to raise an army that was either large or good. Congress provided for a regular establishment, the Continental Line. Though it had two hundred thirty thousand enlistments, so many of these were repeaters that we have no idea how many individuals there were. It was well organized and dependable, but it was poorly equipped and was usually paid in worthless Continental scrip money. Practically all Americans of military age were family men who worked hard for a living and whose crops would not tend themselves. Since they received so little to maintain their families, they had a tendency to take French leave to help with planting or harvest. The indifference of the responsible civil authorities to the plight of the freezing and starving soldiery should do something to excuse the several serious mutinies which Washington had to meet. To the mutineers' credit, however, they refused to be tempted by offers of aid by British agents. Washington, who knew and appreciated the qualities of the Continental Line, wrote of their unparalleled perseverance throughout the war as "little short of a standing miracle." **Continental Line**

It would have been more efficient and less expensive in the long run to have recruited and trained and paid a dependable professional force of fifty thousand men. But that was not what Congress saw fit to do, partly because English experience had been that standing armies were a menace to liberty. The Revolutionary armies, therefore, were swelled by militia units called out for a few weeks or **The militia** months to meet a particular crisis. Americans have never been a militaristic people. Bellicosity is more our style—an emotional splurge, a quick campaign with brilliant victories, not much hardship, and a return home to mother to plant corn, bask in glory, and agitate for a bonus and promote Congressional investigations. This was the nature of many of the Indian wars, and from this standpoint the Spanish-American War was ideal. When the battle began, the militia seldom stood more than the first volley but hastily went home; such action was reasonable, for otherwise how could they have become ancestors of patriotic societies of sons and daughters?

Washington was continually annoyed by the unreliability of the militia. "The collection of the militia," he wrote, "depends entirely on the prospects of the day; if favourable, they throng to you; if not, they will not move." A nose for victory is a very valuable asset, as was proved on several occasions when decisive American victories were won largely by the militia. Indeed, there was nothing inherently cowardly in the Americans, as a number of British commentators noted with some surprise. What they lacked was the training which makes the soldier able to withstand a bayonet charge and the leadership on which they could rely in time of crisis.

The United States had few good generals in the European sense. Most of them had served in the French and Indian War and gained their commissions by political pressure by their state delegates. Most of them at best could be rated only as competent, and they **American leaders** had a tendency toward grandstanding and trying to rank their fellows. However, they usually improved with experience: this category included such men as John Sullivan, Anthony Wayne, Henry Knox, John Stark, Philip Schuyler, and Benjamin Lincoln. A few, notably Benedict Arnold and Nathanael Greene, were natural-born generals. Most of the British and Irish-born generals who had been trained in the British armies were mediocre; among these were Charles Lee, Horatio Gates, and Arthur St. Clair. More significant was a group of European volunteers which included Baron von Steuben, a Prussian, who was the drillmaster of the Revolution; Count Casimir Pulaski and Thaddeus Kosciusko of Poland; and the Baron de Kalb and the Chevalier du Portail, Frenchmen. There were, of course, numerous other volunteers, some of them in search of their fortunes. The Marquis de Lafayette, the first of the French volunteers, was a charming lad whose prestige with the French court made his major-general's commission a good investment; he was a sincere liberal and a courageous and efficient soldier, but he never distinguished himself in his independent operations.

The selection of Washington as commander in chief was one of Congress's few political choices which exhibited genius. If any other man could have done what George Washington did, it is not now apparent who he was. Washington was a younger son of Augustine Washington, a farmer in Virginia's Northern Neck. The family was among the earliest settlers of the colony but would not appear to have been in the top drawer of the socially élite. After a brief schooling Washington became a surveyor for Lord Fairfax, one of the colony's greatest landowners, and it is likely that contact with the Fairfaxes helped to civilize a nature that was naturally rather arrogant and violent. Though he did not have much formal schooling, he was fairly well read in literary and political works, and even more so in agriculture, which was his life-long love. Lawrence, an older brother, had married into Fairfax wealth, and this eventually came to George along with the famous Mount Vernon estate on the Potomac at the head of tidewater. Washington's resources were further increased by his marriage to Martha Dandridge Custis, a widow with two children. Washington himself never had any children.

George Washington (1732–99)

Meanwhile he had served in the French and Indian War and had become brigadier in command of the Virginia troops on Forbes's expedition against Fort Duquesne. Thereafter he retired to manage his estate, though he also served as a county justice and was active in the House of Burgesses and as a militia officer. His interest in western lands was whetted by his bonus claims and by the stark fact that his plantation, like others in Tidewater Virginia, was not as profitable as he could wish, even though he stopped raising the soil-robbing crop of tobacco as early as 1765. He was a shrewd manager and land speculator, and he has been credited with having been the richest man in the colonies; if this was true, he must at the same time have been land-poor. As the Revolution approached, Washington was active among the radical planters; and though he never was ranked as a speaker, the party's confidence in his judgment was such as to win him election to both the First and the Second Continental Congress.

Early career

Washington was well over six feet in height and had a long, strong face, blue eyes, and reddish hair. Though he was athletic in his youth and retained unusual strength and capacity for hard mental and administrative work, he was subject all his life to whatever diseases might be prevalent, and they often laid him low at most inconvenient times. He was ambitious, but his good sense was shown by the fact that he often sacrificed his own opinion or advancement in the interest of harmony, though he was ready to assume responsibility and invariably stood up for the rights of his men. He was a better listener than talker. His intellect probably was not brilliant, but his thought processes usually resulted in sounder judgments than were formed by his more assertive and perceptive fellows. His common

Washington's character

demeanor was cold, partly because he was shy and sensitive, also because he possessed a quick temper which he had to keep under constant guard.

His dignity of bearing was so great that in a lesser man it could only have indicated a stuffed shirt, but even his enemies rarely implied that. The grim line of his mouth was probably due to the fact that his teeth troubled him, and later in life when he wore false ones they were hard to retain. However, he knew how to relax among his social equals and had among them a reputation for wit and charm as well as the ability to win loyalty and affection. His relaxations were the usual ones of cards, wine, balls, hunting, and horse racing. He was an Episcopalian and a Free Mason. He was not democratic in the sense of being equalitarian, either socially or politically, but he possessed the warmth of heart, the sense of duty, and the willingness to work and sacrifice for the public welfare that distinguishes the better aristocrats in every generation.

It is a wonder that Washington was not ground fine between the upper and nether millstones of Congress and the army. He was forbidden to maintain discipline and then criticized by the very same men for not doing so. Impossibilities were demanded, and when deliveries were made they were criticized because they were not miracles. Obviously no military move was made but what someone on the Board of War could have told him better. It is not necessary to insist that Washington was a military genius in order to defend his reputation; indeed, like those under him, he learned his job as he went along, sought to use wisely the few military resources and the little military knowledge he had, and emerged with a creditable though by no means brilliant military record. As a matter of fact, he did not during the whole war win a single full-dress field battle, and on several occasions he barely escaped losing his entire army.

Commander in chief

Washington was something more valuable than a military genius would have been in the American wilderness—a great leader and a great man. In the midst of defeat, with his men starving in their shacks and melting away to their homes, he never lost faith, and this faith was transmitted to most of those about him. He possessed a graven patience and perseverance which in spite of frustrations at the hands of Congress and intrigues against him by subordinates enabled him to keep an army together to betoken resistance. This was a tremendously important object in the first half of the war; for if the army vanished, there would go with it the only chance of winning the foreign support that was absolutely essential to victory. In the chaotic state of the country it was inevitable that Washington should be touted as the dictator who could (and in fact had the duty to) restore national order; on one occasion a Colonel Nicola "offered" him the

Washington's services

crown, but received a stern rebuke for his good offices. Until his retirement in December 1783, Congress seems never to have lost a touch of fear that Washington would yet become "a man on horseback."

The strength of the United States lay in its vast area, which enabled its generals to trade space for time and to keep the British worn out and continually guessing. British generals who ventured far from their coastal bases could expect defeat or at best failure. The weakness of the United States lay in the jealousies and indifference of its people. The true division of American sentiment will never be known, but the best guess is that about one third were enthusiastically rebellious, one third were actively or quietly for the king, and the other third desired to be let alone to hoe their corn. The Independence Party was by far the most dynamic, and it forced action of one sort or another on the others. Many Loyalists found it unhealthy to remain at home and consequently flocked to the cities under British control and into the British army. Tories and neutrals in the interior fled by the thousands from the tar and feathers of their neighbors to Kentucky; there the raids by British and Indians forced them to abandon their principles and take a stand, and the stand they took was naturally in defense of their scalps.

Division of American people

It should be noted that the dynamism of the Patriots was chiefly exhibited in their own neighborhoods, and that they relaxed to the extent of actual obstructionism when the war passed on to other areas. This relaxation made recruiting especially difficult after the French came to the rescue, and the Continental army actually had to draw on prisoners and deserters for recruits. One wag has pardonably exaggerated the situation to the extent of saying that at the close of the war the American army was made up of Britishers and the British army of Americans— that is, British deserters and American Tories. Before the peace the British army had enlisted a total of about 60,000 Americans, which was actually more than double the number that Washington ever had under his immediate command at one time, and probably more (including militia) than ever marched under the American flag at one time except at one high spot in 1776.

The Revolution was no sooner under way than it developed that the Americans objected not only to Parliamentary taxation but to any taxation. The theory was that Congress would make requisitions on the states, but in practice the states rarely honored the requisitions to the full amount; indeed, it was often literally impossible, simply because people would not or could not pay their taxes. Currency was still the great lack, and resort to paper money was inevitable—and so was its train of woes. There was intense suffering among city workmen, price controls broke down, and the black market

Continental finances

flourished. Merchants and landholders made fortunes out of the situation, then plumped for sound money. Nevertheless, paper money in the form of promises to pay was a form of forced taxation, so the people did not succeed completely in shrugging off their financial duty.

Altogether about $450,000,000 of Continental and state currency were floated; after the collapse of Continental paper in 1779 part of it was taken back for taxes at the depreciated rate of forty of paper to one of silver and destroyed; "not worth a Continental" became an apt phrase. Over $60,000,000, chiefly in Continental paper, were received for Continental bonds, which were eventually redeemed. A little under $8,000,000 was borrowed abroad, and foreign gifts amounted to about $2,000,000. The debt was further increased after the war, principally by loans in Holland.

The student of the Revolution must consent to immerse himself in a chronicle of gloom. The bickerings and intrigues in the halls of Congress were imitated in the states, in the army, and among the diplomatic **Ineptness** representatives abroad—or in many cases originated there. **of Congress** That many of these struggles were over vital procedures, **gress** policies, and rights does not invalidate the fact that the greater struggle for independence was set back. Washington complained that "speculation, peculation, and an insatiable thirst for riches seems to have got the better of almost every order of men." At another time he added gloomily: "Virtue and patriotism are almost extinct." Congress was weak because the popular will behind it was weak; finances were straitened in large part because the people were not willing to sacrifice. Trade boomed in spite of the partial blockade, and the merchant class prospered as never before. Franklin in 1779 remarked that "the extravagant luxury of our country in the midst of all its distress is to me amazing."

The political split between radicals and moderates was evident even in the First Continental Congress. During the first five years of the Second Continental Congress the radicals, led by the "Lee-Adams Junto," **Federalism** were usually ascendant. As the name indicates, this was an alliance of Virginia and Massachusetts in which the several Lees and Adamses were respectively the most prominent leaders. They were on the whole the party of democracy, decentralization, agrarianism, and free trade. The last item appealed to some merchants who dealt in staples which would presumably suffer by trade regulation. This party upheld what was then called federalism, by which they meant that the states should retain sovereignty and make co-operation among them no more than the voluntary action of the members of a league.

Such men had noses that could "snuff" tyranny in the moderates' program of aristocratic leadership, centralization, commerce, and regulated trade. Indeed, the moderates favored a degree of nationalization

which scared the Junto. They were ready to eradicate state
lines or at most retain the states as administrative units of   **National-**
a strong national government. They were for the most part   **ism**
members or associates of the commercial community in the North. Their
leader was the merchant prince Robert Morris of Philadelphia. Morris,
who was Confederation treasurer from 1781 to 1784, has probably received too much credit for his work in that office; actually he seems to
have accepted the office only to impose a central financial control and to
line his pockets with the profits of flyers made on the basis of inside
knowledge.

In actual practice, principles were sometimes overshadowed as the
two parties for purely political reasons ranged themselves on opposite
sides of almost any issue. Washington was counted as an adherent by the
nationalists even though he did not go all the way with their
ideas and so became a target of federalist suspicion. It   **The parti-**
seems to have been the Lee-Adams party which backed the   **san conflict**
"Conway Cabal" in the winter of 1777–78 in its abortive attempt to replace Washington by Horatio Gates. This had no sooner collapsed than
Arthur Lee and Silas Deane, former envoys to France, quarreled over
whether the arms furnished by Beaumarchais were a gift (Lee) or a loan
(Deane), and this question became a *cause célèbre* which for years
rocked the American political structure. The federalist ascendance over
Congress began to decline in 1781 as the conservative reaction was felt
in the states.

One must be careful to assess a considerable degree of the failure of
Congress to the unco-operativeness of the states as well as to inexperience and to the too common attitude that an intention is as good as a
deed. Congressmen, of whom most were by no means well-   **Accom-**
to-do, lived hungrily and worked hard. Some things were   **plishments**
done. Considerable effort was made to encourage the manu-   **of Congress**
facture of rifles and gunpowder and to set up iron and brass foundries,
though the supply remained far below the need. About ninety per cent
of the gunpowder had to be imported, but by one means or another there
was usually, after the first months, a sufficient supply; once in 1775
Washington obtained a supply stolen from the magazine of a Bermuda
fort with the connivance of the islanders.

When we turn to the British side of the war effort, the things we see
definitely lighten the gloom of the American picture. British soldiers
were better equipped, better fed, and better paid; and the credit of the
British government held up, though sadly strained. How-   **British**
ever, the British, considering their chances of success, mud-   **leadership**
dled even more than the Americans. Their initial mistake   **inept**
was the same one made by Napoleon and Hitler in Russia: a lack of
comprehension of the significance of great spaces. The British won most

of the battles, but they never conquered the deplorable conditions of transport in America, and so they were handicapped whenever they were drawn far from their bases. Their generals as a whole were even closer to mediocrity than the American commanders. Their dilatoriness, over-confidence, and needless blundering were so apparent that it led to accusations that some of them, at least, wanted to lose the war. Certainly some of them were Whigs and would not have been disappointed at the failure of the Tory program, but it is likely that they merely reflected the defects of their class and training. One must consider also the distaste of the professional soldier for garrison life and for retirement on half pay.

Even more important was the natural penchant of a European-trained army for conducting war according to the book. In this respect, at least, the disorganization of the Americans sometimes actually gave them superior resilience and enabled them to make quick come-backs after defeats. The British also were hampered by detailed but vague and contradictory instructions from a ministry that knew nothing of American conditions. The ministry chose, moreover, to act through the Secretary of State for the Colonies, Lord George Germain, who had been court-martialed and expelled from the army for cowardice, who hated the generals to whom he was dictating, and who was cordially hated in return.

It is an odd fact that, though the British Isles had around ten million people, the government was unable from the first to raise an adequate army. Soldiering was the business of professionals, and the average civil-**The British army** ian patriot gladly left it to them. Parliament had always feared the power and resented the expense of a standing army and insisted on reviewing its status and support in an annual Mutiny Act, and after every war tore down the military structure with an enthusiasm which we have duplicated a number of times. At the beginning of the Revolution the permanent establishment included on paper about 48,000 men, and by 1781 it had climbed to 110,000. Obviously this was not enough to fight a world war even in that day; and since the ministry did not dare risk public displeasure by enforcing universal service, it hired mercenaries from six German princes, eventually to the number of 30,000. They are known in American history as Hessians because most of them and their commanders came from Hesse-Cassel.

In addition, it is estimated that about 60,000 American Tories were enlisted at one time or another in regular and auxiliary bodies; but for years they were distrusted and insulted by the British, and their value was not recognized until it was too late. This, at least, was the claim of the American Tories as expressed by Joseph Galloway. There is reason to suspect that they exaggerated, and that their plan was not to fight in regular bodies but to engage in guerrilla warfare with its opportunities for private vengeance and plunder. At any rate the Tories, it should be noted, were regularly enlisted for long terms and fully trained and so did not vanish from the service after a few weeks or months like the bulk of

QUALIFYING for a CAMPAIN

A British view (1777) of how to train for war in the colonies

American soldiers. The British forces in America probably never reached 100,000 at one time.

An examination of other aspects of the British effort affords no relief. The navy was at the low ebb of the century due to the corruption and inefficiency of its management under Lord Sandwich. It was not until the end of the war that it pulled itself together and delivered some victories. The services of supply in both army and navy were still under the old system whereby the managers reimbursed themselves by taking a percentage of the money that passed through their hands, and they found further and illegal means of increasing their cut, such as sale to civilians and purchase of spoiled and defective supplies.

Corruption in British services

The importance of American access to the sea cannot be overemphasized, for it was by sea that the bulk of their supplies came in; and, moreover, the sea had to be kept open for the transport of French reinforcements. American privateers, three fourths of them from New England, were active all during the war, and their captures constituted one of the main sources of military supplies. Statistics are unfortunately incomplete, but there were around two thousand of them commissioned; they brought in at least as many cap-

Importance of the sea to Americans

tures and in addition did a great deal of blockade-running with supplies. American losses, however, may have equaled captures. The trade in military supplies at neutral West Indian ports was vital to the American resistance, especially during the early years; and the importance of one of them, the Dutch possession of St. Eustatius, was such that when the British Admiral Rodney took it early in 1781 he captured 2000 Americans, about 50 American ships, and £3,000,000 value of goods. However, much of the spoils while in transit to England was recaptured by a French fleet.

With the exception of Delaware and New Jersey, each one of the states had at one time or another a little navy. Their functions were to capture prizes and to protect the coasts against British raiders; many a stout action was fought that has long since been forgotten.

American navy Arnold's little fleet on Lake Champlain, composed chiefly of galleys and gondolas, was effective in delaying a successful entry by the British into the upper Hudson Valley in 1776. Probably it rates as the most important American naval venture of the war, even though Arnold's fleet was defeated and destroyed in the end.

The Continental navy at one time or another included about seventy ocean-going vessels of all categories and made sundry raids on British West Indian islands and even Great Britain itself. It was obviously impossible to meet the British navy in fleet action, so the fleet was gradually reduced almost to the vanishing point after the French entry into the war. Under the new flag, "The Stars and Stripes," it carried on some spectacular raids in European waters, and the victory of John Paul Jones in the leaky old *Bonhomme Richard* over the superior *Serapis* (1779) has become a classic of the sea. On the whole, the naval service suffered in comparison with the privateers, for the latter offered less perilous ventures and greater prize money.

If the survival of the American cause depended upon the ocean, Great Britain lost because of its failure to get control of the sea and keep it. As it turned out, the crucial blow was struck because an incompetent

British fail to use naval strength admiral lost control of Chesapeake Bay and with it lost Cornwallis's army at Yorktown. Indeed, the Englishmen's basic failure from the first was in misapprehending the problem before them. Their element was the ocean, and the mere fact that they had defeated some Hindu rajahs on land did not excuse them for assuming that they could win a land war in a wilderness defended by their own kin. The whale went ashore and exhausted himself in useless marches. Certain observers had seen this from the first and advised the ministry not to try to seize and hold the wilderness but to occupy the chief ports as bases and from them seal the coast with a naval blockade. And yet, despite the costliness of its strategy of land warfare, the ministry might have succeeded in its bull-headed program if it had not been for France. It was the French entry into the war that disclosed the weakness of the whale-on-land strategy and led to the overextension which almost ruined the Empire.

Could the United States have won its independence without French aid? The answer is embarrassingly clear. If the Americans had been as united and as desperate as the Dutch rebels against Philip of Spain, they could have made good their independence in short order **Could the** even against a well-conducted British opposition. Their **Rebels have** effort was favored by strategic advantages and by the mag- **won alone?** nificent leadership of Washington, but it was never united and whole-hearted and only sporadically did it show signs of really grim determination. Congress seems to have assumed almost from the first that independence could be assured only by foreign aid. We would most certainly have been conquered if the struggle had not turned into a world war that was too big for Great Britain to handle by the methods the ministry had adopted.

2   Military and Diplomatic Conflict

Before its close the American phase of the war was so overshadowed by its significance as a world conflict that British diplomats and strategists were willing to write off the struggle with the Thirteen United States as a minor phase of the whole. The object of the continental powers was to trim down the overweening **World war** strength Britain had gained in the Seven Years' War by shearing the Empire of important segments of its colonies, bases, and trade. In the main they succeeded, and the outcome of this war was that Britain sustained her only defeat in the long series of conflicts. Even at that she was able by clever maneuvering to break the full force of the disaster.

Reduced to its simplest terms, Washington's task was to keep an American army in existence and fighting in order to convince Europe that it was worth while to enter the conflict against Great Britain. This entailed two strategic necessities: first, the British coastal armies must be confined to their seaports and not permitted **American** to occupy the interior; second, the American rear must be **strategy** protected by preventing the Canadian British and their Indian allies from breaking through the Appalachian barrier. Within a couple of years of the battle at Lexington a third factor rose: the Americans must win a victory so important that it would warrant hesitant France in entering the fray. The war was won in the East and on the ocean, but we will turn first to contributory events on the frontier.

The vulnerable points in Washington's rear were three. First was the

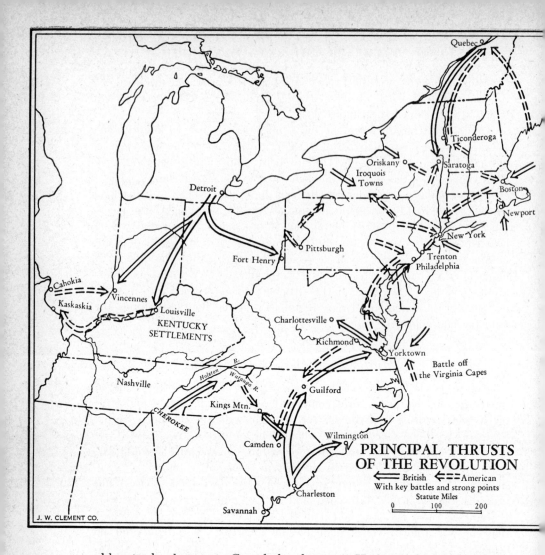

PRINCIPAL THRUSTS
OF THE REVOLUTION

⟸— British ⟸=== American
With key battles and strong points
Statute Miles

J. W. CLEMENT CO.

old water-level route to Canada by the upper Hudson, which led to Lake
Ontario by the Mohawk River and to the St. Lawrence by way of Lake

**Appa-
lachian
gateways**

Champlain. The first was occupied by the Iroquois, now
much reduced in power but still dangerous. The Champlain
route was flanked on the west by the Iroquois and on the
east by the Green Mountain Boys under the leadership of the three
Allen brothers: Ethan, Ira, and Levi. The British stronghold of Detroit
menaced the two widely separated pioneer settlements in Kentucky and
on the Monongahela (around Pittsburgh), both of them then administratively part of Virginia. Both areas controlled portages and paths
across the mountains by which it would have been feasible for light-
armed British and Indians to have fallen on settlements in the Great
Valley and the Piedmont and to have diverted their supplies and man
power from Washington's armies. The third frontier menace was the

252

Cherokee, who lived in the valley of the upper Tennessee and whose natural enemies were in the new white settlements around Watauga and at Nashville.

The Revolution in the West was a story of raid and counterraid, of sieges, massacres, and often fruitless heroism. Though Fort Pitt was occupied by Continental troops and made the key in a line of strong points, it was chronically undermanned and undersupplied. Kentucky and Tennessee were, in general, left to take care of themselves. Pioneer communities usually built centrally located blockhouses to which they could repair when the alarm was given. More ambitious defenses, called "stations," were also community homes; they were great quandrangles enclosed by palisades, cabins, and blockhouses. Woods-wise scouts haunted the warpaths to detect approaching raiders. Small companies of rangers sometimes stood ready for instant pursuit whenever a war party was reported near by.

War on the frontier

The Indian nations of the upper Ohio Valley, especially the Shawnee and Delawares, asked nothing better than to see the British and Americans eat each other up. The habitual highhandedness of the pioneers, however, had by 1777 forced them into war—an end to which the British contributed by bribes, blandishments, and a perpetual guarantee of their hunting grounds. There is good evidence that the Americans would have gladly utilized the Indians (and did at times) but did not have the price; moreover, their record was against them. Though the western frontier settlements were in continual peril, it is of interest that their population increased manyfold: Kentucky rose from a few hundred to possibly ten thousand, and Nashville was settled in 1780 in the midst of the war. Though many of the settlers were Tories or neutrals, they were forced to defend themselves against the raiding parties of British, Tories, and Northwestern Indians which Governor Henry Hamilton of Detroit began sending out in 1777. The British policy of encouraging the raiders by offering bounties for scalps and prisoners greatly embittered the frontiersmen and led to Hamilton's odious and possibly unjust memory as the "Hair-buyer."

The first hostilities began in 1776 in the South, when the Cherokee attacked the frontiers of Georgia and South Carolina with some success but were repulsed from the Watauga and Holston settlements. The next year the Cherokee towns were destroyed by converging white forces, and the defeated nation obtained peace only by considerable land cessions to the Carolinas. Some Chero-

Cherokee Wars, 1776–81

kee and Creek elements known as the Chickamauga kept up sporadic warfare until 1780, when war again became general. Once more the Cherokee towns were destroyed, and the main body of the nation thereafter remained at peace.

By the end of 1777 the raids from Detroit had become so terrible that the settlers of Kentucky and even of the Monongahela country seriously considered abandoning their homes and recrossing the mountains. **George Rogers Clark saves the West** A remarkable young frontiersman named George Rogers Clark (1752–1818) stepped into the breach. Armed with Virginia authority, he gathered a tiny force of less than 200 riflemen in the Monongahela country early in 1778, descended the Ohio, and marched across the southern part of Illinois and seized the British posts at Kaskaskia and Vincennes. The inhabitants in the area were French and gladly supported Clark. When Hamilton moved down from Detroit with eighty men and retook Vincennes, Clark led double the number of Americans and French through midwinter floods, captured the fort once more (1779), and sent the "Hair-buyer" prisoner to Virginia. Clark never succeeded in mustering a force large enough to take Detroit, but by his incessant vigilance and frequent blows during the rest of the war he kept the British in a state of alarm and preserved the vital screen of transmontane settlements. On the other hand, Virginia's military control of the Illinois country became so tenuous that it is a moot question whether it played any part in the American demand for possession of the West at the time of the peace negotiations.

The third frontier episode concerned the Iroquois. The outbreak of the Revolution caused the Tories of the Mohawk Valley to flee, among them the son and nephew of Sir William Johnson, and John and Walter **The New York frontier** Butler, father and son. It was the Mohawk Valley Tories who were chiefly instrumental in defeating the Montgomery-Arnold invasion of Canada. The invasion of upper New York by Burgoyne will be treated later, but a part of the plan was for these Tories to join with the Iroquois under Chief Joseph Brant to attack Fort Stanwix. The result was their repulse at Oriskany (August 1777) by a little army of determined German settlers under General Herkimer.

During the rest of the Revolution a furious frontier war raged in the northern wilderness between Continental troops and settlers on one side and Iroquois and Tory Rangers on the other. The outstanding events were the Tory and Indian attacks on Wyoming, Pennsylvania and Cherry Valley, New York (July and November 1778), which were accompanied by Indian atrocities. The next year Washington sent converging expeditions under General John Sullivan against the Iroquois towns in the Finger Lakes region. Forty towns and 160,000 bushels of corn were burned. A large part of the Iroquois perished in the succeeding winter or fled to Canada, and thereafter the raids weakened.

We return now to the main thread of war in the North and East. When Howe sailed away from Boston to Halifax, it was virtually certain that he would descend next upon New York. It was a Tory stronghold, and even its Whigs were still opposed to independence; it lay at the center of the northern colonies; it controlled one end of the vital Hudson River route to Canada; and since **British plan in 1776** it was located on islands it was considered easy to defend by a fleet-supported army. Obviously it was difficult for Washington to defend New York without a fleet and even without heavy coast artillery, but at the behest of Congress he undertook to do so with a force composed of

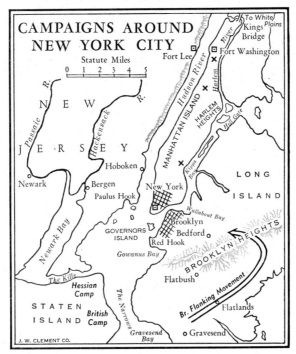

around 20,000 untrained and poorly equipped men. The British plan was for Howe to attack New York by sea and for Carleton to come overland, but the ill-fated American expedition against Canada had so scattered British ships, troops, and cannon that Howe did not appear until the end of June 1776. It will be remembered that this was the summer of Arnold's gallant defense of the back door at Lake Champlain. These were fateful delays which may have saved the cause of independence.

The force which invaded New York consisted of 30,000 troops under Sir William Howe on a fleet of one hundred ships commanded by his brother, Admiral Lord Richard Howe. The brothers exercised joint author-ity both to direct the war and to treat for peace. In the Battle **Campaign** of Long Island (27 August 1776) the British outflanked the **around** American lines, and Washington lost about 1500 men and **New York,** was able to withdraw his forces to Manhattan Island only **1776** because rain and fog gave him cover. Though the British were in control of the water, Washington undertook to defend another island. The inevitable happened: the Americans retreated northward, fighting a series of engagements most of which were lost. When the British threatened New Jersey, Washington divided his forces between the two banks of the Hudson; his object, of course, was to maintain control of this vital gateway to the interior. The Manhattan sector of the American army was largely captured, and Charles Lee with 7000 men in Westchester refused to obey orders and come to Washington's support in New Jersey.

There was nothing for Washington to do with his rapidly diminishing force of less than 5000 troops but retreat across the Delaware into Pennsylvania, which he reached on 8 December. The plan of campaign called for Howe to advance up the Hudson and aid in crushing Arnold, but instead his troops chased Washington across New Jersey and arrived at the Delaware just in time to see the Americans land on the other bank. Washington had made a gallant attempt to defend an impossible position and survived only because Sir William Howe missed several opportunities to write finis to the war. Lee's disobedience was followed by his capture and by a year's imprisonment, during which he engaged in an attempt to "reconcile" the contestants.

A lesser man than Washington would have given up, but defeat only spurred him to recruit the strength of his army. Then on Christmas night he crossed the Delaware through the floating ice, seized the Hessian **Trenton** garrison of Trenton, threw the British up and down the **and** river into panic, and took about 1000 prisoners back to **Princeton** Pennsylvania. He then recrossed the river and near Princeton on 3 January 1777 defeated a British column. After that he occupied the heights at Morristown, New Jersey and so seriously threatened Howe's lines that the British troops were withdrawn to New York. These blows naturally gave American morale a much-needed lift. At the same time Howe's deliberate policy of plunder and maltreatment of prisoners in order to teach the Americans a lesson had quite the opposite effect.

The British plan for 1777 was not very different from that of the year before, but this time it was General "Gentleman Johnny" Burgoyne who was to sweep away the American army in upper New York. At this **British plan** time the politicians of Congress were engaged in a ridicu- **for 1777** lous game of alternating Philip Schuyler and Horatio Gates in command of the army in the North, and there actually were five shifts in the command from one to the other in fifteen months. Burgoyne's task did not seem very difficult to the British ministerial optimists, and they proposed at one fell swoop to do away with one pestiferous American army, cut off New England from the rest of the country, and place Burgoyne and Howe in a position to polish off

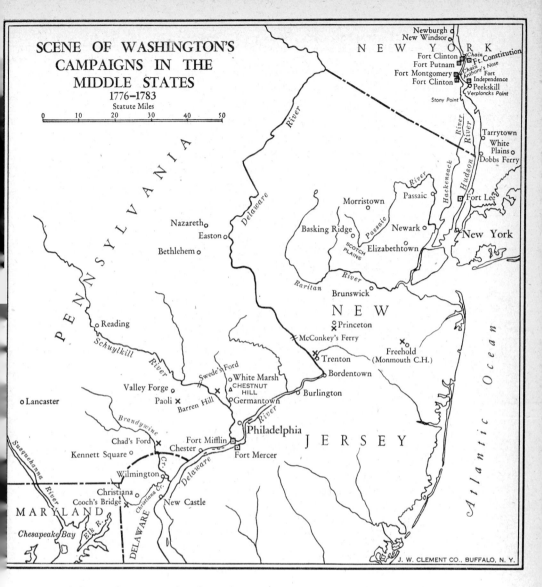

SCENE OF WASHINGTON'S
CAMPAIGNS IN THE
MIDDLE STATES
1776–1783
Statute Miles

remaining resistance. It has been long believed that Howe was to advance up the Hudson to meet Burgoyne but never received the orders. The fact seems to be that Burgoyne was expected to be fully able to care for himself, and that Howe had leave to strike a blow at Philadelphia. Howe was, however, supposed to open the lower Hudson—which he did not do. Howe supposed that he was supporting Burgoyne by occupying Washington's forces; actually Washington seriously weakened himself to send reinforcements to Gates.

This time Howe went by sea, and because the Delaware was well defended he went to the head of Chesapeake Bay. There Washington vainly opposed his advance at Brandywine (11 September). Howe

257

Howe in Pennsyl- vania quickly occupied the capital, found a warm welcome from the élite, and settled down to a snug winter after beating off an American incursion at Germantown early in October. Washington fortified himself at Valley Forge some eighteen miles to the west. There his army spent an unusually mild winter, but hundreds died of disease and malnutrition. "Naked and starving as they are," said Washington, "we cannot enough admire the patience and fidelity of the soldiery."

Disaster now overtook Burgoyne. He must have felt a premonition when St. Leger with his Tories and Indians was defeated at Oriskany, and two large plundering parties comprising over one thousand men **Burgoyne's surrender, Saratoga, 17 Oct. 1777** were defeated separately by the New Hampshire militia under General John Stark near Bennington, Vermont. When the news of these successes was spread, the volatile New York and New England militia hastened to Gates's colors until he had about twelve thousand militiamen in addition to five thousand Continentals. In September and October two actions known variously as the First and Second Battles of Stillwater, Bemis Heights, or Freeman's Farm were fought near Saratoga. Gates was technically entitled to the credit for the victory, but it has been all but universally begrudged, especially by the adherents of Arnold. In fact, both men were inordinately ambitious and not at all averse to contention and intrigue to promote their own power and glory.

At any rate, on 17 October 1777 Burgoyne surrendered 4500 men with the "convention" that they should be shipped back to England and take no further part in the war. Howe planned to recapture Burgoyne's troops at sea and add them to the New York garrison, but Congress did not know this and seized a much weaker excuse to reject the terms. For six years the so-called Convention Army was shuttled back and forth between Massachusetts and Virginia until by the peace half of its number had been lost by exchanges, paroles, hardship, disease, and evaporation.

The surrender at Saratoga was the decisive event of the Revolution. Even before the battle at Lexington French spies had been reporting jubilantly on American events, and the merchants and the court of **French goodwill** France were ready to enter the war as soon as there was a reasonable chance of success. Much more vocal were the intelligentsia, who had been trained in liberalism by Voltaire and the Encyclopedists and now found in American state papers and in the embroidered deeds of American heroes the practical demonstration of their ideals. American ships were permitted to use French ports as bases and refuges. Old Ben Franklin, who had gone over as agent, clad in brown and looking benevolently over his spectacles, padded from one salon to another and enchanted people, intelligentsia and *hautmonde* alike. The courts of both France and Spain had doled out a little secret help through the dramatist Beaumarchais, at that perhaps enough to turn the tide, for the American army at Saratoga was largely armed with weapons from the royal arsenals of France,

Now at the news of Saratoga, Vergennes, the French minister, hastened to act lest the English yield and the golden opportunity be lost. Indeed it would have been but for stubborn George, and even he was willing to give up control of taxation. North introduced a bill to this effect in November 1777, but it rested over a long holiday period and was not passed until 17 February 1778. Meanwhile, on 6 February, the American envoys signed a treaty of commerce and alliance with France, and North's gesture lost its value. This, incidentally, was the only alliance in American history until our own day; and it was very weak, for it only bound us to help defend the French West Indies and not to make peace with Great Britain without the consent of France. Commercial conditions were even more liberal, for France violated mercantile principles by accepting a "most-favored-nation" proviso and agreeing that in time of war "free ships make free goods." **Alliance with France, 1778**

The paradox in the alliance is apparent: by the military and financial strain of war the French monarch hastened revolution and brought himself to the guillotine; the Thirteen States were now joined in alliance with the very power which had for a hundred years been loosing scalping savages on their borders. Perhaps on both sides there was that touch of opportunism if not desperation expressed by Egerton, "when our house is burning, we do not inquire too curiously into the moral antecedents of those who hand the water-buckets." The alliance was a fruitful subject for Tory pamphleteers, and its effect was so apparent that the French minister in America hired Tom Paine as a counterpropagandist. Many Americans were never reconciled to the French alliance, and Benedict Arnold's treason was in some part due to resentment against it.

Hostilities between Britain and France began with a naval action off Ushant in June 1778. Spain hesitated to encourage openly any rebellion of colonies, but she longed to recover Gibraltar and Florida, so in June 1779 she made the plunge. Florida fell promptly, and the British threat against Georgia and the Carolinas from that direction was removed. The British, in order to hamper their enemies' supplies, had revived the Rule of 1756 which forbade neutrals to engage in a commerce with belligerents which the belligerents had forbidden to them in peacetime. Catherine II of Russia sought to counter it in 1780 by forming a League of Armed Neutrality. The league insisted that "free ships made free goods" and that belligerent goods (except contraband) could be carried on neutral ships; contraband was **Europe against Britain** limited to goods already specified in treaties; and blockades of enemy ports to be legal must be close and effective. The league armed its merchantmen to enforce these rules and invited other powers to join. Eventually it included the Scandinavian nations, Austria, Portugal, the Two Sicilies, and Prussia, which last had been looking for a means of getting back at George III ever since he had abandoned her at the close of the Seven Years' War.

Dutch merchants had been active in supplying American military needs, and Holland adhered to the league in the vain hope that it would be some protection against British wrath. At this time Congress adopted a policy, called "militia diplomacy," of sending agents around to the European courts in search of alliances. One of these agents met a Dutch merchant who quite without authority drafted a treaty. When Henry Laurens of South Carolina was sent over as agent to The Hague, he was captured by a British ship. He threw his papers into the sea, but they were fished out, and a copy of this "treaty" was found among them. The Dutch government protested its ignorance of the document, but the ministry, anxious to avoid having to take a stand on the armed neutrality, seized on this excuse to force the Dutch into the war, in December 1780. The league wanted a general war no more than Britain did and abandoned Holland to its fate. The result was that the league became what Catherine called an "Armed Nullity," which promulgated high moral principles but preserved peace by realistic diplomatic arrangements. The provisos of this rather involved league agreement were adhered to by the United States and were to become the basis of our diplomacy during the long Napoleonic Wars.

The campaign of 1778 opened in a new spirit of hope. Sir William Howe at the close of his snug winter in Philadelphia was replaced by Sir Henry Clinton, who was ordered to return to New York largely because of the threat of D'Estaing's French fleet. Washington overtook Clinton on 28 June in New Jersey near Monmouth, and Charles Lee, returned now from captivity, failed to make good an attack; in the end the army was saved from disaster only when Washington took charge after violently reprimanding Lee and sending him to the rear. Eventually Lee was dismissed from the service. Meanwhile D'Estaing joined in an abortive attack on Newport, which had been occupied by the British since 1776. A storm damaged the fleet, and for repairs it put into Boston, where there were the usual waterfront brawls between allies.

Events in the North

Washington invested New York, and the British emerged only to raid the surrounding coasts. The "Neutral Ground" between the armies was haunted by bands of robbers called "skinners," who represented themselves as adherents of either side as it suited their convenience. The one remaining outstanding event of the war in the North was the treason of Arnold. His offer was to surrender West Point as the price of a command in the British army, but he had to flee when some papers found on a British spy (Major John André) disclosed his intention. He got his command and a money grant, but the British were barely polite to him and let him out as soon as the war was over. The rest of his life was spent in fruitless commercial ventures. He died in 1801 at the age of sixty.

The principal scene of warfare now changed to the South, where the British had high hopes of exploiting the strong Loyalist sentiment in that region. Savannah was seized as a base in December 1778. D'Estaing and General Benjamin Lincoln attempted its recapture, but the Frenchman for reasons which seemed good to him abandoned the effort and sailed off to the Caribbean to **War in the South** pick up sugar islands. Clinton brought an army south, and Lincoln allowed himself to be bottled up in Charleston and in May 1780 surrendered with 5000 men. Clinton left Lord Cornwallis in command in the South and returned to New York; by this time D'Estaing's activities in the West Indies had forced Clinton to evacuate Newport and send the troops to bolster the Caribbean garrisons. Nevertheless, British power in the Carolinas was such that American regular forces practically ceased to exist; however, the bitterness of the people caused an acceleration of the savage guerrilla warfare which had been going on for years. But British commanders of Loyalist troops, such as Tarleton, Ferguson, and Rawdon, rode where they pleased. Congress sent Gates south with 3000 troops, but he was overwhelmed at Camden, South Carolina in August 1780 by Cornwallis and Rawdon. Gates fled seventy miles that same day before he even wrote a report. There were extenuating circumstances for the disaster, the usual ones of starvation, lack of equipment, and the unreliability of militia. Gates was permitted to serve for a while at the close of the war, but the public never forgot that his "northern laurels" had "turned to southern willows."

Cornwallis moved into North Carolina and stopped at Charlotte while his parties scoured the country for horses, provisions, and recruits. In October one thousand mountaineers from the Watauga settlements and beyond and led by Isaac Shelby, John Sevier, and others appeared in the Piedmont. After being joined by as many more Carolinians, they attacked a force of about **King's Mountain, Oct. 1780** one thousand Loyalists, who under Major Patrick Ferguson were fortified on King's Mountain. The Loyalists were totally defeated in a bitter battle, practically all of them being killed, wounded, or captured. It was

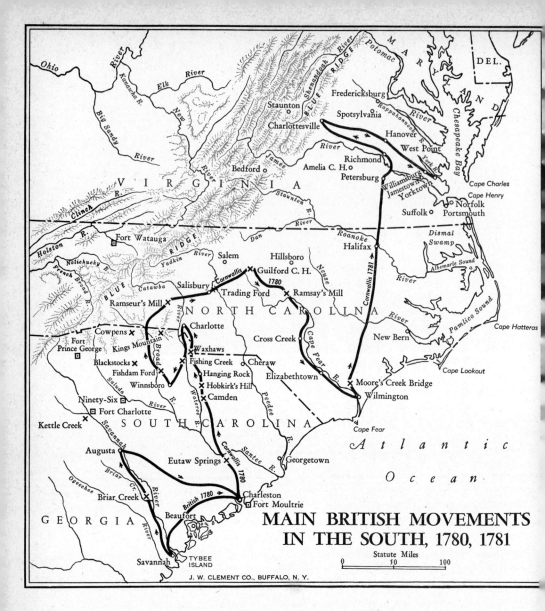

MAIN BRITISH MOVEMENTS
IN THE SOUTH, 1780, 1781

Statute Miles

0   50   100

J. W. CLEMENT CO., BUFFALO, N. Y.

not a great battle, but Clinton wrote that it "proved the first Link of a
Chain of Evils that followed each other in regular Succession until they
at last ended in the total loss of America."

General Nathanael Greene now came south to organize the defense.
Under his direction Daniel Morgan moved into South Carolina, but when
Tarleton appeared he retreated northward and won a brilliant delaying
Greene re- action at Cowpens in January 1781. Cornwallis sought to
takes the prevent Morgan's junction with Greene but failed, and he
Carolinas pursued them to Virginia. While he was congratulating him-
self on controlling the Carolinas, Greene returned to North Carolina and

262

fought at Guilford Court House a battle which was more or less a stale-mate but caused Cornwallis's ragged and hungry army to withdraw to Wilmington for supplies. The interiors of Georgia and the Carolinas now fell to Greene, though every important battle he fought was lost. The inability of the British to maintain themselves away from their bases was never more evident, but the inability of the Americans to take these bases was just as evident. Cornwallis now resolved to carry the war to Virginia, where Lafayette and Arnold, the latter now in command of a British force, had been maneuvering between the Blue Ridge and the Chesapeake. Upon his arrival Cornwallis was ordered to fortify a military and naval base at Yorktown. He protested but was overruled and sulkily undertook the task.

A juncture of events now made possible the allied capture of York-town. A French army of 6000 men under Rochambeau lay at Newport, and Washington with 6000 men was watching New York. As Washington saw, a navy was so essential to victory that it had the cast- **Naval pre-** ing vote in any operations, and he sent an aide to the French **liminaries** court to ask for naval aid. Partly as a result of this request **to York-** a French fleet under De Grasse reached the West Indies in **town** the spring of 1781. Admiral Rodney was so busy counting his prize money at St. Eustatius that De Grasse was able to secure control of the Caribbean and turn his attention northward. Yorktown and New York were the alternative objectives which Washington put up to De Grasse, and the admiral chose Yorktown. Meanwhile Rodney, who was ill, sailed to England on leave, and his fleet was left to Hood. The admiral guessed that De Grasse was going north, and so he followed, looked into the Chesa-peake, and then went on to New York. He missed De Grasse because the Frenchman sailed slowly.

Meanwhile the French fleet at Newport sailed with Rochambeau's siege artillery, but not even on Hood's arrival a few days later did it dawn on Clinton and the senior admiral, Graves, that certain mysterious actions of Rochambeau might mean a movement to Vir- **Battle off** ginia. Rather, it was supposed that the two French fleets **the Virginia** merely had a rendezvous in the Chesapeake, so Graves de- **Capes** parted with nineteen men-o'-war to look for them. De Grasse was already there, with twenty-four ships of the line. On 5 September the two fleets met in an action off the Virginia Capes in which the British received the worst usage; then De Grasse decoyed the British southward for four days while the French fleet from Newport slipped into the bay. De Grasse pro-ceeded to sail for the Chesapeake; and Graves, fearing to tackle him again, abandoned Cornwallis and returned to New York.

The fate of Yorktown was sealed. The French and American armies were brought down the bay in De Grasse's ships, and on 30 September

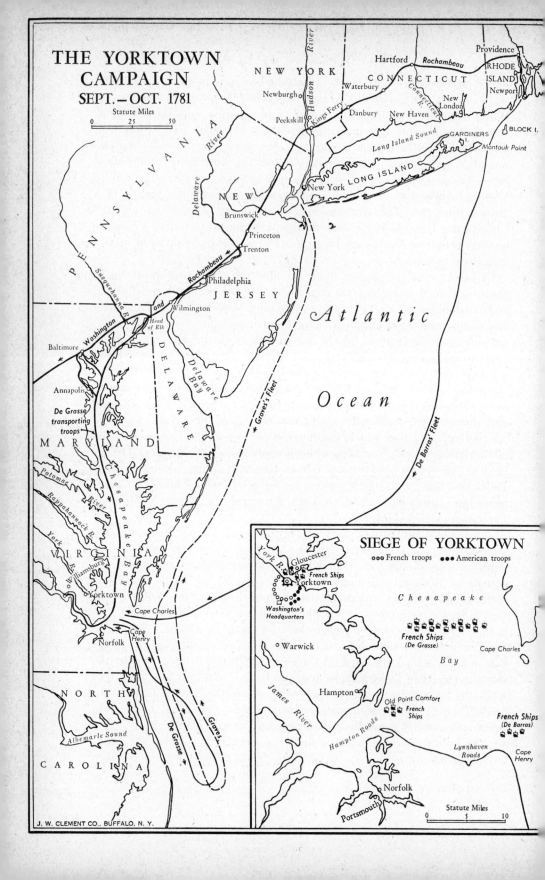

THE YORKTOWN CAMPAIGN
SEPT. – OCT. 1781

Statute Miles

0   25   50

NEW YORK

Newburgh
Peekskill
Kings Ferry
Waterbury
Danbury
Hartford
Rochambeau
CONNECTICUT
New Haven
New London
Providence
RHODE ISLAND
Newport
BLOCK I.
GARDINERS I.
Montauk Point

Long Island Sound

Hudson River

PENNSYLVANIA

Delaware River

NEW JERSEY

Brunswick
Princeton
Trenton
Rochambeau
Philadelphia
Wilmington
Head of Elk
Washington

New York
LONG ISLAND

Atlantic Ocean

Susquehanna R.

Baltimore
Annapolis

DELAWARE

Delaware Bay

MARYLAND

De Grasse transporting troops

Potomac River
Rappahannock R.
York R.
Williamsburg
Yorktown

VIRGINIA

Chesapeake Bay

Graves' Fleet

De Barras' Fleet

Cape Charles

Norfolk
Cape Henry

NORTH CAROLINA

Albemarle Sound

De Grasse

Graves

J. W. CLEMENT CO., BUFFALO, N. Y.

SIEGE OF YORKTOWN

ooo French troops   ●●● American troops

York R.
Gloucester
French Ships
Yorktown
Washington's Headquarters

Chesapeake

French Ships (De Grasse)

Cape Charles

Warwick

Bay

James River

Hampton

Old Point Comfort
French Ships

Hampton Roads

French Ships (De Barras)

Norfolk

Portsmouth

Lynnhaven Roads

Cape Henry

Statute Miles

0   5   10

the siege was begun. The preponderance of strength in this, the final battle for American independence, was French. Rocham- **Cornwallis** beau had about 7000 troops (3000 of them brought from Haiti **surrenders** for the operation) and the fleets had about 24,000 men; **Yorktown,** Washington had only 9000, of whom about 5500 were Conti- **Oct. 1781** nentals. Cornwallis had over 7000 men, but these were not enough to man his extensive fortifications, and he was so ill and confused that he actually abandoned his outer works, the possession of which might conceivably have enabled him to hold out until succor arrived.

The only assault was delivered on 14 October 1781, when two British redoubts were stormed; prominent in the assault was young Alexander Hamilton, recently an aide on Washington's staff. On the 19th Cornwallis surrendered, and his troops marched into captivity with their music playing "The World Turned Upside Down." Graves appeared two days later with reinforcements. Cornwallis and Clinton began a bitter altercation over the responsibility for the disaster which lasted for years. De Grasse had commitments with the Spanish in the Caribbean which made it inadvisable to join in the conquest of New York or Charleston, and so he sailed back to the West Indies. There, the next April, he received a smashing defeat from Rodney in the Battle of the Saints. The French naval ascendancy had lasted just long enough to guarantee American independence.

The desperate plight of Britain is shown by the fact that she found it literally impossible to replace Cornwallis's army. In addition it brought the Parliamentary crisis which had long been threatening. Merchants were hampered by the perils and shortages attendant on **Why** world war and longed for trade to reopen, and the growing **Britain** popularity of the ideas set forth in Adam Smith's *Wealth of* **granted in-** *Nations* made them increasingly indifferent to the political **dependence** allegiances of their customers. The country gentry now found their zeal cooled and instructed their representatives to vote for peace and economy. The fact was that Great Britain's debt was practically doubled, and the country was on the verge of bankruptcy.

There was nothing for the king to do but yield. North now carried out his recurrent threat to resign, and in March 1782 he was succeeded by a Whig ministry headed by Rockingham, Shelburne, and Charles James Fox. They saw just one way to save something from the wreck of the Empire. That was to cut their losses in North America and concentrate their forces on saving the situation in the rest of the world. Essentially that is what happened. Peace negotiations were carried on in Paris, with the British ministry represented chiefly by a Scottish merchant named Richard Oswald.

Congress had four peace commissioners in Paris: Franklin, John

Adams, John Jay of New York, and Henry Laurens of South Carolina. Adams did not arrive from his post at The Hague until October 1782, **American** and Laurens, who was a prisoner in the Tower of London, **peace com-** was even later. The instructions of Congress were that the **missioners** commissioners were to be guided by Vergennes. This order sounded well, but, after all, Vergennes was working for the enhancement of France first and Spain second, and he was (at first) anxious to pro-

Culver Service

"The Reconciliation Between Britannia and Her Daughter America" was a British propaganda cartoon (1782) intended as an aid to the peace talks which were then going on.

long the war until Gibraltar could be taken. Actually Vergennes saw little reason to favor the United States, for since the alliance its people had become increasingly indifferent to the conflict and refused to bear more than a minimum share of the burden.

Now John Jay was a suspicious man. His Americanism made him suspicious even of the Whig ministry; as a member of Congress and minister to Madrid he was perfectly aware of Spain's desire to limit the new nation to the Appalachian ridges to protect Louisiana; **Jay's dou-** and, since he was of Huguenot descent, he had reason to **ble cross** hate France. Before Yorktown Vergennes had intrigued for peace on the basis of *uti possidetis,* which would have given to each side the territory it held; that is, the British would have retained the ports they held, and the United States would have been confined to about the territory Spain wished. Various suggestions made by Vergennes for carving up the Indian country at the expense of the American claim to the West showed that he still placed the old Family Compact with Spain ahead of the welfare of his new American ally. Jay knew, moreover, that Vergennes wished to extend French rights in the Newfoundland fisheries and exclude the United States from them. By the terms of its alliance with France the United States could not make a separate peace, but Jay was not a man to be impressed either by the instructions of Congress or by a paper agreement with France. He proposed to overreach Vergennes and Spain and sign a favorable "preliminary" treaty of peace with Great Britain. In the end he carried Franklin over to his program.

At first the British ministry was apparently willing to cut the United States loose with the free gift of Canada to prevent future friction. But while Jay caviled at diplomatic protocol, the tide of the war began to run in Britain's favor. Rodney defeated De Grasse; the Spanish and French attack on Gibraltar weakened; the **Peace negotiations** French were going broke; and American public opinion was becoming incredibly indifferent to what happened. Actual negotiations did not begin until September 1782, and by then it was too late to obtain Canada, if the ministry had ever seriously considered its cession. Nevertheless, the terms granted were more generous than those that either France or Spain would have supported. The preliminary treaty was signed 30 November 1782, but it did not become technically effective until the general peace was signed at Paris, 3 September 1783.

The peace terms were as follows: 1) Great Britain acknowledged the independence of the United States; 2) the boundary was essentially what the United States now holds east of the Mississippi (except Florida), but it was vague in the Maine area, in the Lake of the Woods area, and along the Florida border; 3) American **Peace terms** "liberty" to fish in Newfoundland and Canadian waters was acknowledged; 4) British merchants were to "meet with no lawful impediment" in collecting their debts; 5) Congress agreed to "earnestly recommend" to the states that Loyalist property be restored.

The meanings of all of the articles except the first were open to doubt and led to long and acrimonious dispute. The last two especially were purposely indefinite because the commissioners knew very well that Congress would accept nothing stronger. The ministry's desertion of the Loyalists was a factor that led to the fall of Shelburne (Rockingham had died), and it was another ministry that signed the definitive peace.

Very little Loyalist property was ever restored, and legal impediments definitely were placed in the way of the collection of debts; the last issue passed through many vicissitudes until finally in 1802 Congress

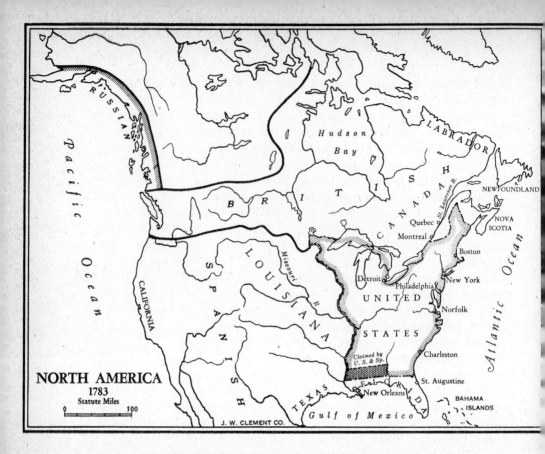

NORTH AMERICA
1783
Statute Miles
0   500

Pacific Ocean

RUSSIAN

CALIFORNIA

SPANISH

LOUISIANA

Missouri R.

Mississippi R.

TEXAS

Hudson Bay

BRITISH

CANADA

St. Lawrence R.

LABRADOR

NEWFOUNDLAND

NOVA SCOTIA

Quebec
Montreal
Boston
Detroit
Philadelphia
New York
UNITED
Norfolk
STATES
Claimed by U. S. & Sp.
Charleston
St. Augustine
Fl.
New Orleans
FLORIDA
BAHAMA ISLANDS

Gulf of Mexico

Atlantic Ocean

J. W. CLEMENT CO.

Both sides break the treaty appropriated £600,000 to be divided among the creditors. An excuse for impediments and delay was found in the fact that Great Britain kept possession of seven military and trading posts—five points on the New York border including Niagara, and Detroit and Michilimackinac—until 1796. There is no doubt that Great Britain deliberately did so in order to keep the Indian trade as long as possible. Another excuse was that the British had carried off many Negro slaves in violation of the treaty. This problem was to survive well into the next century and to be finally settled by arbitration.

Posterity has in general agreed with Jay's view that France was prepared to sell us out and that it would have been foolish not to auction her off first. Apparently Vergennes was not greatly worried. The day **French reaction to American action** before the preliminary articles were signed he congratulated the American commissioners on their favorable terms, then used the American defection as a prod to force Spain to end a war of which France was getting weary. He did not, however, fail to emphasize the moral obliquity of the American action; in a masterly reply Franklin pointed out that the English flattered themselves that they had already divided the allies, and with magnificent effrontery asked for a thwacking big loan to recement the alliance. He got it.

3   *The Social Revolution*

We have seen that a deep fissure separated the two wings of the Revolutionary movement. The moderates (we may now call them con-servatives) opposed independence to the very last because they saw that it would strengthen the advocates of social change, whom **Wings of** they had been fighting long before the issue of imperial **the revo-** control became dominant. It was only with the deepest **lutionary** misgivings that such men as Washington and Dickinson **movement** chose the risk of social chaos to the certainty of imperial regimentation. Thereafter they acknowledged no major issue except that of independence; otherwise things must remain as before. The radicals agreed on the goal of independence but insisted, also, that the dominance of wealth and aristocracy must go and that the people must rule.

Let us examine first the ideas on which the two wings *most nearly* agreed. Their experience with royal tyranny had convinced most of them of the general desirability of placing the principal authority in a local government rather than in a central or national power. **Commonly** They agreed with Tom Paine that government was the **accepted** natural enemy of the people and with Jefferson that if lib- **political** erty were to be preserved the chief powers must be exercised **ideas** by authority close at hand and subject to the immediate veto of the people. Just who should vote and just what should be the precise apportionment of power between local and central authorities was, of course, a matter of conflict. At any rate, most men agreed that the executive must not be permitted the independent powers wielded by the colonial governors. Constitutions must be written, so that there would be a minimum amount of dispute over their provisions, and they should specifically assure civil liberties by a Bill of Rights. Finally, most agreed that political rights must be based on a reasonable economic independence, usually in the form of land ownership, and the citizen who did not have this economic independence was not entitled to vote.

The result of this localism was seen in the Articles of Confederation. Lee had proposed the setting-up of a confederation at the same time he proposed independence. Little time was lost in drawing up a plan (it was largely the work of John Dickinson), but it did not **Struggle** reach a form which pleased Congress until November 1777. **over Arti-** The conservatives, as men of property who were anx- **cles of Con-** ious to repress the radicals with their leveling ideas, **federation** favored a strong government, but the fear of central authority still pressed even on many of them. After all, the issues were much the same as those which had led to rebellion: representation, taxation, commercial regulation, paper money, western lands, and Indian affairs. The result, was that the agrarian localists got their way. Then for reasons which will appear later Maryland refused to ratify it until 1781, after which it went into effect on 1 March. It is easy to misinterpret the character of the new Union because we think in national terms; actually the designers of the Articles avoided any assertion that they were setting up a national government and called their creation "a firm league of friendship."

The Articles of Confederation failed to give the central government effective power to manage common welfare and even left it without an executive and judiciary (except admiralty courts), lest they encroach on the liberties of the states. All national powers were placed **Nature of** in the hands of Congress. Taxes were to be raised by requi- **the Articles** sitions on the states. Control of commerce remained with the states even though foreign relations, Indian affairs, currency, and the army and navy were under the control of Congress. Each state had one vote, and important decisions could be made only by consent of nine states; amendment must be by unanimous consent. The states reserved the concurrent right to issue currency and coin money, they made laws concerning contracts and debts, and finally they could with the consent of Congress exercise many of the very powers so grudgingly given to Congress. Just to make sure that Congress did not overstep its boundaries, the army was to be made up of troops raised, officered, and equipped by the states.

The basic defect was that the Confederation government could not operate on the individual citizen and did not have the strength to coerce the states, so such powers as it had were in some danger of becoming meaningless. It set up very much the same sort of government as the Americans had conceived of the king as exercising over the British Empire. Their mistake was in not realizing that the colonies must be welded into a nation, not an empire. Still, this was probably the best federal constitution the world had yet seen, and if it had been accepted as a basis of evolution it might have worked.

The struggle between conservatives and democrats was best seen in the states. The back-country men had the equal voice in the Revolutionary bodies which had been denied them in the colonial legislatures, **First state** and together with the coastal radicals succeeded in taking **constitu-** over several of the new state governments, notably Rhode **tions** Island, Pennsylvania, Delaware, North Carolina, and Georgia. Constitution-making was usually hastily and rather sloppily done by the state congresses, and only occasionally as in Massachusetts was a constitutional convention elected and the result submitted to the vote of the people. Connecticut and Rhode Island, in fact, simply kept their colonial charters with the king deleted.

Colonial experience with governors led most states to strengthen the legislature at the expense of the executive. This was notable not only in the extremely democratic constitution of Pennsylvania but in the extremely conservative constitution of South Carolina. Economic independence was still the basis of the franchise, and in no state were all officials elected by manhood suffrage. The chief differences that marked democrats over conservatives were three: first, the legislators were chosen in proportion to the population; second, the amount of property necessary to empower a man to vote and to hold various offices was very low; and third, the power of the upper house of the legislature was strictly limited in favor of the lower. Pennsylvania and Georgia, in fact, set up unicameral legislatures.

One of the most significant effects of the Revolution was on the land. Quitrents were abolished, and taxation to support public functions was substituted. Congress had recommended that the lands of open Tories be confiscated and sold, and the money used for the prosecution of the war. It is certain that men with ready cash were able **Land** to buy vast holdings at ridiculously low prices; and indeed **problems** many of them may have stirred up mob action in order to drive out proprietors whose land they coveted. Nevertheless, thousands of small holders were also created by the policy of confiscation. Somewhat different in method was the purchase of the Penns' land claims by Pennsylvania for £130,000 and of the Calverts' claims by Maryland for £10,000.

The story of land speculation in the West is not pretty. Men with money and influence bought up soldiers' land-bounty claims or took advantage of the offer of Virginia's Land Office to receive the state's depreciated paper money in payment for land. The result was that speculators cut out millions of acres which they held **Influence of** vacant for a rise in price while the thin frontier of actual **speculators** settlers fought to develop and protect the country. There was also a recrudescence of the great land companies, among them the Vandalia Company, now split into the Indiana and Vandalia companies; and the Illinois-Wabash Company, a merging of old cessions made by the Indians. The activities of the speculators extended from the Mississippi to Paris and involved Americans, Englishmen, and Frenchmen alike in *sub rosa* intrigues which placed profit before national loyalty and besmirched such names as Franklin, Morris, and Patrick Henry. The decisions of Congress, the loyalty of the West, and even the fortunes of war depended too often upon the self-interest of these land speculators.

It was chiefly due to the struggle between Virginia and her old enemies, the great land companies, that we owe the acquisition of the public

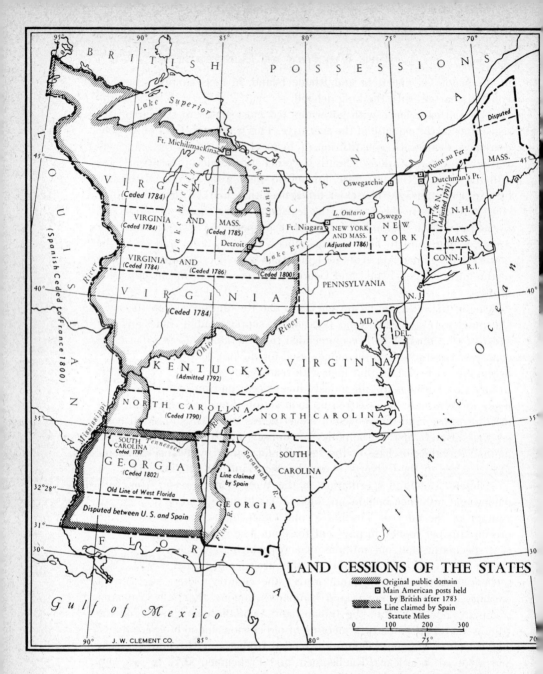

LAND CESSIONS OF THE STATES

- //////// Original public domain
- ☐ Main American posts held by British after 1783
- ▓▓▓▓ Line claimed by Spain

Statute Miles

0   100   200   300

J. W. CLEMENT CO.

domain. The land companies, which were largely owned by citizens of states without western lands, and which had negotiated directly with the Crown were anxious to have the West belong to the Confederation government. The Illinois-Wabash Company, which was largely owned by Marylanders, got Maryland to refuse to ratify the Articles of Confederation until the states with western

Origin of the public domain

lands should cede them to the Confederation. The hold-up was defended on the ground that since the western country had been won by the common blood and treasure, it should not be permitted to belong to a few states and eventually to so swell their strength that they would menace the rest.

The action, of course, was aimed at Virginia, whose western claims covered everything now between Tennessee and the Canadian border and included the claims of New York, Massachusetts, and Connecticut. New York set the example by yielding her claim (such as it was), and Congress helped the good work along by promising to erect the cessions of western lands into states which should be equal to the original thirteen. Virginia, invaded by Arnold's British troops, agreed to cession in the hope that Congress would feel more like sending help. However, the terms of the cession were carefully planned to kill the great companies; so, even after Maryland yielded, the speculators got New Jersey to block acceptance of the cession. Finally in 1784 Congress got tired of the game and essentially took Virginia's terms.

The Vandalia and Indiana companies perished because their claims lay south of the Ohio, and Virginia ceded only the land north of the river; the Illinois-Wabash Company likewise folded, for Virginia's cession was made on the condition that private land claims based on Indian purchases must be given up. All of the states with western claims gave them up, though Georgia held out until 1802 for reasons that will appear in good time. The result of the struggle was that the land companies were defeated, Virginia retired with limited gains, and democracy held the field. Right down to our own day the public domain has been one of the central factors of American history.

The continued existence of a privileged class in the colonies had depended upon the retention in a few hands of great blocks of property. This had been assured by primogeniture, by which all the property of a father who died intestate went to his eldest son; and by **Primogeniture and entail**, which provided that a certain block of property could not be alienated but must descend as an unbroken unit from generation to generation. The Revolutionary years saw a general assault on these two institutions, though both had already been weakened by exceptions and had long been out of public favor. Entail pretty well vanished by 1786, and primogeniture by 1800. The breaking-up of great estates was thus accelerated—though they were far from disappearing— and democracy was strengthened by the increase in small holdings. This victory, however, was soon countered by an increase in industrial and fiscal wealth and by the growth of great estates in the Southwest.

An equally dramatic assault was made on established churches. The Congregational establishments in New England were too firmly planted to be shaken until the next century. The Church of England, on the other hand, was a symbol of British authority and in spite of its roll of patriots harbored what may perhaps have been the majority of overt Tories in both North and South. To work for its disestablishment was therefore regarded by its enemies as a work of patriotism and of democratic sympathies.

Disestablishment and new national churches

The battle was bitterest in Virginia, where Jefferson led the struggle for this reform as he had that for the abolition of entail and primogeniture. As a matter of fact, religious freedom had been almost complete in the colonies; these actions only legalized the situation. The way was now clear for the organization of churches on national lines. The Methodists were first when John Wesley sent over a rule for their governance and Thomas Coke to serve as superintendent along with Francis Asbury, who had come before the war. The colonists had resisted the appointment of an Anglican bishop on the ground that he would be an instrument of tyranny; now that the church was disestablished the way was open for the consecration of James Madison, a cousin of the President, as bishop of Virginia. John Carroll of Maryland was the first Roman Catholic bishop, consecrated in 1790.

The more thoughtful of the Founding Fathers were quite conscious of the inconsistency between their demand for liberty or death and the holding of Negro slaves. Patrick Henry, for example, yielded to the social pattern but refused to excuse himself morally. Congress in 1774 approved a nonimportation agreement prohibiting the slave trade, and by 1798 all the states had forbidden the trade.

Beginning of emancipation of slaves

The first antislavery society was formed in Philadelphia in 1775 by Quakers, and others followed. Rhode Island headed the list of free states in 1774, and in 1780 Pennsylvania provided for gradual emancipation. In the *Quock Walker Case* in 1781 the Massachusetts supreme court decided that slavery could not exist in the state because the Constitution declared that "all men are born free and equal."

By 1804 all of the states north of Maryland had emancipated their slaves or provided for gradual emancipation, and the southern states were debating the problem. Economic conditions made slavery unprofitable in the North, and emancipation posed only a minor social problem; but the South had ninety per cent of the half million Negroes in the country, and they were so intertwined with the social and economic pattern that their emancipation would have posed well-nigh insuperable problems for both themselves and the society in which they lived. Nevertheless, it is likely that slavery would have gradually disappeared even in the South had it not been that the cotton gin provided a powerful economic argument against the developing trend.

Such activities as the foregoing show not only enlightened self-interest but also a broadening moral and intellectual horizon. Though the war had closed many schools, education was recognized as the basis of democracy, and public schools received a fillip in the North and in the West. In 1783 Noah Webster published his speller, and it **Broadening** was followed by a reader; a geography by Jedidiah Morse **horizons** appeared in 1784. Unfortunately public schools were not as well received in the South, and Jefferson suffered one of the great defeats of his career when Virginia voted down his scheme for popular education, though it later on agreed to his plan for a University of Virginia. It was a forecast of the future in the South, for as is natural in an aristocratic society collegiate education has always received more attention than lower public schools. Another evidence of a broadening horizon was the growth of national sentiment, though the accusation might be made that it received more lip service than actual co-operation. At any rate, the people began to emerge from the colonial stage of distrust of the hereditary enemies. France, particularly, became the subject of study; indeed, French fashions and French thought became a fad.

The psychological effects of the Revolution were such as thoughtful people expect after any war. Resentment between soldiers and civilians ran at high tide, each being unfair to the other. Civilians felt that the soldiers were worthless and irresponsible fellows who had **Psychologi-** evaded their economic duties and lived the life of Riley at **cal after-** public expense; soldiers felt that they had shed their blood **math** in defense of an ungrateful nation, and the officers organized the Society of the Cincinnati, not merely to keep old memories fresh but also to lobby for a bonus of five years' pay to make up for their losses by inflation. Resentment on the part of both soldiers and most civilians against war profiteers also ran high, for obvious reasons. The profiteers, on the other hand, ostensibly regarded themselves as public benefactors whose ability to produce the needed goods was worth the modest few-hundred-per-cent profit they had made. Feeling against the Tories was probably worse at the close of the war than at any previous time, and even those areas which had tolerated them now mobbed and robbed them, often at the instigation of "patriot" profiteers who sought to buy in choice Tory property before it was too late. The war psychology, as we shall see, gradually passed away, but its resentments broadened and complicated social divisions and endangered the delicate balance which is essential to ordered evolution.

No less evident were the effects on manners and morals. The newly-rich aped their Tory predecessors, but their crudeness and insecurity led to arrogance and ostentatiousness. Many schools and churches had been closed, and this action may have removed a moderating influence from the behavior of both old and young. Drunkenness and delinquency increased, and the old standards of business and society were weakened. Not least among the losses was that of a certain stateliness and dignity; the old staidness of life passed away, never to be renewed, at least in the same forms.

One of the greatest mistakes made by the conservatives was in allowing and even encouraging the expulsion of the Loyalists. These people were, in the North at least, the ablest and best-educated part of the population, nor were they dastardly enemies of liberty; on the **Fate of the Loyalists** contrary, they simply took the strong side in a controversy to which we today are willing to admit there were two sides. While in general those Loyalists who took an oath of allegiance to the new governments, paid their taxes, and did not encourage the enemy by word or deed were not expelled, those who were lost to the country through death or exile have been estimated as high as one hundred thousand. At any rate, their absence seriously weakened the cause of conservatism during the postwar period.

Most of the exiled Loyalists, of course, suffered economically for their stand and were only partially relieved when the British government allowed their claims to the extent of about £3,300,000. Many Loyalists made a new start in England, remained in the army or navy, or eventually returned to the United States. Many obtained land grants in the West Indies and Canada. The Provinces of New Brunswick and Ontario were chiefly settled by Loyalists; the United Empire ("UE") Loyalists of Ontario and their descendants constituted the ruling element of that province for generations and have always been the staunchest opponents of American penetration. A little-known footnote to history is that a unit of the Continental Line was composed of Canadians who after the war could not return to Canada. In 1801 the survivors were given land in the Canadian Refugee Tract in central Ohio.

In casting up the balance sheets of the American Revolution, it is apparent that out of the war came both a tragedy and a blessing. The seed was sown of a long rivalry between the two nations. American de-**Long-range results of independence** velopment, unchecked either by experienced administrators or by a deeply rooted native aristocracy, entered upon a course of headlong democracy which was often as oppressive as liberating. Perhaps if the Americans had remained part of the British Empire and eventually become part of the British Commonwealth of Nations, the *Pax Britannica* might still dominate the world and encourage orderly growth. There might have been no world wars, no Russia and Germany resurgent in the same senses as in our time, because it would obviously have been foolish to combat so great a combination devoted to the cause of peace and law.

On the other hand, as things turned out, we have seen that democracy can appear in various forms. The United States has been a moderating influence in modern imperialism, both because of its example and because its existence has forced rulers to moderation—as Britain in Canada. It is conceivable that without independence America might have had a saner growth, but it would never have attained the tremendous power which has enabled it to cast a deciding sword into the scale against predatory doctrines.

BIBLIOGRAPHICAL NOTE

The Nature of the War

AMERICAN ARMY: See Louis C. Hatch, *Administration of the American Revolutionary Army* (1904); and Charles K. Bolton, *The Private Soldier under Washington* (1902). Allen Bowman's *The Morale of the American Revolutionary Army* (1943) is fascinating and significant, but it presumes considerable knowledge of the period. Carl Van Doren, *Mutiny in January* (1943) concerns the most serious mutiny, that of the Pennsylvania Line in 1781. Sketches of the chief American military leaders are in Joel T. Headley, *Washington and His Generals* (2 v., 1847). See also John M. Palmer, *General Von Steuben* (1937) and the series on Lafayette by Louis R. Gottschalk.

AMERICAN NAVY: See the following: Gardner W. Allen, *Naval History of the American Revolution* (2 v., 1913); Charles O. Paullin, *The Navy of the American Revolution* (1906); Edgar S. Maclay, *History of American Privateers* (1899); Alfred T. Mahan, *Major Operations of the Navies in the War of Independence* (1913). There are numerous biographies of John Paul Jones; the most detailed is by Mrs. Reginald De Koven. An interesting episode in the history of American supply is told in John F. Jameson, "St. Eustatius in the American Revolution," *American Historical Review*, 8:683–708 (July 1903).

WASHINGTON: Since the first quaint mixture of fact, legend, and hero-worship published by the pack-peddler Parson Weems, in 1800, many eminent historians and men of letters have followed suit. Now being published is Douglas S. Freeman, *George Washington* (6 v., 1948–), which departs from the traditional congealed portrait. Treatments of special aspects include P. L. Haworth on Washington as a country gentleman; T. G. Frothingham, as commander in chief; H. L. Ritter, as a businessman; J. H. Penniman, as a man of letters; C. H. Ambler, in connection with the West; and as the crowning cherry, John C. Fitzpatrick, *George Washington Himself* (1933). Fitzpatrick's edition of the *Writings* (39 v., 1931–44) supplants all previous editions; see also *Diaries* (4 v., 1925).

CIVILIAN ADMINISTRATION: See Edmund C. Burnett, *The Continental Congress* (1941); Charles J. Bullock, *Finances of the U.S., 1775–1789* (1895); Ellis P. Oberholtzer, *Robert Morris* (2 v., 1903); and William G. Sumner, *The Financier and Finances of the American Revolution* (2 v., 1891). The financial historians' view of Morris is unduly worshipful.

BRITISH FORCES: See William M. James, *The British Navy in Adversity* (1926); Edward E. Curtis, *Organization of the British Army in the American*

Revolution (1926); J. F. C. Fuller, *British Light Infantry in the Eighteenth Century* (1925). John W. Fortescue, *History of the British Army* (v. 3, 1902) blames the finagling civilians when military affairs went wrong. For the Hessians see Edward J. Lowell, *The Hessians and the Other German Auxiliaries* (1884). Interesting source materials are R. W. Pettengill, ed., *Letters from America . . . of Brunswick, Hessian and Waldeck Officers* (1924); and *Letters and Journals of the Baroness Riedesel* (1867): the baroness was wife of a German officer.

Military and Diplomatic Conflict

GENERAL WORKS: Most satisfactory is John C. Miller, *The Triumph of Freedom, 1775–1783* (1948). Older and in some respects more detailed are George O. Trevelyan, *The American Revolution* (6 v., 1905–14); Claude H. Van Tyne, *The War of Independence* (1929) carries up to 1778; and Frederick E. Whitton, *The American War of Independence* (1931).

MILITARY HISTORY: To date the old *Field-Book of the Revolution* (2 v., 1851–52) by Benson J. Lossing is unrivaled, but Willard M. Wallace, *Appeal to Arms* (1951) will satisfy the general reader.

MIDDLE CAMPAIGNS: Troyer S. Anderson, *The Command of the Howe Brothers During the American Revolution* (1936) is a useful analysis of ministerial and military points of view; the Howes' program of steady pressure and occupation in force of conquered territory was too costly in men and money for British resources. On New York City during the war see Thomas J. Wertenbaker, *Father Knickerbocker Rebels* (1948). John R. Alden, *General Charles Lee* (1951) defends Lee's actions at Monmouth and while a British prisoner. Leonard Lundin, *Cockpit of the Revolution* (1940) covers the war in New Jersey; Alfred H. Bill, *The Campaign of Princeton, 1776–1777* (1948) portrays a psychological turning point; another crisis is dealt with in Harry E. Wildes, *Valley Forge: Soul of the Revolution* (1938). Alexander Grayson, *Memoirs of His Own Times* (1846) is a valuable personal account.

UPPER NEW YORK: See Francis J. Hudleston, *Gentleman Johnny Burgoyne* (1927); Howard Swiggett, *War out of Niagara* (1933); Hoffman Nickerson, *The Turning Point of the Revolution* (1928); and Samuel W. Patterson, *Horatio Gates, Defender of American Liberties* (1941). The story of Arnold's treason is told in Carl Van Doren, *Secret History of the American Revolution* (1941). The treatment of the Convention Army can be followed in the *Letters and Journals* (1867) of the Baroness Riedesel and in Thomas Anburey, *Travels Through America* (2 v., 1789).

YORKTOWN CAMPAIGN: See Howard L. Landers, *Virginia Campaign and Blockade and Siege of Yorktown* (1931). The part played by the French navy is amply covered in Charles L. Lewis, *Admiral de Grasse and American Independence* (1945). Interesting additional information on the French is in Stephen Bonsal, *When the French Were Here* (1945).

THE WEST: The war in the West and beyond the frontier is covered in Theodore Roosevelt's slap-dash *Winning of the West* (4 v., 1894–96), required reading for all red-blooded American Li'l Abners. Randolph C. Downes,

Council Fires on the Upper Ohio (1940) is a resumé of Northwestern Indian diplomacy from 1720 to 1795. Definitive *Life of George Rogers Clark* (1928) is by James Alton James.

DIPLOMACY: See Samuel F. Bemis, *Diplomacy of the American Revolution* (1935); Gilbert Chinard, *Honest John Adams* (1933); Frank Monaghan, *John Jay* (1935); and the biographies of Franklin by James Parton and Carl Van Doren. Edwin S. Corwin, *French Policy and the American Alliance of 1778* (1916) knocks on the head the idea that the French were solely actuated by friendship to the colonies. Friedrich Edler, *The Dutch Republic and the American Revolution* (1911) deals with a little-known but vital subject. On the whole subject of attempts at reconciliation see Weldon A. Brown, *Empire or Independence: A Study in the Failure of Reconciliation, 1774–1783* (1941).

The Social Revolution

GENERAL: Best treatments are Merrill Jensen, *The New Nation* (1950); and Allan Nevins, *The American States During and After the Revolution, 1775–1789* (1924).

SOCIAL: Classic statement is John F. Jameson, *The American Revolution Considered as a Social Movement* (1926). See also Edward F. Humphrey, *Nationalism and Religion in America, 1774–1789* (1924); Alice M. Baldwin, *New England Clergy and the American Revolution* (1928); Herbert Asbury, *A Methodist Saint: The Life of Bishop Asbury* (1927).

ARTICLES OF CONFEDERATION: Best treatment is Merrill Jensen, *The Articles of Confederation* (1940). For their connection with land speculation see Herbert B. Adams, *Maryland's Influence upon Land Cessions* (1885); and works cited in Chapter VII under the section "Western Lands and the Revolution."

LOYALISTS: See especially Claude H. Van Tyne, *The Loyalists in the American Revolution* (1902). There are numerous treatments of local Loyalists, of which see especially Alex. C. Flick, *Loyalism in New York During the American Revolution* (1901). Arthur G. Bradley, *The United Empire Loyalists: Founders of British Canada* (1932) is good for Canada but must be used with caution in its analyses of American history.

PART II

"NATIONS ARE RENEWED FROM THE BOTTOM."

When I look back on the processes of history, when I survey the genesis of America, I see this written on every page: that the nations are renewed from the bottom, not from the top; that the genius which springs up from the ranks of unknown men is the genius which renews the youth and energy of the people. Everything I know about history, every bit of experience and observation that has contributed to my thought, has confirmed me in the conviction that the real wisdom of human life is compounded out of the experiences of ordinary men. The utility, the vitality, the fruitage of life does not come from the top to the bottom; it comes, like the natural growth of a great tree, from the soil, up through the trunk into the branches to the foliage and the fruit. The great struggling unknown masses of the men who are at the base of everything are the dynamic force that is lifting the levels of society. A nation is as great, and only as great, as her rank and file.

—Woodrow Wilson, *The New Freedom* (1913), 79–80.

THE RISE

OF NATIONALISM

1787–1840

THE TERM AMERICAN REVOLUTION IS IN REALITY A MISNO-
mer, for the war did not change American directions but only accelerated
certain trends which were already evident. These trends, it must be obvious
by now, were toward democracy and nationalism. At the time they were
regarded as inconsistent, and the adherents of each fought for its own
program as the only salvation of the nation. In 1787 they accepted the
Constitution with crossed fingers, each hoping to interpret or mold it to
his ideal. The result was that this became the period in which the battle
for the democratic process was fought and won, with the surprising outcome that the two ideals were found to be not inconsistent but complementary.

The half-century which followed the drawing-up of the Constitution
saw the steady development of American nationalism, nationalism in the
sense of co-operative and aggressive patriotism. When the Constitution
was completed, thirty-five of the thirty-nine men who signed it lived on
or near Atlantic tidewater; sixteen years later that Constitution gave law
to the peaks of the Rockies. The American flag had appeared in the Oregon
country and the ports of the Orient and was soon to fly over the Barbary
castles of North Africa. The rocks of New England and western sectionalism were successfully passed by 1815, but before the end of the period
it was evident that the nation might yet founder on the rock of southern
sectionalism. Nevertheless, this was the period in which the consciousness
of American nationality took hold of so large a part of the people that a
generation later they were willing to offer their lives in defense of the
ideal.

Modern nations are the creation of historical and political forces among which language, race, religion, geography, economics, and culture may have played parts. As a distinct motivating force nationalism was recognizable in a number of European countries before the end of the Middle Ages, but it received its great impetus from the French Revolution. Nations are not likely to spring suddenly into full maturity but usually evolve slowly. This process certainly applies to the United States, for it created the machinery of a national government long before its people were agreed that they constituted a nation. The American people, indeed, long thought of themselves first as citizens, say, of Vermont or Virginia and insisted that the Constitution of 1787 had set up an alliance rather than a nation. This was shown by the common way of referring to the country as "these" United States; it was not until after 1865 that "the" United States became the common form.

Here we shall find evolving nationalism basing itself upon a common vision of expanding democracy and expanding national prosperity and power. But this was the gawky age of America, a time when the operation of the national glands was uncertain and one never knew whether to expect heroism or cowardice, wisdom or shortsightedness, generosity or selfishness in national policy. Tremendous struggles were shaping between rival economic interests as the foundations of industrial and financial empire were laid. The deplorable side of nationalism—its selfishness and intolerance—was too clearly evident. The new was being glorified because it was new, and change was being identified with progress. But the credit side of the ledger was even more evident. Reform was making headway in social, cultural, and intellectual lines. Material advances were raising the standard of living of the common man. Best of all, there had emerged a systematic understanding of the meaning and method of democracy and of the fact that if democracy was to live, the nation must be a unit in its defense.

Chapter IX

THE FORMATION
OF THE FEDERATION

1 *The Confederation Period*

AMERICANS of the Confederation period had definite ideas of why they had fought the Revolution, and they did not propose to lose its fruits by any failure to state their case. For once in American history realism was almost unclouded by any mythus. The propaganda battle of the 1780's was fully as bitter and conscienceless as that of the 1770's. Moral clichés and pious platitudes became the politicaster's stock in trade, and he cited fake statistics to prove that the country was on the verge of chaos unless it swallowed his nostrum. He may not have fooled contemporaries, but he has fooled historians right down to the present. The battle that the men of that day waged was long and loud, but the very multiplicity of the demands at issue forbade a solid victory by any one party.

Realism of the period

It has been customary to divide the contestants between merchants and agrarians; actually the situation was far more complex. True, many merchants wanted navigation acts to assure their own control of imports, exports, and carrying, but they wanted no protective tariffs for manufactures. Such merchants had been black marketeers during the war and had been inveterate enemies of price-fixing; also, they had grown rich. Allied with them in some ways but not in others were the manufacturing interests which had received a fillip from the war. However, in this case investors and "honest mechanicks" joined in wanting protective tariffs.

Partisan issues

Farmers and planters wanted free trade, and they were joined by some merchants who wished to avoid foreign reprisals or who agreed with their planter clients in fearing that navigation acts would be used to promote monopoly and to lower the price of staples. Farmers had suffered from wartime inflation and were now demanding land banks which could loan them money cheaply on mortgage. The money, of course, would have to be paper and legal tender. They demanded, moreover, that prices be controlled and taxes be laid according to wealth. The merchants were naturally horrified at such attempts to limit or control wealth and to interfere with their monopoly of credit. "Money," declaimed Gouverneur Morris, "is of too subtle and spiritual a nature to be caught by the rude hand of the law."

However rudely they might contradict each other on economic issues, these partisans were pretty consistently divided on one thing: they were for or against centralization of the government. Those for it were the "nationalists," in general aristocratic, mercantile, and advocates of sound money and limited credit. Those against it were "federalists," democratic (except for the planters), agrarian, and advocates of easy money and credit. They put their reliance in the sovereignty and dignity of the states and denounced as tyranny any effort to grant to the Confederation any more powers than had been given by the Articles.

"National- ists" and "federal- ists"

The conservative wing of the Revolution had no intention of replacing royal control by democratic control but rather saw the war and independence as ways of securing their own ascendance. They wished to do away with the states or to make them mere administrative units of a strong central government, and during the war they sought to take advantage of popular alarms and necessities to attain their object. The Articles of Confederation did not set up a union strong enough to satisfy them, and the hope of early amendment was dashed by the let-down which followed Yorktown.

"National- ist" pro- gram

Nevertheless, the "nationalists" improved every opportunity. They erected a new bureaucracy with secretaries for Treasury, Foreign Affairs, War, and Posts. They passed ordinances for the organization of the public domain and the sale of its land on generous terms to deserving associates. They were well aware that creditors would tend to support whatever government owed them money, so they worked to have the Confederation assume the state debts contracted in prosecution of the war. They established banks in Boston and New York, and one in Philadelphia (the Bank of North America) which was intended to serve the needs of the Confederation government. They launched new amendments intended to give Congress an independent income and the right to regulate trade. They did not stick even at attaining their objects by force and utilized the discontent of the officers of the Continental Line to promote a plot to set up a government more to their taste. Possibly it was only Washington's address to the army at Newburgh that thwarted the scheme.

The moves of the "nationalists" were by no means lost on the "federalists." They countered by persuading some of the states to take over the payment of soldiers' bonuses and of Confederation debts owed to their citizens. They fought and defeated proposals for amendments to the Articles. They stirred up public antipathy to remaining Loyalists lest they stay in the country and make common cause with the "nationalists"—as did happen. They warned planter debtors that the "nationalists" intended to make it possible for British creditors to collect debts. They told farmers and planters that "nationalist" merchants would seize the monopoly of exports and depress prices. Fortunately for their argument, that was exactly what Robert Morris did when he obtained a monopoly of the French tobacco market. "Federalist" program

Actually the United States of the 1780's was (save for a brief interval) in a boom period. The losses and destruction of the war were being rapidly repaired. The armies had left in their wake three times as much hard money as there had been in the country before the war. New wealth had been created by the public debt, and private manufactures and the standard of living had shot up, at least for many. Societies were being founded to promote research and manufacture of everything from silk to steamboats. Goods were pouring into the country at every port. Shipyards and their attendant industries were bustling with activity. American traders now had the markets of the world in view, and before long they were appearing on the coasts of Oregon and China. Postwar prosperity

The European nations were glad to trade with the United States, and they even partially opened their West Indian ports. Britain was the principal exception to the universal welcome. France now learned that her dream of pre-empting American products and markets was in vain, for the American attachment to British goods was as great as ever. As soon as the British realized this fact, they coldly calculated on making the United States help pay for the war by closing the British West Indies to its commerce and forcing American exports to that area into British bottoms. However, American ships were allowed to carry American products to the British Isles. The motive was to regain the old control of American tobacco, but it was regarded by sound mercantilists as an unusually generous gesture. Trade with Britain

On the whole, British policy was a defeat for Adam Smith. Separate states could not retaliate very well, and those who tried found goods could be run in from a neighboring state. The states refused to obey Confederation commercial treaties and fought among themselves so disgracefully that when John Adams, minister to London, asked for a trade treaty the cynical riposte was to ask him whether he wanted one or thirteen. It was reported in 1787 that of sixty vessels in New York Harbor fifty-five were British, and of one hundred Americans helpless—legally seventy ships engaged in trade with South Carolina one hundred fifty were British. English goods, which could be brought in only in English ships, were dumped on the American market and auctioned off at prices that put many of the new American manufacturers out of business. The British policy was successful; by 1789 trade was back to its prewar value, and the "favorable" balance was running more strongly toward Britain than it ever had before. Once more the drain of specie was resumed as the gold spent in America during the war by the British and French armies was siphoned off to England.

Perhaps the situation was not as bad as shippers wanted the public to believe. The exclusion of American traders from the British West Indies was greatly resented by the planters, who regarded American products as necessary to their existence and hated to pay the higher cost of carriage in British ships. As it turned out, the law permitted emergency shipments in American vessels; emergencies straightway became normal. But this was not enough. American skippers, always adept at smuggling, had taken postgraduate courses during the war and presently had the future Horatio Lord Nelson, then a captain on the West India station, running in nautically disgraceful circles. The postwar boom collapsed in 1784, but by the end of the next year improvement was noticeable. During the decade of the 1780's the United States probably exported more than it imported. Since tobacco could now be shipped directly to consumers (chiefly France), the country probably bought less from Britain and sold her less during the decade than before the war.

It would, of course, be wrong to claim that all was rosy in the 1780's. The decline of the radical faction in Congress only reflected the conservative reaction in some of the states. Here and there the "nationalists" **State con-** accepted state favors because of Confederation inability to **trols of** grant them. Navigation acts and protective tariffs were natu-**trade** ral irritants to foreigners and their American partners, but reciprocity existed between the states save for minor restrictions among New York, Connecticut, and New Jersey.

Meanwhile the farmers were having their way in several states. It was provided that paper currency be accepted at par value as legal tender in payment of debts and that "stay laws" be passed to delay the collection of **Legal ten-** debts. In Rhode Island business practically stopped, and **der and** creditors would have fled the state to escape payment of the **"stay" laws** money owed them but that the law made it possible to discharge a debt by placing the money in the hands of a court. As one observer put it, the debtors triumphantly pursued their creditors and paid them without mercy. The situation lasted until in the case of *Trevett v. Weeden* a court decision declared the law unconstitutional and void.

There was trouble also in the West. The Spanish blocked the West's only commercial outlet at New Orleans. In the long run this blockade would have depressed land values, so land speculators began intriguing with Spain to move over to its protection. Some began to boom the cause of new states: Westsylvania at the head of the Ohio; Kentucky farther downstream; and Franklin, in **Trouble in the West** what is now Tennessee. Curiously enough, the Spanish were at the same time promoting Indian raids on Georgia and Tennessee. The British, who still occupied Detroit, were employing similar tactics. On the one hand they goaded the western settlements with Indian raids, and on the other they intrigued to separate them from the Confederation and bring them back under British protection.

Vermont, which was claimed by both New York and New Hampshire, set up a government and constitution of its own. Back of the action were the great landholders led by the Allen brothers, who were so determined to make good their claims that they actually entered into negotiations with the British to make Vermont a British province. The effort did not cease until the verge of Vermont's admission to the Union in 1791. Meanwhile Connecticut's claim by right of its "sea-to-sea" charter to the northern part of Pennsylvania was leading to bloodshed between grantees of the two states in the last of two so-called Pennamite Wars.

The capsheaf to the troubles of the Confederation came in Massachusetts. There the constitution had been rigged in favor of the mercantile classes, and the burden of taxes had been placed on the agrarians. When protests were unavailing, the malcontents undertook in the summer of 1786 forcibly to close courts in order to save their property from foreclosure; and this movement soon grew **Shays's Rebellion, 1786–7** into an armed uprising under the leadership of a Revolutionary captain named Daniel Shays. An attack on the Springfield arsenal to obtain weapons was repulsed, and in February 1787 an expedition from Boston under General Lincoln defeated and captured or dispersed the dissidents. After the crisis was over the state made reforms, but the damage was done. This final social tumult convinced the remaining doubters among conservatives that a way must be found of strengthening the central government if order and property were to be preserved.

The events which followed called forth unsuspected reserves of national sentiment. It is true that there were dangerous dividing influences: the rivalry between little states and big states, that between the coast and the interior, and the incipient quarrel between North and South over Negro slavery which was one day to split the Union. But the binding influences were stronger and were daily breaking down state differences. First were common **Dividing and binding influences** blood, language, and institutions, and the common possession of the West, where was growing up a generation which regarded itself as American rather than Virginian or Pennsylvanian. Developing economic interests were already cutting across state lines. The interior agrarians from Vermont to Georgia had more in common than their state of indebtedness; they wanted cheap land, transportation, self-government, and protection from the Indians; and the great land speculators agreed with them in all except the first. Even more important, northern merchants and southern commission merchants were finding common ground with bankers, manufacturers, and planters in a determined defense of their property. Perhaps most powerful of all was the memory of the struggle for independence which, however halting and halfhearted it may have been in reality, had already become a heroic legend which bound together men from every state and region in a common determination that their sacrifices should not prove to have been in vain.

The movement for a new constitution began in 1785 when representatives of Virginia and Maryland were scheduled to meet at Alexandria to confer on the problems of the navigation of the Potomac River and

Movement for a new constitution
Chesapeake Bay. At Washington's invitation the meeting was held at Mount Vernon. The problems proved so important that it was decided to ask for a meeting of all the states at Annapolis the next year to adopt uniform commercial regulations, and the Virginia legislature sent out the invitations. The Annapolis Convention (1786) was attended by representatives from only five states, and its only important action was to recommend, on the motion of Alexander Hamilton, the holding of another convention to propose amendments to the Articles of Confederation. Congress, disgusted by the failure of the states to give it workable powers and to pay more than a fraction of their allotments for the support of the Confederation, now called a convention to meet at the time and place proposed at Annapolis.

The events of the winter, including Shays's Rebellion, apparently convinced the state governments that reform was necessary. When Virginia signified its serious intentions and its confidence in the success of the convention by selecting its most brilliant men as delegates, with Washington at the head, most of the other states promptly fell into line.

2 The Second Constitution

The Constitutional Convention met in Philadelphia's Independence Hall, a building which had already seen the making of much American history. The convention was organized on 25 May 1787 with George Wash-

Personnel of the convention
ington in the president's chair. The sessions lasted through a hot and muggy summer until business was adjourned on 17 September.

There were fifty-five members in attendance at one time or another, only thirty-nine of whom signed the final recommendations. Voting was by state delegations as units. The members were remarkable for their youth, their ability, and their property. Twenty-nine of the members were college graduates, five were college presidents or professors, eight had signed the Declaration of Independence, and more than half were lawyers. The average age was forty-two, but the youngest member was twenty-seven, and the average was raised by a few oldsters like Franklin and Washington. On the whole, it was the young men who did the work.

Virginia led with the most outstanding delegation, which besides Washington included George Mason, Edmund Randolph, and the brilliant young James Madison, whose share in the convention was so great that he is known as the "Father of the Constitution." It is to Madison's notes, also, that we are chiefly indebted for our knowledge of the proceedings, for the meetings were secret and the secretary's minutes were poorly kept. Pennsylvania was represented by Benjamin Franklin, Robert Morris, Gouverneur Morris, and the able Scottish lawyer James Wilson, whose contributions ranked next to Madison's. Alexander Hamilton was the most prominent representative from New York, but he was outvoted by two others who opposed a new constitution and so did not attend regularly. Delaware was represented by John Dickinson; Massachusetts by Elbridge Gerry and Rufus King; Connecticut by Roger Sherman and Oliver Ellsworth, a future Chief Justice; Maryland by the radical Luther Martin; and South Carolina by John Rutledge, C. C. Pinckney, and Charles Pinckney. These were the men most prominent in the convention. Among the missing giants of the Revolution Jefferson and John Adams were on foreign missions. Patrick Henry refused to serve because, said he, "I smelt a Rat."

At first the convention made an attempt to follow its instructions and recommend amendments to the Articles but in the end gave it up as hopeless and frankly launched into drawing up a new constitution. To do that successfully it had to solve three problems which had often **Problems** confronted constitution-makers but to none of which history **before the** had as yet offered any satisfactory answers. First was the **convention** necessity of reconciling the interests and jealousies of the large and small states; second, the problem of reconciling the sovereignties of states and nation; and third, the desirability of protecting holders of large property without hampering or antagonizing the holders of small property. These were the basic issues before the convention, and each one of them before it was settled was in danger of breaking down the deliberations.

This situation meant that the Federal system must be invented. It meant that each state must preserve enough self-government and receive a large enough share in the central government for its prestige and dignity to be preserved and for it to fear neither the central government nor its powerful neighbors. At the same time the central **Their** government must be strong enough to carry out its duties of **solution** protecting and promoting the general welfare. The Confederation and other historic confederations had depended on the goodwill of its parts, the states, and in fact the states had reserved to themselves the function of administering the general laws; the inevitable result was that local interests were in a position to block confederate policies and seldom hesitated to do so. The Constitution of 1787 solved this problem by giving local interests a voice in molding policy but assigning the execution of the plans to a general government which by-passed the states and acted directly on the individual citizen.

The Constitution was not an original creation. It was simply the next step in political evolution. Considerable reference was made to Greek confederacies and to the Bible, to Blackstone, and to Montesquieu; but on the whole the Constitution owed its nature to the examples offered by the Articles of Confederation and the constitutions of the states and, most of all, to the Anglo-Saxon genius for compromise.

It was natural that Virginia, having taken so prominent a part in promoting the convention, should be the first to present a new plan of government. This was probably largely the work of Madison. It followed **The Virginia and New Jersey plans** the misinterpretation of the form of the British government presented by Blackstone and by Montesquieu in his *Spirit of the Laws,* that is, it consisted of three mechanically separate and equal divisions: executive, legislative, and judiciary. It was not recognized at the time that the Revolution of 1688 had placed Parliament in a position where it would soon effectively control the entire government. To that misconception we owe the form of our government. Even if it had been recognized, it is possible that the writers of the Constitution, drawing on their experience, would have vetoed the idea of an all-powerful legislature. At any rate Virginia proposed an effective central government, empowered to lay and collect taxes and to defend its rights against individuals and states.

To most of its proposals there was little objection, but its plan for a two-house legislature to be elected by the states in proportion to population was assailed by those, chiefly from the smaller states, who mistrusted a strong government which they could not control or at least veto. To meet this objection the New Jersey Plan was introduced. It proposed a unicameral legislature in which the states had equal votes, and, though it permitted some expansion of the central government's powers, it essentially insisted upon the preservation of the features which had crippled the Confederation.

Fear lay at the bottom of New Jersey's action—fear that strength would necessarily breed tyranny. The basic issue was thus not simply between big and little states, but between a strong and a weak central government. **The Great Compromise** The deadlock lasted for a sweltering month; then the heat broke and the Great (or Connecticut) Compromise, probably the suggestion of Dickinson, was adopted. There was to be a Senate composed of two members from each state, and a

House of Representatives with membership proportionate to population and elected by popular vote. The question of an effective national government was settled, and in settling it the core of modern Federal government had been invented.

The core of the new invention consisted of two parts: (1) the representation of both states and population in the central government, and (2) the right of the central government to operate directly upon the individual citizen without asking the permission of the state. The states **Effects of** could no longer block Federal law because they did not ad- **the Great** minister it, but just to make sure that no state should over- **Compro-** awe the Federal government it was later provided that the **mise** capital city was to be built in a Federal district which should be subject only to the laws of Congress. Though the states were the geographical units of Federal administration and of Congressional representation, they were not to vote in Congress as units, but each Senator and Representative was to vote as he chose. The way was thus open for the formation of alliances that not only cut across state lines but also represented minority interests within the states. At the same time a step had been taken toward compromising the economic struggle, for the House, elected by the people, would represent little property, and the Senate, elected by the state legislatures, would represent the interests of big property. Compromise between them would be essential, for each would have a veto on the other.

Another feature of the Great Compromise was that five slaves were to be counted as three free persons in reckoning the population of the states for apportioning members of the House and for laying direct taxes. As a matter of fact, direct taxes (Federal poll and property taxes) have been laid only five times; so the South gained **The Three-** greatly by the measure. While it is true that the South feared **fifths Ratio** the North's commercial dominance, yet the importance of the struggle over counting slaves has been exaggerated in the light of the later slave controversy; the Three-fifths Rule or Ratio had been used since 1783 by Congress in laying its requisitions on the states.

Following this feature of the Compromise was the problem of how to keep the North from dominating the South commercially, for it was feared that its more numerous population, greater number of states, and commercial facilities would enable it to treat the South as Great **Commer-** Britain had treated the Thirteen Colonies. The Three-fifths **cial com-** Ratio was a part of the answer, and the South, which was **promises** primarily an exporting section, was further protected by forbidding Congress to lay export taxes and by requiring all Federal taxes to be "uniform throughout the United States." At first the South insisted that "navigation" acts must be laid only by a two-thirds vote of Congress but finally accepted majority rule with the proviso that slaves could be freely imported for twenty years. This provision was due to the demand of Georgia and the Carolinas. The South was further protected by the rule that treaties to be approved must receive the vote of two thirds of the Senate.

It was recognized that in order to strengthen the Federal government it must receive the powers which concerned the welfare of all. Actually the word "federal" (Latin *foedus*, league, treaty, compact; akin to *fides*,

Division of powers faith) originally applied to the adherents of a league or compact and in the United States was used about as we now use "confederation." We have seen how "federal" was used by decentralizers to indicate their opposition to a national government. Of course, the authors of the Constitution knew the difference very well but expected to allay public fears of a *national* government by stealing the decentralizers' thunder and speaking of their plan as "federal." As a result the word has taken on new meaning. Enumerated powers were assigned to the Federal government, and all of them (except a few with the consent of Congress) were forbidden to the states. Within its powers the state was sovereign and answerable to no one, and this sovereignty is essentially true today in spite of Federal aggrandizement. Certainly the individual citizen finds his life touched more by the state and its creature, the municipality, than by the Federal government.

The members of the convention seem to have differed in the interpretation of the language assigning powers to the Federal government, and it was inevitable that these differences should later become the subject of long

Interpretation of powers political battles. Americans search for legal excuses—and usually find them. The so-called "sweeping clauses" supplied the arguments that loose constructionists wanted. One of them, in the preamble, declares it the purpose of the Constitution to "promote the general welfare"; a second, in Article I, gives Congress the power to "provide for the common defense and general welfare." The so-called elastic clause has in particular been used to excuse the growth of Federal authority, because after the enumeration of Federal powers it provides that the government shall have the power "to make all laws which shall be necessary and proper for carrying into execution the foregoing powers." From this (as well as from the two welfare clauses) Congress has deduced that its taxing and borrowing power gives it the right to create national banks, emit legal-tender paper money, and erect a system of protective tariffs. The war power has been interpreted to authorize the annexation and government of territory and to make the President a virtual dictator with the consent of Congress. The power to regulate foreign and interstate commerce has been stretched to justify the control of immigration, the building of public works to aid and promote commerce, and the regulation of public carriers and local manufactures by controlling the terms of interstate commerce.

It will be noted that the Constitution provides not only for the division of powers between Federal and state governments but also for the separation within the Federal government of powers among executive, legislature, and judiciary. The state constitutions soon began to follow the same principles both in apportioning state and local powers and within the state government itself. In order to maintain this balance constitutions and customs have provided checks. In the Federal government the President appoints officials and makes treaties with the consent of the Senate, and he may veto legislation. The legislature initiates bills, restrains executive and judiciary by the power of impeachment, and overrides vetoes by a two-thirds vote. The judiciary may restrain executive officials from illegal acts, and it may declare legislation unconstitutional. Though there has from the first been considerable objection to this last power, and in fact it was only slowly and grudgingly accepted, there is now no doubt but that it was specifically envisioned by the framers of the Constitution as a judicial function.

Separation of powers: checks and balances

Another aspect of the balance of powers is found in the way in which the framers sought to balance social forces. Most of the members of the Convention of 1787 had a profound distrust of the people and wished to place their own social class in control. This is not to deny that they loved their country or the sincerity of their belief that they were saving it from chaos when they sought to limit democracy. They could not go to an extreme, however, for it was evident that their document must meet the test of popular approval. They therefore sought to remove the people as far as possible from direct influence on policy: the President was given almost monarchic powers, but he was elected by an electoral college; the Senators were elected by the state legislatures; and the Senate was given the power of approval of treaties and presidential appointments. The popular demand for paper money was spiked by prohibiting the states from issuing it, and it was purposely left out of the powers given to the Federal government; later on it was interpreted back into the Constitution. The deliberate intention was to restrain the people from radical orgies by giving the President and the Senate large powers. Indeed, the only direct control given to the people was in the election of the House of Representatives. English and colonial custom led to the incorporation of the right of the popular branch to initiate money appropriations, but the Senate sometimes manages to get around it. Though in that day the House was regarded as the "arcanum" of the popular will and the Senate as the creature of conservatism, the present tendency is for the two houses to reverse the role.

The Constitution and democracy

Even though the Constitution was not democratic in our modern sense and was not intended to be, it is important to note that like the democratic process it kept the way open for change. This fact is evident in the pro-

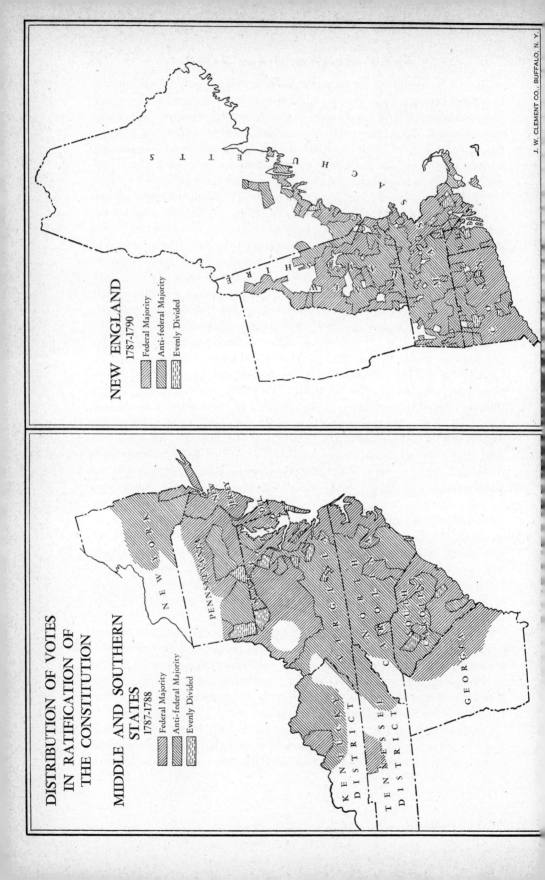

DISTRIBUTION OF VOTES IN RATIFICATION OF THE CONSTITUTION

MIDDLE AND SOUTHERN STATES
1787-1788

Federal Majority
Anti-federal Majority
Evenly Divided

NEW YORK

PENNSYLVANIA

NEW JERSEY

VIRGINIA

NORTH CAROLINA

SOUTH CAROLINA

GEORGIA

KENTUCKY DISTRICT

TENNESSEE DISTRICT

NEW ENGLAND
1787-1790

Federal Majority
Anti-federal Majority
Evenly Divided

MASSACHUSETTS

NEW HAMPSHIRE

J. W. CLEMENT CO., BUFFALO, N. Y.

visions for amendment and for local control of qualifications **Contribu-**
for voting. More important than these was the use or inclu- **tions to the**
sion of three basic American contributions to the democratic **democratic**
process. First, the Constitutional Convention implemented **process**
the compact theory in a practical way, and the method has found world-
wide acceptance. Second, the Federal system found the practical compromise between the age-old rivals, nationalism and localism, and has been
one of the important factors in making possible the growth of the modern
state. Third, the old concept of empire as composed of a metropolis and
permanently subject colonies or possessions was done away with; the
Constitution-makers deliberately provided for the admission of dependent
areas to the same status as the old.

One curious intention of the framers in setting up their system of
checks and balances was to prevent the growth of parties—"factions,"
they called them, though they seem to have used the word also to denote
the pressure groups which today compose a party. Actually **Miscalcula-**
the system has promoted the opposite result, for the balanc- **tions of the**
ing parts of government co-operate well only when they are **framers**
united by party discipline in support of common policies. The requirement
of the consent of three fourths of the states to pass an amendment would
seem not only to have been to win the goodwill of the jealous states which
feared the tyranny of their neighbors but also to hamper change, and indeed the method was so cumbersome that it succeeded until the rash of
speedy amendments in our own day.

On the whole, technical amendments have made but few important
changes. The vital changes have come about through interpretations; the
growth of a body of political and technical customs and usages; and the
arbitrament of arms, as the Civil War's decision of the problem of state
rights. One bitterly contested provision in the convention was the right
of Congress to admit new states on an equal basis with the old; the objection, of course, was based upon the perennial quarrel between the coast
and the interior. Nevertheless, the right was essential to gain the co-operation of the West, which would never have consented to an inferior rank
in the Union.

Obviously the framers could not name the states which would adhere
to the new Constitution, so in the preamble they attributed the document
to "we, the people of the United States." Actually it was regarded as set
up by the states—or the people of the states—and it was to
be approved by especially summoned conventions. The Con- **Battle over**
stitution was to go into effect by the agreement of any nine **ratification**
conventions. The proponents of the new Constitution were speedily known
as Federalists and the opponents (the old "federalists") as Antifederalists.
The battle was bitter and was carried on in press, pulpit, and conventions.

Indeed, it is believed that had the Constitution been put to the direct vote of the people a majority would have opposed it. New York was especially doubtful, and there Madison, Hamilton, and Jay published in a newspaper under the pen name "Publius" a series of eighty-five essays which as *The Federalist* have become the classical commentary on Federal government.

Delaware was the first state to ratify (7 December 1787) and New Hampshire the ninth (21 June 1788); Virginia and New York were tenth and eleventh, but their ratification assured the success of the Constitution.

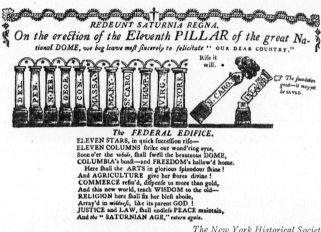

The New York Historical Society

After eleven states had ratified the Constitution, the Massachusetts *Centinel* found reasons for rejoicing.

In general the coast was Federalist, for even the fishermen, artisans, and shipbuilding mechanics hoped for prosperity under Federal trade regulation. On the other hand the inflationists, who included by far the most of the debt-ridden yeomanry of the interior, were Antifederalist. However, in Virginia the Great Valley, eager for interstate commerce, allied with Tidewater to turn the state to ratification. Pennsylvania was carried by a slippery trick of the Federalists, who called the election for the state convention before the western Antifederalists could organize. New York ratified only after New York City threatened to secede from the Antifederalist interior. It seems fairly certain that the votes of the old Tory element were important in swinging the states toward ratification. North Carolina did not ratify until November 1789; and Rhode Island, the home of "the otherwise-minded," acceded in May 1790 when it became evident that the new government in laying its imposts would treat her as potential foreign territory.

One objection to the proposed Constitution was that it had no Bill of Rights which specifically guaranteed the civil liberties of the people against Federal encroachment. Federalist consent to the incorporation of such limitations helped to win the battle for ratification in Massachusetts and doubtless other states. The First Congress submitted proposals to the states which now appear as the first ten amendments: the Bill of Rights.

Bill of Rights

In looking over the Constitution one is impressed by the fears of the framers and the people as expressed by the Bill of Rights, the many compromises, and the elaborate checks and balances. These cumbrous mechanisms were so patently intended to prevent the interference of government in individual affairs and to prevent hasty action that it is almost fair to say that the document was as much intended to prevent government as to implement it. This was inevitable in an unformed nation which had just emerged from a war against tyranny and which was torn by rivalries among localities and between social classes and economic interests. These fears still are with us, but they do not control us as they did our fathers. It has been the mission of our century to carry out the positive functions of the Constitution, for most Americans now agree that they are there, written large not only in the powers specifically granted to the Federal government but in the preamble.

Negative and positive functions

> We, the people of the United States, in order to form a more perfect union, establish justice, insure domestic tranquillity, provide for the common defense, promote the general welfare, and secure the blessings of liberty to ourselves and our posterity, do ordain and establish this Constitution for the United States of America.

3 Hamilton the Force

The Congress of the Confederation had designated New York City as the capital of the new government and named the first Wednesday in March 1789 for the meeting of the Congress. It was not until 6 April that a quorum of the Senate was present and Congress was able to begin business. During the winter Congressional elections had been held, and though they were bitter contests between the two parties they apparently did not greatly interest the mass of voters. At any rate there was a small turnout to the polls, and the Federalists had made the best showing. Their strength is shown by the fact that over half the members of Congress had been active as proponents of the Constitution either in the Constitutional Convention or in the state ratifying conventions. In other words, Congress was dominated by the northern merchant aristocracy, even though at least ninety per cent of the country was agrarian.

Setting up the new government

The Senate counted the votes cast by the states' electoral colleges for President and Vice-President, and as had been generally anticipated Washington was elected by unanimous vote. John Adams of Massachusetts

**Inaugura-
tion of
Washing-
ton**

was elected Vice-President by a much smaller vote, for Hamilton had feared a tie vote in the college and had solicited the electors to throw away some of their votes on other persons. Adams arrived in New York first and took up his duties as president of the Senate. Washington arrived more than a week later after a triumphal progress from the Potomac, and on 30 April on the balcony of Federal Hall on Wall Street took the oath as President of the United States.

There can be no doubt that Washington responded to the call to the presidency only because of that sense of duty which was one of his finest characteristics; he remarked half-humorously that he felt like a culprit

**Washing-
ton's prob-
lems**

who was going to the place of execution. The emotional strain of the Revolutionary years still affected him, and his estate had suffered so grievously that he actually had to borrow money to pay his traveling expenses to New York. Thereafter he remained financially solvent only by selling parts of his landholdings from time to time. The burden he assumed was enormous. The Confederation left him little but a roster of unpaid and discontented clerks, a heavy debt, and a record of frustration. The navy had been disbanded, the army boasted less than seven hundred officers and men, and England and Spain were intriguing for the separation of the West. Even the friends of the Constitution had no great faith in it. Few expected it to outlast their generation, and Hamilton called it a "frail and worthless fabric," quite unaware of his coming deification as one of the galaxy of Founding Fathers possessed of more than human insight and foresight.

Not only did Washington have to work out a complete hierarchy of executive officers, but appointments had to be made, policies and precedents inaugurated, and smooth relations established among three branches of government which the Constitutional Convention had regarded more as checks on each other than as co-operators. And all of this had to be done so fairly that it would not antagonize on the one hand the opponents of the Constitution who, having gone through one revolution, might not gag at another, nor on the other hand the conservatives who regarded government as their private preserve and might not gag at a direct seizure of power. On the credit side were the faith and love that the American people bore toward Washington, and the rather general prosperity of the Confederation period. Even some of those who had opposed the adoption of the Constitution wished the new government well—provided it did not tread on their toes—and were disposed to wait and see.

At the beginning Congress provided for three executive departments: State, Treasury, and War. The Attorney-General was not a Cabinet member until 1814, and the Postmaster-General was under the Treasury until 1829. The existence of the Cabinet was not recognized **Admin-** officially by Congress until 1907; but of course custom had **istrative** set it up long before, and Washington held frequent meetings **foundations** with it. In the hope that the formation of parties could be avoided Washington brought into his Cabinet representatives of the two political extremes—Hamilton and Jefferson. Executive appointments were made only after minute investigation and were calculated as nearly as possible to recognize and placate regions and interests, but also with regard to the fitness of the appointee and his record of service. The Senators soon found that their power of approval of executive appointments gave them political power in their own states, and by the rule of "Senatorial courtesy" they rejected nominations not favored by the Senators from the nominee's home state. It was all a slow process. In July Congress laid a tariff on imports in order to provide a revenue, but it was months before a customs service could begin actual operation.

Washington seems to have taken literally the Constitutional provision that treaties should be made with the advice and consent of the Senate. One day he appeared in the Senate chamber with an Indian treaty and undertook to jam it through while the Senators sat by like **Congres-** awe-struck schoolboys. Finally a motion was carried that the **sional prec-** treaty be referred to a committee, and Washington stalked **edents** out with a "discontented air." Thereafter the President did not consult the Senate until a treaty had been negotiated. The incident encouraged the adoption of the committee system, though that would have come in any case with increased pressure of business. Washington read his messages to Congress in person, but as this proceeding was regarded as a sort of speech from the "throne" the custom was discontinued by Jefferson (who was a poor speaker) and was not revived until Wilson's administration. Adams lamented the insignificance of the office of Vice-President, but he and those after him accepted the office as that of a moderator rather than a parliamentary leader. The Speaker of the House, to judge by the British precedent, should have been also merely a moderator, but the office has so often been filled by forceful men that it has at times almost constituted a dictatorship.

Obviously the powers of the new government could not be enforced until Federal courts had come into being. The Constitution had provided for a Supreme Court but had left the remainder up to Congress. On 24 September 1789 the Judiciary Act laid down pretty much the **The** judicial system which survives to our own day: district **judiciary** courts, circuit courts of appeal, and the Supreme Court of six members. John Jay was made Chief Justice. The act provided that cases involving Federal Constitutional powers or the laws and treaties of the United States might be appealed from state courts, and at least twice decisions of state courts were reversed. On another occasion a circuit court refused to administer a Federal pension law on the ground that Congress had no Constitutional right to pass laws requiring a court to undertake nonjudicial functions. These decisions did not excite much opposition at the time. The provision of the Constitution that citizens of one state could sue another state in Federal courts proved unsatisfactory, and it was changed by the Eleventh Amendment, added in 1798.

In a century which regarded protocol as a mainstay of social stability and the first mark of breeding, it was inevitable that many hearts should burn over titles of address and rules of precedence. John Adams longed to preserve some of the trappings of royalty as a mark of

Problems of precedence

dignity and respectability and sought to introduce into Congress the forms and ceremonies of the British Parliament. Washington himself may have realized that human nature requires a certain amount of pomp and circumstance, and—lacking Hollywood—tried to fill the gap left by the passing of royalty by holding such elaborate levees that his official family and social circle was soon dubbed the Republican Court. Of course good democrats looked askance on all such shenanigans, and Jefferson did away with them when he became President and, in fact, went to the opposite extreme. Nevertheless, an early custom of addressing the President as "His Excellency" has survived, even though Congress after grave searching of soul refused to give it legislative sanction. It is an ironic comment on something or other that Washington is today probably the most precedence-ridden capital in the world.

The burden of organization was too great for the tired Washington, and he turned with relief to the young and vigorous Hamilton, who in September 1789 was made Secretary of the Treasury. It was Hamilton

Alexander Hamilton (1757– 1804)

rather than Washington who organized and channelized conservative interest in the government and made it a tremendous driving force all through American history. This does not mean that Washington was Hamilton's dupe; it was rather that Washington agreed with Hamilton's general principles and accepted his program after making certain alterations.

Alexander Hamilton was born on the West Indian island of Nevis, the son of an unprosperous Scotch merchant and a French Huguenot. It is true that the parents' union was not legal, but the circumstance was due to the rigid divorce laws of the time and the union was in every other respect irreproachable. Both parents were of good blood and education. Nevertheless, the stain on his birth may have been a powerful incentive in Hamilton's struggle for recognition. The brilliance of the boy led some relatives to send him to the mainland, where in 1773 he entered King's College (now Columbia University).

During the preliminaries of the Revolution the lad became widely known for his writings and speeches. The war found him a line officer and then Washington's most trusted aide-de-camp, indeed a sort of executive assistant. Hamilton, however, always regarded himself as a frustrated military genius, and he vented his resentment at his noncombatant role on Washington. Nevertheless, this period of training in public administration was the indispensable step toward his eagerly sought goals of power and prestige. Hamilton was a social climber, like most great leaders of conservative causes. Before he left Washington's staff he consolidated his gains by marriage with the daughter of General Philip Schuyler, one of the richest and most influential of the New York magnates.

Upon leaving the army Hamilton once more proved his brilliance by gaining admittance to the bar after only five months' study of law. After some service in Congress he began the practice of law in New York and quickly became a legal and political power and the champion of New York's Tory élite, which was now being persecuted by the triumphant radicals. It took courage to face a radical mob as he did in behalf of William Samuel Johnson, that Tory president of Columbia College who later served as a member of the Constitutional Convention and Senator from Connecticut. Hamilton's share in summoning the Constitutional Convention has already been noted, and as co-author of *The Federalist* he exerted tremendous force in favor of the adoption of the Constitution; it is scarcely too much to say that he carried hostile New York single-handed.

Hamilton became at once the hope and the idol of the conservatives. He accepted the Secretaryship of the Treasury as his by natural right. Indeed, he was born with all the qualifications of an aristocrat except for the doubt of his right to the actual status. His tastes, his manner, his lightning intellect were all aristocratic. Though he was a small man, he reminded one of a rapier by his elegant slimness, his military erectness, his quick, energetic movements, and his cold, intent blue eyes. His hair was reddish-brown, his complexion clear and ruddy, and his features refined and handsome. Though he was affectionate to his family and intimates, possessed a charming smile and conversational fascination, there was nevertheless no doubt of his willful pride and his thirst to command. He was eloquent, logical, systematic, an abnormally hard worker, and honest and honorable in his business life. On the other hand, he was a director rather than a leader, tactless in management, and intolerant of stupidity. He had a taste for intrigue and would have succeeded in it more often if he had not also possessed a quick temper, which led him to throw away his gains in rash resentments.

Hamilton came into office at the age of thirty-two with his political philosophy already developed and with an economic program for putting

it into effect. The touchstone of Hamilton's life and policy was his fear of
and loathing for the people; it is difficult to escape the con-
Political philosophy clusion that he was frantically striving to differentiate himself from them and was haunted by the fear that his foot
might slip on the ladder and he would be precipitated back to his obscure
origins. *In vino veritas:* one evening when flushed with wine he disclosed
a little of his fear in the famous words, "The people—your people, sir, is a
great beast." He acknowledged that his social ideal was met in Japan: "a
mass of intelligent humanity, reckless of their lives, yet filled with the joy
of life, eager for distinction, hungry for success, alert, practical, and
merry; but at the same time subordinate, humbly and piously subordinate,
to a pure abstraction."

Hamilton favored monarchy and supported aristocracy because they
had nothing to gain by a change; he seems never to have understood the
value of the democratic process, though like all democratic conservatives
(how he would have loathed the tag!) he yielded to the rising counterforce. The British form of government as practiced by George III he
swallowed whole. Even its corruption, he pointed out, was necessary because in order to ensure stability the rich must be bound to the cause of
government by self-interest. While he would not have made serfs of the
people or excluded them completely from political rights, he proposed to
thwart their disruptive demands by seeing to it that the rich were cared for
and thus, having a property interest in the government, would support it
against the storms of democracy. He envisioned the United States as
another England, with great industrial cities, with workers crowding in
from Europe, and ruled over by an aristocracy which because it had everything it wanted could not be subject to temptation. Hamilton knew
nothing of the aspirations and capacities of the poor at his own doorstep,
and nowhere do we find any suggestion that they could be educated into
good citizens. How much less could he know of the democracy of the West
—Jefferson's Piedmont home—where the future of America was taking
shape.

The philosophy of Federalism owes much to John Adams. Born of
generations of New England farmers, Adams graduated from Harvard in
1755, but his original plan of entering the ministry he abandoned because
John Adams (1735– 1826) of his dislike of Calvinist theology. As a lawyer his practice
grew slowly, though his marriage to Abigail Smith allied him
to a number of prominent families. We have seen him serving
in key positions during the Revolution. Though Adams had
enjoyed high honors and was to receive the highest, he never rid himself
of his middle-class inferiority complex and was convinced that his ability
was unrecognized. This conviction was not inconsistent with an inordinate
vanity, which he regarded not as vanity but as a sensible recognition of his

own superiority. His enemies looked upon him as a pooh-bah, for he was that tragic figure, a roly-poly man who is a poor judge of his fellows, humorless, suspicious, and easily angered. Nevertheless he was possessed of ability, good sense, integrity, and courage; and his aristocratic convictions were based upon much deeper thought than Hamilton's.

His principal publication was *A Defense of the Constitutions of the United States* (1787), which was one of the major American contributions to political theory. Hamilton wished to promote commerce and finance; Adams distrusted "paper" wealth and favored the land- **Philosophy** owners. He believed that the basic social struggle was be- **of John** tween rich and poor, and he strung along with the rich only **Adams** because he distrusted them less than the poor. His dictum that government should be by the natural aristocracy of "the rich, the well-born, and the able"—the last obviously including John Adams—was tempered by his ideal of giving both rich and poor representation and having an executive strong enough to hold the balance and a Constitution designed to preserve the status quo. Actually Adams was almost as close to Jefferson as to Hamilton, and indeed it was well known that he opposed Hamilton's financial legerdemain; the result was that he was never trusted by the leaders of his own party.

The Federalists inherited many of the prominent men of the Revolutionary era, but because the party steadfastly regarded itself as a class rather than a political entity it never developed the party organizational genius its opponents did. Its permanent fall from power in 1801 put its leaders in the role of opposition, a place which **Federalist** they had no training or stamina to occupy, and the vital **leadership** importance of which they never grasped. The result was that of the large coterie of really able Federalists few are known to one not a close student of history.

Except for the Virginians George Washington and John Marshall, the leadership devolved chiefly upon New York, South Carolina, and New England. One of Hamilton's principal associates in New York was Rufus King, originally from Massachusetts. He served as Senator, minister to Great Britain, and then perennial candidate for the vice-presidency in 1804 and 1808 and the presidency in 1816. Gouverneur Morris was witty and self-confident, always a favorite of the ladies despite his peg leg. An aristocratic New Yorker, he served in public office from both New York and Pennsylvania during the Revolution. After the war he roamed about Europe for ten years, during which time he authored a remarkable journal, joined an unsuccessful plot to get Louis xvi out of prison, and served as minister to France. On his return he became Senator from New York. The Pinckneys and Rutledges, both numerous families, kept South Carolina in the Federalist column and represented it on the national stage until

Charles Pinckney went over to the Republicans. Thomas Pinckney and Charles Cotesworth Pinckney both ran for Vice-President, and the latter ran for the presidency in 1804 and 1808.

Among the topmost Federalists was John Jay, descendant of rich and influential Dutch and French Huguenot families of New York. He served as peace emissary in Paris, Confederation Secretary for Foreign Affairs, and Chief Justice of the Supreme Court. He could have held other high offices, but he was an unwilling and unambitious politician. Though he yielded to no one in his contempt for the people and faithfully upheld Federalist principles, he was unwilling to countenance much of his party's trickery. Upright, high-minded, and rigidly scrupulous, he had only one outstanding fault: too great satisfaction with himself. Probably that explains his lack of ambition; certainly it was a string on which his diplomatic opponents learned to pluck with results sometimes prejudicial to the country that he sincerely loved.

John Jay (1745– 1829)

The stronghold of Federalism was New England. For an area whose democratic town meetings had shaken the British throne it was strangely and slavishly subservient to the clergy of the established Congregational churches, the magistrates, the lawyers, the merchants, and the other "gentlemen of respectability." Manufacturers sought and found some tariff protection from Hamilton, and he would have given them more had he had his way, but the dominant interest was still merchant capitalism. Social Boston was in a flux as the crude beneficiaries of Revolution—the privateers, profiteers, and receivers of expropriated Tory goods—took over the thrones from which they had toppled the Tory aristocracy and sought to palm themselves off as John Adams's aristocracy of Nature. Nevertheless those of the old aristocracy who had survived or who had returned after the war joined causes with their former ship captains, clerks, and attorneys as lesser evils than the democrats. It was the moment of the merchants' glory: they were paid well for carrying goods; and even the light protective tariff, though it might hamper imports a little, poured the customs duties into their pockets in the form of interest on Federal bonds.

Conserva- tive New England

The clergymen of the established Congregational churches were almost Federalist toadies. The once-proud theocracy was now dependent upon the goodwill of the merchant aristocracy. Indeed, it was frightened. Not only did the growing spirit of dissent threaten the continuance of the state-laid taxes which supported it, but it was disintegrating internally. Three chief divisions had appeared: the old, strict, stand-pat theocratic Calvinists; the "Hopkinsians," followers of Samuel Hopkins, who adopted the evangelical and reforming zeal of Jonathan Edwards; and the Unitarians, who rejected the old theology and sought guidance in human reason and human sympathy. The fact that

Politics and religion

their own Unitarianism was in the long run more dangerous to orthodox Christianity than atheism did not prevent the Unitarian leaders from bitterly denouncing the democrats as anticlerical and even antireligious. It seemed logical to them that the weakening of ecclesiastical control would undermine political order and bring democracy and chaos.

The New England state which was most firmly chained to the Federalist bandwagon was Connecticut. Its nascent democracy had long since been frozen into a social structure that abhorred new ideas like Satan abhors holy water. Its people were prosperous enough to be contented; and when their smug stagnancy (which they called "steady habits") was threatened by any complex **Connecticut: Family Compact** force, their barren piety taught them to look around for a personal devil to blame. At the head of this smug commonwealth was a coterie so interconnected by marriage that it was often known as the Family Compact. At its core were the Dwight brothers, grandsons of Jonathan Edwards and cousins of Aaron Burr. Timothy Dwight, president of Yale, was its "pope," a man who was regarded by his followers as the eighth wonder of the world for his learning and ability, but who survives only as a pontifical wind garlicked with Greek roots. His brother, Theodore, was a Federalist wheel horse in Connecticut. Oliver Wolcott became Secretary of the Treasury under Washington and Adams, but in his later life turned toward democracy.

The Dwights were also members of the literary group, known as the Connecticut or Hartford Wits, which devoted itself to forging verbal lances for tilting at democratic windmills. Most of the members were voluminous writers, and they collaborated in a series of mock-epics which were hailed at the time as the deathblow **Hartford Wits** to democratic pretensions, but which to the modern taste are blunted by heavyhandedness and possess scant literary merit.

More significant than the Family Compact was the Essex Junto—a coterie, not an organization—made up of Federalist leaders, chiefly lawyers and merchants of Essex County, Massachusetts. Most of them bore intricate family relationships to each other. Their political career was launched in 1778, when they defeated John Hancock's democratic constitution for the state, and extended to **The Essex Junto** the close of the War of 1812. The Essex Junto and its espousal of Federalism may have been prompted in part by economic motives, but we must not ignore the psychological factor. The merchants and lawyers who had taken the place of the theocracy believed firmly that they had inherited the original Calvinist mission to look after their neighbors' conduct—and of course the divine seal upon their mission was evidenced by their property. God still prospered the righteous by sending them prizes of war and confiscated Tory estates, and by letting them in on the ground floor when

He intended to pass a miracle by raising worthless government paper to par value.

The leader and most powerful member of the Essex Junto, however, was George Cabot, a merchant of the tight little aristocracy of Beverly, who occasionally condescended to hold public office but preferred to

George Cabot (1752–1823)

devote himself to business and to political manipulation. Along with other aristocrats of decaying Essex County he moved to Boston, and the names Cabot, Lowell, Parsons, Lee, and Higginson have become as Bostonian as scrod. Cabot's ascendance was the natural result of his qualities of leadership; and though he was indolent and at times fearful, his diligence in correspondence with Federalist leaders held the Junto together and made it a continuing influence. Hamilton was the titular head of the party and its guiding genius, but Cabot and his Junto furnished the political punch which made New England a unit in support of the Hamiltonian program.

The brains of the Junto seems to have been Theophilus Parsons, a lawyer of Newburyport who in 1800 moved to Boston and in 1806 became chief justice of Massachusetts. Most prominent legislative wheel horse

Other members

was Fisher Ames, member of the House of Representatives. He was next to Hamilton probably the most brilliant Federalist intellect and certainly was the foremost orator, but ill health forced his retirement in 1796. Next to Ames was Timothy Pickering (1745–1829), a Salem man who served in the Revolution, entered politics in Pennsylvania, and became Secretary of State under Washington and Adams. Pickering then returned to Massachusetts and served as Senator from 1803 to 1811, most of the time a vigorous plotter for disunion. Next should be mentioned the impetuous Josiah Quincy (no Essex man), who served only briefly in Congress but became chief assassin of Jefferson's Embargo. Later on he was president of Harvard and reform mayor of Boston—and founder of a line of Josiah Quincys who became mayors.

Hamilton entered office with the sense of a mission strong upon him. It was well known that the First Lord of the Treasury held in the British Cabinet the position of prime minister, so by analogy Hamilton looked

Hamilton's role as prime minister

upon himself as Washington's prime minister, the general manager not only of the executive departments but of Congressional legislation as well. Washington, who always thought slowly, permitted it, and Hamilton went to absurd extremes. His interest in military affairs led him to take from the Secretary of War, bumbling Henry Knox, the ordering of army supplies. When Jefferson took up his duties as Secretary of State (March 1790), he found that Hamilton expected to dominate foreign affairs also. Indeed, Hamilton made the British envoys his confidants and deliberately muddied the waters of diplomacy by insisting that Jefferson did not represent the actual opinion of the country and was double-crossing Washington.

Hamilton's quick, nervous figure was everywhere: he sat with Congressional committees by day and caucused with his supporters in the evening. The dead hours of the night were spent in composing his famous state papers, the chief of which were his *Report on the Public Credit* (1790) and his *Report on Manufactures* (1791). His power as a speaker was so feared by his opponents that they managed to have Congress insist that he present his reports in writing. This was the first block to Hamilton's plans, for as a British-type minister he would have to have access to the floor of the houses of Congress.

In order to implement his political philosophy it was necessary for Hamilton to insist that the powers of the Federal government as expressed in the Constitution be loosely interpreted. The actions and reactions of that vital period have inexhaustible interest, but their complications permit only a bare outline here without strict attention to separate bills or to timing. Remember that Hamilton's one basic object was to create a governing class. Politics and economics were inextricably intertwined, for he sought to use his political control of Congress to promote an economic system, and he proposed to use the economic system to strengthen and perpetuate his political system. Obviously his plans were altered in detail by both President and Congress, but in the main the credit belonged to the Secretary of the Treasury. **Hamilton's program**

Hamilton's first move was intended to establish the public credit, for without a firm financial base the government could not hope to last. Even the suspicious democrats saw the point and favored the payment in full of the debt to foreign countries. They objected, however, to Hamilton's proposal to pay off the domestic debt of the Confederation at face value to the present holders of the bonds. They pointed out that the bonds had been accepted by the people either for cash or in exchange for supplies, but that they had often sold them to speculators for a fraction of their face value. Let the bonds be redeemed, then, at their market value of about one quarter of face rather than be used as an excuse to enrich a class of men who were already rich enough. Of course, Hamilton's plan no sooner leaked out than agents of those with ready money departed posthaste for the interior to buy up as many bonds as possible before the slow news agencies of the day overtook them. Eventually the speculators jubilantly raked in their profits as Hamilton redeemed and refunded their holdings. **Paying the Confederation debt**

It was one of Hamilton's maxims that "a public debt is a public blessing" because it made the creditors concerned over the political and financial stability of the government. He seems also to have regarded a

Assumption of state debts   thumping big debt as the means of getting into the proper hands the capital necessary for carrying out his dreams of industrialization; probably it was, even if it does sound like the New Deal. Next, the Federal government was to assume the state debts incurred by the Revolution. This time the advantage was not quite as evident to the democrats. Most of the states south of Pennsylvania had paid

"What Think Ye of Congress Now?" satirizes the removal (1790) of the seat of government from New York to Philadelphia. The parade is led by Robert Morris, who had large interests in Philadelphia.

off a considerable share of their debts in paper money and land certificates and now saw no reason why their Federal taxes should be boosted to pay off the debts of the northern states which had remained on a hard-money basis. Though the northern states in general supported Hamilton's scheme, the southern Congressmen defeated it by two votes.

It happened that the Southerners had hoped to have the new capital city and Federal district located in their region. Hamilton saw the elements of a bargain and approached Jefferson, who was not only a Southerner but a leader of the democratic opposition. As a result **The new capital city** Jefferson and his friends agreed to find two votes for assumption while Hamilton agreed to swing his support toward a southern capital. Jefferson later asserted that he had been so short a time in the country that he did not realize all that was involved; the disclaimer is not altogether convincing. The present site of Washington and the District of Columbia was selected by President Washington, and a magnificent city plan was laid out by the French engineer L'Enfant. Meanwhile the capital was moved (1790) to Philadelphia and there remained until the principal government buildings in the new city were ready for occupancy (1800).

Hamilton now pushed through the third item on his agenda, the Bank of the United States. He proposed the charter for twenty years of an institution with a capital of $10,000,000, one fifth of which would be subscribed by the Federal government. His arguments would today be **Bank of the** regarded as sound: it would furnish a convenient depository **United** for public and private funds; serve to transfer money and **States** credit from place to place; it could expand the currency when needful by banknotes; it would stabilize money and credit by furnishing a common policy and standard in all the states; it would advance money in anticipation of taxes; and it would act as agent or purchaser in the disposal of government bonds. There were only three banks in the United States—in Philadelphia, Boston, and New York—and, in fact, banks were regarded with suspicion as agents of economic power and privilege. By this time Hamilton's great objective was common knowledge, and suspicion of his proposed bank was lively because he reserved to the government only partial control (as with the Bank of England at that time) and left the real control and the bulk of the profits in the hands of private investors.

The possibility of manipulation of government funds and the power of issuing banknotes for the benefit of the investors and to the detriment of the people was so obvious that bitter but ineffectual opposition developed. This came especially from representatives of the South and the West, where no banks existed and none were wanted. **Opposition** A national bank, it was asserted, would monopolize the **to the Bank** nation's money and make it hard to obtain and then only at high interest rates. This was not quite true (as was shown in later years when state banks printed money as fast as the presses could work), and the opposition soon shifted its arguments to the indubitable fact that the Constitution did not specifically authorize the creation of a national bank. Hamilton airily waved aside the objection with the assertion that Congress undoubtedly had the right to raise tax money: obviously it must have the right to provide for its safekeeping. The latter came within the meaning of the clause which empowered Congress "to make all laws which shall be necessary and proper for carrying into execution" the specified powers. Hamilton won (1791), but Washington had been deeply impressed by the Constitutional issue and hesitated long before he signed the bill.

It was abundantly evident that this ambitious financial program would require a great deal of money. A light tariff with some restrictions intended to protect American trade had been levied in 1789, but it did not

Question of a protective tariff provide enough revenue. In his *Report on Manufactures* Hamilton proposed a revolt against the free-trade doctrines of Adam Smith's *Wealth of Nations* and recommended a protective tariff which would encourage the growth of manufactures. This, he asserted, would promote national wealth more quickly than agriculture because it would protect American enterprise from foreign discrimination, would widen the field of investment, and by introducing machinery would increase employment and stimulate immigration. The report had little immediate effect, for the Napoleonic Wars soon made agriculture and commerce more profitable than manufacturing, but it was to be the guidebook of later generations. The protective-tariff idea was opposed by the merchant-importers as detrimental to their business and by the agrarian representatives as unconstitutional. To the latter Hamilton replied that tariff protection was an implied power just as was the right to establish a national bank, but he did nothing about it as he had already pushed his luck pretty far and was hesitant to embark on another Constitutional battle, especially one in which his own supporters would be split.

The Constitution did, however, specifically authorize an excise tax; so Hamilton had already proposed such a tax on the distillation of whisky. This would not affect the moneyed classes, who were partial to wines, but **Whisky excise** would descend heaviest on the back-country farmers, who had consistently opposed his program and who needed a demonstration of the power of the Federal government to enforce the laws. Most of the whisky distillers lived toward the frontier, where grain was superabundant but too heavy to transport to market. It was therefore the custom for neighborhood distillers to turn grain into whisky on shares, both because it was the favorite local tipple and because the distiller's share could thus be profitably carried to the eastern markets. Hamilton's excise was thus justifiably regarded as a blow at one of the few sources of cash open to the Westerner and an arrogant tax on his principal social beverage.

Hamilton's main program was undoubtedly a success. United States bonds sold abroad at a premium, and the profits placed in the hands of investors by his program and by the immensely successful national bank **Significance of Hamilton's program** promoted a boom both in speculation and in legitimate development. Hamilton himself carefully abstained from profiting; but his friends plunged, and some were financially ruined. Such abuses are perhaps inevitable. In Hamilton's favor it should be remembered that he scotched inflation, established the public credit, introduced stability and predictability in money matters, and cleared the channels of commerce. While he strengthened the power of economic privilege, the attempt called into organized being the counterforce which was to thwart his attempt to "administer" the Constitution into the form most suitable to himself and to furnish the balance to his concepts all through American history.

BIBLIOGRAPHICAL NOTE

The Confederation Period

Older works on the Confederation period have been displaced by Merrill Jensen, *The New Nation: A History of the U.S. During the Confederation, 1781–1789* (1950). This should be supplemented by Irving Brant, *James Madison: The Nationalist, 1780–1787* (1948). Jennings B. Sanders, *Evolution of the Executive Departments of the Continental Congress, 1774–1789* (1935) is essential for its subject. For Vermont in this period see Chilton Williamson, *Vermont in Quandary, 1763–1825* (1949).

The Second Constitution

The literature on the Constitutional Convention is extensive. Handiest is Max Farrand, *The Framing of the Constitution of the United States* (1913); his *Records of the Federal Convention of 1787* (3 v., 1911) contains the notes made by various members of the convention, especially Madison. Charles A. Beard's *An Economic Interpretation of the Constitution of the United States* (various ed.) is a product of economic determinism but provides a much-needed study of economic influence in the convention. See also Robert L. Schuyler, *Constitution of the U.S.: An Historical Survey of Its Formation* (1928); Charles Warren, *The Making of the Constitution* (1947); and Carl Van Doren, *The Great Rehearsal* (1948). Irving Brant, *James Madison: Father of the Constitution, 1787–1800* (1950) is a careful study both of the Convention and of Madison's part in it.

Hamilton the Force

ADMINISTRATION: In addition to works on Washington, Hamilton, and other figures of the time see Leonard D. White, *The Federalists* (1948); and James Hart, *The American Presidency in Action, 1789* (1948).

CONGRESS: On Congressional methods and evolution see Ralph V. Harlow, *History of Legislative Methods in the Period Before 1825* (1917); George H. Haynes, *The Senate of the U.S.* (2 v., 1938); and De Alva S. Alexander, *History and Procedure of the House of Representatives* (1916). The *Journal* (1927) of William Maclay, Democratic Senator from Pennsylvania, is an interesting account of the early years of the Federal Congress.

JUDICIARY: Of the vast amount of comment and history the following are most useful: Charles Warren, *Supreme Court in United States History* (2 v., 1926); Clarence C. Callender, *American Courts* (1927); Alfred H. Kelly and Winfred A. Harbison, *The American Constitution* (1948).

HAMILTON: There are numerous biographies of Hamilton, none of them definitive. Those biased in his favor are by Henry C. Lodge, John T. Morse, and Frederick S. Oliver; more impartial are others by Henry J. Ford, James Schouler, and William G. Sumner. *The Intimate Life of Alexander Hamilton* (1910) by his grandson, Allen M. Hamilton, has interest. His *Works* were edited by Henry C. Lodge (9 v., 1885–86).

ADAMS: Most recent biography and best reading is Gilbert Chinard, *Honest John Adams* (1933). Besides Chinard, there are biographies by Charles F. Adams (his grandson) and John T. Morse. For his philosophy see Correa M. Walsh, *The Political Science of John Adams* (1915). Of particular value is James T. Adams (no kin), *The Adams Family* (1930) as a study of a family which has contributed outstanding public men to every generation of American history since the Revolution. *New Letters of Abigail Adams, 1788–1801* (1947) is of interest as depicting the trials of a President's wife in the new Republic. His *Works* were edited by Charles Francis Adams (10 v., 1850–56).

FEDERALIST WORTHIES: Frank Monaghan, *John Jay* (1935) is unusually sound and interesting. On the Connecticut coterie see Vernon L. Parrington, *The Connecticut Wits* (1926); Henry A. Beers, *The Connecticut Wits and Other Essays* (1920); Charles E. Cunningham, *Timothy Dwight, 1752–1817* (1942); Richard J. Purcell, *Connecticut in Transition, 1775–1818* (1918). On the Essex Junto see Anson E. Morse, *The Federalist Party in Massachusetts to the Year 1800* (1909); Samuel E. Morison, *Life and Letters of Harrison Gray Otis* (2 v., 1913); Henry Cabot Lodge, *Life and Letters of George Cabot* (1877).

HAMILTON'S PROGRAM: In addition to other works refer to John S. Bassett, *The Federalist System* (1906). On the early years of the First Bank of the U.S. see Burton A. Konkle, *Thomas Willing and the First American Financial System* (1937); and for its entire history see John T. Holdsworth, *The First Bank of the U.S.* (1910).

Chapter X

THE BATTLE FOR
THE DEMOCRATIC PROCESS

1 *Jefferson the Counterforce*

HAMILTON'S program was in its essentials what the country needed if it was ever to become a nation. Perhaps it was in the long view fortunate that the counterforce was not in the beginning well enough organized to block the force. Though the counterforce was represented from the first by such leaders as Madison of Virginia, it failed to get much backing either in Congress

The force calls forth the counterforce

or among the people until the actual results of Hamilton's program demonstrated beyond the shadow of a doubt that a new Tory party had developed and was devoted to promoting the political, social, and economic ascendancy of an aristocracy of wealth and position. Jefferson was the political genius chiefly responsible for giving the inchoate opposition the semblance of party discipline and a party program.

Thomas Jefferson came out of the Virginia Piedmont at a time when it was more authentically western in spirit than California is today. His father came of the lower gentry and as a surveyor and land speculator rose to affluence and prominence. His mother was a Randolph, the *crème de la crème* of Virginia's aristocracy. Thus backed by his father's political and financial position and his mother's social position, Thomas Jefferson was so se-

Thomas Jefferson (1743–1826)

cure among the aristocracy that he never needed to adopt the armor of snobbery so often worn by the socially insecure. And yet, growing up among the buckskins of the Piedmont under the eye of a father who never ceased to be one of the people, and receiving his early education among the dissenting frontier Presbyterians, he imbibed a faith in democracy which was not shaken by his residence as a student at aristocratic William and Mary College and his later study of the law.

He was active in politics from 1769 until his retirement from the presidency in 1809 and comprehended in that forty years enough activity for three careers. As a young Revolutionary leader he undertook the **Career in Virginia** championship of a series of reforms which even Patrick Henry regarded as radical. One after another the laws of primogeniture and entail were abolished and the Church of England disestablished, though he lost his battle to set up a system of public education. By 1779 he had succeeded Henry as the effective leader of the progressive movement, but during a term as governor he disclosed his weakness as an executive. He was hesitant in making decisions, had an excessive regard for Constitutional limitations, and possessed an obvious distaste for the necessary evil of government in any form. In the end he was beaten down by odds which it must be admitted were almost insuperable.

History was to repeat itself during his presidency. Virginia now went conservative for a while, but in later years he was to force upon it a state university in place of hidebound William and Mary. The abolition of slavery was another of his dreams, but like so many of his objectives it was in advance of the times. It was the dreams which came true, not the high offices he had held, which he asked be recorded on his tomb. There they can still be read: "Here was buried Thomas Jefferson, author of the Declaration of American Independence, of the statute of Virginia for religious freedom, and father of the University of Virginia."

Despite his political activities he found time to cultivate a range of interests not equaled even by Franklin. He was passionately fond of music and practiced the violin assiduously, but it was said that only **Universal interests** Patrick Henry was a worse fiddler. He was scholarly but not pedantic. He spoke or read seven languages. His *Notes on Virginia* showed his relative proficiency in the geography, paleontology, ethnology, zoology, and botany of that day; he had a perennial interest in mechanics, invented a plow on mathematical principles, and filled his home with handy gadgets of his own invention; as a garden designer he was acknowledged as tops even in England; he was, like Washington, a tireless investigator of and experimenter in new agricultural methods and was later to fill his pockets with seed rice when he left Italy, even though the penalty if caught was death. As an architect he drew on Roman sources and their French adaptations and actually led the classical revival which was to sweep Europe twenty years later. His home at Monticello near Charlottesville, the state capitol at Richmond, and the campus of the University of Virginia are the best known of his designs, and the style has been followed almost religiously in American public buildings. More than this, however, he was a collector of paintings and sculpture, and he was one of the first Americans to set down his appreciation of natural scenery without hastening to estimate the board feet of lumber in the view.

Jefferson was mellowed and matured in taste, in mind, and in philosophy by five years spent in France as Confederation minister, but with frequent pilgrimages to other countries. Jefferson was at this time a widower with two little daughters, for his beloved wife had died in 1782. The author of the Declaration of Independence and of *Notes on Virginia* was readily received into the social and intellectual world at Paris. He enjoyed the experience, lived elegantly, and entertained often. Came the Revolution, and Jefferson watched with fascination the mobs of Paris and the razing of the Bastille. Later on Jefferson's enemies likened him to the fearsome and bloody Jacobins and asserted that he drew his "democratical" ideas from them. Nothing could be farther astray. Though he found in Physiocratic doctrine a welcome rationalization of his Virginian economic ideas, he took his political ideas to France with him. If anything, it is fairer to say that politically he was the teacher of those very moderates (Girondins) who because of their consistent refusal to use terror in support of liberty were led to the guillotine by the extremist Jacobins.

Jefferson in France

The Jefferson who took up his duties as Secretary of State was fourteen years older than his great rival. He was very tall, slender, and loose-jointed, with red hair, blue eyes, and a long face. No one ever called him handsome, but many observers noted the serenity of his expression. He was shy, and shyness may have caused the characteristic habit of averting his eyes from anyone with whom he was talking; at any rate, it led to the plausible accusation that he was shifty. Slow and calm in his manner, he was reserved on first meeting but was a good talker (except in public), once he got started.

Appearance

It has been argued that he was devoid of a sense of humor, "that sympathetic enjoyment of all the manifold contrasts and incongruities of life." Probably so, for he was too deeply absorbed in the analysis of the incongruity to be able to enjoy it. Yet he did possess sympathy, tolerance, and kindliness; and his frequent patience and tact in large matters and considerateness in small things were indisputable. He was perfectly willing to let others take the credit if he but attained his object. He was seldom rattled or irritable, and he was not a crusader in the emotional sense; the Declaration of Independence is the most emotional of his compositions.

Character

Though Jefferson is rightly called a philosopher and like philosophers dreamed of "the good society," it is notable that he expressed his ideas and his program in concrete, practical terms. Aristocracy in itself was cer-

His philosophy tainly not an object of his hatred, for he sought only to spread its gospel of taste, refinement, education, and competent leadership—but not its abuses. Property was not the enemy, for he sought to spread and increase it, though he did assert that its possession was not one of the Natural Rights. Religion was not the enemy except as it was used to uphold special privileges. Though he was probably a deist, he did not evangelize. On the contrary, he reverenced the teachings of Christ and read His words every evening. He was an Episcopalian and, what is more, attended services more faithfully and contributed more largely than many of his critics. And yet he was hated by Episcopal and Congregational clergymen for his advocacy of the separation of Church and state, and they sought diligently in his scientific writings for proofs of his atheism.

Jefferson was not (at least after the Revolution) a radical bent upon overthrowing established institutions or uprooting the social tree. He believed in working calmly and slowly by education, and that if the people received light they would find their own way. And yet he recognized the danger that popular "whims" might institute a tyranny of the majority. The minority also had rights; the majority to be right must be reasonable. He fought against any attempt to rivet the ideological chains of one generation upon the next. Amendment of the Constitution instead of being thwarted should be deliberately undertaken every twenty years or so. Moreover, freedom was not necessarily synonymous with peace. "The Tree of Liberty," he said, "must be refreshed from time to time with the blood of patriots and tyrants."

Basically Jefferson taught that government is the natural enemy of man, hence his insistence that as many functions as possible must be localized in order that the people might be able to control them directly.

Political tenets Government must not be permitted to do anything for the people that they could do themselves, hence "that government is best which governs least"; by protraction it followed that the cheapest government was the best, an idea which still has exponents. Jefferson opposed the interference of the government to strengthen or enrich a class, especially to give it the subtle and intangible forms of wealth (stocks and bonds) which he believed arose from the exploitation of others.

He opposed this kind of interference because he feared that wealth would sooner or later breed power, and power for the few is a menace to the liberties of the many. Now since power and property are inseparable, he desired that property be scattered as widely and as evenly as possible; in other words, he favored the multiplication of yeoman farmers. Great cities to him were great sores, and he never trusted the proletariat because they were dependent upon the goodwill of employers. For this reason he was willing to break his tenets and use the government to distribute land cheaply and protect the farmer in its ownership. The good society was one of farmers; let the United States remain content in agrarian freedom and import from other countries such products of wage slavery as it must have —and in British ships. He took direct issue with Hamilton's objectives and taught (1) government by the people; (2) the dominance of agriculture; and (3) the literal and strict interpretation of the Constitution. We shall see to what extent time, political necessity, and executive responsibility influenced his thinking.

In his political methods, Jefferson was too practical and too much the opportunist to be a saint. His political machinations were filled with the low cunning which Hamilton tried to equal but never could. Though he was a voluminous letter writer, he possessed that elusiveness so valuable to a politician which hindered his enemies from pinning him down. He prided himself on never having written an anonymous article (in a day when that was the rule), but he was willing to use subterfuge; if he did not encourage scurrility, he at least permitted it. He was accused, apparently with justice, of vindictiveness, and certainly he was persistent in seeking to break his political enemies. Nevertheless, he judged his enemies clearly and often admiringly without underestimating them or wasting his nervous energy in useless raving. **Political methods**

But the secret of his political success did not lie in the use of such commonplace though deplorable weapons. He did not make Hamilton's mistake of organizing an army of generals. He sought to arouse the common people to an awareness of the value of the vote, he sought to break down excessive property qualifications for the suffrage, and he preached party discipline incessantly. He knew intuitively what the people at the grass roots were thinking and was able to build upon it. Even more important, he had that faith in the people which was necessary to inspire them in following him toward the bright goal of human rights which they may have glimpsed but dimly yet accepted because of their faith in him.

When Jefferson entered Washington's Cabinet he had no intention of being the founder of a party. Indeed, a few months previously he had written that if he could not go to heaven but with a party, he would not go at all. In 1789 Hamilton set up John Fenno as editor of *The Gazette of the United States,* and Fenno rapidly slapped down all opposition. Jefferson countered in 1791 by setting up Philip Freneau, the "Poet of the Revolution," as editor of *The National Gazette.* The paper was short-lived, but it vigorously paved the way for a spate of democratic papers. Soon Greek and Roman pen names spattered the pages of the two journals and their imitators as they joined in political combat. **Political battle joined**

That Hamilton wrote copiously for Fenno's paper was an open secret, and his venom was particularly directed at Jefferson in an effort to force his resignation. Washington was distressed by the spectacle and vainly attempted to reconcile his two chief officers. Jefferson offered his resignation, but Washington refused it; on the other hand he permitted Hamilton's attacks to go on—perhaps, indeed, he was powerless to govern the headstrong Secretary of the Treasury. Month by month the situation deteriorated. Clashes in Cabinet meetings became more frequent; and before long even the deliberate Jefferson had lost his calm, and the two men were glaring at each other across the council table "like cocks in a pit."

Growing antago-nisms

Washington's hope of avoiding party strife was clearly bankrupt, yet there was difficulty in organizing an opposition party so long as he publicly supported Hamilton's program. Hamilton and his followers knew this and never hesitated to take refuge from democratic barbs under Washington's coat tails. Indeed, it became standing operating procedure to interpret any attack on Federalist measures as a personal attack on the great man; inevitably this interpretation led to such personal attacks, which the Hamiltonians gleefully found drew the wavering into their ranks. Yet to the very last the Federalists looked upon themselves not as a party but as the political instruments of the ruling class, governing by natural right because they possessed the property. They even denied with perfectly straight faces that they were organized and carefully concealed the strings of management in order to be consistent in denouncing democratic organization.

Federalists' view of their mis-sion

Fisher Ames of Massachusetts departed only a little from the official terminology when he stated that of course there could be but two parties: "the friends of order, and its foes." Even Washington descended into the arena to grasp a cudgel when he deplored pressure groups (he called them "self-created societies") as destructive of Constitutional authority.

The democratic party which Jefferson now seriously undertook to mold was known at first as the Democratic-Republican Party but was soon to be shortened to Republican. The elements from which it was formed had existed in each colony from the earliest days, though they had never acted together until the Revolution. It was they who had settled Rhode Island and the Connecticut River towns, engaged in Bacon's Rebellion, fought the Stuart governors in 1689, comprised the Carolina Regulators, formed the Country Party of agrarian frontiersmen, composed the Lee-Adams Junto in the Revolution, and finally had as Antifederalists opposed ratification of the Constitution. The Jeffersonian Republican Party, therefore, was not in any sense a new creation or a foreign "ism" (as the Federalists pretended) but a legitimate growth of the seed of Eng-

Jefferso-nian Re-publicans a native growth

lish liberties brought to this continent by the earliest settlers, planted in the American soil, and nourished and shaped in its growth by the peculiar conditions of the new environment.

Jefferson was little given to joining schools of thought, but until after 1800 he not only agreed with the Physiocrats that wealth came only from the land, but he (or at least his followers) regarded merchants, capitalists, and manufacturers as parasites. He had little comprehension of the part that capital and labor play in the creation of national wealth and did not learn until later. Physiocratic **Jefferson as a Physiocrat** doctrines titillated the planter because they were designed to dignify and protect great landowners, and the small farmer because they made him the creator of national wealth. Since both planter and farmer were in debt, they naturally agreed that their creditors were parasites who did not deserve to be paid. Bankers and merchants not only drained away wealth without performing any true service in return, but they also flouted the natural law of free enterprise by using the government to carry out their schemes.

Just how much Americans owed to French thinkers is uncertain, for a predominantly agrarian society is sure to develop ideas of the importance of agriculture regardless of what economists may be doing. These ideas have been basic in American history, but there is no term adequate to express them. The word *agrarian* has come to carry little more meaning than *rural;* on the other hand, **American Physiocracy** French Physiocracy was far more subtle and rigid than was the thinking of American agrarians. For lack of a better term we shall adopt *American Physiocracy* to indicate the American form of agrarian laissez faire with its emphasis upon natural law and upon the fundamental importance of agriculture and its consequent right to dominate economics and politics.

A glance at the attitudes of Hamilton and Jefferson toward the powers of government is instructive. The Constitution was designed to provide a government that could not act too decisively, that in effect could not interfere with the current concept that the law of Nature was that business should regulate itself. True, there were **Party attitudes toward strong government** "strong" government men in the Convention, but they had had experience with royal governors and courts and agreed to the checks held by the three branches of government on each other. It is significant that Hamilton was one of the few exceptions who did not fear a strong government. We usually oppose a strong government unless it operates in favor of our particular interest, so it is almost always true that the party in power tends to favor strong government and the one out of power desires weak government. Hamilton and Jefferson were no exceptions.

But the future was concealed from Jefferson and his good friend Madison when they discussed the bases of the new party as they sat by the fire, tramped across the fields, or ascended the Hudson on their famous "bot-

Material for a protest party

anizing" expedition. They saw a country remarkable for its variety of interests, not yet truly conscious of its nationality, and with the underdogs as so often in human affairs quarreling among themselves and unable to find strength in unity. And yet there were certain factors on which party unity could be built. Hamilton had united the mercantile class and its hangers-on, and in the process he had further antagonized the debtor class. Not only did the debtors have to bear their local burdens, but now a Federal burden had been assumed and inflated (they believed) and laid upon their backs in the form of increased taxes. The debtors were usually farmers, and those farmers who were not already debtors feared the milking-away of what they had and a reduction in their standard of living. Though ninety per cent of the population were farmers, Hamilton had ignored them in scattering his largesses, had laid a whisky tax on them, and had promised them nothing save that greater prosperity and an increased industrial population would raise the price of farm products.

New England did not appear to be a promising field for Republicanism. Such Revolutionary firebrands as Sam Adams and John Hancock were flickering out, and younger talent was only slowly developed. At first New

Republicans in New England

England's workingmen, insofar as they were enfranchised, were Federalist, for they had received the pence dropped from the overflowing counting tables of the merchants. Later on they were to move over, at least in part. Most promising timber for the Republican Party was found in the back country between the well-favored river valleys. These farmers at best made a hand-to-mouth livelihood and were chronically exploited by the merchants and their hangers-on. Many of them were dissenters and resented the tax for the benefit of the established church, and the way in which the established clergy called down divine wrath on anyone who got out of line politically. Consequently Jeffersonian Republicanism in back-country New England was recruited from the Methodists, Presbyterians, Baptists, and curiously enough the Episcopalians, who were also dissenters there.

New York had always been aristocratic, but there had grown up within this magic circle two factions which by 1760 had taken on the dignity of parties. One of them, led by the Livingston family, had found allies in

New York politics

the rising middle classes and in the dissenting clergy and was Whig in its tendencies. This so-called "Presbyterian Party" edged toward Revolution and finally took the plunge. The other party was merchant, Episcopalian, and Tory; though it sanctioned protest and even mob action against royal policies, it drew the line at rebellion. During the Revolution this party under the leadership of the De Lancey family had been actively Tory, but after the war many of its members managed to hold on to their property and social prestige. As previously noted, Hamilton had become its legal and political champion.

The war had promoted a democratic movement under the skillful leadership of George Clinton, perennial governor of New York and twice Vice-President of the United States, and his nephew De Witt Clinton. At this time (about 1790) there were only twenty-three thousand voters in New York. Clinton's ascendancy was based upon an alliance of the commoners in the city and the farmers of the Hudson and the Mohawk valleys. After 1790 he was strengthened by the expansion of settlements toward Lake Erie, as the Iroquois in large part went to Canada and their lands were purchased either by the state for disposal as military bounty lands or by private speculators under state authorization. **Settlement of upper New York**

The western part of the state had been claimed by Massachusetts under the terms of its colonial charter, and in 1786 by a compromise arrangement Massachusetts was permitted to sell the land though New York retained the sovereignty. Massachusetts quickly sold off its claims in large blocks to speculators in order to replenish its treasury, and settlers, the bulk of them New Englanders, poured into the old lands of the Iroquois. Hitherto New York City had been hampered in its growth because its distant hinterland was unproductive of much besides furs; now it began a phenomenal growth, a growth which was to be accelerated by turnpikes, canals, and railroads until the city was unchallenged in size and· wealth.

Even before the adoption of the Constitution the two aristocratic wings had begun to draw together under the leadership of Hamilton and of John Jay, who had married into the Livingston clan. That family was at this time led by Chancellor Robert R. Livingston and by his much younger brother Edward. Both brothers had distinguished careers both in state politics and in diplomacy, **Party lines tightened** though the former is usually recalled chiefly as a partner of Robert Fulton in steamboat navigation. Hamilton now performed one of the amazing boners which dotted his career by ignoring the Livingstons in the distribution of patronage. It was the opportunity of a rising young politician, Aaron Burr, the attorney-general of New York.

Aaron Burr was the son of one president of Princeton and grandson of another, the great Jonathan Edwards. Burr graduated from Princeton at sixteen and had a distinguished career in the Revolutionary army, though a few weeks on Washington's staff brought out his unfortunate penchant for indecorous and impertinent behavior, and the two parted with mutual dislike. As a lawyer **Aaron Burr (1756– 1836)** in New York City, Burr was second in prominence only to Hamilton, and he easily surpassed Hamilton in his ability to charm a wide circle of acquaintances. Burr was a man with brilliant intellect and fascinating personality, but like many thus gifted he depended on dexterity rather than profundity, and intrigue rather than *bona fide* leadership. With a mind uncluttered by any hampering notions of truth and honor, he was ambitious, plausible, and outwardly serene, sometimes rash in his judgments, and always unscrupulous; what was worse, he refused to play the hypocrite by claiming scruples he did not possess.

Some of Burr's political friends made their headquarters at a tavern called Martling's Long Room, which was also the meeting place of a pre-Revolutionary radical club called the Sons of St. Tammany, reorganized **Rise of** probably in 1788 as the Society of Tammany, or Columbian **Tammany** Order. Tammany seems to have been intended as a counter-irritant to the aristocratic Society of the Cincinnati and was chiefly a working-class order and benevolent association. It is not likely that Burr ever belonged to Tammany, but it became under his management a potent political instrument and has remained that ever since. Hamilton's alienation of the Livingstons was exactly the opportunity for which Burr was looking. He united the Clintons and Livingstons and had himself elected to the Senate of the United States over Hamilton's own father-in-law, General Philip Schuyler.

New Jersey was normally run by a so-called "squirearchy" and was dependably Federalist, but Pennsylvania was another matter. Philadelphia was still the metropolis of the new country as well as the capital and **Phila-** was marking its fading glory by a last mad fling. Less au- **delphia** · thentically aristocratic than New York, it was a hive of frantic dollar-worshipers (whether dressed in Quaker brown or gayer plumage) who aped the more ostentatious side of Old World society. It was the snob's paradise, for the rich and the newly-rich were drawn together by a common fear of the mob; the entrance requirements were wealth and abhorrence of democracy. The Philadelphia mob was indeed something to be feared; nevertheless, it had respectable directors or at least inspirers, among them the eminent scientist David Rittenhouse; the medico Benjamin Rush; Benjamin Bache, grandson of Franklin and editor of the independent-democratic paper *Aurora;* and others such as Governor Thomas Mifflin, Judge Thomas McKean, Alexander J. Dallas, and the gentle Quaker philosopher George Logan, a close friend of Jefferson.

Beyond Philadelphia lay the neat fields of the Pennsylvania-Dutch farmers, who under the leadership of the Muhlenberg family were beginning to take an interest in democratic opposition to the Federalists. The **Pennsyl-** Scotch-Irish country beyond the Susquehanna was Presby- **vania hin-** terian and therefore democratic, while the mixed population **terland** among the slashings and the already-eroding hills of the

Monongahela country were Antifederalist for hereditary and economic reasons—the whisky excise among the latter. A rising democratic leader in the West was the Princeton lawyer, novelist, and poetaster Hugh Henry Brackenridge, but he was to fall victim to the antipathies bred by the Whisky Insurrection, and William Findley and Albert Gallatin were to dominate the scene.

Gallatin was a Genevan aristocrat who had served momentarily in the Revolutionary army, taught at Harvard, then gone into western land speculation. For forty years he served in legislative or diplomatic capacities and as Secretary of the Treasury. It is difficult to muster **Albert** any enthusiasm over Gallatin the person. He was too humor- **Gallatin** less, too much the adding machine. He kept his mouth shut **(1761–** and stroked fur the right way when possible but was a fox **1849)** in council and a lion in combat when his doctrinaire sense of justice was aroused. Only once did he obey an impulse: when he went overboard for Rousseau and let his search for the state of nature lead him to America. However, that was understandable in a lad of eighteen in strict, Calvinistic Geneva. If the western wilderness was not the paradise that he had been led to expect by his reading of Rousseau, it was at least democratic. "Not only have we neither Livingston nor Rensselaer," he wrote, "but from the suburbs of Philadelphia to the banks of the Ohio I do not know a single family that has any extensive influence. An equal distribution of property has rendered every individual independent, and there is among us true and real equity."

Virginia, at this time the largest state in the Union both in area and in population, was the undisputed leader of the South and the rival of Massachusetts for domination of the Union. Though Virginia bred both Washington and Marshall, there was never any doubt that **Virginia** it belonged in the Republican column. The reason was that **the epitome** it was purely agricultural. True, it had a planting aristocracy **of protest** in Tidewater and a farmer democracy in the interior, but both found a common enemy in the merchant capitalism of the North which threatened to keep them in the same debtor relationship that they had known in colonial days. Even when the war in Europe increased the demand for meat and grain, the stiff competition of the rich Ohio Valley with a downstream outlet to world markets from New Orleans outrivaled the East. Eastern farms were failing, partly because the agrarian traditionalist refused to abandon his wasteful methods for better ones, partly because better techniques in America were still in the experimental stage. The eastern farmer was, he felt, driven to rob his soil to the point of ruin. All of these factors promoted debt. Instead of boldly attacking their problems with brains, the planter and the farmer (even as we) blamed the government. Taxes were collected in cash, and cash was scarce; therefore let the Federal government economize and thus reduce the tax burden which Physiocratic doctrine claimed was always passed on to the farmer, no matter who got the tax receipt.

Virginia bred the chief leaders of Republicanism: Jefferson, Madison, and John Taylor of Caroline. James Madison came from a family of the lesser aristocracy of the Piedmont. At Princeton he paid unusual atten-

James Madison (1751– 1836) tion to history and politics, a training which made him a useful legislator and constitution-maker during the Revolution, and led to his role as the "Father of the Constitution." Madison was a bald, pot-bellied, thin-legged, physically unimpressive little man with mild eyes and a weak voice. Washington Irving once exclaimed, "Poor Jemmy! Withered little applejohn!" Stilted and uninspired in public relations, Madison was in his private relations a well of humor, running over with puns and whimsicalities which kept his friends in stitches. In spite of his unimpressiveness he wooed and won in marriage a Quaker belle whose beauty, vivacity, and social gifts made her famous as Dolly Madison.

Though he lacked political sex appeal, his mental and forensic powers were beyond dispute. In some fields Madison was the instructor of Jefferson. For example, he seems to have been the first to grasp (in No. 50 of *The Federalist*) the technical mission of political parties as the practical expression of changing social alliances, though indeed he erred in expecting them to be temporary. He was Jefferson's closest friend and confidant. The organization of the Republican Party was definitely influenced by his advice and efforts, and he was its foremost public defender. Nevertheless, he was never as convinced a democrat as Jefferson and in that respect was more typical of the planter aristocracy of Virginia than was Jefferson.

John Taylor of Caroline County was a Tidewater planter and lawyer who was as prominent in agricultural experimentation as in political writing. Throughout his life he held consistently to the aristocratic wing

John Taylor of Caroline (1753– 1824) of the Physiocratic doctrines, though he never acknowledged the source of his arguments and indeed seems never to have understood that the planters comprised an aristocracy. Aristocracy to him meant the artificial class of speculative capitalists created by Hamilton, and he rejected utterly the concept that there is such a thing as a natural aristocracy.

Taylor disagreed with the Jeffersonian concept of conflict of balanced social forces and rejected parties as an evil—though if there must be parties the agrarian party was the only one that had justification because agriculture alone is productive. He failed quite completely to see that parties could give way to each other as social alliances changed. Rather, he depended upon the states to hold the balance between a selfish financial aristocracy in control of the central government on one hand and the chaotic tendencies of the people on the other. For that reason the Federal government must be weakened, and such governmental functions as had to be exercised should be assigned to the states. The Constitution was a compact between the states; and the latter, since they had created it, were the judges of its terms. Until 1808 he was a vigorous supporter of Jeffersonianism, and his pamphlets *A Definition of Parties* and *An Enquiry into the Principles and Tendencies of Certain Public Measures* (both published in 1794) were powerful attacks on Hamilton's program. After 1808 the shift of the Republican Party toward business interests led to the publication of certain turbid but influential books which became the foundations of southern sectionalism and the springboard for Calhoun's doctrines of nullification and secession.

These were the outstanding leaders of Republicanism. But there were others only less well known nationally. John Francis Mercer, member of the Constitutional Convention who refused to approve the result, served Virginia and Maryland in turn in Congress. James Monroe of Virginia was partisan and ambitious but destined for the highest office. William B. Giles of Virginia, ungracious and rash, was still a superb floor manager. Not least was the **Other southern Jeffersonians** brilliant John Randolph of Roanoke, a distant cousin of Jefferson, whom we will meet again. In North Carolina was Willie Jones, an aristocrat with the common touch, and Nathaniel Macon, who became Republican leader of the House, but was better at tearing down than building up. In South Carolina there was no one at first, but presently Charles Pinckney, a Federalist in the Constitutional Convention, became a Republican war horse. In Georgia there was James Jackson, whose mouth was bigger than his brain but whose heart was in the right place. Most of these men were originally opponents of the Constitution, and some of them never recovered from the feeling that the people had been bilked.

There is a story that in 1791 Jefferson and Madison on a "botanizing" tour in the Hudson Valley conferred with Burr and Clinton and formed the historic alliance between the South and Tammany Hall which has been the mainstay of the political descendants of Jefferson. Doubtless the exact time and circumstances of the transaction will never be known.

At any rate, when Washington expressed his determination to retire, Hamilton saw that the Republicans were likely to carry the two new western states of Kentucky and Tennessee and all of the South except Maryland and South Carolina; with good luck in New York and Pennsylvania they might elect their presidential candidate. Washington was the only man on whom the two parties could agree, and at the insistence of both Hamilton and **Washington re-elected, 1792** Jefferson he agreed to accept one more term. Even as it was, the Republican electors from five southern states after showing their preference for Washington as President cast their vice-presidential ballots for George Clinton of New York, though they could not prevent Adams from squeezing through again. After bitter local contests in which Hamilton did not scruple to use the prestige of Washington to swing doubtful votes, the Republicans showed perceptible gains in Congress. The arrogant challenge of the Hamiltonians had been accepted, and the counterforce had begun to gather. Let us turn now to the years of rising conflict.

2   The Rising Conflict

History records no reagent that roused the people of the nations as dramatically and effectively as the French Revolution. Its effect even upon the United States was deeply significant, for it stirred the imagination of

Impact of the French Revolution on the U.S. the people and raised the Jeffersonian struggle for democracy from a factional skirmish to a battle between parties. From 1793 until 1815 European events were to shape American domestic politics. Though it would be inaccurate to say that the French Revolution rose out of the American Revolution, it is certainly true that American legal and philosophical concepts were closely studied in France and accelerated a crisis that was bound to come. Since France had been our ally in the War of Independence it was only natural that many Americans should sympathize with the French movement for democracy, and the fact that Lafayette and Tom Paine were prominent in French events furnished a visible link between the two revolutions which promoted in this country an almost proprietary interest. When in 1792 the French threw back the royalist army of Prussia at Valmy, American rejoicing was second only to that of France; and when the French republic announced its mission and purpose to free all peoples, the dramatic defiance to tyrants made us of one kin. Even the Federalists were stirred.

Winter storms cut communication with Europe until April 1793. Then in one package came the news of events that changed the French Revolution from a topic for routine toasts to a vital issue in domestic politics

American opinion divides and foreign affairs. The Girondin friends of Jefferson had taken over the government and were sending Citizen Edmond Genêt to instruct the United States in its duties as an ally. Louis xvi had been tried and guillotined. Most ominous of all, war had been declared against Great Britain and Spain. The effect was almost immediate. The Federalists dropped the mask and denounced the French Revolution. They were not enemies of liberty, they said, but of a license which sought only disorder and blood; as such they must side with England, the traditional home of ordered liberty. On the other hand, the Republicans found that they had much in common with the Girondins.

The French news did in weeks what Jefferson might have struggled in vain for years to accomplish. Its drama roused the indifferent and promoted the separation of the people into two parties—pro-French and pro-British—and Jefferson in estimating the situation must **Effect on** have been haunted by the fear that the issue of democracy **political** had been swamped by sentimental loyalties to foreign pow- **parties** ers. The Americans' penchant for taking vocal sides in foreign quarrels in which they have no serious intention of wielding a cudgel was never shown to better advantage. France had never been as popular among Americans during the Revolution as it was now, and old Tories must have observed wryly that half as much enthusiasm for Britain in 1776 as there was now would have saved America for the Empire. The Jacobin Clubs of France found imitators in a rash of Democratic Societies which declared war on kings and aristocrats, particularly against those of England and their imitators in the United States. They even dropped titles of address as undemocratic and urged everyone to use "Citizen" and "Citizeness."

Almost simultaneously with the news of his coming, Citizen Genêt landed in Charleston and began a leisurely journey northward while the adoring country flocked to the roadside to cheer his passage. By the time he reached Philadelphia the adulation had gone to **Citizen** his head, and he was inclined to regard himself as a pro- **Genêt** consul who would allow the nation to retain its own rulers if they "co-operated," but who if they balked would not hesitate to overturn them and take over the government himself. As a matter of fact, the best cards were in his hands. By the treaties of 1778 the United States was bound upon demand to help defend the French West Indies. In addition each had guaranteed to the other the provisos of the Armed Neutrality that free ships made free goods save for contraband of war, which should not include foodstuffs and naval stores. This guarantee made American neutrality valuable to France, for if American ships could carry food and naval stores through the British fleet it would be of more help than any conceivable navy. At the same time France could hope to use American ports as bases for the French fleet, for the outfitting of privateers, and for the disposal of captured ships and goods.

Washington and his advisers were not so naïve as to miss the fact that France either could insist upon American entry into the war on the basis that the French islands were in danger, or as the price of peace could try to jockey the United States into a position of co- **Washing-** operation which would arouse the ire of Great Britain. **ton's di-** Meanwhile an attempt was made to cool the overheated pop- **lemma** ulace by issuing on 22 April 1793 Washington's Neutrality Proclamation. Though the word "neutrality" was left out at Jefferson's suggestion, it declared the diplomatic independence of the United States by

asserting that we would be "friendly and impartial toward the belligerent powers." When Genêt arrived in Philadelphia the diplomatic management passed to Jefferson, who deliberately played for time. Genêt got nowhere in his attempts to make the United States a cat's-paw for French
policy, but Jefferson was so adroit that the French republic could not take
official offense. However, by one means or another Genêt managed to send
out fourteen privateers, and eighty British prizes were brought into American ports and condemned in French consular courts which, curiously
enough, held extraterritorial jurisdiction by treaty. Americans engaged
in such hostilities were brought to trial but were released by pro-French
juries.

Genêt rode high during the early summer of 1793. The Democratic
Societies, increased in numbers and in boldness by Genêt's encouragement,
led the revolutionary van. Innumerable roasted oxen were consumed in
The the good cause and countless bumpers tossed off in toasts to
Democratic "Liberty, equality, and fraternity." "Louis Capet has lost
Societies his caput," chortled Brackenridge in the backwoods village
of Pittsburgh, and the Democratic Societies introduced the ceremony
of beheading a roast pig at their dinners. Zealous Francophiles actually vilified the sacrosanct name of Washington and scattered crude
prints showing him being guillotined. Genêt's confederates and agents
stirred up the dreaded Philadelphia mob. John Adams many years later
wrote to Jefferson, probably with some exaggeration, that "ten thousand
people on the streets of Philadelphia, day after day, threatened to drag
Washington out of his house and effect a revolution in the government,
or compel it to declare war in favor of the French Revolution and against
England." The rage of the mob did not die down until a scourge of yellow
fever gave "the many-headed monster" something else to think about.
Adams was convinced that the epidemic was all that saved the government
from revolution.

At any rate, it was evident to Jefferson that Genêt was weakening the
Republican cause with the people as a whole, and he and Madison spurred
local Republican meetings into passing resolutions which disclaimed policies partial to any one foreign power. The Democratic Clubs
Fall of saw the abyss of war and revolution yawning at their feet
Genêt and hastened to add their dittos. At this juncture Genêt
made his most colossal blunder. He was so convinced of his popularity
that he actually threatened to appeal over Washington's head to the
masses. He soon saw that Washington's name still bore magic, for when
early in August the President demanded that the French government recall its envoy few voices were so shameless as to protest. Meanwhile the
radical Jacobins had seized power in France and sent the Girondin moderates to the guillotine. They agreed to recall Genêt if Washington would
recall his minister, Gouverneur Morris, who had made himself obnoxious

by his obstructive tactics in Paris. The Jacobins wanted Genêt returned to France, but Washington refused to make a martyr of him. Presently he moved to New York, and there, having escaped the jaws of the guillotine, he entered the jaws of matrimony with Governor Clinton's daughter and lived to a ripe and comfortable old age.

On the last day of 1793 Jefferson retired from office and returned to his beloved home, Monticello, there to dedicate himself to assiduous correspondence with Republican leaders all over the nation in order to weld them in common principles, discipline, and method. His **Jefferson's** record as Secretary of State has been overshadowed by his **diplomatic** party role, but it was significant. Though he favored the **record** French Revolution, he refused to risk American national existence in its defense. Jefferson hated war, but besides that he felt that the hope of the world lay in peace and in that respect, at least, the United States could set an example. The American policy of diplomatic isolation was launched by him as Secretary of State and strengthened by him as President. He made it evident that America was different from Europe, with a different mission and different interests. One of the successors of Genêt expressed this thought in a report to his government: "Mr. Jefferson likes us because he detests England [*although he*] is the friend of liberty and science, [*and*] an admirer of the efforts we have made to cast off our shackles. . . . Jefferson, I say, is an American, and as such, he cannot sincerely be our friend. An American is the born enemy of all the peoples of Europe."

Jefferson was also the father of the historic "will of the nation" test for deciding whether to receive envoys from revolutionary governments. Indeed, the author of the Declaration of Independence could scarcely hold otherwise. "We certainly cannot," he wrote, "deny to other nations that principle whereon our government is founded, that every nation has a right to govern itself internally under what form it pleases, and to change these forms at its own will; and externally to transact business with other nations through whatever organ it chooses, whether that be King, Convention, Assembly, Committee, President, or whatever it be. The only thing essential is, the will of the nation." Jefferson's rule was followed quite consistently until the present century, and its abandonment has plunged us into much diplomatic and military hot water.

While Genêt rusticated as a country gentleman, the fuse he had lighted burned on. American merchantmen sought to run the British blockade into France and the French West Indies. The depredations of Genêt's privateers on British shipping were avenged when two Or- **British re-** ders in Council authorized the British navy to seize Ameri- **taliation** can vessels trading with French ports or carrying French goods. A hundred American ships were seized, and American seamen were thrown into dungeons or impressed to serve on British warships. Federalists pointed out that if a choice had to be made between French and British trade, it was better to keep the latter, which they claimed amounted to about nine tenths of our total commerce. Nevertheless, it was undeniable that the British still occupied posts in our West and that they had egged on the Indians to war against American settlers in the Ohio country. Even the Federalists had to bow to public opinion when Congress embargoed all shipping for two months, an act aimed at England, and began to overhaul the militia. Attention was then turned to a bill to prohibit all purchase of British goods.

Progress toward war with Britain was slowed down when the French foolishly began seizing hundreds of American vessels bound for England, on the ground that the United States should force Britain to permit the

French alienate American opinion passage of American food to France. For once the British showed sense by opening American trade with the West Indies (the Rule of 1756 did not apply to Britain!) and agreeing to pay for confiscated cargoes. At the same time reports of the Jacobin Reign of Terror were alienating moderate Republicans from the support of France. There was evidently something to the Federalist plaint that liberty in the wrong hands would turn to license. Washington seized the chance and spiked the Republican guns by sending (May 1794) John Jay to London to see what permanent adjustments could be made. Then, as though the cloud of foreign war were not enough, rebellion threatened in the backwoods of Pennsylvania. This, however, was something within the competence of the young Federal government to handle.

It will be remembered that Hamilton had laid his whisky excise in defiance of western sentiment. During the next three years the failure to open the Mississippi to western navigation and the dilatory conduct of

The Whisky Insurrection the Indian wars plus the usual resentments against the East gradually brought opinion to a boil, and it was exhibited by the renewal of a Revolutionary custom of erecting "liberty poles." It so happened that under the original excise act noncomplying distillers from western Pennsylvania had to go to York or Philadelphia for trial, a procedure that cost the value of the average western farm. This was changed in June 1794 to make offenses cognizable in state courts, but while the bill was in passage Hamilton took out a score of processes returnable to Philadelphia under the old law. The fact that these processes were not served until July, six weeks after the easing measure was passed, angered the citizens of the Monongahela counties. Certain hotheaded leaders of the local Democratic Societies stirred up a series of riots during which the home of the chief inspector of the excise was burned. A militia march on Pittsburgh (regarded as the regional Sodom) followed, but cool heads prevented damage.

Hamilton now had the excuse he had desired to show the muscular power of the government. Washington called for militia levies from several states to suppress the "insurrection." The rioters were thrown into panic. Several inconclusive meetings were held, and at Washington's demand a vote on the question of submission was taken in the disaffected counties. The submission was so grudging that Washington set the army of thirteen thousand men in motion under General "Light-Horse Harry" Lee, with Hamilton, still thirsting for military glory, accompanying it as a sort of political commissar. When the army reached the Monongahela in November, the culprit leaders had fled; but Hamilton arrested a score of men, apparently selected on the basis of anonymous tips, and they were marched into Philadelphia amidst the hoots of a mob that was now thoroughly Federalist. After a winter in prison they were tried, but not a single one was found guilty. Two belated captives were convicted and sentenced to death but were pardoned by Washington. After less than three weeks in the West the army returned to the East, leaving fifteen hundred men under General Daniel Morgan to hold the area for law and order.

Hamilton attained his object. A series of riots had been blown up to resemble a national crisis, and the heroic Federalist rescuers were rewarded in the elections. Washington cast the onus squarely on "certain self-created societies," and his followers hastened to point out that such appalling exhibitions were inevitable when the sans-culottes tried to rise above their betters. The Democratic Societies refused to be shamed. Were they abettors of treason for having supposed that governments could do wrong? "Self-created societies?" Nonsense! Scarcely a citizen but what belonged to one: Methodists, Friends, Philosophical, or—boldly tweaking the lion's tail—even the Society of the Cincinnati. In the end the whole episode merely confirmed the Republicans in their belief that the Federalists meant to subvert freedom, but at the same time it was evident that they possessed the psychological and the physical advantages and could be beaten only at the polls.

Results of the Whisky Insurrection

One advantage the Republicans did win. Gallatin had boldly opposed the course of his rowdy neighbors, and the more conservative element had sprung him as a surprise candidate for Congress and elected him. He was worth an army to the Republicans. Madison and his colleagues had floundered hopelessly in their attempts to sift Hamilton's financial prestidigitations; Gallatin followed them with ease and was to become the spearhead of the Republican Congressional attack on the highhanded Secretary of the Treasury.

Meanwhile Chief Justice Jay was making the best of a bad situation in London. With nothing to trade, he had to take what he could get. The only concession worth having was an agreement to vacate the frontier

Jay's Treaty, 1794

posts, but British traders were to be permitted to operate in the United States; no promises were made to abstain from backing Indian raids, or to return or pay for slaves carried off in 1783. Instead of getting a settlement of the matters of impressments and ship seizures, he actually agreed to permit the seizure of French goods found on American ships and the confiscation of foodstuffs if they were paid for. This agreement was certain to roil the French and lead to the accusation of broken treaties. Article XII of the treaty permitted American ships of less than seventy tons to trade with the British West Indies, but in return the United States agreed not to export coffee, cocoa, sugar, and cotton. One provision bore some hope: other unsettled questions were to be referred to mixed arbitral commissions. It was the first important occasion for such an arrangement in modern history, and it set the pattern for such solutions in the future. In the end mixed commissions set the sum of British spoliation of American commerce at $10,000,000, and the sums owing to British merchants on pre-Revolutionary debts at $3,000,000.

Britain had signed what she regarded as a bad treaty in order to keep the Americans as customers and to keep them out of the war. However, it had much to do with the rather general American opinion that Britain

The treaty in the Senate

always wins from us in diplomacy. When Jay reached home with his treaty, even his Federalist friends were dissatisfied. The terms were concealed from public knowledge while the Senate argued. Finally at the insistence of Hamilton the Senate approved it without Article XII, then voted that it not be published. Nevertheless, a Republican Senator turned a copy over to Benjamin Bache, and it appeared in the *Aurora*.

The Whisky Insurrection and the Indian war in Ohio had both been ended by glorious victories, and the public was feeling its oats. When the terms of the treaty became known, a simultaneous howl of rage went up

Popular opposition

from Maine to Georgia, even from the Federalists. "Sir John Jay" was hung and burned in effigy a hundred times, the treaty was burned by the public hangmen, and Hamilton for his part in the sellout was stoned by a mob. The mildest accusations were that Jay had sold out for British gold. On a fence in New York someone wrote these words: "Damn John Jay! damn everyone that won't damn John Jay!! damn everyone that won't put lights in his windows and sit up all night damning John Jay!!!" Washington may or may not have agreed with these sentiments, but he and Hamilton saw what the public did not—that the nation was weak and financially unsteady, that the allegiance of the West was uncertain, and that Spaniards and Indians were only waiting to take advantages of national distress. If the treaty were rejected, war with Britain would follow sooner or later. On the whole it was better to take such kicks in the teeth as these and continue to grow. Jefferson forgot his philosophical serenity and his pacifism and accused Washington of having had his head "shorn by the harlot England." But the United States went on growing.

Less than a year later the United States collected an unexpected dividend on Jay's Treaty. Spain had withdrawn from the war against France and, it was evident, would soon plunge in on her side. Madrid viewed Jay's Treaty with alarm as presaging an alliance with Eng- **Pinckney's** land and hastened to offer to the American minister, Thomas **Treaty,** Pinckney, a treaty which yielded nearly everything she had **1795** sought to withhold in the West. The details will be recited in a later chapter; the point to note here is that the threat of western disunion was stilled, at least for the moment. Great Britain and Spain had both yielded more than they would have in time of peace, and Washington could give up the cares of office and retire to Mt. Vernon with a good conscience.

When Washington decided not to seek a third term in the presidency he set a precedent which lasted down to our own day. His valedictory to the American people was published in September 1796. Though he con- **Wash-** sulted a number of friends on its subject matter and Hamil- **ington's** ton was responsible for its language, it was definitely Wash- **Farewell** ington's own thinking. Saddened by the growth of political **Address** parties, he warned against them as destructive of liberty and upheld Constitutional checks and balances, not parties, as the proper safeguard. Nearly everything he said bore upon the world crisis. He warned his countrymen that good faith and justice toward all nations not only were wise policies for a weak nation but were enjoined by religion and morality; certainly in this wicked world they were novelties worth cultivating and in the end might lead to permanent felicity.

Such policies were possible only if the people put virtue above temporary advantage; indeed, the nation's only protection lay in national union. Undue antipathy toward or attachment for any foreign nation would make it a slave to that passion and was a sure road to ruin. The great rule of conduct was to have as little political connection as possible with foreign nations. "It is our true policy to steer clear of permanent alliances with any portion of the foreign world. . . . Taking care always to keep ourselves by suitable establishments on a respectable defensive posture, we may safely trust to temporary alliances for extraordinary emergencies."

A careful reading of the address shows that it was definite advice intended to apply to the peculiar circumstances of that time—and very sound advice it was. Nowhere did Washington intimate that he was laying down a permanent policy for future generations to follow. Why then has he been quoted for a century and a half as warning against "entangling alliances," a phrase, by the way, which was not Washington's but was uttered in Jefferson's first inaugural address. After the War of 1812, when the United States turned its face westward and sought isolation from Europe, Washington's rule for temporary guidance suited the American mood. In the search for sanctified excuses—for we as a people are almost pathologically dependent upon precedent, whether Constitutional or historical—nothing could be more comforting than the words of Washington, who was by now apotheosized as the god of American legend. Consequently his words were mistakenly lifted from their context to explain and excuse the desired attitude. We mistook diplomatic isolation, which was possible for a century, for total isolation, which was not and never has been possible.

3 The Federalist Journey Toward Limbo

Despite Washington's temperate advice the election of 1796 was a tug-of-war between pro-French and pro-British parties. It was no less a struggle between Virginia and Massachusetts for ascendance. The candidates were chosen in each party by a caucus, a secret meeting of its members in Congress. The caucus was to do the nominating until 1824, though from 1804 on it was not secret. The two presidential candidates were Jefferson and Adams, respectively with Burr and Thomas Pinckney as running mates. Hamilton had been passed over because he was too much the exemplar of ultraconservatism; but, though he had left the Treasury in 1795, he continued to be the guiding genius of Federalist and governmental policy.

Election of 1796

Hamilton, feeling that Adams was not a strong candidate, proposed to manipulate the electoral vote in such a way as to keep Adams in the vice-presidency and elect Thomas Pinckney to the presidency. The fact, however, that the brunt of the Republican and French attack fell on Adams, since it was not politic to go all out against Washington, perversely gained support for him, and Hamilton's scheme turned the balance. Some of his supporters among the New England electors dropped their vice-presidential votes to others than Pinckney. Hamilton thus outsmarted himself and made Jefferson, his chief political opponent, Vice-President with 68 votes, while Adams with 71 became "President by three votes."

The Federalists did not appreciate being hoisted by their own petard, and from the redoubling of the vilification of Jefferson in their press it would have been thought that his own plot and not Hamilton's had raised him to office. Conscience made cowards of the Federalists. Philadelphia actually exhibited the sight of the Vice-President of the United States being ostracized by the "respectable" element and of men crossing the street to avoid speaking to him. These were the years of the ill-fated revolt of the United Irishmen, and

Newspaper war

many of those rebels who were not rotating on gibbets were pouring into the United States. Naturally, since the Federalists abhorred rebellion, the Irish joined the Jeffersonians, and their ready wit and ready shillalahs soon made them political powers. On the other hand, the Republicans were by no means wordless, especially when Hamilton was driven to publish a pamphlet in which he confessed to a sordid love affair which had turned out to be a blackmailer's trap. Though the incident did not have a political origin, it was wonderful political ammunition. Verbal insults led to blows; Fenno and Bache fought in the street, and the latter barricaded himself in his office against a Federalist mob.

The literary war must be viewed in the light of the current war fever. Adams had scarcely taken office when the disappointed French government began to show its teeth. Gouverneur Morris had been succeeded as minister to France by James Monroe, who went to the opposite extreme of friendship for the Jacobins and actually appeared before the Convention and received the "fraternal kiss" from its presiding officer. **The French crisis** Monroe had not been properly informed of Jay's mission and in consequence unintentionally deceived the French foreign ministry about its nature and extent; this deception later became the subject of a bitter and prolonged battle when Monroe returned to the United States. Now the French ministry accused the United States of having broken its treaty obligations, and the French depredations on commerce (which had never ceased) were accelerated. In less than a year over three thousand American ships were confiscated and their crews brutally maltreated. Monroe was recalled, and his successor was ordered out of France by the Directory, the new French executive committee.

In a last attempt to preserve peace Adams in 1797 sent Elbridge Gerry, Charles C. Pinckney, and John Marshall to Paris. After a long delay they were approached by three emissaries of Talleyrand, the cynically corrupt foreign minister who informed the Ameri- **XYZ Affair** cans that if they wished to begin negotiations they would have to pay $250,000 to Talleyrand and the Directory, make a thumping big loan to France (which no one pretended would be repaid), and apologize for certain references to France made in a recent message of Adams to Congress. The demand for an apology was probably a bargaining item, and bribery was too common a practice in diplomacy to cause much shock. The monetary demands, however, were too high a price to pay for the opening of negotiations which might end in nothing, especially since the loan was likely to lead to war with England. The President now hotly proposed preparations for national defense but was so vague upon the circumstances of the mission that the Republicans suspected Federalist dirty work and demanded to see the documents. Finally, with seeming reluctance, the pertinent papers were published, with the letters X, Y, and Z substituted for the names of the three French messengers.

A howl of rage went up from press and public, and the red-faced Republicans were compelled to join the outcry. War against France was now even more popular than war against England had been four years

Quasi war with France, May 1798– Sept. 1800

before. An exclamation of Pinckney's was wrested into the stirring slogan "Millions for defense but not one cent for tribute," and the song "Hail Columbia!" swept from the music halls of Philadelphia to the farthest hamlet. Armed neutrality was the policy adopted. Congress voided the treaties of 1778, provided for the issuance of letters of marque to privateers against French *armed* vessels (about a thousand were issued), began to build a small navy, and re-organized a Marine Corps (1798). About eighty-five French armed vessels were taken in two years, and the American frigate *Constellation* won two sharply contested engagements with French naval vessels.

Washington was placed at the head of a new army and, falling victim to Hamilton's intrigues, forced Adams to commission Hamilton second in command and actual executive. Of course, armies and navies cost

The new army

money—as Adams never tired of pointing out—so the Federalists laid a direct tax on houses, lands, and slaves. The result was a piffling protest in central Pennsylvania, called the Fries Rebellion, just riotous enough to give the troops an excuse for brutality. Other such actions as this did not go unnoted by the silent majority, and protests and petitions by the more courageous multiplied, especially since the French did not oblige the Federalists by landing a single invading grenadier on the American shore. Was the army after all being raised as a party and class weapon?

Hamilton was at last in his element. He dreamed of sweeping down the Mississippi to annex New Orleans (held by Spain, the ally of France) and on to Florida. And if those, why not Mexico and why not Peru?

Adams thwarts Hamilton's plans

He got into touch with the Venezuelan revolutionist Francisco Miranda, then in exile, and the two undertook conversations with British emissaries with results that are not at all clear. It does seem that at one time Britain considered lend-leasing a fleet to the United States, perhaps to prevent the building by this country of a powerful fleet of its own. It was in this crisis that John Adams proved his greatness. His party saw the war as a means of advancing political and imperial objectives, but he had sought for a peaceful solution from the first. Fully conscious of the fact that he was bringing on his own political funeral and probably that of his party, he doggedly refused to permit war.

Talleyrand was annoyed by the whirlwind which the unsophisticated Americans had called forth at his routine demand for a sweetener, so he characteristically cut his losses and began again. We know now that he was planning to force Spain to disgorge Louisiana and, with this as a starter, to erect an empire in the Mississippi Valley to which Canada would presently be added by conquest. The grand object, of course, was to contain the United **Talleyrand plans an American empire** States and to win for France the dominant place in the Western Hemisphere, to which Frenchmen had always believed that "Nature" had destined them because of their obvious superiority. Had the United States realized this fact, war could have scarcely been prevented, but fortunately for the cause of peace it was not known.

When Talleyrand intimated to Adams that an envoy would be well received, the President took the opportunity. The Federalists were appalled at this rude awakening, but as the nation was with Adams they did not dare to resist too strongly. By the time the envoys arrived in Paris, Napoleon had taken control of France (and with it Talleyrand's secret plan for Louisiana), and **Convention of 1800** he agreed to allow the abrogation of the treaties if the United States would release him from spoliation claims. This was the basis of the convention signed 30 September 1800 by which the United States assumed $20 million worth of claims on 1853 cases involving about 600 ships. This claim, incidentally, was just twice the claim against the British at the time of Jay's Treaty. Actually the last of the claims were not adjudicated until 1915, and Congress has not yet appropriated all the money to pay them. The day after the convention between France and the United States was signed, France at the secret Treaty of San Ildefonso forced senile Spain to cede Louisiana to it.

Many of the French, English, and Irish immigrants who came to the United States were liberals who had found it expedient to leave because of differences with their governments and they, together with most of the less hurried emigrés, were enthusiastic workers for the Republican Party. In 1798 the Federalists took advantage of the war fever to push through the so-called Alien and Se- **The Alien Acts** dition Acts. The Naturalization Act raised the naturalization period from five to fourteen years; the Alien Friends Act gave the President the right in time of peace to order any "dangerous" alien out of the country on pain of imprisonment; and the Alien Enemy Act gave him in time of war the right to banish or imprison such citizens or subjects of the hostile nation as he deemed dangerous. These acts were in obvious violation of the Bill of Rights because they depended solely on executive action without judicial trial. The laws were never invoked, but they did frighten many aliens into leaving, among them two shiploads of Frenchmen. The Irish, against whom the laws were chiefly aimed, did not frighten as easily.

More important was the Sedition Act, intended to apply to citizens.

We have seen that political writers and speakers of the time resorted to sarcastic, insulting, and scurrilous language. Both sides were equally **The Sedition Act** offensive, but the Federalists, who believed in their natural right to rule, resented Republican criticism. The bill as introduced would have punished Congressmen for criticizing administration measures; France was actually declared an enemy, and anyone saying a word for France would have hung by the neck. Hamilton was thunderstruck and hastily ordered the measure toned down. What must have been the thoughts of Jefferson, presiding blandly and impartially over the Senate debates on a bill at first designed to send him to the gallows and even in its final form plainly intended to nullify his life's work! It was obvious that this was an attempt to entrench the Federalists in power by choking off criticism. If successful, it would have instituted a one-party system. Perhaps his subtle mind saw what the Federalists did not—that this very bill was destined to be one of the means of calling up the rising counterforce which would destroy them.

Since there was no Federal common law, it was defensible for Congress to provide statutory authority for the punishment of riots and conspiracies against the government and its agents, and to define and punish libels. It should be remembered that at the time the country was on the verge of war and that had war actually come, the laws might have been generally regarded as protective rather than oppressive. Certainly the Espionage Act of 1917 loosed a far more oppressive series of executive actions than did the Alien and Sedition Acts. However, the Sedition Act went on to prohibit writings and utterances "with intent to defame" the President (not the Vice-President), Congress, and government or to bring them "into contempt or disrepute." This, again, was in palpable violation of the Bill of Rights. Two concepts were warring here: the old common-law concept that freedom of speech is freedom from prior censorship, not freedom from prosecution after the utterance; the new concept which had been gaining since the Zenger case in 1735 was that truth is a defense. The Sedition Act, indeed, made truth a defense and provided for jury trials.

Of many Republicans indicted for criticizing the government ten, mostly editors and printers, were tried and convicted; juries co-operated rather well, for they were selected by Federal marshals. Federalist judges **Enforcement of the Sedition Act** sometimes overstepped the bounds of propriety in the rulings on the law and their charges to juries and, indeed, delivered from the bench splenetic lectures on the evils of democracy and the depravity of democrats. By far the most prominent victim was Matthew Lyon, a member of Congress from Vermont, who had shocked and delighted the nation by meeting the assault of a Federalist colleague on the House floor, fire tongs against cane. Upon his return home he was convicted under the Sedition Act and thrust into jail. When the Green Mountain Boys gathered to release him, he forbade them through the bars; and they went home and re-elected him to Congress. It was not long until the Federalists realized that they were raising up martyrs to the enhancement of the Republicans, and they abruptly

Congressional Pugilists.

He in a trice struck Lyon thrice
Upon his head, enrag'd Sir,

Who seiz'd the tongs to ease his wrongs,
And Griswold thus engag'd, Sir.

Congress Hall,
in Philadª Febª 15. 1798.
S.E. Cor 6 ᵗʰ & Chesnut

The New York Historical Society

The first physical encounter between members of the House of Representatives (1798) was ridiculously portrayed in various cartoons.

stopped their prosecutions. Fortunately the Alien and Sedition Acts were limited in time and expired by the end of Adams's administration; the Republicans later restored the five-year qualification for naturalization.

The Alien and Sedition Acts brought talk of secession in the Republican strongholds of the South, but Jefferson opposed it on the ground that fission once begun would lead to a replica of the warring Germanies. By now he had clearly in mind the function of parties, and he saw that in order to fulfill that function they must act with restraint. Let the party out of power "have patience 'til luck turns." But some form of effective public protest must be made. The war fever of 1798 had preserved Federalist strength in most of the state legislatures, but Virginia and Ken-

Virginia and Kentucky Resolutions, 1798–9

tucky were safely Republican. Accordingly in 1798 and 1799 the so-called Virginia and Kentucky Resolutions were passed by the legislatures of the two states; the first were written by Madison and the latter, the stronger, by Jefferson. Both asserted that the Federal government was one of limited and delegated powers and, since it could not be the judge of its own powers, the states as its creators were.

The Virginia Resolutions used the word "nullification," but when many years later Calhoun seized upon them as an early example of his doctrine of nullification and state sovereignty, Madison vigorously denied that he had meant or implied any such doctrine. It is interesting to note that a number of state legislatures considered the assertions of the resolutions and replied that the constitutionality of Federal laws should be decided by the judiciary.

As though the tale of the last three years were not enough to ensure defeat, Hamilton now proceeded to make Republican victory certain in 1800. The testy New England President had never appreciated Hamil-

Adams and Hamilton split

ton's gratuitous plots at the time of the elections of 1788 and 1796. Now he discovered that Hamilton was actually instructing two of the members of his Cabinet (Pickering was one) on their executive actions and their advice to the President, and dismissed them; the third (Wolcott) was as guilty as the others but was not suspected. Adams's mission to France wrecked Hamilton's military aspirations, and it was easy to charge that he had sent the mission not to preserve peace so much as to undermine Hamilton.

When the party caucuses nominated Jefferson and Burr on the Republican ticket and Adams and C. C. Pinckney on the Federalist ticket, Hamilton saw that the race would be close. In spite of his best efforts

Campaign of 1800

the Republicans, marshalled by Burr and Tammany, took the New York state elections early in 1800. Perhaps Hamilton honestly believed it was the only alternative to chaos when he wrote to Governor Jay of New York demanding that the Federalist legislature be summoned to take the election of presidential electors from the incoming Republican legislature and place it in the hands of the public, where the Federalists might conceivably have a chance. Jay refused to descend to such an action though both Federalists and Republicans were changing the election laws to their own advantage in other states. Hamilton now wrote a pamphlet reflecting pointedly upon Adams's vanity and accusing him of want of ability and criticizing him bitterly for the actions which had struck hardest at Hamilton's military ambitions and control of the party; then at the end of this chain of jealous insults he recommended his re-election. When Burr got hold of a copy and sowed the nation with reprints, it was evident for all to judge that the Federalists had been split wide open.

Still, a measure of agreement prevailed because there was no feasible alternative. Adams was supported uniformly as the desperate Federalist leaders summoned their "paper" plutocracy, the clergy of the established churches, and "the rich, the well-born, and the able" to ride to the rescue of the country. Old ladies in New England went home from the Sunday sermon and hid their Bibles lest the "atheist" Jefferson confiscate and burn them. When Jefferson was elected, the Rev. Theodore Dwight warned his congregation that "the ties of marriage are . . . destroyed; our wives and daughters are thrown into the stews; our children are cast into the world from the breast and forgotten. . . . Can the imagination paint anything more dreadful this side of hell?"

In most of those states which had popular elections the Republicans showed surprising strength, even in the rock-ribbed Federalist strongholds of New England. Jefferson and Burr each received seventy-three votes, Adams sixty-five, and Pinckney one less. New York plumped into the Republican column by two hundred fifty popular votes and swung the election; highminded John **Election of 1800-1** Jay had defeated his own party. The Constitution provided that in case of a tie the House of Representatives, voting by states, should elect the President. This provision meant that the Federalists, in control of the House until 4 March 1801, would elect the President. A wit has said that Burr's only virtue was that he frankly acknowledged that he had no virtues. It is no wonder, then, that Federalist politicians supposed that they could make a deal with him, especially since Burr was himself a banker and was naturally interested in the welfare of capital. Accordingly they approached him with the proposition that they would make him President if he would agree to continue the Hamiltonian program. Burr stalled.

When Hamilton heard of the plan he was aghast and straightway threw the remnants of his influence against it. Burr, he pointed out, was utterly untrustworthy, "the Catiline of America." Such was his ambition, boldness, energy, and vindictiveness that he might better be expected to turn and rend the Federalists and on the basis of their ruin make himself "First Citizen" as one Napoleon Bonaparte had done recently in France. Burr's election would be introducing a Republican wooden horse into the walls of the besieged Federalist Troy. Jefferson, on the other hand, was not a man to let theories stand in the way of practical solutions and would therefore temporize; therein lay the best chance of saving Hamilton's fiscal structure. Jefferson was at least a sincere democrat with some pretensions to character, and he could be trusted as an enemy.

Meeting for the first time in the new capital of Washington, the House proceeded to business while Adams paced the floor of the unfinished White House, convinced that the country would be ruined if his

Jefferson elected

old friend were elected. For thirty-five ballots Burr's Federalist support prevented a decision, but he refused to commit himself and by thus attempting to carry water on both shoulders lost his chance. On the thirty-sixth ballot the Federalists from three states declined to vote, and this action gave Jefferson ten states. The lesson upon the shortcoming of the method of elections was sufficient. In 1804 the Twelfth Amendment was added to the Constitution, providing that electors should vote specifically for President and Vice-President.

At the last moment the Federalists managed to entrench themselves in the judiciary, a branch of the government which in the more dramatic hurly-burly of political warfare had been little regarded. Even then it is

Federalists entrenched in the judiciary

not certain that the Federalists intended to do more than leave a rear guard which could fight a delaying action until their return in force. The Judiciary Act of 1801, passed by the lame-duck Federalist Congress, among other things set up a panel of circuit judges and almost doubled the number of district judges; some of them were not commissioned until the day before Adams left office, so were derisively called "Midnight Judges." As a matter of fact, the act made needed reforms which had been long in preparation. More important than the "Midnight Judges," however, was the elevation of Secretary of State Marshall to be Chief Justice of the Supreme Court. For a third of a century, long after the Federalist Party had passed into limbo, John Marshall was to continue to mold the nation's institutions after the Hamiltonian ideal.

Jefferson became President through the efforts of his bitterest political enemy. There is something ironic in the fact. And yet Hamilton, whatever his motives, was acting in what we now recognize as the democratic tradition. When the force is defeated and must step down

Hamilton a democrat

to make way for the counterforce, there is often opportunity for it to show restraint in the way in which it arranges the tools for its rival's hands. Hamilton would have scoffed at the thought that he was a democrat, and yet at this moment he proved it by seeing to it that the office went to the man who had won it. This is exactly the restraint which the democratic process envisages, the willingness to yield to the counterforce—of course, in the hope that it will hang itself.

The Federalists never returned to power. The reason is simply that their aristocratic theory of government was already outmoded at least in its mercantile aspect, for the Hamiltonians were to come back in a new

The Federalists' mission and their fate

and surprising guise. And yet the Federalists deserve more than a parting jeer or a romantic tear from posterity. They had done a task which the Republicans could not have accomplished simply because they were not convinced of its necessity nor willing to take risks boldly. It was the Federalists who established the public credit, nursed the fledging Republic through its first perilous decade of foreign embroilments, laid down precedents and customs, and set the feet of public administration on the firm upward path. Hamilton was not gifted in his merchant followers, for they were a decaying class which try as he might he could not make over into an industrial capitalist class. That was the work of the next generation.

After the fall of the Federalists most of the leaders of the party became flabby catastrophists. Only the Essex Junto retained a solid core of resistance, though it was no less pessimistic. Out of the democratic ascendancy, they told themselves smugly, would come chaos and finally a military dictatorship—a divine retribution on the people for having cast their "natural" rulers out of power. When that day came, the Federalist political veterans would shine in a more splendid court than Washington's, while the chastened people would humbly knuckle their foreheads as they passed. Thus dreaming they doddered off life's stage and into the wings from which no man and no institution ever returns. They deserved better of fate, but fate has no pity on those who meet the future with only dreams of the past in their hearts.

BIBLIOGRAPHICAL NOTE

Jefferson the Counterforce

JEFFERSON: Jefferson wrote no weighty summary of his philosophy, but Charles M. Wiltse, *The Jeffersonian Tradition in American Democracy* (1935) is the clearest exposition of his ideas. See also Adrienne Koch, *Philosophy of Thomas Jefferson* (1943). There are numerous biographies, of which two of the best are Gilbert Chinard, *Thomas Jefferson, The Apostle of Americanism* (1929); and James T. Adams, *The Living Jefferson* (1936). Sarah N. Randolph, *The Domestic Life of Thos. Jefferson* (1871) has interest. Series of volumes upon the life of Jefferson have been written or are under way by Dumas Malone, Marie Kimball, Adrienne Koch, and Claude Bowers. Especially useful for this section is Adrienne Koch, *Jefferson and Madison: The Great Collaboration* (1950). Three among the many collections of excerpts from his writings are edited respectively by Edward Boykin, Philip S. Foner, and Saul Padover. His complete *Papers* (estimated to fill 50 volumes) are now appearing under the editorship of Julian P. Boyd. His *Summary View of the Rights of British America* (1774) ranks next to the Declaration. One should also become acquainted with his *Notes on the State of Virginia* (first pub. in 1784), which not only is a storehouse of information on the state, which then extended to the Mississippi, but is enriched by Jefferson's comments and reflections on many matters.

MADISON: There are biographies by Abbott E. Smith, Sydney H. Gay, and Gaillard Hunt. The most extensive is Irving Brant, *James Madison*, now in process of publication. See also *Memoirs and Letters of Dolly Madison* (1886); and Katherine Anthony, *Dolly Madison, Her Life and Times* (1949).

TAYLOR: See Henry H. Simms, *Life of John Taylor* (1932); and Eugene T. Mudge, *The Social Philosophy of John Taylor of Caroline* (1939). Taylor's own writings are so labored and prolix that they are now of little interest to anyone except the specialist. Jefferson seems never to have recognized the vital cleavage between his own ideas and those of Taylor.

BURR: This "finished scoundrel" was fascinating even to his biographers. Most sprightly is S. H. Wandell and Meade Minnigerode, *Aaron Burr* (1925); but James Parton, *Life and Times of Aaron Burr* (1858) is good reading. Nathan Schachner, *Aaron Burr: A Biography* (1937) wields the whitewash brush even more vigorously.

REPUBLICAN WORTHIES: Useful biographies are Lewis Leary, *That Rascal Freneau* (1941); William B. Hatcher, *Edward Livingston* (1940). Henry Adams, *Albert Gallatin* (1879) should be supplemented for the early period by Russell J. Ferguson, *Early Western Pennsylvania Politics* (1938). Other biographies will be noted from time to time.

POLITICAL HISTORIES: On the development of the Republican Party in New England see William A. Robinson, *Jeffersonian Democracy in New England* (1916); and James T. Adams, *New England in the Republic* (1926). On New York politics see New York histories by De Alva S. Alexander and Alexander C. Flick; Dixon Ryan Fox, *Yankees and Yorkers* (1940) and *Decline of Aristocracy in the Politics of New York* (1919); and Morris R. Werner, *Tammany Hall* (1928). A brilliant attempt to find the origins of the Jeffersonian movement in economic conditions is Charles A. Beard, *Economic Origins of Jeffersonian Democracy* (1915). It is not necessary to accept economic determinism unreservedly in order to recognize the significance of economic causes.

The Rising Conflict

FRENCH REVOLUTION AND THE U.S.: Charles D. Hazen, *Contemporary American Opinion of the French Revolution* (1897). Bernard Fäy, *The Revolutionary Spirit in France and America* (1927) traces the literary and psychological relations of France and the U.S. from 1763 to 1800 with rare acumen; probably, however, it exaggerates the pre-Revolutionary influence of France on America.

POLITICAL: By far the most interesting account of the conflict between the two great party leaders is Claude G. Bowers, *Jefferson and Hamilton* (1925); it is almost painfully partial to Jefferson. Albert J. Beveridge, *Life of John Marshall* (4 v., 1916–19) goes almost as far in the other direction. John S. Bassett, *The Federalist System, 1789–1801* (1906) is better balanced. For the Whisky Insurrection see Leland D. Baldwin, *Whiskey Rebels: The Story of a Frontier Uprising* (1939); and for the "self-created societies," Eugene P. Link, *The Democratic-Republican Societies, 1790–1800* (1942).

DIPLOMACY: See Samuel F. Bemis, *Jay's Treaty* (1923) and *Pinckney's Treaty* (1926). Neutrality can be covered in Charles M. Thomas, *American Neutrality in 1793* (1931); and Anna C. Clauder, *American Commerce as Affected by the Wars of the French Revolution and Napoleon* (1932). From this point on refer continually to Samuel F. Bemis, ed., *American Secretaries of State and Their Diplomacy* (10 v., 1927–29).

FAREWELL ADDRESS: Most of the Farewell Address is reprinted in Commager, *Documents*, 169–175. The most complete treatment of the origin is Victor H. Paltsits, ed., *Washington's Farewell Address* (1935). For a discussion on whether the advice was intended to apply only currently see Albert K. Weinberg, "Washington's 'Great Rule' in Its Historical Evolution," in E. F. Goldman, ed., *Historiography and Urbanization* (1941).

The Federalist Journey Toward Limbo

ELECTIONS: For the circumstances of all presidential elections through 1928 see Edward Stanwood, *History of the Presidency* (2 v., 1898, 1928). An excellent account of the election of 1800–1 is in Charles A. Beard, *Economic Origins of Jeffersonian Democracy* (1915).

DIPLOMACY: Among other accounts see the following: Beverley W. Bond, *The Monroe Mission to France, 1794–1796* (1907); for the XYZ Affair, Albert J. Beveridge, *John Marshall*, 2:214–334; George A. King, *The French Spoliation Claims* (1912).

QUASI WAR: Gardner W. Allen, *Our Naval War with France* (1909); U.S. Office of Naval Records and Library, *Naval Documents Related to the Quasi-War* (7 v., 1935–38).

ALIEN AND SEDITION ACTS: James F. McLaughlin, *Matthew Lyon* (1900); John C. Miller, *Crisis in Freedom: The Alien and Sedition Acts* (1951).

Chapter XI

THE ORDEAL
OF THOMAS JEFFERSON

1 *Jefferson the Force*

ON 4 MARCH 1801 in the little Senate chamber in the unfinished capitol building in Washington, Jefferson took the oath of office. His inaugural address was a model of moderation. "We are all Republicans,"

Jefferson's first inaugural

he said, "we are all Federalists. If there be any among us who would wish to dissolve this Union or to change its republican form, let them stand undisturbed as monuments of the safety with which error of opinion may be tolerated where reason is left free to combat it. I know, indeed, that some honest men fear that a republican government cannot be strong enough. . . . I believe this, on the contrary, the strongest Government on earth. I believe it the only one where every man, at the call of the law, would fly to the standard of the law, and would meet invasions of the public order as his own personal concern. Sometimes it is said that man can not be trusted with the government of himself. Can he, then, be trusted with the government of others? Or have we found angels in the form of kings to govern him? Let history answer this question."

What are the essential principles of our government, which consequently ought to shape its administration? "Equal and exact justice to all men, of whatever state or persuasion, religious or political; peace, commerce, and honest friendship with all nations, entangling alliances with none; the support of the State governments in their rights . . . the preservation of the General Government in its whole constitutional vigor, as the sheet anchor of our peace at home and safety abroad; a jealous care of the right of election by the people . . . absolute acquiescence in the decisions of the majority . . . a well-disciplined militia . . . the supremacy of the civil over the military authority; economy in the public expense, that labor may be lightly burdened . . . the honest payment of our debts . . . encouragement of agriculture, and of commerce as its handmaid; the diffusion of information and arraignment of all abuses at the bar of public reason; freedom of religion; freedom of the press, and freedom of person." These principles "should be the creed of our political faith, the text of civic instruction, the touchstone by which we try the services of those we trust."

Jefferson could afford to be moderate, not only in order to draw back those Republicans who had been weaned away by the quasi war but because Europe was plainly on the verge of a general peace, which would at least remove the occasions found in foreign affairs for party quarrels. With Madison in the State Department and Gallatin in the Treasury, Jefferson had executives and advisers who were experienced and trustworthy. **Fate of the Jeffersonian program**

Yet the wisdom of Hamilton was never more strikingly portrayed than in his rejection of Burr and his support of Jefferson for the presidency. Jefferson had honestly intended his accession to mark the beginning of the decline of Federal power. It did not, and for three reasons: 1) Hamilton had set the customs and precedents in the general direction of his desires, had swollen the public debt, and had taken over the judiciary, wherein judges sat for life; 2) international problems complicated the situation and scuttled many of Jefferson's dearest plans; and 3) Jefferson himself, as Hamilton knew, was not a man to thwart a practical solution by sticking to a theory (Hamilton said "principle"). Perhaps Jefferson learned by experience; perhaps, as John Taylor of Caroline asserted, he was a traitor to his principles; perhaps he was like many of us who fight a power when exercised by others but feel safe in assuming it ourselves because, of course, we will not abuse it. There is no proof that Jefferson ever changed his basic thinking, but we see in his actual policies a forecast of the characteristic modifications which inevitably come to victorious liberal movements.

It was fitting that the new administration brought in by the "Revolution of 1800" should be the first inaugurated in the new capital of the United States. Washington City, as it was called to distinguish it from the numerous towns and counties of the same name, was a wasteland beside the Potomac with a few mud traces called streets striking across the stumpy fields and the malarial **The new capital city** swamps. The Capitol on the eastern hill and the White House two miles to the west toward the quaint village of Georgetown were both unfinished. Congressmen lived perforce in boardinghouses, which soon came to be divided between the two parties. Homes and even mansions appeared gradually, and there was some social gaiety during the winter sessions;

but though Congressmen grumbled at the desolation, they characteristically refused to do much for the beautification of the city. True, "the city of magnificent distances" spread in a few decades to the confines of L'Enfant's plan, but it was a shoddy and vermin-ridden hole until national pride and the desire for lucrative building contracts led to its reconstruction after the Civil War.

Jefferson had determined that his administration should be marked by democratic simplicity. He quietly dropped the levees held by Washington and Adams, and in the place of rigid precedence in seating at **Jeffersonian simplicity** table he adopted the rule of pell-mell. Jefferson himself did not don formal "court dress" to receive foreign envoys, and in their pique they doubtless exaggerated the carelessness of his attire. Nevertheless, the White House had the best French chef and the best wines in Washington City, and few diplomats or politicians allowed their resentments to keep them from the presidential board. Every Fourth of July the White House was thrown open to the public, and at other times Jefferson entertained as a Virginia gentleman, that is, welcomed all who were of good social standing. Consequently there was a continual stream of visitors; some of them went away admiring, but others scoffed secretly or openly according to their natures. Jefferson was apparently quite indifferent to scorn. When a distinguished guest, Baron von Humboldt, the great scientist, found on Jefferson's table a newspaper bearing a scurrilous attack on the President, he protested that the editor should be punished. "Put that paper in your pocket, Baron," replied Jefferson, "and should you hear the reality of our liberty, the freedom of the press questioned, show them this paper—and tell them where you found it."

Jefferson's deviation from Jeffersonian principles was not in any primary sense due to irresistible pressure by the Federalists. True, the Federalists had by no means gone out of existence, but their artillery had **Executive actions** been captured except in the judiciary, and they were for a while reduced to sniping with Congressional and journalistic riflemen. The administration began its reforms by doing away with Hamilton's motto that "a public debt is a public blessing" and substituting the principle that "a public debt is a public mortgage." Wherever possible, appropriations, even those for the army and navy, were drastically reduced. The total debt was cut by a third even though the whisky excise was repealed and the government assumed fresh burdens, including in 1802 the payment of $3,000,000 in pre-Revolutionary debts owed to British merchants. Gallatin asked Congress to appropriate specific sums for specified purposes. Congress, perhaps a little lazy, saw no reason for doing the work that Gallatin had been hired to do, and it was not until after the War of 1812 that its laziness was cured by the discovery of the usefulness of logrolling and pork barrels.

Though almost all of the Federal policy-making officials in 1801 were Federalists, Jefferson at the end of his first term had replaced only half of them. Some of the jobs were dispensed with in the economy drive (an astonishing sacrifice of executive patronage), some officials were removed for "sufficient cause," and attorneys and marshals were replaced in order to balance the Federalist ascendancy on the bench. On the other hand, a number of Jefferson's appointees were Federalists.

Jefferson's attempt to remodel the judiciary was only partially successful. Congress repealed the Judiciary Act of 1801 and revived the old system and thus got rid of a score or so of judges with their court attachés. The commissions of the "Midnight Judges" for **_Marbury v._** the District of Columbia had not been delivered but had **_Madison,_** been left on a table in the Department of State. Jefferson **1803** had decided not to deliver the commissions and instructed Madison to that purpose. One of the appointees, William Marbury, now sued for a writ of mandamus [*we command*] to compel Madison to deliver the commission.

The case came before the Supreme Court in 1803. Marshall, who had served concurrently as Chief Justice and Secretary of State, had made out the commission and knew the circumstances well, but it was evident that if he issued the desired writ it would be ticketed as an open political maneuver and ignored by his cousin and enemy, President Jefferson. Marshall therefore decided that Marbury was entitled to the commission. Then he went on to deny that the Supreme Court could issue a writ of mandamus, on the ground that it was not among the powers granted it by the Constitution, and Congress in the Judiciary Act of 1789 had exceeded its authority in naming it among the powers of the Supreme Court. That part of the Judiciary Act of 1789 was therefore null and of no effect.

Marshall had at one swoop struck a blow at Jefferson (but left him no means of retaliation) and declared the right of the Supreme Court to invalidate laws of Congress on the ground of unconstitutionality. By denying a minor power to itself, the Court had assumed **Signifi-** the role of supreme arbiter of executive and legislative acts. **cance of** The Constitutional phase of the decision aroused little atten- **the decision** tion, but Jefferson saw the trap and was prepared to assert that executive and legislature were co-equal with the judiciary in deciding constitutionality and that in reality, as the Virginia and Kentucky Resolutions held, the decision should rest with the states because they had created the Constitution. The Federalists had indeed planned to use the judiciary in molding the Constitution, but Marshall was too canny to engage in open combat. He never applied his principle again, and it was not until the Dred Scott Case of 1857 that it was applied for the second time.

Only one resort was left: impeachment of the judges. Already a dis-

THE BARBARY STATES
Scene of American Campaigns
1801-05, 1815
Statute Miles
0   100   200   300   400   500

J. W. CLEMENT CO.

trict judge who had suffered a mental breakdown had been removed by
impeachment; whatever political animus there may have been, the fact
remained that the Constitution provided no other remedy.

**Impeach-
ment of
Justice
Chase,
1805**

The administration now apparently decided (1805) to make
a test case of a peculiarly vulnerable Associate Justice,
Samuel Chase, who had indubitably used his high office for
purposes of political browbeating during the days of the
Sedition Law. The trial that followed his impeachment was woefully mis-
managed by the "managers" (led by John Randolph) appointed by the
House, and the Senate voted for acquittal. Thus ended Jefferson's attempt
to force the judiciary to "return to the Constitution." Henceforth the
Supreme Court was not directly amenable to political dictation. Nevertheless, the trial threw a scare into the Federalist judges, and thereafter
they became more impartial and less political. That, after all, was what
Jefferson sought.

The words of his inaugural address had scarcely fallen from his lips
when Jefferson found himself confronted by a foreign situation which
made it necessary to break some of his noble pledges. At this time the

**Depreda-
tions by
Barbary
States**

Barbary States of North Africa—reading from west to east,
Morocco, Algeria, Tunisia, and Tripolitania—based their
economies on piracy and on the "presents" which the European trading powers paid them for immunity from cap-
ture. There was no doubt that the greater naval powers could easily have
crushed the Barbary States, but they did not, and there was an opinion
that they found the Barbary States useful in picking off minor competitors. Washington and Adams had felt compelled to follow the European
example, and at the very time when wine glasses were being lifted in
patriotic toasts to "Millions for defense, but not one cent for tribute" an
American ship delivered twenty-six barrels of coin as tribute to the Dey
of Algiers. The ultimate insult was reached when in 1800 the Dey forced
the U. S. S. *George Washington* to lower the American flag and under the
Algerian flag carry an Algerian ambassador and presents to Constanti-
nople. The Dey's reasoning was irreproachable: "You pay me tribute,

by which you become my slaves. I have, therefore, a right to order you as I may think proper."

Jefferson now decided upon a demonstration of strength and sent a squadron to the Mediterranean. Meanwhile the Pasha of Tripoli had declared war, and the American force proved ineffective, largely because it had a succession of timid commanders. It was not until 1803 when a strong fleet under Commodore Edward Preble demonstrated before Tangiers and blockaded Tripoli that the American flag won respect. For two years American ships **Barbary Wars 1801–05, 1815** and sailors harassed Tripolitan shipping and fortifications, and the British navy, whose respect was reserved for those who took their own part, opened its refitting facilities in the Mediterranean to the Americans. Meanwhile an American adventurer, William Eaton, consul at Tunis, raised a motley force of ruffians in Egypt and in 1805 made a spectacular march across the desert to the Tripolitan subject city of Derna. With the aid of a naval force the city was captured, and Tripoli itself threatened. At this juncture the best part of the fruits of the victory were thrown away when a stupid American representative (Tobias Lear) signed with the pasha an unsatisfactory treaty, which was approved by the unenergetic naval commander (Commodore Samuel Barron) and accepted by the Senate.

Upon the withdrawal of American warships the depredations by the Barbary powers were resumed. It was not until 1815 that Stephen Decatur, who had made an enviable record during the earlier expeditions and in the War of 1812, reappeared and imposed humiliating terms on Algiers, Tunis, and Tripoli. Thereafter a fleet was kept in the Mediterranean, and the Barbary States kept within the treaties. While the commanders of the American navy in the Mediterranean (with the notable exceptions of Preble and Decatur) fell short of the decisiveness which the situation demanded, it should be recorded that they were handicapped by Jefferson's innate pacificism and instinct for political straddling. The operations, however, bred a group of brilliant young officers who proved themselves in the War of 1812, and whose exploits on the Barbary coast transcended in popular estimation the blunders of executive and commanders.

Ever since the Revolution the growing power of the West had been exerted to solve the problem of commercial egress from the Mississippi. This problem was so important that it will be treated at length later on; here it is sufficient to say that it was a continuation of the colonial struggle between coast and interior, and that while the Republicans supported western desires the Federalists **Constitution and the Louisiana Purchase** in general opposed them. When in 1803 Jefferson purchased Louisiana from France, he was perfectly conscious of the fact that it violated his interpretation of the Constitution. While the purchase was pending he canvassed his supporters as to the desirability of an amendment to make it legal but met almost uniform discouragement. They argued that the purchase was legal because the Constitution permitted the admission of new states and because of the treaty-making power; Jefferson replied that if they were right, treaties would supersede the Constitution, and it would become "blank paper." If he and his friends, as Henry Adams puts it, "were to interpret the treaty-making power as they liked, the time was sure to come when their successors would put so broad an interpretation on the other powers of the Government as to lead from step to step, until at last Virginia might cower in blood and flames before the shadowy terror called the war power." Nevertheless, Jefferson permitted himself to be overruled and thus took the longest step of his career toward the Hamiltonian doctrine of loose construction.

The extension of the western domain by the Louisiana Purchase brought to a head the Federalist fear of being overwhelmed by the democratic West, for it was evident that the growing number of western **Pickering's** states would soon put them permanently into the shade. **secession** They now became the exponents of strict construction and **plot** even of the doctrines of the Virginia and Kentucky Resolutions and began to confer on the advisability of New England's secession. The decision of the Essex Junto was that the time was not ripe, but Timothy Pickering, now Senator from Massachusetts, in the hope of preserving Federalist power and ideas, at least in the North, became the spearhead of a plot for immediate secession. Burr, excluded from Federal patronage, had continued as Vice-President to play footie with the Federalists; and now he and Pickering struck a bargain. Burr was to get himself elected governor of New York and in that capacity was to carry his state out of the Union with New England and in return was to become chief of the new union. Hamilton, no longer the head of the Federalist Party except for lip service, was aghast when he heard of the plot. He loved his country and the Union and believed it destined to greatness. Once more he proved himself a statesman rather than a politician by throwing himself into the battle against Burr and contributing to his defeat. Pickering's plot died without a struggle.

For two decades Hamilton and Burr, so alike in physique, personality, and ambition but utterly unlike in ideals, had fought each other in the political arenas of New York and the nation. Usually the victory had **Duel** remained with Hamilton, and Burr now coldly determined **between** that the barrier to his ambitions must be removed. Hamil- **Hamilton** ton believed implicitly in the catastrophic theory that Re- **and Burr,** publican government must lead to chaos, and he held him- **1804** self ready to be the rescuer of his country and the restorer of order. Meanwhile his reputation and his courage must be above reproach; so when Burr challenged him to a duel, he accepted. They met early on the morning of 11 July 1804 under Weehawken Heights on the New Jersey shore of the Hudson, where three years earlier Hamilton's son Philip had been killed in a duel rising out of politics. Now Hamilton shot in the air; Burr, whom no one ever accused of magnanimity, shot his opponent through the body. Hamilton died two days later, and the Vice-President of the United States fled south from an indictment for murder and from the storm of indignation that he had raised. Hamilton, no longer an embarrassment to petty politicians, was sanctified by death and has become the conservative face of the Janus-headed saint who rules America.

There had never been any doubt that Jefferson would sweep the presidential election of 1804, and in fact he and George Clinton, his running mate, took one hundred and sixty-two votes and left only a paltry fourteen from Connecticut, Delaware, and Maryland for C. C. Pinckney and Rufus King. The country had pros- **Gradual change in Republi-canism** pered, and Gallatin's careful conservative estimates of the revenue had been exceeded by a third. True, the national debt had been increased, chiefly by the Louisiana Purchase, but in exchange the territory of the United States had been doubled. Gallatin, enemy of the Bank of the United States, had found it very handy in transacting Treasury business and had overridden Jefferson's objections and established a branch in New Orleans in addition to those already existing in Boston, New York, Baltimore, and Norfolk. National pride had been titillated by an enlarged navy and a successful little war. Two years after the election Jefferson was to take cognizance of the crying need for public works and to recommend that instead of a reduction of the tariff (which would discourage developing infant industries) the surplus be put into internal improvements, such as roads and canals. Thus he kowtowed to the protectionists and to the West with its transportation problems, though he salved his conscience by asking a Constitutional amendment and recommending a national university to promote science.

Nevertheless, there were storm signals flying for the observant to see. Lack of experience concealed the fact, now well known, that a conservative reaction is inevitable after a liberal victory. Hitherto the country had been protected by the fact that the War of Independence did not make revolutionary changes but only **The reaction** accelerated a movement already under way. Now the conservative reaction came from an unexpected direction. New England Federalism rigidly upheld the natural right to rule of a decadent aristocracy and tried to make arrogance and slander serve for votes. The result was that the voters went over to the Republicans in droves, but they took Federalist Constitutional and economic ideas with them and pressed them upon the government in Washington.

The developing pressure was not lost upon the Virginia aristocracy, which depended for its own ascendance upon the ascendance of Virginia, and that could be maintained only if the strict letter of the Constitution **Randolph** were followed. It was John Randolph of Roanoke (1773– **and the** 1833), leader in the House, who led the rebellion of the **Quids** southern malcontents. Randolph, brilliant, pain-racked, dulcet in voice, and courtly in manner when he chose, with the features of a boy and the parchment-like skin of an old man, was a master of caustic wit and searing invective; indeed, he relied more on wit than on wisdom. Contemptuously aristocratic, he supported the Republicans only so long as they maintained Virginia's ascendance. Bitter foe of equality and of the democratic West, Randolph was father of the dogmatic southern sectionalists. As House manager he had led the attack on Justice Chase, and the failure of the trial by the vote of the Republican Senators convinced him that the Republican Party had passed under northern and western domination and sold out its principles. Never so happy as when in opposition, Randolph organized the Quids (from *tertium quid*, a third something or other) and turned his venom on Jefferson, whom he labeled "St. Thomas of Cantingbury." John Taylor of Caroline became the philosopher of the Quids, though a little late; in 1808 Monroe was used as a stalking horse against Madison, Jefferson's heir, but repented in time. The Quids, indeed, broke up after their failure but were to reappear in a new guise a score of years later.

2   Measures Short of War

Jefferson's first administration had been fairly smooth, but before its end that bête noire of the early Republic, European war, was knocking at the door. The conflict had gradually run down to a stop in the **Renewal of** Treaty of Amiens (March 1802), only to be renewed a year **European** later (May 1803) between France and England and gradu- **war** ally joined by others. The acquisition of Louisiana had encouraged the export of western grain, meat, and tobacco down the rivers to New Orleans for shipment abroad, and this trade had rapidly become an essential to western economic development. Now the renewal of European war brought back the old problems of neutral commerce with the added factor that the growing West was vitally concerned with their solution. Jefferson, like Washington and Adams, was desperately opposed to war, if for no other reason than that the nation was too weak to stand the buffeting it would receive.

Curiously enough, for over two years neither belligerent interfered seriously with American trade. The French and Spanish once more opened their West Indian islands to American ships, and the British countered by reviving the Rule of 1756. Nevertheless, Yankee shippers built up a lucrative trade between the French and Spanish West Indies and Europe by taking sugar to the United States, paying the duty, reshipping it (and receiving back most of the duty) and carrying it to Europe; this was the "broken voyage." These tactics naturally aroused the ire of British shipping interests, and in the *Essex* case (July 1805) a British prize court ruled that these hauls were actually "continuous voyages" and would be so treated unless a *bona fide* duty had been paid.

Beginning of friction with Great Britain

British squadrons now began an intermittent blockade of American ports, and at times actually operated within sheltered waters—not but what French warships did also when they could, but there were not many of them. The British therefore received the most blame, and it must be admitted that they were needlessly arrogant. Innocent ships were ordered to Halifax regardless of the cost to the owners, and sometimes suspicion was as good as evidence to the British prize courts. Warning shots were fired, and stories went around that an American was killed; even more degrading, an American captain who protested a British search was stripped on his own quarterdeck and flogged. It was evident that the British were determined to use the opportunity to destroy or at least cripple the merchant marine of their greatest rival.

The old British practice of impressment was also renewed. The conditions of service in the British navy were brutal, and most sailors preferred the merchant marine. The conditions of American nautical service were far above those of even British merchantmen, and so it is no wonder that according to Gallatin twenty-five hundred men deserted the British navy and merchant marine annually and sailed on American ships. Nevertheless, England's life depended on the navy, and it took precedence. Press gangs from ships in port seized any able-bodied men or boys and shanghaied them aboard; at sea a shorthanded naval vessel could stop any British merchantman and impress as many men as it saw fit. Now, England denied that her subjects could change their nationality—"once an Englishman, always an Englishman"—and therefore extended the right of impressment to foreign vessels likely to be carrying British sailors in their crews.

Renewal of impressment

British naval captains consequently sent press gangs aboard any American merchantman they chose and seized any man with an English, Scots, or Irish accent, or if there were not enough of them took anyone else they chose. Of course, an American-born would be returned upon complaint of the American minister in London, but there was no seaman's register and years might elapse before the ship in which he served returned to England; then he might be dead or with health and spirit broken. Altogether it was claimed that about ten thousand *bona fide* American seamen were impressed. When the State Department protested, it was held up to scorn not only by the British Foreign Office but by Federalists. Britain, it was pointed out, was fighting for life; the Americans merely wanted to make more money; the British navy was fighting for the world's freedom, and the cowardly Americans as usual were trading with the enemy and prating of neutral rights. The fact that the United States did not resist only raised British arrogance and sank the Americans even further beneath contempt.

It was natural that indignant Americans should use any possible means to thwart the British navy. By Jay's Treaty (which did not expire until 1807) British naval vessels and privateers had the right to resort

American retaliation

to American ports with their prizes. As a result British patrol ships often reprovisioned in the very ports they were blockading. In such cases their deserting seamen were sometimes welcomed by the citizens and provided with fraudulent naturalization or "protection" papers. There is a story that a British officer who left his longboat and crew at the wharf in New York and went to buy supplies returned presently to find that his men refused to man the boat; when he threatened them, they insolently exhibited naturalization papers as "proof" that they were now Americans. On another occasion twelve British naval vessels lay helpless in Norfolk while the crews lounged about the streets and cursed and made snooks at their officers. American officials refused to aid in the return of such deserters, and, when reproached, they truthfully pointed out that British officials also refused to return American seamen who deserted in British ports.

By 1806 the great powers' old toleration of neutral commerce with the enemy was at an end. One neutral after another had fallen prey to force, until at last the United States was the only important neutral

The Continental System

carrying nation left. Britain should have stepped softly, however, in dealing with America, for about one third of her exports went there and, indeed, she at times sold three or even four times as much as she bought. In the battle of Trafalgar (October 1805) Lord Nelson destroyed the combined French and Spanish fleets and gained such complete control of the seas that British men-o'-war actually stopped gun practice. Napoleon's sea power was now represented only by privateers preying on British commerce.

About a month after Trafalgar, Napoleon defeated Russia and Austria at Austerlitz and established his control of Europe. Napoleon knew that England as a shopkeeping nation could be conquered only by crippling her commerce; therefore by the Berlin and Milan decrees he set up the Continental System, which prohibited the entry of British ships and goods into Europe. In addition, he declared a "paper" blockade of the British Isles; of course, he had no navy, but by this means he held a club over any neutral vessels which entered British ports. On the other hand, a series of British Orders in Council established a blockade of the continent from the Elbe to Brest through which neutral commerce was strained as through a sieve. It was an excellent means, and was intended to be, of discouraging American commerce to the continent; on the other hand this was also a "paper" blockade, for Britain did not have enough ships to watch every European port and so adopted the policy of stopping American ships at sea.

Americans were caught in a dilemma. If they visited a British port to obtain a license or submitted to British search on their way to the continent, they were subject to seizure by French port officials. If they were caught at sea by French privateers, it was pretty likely to be assumed that they were headed for Britain or a British colony. On the whole, highhanded and wrongheaded as the British were, it was still possible to do business with them. Prices were such that a few successful voyages would pay for the risk, even if the ship were then captured by the French; the same was even more true in the trade to those parts of Europe where French control was weak. Of course, few shipowners cared that in the end it was the common sailor who took the risk and suffered impressment or the dungeon.

Effects on American commerce

Both British and French had taken the measure of Jefferson and were convinced that he would not go to war; and the Federalists, who were in constant touch with British diplomats and spies, strengthened the opinion in the British. Indeed, Jefferson was fatuously laying up the navy now that the Tripolitan War was over and asking authorization to build flotillas of shallow-draught boats claimed to be suitable for coastal defense and carrying but one gun. It was presumed that they could be easily manned by crews from coastal villages; at any rate, the building contracts were widely distributed, with political results that surprised no one. Jefferson and Madison, both of them superb realists in many ways, nevertheless never understood that he who would sup with the devil must have a long spoon—that power is necessary in order to play at politics with the great powers.

A crisis was bound to occur sooner or later. Early in 1807 a small French fleet sought refuge from a storm in Chesapeake Bay, and one of the ships which ran ashore on the beach was shelled and destroyed by British pursuers. The British then took up their station in Lynnhaven Bay within the Capes of Chesapeake. While they were there, a number of sailors deserted, and word was received that four of them had enlisted on the U.S. Frigate *Chesapeake*, which with Commodore James Barron in command was then

Chesapeake and Leopard, June 1807

fitting for the Mediterranean station. The British commander, Admiral G. C. Berkeley, ordered that the *Chesapeake* be stopped on its departure and the men retaken. Accordingly on 22 June when the American frigate sailed, the British frigate *Leopard* hailed her ten miles off the coast. Barron's deck was littered with stores and the guns unmounted, but he refused to submit to search; the *Leopard* thereupon poured three broadsides into the *Chesapeake* and forced her to strike. The four men were taken off, and one of them (a born Britisher) was hanged; the other three had allegedly been impressed from American ships. After the disgraceful incident the *Chesapeake* limped back to Norfolk, and the *Leopard* nonchalantly returned to its anchorage in Lynnhaven Bay.

The fury that swept the nation had not been equaled since Lexington, according to Jefferson. He was compelled to order British ships out of American harbors, for their own safety if for no other reason. Congress was summoned, but at a date distant enough to allow emotions to cool. Meanwhile the British Foreign Office disavowed the act, and Berkeley was recalled—and promoted to a better station. Monroe and William Pinkney of Maryland, then in London negotiating a treaty to replace Jay's, were ordered by Jefferson to accept no treaty which did not give up the right of impressment. This the British refused to comply with, and so negotiations dragged on until finally the *Chesapeake* outrage became lost in a tangle of issues. More than a year before the incident Congress had passed a Nonimportation Act prohibiting the entry of certain British goods, but its application had been repeatedly postponed in order not to hamper Monroe and Pinkney; now in December 1807 it was put into effect. It prohibited the importation of British glass, metals, and textiles in such categories as the United States could make itself or obtain elsewhere. This was in effect a disguised protection to American manufacturers.

Effect on the nation

The country was not appeased, but Jefferson was determined to avoid war. For all that, French actions were every bit as unreasonable as the British and equally subject to sanctions. Economic sanctions seemed to him a fitting weapon and, indeed, the only one available. Nor was an embargo an idea of the moment. On the contrary, he had urged it as early as 1774 as a substitute for war, especially wars between large nations which were liable to result only in mutual exhaustion and settle nothing. At first glance it might seem strange that an American Physiocrat would expect to gain a point by using the weapon of commerce, but it must be remembered that the chief American exports were agricultural: grain, tobacco, and cotton. In December 1807 the well-disciplined Republican majority passed the Embargo Act. The intention was to force England and France to abandon unreasonable controls by prohibiting the export of American goods by land or sea; the Nonimportation Act, of course, continued to prohibit the

The Embargo

entry of many British articles. As a matter of fact a considerable part of the American merchant marine was unaffected, for of the ships in port as many as could left before the passage of the act, and every effort was made to warn those abroad to stay away. Many ingenious ways were found to evade the terms of the Embargo, and the number of Spanish and

OGRABME, or, The American Snapping-turtle.
The New York Historical Society

The Embargo's hindrance of trade led to its enemies' reversing the spelling and picturing it as a snapping turtle.

Swedish ships entering American ports increased amazingly. Nevertheless the Embargo was favored in almost all the states except those of New England, and even there opposition developed slowly outside the ranks of the Federalists.

The old idea that the Embargo was ruinous to business has been blasted. Even in New England the blow fell upon the laborers and seafarers rather than the merchants; on the positive side, there was a definite movement of capital into manufactures and a consequent improvement of conditions. The Middle States, where manufacturing was already well developed, found themselves booming. The South, most helpless of the sections, suffered because it could not export its staples, but it was willing to suffer for its principles; there is, moreover, more than a hint that many Southerners expected the Embargo to encourage manufactures in their area. In the light of later history, it is tragic that it did not. It is worth noting that Jefferson himself never recovered financially from the effect of the Embargo. The enforcement of the Embargo was fairly successful, though Yankee ingenuity found many ways of thwarting it and carrying on a lucrative trade with Canada.

The measures voted in the Enforcement Act and necessary to impose the Embargo on the North must have made Sam Adams turn over in his grave, and even Jefferson must have blushed when he thought of the high **Embargo** idealism of his inaugural message. Congress had made a **emasculates** gesture toward defense by providing for a new army of ten **Republican** thousand men, but now Jefferson had to use parts of it in **principles** enforcing the Embargo; he must have been haunted by his own propaganda that a standing army is the foe of the liberties of the people. The Federalists, of course, misrepresented the situation for political purposes and even started soup kitchens for the helpless victims of Republican policy. Actually the tariff revenues collected during the Embargo decreased by only about one half, for by the Nonimportation Act the cheaper quality of British manufactures could still be brought into the country indirectly. It is supposed that American exports declined by seventy-five per cent and imports by one half.

Napoleon affected to regard the Embargo as an aid and declared: "War exists then in fact between England and the United States; and His Majesty considers it declared from the day on which England published **Effect** her decrees." The implication was unmistakable. Napoleon **of the** was calling a dog to heel. In England the rise in the price **Embargo** of food and clothing fell most heavily on the workingmen, **abroad** who, however, could make no effective protest. Merchants and shippers were delighted at the removal of competition; though American purchases from England were half those of 1807, England's total exports dropped only seven per cent. Several things combined to pad the blow. The harvest of 1808 was unusually abundant; the reconquest of Spain from Napoleon re-opened that market; and the loss of Spanish control of its American colonies allowed the entrance of British goods. About the same time the Portuguese court threw Brazil open. When Pinkney in England offered to trade the Embargo for repeal of the obnoxious Orders in Council, Foreign Minister George Canning sarcastically replied that he had no complaint to make about it but out of goodwill to the United States he would be glad to facilitate the removal of the Embargo "as a measure of inconvenient restriction upon the American people"—but not in trade for the Orders in Council.

Whatever was the public attitude toward the Embargo, it failed quite completely to shake the Republican hold upon the people. Madison and Clinton ran for President and Vice-President against C. C. Pinckney and **Election** Rufus King and carried two thirds of the electors; though **of 1808** the New England popular vote except Vermont went to Pinckney, it was by a narrow margin. The fact that Jefferson had his way on the national stage did not prevent his party from paying the price that goes with an excess of power and a weak opposition. In New York the Clintons were besieged by rivals within the party, and in Pennsylvania the party was split into two camps; Randolph's Quids have been noted earlier. The result of these and other factional struggles was to weaken the Republicans in Congress, in spite of their overwhelming numbers, and offer cleavages into which the Federalists could insert their wedges.

The Federalists took courage. The propaganda against the Embargo became, if possible, more venomous. The Republicans took heart when a New England judge upheld the constitutionality of the Embargo with arguments that were strikingly like Hamilton's and Marshall's but were downcast when Governor Trumbull of Connecticut addressed his legislature in language closely patterned on the Virginia and Kentucky Resolutions. **New England threatens secession**

Cabot's indolence and lack of ambition made him hesitate to support the measures of a fire-eater like Timothy Pickering; but this hesitation was not evident to the Republicans, and they were thrown into a panic by what they took to be the slow sure measures of a strong man who knew what he wanted. The New England town meetings, ably marshalled, took up the cry against the Embargo. "I felt the foundations of the Government shaken under my feet by the New England townships," said Jefferson in later years. He and George III! The Northern Republicans were convinced that the Federalists meant business this time, and that the only ways to block their secession were by force (which might mean civil war) or by repeal of the Embargo. War with England was conceivably better than civil war, but Jefferson and the agrarian South opposed any war and especially one which would benefit no one but the manufacturers of the North.

When Congress met it was haunted by the specters of war and secession. In vain did Jefferson try to persuade it that Embargo and war were the only honorable alternatives, and that after all Embargo had benefited the nation by promoting manufactures. It only angered the mercantile Federalists—and showed how far Jefferson had departed from his agrarian principles. John Randolph reigned forensically supreme "and like the water snakes in Coleridge's silent ocean his every track was a flash of golden **Repeal of the Embargo, March 1809** fire." Lesser orators recited in masochistic detail the insults the nation had borne. When it became known that the President-elect would yield the Embargo only if war were declared on Great Britain, Congress went wild with fear. It thought only of immediate submission and, egged on by the jubilant Federalists, repealed the Embargo, effective 4 March. Though it substituted a Nonintercourse Act which prohibited commerce with England and France, the law could easily be circumvented by using neutral ships and signified nothing but abject submission to the Federalists and their pro-British policy.

One of the most important attempts in history to find an economic substitute for war had failed. Even more significant, it was the nadir of national disgrace. The Federalists now had the opportunity for construc-

**Signifi-
cance of
the defeat
of Embargo**

tive statesmanship for which they had watched and prayed; but their bankruptcy was complete, and they had no states-manlike program to offer—only submission. Undoubtedly they were right in asserting that England was fighting for such constitutional liberty as the world could boast. But that was not the reason for their submission: they sought commercial profits and pro-tection from democracy. It was inevitable that the scepter should pass to new hands. Neither Massachusetts nor Virginia was to rule, but the new West which in their hearts they both despised. Thereafter step by step the nation descended to war.

Jefferson, as he left the presidency, was a disillusioned man. He had failed even as Washington to imbue public affairs with a spirit of sweet reasonableness. His method of democratic compromise had resulted in

**Jefferson's
failure**

pouring out the baby with the bath. Most of the Republi-can principles of 1801 were now so full of holes as to be unrecognizable. Instead of strict economy, national expendi-tures were greater than ever; instead of a navy at the docks, it had been busier than ever; instead of peace, Jefferson had fought one war and barely escaped another; instead of strict construction and preservation of state rights, the way had been opened for Federal supremacy. Even the hated Sedition Act had been aped by a no less tyrannical Embargo En-forcement Act. Gallatin, the enemy of the Bank of the United States, had become a convert to its convenience and efficiency, and Jefferson had pro-tested mildly, then assented. From an American Physiocratic distrust of manufactures, he had come to view them with pride and even counted them as a good result of the Embargo.

He but reflected the change in his party. Every election strengthened the Republican Party in the North, but the recruits were all but indis-tinguishable from the Federalists in economic principles and rejected only the Federalists' secessionism, merchant enterprise, and decadent aristoc-racy. Federalist principles were making way even in South Carolina as the cotton gin gave a new class of planters visions of busy textile mills. There were definite signs that even the Republicanism of Virginia was weakening; it was that which led the brilliant and erratic John Randolph and his Quids to part with Jefferson and fight a battle of invective for the strict construction of the Constitution. Yet another decade and the Old Dominion leadership even in the South would bow in everything but mere name to that of the Cotton States.

If Jefferson needed any proof of his basic failure, it was found in the long caravans of common farmers who in despair of relief from Republican policy were abandoning their sour and eroded acres and wending across the mountains to the fertile bottom lands of the West. If he needed any proof that his agrarian policies were not those of the developing future, he needed only to look at his followers in North and South who were furtively turning the pages of Hamilton's *Report on Manufactures* and dreaming not of a bucolic paradise but of bustling cities and whirring machinery. It was they who had pulled down the pillars of his Embargo when it was on the verge of success and brought down in ruin his hope of finding a substitute for war.

3   *Hamilton and Jefferson in the Stream of American History*

When Jefferson retired from the presidency he placed his own bust and that of Hamilton facing each other in the great hall of his home at Monticello, and there they still stand, opposite each other in death as in life. Their position is fitting, for they personify the two great forces of democratic evolution. Each was, and is, necessary to the other, just as without protagonist and antagonist there can be no drama. As Jefferson himself said: "The terms Whig and Tory belong to natural as well as to civil history. They denote the temper and constitution of mind of different individuals." In another place he was even more explicit: "In every free and deliberating society, there must, from the nature of man be opposite parties, and violent dissensions and discords; and one of these, for the most part, must prevail over the other for a longer or shorter time. Perhaps this party division is necessary to induce each other to watch and to relate to the people at large the proceedings of the other." *[margin: Protagonist and antagonist]*

We have devoted so much time to the first twenty years of the Republic because this was the period in which the nation set the direction of its development (democratic capitalism) and the method of its development (the democratic process). Hamilton stood for a strong central government, the dominance of commerce and manufactures, and rule by the rich, the well-born, and the able; Jefferson stood for a weak central government, the dominance of agriculture, and rule by the people as a whole. The lesson of the first twenty years is that we find either the two leaders or their followers deliberately contradicting in word or deed every item of their trilogy of principles. It is already evident that these "principles" were merely weapons for political combat and that a party out of power held quite different standards from those it held when it was in power. This fact will become increasingly evident in later generations, so evident that only confusion can result if we try to distinguish the two sides by these superficial tags. *[margin: Significance of the first twenty years]*

The true principles of Hamilton and Jefferson lie much deeper. They can perhaps be best expressed respectively in the two catchwords "order" and "liberty." Hamilton did not reject liberty, of course; he simply believed that it must give precedence to order. Jefferson did not reject order; he simply believed that order without liberty is of no value, and that to preserve or extend liberty its tree must sometimes be refreshed by the blood of tyrants and of patriots. Hamilton was the realist, the practical man of affairs who thought in terms of dollars and cents and saw that they could not be amassed and protected without a high degree of public order. Jefferson was the idealist, the man of faith and optimism who believed that happiness is the end of human existence and the only defensible purpose of government—and how could a man be happy without liberty?

Which precedes, order or liberty?

Both believed that where a man's treasure is, there will his heart be also. Hamilton looked upon order and property as treasures which are responsibly guarded only if they are entrusted to the select few. Property, as the rock of good order, must be preserved from direct injury or from limitations which prevent it from multiplying itself freely. The individual who sought either of these ends was not only trying to upset society but was also attacking the rights of a human being, the owner of the property. Jefferson sought to entrust the treasures of liberty and happiness to the many in the sublime faith that men who are trusted will prove themselves trustworthy. Therein lie the strength and the weakness of democracy. Obviously the Jeffersonians did not reject the holding of property; they simply believed that property should not become an instrument for limiting the rights, snatching the livelihood, or besmirching the dignity of the individual.

It is a curious fact that the philosophies of both Hamilton and Jefferson stemmed from American Physiocracy, though from different aspects: that if the individual were left free by the government to farm, manufacture, and trade, he would find an equilibrium with his fellows. Adam Smith adapted the general idea to trade and manufacture. He sought to smash the barriers of tariffs and governmental regulations and allow individuals freedom of enterprise both at home and in dealing with businessmen of other nations.

Hamilton, Jefferson, and Physiocracy

To find the equilibrium, Smith insisted that neither nation nor individual must seek an artificial monopoly but must honestly obey the law of supply and demand. Hamilton sought to apply Smith's doctrines domestically, but internationally he sought to go back to some phases of mercantilism and have the government manipulate the tariff to protect and promote manufacture and trade. The fact that Hamilton did not live to see his ideas put into effect should not shear him of the honor of paternity. The Jeffersonian relation to American Physiocracy was even more direct. The Republicans (at first) insisted that all wealth springs from the land and that manufacture and trade are parasites. Even before Jefferson's death the movement had split into two wings.

For the sake of clarity it is well to forecast those wings here. Jefferson had sought both the welfare of society as a whole and the protection and expression of individual rights. One wing desired the government to promote public welfare even if it had to limit individual rights; to this now belong the plebeians and such of the farmers, laborers, and intelligentsia as are verging on socialism as they urge the people to add economic to political power. Probably Jefferson never realized that his theories could lead to such a result. The individualist wing has insisted that the government must stand aside and let the individual run his own affairs. In this wing there have been two elements. The rugged individualist, whether farmer or businessman, who has identified democracy with private enterprise, has often insisted that economic power carries the right to political power, and has often preferred Jefferson's weak government to Hamilton's strong government. The other individualist element, fostered by Taylor, Randolph, Calhoun, and the Tidewater aristocrats, was the die-hard, aristo-agrarian state-rights school which opposed business and insisted upon complete laissez faire; it was agrarian and American Physiocratic, and set up the Athenian ideal of a society of citizens erected on an economic basis of slavery. *Splits in the Jeffersonian movement*

Jefferson thought of the small farmers as the bulwark of democracy because in their independence and economic equality he saw the only feasible way of reconciling liberty and equality. If there is complete liberty (individualism), the danger is that those with luck, initiative, or shrewdness will gain an undue share of economic power—and with it will come inequality, because they will have the power to oppress their fellows. If there is inequality to begin with, that is, an undue share of privileges in certain hands, it will be a serious obstacle to the preservation or the attainment of liberty; the alternative of setting up a government to preserve equality immediately shears the individual of part of his liberty to do as he pleases. There has always existed among Americans an opinion that we are free so long as the government is not politically or economically tyrannical; many of us fail utterly to see that tyranny can just as easily come from the overwhelming economic power of individuals or corporations, or from social or religious restrictions. *Relationship of liberty and economic equality*

Jefferson saw what many of us still fail to grasp: that to preserve liberty there must be throughout the nation a considerable degree of relative (*not* absolute) economic equality. It was to promote this end that Jefferson fought and conquered primogeniture and entail in Virginia.

This was why he violated his Constitutional principles: he made the Louisiana Purchase in order to obtain more land for the common man; he fought the Federalist judges because they were concerned chiefly with protecting property rather than liberty; he warded off war by the Louisiana Purchase and by harsh enforcement of the Embargo because he knew that war ordinarily makes the rich richer and endangers the economic equality necessary to democracy.

During his whole life Jefferson was concerned with finding the balance between liberty and equality, for he was not so foolish as to think that a wide distribution of property would be an automatic stabilizer. He proposed a solution that was quite in keeping with his faith in human nature. Let men be educated to their responsibilities, let them restrain themselves from deliberately overturning the balance between liberty and equality, and let them have the courage to fight any such attempts. The form of government was important, but secondary. What counted was the willingness of democrats to live virtuously and deal justly with their fellow men.

The problem of economic equality became acute after the Civil War with the growth of teeming industrial populations who could not live on their own land but were dependent upon the fortunes and the goodwill **Problem transferred to an industrial society** of others. Jefferson in his presidency had forecast the future when he sought to preserve economic equality by breaking his own partisan tenets. Since democracy tries to preserve and promote human happiness by seeking a reasonable balance between liberty and equality, it must create economic equality where it does not exist or has been lost. Thus MacArthur broke up the great corporations and the great landed estates of Japan. For the same reason both Democratic and Republican progressives have sought to enforce competition in manufactures by breaking up monopolistic corporations, and where "natural" monopolies exist they have imposed regulations (as on street railways) or taken them under government ownership (as the post office).

The people of the United States have found in capitalism the promise of popular welfare, and usually its delivery. The abundance of resources has given to our reform movements a color quite unlike that of older countries. Since nearly everyone here has been able to win **Reform is sporadic** some property if he is willing to work and save, the historic combat has not been a straight issue between property and human rights. It would be clearer and usually more accurate to speak of the struggle as between big property and little property.

While it is true that political revolts are always in progress somewhere in the country, the Jeffersonian side of the conflict nevertheless becomes clear in the national scene only about once in a generation (1800,

1828, 1860, 1896, 1912, 1932). The Democratic Party is the one with the *tendency* toward liberalism, but the opposition is never without its liberal wing, and Jeffersonian reforms may be implemented by either party. Lincoln once pungently illustrated this condition with a story: "I remember being once much amused at seeing two partially intoxicated men engaged in a fight with greatcoats on, which fight, after a long and rather harmless contest, ended in each having fought himself out of his own coat and into that of the other." Lincoln himself, though a member of the party of Hamilton, has become a legendary hero of Jeffersonianism.

American political reform movements have never been root-and-branch crusades. They have pared, and altered, and regulated, but in the end the old tree is still alive. The aim has been not to kill our basic institutions but to revitalize them. Little property has sought **Character** to limit the overwhelming menace of big property to demo- **of reform-** cratic equality. Liberal political movements usually have **ism** come on the heels of notable increases in the size or privileges of big property. It is also noteworthy that in a number of cases the rebels have been bought off by a handout of public land. Jefferson had to make recourse to this evasion when he lowered the price and terms of payment of public land. Hamiltonians and Jeffersonians have historically followed pretty much the same methods. Both have desired minimum government interference, though neither has scrupled to call for government aid in a pinch—little property against big property, and big property against labor agitators or foreign competitors. The tendency in this century, however, is for the Jeffersonians to demand regulation of big property or enforced competition.

It was Hamilton who first saw that the United States was poorly balanced economically and that manufacture and commerce needed to be fostered in order to promote prosperity and national security; it was only after years of buffeting that Jefferson got the point, and **Progress** even then his consent was grudging. Certainly in this re- **through** spect Hamilton deserves to be called progressive; by the **conflict** same token Jefferson, with his desire to preserve a nation of small farmers, was a conservative. It is confusing, unless we interpret liberalism and conservatism as political attitudes, not necessarily economic or administrative tags.

Hamilton sought to maintain the political *status quo;* it was Jefferson who forced on him the pattern of democratic evolution through political conflict. Hamilton's legacy was intensely practical, mundane, and a little selfish; he lighted the furnaces of our iron mills, hoisted the sails of our trading ships, and posted the ledgers in banks and counting houses; his was the inspiration that brought us science and technology and that bred mass production and the American standard of living.

Jefferson's legacy was that of faith in humanity; he touched the moral consciousness of men with the spark of inspiration and sounded the trumpet call to battle for human rights. Hamilton was the head, Jefferson the heart. Hamilton was science, Jefferson was democracy; and though they may clash, neither can live long without the other. Hamilton was might, Jefferson was right. Might gives to right the power to survive, and right gives to might the moral reason to fight for survival. Thus in eternal conflict, eternal compromise, and eternal interdependence Hamilton and Jefferson have lived since there were men on this earth and will live as long as men remain.

BIBLIOGRAPHICAL NOTE

Jefferson the Force

POLITICS: It is difficult to find an impartial account of Jefferson's administrations, and probably Edward Channing, *The Jeffersonian System* (1906) is best, though unfortunately colorless. Claude G. Bowers, *Jefferson in Power* (1936) is again a colorful attempt to canonize Jefferson, but it falls down somewhat when compared with Henry Adams, *History of the United States, 1801–1817* (9 vols., 1889–91). See the abridged version by Herbert Agar published in two volumes in 1947 under the title *The Formative Years.* Adams, who was a descendant of two Presidents, wrote to demonstrate that the Republicans had actually put into effect the very Federalist policies which they had fought. He proved his thesis. Jefferson is treated with Jovian pity streaked with Adamsian superciliousness; probably Adams was incapable of appreciating the idealism of Jefferson's philosophy and thought it disproved by his actions in office. The significance of Jefferson lies deeper. Everett S. Brown, *The Constitutional History of the Louisiana Purchase* (1920) is useful in tracing that phase of Jefferson's *volte face.* See also Leonard D. White, *The Jeffersonians: A Study in Administrative History, 1801–1829* (1951).

WASHINGTON LIFE: Claude Bowers and Henry Adams give interesting vignettes. See also Margaret B. Smith, *First Forty Years of Washington Society* (1906); and the journals of William Plumer, Manasseh Cutler, and John Quincy Adams.

BARBARY WARS: See Ray W. Irwin, *Diplomatic Relations of the United States with the Barbary Powers* (1931); Gardner W. Allen, *Our Navy and the Barbary Corsairs* (1905); Charles O. Paullin, *Commodore John Rodgers* (1910); L. B. Wright and J. H. Macleod, *The First Americans in North Africa: William Eaton's Struggle* (1945); Alexander S. Mackenzie, *Life of Stephen Decatur* (1846); and Charles L. Lewis, *The Romantic Decatur* (1937).

PICKERING: For information on this stern and ambitious Puritan, whose dearest hope was to wreck the Union, one must go to hostile accounts such as Claude Bowers, *Jefferson and Hamilton* and *Jefferson in Power,* or to the partisan *Life* (4 v., 1867–73) by his son, Octavius Pickering, and C. W. Upham.

RANDOLPH: Gerald W. Johnson, *Randolph of Roanoke: A Political Fantastic* (1929) is based largely on the more extensive William C. Bruce, *John Randolph of Roanoke, 1773–1833* (2 v., 1922). See also Henry Adams, *John Randolph* (1882); and Russell Kirk, *Randolph of Roanoke: A Study in Conservative Thought* (1951).

Measures Short of War

IMPRESSMENT: James F. Zimmerman, *Impressment of American Seamen* (1925) deals chiefly with the diplomatic phase but includes some interesting statistics. Impressment and also many other phases of Anglo-American relations are treated in Alfred L. Burt, *The United States, Great Britain, and British North America from the Revolution to the Establishment of Peace after the War of 1812* (1940).

EMBARGO: In addition to other references on diplomacy see Louis M. Sears, *Jefferson and the Embargo* (1927); and Walter W. Jennings, *The American Embargo, 1807–1809* (1921).

Chapter XII

THE RISE OF TRANS-APPALACHIA

1 *The Old Northwest*

THE American movement from the Appalachian Mountains to the Great Plains was completed in two generations, roughly between 1755 and 1820. Four general forces were involved: the Indians, aboriginal lords of
Factors in the westward movement the soil; the white settlers, those "new men," the Americans; a succession of European powers whose influence disappeared one by one: France, England, and Spain; and finally the economic and political interests of the Atlantic seaboard. We have seen how New England and Virginia fought over the infant West and made it the pawn of their game of power politics. Virginia had tended to promote the acceptance of the West in the councils of the nation, since common agrarian interests would promote agrarian ascendancy in the Federal government. New England on the other hand, as a mercantile center, opposed the West as financially and politically disorderly and a refuge for men who should have stayed in the East and worked for wages. Gouverneur Morris in the Constitutional Convention struck the keynote of New England's attitude toward the West: "The busy haunts of men, not the remote wilderness, are the proper school of political talents. If the western people get the power into their hands, they will ruin the Atlantic interests. The back members are always averse to the best measures." By 1812 Morris was able to slap his wooden leg and cram a cynical I-told-you-so down the national throat.

The rush of settlers into the Indian country at the close of the Revolution convinced the state and Confederation governments that there would be trouble unless the Indians were bought off. As a result, treaties at Fort
Northwest Ordinance of 1784 Stanwix in 1784 and Fort McIntosh in 1785 extorted from miscellaneous western tribes their claim to the major part of Ohio. Meanwhile speculators and veterans with land

THE SURVEY OF THE PUBLIC DOMAIN

is based upon the Ordinance of 1785. Beginning with the Seven Ranges, this survey was continued across the country, although there still remain, in the mountainous sections of the Far West, over one hundred million acres of un-surveyed land. However, with a few local exceptions, the survey applies in every state in the Union, except in the Thirteen Colonies and in Maine, Vermont, Kentucky, Tennessee, West Virginia, and Texas. From arbitrarily selected east-and-west Base Lines and north-and-south Meridians, the land is surveyed into Ranges of Townships, lying north and south of the Base Lines, and east and west of the Meridians. The Ranges are numbered east and west from the Meridians. The Townships, each six miles square, are numbered north and south from the Base Lines. The diagrams below illustrate the actual survey east of the Sixth Principal Meridian south of a Base Line located on 40° north latitude.

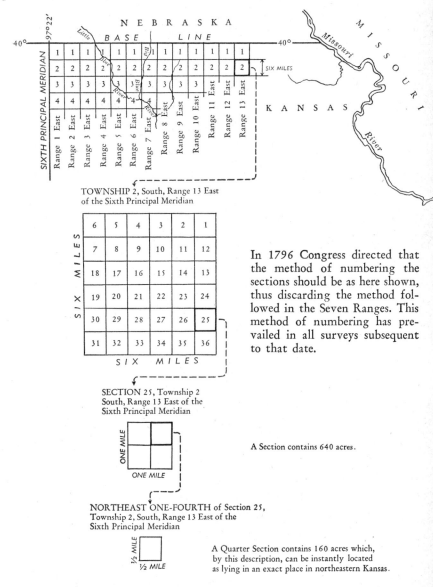

TOWNSHIP 2, South, Range 13 East of the Sixth Principal Meridian

SECTION 25, Township 2 South, Range 13 East of the Sixth Principal Meridian

In 1796 Congress directed that the method of numbering the sections should be as here shown, thus discarding the method followed in the Seven Ranges. This method of numbering has prevailed in all surveys subsequent to that date.

A Section contains 640 acres.

NORTHEAST ONE-FOURTH of Section 25, Township 2, South, Range 13 East of the Sixth Principal Meridian

A Quarter Section contains 160 acres which, by this description, can be instantly located as lying in an exact place in northeastern Kansas.

Adapted from *Atlas of American History*, edited by James Truslow Adams and R. V. Coleman; copyright 1943 by Charles Scribner's Sons; used by permission of the publishers.

claims were demanding that the Confederation Congress provide for the sale of western lands and their political organization. A committee under the chairmanship of Thomas Jefferson introduced in 1784 the first of a series of bills which were to be known as the Northwest Ordinances. Jefferson's proposals drew on the New England model of townships surveyed in squares and provided that the public domain north of the Ohio should be divided into ten territories, each of which should eventually become a state, and from which slavery should be excluded forever. He even proposed names for the new states, such as Assenisippia and Polypotamia. Such names must have helped to kill his proposal, though three of the more pronounceable names, Washington, Michigania, and Illinois, have been used since.

The Ordinance of 1784 was replaced after Jefferson's departure for France by the Ordinances of 1785 and 1787, which laid the foundations of the national land policy. The first act provided for the survey of townships six statute miles square, each with thirty-six sections of one square mile (640 acres). Lines were to be laid out along meridians of longitude and parallels of latitude; surveys were begun almost immediately with the "Seven Ranges," just west of the Pennsylvania boundary and the Ohio River. Half of the land was to be sold in sections and half in township lots at auctions (held in the East), but at not less than one dollar an acre. The government reserved four sections in each township, and one section which was to be sold for the benefit of common schools. A Geographer was appointed to direct land surveys. We may anticipate by saying that he was succeeded by a Surveyor General in 1796; in 1812 a General Land Office under a Commissioner was set up in the Treasury to handle land sales, though the Surveyor General was not placed under him until 1836.

Northwest Ordinance of 1785

The survey features of the ordinance were wise and, indeed, have since become the pattern of many of the world's public land surveys. In other respects the bill was plainly intended to accommodate land speculators, for it was evident that small farmers could neither afford the trip to the New York auctions, nor could they afford to bid in either a whole section or a whole township. Actually it was the work of a group of well-heeled gentlemen, chiefly New Englanders, some of them members of Congress, who proposed to profit by it. Congress, badly in need of money, immediately set aside the auction provisions and sold three great tracts to speculators. Two of them were wangled through the smooth lobbying of the Rev. Manasseh Cutler of Connecticut. The first grant, of a million and a half acres, at about eight cents an acre because it was paid in depreciated currency, went to a group of New England veterans called the Ohio Company of Associates.

Ohio land companies

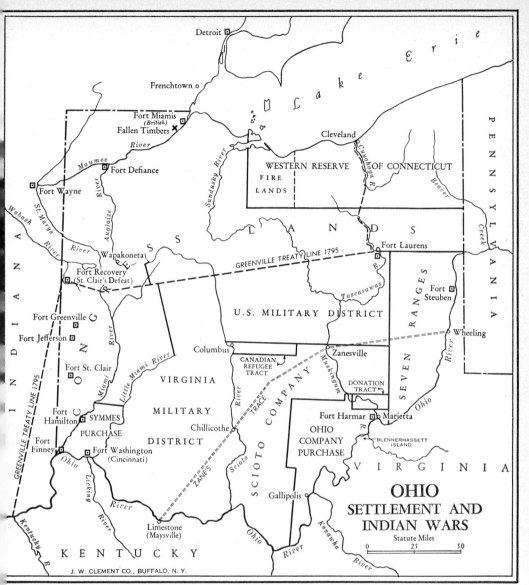

Adapted from *Atlas of American History*, edited by James Truslow Adams and R. V. Coleman; copyright 1943 by Charles Scribner's Sons; used by permission of the publishers.

They founded Marietta, Ohio on their tract in 1788. When they fell into financial difficulties Congress deeded them half the grant for the money already paid. The second grant went to the Scioto Company, which included a number of Congressmen and was headed by William Duer, a New York speculator. Their tract comprised five million acres just east of the Scioto River. The company induced a few French believers in Rousseau's state of nature to settle at Gallipolis—then went broke.

The third grant, of a million acres, lay on the Ohio between the

Miami and the Little Miami rivers and went to another group of Congressmen, headed by Judge John Cleves Symmes of New Jersey; whence it was called the Symmes Purchase. Eventually the syndicate retained only a third of its land. Cincinnati, founded in 1788, was the result of this venture. In addition to these grants Virginia had retained the right to the soil in a large tract with which to pay its soldiers' land bonuses (now largely in the hands of speculators); General George Rogers Clark had another grant opposite Louisville; and Connecticut had retained soil rights in a vast tract called the Western Reserve in northeastern Ohio.

Most of the northern shore of the Ohio as far as Louisville was by 1790 in the possession of speculators. Common farmers resented this and for a time usually refused to pay the inflated prices which were demanded; many of the settlers in Ohio were squatters, who simply cleared and built on land of their choice and frankly defied government or speculators to do anything about it. Indeed, this particular crop of speculators was in difficulties. The prospect of cheap Ohio lands had caused owners of new lands in New York, Pennsylvania, Kentucky, and Tennessee to offer lower prices to attract buyers. They were successful. More than that, it was possible to cross the Mississippi into Louisiana and receive a Spanish grant for the asking and the price of a little perjury.

Settlers bypass Ohio

The Ordinance of 1787 was political in its objectives. Though it owed something to Jefferson's committee, it seems to have owed more to the Rev. Manasseh Cutler, who shrewdly realized the attraction that certain political guarantees would offer. Civil liberties were assured, primogeniture and slavery were prohibited, and education was to be encouraged. The ordinance set up (13 July 1787) a political entity known as the Territory Northwest of the River Ohio, usually known simply as the Northwest Territory. A guarantee was made that the area would eventually be carved into from three to five states. The desired statehood was to be approached in three stages. First, governmental powers were all to be vested in a governor, a secretary, and three judges elected by and responsible to Congress. When the population reached five thousand free white males of voting age, legislative powers would pass to a popularly elected assembly. When any practicable portion of the territory reached a population of sixty thousand, it could apply to Congress for admission as a state. The Ordinance of 1787 was the most creative effort of the Confederation Congress, for it was the model by which was solved the age-old problem of what to do with grown-up colonies. The solution was feasible, of course, because the colonies were directly adjacent to the mother country.

Northwest Ordinance of 1787

The settlement of the Northwest Territory was slow, but as cogent a reason as speculators' pre-emption was Indian hostility. The tribes claimed with reason that the Treaty of Fort McIntosh was not binding, and a subsequent treaty at Fort Harmar (Marietta) in 1789 was also full of holes. The various tribes co-operated loosely under the Miami chief, Little Turtle, and went on with the sporadic raiding which had been going on ever since the Revolution. When in 1790 General Josiah Harmar undertook to chastise the Indians near Fort Wayne, Indiana, his forces were defeated in two severe skirmishes and retreated to Fort Washington (Cincinnati). The next year General Arthur St. Clair, governor of the territory, marched against the Indians with fourteen hundred men, chiefly militia from Kentucky and Pennsylvania, deplorably equipped and fed, undisciplined, and on the verge of mutiny. When Little Turtle struck the army, it was disastrously routed and lost two thirds of its number in killed and wounded. St. Clair was held responsible by the public, but the blame should have rested chiefly on the ineptness of the new Federal government.

Harmar's and St. Clair's defeats, 1790, 1791

The situation in the Northwest Territory was complicated by British trade and politics. While it was true that the value of the fur trade south of the Lakes was decreasing, the British fur traders nevertheless desired to wring out of it the last shilling of profit; and political officials felt under moral obligations to carry out as long as possible the guarantee they had made during the Revolution to protect the Indians' hunting grounds. On the other hand, British home politicians would not risk a war with the United States. The result was that Canadian officials blew hot and cold while waiting for something to turn up. Traders were permitted to furnish the Indians with ammunition, and undoubtedly some of them went on to stir up hostilities. Harmar's and St. Clair's defeats encouraged the British to hope for the chance to mediate between Americans and Indians, and they hoped out of it to fish continued control of the trade or even American cession of the territory.

British policy

Such hopes quickly evaporated, however, when the United States began at last to prepare seriously for war. "Mad Anthony" Wayne, a Revolutionary general with a reputation for rashness and intrepidity, was placed in command of a newly-raised regular force called the Legion of the United States. British officials and traders naturally interpreted war on the Indians as a disguised thrust at the western posts, especially Detroit. It was therefore evident that the war could develop into a conflict with Great Britain, so Wayne (at Washington's insistence) spent nearly two years drilling and equipping the Legion and building as bases a line of forts northward from Cincinnati. The British professed alarm, and Sir Guy Carleton, now Lord Dorchester and Governor of Canada, announced that the two countries would probably soon be at war. To point the statement he ordered Lieutenant Governor Simcoe to send out a force from Detroit to build and

Fallen Timbers, 1794

garrison Fort Miami, near modern Toledo. It was a bitter blow to both British and Indians when Wayne with 1000 regulars and 1600 mounted Kentucky militiamen met and sharply defeated 800 Indians in the Battle of Fallen Timbers (20 August 1794), two miles from Fort Miami. The Indians begged to be received into the fort, but the commandant refused, and the barbarians vanished into the forest.

Meanwhile the British government disavowed Dorchester's speech and in Jay's Treaty agreed to surrender the frontier posts. The Indians, thus abandoned, signed the Treaty of Greenville (1795) by which they surrendered the northeastern corner and the southern two

Ohio

thirds of Ohio. The removal of the Indian menace stimulated settlement, and it was encouraged also by laws passed in 1796 and 1800 which allowed the purchase of tracts as small as three hundred twenty acres, gave four years' credit, and set up land-purchase offices in the West. By 1800 Ohio had become populous enough to be split apart from the rest of the territory, and in 1803 it was admitted as a state—the first new state carved from the public domain.

William Henry Harrison (1773–1841), scion of a prominent Virginia family, became the leader of the Northwest. He had been an officer in Wayne's army, had married the daughter of Judge Symmes, served as

Harrison's policy of encroachment

territorial delegate to Congress, and now became governor of the newly-created Indiana Territory. He obeyed with alacrity Jefferson's instructions to obtain as large land cessions as possible. Jefferson advised getting the Indians into debt, so that they would be willing to sell. Harrison and his fellows in the West knew a few more tricks. By 1811 they had badgered, bribed, and whiskied the Indians into turning over to white settlement all of Ohio, the southern part of Indiana, most of Illinois, and eastern Michigan. Meanwhile Indiana Territory was reduced in size by the setting apart of Michigan and Illinois territories. Their defeat at Fallen Timbers and the British sellout had completely destroyed the Indians' morale. Disease and alcoholism decimated their ranks and further reduced their will to resist. Each land cession that was filled by white settlers drove out the game for a hundred miles beyond, so it was easy to agree to sell that stretch and have a prolonged debauch on the proceeds.

The greediness of the whites led to the last important flare-up of Indian resistance in the Old Northwest. Naturally Harrison attributed Indian resentment to the British, who were now carrying on trade across

Tecumseh's Northwestern Confederacy

the Detroit River at Malden. It is probably true that resistance was encouraged by British traders and by the British superintendent of Indian affairs, Alexander McKee, an old western Pennsylvania Tory. More important, however, was the inspiration of two remarkable Shawnee brothers, Tecumseh and the

Prophet. The latter was a medicine man, considerable of a charlatan; Tecumseh, "The Meteor," was the orator and leader, a warrior with courage and personality, possessed of unusual foresight and organizational ability, and renowned even among the whites for his honesty, temperance, and humaneness.

During the first decade of the century Tecumseh gradually developed the idea that the land belonged to the members of all the Indian nations and that no one of them could cede it without the consent of the others. He saw clearly that the Indians' only hope lay in two policies: cleansing themselves of the white men's vices and uniting in a confederacy to resist all further white advances. The amazing fact is that he actually succeeded in welding together the quarrelsome and debauched remnants of the nations into a fairly general support of confederation and alcoholic prohibition. Under his influence the Indians began to turn to agriculture and to live on what they earned instead of running up bills at the trading posts. The Prophet aided by giving the sanction of religious enthusiasm and the terror of magic.

After 1808 the brothers lived on the banks of the Tippecanoe River in northern Indiana in a sacred village known as the Prophet's Town. Whether or not he was justified in his belief, Tecumseh expected to obtain British aid; certainly it was evident that a war between **Battle of** Great Britain and the United States was in the offing, and **Tippeca-** it may be that tentative promises of help were made. At **noe, 1811** any rate, he received supplies of arms from the royal stores. Though some Indians were already raiding, Tecumseh was not willing to strike without the help of the Civilized Nations of the South and so in 1811 departed for a round of councils in that quarter. Harrison had looked upon the Indian renascence with alarm. Now he took advantage of Tecumseh's absence to gather about 800 troops at Vincennes, his capital, and lead them to the Prophet's Town. Harrison may or may not have intended to force a battle; in any case, the problem was solved for him. Tecumseh had warned his brother against engaging in a battle, but at dawn (7 November) the Prophet's three or four hundred warriors attacked the encampment and were repulsed. The Indians fled and Harrison, after burning the town and its accumulated stores, retreated to Vincennes with a quarter of his men dead or wounded.

Tippecanoe was scarcely in itself a decisive victory; but the ambitious commander represented it as a glorious triumph, and so it has been regarded ever since. At any rate, it made him more than ever the popular hero—"the Washington of the West"—and thirty years **Effect** later made him President of the United States for exactly one month. It is true that the battle of Tippecanoe threw Tecumseh off balance and so had a greater effect than would have seemed warranted by the size of the blow. Neither Tecumseh nor the British had been ready for war; therefore the Prophet's premature resistance destroyed the force of the threats with which Tecumseh had planned to confront the Americans. The members of the confederacy scattered; and, though forays were resumed, Tecumseh's prestige was damaged and the Northwestern Indians never again rallied in great force.

2   *The Old Southwest*

The Mississippi River and its tributaries were the highways of the early West. The power that controlled New Orleans dominated the economic life of the West and held a partial veto on its political actions. In **West open** 1786 John Jay, Secretary of Foreign Affairs, and Gardoqui, **to foreign** the Spanish minister, negotiated a treaty by which the **intrigues** United States surrendered for thirty years the claim to the right to navigate the Mississippi through Spanish territory. Though Congress did not ratify the treaty, the West was alarmed and resentful, and the more mature part south of the Ohio was ripe for the intrigues of England, France, and Spain.

At the close of the Revolution Spain enclosed the United States on two sides—Louisiana on the west and Florida on the south. Spain's policy was aimed at protecting her own colonial authority by weaning the **Spanish** West away from the East, and in doing this she initiated **policies** curiously contradictory actions. The Mississippi was closed to western navigation, and the Creek Indians were permitted (though not exactly urged) to attack Georgia and Tennessee. On the other hand, when restless American traders and land speculators, usually the same individuals, approached Spanish officials with schemes for western secession, they were given verbal encouragement but no promises of aid, at least not before 1795. Americans were in 1787 given the right to export their goods via New Orleans on payment of a considerable tariff and were encouraged to settle on Spanish territory on condition that they become Spanish subjects. This policy seemed to Jefferson like "settling the Goths at the gates of Rome," but it was not altogether stupid. The Spanish believed that the settlers were foreigners, Tories, and refugees from the law, whose hostility to the United States would lead them to accept Spanish rule. As a matter of fact Natchez, though inhabited by British and Americans, was a model of submission and had even rejected an attempt by Georgia to take control. The area was by treaty technically a part of the United States, but Spain had refused to vacate after the war on the logical ground that it was historically a part of West Florida.

Spain, indeed, was leading from weakness. The furs, skins, rice, indigo, and tobacco of Louisiana found little vent in Spain and had to be sold elsewhere. Louisiana needed Kentucky wheat and meat, British textiles, and French luxury goods. The more trade the better, and the French Creoles resented the closure of the river to Americans in 1784 almost as much as did the Americans. **Weakness of Louisiana** As it was, the revenues did not pay the administrative expenses of the province, and the Spanish governors were perfectly aware that their defense rested chiefly on the goodwill of ten thousand French Creoles. They did not dare go too far in antagonizing them or the multiplying thousands of Americans who were spreading swiftly westward from the mountains. Their program was not based on any illusive hope of success but merely on delaying the threat to the more valuable Mexican and Caribbean possessions.

Spain found Tennessee and Kentucky fertile fields for intrigue. When Tennessee separatists made overtures for Spanish support, a number of famous men were involved, notably John Sevier, James Robertson, founder of Nashville, and William Blount, a member of the Constitutional Convention. Many others, including Andrew Jackson, were attracted by the prospect of a free Tennessee **State of Franklin** under Spanish protection. Here as elsewhere land speculation and political faction lay at the bottom of the problem. North Carolina had sought to save the expense of protecting Tennessee by turning it over to Congress, on condition that her land cessions be respected. The Watauga mountaineers distrusted the motives and set up the "State of Franklin," whereupon Sevier and other speculators took control in order to protect themselves.

Their intention was to spread down the Tennessee River to Muscle Shoals and thence dig a canal to the headwaters of the Tombigbee River; in this way, by finding egress at Mobile, they proposed to by-pass the Mississippi and New Orleans in the economic development of Tennessee. Unfortunately Spain refused to permit a scheme which would develop a powerful enemy on her border. The disappointed Franklinites then enabled North Carolina (which had repealed her cession) to regain control by 1789. This was followed by a second cession to the United States, and in 1790 Tennessee was organized as the Territory South of the River Ohio. Washington shrewdly chose William Blount as governor, and placated Sevier and Robertson with political plums. In 1796 the Tennesseeans attained their original ambition and were admitted to the Union.

Kentucky was, if possible, more torn by faction than Tennessee. Though Congress had intended it to be a part of the Territory South of the River Ohio, it actually remained a part of Virginia until its admission

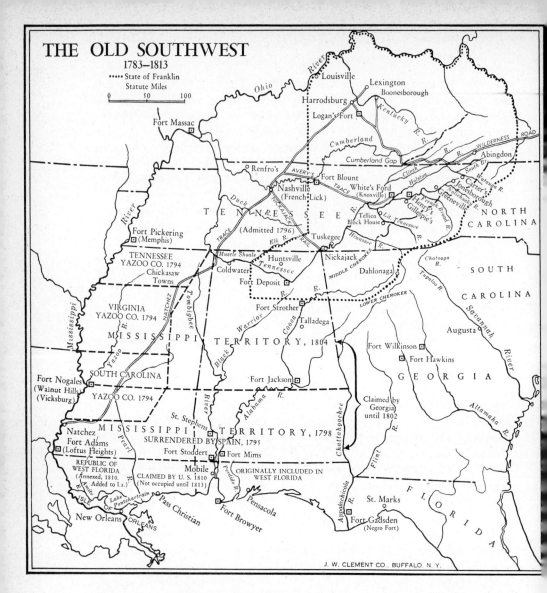

THE OLD SOUTHWEST
1783—1813

••••State of Franklin
Statute Miles
0   50   100

J. W. CLEMENT CO., BUFFALO, N.Y.

Kentucky and the Spanish conspiracy
to the Union in 1792. It will be remembered that rival land claims afflicted Kentucky from the very beginning, and these now found expression in political faction, though all claimants realized that their claims would not attain full value until the Mississippi was opened to Kentucky commerce. The problem, of course, was whether to play along with the Spanish or trust to Congress and the prospect of statehood. Here again it was the Americans who made the overtures to Spain.

Center of the Spanish party was James Wilkinson, a sort of cut-rate Aaron Burr. A career of intrigue and backbiting during the Revolution had won him the brevet title of brigadier-general at the age of twenty.

382

In 1784 he appeared in Kentucky and straightway engaged   **James** in trade, land speculation, and politics. In 1787 he went to   **Wilkinson** New Orleans and there made such an impression on the   **(1757–** Spanish governor that he was given a monopoly of the Ken-   **1825)** tucky trade (which did not last long) and secretly subsidized as a Spanish agent. Though Wilkinson remained in Spanish pay for many years, he tried unsuccessfully to get the British to back an attack on New Orleans. Indeed, Wilkinson's activities were so skillfully devious that it is impossible to assess his real motives beyond those of personal prestige and monetary gain. The gradual strengthening of the Federal government, followed by the admission of Kentucky, was the best possible argument against the Spanish intrigues in the West; so in 1791 Wilkinson reentered the United States army, became second to Wayne, and actually commanded the army from 1796 to 1798 and from 1800 to 1812. His relations to Spain were perfectly well known, but his enemies were never able to find proof; it was not until our own century that the proof was found in the Spanish archives. It will always be a prime mystery how he was able to fool all the Presidents from Washington to Madison.

The outbreak of the French Revolution was soon followed by a French plan to release their French cousins, whom Louis xv had deeded to Spain with Louisiana, and make them the nucleus of a revived French empire in the New World. Not the least of Genêt's projects was to   **Collapse of** raise a western American army and use it to seize Louisiana   **French in-** and Florida. George Rogers Clark, the Revolutionary hero,   **trigue** who had been flouted by Congress and ousted by James Wilkinson from his position of leadership in Kentucky, found refuge in land speculation, whisky, and Spanish intrigue. Genêt's agent persuaded him to take command of the French forces, but the whole plot collapsed when Washington asked for the recall of Genêt and sent orders to have the recruiting stopped.

Spain had first entered the European war on the side of the enemies of the French Revolution but in 1794 was plotting a change of sides. Jay's Treaty with England (1794) had alarmed the Spanish lest it portend common action by England and the United States and   **Pinckney's** the payment of the latter in Spanish territory. At this time   **Treaty,** the puerile Spanish monarch, Charles iv, was under the   **1795** control of Manuel de Godoy, Prince of the Peace, and paramour of the queen. A report that England was preparing an expedition against Mexico alarmed Godoy, and at the same time Spanish discontent with high taxes and military reverses was shown in a palace intrigue against him. Godoy hastily sought to fortify his position by ensuring as much peace as possible under the circumstances. A treaty was signed with France, and it was decided to stop trusting to intrigues and placate the

American Westerners by some solid benefits. The result was Pinckney's Treaty (San Lorenzo, 1795), by which Spain opened the Mississippi to American navigation; granted for three years the right of deposit of American goods at New Orleans for transhipment without payment of duties; and surrendered the disputed area of West Florida from Natchez eastward. The execution of the treaty was naturally delayed by the Spanish authorities, but for a few years the West was almost satisfied.

By this time the Spanish court saw that there was no chance of the western states seceding and accepting the role of Spanish protectorates. Even the policy of settling the Goths at the gates of Rome was a failure, **Spain parts** for not many Americans would settle where there were no **with** civil liberties, where Protestant worship was limited, and **Louisiana** where speculation in land was not permitted. It was evident that sooner or later Louisiana, at least, would fall to the United States. Kentucky riflemen might have made good their threats before this and have seized New Orleans, had it not been that they could not hold it against the Spanish navy. From 1795 on Godoy refused to throw any more good money than necessary after the bad and permitted Louisiana's administration and defenses to deteriorate. As he explained, "You can't lock up an open field."

Spain now turned to France, which dreamed of acquiring Louisiana as the basis of a new empire. The secret Treaty of San Ildefonso in 1800 made the bargain. Napoleon delayed taking possession because he did not dare to risk a British or American invasion of his new colony, so for three years it remained under Spanish administration. Nevertheless, rumors of the transaction found their way to the American West, and the prospect of French acquisition of Louisiana was not pleasant to either western settlers or land speculators. Spain hampered trade and speculation, but it was plainly on the way out; France on the other hand was strong, and its control of New Orleans would pose an obstacle difficult to overcome.

It is almost impossible to follow the intricacies of land speculation in the Old Southwest, or the changing alliances and diplomatic intrigues which accompanied them. Since Georgia claimed the territory disputed **Yazoo** with Spain and now included in Alabama and Mississippi, **frauds** she was perennially concerned with the quarrel over possession. In 1789 Georgia had sold vast tracts in the area to three companies which were known as the Yazoo companies, from the Yazoo River, which empties into the Mississippi near Vicksburg. These companies failed, but in 1795 persistent speculators organized four New Yazoo companies and by the most incredible bribery pushed land grants comprising thirty million acres at a cent and a half an acre through the Georgia legislature. The names involved in the scheme at one time or another formed almost a roster of public men, and the companies' warrants swamped the speculative market in northern cities.

When the people of Georgia awoke to the steal, they cleaned out the legislature and in 1796 repealed the cessions. The result was an unparalleled dog fight. In 1802 Jefferson got Georgia to agree to its present western boundary in the "Georgia Compact"; but when he then **Effect of** attempted to settle the Yazoo claims and avoid ceaseless law- **Yazoo** suits by turning over five million acres to the companies, **frauds** John Randolph was seized by a fit of morality and blocked the move in Congress until 1814. Meanwhile in 1810 in the case of *Fletcher v. Peck* the Supreme Court decided that Georgia could not rescind a contract, even though it was made as the result of fraud. In the end, well over $4,000,000 were paid by the Federal government to holders of Yazoo scrip: by 1815 to wise boys who had bought up the claims for a song. The Yazoo crash in 1796 had knocked the bottom out of land speculation in all directions. Among those who suffered were Robert Morris, who went to debtors' prison; Patrick Henry, who was financially ruined; and Andrew Jackson, who did not emerge from debt for many years.

Others, however, proposed to fight fate. There were many crosscurrents of intrigue, which curiously enough often involved the same men in contradictory schemes. Mostly they centered on a preference for British rather than French control of Florida and Louisiana in the belief that the British government could be reached through **Renewal of** merchant investors. Doddering Spain's most vulnerable **plotting** point in the Old Southwest was her precarious control of the Creek and Choctaw Indians, and her fear was that Georgia and Tennessee traders would wean them away. At this time the Creeks, the most powerful of the Five Civilized Nations, were under the leadership of Alexander McGillivray, an able and civilized quarter-breed, who sought to preserve Creek independence by playing off Spain, Britain, and the United States against each other. The Creeks were a valuable buffer between the Spanish and the Americans, but since Spain lacked the trade goods to preserve their allegiance it was forced to turn the trade over to a British firm of Scottish merchants: Panton, Leslie and Company. The company contrived to operate through the years of war between Spain and England, and its chief, William Panton, was so necessary to Spanish policy in the Old Southwest that he was at times able to dictate his own terms.

Among the American schemers was William Blount, now Senator from Tennessee. He proposed to revive the Franklinite scheme of by-passing the Mississippi River; he would assure control of the mouth of the Tombigbee by seizing Florida and Louisiana and placing them **Blount's** under England. When his scheme was discovered, the Feder- **conspiracy,** alists expelled him from the Senate and sought to tar the **1797** entire Republican Party with the responsibility. A year later Hamilton was plotting with England to seize far more than Florida and Louisiana.

Even more important than Blount's conspiracy was the long-continued attempt to oust Panton from his control of the Indian trade. Core of this scheme was a group of Britishers led by Lord Dunmore, once governor

Bowles's filibusters disrupt Creek unity of Virginia and now of the Bahamas, but at one time or another it involved many Americans, including Blount and Sevier. To give the color of patriotism to their piracy the Bahaman highjackers proposed to use the Creeks in seizing Florida for England. William Augustus Bowles was their tool, and three times between 1788 and 1799 he made unsuccessful filibustering expeditions against Florida; eventually after incredible adventures he died in a Spanish prison. The significance of his activities lay not so much in the alarm he occasioned to Spain, England, and the United States as in the fact that he split the Creeks in their support of McGillivray's diplomacy and opened the way for American conquest.

The Peace of Amiens in March 1802 gave Napoleon the opportunity to take over Louisiana. It is true that Napoleon ignored his part of the bargain, including a solemn promise not to dispose of the province to a

Louisiana's last days under Spain third party, but then Napoleon had his leading ring in the nose of the Spanish bull and forced it to his will. By this time the Louisiana problem had become the prime political bone of contention in the United States. On 18 October 1802 the Spanish intendant at New Orleans suddenly (and temporarily) withdrew the right of deposit from American traders in response to a secret order from Spain. Though complicated exceptions made it possible for American trade to find egress, the order caused an unprecedented furore even in the East. About the same time the fact of the cession to France became known, and it was commonly supposed that Napoleon had dictated the order. It was about this time that President Jefferson wrote the oft-quoted words: "There is on the globe one single spot, the possessor of which is our natural and habitual enemy. . . . The day that France takes possession of N. Orleans . . . we must marry ourselves to the British fleet and nation." Monroe was shipped off to Paris to make an offer to purchase New Orleans.

Before Monroe reached France events had hustled Napoleon into a change of plan. He had hoped to make the food and lumber of Louisiana complementary to the plantation products of the French West Indies in

Why Napoleon sold Louisiana building up French wealth and naval power. But France had lost her most important West Indian possession, Haiti, to a slave rebellion and it was necessary to recover it, not only for its sugar crop but as a naval base. His brother-in-law, Leclerc, had gained a foothold in 1802 despite the heroic resistance of the Negroes under the little coachman Toussaint l'Ouverture, only in the end to lose his own life and to lose fifty thousand troops to yellow fever and war. A relief expedition was frozen in by Dutch ice, and by spring Britain and

France were plainly drifting once more into war. Napoleon resolved to save Louisiana by selling it and to use the money for war. Very likely he had other objectives in mind as well: a desire to avoid trouble with the United States, the hope of building up the United States as a rival of Great Britain, and possibly he expected the designedly vague boundaries of the Louisiana cession to cause contention between the United States and Spain—and they did.

Robert R. Livingston, American minister in Paris, had been discussing the problem of New Orleans, and now (11 April) Talleyrand suddenly asked him how he would like to have all of Louisiana. Livingston managed to conceal his elation, and as soon as Monroe ar- **Louisiana** rived they got down to serious bargaining with Barbé- **Purchase,** Marbois, whom Napoleon had appointed to handle the ne- **1803** gotiations. On the last day of April the Americans agreed to pay sixty million francs plus certain claims of American citizens against France. Two weeks later war began. If the Americans had lost a great deal as the result of European strife, they were at least able to profit territorially by Europe's distress. Jefferson's doubts about the constitutionality of the purchase were overridden by his party lest Napoleon change his mind, and in October Congress approved the treaties—with the Federalists arguing for strict construction! On 30 November a French representative took over Louisiana from Spain and put into effect the Code Napoléon which is still used in the state of Louisiana. On 20 December 1803 Louisiana became a part of the United States.

The Louisiana Purchase has with justice been called the greatest real estate bargain in history—eight hundred twenty-eight thousand square miles at about three cents an acre! The area of the United States was almost doubled, and that for a mere pittance of $15,000,000. **Signifi-** Of course the Federalists cried out that we had become re- **cance of the** ceivers of stolen goods (which in effect we had), that we **Louisiana** had been overreached, and that the area was useless save **Purchase** for a fringe along the Mississippi. Indeed, no one realized the actual value of the cession: the coal, petroleum, timber, and minerals, let alone the vast prospects of grain and cattle. Out of Louisiana as eventually defined there have been carved all or the larger part of thirteen states.

By the treaties of cession it was guaranteed that the people of Louisiana should "be incorporated in the Union of the United States, and admitted as soon as possible, according to the principles of the Federal Constitution, to the enjoyment of all the rights, advantages, **Problem of** and immunities of citizens of the United States." This guar- **new citi-** antee meant that Louisiana would promptly be admitted **zens** as a state but, typically enough, it was a long time before the promise was fulfilled. Meanwhile it became a political football. The purchase was

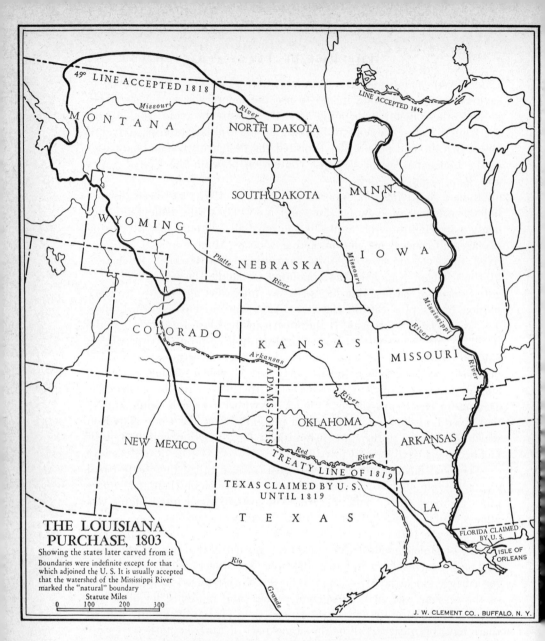

THE LOUISIANA
PURCHASE, 1803
Showing the states later carved from it
Boundaries were indefinite except for that
which adjoined the U. S. It is usually accepted
that the watershed of the Mississippi River
marked the "natural" boundary
Statute Miles
0   100   200   300

J. W. CLEMENT CO., BUFFALO, N. Y.

divided into two territories, each with a complement of officeholders, but
it was not until the people complained vigorously to Jefferson that they
were given self-government. The two divisions underwent various changes
in boundary and name until at last in 1812 the southern part had grown
populous enough to be admitted as a state. The northern part became
Missouri Territory until 1820. Naturally enough many of the French
Creoles resented their "sale" to the brash young Republic, and frictions
developed which were never entirely healed until the older generation
died off.

388

Meanwhile that "finished scoundrel," Aaron Burr, had played his last public role. Like thousands of other men who had been ruined by eastern vicissitudes he hoped to recoup his fortunes in the West. Soon after he left the vice-presidency he traveled beyond the mountains and laid the groundwork for later action, particularly in long conferences with that other scoundrel, James Wilkinson. The next year (1806) he floated in leisurely fashion down the Ohio and the Mississippi with a few armed men, preceded by conflicting rumors. To this day it is not known whether he planned to seize New Orleans and set up an empire in the Mississippi Valley or to conduct a filibustering expedition to Mexico; he himself later claimed that the latter had been his object, but it is certain that he told different stories to different listeners. Whatever he may have intended, he had the goodwill of the West, for three times he was brought before Federal grand juries and three times was acquitted.

Burr's conspiracy

Meanwhile Jefferson had issued a warrant for his arrest. Wilkinson, then in command of the United States army in the South, became alarmed, turned his coat, and zealously worked to fortify New Orleans against attack! When Burr learned of Jefferson's action and Wilkinson's defection, he fled toward Florida but was captured. His hearing was held at Richmond in the spring of 1807 with John Marshall as judge and John Randolph as foreman of the grand jury. The subsequent trial for treason was inevitably a political battle between Jefferson and his bitterest enemy, Marshall. Wilkinson, as usual, played both sides as witness, and in the end Burr was acquitted. To reach this conclusion Marshall casuistically cast aside the English common-law doctrine that "in treason all are principals." Burr might have been guilty of conspiracy to levy war—"constructive treason"—but since he had not actually accompanied his armed forces he was not guilty of treason. Since the indictment was for treason, not conspiracy, he was free. During the next few years Burr was in Europe, chiefly engaged in seeking French support for a western revolt. Disappointed all along the line, he returned to New York in 1812 and resumed the practice of law. He died in 1836.

Burr cleared of treason

There was no doubt that Napoleon had broken his engagement to Spain when he sold Louisiana, and Spain at first warned the United States that it would not recognize the transfer. Jefferson had hoped to get the Floridas with New Orleans but was perfectly aware that they were not included in the bargain. Nevertheless, the acquisition of Florida was essential. It blocked off the mouths of the rivers of the Mississippi Territory and western Georgia; a Spanish garrison still commanded the Mississippi at Baton Rouge; it was an annoying refuge for bandits, runaway slaves, and British traders who remained active among the Civilized Nations; and, not least, it threat-

Jefferson covets West Florida

ened the sea line between New Orleans and the East because it commanded the Florida Strait. Jefferson and his advisers now consulted old maps and treaties and blandly claimed that Louisiana included West Florida as far as the Perdido River and Texas as far as the Rio Grande. It was, to say the least, plausible misrepresentation. Presently Jefferson asked Congress for an army of three hundred thousand men, in an attempt to frighten Spain into selling, and then tried to trade Napoleon into acting as middleman. Instead of getting Florida he got the contempt of Napoleon, the distrust of England, the hostility of Spain, and the well-earned ridicule of the Federalists.

Madison, for once, was more successful. Secret assurances to the American settlers in Baton Rouge resulted in a revolution in 1810 and the establishment of the Republic of West Florida with a lone-star flag.

Annexation of West Florida, 1810, 1813 Madison promptly proclaimed that West Florida as far as the Perdido River was a part of the United States and falsified certain documents to defend his action. As a matter of fact, he only occupied the region as far as the Pearl River, the area that is now the southeastern part of the state of Louisiana. Three years later (1813) Madison calmly latched on to the Mobile Bay area by moving the boundary eastward to the Perdido; appropriately enough, General James Wilkinson was the instrument for this bit of highhanded rascality. Spain fumed and threatened but got nowhere.

3   The Pattern of Western Settlement

There were two principal routes to the West up to the time of the War of 1812. The older one, by way of the Ohio, was dominated by Pittsburgh at the head of that stream. The convenience of floating down-

The rivers and early western settlement stream made it worth while not only for Pennsylvanians but for northern Virginians to take that route; so it was natural that areas near the Ohio River, especially on the Kentucky bank, should be among the first settled. Lexington had been the first metropolis and cultural center of Kentucky, but Louisville's superior position on the Ohio put it in the lead. Louisville in turn was displaced by Cincinnati, which after 1818 became a meat-packing center and as the "Queen City of the West" (or "Porkopolis") reigned over the Ohio Valley.

Boone's Wilderness Road, by way of Cumberland Gap, was the overland competitor as a route to Kentucky for the inhabitants of Virginia and North Carolina. Even at that, the headwaters of the Tennessee River afforded fairly good communication with the West. The Ohio and Tennessee soon became the highways of farther settlement, for emigrants from the East or from the older parts of the West soon spread down the

Mississippi to the French plantations and founded or accelerated the growth of numerous towns, among which Memphis, Vicksburg, Natchez, and Baton Rouge are best known. Upstream they turned St. Louis from a village to a small but important city, and led by old Daniel Boone (who had been euchred out of his Kentucky land) they spread up the Missouri.

The commercial entrepôt of the Mississippi Valley, which easily comprised two thirds of the area of the nation, was New Orleans. At the time of the Louisiana Cession it was a rickety and smelly city of eight thousand. Before the successful introduction of the steamboat (about 1820) New Orleans depended chiefly on downstream **New Orleans** traffic. Even at that, the picturesque French Quarter was being supplemented by rather more up-to-date (but still shoddy) American-built suburbs. The steamboat boomed upstream commerce, and together with the rapid development of sugar and cotton culture accelerated the growth of New Orleans to a hundred thousand in 1840, a babel of French, Spanish, "Kentucks," Germans, Irish, and of course the ever present Negro roustabouts.

Even then steamboats, turnpikes, and canals had begun to turn northern commerce toward the East, but the rapid growth of the Gulf region concealed from all but the most discerning that New Orleans must soon lose its monopoly. New Orleans's gay combination of the tropics and the Latin Old World were in such contrast to the Calvinistic straitness of American society (even in such a worldly center as Charleston) that it exercised a strong hold upon the American imagination. Its gaudy brothels with their octoroon courtesans, its gambling halls, its pickpockets, its picturesque and stinking Vieux Carré, its Mardi Gras, its culinary prowess, and even its moonlight and orange blossoms have entered into the stuff of American romance.

The once-popular "safety valve" theory, that western lands afforded an escape for depression-ridden workmen of the East, seems to be controverted by the fact that migration to the West was most active in periods of eastern prosperity. Thus in the periods of deep depression, roughly 1805–1815, 1819–1821, and 1837–1841, **Periods of migration** migration was reduced to a comparative trickle. The period immediately after the close of the War of 1812 was that of the Great Migration to the West, a time when all the country seemed to be on the move. It was the first mass movement of settlers, though improved means of transportation later on may have brought even larger influxes of immigrants in periods of no longer duration. Despite the arrangement from 1820 to 1850 of admitting free and slave states in pairs in order to preserve the equality of the two interests in the Senate, it is readily recognizable from the following table that the various surges of immigration had their effect in the admission of new states to the Union.

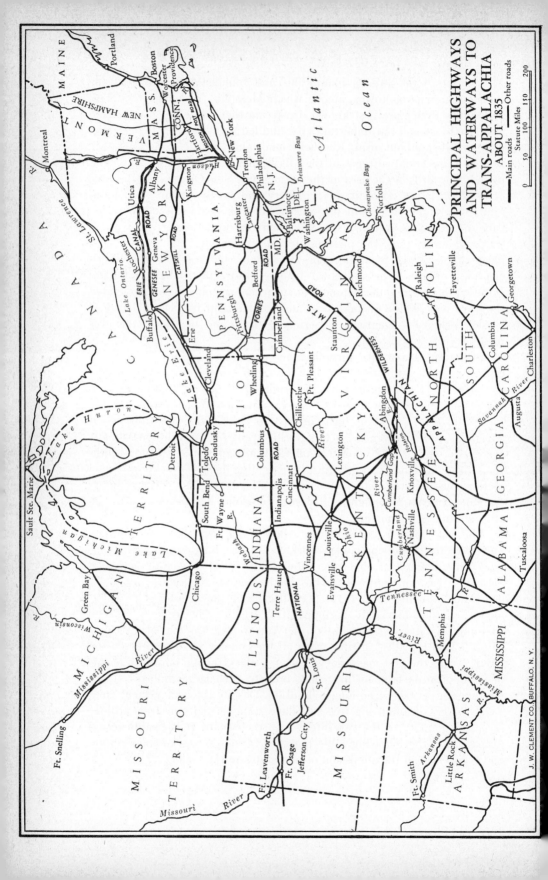

Group I		Group III	
(Vermont	..............1791)	Arkansas	1836
Kentucky	1792	Michigan	1837
Tennessee	1796		
Ohio	1803	Group IV	
		Florida	1845
Group II		(Texas	...................1845)
Louisiana	1812	Iowa	1846
Indiana	1816	Wisconsin	1848
Mississippi	1817	(California	...............1850)
Illinois	1818		
Alabama	1819	Group V	
(Maine	...............1820)	Minnesota	1858
Missouri	1821	(Oregon	.................1859)

Settlers, to a remarkable degree, tended to move westward in a direct line. Thus New England and New York settlers were strong in northern Ohio, Indiana, and Illinois; and after the opening of the Erie Canal they moved into Michigan, Wisconsin, Iowa, and Minnesota. An *Origin and* interesting sidelight is afforded by the partiality of North- *lines of* ern Europeans, particularly Scandinavians, Germans, and *migration* Hollanders, for the later named states. The building of the National Road encouraged citizens of the Middle States, particularly Pennsylvania, to move across the central parts of Ohio, Indiana, and Illinois, though the Ohio River diverted numbers of them southward. It is said that in 1817 a majority of the members of the Ohio House of Representatives had been born in Washington County, Pennsylvania.

Migration from the southern states was rather less consistent. Non-slaveholding Virginians and North Carolinians moved directly west into the more rugged parts of Kentucky and Tennessee or went on to the southern parts of the free states and territories of Ohio, Indiana, and Illinois. While they may have favored slavery as a means of social control of Negroes, as in Missouri, it is also evident that they were attracted to areas where there was a minimum of Negro competition. Nonslave-holding Georgians and South Carolinians tended to move directly west-ward into Alabama, and there they met the overflow from the state of Mississippi, which had been settled by men who had drifted down the river. Planters from the Upper South crossed the mountains to Kentucky and Tennessee or moved southward with Carolina and Georgia planters around the end of the Appalachians into the Gulf states. If they could not acquire public land, they purchased the lands of several small farm-ers who then moved back into the hills or out beyond the Mississippi. Of course, there were numerous small farmers who became successful cotton planters.

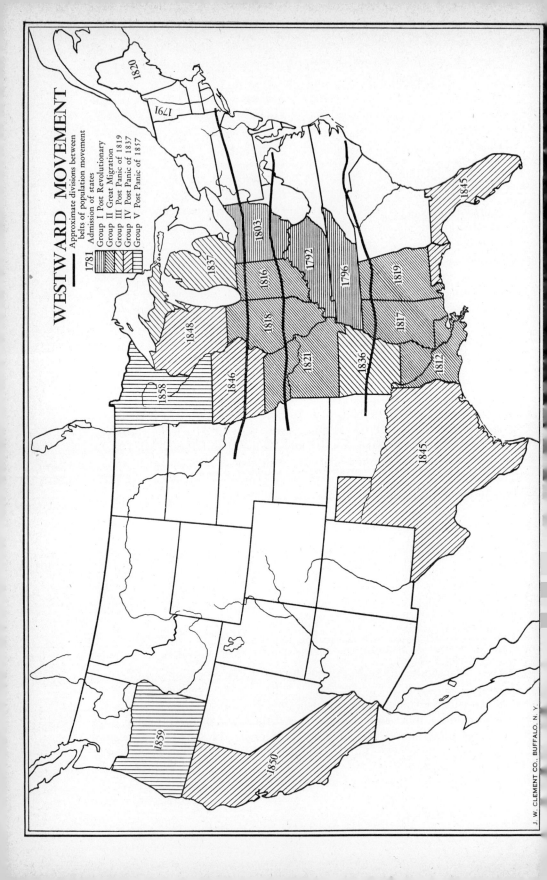

WESTWARD MOVEMENT

Approximate divisions between
belts of population movement

1781   Admission of states

Group I Post Revolutionary
Group II Great Migration
Group III Post Panic of 1819
Group IV Post Panic of 1837
Group V Post Panic of 1857

The foregoing is not intended to deny that numbers of migrants jumped over their thermal lines and settled in regions quite unlike their old homes; it was obviously more common in the case of Northerners who were able to drift downstream to the new plantation areas. It should be remembered also that Europeans usually preferred to settle in free states; the large German element which found its way to St. Louis was discontented from the first and was instrumental in holding Missouri in the Union in 1861. Nevertheless, it is possible to trace out as far as the Great Plains the distinct imprint of each of the three principal sections.

It should be noted here that the New England population and institutional impact had already been felt across New York and northern Pennsylvania, and that it had developed in New York a system of local government which gave some functions to the county but **Institu-** still emphasized the town meeting and township functions. **tional** New Englanders and "York State Yankees" now moved **transfers** across northern Ohio, Indiana, and Illinois, and in an institutional sense practically took over Michigan, Wisconsin, Minnesota, Nebraska, and the Dakotas—at least their "township-county" system was rooted in the latter group of states. At the other extreme the southern emphasis on the county extended westward (passing below Missouri and Kansas, however) and swallowed up the Far West. Between the two regions the states in general followed the Pennsylvania pattern of compromise between county and township, usually with more emphasis on the county. Illinois is significantly split between the county and township systems.

In the East of 1820 (omitting Episcopalians, who spread relatively little to the West) the characteristic churches from north to south were Congregational, Presbyterian, and Baptist, each with its offshoots; the same held true of the West, but the Methodist Church was strong in all three parts, though particularly in the center. Public elementary schools also moved west with the settlers and tended to be most efficient in the northernmost sections, as in the New England homeland. Harvard and Yale men followed the line of settlement and founded academies and colleges in such numbers that nearly every county seat boasted at least one. The South, on the other hand, though it possessed many good colleges, had few good elementary schools; the answer lay not solely in the problem of great distances but in the opinion that education was for the élite.

Again it is worth noting that though New England Federalists tended to change to Democratic-Republicans in the West, when the Whig Party split away from the Democratic-Republicans it nevertheless found a warm welcome in the states of distinctly Yankee origin, and to this day the rural sections of those states tend to be **Political** faithful to the Republican successors of the Whigs. The **transfers** southern states, on the other hand, have always been Democratic, except for certain Whig aberrations. The result is that the great and populous "doubtful" states from Ohio to Missouri have commanded more than their share of weight in national politics—again following the precedent of the Middle Atlantic states before the Civil War. These alignments, research has demonstrated, are to a considerable extent hereditary and not altogether due to economic interests.*

The Great Migration to the West which began in 1815 followed chiefly the Ohio River route from Pittsburgh or Wheeling, and most of the settlers went to states or territories adjacent to that stream or the Mississippi. Kentucky added 150,000 population (by birth and immigration) in the decade ending in 1820 and boasted 565,000 inhabitants; Tennessee rose to 420,000; Ohio rose two hundred and fifty per cent to 580,000 and was the most populous state in the West. Indiana with 150,000 and Illinois with 55,000 were peopled chiefly in the river valleys. Missouri, soon to be a state, had 65,000, which in view of the newness of the region was unexpectedly close to Louisiana's 150,000. Mississippi with 75,000 was outpaced by even younger Alabama, which had about 130,000. Of nearly ten million people in the nation in 1820 about one quarter lived west of the mountains, and of twenty-three states eight were in the West.

The Great Migration

The third wave of migration brought only two states into the Union, Arkansas and Michigan, but it also filled in the gaps between the old settlements and accelerated the growth of the river cities. In 1840 the eleven western states possessed over six million people, more than one third of the nation's total. Ohio, with a million and a half people, was twice the size of Kentucky, its closest western competitor, and was outdistanced only by New York, Pennsylvania, and Virginia. Cincinnati with 46,000 people was the nation's sixth city, three times the population of St. Louis but only half that of New Orleans.

Third wave of migration

Arkansas, with 100,000 inhabitants, was admitted only to balance Michigan, which had more than twice as many. Michigan and northern Ohio owed their growth largely to the Erie Canal, which afforded easy entrance to immigrants and easy exit for grain, meat, and lumber. Settlement was pretty well confined to the southern part of the territory; the northern part enjoyed a few decades of prosperity in lumbering and mining after the Civil War. Detroit, though the oldest and largest town in the territory, scarcely ranked as a first-class city until after the beginning of automobile manufacture. A technicality in the boundary between Ohio and Michigan left the status of Toledo in dispute. Ohio, which was putting Toledo on the economic map with the construction of the Wabash Canal, refused to surrender it.

Michigan

* On the subject of regional transfers see Lois K. M. Rosenberry, *The Expansion of New England* (1909).

The ensuing "Toledo War" brought nothing worse than bruises and national ridicule. Since it occurred in a presidential-election year (1836) Ohio, which had a vote, obtained the advantage in Congress, and Michigan was forced to accept the Upper Peninsula as a substitute; its riches were not then apparent.

Early settlers in Illinois had preferred to clear farms in the wooded regions rather than take up prairie land, which was then regarded as unfit for farming. Presently, however, it was discovered that the prairie was the richest part of the state, and settlers quickly laid **Illinois** it under contribution even though the sod was hard to break and timber had to be hauled in for houses, barns, and fences. When Illinois was admitted to the Union it was given a front on Lake Michigan by the addition of sixty miles taken from what is now Wisconsin. It was in this added territory that the city of Chicago was laid out in 1830 near the site of the Fort Dearborn massacre. The name was taken from the shallow prairie stream called the Chicago River. After a couple of decades Chicago found its mission as a railroad and meat-packing city. St. Louis passed New Orleans in population during the Civil War; soon after 1870 Chicago with well over 300,000 sprinted past St. Louis and has ever since been the principal city of the Mississippi Valley–Great Lakes region.*

Wisconsin began its rise during the 1820's and 1830's. Here again the Erie Canal was by far the most important factor, though it was possible for immigrants to go from Pittsburgh down the Ohio and up the Mississippi by steamboat. Wisconsin's territorial loss to Illinois had taken with it part of the important lead-mining **Wisconsin** area which extended along the Mississippi from Galena, Illinois, northward. The lead-mining boom which began in the late 1820's brought thousands of miners into the area and played some share in the troubles that led to the Black Hawk War. Unfortunately lead was worked out in a few decades; and, partly because it is a peculiar pocket which had not been affected by the glaciers, the area has never prospered in grain growing but has turned to dairy products. Meanwhile Milwaukee had become the chief town of southeastern Wisconsin. When the territory was split off from Michigan in 1836, a compromise between the two metropolitan centers led to the choice of Madison in the beautiful Four Lakes region as the capital. Wisconsin was the first of the states to undertake an official campaign to attract immigrants, and it was so successful that Milwaukee became almost a German city and the back country was strongly influenced by Scandinavians. The admission of Wisconsin in 1848 led to the erection of Minnesota Territory, which in turn was admitted as a state in 1858.

The discovery that prairie land was good land naturally turned cove-

* Wyatt W. Belcher, *Economic Rivalry Between St. Louis and Chicago, 1850–1880* (1947).

tous eyes on Iowa. The Black Hawk War of 1832 afforded an excellent excuse to buy a fifty-mile strip west of the Mississippi. During the next

Iowa

two decades further Indian claims were "quieted" as the rush of northern settlers crossed from Illinois or came by steamboat down the Ohio and up the Mississippi. Congress, as usual, was slow in providing adequate government, and so the farmers organized their own vigilance committees to suppress the lawless lead miners and "watermen." Since the government was also slow in opening land to sale, the farmers simply staked out what they wanted and organized "claims associations" to protect their rights. Iowa was split off from Wisconsin in 1838, and in 1846 was admitted as a state.

Even before the War of 1812 the parts of the New West began to discover varying economic interests. The great corn belt stretches from Ohio through Indiana, Illinois, Missouri, and Iowa into eastern Kansas,

The corn belt

Nebraska, and South Dakota. The soil is the gift of the glaciers, but the addition of hot bright summers makes it the best region in the world for corn. This fact was not immediately apparent to the pioneers, for the eastern part of the area was covered with trees which had to be logged or burned off. The first resort thereafter was to wheat, and Ohio in its late pioneer stage sent over the Erie Canal a large share of the world's marketed wheat. The relationship between corn and hogs became evident in the prairie region by 1850, but it was not until after cheaper wheat began to be produced by the Great Plains states that the eastern corn belt began to make the turning of corn into pork and beef its basic reliance. Even at that, wheat and dairy products are by no means neglected in our own day. During the pioneer period the corn belt depended upon New Orleans as an outlet to the world and upon the Cotton South to absorb much of its food. For this reason the South supposed that the corn belt must support the cotton interests; the fact was otherwise, as we shall see, for the direction of trade began to swing more and more toward the East after the opening of the Erie Canal.

Michigan does not share the blessings of the corn belt, but after the land was cleared it was discovered that the southern portion was even better for vegetables, fruits, and dairying. Michigan's easy accessibility

Fruitland and dairy- land

to the Lakes made lumbering profitable almost from the first. Wisconsin not only had access to the Lakes but could ship its lumber down the Mississippi to the burgeoning cities of the corn belt and the South. With the timber gone, Wisconsin turned to wheat and rapidly exhausted the soil; only then did it discover that it is Nature's own idea of a dairyland. The timbered part of Minnesota has been through much the same evolution.

Though three states (Iowa, Wisconsin, Minnesota) still remained to be admitted, by 1840 the area between the Appalachian Mountains and the Great Plains had taken on pretty much the characteristics which it was to bear in maturity. The political accompaniments of its development will be discussed later: here we are concerned only with certain ecological facts. The Old North-

The Middle West

west had now become the West, or in later parlance the Middle West. Though its rich glacial land insured that it would always be important agriculturally, it was already beginning to take on the industrial characteristics of the East. Meat packing, flour milling, wood working, leather working, and finally textile and metal manufactures began to appear not simply in the cities but in hundreds of villages. The area was unsuitable for plantation products and therefore escaped the blight of slavery and the restrictive effects of an economic and social system built upon it. Enterprising men were able to lay the economic foundations of a society in which the vast majority of the people belonged to the middle class. Meanwhile the steamboat, the turnpike, the canal, and presently the railroad enabled the West to escape from its dependence on New Orleans and to trade with the East.

The Old Southwest had joined the Older South to form the South. This occupied the area below Mason and Dixon's Line and the Ohio River, an area which was largely unaffected by the glaciers and which had a rainfall twice that of the North. Whether without slavery it would have developed its peculiar characteristics

The South

is a moot point. At any rate it was agricultural, based on slavery and for the most part on plantation products: tobacco, rice, sugar, but above all cotton. Except for corn, hogs, and root crops, the Cotton States grew little but cotton; they depended considerably upon the North for food. Socially the South developed the pattern almost always found with slavery, that is, the separation of the free population into a dominant class which looked upon itself as aristocratic and an underprivileged class which was in some danger of becoming submerged.

Cotton influence was dominant in the South, but the fringes had other interests. Florida and the Gulf Coast were not productive of much of anything, except of sugar in Louisiana. The states of the northern part of the South, however, had diverging interests which would probably have turned them eventually toward the North had it not been for the Civil War. Maryland and Virginia

The Border States

were turning from tobacco to general farming at the time of the Civil War. North Carolina was largely an area of small tobacco farms. The mountain areas were given over to subsistence farming and logging. The lower Ohio Valley (central and western Kentucky and central Tennessee) was devoted to grains, stock, tobacco, and some cotton. The Bluegrass area of Kentucky and the Nashville area of Tennessee early became famous for horses. Missouri was divided between the Ozark Mountains and the corn belt, but the large southern element in its population made it psychologically a part of the South. Border States also found themselves owing allegiance to the Cotton States because they made much of their income by exporting Negro slaves, mules, tobacco, and food to them. There was an opinion in the South that because it purchased so much of their goods, Middle West and Border States must maintain a benevolent neutrality in case it left the Union. It was a fatal delusion, for by 1860 the Lakes and the Ohio Valley were already so bound to the seaboard by bands of railroad iron that they were ready to fight for the Union.

BIBLIOGRAPHICAL NOTE

The Old Northwest

SETTLEMENT: Indispensable is Beverley W. Bond, *The Civilization of the Old Northwest, 1788–1812* (1934). See also Randolph C. Downes, *Frontier Ohio, 1788–1803* (1935). Here let us introduce *The Territorial Papers of the U.S.*, edited by Clarence E. Carter, and now in process of publication.

INDIAN WARS: On the earlier aspects see Louise P. Kellogg, *The British Régime in Wisconsin and the Northwest* (1935); Nelson V. Russell, *The British Régime in Michigan and the Old Northwest, 1760–1796* (1939); Wayne E. Stevens, *The Northwest Fur Trade, 1763–1800* (1928); and Harry E. Wildes, *Anthony Wayne* (1941). On Harrison see James A. Green, *William Henry Harrison* (1941); and Freeman Cleaves, *Old Tippecanoe* (1939). On Tecumseh see John M. Oskison, *Tecumseh and His Times* (1938).

The Old Southwest

The ablest account of the diplomacy and intrigues of this period is found in Arthur P. Whitaker, *The Spanish-American Frontier, 1783–1795* (1927) and *The Mississippi Question, 1795–1803* (1934). Of course refer again to Samuel F. Bemis, *Pinckney's Treaty* (1926). Other monographs include Samuel C. Williams, *History of the Lost State of Franklin* (1933); Charles H. Haskins, *The Yazoo Land Companies* (1891); Isaac J. Cox, *The West Florida Controversy, 1798–1813* (1918); and Elijah W. Lyon, *Louisiana in French Diplomacy, 1759–1804* (1934). Pertinent biographies are: James R. Jacobs, *Tarnished Warrior: Major-General James Wilkinson* (1938); John W. Caughey, *McGillivray of the Creeks* (1938); and Elijah W. Lyon, *The Man Who Sold Louisiana* [Barbé-Marbois] (1942). For Burr's conspiracy (or whatever it was) see Walter F. McCaleb, *The Aaron Burr Conspiracy* (1903).

Chapter XIII

THE WAR OF 1812

1 *The Causes of the War of 1812*

BY 1812 the West had become the nexus of the interrelated economic, biological, and psychological forces which were stirring the young Republic. There lived that new man, the American, young, vigorous, and self-confident, and desirous to test his muscles and win wealth and renown. The West had for years talked of war and fili- busters, and beginning with 1810 a series of events worked the West into a lather of expansionist fervor. Americans had for many years been groping toward the imperialist objectives which after 1845 came to be called Manifest Destiny. It now found clear expression in Congress when John A. Harper of New Hampshire declaimed: "The Author of Nature has marked our limits in the south, by the Gulf of Mexico; and on the north, by the regions of eternal frost." The words found ready echo both inside and outside the legislative halls. The West was land-hungry, and Louisiana had not satiated it, for appetite increased with eating.

Western expansion- ism

Ontario lay west of upper New York, where an excess population of second-generation New Englanders was looking for land. What more natural, then, than to represent the between-the-lakes part of Upper Canada (Ontario) as a pistol pointed at the heart of the United States and to cite British support of Tecumseh as proof? The Florida situation was as readily adaptable as an excuse for expansion, for, though the Spanish flag waved over its swamps and sands, it was actually in control of the hereditary enemy, England, which was making herself at home commercially in the Spanish possessions. British traders from Florida were still ascendant over the Civilized Nations, ran smuggling vessels from Amelia Island to the coves of Georgia, and welcomed runaway slaves.

Desire to annex Can- ada and Florida

The average Westerner may have dreamed of an agrarian paradise erected out of unearned profits on land, but even those who planned industrial cities in the Mississippi Valley understood the necessity of "clearing away" the Indians and of controlling the waters of Florida and the Great Lakes. They wanted freedom of the seas for the goods they intended to manufacture of American raw materials, and they despised the pusillanimity of a New England which supinely suffered seizures and impressments if only the hereditary enemy would let it carry on a modicum of trade.

Southwestern dreams of seizing Mexico had not died with Burr's failure, but forerunners, ostensibly engaged in the trade in mustangs, haunted the Texas border and in 1812 undertook an abortive invasion. **Aggression** On the east the Baton Rouge "revolution" was the first step **against** in the movement to clear the Spaniards away from the **Spain** mouths of the Mobile and Apalachicola rivers. Early in 1812 George Mathews, a former governor of Georgia, responded to a carefully fostered rebellion of Americans in East Florida by leading across the St. Marys River a filibustering force which actually included American regular troops and gunboats. Mathews obviously had the backing of Secretary of State Monroe in this attempt at "preoccupancy," but political expediency caused Monroe to withdraw support and the "revolution" fell flat. Meanwhile the rise of Tecumseh had shaken white smugness in the Ohio Valley and revived talk of seizing Canada.

The rising tide of western expansionism swept out half the membership of the House of Representatives in the election of 1810 and replaced them with the radical and rash—sometimes old war horses who loved the **The War** scent of battle (from afar), sometimes youngsters whose **Hawks** self-reliance, optimism, and energy outran their experience. The expansionist fever ran in a semicircle inside the frontier from New Hampshire to Georgia: John A. Harper of New Hampshire; Peter B. Porter of the Niagara frontier; Henry Clay and Richard M. Johnson of Kentucky; old "Nolichucky Jack" Sevier of Tennessee and young Felix Grundy, who had lost three brothers in the border wars; William H. Crawford and George Troup of Georgia; and the brilliant South Carolina trio John C. Calhoun, Langdon Cheves, and William Lowndes, ocular proof that the leadership of the South was passing from Virginia. These were the leaders of the War Hawks, who devoted themselves to vindicating American honor and land claims. Southern War Hawks, indeed, may have been actuated by a motive additional to expansion, for the prices of cotton and tobacco were governed by British demand, and this in turn by continental demand; the commercial struggle between Britain and France was plainly ruining the South, and desperate measures were needed.

The War Hawks were a minority, but by shrewd bargaining they put Clay into the speakership; not yet thirty-five, this magnetic young lawyer and orator had served a short term in the Senate even before he was of legal age, and part of another term later on. If the Federalists needed any proof, they had it now: their dire predictions that the irresponsible West would overbalance the conservative interests of the East were coming true. How could they know that twenty years later Clay and Calhoun would be the idols of a new generation of conservatives!

The energy and optimism of the War Hawks were a welcome contrast to the old order. The old Republicans were still in office, but almost by Federalist default. "Wee Jamie" Madison might be loved by his friends, but he was no leader and had allowed his office to be reduced to impotence by factional fights within the party. **Republican decadence** This situation was clearly shown when a bill to recharter the Bank of the United States was introduced. Gallatin, still Secretary of the Treasury, had originally been an enemy of the Bank, but experience had converted him into a strong advocate. Now the old Republicans united with the personal enemies of Gallatin and the state banking interests (which expected to divide the carcass) to defeat recharter. One of the most telling arguments used was that seventy per cent of the Bank stock was held abroad, chiefly in England. Accordingly the Bank closed its doors in 1811.

Madison was no more successful in handling the problems of neutrality. For an enterprise that was supposed to have been ruined by the Embargo, commerce made a phenomenally rapid recovery. It will be remembered that a Nonintercourse Act, prohibiting trade with Britain and France, had been substituted for the Embargo. **Failure of the Erskine Agreement** Madison negotiated the Erskine Agreement to forbid trade with France and remove all restrictions on trade with England in exchange for the lifting of the Orders in Council against American ships; Canning, British Foreign Secretary, refused to accept, probably because he was convinced that the United States would not defend its interests to the extent of war. He missed a splendid chance to use the United States against France and opened the way for Napoleon and the War Hawks to push us into war against England.

The failure of the Erskine Agreement left Madison and Congress in a quandary. Finally in 1810 Congress passed Macon's Bill No. 2, which repealed nonintercourse but offered to revive it against the enemy of whichever country first repealed its discriminations, provided that **Macon's Bill No. 2 and Napoleon's trap** the enemy did not also repeal its discriminations within three months. As a matter of fact, British actions toward our shipping were increasingly friendly while those of Napoleon were increasingly arbitrary and confiscatory. Napoleon, more long-headed than Canning, now saw an opportunity to use the United States against England. In July 1810 he announced that the Berlin and Milan decrees would be revoked on 1 November, "it being understood that the English are to revoke their Orders in Council." Of course, his object was to force the United States into war against England in case the Orders were not revoked, but Madison fell into the trap. On 2 November Madison gave England three months to rescind the Orders, or he would revive nonintercourse against it. During that time there was no indication that Napoleon had kept his word; on the contrary, French seizures were accelerated.

Nevertheless, Madison with the blind stubbornness of a weak man refused to acknowledge that Napoleon had not kept his word and on 11 February 1811 cut off trade with Britain. Strangely enough, this third **British re-** stab at Britain's trade within four years was effective. Na- **peal Orders** poleon's Continental System was succeeding, at least for the **in Council** moment, and the American market was the largest one left to England except for Russia, which was on the verge of invasion by Napoleon's Grand Army. The English wheat crop failed in 1811, unsold goods were piling up in warehouses, and unemployed laborers were joining in bread riots. Desperate manufacturers and merchants demanded that Parliament do something to recover the American market and to gain access to American foodstuffs. With typical British leisureliness the Cabinet came to a decision, and on 16 June 1812 announced that the Orders in Council would be suspended at once. Two days later the United States went to war. It is certainly conceivable, though not provable, that had the suspension been known the seaboard would have put up a much more effective resistance against the War Hawks.

The Twelfth Congress had met in special session in November 1811. It had scarcely organized before it received Harrison's inflated account of his victory at Tippecanoe and noted that the Indians had received powder and guns from the British arsenal at Malden. Some of **Drift to-** the guns had been received so short a time before "that they **ward war** were not divested of the list covering in which they are imported." A few months before this the frigate *President*, while cruising off New York to prevent impressments by British patrol ships, was fired upon in the dark. Its return fire disabled its opponent, which upon the coming of day proved to be the much inferior British corvette *Little Belt*. It was, however, a victory to chalk up opposite the *Chesapeake* disgrace, and Americans classed it with the battle of Tippecanoe—which after a fashion it resembled. Congress now gave official sanction to the Baton Rouge steal by adding the area to the new state of Louisiana, and about the same time Mathews invaded East Florida.

These actions gave the Americans a degree of self-assertiveness as

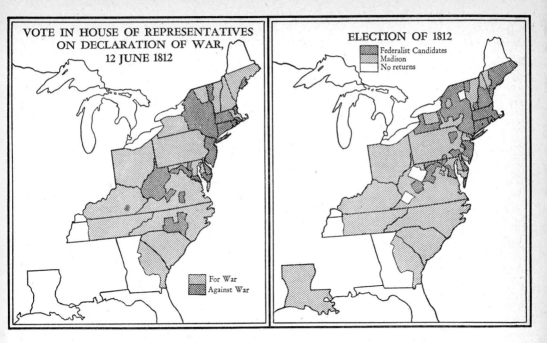

VOTE IN HOUSE OF REPRESENTATIVES
ON DECLARATION OF WAR,
12 JUNE 1812

For War
Against War

ELECTION OF 1812

Federalist Candidates
Madison
No returns

they pondered twenty years of discrimination and insult at the hands of England, and the war spirit rose to the boiling point outside as well as inside Congress. Washington and Jefferson had insisted that the country must suffer insults and injustices until it was grown big enough to take its own part; very well, it was grown up now. Let the British lion beware! The War Hawks, with the West and South pretty solidly behind them, could afford to lay stress on what should have been the grievances of the East, and so they led the van shouting: "Free Trade and Sailors' Rights" and declaiming that the United States could never fulfill its destiny until Great Britain was driven from North America. It would be a short war and a merry one: a six weeks' picnic in the woods.

They voted an army—presumably of picnickers—but recoiled both from strengthening the navy and from laying new taxes. It was plain that the two wings of the War Hawks were jockeying for position. The North wanted Canada, and the South wanted Florida; but each was willing and anxious to thwart the other. Already both were thinking of the rivalry between farmers and planters, between free labor and slavery. In the light of these facts the War Hawks' reckless and uncalculated acceptance of all the odds against them is the more astounding. Wise men saw even before the declaration that this was to be a war managed by men jealous and irresponsible as boys. Madison, for all his faults, realized it. Years later he explained that he had "esteemed it necessary to throw forward the flag, sure that the people would press forward and defend it."

War Hawk
divisions

The Federalists protested and threatened, and John Randolph, always in opposition but right for once (whatever his motives), outdid himself

in brilliant denunciation of the agrarian plotters and canting patriots,
Opposition to war who had "like the whip-poor-will but one eternal monotonous tone—Canada! Canada! Canada!" The opposition
to the War Hawks, indeed, included not only the Federalist
stronghold on the seaboard of New England but the seaboard as far south
as North Carolina, both Federalists and Republicans. The Federalists
rightly regarded War Hawk policy as a blow to liberty and drank to
Senator Pickering's toast, "The world's last hope—Britain's fast-anchored
isle." And yet until almost too late they regarded the war party as mere
braggarts and held with Josiah Quincy that the Republicans "could not
be kicked" into hostilities. Both Jefferson's Embargo and his party's
panicky repeal of it certainly gave color to that contemptuous opinion.

If Madison had been John Adams, he might have saved the cause of
peace and reaped the benefits of the repeal of the Orders. As it was he
wavered, talked about Napoleon's good faith, then seized on a report that
War—and re-election the British government would not repeal the Orders. On
1 June he sent a war message to Congress, and on the 18th
war was declared—but with a number of eastern Republi-
cans not voting. It is difficult to avoid the conviction that Madison tacitly
traded with the War Hawks for the renomination to the presidency; at
least he received it and along with Elbridge Gerry triumphed over De
Witt Clinton, a Republican who was discontented and ambitious enough
to seek the presidency with Federalist support. The pattern of the vote
in Congress on the declaration of war closely resembled the presidential
vote. In both cases the states that touched the sea from Maryland northward were all but solidly against Madison except New Hampshire, which
voted for war. But the War Hawks had their war. It was our first venture
into the sun of Manifest Destiny—and we got more than our noses burned.

2   *The War of 1812 in the North*

There is no use in belaboring the obvious by following in detail the
ineffectivenes of American strategy, the defects in leadership both civil
and military, the weak dependence on militia units which retired to high
Ineffective- ground where they could safely watch the course of conflict,
ness of war and the utter refusal of Congress to support the war by
measures adequate taxation. Neither North nor South would adequately back the expansionist objectives of the other; certainly they
could not unite in seizing Canada, which after all was the only place
where the British were "tangible."

It is probable that the North would have taken Canada if it could
have sold the war to New England. That section, however, still wearing
the nose-ring of the Essex Junto, opposed the war. This attitude was so

clear that until April 1814 (for almost two years) most of **New Eng-** its coast remained unblockaded, while the British fleet **land's atti-** hermetically sealed the coast from Cape Cod southward. **tude** The result was that British goods entered by way of New England and were distributed through the country. At the same time New England manufacturers saw their opportunity and stepped up the manufacture of goods for sale to the other states and to the army. Throughout the war drovers and grain merchants on the northern border carried on a lucrative trade with British quartermasters. Connecticut and Massachusetts refused to muster their militia into Federal service. New England bankers tripled their deposits and held possibly two thirds of the country's specie. They refused to buy more than a minimum of war bonds and, according to Henry Adams, probably loaned more to the British than to the United States. New England grew rich through a war which it constantly sabotaged.

On the other hand, it must be pointed out that not all New Englanders opposed the war. Henry Adams has compared the contributions of Massachusetts and Virginia, greatly to the latter's disadvantage. Massachusetts was not blockaded and therefore naturally furnished far more customs duties, but Massachusetts also did better in other taxes and even in the government loans. In the recruiting of regular troops Massachusetts again led and, indeed, furnished more than any other state but New York; New England troops were in the front at Chippawa and Lundy's Lane. Indeed, the war was lost not because New England did not throw her wealth and power into it, but because most of those parts of the Union which voted for war did not back it wholeheartedly. The only states with relatively clear skirts were New York, Kentucky, and Tennessee—and even they eventually lost heart.

Throughout the war the battles on land and on salt water had little but moral effect upon each other, so it is easy to clear away the naval phase first. It must be admitted even by the most carping critic that the American navy was in good shape: its officers were efficient, its crews well-trained and courageous, and its vessels well **Naval war** outfitted—all seventeen of them. Unfortunately there was **of 1812** not a single ship of the line, battleship to us. The enemy against which the War Hawks vaingloriously sent the navy had a thousand warships, but it could only spare a hundred for the American war. By and large American vessels were well maneuvered, and their artillery was superbly handled; so they gave excellent accounts of themselves in single combat (no fleet actions occurred on the ocean). The victories of the *Constitution* ("Old Ironsides"), the *United States,* the *Wasp,* and the *Hornet* became household topics, and Decatur, Rodgers, and Isaac Hull became national heroes.

By 1813 Britain took her naval task more seriously, and the tide turned with the victory of the *Shannon* over the *Chesapeake* almost within sight of Boston. "Don't give up the ship," the dying words of the *Chesapeake's* captain, James Lawrence, have become the motto of the American navy. Nevertheless, the *Chesapeake* surrendered. Thereafter

JOHNNY BULL in a Fret

Oh these Wasps & Hornets! the dreadful little Insects, how they sting! Oh woe is me! why did I disturb their Nest!!

Baiting Britain during the War of 1812, after several American
sea victories

American naval vessels were picked off one after another or blockaded in port. What with new building, the navy finished the war about as it had begun: seventeen vessels, but all blockaded.

Privateers had become active early in the war, and they were now left unaided to carry the American flag on the high seas. Half of them were unsuccessful, but those with speed and expert commanders did not **Privateers** hesitate to cut merchantmen out of convoys or to attack small British war vessels. Altogether there were about 500 privateers, and they took about 1350 prizes.

Ironically enough, most of the privateers were from states opposed to the war, and Massachusetts merchants were among the most effective when it came to exploiting the opportunity. On the other hand, many of the captures must have been the result of collusion between British and American partners; the method had fascinating possibilities of passing back and forth the same ship with successive cargoes by means of collusive captures. However, there were many *bona fide* captures, and very likely it was New England's privateering activities which caused the British finally to blockade its coast.

At the close of the war, though Europe was in an interlude of peace, American privateers had actually forced up insurance rates in English waters to double or triple the rate when only French privateers were active, and finally in many cases underwriters refused to underwrite. Toward the end of the war the privateers even appeared in the China seas and preyed on the East India Company's richly laden ships. British anger at American successes was so pronounced that the English did not hesitate to violate neutrality to put a stop to American raids, as was witnessed by the attack on the U.S. Frigate *Essex* in Valparaiso and the *General Armstrong* in Fayal.

The thrill of danger and the prospect of easy money were too much for many privateers to resist after the war, and they went into privateering for the Latin-American states or into plain piracy—two activities that were not always clearly distinguishable—and these were joined by many entrepreneurs from the Spanish Caribbean colonies. Between 1814 and 1824 over three thousand piracies were reported, half of them on American vessels, and the American navy was actually busier than it had been during the war.

The War Hawks realized that the sea was Britain's element, but they expected to be superior on land. Actually they should have been. The United States had a population of nearly eight million against a half million in the British provinces, most of them French. The **Strategy of** logical way to conquer Canada was to concentrate all avail- **the war in** able force on Montreal and thus cut off the supplies to Brit- **the North** ish and Indians on the upper waters and at the same time rob Quebec of its inland trade, even though the fortress of Quebec itself might be too strong to be successfully assaulted. Doubtless Madison knew this perfectly well, but it was inexpedient to withdraw the few regulars from the West and leave that politically potent region to furnish its own defense against the Indians. The result was that the scant and scary American forces were split up among four principal frontiers—Detroit, Niagara, the upper St. Lawrence, and Lake Champlain—and ambitious politicians or leisurely and pompous old duffers left over from the Revolution were put in charge.

On the other side the old American Tories (the United Empire Loyalists), who comprised the backbone of the settlers of Upper Canada, rallied with their sons to the defense of the Empire. Theirs is the glory of

United Empire Loyalists having held back the feeble American attempts at invasion until British might could be made manifest in blockading fleets and invading armies. There is poetic justice in the fact that American treatment of its Loyalists in the first war against Great Britain did much to insure its loss of the second war. At the same time it is curious to note that out of eighty thousand inhabitants of upper Canada probably over sixty per cent were Americans who had moved over during the generation after the Revolution. They had been attracted by generous land grants and counted the oath of loyalty to King George a small exchange. Possibly most of them were old Tories or at least indifferent to their allegiance, but disaffection toward British rule was widespread enough in 1812 to make it likely that a few American successes would have made a transfer welcome. At any rate, that did not happen. The war stanched the American influx, and presently the British began actively to encourage emigration from the home islands.

The American strategy in 1812 was to exert pressure all along the frontier and make the main push toward Montreal, with two armies from the St. Lawrence and Lake Champlain converging on Montreal. It was

Defeat in 1812 not really a bad plan under the political circumstances. Unfortunately General Henry Dearborn, who commanded the Lake Champlain column, failed for a number of reasons, not all of them his own fault. The invasion across the Niagara was bloodily repulsed at Queenstown; in this sector part of the common soldiers showed spirit, which pointed up all too clearly the incompetence and cowardice of the generals. The worst blow fell in the West. The fall of Fort Michilimackinac gave the upper lakes to the British, and Tecumseh's Indians forced the surrender of Fort Dearborn (Chicago) and massacred the prisoners. General William Hull undertook a timorous invasion of Canada, then retreated to Detroit and surrendered (16 August) to British General Isaac Brock. Hull had some excuse: his supply route was cut off and he feared Indian massacre, but the West found his surrender disgraceful.

The frontier was now open to Indian attack, and the Ohio Valley suddenly found its yen for war rapidly deflating. The determination to take Canada actually evaporated with the first sting of defeat. Thereafter western leaders fought principally to regain their lost territory in order to lose nothing at the peace. The upper West did little more to win the war than did New England, though its sabotage may not have been as great.

The defeats of 1812 were sobering but not sobering enough. The

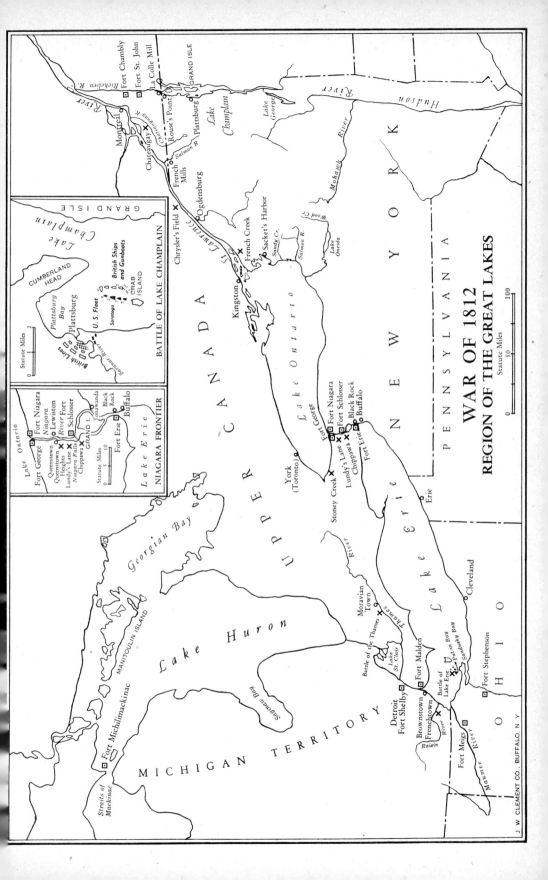

WAR OF 1812
REGION OF THE GREAT LAKES

Statute Miles

0   50   100

BATTLE OF LAKE CHAMPLAIN

GRAND ISLE

Lake Champlain

CUMBERLAND HEAD

Plattsburg Bay

Plattsburg

British Lines

U. S. Fleet

Saranac River

Saratoga

British Ships and Gunboats

CRAB ISLAND

Statute Miles
0   2

NIAGARA FRONTIER

Lake Ontario

Fort George
Queenston
Queenston Heights
Lundy's L.
Niagara Falls
Chippawa
Fort Erie

Fort Niagara
Niagara
River
Fort
Schlosser

GRAND I.
Tonawanda
Black Rock
Buffalo

Lake Erie

Statute Miles
0   5   10

CANADA

UPPER CANADA

Montreal
Chateaugay
Chateaugay R.
Chazy
Rouse's Point
Plattsburg
La Colle Mill
Fort St. John
Fort Chambly
Richelieu R.
River

GRAND ISLE

Lake Champlain
Lake George

Hudson River

NEW YORK

Salmon R.
French Mills
Ogdensburg
French Creek
Sacket's Harbor
Sandy Cr.
Salmon R.
Wood Cr.
Lake Oneida
Mohawk River

Chrysler's Field
St. Lawrence River

Kingston

Lake Ontario

York (Toronto)

Stoney Creek

Fort George
Fort Niagara
Fort Schlosser
Black Rock
Buffalo
Lundy's Lane
Chippawa
Fort Erie

Erie

PENNSYLVANIA

Lake Erie

Cleveland

OHIO

Fort Stephenson

Moravian Town
Battle of the Thames
Thames River
Lake St. Clair
Fort Malden
Put-in Bay
Battle of Lake Erie
Sandusky Bay

Detroit
Fort Shelby
Brownstown
Frenchtown
Raisin River
Fort Meigs
Maumee River

Georgian Bay

MANITOULIN ISLAND

Lake Huron

Saginaw Bay

Fort Michilimackinac

Straits of Mackinac

MICHIGAN TERRITORY

J. W. CLEMENT CO. BUFFALO, N.Y.

opposing naval forces on Lake Ontario were well matched, though they
never came to serious battle. Each took advantage of the other's absence
New York to undertake raids into enemy territory. In April 1813 the
frontiers Americans raided York (Toronto), the village capital of
in 1813 Upper Canada, and wantonly burned the Parliament buildings, an act perpetrated by private soldiers without orders. A British
raid under Sir George Prevost in May on Sacket's Harbor at the other
end of Lake Ontario was repulsed by regulars and militia under young
General Jacob Brown, a militia man himself. Meanwhile events on the
Niagara frontier, bloody but without much strategic importance, brought
to the front another young general, Winfield Scott, who was capable and
courageous if not actually brilliant. In the course of the year James Wilkinson succeeded Dearborn in northern New York. Once more two expeditions, planned to converge on Montreal, failed to converge anywhere.
Wilkinson preened himself before his last court-martial and retired to
write his memoirs.

As before, the most spectacular events occurred in the West. William
Henry Harrison, now in command in that area, moved northward during
the winter. An advance force of nine hundred men was attacked in Jan-
War in the uary 1813 on the River Raisin (near modern Monroe,
West in Michigan) by Colonel Henry Proctor and a force of British
1813 and Indians. Nearly every American perished in battle or in
the subsequent massacre. "Remember the Raisin" became a battle cry to
stir the dying embers of western determination. Proctor improved his
opportunity by capturing a division of militia, but attacks on Fort Meigs
on the Maumee and Fort Stephenson on the Sandusky were repulsed.

Meanwhile it had become evident that success in the West depended
on naval control of Lake Erie. That winter a young naval officer known
to history as Commodore Oliver Hazard Perry succeeded against tremen-
Battle of dous difficulties in building a little fleet at Erie, Pennsyl-
Lake Erie, vania. On 10 September 1813 with ten vessels he met the
10 Sept. somewhat inferior British fleet under Barclay at Put-in Bay
1813 and destroyed it.

This victory opened the way for Harrison. Proctor burned Detroit and
Malden and retreated eastward across Ontario. Harrison, in command of
greatly superior forces, overtook him at the Thames River and defeated
Battle him (5 October) in a battle in which Tecumseh was killed
of the by that fire-eating War Hawk, Richard M. Johnson. The
Thames, 5 battle of the Thames put an end to the Northwest Con-
Oct. 1813 federacy and, indeed, to the War of 1812 in the West. A
land movement across the Ontario wilderness was not feasible, so Harrison returned to Detroit. No serious effort was made to retake Michilimackinac, and in consequence the British were able during the rest of the

war to control the Mississippi as far south as Rock Island and to continue channeling the fur trade to Montreal.

In April 1814 Napoleon signed his first abdication and went into exile on the island of Elba. The British were now able for the first time to concentrate on the American war, and by August veterans of the Peninsular War were pouring into Canada and gathering in the Bermudas and the West Indies. The British intended 1814 to be the year of decision. The blockade was extended to New England. Maine from the Penobscot northward was **British plans for 1814** occupied in September, and the citizens of the conquered territory were required to take an oath of allegiance to George III; there is little evidence that they were reluctant to do so. Farther south Nantucket was occupied as a naval base, and the Cape Cod towns plundered. These actions may have risen from resentment at the activities of New England privateers, but there must have been also an intent to force New England into a more active opposition to the war. At the same time the British planned invasions of the United States by the old Lake Champlain-Hudson River route, by the Chesapeake, and by New Orleans. Among other things, the first was intended to rectify the frontier by annexing a land route across northern New England to the ocean; the second would create a diversion in support of the invasion from Canada; and the last would hamstring the trade of the interior.

The American counteractions when examined in detail seem almost puerile, but the string of successes which barely escaped being fortuitous showed that Providence must have changed sides. Unfortunately in May an unauthorized American expedition plundered and burned Long Point on the north shore of Lake Erie. The officer in charge was court-martialed and censured, but the action **New York frontiers in 1814** (together with the previous burning of York) gave the British an excuse for the plundering activities noted above. In July Brown and Scott won two battles on the Canadian side of the Niagara at Chippawa and Lundy's Lane, but they were fruitless victories.

British General Prevost's invasion by way of Lake Champlain was the crisis of the war. The arbitrary and incompetent Secretary of War, John Armstrong, with a stupidity that amounted to genius, removed most of the defending army to Sacket's Harbor on Lake Ontario. When in August Prevost with ten thousand regulars advanced against light opposition up the west side of Lake Champlain to Plattsburg, the little fleet of Master-Commandant Thomas Macdonough was the only significant **Battle of Lake Champlain, 11 Sept. 1814** force that lay between him and New York City. Once again control of the water proved decisive, for it was practically impossible to supply an army over wilderness roads. The British fleet under Captain George

Downie outclassed the American fleet, but Prevost forced it to attack Macdonough in a disadvantageous position, 11 September, in Plattsburg Bay.

Macdonough took intelligent advantage of the natural situation and drew up his little fleet near the entrance to Plattsburg Bay where the British could attack from only one direction, and then under fire of the Americans' short-range carronades. Macdonough had only one formidable ship, the 26-gun *Saratoga,* but he arranged cables and anchors in such a manner that the ship could be turned around end for end. After two hours of destructive but indecisive battle, during which Downie was killed, Macdonough "wound" his ship and brought his uninjured broadside to bear on the British. The well-planned stratagem turned defeat into victory. As a result the British invasion forces abandoned the campaign and returned to Canada. It is highly probable that Prevost's stupidity and Macdonough's foresight were all that stood between the United States and dissolution.

British naval action in 1813 on the Atlantic coast had taken the form of plundering expeditions in the James River area, and for a year and a half Chesapeake Bay was under British control. It was an opportunity **British** for Chesapeake produce merchants, and they reaped a golden **army in** harvest. In 1814 Admiral Alexander Cochrane with a con- **Washing-** siderable fleet and eight thousand regular troops appeared **ton City** in Chesapeake and chased a flotilla of American gunboats up the Patuxent River; there three thousand troops landed and under General Robert Ross marched on Washington. Soon afterward a British naval force ascended the Potomac and plundered Alexandria. The land raid was a complete surprise, for very few (not even the British up to this point) had supposed it worth undertaking. A hastily gathered force of seven thousand, composed largely of "country people" under a ridiculously incompetent general, was contemptuously brushed aside in a brief action at Bladensburg on 24 August. President Madison, who had been inspecting the lines, was swept along in the rout.

That evening the British entered the Capital City. Private property was little molested, but the torch was set to the Capitol, and General Ross ate the dinner which he found on the table at the President's Palace, then set fire to the building; the white paint later used to cover the fireblack gave the name White House to the structure. Madison and his Cabinet (with Dolly supposed to have been clutching the original copy of the Declaration of Independence) barely escaped. On 26 August the British retired to their fleet. British writers have always been uneasy because of this wanton destruction of a national capitol and have adopted the defense that it was in reprisal for the burning of the government buildings at York; the incidents were scarcely parallel.

The Washington episode gave Baltimore time to prepare its defense, and when the British fleet appeared there Fort McHenry withstood bombardment. It was on the night of this attack (13–14 September) that a Washington lawyer, Francis Scott Key, who had visited **Repulse** the British fleet to arrange for the release of a prisoner, **from Balti-** was detained on board. When dawn disclosed that Fort **more** McHenry still held out, Key in a burst of emotion wrote "The Star-Spangled Banner." British troops had meanwhile failed to carry the defenses of Baltimore, and Ross was killed in the action. Troops and fleet now drew off and, fanning about the Chesapeake, devoted themselves to the most wholehearted season of pillage and burning of the war, then presently sailed to new adventures in the Gulf of Mexico.

One result of the Chesapeake campaign was to force the resignation of Armstrong; Secretary of State Monroe took on as an added duty the supervision of the War Department. The improvement was not remarkable, but Madison was so shaken by the raid on Wash- **Collapse** ington that the government practically devolved on Monroe. **of the war** All the banks outside New England ceased specie payments, **effort** and government credit was practically gone; the army, now about thirty-five thousand men on paper, almost ceased recruiting, its service of supply broke down, and its effectives were reduced to pitifully small forces. The militia, in most cases, was quite undependable, but it would soon be the only defense. Republicans and Federalists alike blocked the raising of an effective army because it was traced in the bloodstream that a standing army was the enemy of liberty. Daniel Webster, then a freshman Representative, won his first laurels in helping to scotch an administration move to conscript an army. National morale literally had reached such depths that nothing could be done in Washington to retrieve the national honor.

Even worse was the specter rising in New England, especially in Massachusetts. In that state seventy thousand superbly trained and equipped militia, untouched by the war, were being held for the day when they would dictate to the Federal government. On 10 Oc- **New Eng-** tober British conditions of peace reached Congress. The **land moves** Northwest must be given up to the Indians; the United **toward sur-** States could have neither a navy on the Great Lakes nor an **render—or** army on their shores; the Newfoundland fisheries must be **disunion** surrendered; and northern Maine must be ceded to Canada. New England's time had come. Massachusetts proposed to bow to these "moderate terms," though a hundred miles of her Maine coastline were in British hands and Nantucket was a British naval station. In her state of mind it was perhaps natural that these facts, even though punctuated by plundering raids on Cape Cod, aroused more resentment against Washington than against Great Britain. A convention of the New England states was called at Hartford, and the November elections were in the nature of a plebiscite on the British terms. The Republicans were defeated. The Essex Junto now took the stage for the last time.

"TO THE GRAVE GO SHAM PROTECTORS OF " FREE TRADE AND SAILORS' RIGHTS"—AND ALL THE PEOPLE SAY AMEN !"

This cartoon, printed in 1814 by the *New York Evening Post*, shows that the Federalists blamed the Embargo for starting the unpleasantness with Britain. President Madison is clutched by a terrapin. Although its head has just been severed, it holds on grimly to the President's ear. "Down to the grave t'atone for sin Jemmy must go with Terrapin. . . ."

When the convention met on 15 December 1814 Vermont and New Hampshire were represented only by volunteer delegates, but the delegates from the three other states were elected by the legislatures. It may

Hartford Convention be that all that saved the Union was the inherent lethargy and caution of George Cabot, who was elected presiding officer. The fire-eaters like Timothy Pickering and John Lowell were smothered by those of Cabot's stripe, who proposed to give the rest of the Union a last chance. Nevertheless, Governor Strong of Massachusetts sent an envoy to Halifax to propose peace and an alliance of New England with Great Britain.

The convention's commissioners now went to Washington with a demand that a part of the Federal revenues be turned over to the states to be expended by them for their own defense; this was in effect an assump-

New England delegation in Washington tion of the central government's war powers by the states and of course meant that Federal authority would be effectively blocked. Extremists hoped that this would really mean the end of the Union. In addition, seven Constitutional amendments were proposed for later consideration. Among them were the proposals that southern representation be cut down by repealing the Three-fifths Compromise, and that new states be admitted only by assent of two thirds of the states.

The program was regarded by Federalists as eminently moderate and was later defended as a wise attempt to save the Union from being forcibly torn asunder by the fire-eaters in the convention and among the people. However, even the first demand could scarcely be acceptable to the other states, and it seems likely that the convention leaders proposed to adopt more forcible means of protecting their interests as soon as the British had struck their final blow at national morale by the capture of New Orleans. Instead of that, the committee was met at Washington by the news that the British army had been decisively defeated at New Orleans and that peace had been declared. The delegates slipped off without mentioning their demands, and New England secessionism vanished like the night of national fear which had nourished its growth.

How was the country snatched from the brink of destruction by a peace of whose terms a wise man would not have dared to dream a brief three months before? The fact that the administrations of both Great Britain and the United States had accepted war with re- **Early attempts at peace** luctance encouraged movements toward an armistice as early as July 1812. The Americans were in effect betting that Napoleon would win, and just at this moment his invasion of Russia and Wellington's reverses in Spain threw the British government into a depression which was not helped by the early naval defeats. Nevertheless, Madison's insistence that Britain give way on the old grounds of impressment and paper blockades made any prospect of an armistice fall through, and England soon found depression giving way to anger. Madison was regarded as the tool of Napoleon, giving England the choice of being stabbed in the back or of committing suicide for America's benefit; the war was in English eyes dastardly treason to the cause of human liberty.

Napoleon's Grand Army was destroyed, and Wellington fought his way back in Spain. Mr. Madison's gamble seemed about to lose in Europe, as it was certainly losing on the Canadian border; he was therefore interested when the Russian Czar, mindful of American foodstuffs, offered early in 1813 to mediate. The British put the offer aside, but they permitted two American delegates, Gallatin and James Bayard of Delaware, to open direct negotiations in London in April 1814. The fall of Napoleon immediately afterward was followed by a British decision to exert its force in America, with the results we have seen.

The negotiations were transferred to Ghent, and there Gallatin and Bayard were joined by Henry Clay, John Quincy Adams, and Jonathan Russell. It was an ill-assorted crew, and all of Gallatin's diplomacy was

Negotiations at Ghent
necessary to preserve smooth relations; in the end, each of these able men complemented the others. When the original British demands were received the American delegation began to pack up, but Clay, who was long remembered as the best poker player in Washington, counseled watchful waiting. As a matter of fact, the British were stalling until they could slap down on the table the accounts of expected victories.

Meanwhile in the United States the news of British demands was producing signs of a renewed fighting spirit outside New England. Then came the news of Plattsburg and of the repulse from Baltimore. Nor was this all. The British taxpayer was fed up with war, food was scarce and high-priced, and American privateers had the mercantile interests quaking with fear. Even more important, the Allied diplomats in the main circus tent at Vienna had fallen out, and the ubiquitous Talleyrand had plumped France down on the side of England and Austria against Russia and Prussia. It looked as though war impended, and indeed it continued to look that way for a decade. The worried British ministry now asked Wellington to take command in America, but he declined on the ground that without control of the Great Lakes he could do no more than Prevost had; he went further and counseled that, since the British army held no important stretch of American territory, it could not demand territorial concessions.

In the end the "dishonors were even." The Treaty of Ghent, signed 24 December 1814, made no mention of impressment or neutral rights, transferred no territory, and did nothing for Tecumseh's warriors. In

Treaty of Ghent, 24 Dec. 1814
effect, as Adams said, it was "a truce rather than a peace . . . an indefinite suspension of hostilities." The only constructive measures provided that later conferences should settle standout problems such as fisheries, commercial relations, and disputed boundaries.

3 *The Jackson Legend*

The foregoing is the story of the War of 1812; events in the Southwest had no discernible effect upon the actual course of the war nor upon the negotiations in Ghent. Yet the fact remains that without a knowledge

Andrew Jackson (1767– 1845)
of what went on in the Southwest one would miss much of the psychological implication of the war. It was the Southwest that produced the war's outstanding national hero, and the story of the war in that area was nothing more than a biography of that man from 1812 to 1815. The man, of course, was Andrew Jackson. Born in the backwoods of South Carolina of Scotch-Irish immigrant parents, Jackson as a lad fought briefly in the Revolution, suffered from smallpox in a British prison, and carried to the grave a

scalp wound received in prison from an officer's sword. These facts, together with the loss of two brothers in the war and of his mother to prison fever while nursing in British-occupied Charleston, made him the life-long enemy of England.

After a period of reading law, Jackson in 1788 moved to Tennessee. He was tall, thin to the point of cadaverousness, red-headed, horse-faced, and a prey to violent tempers which for years kept him involved in feuds and duels. Though he was in origin a plebeian, his yearn- **His rise** ings were toward aristocracy. His activities as a lawyer and land speculator presently enabled him to acquire The Hermitage near Nashville, where he lived in the aristocratic manner, and his charm quickly made him the center of a sparkling social circle. Meanwhile he engaged in Indian wars, became a judge, major-general of militia, and the leader of the "aristocratic" political faction opposed to Sevier—and at the same time found time and money to become a leading sportsman, particularly as a horse-racer. Before 1800 he served in both the House of Representatives and the Senate and was remembered for his irascibility, though it should be noted in his favor that the fairness of his judgments while he served on the bench was never called in question.

He also married Rachel Donelson, daughter of a socially prominent family, who had been married to a certain Lewis Robards. At the time Robards was supposed to have obtained a divorce, and when it developed that he had not until later on, she and Jackson were remarried. Unfortunately Jackson's political ambitions made it profitable for his enemies to keep the scandal alive, and no small part of his feuding activities arose from this fact. Nevertheless, their life together was happy. She died just before her husband became President.

Jackson was first of all a man of will, contentiousness, and intolerance of those who differed from him, but these qualities were scarcely handicaps in a region where men stood up for themselves. In the light of his clearly aristocratic tendencies, it seems strange that he **Character** was destined to become the idol of American democracy **and influ-** even in the East. The answer may be found in these facts: **ence of** he was a natural-born leader, and that was the only sort **Jackson** who could arouse the Westerner's enthusiasm; he sympathized with and became the instrument of a strong policy against Indians and Spaniards; he represented a new phase of local self-determination as opposed to Federal dominance; and, not least, he expressed in his policies the growing leveling tendencies which declared every man a king in theory and a mediocrity in practice. If these factors seem incompatible with the nature of the man, it should be remembered that he was also a politician and knew as well as the next man how to convince the public that the deuce of clubs was the ace of spades.

But even more important than these was the national state of mind when he first sprang into public attention. The secret of his ascendancy over the national imagination can best be understood by contrasting his remarkable feats of will with the depression of national morale in 1814. After two and a half years of war—never mind its origin—the administration was paralyzed, Congress shot through with treason, finances in chaos, military defense all but dissolved, and gloating New England stood poised to fasten her shackles on the nation or give it the alternative of being split asunder. True, the war had disclosed a few competent sailors and at least two other good generals, but none of them were imbued with the greatness which can inspire a nation and turn confused and despairing men into heroes. To give words to a dream of what might have been, it is conceivable that had the war gone on, Jackson's presence in the North might have wrought the same miracle that his tremendous will had caused in the South.

The Jackson legend

In the midst of military collapse and threatened disunion, only the will of Andrew Jackson stood between the nation and the bitter cup of national dishonor. The fact that his greatest victory was won after the peace treaty did not destroy the psychological salvation which he offered. Thereafter the common people gave Jackson an almost mystical acclaim. Whatever we may think of his later political course, that fact must not be forgotten. He was the realization of the common American's dream of himself: the man of will, the builder, the champion of democratic liberties, and the preserver of national honor and safety against the powers of foreign evil.

The early phases of the War of 1812 in the South were chiefly concerned with the Creek Indians, who were relied on by the British and Spanish to block any American push against Florida. Tecumseh's leaven and British intrigue had worked among the Upper (northern) Creeks next to the Tennessee border, but the Cherokee and Lower Creeks were not disposed to war. The war party was known as the Red Sticks. Madison's first move was to make good his claim on Mobile, but his intention of seizing East Florida was blocked by the Senate. Jackson, who had collected troops to carry out this operation, returned home in disgust. Indeed, East Florida was a thorn in the side of the war effort, for the amount of illicit trade that was passing between Georgia and Florida was different in degree rather than intent from that between New England and Canada. This trade was doubtless connected with the British plan of 1814 to capture Savannah. Initial steps were undertaken in January 1815 by the seizure of Cumberland Island and the St. Marys River, but these were of no significance since they came after the peace treaty.

The East Florida problem

By the middle of 1813 the Upper Creeks were ready to begin war

against Georgia and Tennessee under the leadership of William Weatherford, a mixed-blood and a relative of McGillivray. The massacre of five
hundred Americans at Fort Mims on 30 August 1813
brought Jackson back into the field. When he received the   **Creek War,**
1813–1814
call, he was in bed recuperating from bullet wounds received in a brawl with two Benton brothers, one of whom, Thomas Hart
Benton, was to be his future senatorial champion. Jackson took the field
with his arm in a sling, but that was the least of his personal handicaps,
for during the next two years he was seldom free from illness of one sort
or another. His forces were militiamen, little disposed to war and thoroughly disposed to go home on the least technicality. Still, despite continual mutinies and lack of weapons and supplies Jackson kept in the
field a force which was considerably augmented by Cherokee and Lower
Creeks. On 27 March 1814 he met and soundly defeated the Red Sticks at
Horseshoe Bend. In the treaty which followed Jackson split the Creek
nation into two widely separated parts by expelling them from two thirds
of their ancestral lands, an L-shaped swath that now includes one fifth
of Georgia and three fifths of Alabama. Jackson was determined to end
the Indian menace, and in doing it he ruthlessly stripped his Cherokee
and Lower Creek allies along with the Upper Creeks.

The Creek War marked Jackson as an outstanding leader and led to
his appointment as major-general and commander of the United States
army in the South. From the first he had aimed at the conquest of East
Florida, and when the British landed marines in Florida   **Early**
and welcomed the fugitive Red Sticks he supposed the time   **stages of**
had come. At this juncture he received word that a large   **the Gulf**
British fleet and army were headed for the Gulf; New Or-   **Campaign**
leans in the midst of its swamps seemed so unpromising an object of
attack that Jackson presumed the British must be heading for Mobile or
Pensacola. In August (1814) an advance fleet landed at Pensacola; Jackson countered in November by storming the town against British and
Spanish defenders. The British sailed away, leaving the Creeks and
Spaniards disgusted, and joined General Edward Packenham, a brother-
in-law of Wellington, who had entered the Gulf in command of eight
thousand men, chiefly Wellington's veterans.

Meanwhile militia from as far north as Kentucky was converging on
New Orleans, and the French population rallied to the defense, even
including the pirates of Barataria under the brothers Lafitte. It must be
admitted that Jackson, though a great leader, showed defi-   **British pre-**
ciency in generalship. On 13 December the British began to   **pare to at-**
land east of New Orleans on Lake Borgne, and since a vast   **tack New**
swamp lay east of the city the only feasible approach was   **Orleans**
south of the swamp across the open fields along the river bank. At the
moment on 23 December when Jackson learned the facts, the British

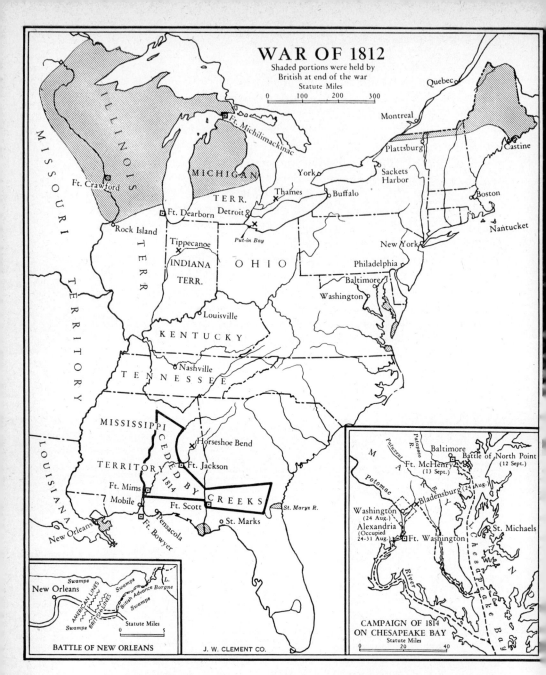

WAR OF 1812

Shaded portions were held by
British at end of the war

Statute Miles

0   100   200   300

Quebec

Montreal

Plattsburg

Castine

Ft. Michilimackinac

York

Sackets
Harbor

Boston

MICHIGAN

Thames

Buffalo

Nantucket

TERR.

ILLINOIS

Ft. Crawford

Ft. Dearborn

Detroit

Put-in Bay

New York

Rock Island

Tippecanoe

INDIANA

O H I O

Philadelphia

TERR.

TERR.

Baltimore

MISSOURI   TERRITORY

Louisville

Washington

K E N T U C K Y

Nashville

T E N N E S S E E

M I S S I S S I P P I

Horseshoe Bend

Ft. Jackson

Baltimore

Battle of North Point
(12 Sept.)

Ft. McHenry
(13 Sept.)

TERRITORY

CEDED BY 1814

C R E E K S

Potapsco R.

Patuxent R.

Bladensburg (24 Aug.)

St. Marys R.

Ft. Mims

Mobile

Ft. Scott

St. Marks

Washington
(24 Aug.)

Alexandria
(Occupied
24-31 Aug.)

Ft. Washington

St. Michaels

LOUISIANA

New Orleans

Ft. Bowyer

Pensacola

Potomac River

Chesapeake Bay

Swamps

New Orleans

AMERICAN LINES

BRITISH LINES

British Advance Borgne

L.

Swamps

Swamps

Swamps

Statute Miles

0   5

BATTLE OF NEW ORLEANS

J. W. CLEMENT CO.

**CAMPAIGN OF 1814
ON CHESAPEAKE BAY**

Statute Miles

0   20   40

were only eight miles away! At dark Jackson gathered two thousand men
and boldly halted the British advance in an action that made the "air
stiff with lead." The next day breastworks and gun emplacements were
thrown up behind a dry canal five miles below the city, and the works
were continued on the opposite side of the river and two ships stationed
to hold the river itself. During the next week the attacks were beaten

back as the feverish work of fortifications continued, while the British brought up artillery from the fleet.

Packenham planned his grand assault for the dark hours before daylight of 8 January 1815; he had at his disposal for the operation close to eight thousand veterans. Miscalculations and mishaps dogged the preparations, and the attack did not begin until after daylight began to dissipate the fog. The only considerable success was on the west side of the river, where Louisiana militia gave ground. The main attack was on the canal fortifications. Jackson's six thousand or more men—sailors, regulars, backwoods riflemen, city Creoles, Santo Domingan Negroes, and Baratarian pirates —stood firm behind their breastworks and traded artillery and small-arms fire to such effect that two desperate assaults were repulsed.

Battle of New Orleans, 8 Jan. 1815

> Behind it stood our little force—
> None wished it to be greater,
> For every man was half a horse,
> And half an Alligator.

In a half hour of action, three of the four British major-generals fell, Packenham, mortally wounded, among them. All together the British suffered two thousand casualties, three hundred of them killed, and the Americans' loss was seventy-one, of whom thirteen were killed. After the main defeat the British withdrew their troops from the west bank but did not begin to withdraw to the ships for ten days. Actually the main battle had been waged between artillery, and that of the Americans had been much the more effective. This should not have been a surprise to the British, for the American handling of artillery both on land and on sea had been one of the few things to which the nation could legitimately point with pride. The story was long told of how the rustic Andy strode through the powder smoke to observe the effect of the artillery fire and gave the order, "Boys, elevate them guns a little lower."

British defeat

The news of the victory at New Orleans reached the East only shortly before news of the Treaty of Ghent, and the banquets and illuminations which swept the nation were double celebrations. People and politicians alike lost sight of facts in their relief and welcomed the treaty and dismissed the war, as Henry Adams says, with the single phrase: "Not an inch ceded or lost!" The market for flour, cotton, and tobacco boomed, and shippers hastened to take advantage of it. The amazing fact is that the weight of national opprobrium was lifted from Madison, and he was hailed as the genius who, next to Jackson, had brought victory. The Essex Junto, suddenly spotlighted by the dazzling sun of "victory," was anathematized

Sudden recovery of national spirit

as a traitorous crew, and the Federalist Party perished with it. For a decade politics almost dropped out of sight, and when it reappeared at intervals it had lost its Federalist and Republican cleavage. "In a single day, almost in a single instant," says Henry Adams, "the public turned

IOHN BULL BEFORE *NEW ORLEANS*

William Charles's cartoon (1815) showing a hulking John Bull, minus his wig, being dragged out of a morass by an American and a Frenchman was the last in a series depicting the troubled days of the War of 1812.

from interests and passions that had supplied its thought for a generation and took up a class of ideas that had been unknown or but vaguely defined before."

The frustration of western expansionism in the War of 1812 had no perceptible influence on the rate of migration into the West. Ontario had not been acquired, but there was plenty of land elsewhere and more could **Florida** be embezzled from the Indians. The Florida problem, how**problem re-** ever, remained acute, largely because of its nuisance value. **mains acute** Creek refugees had joined their Seminole brethren and from time to time raided and plundered white settlements north of the border. In addition, Florida continued to be a handy refuge for runaway Negro slaves who often joined the Indians in their depredations. British merchants retained a foothold in the area, and there was evidence that they encouraged the raids. As if that were not enough, the smugglers of the Georgia border had gone back to their old piratical habits, and Amelia

Island, it was well known, was their headquarters. Spain, unfortunately, was powerless to check any of these dissident elements.

President Monroe, after his inauguration in 1817, opened negotiations with Spain for the purchase of Florida; but Spain, with nearly all of her colonies in rebellion, made it a point of national honor to retain such as she could. Clashes between United States troops and the **First Semi-** Seminole Indians had begun in 1816, and now (1817) Jack- **nole War,** son was sent to command the troops on the border. It was **1816–18** looking for trouble. He wrote to Monroe asking for a hint that the Florida problem should be solved, and in a letter from one of Monroe's friends he thought he received the hint. The army was set in motion early in 1818 and swept across the northwestern part of the province. Pensacola and St. Marks were seized, the Seminole were punished, and two British- ers were court-martialed and executed for promoting Indian raids.

Jackson, with his usual thoroughness, had succeeded in antagonizing both British and Spanish and now confidently demanded government backing. Though the secret was well kept, the administration split wide open, with Secretary of State John Quincy Adams support- **Consequent** ing and Secretary of War Calhoun opposing Jackson. Clay, **diplomatic** Speaker of the House, took the opportunity to trim down **embroil-** the political size of his rival in the hearts of Westerners. **ment** Adams's arguments for a strong course were so cogent that Monroe ac- cepted his advice and refused to punish Jackson. Fortunately the British backed down, and Adams boldly accused Spain of being responsible for the outrages across the border and demanded reparations. Unfortunately Jackson gathered that Adams opposed him and Calhoun supported him; the misapprehension later bore political fruit.

Strange as it may seem, Jackson's raid and Adams's rather unreason- able representations resulted in the acquisition of Florida. Spain was con- vinced that sooner or later it would be seized and decided to get what she could and turn to the far more serious problems posed **Transcon-** by her rebellious colonies. The Adams-Onís Treaty, often **tinental** known as the Transcontinental Treaty, of 22 February 1819 **Treaty of** made a clean sweep of boundary controversies with Spain. **1819** Florida was ceded in exchange for a definition of western boundaries; the United States gave up its manufactured claim to Texas and accepted a boundary which followed the Sabine River, ascended·in steps to the forty- second parallel (the northern boundary of California), and ran thence westward to the Pacific. The Spanish claim to the Oregon country was thus abandoned to the United States. Actually no purchase money was paid for Florida, but the United States assumed $5,000,000 in claims of American citizens against Spain. Despite western objection to the surrender of Texas (Adams was overruled by Monroe in this) the treaty was approved by the Senate, and after considerable delay by Spain. It went into effect 19 February 1821, and Jackson became the first governor of Florida.

The assessment of the War of 1812 has been a fruitful source of contention. The United States army had never had more than 30,000 effectives, it had never been able to place more than 4000 regulars in a single **Situation at** action, and in all its battles it had lost 1877 men. The mili- **the end of** tary history of the war from the beginning to the peace was **the war** one of befuddlement and malfeasance, relieved by less than half a dozen significant victories. At the close of the war we held no British territory, but the British held most of the Michigan and Wisconsin wilderness, northern Maine, and Nantucket. Our navy had been sunk or driven off the high seas.

A third of the population and two thirds of the wealth were dedicated to measures which would quickly bring disunion. Governmental administration and finances teetered on the edge of dissolution. Our diplomacy was bankrupt. Finally, and devastatingly clear, the peace treaty said not one word about impressment or freedom of trade. For years our national weaknesses had been brought out one by one, as by a master puppeteer, and made to dance before a jeering world. The outcome of the war can be honestly claimed at its very best as no better than a stalemate.

Why, then, has it become a cardinal principle of the American creed that "we licked the British twice, and can do it again"? It reminds one of the fabled cock which contended that his crowing brought up the sun. **Stalemate** The explanation lies in the well-known psychological facts **rationalized** that we forget pain and remember pleasure and that we in- **into victory** terpret events to our own credit. The War of 1812, from an obbligato of national dishonor, changed to a causal march of triumph to the tune of which our arms had carried one national objective after another. Occurrences in 1814 and later lent themselves very handily to wishful thinking by the heedless or the shallow. Let us examine them.

(1) The news of Jackson's resounding victory at New Orleans, won *after* the signing of the peace treaty, was followed immediately by news of peace. It was fatally easy to connect them as cause and effect.

(2) The handful of very creditable naval duels was somehow remembered with a pride which had no realistic connection with their significance. The fact that our navy was soon driven off the seas was quietly ignored in American song and story.

(3) Impressment and trade discrimination ceased. Here again completely separate occurrences were connected as cause and effect. The end of the European war in 1814 meant that England cut its navy in two and no longer had reason to impress sailors; at the same time the destruction of commerce by both Britain and France ended.

(4) There were no more significant Indian troubles in the Old North-

west. Historians agree that the battle of the Thames wiped out at one stroke Tecumseh and the last hope of the Indians. Yet Indian troubles had continued that long only because of the possibility of British support. Tecumseh could count only about 4000 warriors, and many of these were disaffected. In contrast there were 200,000 white men of military age in the Ohio Valley alone!

(5) We were now relieved of foreign pressures and were able to turn with easy minds to the conquest of the North American continent. Here again the popular mind pitched upon the War of 1812 as the cause; actually the cause lay in the end of a generation of European wars.

(6) The War of 1812 promoted manufactures and thus gave us our industrial independence. This fact is true (with certain qualifications), but desire for industrial independence was not a cause of war, and industry was accelerated from dire necessity rather than choice. Curiously enough, the movement was most successful in New England, the section most opposed to the war. Still, it was the most valid gain that resulted from the war.

BIBLIOGRAPHICAL NOTE

The Causes of the War of 1812

In addition to Henry Adams, *History of the United States,* see Julius Pratt, *Expansionists of 1812* (1925). Alfred L. Burt, *The United States, Great Britain, and British North America* . . . (1940) covers the field of relations among the three from 1775 to 1818. He argues ably (p. 305–10) that the issue of commerce caused the war and that the American declaration was thus justified; the thesis would be more comforting if it were more convincing. The same general concept is upheld by W. H. Goodman, "Origins of the War of 1812: A Survey of Changing Interpretations," *Miss. Valley Hist. Rev.,* 28:171–86 (1941).

The War of 1812 in the North

MILITARY: For all aspects of the war Henry Adams, *History of the United States* is still unrivaled; to get the full picture of this national perigee one should follow the unabridged edition. For week-end reading see Charles P. Lucas, *The Canadian War of 1812* (1906) or Francis F. Beirne, *The War of 1812* (1949). Benson J. Lossing, *Pictorial Field-Book of the War of 1812* (1868) is about as well as can be done in pictures. For the Northwest woods see Julius W. Pratt, "Fur Trade Strategy and the American Left Flank in the War of 1812," *Am. Hist. Rev.,* 40:246–73 (Jan. 1935).

NAVAL: Best on this side is Alfred T. Mahan, *Sea Power in Its Relations to the War of 1812* (2 v., 1919). Theodore Roosevelt's juvenile opus *The Naval War of 1812* (1882) is still useful, as also are Edgar S. Maclay, *History of the United States Navy* (2 v., 1901) and *History of American Priva-*

teers (1924). See also Charles W. Kendall, *Private Men-of-War* (1931); Samuel E. Morison, *Maritime History of Massachusetts* (1921); Gardner W. Allen, *Our Navy and the West Indian Pirates* (1929); Charles J. Dutton, *Oliver Hazard Perry* (1935); Rodney Macdonough, *Life of Commodore Thomas Macdonough* (1909).

DIPLOMACY: In addition to Henry Adams see Frank A. Opdyke, *Diplomacy of the War of 1812* (1915); and Samuel F. Bemis, *John Quincy Adams and the Foundations of American Foreign Policy* (1949). See also biographies of Gallatin and Clay.

JACKSON: There are biographies of Jackson by John S. Bassett, James Parton, and William G. Sumner. Most recent and interesting is Marquis James, *Andrew Jackson: The Border Captain* (1933). Bassett has edited his *Correspondence* (5 v., 1926–31). Since Jackson's career falls so clearly into two parts, reference will be made later to works on his political life.

CREEKS: Henry S. Halbert and Timothy H. Ball, *The Creek War* (1895).

NEW ORLEANS: The best easily available accounts of the campaign and battle are in Henry Adams and Marquis James, and in Eron Rowland, *Andrew Jackson's Campaign Against the British* (1926). See also Charles F. Adams, *Studies Military and Diplomatic, 1775–1865* (1911). It should be noted that authorities differ on the number of troops engaged and casualties.

FLORIDA: Philip C. Brooks, *Diplomacy and the Borderlands: The Adams-Onís Treaty of 1819* (1939).

Chapter XIV

THE JACKSONIAN ERA

1 *New Men and New Measures*

THE decade after the War of 1812 was a period of reorientation. The War Hawks, though ready to take advantage of the public's belief that the United States had won the war, were keenly aware of the debacle which they had helped to promote and sought for means to **Republican** prevent its recurrence. National strength and national wel- **political re-** fare, it was apparent, could be assured only by nationalist **orientation** political and economic policies. The party of Jefferson, which had laid Hamilton in his political grave, now exhumed his bones and adoringly enshrined them in the halls of Congress—and this with the approval of the aged Jefferson. The Federalists, still maundering into their stocks about the inevitable catastrophe that would follow in the wake of de- mocracy, found their sons refusing to accept the roles of catastrophists and traitors. Young Federalists swarmed into the Republican fold and joined with the reconstructed Jeffersonians to pull the party ship out of its Madisonian doldrums and speed it before the winds of nationalism. The Federalist Party, which in twenty years had run the gamut from rabid nationalism to New England sectionalism, accepted the defeat of Rufus King in 1816 as its death knell and quietly folded up as a national organization.

The election of James Monroe in 1816 ushered in the last of the Vir- ginia dynasty and a period of one-party government somewhat inaccu- rately known as the Era of Good Feeling. The Republicans now copied the Federalists in decrying party spirit. With no conflict **The Era of** between parties, the President declined in significance. **Good Feel-** There was, however, a great deal of sparring for position **ing** among ambitious leaders. Though the young nationalists were distinctly ascendant, it became increasingly evident that there were two wings to the party: the Old Jeffersonian, or Antique Republican, and the Neo-Hamiltonian. It was partly this very cleavage which moved the two wings to renominate Monroe in 1820 and which won for him every electoral vote save one, which was thrown away by a dour dissident who (it was claimed) proposed that Washington should be the only President unanimously elected.

James Monroe was a close neighbor of Jefferson and Madison who had come up through the army, the law, the Virginia legislature, the Confederation Congress, the Senate, and the governorship. Various diplomatic **James Mon-** positions culminated in the secretaryship of state and the **roe (1758–** presidency. Monroe was outstanding neither in his mental **1831)** attainments nor in his personal accomplishments, and his early career was partisan, localistic, and too obviously actuated by ambition. Yet through the years he grew in stature and developed a tact and judgment both in political and administrative affairs which won honor and respect.

The cast now upon the stage was to dominate American history until 1850, when the last of them to survive in the Congressional arena made their swan songs during the debates over the Compromise of 1850 before **Dramatis** an audience of the younger men who were to meet the great **personae of** crisis of secession and war. The period of their activity has **the Silver** with justice been called America's Silver Age, in contrast **Age** to the Golden Age of the Founding Fathers. Jackson, the eldest of the group and the dominant figure in politics for a score of years, owed his position and his availability first of all to the legend which had grown up about him. Younger than he, and without his warlike glamor, were the following names, reading from north to south: Daniel Webster, John Quincy Adams, Martin Van Buren, Henry Clay, Thomas Benton, John C. Calhoun, and William H. Crawford.

Daniel Webster, a New Hampshire farm boy, went by way of Dartmouth College and the law to a seat in the House of Representatives in 1813 as a Federalist. Though he opposed the war viciously, he was not **Daniel** willing to go as far as secession. His view of New England's **Webster** mercantile interests led him to oppose the protective tariff, **(1782–** a stand which he presently had to undergo the embarrass- **1852)** ment of reversing. His removal to Boston in 1816 took him out of the House, though his appearance before the Supreme Court as counsel on the nationalist side of several significant cases kept him before the public eye. He returned to the House from Boston in 1823, and presently (still a Federalist) he was elected to the Senate.

Dark-skinned and raven-haired, Webster was in his youth known as "Black Dan." As he grew older his high forehead and cavernous eyes, added to a talent for the florid oratory then in fashion, gave him a reputation for intellect and statesmanship rather beyond his real capacity;

worshipers called him "The Godlike Daniel." Never a rich man, but with a taste for ease and luxury, his unfortunate speculations made him dependent upon the "best" element for legal retainers and destroyed his chances of building up the popular support necessary for a march to the presidency in a democracy. His later years were hampered by poor health and alcoholism. Nevertheless, his eloquent and consistent support of nationalism (after 1815) made him the personification of national union in the eyes of the people.

John Quincy Adams, the eldest son of the second President, was educated largely in Paris and The Hague, though he added a Harvard degree and a training in law. He was probably, so far as learning and experience were concerned, the best-prepared man ever to reach the **John Quincy Adams (1767–1848)** presidency. After a varied diplomatic career in many European capitals he entered Congress in 1803 as a Federalist Senator from Massachusetts. Too honest and intelligent (and perhaps impractical) to follow the party line, he drifted away and in 1808 resigned rather than oppose the Embargo. He then re-entered the diplomatic service and in 1814 became chief of the American delegation to the Ghent negotiations. After two years as minister to London he was appointed Secretary of State by Monroe in 1817.

The passing of John Quincy Adams from the diplomatic scene marked the beginning of the age of decline in the handling of foreign affairs; headlong democracy now had its innings, and down to World War II foreign missions were political plums rather than significant outworks for the defense of American interests. By 1824 Adams had become the outstanding son of New England in the national scene. Usually recognized as a man of ability, integrity, courage, and learning, he unfortunately antagonized the public by his cold demeanor and politicians by his lack of pliability. Elected President by circumstances, he was unwilling to consolidate his position by trading favors for loyalty. In consequence he was an easy mark for his personal and political rivals, but he accepted their abuse in dignified silence. That he nursed deep hostilities we know from his diary, and its publication was to give him many a posthumous revenge on the pages of historians.

Martin Van Buren, born of thrifty Dutch stock near Albany, became a lawyer by the apprentice method then in vogue and fought his way up in politics as a member of the Clinton-Livingston faction of the Republican Party. Even-tempered, tactful, and personally honest, **Martin Van Buren (1782–1862)** he yet won a well-deserved reputation as a crafty and ruthless political manipulator. De Witt Clinton, heir of George Clinton, was opposed in his Erie Canal program by a Republican faction known as the Bucktails. Though Van Buren voted for the canal, he took advantage of the split to make himself head of the insurgents and won election to the United States Senate (1820).

During his absences in Washington, affairs at Albany were managed by his lieutenants, a hard-headed group of politicians known as the Albany Regency. In this group were many men later prominent in national affairs, including William L. Marcy and two post-Civil War Democratic presidential candidates: Horatio Seymour and Samuel Tilden. The Regency did much to develop the modern political machine with its rigid party discipline, manipulation of conventions, and the deliberate use of the spoils system. It was Marcy who first used in this connection the cynical phrase, "To the victor belong the spoils." Nevertheless the Van Buren ascendance in New York marked fulfillment of the demand for manhood suffrage and made that state the bulwark of the democratic movement. Van Buren was also the real organizer of the modern Democratic Party and the molder of the issues which it normally upheld during the remainder of the nineteenth century.

Albany Regency

Passing to Kentucky, we find Henry Clay, who was born during the Revolution into the family of a Baptist minister in a war-ravaged region called the Slashes, on the Virginia frontier. He studied law in Richmond and at the age of twenty took up its practice in Lexington, Kentucky. Tall, pleasing in appearance even though far from handsome, and a warm and colorful orator, Clay possessed a fascinating personality and remarkable social gifts. Though never more than half-educated he knew human nature, played the game of politics superbly, and inspired an intensely loyal following. Possibly he would have been more successful without so many gifts, for he inspired jealousy as well as loyalty. He was fond of cards, horse racing, and convivial companionship over the flowing bowl, and his sensitivity to honor led him into several useless duels; these traits, so common in his day, played into the hands of his enemies. At any rate, his political rise was phenomenally rapid. He sat in the Senate before the legal age of thirty, served as Speaker during his first term in the House, and on his return from Ghent resumed the speakership. In this advantageous position he was able to promote both his nationalistic ideals and his own ambitions.

Henry Clay (1777–1852)

By no means as significant politically as Jackson and Clay, yet more clearly representative of the West was Thomas Hart Benton. Son of a prominent North Carolina Loyalist, Benton ("*Bayn*-ton, sir") studied law, engaged in Tennessee politics, feuded with Andrew Jackson, fought under Jackson against the Creeks, then moved on to Missouri and became that state's perennial Senator. Benton was a lifelong advocate of cheap land, national expansion, and internal improvements. His championship of hard money led to the coinage of gold ("Benton's mint drops") and gave him the nickname of "Old Bullion," in which he took pride. A strong upholder of the Union,

Thomas Hart Benton (1782–1858)

he edged toward gradual emancipation as a solution of the slavery problem because he felt that slavery was hindering the growth of the West.

John Caldwell Calhoun was the only statesman of the Silver Age (aside from Adams) whose reputation for intellectual depth has come through without serious challenge. Born into a prosperous slaveholding Scotch-Irish family in the South Carolina uplands, Calhoun had the advantage of a Yale degree and of a broad legal training in Tapping Reeve's law school at Litchfield, Connecticut. The rise of the strikingly handsome and able young lawyer was aided by marriage to an aristocratic lowland cousin, for their combined inheritances enabled him to follow his taste for public service with minimum financial worries. Elected to Congress as a War Hawk, he worked assiduously for victory and was called "the young Hercules who carried the war on his shoulders." After the war he accepted appointment as Monroe's Secretary of War, consciously intending to build an administrative record which should lead to the presidency.

John C. Calhoun (1782–1850)

Conviction made him throw himself into promoting the nationalist program, but by 1832 the march of events had thrust him forward as a southern sectional leader. However much he might claim that he had never varied in his beliefs, but that the North was upsetting the Constitutional balance between states and nation, he is remembered as the father of secession. Calhoun had no perceptible sense of humor, and as his years and frustrations waxed he became more than ever cold, logical, intolerant, and rigidly self-righteous. And yet he probably thought of himself as a reasonable and compromising man.

At the head of the pack of ambitious younger men was the Georgia lawyer and politician William Harris Crawford. As Senator he took his place as a leader of the state-rights, antibanking school which swore by the Kentucky and Virginia Resolutions. After service as minister to France and Secretary of War he became Secretary of the Treasury, a position which he held from 1816 to 1825. Crawford was a man of gigantic stature, handsome, able, and affable; he had killed his man in a duel and had suffered the permanent crippling of a wrist. So great was his ascendancy that he was the only rival seriously to dispute Monroe's nomination in 1816, and he was the aspirant regarded as most likely to succeed him.

William H. Crawford (1772–1834)

The Young Republicans agreed rather generally on a four-point program: (1) strengthen the army, navy, and coast defenses; (2) extend internal improvements at Federal expense; (3) set up a Second Bank of the United States; and (4) adopt a protective tariff. Madison acceded to this program though, as it proved, such old "cocked hats" as he and Monroe still had their doubts on Constitutional grounds. At any rate, Calhoun was able to reorganize the

Nationalist program

Military Academy at West Point, to build modest coast defenses, and to increase the regular army to ten thousand men. At the same time the tiny navy was about doubled.

Calhoun championed internal improvements as the only counteractant to sectional rivalry and proposed a network of military highways and canals which would also be useful for posts and commerce. The National (or Cumberland) Road, begun in 1811 to connect East and **Internal improvements** West, was completed from Cumberland, Maryland to Wheeling, on the Ohio, by 1818. Internal improvements, however, received two sharp setbacks. The first was Madison's veto of the Bonus Bill which would have appropriated to internal improvements the $1,500,000 which the Second Bank was to pay into the Treasury. The second shock came in 1822, when Monroe vetoed the Cumberland Road Tolls Bill which proposed to collect tolls on the road in order to pay for maintenance. Both Madison and Monroe were willing to support internal improvements at Federal expense provided they were authorized by a Constitutional amendment, but eastern and southern interests opposed subsidization of the West.

The War of 1812 had clearly demonstrated the chaos of public and private finances. The number of state-chartered banks had risen from four in 1790 to two hundred eight in 1815, but the best of them were in New England and were not disposed to finance the war. **The banking problem** State banks, indeed, rejoiced at the death of the First Bank of the United States, for they expected to get the business. They did. But their operations outside New England were so optimistically (or at times criminally) conducted that they had lost great sums in land speculations, and their paper currency was almost valueless. Since cheap money drives out good, specie had disappeared into private hoards or taken refuge in New England. In spite of this, people in general, especially in the South and West, favored cheap money and opposed a national bank because it would limit available cash (that is, paper currency) and bring hardship on speculators and debtors. New England bankers joined the hue and cry, for they were no more anxious than other local bankers to have their business cut into and perhaps controlled by a great national institution.

Nevertheless, the Young Republicans did not propose that the government should be caught short again, and so in 1816 they authorized the Second Bank of the United States, which came to be known familiarly as **B. U. S.** B. U. S. It was chartered for twenty years; had a capital of $35,000,000, one fifth subscribed by the government and the rest by private individuals; had a monopoly on government business; and could establish branch banks to facilitate exchange. Management of B. U. S. was in a board of twenty-five managers, five of them appointed by the President. For its charter of privileges B. U. S. was to pay into the Treasury of the United States a bonus of $1,500,000.

Hamilton's hope of using a protective tariff to foster American manufactures had fallen foul of the merchant interests of New England and the agrarians of South and West. The Embargo and the War of 1812 by reducing imports had fostered American manufactures to the point where optimists could glimpse early industrial independence. Then at the close of the war British manufacturers dumped their surpluses into the country at absurdly low prices—whether or not they were seeking, as was claimed, to stifle American industry in the cradle. The nationalists retorted in 1816 by a tariff, introduced by South Carolina's Lowndes and supported by its Calhoun, which levied duties of around twenty-five per cent. As events were to prove, it was not effective against British exporters. *Protective tariff*

We have already seen John Marshall as a diplomat, a Federalist politician, and as fighting a rear-guard action from a judicial road block for the defeated Hamiltonian forces. With the rise of Neo-Hamiltonianism Marshall found that his rear guard had become the vanguard of the new nationalism. Marshall, although born and reared on the Virginia frontier, was psychologically allied with the Federalists even more than were his aristocratic kin, the Randolphs. It is perhaps significant that Lord Fairfax, English nobleman and holder of vast lands in Virginia, vitally influenced the lives of George Washington and Thomas Marshall, the father of John. Young Marshall's legal education was interrupted by long and rigorous service as a combat soldier in the Revolution. Black-haired and black-avised John Marshall, though loose-jointed and afflicted with lifelong gawkiness, made rapid headway at the Richmond bar, at that time the most brilliant in the young country. Never profoundly learned in English law, Marshall found this no handicap, for English precedents were temporarily out of favor. He was at his best, in fact, in setting his own common-law precedents and convincing the Virginia bench of their validity. *John Marshall (1755–1835)*

After Marshall's ascent to the Supreme Court, Jefferson's sweeping attack on the Federalist judges seems seriously to have disturbed his self-assurance, and he was actually ready to yield to Congress some of the principles on which his fame is based. The acquittal of Chase, however, bolstered his courage. Thereafter, no matter what fire-eating Republicans the Virginia dynasty might set on the bench, Marshall's clarity of reasoning and charm of manner steadily converted them to his opinions. The two principles steadfastly validated by his decisions were (1) the supremacy of the Federal government and (2) the role of the Supreme Court as the arbiter between states and nation and of the Constitutionality of legislative and *Marshall's Constitutional principles*

executive actions. He did not, of course, draw these Constitutional principles out of the air (though the Old Republicans accused him of it) but
"found" them implied in the Constitution itself.

Though Marshall was inclined to set his own common-law precedents,
other judges saw that the bumptious American sense of legalism would
demand legislative action unless long-accepted common-law standards
Adaptation were observed. It was noted in an early chapter that the
of the Eng- acceptance of Natural Rights, especially in the role of prop-
lish com- erty as the automatic regulator of social order, had resulted
mon law in the freezing of the common law of England, except as
needed to protect property. American patriots, anxious to be independent
in all matters, proposed the formation of a more democratic code of laws,
but the movement was stopped cold by two great jurists. They were
Joseph Story of Massachusetts, associate of John Marshall on the Supreme Court bench, and James Kent, Chancellor of the State of New
York. Their method was to show that English common law was based on
natural law (moral law to the more pious) and must therefore of course
be accepted. Their lives were devoted to fitting the common law of England to the facts, at least the supposed facts, of American conditions.

Now where law is supreme, there is a tendency for the lawyer to become supreme because the law is a "mystery" known only to the initiated.
That the law was chiefly concerned with the protection of individual
The law as rights, principally those relating to property, does not mean
a "mystery" that the Supreme Court was consciously promoting control
by big property, for its decisions were aimed at giving little
business a break as well—and this was then a nation of little business.
The Federal government was defended against the assaults of the states
because the latter were presumably more open to control by wild and subversive interests which would attack property. On the other hand, since
the law is the lawyer's life, he finds it to his interest to preserve it from
heedless executive and legislative encroachments; he watches over it
with a jealous care which the average citizen, even in a democracy, would
never have the knowledge or patience to imitate. On the whole the
method works amazingly well.

To the lawyer, then, principally in the persons of the jurists of the
Supreme Court, goes the credit for making the slightly considered third
branch of the Federal government a decisive instrument for preserving
The balance within that government and between it and the
Supreme states. It paved the legal road for the creation of a nation
Court as in place of the congeries of sovereign states which existed at
creator of the outset of the nineteenth century, and whose rivalries
the nation among themselves and with the Federal government might
have torn the Union apart. Marshall, Story, and Kent also laid the necessary foundations for the growth of industrial capitalism.

Let us indicate briefly the great Constitutional decisions made by the Supreme Court under the influence of Marshall. We have noted already the case of *Marbury v. Madison* (1803), which asserted the right of the Court to pass upon the Constitutionality of Congressional legislation. It is evident now (from British experience, for example) that this is not the only way to handle the problem, but it has won general acceptance in spite of complaints that have continued down to our own day.

Judicial review

The principle that in case of conflict the power of the Supreme Court transcends that of state legislatures was asserted in the case of the *United States v. Judge Peters* (1809). At the request of the Attorney-General, the Supreme Court ordered Judge Richard Peters of the Federal District of Pennsylvania to enforce an old ruling which was intensely unpopular in the state. A Federal *posse comitatus* was gathered to oppose the state militia, and the state yielded. State courts were subsequently declared inferior to the Supreme Court in decisions on Federal rights; the two chief vehicles were cases involving Marshall's own state of Virginia, *Martin v. Hunter's Lessee* (1816) and *Cohen v. Virginia* (1821).

Federal sovereignty

These and other lessons were driven home by the decision in the famous case of *McCulloch v. Maryland* (1819). Opposition to B. U. S. had reached such a pitch that Maryland undertook to tax the Baltimore Branch out of existence and defended its action on the ground that the institution was unconstitutional. When the case finally reached the Supreme Court Marshall upheld Federal sovereignty and Hamilton's doctrine of implied powers. "Let the end be legitimate, let it be within the scope of the Constitution, and all means which are appropriate, which are plainly adapted to that end, which are not prohibited, but consist with the letter and spirit of the Constitution, are Constitutional." At the same time he swept away the states' power to tax Federal institutions and Federally-paid income on the ground that "the power to tax is the power to destroy"; by such means a state might strip the Federal government of any power that it chose. This prohibition still stands, though the Federal government is now self-assured enough to grant to the states limited taxing powers over Federal employees.

Implied powers

Fear of the power of the democratic element over state actions had led the Constitutional Convention to prohibit the states from passing any law "impairing the obligation of contracts." The Yazoo frauds reached the Supreme Court in the action of *Fletcher v. Peck* (1810), and the decision was that contracts made by a state were binding, even if they were fraudulent in origin. This decision was riveted more tightly by the decision in *Dartmouth College v. Woodward* (1819), the famous Dartmouth College Case. The

Federal defense of private property

state of New Hampshire, anxious to democratize the college, had taken it over and abrogated its colonial charter. The old trustees refused to give way; and their case, argued by Daniel Webster, was supported by the Supreme Court on the ground that a charter was a contract which could not be revoked by the state. This decision in large measure freed existing business corporations from state control and was an immense boon to the development of laissez faire. Later generations have found ways of limiting the practically sovereign powers of corporations.

The problems of Federal control of interstate commerce came up in *Gibbons v. Ogden* (1824). Ogden held a license to operate a steam ferry between New York and New Jersey, granted by Livingston and Fulton **Federal** under their New York monopoly of steam navigation on **control of** the Hudson. Ogden's monopoly was assailed by a rival, Gib-**interstate** bons, who was represented by a battery of legal talent **commerce** headed by Webster. The decision was that in granting to Congress control of commerce "among the several States" the Constitution included not only buying and selling but navigation and other intercourse. Since interstate commerce must also necessarily be within the states, no state could limit commerce or navigation which was carried on across state lines. The tremendous effect of this decision will become apparent later on.

The Young Republican honeymoon was too good to last. B. U. S., unfortunately, had engaged in unwise speculations and had sought to destroy a number of state banks by accumulating their currency and then **Panic of** suddenly demanding payment in specie. There were, of **1819** course, other causes also, but 1819 saw widespread business collapse and plummeting prices. Land speculators and *bona fide* settlers suffered; manufacturers, already pressed by British competition, went to the wall. B. U. S. itself had loaned generously on land, and now when it foreclosed the farmers resented its "soulless" behavior and began to call it a "monopoly." Congress passed relief legislation and shook up and reorganized B. U. S., but a movement to protect industry by a higher tariff failed until in 1824 the manufacturers got the support of wool growers by a duty on raw wool.

Monroe's second term was marked by frank jockeying among presidential aspirants. The fact that Crawford had the inside track with Monroe and Congress forced other would-be candidates to oppose the **Rival can-** caucus system. One man after another was put into nomi-**didates in** nation by state legislatures and mass meetings. Neverthe-**1824** less, Crawford led the field until late in 1823, when he was laid low by a paralytic stroke; the illness did his candidacy irreparable damage. Jackson, then a Senator, took the lead. Adams was supported rather reluctantly by New England, but the section had no other man of equal stature to put forth. Calhoun, only forty-two, felt that he could afford to wait and was by general consent awarded the vice-presidential plum.

Clay, the most politically minded of the candidates, realized that growing sectional rivalries were a serious threat to the continuation of the Union, and during the debates on the tariff of 1824 he proposed his American System as a means of reconciling differences by providing something for everybody. He would make the country industrially self-sufficient by a protective tariff. **Clay's American System** More mills would use more southern cotton. More mill operatives would wear more shirts made from southern cotton and eat more western grain and pork. The sale of more cotton and food would enable South and West to buy more shirts and farm tools made in the East. The problem of transportation would be solved by turning the tariff revenues over to the construction of internal improvements. The whole thing had a fallacious ring to many people, like the joke about the mink and rat farm where the minks ate rats and the rats ate the skinned carcasses of the minks. Nevertheless, some such means of living by taking in each other's washing is the way the world actually gets along.

Clay's proposals, intended not only to be constructive but to smoke out his rivals, forced the other candidates to hedge on the issue of tariff and internal improvements. When the electoral votes were counted it was found that each section had pretty well voted for its favorite son, and that only Jackson had drawn significant support outside his own area. Attempts to evaluate public **Election of J. Q. Adams** opinion are useless; in six states the electors were appointed by the legislatures, in only five other states were all four candidates represented by electoral candidates, and in no state did the voters turn out in significant numbers. In the end the electoral vote was: Jackson 99, Adams 84, Crawford 41, Clay 37. Since the House now had to choose from the three highest, Clay was eliminated. Clay and Adams had never been particularly cordial, but since Adams came closest to espousing the American System, Clay threw his support to him. Adams won by the vote of thirteen states, against Jackson's seven, and Crawford's four; New York swung the election by the vote of one representative.

Adams's offer of the State Department portfolio to Clay immediately raised a carefully calculated shout among Jackson's supporters that the candidate of the people had been bilked of office by a "corrupt bargain." John Randolph acidly declaimed that the union of Adams and Clay was the coalition of "the puritan with the black- **The cry of "corrupt bargain"** leg." Clay promptly challenged Randolph to a duel; unfortunately both missed. Jackson was slow in playing up to the opportunity, but presently, when the presidential bug had eaten far enough into his vitals, he added his stentorian cries to the charges of robbery. Clay had earned his bitter hatred by explaining that Adams, as a statesman, was more entitled to support than Jackson, the "military chieftain." There is no clear proof that Clay's support had been purchased; and even if it had been, we would now regard the action as sanctified by custom. Nevertheless, it made a powerful appeal to the little people, already irked by B. U. S., who were becoming resentful of what they regarded as the leaders' manipulation of public policies for their own political ends. The fat was in the fire. Adams's administration was to become an Era of Hard Feeling.

No more high-minded man ever occupied the White House, but probably no President except Andrew Johnson and Woodrow Wilson ever endured more disappointments or ended his term in more bitter frustra-

The greatness and failure of J. Q. Adams
tion. Adams sought diligently to promote internal improvements, manufactures, and the march of science. He wished to make the public lands a source of regular income (particularly for the financing of internal improvements) instead of recklessly throwing them to squatters and speculators; such a policy naturally outraged the West. He even sought to decelerate the waste of natural resources, and the public gasped in wrath or amusement. Adams was indeed far ahead of his time, for he envisioned something very like the modern service state. He wished the government actually to promote and protect the public welfare and to tax away speculative profits and the unearned increment of land because they were the creation of society, not of the individual. It was not until he was out of the presidency and back in Congress as a humble representative—"Old Man Eloquent"—that he found some of the approval and loyalty which he had vainly sought even in New England. The true accolade came only after his death, when the vitriolic Theodore Parker wrote that he was "the one man since Washington, whom America had no cause to fear."

2   Democracy and Sectionalism

The political situation in the 1820's and 1830's was complicated by two trends that were, in that generation at least, quite irreconcilable. One was a movement for the enlargement of democracy; the other was

Irreconcilable trends
the growth of sectional divergencies. This statement is perhaps an oversimplification. Actually the purpose of the democratic movement was to enhance local controls, and to do so it seized the Federal government in order to shear away its powers. The effect (as it had been under Jefferson) was to make the nation stronger, at least in certain ways, and to promote nationalism.

Presently there emerged two wings of the democratic movement. One wing insisted that only by exalting the states could democracy survive; its weapons became state rights and sectionalism and finally southern nationalism. The other wing asserted that the strength necessary for democracy's survival in a hostile world could be furnished only by stressing the Union more than the states. In the struggle between the two the democratic movement faltered, then yielded precedence to the great issue of whether or not the nation should live.

The partial triumph of Neo-Hamiltonianism galled the remaining Old Jeffersonians, and they promoted the resurgence of democracy as a remedy for hard times. The people, looking about for a scapegoat, were ready to find simple causes and to be sold on simple cures. What **Origins of** could be more simple than to assert that the people had lost **the demo-** control of their government since 1800, and what more **cratic revolt** simple cure could be found than to get it back? Politicians scurried to take advantage of popular resentments—undoubtedly they often shared them—and they filled the air with outcries and the newspapers with denunciations. The nationalist program had all been for the benefit of business, so democratic fury focused upon upsetting it.

It has often been the custom to picture this democratic resurgence, called the Jacksonian Movement, as sweeping out of the West like a great wave. Actually it came from all parts of the Union. Look at the numerous local causes of complaint. The West was convinced that **Local** New England was blocking cheap land and internal im- **complaints** provements; the South blamed the Northeast for raising the prices of manufactured goods by the tariff; the Northeast blamed the rest of the country for bringing on the crash by its razzle-dazzle bank currency. Pretty nearly everyone in trouble blamed B. U. S. for its attempt to gain a monopoly of currency and attacked the Supreme Court for promoting national power. Eastern laborers complained that their wages were oppressively low and that employers could cheat them with impunity, for of course a poor man could not afford expensive legal redress. Moreover, membership in unions was punished by loss of the job, and courts went out of their way to prevent and to punish strikes. Laborers did not generally oppose the tariff in itself; they merely saw it as a weapon for the consolidation of the power of their oppressors.

In the East and South state constitutions preserved many earmarks of the conservative reaction of the 1780's, and suffrage was still based on property. State churches survived in New England. Presidential electors as late as 1824 had been chosen by the legislatures in six states. It was inevitable that a movement with so many springs should be amorphous. It was by no means confined to the common people and their political leaders. The ironmasters of Pennsylvania saw a chance to trade votes for a tariff on iron. State bankers saw a rich opportunity to overthrow their enemy, B. U. S. The landed aristocracy, still charmed by American Physiocratic doctrines, joined in the attacks on their old enemies, the merchants and manufacturers. Even the leader of the movement was a poor boy who had fought his way up into the aristocracy and had become its leader in Tennessee.

The democratic wave began in the states and then invaded national politics, though it continued to swell in some of the states even after it had subsided on the national scene. In the states it was led by a remark-
The demo- able galaxy of men, some of them horny-handed tribunes of
cratic move- the people, others ambitious young fellows from the élite—
ment in the one of them the son of Alexander Hamilton!—who rode to
states fame on the tide. Like the Jeffersonian movement before it
and every effective political reform movement since, the leaders were realists who carried daggers up their sleeves and got what they went after, whether it meant trading with the enemy or embracing a political friend and stabbing him in the back. Corruption was as much a weapon of the democratic movement as of the conservatives; and, indeed, it was the democratic leaders who invented the modern machine, fed it on the spoils of office, and manipulated it to seize control of political conventions from the old-line conservatives. The early phase of the democratic movement in the states is too complicated to be followed here, but we can indicate its main features.

The victory of manhood suffrage came in this period. Pennsylvania had taxpayers' franchise from the first, and by 1790 it was joined by Georgia and New Hampshire. Vermont, from its admission, was first to
The march institute manhood suffrage. During the Jeffersonian period
of liberal there was considerable agitation; Maryland removed re-
suffrage strictions, and other states lightened their property qualifi-
cations. All the states west of the Appalachians except Kentucky and Tennessee entered the Union with male suffrage or light tax-paying qualifications, and the exceptions were swept aside in every case before the Civil War. The western example was a challenge to the East, and after bitter fights in most cases manhood suffrage or taxpayers' suffrage was adopted in Connecticut (1818), Maine (1820), New York (1821), and for voting for most offices in Massachusetts (1820).

Virginia was split wide open between the East and the West; and though manhood suffrage was granted in 1850, the long struggle over dominance by Tidewater had so embittered the West that the formation of West Virginia in 1863 was no surprise to the observant. North Carolina kept taxpayers' qualifications as late as 1857. South Carolina, though never regarded as a democratic state, essentially instituted manhood suf-

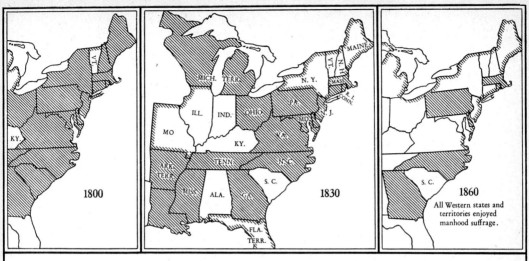

THE MARCH OF MANHOOD SUFFRAGE 1800, 1830, AND 1860

Shaded states and territories reserved the suffrage to property holders or taxpayers. Some of the others set property qualifications but permitted an alternative such as a period of residence.

frage as early as 1810 by permitting a residential qualification as a substitute for property; however, legislative districts were so arranged as to keep control in the coastal area. Most of the northeastern states agreed to a liberal suffrage partly, at least, because they hoped it would persuade labor not to go west. It must be noted, however, that these presumed victories were sometimes vitiated by the retention of property qualifications for candidates for office.

In Rhode Island, where the colonial charter was still in force, industrial workers were largely excluded because they were not freeholders. In 1841 the excluded citizens, led by Thomas W. Dorr, drew up a constitution, elected Dorr as governor, and set up their own legisla- **Dorr's** ture. This was rebellion, and the conservatives twice chased **Rebellion** Dorr from the state and upon his second return tried him for treason and sentenced him to life imprisonment. By this time the state was so aroused that the conservatives set up a new constitution (1842) which granted all but full manhood suffrage and later released Dorr.

Along with the widening of the franchise went a movement for new state constitutions. In general there was a tendency to limit further the power of the governor, to provide for the popular election of judges, to encourage public schools, and to clear the way for state investments in public works such as roads and canals. Along **Other** with this movement went a demand that presidential elec- **reforms** tors be popularly elected, a demand which was granted by 1832 except in South Carolina. Public resentment against "monopoly" promoted the loosening of bankruptcy laws in order to permit the farmer and the small businessman to escape from their obligations and start over. These bankruptcy laws were to prove unexpectedly welcome to big operators with defective consciences. In New England the Congregational was still the state church in four states. The Jeffersonian movement had managed to disestablish the church in Vermont (1807), but elsewhere all citizens who could not prove that they were financially supporting their own church were forced to pay tithes for the support of the state church and its clergy. After bitter battles the tithes were wiped out, and the churches were disestablished in Connecticut (1818), New Hampshire (1819), Maine (1820), and Massachusetts (1834).

In New York the surviving manors of the patroons gave an anachronistic feudal color to the Hudson River Valley by the survival of leaseholds which had to be paid for by an annual tribute of money, labor, or produce. By 1839 the farmers had become so irked with their feudal dues that they rose in a movement known as the **Antirent agitation** Antirent Agitation (core of which was the Helderberg War), tarred and feathered the patroons' collectors, murdered a deputy sheriff, and at times had to be suppressed by militia. Nevertheless, the agitation made political headway. The new state constitution of 1846 and a handy court decision finally put an end to feudal dues, and the ownership of the old leaseholds was converted to fee simple.

The older historians viewed sections primarily as ideological alliances, but Frederick Jackson Turner demonstrated that they were and are at **Sectional shifts: New England** bottom economic and cultural areas. Here let us briefly analyze the changing interests of the sections in the 1820's. New England's commercial interests had backed Hamilton in the 1790's, but they now stoutly opposed the revival of his program. They opposed B. U. S. because they had sound banks of their own and wanted no Federally-licensed competition. They opposed internal improvements at Federal expense because they would be in the West, so New England while sharing the expense could not hope to benefit. They opposed cheap land because it would draw away New England's labor force. Most of all they opposed the protective tariff because it would reduce the imports on which mercantile life depended.

New England was in opposition, and such support as it gave Adams was largely because he was a home boy. The 1820's, however, saw a change. B. U. S. was supported because it promoted sound banking in the nation. Cheap land was still opposed, but immigration became a source of the needed labor. Most significant of all, industries reached the point where they overbalanced merchant interests and forced New England to plump for the protective tariff. Daniel Webster, who had made a name as the champion of sectionalism and free trade, now had to swallow his speeches and become the champion of nationalism and protection.

The Middle States section shifted only to strengthen its support of the tariff. It regarded movement to the West and the cheapening of public lands with disfavor but made the best of them. After all, the West was an important source of raw materials, a tremendous potential market for eastern manufactured goods, and the handling of its agricultural exports to the world was a rich plum for the middlemen. Both New York and Philadelphia definitely planned to reverse the downstream tide of western commerce to New Orleans and bring it pouring over the mountains to their docks. On the whole, New England and the Middle States were approaching the point where, as the Northeast, they could find common grounds for action.

The Mid-dle States

The Older South (or Southeast) had been temporarily shaken by nationalist forces. Virginia's declining fertility enabled South Carolina to displace it as leader of the South. South Carolina itself was menaced by declining fertility, and its brilliant young leaders dreamed of using the South's cotton, water power, coal, and iron to industrialize the area. But setting up factories did not turn out to be easy, nor did Negroes give promise of being efficient operatives; moreover, southern mores looked with disapproval upon a gentleman going into industry. The booming demand from England and New England for cotton after the War of 1812 gave a delusory promise of better times, and anyhow surplus slaves could be sold at good prices to work on the fertile new cotton plantations in the Gulf states. When northern capitalists opposed slavery in the new state of Missouri, South Carolina was offended at their specious assumption of moral superiority. As for the tariff, it was clear that discrimination against cheap English textiles and hardware would lead to English discrimination against cotton.

The Older South

The whole result was that South Carolina resisted Calhoun's arguments and decided to continue growing cotton—and blame the tariff for its low profits. If there were no protective tariff on manufactured goods, it argued, the prices of those goods would decrease because of English competition, and the Older South could still make a good profit. The rivers of the Older South gave it fairly satisfactory transportation, so for a while at least it sought national economy by opposing internal improvements and the cheapening of western land, though strangely enough it only slowly turned against B. U. S. Calhoun, who had led the nationalists, had to choose between the nation and the section. It was probably the bitterest choice an American politician ever had to make, but his roots were in his section and held him there. He did the best he could to show that he had wanted and still wanted a *reasonable* tariff, but the northern trend was against him; he saw himself isolated with his section, and his ambition to become President ended in bitter disappointment.

The West, the vast area between the Appalachian Mountains and the Great Plains, was already beginning to split. True, almost everyone

favored cheap land, and even the speculators wanted internal improvements at Federal expense. Western state banks printed cur-

The West rency in large amounts and loaned generously; they were
called wildcat banks because they were located in out-of-the-way places
where their currency was not likely to be presented for payment, but the
name also carried some concept of their wild way of doing business. Wildcat inflation had its drawbacks, but to a region which badly needed credit
for land purchases and public improvements it was preferable to the
cautious and conservative way in which B. U. S. doled out credit.   . .

The West pretty generally united in opposing B. U. S. Some men, like
Jackson, even went so far as to reject paper currency because it gave
the banker a throttle hold on the credit life of the community, and they
advocated that business be carried on in gold and silver specie. Such hard-
money men did not oppose banks as mere "offices of discount and deposit" but as creators of credit and currency. The real point of dissension
in the West was the tariff. In the heyday of nationalism it had been popular; but as the cotton Southwest grasped the South Carolina doctrine, it
saw that a low tariff would enable it to keep a larger profit. The Ohio
Valley, on the other hand, still expecting to become a manufacturing region—as it did—leaned toward the protective tariff.

With due regard to individual and subregional differences, we can
thus express the desires of each section in their order of importance
about the end of the 1820's.* It will be noticed that slavery as yet played

Sectional no positive part in this line-up, though the Missouri Com-
desires promise of 1820 had given warning of an eventual prob-
about 1828 lem.

Northwest	*Northeast*
Low-priced land	High tariff
Internal improvements	High-priced land
High tariff	Internal improvements
Southwest	*Southeast*
Low-priced land	Low tariff
Low tariff	No internal improvements
Internal improvements	High-priced land

It can readily be seen that here were the elements of political bargains, but until conditions changed, little hope of permanent understand-
ings. The politicians tried, but they seemed doomed to futility. The three
sections (Northeast, Southeast, and West) were in approxi-

Sectional mate balance about 1830. No one section could get what it
rivalries wanted without another's help, so Southeast and Northeast
contended for the aid of the West. The latter section was growing rapidly

* See Raynor G. Wellington, *Political and Sectional Influence of the Public Lands,
1828–1842* (1914).

and seemed destined to control the Union—which it might have, had it not split apart. At any rate, the West was willing to help whoever would help it to what it wanted: low-priced land. After Jackson removed internal improvements from big-time politics, tariff and public lands were linked as political problems. Clay was active in trying to please both New England and the West, but he was unable to make his program palatable. Land sales were booming in the early thirties, and the proceeds were so high that it was proposed that the tariff be lowered. Clay was alarmed, and his Distribution Bill of 1833 would have reduced the surplus by distributing it to the states, thus saving the tariff and giving something to everyone. Jackson was also in the giving mood and contributed a pocket veto.

The majority in the West rejected Clay's program, and after Jackson's time the Federal government was normally controlled by an uneasy alliance of agrarian West and Southeast. At the same time changing directions of commerce and increasing industrialization of the Northwest gradually pulled Northwest and Northeast **Later sectional shifts** together. At the same time the Older South and Old Southwest drew together. We might thus illustrate the sectional changes which developed by 1860.

New England + Middle States = Northeast (East) + Old Northwest = The North.

Older South + Old Southwest = The South (the Old South, Dixie, The Cotton Kingdom).

The election of 1824 had shown that the nation was so well divided between sectional favorite sons that only by political maneuvering could a reasonably clear-cut decision be made in 1828. The Jackson men proceeded to groom their "military hero" as the single person **The Jackson coalition** around whom the nation could rally. The Jackson legend was their ace in the hole. Even Clay, the protective-tariff champion of Northeast and Northwest, never managed to counteract its spell. Crawford, now permanently retired, turned his support to Jackson, hoping that he would uphold state rights. Calhoun threw his support to Jackson on the understanding that he should continue as Vice-President and crown prince and after four years should become Jackson's successor. The master stroke of Jackson's supporters, however, was their annexation of the democratic revolt. The democrats had the issues which appealed to the voters, they possessed the political machines, and they were able to get out the vote; the Jackson men had the nation's only outstanding hero. Together the two were unbeatable. The Jacksonians and the democrats were bitterly anti-British (as the Jeffersonians had been) and by twisting the lion's tail attracted the Scotch-Irish, the Irish, and the Pennsylvania German vote. They opposed British investments and denounced

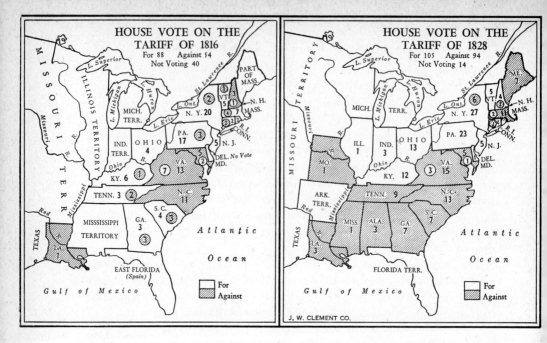

HOUSE VOTE ON THE TARIFF OF 1816
For 88   Against 54   Not Voting 40

HOUSE VOTE ON THE TARIFF OF 1828
For 105   Against 94   Not Voting 14

J. W. CLEMENT CO.

the payment of "tribute" to London bankers. Before long the very name "Democratic Party" (which came into use in the 1830's) was to attract immigrants, and party workers in the cities extended aid to bewildered and browbeaten foreigners and received votes in return.

The chief handicap of the Jackson strategists was that in order to win the presidency they would have to rally both the low-tariff South and the high-tariff North behind their man. Since Adams was the man to beat, they planned to maneuver his tariff support in New England from under him. Early in 1828 a bill, soon to be known as the Tariff of Abominations, was introduced with provisions suitable in general to the Middle States' manufacturers and to the Ohio Valley's wool and hemp growers but not favorable to New England's textile and rope manufacturers. Jackson men of all tariff shades were to unite to prevent New England amendments and then on the final vote to follow their sectional interests. To the amazement of the conspirators, enough New Englanders voted for the bill to pass it, thus marking the swing of New England's balance of power to industry. As a result southeastern low-tariff men felt that they had been sold out by Jackson. Calhoun, one of the engineers of the plot, feared that his chance for the presidency would be ruined if the Southeast abandoned Jackson, and he therefore counseled continued support in the hope that Jackson would remedy the injustice. The Southeast grumbled but yielded. Nevertheless, the two wings of the Republican Party, uneasy together since the days of Jefferson's Embargo, saw the gap widening between them.

Neither side in the campaign of 1828 pulled any punch, however foul. The old scandal of Jackson's marriage was raked over, and it hastened

448

the death of his beloved Rachel in December 1828. A scandal was manufactured in the Adams family, though Jackson sternly protested that he did not make war on "females." Jackson was **Campaign of 1828** portrayed by his followers as a paragon of simplicity in tastes and life, while the White House furniture was listed to prove Adams's aristocracy, and a billiard table and chess set were cited as evidence of gambling! Every effort was made on one side to portray Washington as filled with evil politicians bent on using an all-powerful Federal government to crush the liberties of the people and the states; on the other, Jackson and the democrats were portrayed as enemies of order, liberty, and property who would set up a guillotine before the Capitol. Suspicion was stirred between town and country, employer and worker, educated and uneducated. Each citizen had his reasons for believing that Armageddon was at hand and that perhaps his vote could swing the battle for the Lord.

At any rate, the voters turned out as they never had before, not even in 1800. The march of manhood suffrage and the demand for popular election of presidential electors gave more men the vote, though Delaware and South Carolina refused to go with the tide. Of the other twenty-two states four chose electors by districts; of these **Election of 1828** New York and Maryland divided, and Maine gave Jackson one vote. New England, New Jersey, and Delaware went for Adams, giving him 83 electoral votes to Jackson's 178. The first President from beyond the Appalachians came in by the combined efforts of West, Old South, and most of the Middle States' vote. Nevertheless, Jackson received something less than a landslide in the popular vote, for of about 1,150,000 ballots Adams received about forty-four per cent. Apparently not all the new voters had plumped for the "old hero."

3   The Reign of Old Hickory

The inauguration of Jackson marked a day of dedication, as though the country had been "rescued from some dreadful danger," as Webster put it. A reception at the White House planned for the "gentry" was overflowed by the *hoi polloi*, who stood on the satin chairs with **Inauguration of Jackson** their hobnailed boots, elbowed and fought their way to the refreshment tables, broke the glassware, and stole the silver spoons for souvenirs. Perhaps they were activated more by natural curiosity to see Old Hickory than by any sense of the high import of the day in the history of democracy. At any rate, they were thirsty, for when quick-witted servitors placed tubs of punch out on the lawn the crowd quickly lost interest in the interior of the White House. The scene afforded wry relief to the crushed spirits of many an "aristocrat," for they were as gloomy over the future as the Federalists had been in 1800 and never opened their papers without expecting news of a *coup d'état* by the "military hero." The prevailing alarm was even communicated to Europe, where among the aristocracy there was much satisfaction over the impending failure of the American democratic experiment.

New York Public Library

GERRYMANDERING received its name from an incident which occurred in 1812 when Elbridge Gerry was Democratic-Republican governor of Massachusetts. In order to preserve party control the legislature redistributed the districts with the result that one in Essex County assumed a dragon-like contour. One day the painter Gilbert Stuart saw the district outlined on a map hanging over the desk of Benjamin Russell, editor of the Boston *Centinel*. Stuart added a few strokes with his pencil and remarked that it would do for a salamander. "Better say a gerrymander," growled Russell. The name promptly came into general use.

The inauguration over and the debris cleared from the White House, the nation sat back and waited for the fireworks. None came. The fact was that the Jacksonians came into office with no program. How could such an amorphous movement have a program? Jackson had been elected by advocates and opponents of the tariff, by northern nationalists and southern state-righters, by hard-money men and wildcat bankers, and by land speculators and their victims. The West wanted internal improvements—but that was a National Republican plank. There was old John Marshall still grimly holding on in the Supreme Court, but that Federalist bastion was impregnable until death took its defenders. Indeed, the great reforms of Jackson's administration were undertaken so reluctantly that detractors have implied that they were forced upon him by the moves of his enemies in a complicated political chess game.

Lack of a program at the outset

Look at the record. The great domestic reforms on which Jackson's fame is based are four: (1) removal of the Indians beyond the Mississippi; (2) liberalization of land policies; (3) the Maysville Road Veto; and (4) the war on the Bank of the United States. The first two will be treated in later chapters, but we can note here that the Indians were forced out of the South only when Georgia took matters into its own hands, and that Jackson seems to have been indifferent to land problems and was needled into action only by Benton and his associates.

It looks very much as though the democratic leaders were interested primarily in the loaves and the fishes, though they did sniff out a few minor scandals and tried to make a noise like a new broom sweeping clean. This attempt was demonstrated chiefly by the removal and replacement of about ten per cent of the Federal civilian pay roll, actions which were, of course, attacked as the introduction of Van Buren's New York spoils system. They did open the way for the later introduction of the spoils system in force. Jackson believed in rotation in office, and he defended it not only on the ground

The spoils system

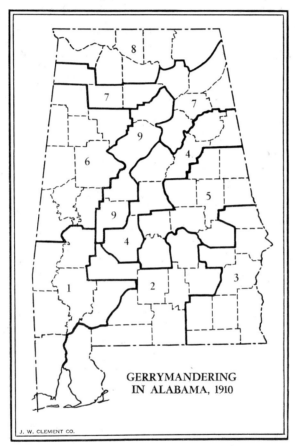

GERRYMANDERING
IN ALABAMA, 1910

J. W. CLEMENT CO.

that one intelligent man was as fit as another for office but on the principle long urged among democrats that rotation would keep officials on their toes and prevent the entrenchment of privilege. Jackson's appointments, however, were not uniformly good, and presently incompetence and sometimes corruption became evident.

Jackson's indubitable honesty and patriotism had given him a powerful popular appeal, but his "Jackson men" were too sophisticated to accept him at legendary value. They saw him as blunt, irascible, intoler-

Jackson's character

ant, obstinate, and politically and economically illiterate. As early as 1825 they persuaded him to retire from the Senate to the safety of The Hermitage, but during the long campaign they were continually haunted by the fear that he would spill the beans. But once he was settled in the presidency, he promptly made it clear that he was boss. He ran his party with an iron hand and preserved his ascendancy in the military manner. As a commander he had listened in council, taken no vote, and chosen his own course. Now he expected absolute obedience from his political followers. On the other hand, age had tempered him, and his famous rages were sometimes put on for effect. Still, with an adoring public at his door and sycophants at his elbow, it was natural for Jackson to accept his role as champion of the people. Anyone who persistently opposed him was obviously an enemy of the people.

At the time of the inauguration Jackson was ill, worn out, and depressed by the death of his beloved Rachel. When he recovered, however, it became evident that his Cabinet was merely political window dressing.

The Kitchen Cabinet

His real advisers, soon nicknamed the Kitchen Cabinet, were made up of those whom he trusted: Secretary of State Van Buren, Secretary of War John H. Eaton, and a shifting group which usually included the newspaper editors Amos Kendall and Francis Preston Blair. It may never be known whether Van Buren, the sly "Red Fox of Kinderhook," or the subtle Kendall was most influential; some historians insist that even from the first Jackson listened to advice but made up his own mind.

If the latter opinion is correct, Jackson showed a singular mixture of nobility and naïvety in the case of Mrs. Eaton. As the vivacious Peggy O'Neale, daughter of a Washington tavern keeper, Mrs. Eaton had been

The case of Mrs. Eaton

the toast of the blades in and out of Congress and the subject of many a sly wink. Two of the boarders at the O'Neale tavern were the Senators from Tennessee, Jackson and Eaton, and eventually there was gossip about the latter and the charming Peggy. After her husband, a naval purser, committed suicide while on service in the Mediterranean, she and Eaton were married. A few months later, when Eaton took over the War Department, the ladies of the Cabinet refused to receive his wife socially. Jackson, always chivalrous and mindful of the unjust scandal whose revival had hastened Rachel's death, sided with Mrs. Eaton. He even besought his Cabinet members to ask their wives to "arrange their parties" so that the world would not get the impression that they were rejecting Mrs. Eaton—a futile request, or have you guessed? The quarrel spread to Congressional and diplomatic circles, and even Jackson's niece, who had been serving as White House hostess, went back to Tennessee rather than accept the outcast. Nevertheless, Jackson steadily refused to give ground.

The career of Vice-President Calhoun, heir-apparent to the presidency, was vitally affected by this tempest in the Washington social cauldron. Mrs. Calhoun, an aristocrat of aristocrats, evidently thought more of a point of etiquette than of her husband's career and refused **Calhoun** point-blank to be sullied by contact with Mrs. Eaton. Cal- **and Van** houn, who also had his pride, refused to interfere, and his re- **Buren** fusal did him no good with the baffled and outraged but still chivalrous old President. Now it so happened that Van Buren was a widower ; so he was perfectly free to please Jackson by paying attention to the lovely subject of contention. Before long the little New Yorker was being called the American Talleyrand, and one may be sure the term was not intended as flattery.

We have already noted that nationalist sentiment in South Carolina was losing ground. The state, not satisfied with Virginia's fainéant leadership, was searching for an active policy and was becoming more partial toward the aristo-agrarianism of the right wing of Jeffer- **Nullifica-** sonianism than it had ever been in Jefferson's time. South **tion** Carolina thinkers began to improve upon the Virginia and Kentucky Resolutions of 1798 by suggesting nullification. By this they meant that since the Federal government was bound by the terms of a compact among the states (the Constitution), it was the privilege of the states or any one state to decide when the instructions had been exceeded and, if necessary, to declare them null and void. Calhoun did not invent it, but he gave it flesh and blood in his *Exposition* (1828), though few knew that it was the work of the Vice-President. The status of slavery was implicitly at the bottom of the movement, though the tariff was the commonly specified ground of grievance. Nullification had its first test in the halls of Congress in the famous Webster-Hayne debates of January 1830, a test which both sides felt they had won.

But such forensics did nothing to solve South Carolina's economic problems. Calhoun, visibly disturbed by the tariff problem and by Jackson's apparent indifference to it, planned a Jefferson's Birthday dinner (actually held on 15 April 1830) as a move toward cementing an alliance between the Older South and the Southwest which should freeze out Van Buren and capture Old Hickory for state rights and antitariff policy. Jackson, probably coached by Van Buren, thought he detected an odor of hostility to the Union, if not actual nullification, and came prepared with a toast furnished by Van Buren: "Our Federal Union—It Must be Preserved." Calhoun's answer was dignified but weak: "The Union—next to our liberty the most dear."

This sparring, which to most Washingtonians was merely political, was taken by Calhoun to portend a serious threat of tyranny by the growing northern majority over a desperate and relatively weakening Older

Jackson's break with Calhoun

South. A month later Crawford, ill and envenomed, disclosed that when Jackson had invaded Florida in 1818 Calhoun, then Secretary of War, had wanted to have the general punished or reprimanded. Jackson unreasonably ignored Calhoun's real services since that time and hotly accused him of treachery —which in Jackson's estimation must have been about the same as lese majesty. Calhoun replied temperately and with dignity, but to no avail. Jackson slapped him down and pointedly broke off relations. Calhoun naturally blamed Van Buren, but it seems established that he had nothing to do with it; it is clear, however, that he profited by it.

The correspondence between the two men had not ended before Jackson undertook a move which, whether intentionally or not, drove another nail in Calhoun's political coffin. After the failure of Calhoun's proposal

Maysville veto, 27 May 1830

for a network of military roads and canals, Congress had with Adams's encouragement adopted the policy of subscribing for stock in private road-building projects. Unfortunately there were ways by which the entrepreneurs could milk away much of the investment (for example, through construction contracts), and many of these roads were intended to open up areas for the benefit of land speculators. At this time there was going through Congress a bill favored by Clay (then in retirement) to take stock in a private road from Maysville on the Ohio to Lexington. The road, though wholly within Kentucky, was promoted as a link in the great Buffalo to New Orleans road which had been one of Calhoun's projects. Hitherto Jackson had not been clear on the subject of internal improvements, but when the Maysville Road Bill reached him he vetoed it, 27 May 1830.

The motives were complex, though Jackson justified his veto by stating that such acts were unconstitutional and by asserting his determination to reduce the public debt. Federal expenditures in the territories he

Effects of the Maysville veto

regarded as legitimate; but if they were to be continued in the states, he demanded a Constitutional amendment. Yet he did not oppose river and harbor improvements with "national objects," and the building of the Cumberland Road was continued. Indeed, annual expenditures all through Jackson's reign were as high as they had been under Adams. Some of Jackson's supporters had been convinced that the veto would weaken him politically, but Jackson's political instinct was right, for a majority of the people agreed that money should be saved and the public debt paid. It is also likely that the people had been alarmed by Adams's plan to sell public lands slowly at fair prices and to use the money for public purposes; so now they were ready to

BORN TO COMMAND.

OF VETO MEMORY.

HAD I BEEN CONSULTED.

KING ANDREW THE FIRST.

A Whig slam at Jackson's autocracy

forego Federal support of internal improvements in order to retain the policy of cheap lands.

One other effect, not foreseen at the time, was that the withdrawal of Federal support from roads left railroad companies to find their own finances with such help as they could get from states and communities and eventually from Federal land grants. The Maysville veto was followed by a series of similar vetoes intended to nail down the policy securely. However honestly Jackson may have regarded it as necessary from the view of constitutionality and economy, the veto was easily interpreted as a blow at both Clay and Calhoun. Clay was overjoyed by this free gift of an issue and the next year re-entered the Senate to take up the battle. The effect on Calhoun, however, was tragic. As a member of the administration he was counted upon by the forces of internal improvement to swing the President to their view. The veto was the proof of his impotence—if further proof was needed—and made Clay the chief of the internal-improvement men. Calhoun, with his northern and western satellites falling away, was forced back more and more upon the Older South for support.

Jackson's sharp break with Calhoun split the Cabinet into two factions. Duff Green, editor of the official *United States Telegraph,* took it over to Calhoun, and Francis Preston Blair set up the *Globe* as an administrative organ. Van Buren, as usual guileless as a new-born babe, showed Jackson the way out. With Van Buren's and Eaton's resignations on his desk Jackson could with propriety ask the other Cabinet members to resign, and did so. Edward Livingston, now of Louisiana, became Secretary of State, and Lewis Cass, a Yankee who had served for nineteen years as Governor of Michigan Territory, became Secretary of War. *L'affaire Peggy* died down, and Van Buren hied away to London as minister. When Van Buren's confirmation came before the Senate and by prearrangement the vote divided equally, Calhoun, with unbecoming ferocity, cast the decisive vote against him. This was even better luck than the little Flying Dutchman could have planned for himself, and he must have smiled with satisfaction as he departed for a continental tour.

Jackson dismisses his Cabinet

It was now December 1831, and no one could complain that the management had spared expense in furnishing fireworks. But they were merely preliminary; it was time for the show to begin in the main tent. Jackson, himself a hard-money man and an enemy of the Bank of the United States, had found that B. U. S. had won support among his official family. There was not the least doubt that Nicholas Biddle, President of the Bank, had promoted a policy of sewing up influential editors, politicians, Congressmen, and members of the administration by judicious loans on which payments were never urged and by legal retainers to such men as Daniel Webster. Jackson believed that B. U. S. by its control of credit was in a position to control business and that this in turn made it possible to bring powerful pressures upon the government. The role of banking in building up a strong economy was apparently a sealed book to Jackson, though he was willing to compromise on a bank owned and operated by the government.

Jackson against the Bank

Now the Bank's charter was due to expire in 1836, and Biddle was anxious to have the question of survival settled as soon as possible. Jackson, though convinced that the people were with him, did not care to thrust the issue into politics; Biddle gladly agreed to let the issue ride until after the election of 1832. Presently, however, he thought that he detected signs of weakness in Jackson's mention of the Bank recharter in his 1831 message to Congress.

Problem of recharter

Clay and Webster, confident that the President could be defeated, urged that a bill for recharter be introduced in January 1832. This action not only violated Biddle's pledge but put the Bank squarely into politics. As anticipated, the bill passed, drawing support from all parts of the country. Jackson straightway vetoed it and, roused to thorough and righteous anger, announced that he would make the question of recharter the main issue in the coming election.

By now no one was under the illusion that the Republican Party was a band of brothers temporarily split by secondary issues. The fission between the wings was made apparent as the followers of Clay began as early as 1828 to call themselves National Republicans, and those of Jackson revived the term Democratic Republican, **Growing party split** first used by the Jeffersonians. Jackson, whose health had been very poor, was now convinced that he must run once more if his party was to win. Calhoun, of course, was out as his running mate, and the "martyred" American Talleyrand was in. Clay was the undisputed leader of the National Republicans and was confident of victory over his senile opponent.

The campaign of 1832 was complicated by the rise of a new factor in American politics: a third party. A certain William Morgan of Batavia, New York, who had published a book which claimed to disclose the secrets of the Masonic Order, disappeared under mysterious circumstances in 1826. The country from Lake Erie to New **Anti-Masonic Party** Hampshire was known as the Burnt District because it was swept so frequently by emotional religious and social excitements. An anti-Masonic frenzy now seized the area and quickly adopted political methods to forward its aim of outlawing secret societies. Because Jackson was a Mason, the Anti-Masonic Party threw its support to Adams in 1828 and sent several members to Congress. Clay, who was an inactive Mason, played footie with the party but in the end failed to gain its official support. By this time a number of young politicians had seized control of the movement and used it to advance their own interests; among them were William H. Seward, Thurlow Weed, and Thaddeus Stevens.

The Anti-Masonic Party, devoted to its interpretation of democracy, held a national presidential nominating convention in Baltimore in September 1831. It set up for the presidency William Wirt of Virginia, a brilliant Constitutional lawyer and Attorney-General un- **National presidential nominating conventions** der Monroe and J. Q. Adams. The Whigs followed suit in December, again in Baltimore, with the nomination of Clay and John Sergeant of Pennsylvania; a few months later a statement of principles, the first official "platform," was adopted. Baltimore saw its third nominating convention in May 1832, when the Democratic Republicans, after adopting the famous Two-thirds Rule, by which the vote of two thirds of the convention members was necessary for the selection of a nominee, approved Jackson and nominated Van Buren for the vice-presidency. The national presidential nominating convention,* first adopted as a democratic gesture and as a means of focusing public attention upon the party and its issues and candidate, quickly supplanted the older methods of nomination and has become ingrained in American political method. It has also become a powerful weapon for control of candidacies by the party leaders.

The campaign of 1832 was if anything more bitter than that of 1828. The vetoes were popular, and several states with Indian problems were weaned from Calhoun's influence when Jackson supported Georgia's case

Campaign of 1832 for Indian removal. The Northwest's approval of Clay's American System was not sufficient to counteract the effect of the above policies. Its Jackson sentiment was enhanced by the Pre-emption Act of 1830, which was supported by Calhoun and Jackson alike, and which gave illegal settlers on certain public lands the first right to buy those lands. Eastern farmers and workmen were enthusiastic over Jackson's Bank and internal-improvement policies, and this enthusiasm was sufficient to override their doubts on land and Indian policies. In the important states Wirt received little support but was sold out by arrangements between the party leaders and Clay. The election showed a popular vote of 690,000 for Jackson against 530,000 for Clay and Wirt. Vermont went to Wirt with 7 electoral votes; Massachusetts, Rhode Island, Connecticut, Delaware, Kentucky, and part of Maryland went to Clay with 49 electoral votes; and South Carolina supported John Floyd, of Virginia, with 11 votes. All the rest, 219 votes, went to Jackson.

Jackson was warranted in regarding the election as the vindication of his past actions and approval of his policies. It was clear that Clay and Biddle would refuse to accept the decision on B. U. S., but the showdown

South Carolina nullifies the tariff was delayed by the rise of a nullification crisis in South Carolina. Detailed discussion of the Constitutional aspects must be postponed, but we can note the principal facts here. Jackson had urged that the Tariff of Abominations be lowered, but the bill which emerged in 1832 was still protective even though it did remove many of the "abominations." Jackson had once more correctly assessed political realities when he signed the bill. South Carolina regarded this as proof that protection had become "the settled policy of the country," and late in 1832 a state convention declared the tariff null and void in South Carolina. Federal customs officials at Charleston were forbidden to collect under its provisions. Battle was clearly joined, and Calhoun resigned the vice-presidency—the only such instance in United

* The first national presidential nominating convention was held in New York City in 1812, when Federalists and disaffected Republicans united to nominate De Witt Clinton; the next national convention was that held by the Anti-Masons.

States history—and the legislature of South Carolina promptly elected him to the Senate to lead the forces of nullification.

Jackson accepted the challenge and reinforced Federal naval and army units in Charleston. Though he believed in state rights and said so, he also believed in Federal rights. He was confident that South Carolina did not want war and was merely bringing pressure to pro- *Clay's* mote a political solution, but this seemed to be disproved *compromise* when Calhoun rejected the Verplanck Bill, which would *tariff* have reduced the tariff to twenty per cent in two years. Clay had dreaded that the crisis not only would disrupt the Union which he loved but might enhance the fame and the executive power of Jackson, whom he hated. Clay found that Calhoun's chief objection to the Verplanck Bill was Van Buren's sponsorship, so he molded a bill which took ten years to reduce the tariff instead of two and thus won enough high-tariff votes to put it through. In return Calhoun's followers allowed the Force Bill pending in Congress to go through, though South Carolina had the last word by declaring it null and void—but after it was no longer needed.

Clay defended his course against the extremists like Webster on the ground that he had saved the principle of the protective tariff; actually this may be doubted, for until the Civil War the United States remained a low-tariff country with the Federal government basically controlled by an alliance of low-tariff South and cheap-land West. Both Jackson and Calhoun claimed the victory in 1833, but in the light of subsequent history it is evident that South Carolina not only had won its tariff contention but had tested and found the threat of secession a valuable aid in getting what it wanted. Whether Clay's action prevented a showdown which might have ended either the Union or the threats of secession is a question that no one can answer.

With nullification out of the way, Jackson now proceeded to renew his "war" on the Bank. He felt that before Biddle would suffer the dissolution of B. U. S., he would try to throw the country into a financial panic which would offer the alternatives of chaos or re- *Renewal of* charter. In any case, the withdrawal of so much credit and *Jackson's* currency from business was sure to pose a delicate problem. *"war" on* Jackson was determined that at least government funds *the Bank* would not be lost nor would they be used to strengthen Biddle's power, and so he planned to withdraw them from B. U. S. and use them to strengthen state banks against the day of trial. But the power of the Bank, or perhaps better, belief in its necessity to a financially stable country, extended into Jackson's official family so far that he had to dismiss two Secretaries of the Treasury who refused to obey his order; the third co-operated. It was Roger B. Taney of Maryland, who had been Attorney-General and a member of the Kitchen Cabinet, and who upon the death of John Marshall became Chief Justice. The deposits were placed in selected state banks which, of course, were accused of having favored Jackson and promptly were dubbed "pet banks."

As a matter of fact, financial stress did come in the winter of 1833–34. Obviously Jackson and the anti-Bank party saw in this a confirmation of their suspicions of Biddle; the truth of the accusation is still being argued. "Go to Biddle" was Jackson's sarcastic advice to the distressed, but Biddle refused to loosen up on credit until forced to it by his own followers. Clay managed to carry through the Senate two resolutions of censure of Jackson for his removal policy. Benton kept up a fight to have the resolutions expunged and was finally able in 1837 to accomplish his object after the Democrats won control of the Senate. This was regarded as the final public accolade on Jackson's Bank policy.

Nevertheless, the financial problem was not solved. The national debt was paid off in 1835, and Jackson as a frugal steward rejoiced. The mounting surplus was a serious problem. High-tariff advocates led by Clay opposed reducing the tariff on the ground that the **Inflationary problems** Tariff of 1833 was inviolate, and they carried the Distribution Bill in 1836, which prorated the surplus among the states. The surplus had led to greater deposits in more and more state banks, while the disappearance of B. U. S. encouraged the issuance of state-bank currency, some of it sound but most of it wildcat. "Old Bullion" Benton championed the demand of the hard-money advocates for more gold and silver specie, but these metals were scarce and could not afford the volume of money needed in business. Wild land speculation in the West, largely based on wildcat currency, was blowing up a bubble which must sooner or later burst. Jackson sought to protect government funds by the Specie Circular of July 1836 (really the third in a series), which directed that only specie should be received in payment for public land.

The Democratic Republicans had by now shortened their name to Democrats, and the National Republicans no longer made any pretense of being Republicans but took the name Whigs. Their reasoning was amusing: since the opponents of executive tyranny before 1776 **Democrats and Whigs** were known as Whigs, it was only natural that the opponents of the executive tyranny of "King Andrew I" should call themselves Whigs. The new party was an incongruous mixture. The controlling conservative element in the North was largely the National Republicans, Federalist fragments, and disgusted right-wing Democrats; in the South it was made up of the remaining nationalists, the commercial classes, anti-Calhoun nullifiers, anti-Jackson antinullifiers, and anyone else who could stand neither Jackson nor Calhoun—plus Calhoun himself. Its northern liberal wing was formed by the absorption of the Anti-

Masons of the frenetically democratic Burnt District and the surrounding states. On the whole, it was primarily an alliance against Jackson and was destined to fall apart when the slavery question became acute. Conservative northern Whigs, however, avowed their relationship to Hamilton. True, they did not attempt to revive the Federalist concept of aristocracy, but they did say baldly that the possession of property was the proof of merit. In their propaganda the owner of property was the burden bearer, while the workingman, free as a bird, could devote himself to the things that mattered!

Jackson's control of the country was so clear that the Whigs did not even bother to hold a convention in 1836 but threw their support in the various sections to favorite sons in the hope of forcing the election into the House of Representatives. Jackson was easily able to dictate the nomination of Van Buren in 1836, and he rigorously cracked the whip over party elements. Richard M. **Campaign of 1836** Johnson of Kentucky was nominated for Vice-President, apparently for no reason any better than that he claimed to have been the man that killed Tecumseh. Doubtless even Van Buren was surprised when he was elected 170 to 124, with the short end distributed among four candidates. Johnson received one half of the vice-presidential votes and presently was balloted into office by the Senate.

No sooner was Van Buren firmly seated than the bubble of land speculation burst, and the Panic of 1837 gripped the country; it did not let up until 1843. Inflation had followed overinvestment and heavy indebtedness in financing land purchases and the construction of turnpikes and canals. Bad crops undercut the purchasing power of farmers, and a financial crisis in England **The Panic of 1837** which forced the withdrawal of English loans made it impossible to sustain the burden. These factors, added to withdrawals from banks that followed upon the Distribution Act, helped the Specie Circular to prick the bubble. Of course the Whigs shouted, "I told you so," and with some justice, for a strong B. U. S. might have mitigated the crisis; on the other hand, Clay had not helped any by his Distribution Act and his heedless ballooning of the spirit of "improvements." The truth was that Jackson and his favored advisers in dealing with money were beyond their depth —as who isn't? Their fear of the power of the Bank may have been justified, but their alternative of a hard-money economy was naïve.

Van Buren struggled against the Whig insistence that a new Bank of the United States be chartered, and in 1840 succeeded in setting up the so-called Independent Treasury System (first outlined by Jackson) by which the government handled its own money transactions through subtreasuries in various cities. B. U. S., which **Independent Treasury System** had been rechartered under Pennsylvania law, had gone under due to Biddle's wild speculations, and his failure reduced opposition to the Independent Treasury scheme and restored some confidence in Jackson's program. The principal drawback to the new system was that when there was a surplus the disappearance of money into the maw of the Independent Treasury disturbed the money market. The Whigs dissolved the Independent Treasury System in 1841, but it was restored in 1846 and lasted until 1921.

The ironic fact was that it was the Whigs who profited from the Panic of 1837: politically as a party; personally because they had the cash and could pick up land and stocks for a few cents on the dollar. The Whigs

Campaign of 1840

entered the campaign of 1840 with confidence, even though Clay was ruled out by the Anti-Masons, now members of the Whig lodge. Old William Henry Harrison, of Ohio, who had done well in the popular vote in 1836, was made the presidential candidate, and to attract the state-rights vote he was given as running mate a Virginia Senator named John Tyler, who had fought for nullification and Clay!

Harrison, though not wealthy, was of aristocratic Virginia stock, but an unfortunate Democratic attempt to portray him as a shiftless "log-cabin candidate" showed the Whigs how to turn him into a democratic hero. They ran the campaign on a simple two-point program; (1) blame the hard times on Van Buren, and (2) turn the Democrats' method of ballyhoo against them. Log cabins and hard cider were featured in Whig parades and rallies, and no opportunity was lost to show how the "old hero" had fought for the popular cause which he loved. "Van, Van," chanted the Whigs, "is a used-up man!" He was. "Tippecanoe and Tyler too" were swept into office 234 to 60. Then, just a month after his inauguration, Harrison, overwhelmed by office seekers and weakened by the strain, died of pneumonia. John Tyler was President, a nullifier and a Democrat in everything but his hatred of Jackson.

It must be evident by now that the Jacksonian movement, never too well integrated, had begun to divide. As we shall see in good time, slavery and problems concerned with the border lands under the control of Eng-

Democratic divisions

land and Mexico hastened the division. In the domestic sphere inflation helped the trend, but the rank and file felt on a number of other counts that it had been sold out by conservative leaders, and after a bitter contest for control the latter were driven over to the Whigs. The battle was especially bitter in the industrial centers, for there inflation hit the workers hard; and when they could not keep control, they organized new local parties. The Working Man's Party ("Workies") grew up in New York and other eastern cities in the early 1830's but never attained national stature and was absorbed by the old-line Democrats when they came out for mechanics' lien laws and the abolition of imprisonment for debt. Northern Whigs were not altogether antilabor, but they did fear the flood of foreigners and free Negroes which was inundating the North.

But protest was perennial. When in 1835 New York City dissidents turned out in force to a Tammany nominating meeting, the old guard turned off the gaslights, a common maneuver in such cases. This time the rebels were prepared; they produced candles which they lit **Loco Focos** with the new friction matches, then called loco focos, and **take over** proceeded to nominate their own candidates. The left-wing **the Demo-** Democrats of New York City were soon known as Loco **cratic Party** Focos. The Loco Focos were hard-money men, wished to curtail banks, and were particularly active in the free-trade, labor, and other reform movements.

Rural New York saw a bitter factional fight within the Democratic Party between the Barnburners and the Hunkers. The former, so called from the Dutchman who burned down his barn to get rid of the rats, were radicals who attacked and overthrew the conservative Regency wing, now called Hunkers because they "hunkered" for the spoils of office. Loco Focos and Barnburners sparked the seizure of the Democratic Party and of President Van Buren by the radicals, who were soon known all over the North as Loco Focos. Van Buren, always the practical politician, saw that the Loco Focos were not strong enough to carry the nation alone. The result was that Calhoun was restored to grace. For the next twenty years the Democratic Party prospered by uniting Loco Focos, Southern state-righters, and western cheap-land advocates. It was a precarious alliance for an era of growing sectional rivalry, and this danger was so well recognized that there was an unwritten taboo against any discussion of slavery. We shall see in good time how well this taboo was observed.

4 *Jacksonian Democracy in the Stream of American History*

Jackson left office grateful for the "happy result" of his reign and regretting only that he could not have shot Henry Clay and hung John Calhoun. There is no indication that he ever thoroughly understood the full implications of his presidency. Indeed, he had signifi- **Jeffersonian** cantly altered Jeffersonian concepts and placed marks upon **and Jack-** American history which have never been erased, even though **sonian de-** they were submerged for a while by the slavery crisis. Let **mocracy** us summarize six of his outstanding achievements.

(1) He turned the presidency into an aggressive force in contrast to Jefferson's belief that the President was the associate rather than the master of Congress. Some of his doctrines have disappeared: for example,

Made the presidency a force
Presidents no longer insist on their co-equal right with the Supreme Court to decide on the Constitutionality of policies. By no means are all Presidents strong and aggressive; but when the strong personality enters office or the crisis arises, the precedent is there.

(2) Jackson made the party a definite, disciplined instrument of policy, in contrast to the old idea that the mission of the party was to rally the unanimous support of the nation. Jefferson utilized the two-party system, though he seems to have learned its nature only gradually. Jackson, who would gladly have hung the leaders of the opposition and forcibly baptized their followers, was probably the unconscious agent of political evolution. The spoils system, of course, was an essential part of the President's control of his party.

Party discipline

(3) Jackson glorified mediocrity by his rule that one intelligent man could hold an office as well as another; Jefferson had believed in the election and appointment of men of experience, ability, and culture to office. Jackson was with the trend of the times. More than that, Americans have ever since preferred mediocrity, as is seen by comparing the brilliant pre-election records of every single President through and including Jackson with the mediocrity of *most* presidential candidates since then, regardless of their performance after the election.

Glorification of mediocrity

(4) The Whig campaign of 1840 was proof of the success of the Jacksonian revolution. The National Republicans had abbreviated John Adams's "rule by the rich, the well-born, and the able" to a short and sharp "rule by the rich." The Whigs now beat the drum for democracy louder and longer than the legions of Jackson ever did. It was a fateful switch in campaign methods, but the only way to keep a conservative party alive. Indeed, the basis of the vote had been so broadened that the privileged caste and its hangers-on could no longer win unaided. Since that time no party has been able coolly to deny democracy and still get elected. Nor is this change of conservative base necessarily cynical even though there always are some cynics among the leaders of any party, and probably many Whig orators talked so often and so eloquently about the beauties of democracy that they convinced themselves. Much more important was the popular pressure for democracy, a pressure carried into the Whig movement by the Anti-Masons and by young men who had grown up in the time of the Jacksonian Movement. It is certainly significant that when we look for the perfect example of the democrat we always think of that rising young Whig politician, Abraham Lincoln.

Politics changes base

(5) Jefferson believed that the vote of a man who could not stand

on his own feet economically—as the land-owning farmer could—would be controlled by whoever controlled his daily bread. Jefferson therefore (until late in his career) distrusted the working classes and **Acceptance** feared their acquisition of the vote as a menace to democ- **of city** racy. Jackson swept away these fears. He divided society **workers** into producers and nonproducers and accepted farmers and industrial laborers into the first classification. He, or rather his eastern followers, basically rejected Physiocratic doctrines and accepted Adam Smith's atomism; he fought monopoly, promoted competition, and tried to keep "fictitious" property (stocks and bonds) from eating up "real" property. He hoped thus to prevent wealth from controlling the worker's vote.

We noted above that Jackson probably failed to understand that the democratic party system seeks a changing balance of interests, not the complete and final victory of one interest. It has been claimed that the Jacksonian movement saw the beginning of the American **Class-con-** class struggle. We do not as yet know enough of the facts to **sciousness** demonstrate such a thesis. In any case, right down to our own day, consciousness of class among wage earners has never been strong, and they along with probably ninety per cent of the total population regard themselves as "middle class." Class-consciousness, indeed, has never been marked except among the propertied—as must be admitted by those who understand the tenets of Federalists, right-wing American Physiocrats like Calhoun, and the leaders of the modern urban rich. Such class-consciousness as existed among the unpropertied was probably pretty much confined to the city "Workies" of the East. They were keenly conscious of the fact that the franchise must quickly be protected by economic measures, or they would be smothered by the mere weight of the capitalists.

(6) Jackson was called upon to choose between the horns of the eternal dilemma, and he did choose whether or not he recognized the fact. He believed in Jefferson's dictum, "That government is best which governs least." He saw himself as called "to heal the wounds **Weak or** of the Constitution and preserve it from further violation," **strong gov-** to peel away the excrescences on the body politic which had **ernment** been created by misgovernment and undue corporate privileges. Once more the Anglo-Saxon pattern was repeated: the desire to return to the purity of the past. But Jackson was caught on the horns of the dilemma: weak government cannot protect individual liberty from other individuals with greater economic power, but a strong government can as easily become the weapon of tyranny as the instrument of public good.

Jefferson had faced the same dilemma and had yielded reluctantly to the pressure for the Hamiltonian method of strong government but never ceased to assert that each exception was merely temporary and that government was still the natural enemy of liberty. He realized thoroughly that every power which he added to government in order to protect the public welfare could also be used by conservatives against the public welfare when they came back into office. Calhoun, who saw the dilemma more clearly than Jackson, chose nullification under the illusion that he was protecting liberty by keeping the national government weakly submissive to the states.

Jackson never admitted to an abandonment of Jeffersonian suspicions, and he expected the Federal government, once it had "saved" the day, to retreat to its narrow sphere; it did momentarily, but thereby left more room for the regrowth of monopoly. Nevertheless Jackson's use of the Federal government to promote the public welfare foreshadowed its enormous expansion during the Civil War and indicated the field in which private business and social reformers would fight after the Civil War. Jackson and Calhoun shared the hope that an order could be set up in which the government would not need to interfere; that hope seems to have gone the way of many other utopian dreams.

The trend of the future was forecast in Chief Justice Taney's decision in the *Charles River Bridge Case* in 1837. Massachusetts had granted a franchise in 1785 to the proprietors of the Charles River Bridge for a toll bridge across the Charles River, but in 1828 it granted a second franchise for a toll bridge which was to become free in six years. The proprietors contended that the second franchise was unconstitutional because it impaired the contract the state had made with the company. After long delays the case was considered by a Supreme Court transformed by Jackson's appointments. The second franchise was upheld. "The object and end of all government," said Taney, "is to promote the happiness and prosperity of the community by which it is established; and it can never be assumed, that the government intended to diminish its power of accomplishing the end for which it was created." This decision, of course, illustrated the Jacksonian opposition to monopoly, but even more significantly it showed that in a crisis the Jacksonians would with Hamilton and John Marshall grasp the strong-government horn of the dilemma.

Taney and the *Charles River Bridge Case*, 1837

It is not likely that Jackson ever understood the dilemma or understood that he had failed to reach his goal of governing least. He was not a thinker but a doer; he reached instinctively for the instrument that would do what had to be done. The confusion of historians over the Jacksonian Movement and the loss of some of its lessons has probably resulted from (1) the fact that there was no political philosopher to systematize its discoveries as Hamilton and Jefferson did theirs, and (2) that the sectional controversy followed so close upon its heels. And yet it would be wrong to belittle Jackson's

The greatness of Jackson

sincerity. A man who for decades was touted as a great democrat, the personification of the will of the people, would be less than human if he had not himself come to believe it. The remarkable thing is that he was right. The old frontiersman had the spiritual dynamism which was necessary to weld inchoate popular discontents into a mighty crusade. He had found a real affinity with the democratic movement, and from it he drew his political sustenance. He was the instrument of democracy in hewing out the shape of the future.

The Jacksonian Movement was not intended as an attack on property but upon the abuse of their power by the owners of property. It was basically the triumph of Little Property over Big Property. The problem then (and the problem now) lay in the definition of abuse. **The West: Little Property versus Big Property** Jackson's answers were too often naïve and prompted by anger at his political enemies. The result was that less progress was made toward solving the problem than serious thinkers had hoped. Western farmers saw the problem chiefly as one of spreading the gravy more evenly. They were not so much concerned with forbidding the means by which some men had waxed rich as they were in obtaining land and other aids to enable them to catch up. The Democrats, therefore, did not have to work out a permanent solution of the problem of monopoly's special privileges; they were able to evade the issue by writing a check for the farmers out of our abundant natural resources.

Eastern city workers, especially those who were unable to depend in part on subsistence farming, took more interest in shearing away the power of the Bank, reducing the expenses of government, stopping capital's abuses of labor, and clearing the way for their right **The East: Human Rights versus Property Rights** to organize for their own protection. They were fighting for Human Rights versus Property Rights—the first time the issue had been boldly flung into the political arena. Even Jefferson had thought in terms of Little Property versus Big Property when it came to the practical political battle. Actually the industrial workers were neither united nor articulate; so, though they obtained a few of their desires, their principal gain was the franchise—a powerful weapon for future conflicts.

BIBLIOGRAPHICAL NOTE

New Men and New Measures

GENERAL: See Gerald W. Johnson's absorbing record, *America's Silver Age: The Statecraft of Clay, Webster, and Calhoun* (1939); and William O. Lynch, *Fifty Years of Party Warfare, 1789–1837* (1931). For an unexcelled contemporary view see the *Diary* (Allan Nevins, ed., 2 v., 1927) of Philip

Hone, a conservative, public-spirited Whig merchant and politician of New York City. In addition to other treatments of the judiciary see Henry S. Commager's little *Majority Rule and Minority Rights* (1943), a brilliant assessment of judicial review. For light on Jacksonian politics and legal ideas see Carl B. Swisher, *Roger B. Taney* (1935).

J. Q. ADAMS: There are biographies by John T. Morse and B. C. Clark. His *Memoirs* (12 v., 1874–77) were edited by his son Charles Francis Adams. See also Samuel F. Bemis, *John Quincy Adams and the Foundations of American Foreign Policy* (1949); and George A. Lipsky, *John Quincy Adams: His Theory and Ideas* (1950). Read also the summary of Adams's hopes for the nation in Brooks Adams's preface to Henry Adams, *Degradation of the Democratic Dogma* (1919).

BENTON: There is a life by William M. Meigs, but Benton's *Thirty Years' View* is one of the great American politicial autobiographies.

CALHOUN: There are biographies by Gaillard Hunt and William M. Meigs. These are supplanted by Charles M. Wiltse's three volumes, *John C. Calhoun* (1944–51). R. K. Crallé edited his works (6 v., 1851–55), and his correspondence appears in government and American Historical Association publications. The *Life of John C. Calhoun* (1843) attributed to R. M. T. Hunter was actually written by Calhoun himself. For an exposition of his ideas see August O. Spain, *The Political Theory of John C. Calhoun* (1951).

CLAY: Carl Schurz, *Henry Clay* (2 v., 1887); Glyndon G. Van Deusen, *Life of Henry Clay* (1937). Bernard Mayo, *Henry Clay: Spokesman of the New West* (1937) carries through "Mr. Clay's War." There are various old editions of Clay's works, none of them complete.

JACKSON: John S. Bassett, *Life of Andrew Jackson* (1911) best portrays the traditional view of Jackson as leader of a western revolt. Claude G. Bowers, *Party Battles of the Jackson Period* (1922) is mawkishly worshipful. Arthur M. Schlesinger, Jr., *The Age of Jackson* (1945) goes to the extreme in supporting the view that the Jacksonian Movement was based on the protest of eastern commoners. Marquis James, *Andrew Jackson: Portrait of a President* (1937) is less partisan than most writers on Old Hickory.

MARSHALL: Best on Marshall and outstanding among biographies is Albert J. Beveridge, *Life of John Marshall* (4 v., 1916–19).

MONROE: William P. Cresson, *James Monroe* (1946); Arthur Styron, *The Last of the Cocked Hats: James Monroe and the Virginia Dynasty* (1945).

VAN BUREN: See Denis T. Lynch, *An Epoch and a Man: Martin Van Buren and His Times* (1929). His uncompleted autobiography is in Am. Hist. Assoc., *Annual Report, 1918*, v. II (1920). In addition see Dixon R. Fox, *Decline of Aristocracy in the Politics of New York* (1919); and D. S. Alexander, *Political History of the State of N.Y.* (3 v., 1906).

WEBSTER: Best is Claude M. Fuess, *Daniel Webster* (2 v., 1930). The picture of the popular hero set forth in Benét's short story "The Devil and Daniel Webster" is unfortunately wide of the mark. Most complete collection of Webster's works is *Writings and Speeches* (18 v., 1903) edited by J. W. McIntyre.

Democracy and Sectionalism

DEMOCRATIC REFORM: In addition to other material cited in the bibliographical notes of this chapter see Kirk H. Porter, *History of Suffrage in the U.S.* (1918); Arthur M. Mowry, *The Dorr War* (1901); Brooks Adams, *Emancipation of Massachusetts* (1915); and Paul E. Lauer, *Church and State in New England* (1892).

SECTIONALISM: See Frederick Jackson Turner, *The Significance of Sections in American History* (1932). The subject will be treated in detail in connection with the sectional conflict.

The Reign of Old Hickory

On some of the political issues see: Queena Pollock, *Peggy Eaton: Democracy's Mistress* (1931), and Peggy's own *Autobiography* (1932); Charles McCarthy, *The Antimasonic Party* (1903); Samuel R. Gammon, *The Presidential Campaign of 1832* (1922); Reginald C. McGrane, *The Panic of 1837* (1924). Best study of B. U. S. is Ralph C. H. Catterall, *The Second Bank of the United States* (1903); it should be counteracted with a dose of Schlesinger, *The Age of Jackson* (1945).

Chapter XV

AMERICAN NATIONALISM ABROAD

1   *Rise of the Latin-American Nations*

THE resurgence of American nationalism after the War of 1812 possessed curiously contradictory facets. Though it soon ebbed in the domestic sphere, it continued to rise in the field of foreign relations. The

Aspects of nationalism abroad latter assumed four general aspects: (1) Canadian problems; (2) trade problems in the Pacific; (3) relations with the revolting Latin-American nations; and (4) territorial

expansion, particularly at the expense of Mexico and Great Britain.

All of these had certain common denominators. The American search for new trade and new territory was in a way the reverse side of our presumed isolation, for we were trying to insure that isolation by build-

Common denominators ing up our power to defend it. Ironically enough, this brought us into intimate contact with world affairs; and, moreover, that power, once gained, would bring responsi-

bility and the inevitable breakdown of isolation. A second common denominator was rivalry with Great Britain. The world-wide nature of British empire and trade was such that no matter where we turned we found ourselves confronted by the British lion. Indeed, the foreign policy of the United States could almost be written in terms of Anglo-American relations. Third, there was a slowly blossoming recognition of common interests by responsible leaders both in Britain and America, and a little fruit was gathered in each decade before the great harvest of our own century. The story of this recognition is so interwoven with our entire history that it can be unfolded only gradually. Here we shall set forth certain beginnings of our relations with Great Britain in Latin America, in Canada, and in the Orient.

The Napoleonic Era brought the crash of that old colossus, the

470

Spanish Empire. Spain had tried to shut off her colonies from the world and, indeed, had succeeded fairly well in this mercantilist program. For three centuries Spanish culture had leavened the Indian masses, but distances were so vast and intercommunication was so scanty that there had been formed not one uniform amalgam, but many. Some of them were clearly like Spain— as Chile and Argentina—but others were vitally affected by other racial elements. Each province was by geographical isolation or cultural peculiarities the seed bed of a nation. In all of them the native white (or almost white) Creoles and the Spanish-born official class were dominant. There was intense antipathy between them, for the Spaniards, who monopolized administrative offices and graft, despised the Creoles as mere colonials, and the Creoles resented the privileges and the arrogance of the peninsulars. Creoles, indeed, had little practice in self-government except at the town level. Spanish rule was unbelievably restrictive, but it always had been; sensible men saw it as the only possible check on the Hispanic yearning for individual domination.

Latin America on the eve of revolt

The liberation of Latin America was accomplished against odds beside which the liberation of the United States is a pastoral tale told on a summer day. The Latin-American independence movement did not arise from political and economic maturity. Only the leaders had come under the influence of the political theorists of France and had read and admired the Declaration of Independence and the Constitution of the United States. They whipped and spurred their fellows into independence and then, when they saw the results, doubted their own wisdom. Once the habit of loyalty to the Crown was destroyed, the colossal individualism of the Latin, together with natural, racial, and social conditions brought on the chaos which only the power of the Spanish king had staved off for three centuries.

Causes and results of revolt

The opportunity of the colonies to rise against the oppressive mercantilism of Spain came when Napoleon invaded the peninsula. The Wars of Independence lasted from 1810 to 1825 and were waged not only between the Creoles on one side and the remnants of Spanish royal administration on the other but also between factions among the rebels. There were three focuses of revolt: Buenos Aires, the old Spanish Main, and Mexico. After 1810 Spanish authority was never established in the region of Buenos Aires, and José de San Martín was able in 1817 to carry aid to the rebels of Chile. Meanwhile the Venezuelan Simón Bolívar established by 1820 the independence of Great Colombia, composed of modern Venezuela, Colombia, Panama, and Ecuador. Northern and southern armies then converged on Peru.

Independence of Latin America

At first Mexico resisted the fever of revolution, but when in 1820 the

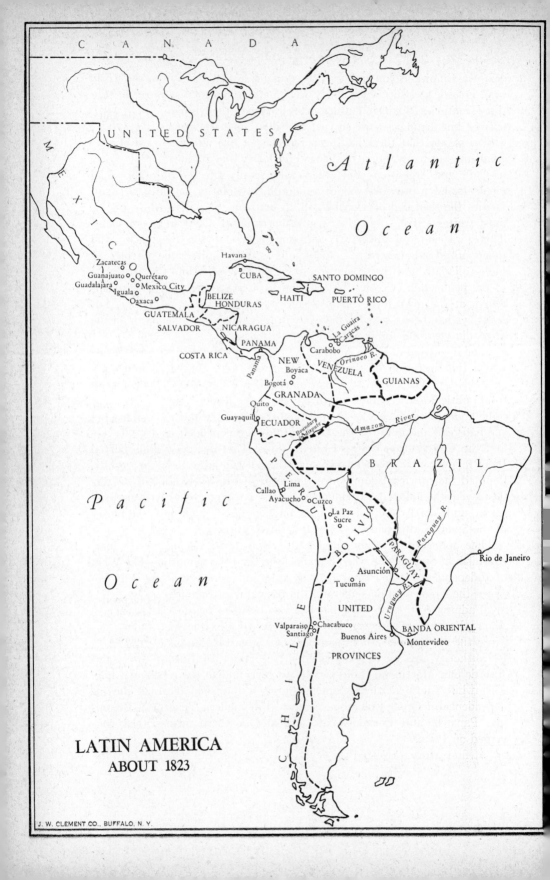

CANADA

UNITED STATES

Atlantic

Ocean

MEXICO

Zacatecas
Guanajuato   Querétaro
Guadalajara   Mexico City
Iguala
Oaxaca

Havana
CUBA

BELIZE
HONDURAS

GUATEMALA

SALVADOR   NICARAGUA

PANAMA

COSTA RICA

SANTO DOMINGO

HAITI   PUERTO RICO

La Guaira
Caracas

Carabobo

Panamá

NEW
Boyaca
Bogotá

GRANADA

VENEZUELA   Orinoco R.

GUIANAS

Quito

Guayaquil   ECUADOR

Boundary
in dispute

Amazon   River

BRAZIL

PERU

Lima
Callao
Ayacucho   Cuzco
La Paz
Sucre

Pacific

BOLIVIA

PARAGUAY   *Paraguay R.*

Rio de Janeiro

Ocean

Asunción

Tucumán

CHILE

UNITED

Uruguay R.

Valparaiso   Chacabuco
Santiago
Buenos Aires

BANDA ORIENTAL
Montevideo

PROVINCES

LATIN AMERICA
ABOUT 1823

liberal Riego revolt in Spain alarmed the privileged classes, they declared independence in order to preserve their control of the country's economic and religious life. Central America had joined Mexico at first, but in 1823 it seceded and soon fell into its component parts. After the fall of Napoleon tiny Portugal attempted to reassert its control over its huge colony of Brazil with the result that the prince-regent, Dom Pedro, declared Brazilian independence (1822) and was proclaimed emperor. Buenos Aires had tried to establish its power over the vast Viceroyalty of La Plata, but Paraguay and Bolivia (named for Bolívar) made their independence good. Uruguay, long a bone of contention between colonial Buenos Aires and Brazil, became the prize of a new series of wars; the acknowledgment of Uruguayan independence by both contestants in 1828 by no means ended the struggle for ascendance.

During the Wars of Independence the Creoles had sought to gain the subject classes as recruits. They freed the Indians from the most onerous taxes and abolished Negro slavery (except in Brazil). The Church, which not only had borne heavily upon the people but had been the chief support of Spanish rule, was made subordinate to the state. The political, intellectual, and economic liberties **The fruits of idealism** inherent in Anglo-Saxon institutions were guaranteed. At first the idealists, with a touching faith in the efficacy of political forms, modeled their constitutions and institutions upon those of the United States; but, since democracy depends more upon co-operation and compromise than upon constitutions, it was inevitable that the stubborn individualism and amazing diversities in each country should plunge it into strife. Elections were usually mere forms; the real elections were by battle and *coup d'état*. For a period which varied from a few years to a century the Hispanic nations were torn by civil wars from which the only rest was the iron rule of the dictator, or *caudillo;* at least in some countries he furnished intervals of the order and peace which enabled wealth to multiply and knowledge to be spread.

The Wars of Independence offered both opportunities and problems for the United States and Great Britain. The destruction of Spain's mercantilist controls was welcomed by both countries, and their trading ships swarmed in Hispanic ports. Britain's commercial and **Britain and the Latin-American revolutions** liberal elements sought to persuade the government to recognize and assist the rebels; on the other hand, the British government was allied with the Spanish *Junta* against Napoleon. As a result Britain was forced to carry water on both shoulders for fifteen years and actually accomplished the feat without undue splashing.

The fall of Napoleon was followed by a century of relative peace, but this knowledge was not given to the diplomats of the 1820's. Numerous problems made them fear a prompt renewal of world strife. Rus-

**The Euro-
pean Sys-
tem**
sian diplomats and secret agents were carrying on in Western Europe activities strikingly like those of our own day.
Liberals, socialists, and nationalists, one or all of them,
threatened revolution in nearly every country. To meet these turbulent
elements the victorious absolute monarchs of Europe drew together in
the so-called Holy Alliance—"neither holy nor an alliance"—under the
leadership of Metternich, the Austrian premier. This group was determined to eradicate democracy, which they regarded as a highly con-
tagious disease, and liberal revolutions in Italy and Spain were ruthlessly
crushed.

The Spanish-American revolts had at first seemed to Jefferson and
Madison a heaven-sent opportunity to reduce European influence in this
hemisphere and to increase the influence and trade of the United States.

**American
alarm**
The close of the Napoleonic Wars, however, brought rumors
that the absolutist countries were toying with the idea of
crushing the Spanish-American rebels and annexing choice
bits of the old Spanish Empire as rewards for their good offices. There
were hints that England and France both wanted Cuba, an island which
pre-empted half of our Spanish-American trade and which many Americans also coveted. The situation was delicate, and we could not afford
to antagonize even puerile Spain, for we wanted Florida and Texas, still
in Spanish hands. To make matters worse, Russian traders from Alaska
were haunting the California coast and threatening to close the United
States off from a Pacific outlet.

Nevertheless, the United States was the first to recognize the belligerency of the rebels, and it sent agents to a number of the rebel cities.
The revolutionists obtained ships and arms in the United States, though

**The U.S.
and Span-
ish-Ameri-
can revolt**
by no means in the desired quantities, and American ships
sailed under revolutionary licenses to harry Spanish trade.
When it became evident that the United States did not
propose to aid them to the extent of risking a war which was
clearly beyond its strength, the revolutionists bitterly denounced its
cowardly caution. Actually there was little ground for recognizing the
revolutionary governments as independent and responsible. Spanish troops
threatened their existence as late as 1824. The governments were intensely
antiforeign, even to the extent of abusing foreign merchants and envoys.
Their privateers were often little better than pirates. Worst of all were
the ferocious civil wars between rival factions, which resulted in such
rapid changes that with the best will in the world the United States
could scarcely have found a government in power long enough to be
recognized.

There could be only one outcome to any rivalry between the United

States and Great Britain for influence and trade in the revolted countries. American consular representatives were too often inept; those of Great Britain were normally experienced and subtle. American **U.S. and** merchants could offer few goods which Latin America **British riv-** could not produce for itself as soon as order was restored; **alry** British merchants offered the finest and cheapest array of manufactured articles in the world. Great Britain had the capital to finance trade and new enterprises, and it had the sea power to protect its commerce in time of war; the United States had neither. Not least, Latin America was under the dominance of an aristocracy which had a natural sympathy with Britain and which feared the runaway democracy of the United States. Nevertheless, the United States did gain a temporary advantage in 1822, when a lull in the storm gave some promise of order and Monroe seized the opportunity to recognize the independence of Argentina, Chile, Peru, Great Colombia, and Mexico.

In the 1820's Great Britain was still run largely by its "ruling classes" —the same combination of aristocrats and merchants that had supported George III during the American Revolution—and their sympathy was with the Holy Alliance. Nevertheless, the British gov- **Britain's** ernment, though it had no official truck with revolution, had **dilemma** protested against Metternich's interference with the right of nations to set up liberal constitutions, and its relations with the nations of the Holy Alliance had become strained. This situation merely reflected the fact that there was rising in Britain a powerful liberal element which opposed the so-called Legitimists, and it was joined by industrialists and merchants who coveted Latin-American markets and conceived them to be in danger from France and the United States. They were aware that Spain could not restore its empire with its closed markets, but they knew that a division of Latin America among the nations of the Holy Alliance would be just as inimical to British trade. George Canning, British Foreign Minister, shared the alarm and sought a means of counteracting the possible plans of the Holy Alliance and of obtaining an ally in case of actual war. At the moment French troops were crushing the Riego revolt in Spain, and Canning feared that France might use this opportunity as a springboard for adventures in Latin America.

Canning hated democrats, republics, and rebels, and regarded the United States as a glaring specimen of all three aberrations. Nevertheless, in this crisis it occurred to him that he might kill two birds with one stone. Accordingly in August 1823 he proposed to Richard **Canning** Rush, the American minister in London, that the two gov- **proposes an** ernments issue a joint declaration that would (1) disounte- **alliance** nance any foreign attempt to seize Spanish-American territory and (2) disavow any intention to take territory for themselves. Rush was willing to sign at once on condition that Canning immediately join the United States in recognizing the new nations. Now Canning still hoped to bluff the Holy Alliance and was not anxious to promote a showdown by so drastic a step as recognition. His intention apparently was to use the United States as a pawn in his European game and at the same time flatter it into a promise to end its territorial expansion. Rush was not fooled, but he sent Canning's proposal on to Washington. By October Canning had become satisfied that France would not use its conquest of Spain as a stepping stone to America and reverted to his anti-American-ism. Rush did not fail to pass on to Monroe information concerning Canning's loss of interest in a joint declaration.

John Quincy Adams, Monroe's Secretary of State, has usually been credited with the authorship of the Monroe Doctrine, but it now seems that Monroe had primary responsibility in its formation. When Jefferson **The forma-** and Madison were consulted, they were of the opinion that **tion of the** it was time for joint action with Great Britain; but now **Monroe** Monroe and Adams learned that Canning had abandoned **Doctrine** his proposal (they also knew why), and they resolved to issue a unilateral declaration of policy, aimed chiefly against France. Fortunately the wrath of Spain could be risked, for Florida had now been transferred.

The United States, as Adams pointed out, could not afford to become "a Yankee cockboat in the wake of the British man-o'-war," and in any case the British navy would stand between Latin America and the Holy Alliance. Lastly, it would not be politically advisable for the United States to adopt a self-denying ordinance regarding territorial expansion, for it was possible that Canning was trying to euchre the United States into a position where it would not dare to annex Cuba. Outside these considerations they seem to have felt that they owed it to the dignity of the United States and to its interest in Latin America to take a stand on the problem of the Holy Alliance. They had no illusion that they could frighten that rather inchoate monster, nor did they anticipate war, but they did hope that an American pronouncement would add the feather-weight of influence which would dissuade it from Latin-American ven-tures. There was the added advantage that such a declaration would now be as much a warning to England as to France and the Holy Alliance.

Monroe's annual message of 2 December 1823 carried the fateful declaration of policy, sandwiched into two widely separated parts as though to obscure its importance. The first part stated the No-coloniza-**The** tion or No-annexation Principle: ". . . the American con-**Monroe** tinents, by the free and independent condition which they **Doctrine** have assumed and maintain, are henceforth not to be con-sidered as subjects for future colonization by any European powers." The second part stated the Doctrine of the Two Spheres, pledged the United States to stay within its own sphere, and warned Europe to exercise a like restraint: "In the wars of the European powers in matters relating to themselves, we have never taken any part, nor does it comport with our policy to do so. . . . The political system of the allied powers is essentially different . . . from that of America. . . . We owe it, therefore, to candor and to the amicable relations existing between the United States and those powers to declare that we should consider any attempt on their part to extend their system [*of government*] to any portion of this hemisphere as dangerous to their peace and safety. With the existing colonies or dependencies of any European power we have not interfered and shall not interfere."

The people of the United States, still fatuously believing that they had proved themselves a great power by winning the War of 1812, complacently hailed Monroe's warning (whenever they noted it at all) as the decisive check to European aggression. This opinion was promoted by the fact that Russia, overextended in Alaska and busy in Siberia, had already stopped its southward advance. Even Mexico's offer to cede California to Russia as a bribe for recognition did not persuade her to try to block the United States from the Pacific—perhaps because the czar wished to build up that country as a counterweight to Britain. In 1824 she signed a treaty with the United States which placed the southern boundary of Alaska at 54°40'.

American reception

Canning was infuriated at having been overreached, since it was evident that the Americans must have counted upon the fact that Britain would have to oppose an aggressive move by the Holy Alliance. Especially did he resent the Doctrine of the Two Spheres, which denied Britain's special interests in America, and every possible means was used to counter in Latin America the idea that there was any affinity between Britain and the United States. Early in 1825 Canning recognized the Latin-American nations, chortling that he had "called the New World into existence to redress the balance of the old." He rightly estimated the value of these recognitions as far greater than those of the United States. "The deed is done," he boasted, "the nail is driven, Spanish America is free, and if we do not mismanage our affairs badly, she is English." England did not mismanage; henceforth Latin America was, next to India, Britain's greatest colony. It was a new sort of colony, an economic domain, in which the imperial power took little political interest but from which it drew a profit at the expense of keeping its naval brass well polished in order to scare away intruders. The struggle that the bearded sailors of Queen Elizabeth had begun was over at last. Spain had lost its empire.

British reception

Latin-American reception of the Monroe Doctrine was mixed, with considerable evidence of suspicion and little of enthusiasm. Latin-American leaders had accused the United States of lukewarmness to human **Latin-American reception** liberty when it did not risk all for them, and now any hope that Monroe's message might presage a change of policy was dashed when the United States rejected an overture for an alliance with Great Colombia.

Meanwhile Bolívar had called a congress of the free nations of the hemisphere to meet at Panama in June 1826, "to deal with the high interests of peace and war"—which meant to provide for a defensive alli-**The Panama Congress** ance, a code of international law, commercial treaties, and for the liberating of Cuba and Puerto Rico. As it turned out, only four out of eight eligible nations attended, and of these not one ratified all the discussions of the congress.

Henry Clay, who envisioned the United States as the leader and defender of the hemisphere, was now Secretary of State and after a prolonged and severe conflict in the Senate obtained the appointment of two delegates to the congress; one of them died en route, and the other arrived after the adjournment. Adams, indeed, had hesitated to participate lest it lead to embarrassing commitments; especially did he seem to desire Cuba to remain on the parental tree until it was ripe enough for American plucking.

The Jackson men made political capital in the South by denouncing the scheme as an attempt to break the color line by making white Americans sit in session with mulatto generals; there was always the danger, as well, that a Haitian ambassador would sully Washington's diplomatic balls with his black presence. All this was a delight to Canning, and the English observer at Panama was able to increase Latin-American antipathy to the United States.

The Monroe Doctrine as stated in 1823 was merely a presidential utterance; it was not binding upon the country because it had not received Congressional approval. Nor was this all. The doctrine sank from **Significance of the Monroe Doctrine** public consciousness until 1895, except for a few brief occasions which we shall note in due course. Even on those occasions it was the President, rather than Congress or the people, who took the initiative in warning away trespassers. What, then, was the significance of the original Monroe Doctrine?

(1) It marked the triumph of isolationism, which (however illusory) was to sway American sentiment for almost a century. No attempt was made to back up the doctrine by alliances even with the nations whose independence was thus guaranteed.

(2) It marked the decision of the United States to bear toward Latin America a responsibility which it would not bear toward the rest of the

world. Thus, the United States refused to take sides in the struggle for Greek independence, an issue which, to a generation that had been educated in the classics, had far more emotional appeal than the Latin-American issue.

(3) It marked the recognition on the part of responsible American leaders of the fact that Great Britain was no longer to be greatly feared —that, indeed, we had much in common. Monroe's defiance to Europe was absurd unless in a showdown it would be backed up by a greater power than ours. That power was the British navy—added, of course, to the jealousies which European powers nursed toward each other and which made each hesitate to grab what it wanted. There is irony in the fact that the effectiveness of our proud isolation depended upon the goodwill and self-interest of the very power which the American people were denouncing as the enemy of human liberty.

2 The North Atlantic Triangle

The existence of a strong British colony north of the United States has been a significant factor in molding modern history. First, had it not been for British power, it is likely that the United States would have expanded to the Arctic as well as to the south and west, and would have become a truly continental power. Second, British strength on the north was a continual reminder to American leaders and people that they must set a limit to their vaulting ambitions; otherwise they might become involved in a first-class war whose issue would at best be doubtful. Third, the existence of British North America has served in the long run to draw Britain and the United States together.

Significance of British North America

On one side, the British pull on Canada has moderated American isolationism. On the other side, the American pull on Canada has moderated British imperial controls and exerted a powerful force in compelling Great Britain to permit the growth of self-government not only in Canada but in all of the British dominions.

The Treaty of Ghent had paved the way for the settlement of outstanding disputes between Great Britain and the United States by conference or arbitration. A commercial treaty of 1815 removed British restrictions on American trade except in the West Indies. The role of Canada as a buffer state was forecast when the Rush-Bagot Agreement of 1817 provided for limitation of naval armament on the Great Lakes; it did not, however, affect land fortifications, so these were maintained and strengthened. The American "liberty" to fish in British North American waters was presumably abrogated by the War of 1812. The Convention of 1818 settled the

Settlement of Anglo-American disputes

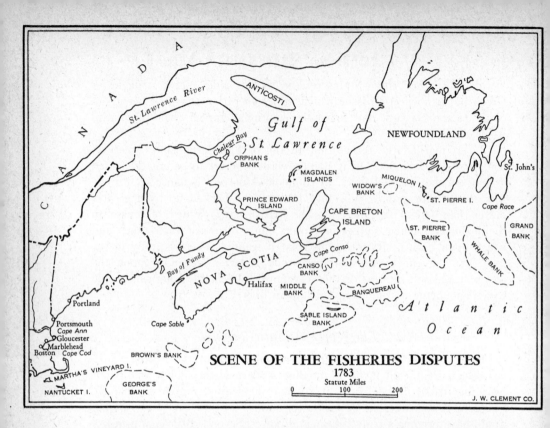

SCENE OF THE FISHERIES DISPUTES
1783
Statute Miles

J. W. CLEMENT CO.

problem of the fisheries along with several others. Americans could fish off Labrador, the northern and western shores of Newfoundland, and the Magdalen Islands (in the Gulf of St. Lawrence) and could also land elsewhere on uninhabited shores, but not to engage in inshore fishing. The old chestnut of the controversy over British removal of slaves at the close of the Revolution was arbitrated by the Czar of Russia, who awarded a compensation of $1,000,000 to the United States. The northern boundary of the Louisiana Purchase was set at the forty-ninth parallel from the Lake of the Woods to the Rocky Mountains. The Oregon country was to be jointly occupied, an arrangement which was renewed until 1846, when it also was divided at the forty-ninth parallel.

The most serious remaining trade problem concerned commerce with the British West Indies. The treaty of 1815 had put British and American ships on an equal footing in commerce between Great Britain and the **Struggle for British West Indies carrying trade** United States. It soon became evident that in practice the trade was falling to British vessels because their monopoly of carrying American produce to the West Indies enabled them to build up a triangular trade so profitable that they could undercut the freight rates of American vessels. Congress retaliated by prohibiting commercial intercourse with British America,

480

and the British government made concessions which enabled American ships to take over nine tenths of the West Indian trade. However, John Quincy Adams was so thoroughly convinced of the dependence of British planters on American foodstuffs and lumber products that he stubbornly insisted that not even British vessels should have any advantage in the West Indian trade. The result was that in 1827 the British closed the trade once more. Adams's mistake told heavily against him in the presidential campaign of 1828. On the other hand, the long fight and the outrageously high prices of supplies did much to ruin British West Indian planters.

Jackson, as one might have expected, threw aside the delicate nuances of protocol for "shirt-sleeve diplomacy." Upon his accession to the presidency he abated his Anglophobia in order to take a crack at Adams. Through Van Buren he announced to the British government that the people had rejected Adams's policy, a public washing of dirty linen which caused scandal and amusement in diplomatic circles. At any rate, in 1830 both countries renounced their restrictions, and a relatively free direct trade between the United States and the West Indies ensued. Another example of Jackson's rough-and-ready diplomacy came soon afterward. France on one excuse or another had put off payment of the claims for Napoleon's spoliation of American commerce, and Jackson's accusations of bad faith and threats of reprisal wounded French pride. One thing led to another until the two nations seemed to be on the verge of war. The situation was finally salved by the British, who persuaded France to take an explanation in place of an apology and to pay the claims.

Jackson's "shirt-sleeve diplomacy"

The settlement of the West Indian problem was basically due to Great Britain's gradual abandonment of mercantilism. The morals of the Wesleyan movement, the laissez-faire economics of Adam Smith, and Jeremy Bentham's urge to positive improvements, all united in a sweeping wave of reforms which washed out British mercantilism with its restrictions on trade and society and ushered in the modern age of free enterprise and social reform. The Reform Bill of 1832 smashed the control of the merchants and aristocratic agrarians and put the great industrialists in the driver's seat. It was not long until the great bankers (finance capitalists) began to weld the industrialists into a vast economic empire which governed world trade, production, and investment.

Great Britain goes over to free trade

The conversion of Great Britain to the doctrines of "economic liberalism" was marked by the downfall of the government planning implicit in mercantilism and by the gradual removal of tariffs and trade restrictions, especially of the "Corn Laws" which had limited the importation of foreign grain. Economic liberals were so sure that England had a natural monopoly of the feast of trade and manufacture that they were quite willing to let other nations gather what fallen crumbs they could. This policy of relative free trade was in proces of evolution during the generation after 1830, and it obtained such a hold upon the British imagination that it was only abandoned in 1931 under the grim pressure of American competition and general world conditions.

These fundamental changes in British attitudes necessarily affected British colonies. The American Revolution had convinced the ministers of the Crown that, while they must never again lay taxes on colonies, they must keep a tight rein on colonial administration. The result was that British North America had been closely bound into the imperial commercial system, and the Crown officials in each colony maintained strict control by building up a conservative interest in the legislatures. Thus Upper Canada (Ontario) was dominated by a clique of United Empire Loyalists called the Family Compact, which was united by land grants, social and economic privileges, and a common hatred of democracy. A similar group, the Chateau Clique, existed in Lower Canada (Quebec). The effect was to unite the Crown and a privileged colonial administrative and legislative oligarchy in a barrier against any breeze of reform which might ruffle the conservative calm of the legislatures. This condition existed in greater or lesser degree in every British North American colony.

Conservative controls in British North America

The conservative strangle hold on colonial affairs was increasingly resented by taxpayers, by farmers who found themselves barred from new lands, and by businessmen who were blocked by established interests. Reformers were smacked down so decisively that extremists began to talk of armed revolt and possible union with the United States. Finally economic depression did touch off abortive risings in 1837, under Louis Joseph Papineau in Quebec and William Lyon Mackenzie in Ontario. Both leaders were defeated and fled to the United States. There they gathered men and supplies, and made puny raids into Canada.

British North American Revolution

Late in 1837 Mackenzie established himself on Navy Island on the Canadian side of the Niagara River, where he was supplied from Buffalo by the American-owned steamer *Caroline.* On the night of 29 December some Canadians crossed the river to the American shore, seized the *Caroline,* killed an American citizen, and sent the steamboat down the river in flames. President Van Buren appealed for neutrality, but public feeling led to a series of retaliations. A Canadian, Alexander McLeod, was arrested in New York and tried by the state for the *Caroline* murder. The Federal government, unable to interfere in a matter of state jurisdiction, was warned by Great Britain

The Caroline Affair

that McLeod's conviction would mean war; fortunately the prisoner was acquitted.

The cause of Canadian independence was espoused by organizations of "Patriots" on the American side; hence the "Patriot War," their abortive efforts to aid the rebels. The issue was kept alive for some years by secret "Hunters' Lodges" of refugees and Irish-Americans. If either country had really wanted war, there were numerous occasions when it might have been started. As it was, Van Buren sincerely strove for peace, and this effort may have been a contributory cause of his defeat in 1840. Papineau and Mackenzie later returned to Canada and had undistinguished legislative careers.

The rebellions, though abortive, were by no means unfruitful. The British government promptly suspended the constitutions of all five provinces, and Lord Durham was sent out as governor to deal with the critical situation. He recognized the truth of the statement made by one of the leading rebels: "We rebelled neither against Her Majesty's person nor her government, but **Colonial reform** against colonial misgovernment." Durham's *Report on the Affairs of British North America* (1839) became in time the inspiration of a complete reorganization not only of Canadian affairs but of the entire system of government of white colonies.

The Crown granted autonomy because it was convinced that white colonies would in time become independent anyhow. Economic liberals placed little stress on political ties but expected trade to flow in natural economic channels. It was better to let the North American colonies go peaceably and maintain the economic ties than to drive them into a serious revolt which must win because of their nearness to the United States. The amazing result was that the colonies, instead of departing, actually sought closer co-operation with the mother country. The conservative oligarchies, with the British props removed, had to give way gradually to popular demands for reform and democratization.

The granting of responsible government to the British North American colonies did not automatically settle all the differences between them and the mother country. Commercial relations and foreign affairs were still under the control of the Crown. When Britain adopted free trade, she admitted serious competitors to Canadian products and destroyed the trade in American products which a more favorable tariff treatment had siphoned from **Canadian commercial independence** the Great Lakes states to Montreal. Nevertheless, the navigation acts remained for some years and limited Canadian trade pretty well to British ships. There followed in 1849 the Annexation Manifesto issued by the merchants of Montreal. It was a flat failure, largely for reasons that originated south of the border. The Cotton States opposed annexation

A general arguing of the MAINE question, or John Bull's Bully, trying to frighten Jonathan out of TITLE & TIMBER.

Jonathan (Uncle Sam in his youth) defies Britain in the controversy over the Maine boundary.

because they did not wish to see the number of the free states increased.

In 1854 the annexation movement was further weakened by the Elgin-Marcy Reciprocity Treaty, which set up free trade between the United States and the British provinces in their principal products without destroying the right of each to lay a tariff on articles not enumerated, chiefly manufactures. In 1859 Canada (that is, the united provinces of Ontario and Quebec) did impose a tariff on manufactured articles of both American and British origin. The British government protested, but without result. Canada made good its claim to commercial independence, and not the least reason for its success was the fact that Britain did not dare to coerce a colony so close to the United States.

The winning of control of foreign affairs took longer, and until World War I Canada lived in fear that the Crown would sell out Canadian interests in order to retain the goodwill of the United States. From the **Failure to win control of foreign relations** Canadian point of view this is what happened after the Revolution and the War of 1812, and in the series of negotiations in the 1840's and 1850's. Nevertheless, these negotiations were important steps in reducing international friction; the very fact that both Canadians and Americans resented the decisions as sellouts probably indicated that they were fair compromises.

The Treaty of Paris (1783) had set the Maine boundary at the St. Croix River and the "Highlands Line," but the official maps marked with the boundary had not been preserved in the United States archives, and the one in the British Foreign office was kept secret. A **Maine** difference of opinion as to which river was the St. Croix was **boundary** settled in 1799 by designating the river which now bears **dispute** the name, and in 1817 the islands at its mouth were divided. The United States claimed that the Highlands referred to the watershed between the Atlantic and the St. Lawrence, which runs very close to the latter. Great Britain, anxious to control a short route from Halifax to Quebec, insisted upon a line far south of the true one. The compromise award of the King of the Netherlands was rejected by the United States in 1831, and in 1838 Maine and New Brunswick lumbermen clashed in the disputed region in the so-called Aroostook War, or War of Pork and Beans. Both sides called out the militia and clamored for war.

When Secretary of State Webster and Lord Ashburton, special commissioner of Great Britain, met in Washington in the summer of 1842 to negotiate, neither one knew of the proof of the American claim but, since the available documents and maps were so contradictory, **Webster-** decided to split the difference. About seven twelfths of the **Ashburton** disputed territory went to Maine, and adjustments were **Treaty,** made in favor of New York and New Hampshire. Maine and **1842** Massachusetts (the latter had certain rights to the soil) were each pacified by a Federal payment.

Webster and Ashburton undertook to settle a number of minor problems between Canada and the United States, but their consideration of the problem of the Atlantic slave trade had nothing to do with Canada. The agitation against slavery in Great Britain had led to **The slave** the stoppage of the slave trade in the colonies in 1807 and **trade** to the abolition of slavery itself in 1833. The British West Indies, rapidly becoming a poorhouse, feared being undersold by countries like Brazil and Cuba, where fresh supplies of cheap slave labor were being imported from Africa. Great Britain thus, for both humanitarian and economic reasons, undertook to put an end to the international slave trade. Slavers were treated by the British, as they were by the United States, as pirates. Most of the European nations were willing to agree that their ships might be searched.

The United States, under the influence of southern slave interests and belligerently conscious of former British searches and seizures, refused to permit either visit or search unless Britain gave up its historic claim to the right of impressment. This she refused to do. There was, more-

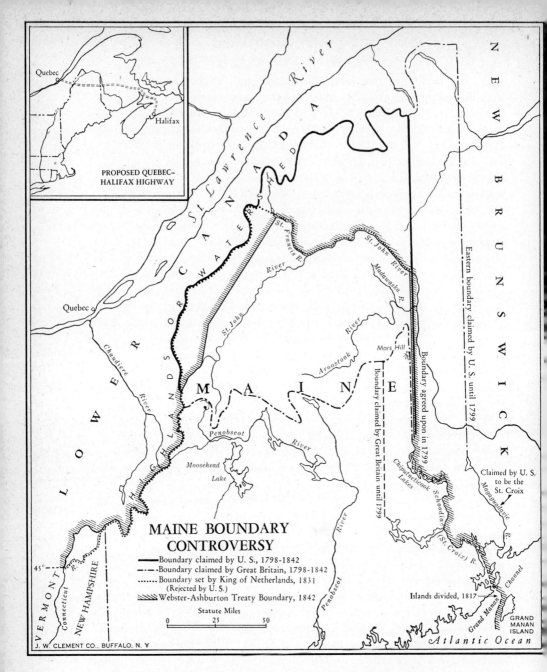

MAINE BOUNDARY
CONTROVERSY
—— Boundary claimed by U. S., 1798-1842
—·—·Boundary claimed by Great Britain, 1798-1842
········ Boundary set by King of Netherlands, 1831
(Rejected by U. S.)
\\\\\ Webster-Ashburton Treaty Boundary, 1842

Statute Miles

0   25   50

PROPOSED QUEBEC-
HALIFAX HIGHWAY

J. W. CLEMENT CO., BUFFALO, N. Y.

over, the accusation—apparently valid—that the British navy sometimes
used its powers of search to remove troublesome competitors to British
commerce. The result was that slavers of any nation had only to run up
the American flag to avoid British interference. Webster and Ashburton
agreed that both nations would keep warships on the African coast, the

Americans to suppress the trade in vessels flying their flag. As it turned out, the United States, which was then ruled by a government sympathetic to slavery, did not live up to its bargain, and it was not until after the beginning of the Civil War that the two countries agreed to mutual right of search.

One of the most difficult problems before the North Atlantic Triangle in the 1850's concerned the fisheries. The Convention of 1818 was fairly satisfactory until about 1840, when the feckless mackerel deserted the New England coast and moved to the inshore waters of the Maritime Provinces. When New Englanders followed, they fell afoul of the prohibition against Americans fishing in-shore. The Elgin-Marcy Reciprocity Treaty of 1854 not **Elgin-Marcy Treaty, 1854** only provided for reciprocal trade but for reciprocal fishing rights. The North favored the treaty in order to advance annexation, and the South favored it on the ground that it would promote Canadian prosperity and block annexation. Skeptics on both sides of the Canadian-American bor-der were finally convinced by a Department of State agent who spent lav-ishly in its behalf, ably aided in Washington by Lord Elgin's racy anec-dotes and his bubbling champagne. One important provision of the treaty was to open the St. Lawrence River to Americans and Lake Michigan to Canadians.

3   The Spread of American Commerce

American shippers not only were merchants and carriers, but they were traditionally salt-water drummers. Most merchants served in their youth as captains of ships or supercargoes (business representatives), but after they retired from the sea to manage their counting rooms their financial welfare depended not only upon their **Salt-water drummers** own acumen but upon that of their agents. Captains and supercargoes either were relatives of the merchant or were by contract entitled to a share of the profits of a voyage. It was their business to study the market in whatever part of the world they might be and to buy and sell in a manner which would bring the largest profit to the house. The goods with which they cleared from the home port might be only a starter, for there might be several turnovers of freight before the ship returned to its base; and if the goods they brought back did not suit the current market situation, the profits of three years of shrewd trading might be swallowed up in the terminal loss. Add to these risks the ordinary dangers of the sea such as shipwreck, disease, piracy, and the possibility of seizure by warring powers, and it will be seen that American shippers were by no means betting on a sure thing.

On the other hand, certain factors favored American enterprise. For twenty years the United States was the only large neutral carrier, and its ships came and went among the warring powers with a loss from

Rivalry with Great Britain seizure which was small in relation to the gross business. The only rival carrier which consistently had access to the sea was Great Britain, but here again circumstances favored the United States. The British merchant marine was for the most part made up of slow, unseaworthy vessels, poorly commanded and wretchedly manned. The East India Company ("Honourable John Company") had a monopoly of British trade in China until 1834; but though its ships were better commanded and manned than those of the merchant marine, they were sluggish, kettle-bottomed craft; protected by the navigation acts, the Honourable John's captains never tried to beat competitors to market and habitually lingered long in port and when at sea slowed down at night. American ships were light and swift, and their masters were not only shrewd bargainers in port but skillful sailors and navigators who knew how to outsail their rivals. The result was that until the triumph of steam American ships and shippers had the edge.

It was not until the 1830's that the British Parliament awoke to the situation and began to improve the merchant marine and to awaken the East India Company by allowing other Britishers to compete with it.

Reform of British trade In 1849 the final logical step was taken of opening the ports of the Empire to almost unrestricted foreign competition except for the coastal trade, and even that restriction was presently loosened. The result was the phenomenal growth of the British merchant marine both in size and in efficiency. The American flag all but disappeared from the seas except for its monopoly of the American coastal trade.

New York, Philadelphia, and Baltimore were by no means negligible home ports for American ships, but until a decade after the War of 1812 Massachusetts led the parade. The Oriental trade of the United States has

American Oriental trade received perhaps more attention than its monetary value warrants, for up to 1860 it probably amounted to less than five per cent of the total; trade with Europe, ranging between one half and three fourths, or with either North or South America was far more important. The Oriental trade was, however, a welcome substitute for the lost West Indian trade, and its influence on American foreign relations would be hard to overestimate, for here was (as we can see now) a clear portent of the future. American agents established American interests everywhere in Asia's ports and the Pacific's islands. Boston and Salem roughly divided the Orient between them, the former taking the North Pacific and China, and the latter the South Pacific, the East Indies, the Indian Ocean, and Africa.

The American flag first appeared in China in 1784, flown by the New York merchant ship *Empress of China,* and six years later Robert Gray in the *Columbia* of Boston was the first to carry the flag around the world. Since China had little need of Occidental goods, the **Boston's** East India Company had been forced to pay in cash for tea, **Pacific do-** silk, and chinaware, or to eke out the exchange by sales of **main** opium from India. Boston merchants soon found that the Chinese would gladly take the sandalwood of Hawaii and the sea-otter furs of Oregon, and they arranged to help the Hudson's Bay Company break the East India Company's Chinese monopoly by carrying its furs to Canton. Ginseng, and later on cotton goods, were also exported to China. When the Oregon fur trade declined (about the 1820's), Boston ships began loading cargoes of hides in California, Chile, and Buenos Aires for the use of the growing shoe manufactories of Massachusetts.

One curious illustration of Boston initiative was Frederic Tudor's creation of a demand in the tropics for New England's ice, a trade which gave Boston welcome exchange in areas such as India and Persia which would otherwise have been hard to enter. The far waters of the world were better known to Bostonians than was the Hudson River. To the Perkins, Crowninshield, Forbes, and Amory families "the Coast" was Oregon and California, and Hawaii was familiarly known as "the Islands."

Boston ships rounded Cape Horn to enter their empire, but those of Salem sailed eastward around the Cape of Good Hope. The spice trade was their main reliance, and Salem was for a time the pepper capital of the world. However, Salem's ship captains, even more than those of Boston, were salt-water drummers, and the cargoes **The Salem** which they brought home were more diverse. They fished in **East Indies** Micronesia for trepang and climbed cliffs for edible birds' nests and traded them for Chinese tea. Sugar, hemp, indigo, and tin from the East Indies, coffee from Arabia, carpets from Persia, silk and cotton prints from India, hides from Argentina, rubber overshoes from Brazil, copal from Zanzibar, gold dust, ivory, and camphor wood from West Africa, and wines from Madeira and the Azores were exchanged for butter, beef, rum, codfish, tobacco, and missionaries. It was a Salem vessel, the *Friendship,* which in 1831 was captured by Malays at Quallah-Battoo in Sumatra, an incident which led to a punitive naval expedition which the next year bombarded the town in retaliation. The names of Salem's great trading families, Derby, Peabody, and Prince, ranked with those of any city of their time.

By 1830 it had become evident that Massachusetts was losing to New York in its relative share of foreign trade. New York's superiority as a distributing center, especially after the digging of the Erie Canal and the

Boston loses to New York development of railroads, was undoubted. The large packet ship was now supplanting the small salt-water drummer all over the world; and the smaller Massachusetts ports, less suitable than Boston for the larger ships, yielded slowly to the capital city and went into the manufacture of textiles and shoes or revived the fishing industry. Shipbuilders also moved to Boston and New York. Out of the new state of affairs Boston managed to retain a considerable part of its Russian and East Indian importing business and the Mediterranean fruit trade, but even in these lines Boston-owned ships often were sent into New York. The final pay-off was clearly foretold when Boston merchants began to move into New York, and New England merchant capital began to pour into industry. By 1845 New York's merchant fleet had passed that of Massachusetts. New York, as well as other ports, built up the profitable "cotton triangle" trade carrying manufactures to the South, cotton to Europe, and manufactures and immigrants back to the home port.

The generation after the War of 1812 saw a radical change in the type of merchant seamen. From olden times young farmers and townsmen had gone to sea to save a nest egg to set themselves up in business or matri- **Deterioration of American seamen** mony. The West and the city now began to lure these young men, and the pull was all the greater because sailors' wages had been reduced by the bitter competition that followed the end of the Napoleonic Wars. Probably there was also a growing independence among Americans which caused them to refuse to submit to the ill-treatment traditional on ships.

However, native Americans were still plentiful in coastal shipping, a service which was by the Navigation Act of 1817 practically reserved to American owners and seamen and in which seamen's laws were more strictly enforced. Before long a flood of foreign seamen from all nations invaded the American blue-water merchant marine, attracted by standards which seemed adequate to them, and most of such Americans as it held were the scum of the seaports. The crimp became important for the first time in American shipping, and numbers of landsmen or coasting seamen were shanghaied for blue-water service. It should be noted that the efficiency of merchant officers had never been greater, but neither had their brutality—as indeed the quality of their crews demanded.

The coming victory of steam was already evident to the discerning when American designers gave to sailing ships their highest development and a parting taste of glory in the famous clippers, which could actually outsail the steamships of that day. The clipper was essen- **The clipper ship** tially a large ship (around 4500 tons as compared to the 300 tons of earlier merchant vessels) built with the lines of the small, speedy schooner; its superiority was due not only to the design of its hull but to its lofty sails and to its handling by sailors whose daring and skill had never before been equaled.

The first renowned clipper was the *Rainbow,* designed by John Willis Griffiths of New York and launched in 1845. The *Rainbow* made the round trip to Canton in less time than other ships took for one way and brought back a cargo of tea which, because its flavor was unspoiled by a long voyage, paid double the cost of the ship. Griffiths's next clipper, the *Sea Witch,* actually sailed from Canton to New York in seventy-three days. Before long Donald McKay, a Nova Scotian shipbuilder settled in Boston, launched the *Flying Cloud,* the fleetest of all clippers. It made the voyage from New York around the Horn to San Francisco in eighty-nine days. Another of McKay's ships, the *Lightning,* logged four hundred thirty-six nautical miles in one day. The California and Australian gold rushes gave the clipper ships a truly golden opportunity, and the repeal of Britain's navigation acts (1849) put the world's tea cargoes into their holds. British shipwrights adopted the new form, but they preferred a "medium" type which carried less canvas and shipped smaller crews. Until about 1875 the clippers carried the fast freight and passenger traffic of the world.

Isaac Wright of New York was the first to establish a transatlantic packet line. This was the famous Black Ball Line, which in 1819 began plying between New York and Liverpool. Black Ball ships reduced the six-weeks' horror of the passage as much as the techniques of the time permitted; they were specifically designed for **Packet lines** the safety and comfort of the first-class passenger and made the crossing with amazing regularity in just under three weeks. During the next few years lines from New York and other American ports set up packet competition, followed in 1835 by Edward Knight Collins's Dramatic Line, which offered the crack transatlantic service of the ante-bellum years. In 1838, however, two British steamship lines began packet service with the liners *Sirius* and *Great Western,* and two years later the Nova Scotian Samuel Cunard founded the famous British Cunard Line. Collins obtained a Congressional subsidy and with a new fleet of steamers beat Cunard at his own game. However, the strain was too great. Two of Collins's magnificent steamers were lost, and the Cotton States, which resented Federal support of navigation, succeeded in killing the subsidy. Collins ceased operations in 1858.

By and large the triumphs of American trade were gained without government aid, unlike those of Great Britain. The Navigation Act of 1817 confined coastal trade to American ships and largely to American sailors, but no system of subsidies ever continued very long. **Scientific** Congress was even grudging in its support of coast surveys, **aids to nav-** aids to navigation, and life-saving. However, Matthew Fon- **igation** taine Maury, a Virginia naval officer and father of the science of oceanography, was given a post at the Naval Observatory as an aid to his researches. His close study of innumerable ships' logs and sailing records enabled him to point out to shipmasters new routes which saved time by taking advantage of winds and currents. Thus he made it possible even for the old type of ships to cut almost seven weeks from their average sailing time between New York and San Francisco. In 1853 at an international congress at Brussels he persuaded the nations to adopt a uniform system of recording oceanographic data. His work also provided the information essential to the laying of the Atlantic cable and was significant in the development of weather forecasting. Only less important than Maury was Nathaniel Bowditch of Salem, whose *New American Practical Navigator* of 1802 improved on an English model and went through sixty-six editions and reprints.

The American merchant marine had never been larger or more prosperous than it was in the early 1850's, and at the beginning of the Civil War in 1861 it included about 2,500,000 tons engaged in foreign trade, Decline of and in all categories 5,350,000 tons, a total very close to that American of Great Britain. Nevertheless, Collins's failure was merely merchant the most obvious indication of the impending decline of the marine American merchant marine. The reasons were several. The British government realized the vital importance of shipping to the imperial economy and lavishly supported its shippers in the race for maritime supremacy. British shippers early recognized that the iron ship and steam would supplant wood and sails and took the lead in technological development, though it was 1889 before the White Star Line led in cutting loose from sails and trusting solely to steam.

In the United States the rising conflict between North and South blocked Federal subsidies to steam-shipping, and the rapid development of manufactures and of the Mississippi Valley offered more attractions to private capital than did the sea. American shipbuilders, favored by cheap timber and with shipyards chiefly adapted to wooden construction, were also bemused by the fleeting success of the clipper ship and failed to recognize the coming victory of iron and steam; the sudden demands of the 1850's (wars, gold rushes, etc.) resulted in the accelerated production of wooden ships—as high as five hundred thousand tons annually. That this was overproduction became quickly evident when in the depression of 1847 steam proved more economical and dependable than sails.

The proportion of American exports and imports carried in American ships had been decreasing ever since 1825, but with the coming of the Civil War it dropped by half—then continued dropping until 1914. The

Confederate commerce raiders loosed by British policy during the Civil War destroyed almost three hundred ships and drove many more to take refuge under the British flag, as the British intended. By the close of the Civil War the merchant marine engaged in foreign commerce had been cut in half. The decline continued until little but the coastal trade was left under the American flag.

Among the most important of American enterprises in the heyday of maritime prosperity was whaling. Whale oil was a valuable illuminant and lubricant to a world ignorant of petroleum, and whalebone was useful in stays, riding crops, and other articles that required resili-

ence. The islands of Nantucket and Martha's Vineyard and **Early whalers** the towns on Buzzard's Bay early entered the business of offshore whaling, taught by the local Indians, who remained prominent as harpooners until the passing of the industry in our own century. The barren island of Nantucket was the leader in developing whaling technology and in ranging abroad to the whaling grounds. Nantucket suffered greatly during the Revolution and the ensuing wars, since it could not, like the mainland ports, keep its ships at home and sit out the conflicts. Nantucketers in British service found their way to the Pacific as early as 1787, and other whalers followed in increasing numbers. With the coming of the War of 1812 Pacific whalers were harassed by British cruisers until Captain David Porter of the *Essex* appeared in 1813 and wrought havoc among the depredators. After wintering with his prizes at Nukahiva in the Marquesas Islands and taking possession of it for the United States, Porter returned to Chile; there, within the neutral port of Valparaiso, the *Essex* while disabled was attacked by two British ships and cut to pieces. As a result of the War of 1812 Nantucket lost four fifths of its fleet.

The recovery of whaling after the war was phenomenal. By 1847 American whalers, almost wholly from the general region of Buzzard's Bay, comprised seven hundred twenty-two of a world total of about nine hundred ships and employed around twenty thousand men. **Heyday of** Thirty well-recognized whaling fields existed in the three **the whale-** great oceans, and New Zealand and the Hawaiian Islands **men** were constant resorts for the whalemen for refitting. Nantucket long led in the number of ships, and its captains gave their names to remote Pacific islands such as Starbuck, Coffin, and Folger. Nantucket was a realm to itself; one old whaling captain had never been in the United States but knew the Pacific Ocean like the palm of his hand. After 1830 Nantucket fell behind, partly because its harbor was shut in by a sandbar, partly because its captains would hunt only the increasingly scarce sperm whale of the tropics and refused to seek the bowhead and right whales in the Arctic Sea beyond Bering Strait. Nantucket's rivals, however, moved into the Arctic, and by 1860 New Bedford boasted that it was the home port of about half the world's whaling ships.

The decline of whaling after the Civil War was due to a number of factors. Forty old whaling ships—"The Great Stone Fleet"—were sunk in an attempt to block the harbors of Charleston and Savannah during

Decline of whaling
the war. Confederate raiders accounted for as many more, setting fire to the first prizes and potting others as they came to the rescue of their comrades. Thirty-three were lost in the Arctic ice at one blow in 1871, and twelve more in 1876. These losses might have been replaced, but the scarcity of whales and the leaping competition of petroleum products had taken the profits out of the business. By 1900 whaling had all but disappeared. It survives today in a few floating factories which serve the meat- and fat-starved nations of Europe.

Whaling, indeed, was a more sweated industry than any on land, for its profits were rarely more than modest. Whaling crews served on shares, but cheating captains and owners made it common for a man after a suc-

Conditions of whaling crews
cessful cruise of three or four years to find himself back in Buzzard's Bay, still in debt to the outfitter. It was a rugged life, alternating among peril, boredom, and back-breaking labor. Quarters were cramped and stinking, food vile, and officers sadistic. The result was that self-respecting sailors refused to serve on whalers, and the crews were filled with depraved and criminal men, stretched out by green hands from inland farms and Negroes, Indians, Azoreans, and Kanakas.

Thousands vanished into the maw of the Pacific: dead, deserters, or left ashore by cheating captains to become beachcombers. Whaling men were notorious for their brutal and licentious behavior on shore, especially in the South Seas, and often paid for their crimes by being killed and eaten by the resentful natives. On the other hand, few attempts were made to protect maltreated seamen. Laws were vague and inapplicable, and the courts prejudiced in favor of masters and owners. Even American consuls, legally the protectors of seamen, eked out a living by merchandising or ship-chandlering and so were obsequiously on the side of the masters.

Let us turn now to the slow growth of American diplomatic relations with the Orient. Until after 1840 Western merchants—and merchants of any ilk were peculiarly despicable to Chinese—were in Canton only by

American merchants in China
favor, being graciously permitted to export the tea which according to Chinese ideas was necessary to keep human beings alive! American merchants, since they knew there was not the faintest chance of naval backing by their government, earnestly sought to conciliate Chinese officials during the generation after their first coming in 1784. Meanwhile Christian missionaries were

infiltrating the Canton area, making converts and adding to Western knowledge of China, and at the same time the illicit importation of Indian and Turkish opium had reversed the balance of trade and begun to drain specie from China. Both actions were deeply resented by the Chinese. American merchants were involved in the disgraceful opium traffic, though of course it could be carried on only by the connivance of Chinese officials.

The Chinese government now shrewdly combined into one package an antiforeign campaign, a curb on the export of specie, and a moral reform, tying them all together by an attempt to destroy the opium trade. The result was the Opium War (1839–42), in which the **The opening of China** British seized Hong Kong, opened to trade five ports, including Shanghai, and ended the tributary status of their merchants. The Chinese government, anxious to balance the British by other foreign interests, quickly gave most-favored-nation privileges to other powers. The United States, as the British complained, thus moved into China behind British guns without having to spill a drop of blood. Caleb Cushing, a brilliant Massachusetts lawyer, after shrewd bargaining signed in 1844 the Treaty of Wanghia, which among other things set the precedent of extraterritorial jurisdiction for foreigners in China, that is, exempted them from prosecution in Chinese courts and subjected them to the jurisdiction of consular courts.

During the next twenty years foreigners steadily enlarged their privileges and their trade, aided not a little by the internal chaos of the country. Most serious of China's troubles was the Taiping Rebellion (1850–64), reputed to have taken twenty million lives. The Man- **Foreign privileges extended** chu dynasty, regarded as foreign by Chinese, was threatened along with Westerners. Strangely enough, Hung, the fanatical founder of the movement, was profoundly affected by Christian missionaries, particularly Issachar Roberts, a Tennessee Baptist who later on became the Taiping foreign minister. The pseudo-Christian nature of the movement roused considerable Western sympathy.

In two sharp wars (1856–60) against the emperor, culminating in the sack and burning of the Summer Palace at Peking, the British and French dictated treaties which established diplomatic relations with China, opened more ports to trade, legalized the opium traffic, and placed Chinese customs under foreign control. Russia seized the opportunity to force Chinese cession of southeastern Siberia and later added special privileges in Manchuria. Now that the British and French had the imperial government under their thumbs, they backed the Salem-born soldier of fortune Frederick T. Ward, who with a motley horde of adventurers began the suppression of the Taiping rebels.

Evidences of psychological clash between China and the West were too numerous to be treated here. These included a natural objection on the part of the Chinese to permit their civilization to be contaminated by "barbarian" customs and religion, and vigorous opposi-

**Psychologi-
cal clash** tion developed even to selling or leasing land to foreigners. Extraterritoriality was a perennial cause of friction, though in the light of the radical differences between the two ideas of justice there was perhaps no other way to settle the problem. Most prominent of all was the problem of the kowtow. Chinese regarded their country as the center of civilization, the sun around which the peoples of the world revolved, and so treated foreign diplomats as tribute bearers. In addition they insisted upon the kowtow to the emperor, by which the foreigner knelt and knocked his forehead nine times on the floor as a sign of submission. Foreign diplomats of course refused to kowtow and in consequence had no audiences with the emperor. It was not until 1890 that the court ceased to demand the kowtow as an imperial right. On the other hand, there is no doubt that many foreigners (even some missionaries) by their arrogance were fully as unreasonable and provocative in their attitudes toward China.

The United States, preoccupied with coming civil war, had refused to act in concert with England and France—but did not neglect to profit by their aggressiveness. Anson Burlingame (1820–70), a Massachusetts

**Burlin-
game's work
in China** politician, was in 1861 appointed minister to China. A man of unusual charm and ability, Burlingame soon became leader of the new legations in Peking and succeeded in winning foreign tolerance when the Chinese government was unable to carry out all its treaty obligations because of civil war and the traditional autonomy of the provinces. It is possible that Burlingame prevented the partition of China by the irritated powers. At any rate, he so won the confidence of the Chinese government that he was able to persuade it to send a diplomatic mission to the West (1868–70), a mission of which Burlingame himself became the mouthpiece and titular head. While in the United States the mission signed the Burlingame Treaty of 1868 (drafted by Seward), which guaranteed to China a continuance of unrestricted emigration to the United States. The clear fact that the United States wanted no territory in China was a forecast of the later Open Door policy, and early resulted in a preference on the part of the Chinese government for American technical advisers.

The United States rode into China on the coattails of the British, but the procedure was reversed in the opening of Japan. After a term of contact with Christian traders and missionaries in the sixteenth cen-

**Japanese
isolation** tury, Japan closed its doors to the West except for a single Dutch foothold on the island of Deshima in Nagasaki harbor. The emperor of Japan, called the mikado, had long

been a mere figurehead, but now his mayor of the palace, the shogun (or tycoon), became in turn a figurehead for a group of feudal lords. Japan by 1850 teetered between a return to feudal chaos or an advance toward the Western institutions which a considerable group of liberal leaders had glimpsed through the porthole of Deshima.

The United States had a peculiar interest in Japan. New England's textile manufacturers wished to find an unexploited market. American whalers had frequently been cast on the shores of Japan by storms; sometimes they were slaughtered or imprisoned or exhibited in **American** cages, and occasionally they were turned over to the Dutch. **interest in** The American occupation of Oregon and California with **Japan** their promise of trade with the Orient brought the Great Circle route into use, and in addition the rise of steam navigation made coaling stations necessary somewhere along this route. Since American policy did not favor territorial annexation in the western Pacific, it was hoped that coaling rights could be obtained in Japan. Russia, England, and the United States had made abortive attempts to open trade with Japan, and in 1846 Washington had sent Commodore James Biddle to Tokyo. Biddle, anxious to avoid provocation, had failed to resent a push by a Japanese soldier; this was taken as a proof of cowardice, and Biddle was peremptorily ordered away.

President Fillmore was quite hospitable to expanding American power and commerce everywhere in the world, and he now determined to see what an intimation of force would do. In July 1853 Commodore Matthew C. Perry, a brother of the victor of Put-in Bay, appeared in **Perry** Tokyo Bay with four warships. Perry left a written proposal **reopens** to negotiate, then steamed away with a promise to return. **Japan, 1854** Perry's black warships, belching streamers of smoke, terrorized the Japanese and recalled an old folk song:

> Through a black night of cloud and rain
> The Black Ship plies her way—
> An alien thing of evil mien—
> Across the waters gray.

In the argument which followed among Japanese leaders the liberals won, partly because of the pressure of a growing commercial class, partly because of the opinion that Japan must arm itself in the Western manner in order to escape the fate of China. Even this early their particular fear was Russia, which was encroaching on Sakhalin. As a result, when Perry returned with an augmented fleet in February 1854, the Japanese were willing to sign a treaty which provided for most-favored-nation treatment, opened two minor ports to American trade, and provided for proper care of shipwrecked sailors.

The Perry treaty has been rightly called merely a foot in the door. Indeed, Perry had come at the psychological moment; otherwise he might have had to blast down the door as the British had done in China. Mr.

Harris in Japan

Dooley, that profound commentator on men and affairs, hit the truth in his remark: "Whin we rapped on the dure, we didn't go in, they come out." It was Townsend Harris who as the first consul general was responsible for the real opening of the door. Though little known in the United States, Harris has loomed large in Japanese history and has even become a figure of drama and legend. From 1855 to 1862 he gradually overcame suspicion and hostility and won vastly increased trade and residence rights as well as extraterritoriality. All this he did without threats, using as his trump the argument that the United States, unlike other Western nations, did not desire territory. Harris was followed by Robert H. Pruyn, another able man.

Meanwhile other nations had followed in American steps. Western entrance was not universally approved, and first British then American ships undertook to bombard dissident lords, who were utilizing popular

Westernization of Japan

hostility to foreigners to overturn the shogun and elevate the power of the mikado. Hostilities continued in the Strait of Shimonoseki; and since the shogun was unable to enforce the treaties he had made, the Western powers sent a naval expedition, including one American vessel, which in 1864 reduced the city of Shimonoseki to rubble. The shogun paid an indemnity of $4,000,000 of which the American fifth was so clearly disproportionate to the damage sustained that in 1883 Congress returned it to Japan. These various bombardments were convincing arguments that Japan could not adhere to its traditional isolation, and after a term of jockeying among political factions the shogunate came to an end in 1867.

A new emperor fostered the rapid Westernization of Japan and the centralization of governmental powers. From the first there was a bitter struggle for control of national policies between the warrior class and the bureaucratic class, which placed emphasis upon commerce and industrialization. The theory that the Japanese emperor was by right the ruler of the world was firmly fixed. As early as 1858 the shogun's prime minister pointed out to the mikado that the world was split up among many nations and sadly needed a universal ruler. He then urged that "the nations of the world will come to look upon our Emperor as the Great Ruler of all the nations, and they will come to follow our policy and submit themselves to our judgment. . . . Now is the opportune moment . . . to seize the opportunity for realizing the great destiny awaiting our country."

The policy of the United States in the Far East was in striking contrast to the policy of isolation from Europe's affairs. On a number of occasions it co-operated with other powers in working out Oriental trade

and diplomatic problems, and it resorted to force against **Open Door**
Japan (1864) and Formosa (1867). An attempt in 1871 to **foreshad-**
open Korea by force was a dismal failure, and that kingdom **owed**
was not opened until 1882. This "gunboat policy," however, was far
less characteristic of the United States than of the other powers, though
that may have been due less to official forbearance than to hostility
of the people at home to Far Eastern ventures. The United States

Ivan and Uncle Sam reaching Asia by opposite routes, drawn
by Frank Bellew for *Harper's Weekly* in the 1870's

navy has historically been a powerful urge to imperialism, a fact little
known to the American people, and it persistently sought to commit the
country to annexation in the Marquesas, the Bonins, Formosa, Samoa,
Hawaii, and other places. Especially after the rise of the need for coaling
stations, the navy may be credited with having had a clearer view of
reality than Congress or the State Department, but it was so rudimentary
in both size and influence that it was unable to overcome home inertia.

Missionaries, by now numerous in the Pacific and the Orient, and
through their home churches a powerful political pressure group, were
opposed to annexations because they disturbed the peace and stirred up
bitterness; the only important exception was Peter Parker, a medical

missionary to China turned diplomat. The United States was thus committed to peace, to opposition to annexation, and to the most-favored-nation principle. These clearly foreshadowed the later Open Door policy. The natural consequence was that the United States sought not only to preserve the independence of Oriental nations but to make them strong enough to defend themselves. However selfish the policy in origin, it bore the fruits of altruism and paid off in goodwill.

One of the results of the activities of American merchants and whalers in the Pacific was the Americanization of the Hawaiian Islands. These volcanic islands, of which nine are inhabited, are about the area of Con-

**Americani-
zation of
Hawaii**
necticut and Rhode Island and lie about twenty-one hundred miles southwest of San Francisco. They were discovered by Captain James Cook in 1778. During the next generation the Polynesian peoples of all of the islands, about two hundred thousand in number, were conquered and united by a great native conqueror, Kamehameha I. Oregon traders and whalers found that the islands were convenient refitting stations, and the sandalwood trade with China afforded an additional economic resource. At the same time American merchants, ship chandlers, and beachcombers were destroying the native way of life without offering an adequate substitute.

Hawaii's monarchs made shrewd use of American advisers to maintain the independence of the islands against Great Britain, Russia, and France, and upon the coming of New England missionaries in 1820 rapidly turned the people to Christianity and to Western institutions. The natives, drawn into the severe school of New England Calvinism and prey to rapacious merchants and seamen, began to languish and decrease in number. Honolulu itself was often described as a New England village. Mission schools were so excellent and so successful that many Americans in Oregon and California sent their children there to be educated.

Presently the sons of the missionaries, as Hawaiian subjects, began to take over the ownership of the land from the artless natives and to build up sugar plantations and a thriving commerce with North America.

**The U.S. re-
fuses to an-
nex Hawaii**
Their desire was annexation to the United States, but Washington stalled until 1898, though in 1842 Secretary of State Webster did make clear to the world his country's opposition to annexation by any other power. The peculiar interest of the United States in the islands was soon exemplified when vigorous protests were made to London and Paris against fresh attempts at British and French annexation. The alarmed Hawaiian monarch asked in 1851 to have his country annexed to the United States, but the request was refused because it was politically impracticable. Nevertheless, by this time the American domination of the legislature and of Hawaiian business life was so great that, added to the recent American acquisition of

Oregon and California, it was evidently only a matter of time before Hawaii should pass under the Stars and Stripes.

BIBLIOGRAPHICAL NOTE

Rise of the Latin-American Nations

REVOLUTIONS: Salvador de Madariaga, *The Fall of the Spanish American Empire* (1948); William S. Robertson, *Rise of the Spanish-American Republics* (1918); Charles C. Griffin, *The U.S. and the Disruption of the Spanish Empire, 1810–1822* (1937).

MONROE DOCTRINE: Arthur P. Whitaker, *The U.S. and the Independence of Latin America, 1800–1830* (1941); Dexter Perkins, *The Monroe Doctrine, 1823–1826* (1927).

The North Atlantic Triangle

See especially John B. Brebner, *North Atlantic Triangle: The Interplay of Canada, the U.S., and Great Britain* (1945); C. P. Stacey, "The Myth of the Unguarded Frontier, 1815–1871," in *American Historical Review*, 51:1–18 (Oct. 1950); F. Lee Benns, *The American Struggle for the West Indian Carrying-trade, 1815–1830* (1923); Albert B. Corey, *The Crisis of 1830–1842 in Canadian-American Relations* (1941); Lester B. Shippee, *Canadian-American Relations, 1849–1874* (1939); and Hugh G. Soulsby, *The Right of Search and the Slave Trade in Anglo-American Relations, 1814–1862* (1933).

The Spread of American Commerce

GENERAL: Emory R. Johnson, *History of Domestic and Foreign Commerce of the U.S.* (2 v., 1915); Samuel E. Morison, *Maritime History of Massachusetts* (1921); Ralph D. Paine, *Ships and Sailors of Old Salem* (1912); James D. Phillips, *Salem and the Indies* (1947). For the rise of the Port of New York see Robert G. Albion, *Square-riggers on Schedule* (1938). Among numerous contemporary accounts of life at sea is Richard H. Dana, *Two Years Before the Mast* (1840). On the subject of the navy's attempt to develop its own foreign policy see Charles O. Paullin, *Diplomatic Negotiations of American Naval Officers, 1778–1883* (1912); obviously many of these negotiations were authorized. The curious ice trade to the tropics is covered in Richard O. Cummings, *The American Ice Harvests* (1949).

CLIPPERS AND WHALERS: On clippers the classic is Arthur H. Clark, *The Clipper Ship Era* (1910); see also Carl C. Cutler, *Greyhounds of the Sea* (1930). Elmo P. Hohman, *The American Whaleman* (1928) affords not only an excellent summary but an exhaustive bibliography. Herman Melville's classic novel *Moby Dick, or the White Whale,* was written by an experienced whaler.

U.S. AND CHINA: On the whole subject see Tyler Dennett, *Americans in Eastern Asia* (1922); Kenneth S. Latourette, *History of Early Relations Between the U.S. and China* (1917); and Foster R. Dulles, *China and Amer-*

ica (1946). On individual Americans see Claude M. Fuess, *Life of Caleb Cushing* (2v., 1923); Holger Cahill, *A Yankee Adventurer* [Frederick T. Ward] (1930); Frederick W. Williams, *Anson Burlingame and the First Chinese Mission to Foreign Powers* (1912).

U.S. AND JAPAN: Inazo Nitobé, *Intercourse Between the U.S. and Japan* (1891). On Perry's expedition see Payson J. Treat, *Diplomatic Relations Between the U.S. and Japan, 1853–1895* (2 v., 1932); and Arthur C. Walworth, *Black Ships off Japan* (1946). On Townsend Harris see Carl Crow, *He Opened the Door of Japan* (1939).

U.S. AND HAWAII: Of particular value is Harold W. Bradley, *The American Frontier in Hawaii* (1942). See also Theodore Morgan, *Hawaii: A Century of Economic Change, 1778–1876* (1948).

Chapter XVI

THE INDIAN SIDE
OF THE FRONTIER

1 *The Indians' View of the White Advance*

THE lad from the agency stood respectfully silent by the little campfire made of a few meager sticks until the old Indian chief slowly removed his redstone pipe from his lips and looked up. The boy raised his clenched right hand with the knuckles outward and spoke the word of greeting, "How!" The Indian, without rising, made the same sign and repeated the word, then with a barely perceptible motion of the hand indicated a buffalo robe. The boy sat down and composed himself solemnly to patience, while the old man returned the pipe to his mouth. Ten minutes passed without another word or without any motion from either, except as the Indian removed his pipe and blew smoke into the morning air. Then the old chief spoke, looking at the fire.

"White man make big fire. Much smoke. Not much heat."

The white boy listened gravely and pondered. The chief extended his redstone pipe in a short gesture.

"White man's pipe big at top. Tobacco soon burn out. Indian pipe deep. Little hole burn long."

"Blue Horse," said the boy, "I dreamed last night that you told me the tale of the coming of the white man."

"It is well," grunted Blue Horse in approval of the white lad's good breeding. "Who am I to make a liar of your manitou?"

He threw the blanket off his shoulders, for the sun was getting high. Then he gently knocked the ashes from his pipe, produced a twist of tobacco from his pouch, cut off some shreds with his hunting knife, rubbed the dried leaves between his hands, and refilled the pipe. When it had been lighted with a brand from the fire he leaned back, his eyes twinkling.

"Great Spirit make all men—all one time under the earth. Make Lenni Lenape [*Delawares*] first. Use best clay first, then last thing make white man from what left over. Black man find way out first; long time under sun, very much burned. Indian next; sunburned too. Then came yellow man, and long time after white man. He very palefaced from the dark. Very young and foolish. Camp in wet places. Build fires of rotten wood—make smoke all night. Maybe use chestnut—sparks burn holes in blankets. Always lose things at camp—maybe knife, maybe bullets, maybe money. Very proud. Always hunt riches because he think rich man great. Rob, steal, cheat, put lock on door. Maybe he think Great Manitou let him in hunting ground because he rich. Maybeso white man foolish, Great Spirit give him Book which tell what he should do, but white man never do it.

"Indian not have iron for hatchet or kettle. Use stone knife, hatchet, clay pot. Not have cloth or blanket. Use skins, furs, weave bast. Not kill all the game—only what he need. Get along all right. Never cheat, lie, steal, get drunk. Never fight about religion. Never hang witches. Never refuse food to hungry when it is in his lodge. Take what the Earth Mother provide and give thanks to the Great Manitou, whose children we are."

Blue Horse was silent for a moment as though dreaming of the day when the Indian was lord of the continent. When he went on there was a note of bitterness in his voice.

One day a great canoe with spreading wings appeared on the salt-water-lake-with-no-farther-shore, and white men clad in strange garb came out of it. The wise men gathered the Indians and said to them, "See, here are those whose coming we have foretold; they are manitous come to visit us." Then the Indians prostrated themselves and the white manitous gave to them knives and hatchets of strange metal and warm shirts and blankets, and in exchange accepted gifts of the winter catch of furs.

For a while all went well. The white manitous now expressed a desire to share the Indians' hunting grounds, and in exchange they gave much goods. Now this was foolishness, for the land was the gift of the Great Spirit to all his children but the white manitous seemed to set great store upon the exchange and prepared certain talking leaves which spoke to the minds of the initiated when consulted. Then the white manitous desired the Indians to mark the talking leaves in witness thereof. The goods which the white manitous offered were of great value, which seemed strange, for the land could not be eaten or carried away, but the chiefs after consultation together agreed that it was only polite to accede to the strangers' wishes, so they made their marks even though the talking leaves spoke no word to them.

Then the white manitous brought their women and children and built strange lodges. Always they were gabbling like crows in spring, even when in council they should have been grave and dignified. But the Indians were tolerant, and when the white manitous became hungry the Indians gave them corn and venison, showed them how to fish and hunt, and when the trees became green showed them how to plant corn with a fish in each hill. Then they began to demand more skins and furs; they gave the Indians firesticks and sent them to hunt in the forests of other nations, not seeming to know that the guns scared away the game and warned the people of that land that an enemy was near. Then there was war, more bitterly fought than in the old days, and the white manitous paid goods for the scalps and furs taken, for presently the Indians forgot their old crafts and depended upon the white manitous for knives and guns and blankets.

There came a time when the winter was heavy on the hills and valleys and starvation stalked the land. The Indians went to the white manitous and asked for food, as is the right of all men. Then the strangers laughed with the lips (but there was no laughter in their eyes) and said to bring them furs, which was impossible, for the furred creatures could not go abroad but starved in the heavy snow. Nevertheless, the white manitous refused them food, though there was food in their lodges, and when the Indians would have taken it they were brought before the elders of the whites who consulted the talking leaves and took the Indians' garden plots and announced that henceforth the Indians and their women and children were slaves and must work daily in the fields for their food and be beaten with many stripes.

Now this was unbecoming to warriors and, moreover, was not according to the way the Great Spirit had taught the red men, so they agreed with their friends of the forest and rose in defense of their families and their hunting grounds. Then the white manitous came upon their villages at night and slaughtered them, raping their women and holding aloft their infants on pikes, and those whom they did not kill they put in chains and sold across the salt-water lake.

For the white manitous were not manitous but men, more greedy and unjust and terrible than the warriors of the Five Nations. They multiplied like the locusts, and like the locusts swept everything before them. The trees fell before their bright axes and the game fled two-nights' journey into the forests. Then the white men sold the Indian firewater to give him the comfort of a moment's madness, and when he awoke the white man had cheated him of his poor belongings and showed him a talking leaf with an x mark upon it by which it was witnessed the Indian had sold yet more of his hunting grounds. The white traders followed the old trails and wore them by their heavy boots so that in the life of one man they were gullied by the rains and no longer of any use. And there fell upon the Indian the white man's terrible diseases, brought by the traders in their blankets—the measles and smallpox which carried away thousands, the coughing sickness from which even the young and strong wasted away, and running sores got by the young women who lived with the traders and which caused the children to be born blind or with bones already old and decayed.

This was the work of the white men who had been at first welcomed as manitous. But there were among the white men those with long faces bearing the Book and wearing black robes or some of them long coats. And they spoke to the Indians saying that it was set down in the Book that the Indian must give over blood and fighting and when an enemy smote him on the cheek he must turn the other cheek also. Then the Indian marveled that the white preachers would think him so simple as not to see the trap. For the white men fought among themselves with great ships and guns and lines of red and white-coated men, spoiling each other of goods and torturing their prisoners with curious engines. And when there was no war, so great was their lust for blood that they chose from among them old men and women who must be pressed to death under great weights, have their bones broken on great wheels, or be hung and cut asunder and the parts placed on the gates of their towns while the people looked on shouting. This might have been expected of men and women in the heat of war, but there was no war. When the Indians asked why it was, the bearers of the Book answered that it was because they worshiped the wrong god, and some said they worshiped devils.

Then the Indian made his choice of the old manitou and went beyond the mountains to live. Then came the white governors, who spoke honeyed words and made the chiefs drunk so that they went against the will of the nations and sold their lands by making their marks on the talking leaves. Even before the governors there had come white hunters and trappers, and now came the axmen and the turners of the soil, who passed beyond the land allotted them by the frauds of the governor, seized the Indians' plantations of corn, and when they protested the interlopers laughed and killed the men, raped the women, brained the children, and cast out such as survived with no food or guns or raiment.

Many preachers arose among the Indians, saying that the old spirits of the land were offended, and would not be appeased until the red men threw away the white man's knives and guns and blankets, and went back to weapons of stone and clothing of skins and bast. But that was no longer possible, for the knowledge of the old ways had passed, and the spirits of the land had cast a blight on the game. So the Indians rose against the axmen and turners of the soil, and they fled with their women and children to great wooden houses. When they came out and marched against the tribesmen they were easily frightened, for they were cowards and knew nothing of the forest, and many yellow scalps were taken.

Presently there came from the direction of the Thirteen Fires a great warrior, the Black Snake [*Wayne*] with men in blue coats armed with firesticks and long knives. These men were not like the cowardly axmen and turners of the soil but stood together and defeated the Indians. Then the Black Snake, saying that the Indians had broken the treaties, set down on the talking leaf that they must move into the forest a journey of six nights. They had not broken the treaties—that was the work of white men—but the Indians were silent because they were ashamed and without power.

The redstone pipe was cold, forgotten by the old man in the fervor of recounting the glory and the shame of other years. Slowly the fire died from his eyes, and the old shoulders sank. The sun was high, but he pulled the blanket about him as though he were chilled.

"Always the same," he said finally. "White man always break treaty —Indian never. Many times we fight—always lose when soldiers come. Many majors [*agents*] come—much firewater—bribe chiefs sell much land. Always say we break treaty, but they lie. Young men die in battle or kill each other when the whisky in them. Women die with coughing sickness. Children not born, or die when winter come. Old people starve. Indian lie, cheat, steal for firewater. Me young man leave my people go fight with Black Hawk. Indian no want fight—want to surrender. White men shoot at white flag. Kill women and children on raft. Many, many killed. White man give us land. Say farm. We try. Then white major say move on to new farm. We begin again. But always we must go. Now Lenni Lenape on plains, far from old hunting grounds. Land poor. No good farm. Wild Indians steal horses, steal women. No buffalo no more. White majors steal rations before your pa came."

Blue Horse drew the twist of tobacco from his pouch and went through the ritual of filling and lighting the pipe, then carefully mended the fire.

"Me born Wolf Clan of Lenni Lenape. White man say how can Indian come from wolf? Me ask how can white man come from monkey like Four-Eyes-Who-Gathers-Herbs say? Wolf Clan live long ago by salt-water lake near river white man call Delaware. Me born on Tippecanoe in Prophet's Town. Father born Coshocton—his father Logstown when Redcoats fight Whitecoats on Ohio. Before him come the first of my family from the shore of salt-water lake. Four lives, and the Wolf people only handful."

The rheumy old eyes seemed now to look inward, and the voice was scarcely audible. The old man was no longer conscious of the white boy but was speaking to his manitou, not in English but in his native tongue.

"Why does the Earth Mother give corn no more? Why has the Great

Manitou hidden his face from his children? Surely we must have disobeyed, but how? Did the Lenni Lenape ever drive off the game that the Great Spirit sent, or did they kill more than they needed? Did they ever turn the hungry from their lodge when there was food to eat? Did they ever kill those who called the Great Spirit by another name? Or hang witches? Or rape their captive women? Did they make firewater to steal their brains? Or did they lie and cheat and steal before the white man came among them to rob them of manhood?

"Great Spirit, I am old and useless. My hand cannot lift the rifle or hold the plow. But I can hear Thy voice if Thou wilt speak. Tell me wherein we have strayed that I may warn the remnant of my people before I go to the long sleep. Speak, Great Spirit. I await Thy will."

The old man's eyes were closed, and the smoke rose in futile curls from the redstone pipe where it had fallen on the grass. Quietly the white boy rose and, respecting the old man's reverie, moved away with noiseless steps.

*   *   *

Yes, the historian has permitted himself the license of making an allegory to show a point of view. The tale that Blue Horse told may have been lacking in sophistication and universal understanding, but it was spoken in sincerity and was not without shrewdness. True, there were discrepancies. How could the boots of the white men do more damage to the trails than the sharp hooves of the buffalo? Was the Indian never arrogant in his pride of race, or high-handed, or greedy for the spoils of the white settlements? Was it true that the Indians *never* broke treaties, especially in view of their complete individualism and of the absence of tribal enforcement machinery? Moreover, he must have glamorized the first state of his people; but which of us (with a Fourth-of-July oration booming over the radio) can cast the first stone? Here then is the story of the side of the frontier on which the Indians lived.

2   The Passing of the Woods Indian

When one recalls that during the Revolution the western Indians kept the Pennsylvania and Kentucky settlers pretty much on the defensive, it is easy to understand the amazement of those Indians at finding their hunting grounds deeded over to the "Thirteen Fires." The British sought to break the blow by delaying evacuation of the posts on American soil which had become centers of the fur trade. This policy of delay was confirmed largely because of the pressure of the North West Company, a new monopoly founded in 1784 by the Scots factors of Montreal. By 1794 they had

British desire to retain the West

built up a trade which was taking out of the interior furs worth $1,000,-
000 annually. The Scots merchants and their British political associates
and French employees were fully aware of the land hunger of the American pioneers and of its threat to the fur trade, and they coldly proposed
to thwart it as long as possible by subsidizing Indian war on the American settlements.

The Indians were in a quandary, for they were not fooled by dulcet
words about keeping bright the chain of friendship. They had long
sought to hold the balance between warring white nations, but now that
resort was almost played out; the French were gone, the **Breakdown**
Spanish were weak, and the English had been defeated. It **of Indian**
was evidently only a matter of time until the rapacious **diplomacy**
Americans had their way. It is supposed that between the Ohio River and
the Great Lakes there were after the Revolution less than ten thousand
Indian warriors. Alcohol, tuberculosis, smallpox, and syphilis were steadily reducing their number, and the fall of the forest was driving out the
game upon which they chiefly depended for food. And yet the Indians
could not do without the white men, for they had lost their Stone Age
skills and depended upon European weapons, utensils, and textiles, and
upon white blacksmiths to keep their guns repaired. Indian leaders were
shrewd enough to recognize this fact. The more intelligent thought to
weld the Indians into a confederacy which would limit white expansion
without interrupting trade; the more demagogic urged their followers
to avoid dependence upon the whites by returning to the ancestral tools
and methods. Both were futile.

Two ways of life were in conflict. The American economy was agricultural and was based on individual ownership of definite tracts of
land: the Indian was chiefly a hunter, and land ownership lay with the
totem. Superficially the Indian problem lay in the decision **Clashing**
whether to allow themselves to be forced out of their lands **ways of life**
to the wild country beyond the Mississippi; to try to adopt
the white man's ways in the hope that they could cling to a few acres; or
to yield their homes and their lives in bloody holocaust. No Indian nation ever united in a single policy, and indeed any one was about as
futile as the others. The fact that the Five Civilized Nations of the
South made a rather successful attempt to assimilate white institutions
did not save them, for they were confronting a conquering horde which
was possessed of greed and racial arrogance and armed with a superior
technology. The Indians also were greedy and arrogant, but they lacked
technology, organization, and unlimited reserves.

There is every reason to believe that the Federal government sincerely
wished the Indians well. Nevertheless, it regarded force as an element of
the problem and placed Indian affairs under the War Department. There

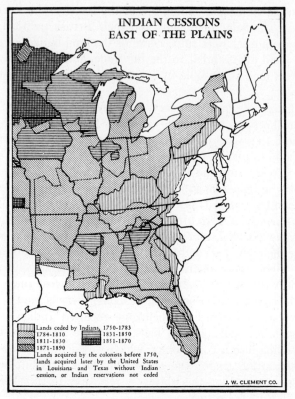

INDIAN CESSIONS
EAST OF THE PLAINS

Lands ceded by Indians, 1750-1783
1784-1810   1831-1850
1811-1830   1851-1870
1871-1890
Lands acquired by the colonists before 1750,
lands acquired later by the United States
in Louisiana and Texas without Indian
cession, or Indian reservations not ceded

J. W. CLEMENT CO.

Adapted from C. O. Paullin, *Atlas of the Historical Geography of
the United States,* 1932. Carnegie Institution of Washington.

Federal
Indian
policies
they remained until the creation of the Department of the
Interior in 1849; the Bureau of Indian Affairs was not
organized separately until 1824, and its administrator was
made commissioner in 1832. The procedures of Indian affairs were
modeled upon those of Great Britain and the colonies. The title to the
soil lay with the occupying Indians, and it could be extinguished only by
Federal purchase or conquest. Treaties were negotiated with the Indian
nations and had to run the gantlet of the Senate just as did treaties with
Great Britain or Spain. Unfortunately the Indians were not equipped
to hold their own diplomatically. Their status should have been that of
wards for whose welfare the government was responsible, just as a guardian is responsible for a minor.

The more advanced Indians recognized this fact and sought through
the Supreme Court to force the government to protect them; but when
in a series of decisions (notably the *Cherokee Nation v. Georgia*) the
Court confirmed their status as "dependent domestic nations," President

Jackson refused to assume any responsibility for protecting them, in this case against the state of Georgia. Political exigencies forced the interpretation of "dependent domestic nations" as meaning anything or nothing. It was not until 1871 that Congress abandoned the policy of regarding the Indian nations as independent.

Land was not legally open to white settlement until it had been purchased by the Federal government, surveyed, and opened to entry. The land hunger of settlers and speculators, added to Jefferson's belief that this should be a land of free farmers, forced territorial governors and Indian agents to get land cessions by hook **Land purchase** or crook. If it was impossible to get land by fair purchase, these agents knew how to make whisky work for them, how to threaten, how to alter phraseology, and how to bribe into complaisance selected Indians who had no right to speak for the nation. When the remainder of the nation showed its resentment by taking a few scalps, waves of righteous indignation swept the white settlements at the way in which Indians broke treaties. The result was that troops moved in, and the beaten Indians confirmed the brummagem treaty and sold more land.

When the government refused to purchase wanted land, there were ways of forcing its hand. Ruffians moved into the Indian country and appropriated what they pleased, often ejecting the Indians from their clearings with accompanying outrages. The war that followed was of course fought to protect the settlements. There was no intention of *seizing* land, but nevertheless the Indians *sold* it. The Indians rarely if ever broke their treaties; the white men rarely if ever kept theirs. The Indians were perfectly aware of their dilemma, and white speculators and settlers were perfectly aware of their power.

Indian lands were paid for in goods, usually over a period of years, or money payments were invested and the income doled out from time to time. The giving of presents, rations, and annuities was an easy policy but scarcely a wise one. However much it may have been **Rations and reservations** prompted by altruistic motives—and doubtless it sometimes was—the Indians were seldom grateful but regarded it as a pusillanimous attempt to gain their favor. It tended, moreover, to break down the Indians' self-reliance and to make them lazy, arrogant, and discontented.

The reservation system was intended to give the Indians permanent homes, but it hardly ever did. As the result of white demands for reservation lands, the Indians were hustled from one reservation to another in advance of the white settlers, and any chances they might have had to adopt white ways were frustrated and destroyed. Occasionally specific lands were guaranteed to certain heads of Indian families; the white neighbors knew how to take care of such exceptions. The Indian agent was in an anomolous position, for if he got the co-operation of the Indians, he could not too baldly push the desires of white politicians and traders; on the other hand, if he did not, he might lose his agency and with it whatever chance there was to do good. Naturally there were many good agents despite the fact that some others browbeat their charges into land cessions, sold the goods they were supposed to distribute for treaty payments, and winked at the whisky trade for a cut of the profits.

At the instance of Washington, who had no love for the Indians but desired to do them justice, the Indian Factory System (under "factors") was set up in 1795 and lasted until 1822. These were government-op-

Factory system, 1795–1822 erated trading posts established along the frontier, where the Indians could obtain honest goods at honest prices. Unfortunately Congress in the true political tradition handicapped the system's operations so radically that with the best will in the world the superintendents were not always able to sell reliable goods or to sell them at reasonable prices. Private traders, licensed and unlicensed, also remained in business and found the liquor trade very profitable in spite of government prohibition. Naturally they resented the factories, opposed them on every occasion, and brought such powerful political pressure to bear that they finally killed the system.

Americans were quite conscious that the Indians had little chance of acquiring white ways, but many of them proposed to see to it that the Indian should find every obstacle in his path to improvement. The In-

Deliberate debauchery of the Indians dian was notorious for his simplicity in business affairs and his inability to understand the value of money, the ownership of land, and the necessity of saving for the morrow. Grog sellers found it easy to implant the taste for liquor by giving free drams and easy credit; then they mulcted the drunkard they had made of all he possessed—furs, horses, land—and finally acted as receivers of stolen goods. When the victim left off hanging about the settlement cadging drinks and took to the warpath to rectify an injustice whose origin he only dimly understood, the very man who had undermined his undoubted virtues pointed to him as proof that red men were improvident, thievish, and treacherous.

It was all very well for the rich Federalists in the coastal cities to utter pious platitudes about poor Lo, but on and near the frontier public opinion regarded the pioneer as a crusader in the cause of civilization. In

White racism every community there were men who had "fit the Injuns," or convinced themselves that they had, and perhaps had lost a brother to the "red varmints." That the brother might have been slain for raping a squaw, or cheating in a trade, or evicting an old Indian couple from a desirable corn patch had nothing to do with the case. The lordly white man regarded the rights of Indians no more than the rights of wolves. So kill, and burn, and rob! The only good Indian was a dead Indian. And kill the papooses too, for nits make lice.

But let the desperate survivors of a foray on an Indian family or village come back for revenge, and the frontier was aflame with fear. Wails of aggrieved innocence went up from the crowded blockhouses, and demands were sent out posthaste for troops. A few raiders *White reactions to Indian retaliations* were sometimes enough to paralyze settlements holding a hundred times their number of whites. After all, the business of the average white man was to farm and manufacture; on an Indian expedition he was too likely to slip away home and leave the danger to the Boones and the Wetzels. The pioneer was nearly as unco-operative as the Indian and strongly resented taxes, military service (except on parades), or any attempt at regulation. The business of government was to leave him to his own devices and never to show strength except when it was needed to get him out of a jam.

These attitudes were not regarded as inconsistent or selfish. The prevailing Calvinist economic psychology was that the land belonged to those who could best use it. Certainly the Indian would be lazy, thievish, and poverty-stricken until he acquired "the stimulus of physical exertion and intellectual exercise" found in John Locke's principle that the process of acquiring and protecting property was the stabilizer of society. When one considers that a considerable proportion even of whites has failed to measure up to the Lockian standard, it is evident that an impossible task was being set for the Indian.

Given the unalterable economic and psychological conditions, it is difficult to see any way in which conflict could have been avoided. Democratic pressures on the Federal government were not solely responsible, for the absolutist French and Spanish governors were only *Conflict inevitable* slightly more successful in averting frontier wars even with the help of missionaries and even where there were no foreign pressures. Conflict seems to be the inevitable result when two cultures meet and one or both cannot or will not assimilate to the other. Bewildered by white brutality, inconsistency, and sharp practice, our Indians were beaten down but never reconciled. Those who would have turned to civilization were brutally kicked aside, and it is only in our own day that the admixture of white blood and the institution of more reasonable land and educational systems are pointing toward a solution; there is doubt even of that.

3   *The Fur Traders' Frontier*

The entry of the Americans into the fur trade of the West was only one part of the many-headed conflict which was going on for the diminishing North American wilderness. The Pacific Northwest was the center

The Oregon country of one of the bitterest aspects of this conflict. For two centuries the Spanish had claimed the area, and from time to time explorers or shipwrecked seamen landed there. After Vitus Bering's discovery for Russia in 1728 of Bering Strait and his voyage of 1741 to Alaska, Russian fur traders began to move down the American coast to the Oregon country. The Spanish were alarmed and according to their habit in such cases began to rush missionaries into California in order to convert the Indians and make them a bulwark against Russian encroachment.

In 1778 Captain James Cook visited the region on an official reconnaissance. When he touched at Canton on the way home, he found that some sea-otter skins brought from Oregon were so highly valued by the

British and American entry Chinese that they would command in exchange unheard of quantities of tea and silk. British merchants at once entered into the trade, and the Spanish hastened to forestall them. In 1789 both Spain and England tried to plant their authority by seizing Nootka Sound on Vancouver Island, and the clash led to a short-lived international crisis and to a British triumph. Boston merchants had meanwhile entered the trade in sea otter and other furs, and in 1792 Captain Robert Gray rediscovered the mouth of the Columbia River, which was hard to descry from the sea, and named the stream for his ship. Later the same year George Vancouver on behalf of the British government began an extended survey of the coast from California on north. While he was still on the coast a Scot named Alexander Mackenzie, an explorer for the North West Company, crossed the Rocky Mountains and emerged on the Pacific (1793) north of Vancouver Island. This was the same Mackenzie who in 1789 had descended to the Arctic Ocean the river that now bears his name.

The Russian exploitation of Alaska had been poorly organized and controlled. Robbery and massacre had been the regular procedure among the beautiful fiords as these seagoing Cossacks drove the native Aleuts

Russians in Alaska into the perilous currents and slippery rocks of the coast in the hunt for otters. By 1799 Russian ships had worked down the coast to island-studded Sitka Bay. There they came into contact with the Tlingits, a much more assertive breed than the Aleuts. With Russian companies fighting each other and natives actively resenting white insolence, the turmoil on the coast became so notorious that even remote St. Petersburg took alarm.

The Russian American Fur Company now received a monopoly of Alaska and sent out the merchant Alexander Baranov as manager. One of the first problems he had to meet was a great rising of the Tlingits, who

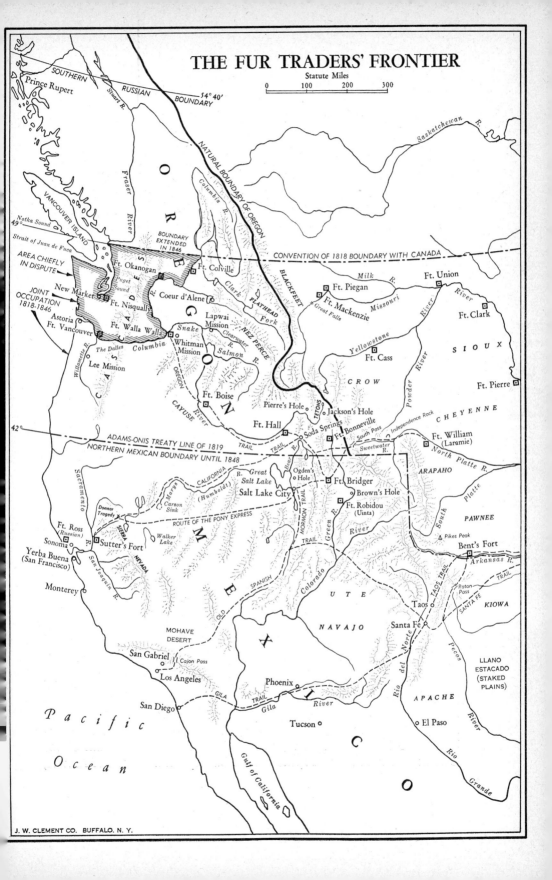

THE FUR TRADERS' FRONTIER

Statute Miles
0   100   200   300

SOUTHERN
Prince Rupert
RUSSIAN
BOUNDARY
54° 40'
Stuart R.
NATURAL BOUNDARY OF OREGON
Saskatchewan R.
O
R
E
Fraser River
Columbia R.
49°
Notka Sound
BOUNDARY
EXTENDED
IN 1846
Ft. Colville
CONVENTION OF 1818 BOUNDARY WITH CANADA
Strait of Juan de Fuca
Ft. Okanogan
Milk R.
Ft. Union
AREA CHIEFLY
IN DISPUTE
New Market
Puget Sound
Ft. Piegan
BLACKFEET
Ft. Mackenzie
Missouri River
Ft. Clark
JOINT
OCCUPATION
1818-1846
Ft. Nisqually
Coeur d'Alene
Clark Fork
FLATHEAD
Great Falls
River
Astoria
Ft. Vancouver
Ft. Walla Walla
Lapwai
Mission
Clearwater R.
NEZ PERCE
Yellowstone River
SIOUX
The Dalles
Columbia
Snake
Whitman
Mission
Salmon R.
Ft. Cass
Ft. Pierre
Lee Mission
O
N
Willamette R.
CASCADES
Ft. Boise
OREGON River
CROW
Powder River
CHEYENNE
42°
CAYUSE
Pierre's Hole
TETONS
Jackson's Hole
Independence Rock
Ft. William
(Laramie)
ADAMS-ONIS TREATY LINE OF 1819
TRAIL
Ft. Hall
Soda Springs
Ft. Bonneville
South Pass
Sweetwater R.
North Platte R.
NORTHERN MEXICAN BOUNDARY UNTIL 1848
TRAIL
Bear R.
CALIFORNIA
Sacramento R.
Ogden's
Hole
Great
Salt Lake
ARAPAHO
R. (Humboldt)
Carson
Sink
Salt Lake City
Ft. Bridger
Brown's Hole
Platte River
Donner
Tragedy
MORMON TRAIL
Ft. Robidou
(Uinta)
South Platte
PAWNEE
ROUTE OF THE PONY EXPRESS
Green R.
Pikes Peak
Ft. Ross
(Russian)
Walker
Lake
SIERRA
NEVADA
M
TRAIL
River
Bent's Fort
Sonoma
R.
Sutter's Fort
San Joaquin R.
UTE
Colorado
Taos
TAOS TRAIL
Arkansas R.
TRAIL
Yerba Buena
(San Francisco)
E
Raton
Pass
KIOWA
Monterey
X
SPANISH
NAVAJO
Santa Fe
SANTA FE
Pecos River
LLANO
ESTACADO
(STAKED
PLAINS)
MOHAVE
DESERT
Cajon Pass
San Gabriel
OLD
I
Phoenix
APACHE
Rio del Norte
Los Angeles
GILA
TRAIL
El Paso
San Diego
Gila River
C
Tucson
Rio Grande
Pacific
Ocean
Gulf of California
O

J. W. CLEMENT CO.   BUFFALO, N. Y.

Russian American Fur Company burned Sitka and massacred most of its inhabitants. Baranov soon appeared with a fleet, however, and after bombarding the natives built a tremendous log fortress. About this and its neighboring shops, warehouses, and dwellings ran a great stockade. High above on a hill stood Baranov's Castle in which the governor lived in viceregal state, surrounded by books and paintings and entertaining visitors from the outside world. Profits began to come in. Aleuts hunted sea otters as far as Lower California, posts were established at strategic points along the coast, Russian farmers and laborers were brought in, shipbuilding was promoted, and trade was opened with the Hawaiian Islands. Frequent ship losses in the treacherous fogs and currents of the coast offered the chief discouragement.

With the ships of three nations pouring sea-otter furs into China, the price fell disastrously, and after 1800 the British practically withdrew. Since the Americans had no designs on Alaska but brought cargoes of **American trade in Oregon** food to exchange with the Russians for furs, the two nationalities got along quite well. Unfortunately these New Englanders were a turbulent lot who cheated and mistreated the natives and, since they also persisted in selling rum and arms to the very men they abused, sometimes paid a severe score to native vengeance.

Jefferson, who had been Secretary of State at the time the Nootka Sound crisis threatened to grind the United States between England and Spain, saw the importance of the Oregon country to American trade—not **Lewis and Clark Expedition, 1804–06** simply the sea-otter trade with China but trade in the Rocky Mountain beaver furs which were beginning to appear at St. Louis. Jefferson had for years been interested in a possible route between the headwaters of the Missouri and the Pacific. The Treaty of 1783 had given Britain the right to navigate the Mississippi, and, now that it was known that the river did not rise in Canada, Britain was looking for an excuse to move the boundary southward. Jefferson had hopes that an American-controlled route between the Missouri and Columbia rivers would help to block this scheme.

Accordingly early in 1803, when Louisiana was still Spanish, Jefferson obtained Congressional authority for a military scientific expedition to cross the plains and mountains to Oregon to search out routes for American fur traders. For this purpose he chose a Virginia neighbor, Meriwether Lewis, and William Clark, younger brother of George Rogers Clark. Early in 1804 the expedition of about forty-five, chiefly army personnel, began a leisurely ascent of the Missouri. The winter was spent near the site of Bismarck, North Dakota. The journey was resumed in April, the Bitter Root Mountains were crossed to a branch of the Columbia, and in November 1805 Lewis and Clark reached the mouth of the Columbia. The winter was spent at Fort Clatsop (near the site of Astoria,

Oregon), then in 1806 the six-months return journey was begun. Lewis later served as governor of Louisiana Territory and was murdered on the Natchez Trace. Clark, the Red Head Chief, as he was called by the Indians, served as an Indian agent and governor of Missouri Territory.

Though the Lewis and Clark expedition was by no means first in the Oregon country nor first across the continent, it nevertheless reinforced an American claim to Oregon, gave a fillip to the fur trade, and encouraged other explorations. In 1806 General James Wilkinson sent Zebulon Pike, a young army officer, to explore the Southwest. His course led near Pikes Peak and on into New **Further exploration** Mexico; there Spaniards seized him and took him to Chihuahua, confiscated his papers, and sent him back to Louisiana. From this time on exploring and scientific expeditions became almost army routine; especially notable was that of Major Stephen Long up the Platte River in 1820 to the Rocky Mountains in Colorado and back by way of the Arkansas River.

The giant of the American fur trade and the only considerable rival of the two great British companies was John Jacob Astor, a German immigrant. He was already the leading American fur dealer, active both in the Northwest Territory and in the China trade, when the Louisiana Purchase stirred his imagination and lured him **Astor's fur enterprises** into competition with the British on the upper Mississippi. With the return of Lewis and Clark he began to plan a line of posts up the Missouri and down the Columbia, together with a fleet of ships plying between Oregon and China. The American Fur Company was incorporated in 1808 and was instrumental in forcing the North West Company to share the trade of the Great Lakes region. Competition with the powerful Spanish and French traders of St. Louis had reached no decision before the War of 1812 interrupted normal operations. Meanwhile the Pacific Fur Company had been organized (1810) to draw the Rocky Mountain furs down the Columbia, whence they would become the basis of a trade to China, Europe, and New York. The know-how was largely supplied by partners enticed away from the North West Company.

In 1811 an Astor ship reached the Columbia and founded Fort Astoria. Shortly afterward the ship was blown up, and part of the crew was massacred by Indians. Overland and seaborne reinforcements arrived, and a good start was made in trade before an expedition from the rival North West Company arrived and set up shop. **Astoria** When news of the War of 1812 came early in 1813, there came also word that the British admiralty was preparing to send a frigate to capture Astoria. Astor's commandant thereupon sold the fort and its supplies to the North West representative. The Pacific Fur Company was a failure, but the Treaty of Ghent restored the *status quo ante bellum* so far as political ownership was concerned, and in 1818 the two countries agreed to joint occupation for ten years—an arrangement which was renewed in 1828 for an indefinite period. The North West Company, which under David Thompson had been trading on the upper Columbia since 1807, now controlled the trade of the whole valley. The fact that it was British excluded it by law from competing with British monopolies in the Orient, so in the end it was glad to arrange with a Boston firm to carry its furs to Canton.

This was the great day of the North West Company. Its tough Scots factors, scarcely emerged from Gaelic barbarism, were well equipped to carry out its policy of ruthless exploitation. Once a year at Fort William

Ascendance of North West Company on Lake Superior the fur brigades gathered for a grand spree. It was held in a great log hall which could hold two hundred feasters, and which was adorned with portraits and a big map drawn by David Thompson on which appeared the names of the company's seventy-eight posts where its two thousand men lived. Far away in Montreal the gold-laced partners gathered in the Beaver Club to partake in reminiscent mood of pemmican brought at great expense halfway across the continent. After having dined and wined well, they sat in a long row on the floor as though they were in canoes again, and with swords, fire tongs, and walking sticks for paddles they dipped and weaved while they roared the old boating songs of the Great Plains.

But rivalry between the North West Company and the Hudson's Bay Company, immediately to the north, brought the end of this saga. In the competition the Indians were plied with liquor to denude the land of

Merger of Hudson's Bay and North West companies game, and robbery and murder became common business methods. Then in 1811 the Bay Company granted to Lord Selkirk for agricultural purposes a tract of land on the Red River of the North which lay across the Nor'Western route to the Rockies. Massacre and civil war followed but were suddenly cut short in 1821 when the British Parliament forced a "voluntary" merger. Thereafter the Hudson's Bay Company ruled the roof of the world with Sir George Simpson as the viceroy of the realm, and on the Columbia a Canadian medico named John McLoughlin ruled as his satrap.

The failure of the Pacific Fur Company by no means put an end to Astor's fur-trading activities, for he still owned the American Fur Company. During the war he made a killing in government loans and now had

American Fur Company plenty of capital. In 1816 he persuaded Congress to prohibit aliens from engaging in the fur trade, except as employees, and quickly took over the British posts south of the forty-ninth parallel. In 1822 he led the movement to abolish the government's

Factory System which, though it was not in a position to prevent private trade, offered the Indians too high a standard for comparison.

The American Fur Company had its western entrepôt in St. Louis and operated on and pretty well monopolized the upper Mississippi and upper Missouri. In the latter area it carried on a bitter and at times bloody struggle with its St. Louis rivals and gained a reputation for rascality which was probably all the greater because the company got results. By the 1830's fashions in hats were changing from beaver to silk, and none too soon, for the beavers were becoming scarce. Over a period of years Astor's profits had been disappointing, so in 1834 he sold the western interests of the American Fur Company to his St. Louis rivals, the Chouteaus, and disposed of the Great Lakes interests to his partners. He then devoted himself to Manhattan real estate in which, rather than in furs, lay the foundations of the present Astor fortune.

Meanwhile Astor's competitors south of the Missouri had enacted a colorful phase of American history. Though the companies came to rely chiefly upon white trappers, it was nevertheless necessary to make friends with as many of the Indian nations as possible. Nor did they hesitate to use Indians against their rivals; the record of diplomatic intrigue and mutual robbery and murder is **The St. Louis fur trade** obscure but undoubted. The capitalists and managers of these companies were among others the Chouteaus and Sublettes of St. Louis, William H. Ashley of Virginia, Andrew Henry of Pennsylvania, and the young Irishman Thomas Fitzpatrick, whose adventures read like fiction.

Actually most of the so-called companies were more or less temporary joint ventures, and names re-appear in numerous combinations. The fur business was highly speculative, for luck and Indians were never twice the same. Both companies and "free trappers" depended on long-term credit, and it is said that it was four years from the time the trade goods left Europe to the final sale of the furs received in exchange. Sharp practice was the rule, and the shaggy "mountain men" who brought their catches to St. Louis or the upper posts were usually jockeyed out of most of the value; they blew the rest in a spree and went back across the plains to their trap lines.

Indians were always a potential menace to the fur trade, and the stocks held at permanent posts were an invitation to attack; moreover, they were an expense, for garrisons had to be maintained, much of the time in idleness. Posts remained in use and were the beginnings of many modern cities, but in 1824 a partial substitute **Trappers' rendezvous** came into use, when the Rocky Mountain Fur "Company," at the suggestion of Ashley and Henry, abandoned the trading-post system and held a *rendezvous,* or fair, at a designated spot in the mountains. Brigades from St. Louis brought in trade goods, and there the

Indians and the trappers, whether working for themselves or the "Company," brought their furs for exchange—at the usual ruinous discount. The rendezvous remained the most colorful and turbulent institution of the fur trade until its cessation about 1840. At the rendezvous the representatives of the companies met on common ground; it was a time not only of barter and bargain but of intrigue, settlement of feuds, and wild revelry. Anything might happen, and usually did, from wife-trading to Indian raids. Actually the rendezvous system laid a premium on rapid exploitation of the game resources, but conservation, if it was ever thought of, was left to the future to worry about.

Transportation of trade goods and furs was carried on by the fur brigade, which might contain as many as several hundred men. When possible, travel was by water in canoes or, if necessary, great skin "bull-boats," but in the mountains the brigade might use hundreds of pack horses. The rank and file of the brigades were the mixed-breed Indian-French-Canadian *engagés*, or contracted men (once known as *voyageurs*), who possessed an amazing capacity for starvation, hard work, and dissipation. Withal a merry and optimistic race, the bits of metal they wore on their hunting shirts jingled a melodious accompaniment to their light-hearted songs as they plied their paddles on every stretch of water from New Orleans to the Arctic Ocean. The leader of a fur brigade was called the *bourgeois,* and he ruled his men as a feudal baron ruled his villeins, acting as leader, patron, protector, and god. Surging through the summer wilderness in their bark canoes, the brigades sometimes traveled as much as a hundred miles a day across the vast interior, winning over the Indian tribes with exactly the proper mixture of servile attention and grave courtesy.

The fur brigade

Perhaps even more important were the mountain men, the free trappers or company employees who flourished especially in the era of the rendezvous. Some of them were French-Canadian *engagés* who had left the rivers, but the most famous mountain men were Americans: wandering boys from Missouri farms, quarrelsome keelboatmen displaced by the steamboats, boisterous and boastful Kentuckians, and silent outcasts from the mountains of Pennsylvania. Probably there were never more than a thousand of them. These were the men who explored the mountain passes from Mexico to Canada and came into increasingly bitter relations with the Bay Company's Oregon trappers and with the Mexican governors of New Mexico. Their names mean little today: Kit Carson, who found his way by instinct and was respected by the Indians because he never broke his word; Jim Bridger, who carried a map of the Rocky Mountains in his head and could smell his way where he could not see; Jedediah Smith, who

Mountain men

always traveled with a Bible; John Colter, who guided Lewis and Clark and was laughed at for his tales of hot springs on the Yellowstone that shot water a hundred feet into the air. When in the 1840's the demand for beaver faded, the mountain men left their trap lines and became traders, buffalo hunters, army scouts, or immigrant guides.

4 *The Permanent Indian Frontier Policy*

The War of 1812 saw the end of effective Indian resistance east of the Great Plains; the so-called Black Hawk and Seminole Wars scarcely deserve notice except for their exhibitions of white arrogance and perfidy. The bellicose Indian faction had lost out, and it joined one of the other two factions: those who were quietly moving west or those who were attempting to assimilate white ways. Despite all discouragements surprising progress was made toward civilization. Even the old Ohio-country nations, the Delawares, Shawnee, Miami, and the rest, though they were pushed from reservation to reservation from Illinois to Oklahoma, doggedly applied themselves to improving their farms with skill and energy. The Creeks, Seminole, Choctaw, and Chickasaw had been basically agricultural from the first, and they had acquired white ways so well that they were often better farmers and stock raisers than the whites who coveted their lands. *Indian attempts to assimilate white culture*

Pioneer opinion held that trees were one indication of fertility, so it was natural that Pike, Long, and other explorers of the Great Plains should regard them as deserts fit only for buffaloes and Indians. There thus grew up the myth of the Great American Desert, which can still be seen indicated on old maps as extending from the Rocky Mountains to the western borders of the first tier of states beyond the Mississippi. Far from regretting the condition, many people hailed the plains as a providential limit to white settlement; as late as 1849, on his way to be inaugurated as President, Zachary Taylor (who should have known better) told Polk that the two segments of the United States were so completely separated by the Great American Desert that each would have to go its own way. It is easy to be generous with something one does not want or cannot use. The existence of this vast area, supposedly of no use to white settlers, bred the project of setting it aside as a permanent home for the Indians, one to which eastern Indians would be encouraged to migrate. Between it and the settled states would exist the Permanent Indian Frontier, marked by a road and a line of forts west of which no whites would be permitted to settle. *Permanent Indian Frontier*

This plan was the answer to several problems. By the Georgia Compact of 1802 the Federal government had agreed to move the Creeks and

Cherokee, but had never done anything decisive about it. Georgia was not
Beginning the only complainant, for every other state with Indians
of removal was clamoring to have them moved out. It was therefore
policy proposed to offer the Indians such generous inducements
that they would be glad to move on to the area to which, in fact, segments of most tribes had already gone. Dreamers like Jefferson had been
promoting the idea of an Indian state, presumably to be admitted to the
Union eventually, and the removal project thus received their blessing.
John C. Calhoun as Secretary of War recommended the project to President Monroe early in 1825; and, though Congress did not finally provide
for land exchanges until 1830 by the Removal Bill, the War Department
immediately began making new treaties to put it into effect.

For the most part the despondent northern Indian nations moved
quietly westward, step by step as the government directed. The only
serious protest was the so-called Black Hawk War of 1832. At this time
Black Hawk Iowa was inhabited by the Sauk and Fox Indians, part of
War, 1832 whom lived east of the Mississippi on and near Rock Island,
an area which in 1804 Harrison had acquired from some
drunken chiefs. Late in 1831 the latter were expelled with loss of their
corn crop. Starvation followed, and when the next spring somewhere near
a thousand men, women, and children returned to Illinois to raise food
in the old fields, the governor of Illinois called for volunteers to repel an
Indian invasion. The first "troops" fled at the sound of the war whoop,
and the elated Indians scattered and took a few scalps. But the gathering
regulars and militia were too numerous to be defeated; so Black Hawk's
tribesmen fled northward, then descended the Wisconsin River to the
Mississippi. There they tried to surrender but were caught between the
pursuing militia and an armed steamboat, the *Warrior,* and pitilessly
slaughtered in the "battle" of Bad Axe. Only about a hundred fifty
survived. Black Hawk's tribesmen were forced by General Winfield
Scott to give up a fifty-mile strip along the river in Iowa.

Several of the removal treaties with the Civilized Nations were
deliberate breaches of contracts with the nations, and all of them were
forced upon the Indians by threats and bribery. There is good reason to
Abuses of suppose that Jackson was perfectly cognizant of the method
the removal and may have promoted it in the treaty with the Choctaw
policy which he personally initiated. At any rate, the treaties had
not been ratified by the Senate before land speculators and grog dis-
pensers rushed into the Indian country to mulct the Indians of their
lands and money payments. The treaties guaranteed the Federal troops
would keep such white men away, but Federal agents had neither the
strength nor the will to enforce the guarantees. State rights lay at the
root of the trouble. Jackson and his agents believed in state rights, and

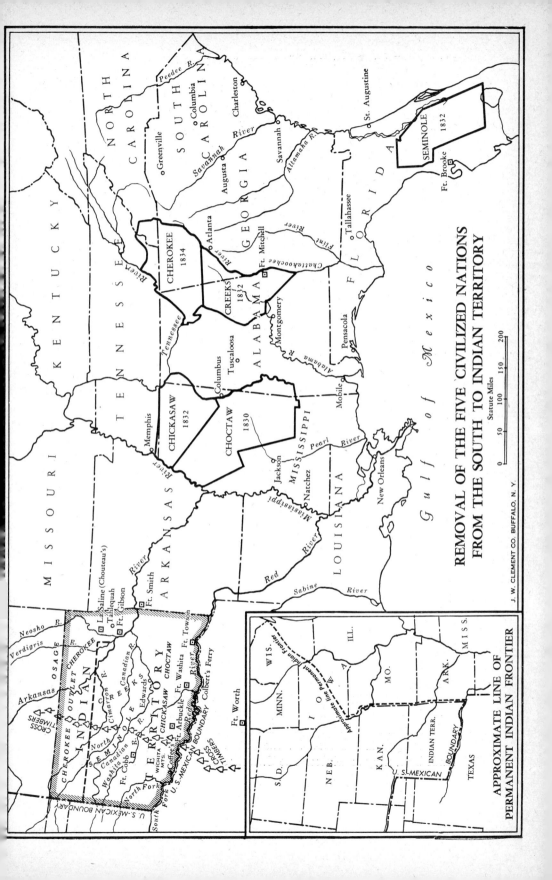

REMOVAL OF THE FIVE CIVILIZED NATIONS
FROM THE SOUTH TO INDIAN TERRITORY

Statute Miles

0   50   100   150   200

J. W. CLEMENT CO. BUFFALO, N. Y.

APPROXIMATE LINE OF
PERMANENT INDIAN FRONTIER

for both political and psychological reasons felt no call to clash with the states in defense of a few thousand "savages," even though the state courts were upholding swindlers and murderers.

The Choctaw and the Chickasaw of Mississippi were successfully removed during the 1830's, but though they suffered less from white exploitation they were decimated by disease and hardship. The smallest of the Civilized Nations, the Seminole, were the hardest to oust. Under the leadership of Osceola, a mixed-breed with high qualities of leadership, they retreated to the swamps of Florida, whence their raids became the terror of planters and soldiers alike. Their resistance, which began with sporadic raids in 1832, did not end with the seizure of Osceola and his death in prison but went on until 1842. In the end the United States at the cost of $20,000,000 and the lives of 400 soldiers dragged 3000 Seminole out of the swamps and sent them to Oklahoma. Even at that, a remnant remained in Florida, and their descendants are there to this day.

Second Seminole War, 1835–42

Most amazing, however, were the Cherokee, whose home was chiefly in Georgia though there were villages in North Carolina and Tennessee. Part of them, called Cherokee West, had moved beyond the Mississippi. After a last sharp war the Cherokee seriously sought to adapt themselves to white civilization. They welcomed New England missionaries and government handicraft instructors and embraced Christianity and the arts of peace. They parceled out land to individuals (though basic ownership remained with the nation), adopted agriculture and stock raising, took up spinning and weaving, rebuilt their villages on white models, and centralized and strengthened their government by adopting (1827) a constitution patterned on that of the United States. They even adopted some of the white man's prejudices, notably discrimination against Negroes. About 1821, Sequoyah, a mixed-blood who knew little English and could neither read nor write, introduced a system of characters for writing the syllables of the Cherokee language. Another Cherokee, Elias Boudinot, used the system in a newspaper, the *Cherokee Phoenix,* and translated and published a number of books.

The Cherokee

The initiation of the removal policy split the Cherokee into factions. Unfortunately for their own good, the standpat faction of the Cherokee gained the ascendance and kept it. The discovery in 1829 of gold at Dahlenega, Georgia caused a rush of white and Indian diggers, all of whom showed a laudable understanding of the institution of private property but strengthened Georgia's determination to oust the Indians. Georgia now baldly asserted its sovereignty and provided for the distribution of the Georgia Cherokee lands by lottery to whites. The Cherokee sued before the Supreme Court

Cherokee resistance to removal

(*Cherokee Nation v. Georgia*) for an injunction to restrain Georgia from interference. Georgia refused to defend itself in the suit, and the Supreme Court denied a trial on the ground that the Cherokee was a "dependent domestic nation"—not a foreign, independent state—and therefore could not sue. Georgia now arrested and imprisoned eleven white missionaries to the Cherokee for residing among the Indians without taking a prescribed oath of allegiance to Georgia. In the case of *Worcester v. Georgia* (1832) two of the missionaries won a decision by the Supreme Court that the Cherokee were under Federal protection and not subject to Georgia.

It was a victory, but a Pyrrhic one. Georgia ignored the decision, and Jackson was reported to have remarked sarcastically: "John Marshall has made his decision—now let him enforce it!" When the Cherokee refused to move, the government agents persuaded a pick-up group of Cherokee to sign a treaty, the Senate ostentatiously ratified it, and the United States army was moved in (1838). As files of soldiers marched Cherokee families to the collection centers, white families were in many cases waiting to take over their houses, fields, and stock. Nearly a fifth (about four thousand) of the Cherokee Nation East died of sickness and hardship on the "Trail of Tears" to the West.

Meanwhile Georgia had been carrying on similar outrages against the Creeks and had been reinforced by Alabama, which desired to get rid of the Creeks. By the removal treaty of 1831 individual Creeks retained certain acreages which they could live on until the removal or could sell. White land speculators gathered in like vul- **Creek resistance** tures, for the Indians had little knowledge of land values and in any case could be easily plunged into debt for purchases of food, gewgaws, and whisky. Every card was stacked against the Indians: even when white men fraudulently seized their property they could not legally testify in state courts on their own behalf. Federal officials were weak and indifferent.

When Secretary of War Cass, an old Indian hater, finally got around to investigating the land frauds, the unscrupulous swindlers found means of stirring the gullible Indians to hostilities. The plot succeeded; Cass ordered the investigations stopped and all of the Creeks removed at once (1836). Fifteen hundred Creeks who refused to go and took to the warpath were rounded up by 11,000 troops (1800 of them Creeks) and forwarded willy-nilly. As late as the 1850's an additional 4000 were sent off, many of them in irons. It is claimed that of the nation of about 25,000 only half survived the starvation and debauchery of the last years in Alabama and Georgia and the hardships of the removal.

The fact remains that not all the Indians were removed. Pockets of them remained in nearly every eastern state, the small reservations of the Iroquois in New York and the Cherokee villages in North Carolina

Those who stayed behind being examples. At the time it was estimated that approximately 12,000 remained behind. It is known also that thousands of mixed-breeds successfully held their ground and eventually merged with the white population. The process of amalgamation had been under way for generations among the wandering *voyageurs,* the *habitants* settled around the French forts, and the British and American fur traders and blacksmiths in the Indian country. The advance of the frontier by no means swept all the undesirables before it. Accounts of the nineteenth century bear witness that in numerous communities among the shiftless element pushed out to the hard-scrabble hills and valleys there was often a perceptible amount of Indian and Negro blood. From these various sources the social ferment must have resulted in the transmission of Indian and Negro blood to millions who today are ignorant of the fact.

Removals were usually by steamboat and keelboat and were carried out under military supervision by contractors at specified rates. Scarcely a single one of the scores of caravans escaped epidemics and starvation. **Hardships of the removals** Those who reached the new lands were confronted by rigorous winters and were in some cases all but devoid of resources. The spirit of co-operation was often lacking between the newcomers and those of their nation who had preceded them, and political and economic rivalries sometimes ended in armed conflict. Even more serious, the immigrants found that they must accustom themselves to plains warfare, for the wild Kiowa, Comanche, and others were inveterate raiders and horse stealers. In time they learned, and the descendants of the Delawares who had danced in council with William Penn at Shackamaxon and of the Cherokee who had besieged the environs of Charleston now fought the Plains Indians on equal terms and went on hunting and trading expeditions to the Rocky Mountains.

The Permanent Indian Frontier policy was essentially in effect by 1840. The frontier ran across northern Wisconsin to the Mississippi, down that stream to northern Iowa, whence it struck inland to the Missouri border, thence along the borders of Missouri and Arkansas **New policy in effect** to Texas, not then a part of the United States. The line of forts along the frontier had materialized, but not the road. The Indian Intercourse Act of 1834 had sought to put into effect the government's ideas. White entry into the Indian country was forbidden, the sale of liquor was prohibited, and the agency system was overhauled and improved. Missionaries were encouraged to teach Christianity and the arts of peace, and government subsidies were distributed among the missionary schools. A beginning was made at allotting lands to Indian families in order to prepare them to take their places as citizens.

The shortcomings of Federal Indian policy are clear, but it is unfair to accuse the government of deliberate cynicism and brutality. Its worst faults rose from ignorance and political exigencies. Very often it was poorly served. Indian agents were often corrupt, filled with impractical do-goodism, or incapable of understanding Indian psychology; it is arguable that one is as destructive as the others. The heritage of fear and hatred and the con- **Shortcomings of U.S. Indian policy** sciousness of cultural incompatibility sat with the conferees at every council fire. Sheer frustration and weariness bred halfway measures. For example, it is probable that down to 1850 Indian wars cost the United States $200,000,000 in direct expenditures, and that civil disbursements for land cessions, presents, pensions, etc., cost $60,000,000. It is no wonder that by 1850 it had come to be believed that it was "cheaper to feed the Indians for a year than to fight them for a day."

It is apparent today (1) that it was a mistake to treat with the Indian nations as possessing sovereign powers when in actuality they had neither the understanding nor the political machinery to act as such, (2) that frequent removals bred social dislocations and discontents, (3) that the great areas assigned to the nations fostered the false hope that they could preserve their traditional way of life, and (4) that the system of payment for land cessions encouraged arrogance, spendthrift habits, and the feeling that the government owed them a living. These facts bred wars, no matter how much they might cost.

But there was a brighter side. It should be emphasized that the removals, even though they bore the curse of political feasibility, were intended to enhance the welfare of the Indians. This intent applied not only to the eastern Indians but to those already in the West. **Favorable aspects of U.S. Indian policy** Indeed, the entire policy was the culmination of a long battle on the part of the government to do its duty by the aborigines. The recognition of the Indians' right to their land set a standard of moral obligation which conquering nations have too often ignored. The money paid for lands was invested and honestly administered. Famine and winter were often mitigated by government gifts, and epidemics were often fought by army surgeons. Orphans were maintained. Missionary schools were subsidized to teach the white man's ways, and tools, seeds, and livestock were distributed. Criminal jurisdiction was extended to protect the Indians, and the Federal courts regarded themselves as the red men's guardians. Even the military forces, however often they were highhanded, frequently protected peaceful Indians against hostile red and white men.

Indian Territory, the last home of the eastern Indians, domiciled possibly forty thousand Indians of the Five Civilized Nations by 1840. They

were little self-governing republics, and all but the Seminole had written
Failure of the Permanent Indian Frontier policy constitutions and laws. The good intents inherent in government policy were to an alarming extent swept aside by the events of the 1850's. Already the Santa Fe traders had seen that the Great Plains, especially the eastern part, was not a desert but was capable of sustaining stock farming if not actually agriculture. Long caravans of Oregon and Mormon emigrants and California gold seekers crossed the Indian country, chiefly through Kansas and Nebraska, and their highhandedness upset the fairly stable Indian relations of the fur empire. The government now had to acquire the right to lay out roads, and this meant removal of the Indians whose lands lay across the overland routes. The new policies were carried out under new auspices. The rising tide of western anger forced the creation of the Department of the Interior in 1849 to initiate western policies in the control of public lands and Indians affairs. The War Department had made many mistakes, but it had often in the administration of the Indian Bureau opposed western highhandedness. With the removal of the Indian Bureau to the Department of the Interior the groundwork was laid not only for western landgrabbing from the Indians but (since the War Department still controlled the army) for added inconsistencies, misunderstandings, and wars. Fortunately for whites and eastern Indians alike, great epidemics swept the Plains nations in the 1830's and seriously reduced their numbers, so that the era of great wars did not begin until the 1860's.

BIBLIOGRAPHICAL NOTE

The Passing of the Woods Indian

There is need for a well-integrated survey of Indian-white relations; as it is, one must depend upon numerous studies of epochs and phases, the majority of them so detailed that one cannot see the woods for the trees. For general reference see William C. Macleod, *The American Indian Frontier* (1928), useful but diffuse; and Frederick W. Hodge, ed., *Handbook of the American Indians* (2 v., 1907–1910).

The Fur Traders' Frontier

GENERAL: The classic account of the American fur empire is Hiram M. Chittenden, *The American Fur Trade of the Far West* (3 v., 1902); see the same author's *History of Early Steamboat Navigation on the Missouri River* (2 v., 1903). The exploration phase is treated in Edmund W. Gilbert, *Exploration of Western America, 1800–1850* (1933); and C. A. Vandiveer, *The Fur Trade and Early Western Exploration* (1929). There are many journals and reminiscences of travelers, company managers, and independent entrepreneurs. Among these the following have been reprinted in Reuben G. Thwaites, ed., *Early Western Travels* (1904–07): Henry M. Brackenridge;

John Bradbury; Thomas J. Farnham; Gabriel Franchere; Maximilian, Prince of Wied; James O. Pattie; and Alexander Ross. For further sources see H. R. Wagner, *The Plains and the Rockies: A Bibliography of Original Narratives of Travels and Adventure, 1800–1865* (1921).

CANADIAN COMPANIES: See Gordon C. Davidson, *The Northwest Company* (1918); Louise P. Kellogg, *The British Régime in Wisconsin and the Northwest* (1935); Arthur S. Morton, *History of the Canadian West to 1870–71* (1939); Robert E. Pinkerton, *Hudson's Bay Company* (1931); Grace L. Nute, *The Voyageur* (1931); and of course many others.

OREGON: Adele Ogden, *The California Sea Otter Trade, 1784–1848* (1941); Hector Chevigny, *Lord of Alaska* [Baranov] (1942); Kenneth W. Porter, *John Jacob Astor, Business Man* (2 v., 1931); Arthur D. H. Smith, *John Jacob Astor, Landlord of New York* (1929). Washington Irving's *Astoria* (1836) and *Adventures of Captain Bonneville* (1850) still have absorbing interest. There are numerous accounts of the Lewis and Clark expedition, all of course based on the journals kept by members. Latest and one of the best is John Bakeless, *Lewis and Clark: Partners in Discovery* (1947). The *Original Journals* were edited by Reuben G. Thwaites (8 v., 1904–05).

MOUNTAIN MEN: In addition to some of the titles cited above see Stanley Vestal, *Mountain Men* (1937), *Kit Carson* (1931), and *Jim Bridger* (1946); Noel J. Breed, *Story of Jedediah Smith* (1926); Alpheus H. Favour, *Old Bill Williams* (1936); LeRoy R. Hafen and William J. Ghent, *Broken Hand: The Life Story of Thomas Fitzpatrick* (1931); Bernard De Voto's lavishly illustrated *Across the Wide Missouri* (1947); and Robert G. Cleland, *This Reckless Breed of Men: The Trappers and Fur Traders of the Southwest* (1950). Another collection of western drawings is in *The West of Alfred Jacob Miller* (1951).

The Permanent Indian Frontier Policy

GENERAL: Best on the period covered is George D. Harmon, *Sixty Years of Indian Affairs, 1789–1850* (1941).

BLACK HAWK: See *Autobiography of Black Hawk* (various ed.), a classic of Indian history; and Frank E. Stevens, ed., *History of the Black Hawk War* (1908).

REMOVAL: Annie H. Abel, *History of Events Resulting in Indian Consolidation West of the Mississippi* (1906); and Marion L. Starkey, *The Cherokee Nation* (1946). Grant Foreman has become principal historian of the Civilized Nations. See especially his *Indian Removal* (1932) and *Advancing the Frontier* (1933); and for the period after the removal *The Five Civilized Tribes* (1934).

Chapter XVII

THE WHITE SIDE
OF THE FRONTIER

1 *The Significance of the West*

AMERICAN historians of the nineteenth century were overwhelmingly Easterners, or at least obtained their training in the East or in Europe. More than this, those of the first rank were for the most part

Northeastern bias of historians New Englanders; even the exceptions usually lived no farther away than New York. The natural result was that formal United States history had an incorrigibly northeastern bias, and textbooks emphasized Plymouth Rock at the expense of Jamestown. Boston, often jokingly called the Hub of the Universe, was seriously presented as the center of most that was worth while in American political, economic, and cultural history. The point of view had a superficial plausibility simply because no one had yet tied into the national pattern the tremendous forces of the South and the West.

The role of the South in American history was thrust upon public attention by the Civil War. The West came into its own with dramatic suddenness in 1893 at the World's Columbian Exposition in Chicago

Turner's hypothesis when Frederick Jackson Turner (1861–1932), born in Wisconsin and trained at Johns Hopkins, read to a small group of historians a paper on "The Significance of the Frontier in American History." The famous Frontier Hypothesis, thus launched, held that the abundant free lands at the edge of the settlements not only caused the rapid advancement of the frontier to the Pacific but was instrumental in developing (from eastern and European seeds) American democracy and nationalism and in giving us a host of characteristics, such as individualism, inventiveness, freedom of opportunity, energy,

530

equalitarianism, and exuberance. Hundreds of students sat under Turner's spell at the University of Wisconsin and at Harvard, and before long the effects of his hypothesis began to be felt not only in the historical field but in the other social studies and even in literature.

For a generation it was orthodox to present the West as the paramount molder of American institutions—indeed, Turner's followers were more dogmatic and sweeping in their claims than he ever was. Then the reaction set in. The political, social, economic, and cultural influences of Northeast and South upon the West began to **Reaction** be stressed. More than this, the heritage of the English democratic process was emphasized, and the bitter struggle of the honest mechanics of eastern cities for their democratic rights was shown to have been little influenced by the West. Probably the pendulum has gone too far to the opposite extreme, and the truth will eventually be found to lie somewhere between. At any rate, the present-day historian approaches the analysis of the West and its influence with reservations; certainly as yet he does not expect to find the answer to all his questions.

Turner seems to have used the words *frontier* and *West* as synonyms; there is something to be said for this, for certainly the two blend into each other so gradually that it is not always easy to tell where one leaves off and the other begins. Nevertheless, in this work we have tried to preserve the distinction between the frontier as the **The changing West** area of contact and conflict (trading and crudely agricultural) between civilization and wilderness, and the West as the sparsely inhabited area of agricultural settlement; at times the West has also included mining and cattle raising. Turner also used the two words to denote a state of mind prevalent in those areas, either at the time of their existence or as passed on to later generations. The usage is well justified, for the *frontier* and the *West* had tremendous effects upon national psychology, but one must be careful in general reading to note the context in connection with each word. Eventually the term West was gradually shifted to the Great Plains states and to the Pacific Coast (or Far West), and these areas because of their special and irreconcilable interests are the closest thing we possess to the West in its old meaning as an economic and cultural area and as a state of mind.

The West has always been recognizable by its problems. Most obvious problem was the Indians; even when the Indians were not on the warpath, the people of the West were concerned to get them pushed farther on in order to make more land available. Second was the **Problems of the West** problem of how to get control of land quickly, cheaply, legally, and in generous quantities. Third was the problem of transportation, for the pioneer's grain, meat, and lumber were too heavy to be carried far by primitive methods; even with the coming of the steamboat and the railroad, rates were so high that transportation remained a live problem. Fourth was the fact that the West was always a debtor area, for its products never brought enough to develop its resources and public utilities and leave enough for the people to live on in the style to which they wished to become accustomed.

As a result eastern capital was invested, but since the risk was great it charged all the traffic would bear and took much of its earnings out of the area; the effect was to reduce the circulation of cash, just as had happened in the Thirteen Colonies. There were many other western problems, but it will be sufficient here to name cultural sterility. This arose from several causes: the bitter struggle against Nature left little leisure for self-improvement; poverty in the pioneer era made it difficult to support colleges, churches, libraries, welfare agencies, and even common schools; and distances made social and institutional contacts difficult.

The West had a wealth of positive qualities. The first one that struck the traveler was the well-nigh universal optimism. The Englishman on the steamboat who listened to the native describe the great and beautiful

Optimism and materialism city around the next bend was disappointed to find a collection of hovels with a few fever-racked inhabitants. The American probably had not been lying; the vision of the future had so filled his mind that he quite failed to see the reality, and what he described was merely what he saw in his mind's eye. The American of the pre-Jeffersonian era, it has been quite generally held, was indolent and indifferent. If that was true, something must have stirred him up by the time the War of 1812 was over—perhaps the hopes and visions offered by a continent full of opportunities. Except in certain backward and malarial regions he now became a live wire. He attacked his problems with intelligence, energy, initiative, and without undue scruples; he took calculated risks, and if he lost he picked himself up and tried again. He was materialistic, as was natural, for it was a material problem which he had set out to conquer. The whole country, it may as well be acknowledged, evidenced optimism and materialism, but these qualities were focused most sharply in the West.

The West was an economic opportunity rather than a stamping ground of freedom. Its citizens often worked hard to raise its religious, educational, medical, and cultural standards, but the standards they had

What the West was and was not in mind were imported from the East or from Europe. The Westerner quite sensibly looked at his problems primarily in economic terms, for economic disputes can be compromised; when they are transmuted into moral principles, they never can be. Lincoln was best illustrative of this attitude in his steadfast refusal to accept slavery as a moral issue. The Westerner refused to make sweeping reforms. He was democratic, but he did not give the vote to women,

Negroes, or Indians; he agreed reluctantly to emancipation but preferred to leave the details to the South. He belonged, of course, to churches, missionary societies, temperance societies, abolition societies, and prison-reform societies, but these movements started in the East and for a long time were struggling and imitative in the West. The Westerner was not out to build a new Jerusalem but to duplicate settled areas on a somewhat better scale. Considering the obstacles, that gave him quite enough to do.

It has been the habit of the extreme proponents of the Frontier Hypothesis to claim everything in sight for the West. Not only were the breezes that blew from the West fresher and more invigorating than those from the East, but they bore on their wings all good gifts of politics, economics, and society. Unfortunately for the reliability of these interpreters, the West in its pioneer stage was all but sterile of new ideas in all three. The West was politically democratic, largely because at first its people were pretty much on an economic level, but it was equalitarian rather than socially conscious. The West itself was ostensibly convinced of its own superiority, but the heat of its protestations rose from a basic inferiority complex. It was jealous of eastern and British advantages and showed it by ridiculing and at times smashing manifestations of culture, luxury, and good manners.

Contrary to popular opinion our various Wests have not always been areas of progressive revolt; basically they have always upheld capitalism: their intention was simply to extend its blessings to themselves by pruning off the privileges which enabled eastern capital to drain away their surplus. Economic radicalism, indeed, is nearly always characteristic of agricultural areas, but it usually takes the form of panaceas (such as inflation by free silver) and is preached with the emotional zeal of crusades. Again, the Wests have contributed but few mechanical inventions, though they eagerly accepted and sometimes improved agricultural machinery; unfortunately, either because of circumstances or innate conservativeness, this tolerance was not for some time extended to scientific farming methods. The Westerner was an expansionist, but only in North America and certainly no farther than the Caribbean; he was an isolationist, but with a touchy sense of national honor; and a nationalist, but sometimes with his fingers crossed on policies (such as the tariff) which the East thought essential to national welfare.

Though the West may not have played quite the dominant role that its admirers would insist, it nevertheless had tremendous significance. Its drama has pervaded American literature, song, and story. Its psychological characteristics have strengthened certain trends in the pattern of national thought and action which would **Significance of the West** otherwise have been less pervasive; we shall find ourselves concerned with these throughout the remainder of the American story. The West turned national attention inward and bred an illusion of isolation and self-sufficiency; at the same time the cotton and grain of the West slowed down the growth of an industry which might have given us an enlightened interest in world trade and consequently in world affairs. As it was, the tremendous domestic market afforded by the West (and the South) delayed an interest in world affairs even after industry had grown to almost unprecedented size.

The West drew surplus eastern farmers and thus by lowering the pool of prospective native industrial laborers raised wages and stimulated the flow of European labor; this in turn bequeathed to us the problem of the melting pot and delayed the integration of American culture and the solidification of social and economic classes. Lastly, this vast agricultural empire (cotton, corn, and wheat) has had decisive political influence. Even though population in industrial states has outgrown that of agricultural states, the number of the latter under our Constitutional system has given them a preponderance in the Senate. This has enabled them from time to time to check the arbitrary rule of industry, to enhance the growth of individual political rights, and finally to join in enhancing the growth of the individual's social rights.

2 Life in the West

The method and conditions of the journey to the West varied with the resources of the pioneer, the route followed, and the generation in which it was performed. Those who came first across the mountains sometimes actually brought little more than a rifle, an ax, a **The pioneers** hoe, a frying pan and cups, and a bag of seed corn; if they were fortunate, they brought a horse or a cow laden with spare clothing and blankets, a spinning wheel, a few iron pots and pans, and such extra tools as adzes, augurs, stone chisels, hammers, nails, and plow points. Since roads were nothing more than traces, the pioneers used the rivers whenever possible. The immigrant's boxlike flatboat carried equipment, provisions, and livestock which would otherwise have been difficult to transport; and the flatboat itself furnished lumber for the new home. Of course, elaborate equipment was helpful, but in the long run more depended upon luck and skill. It was literally possible for a woodswise pioneer with nothing but an ax and a hunting knife to build and furnish a cabin, put a field under cultivation, and by clever use of traps provide his family with leather and fur clothing.

Ordinarily immigrants traveled in caravans or flotillas for protection against Indians and robbers. Sometimes they were chance assemblages, sometimes they were neighbors or even congregations led by their pastor.

Most pioneers took up land in a "settlement"; that is, the clearings were dotted about at intervals of a mile more or less, **Early settlements** as soil and water dictated, but were reasonably accessible to a central farmhouse which had been "forted" or to "stations," real forts with log blockhouses and palisades within which the settlers and their stock could take refuge.

By the time of the War of 1812 conditions of migration had improved remarkably. A farmer could now load his most important equipment and some furniture on his wagon and drive to the West over roads that were at least passable. It was now possible to go west by public **Later migration to the West** conveyances or private carriages and purchase needed equipment near the place of settlement. Of course, poor people often traveled in the old way, carrying all they possessed or loading it on a horse or a cow. However, the extension of roads brought the pushcart mover: the husband harnessed himself to a handcart loaded with goods and infants while the wife pushed on the hills. Forts were no longer needed except on the northern and southern flanks, where Tecumseh and the Creeks made occasional raids. After 1825 the opening of the Erie Canal and of canals in Ohio, plus the multiplication of steamers on the rivers and the Great Lakes, made transportation of passengers and goods easier and cheaper than ever before and led to phenomenal growth.

The knowing pioneer in selecting a new locality considered soil, wood, rain, and water power. Rain was usually dependable east of the Great Plains, but the other factors were not always easily obtainable. Water power meant that there must be a stream of water large **Choosing a location** enough and constant enough to run a neighborhood grist-mill. When possible, the cabin was built near a spring or "branch"; but, as it was, the settlers often had to carry water long distances, especially in dry seasons. Wood was usually so abundant as to be a nuisance, but it was none the less important. The pioneer preferred the labor of clearing land to settling on a prairie distant from trees. There was also, in pioneer lore, a direct connection between the presence of trees and soil fertility; some pioneers even claimed to be able to judge the soil by the kind of trees, herbs, and grasses. As it was, settlement was spotty. Clearings were made in locations chosen for their supposed fertility, while in between the forest reigned undisturbed. The Indians were continually puzzled by this procedure and accused the whites (with justice) of refusing to utilize any but the best land and so of always wishing to push the Indians farther on.

Travelers' accounts of newly-settled areas agree that farms kept a ragged appearance for years. Usually the pioneer first girdled trees by cutting away the bark on a ring around the trunk, thus killing the tree

Evolution of the farmstead and letting the sun in to a hastily planted corn patch. Even after the trees were felled, the fields were dotted with stumps and the immediate surroundings were disorderly "slashings" from which the trees had been cut away and the brush left to grow. Sometimes the pioneers passed their first winter in a "lean-to," a bower of saplings and brush built against a log or a bank. After that came a one-room cabin built of round logs with the crevices filled with mud and moss; the chimney was made of sticks, stones, and mud and was constantly in danger of catching fire. Cattle, horses, and hogs roamed the woods or were stabled in the roughest of open shelters.

The second stage of development came in from five to ten years, if the pioneer was industrious. The stumps were pulled out and the slashings cleared and turned into fields, meadows, or orchards. "Stake-and-rider" fences were built of rails, a new squared-log house with two or three rooms was built, and the old cabin was turned into a stable. The third stage might or might not be reached in the lifetime of the original settler. The meadows and crop fields and fences were extended, the stock increased and adequately stabled and fed in the winter, a spring house built, and the house covered with clapboards or perhaps replaced by a frame structure. In a few cases brick houses and enormous barns marked the farms of especially enterprising and successful farmers.

Crops were not greatly varied, and for some time there was little understanding of the value of rotation or of liming or manuring the fields. Indeed, so long as land was abundant, some farmers preferred to mine the soil for a few years, then move on. Obviously such **Farm products** farms did not pass out of the stump-and-slashings stage until a more careful farmer took them over. Until the fields were clear of stumps the pioneer relied upon corn and potatoes; hogs and cattle were branded and allowed to run loose until butchering season, when they were driven in and slaughtered. Such methods did not produce the best beef and pork, so as soon as he could the farmer fenced in his stock and fed them corn. Wool was in demand, so sheep were raised.

Open fields also enabled the introduction of hay, clover, hemp, flax, and wheat. In this stage the farmer was almost self-sustaining, except for iron and salt. He grew his own beef and pork, ground his wheat and corn at a neighboring mill, produced the wool and flax which his wife spun and wove, made his own hominy and cheese, and perhaps distilled his own whisky. Orchards were precious, for tree nurseries did not exist, and anyhow young trees would have been beyond the means of the cashless pioneer. A half-demented New Englander named John Chapman made it his mission to supply the lack by planting fruit seeds all over the Ohio wilderness, principally apple seeds brought from the cider mills of the Pittsburgh area. He attained fame in pioneer rhyme and legend as Johnny Appleseed.

Presently, as markets and arteries of commerce began to open up, the farmer sold more of his produce, purchased more of his necessities, and added to his luxuries. Hogs and cattle were if possible driven to the slaughterhouses in the river towns; sometimes they were actually driven across the mountains to Baltimore and **Marketing** Philadelphia. A common procedure was for one or more farmers to build a flatboat near a creek. When the spring flood came, they launched it and loaded it with flour, meat, cider, and other produce and floated it downstream to Natchez or New Orleans. This custom continued into the steamboat era and ended only when the railroads offered effective competition.

Upstream transportation until about 1825 was meager and depended largely upon keelboats, which were rowed, pulled by a towline, or poled in shallow water. The keelboatmen were the offscourings of the West, and their brawling and cantankerous conduct made them feared, hated, and admired. Keelboats, however, could furnish only a minimum of luxury goods; most people therefore had to depend on local manufactures or do without until steamboats, canals, and railroads raised the volume of commerce and the standard of living. Much of the western demand for internal improvements (roads, canals, and railroads) came from areas which had no access to navigable water and consequently could not keep pace with the farms and towns along the rivers.

It has been the custom to speak of the pioneers as men and women with unusual health and endurance. Now we are not so sure but what their endurance rose simply from necessity. Though western adults were younger than the national average, it would seem that they had worse health. Swamps and forests promoted malaria **Pioneer** (fever and ague), undulent fever (milk sickness), and rheu- **health** matism. Plagues like cholera and yellow fever were frequent. Poor medical and dental attention allowed minor "miseries" to develop into serious organic and inflammatory conditions. Exposure led to a high pneumonia rate, and the lowering of resistance added to malnutrition made tuberculosis a scourge in nearly every family. Medicos usually received their training as assistants to a practitioner and used only the simplest medicines and instruments. Just the same, in passing, one should note that there were a number of western physicians who made excellent contributions to medical and surgical science.

Even with the best of intentions it was hard to avoid filth. Bacteria were unsuspected and so were not guarded against, soap was homemade and harsh, clothes were stiff and irritating, and only the wealthy possessed underwear. During the Civil War the army intro- **Sanitation** duced underwear to the troops; indeed, it had to be forced on them in many cases, for the conservative soldier resented such cultural innovations. Bathtubs were unheard of—there was a national scandal when in 1850 Mrs. Fillmore insisted on installing them in the White

House—and in western cabins even the Saturday-night bath was still to come. One suspects that there was something more than a joke behind the institution of the Fourth-of-July bath. Bathing in the creek was pleasant in the summer, but it was not done when the ice had to be broken.

Social life in the pioneer days had a rough similarity all through the West. When neighbors gathered in to help raise a house or barn, husk corn, make maple sugar, or slaughter, a virtue was made of necessity by **Social life** adding festivities to the occasion: a picnic, wrestling, foot-races or horse races, and square dances. Other gatherings occurred on election days, court days, and the Fourth of July. On muster days men of fighting age were supposed to meet to elect officers and to receive instructions in handling weapons and in drill, a perfunctory performance which was a favorite butt of ridicule by cartoonists and humorous writers.

Religion was another social vent. The sordid truth is that western religion (as in the Piedmont) was often so primitive that it was scarcely more than cults that recognized and utilized magic and superstition. The **Religious life** witch and the evil eye were widely feared. The Methodists and Baptists, the most popular denominations on the frontier, did not have a learned clergy, and their church services were often orgies of emotion with shouting, hysterics, and trances. Fires of religious excitement swept down and across the frontier from Vermont to Georgia, and these emotional debauches were accepted by the shallow as seasons of purification. The Great Revival (1797–1805) centered in Kentucky, and its zenith was a camp meeting held in 1801 at Cane Ridge, attended by at least ten thousand persons and accompanied by unprecedented emotional orgies.

Such revivals greatly strengthened the evangelical sects, largely to the good, as these churches upheld and practiced good social and moral standards and permitted the entrance of education, and were therefore far better influences than the primitive cults. There were, of course, many other denominations in the West, but the Presbyterians can stand for those that insisted upon a high educational standard for their ministers and looked with disfavor on emotionalism. Among the Presbyterians there was a split between those who held to the old theology and those who opposed the rigid Calvinist doctrine of predestination. Such factionalism has always been characteristic of Protestantism, and in the West it was promoted by the individualism which made it normal for any strong leader to break away from an organization which he could not control.

Western ministers were few in number in the rural areas, and this scarcity also promoted in many localities the emergence of men who felt "called" to preach. Rural congregations were organized in circuits, and they might be visited every few weeks or months by circuit riders, that is, ministers who preached in regular order to these congregations. The visits of the minister were so rare that he usually had waiting at each place a number of baptisms to preside over and marriages to perform. In some cases social approval was given to the custom of couples setting up housekeeping together, then being married during the circuit rider's next visit. Ministers probably did not approve of such customs but had to accept facts. Ministers were natural-born leaders, men with a shrewd knowledge of human nature even if their wisdom was not beyond reproach. They fought the drunkenness, lechery, brutality, and sharp dealing of pioneer society with threats of hell fire; and by picturing the rewards of heaven they sought to implant the virtues of sobriety, diligence, thrift, fair dealings, and good order. Their medicine was doubtless strong, but it was suited to a rough society.

Circuit riders

Attempts to prove the significance and originality of western culture are not very convincing, except possibly as to its psychological effects. It seems fair to say that the first generation reared in the West was lower culturally than its immigrant parents. Its culture was not peculiarly western but a simpler and cruder version of the East. Sober citizens of the East realized that cultural and religious deterioration in the West was a menace to the entire country, and so they organized missionary societies which supported ministers in the West and distributed Bibles and religious literature. There was a direct connection with economic and political conservatism, for it was felt that a society either with no religion or with an overly emotional brand of religion was bound to be radical in politics and economics, but that proper religious views would necessarily breed proper views in all other matters. Thoughtful Westerners welcomed eastern missionaries as positive aids in the struggle to raise religious and cultural standards.

Western culture

Unfortunately the majority of the people saw little value in education beyond the three R's, especially if it meant higher taxes. Rural public schools were one-room log cabins, and attendance was confined to seasons when farm work was slack. Teachers were usually poorly prepared and poorly paid. Textbooks and other school equipment were scarce in the early days, but after the War of 1812 western printers began issuing spelling books and arithmetics, and William Holmes McGuffey's famous readers began to appear in 1837 and reinforced the tendency to make moral precepts and stories with a moral the substance of education.

Education

Northern schools, especially in the area of New England settlement, were fairly good in the context of the times, but the school standard tapered off the farther south one went. This condition was not the fault of Congress, for from the very first it had set aside in each township certain sections of land which were to be sold for the benefit of public common schools. As the nineteenth century advanced, eastern college men set up academies in western population centers. These were usually a sort of high school which prepared young people for college and for teaching in rural public schools. Some of these academies developed into normal schools and colleges, but for the most part this development occurred after the pioneer stage had passed.

Success was not attained in the West merely by working and waiting. Red men were the least of the dangers. Even if the pioneer's chosen spot was fertile, it could be situated off the developing arteries of transporta-

Obstacles to success tion, or lost in a law suit, or prove to be inescapably malarial. Disease, malnutrition, exposure, and accident always plagued the pioneer. Few families failed to lose children; few men and women reached old age with the same spouse with whom they had begun adult life—and death, not divorce, was the great separater. Probably a minority of those who took up western land had reason to rejoice when they came to cast up life's balance, except for the one fact that their surviving children had a better start than they would have had in the East. Yes, the ordinary men and women of the West were heroic, but not in any dramatic sense. They lived (in the words of Thoreau) lives of quiet desperation. They were heroic because for a generation, perhaps all their lives, they doggedly fought adversity and monotony and forced both to yield a few grudging conveniences. They were tragic, also, not because they were smitten with sudden disaster but because through the years good crops and good prices seldom came together, because of the lengthening row of graves in the field beside the cabin, and because the years bowed their shoulders without giving them their hearts' desires.

So far as the frontier was concerned, the Revolution and the Indian wars which continued through 1794 were one. Pioneer methods of defense had developed during the Indian wars of the seventeenth century and

The fighting frontier were refined on the Applachian frontier. Strong points were of various forms. At the least, every community tried to have a home in a central location built and equipped for defense; usually it was of squared logs, and sometimes the upper story projected in such a way as to make it possible to shoot down on assailants or to pour hot water on them. Here the settlers from the surrounding region could rally for safety whenever Indians invaded the vicinity. More ambitious were the forts or stations built as long-term community homes and refuges. These consisted of quandrangles, enclosed by cabins and log stockades, with room enough for a corral inside. A third type of strong point was an engineered fort equipped with artillery and garrisoned by regular troops; Fort Pitt was one such, but there were few others, at least during the Revolutionary period. Anyhow, in such instances the settlers lived outside the fort in a village. On the frontier every able-bodied man and half-grown boy was regarded as a member of the militia and was obligated to turn out at the alarm. The cutting edge of settlement was usually made up of men skilled in woodcraft and the use of weapons, but their organization as military units was so democratic that men could often obey orders or not as they chose, and since they were given to rashness, they suffered occasional disastrous defeats.

The New York Historical Society

A Philadelphia caricature of 1829 ridiculing the country's traditional reliance on the militia

Two decades of continuous crisis during the Revolutionary period brought to the front a number of men remarkable for leadership and/or individual prowess. Daniel Boone, born in Pennsylvania and an adopted North Carolinian, was a "long hunter" of renown. He aided in the settling of Kentucky and was a tower of strength in **Indian fighters** defending it against the Indians, though disregard of his advice led to the disastrous Kentucky defeat at Blue Licks in 1782. Rooked out of his land claims by speculators, he departed in 1798 or 1799 for Missouri, then under Spanish rule. A sometime associate of Boone was Simon Kenton, who remained an active warrior through the War of 1812. Lewis Wetzel, a morose and merciless killer, operated out of Wheeling and usually hunted Indians alone. Ebenezer Zane, head of a famous family, was the founder and defender of Wheeling and later a prominent settler of Ohio. No less important than these was Simon Girty, who took the British side. As the leader of Indian war parties he was hated and feared for his cruelty to his former comrades and became known as the Great Renegade. One of his exploits was the bloody defeat of a western Pennsylvania expedition against the Indian towns at Sandusky and the subsequent torture and burning of its commander, Col. William Crawford.

The frontier was one thing—the West quite another. Writers of romances have often given a quite erroneous picture of the fighting men of the West. When the frontier passed on and the West began to fill up with

The pioneer as a fighter peaceful agriculturists, ignorant of forest ways, and often unarmed (for a good rifle cost as much as a small unimproved farm), the amorphous country militia was of even less use on the occasions when Indian raiders were to be pursued or incursions were to be made into the Indian country. They were men of the soil, not of war, slow men who did not know how to act together except when sparked by a leader. Much has been made of pioneer co-operation in harvests and house raisings, but these were traditional and were not concerned with crises. Even the powerful community operation known as "hating out" an unwanted neighbor was probably tacit rather than planned. The western military record, then, was not due to simple cowardice but to the mistakes and fears engendered by inexperience, faulty organization, and incompetent leadership, for the militia was neglected by legislatures and commanded by politicians. That militiamen could serve creditably was shown by the fact that Wayne, Harrison, and Jackson managed to lick volunteer units into serviceable troops.

Indeed, it is time to limit and define the mythus of pioneer individualism. Most admirable of the frontier individualists were the mountain men, who sought for freedom and elbowroom rather than dominance.

The mythus of individualism They loved the freedom of the wilderness, accepted its dangers, and in the end often died violent deaths. Closer to the frontier were the fort traders and the liquor runners, men who lived by frankly exploiting the needs and greeds of their customers. Individualism to them was not an expression of human dignity but an assertion of their right to flout the law and to undermine and exploit the dignity and the rights of others. A third individualist, this time on the white side of the frontier, was the man whose egotism found outward manifestation in a touchy sense of "honor." Among the rough-and-tumble element, personal dominance was asserted by fist fights and gouge fights. The latter, imported from Yorkshire where it flourished well into the nineteenth century, had as its purpose to gouge out an opponent's eye. Personal combat was often preceded by an exchange of threats and boasts known as "brags," which became a part of the ritual of the struggle for dominance. Among the self-styled gentry there were also brawling and blackguarding, but the "code of honor"—that is, the duel—made considerable headway. It enabled the expert pistoleer to rule by the threat of death, for anyone who refused a challenge was a social outcast.

The foregoing exhibitions of individualism were also, some of them at least, exhibitions of lawlessness. The Saturday-night reign of terror is an institution that has not yet altogether disappeared. The ducking of teachers, the stoning of preachers, and the plaguing of wed- **Lawlessness** ding parties were common forms of lawlessness. Along the rivers property, and sometimes life, were not safe because of the maraudings of boatmen. Scarcely a pioneer community but what has a tradition of gang robbery at some time or other in its past. Some river cities now bear an aura of romance—"crime in the past tense"—as centers of robbery, crooked gambling, and revelry.

Before the steamboat furnished a cheap and speedy means of transport upstream the farmers from the upper river, who floated their produce to Natchez and New Orleans on flatboats, had to return home with their money across the wilderness by the Natchez Trace. Here robbers found a lucrative hunting ground and extended loose organizations to cover both river and Trace. Horse stealing and Negro stealing were added to their repertoire, horses and Negroes being passed along to strange communities and sold. In the end, the power of the law and the rapidity of communication put an end to organized activities. The last of the great "land pirates" was a megalomaniac, one John Murrell, who was said to have planned a slave uprising which would afford an opportunity for wholesale plunder by the underworld. He was caught in 1834 in Tennessee and sentenced to the penitentiary. The accidental discovery of plans for a slave rebellion soon afterward seemed to prove the rumors of his intentions, and the whole area was thrown into terror. There was rioting in the river towns between the respectable sections on the bluffs and the denizens of the red-light districts "under the hill" along the river banks, and a number of white suspects were hanged by "regulators."

Great champions either as fighters or hunters became the subjects of tall tales and presently were enshrined as folk heroes. Earliest of these was Mike Fink. Brought up near Pittsburgh, Mike became an army scout in the Indian wars, then became a rough and tough **Folk heroes** keelboatman. A fighter, drinker, and practical joker, he quickly became famous and probably was made the hero of many incidents and crimes attributable to other men. One of his favorite relaxations when drunk was to shoot tin cups from the heads of his friends. With the coming of the steamboat Mike retired up the Missouri and there was shot as the result of a quarrel. David Crockett, the hero of Tennessee, knew how to hold his likker and take care of himself in a fight, but his chief fame arose from his luck and skill as a bear hunter. He fought under Jackson in the Creek War and held minor political offices. Finally the Whigs picked him (as a popular hero) to send to Congress, and there he became renowned for his stories and his homespun wisdom. However, he was unable to buck successfully that other popular hero, Andy Jackson; so he went off to Texas, probably with the hope of raising his political stock. There he was a member of the band which fell in the defense of the Alamo. There were, of course, other frontiersmen who had performed great deeds: Lewis Wetzel, Simon Kenton, and Daniel Boone, not to mention the roster of mountain men—but for some reason Mike Fink and Davy Crockett struck the popular fancy and were immortalized in western story.

The West sought to limit predatory individualism by demanding adherence to a concept of strict equality. This had as much to do with the development of modern American psychology as the land and the resources of the West have had to do with the growth of American power. A story is told of a pointed incident when some officials, trying to get through a crowd to the speaker's platform, shouted self-importantly:

Concept of equality

"Make way for the representatives of the people!"

"Make way yourself!" answered a voice from the crowd. "We *are* the people."

The spirit of equality found practical application in opposition to aristocracy, and it became so marked a characteristic of the West that it was transmitted without much dilution to later generations. Actually the aristocracy which was so distrusted was a plutocracy of slave-holding planters, land speculators, or industrial and investment magnates. In tracing the division of political parties one must recognize the fact that at least until about 1840 they were drawn more nearly on social and economic lines than they have ever been since. The alignment of sections in the Civil War was vitally affected by the antiaristocratic movement: in the Northwest the farmers were influenced by antipathy to the southern "slavocracy"; in the Southwest the poor white was influenced not simply by the social menace of abolitionism but by the old Jacksonian antipathy for northern capitalists. Politicians have known for generations how to win votes by invoking the little red schoolhouse and birth in a log cabin. Even in our own day red galluses and hill-billy bands are standard equipment of some southern politicians, and northern politicians have to shout down banks and corporations and extol the old American virtues, which they represent as having survived chiefly in the breasts of wage earners.

Opposition to aristocracy

The turbulent individual's demand for personal dominance was in the end quelled by social pressure. The West's demand for conformity to a pattern of equality was so strict that mediocrity was glorified. To be socially acceptable, a man could not afford to rise above his neighbors; to show the marks of education and culture, to **Conformity** dress well, or to build a mansion was in many communities known as "putting on airs." The dead weight of public opinion favored the stodgy humdrum virtues, mediocrity, and complete predictability, and it made headway against the more self-assertive and lawless elements. The phenomenon is still familiar in small towns. It is no wonder that professional men, bored and frustrated by the sterile life about them, often drank themselves to death. The standard of success was property, not education, culture, travel, or work for building a better community in any except a strictly material sense. Everyone was perfectly free—to do the socially acceptable thing. As Jefferson put it: "The inquisition of public opinion overwhelms in practice the freedom asserted by the laws in theory."

All this shows nothing if not an innate conservatism in the West. Progress was a fetish, but it was strictly material progress; any other kind of change had to fight its way against general suspicion. The result was that the individualist threw himself into making money **Conserva-** and amassing property and in the end brought about the **tism** very inequality which Jefferson had dreaded, and which now in fact menaced liberty. Western equality had failed to obtain a dead level of economic conditions and was in danger of being overturned. The successful were out to benefit themselves and were perfectly willing to let the devil take the hindmost.

3   The Land

Insatiability is the word which most readily comes to mind in connecting the Westerner with the land. Land was involved in the causes of all the colonial, early national, and Indian wars. Speculations in land, oversettlement, and sometimes overproduction were directly **Significance** related to our booms and busts. From colonial times in- **of land** satiability for land exercised a powerful political pressure, **problems** and the satisfaction of this demand has vitally affected the growth of the democratic process, population shifts, foreign immigration, race relations, cultural indigestibility, growth of corporations and technology, American psychology and philosophy, and the present political pattern. The land was obviously not the only factor in American development, but if it did not affect all other factors the exception is not readily apparent.

We have seen how the land was the capital stake which the government offered to the settler and the speculator, and we should add the

miner, the lumberman, and the cattleman. The settlers themselves were
The land as young people or foreign immigrants seeking a stake and
a capital farmers who had lost or worn out their land. Naturally
stake settlers preferred fertile soil, so they left much unappropriated land between their holdings and added their political pressure to
that of the speculators to force the government to buy more land from
the Indians. There was, from the first, agitation for free land—"Vote
yourself a farm"—but the policy was so clearly politically impractical
that settlers had to content themselves by seeking more and better land
at lower prices; on the other hand, speculators were hoping to make a
killing by holding land for a rise. Though at one time or another most
men with initiative or gullibility took a flyer in land speculation, the
large-scale holder of "unseated" lands was all but universally hated,
especially if he was successful and an absentee. Both the settler and the
speculator wanted land, but under different conditions, and it may be
said here that on the whole Congress was more responsive to the needs
of the actual settler. However, since the first business of a politician is to
get elected, Congressmen sought diligently to apportion the public domain
to all interests as a capital stake for their ventures. Government gifts to
private interests are not the creation of our own day but have been a
historic American policy.

A lenient policy toward the actual farmer-settler developed during the
early 1800's. Harrison's Land Law of 1800 provided that land offices be
set up in various western towns and that a certain part of the public
Land laws lands offered for sale be sold in half-sections. Though they
of 1800 and were to be sold at auction and at a minimum price of two
1820 dollars an acre, it was nevertheless possible to purchase half
a section on four years' credit with a down payment and fees that totaled
around $175. An act of 1804 reduced the minimum purchase to a hundred
sixty acres, and another of 1817 reduced it to eighty. The hard times,
which were almost endemic in the West from 1800 to 1820, made it difficult for farmers to complete their payments and led to a demand for
relief. The West wanted free land for actual settlers, but the East was
inclined to use the public lands as a source of revenue and, moreover,
wished to slow down the drain of population to the West. Congress
temporized with a long series of relief bills until 1820, when the land
laws were overhauled. Credit was abolished, the minimum price at auction was reduced to $1.25 an acre, and the minimum sale of eighty acres
was retained. Remaining defaulters received as much land as their payments would buy at the new rate.

During this period timber was such a nuisance that lumbermen were
free to cut on the public domain; it was not until 1831 that a beginning
was made toward the present policy of preserving trees on public lands.

Saline lands, those having springs from which salt was obtained by evaporation, were reserved. Mineral lands were leased until 1829, when a
policy of selling them at low prices was begun. However, no adequate
general mineral law was passed until after the Civil War.

The West remained unsatisfied and continued to advocate free land.
The immediate problem, however, lay in the ability of the speculator to
outbid the settler. Indeed, there were quirks in the law by which a man
could bid the price up to any sum; when he defaulted the
land was quietly turned back to the government, and his **Pre-emption**
associates, who were in the plot, could snatch it up at the minimum price.
Then there was the fact that great tracts of public land had been settled
by individuals before it was offered for sale. These pre-emptors, or squatters, were usually poor men and frequently found when the sale was held
that they were outbid on their holdings by speculators or perhaps by
bona fide settlers.

As a result there arose in these unsold areas extralegal "claims associations," devoted to the enforcement of "squatters' rights." When government auctions were held, the associators saw to it that no one put in a
bid on a certain tract except the squatter who actually occupied the land.
As a matter of fact, government agents seldom tried to evict squatters
simply because it was physically impossible and politically unwise. Congress tried to meet the problem by a series of pre-emption acts applying
to specific areas which gave squatters the right to purchase their land at
the minimum price. The Pre-emption Act of 1841 (with later amendments) made this right general to the extent of 160 acres, providing that
the purchaser would not thereby own more than 320 acres or exercise his
right more than once.

The land problem entered into most political issues before the Civil
War; and, if it did not, the West was pretty likely to drag it in with the
offer to exchange its political support for more liberal land policies. The
outstanding western leader in the battle was Senator **Proposed**
Thomas Hart Benton of Missouri. His first choice of policies **solutions of**
was *cession,* by which public lands would be turned over to **the land**
the states in which they lay, on the presumption that they **problem**
were entitled to the revenue and would be complaisant toward local interests and pressures. Next Benton upheld *graduation,* by which the price
of the land would be reduced each year until after a specified time what
remained would pass to the state in which it lay. *Distribution* proposed
to divide the money received for the land among the states according to
population; it was fairly popular in the populous Northeast, but since
Clay proposed to link it with a high tariff it got nowhere in the South.
Pre-emption, as we have seen, went into effect gradually. The settler had
to be satisfied with it, until the departure of southern Congressmen at the

beginning of the Civil War enabled Congress to pass out free land by the Homestead Act.

Benton never got all he wanted, but it is noteworthy that Congress granted to the states about 360,000 square miles of land, an area approximately equal to the part of the United States east of the Appalachian **Federal** mountains. It specified that some grants were to be sold **subsidies to** and the money applied to education or internal improve- **states** ments. The Pre-emption Act of 1841 introduced the policy of endowing new states with half a million acres. Here is a resumé in millions of acres of the chief grants to the states; though some lands were turned back to the government, minor grants balance them.*

Roads, bridges, etc.	3.2	Education	118.0
Canals	4.6	Swamplands	64.0
River Improvements	2.2	Total	229.8
Railroads	37.8		

These figures are approximate totals to the present. "Swamplands," it should be explained, were for the most part actually good lands which the states, using the occasion of the Federal grant of swamplands, appropriated. The railroad grants do not include the grants made to private corporations, chiefly after the Civil War; the above figures include the lands which Congress gave the states with authority to turn over to private corporations. The Illinois Central Railroad was one enterprise which was partly financed in this manner. While in some cases the states wasted much of the income derived from the grants, the grants nevertheless were of incalculable benefit in economic and cultural development. At any rate, Federal subsidization of states and private enterprise was a firmly established policy before the Civil War. Our "dollar-matching" is merely the modern form necessitated by the fact that the Federal government now has no agriculturally valuable public lands to turn over to the states.

The public domain was a tremendous natural endowment, the most valuable that any nation (with the possible exception of Russia) has ever had. Hamilton and many Easterners hoped that the land could be doled **Public do-** out slowly at reasonable prices and would thus supply much **main not a** of the money needed to run the government. Since the pro- **source of** gram was politically impossible, the hope was never real- **profit** ized; and only in 1836 and 1841 did land sales yield such a Treasury surplus that it was distributed to the states. In most years surveys and administration actually cost more than land sales brought in.

The reasons are not far to seek. The people (meaning not only settlers but lumbermen, miners, speculators, and manufacturing and transportation entrepreneurs) asserted that the public land was their heritage and

* Benjamin H. Hibbard, *History of the Public Land Policies* (1924): 228–88, 305–46.

that actually it had no value until their labor and enterprise subdued it. They demanded and obtained land in vast quantities at very low prices. Fraud on the part of individuals, corporations, and states cut into the income from the public domain and was often condoned as necessary, if the heir was to enter into the enjoyment of his heritage. Congress was perfectly aware that land disposal was honeycombed with fraud but had to deal with it in a gingerly and usually ineffective manner.

Before criticizing the amorphous Federal land policy and the frauds which all but ruined what planning there was, it is well to consider their effects. A more reasoned and frugal administration of public lands would probably have slowed down the cultural and institutional growth of the states and have hampered the growth of American population and power. At any rate, the political and economic power of the United States in the present world crisis would have been less. It is possible in that case that government enterprise as against private enterprise would have been far more important; even as it was, the trend was reversed chiefly by the hardheadedness of Andrew Jackson.

Public-land statistics are notoriously inaccurate, but up to 1904 (as nearly as we can tell) about 277,000,000 acres were sold and about 364,-000,000 were acquired by states and private corporations through grants. Such grants, of course, were expected to be offered for sale, but great areas were reserved by the owners for the **Land speculation** value of their timber and minerals, or possibly because no one found them worth buying. The prospective purchaser, then, found it possible to buy directly from the government, from the state, or from corporations. Nevertheless, the volume of sales of government land gives a clue to the inflation of land values. Until after the War of 1812 the normal annual sale was well under a million acres. The Great Migration to the West boomed it to 3.5 million in 1818, then the sale dropped back until 1828. The land price inflation of the 1830's brought the peak sale of 20 million acres in 1836, followed by the rapid drop back to less than 3 million. Another boom came in the middle 1850's, and nearly 16 million acres were sold in 1855. After the Homestead Act of 1862 speculation in public lands never again attained such dramatic heights.

The speculators of the 1790's were to a considerable extent men of fortune who combined in great companies and dealt in scores of millions of acres. One of their hoped-for outlets was in Europe, and a number of land agents were kept there, among them those two prominent American statesmen Gouverneur Morris and Joel Barlow. Sometimes speculators sold (especially in Europe) land **Early land speculators** they did not then possess and which they took a chance of getting. This was known as "dodging." All sorts of other frauds were practiced, as selling land held by Spanish patents that had never been legalized or duplicating military land warrants so as to sell the same tract to several suckers. New England may have opposed the West, but its leaders often plunged into land speculation, even the saturnine, West-hating Pickering. It is amazing how gullible speculators snapped up "bargains" without looking at them, perhaps often in the expectation of finding purchasers even more gullible than themselves. The speculators of this period, at least the Easterners, aimed solely at skimming off the unearned increment and were crushed by the collapse of 1795 and 1796. Many, perhaps the majority of eastern speculators, died poor or eked out a living by other methods.

Western speculators were much more likely to be concerned with doing something to earn their increment. The passing of the great eastern-controlled land companies left speculation chiefly in western hands.

Later land speculation Western moneyed men promoted metaled roads and river improvements, built mills, and led the way in agricultural experiment. They were not very wealthy and their transactions were small, but their financial success (if any) came because the boom in settlement was actually under way, especially after 1815.

The government requirement that land be sold at auction may have had some effect in discouraging speculation, but there was a great deal of competitive land available. The speculator, after 1820, offered two advantages that the government did not: liberal credit and "town jobbing." In 1818 town lots in the "paper town" of Florence, Alabama leaped as high as $3500 apiece. Towns with high-sounding names were laid out in every favorable location, though there was little to show for them but gaudily colored plats and lying prospectuses. Rumor has it that at one time most of northeastern Illinois was laid out in town lots. Probably nine of ten such projects sank without trace; the rest might have survived as hamlets, while a minute number became towns and cities.

Liberal credit extension depended chiefly upon the existence of complaisant banks willing to loan money at easy rates; this function was fulfilled by the wildcat banks, which have already been noted in connec-

Panic of 1837 promotes power of moneyed interests tion with Jackson's War on the B. U. S. When by the Specie Circular the government refused to accept the banknotes of the wildcat banks, the speculators lost their advantage and the land bubble burst. It is interesting to note certain sequels of the Panic of 1837. Jackson had meant to hamper the growth of financial power based on paper money, and he did succeed in wiping out the little fellows who were operating chiefly on borrowed capital. The government's income was reduced to the danger point, and millions of acres reverted to the Land Office. On the other hand, men with sound resources—ironically enough, usually Whig enemies of Jackson—bought up lands and other assets at a song and for the first time actually constituted the western moneyed power which Jackson had so feared.

The growth of western towns is fascinating in retrospect. Let us follow a hypothetical instance, it doesn't matter much where. After one of the Indian wars a lad named Andy Brown, who had been a captive among the Indians and had been restored to his family by one of the perennial treaties, decided that he liked Indian life better than white. So he became a trader, traveling among **Brown's Crossing** the nations. Presently he fell in love with the beautiful mixed-blood daughter of a chief and settled down at a point where a trace crossed an important river, to keep store, tavern, post office, and ferry at what came to be known as Brown's Crossing. When the Indians went west, Andy Brown bought up all the land he could from them, using his wife's brothers as stooges and partners in fraud. Then the brothers went on to Oklahoma, and Brown was stuck with several thousand acres of choice land. To his dying day he insisted (and finally came to believe) that he had taken it only as a favor to his Indian acquaintances and relatives. True, there had been trouble with an overconscientious Federal land agent; but when it was discovered that the fellow had been taking bribes, dozens of protests (with strangely similar affidavits) were poured into Washington, and he was recalled. He died soon afterward of a broken heart. For a man who had received at least $10,000 as witnessed by sundry affidavits, he left his wife and family singularly destitute.

One evening an itinerant surveyor stopped at Brown's tavern and readily agreed to lay out a town in exchange for board, a horse, and some equipment. Brown happily carried the chain and drove stakes. A week later when Brown stood before the door of his log store and cabin with the boldly colored plan of the new town in his **Brown's Landing** hand he saw, not a wide streak of mud but a paved street, and along it were a town hall, a court house, a market, a school, and even a place for a "seminary" of higher education. Brown now built a warehouse in which to store produce which he took on a commission basis from neighboring farmers, and he took a share in a little keelboat which plied the river and brought in manufactured goods and carried the produce away.

The forehanded Brown, aware of coming needs, set up a sawmill in order to be ready. Other people began to see the advantages of Brown's Landing, as it was being called, and bought lots and put up cabins or farmhouses. A blacksmith, a cobbler, a joiner, a physician, and a preacher moved in, attracted by promises of free lots by public-spirited Citizen Brown; a young fellow named Green, fresh from Judge White's law office over in Heliopolis, moved in and put up his shingle; a slick-looking operator named Black, in a new-fangled silk hat, came along and set up a bank which dispensed paper money to anyone who would promise to pay interest; an ingenious mechanic (backed by Citizen Brown) borrowed some of the money and in succession set up a gristmill, an oil mill, and a distillery. Then the township put up a log schoolhouse and snared an itinerant teacher.

Brown and Black now saw that settlers in the back land needed access to the river, and so they organized a company to build a turnpike. Next they got Lawyer Green (who had just married Brown's second daughter) elected to Congress, and he logrolled a bill through the national legislature which obligated the Federal government to buy a block of stock in the company. Brown and Black then set up their own construction company to build the road and as soon as it was finished sold out their turnpike stock before it took the inevitable nose dive. It was sharp practice, in a way, but there was the turnpike as solid evidence of their public spirit. Even the most carping critic had to admit that Banker Black, after his first days as a land speculator, turned to the promotion of sound, community-building manufacturing enterprises. Not so well known was the fact that he quietly aided many a bright country lad to an education, for he saw more clearly than Brown that there was more to a community than houses and factories.

By now the "gov'mint" could hold out no longer against popular pressure and moved the land office from inland Heliopolis to Brownstown, as the place had come to be called. At this point there was a successful struggle to have the county court moved over from Heliopolis. The fact that turned the scale was the simultaneous announcements that Brownstown was to become the terminus of a new state canal (financed by the sale of a gift to the state of Federal land obtained through the skilled efforts of Congressman Green), and that Citizen Brown had bought a steamboat and was planning a brick works. A fine new brick court house was erected (guess who got the contract), and the learned Judge White built a brick "mansion" at the edge of town on a spot of high ground. The judge proved to be such a remarkable judge of character and real estate that within ten years he had acquired mortgages on a large percentage of real estate in the county. The town was no longer Andy Brown's personal property. He was a realist, however, and followed the western motto, "If you can't lick 'em, jine 'em." He furnished the common touch for the court-house gang over which Judge White presided with dignity and suavity, for which Congressman Green fronted with glad hand and orotund speeches, and which Banker Black manipulated from his mahogany desk in the office in the back room of the bank.

Brownsville—the judge thought the form an advance in dignity—

Browns-
town

grew, whether because of the court-house gang or in spite of it. Two newspapers were begun, one Whig and the other Democrat, and their weekly tirades at each other were eagerly awaited events.
Brownsville
More mills, shops, and stores, and a couple of wildcat banks were established; several more lawyers and medicos appeared, and additional tavern keepers made a living by providing the whisky they needed to drink themselves to death in disgust at life's futility. An academy was begun by a Yale man, and there the broadclothed sons of the town's "gentlemen of respectability" dug for Latin roots beside a few linsey-woolsied lads from the surrounding country.

Brownsville had its ups and downs, but Banker Black's conservatism saved his bank in 1837 when the rival wildcat banks were wiped out. As a result the court-house gang survived unhurt, and its members even increased their personal holdings. A few years afterward, and this was the crowning glory, came the railroad. True, the town and the county both mortgaged themselves to the gills to entice it, but when Congressman Green came in on the first train he told the assembled citizenry that it was worth it. The speech he made was confidently compared by the town's leading paper (Whig, of course) to the best efforts of "The Godlike Daniel"—or Henry Clay, if you preferred. That night a sour-bellied lawyer pointed out to his tavern cronies that though Black and White and Brown and Green had bought railroad bonds in generous amounts, they had nevertheless already sold them; and he darkly revived the scandal of what had become of the funds from the land which had been sold to finance the canal which had never reached Brownsville. But then he was an old Heliopolis boy and had never become reconciled to its rival's victory.

Brownsville was now a metropolis. It was true that there was not a paved street in town, that the only sewer advertised its openness to the sky, and that hogs were tolerated on the streets as garbage collectors. These, however, were minor matters to loyal citizens, and
Brown City
nothing less than Brown City would do for its proud inhabitants as they gathered on the porch of Leading Citizen Brown's store to spit tobacco juice at the cracks in the floor and do a good pre-Lion job of local roaring. Old Andy Brown was among them, as drawling and horny-handed as when he had tugged at the ropes of his ferry, and outspitting them all in spite of the stack of deeds and mortgages in the tin box under the post-office window. But his youngest son (by his third wife) was away at Yale College preparing to be a "catch" for the judge's daughter; and his second daughter, Mrs. Congressman Green, was such a social light in Washington that there was talk of offering her husband a Cabinet office.

BIBLIOGRAPHICAL NOTE

The Significance of the West

Turner wrote but little, and his publications are chiefly collections of articles. The paper named in the text contains statements of most of his ideas about the West; it is to be found in *The Frontier in American History* (1920). Turner's thinking on the West led naturally to comparisons with other sections and eventually to clarification of the meaning of sectionalism as set forth in his *Significance of Sections in American History* (1932). These two contributions (regardless of whatever modifications may have been made since) entitle Turner to rank as the greatest of American historians.

For a temperate presentation of the history of the frontier and an analysis of present opinion of the Turner Hypothesis see Ray A. Billington, *Westward Expansion* (1949). George R. Taylor ed., *The Turner Thesis* (1949) offers a convenient collection of critical essays.

Life in the West

GENERAL: Most useful of original accounts of pioneers is Joseph Doddridge, *Notes on the Settlement and Indian Wars of the Western Parts of Virginia and Pennsylvania* (reprinted 1912). A secondary account applicable to the pioneer years of most parts of the West is John E. Wright and Doris S. Corbett, *Pioneer Life in Western Pennsylvania* (1940). For the southern frontier see especially Everett Dick, *The Dixie Frontier* (1948). One of the most temperate views of the early West was *Recollections of the Last Ten Years* (1826) written by Timothy Flint, a missionary. For keelboats and flatboats see Leland D. Baldwin, *The Keelboat Age on Western Waters* (1941). An amusing and informative picture of *homo occidens* is given in Thomas D. Clark, *The Rampaging Frontier* (1939). Among the numerous descriptions of pioneer adversities see the account of Seth Hubbell's removal to Vermont in June B. Mussey, *We Were New England* (1937). The books cited below under CULTURAL have much general coverage.

RELIGIOUS: Winifred E. Garrison, *Religion Follows the Frontier* (1931); Colin B. Goodykoontz, *Home Missions on the American Frontier* (1939); Catherine C. Cleveland, *The Great Revival in the West* (1916); Herbert Asbury, *A Methodist Saint* [Bishop Asbury] (1927); and Peter Cartwright's ever pungent and delightful *Autobiography*.

CULTURAL: James M. Miller, *The Genesis of Western Culture* (1938); Beverley W. Bond, *The Civilization of the Old Northwest* (1934); Solon and Elizabeth Buck, *The Planting of Civilization in Western Pennsylvania* (1939). Outstanding is R. Carlyle Buley, *The Old Northwest: Pioneer Period, 1815–1840* (2 v., 1950).

HEROES AND VILLAINS: Among numerous others see John Bakeless, *Daniel Boone* (1939); Thomas Boyd, *Simon Girty* (1928); Walter Blair and Franklin J. Meine, *Mike Fink: King of Mississippi Keelboatmen* (1933). A book purporting to be the autobiography of Crockett was published under various titles; doubtless it was a fake, but it nevertheless is delightful reading.

Johnny Appleseed has been covered in books by William A. Duff and Henry Chapin. Meine's collection of *Tall Tales of the Southwest* (1930) has many contemporary stories of western life. For the history of crime in the early West see Otto A. Rothert, *Outlaws of Cave-in-Rock* (1924); Robert M. Coates, *The Outlaw Years* (1930) carries the story through Murrell.

The Land

There are four outstanding general treatments of public lands: Thomas Donaldson, *The Public Domain* (1884); Benjamin H. Hibbard, *History of the Public Land Policies* (1924); on the period chiefly covered in this section, Payson J. Treat, *The National Land System, 1785–1820* (1910); and most recent and most satisfying to the general reader, Roy M. Robbins, *Our Landed Heritage: The Public Domain, 1776–1936* (1942). Popular in its approach but very informative on land speculation is Aaron M. Sakolski, *The Great American Land Bubble* (1932). For contemporary accounts of land speculation and town booming see Dickens, *Martin Chuzzlewit;* and Joseph G. Baldwin, *Flush Times in Alabama and Mississippi* (1908).

Chapter XVIII

THE MATERIAL SCENE

1   *The Rise of American Technology*

IT IS a general misapprehension among Americans that historically we have been the most inventive of nations. This is not quite true. Nor have we been until this century a leading scientific nation: American history before 1900 offers only three notable "pure scientists"—

The meaning of invention Benjamin Franklin, Joseph Henry, and Willard Gibbs. The word *invention* has several meanings. It may, as is popularly supposed, refer to the sudden production of something new and useful. It may refer to a process to which numerous men each add a little, a process that may take many generations. Again, invention may refer to carefully planned and integrated technical research and experiment by a team or corps of men.

Inventions are of two kinds: basic inventions and improvement-inventions. In the beginning it is likely that both were the result of accident or of a technique of trial-and-error made necessary by ignorance of scientific principles. The Greeks, however, made some inventions

Science, invention, and technology by consciously applying scientific truths, and in modern times this method has become much more common. Nowadays the creation of useful machines and processes usually comes through three steps: the pure scientist discovers the principles; the inventor combines and applies them; and the engineer-technologist adapts and refines the invention. Indeed, the two last steps may sometimes be identical, for very often the inventor is simply an engineer or chemist with an imaginative and experimental flair. It is in the third step, that of technology, that the United States has historically held primacy, though it also has a proud record in the second. Many of our supposed inventions were really engineering refinements of inventions already made abroad; among these were the cotton gin, the rotary press, and the automobile.

556

Though many improvement-inventions are made by men who are conscious of the needs, it would be an error to suppose that mere need is enough to bring forth the mechanical solution. The Roman Empire had dire need of efficient and speedy transportation and com- **The soci-** munication, but the steamship, railroad, and telegraph **ology of** failed to appear, and the empire broke up. It is a common **invention** saying that necessity is the mother of invention; in more cases invention is the mother of necessity, for the invention brings such changes in society and economy that it cannot be dispensed with.

The need for inventions cannot be perceived, nor can the invention be made until the component parts have been invented. This fact is so clear that inventions seem almost to be plucked from the atmosphere of the time. Many inventions are duplicated in two or more places by the work of men or teams who have never heard of each other. The classic example is that of Elisha Gray, whose *caveat* on the method of the telephone reached the patent office only two hours after the application for a patent on the completed invention was filed by Alexander Graham Bell. Modern inventions do not necessarily improve the quality of the work; metallurgical products are superior, but some other articles—such as linens and cut gems—are no better now than they were in ancient Egypt. The principal effects are social and economic in as much as modern methods reduce costs and increase production.

Most of the inventions fundamental to early nineteenth-century industry were a part of our European heritage or were imported soon after they were made. The steam engine, based on principles familiar from the time of the ancient Greeks, was utilized in simple forms in **Borrowings** France and England for pumping water from mines. The **of the tech-** invention, in fact, was essential to the coal-mining industry, **nical revo-** for otherwise mines were invariably flooded and rendered **lution** useless. James Watt, a Scottish instrument maker, turned the simple mine engine into a mighty force by adding the condenser, the steam jacket, and the cylinder head, all of them patented in 1769. Textile machinery was the work of a series of brilliant English inventors. Machine tools had made headway on the European continent after 1450 but were vastly improved in England, largely due to the necessity for precision work in the building of steam engines. English industry was built on steam power; that of the United States chiefly on water power, at least in the early stages. The long dominance of water power made New England a permanent industrial area and has infected the American engineer with a yearning to harness rivers and waterfalls even when they are not the cheapest source of motive power.

Americans have long been justly famed for mechanical ingenuity; most significant have been the contributions of New England, which, be-

cause it was not well adapted to agriculture, had taken up wood and
Isolation of metal working, and where machinery of a sort had been in
early Amer- use almost from the time of settlement. Even before the
ican tech- Revolution the British prohibition of the export of iron-
nology working machinery threw Americans in that industry on
their own resources. After independence Parliament not only widened
the embargo on machinery and plans but forbade the emigration of mechanics. Americans were thus stimulated to make their own developments, and with certain important exceptions technical progress was of
native growth up to about 1840.

America was a raw continent with all the heavy work of building a
civilization to be done and but few inhabitants to do it; in these straits
it was perhaps natural for an American to see the uses of steam in lifting,
Oliver Ev- moving, hauling, sawing, crushing, and grinding. Oliver
ans (1755– Evans, a mill mechanic in the wheat region along the Dela-
1819) ware River, saw that Watt's low-pressure engine did not
generate enough power to perform heavy duties, and so in the 1780's he
worked out plans for a high-pressure engine. This engine he adapted to
many practical uses. One of them was to power a new series of machines
which revolutionized the flour-milling industry by making it all but completely automatic. Though investors were in no haste to avail themselves
of the fruits of Evans's genius, he persevered. On one occasion in 1804,
in order to move a steam dredge, he actually built a steam-driven machine which not only traveled over land but took to the water and pad-
dled to its destination.

One of the earliest and most significant American inventions was the
cotton gin, or engine. British improvements in textile machinery had
caused an unprecedented demand for cotton; the trouble was that there
The cotton was no efficient means of separating seeds and fiber. Much
gin cotton was cleaned by hand, though a crude roller gin
(*churka*) had been brought from India by way of Brazil or
the West Indies and was useful in seeding the long-staple (black seed)
sea-island cotton grown on the coastal islands. Unfortunately short-staple
(or green seed) cotton, which adhered to the rough seeds, was the only
kind that would grow inland, and the roller gin did not clean it efficiently.
In 1793 Eli Whitney, a Connecticut Yankee on a visit to South Carolina,
invented the spike-toothed cotton gin, which successfully cleaned inland
cotton. The machine was so simple that he could not successfully defend
his patents, and he eventually returned to New England and took up gun
manufacturing.

The effect of Whitney's gin on history has been tremendous. Cotton
had never been an important crop in the Thirteen Colonies, and as late

as 1794 John Jay agreed not to export cotton—apparently ignorant of the fact that it was grown in the United States! Most British **The cotton** cotton had come from India and the West Indies; in 1790 **gin and** the United States exported only what would now be about **history** three hundred eighty bales. Not only did the production of short-staple cotton now leap, but it became the economic basis of most of the South and put the profits back into slavery, which had apparently been a dying institution. The result was the Cotton Kingdom, a powerful agricultural domain devoted to slavery and to political reaction, which was regarded by its enemies as a dragon blocking the path of progress. The greatest internal crisis in American history was the result.

Even before the invention of the cotton gin a number of Northerners had attempted to make a go of cotton textile manufacturing establishments, but none of them succeeded until an English textile mechanic named Samuel Slater escaped from England in disguise and **Growth of** from the plans which he had memorized built the first **the cotton** successful American spinning mill in 1790 at Pawtucket, **textile in-** Rhode Island. Thereafter the American textile business was **dustry** mainly on its own; but when freedom of interchange with England began, the Americans were found to be ahead in their technology. American cotton cloth by 1860 was able to compete with the British product, and considerable quantities were finding their way all over the world. The manufacture, and that of woolens also, was pretty well concentrated in New England where labor was cheap and water power plentiful, though there were competitors farther west and even a few in the South.

By the Revolution ironworks had been set up in every colony except Georgia. One seventh of the world's iron was being produced in the colonies. Pennsylvania's rich ores, especially the deposit still being exploited at Cornwall, made it the chief center of production. Though iron smelting required vast quantities of charcoal, **Iron** wood was so plentiful and cheap that coke and anthracite **production** coal did not come into use until the 1830's. Ironworks then began to grow in size and to be concentrated in urban areas. Iron production, moreover, moved into and over the mountains, especially into western Pennsylvania, where the great Pittsburgh Coal Seam, among the finest coking coal in the world, gave Pittsburgh a permanent place in the iron and steel industry. The Bessemer process of making vast quantities of mild steel (useful in rails and structural beams) was developed in the 1850's in England; the same process, however, was developed a little earlier in Kentucky and Pennsylvania by William Kelly.

The abundance and cheapness of wood made it the favorite American fuel almost up to the Civil War, not only in homes but in many indus-

tries. The increasing use of steam engines in eastern centers, however,
made wood scarce in those areas and led to a growing de-
Coal mand for coal. It is estimated that twenty thousand tons of
coal were mined in 1820 and fourteen million in 1860. The increase was
made possible by improved means of transportation, in which coal itself
played a large part. As it was, industrial power reflected the resources of
its area: New England relied on water power, the Hudson and Delaware
valleys on anthracite, and the West upon western Pennsylvania's bituminous coal. The use of anthracite lagged because it requires elaborate draft
controls to burn efficiently, but technical and psychological objections
were overcome before the Civil War. Bituminous coal had made Pittsburgh a grimy manufacturing center by 1812, and coal was floated down
stream in flatboats to the manufacturing cities of the Ohio Valley.

All the magnificent array of modern machinery would be quite impossible without the lubrication afforded by petroleum or its mineral
equivalent. In the early days animal and vegetable oils had to be used for
lubrication, but they were easily broken down by heat. Now
Petroleum there had grown up in the Ohio Valley a technology for
drilling salt wells, and on many occasions petroleum had bubbled forth
and spoiled the brine. Oil obtained from these wells or skimmed or soaked
up in blankets from the top of "oil springs" had long been used as a
medicine. A number of attempts were made to obtain this oil in larger
quantities and to rid it of odor and impurities by refining. The principal
purpose was to obtain a cheap illuminant, for whale oil was becoming
more expensive every year as whales became scarcer; coal oil, or kerosene,
a substitute extracted from coal, had not proved entirely practical.

Early in the 1850's George H. Bissell, a lawyer of New York City,
was among those interested in introducing petroleum. He induced Professor Benjamin Silliman, Jr., a Yale scientist, to analyze the oil and
suggest practical methods of refining it. As a result Silliman separated
from petroleum its illuminating oil, lubricating oil, paraffin, and illuminating gas; gasoline was the only fraction for which he could suggest no
use. Encouraged by this research, Silliman, Bissell, and some New Haven
investors organized the Pennsylvania Rock Oil Company and sent Edwin
L. Drake to drill for oil near Titusville, utilizing the salt-well technique.
Drake luckily hit the right spot and in 1859 struck oil. The first oil boom
ensued. The demand brought by the Civil War continued the boom at
fever pitch, but even in those mad days few could have dreamed of the
tremendous role that petroleum was destined to play in the next century.

The technology of timber cutting and sawing was of importance in a
country which depended greatly on wood. The awkward colonial broad-
axes were reduced in size and improved in balance, and shaped handles of

hickory gave unsurpassed "spring." The original iron heads were improved by inserting and welding in cutting edges of steel. The canthook, or peavey, for use in rolling logs, seems **Lumbering technology** to have been invented about 1858 by Joseph Peavey of Maine. Originally boards were cut over saw pits or on scaffolds, one man below and one above dragging on a big saw; sometimes the saw was run by water power. Efficiency, however, came with the invention of the circular saw, first in England, then in America about 1814. The bandsaw may have been first invented in France, though it also seems to have been invented in the United States about 1808.

Lumbering was practiced, of course, wherever there was a demand, but Maine and Nova Scotia were most active in developing its technology. Cutting was done in the winter and the logs floated downstream on the spring freshets to the mills; the next step was to store water in dams. Where great distances were to be traversed over reliable waters (particularly in the West), rafts were formed of logs bound together. Mills kept reserve supplies in quiet pools enclosed by heavy lines of logs called booms. The greatest of the booms, at Williamsport, Pennsylvania, in its half-century of existence held six and a half billion board feet of lumber.

In 1830 a practical sewing machine was patented in France, but successive installations were burned by mobs. Elias Howe, a native of Massachusetts and one of those traditional inventors who starve in a garret, patented a machine in 1846. Presently other machines appeared, but whether they were infringements or independent inventions was a point bitterly disputed at law. **The sewing machine** At any rate, improvements made by Isaac Singer were so decisive, and Singer's sales genius was so remarkable, that Singer had become a synonym for sewing machines over much of the world. Variation and improvements multiplied as the sewing machine was adapted to the ready-to-wear clothing industry and to shoe and harness making. Great factories were pushed into production during the Civil War, and somewhat to the sorry rise of the owners the demand for ready-made clothing and shoes continued almost unabated after the war.

For a long time attempts had been made to utilize the waterproofing qualities of rubber for rain shoes and rain capes, but the least heat, even sunlight, would reduce it to a gluey mess. Charles Goodyear, a New England hardware man settled in Philadelphia, broken in health **Vulcanization of** and fortune, began experimenting for a means of hardening **rubber** rubber. He was actually in jail for debt at the time. Quite without scientific knowledge Goodyear continued his efforts, in jail and out, for five years. Then one day in 1839 he accidentally dropped a ball of rubber mixed with sulphur on top of a hot stove. It was the great discovery! The process was immediately adopted far and wide in making waterproof clothing, toys, and gadgets, but in the long run Goodyear profited but little. When in 1852 Daniel Webster received $25,000 from a Goodyear licensed company to defend its rights, he made more money out of rubber than Goodyear ever did.

Americans made few contributions to the technology of printing until after 1820. Thereafter they came fast. While job presses were perfected, the most remarkable progress was in newspaper presses. Robert Hoe, an

The Hoe presses English immigrant and founder of a family of remarkable inventors of printing machines and processes, was among the first to build power presses in America. His son Richard invented in 1846 the "type-revolving" press in which the type was placed on a cylinder to which sheets of paper were fed by four impression cylinders. This made eight thousand impressions an hour, and he speeded it up by adding more impression cylinders. Out of this cheap and rapid process came the "penny press." Invention by other men of the curved stereotype plate and of the use of a continuous roll of paper made it possible by 1871 for Richard Hoe to develop his steam-driven rotary press which would print eighteen thousand papers an hour. This was only the beginning. Modern developments are almost unbelievable.

The first half of the nineteenth century saw the groundwork laid for the later development of American mass production. Most significant features of the new era were the adoption of power to machinery, the

Machine tools amazing growth of the use of machine tools, the invention of the principle of the interchangeable part, and the utilization of semiskilled labor. The last three developments were chiefly the work of a galaxy of New Englanders, most of them gunmakers of Massachusetts and Connecticut. Though the interchangeable part had been used in England in making marine blocks and in France for muskets, it was not carried to perfection. Eli Whitney and Simeon North separately worked ot the principle in their gun factories about 1800. Whitney, however, showed more genius as both an inventor and an organizer. Before he turned out a single weapon he spent two years at his factory near New Haven, building special machines and training green workmen to do specific jobs. Then one day late in 1800 he dumped a box of parts upon the floor of the Secretary of War's office and picking them up at random put together ten muskets, which stood the tests.

Other gunsmiths prominent in the machine-tool business were Thomas Blanchard, inventor of the copying lathe for making articles of eccentric shape, such as gun stocks; Samuel Colt, inventor (or at least perfecter) of the revolver; and Elisha King Root, an associate of Colt, who perfected the drop hammer and the die forge and also designed numerous other tools. Equally important in developing the machine tools of the textile industry was David Wilkinson of Pawtucket, brother-in-law of Samuel Slater.

The names of inventors and improvers could be greatly extended; suffice it to say that long before the Civil War the machines of New England were pouring forth a steady stream of bolts, nails, tacks, screws, wire, small tools, and other objects too numerous to mention. The crowning achievements of Yankee ingenuity were **Large-scale production** the turret lathe, the grinding machine, and the universal milling machine; with these it was possible to attain automatically a precision hitherto undreamed of. One amusing illustration of the growing significance of American industry will serve to illuminate the whole. Before the 1830's wooden clocks had cost five dollars and metal clocks as much as fifty, but in 1838 Chauncey Jerome of Connecticut utilized the system of interchangeable parts to produce brass clocks which sold for fifty cents. When a shipment of his cheap clocks reached England the British customs officials, thinking that he was trying to beat down the amount of the duty, decided to punish him by buying in the clocks at the invoice price of $1.50 apiece. Jerome was delighted and sent another shipment. It was also seized and prompt payment made. It was not until the third shipment of brass clocks arrived at the same low invoice price that the British discovered that they had been had by the Yankee clockmaker.

Patents were originally monopolies granted by kings to individuals to produce or sell certain articles or services quite without regard to their origin. In 1624 by the Statute of Monopolies the English Parliament confined monopolies to the inventors of new processes and **Patents** articles. The patent laws of the United States, based upon the authorization in the Constitution, stemmed from this English act. Mental ideas and discoveries in pure science are not patentable; patents will be granted only to owners of new and tangible utilizations, expressible in drawings or models, of ideas or scientific discoveries. (Under certain conditions ornamental designs and new varieties of plants are patentable.) The patent laws of the United States have on the whole been far more generous than those of other countries, particularly in permitting the patenting of improvements on processes already patented by someone else, and in granting to the owners longer periods of monopoly use.

During the nineteenth century patents were of some value to inventors and manufacturers. However, the complex resources now at inventors' command mean that a desired objective can usually be attained by a method other than the one patented; if not, there is always the possibility of infringement and utilization of the law's technicalities and delays. The value of the patent system is now seriously open to question. Competition seems to be chiefly useful in promoting improvement-inventions and to have little effect on basic inventions.

Even today technical advances are occasionally suppressed by manufacturers who have heavy investments in old processes, or opposed by highly unionized crafts. Such tactics have been even more the rule in the

Fate of the inventor

past. Spinners and weavers broke up textile machinery, tailors destroyed sewing machines, and printers fought the steam rotary press and the linotype—these are only a few examples that might be extended indefinitely. By far the most inventors failed to get adequate financial backing, and many of them died in poverty. Even when they overcame the pressure of vested interests and the skepticism of prospective backers, they almost invariably found their patents infringed on every side. A few had the luck to possess financial acumen or to get partners who had it. Few fortunes were made by mere control of patents; they came from superior manufacturing and business prowess. Patents, as someone has remarked, merely give the government's permission to use the courts in defense of one's invention. In our century it is becoming doubtful if doing even that is worth the trouble and expense.

Engineers in the eighteenth century were either military siege experts or empirical cutters and fitters. With the rise of specialization in the next century we find architects and civil and military engineers gradually

Engineering education

drawing apart. Military education had for some time centered at West Point. The United States Military Academy, the first engineering school in the country, was authorized in 1802 for West Point, but it was sadly neglected until 1817. Naval officers continued to be trained on ships of war until the establishment of the Naval Academy at Annapolis in 1845. The second American engineering school, and the first devoted primarily to civil engineering, was Rensselaer Polytechnic Institute, at Troy, founded in 1824. The Sheffield Scientific School at Yale and the Lawrence Scientific School at Harvard rose from technical schools begun in the 1840's.

The childlike eagerness with which technical advances and new products are now received by the general public is in striking contrast to its former attitude. In 1807 Fulton was called a fool for insisting that he

Contrast in public attitudes

could propel a boat by steam; it would be a hardy skeptic now who would deny that men may soon set foot on the moon. Many people, gullible enough in other ways, sought to show their sound sense by guffawing at nearly every attempt at basic technological improvements. The railroad was opposed because trains scared horses and prevented cows from letting down their milk, and sparks set fire to crops and forests. There was, moreover, a perceptible opinion that if the Lord had intended men to travel in this outlandish fashion He would have equipped them with wheels, steam engines, and bells. Not only did people oppose inventions because of inertia, but religious, social, and economic training made many suspicious of any change that threatened vested interests—not merely vested financial interests but vested interests in established prejudices and opinions, and in social position or prestige, actual or hoped for. Even the tolerant and intelligent did not always understand what was going on. In 1838 the chief clerk in the Patent Office resigned. His reason was that steam and electricity were the ultimate secrets of nature; all inventions worth making had been made, and he wished to find a job with a future!

2 The Revolution in Transportation

The conquest of distance was on the whole the most serious problem that confronted Americans, for the United States was not compact like England or France but even in its infancy sprawled over nearly a million square miles. Roads received little attention in the colonial **Problems of** period and were, according to season, streaks of heavy dust **distance in** or quagmires and in any case unbelievably rough and dan- **America** gerous. Travelers in the East, if they were wise, moved from city to city by packet sloops. Freight, of course, was carried by sea far more quickly and cheaply than by road. Industrial growth in all parts of the country was clearly doomed to be limited until some means was found of carrying on cheaply and efficiently the necessary interchanges of manufactures and agricultural products.

The most obvious answer was a boat driven by steam. The problem before engineers was not so much one of invention as of the development of refinements which would assure economy and efficiency. In the end these refinements were separately made in at least three **Who in-** nations: the United States, Great Britain, and France. The **vented the** United States was first by a few years. The first steamboat **steamboat?** enthusiast to meet with relative success was John Fitch, a Connecticut Yankee, who actually built a series of steamboats on the Delaware. One of these, propelled by steam-driven oars, plied regularly between Philadelphia and Trenton during the summer of 1790. Failing to get financial backing and popularly supposed to be crazy, Fitch finally committed suicide.

Other men took up where Fitch left off. The unfortunate inventor had been granted monopoly rights to steam navigation by the legislatures of various states, including New York and New Jersey. The New York rights now fell to Chancellor Robert R. Livingston, who **John Ste-** formed an association with his brother-in-law, John Stevens, **vens and** a Hoboken engineer, and Nicholas J. Roosevelt. The three **the *Phoenix*** men built a boat which, however, was too slow to be practicable. Livingston now went to France as American minister, and though the partnership was broken up Stevens continued his experiments. After trying out a screw-propelled vessel in 1804 he turned to side-paddle wheels, and on 9

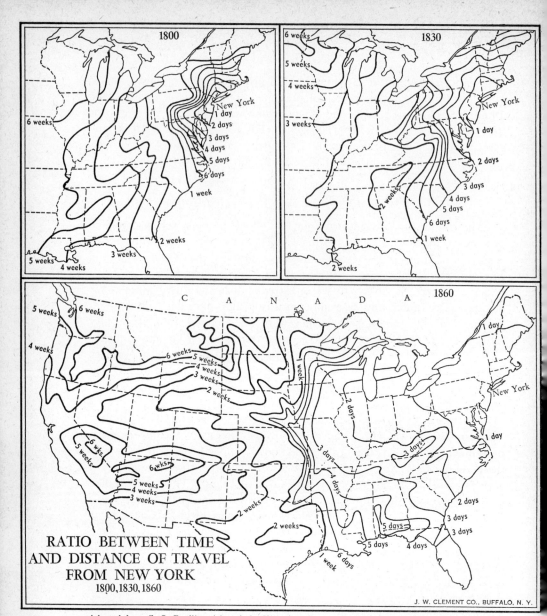

RATIO BETWEEN TIME
AND DISTANCE OF TRAVEL
FROM NEW YORK
1800, 1830, 1860

J. W. CLEMENT CO., BUFFALO, N. Y.

Adapted from C. O. Paullin, *Atlas of the Historical Geography of the United States.* 1932. Carnegie Institution of Washington.

April 1808 launched the *Phoenix,* which made a cautious trip by sea to the Delaware and operated on that river for six years. Not only was the *Phoenix* the first steamboat whose design and engineering enabled it to operate successfully for more than a brief period, but it was the first one to undertake a sea voyage. Stevens's four sons all became engineers, and one of them, Robert L. Stevens, was acknowledged to be the leading marine and railroad engineer in the country.

Chancellor Robert R. Livingston while minister in Paris came into contact with a young Pennsylvanian named Robert Fulton, who was trying to interest Napoleon in his ideas for submarines and torpedoes. Livingston and Fulton found a mutual interest in steamboats. **Fulton and** In 1807, with Livingston's backing and under the protection **the *Cler-*** of his monopoly, Fulton built a steamboat which he regis- ***mont*, 1807** tered as *The North River Steamboat of Clermont ;* the North River was the usual name given to the lower Hudson, and Clermont was Livingston's estate. By contemporaries the boat was called "Fulton's Folly," and it is known in schoolbooks as the *Clermont.* It was a sidewheeler which in August 1807 ascended the Hudson a hundred fifty miles to Albany in thirty-two hours. Fulton has usually received the credit for having built the first successful steamboat, but the *Clermont* was more a promise of success than an actual delivery. Its hull and engine were so crazy that after six weeks' service it had to be withdrawn and rebuilt, but even after that it never gave satisfaction. The Hudson, however, is one of the most co-operative rivers in the world for steamboats, and in his later boats Fulton learned what must be done. There was plenty of time, for he had the monopoly of steam on the river. This was why the *Phoenix* had to go to the Delaware. The monopoly, however, was broken up in 1824 when Marshall and the Supreme Court decided in the case of *Gibbons v. Ogden* that control of interstate commerce was a Federal function.

Long before this Livingston, with the aid of his brother Edward, had obtained a monopoly in Louisiana. The *New Orleans,* constructed at Pittsburgh under the superintendence of Fulton and Roosevelt, descended the Ohio and Mississippi in 1811. Unfortunately its low- **Steamboats** pressure engines were not powerful enough to enable it to **on western** breast the current successfully ; its ship's hull, quite suitable **rivers** for the Hudson, handicapped it in the swift western currents and grounded it frequently during times of low water. Several Fulton boats built on the same principle had to confine themselves pretty much to the deeper waters of the lower course of the Mississippi. Then in 1814 Henry M. Shreve built the *Washington.* It had a flat, shallow hull so that instead of cutting the water it floated on top like a scow ; moreover, it had a high-pressure engine mounted on the deck instead of below the water line as in Fulton's boats. The problem of upstream transportation on the western rivers was licked. Though the monopoly sued, it lost out as a result of the Supreme Court decision in the case of *Gibbons v. Ogden.* The 1820's saw a phenomenal multiplication of western steamers, and presently came the magnificent river palaces which still live in song and story.

The application of steam to ocean transportation was the work of the engineers of many nations, though two American-built ships led the

parade across the Atlantic. They were the *Savannah,* in 1819, a sailing
ship with auxiliary engines and collapsible paddle wheels,
The ocean and the *Great Western,* in 1838, a steamship with auxiliary
steamship sails. On the whole, the British were most active in improving the ocean steamer; in the 1840's and 1850's American merchants and
builders were bemused by the clipper ship. It was also the British who
brought in the iron ship and developed the screw propeller along lines
first used by John Stevens. They also invented or adapted the double
bottom, water-tight bulkheads, bilge keels, and antifouling paint.

The steamboat was a practical solution for the problem of transportation on rivers, lakes, and ocean, but there was still the problem of hauling
passengers and freight over land. The easiest answer was the hard-sur-
faced road, constructed after the principle of the Scots road
The turn- engineer John McAdam. Pennsylvania led in 1794 with a
pike era privately built road from Philadelphia to Lancaster, called
a turnpike or pike because at the toll houses the road was barred by a
pole which was swung aside when the toll was paid. The financial success
of the Lancaster Pike led to the chartering of hundreds of other toll-road
projects. The rise of canals and railroads took most of the profits out of toll
roads. The 1850's saw the brief rise of plank roads which were really
nothing more than giant board walks, but they failed also because they
were expensive to keep in repair. With certain local exceptions American roads sank back into the mud, not to emerge until the coming of the
automobile.

The only important hard road built by the Federal government was the
National Road, opened in 1818 from Cumberland, Maryland across the
mountains to Wheeling, Virginia, on the Ohio River. The road was planned
to reach St. Louis, but only parts of the western end were
The Na- completed by Federal funds. Upkeep was so expensive that
tional Road in the end the road was turned over to the states and became
a toll road. The importance of the road as an artery between East and West
can hardly be overestimated. In certain seasons one was not anywhere on
the 130 miles of the road out of sight of the great canvas-covered Conestoga freight wagons or the innumerable droves of horses, cattle, swine, and
sheep.

The story of transportation across the Applachians was tied in with
the commercial rivalry between the three great seaboard cities of New
York, Philadelphia, and Baltimore. The latter two were well served by
turnpikes which led across the mountains from the Ohio
The Erie River. New York, under the leadership of Governor De Witt
Canal, 1825 Clinton, now proposed to tap the interior by digging a canal
from Troy to Buffalo, through the Mohawk Valley pass, and across the
fairly level plain of upper New York State. The result was the state-

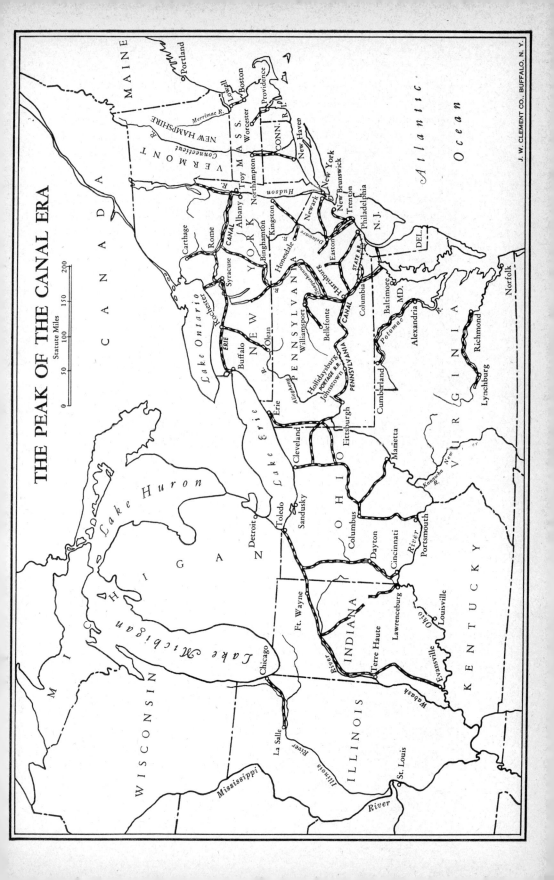

THE PEAK OF THE CANAL ERA

Statute Miles

0   50   100   150   200

owned Erie Canal, opened in 1825. The effect of the canal was phenomenal. Within a generation New York City had become the queen of the seaboard and had outstripped all her rivals in wealth and population. The ease of transporting wheat from the interior actually made western New York flour deposited in Charleston cheaper than that brought from the Carolina uplands. Lake traffic boomed, and Buffalo became a thriving city.

New Orleans, which had confidently planned to engross the trade of the Ohio Valley, saw a network of state-owned canals spreading north of the Ohio River and diverting the manufactures and produce of the Old

The canal era

Northwest to New York. The Lakes states became for a while the granary of the world, and the merchant mills of the Delaware sank into relative insignificance before those of the West. Philadelphia, in desperation, constructed a new channel to the Ohio, partly railroad and partly canal, even though the canalboats had to be lifted over the mountains by inclined planes. Baltimore found that the National Road no longer gave it pre-eminence in western trade, and its capitalists undertook to construct the Chesapeake and Ohio Canal along the Potomac River. The rise of railroads caused the work to lag, and it finally stopped at Cumberland without attempting to pierce the mountains.

Canal building, indeed, became such a craze that several western states overbuilt. Part of the money came from Federal land grants, part was borrowed in Europe and the East, and part came from taxes, tolls, and lotteries. The Panic of 1837 toppled this financial structure, and the threat of the railroad dissipated the canal builders' rosy dreams. For these and other reasons eight western and southern states defaulted in the early 1840's. European investors not unnaturally (and with some justification) thought they had been bilked; it is said that the descendants of British holders of the defaulted state bonds still hold annual dinners at which they bemoan their plight and consider ways and means of getting payment. One result of the episode was to strengthen public sentiment against state ownership and thus further insure private construction of railroads.

The steam locomotive, like the steamboat, was a development. However, it definitely was Oliver Evans's high-pressure engine which made possible the success of George Stephenson, the builder of the first significant English locomotives and railways. Meanwhile Ameri-

The steam locomotive

can engineers were experimenting with the locomotive, among them John Stevens and his son Robert, who in 1826 built a locomotive and ran it on a track on their Hoboken estate. Several American railways had been built to haul stone from quarries and coal from mines, but they utilized cables, gravity, or mules as motive power.

Some of the early railroad builders planned on having their tracks used as highways by farm and freight wagons, presumably with flanged wheels. Where this was actually tried, the confusion can readily be imagined. When it became evident that the owners would have to furnish and operate the rolling stock, serious experiments were made with sails and with motive power furnished by a horse on a treadmill.

Heavy steam locomotives were indeed risky on light wooden rails protected by strap iron. The little anthracite line, the Carbondale and Honesdale Railroad, received a Stephenson locomotive and made a few trips in 1829, but it was too heavy for the rails and had to be discarded. American engineers were now forced to design and build lighter locomotives. No one then dreamed that one day American freight locomotives would be the heaviest and most powerful in the world.

The rise of railroads was clearly a menace to the supremacy of canals, and Baltimore now planned by this modern means to fight its old rivals, New York and Philadelphia. The first section of the Baltimore and Ohio Railroad (some thirteen miles from Baltimore to Ellicott's **The first** Mills) was opened to traffic in 1828, but it was not until **American** 1831 that the line definitely adopted steam locomotives. The **railroads** delay was due to the fact that in 1830 the miniature *Tom Thumb,* in running a race with a horse-drawn car on a parallel track, had a mechanical failure and lost the race! The Baltimore and Ohio did not reach Wheeling until 1853. Meanwhile Charleston, in an attempt to draw trade from Savannah, had built the Charleston and Hamburg Railroad, probably the first railroad in the world to be specifically designed to place reliance on steam. The New York-built locomotive *Best Friend* was placed on the tracks late in 1830 and amazed the world by a speed of thirty miles an hour. The *De Witt Clinton* was put in service in 1831 on the Mohawk and Hudson Railroad between Albany and Schenectady.

The railroad era now came in with a rush. From 1830 to 1860 rapid improvements were made. The opposition of turnpikes and canals was ruthlessly crushed. Public opposition soon passed, and enthusiasm took its place. Engineering difficulties were pretty well overcome. The tendency of locomotives to explode was conquered; coal **Difficulties** was substituted for wood fuel; the carriages modeled on **overcome** stagecoaches were replaced by more roomy and utilitarian designs; sleeping cars were introduced; the wood and strap-iron rails were replaced by iron T-rails designed by Robert Stevens; and tremendous steps in efficiency of management and dispatching were made possible by the invention of the telegraph. A standard gauge for tracks was not adopted until 1886.

True, most of the railroads were short; even though by 1842 it was possible to travel from Albany to Buffalo by rail, one had to travel on

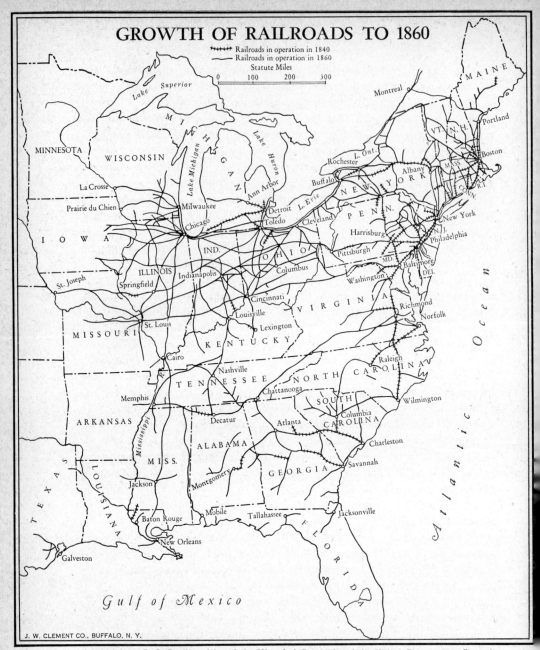

GROWTH OF RAILROADS TO 1860

++++++ Railroads in operation in 1840
———— Railroads in operation in 1860
Statute Miles

0   100   200   300

MINNESOTA

WISCONSIN

Lake Superior

MICHIGAN

Lake Michigan

Lake Huron

MAINE

Montreal

VT. N. H.

Portland

La Crosse

Prairie du Chien

Milwaukee

Ann Arbor

Rochester

L. Ont.

Albany

MASS.

Boston

IOWA

Chicago

Detroit

Toledo

L. Erie

Buffalo

Cleveland

NEW YORK

CONN.

R.I.

New York

St. Joseph

ILLINOIS

Springfield

IND.

Indianapolis

OHIO

Columbus

Harrisburg

Pittsburgh

PENN.

MD.

Philadelphia

Baltimore

DEL.

Cincinnati

Washington

MISSOURI

St. Louis

Louisville

Lexington

VIRGINIA

Richmond

Norfolk

Cairo

KENTUCKY

Nashville

Raleigh

Memphis

TENNESSEE

Chattanooga

NORTH CAROLINA

Wilmington

ARKANSAS

Decatur

Atlanta

SOUTH CAROLINA

Columbia

Charleston

ALABAMA

Montgomery

GEORGIA

Savannah

MISS.

Jackson

Mobile

Tallahassee

Jacksonville

TEXAS

LOUISIANA

Mississippi R.

Baton Rouge

New Orleans

FLORIDA

Atlantic Ocean

Galveston

Gulf of Mexico

J. W. CLEMENT CO., BUFFALO, N. Y.

Adapted from C. O. Paullin, *Atlas of the Historical Geography of the United States.* 1932. Carnegie
Institution of Washington.

seven or eight different railroads, each of them with its own track gauge.
The first single railroad to connect the seaboard with the
West was the Erie, which reached Dunkirk on Lake Erie in
1851. The next year the Pennsylvania connected Philadelphia and Pittsburgh, and in 1853 the Baltimore and Ohio reached Wheel-

**Consolida-
tion of rail-
roads**

572

ing, and the New York Central began to weld the upper New York lines into one system. Connections and amalgamations were eventually made between the transmontane railroads and those which had meantime been built in the West. Unfortunately, after its handsome beginning in South Carolina, railroad building in the South lagged behind the rest of the country, partly because of the many navigable southern rivers. The South thus lost an opportunity to bind the West to itself, a fact which was to have great significance in the coming crisis of secession. Most of the great cities east of the Mississippi and north of the Ohio and Potomac were linked by rail before 1860, and in that year the nation boasted a total of thirty thousand miles of railroads. New York's natural advantages, to the disappointment of its rivals, were only reinforced by the railroad age.

Cities like Columbus and Indianapolis literally owed their significance to railroads. Chicago's position at the southern end of Lake Michigan made it (with some political assistance) the hub through which most traffic from all directions in the interior of the continent **Economic** had to pass; this advantage was enhanced by its proximity **effect on** to the great lumbering, dairying, wheat-growing, and stock- **the West** feeding areas, and by its position midway between southern Illinois coal and Minnesota iron ore. The coming of the railroad struck the final blow to New Orleans by accelerating the growth of business connections between East and Northwest which had been begun by the Erie Canal.

The problem of financing railroads was acute. State legislatures and Congress pretty well steered clear of stock purchases, but the first sometimes gave loans or grants-in-aid, and the latter granted land subsidies. The first land grant was made in 1850 to the state of Illinois for transmission to the Illinois Central Railroad; all to- **Railroad** gether, about twenty million acres were passed out to rail- **finance** roads by 1860. Cities and counties through which the railroads ran made gifts or loans; those that refused might find themselves left off the line or with the closest station located far out in the country. New England investors, as ocean shipping began to decline, turned their attention inland. Presently European capital began to flow in. It was chiefly by its holdings in American railroads that Britain exercised its economic power in the United States.

Rate wars between railroads on one side and canal and steamboat lines on the other were common and were perhaps the only way by which the railroads could establish themselves. Cutthroat methods were also used in forcing independent lines into the large consolidations. However, cutthroat tactics did not stop there. Wherever consolidation formed competing lines between important points, merciless rate wars began between them. Unscrupulous managers and investors also discovered the blessed fact that the financial structures of railroads lent themselves to sharp practices, and the "milking" of railroads had become a well-known profession even before the Civil War.

One of the most important inventions of the nineteenth century was the electric telegraph. Strangely enough, it was separately and simultaneously invented in England, Germany, and the United States. The **The telegraph** American system, because it was based on superior principles, eventually was universally accepted. The American inventor, a native of Massachusetts, a portrait painter, and founder of the National Academy of Design, was Samuel F. B. Morse. Though he was a tyro in electrical science, his ardent research was rewarded, and in 1837 he announced his invention. After numerous disappointments Congress provided in 1843 the money to erect a line between Washington and Baltimore. Public interest lagged, but the railroads found it invaluable, and it gradually won acceptance as a means of transmitting news and private messages. In 1856 Hiram Sibley organized the Western Union Telegraph Company and began to amalgamate a nationwide telegraph system. It was Sibley who, when his associates turned the project down, undertook with a Congressional subsidy the transcontinental telegraph which was completed in 1862.

Meanwhile short underwater cables had been laid on both sides of the Atlantic. Cyrus W. Field, another Massachusetts man, interested New York and English capital in an Atlantic cable, and after two unsuccessful **The Atlantic Cable** attempts one was laid in August 1858 between Newfoundland and Ireland. Faulty operation burned it out a month later. Field refused to be discouraged, and in 1866 yet another cable was laid. This time it worked, and the submarine cable, even in this day of radio, still carries the burden of transoceanic communication.

3 *Capital and Labor*

The merchant capitalist was primarily a trader and financier. Even when he became rich either by trade or banking or perhaps (as the agrarians insisted) by manipulation of government favors, his riches were **Merchant capitalism** modest. The typical rich merchant of New York in 1850 had around $150,000. His traditional interest in speculation and place utility was shown by his investments in turnpikes, canals, river steamboats, and railroads. Even in these he often justified the agrarian accusation that he was a parasite, when he insisted on state and Federal support in money and land. The land, in fact, was quite an object, for he expected to make his real profits from it after his canals or railroads had raised its value.

The merchant capitalist financed some production, but he did it with little vision. Country people produced surpluses of homespun or barrel staves over what they needed, and such surpluses were collected by the merchant and traded in the city or in foreign parts. Such people were encouraged to produce greater surpluses, and sometimes they became "cottage" workers chiefly engaged **Merchant production** in the production of handmade articles such as textiles, shoes, hats, and nails. The next stage brought the mill, which performed by machine one or more of the steps in hand manufacture. Thus, Slater's spinning mill in Pawtucket was operated by children who spun thread which was used by their parents in cottage weaving. Just as typical was the system of payment in kind, which had been handed down from time immemorial and which was a real service in rural vicinities, but which came to be resented as giving the merchant capitalist two profits. These methods were dominant at least until 1850. The factory with its integration of the manufacture of the finished product in one continuous, supervised operation was the exception until the Civil War suddenly called into use the technologies which had been developing.

The failure of the American merchant capitalist to win a clear-cut victory over the agrarians was natural. A rather similar condition had existed in Great Britain at the time of the American Revolution. In that country, however, the Industrial Revolution had bred a class of industrial capitalists who devoted themselves to producing goods. Their early start gave them the rewards of world **Rise of industrial capitalism** trade, and the huge governmental purchases of the Napoleonic Wars made them financial giants. Resistance to them was no longer effective, and by the Reform Bill of 1832 the industrial capitalists ousted the agrarian nobility and the merchants from political control. American industrial capitalists grew by markedly similar methods. The gold of California helped to finance them, the Civil War mushroomed their power, and the Fourteenth Amendment to the Constitution aided in fastening their political hold on the nation. The details are so closely bound up with the sectional struggle over slavery that their recital had best be delayed. At this time, however, we can examine some of the philosophical and practical backgrounds of industrial capitalism.

British economic theorists, convinced that their country, because of its resources and its early start, was destined to monopolize world manufactures, heartily agreed with Adam Smith's dictum that industry should be permitted to develop where it had the natural advantages. **Laissez faire becomes a political issue** Southerners approved of this doctrine of laissez faire, since it meant that they should buy their goods in the cheapest markets. The would-be manufacturers of the North and West, however, were aghast and sought to find some way of thwarting Adam Smith. Hamilton came to their rescue in his *Report on Manu-*

factures, and presently a school of economic writers began making the necessary amendments to the English economists chiefly by upholding the protective tariff.

Mathew Carey, a Philadelphia publisher who had been born in Ireland, wrote *Essays on Political Economy* (1822), in which he linked together the protective tariff and internal improvements at Federal expense and gave Clay the cue for the American System. Carey's son, Henry, followed in his footsteps. Closely associated with them was Hezekiah Niles, whose *Weekly Register,* published in Baltimore from 1811 to 1849, was the champion of protection and of other nationalist policies. Friedrich List, a German resident in Philadelphia during the 1820's, absorbed Mathew Carey's argument. When List returned to Germany he took with him the American economic doctrines, and they became a powerful factor in the growth of German industry and nationalism. Late in the century, partially transformed and very much criticized, they were returned to the United States and influenced the modern American science of economics.

Mathew Carey aimed at more than profits for manufacturers or even national self-sufficiency. If democracy were to be realized, he held, it must offer wider opportunities. As the country then was, the ambitious young **The Careys'** man was limited in choice to a few callings, and these could **ambitions** be increased only by trading simplicity for complexity. Wider **for America** opportunities could be created by industrialization, and that could come only when England's throttling hold on the American market was pried loose. Then talent and ingenuity would be rewarded, general prosperity enhanced, and personal life cultivated and enriched. Carey gave battle on multiple fronts. He attacked the smug conservatism of the merchant capitalist, the traditionalism of farmer and planter, and the desire of the industrial capitalist to keep benefits for himself rather than to share them with his employees.

Henry Carey was no less zealous and much more logical. Laws, he insisted, are unitary, so economic law must agree with moral law. Away with the Economic Man of the English school, devoid of altruism and shaped only to pursue wealth! To bring in the Real Man he proposed the "principle of association"—much the same as national planning—by which each nation should shake off the shackles of England and develop its own economy and culture. The mission of the United States was to hasten this day by its own example. Only when by such means the economic problems of humanity had been solved, could there ensue harmony of interests and the universal reign of tolerance, peace, and morals.

A considerable body of economists of our day believe that the United States would have won industrial power regardless of the Hamiltons, Careys, or Clays, simply because it had the resources and conditions.

(1) The American economic climate was capitalistic **Industrial** from the first. The weakness of state churches permitted **capitalism's** freedom of education and thought. We had no guilds to **advantages** monopolize crafts and to limit and control production, wages, and labor; on the other hand, we did have the psychology of Calvinism with its stimulus to industry, thrift, and initiative, its approval of wealth as a proof of righteousness, and its urge to remake society.

(2) American resources were so abundant that equality of opportunity all but became a reality. Land, timber, and minerals were available almost as gifts, especially to the shrewd; and, since capital was scarce, most enterprisers were on a rock-bottom status of financial equality. It was personal qualifications (often including unscrupulousness) that brought success.

(3) From the time of the Revolution both state and Federal governments were shorn of their power to interfere with individual business. Government planning was abhorrent to all but a few theorists like Henry Carey and John Quincy Adams. The nationalist decisions of Marshall were chiefly aimed at undercutting the states' attempts to interfere with private business and at enhancing the Federal power to promote private business by granting gifts and privileges and setting up a bank.

Mercantile organization was usually simple. Ventures too extensive for the resources of one merchant were undertaken by two or more in a partnership which might be confined to the one venture or prolonged for years. No authorization by the state was necessary, but usu- **Business or-** ally there were private articles of agreement which might in **ganization:** case of dispute become the basis of suits at law. The joint- **Partner-** stock company was merely an undertaking with many part- **ships** ners, each of whom contributed a share of the capital and received shares of the profits. Merchandising, manufacturing, and private banking could be conducted by these private partnerships. Their shares were not bought and sold on the market but were transferable.

Presently joint-stock companies sought state charters, which set them up as legal persons known as corporations. The form was of obvious value in such ventures as insurance companies, which required a longer span of life than it was likely the founders would enjoy. In addi- **The corpo-** tion they could sue and be sued as legal persons; manage- **ration** ment was simplified and placed under the control of the holders of a majority of the stock; and shares could be sold on the market and bonds floated. Scattered capital seeking investment in ventures which freed the owners from the cares of management had hitherto been confined to the purchase of government securities or to "sleeping" partnerships. Now it found investment in banks, insurance and manufacturing companies, turnpikes, canals, and finally in railroad companies. Even small sums were welcome and found proportionate returns. Private partnerships, however, remained the dominant form of business organization until the Civil War.

At first each corporation was chartered by a special act of Congress or a state legislature. Only about three hundred thirty-five had been created up to 1800, about ninety per cent of them in the previous decade. **Monopoly and speculation** The privileges they enjoyed led to accusations of monopoly —which were more or less true in the case of quasi-public institutions such as canal and railroad companies and banks. Gradually, however, the states passed laws which granted free privileges of incorporation to all who wished it, usually with certain regulations over their way of doing business. Most significant was the development of the limited-liability provision by which an investor could in case of the corporation's failure lose only the amount invested, or perhaps (chiefly in financial institutions) a like sum through an assessment called "double liability."

It is now clear that the corporation device has been an essential instrument of progress, but unfortunately it has lent itself to control by a group of insiders and has enabled them on occasion to milk the financial structure or perhaps use it as a powerful weapon in aggressive financial warfare. We have seen how this weakness was recognized as early as the First Bank of the United States and became a bitter issue in political campaigns. Trading in securities led to the formation of a Board of Exchange in New York in 1792, which met under a buttonwood tree at 68 Wall Street. The pouring of railroad shares into the market gave substance to trading, and by the 1850's the Stock Exchange had developed not only as the scene of necessary trading but as the theater in which the bulls and bears maneuvered their meteoric rises and spectacular crashes.

The average laborer and mechanic in early nineteenth-century America lived in a semirural community where he could dovetail agricultural work with his wage earning. Panics and depressions might pinch him, but his family did not starve. A growing number of industrial **Labor conditions** workers, however, lived in cities or mushrooming mill towns and had no farms or garden patches. Their living and working conditions (with certain exceptions) were unsanitary and unhealthy. The average industrial employer was indifferent to safety precautions, and the injured employee received no compensation or only such as the goodwill of the owner dictated. Women and children were commonly employed at unsuitable tasks and for long hours under brutal conditions. Work hours, which ran as high as fifteen a day, left little room for recreation or self-improvement. Long hours were not confined to industrial laborers, but foremen, tradesmen, businessmen, and farmers put in just as many. Employers, especially contractors, often bilked their employees.

Much of the supposed riotousness among foreign workers, especially the Irish, was simply the result of their resentment at broken promises and cheating in the payment of wages.

Here and there farsighted entrepreneurs strove to give their employees good homes and working conditions. The young women employed in the textile mills of Lowell, Massachusetts, though they worked long hours and were poorly paid, lived in dormitories under strict chaperons who ostentatiously emphasized religion, morals, and education. Most mill towns, however, were hastily thrown **Industrial towns** together, and pauperism, drunkenness, vice, and crime were common. The rise of factories caused these towns to mushroom all the faster, and it is to be feared increased their social problems. The weary round between whirring machines and slatternly homes, unrelieved by adequate leisure and too seldom penetrated by beneficial influences, made life in these grimy factory towns a fate to be abhorred.

Despite grumbling in certain quarters, especially in times of depression, industrial entrepreneurs were rightly regarded as public benefactors. Obviously they were increasing the national wealth and self-sufficiency. At first they made few inroads on male laborers who were already employed at the going wage but found operatives **Sources of labor** among women and children. Few were shocked by this practice, for child labor had been traditional ever since work began, and work was regarded as the normal lot in most American homes. It was a part of the educational process and a necessary part of making the family living. Child labor is merely a sign that there is not enough mature labor to perform the work or that the labor cost of products is high. The only practical cure is reduction of costs by mechanization. Manufacturers gave employment to widows and orphans and thus relieved the community of their support. They provided work for town children who otherwise would be "wasting" their time in school, play, or mischief.

That long hours were oppressive, that the whip was used to urge on weary or fractious children, that lazy or greedy parents sent their children out to labor—all these are beyond doubt. It was not a humanitarian age, however, and doubtless as serious abuses existed outside the mills. There was, in fact, a rather general sentiment among employers and the public that leisure was the same as idleness and bred drunkenness and crime—the devil would find work for idle hands to do. Actually there was some justification for the opinion, for the grogshop was the townsman's only practical evening refuge from boredom unless he chose to go to church or night school.

Wages as late as 1850 ran in general from $4 to $10 a week for skilled workers. They had gone up since colonial days, but it seems true that the workingman's purchasing power had not risen in proportion: the familiar difference between "dollar" wages and "real" wages. Workingmen, especially in the cities, regarded themselves as very badly exploited, and perhaps they were in the light of what should have been. Still, their conditions, though far from enviable, were better than those in similar occupations in Europe. Wages which seemed low to Americans were eagerly accepted by immigrants, either because they were desperate or because the pay seemed generous. Foreigners, indeed, swamped the mill towns from the 1840's onward. Irish laborers did the construction work of the country, even in the South, and in the seaports Irish and Negro dock workers fought for jobs.

Organized labor did not get under way effectively until after the Civil War. There were numerous reasons. Public opinion opposed unions on the grounds that they raised prices and interfered with the owner's right to administer his own property; if a workingman was dissatisfied with his wages or conditions of labor, let him get another job or go west. In the beginning relations between employers and employees were close, and this closeness doubtless reduced friction. Nevertheless, labor organizations began to rise in the cities, usually confined to handicrafters such as the carpenters, printers, and cordwainers (shoemakers), but at first they were chiefly devoted to insurance benefits and only cautiously touched the problems of their relations with capital.

Labor organizations

There were a few sporadic strikes from 1776 onward, and each side gradually stiffened its policies. In 1805 when the Philadelphia cordwainers went on strike, a court applied the British interpretation of the common law, which held that a strike was a conspiracy against the public welfare and therefore a criminal offense. The decision aroused bitter protest among workers, but it was ruthlessly used as a precedent during the next generation. Still, one must not overrate the strength of the labor movement, for there were only about twenty-four strikes up to 1835.

Labor organization entered a new phase in 1827, when the Philadelphia crafts set up a central association. The movement spread to other cities, and in several cases the city associations became the core of local political workingmen's parties. These flourished modestly in prosperous times, but scarcity of jobs during times of depression gave employers a weapon against them, and caused heavy mortality in the roster of party workers and voters and cut down the number of unions. Workingmen's parties pushed many useful and much-needed reforms but were successful chiefly in promoting free public education, the abolition of imprisonment for debt, and the passage of mechanics' lien laws.

Workingmen's parties

Presently there arose a demand for a shorter work day and for the regulation of the labor of women and children—chiefly from a desire to spread the work and to reduce the competition of women and children, though there was also a perceptible desire for more leisure for amusements, education, and home occupations and recreations. Eventually the ten-hour day was adopted in New Hampshire (1847) and Pennsylvania (1848), and Massachusetts (1843) and Pennsylvania (1848) regulated the employment of children under twelve. The Federal government had also adopted the ten-hour day for its laborers and mechanics in 1840. Actually much of the credit for these advances must go to the Democratic Party, for its leaders sought to absorb the workingmen's parties by adopting selected parts of their program.

The most significant labor advance, however, was made against the law of conspiracy. The tide began to turn in 1842 when the supreme court of Massachusetts under Chief Justice Lemuel Shaw, in the case of *Commonwealth v. Hunt*, reversed the direction of judicial treatment of labor. The Boston cordwainers had struck to impose a closed shop, and the commonwealth had taken legal *Commonwealth v. Hunt* action against them. By the decision labor unions were accepted as lawful in so far as their means were "fair or honorable and lawful"; the strike was declared a lawful weapon for gaining a closed shop and better wages and working conditions; and it was held that union members could not be held collectively responsible for the unlawful acts of individual members. It was an epochal decision and gradually won acceptance over the nation.

4 *The Agricultural Scene*

We have frequently referred to the agricultural backwardness of Americans. The high cost of labor and the lack of capital were such that few farmers felt they could afford the time and money to preserve the fertility of their farms; those who mined their soil and moved on sold more cheaply and made higher profits. This *Deterioration of the soil* practice bore hardest upon the eastern farmer, who had to compete with the rich soil of the West, but it was also true in the West. Reliance upon staple crops such as cotton and tobacco, without rotation or fertilization, robbed the soil. The prevalence of hill and row crops enabled rain to leach and erode the naked soil. In the early years, the difficulty of marketing made it useless in many areas to seek large crops or efficient methods. Add to these the farmers' distrust of newfangled methods and the firm belief in the concept of the infinity of land resources. The inevitable result was that vast areas of the East and Old South were eroded, or the soil was so sour that it would grow only weeds and pines.

The groundwork for improvement was laid by the growth of cities and the development of transportation. As the nineteenth century advanced, specialization became profitable. The enlarged demand of the cities for

Growth of specialization   flour, beef, pork, dairy products, poultry, eggs, and vegetables affected the farming areas vitally. Corn-belt grain and stock made it better for eastern farmers to specialize in fruit, dairy products, poultry, and vegetables, and to recover some measure of prosperity. The rise of the wool industry promoted sheep raising, especially in New England and the Ohio Valley. Increased world demand for tobacco and the introduction of a new variety and of new curing and manufacturing processes helped to bring back the lagging profits of the tobacco crops of Virginia and North Carolina and, indeed, several other states. The cotton textile industry made cotton the staple of the South. Unfortunately specialization did not always promote efficient care of the soil. This was most evident in the Cotton Kingdom, where great areas of eroded, weed-choked, and abandoned land forecast the coming economic crisis of the Civil War.

The eighteenth century saw the beginning in Europe of the Agricultural Revolution, which sought the application of science to the general improvement of the soil, improvement of stock breeds and crops, and im-

The Agricultural Revolution   provement of equipment. American agricultural leaders early became aware of European progress and tried to adapt the new knowledge to American conditions. Prominent among these leaders and experimenters were Washington and Jefferson in Virginia, John Beale Bordley in Maryland, George Clymer and Richard Peters in Pennsylvania, Rufus King and Robert R. Livingston in New York, and Elkanah Watson in Massachusetts.

The most amazing agricultural progress in America was probably that of Virginia and Maryland, where ignorance, neglect, and the one-crop system had turned once-fruitful tracts into wastes, and slavery had be-

Rehabilitation of Virginia and Maryland   come so unprofitable that planters became little more than breeders of slaves for export to the New South. It was in this scene that Edmund Ruffin (1794–1865) of Virginia undertook his painstaking experiments with restoration of the soil by the use of lime (in the form of marl), crop rotation, fertilizers, drainage, and improved plowing. By 1840 his suggestions had begun to be adopted in Virginia and Maryland, and the result was an agricultural renascence which by 1860 had brought back prosperity, at least to the Tidewater. Increased production of tobacco was made possible, but even more marked was the way in which both states turned toward the northern pattern of general farming. Probably in time these states would have become assimilated to the North in other important ways, but the Civil War came early enough to block the psychological shift and to continue Virginia, at least, as an integral part of the Solid South. Unfortunately the war also in large part destroyed Ruffin's agricultural work.

Except in Virginia and Maryland scientific farming, at least in so far

as care of the soil was concerned, made slight progress. There was too much land available to make it popular, and in any case the margin of agricultural profit was too low to encourage general expend- **Limited** iture for imported guano fertilizers, lime, and drainage. **agricultural** Crop rotation made gradual entry in the North, however, **improve-** and as the cattle were brought out of the woods and win- **ment** tered in barns, more manure was available. New plants and varieties were introduced, notably alfalfa and Mediterranean wheat; the last was important because it was resistant to rust and the Hessian fly. New breeds of farm stock were gladly accepted in most areas. The merino sheep of Spain, noted for their heavy wool, replaced the "rat-tailed" sheep of the colonial period. The undersized all-purpose cattle of the slashings were improved and bred separately for beef or milk. The corn belt gradually found its true vocation as a stock-feeding area, and the Lakes states began to discover fruits and dairy farming. The nondescript breed of farm horses was improved by crossing with imported stallions, and famous strains of draught and race horses were started. Lastly the mule, hardy farm and draying animal, was bred in the Border States and exported in droves to the cotton fields.

Agricultural societies multiplied, especially in the East, and agricultural books and periodicals appeared. However, they found few readers among farmers and were not often believed by those who heard their ideas. More important as a disseminator of knowledge was **Agricultural** the county fair. The fair of the eighteenth century had been **education** little more than a market. Now, largely due to the efforts of Elkanah Watson, it became an exposition where farmers could see with their own eyes better breeds of stock, new agricultural machines, and the results of improved methods of cultivation. Prizes were given for the best stock and farm produce, contests were held between rival makes of farm machinery, there were contests of strength and skill, horses were raced around an oval, and at the end came a "grand agricultural ball." The next step, of course, was the state fair. The mounting impact of private promotion gradually led to a demand for state and Federal support of agricultural research and education. The first American school of agriculture was the short-lived Gardiner Lyceum, founded in 1823 in Maine by Robert H. Gardiner. The first permanent institution was Michigan Agricultural College, founded in 1857.

Meanwhile new types of agricultural machinery were slowly coming into use. Fundamental, of course, was the plow. The colonial plow was of wood, sometimes reinforced with iron, and so heavy that it was best drawn by oxen—hence the name "bull plow." In 1797 **Evolution** Charles Newbold of New Jersey completed and patented a **of the plow** cast-iron plow, but it broke easily and, moreover, farmers refused to accept it because they believed that iron poisoned the soil. In 1819 Jethro Wood, a New York Quaker, devised an iron plow cast in several parts so that broken parts could be replaced; by this time farmers were ready to accept it. Presently pioneers on the Illinois prairies found that they needed a tougher instrument to break the sod and some way of ridding the plow of the sticky black mud which clung to the moldboard. In 1837 John Deere began to put out a plow with a steel moldboard which not only cut the tough sod but was self-polishing. The next improvement was the chilled-steel plow (1868) of James Oliver, a Scottish immigrant, "the plow that broke the plains."

The reaper ranks with the plow as an instrument of agricultural mass production. The traditional sickle used for cutting grain and hay gave way to the scythe only about the time of the American Revolution. Scores **The reaper** of attempts were now made to invent mechanical reapers, but the first reasonably successful one came out in 1833 and was the product of Obed Hussey, a Nantucketer resident in Cincinnati. Even more successful, and destined to eventual triumph, was the reaper invented about 1834 by Cyrus Hall McCormick, a Virginian. McCormick, who was a business as well as a mechanical genius, set up a plant in Chicago, made use of installment buying, and advertised by challenging his competitors to trials under practical conditions. He did not have a monopoly of genius, and others soon made improvements which gave McCormick effective competition.

The foregoing inventions were only the most important and dramatic. Harrows, grain drills, corn planters, mowers, and threshing machines all appeared in more or less crude forms before the Civil War, and experi- **Slow progress of the machine** ments were made in the use of steam power. It must not be thought that the United States took the initiative in the invention of agricultural machinery, for many American machines were duplications or improvements of others already in existence in Europe. Nevertheless, American machines were on the whole cheaper, simpler, and lighter than those of Europe. Even as it was, old methods remained in general use because farmers were conservative, because they could not afford machinery, or because machines were unsuitable to hillside farms. The Civil War, by boosting the demand for wheat and other products at the same time that it drew farm hands into the army, led to a leap in the demand for machinery, especially on the level farms of the West. The day of the agricultural machine had arrived.

BIBLIOGRAPHICAL NOTE

The Rise of American Technology
GENERAL: Waldemar Kaempffert, ed., *Popular History of American Invention* (2 v., 1924) treats at length the rise of American technology in its industrial,

agricultural, and transportation phases. On the industrial phase see also Robert M. Keir, *The Epic of Industry* (v. 5 of *The Pageant of America*). Roger Burlingame, *March of the Iron Men* (1938) is a study not only of technology but of its effect to 1865 in unifying the nation; on the early stages of mass production see his *Backgrounds of Power* (1949). See also Chelsea C. Fraser, *Story of Engineering in America* (1928); and William B. Bennett, *The American Patent System* (1943). Useful biographies are Greville and Dorothy Bathe, *Oliver Evans* (1935); Thomas Coulson, *Joseph Henry* (1950); and Lynde P. Wheeler, *Josiah Willard Gibbs* (1951).

SEPARATE INDUSTRIES: For textiles see J. A. B. Scherer, *Cotton as a World Power* (1916); Caroline F. Ware, *Early New England Cotton Manufacture* (1931); A. H. Cole, *American Wool Manufacture* (2 v., 1926). For iron, Joseph R. Smith, *Story of Iron and Steel* (1908). For petroleum, Paul H. Giddens's superlative *Birth of the Oil Industry* (1938). Chauncey Jerome wrote the lugubrious *History of the American Clock Business* (1860), which let the cat out of the bag on then-current business practices.

The Revolution in Transportation

GENERAL: Seymour Dunbar, *History of Travel in America* (4 v., 1915) is the indispensable account of the American conquest of distance. See also Robert M. Keir, *The March of Commerce* (v. 4 of *The Pageant of America*); and George R. Taylor, *The Transportation Revolution, 1815–1860* (1951).

STEAMBOATS: James T. Flexner, *Steamboats Come True* (1944); Thomas Boyd, *Poor John Fitch* (1935); Archibald D. Turnbull, *James Stevens, An American Record* (1928); Florence L. Dorsey, *Master of the Mississippi* [Shreve] (1941). On the question of the priority of the *Phoenix* or the *Clermont* see S. Colum Gilfillan, *Inventing the Ship* (1935). Louis C. Hunter, *Steamboats on the Western Rivers* (1949) definitively tells their story.

HIGHWAYS: Archer B. Hulbert, *Paths of Inland Commerce* (1920) and *Historic Highways of America* (16 v., 1902–05); Philip D. Jordan, *The National Road* (1948).

CANALS: Alvin F. Harlow, *Old Towpaths* (1926); Reginald C. McGrane, *Foreign Bondholders and American State Debts* (1935).

RAILROADS: Agnes C. Laut, *The Romance of the Rails* (2 v., 1929); John A. Miller, *Fares Please: From Horse-Cars to Streamliners* (1941); Slason Thompson, *Short History of American Railways* (1925).

TELEGRAPH: Alvin F. Harlow, *Old Wires and New Waves* (1936); Carleton Mabee, *The American Leonardo* [Morse] (1943); Robert L. Thompson, *Wiring a Continent* (1947); Isabella F. Judson, *Cyrus W. Field* (1896).

Capital and Labor

GENERAL: George R. Taylor, *The Transportation Revolution, 1815–1861* (1951) deals with labor, capital, and commerce as well as transportation. Joseph Dorfman, *The Economic Mind in American Civilization, 1606–1918* (3 v., 1946–49) is concerned chiefly with the attitude of the government toward business. Thomas C. Cochran and William Miller, *The Age of Enterprise* (1942) begin their incisive account of American business mores with an examination of the early scene.

CAPITAL: Best treatment of the changing forms of American capitalism is Louis M. Hacker, *The Triumph of American Capitalism* (1940). The international picture is best set forth in Norman S. B. Gras, *Business and Capitalism* (1946). For an exposition of early economic ideas see Kenneth W. Rowe, *Mathew Carey* (1933); and Walter B. Smith and Arthur H. Cole, *Fluctuations in American Business, 1790–1860* (1935).

LABOR: See particularly the early volumes of John R. Commons and Others, *History of Labour in the U.S.* (4 v., 1918–35). See also Norman Ware, *The Industrial Worker, 1840–1860* (1924); Edith Abbott, *Women in Industry* (1910); Charles H. Wesley, *Negro Labor in the U.S., 1850–1925* (1927); Henry W. Farnam, *Chapters in the History of Social Legislation in the U.S. to 1860* (1938); U.S. Bureau of Labor Statistics, *History of Wages in the U.S. from Colonial Times to 1928* (1929); Edgar W. Martin, *The Standard of Living in 1860* (1942).

The Agricultural Scene

GENERAL: Ralph H. Gabriel, *Toilers of Land and Sea* (v. 3 of *The Pageant of America*); Percy W. Bidwell and John I. Falconer, *History of Agriculture in the Northern U.S.* (1925); Lewis C. Gray and E. K. Thompson, *History of Agriculture in the Southern U.S. to 1860* (2 v., 1933).

AGRICULTURAL REVOLUTION: Avery O. Craven, *Edmund Ruffin, Southerner* (1932) and *Soil Exhaustion as a Factor in the Agricultural History of Virginia and Maryland, 1606–1860* (1926); Fowler McCormick, *Development of Farm Machines* (1941); William T. Hutchinson, *Cyrus Hall McCormick* (2 v., 1930–35); Edward Wiest, *Agricultural Organization in the U.S.* (1923); Albert L. Demaree, *The American Agricultural Press, 1819–1860* (1941); Wayne C. Neely, *The Agricultural Fair* (1935).

Chapter XIX

MOLDING THE AMERICAN MIND

1 *The Aristocratic Ascendance*

PEACE and independence brought the desire to provide at home the means for a complete education in arts and professions free from the decadent influence of European social and national ideas. New colleges and professional schools sprang up all over the country, even in the new West. Learned societies revived and increased. There was in this a consciousness of the necessary connection between liberty and intellectual progress. As early as 1771 we find Freneau and Brackenridge celebrating their graduation at Princeton with a commencement ode on *The Rising Glory of America,* and invoking

Revival of learning

> . . . sweet liberty!
> Without whose aid the noblest genius fails,
> And Science irretrievably must die.

The influence of the Enlightenment was strengthened. Deism, promoted actively by Thomas Paine and Elihu Palmer, gained acceptance on the ground that revealed religion was a means used by the aristocracy to deceive the people and hold them in subjection. Many men of the humbler classes were convinced of this thesis, and in the 1790's it was promoted by a number of Democratic Republican newspapers. The idea of progress was welcomed from France because it seemed to fit the facts of the conquest of the wilderness and of the rising status of the common man.

Belief in Natural Rights was almost universal, but its validity seemed to be challenged by the visible facts of inequality among classes and races. Environmentalism sought to explain this inconsistency by pointing to social and economic abuses and to differences in institutions and training. A ready illustration of the last was the condition of women, and Aaron Burr disproved the idea that women are mentally inferior by educating his daughter Theodosia until

Environmentalism

587

she was the superior of most men. Political liberals accepted environmentalism as championed by Burr and such a scientist as Benjamin Rush. Conservatives, whose wealth and privileges were based on heredity, preferred to reject it and to rest their understanding of Natural Rights upon Locke's central pillar of property rights as the stabilizer of society. Nevertheless, environmentalism caused liberals to question such institutions as slavery and to hold that its violation of Natural Rights would poison the springs of liberty. Other aspects of humanitarianism were also promoted. Prison reform (after the examples of the Italian Beccaria and the Englishman John Howard) was gradually introduced. Cruel and unusual punishments were abated, and imprisonment for debt was gradually abolished.

Conservatives viewed deists with horror as termites gnawing at the foundations of society but were themselves yielding to even more insidious doctrines. Universalism, transplanted from England, found open expression in New England during the Revolution. It taught that since God is good He must save all men, and men could co-operate in seeking salvation through the cultivation of character. Unitarianism, springing from New England's own Puritan roots and encouraged by English importations, was even more widespread in the North. Americans had wrought their own political salvation in the Revolution, why could they not by their own efforts promote their soul's salvation? Calvin's dour doctrine of predestination fell into disfavor. Unitarianism rejected much of the old theology, including damnation and the Sonship of Christ, but retained God, divine revelation, and the individual conscience. Unitarianism was a comfortable compromise between deism and the searing theology of Calvin, and it found such ready acceptance in the prosperous and satisfied upper classes that it was called the "cult of the arrived." Unitarianism, it has been said, took a great weight from the soul of New England. Certainly it prepared the way for the flowering of transcendentalism in the next generation. Many Unitarians agreed with the deist belief in progress through science and enlightenment and sought to do away with evils by reforms.

Unitarianism

The Federalists formed a core of resistance during the 1790's to the more liberal aspects of the Enlightenment. By 1800 the excesses of the French Revolution had given them the victory, and we have the curious situation of a country going liberal politically and conservative intellectually. This conservatism was to remain dominant until the Jacksonian victory in 1828. Though conservatism's political leaders were patricians who were quietly deistic and Unitarian, it nevertheless found allies in the Calvinist churches and ministers who still distrusted the depravity of the human animal. Even more significant was the support of those among the evangelical sects who could

Conservative victory

not stomach Thomas Jefferson's deism, and who saw the conservatives as the supporters of revealed religion and of the traditional attitudes and virtues.

The effect of the conservative ascendancy on the American scene was not long in developing. Though secular education was honored in theory, it dragged in practice. Morals became the core of the curriculum and gave it a distinct odor of sanctimoniousness. Science was all too **Doldrums** frequently deplored, and this attitude had an effect both **in educa-** upon practical inventions and the popular resistance to **tion** them. The study of Christian evidences and of systematic theology was revived in the colleges, and they were taught by the outstanding lecturers. Advanced education, in fact, was now intended for the élite, though in the West many lads from the *hoi polloi* managed to sneak into the halls of learning. Even the nature of reform was changed, and humanitarianism gave way to moral crusades against alcohol and in favor of Sunday schools and missions. "Culture," says the historian Schouler, "was squeamish, affected, finical, full of classical pretensions, the toad-eater of the rich and patronizing to the poor, inane, wholly out of sympathy with American democracy and imitative of English authors." The literature of the time has aptly been called "twittering."

The moralism of the period found one of its principal vents in the movement for home and foreign missions. A spate of organizations in both fields around 1800 resulted in much confusion, rivalry, and waste until in 1810 the interdenominational American Board of Commissioners for Foreign Missions appeared in one field, **Rise of** and in 1826 the American Home Missionary Society ap- **missions** peared in the other. Obviously neither one held complete control, for denominational boards often persevered and, indeed, by the time of the Civil War were far more powerful. Early missionary enterprise was little inclined to find good in non-Christian cultures but expected to remake the world by the introduction of Christian ethics and theology. A powerful aid in this endeavor was the American Bible Society, organized in 1816, which by now has translated and published the Bible, or parts of it, in almost a thousand languages and dialects and has distributed half a billion copies of the Bible or the New Testament.

Though there was an amazing jump in the number of printing establishments, the production of books and newspapers was handicapped by the high cost of paper and printing and by high postal rates. An annual subscription to a newspaper would cost a farm hand a month's pay. Magazines were numerous, poorly supported, **Literary** and short-lived. The best was the *North American Review* **scene** of Boston, which from its foundation in 1815 kept up a high standard in spite of its poor subscription list; to it many celebrated American writers owed their introduction to the public, one of the first being the young poet William Cullen Bryant. The reading public was not numerous or rich enough to make it possible for a writer to earn a comfortable living, except as the author of textbooks. The writing career, however, enjoyed esteem, and many professional men and merchants wrote on the side. Publishing was more remunerative, chiefly because the lack of copyright arrangements between the United States and Britain made it possible to pirate popular British authors like Scott and Dickens.

"To America," wrote Franklin, "one schoolmaster is worth a dozen poets, and the invention of a machine or the improvement of an implement is of more importance than a masterpiece of Raphael. . . . Nothing is good or beautiful but in the measure that it is useful: yet all things have a utility under particular circumstances. Thus poetry, painting, music (and the stage as their embodiment) are all necessary and proper gratifications of a refined state of society but objectionable at an earlier period, since their cultivation would make a taste for their enjoyment precede its means." This explanation, though cold comfort to the intervening generations, at least helps to show why there has been a lag in the arts in the United States.

Lag in American art

The theater slowly gained in popularity. Most of the actors were English, but the Americans Edwin Booth, Edwin Forrest, and Charlotte Cushman are still remembered in theatrical circles, chiefly for their Shakespearean offerings. Authentically native were the stage Yankee, the stage backwoodsman, and most of all the blackface minstrels with their "Ethiopian operas." Thomas D. Rice began the vogue with his "Jim Crow" dance, and it was carried on by Dan Emmett, composer of *Dixie*. Outside of such presentations, the dance was social rather than artistic. Music without words fared somewhat better, especially in cities where German immigrants had settled.

Theater

A few early artists are still well known, chiefly because they painted historic personages. Gilbert Stuart left a hundred canvases of Washington. Charles Willson Peale added sixty more portraits of the father of his country, and his sons Rembrandt and Raphael were perhaps better artists than their father. John Trumbull specialized in Revolutionary scenes. John Singleton Copley and Benjamin West belonged more to England than to America. Chester Harding, of the younger generation, showed more insight than his masters. Other younger men, competent but not exactly inspired, came to the front after 1815, among them Samuel F. B. Morse, founder with the elder Peale of the National Academy of Design (1825), but better known for his invention of the telegraph. The so-called Hudson River School painted dreamily romantic scenery. Sculptors were few and mediocre. Hiram Powers scandalized and fascinated the public with his nude *Greek Slave,* and

Painting and sculpture

Horatio Greenough emitted for Congress a colossal statue of Washington seated half-nude on a throne; the work is now in the cellar of the United States National Museum of the Smithsonian Institution carefully screened by other exhibits.

American medicine did not make many startling original advances before the Civil War, though numerous secondary contributions were made to medical science by observant physicians. Anesthetics, though known and discussed in Europe, came into general use in America first. Probably Dr. Crawford W. Long of Georgia **Medicine** was first to use ether, in 1842. A Hartford dentist, Dr. Horace Wells, repeatedly used nitrous oxide in dental operations, and in 1846 a Boston dentist, Dr. W. T. G. Morton, used ether in an operation. For some reason a hitherto indifferent medical fraternity took notice, and anesthetics rapidly came into use. A Kentucky physician, Ephraim McDowell, was a pioneer in ovarian surgery. Oliver Wendell Holmes, Sr., a Harvard medical professor, poet, essayist, and raconteur, fought the good fight for antisepsis in the care of childbirth—and was later confirmed by Lister and Pasteur. Dentistry made far more progress in the United States than in Europe and was eventually to change the snaggle-toothed nation of 1800 to the one with the best cared-for teeth in the world.

The vogue of laissez faire prevented wholehearted government support of cultural activities, for it was felt that the author, the educator, and the researcher should be governed by the same competitive rules as business. Nevertheless, there were honorable exceptions. We **Govern-** have seen how Congress voted land subsidies to states for **ment sup-** educational purposes, but it never got around to establishing **port of** a national university. A coast survey bureau was begun in **knowledge** 1807 but was poorly supported for a generation. Matthew Fontaine Maury was the founder of the science of oceanography and received a naval post in Washington as an aid to his studies. The activities of the army in exploration have been noted before, and the navy made important explorations in the Pacific, the Arctic, and in South America. Unfortunately the Library of Congress, twice destroyed by fire, though reinforced by the acquisition of Jefferson's library in 1815, limped for generations.

The American Philosophical Society of Philadelphia, founded in 1743 by Franklin and others, was reinforced in the scientific field by the Columbian Institute, founded in 1816 in Washington and intended to integrate American scientific interest. It received some government favor and did some good but was later merged with the National Institute, which in turn went over to the Smithsonian Institution. When in 1829 James Smithson, an Englishman, left $600,000 to the United States to be used in establishing an institution for the "increase and diffusion of knowledge," the money might well have been dissipated in piddling projects had not John Quincy Adams fought the battle which resulted in the foundation of the Smithsonian Institution.

In an administrative and scientific sense the Smithsonian Institution was the creation of the physicist Joseph Henry, who utilized its limited funds to launch it into an astonishing variety of scientific activities. The Indian Service supported the investigations of Henry R. Schoolcraft into Indian lore and customs. The researches in geology of Joseph Le Conte of Georgia were of great aid to government scientists, as was Louis Agassiz, Swiss naturalist and Harvard professor. The *American Journal of Science and Arts,* founded in 1818 by the Yale chemist Benjamin Silliman, Sr., was for a century edited by a dynasty of scientific Sillimans. By 1848 science had reached the stage where its high priests could form the American Association for the Advancement of Science, which still leads in its realm.

In spite of the dominance of conservative ideas in the intellectual field, progress was made in the popularization of knowledge. Americans read not only native and foreign sentimental fiction and poetry but technical **Populariza-** manuals on cooking, carpentering, farming, and medicating, **tion of** and a mass of pamphlets on religious controversies, scare- **knowledge** head confessions, and odd theories like phrenology. Library associations and book peddlers multiplied. Textbooks were increasingly easy to come by. Museums appeared in the cities, stuffed with curios and exhibits of not too severely educational nature. Private academies increased until probably every county boasted at least one. Elementary education gradually improved. Even in hard times when financial support flagged, the Lancastrian system enabled a teacher to multiply himself by setting the older children to teach the younger; doubtless there was a great deal of parroting, but it was better than nothing. Not least in the spread of knowledge and culture was the fact that the lack of sharp caste distinctions led to frequent contacts between classes and to learning by osmosis. Foreigners noted that even laborers were more intelligent, better informed, and readier to experiment with the new than were those of Europe.

During the first half of the nineteenth century the United States shared with the rest of Western Civilization an admiration for florid oratory. Most of the Founding Fathers were men of profound wisdom, who spoke simply when they spoke at all. The contrast after the **The craze** War of 1812 is startling. Calhoun, Clay, Webster, J. Q. **for oratory** Adams, Benton, and Randolph were orators, but only Calhoun and Adams can be accused of having been profound. The taste for oratory extended down to the county courts. It has been held that Americans "lawed" so vigorously not simply because they were cantankerously determined to have their rights, but also because they wished to give their favorite lawyers excuses to "norate." Oratory—not mere "public speaking"—was the favorite study and diversion of college students, and successful public careers were freely prophesied for the adept. It may be suspected that Americans had come to admire form, color, and emotion rather than substance; certainly a political leader sometimes found oratorical charm more important than ability.

This love for the florid in oratory was merely one phase of our national growing pains which arose in general from the European philosophy, or rather mood, which has been called romanticism. Perhaps it was a revolt against the strait jacket of natural law and the grim realities of developing industrialism. Romantics muted Nature's basic savagery to a wild and melancholy music which **Romanticism** sent delicious chills up their spines and brought tears to their eyes but never reached their hearts. They were deliberately and sometimes blindly optimistic. They rode forth against a threatening universe armed with moral clichés and soothing "romantic" ideals. Escape from the present reached its English poetic flower in Byron and its prose flower in Scott.

Old-line American conservatives distrusted romanticism's undermining of discipline and convention, but the country's nostalgia for a romantic way of life is seen in the sale of five million copies of Scott's novels in the decade beginning in 1813. Even the Federalists welcomed him because he portrayed the aristocratic society for which they yearned. The would-be aristocratic South took him so seriously that Mark Twain quipped that Scott was the cause of the Civil War. Certainly the frontier and sea novels of James Fenimore Cooper strikingly exhibit the influence of romanticism. Cooper later became a bitter critic of the excesses of democracy and denounced the idea of progress as a wishful and optimistic misrepresentation of mere change.

The romantics recognized realities but turned away to a pleasing mythus. A step lower in the scale were the sentimentalists who either deliberately refused to recognize or were incapable of recognizing reality, but embraced the mythus.* It is, of course, characteristic of the mentally or psychologically immature. Cooper **Sentimentalism** showed great awareness of the problems of his generation, but the historian and essayist Washington Irving passed through them with sublime unawareness. Sentimentalism became characteristic of a large part of the people (particularly the prosperous and satisfied) who refused to recognize the real sores on the American body and answered complaints with smug moral and inspirational clichés.

A continuing phenomenon in the Federalist era and in the democratic

---

* This distinction follows Edward D. Branch, *The Sentimental Years, 1836–1860* (1934), a stimulating and amusing analysis of the culture of the period.

THE LAND OF LIBERTY—A BRITISH VIEW IN 1847

Britishers sometimes retaliated for American antipathy by such
cartoons as the above from *Punch*. It was all the more irritating
because it had a certain basis in truth. Brother Jonathan,
equipped with pistol and slave driver's whip, places his foot in
Washington's face and dreams with leering satisfaction of scenes
of violence and injustice.

era that followed was xenophobia, that is, fear of strangers, or antifor-
eignism. It may rise from a number of sources, but most common are
Xenophobia　the fear that foreigners may be strong enough to menace
and　　　　one's liberty or way of life and jealousy of the foreigners'
xenophilia　power, wealth, culture, or living standards. Townsend Harris, one of America's great diplomats, was probably close to the average
in his generation in as much as his mother brought him up "to tell the
truth, fear God, and hate the British." Accompanying xenophobia is its
obverse side, xenophilia. The civilization of the United States obviously
derived from that of Europe, particularly Great Britain, but instead of

calmly accepting the fact the xenophobe sought to deny or minimize European influence while the xenophile slavishly aped Europe. It was perfectly possible for the same person to do both. One of the most curious and significant illustrations of Americans' dependence upon Europe was found in their breathless attention to British travelers and their books. Great Britain became to a morbid degree the object of American xenophobia and xenophilia.

British travelers were by no means all of them anti-American, but American sensitiveness made them most conscious of the travel books which were most critical. Let us look at American society as these sensitive patriots thought the British portrayed it. A nation of **American** sallow, unhealthy-looking specimens, with bad teeth, slur- **views of** ring nasal speech, slovenly clothes and unclean habits, over- **British** run with bedbugs and cockroaches, glum and frigid in man- **views of** ners, eating voraciously of a destructively heavy cuisine, **America** swilling iced drinks, drunk in the afternoon, eternally whittling, rocking, staring, and chewing and spitting tobacco so liberally that sidewalks, steamboat decks, and hotel lobby floors were stained brown by the ceaseless expectorations of bootblacks and statesmen—the American national emblem, said one humorous observer, should be not an eagle but a spittoon. Curious to the extent of impertinence, reading newspapers avidly but gleaning more prejudices than facts, swept by religious orgies at camp meetings and revivals, brutal to slaves, but moral except in business, politics, and such items as gouge fights and murders. Women were dependent on their menfolk for all decisions, took no exercise, and possessed only ornamental accomplishments. Children were brats.

Above all was a sense of insecurity which imbued the nation with a strange unrest, a haste to get things done which set men to chasing dollars as evidences of accomplishment, made them build museums as evidences of culture, and bred a "servile and jealous admira- **American** tion of the Old World [*which led*] to attempted imitation, **insecurity** uncouth and clumsy." This was often shown in amusing ideas of propriety. For instance, the word *legs* was not used; the Englishman Captain Marryat told of seeing in a young ladies' academy a piano with legs modestly swathed in frilled pantalettes. Yet Lady Gough, a countrywoman of his, laid down the rule that the books of male and female authors, unless they happened to be married, must be properly separated on the shelves. Growing prudishness led to the introduction about 1850 of chaperonage in polite society. Powers's nude statue *Greek Slave* was not permitted to be shown in Cincinnati until it had been partially clothed.

Most Americans were full of national and race prejudices, of Yankee tricks, and of oratory which was flatulent and turbid, redundant with

classical allusions and historical illusions. Even more obvious and universal, however, was the lick-all-creation spirit. It was the common impression that America had cornered all wit, goodness, and intelligence, that
all blessings rose from the excellence of our institutions, and that Europe
was rapidly sinking into decrepitude and senility. "We air a great people,
and bound to be tolerable troublesome to them kings," boasted one yokel.

Historical Society of Pennsylvania

"The Trollope Family" from a sketch taken from life, made
in Cincinnati, 1829, may have had something to do with
Mrs. Trollope's caustic comments on America.

Travelers, of course, each saw what it was in his nature to emphasize,
just as Americans saw in travel books the points on which they were
most sensitive. Frances Trollope in *Domestic Manners of the Americans*
(1832) wrote chiefly of Cincinnati, then in its rawboned
adolescence, where she had lost her money in a mercantile
British bias
venture; she was so snobbish and vicious in her portraiture that the
furore over her book was said to have surpassed even the excitement over
South Carolina's nullification and Jackson's War on B. U. S. Charles Dickens was a reformer, and in his *American Notes* and *Martin Chuzzlewit*
it was his nature to attack abuses; nevertheless, it was untactful repay-
ment for unprecedented lionizing and hospitality, however annoying they
may have been at times.

On the whole, it would seem that Britishers were alarmed by the growing power and conceit of America and slandered its democracy in order

to dam the wave of reform then sweeping Great Britain and threatening to undermine privilege in society, politics, commerce, and colonial administration. "In the four quarters of the globe," jeered Sidney Smith in 1820, "who reads an American book? or goes to an American play? or looks at an American picture or statue?" The truth in such a taunt could scarce be turned aside by such retorts as Lowell's "On a Certain Condescension in Foreigners" (1869).

Many Americans were not in a mood to admit they could be improved, though of course they sought that end most diligently. If they had been willing to recognize compliments, they could have found plenty of them in Dickens's *Notes,* in Harriet Martineau's judgments, and especially in Alexander Mackay's penetrating and sympathetic *Western World* (1849), where he expressed admiration for American institutions and society. Basil Hall noted that while slaves were sometimes brutally treated, he had seen worse treatment in the British army, navy, and schools. The Frenchman De Tocqueville, while aware of the pitfalls of democracy, was as fully alive to its desire to elevate the common man. American superficiality was recognized ("We teach all the branches of knowledge," admitted Thoreau, "and none of the roots"), but it was also recognized that the American workingman was keener and better informed than his European counterpart. Americans were patient under the inconveniences of noise, mud, and discomfort in travel. They were genial to strangers and pitilessly hospitable. The church and the clergy were honored. Family life was full of affection and simple pleasures. Equalitarianism, while it bred mediocrity, recognized the worth of the individual rather than that of his ancestors; it was what was above ground, not underground, that counted. Foreign land-lookers were almost always pleased by what they found. The United States was "the poor man's country" where low taxes made it seem like heaven to the immigrant, and "plainness and simplicity of manners, equality of condition, and a sober use of the faculties of the mind" made classes not static but fluid—and gave promise of a bright future.

Foreign sympathy

2   *The Roots of Change*

The ideal and practical streams in American history may be called by the names transcendental and pragmatic. American reform sentiment has thus been divided into two wings: the transcendentalists, who proposed to make a clear sweep, and the compromisers, who proposed to find a middle ground between the practical "evil" and the ideal "good"—to keep the advantages of the old while they tried out the new.

The ideal and practical streams

In the main, Americans have sought ideals, but their method of getting there has been by the compromiser's gradual and practical approach. Thus, when an issue reaches the political realm the problem becomes one **Politicians** of "how" and "how much?" This is where the politician **seek** comes in. He is a man who has made a lifelong study of **compromise** methods of reconciling differences. That is why a politician as President is usually preferable to an engineer or a soldier. We pay politicians in the coin of prestige and power; but, if they make compromises which we regard as ill-judged or crooked, we pile on abuse even before we know the facts of the case.

The typical politician is as jittery as a man going into battle. The politician must straddle issues judiciously in order to win enough votes to get himself elected. Cynical observers say that the politician is trying to deceive the people; an even better case can be made that he is trying to guess what the people want. At any rate, politicians prove their usefulness by finding the ground on which the ideal and the practical can meet. Actually what politicians do is to refuse to recognize either as a moral ideal, for of course a principle cannot be compromised. If one side or both in an issue insist that it is upholding a moral ideal, there can be no practical political compromise, and war is likely to follow as it did in 1861.

The United States of 1830 was shot through with romanticism and sentimentalism. Even the Jacksonian Movement was sentimental in its self-deception as to the ease with which the democratic millenium could **Stimuli to** be whistled into the parlor and house-broken to live in civi- **reform** lized society. There were, however, many Americans who proposed to hew reality to their ideals. During the 1820's certain of the more liberal Unitarians were strongly affected by a number of influences too numerous and complicated to be analyzed here in detail. Classical philosophers, medieval mystics, and Oriental thought were all explored. The belief of the French Revolutionists in human perfectibility was appropriated. The idealism of Kant and his German followers was dissected and selections made. The English Lake Poets were laid under tribute. All this at a time when we would have it that Americans were living to themselves in splendid isolation! Most significant, of course, were the twin streams of the American heritage: on one side the idealism and the Calvinist conscience which were related to these European borrowings; and on the other the self-reliance, common sense, optimism, and restless experimentation which were finding expression in the Jacksonian Movement.

Transcendentalism was not the creation of any certain group at any certain time, but it found its most famous focus in the meetings of the

Transcendentalist Club which began in 1836 in Boston. Its members at one time or another included Ralph Waldo Emerson, William Ellery Channing, Theodore Parker, Henry Thoreau, Margaret Fuller, Orestes Brownson, George Bancroft, and Bronson Alcott. Among such a galaxy of individualists it was inevitable that there should be great differences of opinion, and these were freely expressed in a little magazine called the *Dial*. Nevertheless, there were fundamental agreements. They believed that knowledge of truth transcends experience and reason and is implanted by God in the human heart. Knowledge of the ultimate truth (the Absolute) is thus possible to the individual who will listen to the voice within him. Since they were Americans, the transcendentalists felt the obligation of action, the necessity to preach and experiment and to put their God-given ideals into practice. Though they thus accepted the idea of progress, the relationship to Calvinism's self-righteousness is readily apparent. It is just as apparent that the expression of unalterable moral principles would cause trouble when they reached the political arena with its demand for compromise.

Transcendentalism

Nevertheless, transcendentalism had a relationship to democracy. Its emphasis upon courage and restraint, its glorification of self-reliance and social consciousness, and its belief that man is naturally good and that his divinely implanted instincts afforded reliable guides to judgment and action—all these were inherent in Jefferson's democratic philosophy. With Jefferson it distrusted too much government and denounced industrialism as materialistic and destructive of man's independence. Theodore Parker, appalled by industry's effect on the working class, led the attack and sought a social solution.

Transcendentalism and democracy

Henry David Thoreau, too much the complete individualist to be a loyal transcendentalist, pointed with alarm at the state, nationalism, and the machine. He wanted to stop them cold, not mold them into stepping stones to a better life; and he went to live in the woods at Walden Pond near Concord to show how it should be done. His *Civil Disobedience* is a purge for the overly co-operative. "My thoughts," said he, "are murder to the state and involuntarily go plotting against her." He believed what he said; and when as a practical protest against government support of slavery he refused to pay a poll tax, he was thrust into jail. Emerson visited him and asked sadly through the bars: "Henry, why are you here?" Thoreau's answer was transcendentally direct. "Waldo, why are you not here?"

Henry D. Thoreau (1817–62)

Ralph Waldo Emerson, the greatest of the transcendentalists, yet stood aside from its extreme manifestations. Scion of a long line of ministers, he himself had retired from the Unitarian ministry to work out

Ralph Waldo Emerson (1803–82) his attitude toward God and his fellow men. The world, as he saw it, was throttling law, progress, and individual freedom, and he devoted his life to the battle for individual salvation. "Let men but stand erect," he said, "and they can possess the universe." Serene, high-minded, often accused of pallid thinking, he traveled and lectured untiringly. No settlement was too remote nor its fee too small to divert him from his duty. Concord became the home of a coterie of thinkers who warmed themselves at Emerson's flame but were in no sense subservient disciples. Emerson vigorously championed Jeffersonian democracy but was repelled by the "impudent vulgarity" of the Jacksonians. Nevertheless, he retained his optimism and expressed the faith that some day there would emerge from the racial and social welter of America "a new race, a new religion, a new state, a new literature, which will be as vigorous as the new Europe which came out of the smelting-pot of the Dark Ages."

The American people were too apt to regard democracy as a revealed faith and to sink back in the secure belief that it would bring Utopia without too much effort on their part. Cooper has been mentioned as a **Doubts of the democratic revelation** critic of democratic excesses and of the idea of progress. Nathaniel Hawthorne, born in the decaying old seaport of Salem, in his novels pointed out the truth that pain and sorrow and struggle are the human lot, and that there is no pleasant and secure railroad to Utopia. Edgar Allan Poe, a gloomy and gifted Virginian, master of the romantic mood, inspired writer of poetry and short stories and inventor of the detective story, was the literary American of his generation to receive highest acclaim in Europe. To the tragedy of Hawthorne and the "blasted hope" of Poe one is tempted to link the pathos of Pittsburgh's Stephen Collins Foster, the composer of enduring folk songs of a downtrodden race. All three were out of step with the heedless optimism of democratic America, and each sought refuge in a world of his own far from the self-assurance of transcendentalism.

The most slashing critic of the democratic dogma, however, was Herman Melville. As a runaway sailor on a Pacific isle he had seen the idyll of native life and also glimpsed the ugly cannibalism beneath. Now in **Herman Melville (1819–91)** his tremendous allegory, *Moby Dick,* he sounded the warning that there are no automatic guarantees of human progress. Man is fate's lieutenant; good and evil are eternally with us. Captain Ahab must always pursue the white whale. Our purpose on earth is to engage in the strife; this is our delight and the expression of our individualism, even though in the end we go down like Captain Ahab before the fury of evil. Man's alliance with good against evil, the everlasting search for truth even though we may be destined to know it only in part—these were the facts of life as Melville saw them. Ralph H. Gabriel succinctly points up the two wings of democratic thought: "Emerson said: Trust thyself because God is in you. Melville replied: Trust thyself because no god will aid you." Some of Melville's novels attained success, but *Moby Dick* was received with silence or misunderstanding. America was not ready to be jolted from its smug security by such warlike realism.

The democracy of the 1850's was an incongruous and contradictory mixture without philosophy or direction. In the South it was Athenian in nature, based on slavery. In the North it was smug and contented, overgrown and soft, ready to be bent to selfish purposes. Jeffersonian democracy, suitable for a simple agrarian society, was out of date in the developing industrial society, and **Democratic confusion** its doctrine of individualism was to be the support of the very interests Jefferson had sought to overthrow. These were the men of action, the builders and money grubbers who saw democracy as the pillar of their own power. Such men are necessary for material progress, but society in taking the gifts they offer in one hand must be wary lest the other hand lift the watch and fob of eternal values.

Hawthorne and Poe could offer little but resignation, noble or delirious. Melville's trumpet call to battle was sounded for the heroic, but few of us are heroes. Emerson saw the confusions and contradictions and gave self-reliance and dignity to the American spirit—which was all very well but quite useless without integrated dynamism. For a few years the Civil War gave purpose to democracy, but with the apparent passing of the crisis the old smugness returned. It was the mission of Walt Whitman to strike the spark which has kindled the watch fires of democracy in our generation.

Walt Whitman was a New York Quaker, a carpenter, typesetter, and journalist who knocked about from job to job. Fired by Emerson's faith in man, he applied himself to forging the declamatory poems which he set in type and issued in 1855 as the first edition of *Leaves* **Walt** *of Grass*. The book was an immediate and undoubted fail- **Whitman** ure, and it was not until praise found its way back from **(1819–92)** England that the country awoke to his great gift. Meanwhile he added to his poems, served as an army nurse during the Civil War, and clerked in a government office in Washington. It seems to have been Whitman who first used the phrase "democratic faith"; certainly no more joyous nor impassioned affirmation of it has ever been written than appeared in his work. Van Wyck Brooks has said that he "precipitated the American character." Rude, impulsive, and affirmative, he lived among people and loved them. He looked upon himself as a primitive poet whose function it was to focus tribal aspirations and stir the people to action. He spurned the pallid, unimaginative, duty-bound reformism of the transcendental-ists and put iron tonic in the veins of their self-reliant man. He gathered together the disparate, warring elements of democracy and gave them organic being and dynamism. There he stuck, for he was not a man of ideas and did not know how to build the democratic future. That has been the task of our century, in so far as it has been done.

The men we have been discussing did not necessarily exert direct effect upon the common people but were read and interpreted by the leaders and teachers. Probably more direct was the power exerted by **Bancroft,** George Bancroft, the historian. In the florid style then in **Webster,** vogue his *History of the United States* vigorously cham-**Everett** pioned democracy and found many instances in which Providence had intervened to protect and mold it. Bancroft profoundly influenced statesmen, teachers, and editorial writers, though his views were after all but reflections of American popular opinion. No less sig-nificant in the growth of democracy were the orations of such statesmen as Webster and Everett which were printed in the newspapers, reprinted in readers, and recited in schoolrooms. Webster, in particular, was re-garded as the champion of union, which was in the North regarded as an aspect of democracy, and his "Reply to Hayne" was recruiting men for the Union Army a generation before the Civil War.

3 *The Immigrant Tide*

The role of immigration in American national history has been a subject of lively and sometimes bitter discussion. The claim has been made that if the last immigrant had landed in 1776 the population of **Significance** the United States would today be fully as large, a great deal **of immigra-** better integrated, and more mature. This may be true, but **tion** it was not the way things happened. As it was, the immi-grant played a very important part in schoolroom, legislature, factory, field, and military life. Moreover, his cultural contributions have af-fected the American pattern, not perhaps in any single important way but in numberless small ways which, taken together, have made signifi-cant alterations. To see this one need only look at religion, music, the theater, architecture, and even the American menu.

Until 1885 immigrants came largely from northwestern Europe, par-ticularly Germany and the British Isles. Thereafter the tide set in from the Slavic and Latin countries, though the "Nordic" wave by no means **The Old** decreased in actual numbers. The majority of immigrants **Immigra-** became manual workers; even those with professional skills **tion** frequently had to earn their living with their hands because of their unfamiliarity with the new language and customs. Usually the people of the Old Immigration followed certain patterns in the work they undertook. Irishmen became roustabouts and construction workers; Welshmen went into lead and coal mines; Scandinavians went into farming and logging; and Germans divided between farms and city industries. Englishmen and Scots became farmers, sheepherders, and mechanics, but their possession of education and capital enabled many of

"Welcome to All!" by Joseph Keppler in *Puck* (28 April 1880) shows the various backgrounds of immigrants of the period as well as the prevalent American attitude toward them.

them to go directly into business and the professions. All of these elements were speedily Americanized, but Germans and Irish clung longest to their distinctive traditions and psychology without seeming to find it a hindrance to their new loyalty.

From the beginning of the Revolution to the close of the War of 1812 immigration was not large, possibly a quarter million all together. The result was that for about forty years the United States was able to devote itself to the absorption of the diverse colonial elements and to work out a national pattern. Doubtless this period of **Slow** integration was partly responsible for the wave of national- **beginnings** ism which swept over the country immediately after the close of the War of 1812. The years immediately after 1815 saw economic changes, crop failures, and increasing hardship among the European peasantry. The tide of immigration to the United States set in strongly—thirty thousand came in 1817 alone—and served to fill the vacancies left by

American farmers and laborers who joined the Great Migration to the West.

The industrial collapse of 1819 reduced the influx to a trickle for almost a decade. European landowners and industrial employers seized with avidity upon tales of American crime, disease, and natural calami-

Effects of Panic of 1819 ties to discourage the departure of their laborers and for a while turned the popular picture of America from a land of promise to a land of starvation and disaster. The collapse of 1819 had three important effects. It ruined the brokers who had fattened off the importation of redemptioners; thereafter immigrants came only when they could obtain the means to pay their own fares. Congress passed (1819) the first immigration law, a measure designed to control the number of passengers carried by ships and thus reduce the danger of pestilence in crowded steerages; by the same law a beginning was made of preserving statistics of immigration at the ports of arrival. Lastly, depressed wages and pauperism led to the hiring by mill owners of immigrants at scandalously low rates and brought on the first serious antiforeign agitations.

The upswing of the late 1820's in the American economy with its demand for labor coincided with another wave of hardship in Europe. The European revolutions of 1830 were crushed, and with their failure

Beginning of mass immigration perished the hopes of many liberals and, even more important, the hopes of peasants for relief from bad crops and crushing debts. A resurgence of anti-Semitism in Germany led to the first mass exodus of Jews, and it continued even after the agitation died down. Meanwhile the overhauling of the antiquated English Poor Law in 1834 took thousands off the dole and pushed them into the labor markets of farms and cities. New troubles in Ireland started a new migration from Ulster, as the dispossessed crowded in and bid up the rents. The demand of industrial England for beef and mutton had been converting Scottish farms into pastures, and this urge to the emigration of displaced farmers was accelerated by the failure of the potato crops in 1836 and 1837. For these and other reasons the exodus from Europe to the United States had reached fifty thousand a year by 1832, and only twice thereafter did it fall below that mark. The Panic of 1837 decelerated the flow the next year, but only temporarily.

As a matter of fact, conditions both in Germany and in Ireland became so miserable by the middle 1840's that any change was regarded as far better. Ireland was a rich agricultural land, but it was largely owned

Agricultural conditions in Ireland by landlords who were interested only in rents. The peasants had to sell most of their wheat, pork, and butter to meet rent and taxes, and subsist their families mainly on potatoes. So rigid was this custom that it was later found that the peasantry when given flour to save them from starvation did not know how to prepare bread. Even as it was, potatoes did not keep well, and in any case the crop was never large enough to last through the summer. The women and children were reduced to semistarvation while the men journeyed to England to work in the harvest fields. Nevertheless, the potato, precarious a resource as it was, had actually enabled a population of nearly nine million to grow on an island that today accommodates only half as many.

In 1845, 1846, and at intervals thereafter a blight ruined the Irish potato crops, and typhus followed among the starving populace. Famine relief was slow in arriving, and hordes of those who could rake up the fare fled to America; hundreds of thousands of those who could not get as much together crossed to England to find refuge **Famine in** in tenements and hedgerows. The decade that began in 1841 **Ireland** saw nearly 800,000 Irishmen reach the United States, and the next decade brought 900,000; this does not include those who crossed from Canada and the Maritime Provinces, presumably coming that way because their fares were paid by the overseers of the poor.

Emigration would have been inevitable in any case. British industrialists to get cheap food for their labor had used the Irish famine to hasten the repeal of the Corn Laws, which had protected British and Irish grain from foreign competition. With the repeal of the Corn Laws, European grain flooded the market, and landowners turned more and more to sheep and cattle. The dispossessed peasants of the British Isles had little choice but to join the pool of excess labor in the cities or to emigrate.

The potato blight hit the German peasants hard, but since the potato was not the chief article of diet the crisis was passed without starvation. Nevertheless, the blight was an important factor in precipitating an economic and political crisis. Since the fall of Napoleon crop **Economic** failures and economic dislocations had been plunging the **stress in** German peasants more deeply into debt, for the rents they **Germany** owed to the nobility and the taxes they owed to Church and state were unduly oppressive, and arrears were piling up. The wave of revolutions which swept through the cities in 1848 frightened the German rulers, and they lost no time in setting up land banks from which the peasants could borrow money with which to amortize their debts and purchase their farms. But the peasant found the impersonal land bank no better a landlord than the noble. Crops continued to be precarious, and increasing numbers sold for what cash they could get and emigrated. British textile manufacturers were also adding to German economic stress by undercutting the home industries of spinning and weaving.

Americans were again moving west, this time to Wisconsin, Iowa, Minnesota, California, and Oregon, and the Germans found a hearty welcome to the jobs that had been vacated, bought up abandoned farms,

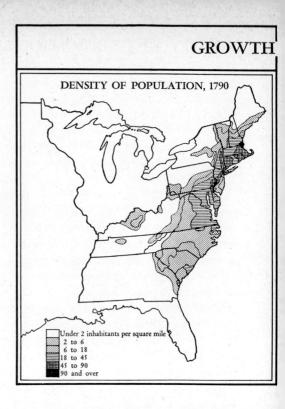

DENSITY OF POPULATION, 1790

Under 2 inhabitants per square mile
2 to 6
6 to 18
18 to 45
45 to 90
90 and over

German settlement

or moved on to the new lands of Wisconsin. Germans, unlike most other immigrants, settled in considerable numbers in the slave states. An attempt was made in 1844 to plant a German colony at New Braunfels in the Republic of Texas, but it failed. Nevertheless, twenty-five thousand Germans found their way to Texas in the 1850's, and other thousands founded homes close to the beer gardens of Cincinnati, St. Louis, Chicago, and Milwaukee. The German political refugees who came soon after 1848 unfortunately were an exception to the rule of easy Americanization and actually undertook to remake the "barbarous" American pattern and even to set up a separate German state. Their strongest opponents were found among previous German immigrants and among the German agrarians. Carl Schurz, himself a "Forty-Eighter," was a strong advocate of Americanization; he became an organizer of the Republican Party, a Union general in the Civil War, and eventually Secretary of the Interior.

Not one of the incoming elements failed to make cultural contributions to the American scene. The English and Scots because of their similarity to Americans left the least trace; the Irish had little to offer

German cultural contributions

that was unique intellectually, though their share in song and drama is evident; the Scandinavians and Hollanders were for the most part solid people of the lower classes, religiously conservative and quietly interested in education and culture. The Germans made the greatest impression. Many of

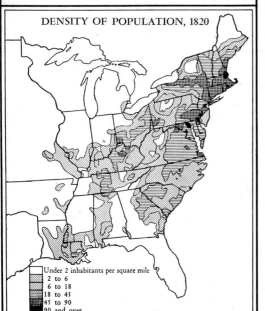

DENSITY OF POPULATION, 1820

Under 2 inhabitants per square mile
2 to 6
6 to 18
18 to 45
45 to 90
90 and over

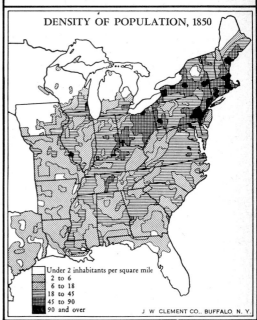

DENSITY OF POPULATION, 1850

Under 2 inhabitants per square mile
2 to 6
6 to 18
18 to 45
45 to 90
90 and over

J W CLEMENT CO., BUFFALO N. Y.

Adapted from C. O. Paullin, *Atlas of the Historical Geography of the United States*. 1932. Carnegie Institution of Washington.

them were educated men, leaders of liberalism in German thought, politics, and professions. They looked upon American puritanism and its peculiar reformism with distaste and fought the temperance movement, blue Sundays, fossilized theologies, the lack of dignity and depth in politics, and the bleakness and mediocrity of American life. There was a great deal of misunderstanding and underestimation of American ways, with much resultant bitterness, but in the end the German critics did more good than harm by their precepts and examples.

German teachers, theologians, engineers, architects, scientists, foresters, horticulturists, and brewers left broad streams of influence in their lines of activity. They were long prominent in the trade-union movement, and socialism as a political manifestation was regarded as a German importation. German societies, such as the *Turnvereine,* were not only active in adult education but helped to turn the American mind toward scientific physical training and organized sports. Most impressive contribution, however, was in music. In the American West the best fiddler was the one who finished the tune first. When little German bands and orchestras appeared, the puzzled Americans found each member playing a different "tune." Orchestras and choral societies spread from German communities, and presently musical conservatories began to appear. Germans were indispensable teachers, impresarios, conductors, composers, and, not least of all, musical instrument makers.

The 1850's saw an astonishing increase in immigration, with Germany and the British Isles furnishing the bulk of the newcomers. Swiss immigration, customarily financed by the cantons, continued. Norwegians, dis-

The Great Migration of the 1850's contented under Swedish rule, furnished part of the Scandinavian element, but it is said that one million Swedes—a quarter of Sweden's population—came to America. Scandinavian settlements in Wisconsin and Minnesota were populous, but since many of these settlers came by way of Canada and the Great Lakes their numbers will never be known. Dutch settlers gave a pronounced Dutch cast to certain counties in Iowa and Wisconsin, and to southwestern Michigan; the descendants of the latter group, in particular, have contributed largely to American professional and political ranks. During the 1850's about 2,600,000 immigrants were recorded as entering the country. By 1860 there had entered 1,600,000 Irish; 1,300,000 Germans; 100,000 French; and 400,000 English. Of a population of 32 millions, one eighth were foreign-born.

The decline of the business of bringing in redemptioners posed a problem for millions who wished to come to America. Sometimes local authorities paid the fare of paupers to avoid the expense of supporting

Paying the fare them. Others sold what property they had for what they could get and launched forth. By the middle of the century, however, it had become the custom for those who had gone ahead to send back money to bring over their friends and relatives. One young man might be sent by his family with this purpose in mind. As relatives and neighbors arrived in America and set to work and save for the passage of the next in line, the process of pyramiding can be readily grasped.

This was made easier as organized services took over the business of transporting emigrants. Fares dropped from $50 to as low as $10 within a generation. The necessity of waiting at the port of embarkation until a

Immigrant service captain could be found to accommodate the emigrant was replaced by 1840 by the sale of tickets which guaranteed passage at specific times. Bremen built its nineteenth-century prosperity upon the emigrant business, and Hamburg followed with a rival service which offered the attractions of a shorter and more interesting journey across England and departure from Liverpool. Le Havre became the goal of many Germans who drove across France and sold their horses in the Paris market; the building of railroads gave Le Havre an additional advantage in the German immigrant service.

Unfortunately the conditions of passage in steerage can be regarded as good only when compared with slaving ships. Voyages were at least shorter than in colonial days, but "ship fever" (typhus) and other diseases

Conditions of immigration took an appalling toll. Decks were low, quarters were close, and the air, always bad, was cut off when the hatches were closed during storms. Legislation to provide better conditions was not well enforced. Steerage passengers had to bring their own food, and they found that it spoiled quickly and that cooking facilities were not adequate and were not intended to be. The custom of furnishing food to passengers did not become general until after the middle of the century. Privacy was not always provided either for individuals or for each sex, and robbery and rape would seem to have been common. Improvements finally began to make headway because governments on both sides of the Atlantic saw that they were necessary in order to prevent the spread of plague.

The immigrant's perils, however, were not over when he stepped ashore, for he had still to fight off the vultures of his own nation who dragged him off to boardinghouses and jobs with the intention of swindling him. The law of the land took little notice of such conditions, but private charitable societies did their best, and Tammany Hall received the gratitude (and the votes) of many immigrants who but for its aid would have starved in a strange land.

European ignorance of America was abysmal in the earlier years, and such information as existed was often drawn from Cooper's novels, which were translated into many languages. Even Britishers sometimes failed to grasp that Virginia or Ohio were parts of an independent United States; to this day there are ignorant Englishmen **Knowledge of America** who do not realize that the United States and Canada are two different countries. Misconceptions were increased by the way in which some British travelers set forth their experiences; these books usually were translated into German. Around 1830, however, strictly factual guidebooks for immigrants began to appear, and these did much to correct romantic or hostile views. Most important of all were the letters —"American letters"—written home by immigrants. The appearance of a single such letter in a community might spread the "American fever" for emigration and strip it of able-bodied citizens.

In spite of undoubted drawbacks, the romantic view of America remained deep-seated. Laziness, bad management, or bad luck might tell against the immigrant, but usually industry and reasonable shrewdness were rewarded. Letters are evidence of the awe-struck amazement of the immigrants at the opportunities offered by America. The Irishman, lately starving on his blighted potato patch, found that he could have meat three times a day. A German farmer could sell his land, buy tickets to America, and still have enough left to buy a cleared farm with buildings for himself and each of his three sons. True, the farms were sometimes in poor condition, but Germans knew how to restore their fertility and were not afraid of work. Those who had no resources found that wages were so high that after two or three years of careful saving they could buy the coveted farm.

Faith in Europe was gone, and even those who could have lived comfortably at home often left because they felt they could do better abroad. "America," wrote Goethe, "thou hast it better." In America there **The land of equality** was no enforced service in the army, taxes were negligible, and so great was the government surplus that Congress was actually troubled by what to do with it. Peasants who had lived under extortionate taxes, rents, and tithes, and had been harassed by government spies were amazed to find that government cost so little and interfered so little with the citizen. One observer who asked German emigrants why they were going to America received from them all the same answer: "There is no king there." No white man in America, the immigrants found, acknowledged a master. Farm hands and housemaids sat at table with their employers, and American women were not accustomed to field drudgery. "There are no large estates," wrote a Swedish newcomer, "whose owners can take the last sheaf from their dependents and then turn them out to beg." Another Scandinavian recounted his blessings, then added the simple truth so telling to the people at home: "Neither is my cap worn out from lifting it in the presence of gentlemen."

BIBLIOGRAPHICAL NOTE

The Aristocratic Ascendance

GENERAL: See John A. Krout and Dixon R. Fox, *The Completion of American Independence, 1790–1830* (1944); and Carl R. Fish, *The Rise of the Common Man, 1830–1850* (1927). See also Herbert M. Morais, *Deism in Eighteenth Century America* (1934); Arthur A. Ekirch, *Idea of Progress in America, 1815–1860* (1944); Oliver W. Elsbree, *Rise of the Missionary Spirit in America, 1790–1815* (1928); Kenneth S. Latourette, *History of the Expansion of Christianity* (7 v., 1937–45).

THE ARTS: Oral S. Coad, *The American Stage* (v. 14 of *The Pageant of America*); Carl Wittke, *Tambo and Bones* (1930); Arthur Hornblow, *History of the Theatre in America* (2 v., 1919); Frank J. Mather, *The American Spirit in Art* (v. 12 of *The Pageant of America*); Oliver W. Larkin, *Art and Life in America* (1949).

CONTEMPORARY: On foreign observers see especially Henry S. Commager, ed., *America in Perspective* (1947); André Morize and Elliott M. Grant, eds., *Selections from French Travelers in America* (1929); and Allan Nevins, ed., *America Through British Eyes* (1948). Each has a valuable bibliography. The reader should by all means become acquainted with Alexis de Tocqueville, *Democracy in America* (various eds.). See also George W. Pierson, *Tocqueville and Beaumont in America* (1938); and Jane L. Mesick, *The English Traveller in America, 1785–1835* (1922).

The Roots of Change

TRANSCENDENTALISTS: Van Wyck Brooks, *Life of Emerson* (1932); Henry S. Salt, *David Thoreau* (1896); Mark Van Doren, *Henry David Thoreau: A*

Critical Study (1916); Henry S. Commager, *Theodore Parker* (1936). Francis O. Matthiessen, *American Renaissance* (1941) concerns Emerson, Thoreau, Hawthorne, Melville, and Whitman. See also Van Wyck Brooks, *The Flowering of New England, 1815–1865* (1936).

NOT SO TRANSCENDENTAL: Van Wyck Brooks, *The World of Washington Irving* (1944) concerns Irving, Cooper, and Poe, among others. The commentaries on the literati of this age are growing alarmingly. On Poe see Hervey Allen, *Israfel* (1926); on Hawthorne, the studies by Lloyd R. Morris and Mark Van Doren; on Cooper the studies by John F. Ross and Robert E. Spiller; on Melville, the studies by Lewis Mumford and Leon Howard; and on Whitman, those by Henry S. Canby and Hugh Fausset. Add to the above Russell B. Nye, *George Bancroft, Brahmin Rebel* (1944).

The Immigrant Tide

Most clearly devoted to the Old Immigration is Marcus L. Hansen, *The Atlantic Migration, 1607–1860* (1945); wider in scope, but of scarcely less value to this period, are George M. Stephenson, *History of American Immigration, 1820–1924* (1926); and Carl Wittke, *We Who Built America* (1939). On the Irish see William F. Adams, *Ireland and Irish Emigration to the New World: From 1815 to the Famine* (1932); on Norwegians see Theodore C. Blegen, *Norwegian Migration to America* (1940) and *Grass Roots History* (1947); on Swedes, George M. Stephenson, *The Religious Aspects of Swedish Immigration* (1932); for Germans, A. E. Zucker, ed., *The Forty-Eighters* (1950); for locality studies see Oscar Handlin, *Boston's Immigrants, 1790–1865: A Study in Acculturation* (1941); and Robert Ernst, *Immigrant Life in New York City, 1825–1863* (1949). See also the bibliographical note at the close of Chapter 5, Section 3.

Chapter XX

THE TRANSCENDENTAL PROTEST

1 *The Age of Reform*

WHEN in 1776 Jefferson laid his Declaration of Independence before Congress an effective majority of the country was ready to accept its political implications. Two generations later (1837) Ralph Waldo Emer-

Emerson's declaration of independence son stood before a Harvard audience and issued an intellectual declaration of independence. "We have listened too long to the courtly muses of Europe," he said. "We will walk on our own feet; we will work with our own hands; we will speak our own minds." Conservatives, anxious to preserve their special social and economic privileges, were aghast at this call to break with tradition, and he was in effect outlawed for the next forty years. The struggle that followed his declaration was longer and more bitter than the war which put Jefferson's Declaration into effect; indeed, it still goes on.

The groping so evident among the American intellectuals of the middle of the nineteenth century was also partly due to the early phases of a dilemma which was not to become clear until our own century. Here

Status versus change we can only forecast what we will analyze at length later on. The American *vernacular,* or native, workmanship was finding expression in the artifacts of the American artisan and in the functionalism of the new machines. On the other hand, European art was rooted in the cultivated tradition which had developed with more or less symmetry from classical times to the Industrial Revolution. The two were quite incompatible, and each stubbornly refused to give way; it was in effect a struggle between the aristocratic élite of the cultivated tradition and the democratic vernacular which sought to exploit the machine to defeat the élite and elevate the masses. The first promised static order; the latter threatened change with all its danger of bringing chaos. We know that status sooner or later brings revolution, but that was not so apparent to men in 1850. Hence, American intellectuals were torn between the supposed security of status and the democratic demand for change.

The bourgeoning of reformism in the 1830's and 1840's was the most remarkable phenomenon in the social history of that generation. Scarcely a field was left untouched. Emerson, who as a truly self-reliant man maintained a rather supercilious attitude of aloofness to- **Chaotic** ward programs, attended in Boston in 1840 a convention of **reformism** the Friends of Universal Reform and recited with some humor the roster of causes represented:

> If the assembly was disorderly, it was picturesque. Madmen, madwomen, men with beards, Dunkers, Muggletonians, Come-outers, Groaners, Agrarians, Seventh-Day Baptists, Quakers, Abolitionists, Calvinists, Unitarians, and Philosophers—all came successively to the top, and seized their moment, if not their hours, wherein to chide, or pray, or preach, or protest.

The reform which in the long run was to prove most fundamental and most significant was in the field of education. It was promoted by nearly all reformers in the conscious hope of building a more enlightened democracy. As a matter of fact, parsimony had combined with **Rise of free** prejudice to hamper the growth of common schools. The **public** revolution in education began in 1823 when Samuel Read **schools** Hall established a little normal school in Vermont. Hall developed many of the features now familiar in teacher training, held conventions, wrote textbooks, and devised teaching aids. The movement spread rapidly. Horace Mann in Massachusetts and Henry Barnard in Connecticut became evangelists in the new cause. One of the most serious obstacles to taxation for the spread and betterment of free schools was the objection that it was a violation of the rights of property; another objection came from the churches, which had traditionally considered education their private field, though they had not cultivated it very thoroughly. The issue was bitterly fought everywhere, but particularly in Pennsylvania, where a dour, club-footed ironmaster named Thaddeus Stevens led the battle for free public schools. By the 1850's the opponents of free schools were losing nearly everywhere. Unfortunately the Civil War seriously handicapped the movement in the South.

Secondary schooling was chiefly college preparatory in nature and was furnished by "Latin Schools." A broader curriculum presently began to be offered by private seminaries and academies. Most of these disappeared after the Civil War with the introduction of public high schools,

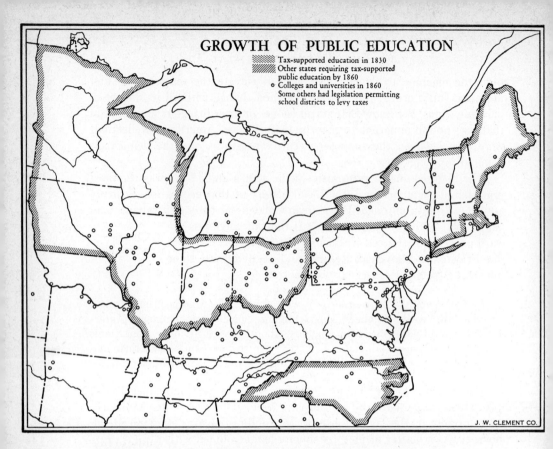

GROWTH OF PUBLIC EDUCATION

Tax-supported education in 1830
Other states requiring tax-supported
public education by 1860
o Colleges and universities in 1860
Some others had legislation permitting
school districts to levy taxes

J. W. CLEMENT CO.

though some continued especially in the East and South, and others became colleges.

Before 1830 colleges were little more than glorified high schools, and boys graduated before they were out of their teens. The curriculum was dull, and since there were no athletic activities to reduce the pressure of **Colleges** youthful spirits it was common for students to engage in drinking bouts and riots. During the 1820's there began an influx of young teachers who had studied abroad, and the slow process of strengthening and enlivening the curriculum was begun. Democratic sentiment favored the growth of state universities at public expense; but conservatives feared public control of higher education, and they were joined by the churches, which insisted that state colleges would be godless. Private control was triumphant, as evidenced by the Dartmouth College Case of 1819, but the state universities did not go out of existence. Northeastern colleges were on the whole the most liberal and progressive in the country. In the South and West the churches had a throttle hold on higher education.

There is doubt as to how many of the institutions calling themselves colleges were entitled to the name. A fairly strict estimate would give fifty-six colleges in 1830 and about 23,000 college graduates, about one fourth of one per cent of the population—quite a contrast to the present five per cent. By 1860 there were two hundred three colleges, of which only seventeen were state controlled or state supported. Apparently the country was now ready to admit that women could be educated, for Mary Lyon founded the first American women's college, Mount Holyoke, in 1837. It must not be thought, however, that women were being trained to become rivals of men. They were expected to become wives and mothers, and the farthest they were permitted to venture into the big bad world was as teachers. Their training was even more strictly moral and religious in character than that of young men.

Very encouraging was the leap in the popularization of knowledge after the Jacksonian victory. Books and periodicals were cheaper, libraries multiplied, night schools were set up, and more lyceums offered more night courses, lectures, concerts, and musical instruc- **Popular** tion. The working classes, particularly young men and **education** women in the towns and cities, seemed consumed by a thirst **and the** for knowledge. One of the most significant aids to the spread **mails** of knowledge was postal reform. Postal rates had always been high and service slow, and with the coming of the railroad the competition of private express companies threatened the breakdown of the supposed Constitutional monopoly of the post office. The example of British postal reform led to a similar movement in the United States; and beginning in 1845, after bitter opposition, Congress began to slash the rates, and within eighteen years a standard rate of three cents a letter had been adopted. The effect on letter writing and the circulation of periodicals was revolutionary and a severe defeat for the enemies of popular education.

Next to the educational reforms the one destined to make the greatest stir in the world was the abolition of slavery. Since it was so closely allied to sectionalism and civil conflict, we shall defer it to a later chapter. Other aspects of institutional reform rose both from the **Institutional** impetus of the Enlightenment and from the philanthropic **reforms** impulses of earnest Christians, both the transcendentalists and the Quakers. Environmentalism, by accenting the effect of social conditions upon human behavior, naturally led to attempts to better the conditions. American reformers profited by European examples and were often inspired by them. The English emphasis upon social rather than legal responsibility in showing the way to reform was accepted in America, and there was no branch of reform but which was persistently promoted by a rash of voluntary associations.

Philadelphia, for long the most enlightened city in the country, led in agitation for the reform of prisons and the penal code. American prisons, crowded, noisome, and maladministered, became even more inadequate

Prison reform

as confinement was substituted for other punishments such as the pillory, the stocks, the whipping post, branding, and ear cropping. Reform came slowly in spite of earnest efforts to bring it. New York, after 1815, built a penitentiary at Auburn which provided a cell for each of the prisoners and utilized their labor in workshops. Perhaps because the prisoners thus paid for their own upkeep, the system was generally preferred to the solitary confinement of Pennsylvania institutions. Some start was made toward separating juvenile offenders from hardened criminals, and self-government was tried out in at least one reform school. A curious commentary upon the slowness of reform is seen in the fact that imprisonment for debt, often for paltry sums, was the rule until 1821. Even after the reform got under way, it took a generation to wipe out this futile form of punishment.

Orphanages and poorhouses increased in number, but conditions were deplorable because of inadequate finances and sometimes because of sadistic attendants. The usual custom was to bind orphans out to service and to give a small allowance to paupers and the aged or to board them out. The insane were removed from prisons, where they were often brutally mistreated, and segregated in asylums. The apostle who fought the good fight in defense of the insane was Dorothea Dix, a gentle, ailing spinster of Boston. Thomas H. Gallaudet devoted himself to the education of deaf-mutes, adopting methods then in use in France. His work was continued by his son, Edward Miner Gallaudet, who did much to introduce speaking and lip reading to deaf-mutes. Equally important to the blind was the devoted Samuel Gridley Howe. He was the first to teach a deaf-blind child to speak, and he pioneered in the training of the feeble-minded. These reformers and their followers traveled far and wide, lectured and lobbied persistently, and were on the whole extraordinarily successful in arousing the people and legislators to provide institutions for care and education of the unfortunate at public expense.

Charitable institutions

In looking about for the causes of the evils that they were attacking, reformers could scarcely escape the conclusion that alcohol lay very near to the roots. They pointed out not only that drunkenness encouraged crime and social diseases, but that a besotted citizenry would be in no condition to perform its duties as enlightened and responsible rulers of a democracy. In hard times they showed that liquor promoted poverty, and in good times they pointed out to employers that it destroyed the efficiency of labor. Though the evangelical churches gradually began to advocate temperance, the movement had little success until after 1825.

Origins of temperance movement

Before long, however, the advocates of temperance and "teetotalism" fell out, and the movement was crippled. Then in 1840 the Washington

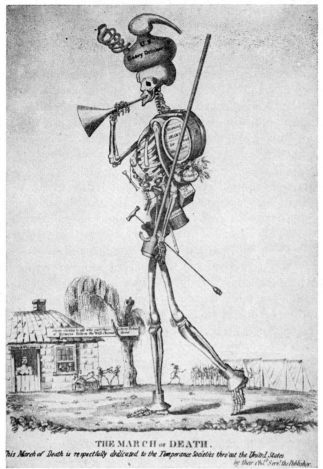

THE MARCH OF DEATH.

This March of Death is respectfully dedicated to the Temperance Societies thro'out the United States
by their Obt. Serv. the Publisher.

Historical Society of Pennsylvania

The rise of Temperance Societies in the early years of the nineteenth century inspired humor of the kind shown here.

Temperance Society, announced itself as made up of "reformed drunkards" and led an emotional crusade which swept the North. **The first** Other organizations adopted its flamboyant methods. Local **prohibition** option was introduced and made some headway. Maine **movement** went dry in 1846. All of New England except Massachusetts followed, and then came Ohio, Delaware, Tennessee, Indiana, Illinois, Michigan, Wisconsin, Iowa, and Minnesota. Except in Maine and Vermont prohibition was short-lived, either losing out in the courts or being repealed. The methods and many of the leaders survived, however, and the crusade was to be renewed after the Civil War.

The conditions of American pioneer life had fostered equality of the sexes, even to the franchise in New Jersey and Virginia. After the Revolution, however, the dependent and protected status of women was emphasized. In a legal sense a woman was a perpetual minor, with her property and wages at the absolute disposal of her husband. Also he had the right of chastisement; halfway through the century he had the legal right to beat his wife with a reasonable instrument, which in one case was adjudged to be a stick no thicker than a man's thumb. Widows and unmarried women had more extensive rights over their own property and their own actions, but courts were not inclined to favor them.

Status of women

It would seem natural that women should from the first have been interested in reform movements, but to the overwhelming majority of nineteenth-century men such activities should have been the property solely of males. Mary Wollstonecraft and Frances Wright led their British sisters in the demand for equal rights in social and political life, and the latter carried the revolt to America, where as Fanny Wright D'Arusmont she scandalized the public by openly flouting the conventions. Quaker acceptance of sex equality (especially by the liberal Hicksite branch) promoted the rise in the reform movements of Lucretia Coffin Mott, Abigail Kelley Foster, Susan B. Anthony, and the Grimké sisters of South Carolina, Sarah and Angelina. The transcendentalist wing was represented by the wives of a number of the great New England reformers, but particularly by Margaret Fuller, whose *Women in the Nineteenth Century* was a powerful argument for equality. Other champions of reform among women were Sarah Buell Hale, authoress of "Mary's Little Lamb," who cautiously preached equality in her fashion magazine *Godey's Lady's Book;* Jane Grey Swisshelm, a belligerently reformist editor of Pittsburgh and St. Cloud, Minnesota; Anne Royall, grim and eccentric writer of Washington City, who had statesmen shaking in their boots; Elizabeth Blackwell, who devoted her life to winning for women a place in the medical profession; and Amelia Bloomer, who championed the combination of skirts and Turkish trousers which became known as the bloomer costume.

Women and reform

These women persevered in their work despite abuse and insults not only by the public but by many smug male reformers who sought to refuse them the right to speak in public. The crisis came in 1840 when in London the World's Antislavery Convention refused to seat American women delegates; as a result, some of the American male delegates refused to take their seats but watched proceedings from the gallery with their womenfolk. It was now apparent that the root of the trouble was the unequal status of the sexes, and the result was increased interest in the movement for equal rights for women.

Women's rights

Better-balanced reformers lost interest in those movements which refused to receive women, and perhaps to this may be attributed the damaging emotionalism of the temperance movement. The advocacy of votes for women began its active phase in 1848 in the Seneca Falls Convention called by Lucretia Mott and Elizabeth Cady Stanton. Close to them in leadership was Lucy Stone, a great soul in a tiny body, and the redoubtable spinster, Susan B. Anthony, who hurled the thunderbolts

Culver Service

"The Age of Iron, or Man as He Expects to Be" is one of the more amusing of the comments on the Women's Rights movement.

that Mrs. Stanton forged. Horace Greeley, the liberal editor of the *New York Tribune,* headed a growing list of journalistic advocates of women's rights, and from 1848 onward the state legislatures began to modify the married woman's property laws. The decisive phase of the movement, however, did not come until well after the Civil War.

The American peace movement received its original impetus from the Quaker Anthony Benezet and that universal reformer, Benjamin Rush. Its leadership was taken up later by William Ladd, who formed the American Peace Society, and by Elihu Burritt, the "learned blacksmith," but it found little favor among combative re- **The peace movement** formists. As for the people, they were too snugly secure behind the Atlantic moat and the *Pax Britannica* to give much thought to the subject. The conflict between pacifist nonresisters and those who admitted "just" or defensive wars split the peace movement asunder, and showed up the nonresisters as Christian anarchists. Burritt, a nonresister, departed for Europe and aided in promoting a League of Universal Brotherhood and several international conferences. The movement, however, collapsed with the European wars of mid-century. In the United States the peace movement was weakened by the defection of prominent Abolitionists, who saw in the coming Civil War a means of accomplishing their favorite reform.

One of the most unexpected outcomes of transcendentalism was the strengthening of American Roman Catholicism. Catholic increase was largely by immigration, largely Irish and German, and largely centered in the cities; the number rose from thirty thousand at independence to a million in 1840 and to three million in 1860 —ten per cent of the population at the latter date. Native-American distrust of Catholics grew with their number and was probably based more on the economic competition of the foreigners than on their religion. Nevertheless, Catholics were often regarded as enemies of democracy, and proof was sought. Catholic desire to receive a share of school taxes for their parochial schools was used to strike a shrewd blow at all church control of common-school education. Inevitable maladjustments to American social and economic life were cited as proof of the foreigners' unfitness for democratic rights, but the tendency of some American employers to exploit immigrant labor was ignored. Even more significant was the growing power of nationalism which, like most self-centered ideologies, requires a scapegoat and found it in Catholics, who were represented as owing primary allegiance to the Pope.

Rise of anti-Catholicism

These issues became topics of public interest and debate by the 1830's. When the Catholic leaders showed superior logical ability and knowledge of facts, many Protestants unfortunately descended to verbal abuse and then to riotous destruction of Catholic church property. Unscrupulous men published fake exposures of nunneries and papal history by the millions of copies. Protestant and Catholic gangs began to clash in the cities, and both sides began to exert political pressure. These exhibitions fluctuated with circumstances, but the influx of Catholic immigration which followed the Irish potato famine and the disastrous German Revolution of 1848 brought on a crisis. Scores of nativist secret societies sprang up; and because immigrants were usually political liberals, their opponents tended to be conservatives. By 1852 these secret societies had found expression in the Native American Party. Its members were popularly called Know-Nothings, because when asked what they stood for they replied that they did not know. Though it was definitely a minority movement, the party (like the Anti-Masons of the 1830's) fell into the hands of ambitious politicians.

Nativism

Prominent among the New England transcendentalists was Orestes Brownson, one of those tortured souls who had sought truth in many different religious pastures. His principal social interest lay in elevating

A DEMOCRATIC VOTER

The New York Historical Society

A Democrat of the late 1830's is caricatured as a nondescript
Irishman offering to vote "according to conscience and for him
as tips most."

the laboring classes, and as lecturer and editor he became
the leader in this aspect of transcendentalist effort. Then
suddenly in 1844 he announced his conversion to Catholicism. From a champion of the self-reliant soul he passed to
**The Ameri-
can current
in Catholi-
cism**
championship of the mediatorial Roman Catholic Church. A few months
before this his young protégé, Isaac Hecker (1819–88), had led the way
into the Catholic fold. Both men were destined to be powerful influences
in reconciling American individualism with Catholicism. They sought to
show that the Catholic Church was democratic, but they emphasized
democratic responsibilities rather than privileges. Hecker, by far the more
liberal and influential of the two, became the founder of the Paulist
Order, which devoted itself to preaching and teaching in the United

States and acclimating immigrant Catholics to American democracy. In 1894 Archbishop Ireland thus summed up the work of Father Hecker:

> He looked on America as the fairest conquest for divine truth, and he girded himself with arms shaped and tempered to the American pattern. I think that it may be said that the American current, so plain in the last quarter of a century in the flow of Catholic affairs, is, largely at least, to be traced back to Father Hecker and his early co-workers. It used to be said of them in reproach that they were the 'Yankee' Catholic Church; the reproach was their praise.*

Reformism was mainly the child of the Northeast, of Quakers, Unitarians, and free thinkers. Because of its emphasis on abolition of slavery it made little headway in the South, and of the western states only Ohio

Shortcomings of reformism was far enough removed from pioneer days to offer soil for the full growth of reform. New England, New York, Pennsylvania, and Ohio thus were the breeding ground of reform.

This regionalism promoted a recognition of common interests among reformers. Scarcely a one, whatever his or her principal devotion, but what was also prominent in several movements. In looking back one is likely to see these reformers as single-minded fanatics, inspired snoopers concerned only with managing their neighbors' business. Perhaps they were, in basic motivation, and therein lay the danger of the movement, but that is only a partial view. They accepted the traditional Anglo-Saxon belief that the responsibility for reform lies with the people, and that it will become expressed in law only after its champions have forced it upon the public conscience. Perhaps the fierce joy that the reformers took in battle was a necessary part of their equipment, if they were to overthrow entrenched conservatism.

The reformism of the period has often been accused of sterility; it might be more accurate to say that it bred more problems than it cured, at least in its own generation. The reasons should be suggested rather than asserted. For one thing, its roots could not be thrust deep because the soil was strewn with the stones of romanticism, sentimentalism, and shortsighted self-interests. The parable of the sower has had no more striking illustration. The strength of the evangelical churches lay in emotional rather than in realistic values; hence the sweeping success and prompt failure of the prohibition movement, and hence the frequent evangelical opposition to reforms which were led by individuals whose theology or habits were unconventional. Another weakness lay in the proneness of the transcendental wing to insist on all or none. Such tactics were outside the Anglo-Saxon tradition of compromise and only gained allies for vested interests, whether slaveholders or industrial capitalists. We shall see how this fact promoted the great conflict over slavery

* Walter Elliott, *Life of Father Hecker* (1891), ix–x.

which fastened upon us a permanent race problem and a long-term preponderance of industrialists. Nevertheless, a few seeds did fall into good ground and eventually brought forth fruit manyfold.

2 American Utopianism

From the foundation of the English colonies we find socialistic threads running through the warp and woof of American life. They became evident at the very beginning when the settlers of Plymouth, as members of a corporation, worked for the community, and the fruit of their labor was placed in the common store. At Jamestown the settlers were technically employees of a corporation. **Socialism in the colonies** Though these systems were replaced by individual enterprise as soon as practicable, the coastal communities in the pioneer stage never surrendered their right to supervise the settlers' use of their property. Though the land was claimed by the Indians or by the great real-estate operators, the settler rejected both claims and asserted that the land belonged to him because he would put it to productive use, and his labor would give it value. The labor theory of value lies at the bottom of socialistic doctrine, and perhaps logically socialism should have developed, but there was so much land available that a strict doctrine of private property developed. This was promoted also by the strength of Calvinist ideas (regardless of theology), which glorified industry, initiative, and individual success. Nevertheless socialism kept cropping up, usually connected in some way with religion. As early as 1680 the Labadists of Maryland practiced community of goods, and similar enterprises sprang up among the Pennsylvania Germans. The most successful was the Ephrata Cloister, which prospered modestly and was the best musical center of the colonies; it lasted until after 1900.

The heyday of American socialist experimentation came during the generation before the Civil War. Developing industry had been slow in fulfilling its promise of a better living for the masses, and life in factory towns too often had the grimness of a nightmare. In Europe reaction to the French Revolution had tightened social and religious controls. Oppression and misery in Europe **Causes of popularity of socialism** and bleak living and emotional starvation in America made the people anxious for any release. History shows that when society reaches the depths of economic or psychological misery, release often comes in the form of religious excitement. Pietists on both continents, longing for the day of salvation, thought they saw in Biblical prophecy the promise of the early return of Christ to earth—the Second Advent—which would begin the millenium, that is, a thousand years during which Christ would reign in peace on earth.

The effect was to tighten the bonds of Christian brotherhood and to introduce celibacy as a sort of purification for the Second Advent. Economic distress and religious hope prompted pietists to find a way of living apart from the sinful world, and because they were poor men, their best opportunity lay in pooling their resources and (if they were Europeans) moving to the New World where land was cheap and, moreover, government was tolerant. This type of socialism was often known as communism, because it supported community of goods; it had none of the political or terroristic earmarks of modern communism.

German pietists formed a number of successful communities. The Harmonists, or Rappites, under the leadership of George Rapp began in 1803 to build the village of Harmony north of Pittsburgh. In 1815 they **German** moved to New Harmony, Indiana, on the banks of the **communi-** Wabash, and in 1825 back to Economy near Pittsburgh. The **ties** society remained in existence until 1905. The Bethelites, composed first of Harmony seceders, settled at Bethel, Missouri and later established a second community at Aurora in Oregon. Other pietists founded in 1817 a community at Zoar, Ohio, and the Amana Society, beginning in 1843, founded communities in New York and then in Iowa. These communities lived quietly for the most part and prospered as the result of industry and wise leadership. The emphasis on celibacy, however, tended to drive away the young people and reduce the strength of the communities. Germans were almost uniformly successful in the early years of their socialistic enterprises because they were docile, obedient, industrious, and possessed of technical skills. An instructive contrast is offered by the Swedish settlement under Eric Janson at Bishop Hill, Illinois (1846–60). Leadership and co-operation were bad, and the community was decimated by disease, robbed by swindlers, rent by quarrels, and finally had to break up.

The history of the Millennial Church or United Society of Believers, usually called the Shaker Society, shows that the seeds of socialism were sprouting in America. Imported from the Rhone Valley by way of England, this pietist movement was distinguished by strange **The Shakers** jerks and other physical manifestations. Its theology was millennial and Quaker with esoteric trimmings, and eventually its physical manifestations were subdued and formalized into the peculiar Shaker "dances." Shakerism was introduced into America in 1774 by Mother Ann Lee, who founded a community near Albany. The society soon became thoroughly American, and at one time numbered about a score of communities in seven states. It was blessed with a corps of able leaders, especially Frederick W. Evans, who fostered its material as well as its spiritual welfare. Shakers lived celibate lives, wore distinctive garb, and are today remembered for their beautifully utilitarian buildings and furniture. Despite its long success, Shaker communism proved unsuited to modern society, and now has all but disappeared.

There was a natural connection between socialist experimentation and transcendentalist revolt. The Hopedale Community (1841–56) was founded by Adin Ballou near Milford, Massachusetts. Though a joint-stock device was used to facilitate entrance and departure of members, it was socialistic in intent. Another experiment at Fruitlands in 1843 was short-lived and is remembered only because it was led by the idealistic but impractical Bronson Alcott, one of the foremost transcendentalists. More successful was Brook Farm (1841–46) near West Roxbury, Massachusetts, led by George Ripley. It was a joint-stock enterprise whose nature was explained by its name, Brook Farm Institute of Agriculture and Education. Though the leading transcendentalists viewed it with tolerant skepticism, it succeeded fairly well as a center of progressive education and civilized living but disbanded when the main building was burned down. *Transcendentalist experiments*

The Oneida Community, near Seneca Lake in New York, was the creation of John Humphrey Noyes, a remarkable reformer from Vermont. The community, founded in 1848, was unique in that first reliance was placed on manufactures rather than agriculture. Equality of the sexes was emphasized, and women cut their hair and wore bloomer costumes. Every effort was made to eliminate competition, in both work and sexual relations, and to build up a completely co-operative, "perfectionist" way of life. For a generation, under the wise guidance of Noyes, the community was happy and successful. Nevertheless, certain practices akin to free love hampered the wider acceptance of its tenets, and Noyes's influence began to wane. In 1881 socialism was dropped, and the venture was reorganized as a corporation. It still exists as the manufactory of Community silver plate. *Oneida Community*

Meanwhile socialism as an economic doctrine began to take form in Europe, chiefly in France. Saint-Simon proposed a world association of industrial states organized and ruled by scientists. Auguste Comte, the father of sociology, proposed to lay firmly the foundations of the better world by a scientific search for the laws of social institutions and progress. Robert Owen, an English industrialist, and Charles Fourier, a Frenchman, proposed that competition be eliminated and socialism instituted by the organization of associations (called phalanxes by Fourier) which should become the centers of their members' social and economic life. They expected to do away with competitive drives by abolishing private property, religion, and marriage. They were absurdly impractical, but they helped to build up class-consciousness and give direction to the workingman's demand for better treatment. Before 1830 revolutions were the work of the middle classes *Growth of socialist theory* (the *bourgeois*) ; now the Chartist movement in England and the wave of revolutions on the continent in 1848 were working-class in origin.

The tolerance of American government and the cheapness of land made the United States the scene of a number of nonreligious socialist experiments. Robert Owen's purchase in 1824 of New Harmony from the

Robert Owen and New Harmony Rappites gave him a ready-made community, and here and in subsidiary communities he gathered a thousand poorly selected idealists who engaged in co-operative enterprises. Even Owen's role as financier and leader could not prevent dissension among the rather high-brow New Harmonists; and when Owen tried to abolish private property, marriage, and organized religion, the community failed. Owen lost most of his fortune and returned to England; his two sons remained and became prominent Americans. One of them, Robert Dale Owen, clearly stated the reasons why co-operative enterprises did not usually flourish in America: land was too cheap and wages too high.

Charles Fourier's creation from dream-cloth of elaborate industrial phalanxes found an American propagandist in Albert Brisbane. He interested a number of "universal reformers" in the scheme, but particu-

Fourierism larly Horace Greeley, a Vermont farm boy who was rising rapidly as editor of the *New York Tribune*. Fourierism, thus popularized, was tried out at Brook Farm, and in forty or fifty other places. None of the experiments was adequately financed or directed, and their citizens were too often impractical idealists or desperate down-and-outers. All of them failed, but the *Tribune* went on its way and gained stature as an honest though indiscriminate advocate of reformism, anchored only by the rather erratic sympathies of its editor.

The area between Vermont and Lake Erie had been swept by so many religious fires that it was known as the Burnt District, and as we have seen, New York and Vermont were seeding grounds for a number of

The Burnt District socialist enterprises. Here gathered all sorts of religious extremists, whether sincere believers or fakers, Swedenborgians, Shakers, vegetarians, wielders of divining rods, and even a sect of men who refused to wash or shave and would wear only bearskin tunics. A curious phenomenon of this district was the "millennial dawn" preaching of William Miller, another New Englander, who prophesied the Second Advent of Christ in 1843 or 1844. Hysteria and panic followed among the poor and ignorant. When the time limit passed without fulfillment, it was natural for extremists to insist that Christ had come but had chosen to remain invisible. The Adventists and Jehovah's Witnesses are present-day relics of this movement. Fully as remarkable was the spiritualist movement, which was set off by the pranks of two sisters named Fox who claimed to be able to communicate with the spirit world. Even when they confessed that their spirit rappings and table tippings were hoaxes, the movement refused to decelerate.

Most remarkable product of the Burnt District, however, and most successful of American utopian movements was the Church of Jesus Christ of Latter-day Saints, usually known as Mormons. About 1820 Joseph Smith (1805–44), born in Vermont and member of a shiftless family near Fayette, New York, began seeing visions. In 1830 he published his revelations in the *Book of Mormon*, a work which shows to an amazing degree the cross currents and soul searchings of the Burnt District. Whatever his social origin or the source of his revelations, the Prophet Joseph Smith became a magnetic leader. Missionaries traveled in all directions and made thousands of converts; even England and the European continent became fruitful recruiting grounds. **Joseph Smith and the Mormons**

The two Mormon centers in Ohio and Missouri had to be abandoned because of local hostility, and a third site was found at Nauvoo, Illinois, on the Mississippi. Here the Mormons became so politically potent that they held the balance of power in the state, and their opinion that they were a people chosen by God did nothing to make them popular with their neighbors. Probably there was also jealousy of their prosperity and resentment that their city charter (granted by the state) practically legalized the supposed despotism of the Mormon elders. Unfortunately they were joined by rough elements which gave color to the accusation that Nauvoo was a rogues' harbor. Joseph Smith's announcement that polygamy would be added to Mormon practices crystallized resentments. In 1844 Nauvoo was mobbed by the uncontrollable militia, and Joseph Smith was murdered.

Mormonism was probably saved from extinction by a second remarkable Vermonter, Brigham Young (1801–77), who deserves to rank among great Americans. In 1847 he led the broken and fleeing Mormons across plains and mountains to the shores of the Great Salt Lake, then in Mexican territory. To this isolated area, free at last from persecution, the Mormons gathered from many lands and by industry and ingenuity subdued the desert to agriculture. During the first years both agriculture and industry were carried on co-operatively under a direction that was almost necessarily despotic, and the Mormon Church still holds vast corporate interests in both lines. **Brigham Young and the settlement of Utah**

If these experiments prove anything, they prove that socialism cannot be suddenly put into effect (at least in a complex society) except when those concerned are skillful and industrious workers ready to yield

Significance of American utopianism obedience to a wise and practical leader whose ascendance amounts to absolutism. Nor could they live a completely self-sufficient existence; indeed, in most cases they succeeded only when their idealism was sparked and disciplined by deep religious feeling. Van Wyck Brooks suggests that the utopianism of Vermont was, after all, the legitimate offspring of New England's Calvinist theocracy, of its search for the City of God and its determination to bend mankind to conformity to the divine plan; but at the same time it was the child of revolt against the individualistic transcendentalism of Concord, which was to become the apologist for the philosophy that "the business of the United States is business." They show that the American spirit is not unassailably competitive—even in that most American of all the states, Vermont. It yearns for a peaceful and co-operative order of society and is sometimes optimistic (or foolish) enough to launch into bold experimentation in the search.

3   The Emergence of American Character

The generation of the War of 1812 saw the emergence of the American character in the form it was to bear for a century with only minor changes. We usually have been materialistic, vaguely idealistic, rashly optimistic, emotional, sentimental, and easily diverted from **American immaturity** the pursuit of difficult objectives—in other words, immature. These characteristics in an older nation would rightly be called psychopathic; of course nations, no more than individuals, exhibit all the characteristics of maturity. In this immaturity lies the explanation for many of the vagaries which have marked our social, economic, and political policies as a people.

American humor of the early nineteenth century showed the national immaturity in its ostentatious robustness and utter callousness. It challenged the giant wilderness with gargantuan fantasies, for those were the **Changing standards of humor** days when Davy Crockett carpeted the Mississippi Valley with bearskins, when Mike Fink roared up and down the rivers, when black John Henry wrestled cotton bales and drove railroad spikes with one blow, and when Paul Bunyan was born in the north woods. It was the day when personal combat was preceded by a ritual of poetic "brags," and Westerners spoke in words chosen for onomatopoeia and mock pomposity.

The decades before the Civil War saw an undercurrent of change, though scarcely the beginnings of subtlety or understatement. Life had not yet beaten the American down, but he was dimly aware that its complexities would not vanish before sound and fury. Nor was American humor standardized. The crackle of Irish wit rose up against Celtic giantism. Burlesque was sometimes softened to satire. The New England Yankee, masking his thoughts behind his native caution like a fox peering from a burrow, carried his wooden nutmegs and ironic jokes over the country. He became the picaresque hero, the butt, and the instructor of the frontier humorist. Humor came more often to lie in the manner of telling rather than the matter. A gust of the primitive, however, lived on in the practical joke, designed to injure or embarrass; the modern "hot foot" is an example. A more refined sadism lay in the seemingly harmless tale or apparent compliment told in a straightfaced and guileless manner with the brutal barb suddenly disclosed at the end. Lincoln was a master of the barb. Once when he spoke from the same platform as the rotund and bibulous Stephen H. Douglas, he referred to the latter's statement that the elder Douglas had been a cooper. "I am certain that he was a very good one," said Lincoln, bowing to his opponent, "for he has made one of the best whisky casks I have ever seen."

One of the most striking and significant American characteristics has been rootlessness: the lack of attachment to any certain place. The European peasant's chief quality is a love and respect for the soil. Historically this has existed in the United States principally in areas where the European peasant managed to preserve some **Rootlessness** measure of aloofness, as among the Pennsylvania-Dutch or the German and Scandinavian settlers of the Northwest. Americans have rarely loved the soil, despite the spoutings of sentimental novelists. We have "wrested a living from the soil"; we have been subduers of nature, not children and partners. Because the forest and the tough sod of the plains were seen first as enemies, it was difficult to develop an affection for the acres that had been won with suffering, and they were frequently abandoned for any reason or no reason. Wondering European observers early noted that American affection and loyalty turned instead toward institutions, specifically our social and political systems. Had Americans had the characteristics of peasants, it would have made more difficult the ruthless exploitation of nature which has made possible the tremendous physical power of the United States.

Another fundamental trait, which we have had occasion to mention frequently, was dualism. This struggle exists, of course, in all human beings, but its emphasis in the Englishman was reinforced in America because we were not mature and well-balanced. The demo- **American** cratic process, moreover, prevents the reaching of a perma- **dualism** nent social or psychological balance because it will not accept any current condition as perfect but insists on further changes to meet changing situations. Let us examine a number of these conflicts and suggest—rather than assert—how they influenced American character.

The conflict between individualism and community controls went on

in the East as well as the West. Now individualism was sometimes law-lessness, but it was also the basis of that courage which is so essential in
Individual- a democratic society. A man could make his own decisions;
ism versus if he thought the law was unjust, he defied it or took it into
social con- his own hands, though of course he accepted the conse-
trol quences. That such actions may be necessary if salutary
changes are to be made was recognized by Thoreau when he went to jail
rather than pay an unjust tax. Joseph Palmer, one of the "universal re-formers," wore a beard in a day when beards were practically unknown
and spent a year in jail for "inciting" a riot among those who gathered to
cut it off. It was such courage that prevented the growth of an American
proletariat, that is, workers with the slave mind. Even our Negroes are
marshaling their social and political weapons like free men.

On the other hand, society countered by laying emphasis upon the
humdrum virtues. Proposed social and political changes had to be ex-amined in the light of their morality, and reformers had to insist that
Stress on they wanted reform in order to promote the reign of moral-
morality ity. Even Bob Ingersoll wanted America to become atheistic
and medi- in order to promote the homely virtues! The intellectual
ocrity stimulus to progress too often failed to crash through this
rigid social and moral system. Mediocrity was the result. As Mark Twain
said: "We have freedom of spirit, freedom of conscience, and the pru-dence never to practice either of them." This was exhibited in social dis-approval of any manifestation of better than average education or refine-ment of taste—that was "putting on airs." Such manifestations were
called "aristocracy," though actually they were no more than the vague
and inexpert gropings of the plutocracy for something higher. The will
of the majority was accepted, not so much because it was right (there
was always vigorous opposition to that idea) as because it would in-evitably prevail until a new majority arose to overthrow it.

Social insistence upon conformity and mediocrity meant that men who
would otherwise have led truly progressive movements had to devote
their lives to strengthening the tribal mores. A few broke away and
Materialism despite taunts and mobbings sought to smash their prison
barriers; they were the great reformers, or the faddists and
fakirs. For other individuals with initiative and ability there was still one
exit open: the road to the amassing of wealth. Probably this road was
left open because the material needs of a new continent were so clearly
evident, even though there was risk that the one who gained wealth
would break through the crust of mediocrity by his mere economic
strength and destroy the careful barriers against individualism. At any
rate, that is what happened. Since material gain afforded the one road of

exit, it was well traveled; and those who reached the mansion at its end were regarded with admiration, a little suspicion, and in time growing hostility. This materialism should not be confused with realism; the latter is a proper grasp of *all* the factors in a situation—material, psychological, and idealistic.

And yet just as plain was the existence of idealism, so close beside materialism that the two seem joined together. The materialist dreamed of factories, cities, and railroads, and he made them come true. He dreamed of setting the American flag in the Pacific, and he did. These accomplishments to him were not solely material, **Idealism** for over them all was spread the mantle of equality of opportunity and free institutions. He knew nothing of art or literature, but he did know something of an idealistic way of life, and he coveted it for his children's generation. His own peccadilloes he saw as temporary and necessary in the rough beginnings of civilization; once the material basis was laid, those who came afterward could go on to higher things. Money was simply a measure of accomplishment and perhaps of power.

Another significant contradiction lay between our inferiority complex and our complacency. It is a well-known psychological fact that one boasts in order to offset a feeling of inferiority. We could not match the art, the traditions, or the elegance of Europe, but we did **Inferiority** have size. Therefore we found something incomparably ad- **versus** mirable in size, mass, weight, quantity, and numbers. Amer- **compla-** ican accomplishments became unique, simply because they **cency** were American. Boastfulness easily became complacency. The crude bumpkin, Yankee Doodle, and the slippery Brother Jonathan (both British characterizations) became the shrewd, tolerant, and benevolent Uncle Sam. With peace and prosperity came greater self-confidence. God must be on our side or we would not have prospered so mightily. Edward Everett remarked smugly that "our government is in its theory perfect, and in its operation it is perfect also. Thus we have solved the great problem in human affairs."

The average American was too often bored by other cultures and contemptuous of other ways of life; this attitude gave him an air of confidence and relaxation, which was often interpreted as the consciousness of power and has even passed muster as sophistication. Indeed, the American has been a strange mixture of loneliness and gregariousness, of naïvety, curiosity, shrewdness, and of contemptuousness of what he cannot understand or cannot have, even though he may have cloaked his feelings in good-humored ridicule. Americans have had a sort of swaggering air, which moved Chesterton to remark that they were born drunk. Sometimes we have been thin-skinned and suspicious; again, we have been bumptiously self-confident or friendly as Newfoundland pups. Kipling, perhaps, was not far wrong when he described an American in these biting lines:

> Enslaved, illogical, elate,
> He greets the embarrassed Gods, nor fears
> To shake the iron hand of Fate
> Or match with Destiny for beers.

This brings us to the closely related but equally amazing contradiction between the American desire to dominate and the desire to be loved—or, if you prefer, to be accepted and depended on. Both were natural human traits but were accentuated by our circumstances. Americans had usually themselves or in the persons of their ancestors fled from an unequal contest in Europe. They brought with them a host of resentments, for instance, their fear of aristocracy, of established churches, and of standing armies, and they sought to prove their own worth by winning a position of dominance. Unfortunately Europe persisted for the most part in regarding its lost sons and daughters as barbarians. Naturally we were puzzled, hurt, resentful, and at times unreasonable. Suspicion marked our private and public actions. We laugh at the Japanese classification of foreign nations into friendly enemies, neutral enemies, and hostile enemies; actually we have had rather similar feelings all through our history.

Desires to dominate and to be loved

We were conscious, nevertheless, of our inexperience and uncomfortable because our great wealth bred jealousy abroad. We tried to purchase goodwill by unparalleled gifts. We poured out our money like water in the support of missionaries and for famine and earthquake relief, and we were naïvely puzzled that the world loved us so little. Even today we have still to learn that the rich and powerful are seldom loved, no matter how generous or helpful they are; the world calls such manifestations arrogance and shows jealousy and resentment. The best we can expect—and, indeed, far more useful than love—is respect, and then only when we have earned it, not bought it.

This pathetic desire to be loved was shown sometimes by the way in which we rejected our prospective friends before they had a chance to reject us. Perhaps we used it to cover our own fear and hostility. The history of our foreign relations is haunted with illustrations of our fear of being rooked, especially by England. The clearest example, however, occurred in 1782 at the close of the Revolution. We had by the terms of our alliance with France agreed not to make peace without French consent, but John Jay, fearful that France would deny us the trans-Appalachian West, hastened to get in the first double cross by making an arrangement with England to get that West; his argument was dubious, but Congress accepted its benefits.

One of the most striking inconsistencies in American character was the simultaneous existence of tolerance and intolerance. We believed in free institutions and equality of opportunity, and by and large we probably had the highest batting average of any great nation. **Tolerance** On the other hand, it is a very human tendency for the pleas- **versus** antly situated to regard their society as the permanently **intolerance** desirable one. We have never, therefore, been without bases of intolerance both on the part of those who want change and those who resist it. One such controversy rages over whether to accept Orientals and Negroes as first-class citizens, and it breeds the view that they should be accepted at once without regard to their fitness, and on the opposite extreme the view that they should not be permitted to prepare for acceptance. When it is asserted that capitalism is synonymous with democracy, both capitalists and socialists rush to take their place in the battle lines.

Optimism has been the key to American history, optimism because of past successes and future prospects. The American accepted the idea of progress without serious cavil. The shortcomings of the past did not worry him; this was not the land of his fathers, but of his chil- **Optimism** dren. James Wilson, who helped to write the Constitution, **versus** regarded it as setting up a nation founded on men's like- **pessimism** nesses, not their differences as in other nations. Democracy is an act of faith, and the very boldness of its optimism calls forth a response in the people. They obey the laws because they make them. "It is really an incredible thing," said De Tocqueville, "to see how this people keeps itself in order through the single conviction that its only safeguard against itself lies in itself." At the same time our optimism asserted that all problems have a solution, and this very assertion prevented deep understanding. We had a strong tendency to oversimplify, partly because we were bored by what we could not understand, partly because we thought in terms of black and white. In American novels and movies the hero and the villain have usually been sharply distinguished. When we looked at troubles in a foreign nation we saw only two parties, the one that was right and the one that was wrong—unless we decided both were wrong—and we took sides with the "oppressed."

Pessimism, save when used for dramatic effect, has been the unforgivable sin, and yet it has never been far from the surface. The Federalists, it will be remembered, fervently distrusted human nature; and in the end they vanished, at least partly because the country got tired of their glooming. The conservatives learned their lesson and since then have concealed their pessimism. They became professional optimists, and their booster clubs have given a rather desperately determined air to American optimism. Nevertheless, both optimism and pessimism are basically expressions of Calvinism's doctrine of predestination. Everything will turn out all right because God is on the side of America; the majority is right, or if it is not it will be succeeded by one that is, because the peoples' hearts are open to truth and justice. Or conversely, everything will turn out wrong because human nature is depraved, and the masses will be too strong for the enlightened few and eventually will bear them down in a vast Ragnarok.

These conflicts and contradictions in American character caused us to vacillate between extremes and rightly laid us open to the charge of being inconsistent and unpredictable. Emotionalism was illustrated in religious

Emotionalism
excitements, in reformist fads, and foreign relations. Our anger was easily stirred by real or fancied insults to national honor. Our sympathies were easily evoked by the sight of hardship and oppression. We repeatedly put our hands to the plow of responsibility, then proved ourselves unfit for the kingdom by looking back and wandering off to hunt for birds' nests. Such wisdom as there was in foreign policies was of executive creation, often against the will of Congress, and such responsibilities as we shouldered were thrust upon us by sudden crises or by catastrophes such as Pearl Harbor. We have been unusually susceptible to newspaper propaganda and to slogans such as "Remember the Maine!" and "Fifty-four forty or fight!"

Too often we found relief from emotionalism only by taking refuge in sentimentalism—the refusal or inability to recognize reality and the embracing of a myth. It was illustrated above by Everett's statement

Sentimentalism
that "we have solved the great problem in human affairs," a statement made at the very time when the operation of democracy had never been so seriously threatened. Sentimentalism governs whenever we refuse to look at the facts but nevertheless boast of perfection in civil rights, social equality, and freedom of opportunity. Sentimentalism thus excuses our evasions and permits our sores (foreign and domestic) to strike inward until such major operations as world wars are necessary. And even if the operations are successful, the patient may die.

The American has been, perhaps more than anyone else, a man of conscience. It is commonly said by cynical critics that the "American way" is one of intolerance, race prejudice, and legal and economic oppression. Noth-

Conscience
ing could be more wrong. American history is concerned with those problems not because they are more common here than in other nations but because we have refused to become reconciled to them and have never for long given up the fight against them. The tremendous part played in American history by conflicts over land, abolition, race equality, and economic concentration are but outward manifestations of bitter inner tensions, which rise from the refusal to be

reconciled to what is regarded as wrong. Conscience, in its social sense, rises from the ability to look in two directions at once—toward the practical program and toward the ideal—and from the realization that the ideal program cannot succeed unless it has yielded enough to the practical to give it a firm foundation. Hence the bitter struggle all through American history over what shall be the terms of the compromise between the practical and the ideal. Hence also the necessity for defenders of slavery to rationalize it as a public, private, and moral good, and hence Ingersoll's rationalization that atheism would promote the homely virtues. The cynic (one who denies the existence of moral standards) was rare in America until the twentieth century.

The American has seen this struggle as part of the universal search for moral values. Hence the American mission. We have pointed out that the contradictions in the American character arise both from national immaturity and from the opportunism of democracy. So long as we are democratic we can never settle down to a completely predictable pattern, nor should we desire to. **American sense of a mission** Nevertheless, we have possessed from the eve of the Revolution to the present day a distinct sense that we have a national mission. Every nation convinces itself that it has something good to offer the world and usually it has, though not always the thing it prizes most highly. Our mission is to spread the gospel that in the democratic process we have found a universally applicable way of life; our youthful optimism and reformism make us certain that sooner or later the world will accept it.

It was obvious to our ancestors that God had designed North America, or at least the better part of it which was bound together by the Mississippi River system, to be one nation. There was a smug sense of security. As that arch-Federalist, Timothy Dwight, put it in an optimistic moment:

> See this glad world remote from every foe,
> From Europe's mischiefs, and from Europe's woe.

The Calvinist concept of a chosen people flourished vigorously. "We are the peculiar people," said a Charleston editorial writer in 1845, "chosen of the Lord to keep burning the vestal flame of Liberty, as a light unto the feet and a lamp unto the path of the benighted nations, who yet slumber or groan under the bondage of tyranny." This was uttered in blank disregard of the existence in Charleston itself of a class which "slumbered or groaned" under the bondage of slavery! Such quotations could be multiplied until they would fill the remainder of this volume. As level-headed a man as Lincoln shared the sentiment. The Declaration of Independence, said he, gave "hope for the world for all future time. It was that which gave promise that in due time the weights should be lifted from the shoulders of all men, and that all should have an equal chance."

It is obvious that however sincerely Americans have held to their sense of a mission, and however significant and useful a factor that mission may be in world history, it nevertheless rose not solely from our security but from our insecurity. Separated from the main stream of Western Civilization, we sought a means of unifying ourselves around a concept that would give us world significance. Because we were rootless we had to build our own contribution, and we found it in the glorification of our free and equal institutions. This has at times taken on the character of Pharisaism: one of the defenses of isolationism was that we could not afford to soil our pure democratic robes by intimate contact with the wicked world. It has never been a conscious intention to force our institutions on others (with the possible exception of Japan), but we have sought to teach by example. One cannot read widely in American history without being struck by the real anxiety in every time of crisis lest democracy be stamped out and the hope of the world vanish with it. There is about it the naïvety and charm of youth, but more than that, the splendid idealism of youth. Let us hold fast to that fact as we wade through the sordid puddles of selfishness and irresponsibility which lie here and there across the path of American progress.

BIBLIOGRAPHICAL NOTE

The Age of Reform

GENERAL: Best of the numerous treatments of reformism before 1860 is Alice F. Tyler, *Freedom's Ferment* (1944); it contains excellent bibliographies of each phase. See also Donald O. Wagner, *Social Reformers* (1934); and of course Vernon L. Parrington, *The Romantic Revolution in America* (1930, v. 2 of *Main Currents in American Thought*).

EDUCATION: Joy E. Morgan, *Horace Mann* (1936); Bernard C. Steiner, *Henry Barnard* (1919); Donald G. Tewksbury, *Founding of American Colleges* [to 1860] (1932); Wilbur H. Phillips, *Oberlin Colony* (1933); Thomas G. Woody, *History of Women's Education in the U.S.* (1929); Frank L. Tolman, *Libraries and Lyceums* (1937).

INSTITUTIONAL REFORM: Harry E. Barnes, *The Repression of Crime* (1926) and *The Story of Punishment* (1930); Helen E. Marshall, *Dorothea Dix* (1937); Albert Deutsch, *The Mentally Ill in America* (1937).

WOMEN'S RIGHTS: Gamaliel Bradford, *Portraits of American Women* (1919); Belle Squire, *The Woman Movement in America* (1911); Richardson L. Wright, *Forgotten Ladies* (1928).

PEACE MOVEMENT: Merle E. Curti, *The American Peace Crusade* (1929); *Peace or War: The American Struggle* (1936); and *The Learned Blacksmith* [Burritt] (1937).

CATHOLICISM: Walter Elliott, *Father Hecker* (1891); Arthur M. Schlesinger, Jr., *Orestes A. Brownson: A Pilgrim's Progress* (1939); Ray A. Billington, *The Protestant Crusade, 1800–1860: A Study of the Origins of American Nativism* (1938).

American Utopianism

GENERAL: Old and in some respects outdated, but still good is Charles Nordhoff, *Communistic Societies of the U.S.* (1875). More general and of broader coverage is Morris Hillquit, *History of Socialism in the U.S.* See also Harriet E. O'Brien, *Lost Utopias* (1929); and Arthur E. Bestor, *Backwoods Utopias* (1950).

EXPERIMENTS: On Brook Farm see John R. Codman, *Brook Farm* (1894), and Katherine Burton, *Paradise Planters* (1939); on Oneida see Robert A. Parker, *A Yankee Saint* [Noyes] (1935); on the Shakers, Marguerite F. Melcher, *The Shaker Adventure* (1941); on New Harmony, G. D. H. Cole, *Life of Robert Owen* (1930), and George Lockwood, *The New Harmony Movement* (1905); the Burnt District, Whitney B. Cross, *The Burned-over District* (1950); the Mormons, Morris R. Werner, *Brigham Young* (1925).

The Emergence of American Character

Few American historians have delved into American character deeply enough to come up with much but glib praise. For the most significant analyses we must turn to literary critics, particularly Van Wyck Brooks, Constance Rourke, and Bernard De Voto (the latter is also a historian). See especially Rourke, *American Humor: A Study of the National Character* (1931) and *The Roots of American Culture and Other Essays* (1942); and sundry essays (read with due caution) in Brooks, *Three Essays on America* (1934) and *Sketches in Criticism* (1932), including "The Tradition of Rootlessness" in the latter. Best-balanced of extended treatments is still the second volume of James Bryce, *The American Commonwealth* (various eds.). On the South see that truly remarkable study by Wilbur J. Cash, *The Mind of the South* (1941). Three of the most useful aids in the study of American democratic ideas are Merle Curti, *The Roots of American Loyalty* (1946); Arthur A. Ekirch, *The Idea of Progress in America, 1815–1860* (1944); and Ralph H. Gabriel, *The Course of American Democratic Thought* (1940).

PART III

"A NEW BIRTH OF FREEDOM."

Four score and seven years ago our fathers brought forth on this continent a new nation, conceived in Liberty, and dedicated to the proposition that all men are created equal.

Now we are engaged in a great civil war, testing whether that nation or any nation so conceived and so dedicated, can long endure. We are met on a great battlefield of that war. We have come to dedicate a portion of that field, as a final resting place for those who here gave their lives that that nation might live. It is altogether fitting and proper that we should do this.

But, in a larger sense, we can not dedicate—we can not consecrate—we can not hallow—this ground. The brave men, living and dead, who struggled here, have consecrated it, far above our poor power to add or detract. The world will little note, nor long remember what we say here, but it can never forget what they did here. It is for us the living, rather, to be dedicated here to the unfinished work which they who fought here have thus far so nobly advanced. It is rather for us to be here dedicated to the great task remaining before us—that from these honored dead we take increased devotion to that cause for which they gave the last full measure of devotion—that we here highly resolve that these dead shall not have died in vain—that this nation, under God, shall have a new birth of freedom—and that government of the people, by the people, for the people, shall not perish from the earth.

—Abraham Lincoln, *The Gettysburg Address,* 19 November 1863

THE

SECTIONAL CONFLICT:

1820–1877

We turn now to the great conflict between the sections which has been justly called the ridgepole of American history. The world today looks upon it as a great struggle over the moral issue of slavery, in which right triumphed. Perhaps so. The most difficult thing for any reader of history to grasp is that men of the past did not have our advantage of hindsight, that those who fought against what we now regard as morally right were firmly convinced that their own side was the champion of eternal truth.

The men on both sides in the Civil War regarded themselves as crusaders for Christianity, justice, democracy, and humanity. Sometimes each side had difficulty in realizing the sincerity of its enemies. Tales have been told of the prayer meetings in Stonewall Jackson's army which turned the camp into one great shouting revival. Such manifestations did not occur in the Union army—and yet listen to this.

Lee's army had known a year and a half of such victory that its men never doubted of final triumph when on 13 December 1862 Burnside's army found it firmly anchored on impregnable Marye's Heights above Fredericksburg. That day the Union forces proved their mettle, forming again and again for the charge, and falling in windrows with their faces to the South. Then, as they formed for the last charge, the words of a new song were wafted across the stricken field and rose above the screams of the wounded up to the listening heights.

Mine eyes have seen the glory of the coming of the Lord;
He is trampling out the vintage where the grapes of wrath are stored;
He hath loosed the fateful lightning of His terrible swift sword.
His truth is marching on.

Glory, glory, hallelujah!
Glory, glory, hallelujah!
Glory, glory, hallelujah!
His truth is marching on.

The men in blue sang those strange and terrible words as Cromwell's Ironsides must have chanted Psalms, like "men who made some conscience of what they did." That charge was a bloody failure; Marye's Heights was not taken. But that day the Confederates who listened to *The Battle Hymn of the Republic,* as they crouched behind their breastworks, knew their first doubt of victory.

The South of the mid-nineteenth century was a great backwater wherein was being preserved the older way of life with its rural conservatism and stability, its gracious cultural values, and its relaxed social intercourse. Unfortunately it also preserved the old American Physiocratic narrowness, the stubborn localism of the early Republic, a considerable degree of intolerance for intellectual change, and a growing advocacy of rigid barriers between social classes—especially in the insistence upon retaining Negro slavery. It was probably inevitable that Northern and Southern values should clash, though not necessarily in war. It was also probably inevitable that Northern values should triumph, simply because they were in the stream of history; it is not likely that the South could have long remained apart from this stream, even had it won independence.

Whether moral values were involved and whether right or wrong triumphed is, as we have pointed out, another question. Historians, like people as a whole, once thought of sectional conflict in terms that were primarily moral and ideological, but Frederick Jackson Turner taught us to search for economic and cultural factors as well, and to accept sectionalism as sometimes beneficial in its preservation of diversities and in its social and economic experimentations. Thus, the defeat of the South by no means solved the problems of sectional conflict. It only strengthened Southern determination to preserve certain of its most cherished values, and these have continued down to our own day vitally to deflect and modify the stream of American history.

Chapter XXI

BACKGROUND FOR CONFLICT

1 *The Cotton Kingdom*

By ABOUT 1840 the South—now often known as the Old South—had taken its place on the American scene. The new section found its principal economic basis in slavery and cotton culture; its social basis in class distinctions; and its political basis in the championship first of state rights and then of sectional rights. Like most agrarian civilizations, the South was conservative. The old was preferred to the new; stability was put ahead of progress.

Emergence of the South

A close examination of the South shows far more diversity than is usually recognized, and this not solely in obvious geographical factors. It is true that there were thousands of plantations, large holdings using slave labor and devoted to raising staple crops such as cotton, tobacco, sugar, and rice. However, small farms dominated in the Border States and thrust deep into the Gulf States along the Appalachian highlands and along the Ozarks into Arkansas and Louisiana. Small farmers, indeed, furnished the bulk of the white population in every state, and there were in addition the cattle ranches of Texas and the Gulf region. Cotton was the single most important cash and export crop, but tobacco, rice, sugar, hemp, wool, wheat, corn, and stock were in the aggregate more remunerative.

Southern diversity

Jacksonian democracy had brought about a degree of political equality at strange variance with the usual picture of aristocratic domination. But there were also numerous antagonisms, usually the back country against the cities or the lush plantation areas or both. The South was by no means united in support of state rights, for by 1850 there was a clash between the traditional state-rights doctrine of the Older South and the growing demand for sectional unity on the part of the Old Southwest. Even free trade had its enemies in the South, notably the sugar growers of Louisiana and the hemp and wool growers of the Border States. No city provided a focus for the business, cultural, and social life of the South, but each area gave such allegiance as it chose to its own urban centers. No city, not even New Orleans, was so important to the business and cultural side of Southern life as was New York.

The unity of the South was nevertheless clear. Its boundaries were set by common interests which are easily discernible, however complex the pattern they formed. Foremost was the presence of the Negro both as **Southern** black man and as slave, for this encouraged race- and class-**unity** consciousness. The historian Ulrich Bonnell Phillips found the "central theme" of Southern history in the determination of all whites to preserve white supremacy. The South was overwhelmingly agrarian, and it depended on exports and imports, that is, the exchange of its agricultural products for the manufactured goods of the North and of Europe. Its religious life was dominated by conservative evangelical sects, and its intellectual life by conservative aristocrats. Little affected by direct industrialization or by European immigration or cultural currents, its institutions were still primarily Anglo-Saxon. Nativism, family-consciousness, and localism were still strong. On the whole, the South was satisfied with things as they were, so well satisfied that change was regarded with distaste and finally with fear. In the end the preservation of the *status quo* became the tie that bound the South together in a grand movement for independence.

The South was inveterately agricultural, and yet it was economically created by the Industrial Age. British spinning and weaving inventions and Eli Whitney's cotton gin raised American cotton production from two **The mod-** million pounds in 1791 to two billion in 1860. A vast area **ern age and** which might have proved hospitable to small farms, free **the Cotton** labor, and industrialization was suddenly turned toward cot-**South** ton, slavery, the plantation system, and active opposition to industry. The haste to get land into cotton resulted in unnecessary exploitation of the soil and finally in overproduction. When prices plunged (around 1840) the cotton planter knew no cure but greater production, which led to worse exploitation of the soil, decreasing profits, and to the demand for new cotton lands. Industry had given to cotton the power to mold a peculiar civilization, but now that civilization had to fight for its life or submit to appalling social and economic disruptions.

The peculiar cotton economy and civilization of the South would have been impossible without the power-driven machines and the amazing rise in the world standard of living, which were brought by the Industrial Rev-**King** olution. The South, however, stoutly insisted that the cause **Cotton** lay in the other direction: that industrialization and the rise in living standards would have been impossible without Southern cotton. The fact that cotton production in Brazil, Egypt, and India had for half a century lagged far behind the United States was mis-

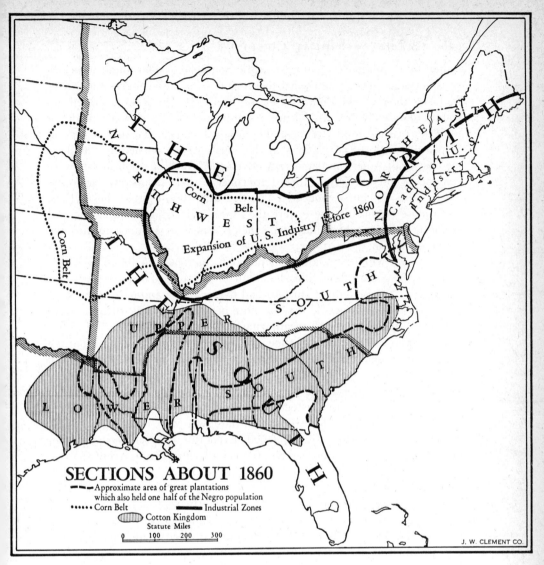

SECTIONS ABOUT 1860

— — — Approximate area of great plantations
which also held one half of the Negro population
••••• Corn Belt   **——** Industrial Zones
Cotton Kingdom
Statute Miles
0   100   200   300

J. W. CLEMENT CO.

read to mean that the South had a natural monopoly on the growth of cotton and could dictate its own terms to the textile manufacturers of Europe and the United States. "Cotton is King" became the watchword of the South, and it was asserted that the fall of textiles would bring down the entire industrial structure and involve the world in ruin.

It has long been a popular opinion that the ante-bellum South was a land of great plantations and pillared mansions presided over by a wealthy aristocracy of Cavalier lineage, broad culture, impeccable manners, and unsurpassed hospitality. The women were invariably gra-   **Southern** cious and beautiful. The men were equally at home in the   **aristocracy:** hunt or under the dueling oaks, riding beside their overseers   **the legend** or declaiming in the halls of Congress, and in their libraries or at fashionable watering places. The remarkable thing is that the legend was ac-

645

cepted by contemporary nonaristocratic Southerners who found vicarious satisfaction in presenting the aristocrat as typical of the South. Such wish-fantasies affected the South's view of itself and led to exaggerated accounts of its chivalry, its culture, its gracious living, and even made an idyll out of the life of the slave. The mythus was carried to Europe and helped to convince the gentry that the South was untouched by the bleak mediocrity of American democracy. Even the Northern abolitionists were convinced and scarcely bothered to conceal their democratic jealousy. There were, of course, Southern families who almost fitted the mythus. Even more important, these were the ideals which most planters desired to meet, a desire which must have helped them to advance toward the actual condition.

The total white population of the South in 1860 was about 8,000,000. Out of 1,500,000 white families, less than 384,000 owned or hired slaves. Of

Southern aristocracy: the facts these only about half had five or more, and only about 8000 possessed the fifty or more necessary to rank them as slave magnates. Even allowing for overseers and other white retainers (who had no slaves of their own but received their living from the institution), something like two thirds of the white families of the South had no direct connection with slavery, and the greater number of those who did had to act as their own overseers or even worked in the fields beside their slaves.* The actual aristocracy of the South, therefore, even allowing for younger sons in the professions and those who were down in their luck probably numbered less than 100,000. Even this number must have included many families who had the requisite wealth but scarcely the cultural background, the so-called Cotton Snobs. One Southern writer insists that there were no more than 500 families of "proper aristocrats." We also know now that even those families who rightly regarded themselves as aristocrats were not often descended from Cavalier stock, as they so fondly believed, but had largely risen from the ranks of yeoman and redemptioner immigrants.†

If there were eight thousand slave magnates in the South who lived after the aristocratic tradition, there were certainly many times that number who lived in log or clapboard houses, struggled with failing land and failing cotton prices, and had no leisure or money to devote

Small planters to cultural pursuits and to long vacations at Northern watering places. Their plantations were often run down, the yards weed-choked, the roofs leaking, the windows broken, and tools and furniture scattered about in careless confusion. They looked as though

* These figures are drawn from the tabulations in James G. Randall, *The Civil War and Reconstruction* (1937), 61.
† Thomas J. Wertenbaker, *Patrician and Plebeian in Virginia* (1910) knocks such wishful thinking in the head. Anyhow, what makes genealogists so innocently confident that all ancestral wives have been faithful?

their owners were only camping—as was often the case, for many small planters deliberately planned to wear out their poor acres and move on.

Squeezed in among the planters or occupying greater areas in the less desirable regions was the yeoman. Working in the fields beside his few slaves or without the help of slaves, he was quite unaware that the white man could not endure the Southern sun. His cash income **The** was low, but his food crops were bountiful. He may have **yeomanry** been hotheaded and intellectually narrow, but he was hospitable, courteous, sometimes pious, and possessed of a self-respect, courage, and salty common sense which made him the backbone of the South. Sometimes his sons became mechanics or tradesmen in the towns. On the whole, the yeoman was held back by the competition of slave labor, by his inferior lands, and by poor transportation facilities which made it difficult to market his produce. His chance came with the end of slavery, but even before the Civil War he had produced leaders who rose into and ranked with the aristocracy, among them Andrew Jackson and Jefferson Davis. Others with yeoman background were Abraham Lincoln and Andrew Johnson.

Somewhat akin to the yeomanry but even more cut off from the world were the Appalachian mountaineers or Southern highlanders. Their way of life was that of the pioneers, and their dialect and their songs had a flavor of Elizabethan times. Slavery did not touch them, and **The moun-** black faces were a rarity among them. Though they pre- **taineers** served many of the superstitions and customs of earlier days, their choice was deliberate. They despised the effeminate trappings of the outside world and the mad pursuit of progress and regarded their own crude, simple, rugged life as more satisfactory. Though they had little use for courts and laws and were not opposed to slavery as an institution, they nevertheless rather generally took the side of the Union during the Civil War.

At the bottom of the social and economic scale, and despised even by the Negro slaves, were the poor whites. Though they had swarmed from the same hives as the rest of the South, bad luck, shiftlessness, or actual choice made them inhabitants of swamps, pine barrens, pal- **Poor** metto wastes, or the sterile hills between the river valleys. **whites** There they lived in tumbledown shacks, hunted, fished, farmed a little, raised big families, and fell prey to hookworm and malaria. Dietary deficiencies resulted in pellagra and in the peculiar habit of clay eating. Sallow, lanky, misshapen, shambling in gait, and morally defective, the "po' white trash" were properly named. The terms hillbilly, sandhiller, and cracker were first applied to poor whites but have since been extended to other classes. Contented with little, they asked only to be let alone and took little part even in such popular pastimes as politics. Poor whites, it should be added, existed in other sections, and even in the South they were a distinct minority whose number is estimated as anywhere from a few thousand to a few hundred thousand. Obviously the line between poor white and yeoman was not clear, and the observer drew it wherever he chose.

Sentimentalists have greatly exaggerated both the romance and the oppressiveness of the Negro slave's lot. The whippings, brandings, and burnings alive set forth in abolition literature may well have occurred, **Misconceptions of slavery** plus innumerable unrecorded routine brutalities. On the other hand, there is just as much evidence that slaves were able to impose upon the good nature of their masters, and that they were spoiled more by lenience than by cruelty. Slavery breeds in the slave a measure of laziness and irresponsibility which by turns goad the master to severity or wear him down to indifference.

Actually the slave's economic condition was superior to that of most of the world's free labor and even of millions of contemporary whites in the United States. Slavery was a system of social security which covered the slave "from the cradle to the grave." Barring certain knotty **The lot of the slave** philosophical problems concerned with the desirability of liberty, it is likely that most slaves were nearly as well off economically as their masters. Of course, slaves bowed low in the presence of the superior race, and when addressed roughly and imperiously they humbly held their tongues and cast down their eyes. Of course, there was the pain of being torn from parents or children, the occasional terror of sadistic beatings, the frustrations of being mere chattels, and the hopelessness of freedom on this side of death. The lot of the slave is never enviable even though he is physician to an emperor or commander of the armies of the Grand Turk.

Slave families usually lived in log cabins, "the quarters," grouped together at some distance from the master's dwelling. Rations of cornmeal, pork, molasses, and other staples were issued regularly, and the slaves were encouraged to have their own poultry and gardens. Clothing was rough and cheap, but most slaves managed to provide themselves with gala attire. The most intelligent and presentable slaves were employed about the mansion (if there was a mansion), and the others were field hands. Working hours in the busy seasons were from daybreak to sunset with liberal time off at noon. Tasks were set by the master or overseer, and the field labor was performed by gangs under the immediate supervision of slave straw bosses called "drivers." Women and children were employed at the lighter tasks, and due allowance was made for expectant mothers; sometimes day nurseries were provided. Slaves who became ill were attended by white physicians, and usually the mistress added nursing to her household duties.

Masters and overseers were perpetually concerned with slave morale. There were rewards as well as punishments, for on the whole the Negro was regarded as a child. A long stint of labor would be followed by a feast and a dance, sometimes shared by the slaves of several plantations. Churches were established and camp meetings held, though they were increasingly subject to the supervision of white ministers. Slaves were encouraged to form permanent marriage unions; but slave marriages were not legally recorded, and divorces could be granted by the owners. Unfortunately chastity was rare among slaves, and white men often set so poor an example that miscegenation was evident everywhere; just how much is hard to say. There were many crimes of violence, both against fellow Negroes and against whites. Petty thievery was even more common and, indeed, became so normal that it was overlooked as long as it was not carried to an extreme.

Slave morale

One of the most remarkable features of Southern slavery was the relative degree of contentment exhibited by the slaves. Most runaways were simply impulsive absentees, perhaps tired of work or protesting against a speed-up, though of course some were seeking to return to old homes or to get back to their families. Despite the assistance of the abolitionists, it is estimated that only about seventy-five thousand Negroes got away to the North, though doubtless more tried it. Though a number of projected slave revolts were detected, the only one which caused serious trouble was that of Nat Turner in 1831, in which nearly sixty whites were killed in Virginia's Southside. At any rate, whites all over the South were alarmed, and the slave codes were tightened. Conspirators were brutally punished, slave gatherings were limited or prohibited, slaves were confined to their plantations unless provided with passes, and it was forbidden to teach Negroes to read or write. Actually it would have been impossible to enforce such rules rigorously. Slave men found it easy to slip away to the swamps or to visit their inamoratas on neighboring plantations, and they were seldom caught by the white patrols which occasionally rode the highways. Many of the more intelligent Negroes learned to read and write, often taught by members of their owners' families.

Slave codes

The decay of the plantation system in Maryland and Virginia left owners in those states with surplus slaves for whom they could not find employment, and who were in the current term "eating their heads off." Naturally many masters sold their surplus slaves for export to the Cotton States. Abolitionists accused them of "breeding" slaves for export, but actually Negroes and whites were increasing at about the same rate. The increasing price of slaves in the newer Cotton States made slave trading a lucrative business and led to a futile demand for the reopening of the African slave trade. That South-

The slave trade

erners suffered some twinges of conscience may be guessed from the way in which slave traders were universally despised. In truth, the way in which traders tore slaves from their families, herded them into stockades, chained them in coffles, and plied them with whips on the march—all of these actions could only be distressing to humane observers.

Free Negroes had been common in the South from colonial times. Some of them managed to attain financial success and even held slaves of their own. The rising fear of slave revolt and the irritations engendered **Free Negroes** by abolitionists increasingly laid strictures upon the conditions of emancipation and handicapped free Negroes, especially in the lower South. In that area their number did not increase greatly in the decades before the Civil War. Of about five hundred thousand free Negroes in the United States in 1860 half were in free states and half of the remainder in Maryland and Virginia. There simply was no secure place for free Negroes. Those in Northern states were limited in exercising the rights of citizens but were well off compared to those in the South, who almost always lost to white complainants. Even worse was the way in which slave catchers in the South were able at will to charge free Negroes with being runaways, and to make the charges stick. It has been claimed that for every slave who got away to the North a *bona fide* free Negro was reduced illegally to slavery.

It is apparent that until the very eve of the Civil War most American whites differed but slightly in their attitudes toward slavery. The Northeastern states had freed their slaves, but the current opinion in that area **Attitudes toward slavery** that Negroes were irresponsible and incompetent made most people appreciate the tremendous social problem that would follow upon emancipation in the South. The southern parts of the tier of states north of the Ohio had been largely settled by Southerners, and the state legislatures remained friendly to slavery until the influx of Northerners swung the balance of opinion; indeed, actual slavery existed in Illinois and Indiana until 1840. As for the nonslaveholding yeomen and poor whites of the South, they usually regarded slavery as the natural condition of Negroes and bitterly opposed emancipation as a social menace. Even the North yielded to emancipation reluctantly, and then only as a war measure, for it also feared social chaos as a result. Reconstruction confirmed most Northerners in their opinion, and in the end they tacitly left the management of the freedmen to white Southerners. At no time either before or since the Civil War has any appreciable number of white Americans, Northern or Southern, been willing to yield white supremacy.

These powerful psychological considerations helped to override the increasingly apparent fact that slavery was not the unalloyed economic success that some of its proponents claimed. The cost of slaves was high and land was cheap, therefore the tendency was to exploit **Decrease of** the land and when it wore out to demand new lands. It was **plantation** not until the middle 1830's that the Gulf states overtook **profits** the South Atlantic states in cotton production, but by 1860 the former were producing twice as much as the latter. The shift was largely responsible for the fact that the price of slaves continued rather consistently to rise, even though the price of the cotton they grew declined. Cotton was being grown in the Old South at what amounted to a loss, and even in the new Cotton States profits declined after 1850 and were seldom more than two per cent. Most planters, however, were innocent of cost accounting and failed to recognize their serious situation. Those who did recognize it often strove mightily to restore soil fertility and with it the profits of slavery, but in the long run they had to abandon the defense of slavery on economic grounds and pass on to social grounds.

Actually cotton could be produced as cheaply by free labor on a fertile small farm as by slave labor on a fertile plantation. Why, then, did the plantation system persist? For one thing, even though the slave might produce less than a free man, the surplus above mainte- **Persistence** nance belonged to the master and gave the owner of a plan- **of the** tation a presumptive advantage over the owner of a one-man **plantation** farm. Cotton kept the hands fairly well occupied for about **system** nine months a year, and the other three months could be used in clearing new fields; moreover, the fact that it required little skill made it suitable for slack slave labor. Again, social prestige in the South had always been accompanied by ownership of plantations, and, indeed, trade and manufacture were regarded as ungentlemanly. Therefore social as well as economic climbers tried to develop large plantations, and those who had them tried to keep them. Lastly was the power of inertia. Even if it had been socially respectable to abandon agriculture and go into industry, and even if the original capital could have been salvaged or the slaves trained to run machinery, the shift would have entailed serious risks for the ignorant entrepreneur; it was better to remain in a business whose pitfalls he understood, however precarious it might be.

Of course, this does not tell the whole story. The Southern way of life had a special attraction for all classes, each after its own fashion, but with certain fundamental values in common. It was these values that helped to balance the picture of economic loss in the minds **The South** of individuals. They believed that the unique rural civiliza- **as a rural** tion of the South had stemmed from England, but that it **civilization** had been improved and stabilized by the new milieu. To the more obvious joys of politics, hunting, and social gatherings they added the rich texture of days passed in unhurried pursuit of business or of frankly relaxed leisure. "Southrons" saw themselves as individuals first, and only secondarily as members of society, and they took such pride in this attitude that they held an erroneous picture of the Northerner as a wage slave, a mere robot. Only Southerners knew how to "live," and they regarded any change as dangerous to their perfect existence.

The South clearly had a poorly balanced economy, and most of its ills rose from this fact. Since cotton's margin of profit was so narrow, it had to exploit the soil and go on to new; when suitable cotton lands were **The** used up, disaster was sure to follow, barring the little-**Southern** expected interposition of science. The planter was extrava-**dilemma** gant, and low prices merely spurred him on to greater pro-duction. Instead of growing all of his own food, he purchased much of it; and instead of patronizing Southern yeoman farmers, he purchased from the corn belt, whose products were more easily accessible. Thus, the poor whites and many yeoman farmers were largely self-sufficient and bought little of either home or foreign products. The cotton planter was over-capitalized, but he could not easily reduce his labor force. Even if he were willing to defy social taboos and go into manufacture or transportation, he would have found it difficult to transfer his capital; and in any case the result would have been to undermine the way of life of which South-erners were so proud. It was begging the question to lay the entire blame for the South's economic subservience upon either slavery or Northern exploitation. It was a Gordian knot which could be done away with only by the sword of a Grant—or by the passage of time.

2 Machine Tools and Corn Belt

It was for a long time the fashion to regard the Civil War as an "irrepressible conflict" drawn upon the stage by a destiny as inexorable and inescapable as the web which the Fates wove about the characters **Hindsight** in a Greek play. We are not so certain now. Indeed, it would **and the ir-** seem that more intelligence and restraint on both sides **repressible** would have forestalled conflict. But we have the advantage **conflict** of hindsight. We might suggest that the plantation South was a casualty in the greater struggle between merchant and industrial capital: a casualty because it did not succeed in playing the two off against each other but ineptly managed to combine them against it and to give them the aid of its own ally, the agrarian Northwest.

The merchant capitalists of the North had early gotten under the skins of Jeffersonians by their demand for dependability in business conditions, chiefly through reliable banks and sound currency. By the 1830's most Southern planters had come to approve of much **The cotton** the same policy, and many of them came to the rescue of **triangle** the Second Bank of the United States. Indeed, a third of the Bank's stock in American hands was held in the South, and a quarter of its currency was circulating in the South. An even stronger tie between the South and the Northeast was cotton. New York merchants had built up the "cotton triangle"—which included rice, sugar, and naval stores—by establishing shipping lines, chiefly to Charleston, Savannah, Mobile, and New Orleans, which carried Southern cotton to the North and to Europe, brought manufactured goods from Europe to New York, and distributed them to Southern ports. It was in reality the cotton triangle which gave New York its overwhelming commercial importance, for the grain of the West was not yet moving to Europe in sufficient quantities to provide profitable eastward cargoes.

Northeastern sympathy with the South was further enhanced by the dependence of New England's textile mills upon cotton and by a growing fear of inundation by foreign labor, a fear strikingly akin to the South's fear of servile revolt. Taken together, New York merchants and New England textile manufacturers constituted a **Cotton Whigs** powerful interest which opposed any attempt to widen the breach between the sections and which for a long time dominated the Northern wing of the Whig alliance. So clear was their sympathy with the South that they were known as Cotton Whigs. By 1837, however, the plantation South awoke to the fact that New York controlled its commission houses and its shipping so tightly that it was able to set freight rates, insurance premiums, interest, and commission merchants' charges. Merchant capital was accused of working its old trick of squeezing the customer for its service of place-utility. By this time New York's throttle hold on the cotton trade was so tight that any Southern rivals who might try to buck the monopoly would only lose their capital. Instead of being allies of the Cotton Whigs, the plantation South saw itself taking a position of subservience.

Merchant capital had received repeated discouragements from the time of the Embargo, and some of it had begun to shift even before the War of 1812. Merchant capital was traditionally interested in "nonproductive" enterprises such as money exchange, speculation, **Change-** and place-utility, and as seaborne commerce began to de- **over of** cline it turned toward banking, real estate, canals, and rail- **merchant** roads; thus it laid the groundwork for its later rebirth as **capital** finance capital. Since American commerce was going over to foreign bottoms, Northern merchants could less than ever afford to sacrifice or even share their control of the cotton trade.

Meanwhile the rule of merchant capital was falling before industrial capitalism. The attempt of industry to obtain a protective tariff which would give it a monopoly of the domestic market had been thwarted in 1833 by South Carolina with the aid of Northern merchants, **Sources of** but industry was far from being arrested in its growth by **industrial** that fact. Industrialists, refused the domestic monopoly, **capital** handicapped by the death of B.U.S., and avoided by European lenders who had been bitten by the canal bust, scrabbled elsewhere for capital. The government's policy of disposing of minerals and timber at give-away prices constituted a subsidy of incalculable value, not the least aspect of which was the gold of California. Just as important was the habit of small manufacturers' keeping what labor regarded as an undue share of the profits in order to plow them back into the enterprise. In the long run this self-dependence was an invaluable stabilizing factor.

The decline of the American carrying trade, it has been noted before, was in part caused by Great Britain's heavy subsidization of its own merchant marine. American carriers obtained modest Congressional subsidies, **Interpretations of laissez faire** but in the end the South vetoed them and helped to drive the merchant capitalists over to the side of the industrialists. Northern industrialists prated of their allegiance to laissez faire. What they meant was that foreign competition should be excluded from the American scene, and that American industrialists should compete without government interference, though of course government favors such as protective tariffs, cheap raw materials, and subsidized transportation systems were not government interference. They reinterpreted democracy as naked individualism. Each preached that the strongest should win —often meaning the shrewdest, most efficient, and most unscrupulous— and that government aid should be given to him freely but withheld from rivals and laborers. Cotton Whigs were aghast at any interpretation of laissez faire which would have enabled the South to buy in the cheapest foreign market and heartily approved Marshall's decisions, which sheltered commerce and industry under Federal wings and forbade state interference. Actually the South was more consistently laissez-faire than the North. It favored competition both domestic and international, and it opposed government subsidies except, as we shall see, for the extension of slave territory and the reopening of the African slave trade.

Marshall had interposed his decisions between rising capitalism and the attempts of the states to limit its rise, but the states through Congress had continued to seek to limit Federal subsidization of capitalist enterprises. **Substantive due process of law** Capitalists now began to see that the Federal government not only must be persuaded or forced to subsidize them more freely by tariffs and cheap raw materials but must be prevented from substantively limiting their growth. The Fifth Amendment to the Constitution had declared that no person should "be deprived [*by the government*] of life, liberty or property, without due process of law." The South claimed that this clause should protect the slaveholder's property in slaves in the territories, which of course were subject to Federal law; the North claimed that it should protect the Negro from being subjected to or held in slavery in the territories. In these contentions both had passed from "due process of law" as mere procedural guarantees of a fair trial in the courts to "due process of law" as a substantive limitation of Federal legislative right to deal with slaves as property. But one looked upon the problem from the standpoint of the slaveholder, the other from that of the Negro.

However, on the whole the South was concerned to limit "due process of law" to procedural guarantees of a fair trial. It had good reason. The progress of the concept of law as an expression of natural law had finally reached the place where lawyers could seriously hold that the Higher Law laid certain ethical prohibitions upon legislatures, regardless of constitutions or customs. That is, "due process of law" examined not only the *how* of a law's application but *what* it was. The rising capitalists of the North, frustrated by Southern vetoes of internal improvements, protective tariffs, and banking legislation, began to sense (though not clearly at first) that "due process of law" could be invoked not only to guarantee fair trials but to prevent substantive encroachments by Southern agrarians upon the "rights" of property in commercial and industrial enterprises. Bear this in mind, for the Civil War by its defeat of the planting South was to open the door to a new day of capitalist domination. That neither side was without its motives is shown also by the way in which Southerners, after burning abolition literature in the mails, defended the act on the ground that the welfare of the community should be placed above the law, meaning above procedural guarantees.

Meanwhile the Old Northwest was becoming more clearly differentiated from its partner, the Old Southwest. Actually it comprised two areas. The southern parts of Ohio, Indiana, and Illinois had been settled chiefly by Southerners and now were in fellowship with Kentucky and Tennessee. The Ohio Valley was a vast border region which was torn between the Cotton South and the Great Lakes region and like its great son, Henry Clay, preferred any compromise to the disruption of the Union. The Great Lakes region, settled primarily by New Englanders and European immigrants, was nationalist, antislave, conservative Whig, and influenced by Eastern reformism.

The Old Northwest

The distinctions between the two parts of the Old Northwest did not destroy its essential unity, especially as the northern parts of Ohio, Indiana, and Illinois became more populous. Its people hesitated to tamper with slavery where it already existed and were a unit in favor of white supremacy. They wanted public improvements and free land and, in general, favored annexation of Texas and other Western areas. The gracious soil of the corn belt was covered with prosperous farms from Ohio to Iowa, actually small individual aggressively capitalistic enterprises whose owners had not yet fully grasped the fact that their interests might differ from those of

Decline of Northwestern agrarianism

industrial capitalists. In the middle 1840's about ninety per cent of the Northwest's exports of corn, meat, and whisky went to the South; and milling, packing, distilling, and leather, wood, and metal working were becoming important industries.

When the spread of canals and railroads filled the Great Lakes region and turned its produce toward the East, the influence of the small farmer and processor was strengthened. In 1860, though the total exports to the South had increased and were still very important to the Ohio Valley, a far greater proportion of the Northwest's produce was finding its way to the East and to Europe. When Cyrus McCormick began manufacturing his reapers at Chicago and there was a leap in the export of wheat to Europe, it only accelerated the growth of the consciousness that the future of the Old Northwest lay in commerce and manufacture as well as in corn and hogs. Its people were now incorrigibly middle-class and looked upon the farm, free labor, and the self-reliant industrialist as part of the order of Nature. It was another harbinger of ill to the agrarian South.

3 *The Antislavery Impulse*

When we treated Northern reformism in the generation before the Civil War, we pointedly omitted abolition. It is now our task to turn back and examine the way in which the cocksure transcendentalist helped to change American history. It was the black abolitionist angel that stirred the economic and social waters into moral motion. It is now less than two centuries since any important segment of mankind began to look upon human slavery with any appreciable degree of abhorrence. Granted that it is morally reprehensible in our modern context, the fact remains that the nations were not willing to part with the institution until it had become unprofitable or interfered with profits in some ways. Even Northern sentimentalists waited until then to make their monumental discovery that slavery in one part of the nation interfered with the proper working of democracy everywhere.

In the great days of antislavery agitation there was a sentimental tendency to see slaves only where slavery existed in *legal* form. Actually slavery can take other forms: social, economic, political, and psychological. The South, in defending legal Negro slavery, was quite correct in pointing out that the North held slaves as truly even if not as obviously in the persons of apprentices, many wage earners, and women who did not control their own lives and property. The fact that the Negro slave had a higher standard of living than many free white men was tossed aside by abolitionists on the ground that a man's economic condition meant nothing unless he had the political and civil rights to defend it. This fact

Slavery and sentimentalism

was true, yet again the South was correct in pointing out that the North did not have clean hands, that Northern Negroes were the victims of all types of discrimination only a little less than Southern slaves.

Objections to Negro slavery had been voiced almost from the time of its introduction, but the most continuous protest was made by the Quakers of the Philadelphia area, who regarded it as inconsistent with Christian principles. Foremost was John Woolman, the modest Quaker whose *Journal* has been called "the sweetest and purest autobiography in the language." Woolman was followed by **Origins of abolitionism** Anthony Benezet, a French-born Quaker teacher whose antislavery pamphlets furnished the impulse behind the British crusade for emancipation. The ideas of Natural Rights and of liberty pricked the conscience of many patriot leaders, and even in the South emancipation had many supporters until cotton began to offer its economic arguments. Prominent during this interim period was Benjamin Lundy, another Quaker, who was connected with a series of abolition papers, of which the best-known, *The Genius of Universal Emancipation*, was published wherever he happened to be. It is a striking fact that of Lundy's one hundred thirty abolition societies (up to 1827) one hundred were in slave states and included four fifths of the total membership. North Carolina alone had ten times as many members as New England plus New York.

The American Colonization Society, whose life extended from 1817 to 1912, was founded to return free Negroes to Africa "with their consent." All together it did return about twelve thousand persons, either free or emancipated for the purpose. The motives of the founders and supporters of the society were curiously mixed. Basically it pandered to the general belief that the Negro was biologically inferior and could not be adapted to civilization; by returning free Negroes to Africa it claimed that at **The American Colonization Society** one stroke the institution of slavery would be stabilized, a social menace would be removed, and a practical means would be offered of lessening a deep moral stain. It is not remarkable that the society never summoned any considerable body of opinion to its support, was poorly financed, and in the end was regarded by abolitionists as a supporter of slavery and by proslave men as abolitionist.

The abolitionist movement owed its dynamism to a marriage of New England's transcendental reformism and the evangelical zeal of New York's Burnt District. In western New York a lawyer named Charles G. Finney suddenly turned into a flaming evangelist and in the 1820's and 1830's conducted a movement often called the Great Revival. Among Finney's "holy band" of evange- **Theodore Dwight Weld (1803–95)** lists was Theodore Dwight Weld, born in Connecticut and reared in upper New York, a young man of unusual maturity, intelligence, and charm, and a scion of the famous New England families of Edwards, Dwight, and Hutchinson. Gifted with a magnificent physique, a handsome countenance, melodious voice, and rare courage, Weld was expected to accomplish great things. Yet he was self-effacing, abhorred conventions and the holding of office and titles, published little in his own name, and took little part in the controversies which rent the reform movement. Even before he met Finney in 1825, Weld had been an advocate of temperance and women's rights. Finney's converts were usually abolitionists, but in Weld abolition found a crusader. His innate modesty could not conceal the fact that he was transcendentally certain that he had truth by the tail. And yet he had no personal enemies and no public ones except the enemies of his cause.

The factor most influential in rousing American interest in abolition and in promoting a movement for centralization of local abolition societies was the British crusade for emancipation which culminated in **The American Anti-Slavery Society** success in 1833. In the same year local abolitionist societies were united into the American Anti-Slavery Society, founded upon the British model and looking to British emancipation leaders for inspiration and approval. The society was formed chiefly under the patronage of the two Tappan brothers, Arthur (1786–1865) and Lewis (1788–1873), pious and wealthy silk merchants who had long been promoting good deeds through the New York Association of Gentlemen. The objective of the new organization, "immediate abolition, gradually accomplished," was interpreted to mean that agitation for eventual emancipation should be commenced at once.

Unfortunately the phrasing lent itself to the accusation that the organization sought to free the slaves at once, regardless of the cost to society. That was not intended to be the meaning of the phrase, but there is no doubt that it was what many abolitionists wanted. Current opinion of Negro capabilities was so low that abolitionism immediately became anathema, even in the North, and was almost universally denounced in press and pulpit. Mob action followed, and leading abolitionists suffered in person and in property. The effect in the South may be imagined.

One of Benjamin Lundy's co-workers in Baltimore had been a half-educated printer of Newburyport, William Lloyd Garrison. Garrison presently went to Boston and on 1 January 1831 issued the first number **William Lloyd Garrison (1805–79)** of his famous weekly *The Liberator*, devoted to abolition, immediate and absolute. The leading article ended on this intransigent note: "I am in earnest—I will not equivocate— I will not excuse—I will not retreat a single inch—and *I will be heard*." Garrison never abandoned this note. He was a pacifist— but a militant fighter; a moralist—but an enemy of orthodox Christianity; a theorist—who demanded immediate results; and a patriot—who damned the Constitution as a covenant with death and an agreement with hell, and rather than truckle to the slave states urged the destruction of the Union.

Garrison was a maverick who would not run with abolitionists unless they knuckled under to his leadership. Reformers are a notoriously contentious crew; so for years Garrison numbered only a few well-known names among his followers, chief of them Wendell Phillips, the eloquent Boston lawyer who supported Garrison's demand for division of the Union. Yet Garrison was regarded then by outsiders as the leader of the abolitionists, and the opinion has persisted. Actually *The Liberator* never

The exhortatory main head of *The Liberator*

sold more than three thousand copies an issue, but Garrison's quotable invective found an immediate hysterical response in the South, which served to make him the symbol of abolition. The State of Georgia set a standing offer of $5000 reward to anyone who would kidnap him and bring him into Georgia's jurisdiction for trial on the charge of instigating servile revolt. In 1835 in Boston itself he barely escaped being strung up by a mob of frock-coated Cotton Whigs. He loved it.

Garrison's rancorous diatribes did more to hinder than to advance the cause of abolition. The real work of the crusade was done by quite another element than the Garrisonians. Arthur Tappan's interest in Christian education was stimulated by the existence of a large body of young men, chiefly Finney's converts, who thirsted **Lane Seminary** for theological training. He now proposed to establish a theological seminary for the education of ministers and with Weld's approval endowed a half-formed institution in Cincinnati called Lane Seminary. The seminary opened its doors in 1833 under the presidency of Lyman Beecher. It had a large body of mature students of whom Weld was the leader, and most of whom had been seasoned by service in Finney's "holy band" or in some of the numerous reform movements then sweeping the country. Beecher was the leader of a group of popular preachers in New England who had further weakened Calvinism by craftily reconciling the old theology with the new liberalism and preparing the masses for the leaven of reform.

Lyman Beecher, always eager to campaign against sin but loath to be too specific, sought to reconcile abolitionism and colonization. Soon after he entered upon his duties at Lane Seminary he found that his student body (many of its members Southerners) was, under the influence of Weld, going over to abolition as the result of a "debate" which lasted for eighteen days and was accompanied by much prayer and soul-searching. This debate attracted wide attention in the reformist press, and further interest was aroused when the students successfully set up an educational program for the free Negroes of Cincinnati. By now the example of the Lane students was starting an agitation in other colleges, and in the summer of 1834 a meeting of college executives hastily passed a resolution calling for the suppression of the antislavery movement among students.

The Lane "debate"

A struggle ensued between the Lane trustees and the student body while the nation looked on with bated breath. Finally in 1835 the students, backed by Tappan, moved to the new college of Oberlin, thereby giving that institution its character as a center of abolitionism and Negro education. Presently Finney joined the Oberlin faculty, and the remainder of his life was devoted to the movement which had sprung from his spiritual loins, though he went along with a heavy heart because he foresaw civil war. Weld was not impressed by his mentor's fears but rejoiced at the vision of the "storm blast with God in the midst." At first even abolitionists seem to have regarded the Lane rebels as juvenile idealists; actually they included the coming leaders of the abolition movement. Beecher alone seems to have recognized that their deep evangelical zeal was a far more dangerous weapon than the scornful futility of Garrison. His daughter Harriet was a fascinated listener to the stories of cruelty presented as evidences of the sinfulness of slavery, and her novel *Uncle Tom's Cabin* was a belated fruit of the great "debate."

The Lane rebels

The next summer one of Weld's converts, a lawyer and planter of Kentucky and Alabama named James G. Birney, organized the Kentucky Society for the Gradual Relief of the State from Slavery and proposed to found an antislavery paper in Danville. In July a highly "respectable" mob seized Birney's press and forced him to leave the state. He now joined forces with the Lane rebels, and together they embarked upon a crusade for abolition, with academic freedom and freedom of the press as the essential weapons of their campaign.

James G. Birney (1792–1857)

The methods which the Oberlin Volunteers used were primarily religious, patterned upon Finney's evangelism. Their arguments in this phase were not filled with hatred nor often with stories of cruelty; their one aim was to convince the national conscience that slav- **The** ery was a sin and should therefore be abolished. Regardless **Oberlin** of whether it was Constitutional, it violated a Higher Law, **Volunteers** one before and above the Constitution, the natural right of men to own their own bodies, participate in their government, and mold their opinions and acts by the dictates of their own consciences. Abolitionists suffered for their faith. Birney's press was destroyed by a Cincinnati mob. The abolitionist temple in Philadelphia was burned. Elijah Lovejoy, publisher of an abolitionist paper in St. Louis, was driven from the city; when he settled across the river in Alton a succession of presses were destroyed, and finally he was shot by a mob. Abolition evangelists seldom escaped being rotten-egged or stoned, but they were preaching a cause in which they believed, and within five years of the Lane secession they had covered the North and had planted the seeds of abolition everywhere in the form of antislavery societies. Weld in Ohio alone can be credited with the conversion of three men who were to become abolitionist giants: Joshua Giddings, Edwin M. Stanton, and Benjamin F. Wade.

The American Anti-Slavery Society at first undertook a zealous pamphleteering campaign. This stirred such anger in the South that bundles of pamphlets were taken from the mails and burned, an action which was finally condoned by President Jackson. By 1836 the success of Weld's method was so evident that the society reduced its appropriations for pamphlets and increased its support of abolition evangelists: Weld's famous "seventy." At Weld's direction the movement sought a firmer basis by working in rural sections, and there abolitionism grew quietly yet rapidly, all but unobserved by the city newspapers.

The literary aspects of the abolition movement were not confined to pamphleteering. A growing demand for more solid food led to the preparation of a long list of testimonies and arguments. The first sort is best illustrated by Weld's *Slavery As It Is: Testimony of a* **Literature** *Thousand Witnesses* (1839), a collection of anecdotes about **of abolition** the brutalities of slavery which was circulated by the hundreds of thousands. The great importance of Bible arguments to a pious generation led to the publication of numerous exhortations against slavery on the grounds that the Bible was against it. Pious and profane alike were titillated by stories of miscegenation and lustful orgies between masters and slaves. Abusive terms, such as "The Slave Power" and "Lords of the Lash," were applied to the South and to Southerners and came to be reflexive images in many Northern minds.

Abolition journals were legion, and they gave circulation to yet another type of propaganda, the antislavery poem. Most significant of abolitionist poets was John Greenleaf Whittier, a New England Quaker

Antislavery poets

of delicate health and retiring disposition. He earned a meager living in various editorial positions, chiefly on reform publications, was active in antislavery politics, and directed his poetic talents so unstintingly in the service of abolition that he has been called the poet of human freedom. Scarcely less significant to the abolition cause was James Russell Lowell, Boston Brahmin, literary critic, and editor of the *Atlantic Monthly* and the *North American Review*. Though he published occasional antislavery poems, his chief service lay in the powerful political satires collected as the *Biglow Papers*, which first appeared in opposition to the Mexican War and the extension of slavery. By that time the intelligentsia had in general joined the antislavery (if not the actual abolition) forces; one of the first was the influential Ralph Waldo Emerson.

The abolitionist movement was now divided into three wings. The Garrisonians demanded abolition, immediate and absolute ("immediatism") regardless of the consequences, but they were weakened by their

Abolitionist wings

leader's rancor and by his growing hostility to the churches, which almost without exception refused to march under his banner. The Oberlin evangelists preached that slavery should be abolished first and foremost because it was a *sin*, but they were vague about time and manner. A third group, which Beecher represented and sometimes dominated, taught that slavery was an *evil* but not a sin; they were concerned with making headway in the South, an impossible feat if they insisted that slavery was a sin. Actually the last two wings publicly supported gradual approach to emancipation, but it was easy for proslavery men to damn them in the eyes of the American public by tarring them with Garrison's immediatism. Few abolitionists had thought the problem through to the extent of advocating a practical program by which emancipation could be instituted without plunging the country into chaos.

Abolition broke into politics in 1836 with the Congressional struggle over the right of petition. The existence of slavery in the District of Columbia, however miniscule its importance, was resented by abolitionists,

The Gag Rule

and for years they had delighted to plague Congress with petitions for its abolition. In 1836 (a presidential year) the number of petitions had so increased that Congressional business was all but stopped. Finally the House voted to lay such petitions on the table; the gag was renewed annually until in 1840 it was made a standing rule with the added proviso that all antislavery petitions should likewise be tabled.

The abolitionists were delighted. They claimed that their opponents had openly denied the right of petition guaranteed by the First Amendment, and the result was seen immediately in added support of antislavery organizations. An unequaled subject of agitation had been offered the abolitionists, and the nation had to sit up and take notice; the effect was to enable them to regain **The right of petition** most of the ground lost by the public's misunderstanding of the Tappans' immediatism. Of course, there were two sides to the issue; certainly Congress could not drop all other business and devote itself exclusively to antislavery petitions. But the Gag Rule only increased the flood, and ingenious ways were found of needling the proslavery cause by sending in petitions on subjects not covered by the gag.

John Quincy Adams, now a Congressman from Massachusetts, made it his business to lead the fight against the Gag Rule, and he was joined by Northern Whigs who wished to embarrass the Democratic majority. So far as the struggle in the House was concerned, Adams bore the brunt of the fray. Day after day he took up the hours in presenting petitions, dodging points of order, bursting forth in brief invectives so quickly concluded that **J. Q. Adams supports the petitions** there was not time to call him to order, then going on to the next petition amidst shouts from the opposition, ranging from "vindictive spite to the noblest heights of feeling" until his tired old shoulders hunched wearily over his desk. But he accomplished his purpose of keeping the antislavery issue before the public and of smoking out the sections on what he sincerely believed was the cause of human freedom.

Even though the Whigs continued the gag in force when they came into power, their action did not affect the problem. The right of petition and abolition had been linked as a sectional issue. An aroused electorate in the North was questioning candidates as to their views and was even going forward to agitate in the state legislatures against the "black laws" which discriminated against free Negroes. At the same time proslave sentiment in the South was drawn together and strengthened by Adams's challenge.

Antislavery sentiment was growing by leaps and bounds, and by 1840 there were two thousand societies with close to two hundred thousand members. The central direction, however, had broken down, for the movement was torn among differing opinions and rival leaders. The zeal of the Great Revival was passing, and abolitionists were now hating the sinner as well as his sin **Abolitionist dissensions** and casting the blame on the South. Northern mobs were fewer, but the fury of Southern and Border area mobs increased as Southern resentment grew. The Panic of 1837 struck a severe financial blow to the tottering structure of the American Anti-Slavery Society, and it was scheduled to be dissolved at the annual meeting in 1840. Garrison ran an excursion steamer loaded with Lynn abolitionists to the New York convention and took over the society, lock, stock, and barrel. Thenceforth it was his shadow—and it had little more substance than a shadow. The Tappans formed the American and Foreign Anti-Slavery Society and in 1840 supported James G. Birney on the Liberty Party ticket for the presidency.

It now remained to establish abolition in the political arena, for Birney's Liberty Party gave no omens of success and Adams was too old for sustained conflict. Adams had been backed by a tiny coterie of abolitionist representatives led by Weld's convert, the uncompromising, severely moralistic Joshua Giddings. In 1841 Giddings and his Select Committee on Slavery took over active direction of the petition campaign and brought Weld to Washington as lobbyist and researcher. Weld was not among strangers, for his boarding hall, soon known as Abolition House, was filled with his converts, both Congressmen and visitors. With Giddings planning the strategy and Weld furnishing the ammunition, the abolitionists deliberately sought to interject the slave issue into every possible opening.

The Great Revival reaches Congress

Presently the *Creole* case played into Giddings's hands. In 1841 some slaves being transported in the ship *Creole* by sea from Hampton Roads to New Orleans had seized the ship, killed one of the owners, and taken refuge in Nassau; there the British released all but those charged with the murder and refused to surrender them upon the demand of Secretary of State Webster. Giddings at Weld's suggestion now asserted in the House that since slavery could exist only by state laws, slaves were free once they reached the high seas where Federal law ruled the ship. The House stopped Giddings and censured him. He resigned, was triumphantly re-elected by his district, and upon his return to Congress promptly finished his speech. Thereafter slavery was subject to open discussion in Congress and no longer needed to be covered by agitation for the right of petition. Two years later Adams won his long fight, and the Gag Rule was revoked. Even more important, the abolition issue had escaped the control of party leaders. Its leadership had passed from private societies and agitators and had been lodged with the politicians. Abolition as a matter of conscience was now represented in Congress; the next step was the formation of the Conscience Whigs, but that was a later story.

Giddings forces the slave issue on Congress

4   *The South as a Conscious Minority*

The Federal census of 1790 showed that the population of the United States was almost evenly divided between North and South, though of course about seven hundred thousand people in the South were Negro slaves. The Three-fifths Ratio gave the North a slight advantage in the House of Representatives, but there seems to have been a confident expectation in the South that population growth would soon place the control of the Union in the hands of that section; otherwise, as some candid souls admitted, the South would not

The South a minority

have approved the Constitution. By 1810 the North had unmistakably forged ahead in population, and in 1820 in the House it enjoyed 123 Representatives against the South's 90. Only in the Senate were North and South equal.

The slavery issue was thrust into national politics with dramatic suddenness in 1819. Northerners, especially the commercial men of the Northeast, had long resented the Three-fifths Ratio and were anxious to find a way of attacking it. When Missouri petitioned for admission to the Union, Congressman James Tallmadge of New York proposed, as an amendment to the enabling act, that no more slaves be brought into Missouri and that those already there be gradually emancipated. The clear intention was to prevent the Three-fifths Ratio from being applied to any more states and to weaken the agrarian alliance between South and Northwest. Southern insistence on equality in the Senate did not bring on the conflict, nor did the moral aspect of slavery, so far as we can tell, have any part in the origin of the amendment though, of course, the moral drums were stoutly beaten in rallying its defenders. *(Tallmadge Amendment, 1819)*

The emergence of the slavery issue struck a chill to the heart of every man whose first love was his country. The aged Jefferson wrote that it came "like a fire bell in the night." All over the country the Constitutional and moral aspects of slavery were fiercely debated, and the arguments in Congress forecast many a bitter struggle to come. Finally the House adopted the Tallmadge Amendment, but when Maine obtained the consent of Massachusetts to apply for admission as a state, the raw materials of a compromise were available. The names of Maine and Missouri were not combined in one bill, but it was well understood that they were to balance each other. The compromise was technically the provision that the Louisiana Purchase north of 36° 30′ should, except for Missouri, be regarded forever as free from slavery. *(Missouri Compromise, 1820)*

Missourians were irritated by the Congressional debate because they held with the South that Congress could not lay conditions on new states as the price of admission. Presently they retaliated by drawing up a rabidly proslave constitution which forbade the legislature to pass any act emancipating slaves without the consent of their masters, and which prohibited the entrance of free Negroes into the state. The latter proviso was inconsistent with the Federal Constitution, which provided that the citizens of each state should "be entitled to all privileges and immunities of citizens of the several states." The wrangle was renewed in Congress but died down when Clay persuaded the Missouri legislature to agree to observe the Federal proviso. It was this which earned for Clay his proud title, "Pacificator." *(Little Missouri Compromise, 1821)*

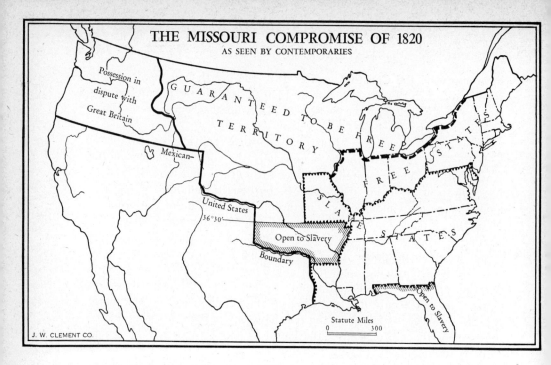

THE MISSOURI COMPROMISE OF 1820

AS SEEN BY CONTEMPORARIES

Possession in dispute with Great Britain

GUARANTEED TO BE

TERRITORY

FREE STATES

Mexican-

United States
36°30'

FREE
SLAVE STATES

Open to Slavery

Boundary

Open to Slavery

Statute Miles
0   300

J. W. CLEMENT CO.

The current opinion that the Great Plains were not fit for white habitation made the division of territory under the Missouri Compromise seem more equable than it finally proved to be. The immediate effect of **Effects of the Missouri controversy** the Missouri Compromise was to crystallize the attitude of Southerners toward their special interests, especially slavery. Though for some time the slavery issue did not openly reappear in Congress, its existence was disclosed by the stiffening of Southern resistance to encroachments on all its interests and by the bitter argument over the matter of sending emissaries to the Panama Conference. The effect of the compromise was strengthened by growing abolition agitation in the North and by the discovery in 1822 of the Denmark Vesey plot for a slave insurrection in Charleston. Since Vesey was a free Negro who had apparently been influenced by abolitionist literature, it was proposed to restrict relations between slaves and free Negroes. South Carolina even provided that free Negro seamen on visiting ships must be imprisoned, and it made the proviso stick in spite of the Federal Constitution.

The reaction was under way. When in 1825 eight Northern state legislatures proposed emancipation at Federal expense, the plan was harshly rejected by the South. From now on the South devoted itself **Southern defense of special interests** to: (1) the search for some Constitutional means of guarding its special interests; (2) the moral defense of its special interests; and (3) the stabilization of the *status quo*.

The Southern search for a Constitutional means of guarding its special interests passed through four stages: (1) local self-

666

government, or state rights; (2) the concurrent voice; (3) Constitutional guarantees; and (4) independence. We have already fol- **Weapons of** lowed through much of the first and second stages in tracing **Southern** the growth of American nationalism and, in particular, **section-** have seen how these weapons were used by New England **alism** Federalists when they were a minority. Here we shall be concerned with their use as weapons of Southern sectionalism.

The weapon of local self-government was wielded by the states either in single or group opposition to the Federal government. State rights were never invoked in a vacuum, that is, they received little allegiance as mere abstract principles unconnected with practical problems. If **State rights** the state or the section was politically ascendant, it saw its interests as those of the nation and was inclined to be nationalist; if it was out of power, it tended to uphold state rights as a protection against the tyranny of the majority. The weapon was brandished by the Virginia and Kentucky Resolutions and used by the New England states during the War of 1812, by Georgia in its defiance of decisions made in the Cherokee Indian cases, and by Ohio in its five-year effort to thwart the Bank of the United States.

Jefferson had sought both the welfare of society as a whole and the protection and expression of individual rights. From these developed two wings of the democratic movement: the plebeian farmers who desired the government (chiefly the states) to promote public welfare **Review of** even if it had to limit individual rights, and the individua- **Jeffersonian** list wing which insisted that the government must stand **splits** aside and let the individual run his own affairs. The latter wing in turn divided into two elements: one the rugged individualist of "big business," and the other the aristo-agrarian individualist fostered by John Taylor and eventually Calhoun.

John Taylor of Caroline rejected Jefferson's concept of conflict between balanced social forces and depended upon the states' holding the balance between a selfish financial aristocracy in control of the central government on the one hand and the chaotic tendencies of **John** the people on the other. The Constitution was a compact **Taylor's** between the states, and the latter were the judges of its **concepts** terms. Taylor authored a long stream of books, articles, and pamphlets, but the most significant in his later career was *Construction Construed and Constitutions Vindicated* (1820), which countered implied powers with the compact theory and asserted that the real issue in the Missouri controversy was the balance of power between the sections. This was followed in 1822 by *Tyranny Unmasked,* a prolix argument against the protective tariff and its creation of an industrial and financial monopoly.

Taylor adapted American Physiocracy to the plantation system. It opposed tariffs, banks, and "paper wealth" and rapidly approached Athenian democracy—a society of aristocrats (or at least citizens) erected on

The "Antique Republicans" an economic basis of slavery. As common interests of the Southern states drew them together to resist Northern attacks, the localism of Jefferson and the compact theory of John Taylor were united into a dogma which a group of embittered Southerners, led by John Randolph, preached in Congress and spread throughout the South at dinners, barbecues, and private gatherings. The rise of the young nationalists during and after the War of 1812 drew the "Antique Republicans" of the South into a desperate little band of "statriots" determined to sell their lives dearly. Actually the economic and psychological tides of the South were running in their favor. The tobacco and cotton kingdoms were drawn together, and the latter took command. South Carolina leadership supplanted Virginia. Intellectual core of this leadership at first were Langdon Cheves and Thomas Cooper. The latter was an Englishman who had exiled himself with Joseph Priestley and had been active in the Jeffersonian conflict. He was now president of the College of South Carolina and author of the pro-Southern *Lectures on the Elements of Political Economy* (1826).

It was not until Calhoun was driven over to the ranks of the localists by the events of Jackson's first administration that the faction was able to develop the discipline of a party and the dynamism of a political pro-

Calhoun takes command gram. To be sure, Calhoun was defending a status, but in the process he became probably the only really original political theorist of the so-called middle period of American history. His chief works are the *South Carolina Exposition*, published anonymously in 1828, and the *Disquisition on Government* and the *Discourse on the Constitution*, not published until after his death.

The freedom of the ballot, said Calhoun, was no guarantee of liberty, for it instituted the tyranny of the *numerical majority*. Only when every interest exercised a check on the others and decisions were watered down

The concurrent voice and compromised until they satisfied all, only then was there a *concurrent majority,* the one effective guarantee against tyranny. Every public decision must be tailored to the satisfaction of the minority, not of the majority. No majority (meaning the North) could institute a policy such as the protective tariff, which injured the interests—which might merely mean desires—of a considerable minority (meaning the South). To prevent such injury the minority was entitled to "a concurrent voice in making and executing the laws, or a veto on their execution." The veto could be overcome only if the minority upon reflection and investigation withdrew it. The concurrent voice has reappeared in our own day, first in Wilson's idea of the self-determination of peoples, and more strongly in the veto in the United Nations. The con-

A POLITICAL GAME OF BRAG .
Or the best hand out of four.

American Antiquarian Society

Brag was the early name for poker. Notice that nullification and antitariff cards are held under the table in this cartoon of 1831. Clay, Calhoun, William Wirt (Anti-Masonic candidate for President), and Jackson are the players.

current voice is the weapon of a minority not simply to protect its rights but to enforce its will.

The concurrent voice found practical expression in the unwritten law which arose from the Missouri Compromise that there must be a balance between slave and free states so that one might check the other in the Senate. There was still the menace of a Northern President, and this Calhoun proposed to meet by having a dual execu- **Nullifica-tion** tive, two Presidents, one from each section, and each en-titled to disallow the acts of the other and to veto Congressional legisla-tion. However, the specific mechanism which Calhoun proposed to use in finding the concurrent voice or in interposing the veto he called "nullifi-cation"; and while he may not have been its inventor, he certainly ranks as its greatest champion.

Any state which felt that its interests were being injured by Federal acts or legislation should call a special state convention which could declare the obnoxious acts or legislation null and void within its borders. The Federal government could (1) yield and withdraw the offense, or

(2) propose a Constitutional amendment giving to itself the disputed power. If the amendment were rejected by the states, the Federal government could not exercise the power. If it were accepted, the objecting state would be overruled; it must submit or consider the course of secession from the Union. Thus, said Calhoun, the creators of the Constitution (the signers of the compact) decided what it meant. Actually the decision was to be made by a minority composed of one fourth of the states plus one, the number necessary to defeat an amendment. The South would have a permanent strangle hold on the Union, which was what Calhoun basically desired, whether or not he saw it in those terms.

Nullification made its entry into Congress in one of the typical political *non sequiturs* so often seen in that body. Late in 1829 the Foot Resolution called for a Senate investigation of the advisability of restricting

The Webster-Hayne debate, 1830 sales of public land—an obvious attempt to limit the growth of the West. Senator Robert Y. Hayne of South Carolina saw an opportunity to strengthen the antitariff forces by winning the goodwill of the West, and on 19 January made an eloquent attack upon the tendency of New England to build up the power of the central government. There was, he hinted darkly, a remedy. Daniel Webster on the 20th came to the rescue of New England in his "Rope of Sand" speech, in which he denied any intention of tyrannizing. As for a remedy, however, there could be none but by the will of the nation; he defied Hayne to show that there was any system by which a state or section could nullify the laws of Congress without making the Union a rope of sand. Hayne accepted the challenge to move to new ground. Parts of two days were occupied in setting forth the first complete exposition in Congress of the remedy: nullification. To the Southerners who listened it was the perfect answer; there was nothing more to be said.

But Webster, who had cleverly led Hayne to make this exposition, had a great deal more to say. On the 26th he rose in the little semicircular Senate chamber, long since abandoned for a more spacious wing, and,

Webster's "Reply to Hayne" speech facing the grizzling Vice-President Calhoun, delivered the most telling defense of Federal sovereignty ever uttered. The magnificent peroration with which he closed his speech was re-echoed in a thousand schoolrooms, and its concluding words became the blood-stirring slogan of the Northern generation which was to fight the Civil War.

> When my eyes shall be turned to behold for the last time the sun in heaven, may I not see him shining on the broken and dishonored fragments of a once glorious Union; on states dissevered, discordant, belligerent; on a land rent with civil feuds, or drenched, it may be, in fraternal blood! Let their last feeble and lingering glance rather behold the gorgeous ensign of the Republic, now known and honored throughout the earth, still

plague originate in the North," said a Virginian phrase maker, "it is sure to spread to the South and to invade us sooner or later: the influenza—the smallpox—the varioloid—the Hessian fly—the Circuit Court system—Universal Suffrage—all come from the North—and they always cross above the falls of the great rivers." The last statement was a crack at the mountaineers, who were not thoroughly loyal to Southern interests.

Both before and since the Civil War it has been a common contention that the South ruled the nation up until 1861 and seceded at that time because it saw its rule threatened. It is certainly true that the South, whatever the proportion of its population, had furnished most of the national leaders. To 1861 nine of the fifteen Presidents had been native or resident Southerners, and all but three of the Northern Presidents had been Southern sympathizers; indeed, the presumably anti-Southern Presidents (the Adamses and Van Buren) had been in office only twelve years out of seventy-two. Four fifths of judicial business originated in the free states, but the Supreme Court had been under a Southern Chief Justice ever since 1800, and eighteen out of thirty-one Associate Justices had been Southerners. The South had furnished two to one the Speakers of the House and presidents *pro tempore* of the Senate. Somewhat the same proportions extended into the executive departments, the diplomatic service, and the officers of the army and navy. Of forty-one Americans rated by the editors of the *Encyclopedia of the Social Sciences* as important in domestic affairs, twenty-seven were Southerners; over half of the men significant in the development of political theory were from the South.

Did the South rule the nation?

These facts show conclusively that the political rulers of the nation were Southerners. They do not, however, prove that the South possessed the economic and intellectual ascendancy, and, indeed, the Civil War was at least in part an attempt to place the political rule in the hands of the economic majority. There were plenty of Southerners before 1860 who denied that the South possessed anything but the appearance of dominance. On the whole the North was on the offensive from 1789, and Southern strategy had to be based on the direction of attack. The South got the best of the tariff struggle, but it lost most phases of its battle to exclude the Federal government from setting the controls (or lack of controls) of business, and the best it could get on the extension of slavery was a compromise. Equality in the Senate was lost, the Supreme Court was shouted down when it tried to protect the South, the Fugitive Slave Laws were nullified in the North, and there was always the fear that an anti-Southern President might some day join forces with an anti-Southern Congress. There was defensible ground for the claim that the South got the honors and the North got the benefits of government.

In view of the South's devotion to the ideal of stability and its refusal to see that the moral atmosphere of the world was changing, it is curious that the Jacksonian impetus toward democracy actually gained **Democratic gains** ground as the positive-good advocates emphasized the line between slaves and freemen. County governments were reformed, legislative districts more fairly drawn, and property qualifications for the suffrage reduced or abolished. Contrary to a common belief the political influence of aristocracy declined, especially in predominantly white areas. Mediocrity was emphasized, and the candidate for office had to cultivate the art of demagoguery, sometimes by chasing lice in the hair of the elector's children. At the same time the new democrats were the loudest advocates of slavery and inveterate enemies of free Negroes; by 1835 North Carolina, the last Southern state to act, had excluded free Negroes from the suffrage. The states which resisted the democratic trend most successfully were South Carolina and Virginia, but even there the resistance showed signs of early cracking at the time when the Civil War began.

The old prejudice against popular education remained strong in the South. About twenty per cent of Southern native-born whites were illiterate in 1850—that is, could not sign their own names—as against less **Education** than three per cent in the North. After 1840 there was a growing demand for libraries and newspapers, and this either caused or accompanied a new interest in public schools; unfortunately the Civil War killed the movement. Despite the paucity of common schools there was no shortage of academies and colleges in the South, and the region boasted half the colleges and half the college students of the nation. Of course, few American colleges outside New England were more than glorified academies, and their graduates were frequently still in adolescence. There was a certain interest in science but even more in the classics and in oratory. Still, what might have turned into a renascence was nipped by the growing slavery controversy. Critics of slavery were weeded out of the faculties, and for good measure religious "skeptics" in faculties and student bodies were disposed of wherever possible. The Southern college became primarily a center of proslave and puritan indoctrination.

Growing conservatism was illustrated in other directions. Nat Turner's Insurrection led to the last serious Southern examination of the slavery dilemma, then abolitionist activity put an end to it. Thereafter few **Curtailment of freedom of thought** Southern editors and public men noted the issue save to fulminate against abolitionism or anyone who did not actively champion slavery. Occasional crusaders for some sort of emancipation remained in Border States, and even a few in Virginia, North Carolina, and Tennessee; some went to the North and became abolition leaders. The laws against the education of Negroes were strengthened. Negro preachers were forbidden to preach or limited in their ministry. Laws were passed prohibiting criticism of slavery and punishing the distributors of incendiary literature; there was a certain justification for this action because abolition literature had almost surely helped to promote Negro unrest and revolt. For the most part the courts were temperate in their treatment of local citizens brought before them for prosecution under laws limiting civil liberties. Nevertheless, the South, while demanding a concurrent voice in the affairs of the nation, had prohibited it within its own borders.

At the same time the South was deepening its religious conservatism. As cotton culture spread, the Episcopalian and deistic planter aristocracy was penetrated by the more "God-fearing" denominations of yeomen who rose into their ranks. The effects of the recent frontier revivals were strengthened by the realization that the Bible, as **The puritan** the bulwark of slavery, deserved Southern adherence. The **South** liberal sects were all but nonexistent in the South, and most of such deists as remained concealed their beliefs. The North, far from hospitable to skepticism, was tolerant by comparison. Southerners correctly identified abolitionism with "universal reform" and endeavored to stop all "isms" at the border, with the notable exception of temperance. On the whole the conservative program was successful. The luxuries and necessities of the North and of Europe were imported, but not their liberal ideas. Presently the churches emphasized their stand by splitting away from their Northern brethren, the Presbyterians in 1838, the Methodists in 1844, and the Baptists in 1845. Technically the split was over slavery. Actually it was just as much an assertion of Southern orthodox rejection of "new light" in theology. The South was now the citadel of puritanism. The angry God of Massachusetts had become the tribal deity of the South, and rising planters accepted with Calvin the belief that prosperity was the test of righteousness.

Newspapers flourished in the Old South, and so bitter were the political conflicts and so touchy the Southern sense of honor that their editors had to be as skillful with the pistol as with the pen. One Vicksburg paper had five editors killed in thirteen years! Magazines were numerous and short-lived. Only three enjoyed a considerable **Literature** measure of success. *De Bow's Review (Commercial Review of the South and Southwest)*, published in New Orleans from 1846 to 1880, was founded by J. D. B. De Bow and was the business voice of the Cotton South. *The Southern Literary Messenger,* published in Richmond from 1834 to 1864, had the advantage of a start with Edgar Allan Poe as editor and went on to become the leading periodical of Southern thought. *The Southern Quarterly Review* (1842–1857) was edited in Charleston by William Gilmore Simms. Simms, the one outstanding Southern literary light of the ante-bellum decades—unless Poe is also rated a Southerner—was a notable victim of the South's neglect of its own literary talent.

The region, despite an educated upper crust, was not ready to stand on its own literary legs. Its people turned to New York, Boston, and London for their provender, quite unconscious of the rich possibilities at their own door, though Simms was limning them in a series of brilliant local-color novels. Simms sacrificed his time, his income, and even his literary integrity in zealous defense of the cause of South Carolina, but he was snubbed to the last as a social inferior—and therefore inferior in everything else.

Here, at the risk of giving aid and comfort to the "great-man" theory of history, one must put a query concerning John C. Calhoun's responsibility for the hastening crisis. Would there have been a war without him? **Question of Calhoun's responsibility** Even in the South many thought that he was using the slave issue as a mere mounting block to power. Of course, it is possible that South Carolina's road to secession was irreversible; nevertheless it was he who watered the seeds of Antique Republicanism and gave form, substance, and strategy to South Carolina's order of battle. Even further, still freely granting that Calhoun was as honest and public-spirited as a politician can be, there is no doubt that much of the Southern impulse to resistance came from him and was directed by him. He created the South's picture of itself as an underdog. His was the voice and the pen that fostered the morbid sensitivity of the South, that harped on Southern rights, white supremacy, and slavery as a positive good, and who consistently exaggerated Northern hostility to the South and to slavery. His emphasis upon Southern honor was a shrewd appeal to Southern romanticism, romanticism in its most invidious sense of rejecting the distasteful fact and accepting the pleasing mythus.

At some time around 1845 the embittered Calhoun seems to have decided that he no longer had a chance for the presidency. Whether or not these were effects, he seems to have decided about the same time that **His methods** secession was both desirable and inevitable, and that the sooner it came the better chance it had of success since the South was losing strength relative to the North. Thereafter Calhoun devoted himself to hastening the showdown, either by forcing the Democratic Party into the Southern camp or by splitting it on sectional lines. His platform was composed of three planks: state sovereignty, Negro biological inferiority, and American Physiocracy. He had none of the arts of the demagogue, but he had other resources. He embodied his metaphysical principles in resolutions, introduced them into the Senate, and launched into exhaustless speeches which were re-echoed throughout the South. Everyone with whom he came into contact was screwed up to high tension by the fierce old man. His was a deadly realistic program, but he was too much the theorist and the fanatic to win immediate general support anywhere in the South except in South Carolina. Southern politicians were concerned with preventing rather than hastening disunion. "Calhoun," said one of them in 1849, "is our evil genius." The last years of his life were thus devoted to protecting the *status quo* by obtaining for the Southern minority either a veto on national policies or independence. "Calhoun," says the Southern historian W. E. Dodd, "died the greatest reactionary of his time."

The fact that Calhoun's fruit was borne after his death and that in the end that fruit was Apples of Sodom should not blind us to his place as one of the greatest figures of American history. Says Gerald Johnson*:

> There is an immensity about Calhoun that compels respect. **His**
> Whatever else he may have been, he was not small. His aspi- **immensity**
> rations were lordly, his range of thought was gigantic, his sense of honor
> was august, his sense of duty was sublime. And his errors were titanic. One
> is tempted to believe that the very excess of his virtues combined into an
> appalling vice. It is by no means certain that it is altogether desirable for
> the political leader of a population of sinful men to be stainless. It may
> lead to arrogant refusal to take into account the weaknesses of ordinary
> people.

We prefer men like Webster and Clay, who, though they had more peccadilloes, also had more humor and tolerance.

We have seen that whether there was a considerable Southern aristocracy is a problem that has occasioned a great deal of heartburning. In any case the aristocratic ideal was sought by the rising mass of Cotton Snobs, and after 1840 there were signs that aristocracy might **The aristo-** flower, if it did not lose its economic basis. Men born in fron- **crat: ideal** tier cabins to the accompaniment of Indian war whoops now **and real** sedulously nursed faint blood connections with Virginia and South Carolina Tidewater gentry and eagerly seized upon the fruits of the family genealogists' naïve search for noble ancestors. The Tidewater influence on manners in the Cotton States was marked, but the Cotton Snob, torn between aristocratic restraint and the self-assertion of frontier individualism, was unsure of himself. The result was that his behavior ranged from the pompous to the overbearing, and the dueling pistols were in constant use. The would-be aristocrat was romantic, hedonistic, violent, leisurely, and wasteful, yet paradoxically terrified of the wrath of a just God. Lastly, the new man accepted aristocratic responsibility, but this was a personal responsibility, not an urge toward a united effort to build a better society. The Southern aristocrat never saw his basic responsibility for the unpro-

* Gerald Johnson, *Secession of the Southern States* (1933), 65.

gressiveness of his section; some bitter Southerners insist that he still does not.

"In its secret heart," says Wilbur J. Cash, the South "always carried a powerful and uneasy sense of the essential rightness of the nineteenth century's position on slavery." But the social and psychological difficulties **Southern** of emancipation made it seek a defense mechanism. It be-**defense** came completely romantic, that is, it knew the truth but **mechanism** rejected it for the mythus. It sought justification by insisting that the ideal had been attained. Slavery was prettified, and the Negroes, quick to recognize their part in the play, took on the role of loyal and contented retainers. Not the least crime of the South was the way in which some white men exploited the complaisance of Negro women. White women were supposed to be blind to the obvious, and for playing the game they were enshrined as madonnas, perpetuators of the sacred mission of white supremacy. The Civil War, in fact, was by some Southerners soberly interpreted as a crusade to save Southern womanhood from a Northern attempt to force them to bear colored children.

Since the Southern way was perfect and its culture the highest of all time, the aristocracy gave itself to political defense against the North rather than to the search for the solutions which might have forestalled **Affirmation** disaster. The aristocrat's political power declined during the **of Southern** generation before the Civil War, but his influence increased. **perfection** Growing Northern pressure and the South's refusal to examine itself were welding Southern white men into an organic whole: a white brotherhood. As the apex of a perfect system, the aristocrats (old and new) were called upon as leaders. The mythus was accepted by all classes of whites, and all alike felt its purifying accolade. By 1840 the South, at least its leaders, had become so clearly conscious of its separate interests that many observant men confidently expected the growth of Southern national consciousness.

Charles S. Sydnor has expressed superbly this affirmation of Southern perfection:*

> The champions of the Old South claimed that theirs was the ideal social order and the only permanently founded democracy, all because it had, with God's blessing, slavery. Surely, Southerners had come a long way from Jefferson and a long way out of reality. Fighting to defend their way of life they had taken refuge in a dream world, and they insisted that others accept their castle in the sky as an accurate description of conditions in the South. . . . It would be fruitless to point to fallacies in their reasoning and to the great contrast between the perfections they described and the imperfections that lay all about them. It would be impossible to guess how many Southerners agreed with these spokesmen in their ex-

* Charles S. Sydnor, *The Development of Southern Sectionalism, 1819–1848* (1948), 338–39.

travagant claims and boastings about the perfect society of the Old South. It is enough to recognize that before the middle of the century there were some Southerners whose minds, under the impact of a long train of bitter criticism of their region and with a realization that the power of their opponents was growing, had turned into this curious, psychopathic condition. And one thing else must be recognized. Even though the idealized portrait of the South was false, it was to be a strong and living force in the years ahead. In the long run, the vision of the perfect South was to supply a substantial element in the construction of the romantic legend about the Old South. In the nearer future, it was to give the Confederate soldier something to die for.

BIBLIOGRAPHICAL NOTE

The Cotton Kingdom

GENERAL: Best one-volume survey is James G. Randall, *The Civil War and Reconstruction* (1937); more detailed and limited in chronological scope is Allan Nevins, *Ordeal of the Union* (2 v., 1947).

SLAVERY: See Ulrich B. Phillips, *American Negro Slavery* (1918) and *Life and Labor in the Old South* (1929); Frederic Bancroft, *Slave-Trading in the Old South* (1931). On free Negroes in the North see Frank U. Quillin, *The Color Line in Ohio: A History of Race Prejudice in a Typical Northern State* (1913).

ECONOMICS: See Emory Q. Hawk, *Economic History of the South* (1934); Allan Nevins, *Ordeal of the Union*, v. I; William C. Bagley, *Soil Exhaustion and the Civil War* (1942); and John G. Van Deusen, *Economic Bases of Disunion in South Carolina* (1928).

Machine Tools and Corn Belt

On the whole subject of the economic springs of the Civil War see Louis M. Hacker, *Triumph of American Capitalism* (1940); and Allan Nevins, *Ordeal of the Union* (2 v., 1947). On the cotton triangle see Robert G. Albion and J. B. Pope, *The Rise of New York Port* (1939). Follow substantive due process of law in Alfred H. Kelly and Winfred A. Harbison, *The American Constitution* (1948), 370, 383, 389, 394, 462.

The Antislavery Impulse

GENERAL: This section follows in the main Gilbert H. Barnes, *The Antislavery Impulse, 1830–1844* (1933); and Dwight L. Dumond, *Antislavery Origins of the Civil War in the United States* (1939). See also Russell B. Nye, *Fettered Freedom: Civil Liberties and the Slavery Controversy, 1830–1860* (1949).

EARLY EMANCIPATIONISTS: Janet Whitney, *John Woolman, American Quaker* (1942); Early L. Fox, *The American Colonization Society, 1817–1840* (1919). On the early period see also William S. Jenkins, *Proslavery Thought in the Old South* (1935).

ABOLITIONISTS: On Weld see Benjamin P. Thomas, *Theodore Weld, Crusader for Freedom* (1950); G. H. Barnes and D. L. Dumond, eds., *Letters of Theodore Dwight Weld, Angelina Grimké Weld, and Sarah Grimké, 1822–1844* (2 v., 1934). On Birney, D. L. Dumond, ed., *Letters of James Gillespie Birney, 1831–1857* (2 v., 1938). On Lyman Beecher see Lyman Beecher Stowe, *Saints, Sinners and Beechers* (1934). On Giddings see George W. Julian, *Life of Joshua R. Giddings* (1892). There are several biographies of Garrison, all bad.

The South as a Conscious Minority

CONSTITUTIONAL DEFENSE: The above Constitutional analysis follows chiefly Jesse T. Carpenter's penetrating study, *The South as a Conscious Minority, 1789–1861* (1930). The Three-fifths Ratio is best handled by Albert F. Simpson, "The Political Significance of Slave Representation, 1787–1821," in *Journal of Southern History,* 7:315–42 (1941).

DEFENSE OF SLAVERY: Most thoughtful assessment of Southern attitudes toward slavery and source of much given above is William S. Jenkins, *Pro-Slavery Thought in the Old South* (1935). On the expulsionists see E. Merton Coulter, *John Jacobus Flournoy, Champion of the Common Man in the Antebellum South* (1942); and Hinton R. Helper, *The Impending Crisis* (1857).

CONSERVATISM: For extended treatments see Clement Eaton, *Freedom of Thought in the Old South* (1940); Charles S. Sydnor, *The Development of Southern Sectionalism, 1819–1848* (1948); and Wilbur J. Cash, *The Mind of the South* (1941)—three of the most brilliant works yet to appear on the South. On the political aspects see Gus W. Dyer, *Democracy in the South Before the Civil War* (1905); and Arthur C. Cole, *The Whig Party in the South* (1913). Literary aspects can be traced in William P. Trent, *William Gilmore Simms* (1892); and John D. Wade, *Augustus Baldwin Longstreet* (1924); both are far more than biographies. On the growth of the Southern mythus see also Rollin G. Osterweis, *Romanticism and Nationalism in the Old South* (1949).

BIOGRAPHIES: On Calhoun see Frederic Bancroft, *Calhoun and the South Carolina Nullification Movement* (1928); and Charles M. Wiltse, *John C. Calhoun: Nullifier* (1949); Calhoun would prefer Wiltse. Other pertinent biographies are Dumas Malone, *Public Life of Thomas Cooper* (1926); and Theodore D. Jervey, *Robert Y. Hayne and His Times* (1909).

Chapter XXII

MANIFEST DESTINY

1 *The Psychology of Agrarian Imperialism*

A STORY is told about a party of Northerners who met in Paris at the close of the War between the States, to celebrate their victory with those sententious toasts characteristic of the day. Presently a Bostonian arose and in cultured accents offered the following:

The universal Yankee nation

"Here's to the United States, bounded on the north by British America, on the south by Mexico, on the east by the Atlantic Ocean, and on the west by the Pacific."

Next came a Chicagoan. "My eastern friend has too limited a view," said he. "We must look to our Manifest Destiny. Here's to the United States, bounded on the north by the North Pole, on the south by the South Pole, on the east by the rising, and on the west by the setting, sun."

Prolonged and boisterous applause followed, but the next gentleman, a Californian, considered the toast too moderate. "With Manifest Destiny in our favor," he cried, "why limit ourselves so narrowly? I give you the United States bounded on the north by the Aurora Borealis, on the south by the Precession of the Equinoxes, on the east by Primeval Chaos, and on the west by the Day of Judgment!"

The exuberance of the Californian typified the great era of American territorial expansion. The words Manifest Destiny seem to have been used first in July 1845 by John L. O'Sullivan, editor of the *Democratic Review* of New York, in an article on the Texas annexation question which decried the attempts of European powers to "check the fulfillment of our manifest destiny to overspread the continent allotted by Providence for the free development of our yearly multiplying millions." This was not by any means the origin of the *idea* of Manifest Destiny, for we have seen how it infected the Revo-

Origin of term: Manifest Destiny

lutionary generation and how it played the major role in bringing on the War of 1812.

The new wave of territorial aggression, which began to rise in the 1830's and reached its crest with the Mexican War, reflected in its origins the growing complexity of the American scene. The movement was still **Agrarian imperialism** basically agrarian. Of course, there was plenty of second-quality land left and, strictly speaking, Oregon and Texas were not needed yet. The planter wing of the agrarian imperialists feared that unless slave Texas were admitted the slave states would leave the Union and unite with Texas. Exponents of state rights felt that expansion and the admission of new states would weaken Federal power to interfere with local institutions, and they pointed out that the abolitionists, the foremost advocates of Federal aggrandizement, were the bitterest opponents of annexations. The proslave argument, offered without humor or intentional deceit, was that the expansion of slave territory would also expand the territory of freedom.

The second great cause of the resurgence of Manifest Destiny lay in fear: American fear of Europe and European fear of the United States. The chancellories of conservative Europe were fully aware of the sprawl- **European fear of the U.S.** ing inefficiency of the United States in its gawky democratic youth, but the lesson of the country's inherent power had been driven home by De Tocqueville's half-admiring, half-horrified, but altogether fascinated analysis of the American scene. The rising industry of the Northeast was regarded as a menace to Manchester and the industrial belt of Paris. The cold-eyed Yankee merchants of New York were molding a financial and commercial wall about the United States which Britishers would soon be unable to pass without their permission. The Cotton South was arrogantly boasting that it could at a word bring civilization down in chaos. Worst of all, the success of the American democratic experiment was encouraging restiveness of the European masses under their kings and nobility.

Just as strong was American fear of European interference. Industrialists feared direct competition. New York feared that Europe not only would breach its wall but would carve out private domains on the Pacific **American fear of Europe** coast and in Latin America. The South feared that its rule of cotton would fall before the competition of the vast prospective cotton lands of a British-controlled Texas. Along with these separate fears went one which shook the nation. A threat to the United States or its welfare was a threat to the existence of democracy and to the American democratic mission. The very least to be expected, proslave men and abolitionists agreed, was the weakening of democratic purity. The welfare of democracy came first; this was the "higher law" of Manifest Destiny.

This view was supported by a series of curious rationalizations: democracy's rights were superior because it was democracy; the necessity for new lands gave a natural right to them and, moreover, Americans would make better use of them than their present barbarous owners; these lands were sparsely occupied, were contiguous to our borders, and were within our "natural" boundaries— **Rationalizations** boundaries which the God of Nature and of nations had marked for our own. The last argument soon developed until its advocates likened the growth of a human political society to the biological growth of plants and animals which ruthlessly overrun or devour weaker competitors. The resemblance to the philosophies of modern dictatorships cannot be escaped. It is a psychology which is common to nations which are building empires, along with the usual protraction that its political and economic and cultural institutions are superior to those of decadent peoples. From this was drawn the curiously inconsistent corollary that therefore it is the "duty" of the strong to "protect" the weak, to bring them the blessings of superior institutions, and to eliminate the international nuisances which exist in the behavior of primitive or decadent nations.

Europeans and Latin-Americans were dismayed by the remorseless progress of the American pioneers, so like the march of faceless and conscienceless soldier ants. Mexicans were particularly alarmed and early analyzed to their own satisfaction the method of American advance by finding the common factors in the absorption of **Mexican view of Manifest Destiny** Louisiana, Natchez, Baton Rouge, Mobile, and finally Florida. Lucas Alamán, a leading conservative historian and statesman, thus epitomized it before the movement for Texan independence and long before its greatest application in the "purchase" of 1848 from Mexico:

They commence by entering the territory they covet, upon pretense of carrying on commerce, or of the establishment of settlements, with or without the consent of the government to which it belongs. The settlers grow, multiply, become the predominant party in the population, and as soon as a foundation is laid in this manner, they begin to set up rights which it is impossible to support in a serious discussion, and to bring forward ridiculous pretensions, founded upon historical facts which are admitted by nobody. . . . These pioneers excite, by degrees, movements which disturb the political state of the country in dispute. When things have come to this pass, the diplomatic management commences; the unrest they have excited in the territory in dispute, the interests of the settlers there, the incursions of adventurers and savages instigated by them, and the persistence with which the opinion is set up as to their right of possession, become the subjects of notes, full of expressions of justice and moderation, until, with the aid of other incidents, which are never wanting in the course of diplomatic relations, the desired end is attained of concluding an arrangement as hard on one party as it is advantageous to the other.*

Here, then, were the two sides of Manifest Destiny. As we shall see, it is impossible to assess to each the exact justice of its arguments. One thing sure is that no party, European, North American, or Latin-American,

Manifest Destiny and the Civil War   approached the court with the first requirement of equity, that is, with its own hands clean. Each party had its own "higher law," carefully tailored to its own needs, and insisted upon its priority. Now it so happens that such "higher laws" are in a practical sense enforced only by the judicial administration of the sword, hence one important cause of the Mexican War. It was in this process, however, that there arose within the United States a struggle over how the welfare of democracy was best to be promoted, and this is what turned the expansionist movement into a quarrel over slavery.

2   *The Borderlands*

Though the Oregon country was technically occupied jointly by Great Britain and the United States, it was, for a generation after the failure of the Astoria enterprise, actually in British hands. Fort Vancouver, on the

McLough-lin's rule in Oregon   site of Vancouver, Washington, was opened for trade in 1825 by the Hudson's Bay Company. There John McLoughlin (1784–1857), the chief factor, ruled a trade empire that extended from San Francisco Bay to Alaska and included around a score of subsidiary posts. The log forts of the company were in several cases the nuclei of future cities and in that day were surrounded by shops and farms and fisheries, for they were so far from civilization that they had to be as self-sufficient as possible. Ships plied to Alaska with flour, to the Hawaiian Islands with lumber, to Canton with furs. Company factors even poached on Russian-American territory until the nonplused Cossacks agreed to a lease. McLoughlin, the lord of this domain, was a huge, white-crested Canadian medico, who ruled with strength and benevolence.

The old medico entertained in hospitable fashion in his log palace, but except for the American ships off the coast he allowed no trade competition. Nevertheless, companies of mountain men began to find their way

American infiltration   over the mountains and were followed by others. In 1833 Nathaniel Wyeth, a Massachusetts ice dealer in search of romance and fortune, blazed the Oregon Trail. Meanwhile in 1831 a delegation of Idaho Indians had appeared at St. Louis to make inquiry about the white man's "medicine," the Bible. As a consequence the Methodists sent out Jason Lee with Wyeth's expedition of 1834, and with

* This is a clarification and abbreviation of the version that appears in *House Executive Documents,* 25 Cong., 2 Sess., No. 351: 312–22.

McLoughlin's aid a mission was established in the Willamette Valley. The next year Marcus Whitman and others sent by the Presbyterians settled near modern Walla Walla, Washington. Canadian Catholic missionaries were not far behind.

The missionaries now began to publicize the beauties of Oregon, its mild climate, and its fertile soil. Oregon emigrant societies were formed, and missionaries returning from furlough by way of Cape Horn brought farmers and craftsmen with their families. Their efforts were reinforced by Washington Irving's popular *Astoria* and *Adventures of Captain Bonneville* and by the writings of Hall **The Oregon fever** Kelley of Boston, who seems to have inspired Wyeth's expeditions. The first wagon train of about seventy emigrants came over the Oregon Trail in 1841. The trail ran from Independence, Missouri to and up the North Platte, through South Pass (Wyoming), across southern Idaho by the line of the Snake River, across the Blue Mountains to the Columbia, and thence by raft to the Willamette. The route was two thousand miles long and took at least six months of arduous travel. Half of the first train split off in Idaho and followed the California Trail to the San Francisco Bay area. Other trains followed in succeeding years. About a thousand persons entered Oregon in 1843, and the tide rose to three thousand in 1845.

These caravans, the stuff of which American legend is made, were usually piloted by one or more of the mountain men who had hunted and trapped and fought Indians in the Rockies until the passing of the beaver hat. During these years explorations along the Oregon Trail marked out better routes and eliminated the perilous Columbia River voyage. Active in this work was a young Georgia-born army officer named John Charles Frémont, who with the aid of his talented wife Jessie, daughter of Senator Benton, wrote a fascinating report which earned him the name "The Pathfinder." On this basis he was to build a flashy and erratic career. McLoughlin's orders from the Hudson's Bay Company were to refuse aid to immigrants, but he contented himself with persuading them to settle south of the Columbia. Indeed, but for his help the sick and half-starved settlers who came down the Columbia might well have perished.

McLoughlin, as chief factor of the Hudson's Bay Company, was law-giver to British subjects in Oregon, but not to Americans. As early as 1838 the mission settlements on the Willamette formed a simple government of their own and petitioned Congress for a regular adminis- **Early government of** tration. A more formal government was established in July **Oregon** 1843, when in the traditional American manner the settlers claimed jurisdiction over the country south of the Columbia, drew up a constitution, swore in an executive committee of three, elected courts and a legislature, marked off counties, organized a militia, and provided for the recording of land claims. On the whole the provisional government was successful, as was presently witnessed when the Hudson's Bay officials north of the Columbia acknowledged its jurisdiction. Meanwhile Indian troubles arose, due to the usual causes plus a plague of measles which they blamed on the whites. The Cayuse rose in 1847 at Walla Walla and massacred fourteen members of the Whitman mission settlement. The provisional government moved promptly to chastise them. One result was that Congress finally erected Oregon Territory (1848) and sent out regular soldiers who overawed the Cayuse. Unfortunately Oregon was disturbed by other wars, the origins of which were not complimentary to the settlers. Oregon was admitted to the Union in 1859, and the remainder of the territory took the name of Washington.

New Mexico was a buffer against the Apaches and Comanches, founded in 1598 by Juan de Oñate. Santa Fe was built in 1609 when Franciscan missionaries were well along with the Christianization of the Pueblo Indians. Then in 1680 an uprising wiped out the missions and **New Mexico** haciendas of the upper Rio Grande, and El Paso became the outpost of Spanish dominion. A few years later the advance of French traders across the plains necessitated the reconquest of New Mexico in a bloody five-year war. The area settled down to its role as a backwater of Spanish culture and by 1840 had a population of about a hundred thousand, chiefly Hispaniolized Indians and mestizos. Santa Fe and Taos became trading towns whence every year traders drove their pack trains to Texas, Kansas, and Utah. The great Taos fair became a regional resort for the exchange of breeding horses and manufactured goods for furs and skins. Captive children brought in by the wild tribes of the plains were an important article of commerce, for the government brought them up as Christians, formed them into the picturesque bands of scouts known as *genizaros* (from the Turkish Janizaries), and used them as the province's chief defense against marauders.

Texas owed its inception as a Spanish colony to the French threat. Explorations were undertaken by the Spanish to counter La Salle's activities, and the area received its name from the Tejas Indians. Attempts **Texas** to found Franciscan missions in East Texas were abortive because of Indian hostility, but before 1700 the frontier of the province of Coahuila was pushed eastward to the Rio Grande. Another attempt followed upon the French advance to Natchitoches on the Red River. San Antonio was founded in 1718, and Los Adaes (twenty miles west of Natchitoches and within present Louisiana) was made the capital of the new province of Texas. The Texas settlements grew, and new ones were added until by the middle of the century they were able to fend for themselves against the Comanches.

Meanwhile along the Sierra Madre Occidental, Jesuit missionaries were working their way into Sonora and Arizona. Head of the missions was the devout Father Eusebio Kino, now as much renowned for explorations as conversions. One of his missions in Arizona which still stands was San Xavier del Bac, founded in 1700 near Tuc- **Arizona** son. A silver rush in 1736 to Arizonac, now within the Sonoran border, gave a name to Arizona.

When the Russian sea-otter hunters began to move down the coast from Alaska and threaten to take over California, the Spanish again resorted to their traditional use of missions as buffers against intruders.

The settlement of Upper California was projected in 1768 by José de Gálvez, Viceroy of New Spain, and carried out the next year under the civil guidance of Don Gaspar de Portolá and the religious guidance of the Franciscan Fray Junípero Serra. Supplies and settlers were drawn from the missions in Lower California, stripping them **Upper California** in the process. Part of the colonists went by sea while others, driving domestic animals, marched northward across desert and mountain.

When the various parts of the expedition met at San Diego, it was found that well over half of the original three hundred had died or deserted. Nevertheless, Portolá pushed on by land to his destination at Monterey while Father Serra remained behind to found the mission of San Diego. By some mischance Portolá passed inland from Monterey Bay and quite by accident found San Francisco Bay. For two centuries Spanish and English voyagers had passed up and down the coast of California without ever becoming aware of this, one of the most magnificent bays in the world!

The missions at San Diego and Monterey were eventually joined by nineteen more. The hardships from disease and starvation were terrific, and it was not until Father Francisco Garcés found a way from Tucson to California that a fourth great pioneer, Captain Juan Bautista de Anza, was able to bring new soldiers, colonists, and cattle from Mexico to a new settlement at San Francisco (1776). El Pueblo de Nuestra Señora la Reina de Los Angeles de Porciúncula—Los Angeles to you—was founded in 1781 by two Spaniards, ten Indians and mestizos, ten Negroes and mulattoes, and a Chinese; Santa Barbara was founded the next year, probably by similar old Spanish stock.

The pattern of Spanish colonization was basically, though not unalterably, the same from Texas to California. The civil and military core was the *presidio,* or garrison; the religious center was the mission; and close by these was the *pueblo,* or Indian village. These **Pattern of** colonies were the centers of fields, vineyards, and olive **Spanish col-** groves; and farther out were the herds of long-horned cattle **onization** tended by *vaqueros* (the tutors of the American cowboy), and on the hills were flocks of sheep and goats. The remoteness of these settlements forced them to become manufacturing centers, and the missionaries were not only

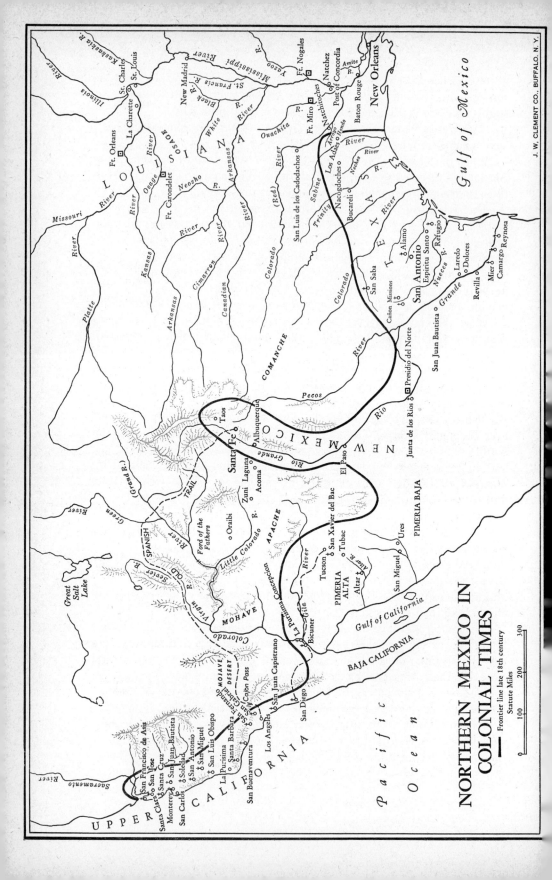

NORTHERN MEXICO IN
COLONIAL TIMES

—— Frontier line late 18th century

Statute Miles

0   100   200   300

J. W. CLEMENT CO., BUFFALO, N.Y.

religious teachers but instructors in agriculture and handicrafts and the managers of great business enterprises. The endeavor of the friars was to spread the Catholic religion and Spanish culture by gathering the wild Indians around the missions and instructing them. As time went on, some settlers obtained royal land grants and built up great haciendas and ranchos. Most of them preferred rural life, and oftentimes they resented the friars' control of the Indians and wished to draw the latter off as workers. Unfortunately the idyllic picture of California's colonial days is pretty much the creation of Hollywood.

The Mexican revolt from Spain was a calamity for Upper California. Sentimentalists deplored the military force sometimes necessary to keep the Indians attached to the missions and demanded that the missions be secularized. They were joined by those who hoped to be able to seize for themselves the use of mission property and la- **Chaos in California** borers. The result was that in 1833 the process of breaking up the missions was begun. What was meant to be a gradual and rational process soon deteriorated into a free-for-all of plunder. The Indians scattered, the remains of the missions were auctioned off, and a relatively few families emerged with great wealth. Vast ranches were put together on the basis of Spanish and Mexican grants, and the province probably possessed a million cattle. All together there were probably about seven thousand Californians of Spanish or Mexican antecedents.

Americans began to enter California early in the nineteenth century, some coming on Boston trading ships and others coming over the mountains to trap beaver. Some became Catholics and married into California families. When in 1836 Juan Bautista Alvarado decided to throw off Mexican rule, he called upon Americans for help. **American intruders** The revolt failed, but Alvarado managed to hold on to the governorship. He now in turn became fearful of an American revolution and arrested a hundred foreigners. Nothing came of it but ill will. One foreigner whom Alvarado delighted to honor was a delightful Swiss immigrant, John Augustus Sutter. With an enormous grant in the Sacramento Valley Sutter built a fort named for himself on the site of Sacramento and apparently plotted to set up the free republic of New Helvetia.

By 1840 California's beauties were rivaling those of Oregon in the American imagination, and part of the first wagon train to Oregon split off to California, though the wagons were abandoned en route. Each year saw a handful of Americans cross the deserts, usually by the California Trail. One group, the famous Donner party, tried a short cut late in 1846, was snowbound in the high Sierras, and resorted to cannibalism before it was rescued. Before the beginning of the Mexican War the Bay region had become the home of about eight hundred Americans who were waiting impatiently for a chance to "play the Texas game." American impatience to acquire California was proved in 1842 when Commodore Thomas ap Catesby Jones, hearing that Mexico and the United States were at war, seized Monterey and ran up the American flag. His information, of course, was incorrect, and he had to haul down the flag and put Washington to the embarrassment of making profuse apologies to the Mexican government.

The long journey across the Great Plains from the Missouri River to Santa Fe had been made by French traders as early as 1739, and after 1800 a number of Americans tried it; usually they ended up in the Spanish calaboose. When the Mexican Revolution swept away trade **The Santa** restrictions, Missouri traders began to wagon goods to Santa **Fe trade** Fe; the first wagon train, which belonged to William Becknell, traversed the Santa Fe Trail in 1822. The usual articles received in trade were mules, furs, and silver. Indian depredations were discouraged by Federal troops. The usual departure point was the famous frontier "jumping-off place," Independence, Missouri, and occasional trains passed Santa Fe and went deep into Mexico. Sometimes Americans stayed in Santa Fe or Taos, and by 1840 there had grown up a considerable number of Anglo-Saxon communities, many of their members old mountain men who had come out of the Rockies to spend their declining years in the sun. Around twelve hundred men were engaged in the trade, and the value of goods exchanged was important for that day, but even more important was the realization that the country traversed was fertile and fairly well watered. This was one of the factors that helped to break down the Permanent Indian Frontier Policy.

Texas was to be the scene of the first serious clash between Americans and a Spanish-succession nation. The province of Texas, between Louisiana and the Nueces River, was a land of forests, savannas, and prairies, teeming with game and all but unoccupied by civilized men. **Americans** As early as the 1790's American traders were bringing **in Texas** mustangs from Texas to the Mississippi, and these expeditions presently developed into a series of storming filibusters which were all defeated, but in which the odorous General James Wilkinson was a common denominator. After the establishment of Mexican independence (with the aid of American adventurers, it should be added), a policy was adopted of encouraging the settlement of foreigners on the vast vacant areas of public land. Thousands of American families flocked to Texas to take advantage of a state law of 1825 by which a man could purchase a *sitio* of 4428 acres for $200—less than the cost of 160 acres of public land in the United States.

In order to hasten settlement, vast grants were made to agents called "empresarios," who agreed to bring in and settle within six years a certain number of families as a condition of receiving titles. The result was that by 1829 most of Texas was covered by the conditional grants to empresarios, which forced would-be purchasers to deal through them or squat in a remote section after the good old American custom. At any rate, the American immigration was so heavy that the population is said to have risen from four thousand (almost all mestizo) in 1820 to twenty thousand in 1830. In the end, most of the empresarios failed to fulfill their contracts. One who did fairly well was Stephen F. Austin, who had inherited a contract from his father, Moses. The capital of Texas was named for the family, and Stephen was the undoubted leader of Texas until the revolution. He was a patient, upright gentleman who sought to live up to his oath as a Mexican official and joined the Texas revolutionary movement only when he was convinced that no other honorable course remained.

The empresarios

Most of the Americans seem at first to have promised to take on the duties of Mexican citizens, even though in so doing they agreed to become Catholics, to use only Spanish in public business, and to submit to laws which they regarded as subversive of self-government. When in 1826 an empresario in East Texas tried to oust the Mexicans and set up the Republic of Fredonia, the Americans marched beside the Mexicans to suppress the revolt. Whether the Mexican government even with the most tactful treatment could ever have made good Latins of the Americans is open to question. Actually they had laid aside little of their Americanism: their colonies, remote from Mexico, were so far as possible run on Anglo-Saxon patterns, and their attitude toward Mexican land laws was based upon the frontier maxim that land belongs to him that gives it value.

Texas attitudes

At this time Mexico was definitely under the rule of the aristocracy. There were, however, numerous cliques among the aristocracy; how much principle there was in each element is open to examination. At any rate, Mexico fell into chaos, with fleeting administrations succeeding each other. The tin-pot Fredonian uprising startled the rulers in Mexico City, and, ignoring the loyalty of the majority and heeding the warnings of Lucas Alamán, they hastened to prohibit further immigration, restrict imports, and abolish slavery. Texans were able to evade the last by making contracts with their slaves, but irritation grew on both sides. Attempts by United States envoys to settle the problem by purchasing Texas were rejected by Mexico with blazing scorn. More than this, American minister Joel R. Poinsett was amazed to find Mexico actually asserting that it was entitled to the Louisiana Purchase on the ground that the Spanish king had no right to dispose of his crown lands. Poinsett, brilliant as the flower which bears his name, was yet a crude and tactless diplomat. Among his mysterious actions was the introduction of York Rite freemasonry into Mexico, presumably as

Mexican repercussions

pro-American rivals to the older Scottish Rite. The inevitable result was a Mexican request for his recall; but his successor was, if possible, even more inept.

By 1830 the Mexican government was ready to impose strict authority on Texas. An army, largely drawn from the prisons, was distributed over the area in convenient garrisons. A squabble over customs regulations on the coast grew into a revolt. It so happened that at this juncture a new star was rising in Mexico. Antonio López de Santa Anna was a frail, thin man with a big head and facile tongue, who gave an impression of simplicity and guilelessness; this was misleading, for he had the energy of a barreled wildcat and the shrewdness and unscrupulousness of a Machiavelli. The Texas rebels, led by Austin, jumped aboard the Santa Anna bandwagon and helped drive it to success early in 1833. Austin then carried to Mexico City the Texan request for a specific reward: the separation of Texas from the state of Coahuila-Texas. Now Mexicans were thoroughly convinced that Washington had planned the Texas revolt as a step toward annexation, so the petition was refused and Austin was put in jail for treason.

Enter Santa Anna

One night in 1835 near Anahuac a group of Texans with ostentatious furtiveness passed a customs patrol with a box. When the patrol ordered them to halt they put up the pretense of a fight, in which one of them received a gunshot wound. Then the box was opened and found to be full of rubbish. Unappreciative of Texan humor, the local commandant asked for reinforcements; they were promised in a letter which fell into Texan hands when a courier was stopped and searched. Thereupon the commandant was forced to leave Texas. Santa Anna ordered the arrest of five of the ringleaders, the Texans flew to arms, and a skirmish occurred near Gonzales. By this time Austin was out of prison, and as chairman of the Texas Committee of Safety he reluctantly took command of a force which besieged a small Mexican army in San Antonio. At this time the population of Texas was probably about twenty-five thousand.

Steps to revolution

In November 1835 a meeting of representatives, called the Consultation, undertook to direct the revolt. As in 1775, the purpose was not independence. What Texas was opposing was Santa Anna's destruction of state governments and their replacement by military tyranny, and a truly deplorable series of duplicities which had ruined all faith in Mexican honor. The local Mexicans, indeed, rather generally joined the revolutionists. Henry Smith, a would-be seceder, was elected governor of the provisional government, Austin was sent to the United States to get help, and Sam Houston was put in command of the army.

The Consultation

Sam Houston, one of the most colorful men in American history, was

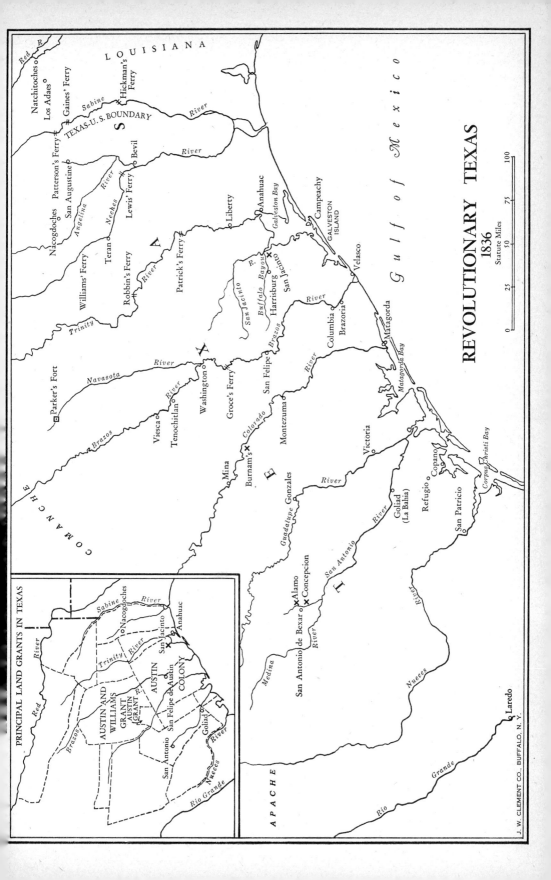

a Virginian by birth and a Tennessean by adoption. His military career began in the Creek War under Jackson, and he was first over the barricade in the charge at Horseshoe Bend. After the war he became governor of Tennessee. A brilliant future seemed to be opening up when suddenly in 1829 his bride of a few weeks left him under circumstances which are still a mystery; Houston resigned the governorship and went to live among the Cherokee on the Texas border. He took no part in the events which brought on the revolution but was present when he was needed.

Sam Houston (1793–1863)

The many hastily organized companies of armed Texans did not propose to submit to the leadership of a commander not of their own direct choice, even so redoubtable a person as Sam Houston. Without plan or common direction they fell upon the Mexican garrisons. In San Antonio the attackers punched their way through the adobe walls of the houses, and in December they forced the garrison to surrender and withdraw to Mexico. While the defenders of Texas were scattered on various foolish ventures, Santa Anna suddenly appeared in Texas at the head of at least 6000 men. Two Texan bands of nearly 500 men were trapped, and nearly 400 of them were massacred after they surrendered. The mission church of the Alamo, across the river from San Antonio, was defended for thirteen days by 188 men, including David Crockett, the Tennessee politician and bear hunter who has become a frontier legend. On 6 March 1836 Santa Anna's trumpets sounded the *degüello*, the dreadful "no quarter" call, and his thousands charged the garden walls, wave after wave, and finally broke over them. Not a Texan remained alive; perhaps 400 Mexicans perished.

The Alamo

While the siege of the Alamo was in progress the Consultation met at Washington, on the Brazos River, and declared Texan independence as of 2 March 1836. David G. Burnet was elected president and Lorenzo de Zavala vice-president. Stimulated by the prospect of liberal land grants, Americans had been pouring money and arms into Texas, and hundreds of volunteer fighters had arrived singly and in groups. Many of the massacred men had arrived shortly before. At last Houston got the remaining bands of the Texas army to listen to reason, and he ordered them to retreat eastward. Ahead of them, traveling on foot or riding whatever beasts or vehicles could be found, trudged the pathetic thousands of Texas women and children: "the runaway scrape." Behind them came the triumphant Santa Anna, burning the towns and homesteads and slaughtering the cattle. Making their way across the swollen rivers as best they could, all Texas poured toward the Louisiana boundary during those fateful weeks of March and April.

Independence; "the runaway scrape"

The only bright features on the Texas side were the superb personal leadership of Sam Houston and the yeoman work of the tiny Texas navy, which was able to disrupt Santa Anna's service of supply. Santa Anna, anxious to overtake the rout, hastened forward with fifteen hundred men and near the San Jacinto River insolently en- **Battle of** camped on a low hill and retired to his tent for a siesta. **San Jacinto,** Then (21 April) Sam Houston and his eight hundred men **1836** **21 April** marched out of the live oaks, with a fife screaming an obscene song, and piled over the breastworks shouting: "Remember the Alamo!" About six hundred Mexicans were killed, and Santa Anna and most of his army were captured. Only a handful of Texans were lost.* Burnet and his cabinet, who had taken refuge on Galveston Island, negotiated the Treaty of Velasco with Santa Anna, by which he withdrew his troops beyond the Rio Grande and agreed to use his influence to win Mexican recognition of Texan independence and a boundary along the Rio Grande from mouth to source. The southern boundary of Texas had historically been the Nueces River.

Houston, who became president for a two-year term (October 1836– December 1838) strove to set the new nation on a firm basis. The Texas war had brought in thousands of turbulent Americans, who turned the army into a mob and clamored for the execution of Santa **Houston's** Anna and the invasion of Mexico. Texas was a frontier na- **first admin-** tion if there ever was one, and its social and financial diffi- **istration,** culties were the old ones of any frontier. Houston tamed **1836–38** the army, refused to goad Mexico, and sent the captive Santa Anna home. Santa Anna promptly went back on his agreement. It signified little, for Mexico, though at the moment torn by internal strife, was not disposed to recognize the fact of Texan independence and announced categorically that American annexation would mean war. The United States cold-shouldered all suggestions of annexation, though early in 1837 it recognized Texan independence, perhaps to beat England and France to the draw. Texas bonds sold poorly because of the Panic of 1837, trade languished, sales of public lands even at bargain prices brought in little revenue, and finally the Texas congress resorted to paper money.

In the light of its problems it was little short of a continuous miracle that Texas was able to preserve its independence for the ten years that it lived under the Lone Star flag. Mirabeau Buonaparte Lamar, a Georgian, succeeded Houston as president (December 1838–December **Lamar's ad-** 1841). He was a man of intelligence, force, and courage **minis-** but with less judgment and character than was needed to **tration,** ensure order in his turbulent country. The Mexicans were **1838–41** no help. Indian unrest at Texan encroachments was easily turned into bloody frontier war. Texan adventurers mixed into Mexico's internal wars,

---

* Warning is hereby given that statistics on the Texas Revolution are not calculated to hide the Lone Star under a bushel.

and in 1841 Lamar sent the McLeod Expedition to seize Santa Fe, which Texas claimed because it was within the asserted Rio Grande boundary. The expedition was so disastrous that it amounted to national disgrace. Lamar's return gesture was to rent the little Texas navy to Tabasco and Yucatán revolutionists!

Houston's second term (December 1841–December 1844) was opened by two Mexican invasions which reached San Antonio before they were repulsed. He was determined, however, to follow peace and retrenchment.

Last years of Texan independence

To get rid of the navy, which was now blithely carrying on a war of its own against Mexico, the congress in secret session voted to sell it, and it was saved only by the commodore's refusal to turn it over. However, Houston managed to play off Great Britain and the United States against each other, thereby whetting the American appetite for annexation. The British resented Southern control of their cotton supply and the United States tariff on British manufactured goods. They now proposed that they take Texas under their wing, refinance it, and get Mexico's recognition of independence with the boundary at the Rio Grande in exchange for cotton, free trade, and the abolition of slavery; France agreed to the plan and was to share its benefits. When Houston left the presidency he put into the office his secretary of state, Anson Jones, a Massachusetts medico. Jones favored the continued independence of Texas under British protection and was able in July 1845 to lay before a special convention two offers: one of American annexation, and one of Mexican recognition and British protection. The convention overwhelmingly voted for the first. Incidentally, it carried the provision that Texas might divide itself into as many as five states. Late in 1845 Texas became a state in the Union, and on 19 February 1846 President Jones turned over his authority to a newly elected governor.

3 The Approach to War

The Jacksonian reforms, like nearly all other reform movements in American history, foundered upon the rocks of foreign problems. It was a complicated situation, which was made only a little simpler by the presence of British interests in every direction. The Canadian aspects were settled by the Webster-Ashburton Treaty of 1842, but Britain still held joint control of Oregon; there were rumors (which became true by 1846) that Mexico had offered California to England for aid against the United States; Mexico itself was a British economic sphere; Texas was coveted by Britain for its cotton and its market; and there were

British share in American foreign problems

signs that Britain was preparing to take over Cuba to keep it from falling into the hands of the United States.

Henry Clay naturally assumed that the triumph of the Whig ticket in 1840 was the public seal of approval upon his American System. He was jubilantly preparing legislation to implement his ideas when Harrison's death raised to the presidency a man who was not a real Whig but an anti-Jackson, nullification Democrat. This was the first time that a President had died in office, and some of the Whigs hoped to restrict Tyler to a limited role as Acting *John Tyler (1790– 1862)* President, but he promptly made it clear that he intended to be President in every respect. John Tyler, a widower when he became President, was a Virginia aristocrat of the John Taylor of Caroline school, honest, dignified, courageous to the point of obstinacy, and so consistently faithful to his "principles" that he can be accused of a sort of narrow-minded vanity. He accepted the risk of throttling his own career and took his punishment like the gentleman of the old school that he was. Nevertheless, in going down he took with him his two chief enemies, Clay and Van Buren.

Tyler was at first disposed to keep the peace and to retain Harrison's Cabinet. Then Congress met in special session to solve the economic problems that had followed on the Panic of 1837, and Clay undertook to shove through his program. He did succeed in killing the Independent Treasury. The dire need for revenue won a rise in the tariff, and the clamor of the West resulted in passing a pre- *Tyler and the Whigs* emption act. On the matters of internal improvements and the establishment of a new bank, however, Tyler proved adamant. As a result the party was thrown into discord: Tyler was read out of the party, and his whole Cabinet resigned with the exception of Webster, who remained partly to spite Clay and partly to finish his negotiations with Ashburton. A deadlock ensued between President and Congress.

Among Tyler's principles he numbered proslavery sentiments and Manifest Destiny, and he was perfectly conscious that Great Britain was bent on thwarting both. It was natural, therefore, that he should strive for the annexation of Texas. By April 1844 Calhoun, now Secretary of State, had signed a satisfactory treaty with Texas, but abolitionist resentment was so clearly reinforced by Mexico's threats of war in case of annexation and by various factors of political expediency that the treaty was soundly defeated. Tyler consoled himself by taking a second wife, as he said, without the advice or consent of the Senate. Eventually he was able to boast of having fourteen children.

The Whig convention, which was held first, did not even consider "His Accidency" and nominated Clay with little opposition. In the Democratic convention proslavery men, annexationists, and the adherents of favorite sons like Lewis Cass of Michigan were able to block Van Buren by use of the Two-thirds Rule. On the ninth ballot, James K. Polk of Tennessee, who was acceptable to the Tyler and Calhoun factions, swept the convention though he had not received a single vote on the first seven ballots. Thus was nominated the first "dark horse"—an inconspicuous candidate for the nomination who may win because of a deadlock among the leaders. George M. Dallas of Pennsylvania was nominated for the vice-presidency. A ringing declaration was then adopted advocating the "reoccupation" of all Oregon and the "reannexation" of Texas. It was a shrewd move to win both free- and slave-state annexationists, and presently Tyler withdrew from the race and gave his approval to Polk. Democrats won away thousands of Clay's supporters by their cry: "Fifty-four forty or fight!" Clay quickly sought to straddle and thereby probably reduced the severity of his defeat, even taking Tennessee from Polk. On the other hand, James G. Birney's Liberty Party took enough votes in New York to throw the thirty-six electoral votes of that state to Polk and ensure his victory, 170 to 105.

Campaign of 1844

Polk believed firmly that his election was a mandate for the annexation of Oregon and Texas. Tyler believed that also. He therefore proposed to by-pass the problem of getting two thirds of the Senate to agree to a treaty of annexation with Texas by asking for a joint resolution of the two houses agreeing to the admission of Texas as a state. Congress passed the resolution, though the change of one vote in the Senate would have defeated it. Texas was by this resolution assured that it could keep control of its public lands and could divide itself into five states, while slavery was protected by extending to Texas the terms of the Missouri Compromise. Texas was to pay its own debt, but its extreme claim of the Rio Grande border was to be adjusted later. The joint resolution was signed by Tyler 1 March 1845, three days before he left office, but actual admission did not occur until 29 December.

Admission of Texas

James Knox Polk was by birth a North Carolinian and, like Jackson, a Scotch-Irishman. As an adherent of Jackson he served in the House of Representatives for fourteen years, four of them as Speaker, and as governor of Tennessee. Though far from being unknown to the public, he was certainly the least-known man as yet to be elected to the presidency. He was a painfully methodical man who relentlessly drove himself to his duty, rarely took any time off for pleasure, kept the Sabbath rigidly, and unceasingly strove to carry out the will of the people. He had little personality, few close friends, no sense of humor, and was amazingly cold and secretive. Mrs.

James K. Polk (1795– 1849)

Polk, one of the most queenly women ever to reign in the White House, was popular even among her husband's enemies in spite of the fact that she was a puritan of the strictest Presbyterian views and permitted no dancing or card playing.

Polk chose strong party men for his Cabinet—Buchanan for State, Marcy for War, Bancroft for Navy, and Robert J. Walker for Treasury —but he expected to make his own decisions, and in most important matters the policies adopted were his own. Few Presidents have had Polk's record of success. Besides the annexations **His record of success** for which he is chiefly remembered, he carried out his two domestic ambitions. They were the re-establishment of the Independent Treasury System and the reduction of the tariff to eliminate its protective features; the last was accomplished by the Walker Tariff of 1846. His success, however, was won at a fearful price, for he broke his health by overwork and died a few months after leaving office.

It was regarded as possible that the admission of Texas would bring on war with Mexico; so during the summer of 1845, while Texas was making up its mind whether to become an American state or a British protectorate, Polk undertook to clear the decks by settling the Oregon question. It had been proposed as early as 1826 **The Oregon settlement** that the boundary be extended along the forty-ninth parallel to the Pacific. Polk now with the previous advice of the Senate resurrected the plan, and after some months of stalling Britain agreed. On 15 June 1846 a treaty was signed. Polk obtained more of Oregon than the United States had a technical right to hope for, but after all the ruckus about "Fifty-four forty or fight!" many Northerners felt that he not only had gone back on a campaign promise but had sacrificed the national welfare in order to protect Southern interests.

Northern dissatisfaction was compounded by another episode. In the summer of 1846 Calhoun made his last attempt to push internal improvements in a bill which would have greatly benefited the Great Lakes region and the adjacent parts of the Ohio and Mississippi valleys. Unfortunately the South opposed it, and when it reached Polk he vetoed it for Constitutional reasons. The Northwest was infuriated and blamed the South, and the recoil fell upon Calhoun.

Precisely what were the motives of Polk's diplomacy? Abolitionists hated him and insisted that he was the instrument of a deep-laid plot for the extension of slavery. There is no doubt that many Southerners clamored for Texas in order to extend the Cotton Kingdom **Polk's** and were trembling lest it become a British protectorate **diplomatic** and a cotton rival. However, New York merchants regarded **motives** the British menace with dismay for the same reasons and also because they feared that free trade in Texas would breed discontent in their cotton allies. There is, however, no evidence that Polk regarded his annexations from the Southern point of view. He opposed sectionalism and abominated the sectional extremists; Calhoun he rated the "most mischievous man in the Senate." His objects were purely national. California he wanted in order to round out the territory of the United States. Above all he felt that unless the English encirclement was broken, the United States would be forced into a major war. A war with Mexico was a cheap price to pay for the exclusion of Great Britain from California and Texas. He was willing to go further if necessary. "Mr. Monroe's Doctrine" was innocuous beside the Polk doctrine, which now proposed to prohibit foreign interference in Latin America, and which in 1848 he used vigorously in warning Britain and Spain away from Yucatán when that Mexican state applied to each in turn for annexation.

There is no clear proof that Polk felt at first that war with Mexico was inevitable. Though the Mexican minister withdrew as Texas was admitted into the Union, Polk felt that he had a solution which would satisfy both nations. The chaos in Mexico and that country's special antagonism toward the United States had resulted in the piling up of a long list of financial claims by American citizens; but though Mexico acknowledged these claims, she failed to pay them; true, she did not have the money, but there was a distinct disinclination to obtain it. Polk now sent John Slidell to Mexico with instructions to offer to assume all claims in exchange for the full Rio Grande boundary and to offer five million dollars for the rest of New Mexico and any sum up to twenty-five million dollars for California. Polk had woefully overrated his trump; indeed, in the light of Hispanic conceptions of dignity and honor, it was not a trump at all. When Slidell's mission became known the Mexican "people" rose in wrath at the insult, and the government in office (though it refused to receive Slidell) was swept out by what was in effect an anti-American revolution.

Slidell's mission

It seems that before Slidell's return from Mexico Polk lost his hope of avoiding war. His problem now became to engineer the outbreaks in such a way as to gain the support of the Whigs. As early as January 1846 he had ordered General Zachary Taylor with a few thousand regular troops scraped from widely scattered garrisons to the disputed area between the Nueces and the Rio Grande. There Taylor undertook the heartbreaking task of gathering supplies and equipment and licking his half-trained soldiers into shape. President Paredes of Mexico regarded the movement as an invasion of Mexican soil and an act of war, and his congress declared war on 23 April.

"A state of war exists," 13 May 1846

By May Polk had resolved to clarify the situation by asking Congress to declare war. While engaged in writing his message he received a report that Mexican forces had crossed the Rio Grande and had on 25 April killed or captured a party of American dragoons. His message was altered to include the assertion that "Mexico has passed the boundary of the United States, has invaded our territory and shed American blood upon the American soil. . . . War exists, and notwithstanding all our efforts to avoid it, exists by the act of Mexico herself." A bill was introduced which acknowledged that "a state of war exists," and after some Whig hedging it was overwhelmingly passed.

It was long the custom of American historians to interpret the Mexican War as an unprovoked attack by the United States. This was the natural result of the attempt of Northerners to represent the Mexican War as part of a Southern conspiracy to extend slavery and a **American** long step toward that greater "Southern conspiracy," the **reasons** Civil War. Justin H. Smith, the historian responsible for the **for war** reversal of opinion concerning the disgracefulness of the war, sums up the long series of incidents which are too numerous to recite here :*

> The American public noted . . . the entire long series of our grievances: our flag insulted, our minister traduced and threatened, our consuls maltreated, our government officially maligned, agreements broken, treaties ignored or violated, citizens persecuted and imprisoned, property confiscated, trade hampered and ruined, complaints more or less politely mocked, positive demands adroitly evaded, valid claims fraudulently defeated; and heard that such offences were not merely committed now and then, but repeated over and over again with apparent deliberation and malice. The highest Mexican authorities were found encouraging prejudice and ill-will against our citizens, exerting themselves to make foreign nations distrust and hate us, misrepresenting our efforts to conciliate them, and describing our honest wish to be on friendly terms as hypocrisy and craft. Our people saw the legitimate results of Mexican misgovernment charged against this country; proceedings of the authorities, fully warranted by the facts, protested against; threats of war freely made to influence our national conduct; and measures looking toward hostilities openly advocated and adopted in the most offensive manner. . . .
>
> Mexico . . . seemed likely to sell California to some European rival of ours . . . refused to pay even her admitted debts to us, claimed the privilege of applying to our government publicly the most opprobrious epithets in the vocabulary of nations, designed to keep our people in a constant state of uncertainty and alarm, intended to cause us the expense of maintaining for defensive purposes a large army and a large navy, planned to destroy our commerce by commissioning privateers. . . . She had informed the world that it was her privilege to keep on harrying Texas from generation to generation; and on a broader scale, but in a manner precisely analogous, it was now proposed to hang upon the flank of the United States.

* Justin H. Smith, *The War with Mexico* (2 v., 1919), 1: 118, 136.

Polk made his most serious mistake in supposing that subjects of dispute with Mexico could be settled by reason and compromise. As for New Mexico and California, they were vast and all but uninhabited tracts

Temperamental clash

which with typical Anglo-Saxon obtuseness he supposed could be obtained by chaffering; it never occurred to him that Mexico seriously supposed that her "honor" was involved. Actually he was dealing with something that few Americans understood: the colossal egotism of the Hispanic character. If Polk had yielded the claim to the Nueces boundary, the next Mexican demand would have been for all Texas; with that yielded, there would certainly have been some Mexicans, at least, who would have demanded the Louisiana Purchase and Florida.

On the other hand Mexicans represented Americans as being brusque to the point of arrogance, brutal, hypocritical, heretical, and so mercenary that anything was for sale if the price was high enough. Mexicans, however, were frank, friendly, gentle, and possessed of dignity, generosity, and an unparalleled sense of honor. Politicians, as is the nature of the critters, spread such prejudices zealously and plucked the feathers of the American eagle just for laughs and votes, quite unconscious of the fact that the same game could be played on the Mexican eagle. The United States, they said and were believed, intended to swallow Mexico a bite at a time, and Mexican conservatives, which included most of the "people" —that is, the rich and educated classes—trembled at the thought of the entry of democracy, Protestantism, and freedom of thought.

Mexico's actions were in Anglo-Saxon eyes like those of a spoiled and vicious brat, and they served to becloud certain legitimate Mexican complaints. Mexicans unjustly blamed the United States government for the

Mexican justification for war

secession of Texas, but certainly the movement had been planned and executed by Americans. California and New Mexico were now being similarly menaced by Americans. Public desire for annexations at Mexican expense had finally been reflected in a presidential campaign and in the election of an annexationist. In truth, there was a distinct menace to Mexico in the existence of a vigorous power in the North. Under the circumstances an automatic declaration of war upon an American annexation of Texas was not without justification, however futile a gesture it might be.

Yet Mexico, far from being picked upon by a big brute, was spoiling for a war and was supremely confident of victory. Americans in the Mexican view, says Smith, "had been abject as well as knavish, stealing her

Mexican self-confidence

territory and then trying to buy off her anger, submitting to be gulled, flouted and lashed, and each time going back for more of the same treatment; and it seemed hardly possible that we should suddenly adopt a bold, positive, unflinching course." Other nations have made the same miscalculation! Mexicans went on to argue that war would offer a prime opportunity for a Whig and abolitionist revolt. But even without that there was nothing to fear. The United States army and navy were weak, undermanned, and inexperienced; and volunteers were beneath contempt, as the War of 1812 had amply proved. Mexicans, on the other hand, were the best soldiers on earth, and continual warfare had given them experience and toughness; Santa Anna even offered to conquer the United States and hoist the Mexican eagle and serpent on the Capitol in Washington!

Then, the United States Treasury was almost empty—as was perfectly true. When it was pointed out that the Mexican treasury was even emptier, it was answered that a patriotic nation would rally around and fill it, not only with its abundant natural resources but with family plate and ladies' jewelry. Lastly, Europe was expected to interfere, not simply with hundreds of commerce raiders sailing under Mexican commissions but with full naval and military strength. It is interesting that European papers, even the lordly London *Times,* agreed with Mexico and expected an early American fiasco in the deserts, mountains, and jungles of the South.

It should be evident by now that in considering the causes of the Mexican War we cannot simply put justice on one side and injustice on the other. It is futile to speculate about what proportions of each should be assigned to the two sides. Each country had been injured **Difficulty** directly or indirectly by the other. Both were afflicted by **of assessing** demagogic politicians, national prejudices, and touchy public **the blame** opinion, but it would seem that the United States had the edge in patience and good faith.

4   *The Mexican War*

Observers confidently expected Mexico to win, and probably it would have if its leaders had been able to submerge their personal ambitions and work together. It was their failure to do so that disgusted soldiers and people and presently shattered the national morale. One **Mexican** might go even deeper and suggest that the Achilles' heel of **mistakes** the Mexican war effort was the thirst of the generals for glory. To win glory, they had to offer battle; they did so and lost. Mexico was designed by nature for guerrilla warfare, but there was no glory in that, and when it was tried after the defeat of the regular armies it was too late for a united effort.

Besides being favored by this basic Mexican blunder, the invaders had certain other advantages. Probably foremost were the superior steadfastness and the resourcefulness of the individual American soldiers, aided by the industrial superiority of the United States and the **American** naval blockade of the Mexican coast. The British govern- **advantages** ment and press were anti-American but did not advocate active interference. Presently the American policy of admitting European goods to Mexico with very low tariff payments and of giving them naval and military protection had their effect. By the end of the war it seems likely that the British would have welcomed the American annexation of all Mexico as a boon to British trade!

The disadvantages under which the Americans labored were probably even greater than the advantages. Polk, irked by the predominance of Whigs among the regular officers (particularly Winfield Scott, now the **American disadvantages** general in chief, and Zachary Taylor), supplemented them with sound Polk Democrats who had their eyes on the political cash value of a brilliant military record. More than that, these officers felt it necessary to curry favor with the volunteers under them; naturally discipline suffered, and sometimes garrison life degenerated into one long round of riotous living. Polk shared the usual American illusion that wars could be easily handled by civilians in uniforms, and when Scott tried to point out some of the difficulties he wrote the general down as too "scientific and visionary."

There was certainly very little that was scientific about the preparations for war. The recruiting of troops and the ordering and collecting of supplies was for the most part a catch-as-catch-can procedure. Boats were difficult to obtain, and liaison between the army and navy was disgraceful. Newspapers regularly published the most cherished secrets from both Washington and the front. Quarrels among the generals, particularly between the professionals and the politicians, were endemic. Worst of all, however, in a day when preventive medicine was almost unknown, were the climate, the insect plagues, and the diseases of Mexico. Yellow fever, typhus, and plain and fancy dysenteries were never absent from the camps; it was nothing unusual for three fourths of a regiment to be knocked out by disease at one time. Out of about 90,000 troops who served in Mexico, 11,300 died of disease and accident and 12,250 had to be discharged because of physical unfitness: a loss of about a quarter, though of course some of these must have been disabled by wounds. This contrasts with 6750 desertions and 1550 killed in combat.

At first the nation seemed to be enthusiastically behind the war, but within a year political obstructionism ran rife. Webster, Clay, Calhoun, Van Buren, and a galaxy of abolitionists and high-tariff men vied in their **Opposition to the war** denunciations of "Jimmy Polk's War." These thoroughly diverse factions formed a strange union to defeat military appropriations and the authorization of troops, especially strange in view of the fact that Webster and Clay each lost a son in Mexico. James R. Lowell loosed almost unbridled sarcasm against the war through the Yankee drawl of his Hosea Biglow, who averred that Manifest Destiny was half ignorance "an' t'other half rum." Abolitionists joined in giving to Mexico a glorification which it by no means deserved. Polk's claim that "war exists by the act of Mexico herself" became the butt of Whig ridicule and earned him the enduring epithet of "Polk the mendacious." Abraham Lincoln, then a Whig Congressman from Illinois, went so far as to introduce the so-called "Spot Resolution," which called upon Polk to name the spot on American soil where American blood had been shed.

This reached a climax in February 1847 in the speech prompted by Webster and delivered by Senator Thomas Corwin of Ohio, which bitterly attacked Manifest Destiny as the plea of every robber chief since Nimrod. "If I were a Mexican," he cried, "I would tell you, 'Have you not room in your own country to bury your dead men? If you come into mine, we will greet you with bloody hands and welcome you to hospitable graves.'" This was treason, and there was such a storm of public protest that Corwin's abettors left him to hold the bag. The effect upon the troops in the field may be imagined, and they frequently sought expression by burning Whig orators in effigy. Such orations inevitably found their way into Mexican papers and rekindled the hope that internal revolt would force the United States to withdraw from the war. The Whigs were in an anomalous position: political expediency demanded that they criticize the conduct of the war, but the chiefs of armies were Whigs, and it was evident that one of them would have to be nominated in 1848 if the Whigs were to win the election.

Polk notably failed to rise above partisan politics and weld the national effort. He mulishly forced the reduction of the tariff, and the consequent Treasury deficit was remedied piecemeal by issues of Treasury notes and bonds until an unexpected public spending spree began to boost imports. At the same time the Irish and **Finances of the war** German famines and growing colonial textile markets caused a sudden European demand for wheat and cotton. It is difficult to say what the war cost the United States, though it may have been around $100,000,-000 including the sums paid Mexico at the peace.

Polk did, however, yield to one amazing brainstorm which changed the entire course of the war. After his fiasco at San Jacinto, Santa Anna had gone into retirement. In 1838 a French expedition occupied Vera Cruz in retaliation for the destruction of a French bakery; and in the "Pastry War" which followed, Santa Anna had the **Santa Anna again** good fortune to lose a leg. Posing as a hero he re-entered politics, became president again, buried his leg with full military honors, and was dubbed the "Immortal Three-Fourths" by the wits. In February 1846, however, he was again out of power, vegetating in Cuba, when a friend of his approached Polk with the proposition that if Santa Anna could restore himself to power, he would treat with the United States on a reasonable basis. Further negotiations led to Santa Anna's agreement

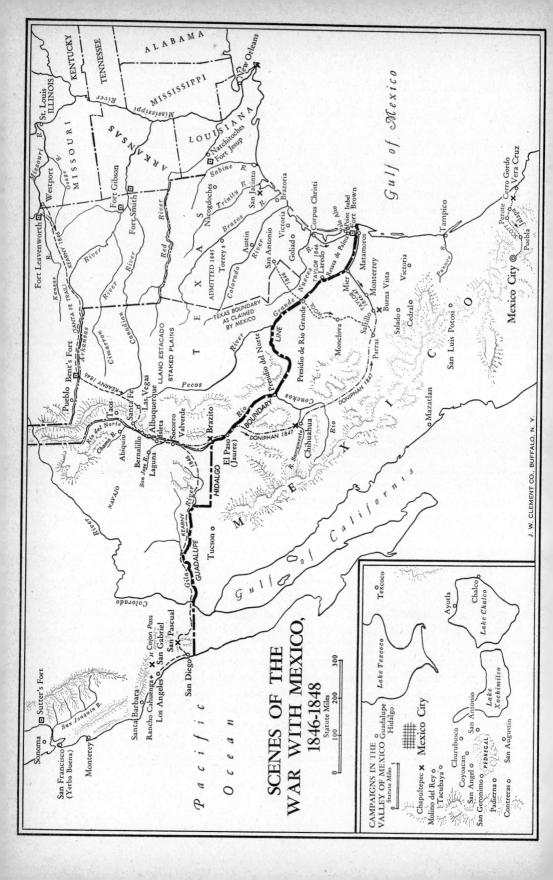

SCENES OF THE WAR WITH MEXICO, 1846-1848

Statute Miles
0 100 200 300

J. W. CLEMENT CO., BUFFALO, N.Y.

CAMPAIGNS IN THE VALLEY OF MEXICO

Guadalupe Hidalgo

Mexico City

Statute Miles
0   5

Chapultepec ✕
Molino del Rey ○
Tacubaya ○
Churubusco ○
Coyoacan ○
San Angel ○
San Geronimo ○   PEDREGAL
Padierna ○
Contreras ○   San Augustin ○
San Antonio ○

Lake Tezcoco
Texcoco ○

Ayotla ○
Chalco ○
Lake Chalco

Lake Xochimilco

Principal place names on map

Gulf of Mexico
Gulf of California
Pacific Ocean

ALABAMA
KENTUCKY
TENNESSEE
MISSISSIPPI
LOUISIANA
ILLINOIS
MISSOURI
ARKANSAS
TEXAS
ADMITTED 1845
NAVAJO

New Orleans ✕
St. Louis ○
Westport ○
Fort Leavenworth □
Fort Gibson □
Fort Smith
Natchitoches
Fort Jesup □
Nacogdoches
San Jacinto
Brazoria
Corpus Christi
Victoria
Austin
San Antonio
Goliad
Torreys ○
Pueblo ○
Bent's Fort □
Taos
Santa Fe
Las Vegas
Albuquerque
Isleta
Socorro
Valverde
Bernalillo
Abiquiu
Laguna
Brazito ✕
El Paso (Juarez)
Tucson ○
San Diego ○
San Pascual ✕
San Gabriel ✕
Rancho Cahuenga +
Los Angeles ○
Santa Barbara
Monterey
San Francisco (Yerba Buena) □
Sutter's Fort □
Sonoma □
San Luis Potosi ○
Mazatlan ○
Chihuahua
Presidio de Rio Grande
Presidio del Norte
Monclova
Saltillo
Parras
Cedral ○
Salado ○
Buena Vista
Monterrey
Mier
Matamoros
Laredo
Resaca de Palma
Palo Alto
Point Isabel
Fort Brown
Tampico ○
Vera Cruz ✕
Cerro Gordo ✕
Perote
Puebla ○
Mexico City ◎

TEXAS BOUNDARY AS CLAIMED BY MEXICO

STAKED PLAINS
LLANO ESTACADO

BOUNDARY LINE

KEARNY 1846
KEARNY 1846
TAYLOR 1846
TAYLOR 1847
DONIPHAN 1847
DONIPHAN 1847
(SANTA FE TRAIL)

HIDALGO
GUADALUPE

Rivers: Missouri R., Osage R., Kansas, Arkansas, Cimarron, Canadian, Red River, Sabine R., Trinity R., Brazos, Colorado, Nueces R., Rio Grande, Pecos, Conchos, R. Sacramento, Rio del Norte, Chama R., San Jose R., Gila River, San Joaquin R., Panuco R.

to terms substantially like those that were adopted after two years of war. Polk swallowed the bait, for he was convinced that even if Santa Anna did not regain power, the resultant civil war would weaken Mexico. In August 1846 Santa Anna was slipped through the fleet and by September was in control of the government of Mexico. He hastened northward to raise an army to oppose Taylor.

Meanwhile war had begun in earnest. The first Mexican foray across the Rio Grande was followed by an invasion in force, which was repelled in two sharp actions at Palo Alto and Resaca de la Palma, on 8 and 9 May. A few days later Taylor crossed the river and occupied Matamoros without opposition. These advantages had been won against a force about double that of the Americans, but now the short-term enlistments were expiring and new regiments of volunteers were piling in. These had to be licked into shape, a process which they did not approve. Taylor, who was no martinet and was already bitten by the presidential bug, let discipline relax and Matamoros became a hell hole. In September he continued his invasion of Mexico and in a three-day battle (21–23 September) took Monterrey, the key to northern Mexico. However, his forces were so battered that he was glad to let the Mexicans march out with their arms. *Taylor's campaign of 1846*

Taylor's advice to Polk was to hold a line that would run from Tampico (now in the hands of the fleet) to Monterrey and Saltillo; thus the expense and blood of a full-scale invasion would be saved, and the United States would hold enough territory to reimburse itself if Mexico refused to treat. Polk and his Cabinet, however, decided that this would simply repeat the situation of war by foray such as had existed for ten years on the Texas border. Something positive must be done, if for no other reason than to keep the political initiative, for the Congressional elections of 1846 had sadly reduced the Democratic majority. As a result, it was resolved to send Scott to seize Vera Cruz and ostensibly threaten Mexico City. Haste was necessary, for to avoid yellow fever the invading army must seize Vera Cruz and get away to the hills by 1 April. Scott accordingly stopped in at Matamoros and drew off most of Taylor's experienced regular troops. *Change in American strategy*

Taylor, left with 5000 recruits, now undertook for the third time to whip an army into shape. Before he could possibly be ready Santa Anna suddenly came up from the south with 15,000 troops. On 22 February 1847 the armies clashed in a rugged mountain pass south of Saltillo, near the hacienda of Buena Vista. The ensuing battle was better handled by Santa Anna than by Taylor, but after two days of surging back and forth the Mexicans broke and fled. The American loss was 673 killed and wounded, and the Mexican perhaps three times as great. Santa Anna left his troops to struggle back across the desert as best they could and fled south, pro- *Battle of Buena Vista, 22–23 Feb. 1847* claiming that he had beaten Taylor and was now on his way to beat Scott. So great was his prestige that he was actually believed!

Buena Vista saved the northern expeditionary force from disaster and probably did the same for Scott at Vera Cruz. Not least of all, it made a President. Zachary Taylor, born to an aristocratic Virginia family, was Zachary Taylor (1784–1850) raised on the Kentucky frontier. He had entered the army before the War of 1812, had seen service in that war, on the prairie, and in the Second Seminole War. His home, recently established, was in Baton Rouge. Grizzled, rough-hewn, streaming picturesque oaths, he was lovingly known and worshiped as "Old Rough-and-Ready." Taylor was not, however, a good general; even his friends knew he was not. He was forceful, an inspired leader, and a superb fighter, but he was not an organizer nor disciplinarian, was woefully ignorant of the professional aspects of military life, neglected details, planned poorly, and continually underestimated the enemy. Nevertheless, even before Buena Vista he was touted for the Whig nomination in 1848 by a group of Congressmen which called itself the "Young Indians." Taylor was convinced, rightly, that the administration wished to knife him; even more to the point, the American people also believed it. In November 1847 he went on an extended leave to mend his political fences and never returned to military duty.

At almost the moment of Buena Vista, American forces had completed a strangle hold on New Mexico and California. In August 1846 an expedition of about 1660 regulars and Missouri volunteers under the command of Campaigns in New Mexico and Chihuahua Gen. Stephen W. Kearny, an experienced and able frontier commander, entered New Mexico without opposition. After taking possession Kearny organized a military government at Santa Fe; then, with a force eventually reduced to 100 dragoons, he departed for California. Col. Alexander Doniphan took El Paso late in December after a brush at Brazito. He then pushed on to Chihuahua with about 200 men and occupied the city on 1 March 1847, after fighting a stiff action at Sacramento a few miles out on the El Paso road. The intention had been to join Gen. John E. Wool, who was to have advanced across country from San Antonio but had been diverted to Buena Vista. Since his men were nearing the date of their discharge, Doniphan now abandoned Chihuahua and joined Taylor at Saltillo. Meanwhile Sterling Price, one of Polk's political generals, had let his men run wild in New Mexico; his administration and the disorderliness of his men were no worse than under the Mexican government, but they were Americans. The result was a brief revolt in January and February 1847, which was quickly suppressed. The New Mexicans sank into sullen resignation.

The situation in California at the beginning of 1846 was hopelessly muddled. Factions formed around the British and American consuls, and

another one opposed both and favored independence. Most native Californians were torn between their desire for independence   **Conquest**
from Mexico and their fear of what the foreign residents   **of Cali-**
might do. The ubiquitous Captain Frémont, on another of   **fornia**
his exploring expeditions, was hovering in the north, and it was suspected
(erroneously) that he bore secret orders from the United States government. A misunderstanding between Frémont and a Mexican official convinced the American residents of the Bay area that they were about to be
expelled. In June 1846 the Americans seized the local capital town of
Sonoma, raised a rudely sewn "Bear Flag," and declared that California
was an independent republic. Meanwhile Commodore John D. Sloat of
the Pacific Squadron, who bore secret orders to occupy Californian ports
in case of war, heard rumors that war had begun and sailed for Monterey.
On 7 July, fearful that an approaching British squadron might act first, he
landed marines and took possession of Upper California. Two weeks later
Sloat turned over the command to Robert F. Stockton, a younger and
more vigorous man, just as Frémont appeared in Monterey at the head of
a company of Sonomans.

Stockton and Frémont now briefly visited the Los Angeles area, received the surrender and parole of the Mexican army officers, and set up
a military administration. However, in September the parolees led a revolt of Los Angeleños, and San Pedro and San Diego were besieged.
In December Kearny with his one hundred dragoons barely escaped the
clutches of the Mexicans at San Pascual and entered San Diego. Early
in January Stockton and Kearny sallied forth and seized Los Angeles
after a couple of skirmishes at San Gabriel and La Mesa.

Frémont, who had been moving overland from the north with a strong
force but carefully avoiding action, now moved in and signed with the
defeated Mexicans the so-called Treaty of Cahuenga. In this Frémont,
anxious to be popular, ignored the broken paroles and
granted the defeated party everything they could wish. This   **Frémont**
action was a deliberate slap in the face to Kearny, who was   **and Kearny**
a superior officer and governor-designate, but Frémont now went on to
assume the governorship with Stockton's support. Two months later
Kearny assumed the office on direct orders from Washington. Frémont
was sent East, virtually as a prisoner, and eventually was convicted of
mutiny by a court-martial and sentenced to be expelled from the army.
Polk remitted the sentence, but Frémont resigned. Not the least result
was that Frémont's father-in-law, Senator Benton, became a violent
enemy of the administration, and the Pathfinder became more than ever
the debonair hero of the people.

California, New Mexico, and the northeastern states of Mexico were
now in American hands, but so little were these gangling parts connected

with the vital center of the country that their loss was far from driving
home to Mexicans the need for peace. It was Scott's mission

Winfield Scott (1786–1866)

to convince the Mexicans of their defeat by stabbing toward the vitals of the country. Winfield Scott, now past sixty but with his six-foot-four figure unbowed, had had a significant career since he had left his Virginia home and made a brilliant debut as a commander in the War of 1812. Almost every problem which had involved the possible use of force had found him present, and because he had worked intelligently and diligently for peace he had earned the title of Pacificator. He may have been pompous, egotistic, and petulant (he was often known as "Great Scott" or "Old Fuss-and-Feathers"), but he possessed good sense, firmness, generosity, and ability. That his knowledge and practice of military science were sound is shown by the brilliance with which he carried out a campaign which so distinguished an authority as the Duke of Wellington considered doomed to defeat.

Vera Cruz fell late in March 1847 after a severe bombardment, and Scott, with 8500 men, lost no time in moving inland. On 18 April he encountered Santa Anna, who with 12,000 men was holding a fortified moun-

Advance from Vera Cruz

tain pass near Cerro Gordo. A young engineer, Robert E. Lee, found a path through the jungle, and the Mexicans were outflanked and sent flying with the loss of 1000 killed and wounded and 3000 prisoners. The next day the army entered Jalapa, and here in strange tropical surroundings it halted. As a matter of fact, between disease and the expiration of enlistments, Scott's army was melting away, and he could not afford to attack Mexico City without reinforcements. Re-enlistments were few, for the men had "seen the elephant," as they put it, and were satisfied and ready to go home. By this time Santa Anna's deceptions had begun to find him out; the Church turned against him, and Scott, risking an advance force in Santa Anna's wake, found clerical Puebla ready to surrender. The American vanguard was now about seventy miles from Mexico City.

Meanwhile the situation in Mexico City was one of bewildering confusion. Santa Anna, energetically raising a new army, had plenty of enemies, but they could not unite against him. As the fates would have it,

Failure of Trist's mission

there had now arrived in Mexico as Polk's special representative Nicholas P. Trist. Trist had studied law under Jefferson and married his granddaughter, had been secretary to Jackson, and was now chief clerk of the State Department. He had served eight years as consul at Havana and knew the Spanish language and character —which was more than Polk and Buchanan knew. He was now authorized to present peace demands to the Mexican government, roughly the recognition of the Rio Grande boundary and the sale of California and New Mexico. Trist, who had exalted notions of his destiny, gave Scott the impression that he was a political commissar, and they did not at first get along very well. Trist got in touch with Santa Anna and persuaded Scott to advance a $10,000 bribe to the Mexican, with the promise of a million more upon the ratification of peace. But it soon became evident that Santa Anna was sparring for time, and that any hope that the Mexicans would treat was delusory. Yet, paradoxically, civil affairs were in such chaos that one of Scott's most serious problems was how to carry on the war without breaking up the government and thus leaving no power with which to treat.

By the beginning of August 1847 Scott had approximately 11,000 effectives and 3000 invalids who might or might not later become effective. Accordingly he led his army across the mountains and down into the storied Valley of Mexico. After probing various **Campaign** routes he passed south of the intervening lakes, near what **in the** is now the floating Gardens of Xochimilco, and turned north **Valley** toward Mexico City. Here an impassable lava field called **of Mexico** the Pedregal flanked the line of march on the west, and Churubusco in the front was heavily fortified. At this juncture Robert E. Lee again came to the rescue by finding a tortuous path across the southwest corner of the Pedregal. On the 19th a force moved across the lava and struck the Mexican guardians of the back door at Contreras. The first action was a defeat, but the next day reinforcements reversed the tide and, catching the Churubusco defenses in the flank, sent the defenders pell-mell up the road to Mexico City. In one day Santa Anna lost one third of his army and was driven back to the immediate suburbs of the capital city.

Instead of forcing his way into the city, Scott seized the opportunity to propose an armistice and peace negotiations. Santa Anna consented but, taking it as a sign of weakness, blocked agreement and used the time to prepare for a renewal of hostilities. When this plan became evident, Scott returned to the attack. In eight days (8–15 September) a sharp action was fought at Molino del Rey, the key fort on the hill of Chapultepec was seized, the Americans stormed into the city, and a vicious resistance by citizens and released criminals was sternly crushed. Meanwhile Santa Anna had resigned the presidency and marched off with 4000 men in the forlorn hope of cutting off Scott by seizing Puebla, which held 1800 invalids guarded by 400 men and was already besieged by guerrillas. Even here Santa Anna was repulsed, and presently his men were scattered by reinforcements marching up from Vera Cruz. After a month of one of the most gallant defenses in American history Puebla was relieved. Santa Anna returned to exile.

Trist renewed negotiations with the Mexican provisional government in October. Mexico was apparently on the verge of falling apart, and there was a strong sentiment among Mexicans for annexation to the United

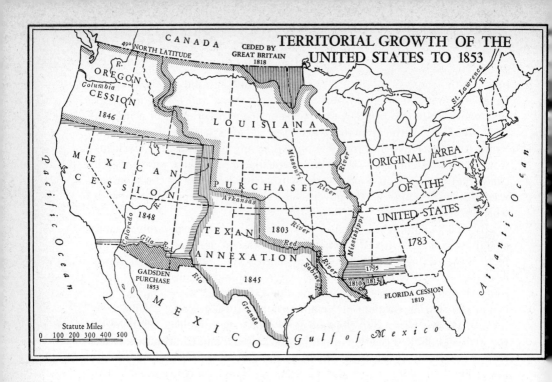

TERRITORIAL GROWTH OF THE UNITED STATES TO 1853

Treaty of Guadalupe Hidalgo, 2 Feb. 1848

States, not for love of the Americans but in the hope that the perpetual civil wars would be ended, reforms made, and trade revived. Meanwhile in Washington the opinion had been growing that Mexican intransigence was increased by the evident American anxiety for peace, and that the way to solve the impasse was to annex the whole country. So Polk, influenced also by some marplot reports from Mexico, recalled Trist. The Mexican government, alarmed at the thought of having the negotiations transferred to Washington, begged Trist to remain, and after some hesitation he acceded, though as a mere private citizen he laid himself open to severe punishment.

Even at that the Mexican negotiators characteristically continued to stall, and it was not until 2 February 1848 that the treaty was signed in the village of Guadalupe Hidalgo, the shrine of the Virgin of Guadalupe, the patroness of Mexico. The Rio Grande boundary was recognized, and in return for Upper California and for Arizona and New Mexico above the Gila River the United States paid $15,000,000 and assumed $3,750,-000 in claims of American citizens against Mexico. Unflattering to Mexico was the way in which the United States followed the pattern already set with the Indian nations of preserving the legalities but forcing the sale. Trist was politically ruined by his action, but upon reflection Polk decided that he could not force the Senate to agree to his larger desires, and so he submitted the treaty as it was. Nearly all the Senators opposed the treaty as either too much or not enough, but in the end they canceled each other and agreed to accept it with minor changes. Ratifications were exchanged at Querétaro on 30 May. The war was over.

Scott's discipline over his troops was strict, so there was little of the terrorism that Taylor permitted in the north; even there the Americans were no worse than the native troops had been, but of course people most resent harshness from a stranger. Scott, indeed, became **The Amer-** popular in Mexico City and was seriously invited to become **ican occu-** dictator. However, in April he was on his way home, con- **pation** scious that his political generals had finally succeeded in knifing him; it was not until 1852 that he received his reward by being made lieutenant general, the first since Washington. The American occupation for the moment gave to the garrison towns some of the air of American streets, what with restaurant signs in English and saloons filled with roaring soldiers. There were even army newspapers, soldiers were sometimes received into private homes, and international social occasions were common. Nevertheless the "I wanna go home" attitude prevailed; fortunately it was easily gratified, for on 12 June Mexico City was evacuated, and during the next month the last boatload of the expeditionary force left Vera Cruz. For over a century captured Mexican battle flags were displayed at Annapolis and West Point, then in 1950 in a gesture of goodwill were returned to Mexico.

The war had taught many lessons about foreign war and occupation, but they unfortunately were forgotten by the time they were needed. Better heeded was the military training, for most of the prominent leaders in both the Union and the Confederate armies received their baptism of fire in Mexico. England learned with a **Results of** sense of shock that the United States was not to be deflected **the war** from its course by harsh words and diplomatic intrigues but, on the contrary, might be spurred on by them. As for Mexico, whatever the morals of the issue, the loss of its northern territories at least filled its treasury and hastened the integration of the country around its economic and political heart. Those Mexicans who could not forget were soon to have their revenge—the American Civil War.

BIBLIOGRAPHICAL NOTE

The Psychology of Agrarian Imperialism

Albert K. Weinberg, *Manifest Destiny: A Study of Nationalist Expansion in American History* (1935), though marred by a certain turbidity, is a thoughtful and penetrating work of first importance.

The Borderlands

OREGON: For the entire area see George W. Fuller, *History of the Pacific*

Northwest (1931); and Agnes C. Laut, *The Conquest of the Great Northwest* (2 v., 1908). There are useful biographies of McLoughlin by Robert C. Johnson and Richard G. Montgomery. See also Allan Nevins's brilliant *Frémont, the West's Greatest Adventurer* (2 v., 1928).

NEW MEXICO AND ARIZONA: Alfred B. Thomas, ed., *After Coronado* (1935); R. L. Duffus, *The Santa Fe Trail* (1930); Francis C. Lockwood, *Pioneer Days in Arizona* (1932); Herbert E. Bolton, *Padre on Horseback* (1932) and *Rim of Christendom* (1936).

CALIFORNIA: Charles E. Chapman, *A History of California: The Spanish Period* (1921); Julian Dana, *Sutter of California* (1934).

TEXAS: Herbert E. Bolton, *Texas in the Middle Eighteenth Century* (1915); Eugene C. Barker, *Mexico and Texas, 1821–1835* (1938); Carlos E. Castañeda, *The Mexican Side of the Texas Revolution* (1928); John M. Myers, *The Alamo* (1948); William C. Binkley, *The Expansionist Movement in Texas, 1836–1850* (1925); Justin H. Smith, *The Annexation of Texas* (1911); Ephraim D. Adams, *British Interests and Activities in Texas, 1838– 1846* (1910); Joseph W. Schmitz, *Texan Statecraft, 1836–1845* (1941); Jim Dan Hill, *The Texas Navy* (1937). Useful biographies are Eugene C. Barker, *Life of Stephen F. Austin* (1925); J. Fred Rippy, *Joel Roberts Poinsett, Versatile American* (1935); Wilfrid H. Callcott, *Santa Anna* (1936); Marquis James, *The Raven: A Biography of Sam Houston* (1929).

The Approach to War

LIVES AND TIMES: For the career of Clay in the post-Jackson period see George R. Poage, *Henry Clay and the Whig Party* (1936). For Tyler see Oliver P. Chitwood, *John Tyler, Champion of the Old South* (1939). On Polk see Eugene I. McCormac, *James K. Polk* (1922); Polk's self-revelations in *The Diary of James K. Polk* (4 v., 1910), and in Allan Nevins's abridgment, *Polk: The Diary of a President, 1845–1849* (1929).

DIPLOMACY: The classic is Justin H. Smith, *The War with Mexico* (2 v., 1919), but see also James M. Callahan, *American Foreign Policy in Mexican Relations* (1932); J. Fred Rippy, *The U.S. and Mexico* (1931); and Louis M. Sears, *John Slidell* (1925).

The Mexican War

See again Justin H. Smith, *The War with Mexico* for the saltiest and most detailed account. More recent, but offering little that is new, is Alfred H. Bill, *Rehearsal for Conflict* (1947). On the generals see the biographies of Taylor by Brainerd Dyer (1946) and Holman Hamilton (1941); of Scott, by Charles W. Elliott (1937); and of Frémont by Allan Nevins. John D. P. Fuller, *The Movement for the Acquisition of All Mexico, 1846–1848* (1936) covers a little-known aspect. For the early moves in the north Bernard De Voto, *The Year of Decision: 1846* (1943) resembles the prologue to a Greek drama in its sense of fate on the march; De Voto writes like an inspired but slightly confused angel. The Mexican side of the war is portrayed in José Fernando Ramirez, *Mexico During the War with the United States* (1950).

Chapter XXIII

THE PREPARATION
OF THE SOUTHERN
MIND

1 *The Compromise of 1850*

THE decade of the 1850's saw the final tightening of sectional lines and the final movement toward secession. There was about this evolution something apparently so fateful and inexorable that it is no wonder the next generation regarded the war that followed as an **Political** irrepressible conflict. Actually it was no such thing. It was **extremes** merely an unhappy illustration of the way in which two **crush the** determined and sizable extremes can crush the reasonable **center** center between them as grain is crushed between the upper and nether millstones. The methods used have become familiar in our own day: lies and distortions to implant prejudices and rouse emotions, specious calls to patriotism and love for human liberty, and sobbing appeals to high and holy religious standards. Calhoun had accepted a puny abolitionist challenge and turned a Constitutional and economic problem into a moral one. The abolitionists, like all fanatics, knew how to fatten on moral issues; and designing politicians showed them how to pursue the moral objective by appealing to the masses through political means.

To their eternal credit let it be said that the rank and file of both Northern and Southern politicians yielded only slowly and grudgingly. Their business was compromise, and they saw clearly that once slavery was accepted as a moral issue it could not be compromised. **Politicians** They fought courageously against the formation of sectional **oppose sec-** parties, and some of them were ready to pour out the baby **tionalism** with the bath in the desperate attempt to preserve the traditional inter-

717

sectional parties. In the end they were overwhelmed and went with their sections, but for looking over their shoulders toward peace some of them were punished by being turned into political pillars of salt.

There was in those days a general opinion that the morally superior should lead; that is why such spotless heroes as Calhoun and Sumner came at last to crystallize in themselves the essence of sectional attitudes. "It is disconcerting to read in the record," says Gerald Johnson,* "how almost all the men who were most active in giving to the country a red harvest of mangled corpses and a fearful legacy of ruin and shame and woe were men of the loftiest moral character."

We will not be concerned with deciding what amount of philosophical justice lay on each side; that would be futile. Each side sought not for truth but for arguments and used the arguments to convince itself that it was right, and each paid a terrible price for its insistence upon its rightness. The responsibility, as always, lay heavy upon the leaders. Sometimes in this imperfect world of ours opinions *must* be turned into principles, "for it must needs be that offenses come; but woe to that man by whom the offense cometh!"

We have noted before how the marriage of New England's transcendentalism and New York's Burnt District produced the abolition movement. The ultra-Jacksonian Loco Focos of New York City had found an echo all over the North, but they were particularly powerful among the so-called Barnburners of upper New York. The Barnburners were political realists who found their platform in the Natural Rights doctrines of the Declaration of Independence and in the Emersonian and evangelical exhortations to follow conscience, the divine guide to what is right. If the Constitution or the laws fell short of what was right, then, said these "Methodists of Democracy," it was their duty to follow the Higher Law of God, which transcends all man-made constitutions and laws. And among the Higher Laws was the prohibition of human slavery. Most of the Barnburners, however, were realistic enough to see that abolition was not an immediately practical program. So they became free-soilers, determined to enforce the Higher Law at least to the extent of preventing the spread of slavery to the Mexican Cession.

Even the Whig Party in the Burnt District was affected by the doctrine of the Higher Law, which is not surprising when we recall that the New York party was closely related to the rabidly evangelical Anti-Masonic Party. Those young politicians who had been lifted to prominence by the anti-Masonic movement now (older and even more shrewd) became the inspirers and leaders of the Conscience Whigs in New York and the allies of the Conscience

The Barnburners and the Higher Law

The Conscience Whigs

* Gerald Johnson, *Secession of the Southern States* (1933), 66.

Whigs elsewhere. Their program, like that of the Barnburners, ranged from abolition to free-soilism, and their allies were scattered all over the North, though perhaps chiefly in Massachusetts and Ohio.

Abolition and free-soilism had thus entered both parties. Already Adams and Giddings had carried the struggle for abolition into Congress, but it was not an issue that appealed to the common sense of the rank and file, who were disposed to see slavery as the business of **Effect of** each state. The amount of the Louisiana Purchase left open **the Mexi-** to slavery after 1840 by the Missouri Compromise was so **can Cession** small (only Oklahoma) that extremists had little chance of forcing battle on the great center group. It was the Mexican Cession which suddenly added an enormous new public domain and gave the free-soil issue an immediate appeal to the masses by linking the territorial gains of the war to the slavery issue. The fuse which ran from the lighted Loco Foco of the North to the open powder barrel of Southern Rights was the Wilmot Proviso.

The Wilmot Proviso was introduced into the House of Representatives in August 1846 by David Wilmot of Pennsylvania as an amendment to a military appropriation bill and proposed that any territory acquired from Mexico should be closed to slavery. Wilmot was a Polk **The Wil-** Democrat who had lost ground with his constituents for his **mot Pro-** support of the Walker Tariff, and he may have been trying **viso, 1846** to regain the goodwill of his free-soil district. Whatever the motive behind its introduction, the Wilmot Proviso immediately served as the reagent to divide North and South. Party lines were transcended. Not only did abolitionists and free-soilers support the measure, but also protective tariff Whigs.

Most significant supporters of Wilmot were the Barnburners, who now found a practical way to express their opposition to the extension of slavery, and Western Democrats, who now got revenge for Polk's veto of the internal-improvements bill. Polk, they asserted, had sold out Northern expansionists by his Oregon deal and now planned on giving Southern expansionists all they wanted. The Wilmot Proviso was passed by the House (in which the North predominated) but was rejected by the Senate. Thereafter the Wilmot Proviso became a standard attachment to House bills, though it was invariably turned down by the Senate. Lincoln, who served one term in the House, beginning December 1847, said that he voted for the Wilmot Proviso at least forty times. The issue, of course, was as bitterly discussed in the press as in Congress, and public opinion was aroused in all sections of the country.

Wilmot does not seem to have learned until later that the Mexican Cession was not suited to slavery, but Calhoun, who was well aware of the geographical situation, regarded the Wilmot Proviso as a gratuitous in-

CHRONOLOGICAL DEVELOPMENT
OF AMERICAN PARTIES TO 1868

Hatched lines indicate official descent. Broken lines indicate principal
migrations of factions or remnants. Dates cannot always be precise.

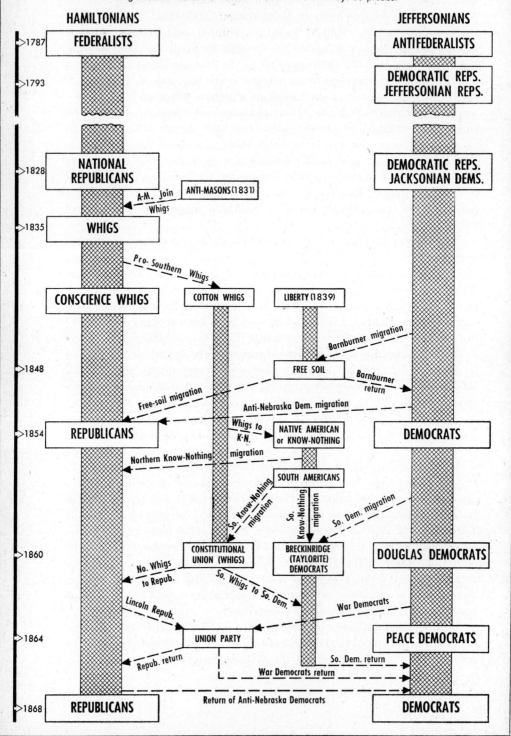

sult to the South. He therefore decided to accept the challenge and regain the initiative for his section. Until this time few had questioned that Congress could control slavery **Platform of the South** in the public domain, and Calhoun, as a member of Monroe's Cabinet, had approved the constitutionality of the Missouri Compromise. However, the situation was now different, and in February 1847 Calhoun summed up the Southern argument in five resolutions which he introduced into the Senate. The gist of these was that all the states held equal rights in the public domain; that their citizens had the right to move there with their property (meaning slaves); that Congress had no right to regulate this migration of property; and even the people of the territory could not decide on slavery or freedom until they came to write their constitution as a preliminary to admission to the Union.

Actually the resolutions never reached a vote, but they accomplished their purpose of publicizing the Southern view, and in the form adopted by the Virginia legislature became known as the Platform of the South. The next year the Democratic state convention of Alabama adopted the Alabama Platform, which went beyond Calhoun to assert that Congress must protect slavery in the Mexican Cession. It was evident that the South did not object to Congressional interference provided it was in favor of slavery. Calhoun saw the logical trap and tried to spring it by claiming that Congress had the power to *protect* property but not to *destroy* it.

It was by now clear that both the Whig and the Democratic Party teetered on the edge of destruction. Northern Whigs were divided into pro-South Cotton Whigs and Conscience Whigs, of which the latter were either abolitionists or free-soilers. Southern Whigs were ei- **Approach-** ther out-and-out Southern Rights men or moderate compro- **ing breakup** misers. Northern Democrats were Loco Focos, who ranged **of parties** from abolitionism to free-soilism, and moderates who were willing to yield to the South to insure peace and as a result were called "Doughfaces"— Northern men with Southern principles. Southern Democrats, however, outside of old Sam Houston had few prominent compromisers; their leaders were for the most part violent partisans of Southern Rights, such men as Calhoun.

The business of politicians is to find practical compromises, and the more temperate leaders knew this. Two principal compromises were proposed. One was to run the Missouri Compromise Line of 36° 30′ on west to the Pacific. The other was to leave the choice between **Proposed** slavery and freedom to the people of the territories con- **compro-** cerned; this proposal, the work of Lewis Cass, became fa- **mises** mous as "popular sovereignty," a term which in ridicule was often changed to "squatter sovereignty." Both solutions were opposed by extremists, and as a result little could be done in the way of organizing the new territories. California and New Mexico were left under military government, and Utah, now settled by Mormons and asking admission to the Union as the State of Deseret, was also left to wait. Only Oregon was given a territorial government, and that because it was so far north that there was no hope that slavery could enter there. Strangely enough, Oregon later showed more sympathy to the proslave cause than any of the others.

A dangerous weakness of our Constitutional system was disclosed by the way in which the growing acuteness of the slavery issue forced party conventions to compromise on weak presidential candidates from Van Buren onward to 1860. This was at the very time when one

Campaign of 1848

or more strong and impartial Presidents might have averted the catastrophe of the Civil War. The Democratic convention chose as their standard bearer Lewis Cass of Michigan, who, whatever he might have been in his youth, was now slow, stodgy, consumed with petty prejudices, and pathologically fearful of the South. The Whigs, as had early been foreseen, nominated Zachary Taylor, the "Hero of Buena Vista" and a Louisiana slaveholder. To make the ticket more palatable they added Millard Fillmore, a lawyer and former Congressman of Buffalo, who was expected to attract Clay and Conscience Whigs. Both the Democrats and the Whigs evaded the free-soil issue.

The Barnburners, angered by the nomination of Cass, united with the Liberty Party and a fragment of the Conscience Whigs to form the Free-Soil Party and put up Van Buren for President and Charles Francis Adams, son of John Quincy Adams, for Vice-President. As it

Free-Soil Party

was, most of the Whigs stayed with Taylor, but the Free-Soilers tipped the scales in perhaps a half-score of states; at any rate they took enough votes to defeat Cass in New York and carried Taylor to victory, 163 to 127. The Free-Soilers, moreover, held the balance of power in the House of Representatives and forced the election of one Senator, the outstanding Salmon P. Chase of Ohio. Chase was humorless, opinionated, self-righteous, and pompous; and a drooping eyelid gave him an air of craftiness. A cultural and religious snob, he was a pietist in the narrowest theological sense of being ritualistic and sanctimonious and always tormented by a sense of eternity. On the other hand, he had a magnificent physical presence, was able, personally honest, and had the moral courage to sacrifice anything in his devotion to the cause of emancipation.

Calhoun regarded the election of Taylor as a defeat for Southern Rights, and in January 1849 laid his Southern Address before a caucus of the slave-state members of Congress. It was a clarion warning to the

Calhoun's Southern Address

South that it must unite, for it was on the verge of being overwhelmed by the growing industry and population of the North; the existence of the institution of slavery was at stake, and unless some way was found of checking the North, a tremendous struggle over emancipation would come and the South, defeated and powerless, would be ruled by black barbarians acting as satraps of Northern vengeance and avarice. The effect on the practical politicians of the South was disheartening to Calhoun, for the address was accepted only by a part of the Democratic delegation. Southern Whigs were convinced that Calhoun did not want a settlement of the territorial issue except by total victory of the South, and that his object was to rend asunder both parties and build a Southern Rights Party as a step toward either secession or the complete subjugation of the North.

The dire periods of the Southern Address were still running across the nation when Taylor came into the presidency. He was a political innocent, confronting a crisis that would have taxed the genius of a Julius Caesar. After a period of floundering about, Taylor suddenly became deplorably self-confident; he decided executive problems with military promptness and ignorance of the circumstances and spent much of his time hobnobbing democratically with adoring callers. Taylor was a slaveholder, but as Calhoun had suspected he was not impressed by the urgency of the slavery crisis. His Cabinet was predominantly free-soil, and free-soilers talked of the possibility of passing the Wilmot Proviso with the blessing of the President. **Taylor as President**

As the summer advanced Taylor fell under the dominance of his two original backers, Weed and Seward of New York. Thurlow Weed, an Albany editor, had been a Clinton Democrat, an anti-Mason, and now was the astute manipulator of New York Whiggery. William H. Seward came up through the same channels, and as front man for Weed he was elected governor at the early age of thirty-seven. Having won his spurs, Seward was accepted by Weed as partner, and for thirty years they normally dominated the conservative party of New York. Seward's strength with Conscience Whigs and Barnburners won him election to the Senate in 1848. **William H. Seward (1801–72)**

The man deserves more than passing mention, for he was destined to become one of the greats of American history, though only after long experience and self-discipline. Short, slight, red-headed, clean shaven, hawknosed, and with piercing eyes, Seward was a self-confident egotist but an intelligent one, who could and did learn in time to exercise good judgment and to free himself from dogmatism. While not without principles, he saw the necessity of opportunism and placed moral crusades second to practical programs. He was a monotonous speaker but learned to gain attention by speaking seldom and then saying something worth hearing. He was pleasant and companionable and made it a point to maintain good personal relations even with political enemies; the time was to come when for a few weeks he confidently relied on these relationships to pave the way to the saving of the Union.

The crisis was at hand when the new Congress met in December 1849, and the House after three weeks and sixty-three ballots elected as Speaker Howell Cobb of Georgia, a Democrat. The Congressional hopper was filled with conflicting bills, and the two extremes united to prevent **The national crisis** action. Most urgent problem was California. In January 1848 James Marshall, while building a sawmill for John Sutter on the American River, had discovered gold in the tail race. Within a few months hundreds of eager men were digging and panning the mountain sands. The next year the Forty-Niners rushed to California from all parts of the globe, crossing the Plains and the Rockies, sailing around the Horn, or cutting across Panama or Nicaragua. By the end of 1849 California boasted 100,000 white inhabitants, had drawn up a constitution, elected Frémont as a Senator-designate, and was knocking at the door of Congress for admission as a free state.

There was the rub. California would upset the balance in the Senate, but Taylor saw no harm in this situation and, indeed, had encouraged California's hopes. The extreme groups, however, disregarding the fact that the Mexican Cession was not suitable to slavery, each resolved to have its way, and extreme Southern Whigs and Democrats alike demanded either secession or a clear-cut victory for Southern Rights. Calhoun, confident that his ambition was on the verge of achievement, refused all compromise. The extension of the Missouri Compromise line to the Pacific could probably have mustered a majority in each house if he had agreed to it, but he had now decided that the Missouri Compromise was unconstitutional. Southern extremists looked forward to a Southern Rights convention, called to meet in Nashville in June 1850, and confidently expected it to initiate secession.

Clay, Webster, and Calhoun were now the elder statesmen of the Senate, and each had at one time or another contributed to swell the passions now striving for mastery. And yet, with the House lost to all sense of **Clay's Omnibus Bill, 29 Jan. 1850** shame, the burden of solution lay upon the Senate. Clay, who had taken little part in the recent scene, now introduced his famous Omnibus Bill. It was a collection of measures, largely borrowed from Senator Stephen A. Douglas, Democrat of Illinois, which taken together compromised the problems at issue by apportioning something to each section. These were his proposals:

(1) California be admitted as a free state.

(2) Utah and New Mexico be set apart as territories, without mention of slavery since the institution was not likely to enter there.

(3) New Mexico east of the Rio Grande be cut off from Texas. (This would please free-soilers, who resented the pretensions of slaveholding Texas.)

(4) In return the Federal government assume the burdensome public debt of Texas.

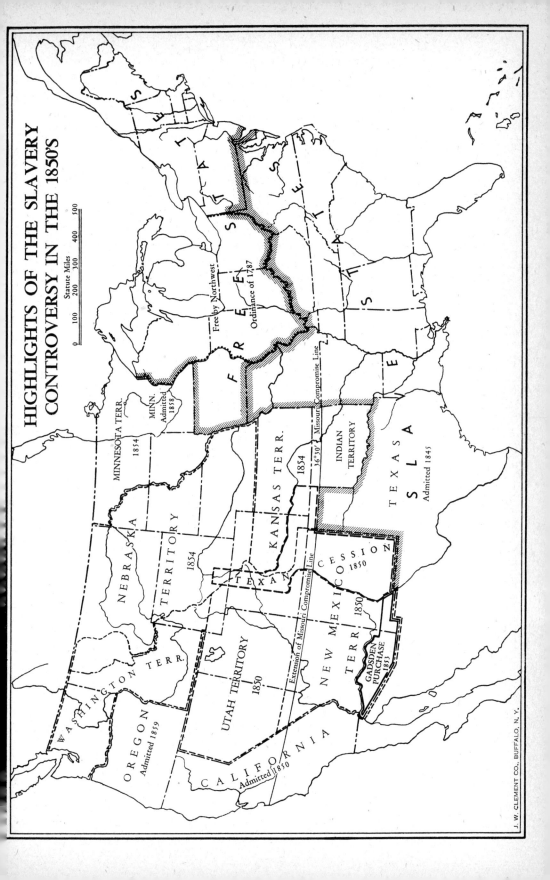

HIGHLIGHTS OF THE SLAVERY CONTROVERSY IN THE 1850'S

Statute Miles
0 100 200 300 400 500

Free by Northwest Ordinance of 1787

F R E E

S L A V E

MINNESOTA TERR. 1854

MINN. Admitted 1858

KANSAS TERR. 1854

36°30' Missouri Compromise Line

INDIAN TERRITORY

TEXAS Admitted 1845

NEBRASKA TERRITORY 1854

TEXAN

Extension of Missouri Compromise Line

NEW MEXICO CESSION 1850

WASHINGTON TERR.

UTAH TERRITORY 1850

NEW MEXICO TERR. 1850

GADSDEN PURCHASE 1853

OREGON Admitted 1859

CALIFORNIA Admitted 1850

(5) Slave depots be abolished in the District of Columbia in so far as they served the out-of-district slave trade.

(6) Slavery and local sales should continue in the District and should never be abolished without the consent of the people of Maryland and the District or without compensation.

(7) A strong fugitive slave law should be passed.

(8) Congress should formally acknowledge that it had no power to interfere with the interstate slave trade.

Though gaunter and feebler than when he had been the magnetic Harry of the West, Clay was still erect and self-confident when he rose on successive days to champion his proposals. With the latitude permitted

Clay's speeches

an elder statesman he chided and soothed both North and South and pointed out to the latter that secession would lose for it the very privileges which it sought in the District of Columbia, in the territories, and by the restoration of fugitives. As a result of his solemn warnings Unionists were rallied, and many hot-headed extremists were drawn back from the brink of ruin. The reaction of the nation was decidedly favorable, but Taylor, encouraged by Seward, mulishly insisted that all anybody needed to do was to ignore the situation— and this despite the approaching Nashville Convention and the fiery resolutions for disunion pouring in from the South and even from the Garrison stooges in Massachusetts.

For months while the Omnibus Bill lay before the Senate or in committee Senators rose to have their say, and the gallery of the little Senate chamber teemed with visitors whenever the word went out that a favorite

The Southern attack: Davis and Calhoun

orator was to be heard. One of the first was Jefferson Davis, leaning on his cane because of a wound received at Buena Vista. Though he had little to say upon the compromise, he set forth a vigorous defense of the South and a ringing challenge to the North. From that time on he was a marked man, never out of the public eye. Next was Calhoun, too ill to speak but carried into the chamber to sit, haggard, emaciated, but with eyes burning like coals while his address was read by a friend. It was his last effort. Ignoring the compromise, he summed up the gospel which he had long been preaching—the guilt of the North—and demanded the restoration of all the rights claimed by the South and a Constitutional amendment giving to the South a guarantee of perpetual balance.

This meeting was on 4 March. Before the month was out Calhoun lay dead, slain no doubt by the racking intensity of the crusade to which he had given the last twenty years of his life.

But before this Daniel Webster also had made the supreme effort of his career. Defeated and frustrated in his great ambition to be President, he now deliberately sacrificed on the altar of the Union whatever chance was left. Wrecked in health as he was and sustained only by **Webster's** drugs, he could summon only flashes of the old oratory. And **Seventh of** yet his Seventh of March Speech survives as his most mem- **March** orable. Standing at the departing threshhold of life, he re- **Speech** viewed the long course of the sectional conflict, assessed its bases, and demonstrated the artificiality of the present quarrel over territory. Since slavery could not exist in the Mexican Cession, why insist on the Wilmot Proviso? Why "re-enact the will of God?" Gently he sympathized with the grievances of both North and South, then went on to assert that the Union could not be sundered without war, for the sections were joined by social, economic, and cultural interests so close as to constitute a common blood stream. As he must have expected, the name Webster became anathema to extremists of North and South alike. And yet it is likely that it was he who turned the tide firmly toward compromise. The sight of those old rivals Clay and Webster, the two best-loved men in America, standing shoulder to shoulder in defense of the Union, won both North and South. From that time on, the success of the compromise was assured, especially when the death of Calhoun deprived the secessionists of their principal leader.

True, the bill lagged in the Congress. Seward, speaking for the anti-slavery North, in the name of the Higher Law, refused all concessions and confidently foretold the doom of slavery. Seward with his calm arrogance enraged the South more than had any other speaker, and even Clay demanded, "Who are they who venture to tell us **Other** what is divine and what is natural law? Where are their cre- **events** dentials of prophecy?" Cass now offered his nostrum of popular sovereignty, and Douglas supported it with a cogency which foreboded his later rise and fall on that very issue. Benton, opposing compromise because he did not believe the South would abide by it, was so out of step with his state that the Missouri legislature failed to return him to the Senate after thirty years' service in that body. Benton was a Westerner who failed to become a Southerner with his section.

Taylor, whose jealousy of Clay was patently growing, made things worse by encouraging underpopulated New Mexico to apply for admission as a state with boundaries including a part of the Texas claim. A clash between Federal and Texas troops seemed imminent, and Taylor further antagonized Southern leaders by asserting his determination to defend the Union by force and hang the leaders of any secession. Nevertheless, the Nashville Convention failed to follow the will of the South Carolina delegation, which wanted secession, but adjourned until November to await the outcome of the Congressional debate.

Suddenly the threat of Taylor's veto of the compromise was removed by the death of the President on 9 July as the result of complications

following heat prostration suffered while attending a ceremony at the
Washington Monument. Millard Fillmore (1800–74), who
now became President, was a handsome and able man who
had come up from the farm through hardships. Prudent, dignified, unpretentious, and conciliatory, he had presided over
the debates on the compromise and was convinced that moderation should
prevail. His attitude was shown by his reconstruction of the Cabinet to
give the South a proper voice and by his exertion of his new power to
whip as many as possible of the Northern Whigs into line with moderate
elements of both parties. Both extremes united and on 31 July forced the
Senate to amend every provision out of the Omnibus Bill except the one
on Utah; wits observed that the rough going had jolted out of the omnibus all the passengers but one. By now it was evident that the compromise as a whole could not muster a majority, but that each part could
rally enough supporters to pass. Clay, exhausted by the battle, went off
to the New England seashore, and Douglas by masterly leadership pushed
through the first seven parts of the compromise as five separate bills. The
House soon added its approval.

Passage of Compromise of 1850

The tremendous pressure under which the actors on the Washington
scene had been working was shown by the unprecedented and prolonged
binge which knocked Congress out of commission. Who can blame them?
Manifest Destiny had not proved fatal after all. Reason and
democratic compromise had routed sectional extremists, and
the Union was saved. The tipsy Webster, now Secretary of
State, was held erect on his balcony while to the jubilant torchlighted
throng he declaimed: "Now is the winter of our discontent made glorious
summer by this sun of York." A little later he more sedately expressed
the national sense of relief when he wrote: "I can now sleep of nights. We
have now gone through the most important crisis that has occurred since
the foundation of this government, and whatever party may prevail, hereafter, the Union stands firm. Disunion, and the love of mischief, are put
under at least for the present, and I hope for a long time."

General sense of relief

2 *The Southern Struggle Over Compromise*

The Compromise of 1850 ushered in a three-year intersectional truce.
Calhoun had sought protection of Southern Rights in the concurrent voice.
The admission of California had upset the balance between the sections,
and the South now retreated to another trench: reliance on
Constitutional guarantees. So far as we can judge, the South
was right in holding that the Constitution recognized slavery, but that does not prove that the Constitution was not
out-of-date.

Southern reliance on Constitutional guarantees

The Compromise of 1850 was not tamely accepted by either sectional extreme, but it was within the Cotton States that the first serious political reactions occurred. Each of these states had at least one outstanding leader who was bent on immediate secession, regardless of what its neighbors did. These Immediate Secessionists regarded themselves as the inheritors of Calhoun's mantle, and so insistent and fiery were their demands for action that they soon became known as Fire-Eaters. They were able to pre- **Southern struggle over the compromise** cipitate a sharp conflict, but within a year their movement had been defeated in each state by a coalition of Unionists and Co-operative Secessionists. The last were men like Jefferson Davis, who perhaps favored eventual secession but realized that the South was not ready either psychologically or economically for such action nor for the war it might bring. The Unionists were by no means submissionists. Their Georgia Platform was a clear warning that the South remained in the Union only because the North had agreed to certain pledges to protect slavery; if these pledges were broken, the South would no longer consider itself bound to its part of the bargain.

The Fire-Eater program was eminently unrealistic in the context of the South in 1851. The fact was that Southern regional consciousness was not yet strong enough (though it was growing) to overcome the traditional love for the Union. The South, along with the rest of the nation, was concerned with its tremendous economic growth and welcomed the compromise and subordination of the slavery issue. Indeed, the impetus given by the settlement to enterprise and investment, together with the gold of Cal- **Why the South favored the compromise** ifornia and an unusual European demand for American products, brought on an era of unprecedented prosperity. Both parties were still intersectional and were led by moderate men who were even ready to break party lines to defend the Union. Lastly, and this was the basic reason for the Fire-Eaters' haste, parts of the South were finding affinity with the North. Commercial and industrial interests, particularly in the seaboard cities, were leaning toward protective tariffs and a stronger central government. Even more serious, the rise of general farming in the Border States and the Upper South was linking them to Northern markets; moreover, slavery was perceptibly weakening and had even entered a "hiring-out" stage which might well portend emancipation.

The Unionists, who had won a temporary victory, trusted the North to obey the Constitution and stand by the Compromise of 1850. Both Immediate and Co-operative Secessionists asserted with varying degrees of conviction that it would not. They pointed out that the Con- **Unionists versus Secessionists** stitutional requirement that amendments be made only with the consent of three fourths of the states had been so thoroughly nullified by the doctrine of implied powers that no amendments had been necessary since 1804. When the Unionists showed that slavery in the states could be abolished only by amendment and that fifteen out of thirty-one states were slaveholding, the Secessionists retorted that the North could and would create enough new states by joint resolution to give the necessary three fourths. The Secessionists knew perfectly well that the territories were not suited to slavery, but by demanding its admission they hoped to keep the field of action outside the citadel where slavery already existed; they knew that the free-soilers were only attacking the outposts preparatory to a siege of the citadel.

The fire-eating Immediate Secessionists were Calhoun men, devoted to state rights, who thought of the coming Confederacy as a congeries of sovereign states governed by the concurrent voice in the best Calhoun tradition. Liberty, they asserted, could exist only if the authority **State rights versus Southern nationalism** of a central government were reduced to the vanishing point, and they refused to be disturbed by the problem of how the seceding states could be held together and defended. Most of them, in fact, later became state-rights thorns in the side of the Confederacy. More practical were the Co-operative Secessionists, who were not quite so much opposed to central power as they were to its use against the South. They wished to found a Southern *nation*, wherein the central power would be wielded by sympathetic officials and for the benefit of the country (the South) as a whole.

The Whigs had been responsible for the Compromise of 1850, but the result had been to split them wide open. The Conscience Whigs refused to be reconciled to the new Fugitive Slave Law, and the party lost more of its cohesive power with the passing of Clay and Webster in **Campaign of 1852** 1852. By the time of the presidential sweepstakes of 1852 the Democrats had suppressed their Southern revolt and, aided by a reconciled Van Buren, were enthusiastically championing the compromise. Reconciliations were purely formal and temporary; they were not even that in New York, where the return of the Barnburners to the parental rooftree had split the Hunkers into two factions: the Soft Shells, who were willing to receive the prodigals, and the Hard Shells, who were not.

When Cass, Benton, Buchanan, and Douglas had fought each other to a standstill in the convention, the party once more resorted to a dark horse. This time it was Franklin Pierce (1804–69), a charming, shallow, and weak-willed Doughface from New Hampshire, who had been one of Polk's political generals. William R. King of Alabama was nominated for the vice-presidency. The desperate Whigs, unable to unite in more than lukewarm approval of the compromise, sought public favor with a military hero, Winfield Scott. But the old war horse was no match for the dark horse. Pierce won 254 to 42, though he drew only about two hundred thousand more popular votes than Scott. The Free-Soilers' John P. Hale did not even show. Pierce selected a carefully balanced Cabinet—with Jefferson Davis as Secretary of War—and planned an administration which should appeal to the commercial North and the expansionist South.

The Democratic victory of 1852 was a lesson to politicians. The Fire-Eaters saw that their hope of immediate secession was an illusion, but they also saw that the Whig Party was hopelessly split along sectional lines and that the Democratic Party could retain its national character only by running an appeaser for President. If something should happen to crystallize sectional attitudes, **Effects of campaign of 1852** it was evident that the Conscience Whigs, the Free-Soilers, and Free-Soil Democrats would be drawn together into a Northern sectional combination. At the same time the Southern Whigs and perhaps the Cotton Whigs would be forced to enter the Democratic Party, which by its championship of the compromise had put itself in the way of serving as the mouthpiece and cat's-paw of the Southern Rights leaders. Northern Democrats like Douglas did not welcome the role, but they saw it as the only way to preserve the Union. Indeed, the people as a whole, far from seeing subtle implications, hailed Pierce's victory as the seal of approval on the compromise and turned with relief to their ordinary affairs.

Secessionists now turned toward a program of practical preparation of the day of crystallization. The failure of secession, they agreed, was due to the lack among the people of the consciousness of Southern separateness. The battle had been fought and lost on a political plane because the people refused to recognize that the issues were moral. Let this situation be remedied as soon as possible. **A decade of preparation for secession** Let the gospel be preached of Southern economic self-sufficiency, Southern intellectual independence, and of the evil Northern forces gathering to plunder the fair Southland and reduce it to the status of a mulatto colony. As might have been expected, the Fire-Eaters were the principal agitators, the Sam Adamses and Patrick Henrys of secession; and like Adams and Henry they were to know the bitterness of being thrust aside by "sound" men when the day of revolution was at hand. Because they were the real fathers, after Calhoun, of the Confederacy, it is worth while to pause to note the three outstanding Fire-Eaters: Rhett, Yancey, and Ruffin.

Robert Barnwell Rhett of South Carolina had a distinguished career in South Carolina politics and in Congress. Always a man to think in terms of black and white, action followed immediately on conviction. He seems to have been converted to secession as early as 1827, and it was only with difficulty that Calhoun broke him to heel during the nullification controversy. Indeed, his fiery independence continued frequently to burst forth, and in **Robert Barnwell Rhett (1800–76)** 1844, in defiance of Calhoun, he led the abortive "Bluffton Movement" to nullify the Tariff of 1842 in South Carolina.

He succeeded to Calhoun's Senate seat, but, upon the defeat of immediate secession in South Carolina, he resigned. Always the crusader, he was soon trying to precipitate a crisis by undermining the Democratic Party, the only remaining link between the sections. It was Rhett who forced South Carolina—Rhettsylvania, his enemies called it—to secede immediately after the election of 1860 and thus precipitated the crisis which helped to bring on war. Pointedly ignored by the Confederate government, he became its bitter critic (though not necessarily from mean motives) and was reluctantly put aside by his native state. Defeat and reconstruction did not destroy his faith in Southern "civilization," and he died believing that the South would yet be "separate and free."

William Lowndes Yancey, though born in Georgia, was reared by his stepfather in the Burnt District of New York, where he came into contact with such zealots as Finney and Weld. Upon his return to the South to

William L. Yancey (1814–63) study law he became the Unionist editor of a South Carolina paper during the nullification controversy. Presently he removed to Alabama, became a leading lawyer, and was sent to Congress. Yancey resigned from the Senate in 1846 because he could not stomach political compromises and thereafter devoted himself with rare consistency to the promotion of secession. The Alabama Platform was written by him, and its demand that Congress protect slavery in the Mexican Cession was widely adopted by state legislatures and conventions.

Perhaps less extreme than Rhett, he yet seems to have had no hope that the North would do justice to Southern Rights, but consented to stay in the Union until the South could learn to act as a unit. Meanwhile, though a long-time enemy of the party system, Yancey was so clearly champion of the ideals of Alabama that he became the leader of the Democratic Party in the state. Finally in 1860 he was able to act a vital role in splitting the Democratic Party, in nominating a Southern presidential ticket, and in leading Alabama out of the Union. After serving as Confederate commissioner in Europe he entered the Confederate senate and, as might have been expected, ended his days in opposition to the centralizing tendencies of the Davis government.

Edmund Ruffin, though a native of moderate Virginia, was one of the earliest secessionists. His chief claim to fame was the development of a practical method for restoring the fertility of the soil, which brought about

Edmund Ruffin (1794–1865) the astonishing economic recovery of Maryland and Virginia in the twenty years before the Civil War. Ruffin's basic intention, however, was to enable the South to stop the loss of population to the West and to preserve its political and economic strength either in a balanced Union or as an independent country.

An early associate of Rhett and Yancey, he gave his time unstintingly to writing and speaking on Southern Rights and to the development of Southern consciousness. When John Brown was captured at Harpers

Ferry, Ruffin hastened to secure some of his pikes and send them to the governor of each slave state as emblems of the Northern threat of servile revolt. His also was the hand that pulled the lanyard that sent the first shot against Fort Sumter, and as a "temporary private" at Bull Run he helped to hasten the Yankee flight. Too old to serve long in the army, he saw his land ravaged by war, witnessed the frustration of his cherished dream of an independent South, and then, brokenhearted, took his own life.

The outstanding leader of the Southern nationalists was Jefferson Davis of Mississippi. Born in Kentucky of yeoman stock, he knew what hard work was before an influential older brother got him admitted to West Point. While serving in the frontier army he married the daughter of Zachary Taylor (she soon died of malaria) and retired to become a cotton planter. As colonel of the Mississippi Rifles Davis played a vital role at Buena Vista and received his reward by being sent as a Democrat in rapid sequence to the House and the Senate. He was slight in body, ascetic in appearance, and hampered by poor eyesight, neuralgia, and nervous indigestion. Though he was sensitive and imaginative, he was wholly lacking in a sense of humor, was quick-tempered and egotistic, and never ceased to be a frustrated military genius. He was not consistently faithful to the idea of secession but for a time hoped to strengthen the South economically and territorially so much that it could balance the North. For this reason he was an active champion of expansion into the Caribbean, promoted a New Orleans–Pacific railroad, and inspired the Gadsden Purchase from Mexico to give it a right of way. *Jefferson Davis (1808–89)*

Even farther to the right than Davis were such men as Sam Houston of Texas, Henry S. Foote of Mississippi, and Andrew Johnson of Tennessee. Houston both as Senator and as governor consistently upheld the Union, and in the end he was deposed from the governorship and placed in Coventry by many of his neighbors. Johnson, trained in the school of Jacksonian democracy, rose from a lowly station in life, became Representative, governor, and Senator. His neighbors in the mountainous country of east Tennessee were notoriously out of harmony with the remainder of the state and in general agreed with the West. Unionist sentiments were therefore natural to the region and to Johnson, its spokesman. Foote as Whig Senator had championed the Compromise of 1850. The next year he ran on a Union ticket for governor, forced the retirement of secessionist John A. Quitman (another of Polk's political generals), and defeated the co-operationist Davis, who took Quitman's place. Foote unhappily acceded to secession in 1861, but was such a thorn in Davis's side that he was imprisoned; later he made his way north and sat out the rest of the war in Europe. Of course, *Southern Unionists* it should be understood that Southern Unionists upheld slavery, hated abolitionism, and believed in state rights. Their contention was that the South had nothing to gain by secession but much to lose.

Even more prominent than the above men was the famous Georgia trio: Alexander Hamilton Stephens, Robert A. Toombs, and Howell Cobb. Stephens came of yeoman stock and fought his way up by hard physical labor and mental and forensic ability. He was a Whig, and his abnormally cadaverous figure and parchment-like face were long in the forefront of state and national political battles. He fought secession to the last ditch, and though elected Confederate vice-president he spent much of the time in retirement and emerged chiefly to uphold state rights against Davis's encroachments. Toombs and Cobb, respectively Whig and Democrat, both came from the planter aristocracy, but they united with Stephens in 1850 to form the Georgia Constitutional Union Party, which successfully upheld the Compromise of 1850. Toombs finally went over to secession, became for a while a Confederate general—during which interval he challenged his commander to a duel—and fought Davis's policies. Cobb became Speaker of the House and Buchanan's Secretary of the Treasury. He also went over to secession and became a general but strongly supported Davis.

The Georgia trio

Rhett, Yancey, and Ruffin labored with voice and pen in preparation of the Southern mind. They organized Southern Rights Associations and Leagues of United Southerners to spread the gospel and to strengthen contacts among the Southern states. They organized committees of public safety on the pattern of the American Revolution and perfected the detailed steps which later led to secession and confederation. Even while they were preaching liberty they did not balk at deepening slavery by agitating for the reopening of the slave trade, on the plea that the blessings of slavery should be wider spread. "All my aims and objects," said Yancey, "are to cast before the people of the South as great a mass of wrongs committed on them, injuries and insults that have been done, as I possibly can. One thing will catch our eye here and determine our hearts; another thing elsewhere; all united may yet produce spirit enough to lead us forward . . . to drive the foe from the city of our rights."* Of course, it is impossible to be sure just how much outright secessionists were responsible for sectional consciousness and how much of it would have developed without their aid. Actually Southern unionists were just as anxious as secessionists for economic self-sufficiency, though not as a step toward political independence.

Planning for secession

Southern leaders also dared to run counter to the prejudice against manufactures and to insist that the South must rid itself of economic dependence on the North. Their aim was self-sufficiency and no more, lest

* Jesse T. Carpenter, *The South as a Conscious Minority, 1789–1861* (1930), 171.

it vitiate Southern civilization; one is entitled to wonder **Southern** how they could stop short at that magic moment. A rash of **economic** commercial, industrial, and agricultural conventions fol- **revolution** lowed, and all possible means of attaining economic self-sufficiency were explored. The chief promoters and publicizers were J. D. B. De Bow of New Orleans, whose *Review* has been mentioned, and William Gregg. Gregg opposed political separation but gave a practical demonstration in his South Carolina cotton manufactory that the South could make its own textiles. Manufacturing and processing were so successfully promoted that in the decade of the 1850's their value almost doubled, and invest-ments shot up about seventy-five per cent, especially in industries that competed with the North. Even more successful were the extension of railroads and the consequent growth of such inland centers as Atlanta.

Closely allied to these efforts was the propaganda for Southern intel-lectual independence. The leading churches had already split off from their Northern wings and were diligently promoting ideas of Southern separate-ness and moral superiority. Attempts were made to break **Demand** the reliance on Northern textbooks, of which many, espe- **for intel-** cially geographies and histories, were outrageously preju- **lectual in-** diced against the South. Perhaps it was natural that anti- **dependence** Yankee prejudices should be hauled into Southern textbooks. *Elements of Algebra* written by D. H. Hill, who later became a Confederate general, had this priceless problem:

> The Buena Vista battlefield is $6\frac{1}{2}$ miles from Saltillo. Two Indiana volunteers ran away from the battle at the same time; one ran half a mile faster than the other, and reached Saltillo 5 minutes and $54\frac{6}{11}$ seconds sooner than the other. Required: their respective rates of travel.

Efforts to keep Southern youth in Southern colleges met with consider-able success, and mountain and Gulf summer resorts began to supplant such places as Saratoga Springs as vacation spots. There was, however, a notable failure to supplant Northern books and magazines, for, as two Southern observers remark, "the culture of the Old South at its best was much more appreciative than creative." Such appreciation, however, was not extended to Southern talents such as Simms and Timrod.

The economic revolution failed to alter current trade conditions very greatly. Northern merchants, who had largely favored the Wilmot Proviso, were now alarmed lest Southern independence be made good, so swung their support to the Compromise of 1850. The more or less **Northern** *sub rosa* African slave trade to Brazil, Cuba, and Southern **merchants** ports was financed largely by New York merchants, and **and South-** investors in such merchandise were naturally sympathetic **ern ex-** to the South. Some merchants, anxious to placate the South **tremists** and preserve the existing pattern of trade, became openly proslave and were even willing to put out cash to advance Southern interests and win Southern goodwill. The dynamic secessionists saw their chance. The result was a curious alliance of some Northern merchants with Southern extremists to promote the expansion of slavery (and trade) to Cuba, Mexico, and Central America. Paradoxically the effect was to encourage Southern plans for the early rejection of the Compromise of 1850.

The weak Pierce immediately fell largely under the domination of this coalition, and the choicest Cabinet and diplomatic posts went to it while it prepared to renew an aggressive foreign policy. Actually the movement

Renewal of aggressive foreign policy
had already started under Fillmore and was to be continued under Buchanan. This was the period of Perry's opening of Japan (1853), of expansion in China, of entrenchment in Hawaii and the abortive treaty to annex the islands, and also of naval and whaler imperialism in the Pacific. The Reciprocity Treaty of 1854 with Canada was hailed as a victory both by Northern advocates of Canadian annexation and by Southern opponents. The clipper ship entered upon its brief challenge to the British carrying trade. Pierce, under the domination of Jefferson Davis and the ardent Doughface, Caleb Cushing, fostered a group of expansionists who were little better than highbinders in their projected seizures. Among them were John Slidell and Pierre Soulé of Louisiana; John A. Quitman, the Mississippi politician; and John Louis O'Sullivan, the New York editor who had coined the phrase Manifest Destiny.

American commercial, investing, and governmental interest was particularly involved in Cuba. We have seen how Spain had lost all its American possessions but Cuba and Puerto Rico, and how Great Britain, France, and the United States all coveted them. The American desire

Interest in Cuba
for Cuba was not solely due to its suitability to sugar, tobacco, and slavery, but also due to its strategic control of the entrances to the Gulf of Mexico. Spain, of course touchy because of its loss of empire, was determined to retain what was left and rebuffed American overtures for the purchase of Cuba. Spanish corruption and exploitation had never been worse, and the Cubans themselves would have welcomed the interference of any foreign power. As it was, refugees in the United States entered into conspiracy with expansionists and backed three abortive filibustering expeditions against Cuba.

In 1853 Pierce, probably influenced by Jefferson Davis and over the protest of Secretary of State Marcy, a New York Soft Shell, sent Pierre Soulé as minister to Spain to negotiate for the purchase of Cuba. Soulé

Ostend Manifesto
was a Frenchman who had left his native country because of his rabid republicanism and as Senator from Louisiana had been a notorious expansionist. He was a poor selection for the task, both because of his record and because of his hot-headedness,

and he promptly and picturesquely managed to ruin all chances of accomplishing his mission. Spain retaliated by suddenly tightening shipping regulations in Cuba and seizing the ship *Black Warrior* for their infraction. Soulé dramatically slapped an unauthorized ultimatum on the Spanish government. Fortunately he was not taken seriously, and the *Black Warrior* affair was settled with the owners.

Nevertheless, Secretary of State Marcy directed our ministers to England, France, and Spain to consult on the problem of how to get Cuba. In October they met at Ostend—James Buchanan, John Y. Mason, and Soulé—and recommended in the famous Ostend Manifesto that if Cuba was in danger of falling to France or England and could not be purchased, "then, by every law, human and divine, we shall be justified in wresting it from Spain." The furor from Europe was echoed by the antislavery press, and Marcy felt obliged to repudiate the manifesto. Soulé, who rightly held that the manifesto was merely a copy of his instructions as minister to Spain, resigned in a huff. Cuba was lost, but already railroads were undermining the value of Gulf commerce, and the renewal of the free-soil argument was overshadowing expansion.

Events in Central America were related in origin to the Cuban *putsch*. At this time Panama was a part of Colombia, and the latter country, fearing British encroachment on the isthmus, by the Bidlack Treaty gave the United States transit rights in return for a guarantee to keep the isthmian route open and neutral (1848). British interests, indeed, were rapidly expanding, and claim was laid to **Caribbean clash** Belize (British Honduras) and the Mosquito Coast of Nicaragua. In the latter area Greytown (now San Juan) was a British commercial center and the key to the San Juan River-Lake Nicaragua-Lake Managua route across the Isthmus of Nicaragua. Now Panama and Nicaragua were both feasible routes for an interocean canal, long an American dream. Suddenly in 1849 a British naval officer seized Tigre Island in the Gulf of Fonseca, and, though the action was quickly disavowed, the fat was in the fire. American public resentment was so high that war seemed imminent.

Secretary of State John M. Clayton promptly entered into negotiations with the British minister, Henry Lytton Bulwer. The resulting Clayton-Bulwer Treaty (1850) had to hedge in the matter of British territorial expansion since neither side would yield, but the document **Clayton-** certainly seemed to agree that neither would extend its Cen- **Bulwer** tral American possessions and that any canal would be open **Treaty,** to all nations and would remain unfortified. This treaty has **1850** always been regarded as the clearest proof of the slick way in which British diplomats have put it over on the ignorant Americans. It is certainly true that the United States failed to get what it wanted; yet in the light of the relative strength of the two powers and of the value of their interests

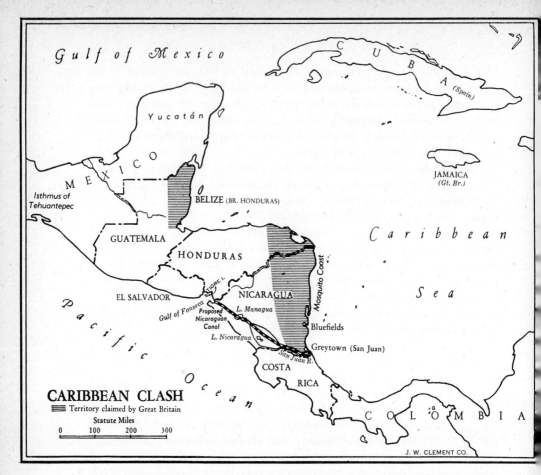

CARIBBEAN CLASH

≡ Territory claimed by Great Britain

Statute Miles

0   100   200   300

J. W. CLEMENT CO.

Map labels: Gulf of Mexico · CUBA *(Spain)* · Yucatán · MEXICO · M E X I C O · Isthmus of Tehuantepec · BELIZE (BR. HONDURAS) · JAMAICA *(Gt. Br.)* · GUATEMALA · HONDURAS · Caribbean · EL SALVADOR · TIGRE I. · NICARAGUA · Mosquito Coast · Sea · Gulf of Fonseca · Proposed Nicaraguan Canal · L. Managua · Bluefields · L. Nicaragua · Greytown (San Juan) · San Juan R. · COSTA RICA · Pacific Ocean · COLOMBIA

in the Caribbean, it can be interpreted as an American victory. By the treaty Britain agreed to Monroe's No-Colonization Policy, though of course she interpreted it to mean no *further* colonization; the possibility, then very real, of an exclusively British canal was averted; and, not least of all, the serious threat of war was dissipated. The treaty was in effect a holding action and was to be radically amended in 1900, when conditions had changed.

The Clayton-Bulwer Treaty settled the principal governmental frictions, but it did not satisfy the expansionist part of the American public, particularly the slavery expansionists and the metropolitan commercial **Walker's** expansionists. An American naval commander bombarded **Nicaragua** Greytown in 1854, and Pierce felt able to refuse a disavowal **filibuster** because England was busy with the Crimean War. Meanwhile there had begun the meteoric career of William Walker (1824–60) of Tennessee, the "grey-eyed man of destiny." A homely, ungracious, little bantam, Walker was opinionated, irascible, ruthless, and quite without military genius. Yet he symbolized Manifest Destiny in the Caribbean. After an abortive filibuster in Lower California he appeared in 1855 in

slaves from station to station across the Northern states to Canada. Hideouts were in barns, attics, cellars, and swamps, and transportation was by wagon or, if effective disguise could be provided, by public conveyances. Some men and women actually went deep into the South to aid the escape of slaves. Hundreds of fugitives found their way northward as stowaways on ships. It is supposed that all together about seventy-five thousand slaves escaped, most of them in the 1850's.

Resentment was not confined to secret operations. Protest meetings were held in the upper parts of the North. Slave catchers and Federal officials were occasionally intimidated. In the Burnt District, Seward went bond for some indicted rescuers of the slave Jerry and ob- **Forcible** tained the acquittal of all but one. Then the deputy marshal **rescues** who had arrested Jerry was indicted under state law for kidnaping! In Boston a mob broke open a jail to rescue a certain Shadrach, who was hurried on to Canada. In 1854 Theodore Parker, Wendell Phillips, and Richard Henry Dana (author of *Two Years Before the Mast*) led a mob which failed to rescue the fugitive Anthony Burns, though a marshal was killed in the scuffle. Federal troops and militia were called out to guard the way from the jail to the ship which was to take Burns back to Virginia. It was a day of mourning in Boston; church bells were tolled, flags were at half-mast, and business houses were draped in black as a cursing and reviling throng watched the procession pass. The return of Anthony Burns to his master cost the Federal government $100,000—and this in the very same city in which only nineteen years before a mob of top-hatted Cotton Whigs had sought to string Garrison to a lamp post!

Northern resentment found expression in at least thirteen states in a series of enactments known as Personal Liberty Laws. Some of these were quite as openly aimed at nullification of Federal law as any Southern state acts had been, and in fact the Wisconsin supreme court **Personal** boldly declared the Fugitive Slave Law void and calmly ig- **Liberty** nored the subsequent appeal to the United States Supreme **Laws** Court (*Ableman v. Booth*, 1859). The Personal Liberty Laws, both in letter and interpretation, varied greatly in severity from state to state but were rather generally strengthened as the sectional controversy became more bitter. The tendency was to prohibit the use of state facilities, such as jails, to slave catchers and Federal officials engaged in restraining a fugitive; state officials and ordinary citizens were forbidden to aid those engaged in the apprehension of slaves; habeas corpus and jury trials were provided for; and the burden of proof was placed upon the pursuer, and failure to win might lead to a charge of kidnaping. The Higher Law was now above the Constitution. Disobedience to the Fugitive Slave Law, said Salmon P. Chase, was "obedience to God."

The campaign initiated in the 1830's by the Tappan brothers and

Theodore Weld had never slackened. "Reformed" slaveholders like James
G. Birney were especially valuable both as evangelists and as exhibits of
Abolition the power of salvation. Another favorite exhibit was the
campaign escaped slave. Some of them, such as Frederick Douglass, a
heightened runaway from a Maryland master, possessed the gift of
oratory and were able to move audiences to emotional heights. As the
1850's advanced and abolitionists glimpsed success, their campaign took
on the frenetic surge of a great revival which sometimes actually throws
into convulsions anyone who comes within hearing.

We have already noted that the abolitionists were sowing the country
with propaganda literature which was in large part filled with, to say the
least, deliberately slanted misrepresentation. This propaganda, however,
Uncle did not strike home until events forced it into the public
Tom's consciousness. Far more important than pamphlets filled
Cabin with fancy and assorted horrors was the novel *Uncle Tom's
Cabin,* written by Harriet Beecher Stowe. Harriet Beecher, daughter of
Lyman Beecher, had seen slaves in Kentucky and fugitives in Ohio and
had listened to the debate at Lane Seminary. She now published her
answer to the Fugitive Slave Act, intending after the manner of Weld to
condemn the sin rather than the sinner; her brutal, slave-driving Simon
Legree was even pictured as a Yankee. Though the novel was based upon
fact, it showed poor comprehension of the slave system. The unctuous,
too-perfect Uncle Tom was cloying, the characters were stilted, the dialect
defective, and the descriptions inaccurate. Nevertheless, the melodrama
and sentimentalism of the novel made it beloved of a mawkish age and
fastened in the public mind a picture of the South as romantic, decadent,
and corrosive. In the first year (1852) three hundred thousand copies were
sold, and presently it leaped the seas to mold foreigners' impressions of
the United States. When it was dramatized, it drew even strict church
members to see it and did much to render the theater respectable. All together it was the most influential novel ever published in this country and
gave to its author a reputation which caused Lincoln to greet Mrs. Stowe
as the little woman who had caused the Civil War.

Uncle Tom's Cabin and the spate of similar works which followed
showed that the abolitionist and free-soil attacks on the South were at last
being transformed into moral and emotional appeals and as such were
Growing sinking into the minds of the masses. Nor was this process
sectional by any means confined to the North. The effects of extrem-
emotion- ist propaganda in either section not only inflamed its own
alism people but also served to irritate those of the other side.
The worst diatribes of Garrison found circulation in Southern papers as
illustrations of the Black Abolitionist determination to reduce the South
to social and economic equality with its own slaves. The secessionism of

Calhoun and Yancey was gleefully cited in the North, and Fitzhugh's highhanded recommendation that Northern laborers be reduced to slavery for their own good was quoted as typical of the Lords of the Lash. Where each side deliberately wrests its opponents' words and cites the abnormal as the average, there will be built up two essentially erroneous, but none the less powerfully effective, pictures.

The North had a clear and concise—but quite wrong—picture of the South as a land of aristocratic planters, slaves, and poor whites. The aristocrats lived in idleness and vicious dissipation in great pillared mansions and arrogated to themselves the benefit of all educational and political powers and the control and ownership of all property worth having. Other whites lived in ignorance, filth, disease, and poverty, voted as they were told to vote, and believed what the aristocratic lords of the soil told them. The slave, in between, lived coarsely (as was true), and worked himself to death, was beaten at the mere whim of sadistic drivers, and found solace only in religion and clog dancing. **Northern picture of the South**

The Southern view of the North was scarcely more accurate. The region was dominated by a class of vulgarians known as bankers, merchants, and manufacturers, who had no time for the cultured leisure typical of the South. Below them were the working masses, pale, overworked, living from hand to mouth, driven mercilessly until they broke down, then cast out to starve or live on charity. At the beck and call of the business interests were the farmers, completely dependent upon the market, which was manipulated in various shifty ways. Somewhere between them was a rabble of reformers, preachers, teachers, and newspapermen, each in his own sphere serving the devious and sinister plans of the rulers to reduce the fair women of the South to a fate worse than death. **Southern picture of the North**

The psychological state in both sections was bad enough, but a variety of economic explosives was lying about loose and adding to the peril of the situation. The Southern public, awake at last to the perils of the Cotton Triangle, refused to see that New York's merchants were slavishly eager for any arrangement that would preserve peace and trade—even to the length of permitting disunion. **Economic explosives** The Walker Tariff of 1846 revised duties downward, and the Tariff of 1857 all but instituted free trade; nevertheless, Southerners were still dissatisfied and habitually spoke of themselves as slaves to Northern interests. On the other hand many industrialists, particularly the ironmasters of Pennsylvania, considered that they were being sacrificed to the inefficiency of Southern planters. At the same time the West's granaries and cattle pens were bursting with a surplus which was unmarketable because there were no facilities for export. Polk's veto of the Harbor and River

Bill was regarded as a Southern slap at the West and encouraged a growing Northwestern belief that the Walker Tariff was a tax paid by the farmer "to this Southern nabob who has countless slaves to watch him when he sleeps and fan him when he wakes."

Most explosive issue of all was still that of slavery in the territories, for the common farmer thought he saw the possibility of being excluded by slave competition from moving to the Mexican Cession. The Compromise of 1850, however, left untouched the great area north of 36° 30′ which had been devoted to freedom by the Missouri Compromise and which the country was now aware was suitable for settlement. The tremendous growth of the West in the 1850's was aided by the railroads, which had tied Northeast to Northwest and were now hurrying toward the Mississippi to lay the prairies under tribute. Congress was already studying the need for a transcontinental railroad, but, since it was not likely to be financially profitable because of the enormously long haul and the scarcity of freight, it would clearly have to be built from government subsidies of land or money. Chicago, which it was evident could become the railroad center of the country, dreamed of extending its tentacles to San Francisco Bay and even to Puget Sound. Chicago, however, had rivals for control of the transcontinental railroad: St. Louis, Memphis, and New Orleans. The logical solution was to build four railroads, but few dreamed that four could ever be used.

Rivals for a transcontinental railroad

James Gadsden of Charleston, an ardent Southern nationalist and one of the greatest builders of Southern railroads, was the chief promoter of the railroad from New Orleans to the Pacific. When he found that the most practicable route lay in part through Mexican territory, his friend, Secretary of War Davis, had him appointed minister to Mexico. At this moment Santa Anna, in power for the sixth and last time, needed money and was willing to sell territory to get it. Though Santa Anna did not dare to part with Lower California and an outlet on the Gulf of California, he did sell an area the size of Pennsylvania for $10,000,000. This acquisition is now the southern parts of Arizona and New Mexico. Of course, antislavery Senators objected to the purchase, and it was open to attack as a worthless piece of desert acquired for the benefit of railroad speculators, but the treaty finally went through in 1854.

The Gadsden Purchase, 1854

2 Douglas and Nebraska

The problem of a transcontinental railroad, as it proved, bore the seeds of a renewal of the struggle over slavery in the territories. Stephen Arnold Douglas, chairman of the Senate Committee on Territories, was

the unfortunate author (and victim) of this renewal. Doug- **Stephen A.**
las had been born in Vermont but had come to Illinois at **Douglas**
the age of twenty. Though his herculean body and head con- **(1813–61)**
trasted with his short legs, and his snub nose destroyed dignity, he quickly
won a place for himself in law and Democratic Party politics and the
affectionate title of "Little Giant." He was indeed a born politician, cocky
and extrovertive, slow to recognize principles and shrewd in compromise,
a magnificent floor leader, a formidable legislative opponent, a popular
orator, witty companion, and man both of the world and of the people.
He was as shrewd an operator in business as in politics, and he managed
to utilize the two careers to win a fortune, chiefly in land speculation.

Though a New Englander born, and a resident (after 1847) of Yankee
Chicago, his strength lay in the southern part of the state ("Egypt")
where the settlers were chiefly from the South, and though they inclined
to oppose extension of slavery to the territories they were
definitely not opposed to slavery where it already existed. **Douglas**
Douglas thought likewise and resolutely refused to adopt **and slavery**
either extreme: "I have no sympathy for abolitionism," he warned the
South, but "if slavery be a blessing, it is your blessing." Douglas was an
expansionist, and (for once opposing a compromise) he fought the Oregon
settlement and had been one of the defiant band who marched past the
Senate teller shouting: "Fifty-four forty forever!" During the following
years he became the leader of the Young America wing of the Democrats
(as opposed to the Old Fogies), which favored expansion in territory and
trade and an active encouragement of democratic movements abroad. As
we have seen, he played a prominent part in initiating and passing the
Compromise of 1850.

Clashing interests had up to 1853 prevented Congress from organizing
the Nebraska area west of Missouri and Iowa as a territory. Indian claims
were not "extinguished" until that year. The South insisted that the Missouri Compromise was unconstitutional and refused to per- **The Ne-**
mit a step which might lead to the creation of another free **braska**
state. Missouri slave owners, chiefly hemp and cotton grow- **problem**
ers, were alarmed at the decreasing significance of slavery in the state
and at the prospect of being hemmed in on three sides by freedom. In
their wrath they rose and threw free-soil Benton out of the Senate and
out of political power and made proslave Senator David R. Atchison
leader. The latter now proposed to repeal the Missouri Compromise in
order to open the Nebraska area to his slaveholding constituents. Benton,
who had obtained election to the House, fought him bitterly.

Not the least of the factors involved was the rivalry between St. Louis
and Chicago. Each of them hoped to push its transcontinental line straight

west, and in 1853 the representatives of two kangaroo governments organized by the settlers of the respective spheres of influence in the Kansas River and Platte River valleys knocked at the doors of Congress. Douglas had been long interested in railroads, both as private investments and as public improvements, and he had been active in organizing the Illinois Central and obtaining its land grant. As a resident of Chicago and a railroad stockholder he was anxious to see his city become the terminus of a transcontinental railroad. This, however, would require the building-up of the intermediate Nebraska country; that would require a territorial organization, and that in turn would require Southern votes—and those votes would have to be purchased by concessions.

When Congress met in December 1853, the Pierce administration was plainly rudderless, and, though no serious questions seemed to impend, there was a chance for a bold pilot to take control. In January Douglas, **Kansas-Nebraska Bill, 1854** as chairman of the Committee on Territories, amended a bill already before the committee and re-introduced it; this was to be known to history as the Kansas-Nebraska Bill. It sidestepped the problem of the constitutionality of the Missouri Compromise but altered the intention of the compromise to insure free states north of 36° 30′ by providing that the new territory would decide the slavery issue when it was admitted as a state. This provision was intended by Douglas to induce the South to vote for the bill. Atchison was president of the Senate—Vice-President King had died—and with Southern backing persuaded his friend Douglas to add a clause which gave the people of the territory the right to decide on slavery or freedom while Nebraska was still a territory. Popular sovereignty would thus be put into effect, but the status of the Missouri Compromise remained vague.

Certain leaders of the Southern forces now saw their chance. They pointed out that unless the Missouri Compromise were repealed, slavery would not have a chance to enter Nebraska; popular sovereignty would **Douglas trapped** be a delusion, for since the territory was free the state would be free. Douglas saw the logical alternative: if slavery were permitted to enter, popular sovereignty would be a delusion, for since the territory was slave that state would be slave. He tried to stall but was overridden; a clause specifically repealing the Missouri Compromise was added. Then he made the best of the situation by trying to give something to both free-soilers and proslave men and to the rival railroad interests. The territory was divided into two parts: Nebraska included the northern or Platte River district, and Kansas included the southern or Kansas River district. The latter part, it was supposed, was suitable for hemp and tobacco and would become slave. The southern boundary of Kansas was placed at 37° to avoid dividing the lands of the Cherokee.

What were the motives of Douglas? There is no reason to suppose that he was solely moved by a desire to gain control of the Democratic Party as a step toward the presidency, or by a desire to boost Chicago railroad stock. The trans-Missouri area needed to be organized, and a transcontinental railroad needed to be built. **Motivations** Moreover, he seems to have believed sincerely that the Missouri Compromise was unconstitutional and that in any case the principle of geographical lines between free and slave soil had been displaced by popular sovereignty under the Compromise of 1850. Still, once he had entered on his course, he could scarcely avoid further steps. Apparently he failed to see that moral issues would be raised, and he underestimated the determination of sectional extremists. The result was a resounding Southern victory, which the South had not expected and which Douglas had not foreseen. In the cataclysm that followed, the transcontinental railroad was shuffled into the background, the ambitions of Douglas himself were frustrated, and the slavery controversy was reopened with heightened bitterness.

Though there was from the first little doubt that the bill would pass, the House proved obstreperous. Four months of battle followed, and all the old Congressional artillery of prejudice and misrepresentation was hauled out. There was, however, a marked difference in the **Repeal** public reception of the bill in the two sections. Southerners **of the** generally, though not invariably, favored it but were not **Missouri** inclined to get excited. The North, on the other hand, blazed **Compro-** up even before the completion of the bill, and Senator Chase, **mise** now a Free-soil Democrat, issued an "Appeal of the Independent Democrats in Congress to the People of the United States." Though full of exaggerations and misrepresentations, the "Appeal" served its purpose. Great numbers of Northerners were convinced, rightly or wrongly, that the Kansas-Nebraska Bill was a foul slavocrat plot and that Douglas had become cat's-paw for the South. The dramatic Anthony Burns incident, which occurred in May, pointed up the lesson.

Even some Southerners resented this breach of the armistice declared by the Compromise of 1850; Benton, Houston, and Bell of Tennessee were among a little group of Southerners who strongly opposed adoption of the bill. Other Southerners felt that neither Congress nor a territorial legislature could constitutionally exclude slavery from a territory. Their interpretation of the bill was that a territory could not legislate on slavery until the moment of admission to the Union; the Douglas-Cass view was that it could legislate at any previous time. Those Southerners who voted for the bill were simply taking what they could get—the repeal of the Missouri Compromise—and resolving to block the payment of the Douglas-Cass price for the repeal. In the end the advocates of the bill were able by threats and administrative pressure to swing Congress into line, and at the end of May it became law. The diligently spread word that Kansas could not possibly sustain slavery helped the passage in the House.

The Kansas-Nebraska Act with its repeal of the Missouri Compromise was perhaps the most fateful bit of legislation in American history. It put the cap on a structure of opinion that had long been growing in the North. **Effect of the Kansas-Nebraska Act** Unfortunately the same session of Congress saw the defeat by Southern votes of a new homestead law and the veto by Pierce of a new river-and-harbor bill. Northern men added up the list of what they believed to be Southern aggressions: free land withheld, the tariff lowered, internal improvements blocked, half of Oregon surrendered, continued efforts to expand into Cuba, Mexico, and Central America, and now the area north of 36° 30′ turned back to slavery with its discouragement of free farmers. The West was particularly irked, and even the upland Southerners in the area just north of the Ohio began to see the light. The moral Higher Law which had convinced the Northeast and the Lakes Region was reinforced by a practical demonstration that slavery was impeding progress. Sooner or later the roadblock would have to be removed from the American path to greatness.

3 The Republicans and Kansas

When Douglas went home after the fateful Nebraska session he traveled to Chicago, he said, by the light of his burning effigies. A little later, when he tried to address a mass meeting in that city, he was **Anti-Nebraska fusionist movement** drowned out by groans and catcalls and had to leave the platform. Indeed, the political situation had deteriorated with dramatic and alarming suddenness, even before the final passage of the Kansas-Nebraska Bill. Abolitionists and Free-soil Whigs and Democrats had frequently made common cause, but now, during the summer of 1854, a fusionist Anti-Nebraska movement swept the North. In the Northwest it all but wiped out the Whig Party, and even in the Northeast it gave the party a definite Anti-Nebraska color. Only in the Border States did Whiggery survive in recognizable form.

The summer of 1854 was notable for the rise of two parties: the Republicans and the Know-Nothings. It will always be disputed as to exactly how and where the Republican Party originated. Certainly as early **Rise of the Republican Party** as 9 May a caucus of Anti-Nebraska Congressmen in Washington proposed the organization of a new party, and the name Republican was suggested. The first adoption of the name, so far as we know, was by a fusionist mass meeting in an oak grove at Jackson, Michigan on 6 July. Other adoptions by conventions and mass meetings followed in rapid succession in Ohio, Wisconsin, Massachusetts, and Illinois. The name Republican appeared on the ballot in various states in the fall elections of 1854, but it was not until February 1856 that a national organizing convention met in Pittsburgh.

The Republican appeal to the tradition of Jeffersonian Democratic-Republicanism is self-evident. The movement was opposed to Federal interference either to weaken civil liberties in the states by the Fugitive Slave Law or to shore up the slave interest in the territories. Many state-rights Democrats were therefore strong supporters of the Anti-Nebraska movement. Indeed, there was **Foundation principles** more than a tinge of the populism of Jacksonian democracy about the early Republican Party; it was in considerable part a protest against the "aristocracy" of the South, which was accused of trying to hamper free labor not only by slavery in the territories but by its opposition to free land, to improved marketing facilities for the corn and wheat farmer, and to a tariff which would protect industrial labor.

Prominent in the movement was the old Jacksonian war horse Francis Preston Blair and his two sons, Francis Preston, Jr. of Missouri, and Montgomery of Missouri and Maryland, all prominent free-soilers even though they were slaveholders. Though the political roots of the family were in Missouri and were never withdrawn, **The Blairs** their headquarters until 1853 were in Blair House, across Pennsylvania Avenue from the White House. In 1853 the elder Blair moved to Silver Spring, a magnificent sylvan estate just outside the District, and it quickly became a refuge for politicians of all parties; for however inimical they may have been in debate, they flocked together in their hours of ease. More than this, however, Silver Spring may well be regarded as the place of conception of the Republican Party, just as Pittsburgh was its birthplace and Philadelphia its cradle. Silver Spring was also a favorite haunt of Lincoln during the war years. The Blairs were a tightly knit clan, allied by marriage and association with prominent families, and their influence in both Maryland and Missouri was an asset to be reckoned with by other designing politicians.

The Republicans were quite frankly a sectional party, and it was hard to deny (though abolitionists tried it) that they were serving sectional interests. The Democrats never let them forget it; the latter, however, ignored the increasingly apparent fact that their own party, **The Republicans and centralization** though still preserving the illusion of being national, had actually become chained to the sectional interest of slavery. There was a growing Northern demand for governmental centralization, and it was evident to many that the real tussle between North and South would be over control of the Federal government. Willingness to use the Federal government gained ground in Republican ranks as Whig leaders came into the party and brought with them the gospel of Alexander Hamilton's *Report on Manufactures* and Henry Clay's American System. The cement of opposition to the extension of slavery was strong enough to hold the party together during the ensuing crisis; but when after the Civil War the Hamiltonians prepared to use the party for their own purposes, the Jeffersonians shook its dust from their feet and returned to the Democratic Party or organized new parties such as the Greenbackers and Populists.

It is a striking fact that during the entire decade of the 1850's and right up to the Emancipation Proclamation most free-soilers heatedly denied that they were also abolitionists. Nevertheless, the South was right **Free soil,** in its claim that the free-soilers were at least antislavery, **abolition,** and as such their logical goal was abolition. We can go even **and popu-** further and admit that Douglas's popular sovereignty, far **lar sover-** from being neutral, would have doomed slavery. Its appeal **eignty** to the public—and Douglas must have recognized this—was that it gave free settlers the advantage and all but automatically excluded slavery. The slaveholder would have been foolish to bring his slaves into a popular-sovereignty territory which was not clearly and definitely adaptable to the growing of plantation products. So true was this that in 1855 Kansas showed only 242 slaves out of a total population of 8500; in 1860, out of 107,000, it showed only two. Republican leaders saw clearly the hopes involved in the Northern Democracy's doctrine of popular sovereignty and outbid it by the promise to every needy American of a free homestead of one hundred sixty acres.

Fully as spectacular as the rise of the Republicans was that of the American Party. The nativist movement was not new, but the spurt in immigration during the 1840's and the decay of the old parties gave it un- **Origin of** usual opportunities. Resentment toward the economic com- **Native** petition of foreigners had led to the formation of a number **Ameri-** of picturesquely named secret societies, chiefly in the cities, **canism** devoted to nativist and nationalist principles. On one hand many Americans resented the radicalism of certain German and Irish elements, while on the other hand they resented the conservative, anti-democratic principles then attributed to the Roman Catholic Church. Particularly feared was the claim of papal supremacy. Horace Greeley warned that most Catholic writers "maintain not merely the pope's supremacy in spirituals, but his authority to draw the line between spirituals and temporals, and when that is conceded, there is very little left."

Americans of that day inevitably made their protests known by political action. By 1854 the nativist secret societies had united into the American Party. Since they were oath-bound, party members answered questions about their principles by a simple "I know nothing" **Rise of the** —hence the popular name of Know-Nothing. The new party **Know-Noth-** had few prominent leaders and was obliged to trade votes **ing Party** for candidates; the result was a welter of local alliances. Prohibitionists resented the reluctance of the Democratic Party and of the Catholic Church to join their crusade; abolitionists bore a grudge against the same institutions, for it was well known that the Democratic Party wooed foreigners, and Catholic Irish laborers not only rioted against Negro labor but openly favored Negro slavery.

The Know-Nothing Party, therefore, became a refuge for homeless elements. For a time nationalists had some hope that the American Party could persuade Americans to ignore the slavery issue and unite in defense of Americanism. The weaknesses of the party, however, were greater than its strength. It went counter to the very considerable opposition to secret societies which had found expression in the Anti-Masonic Party; it was unable to stem the growing flood of the slavery controversy; and, worst of all, it too clearly rejected the American dogma of tolerance. Whether Know-Nothingism harmed the antislavery movement or served as a handy halfway house on the way to Republicanism is still open to argument. At any rate it had a strong if not decisive influence in 1854 and 1856.

The bankruptcy of Pierce became evident in 1854. Anti-Nebraska-Know-Nothing fusionists swept New York and set Weed and Seward to considering ways and means of getting aboard the band wagon. Simon Cameron, Pennsylvania ironmaster, Senator, and rival of Buchanan, went over to the Know-Nothings and carried **Elections** most of the state's Congressmen with him. Massachusetts **of 1854** and Delaware also came over to the Know-Nothing side, while Republicans and Know-Nothings between them controlled every Northwestern state. Even distant California went American. The party boasted that all together it had elected nine governors and 104 out of 234 members of the House of Representatives; actually most of those claimed were elected by coalitions. At any rate, the bloom soon disappeared from the mushroom. In 1855 a wave of bloody riots between Americans and foreigners (chiefly Irish) swept through the Northern cities and made voters hesitate to support such extremes. Even more decisive, in the same year the national convention split wide open on the Nebraska question, and hope of ignoring the slavery issue quickly disappeared. The Republican Party, which faced the issue boldly, began to collect in the state elections that year.

The clarification of the political scene in favor of the Republicans was in no small part the result of the dramatic struggle which was meanwhile going on in Kansas. Even before the adjournment of the Nebraska **Rival plans** session of Congress, Seward and Chase had accepted the **to capture** challenge to battle for the possession of Kansas. The new **Kansas** territory sloped from the high, semiarid plains at the foot of the Rockies to as fertile and beautifully diversified an area on the Missouri border as the continent offered. Now Missouri slavery was deepest entrenched among the hemp growers of the western part of the state, and, under the leadership of Atchison, they planned to make Kansas a slave state.

There seems to have been a measure of desperation in this planning, for slavery was on the defensive in Missouri, and any removal of slaves to Kansas would have weakened it further unless replacements were brought in from other slave states. There was little hope of this action, for slaveholders were supersensitive about risking their capital and property in an uncertain psychological and economic climate. On the other hand, Northern abolitionists and free-soilers organized "emigrant aid" companies and planned to pour free settlers into Kansas. They were for the most part immediate and undoubted failures, but the noise of their bursting was mistaken in the South for success. The free settlers actually came to Kansas, but for the most part they came from the Middle Atlantic states or the Ohio Valley, and they came under their own steam. Most of them, it may be added, though they were free-soilers, denied that they were abolitionists.

The rivalry between slavery and freedom for Kansas lent itself so neatly to rival land interests that it is often impossible to distinguish where land speculation ceased and the moral issue began. Generations of ex-**Kansas, the** perience in land manipulation had bred a class of bold and **land spec-** ruthless operators who poured into the territory as soon as **ulators'** it was opened. Those next to the Missouri border had the **paradise** earliest start and on the whole were the most turbulent. When the first governor did not play along with them, they used his own speculations to undermine his prestige in Washington and for that and other reasons obtained his dismissal. Thereafter they boasted openly that they would break any governor who opposed them, and the record shows that they did so. Their rivals, mostly free-state men, were not so shrewd in their actual operations, but they did manage to set up a government of their own, and they were more successful in their appeals to public opinion in Kansas. Claim jumping was a common practice, and often the real reason for bloodshed lay there rather than in any quarrel over slavery.

The first governor of Kansas was Andrew H. Reeder, a small-bore politician from eastern Pennsylvania. Reeder intended to be fair, but the cards were stacked against him. Voters on the frontier had seldom regarded regulations about length of residence but frequently **Territorial** had taken the right to vote because of the ownership of a **government** tomahawk claim. So it was that on election day in November **of Kansas** 1854 about seventeen hundred Missourians poured across the border to vote; some of them did not even trouble to assert land claims. Actually the same thing was going on in Nebraska, where Iowans flocked in to vote; but slavery was not an issue there. With the territorial vote of Kansas thus suddenly doubled and weighted on one side, the proslave party was in undoubted control. Proslave settlers were most numerous close to the Missouri border, and their chief town was Atchison. Free-soilers occupied the area southwest of them, with Lawrence as their center. Another election on 30 March saw the same tactics used even more brazenly. Free-soilers were either intimidated or indifferent, for they mustered only 800 against 5400, but of the last 4900 were later declared illegal. Nevertheless, proslave members completely controlled the legislature.

Reeder hastily went east to protest to President Pierce that the election was illegal but was coolly received. Upon his return, the jubilant legislature set up shop at Shawnee Mission near what is now Kansas City and proceeded to confine offices to proslave men and to **Rival gov-** vote to punish abolition activities with death. Reeder vetoed **ernments** in vain and presently was dismissed by Pierce for his un- **in Kansas** co-operativeness. Reeder was succeeded by Wilson Shannon, an openly proslave politician of Cincinnati. The free-soilers now held a convention at Big Springs, followed it by a constitutional convention, accepted the constitution by popular vote, and held elections for a free-state government. Forces of the two sides faced each other near Lawrence in the "Wakarusa War" in December 1855. The alarmed Shannon repented just in time and managed to avert open strife. Even Atchison saw the logic of retreat, for civil war might result in the election of an abolitionist President.

Meanwhile the Congress elected in 1854 had begun its session. Though the Democrats still controlled the Senate, they had only 83 in the House against the Republican 108 and the Know-Nothing 43. In those days no business could be performed in the House until a Speaker **The House** was chosen because the Speaker appointed the committees. **investigates** After two months of bickering, Nathaniel P. Banks, a Know-Nothing free-soiler of Massachusetts, was elected Speaker on the 133rd ballot. He proved to be a tactful and fair-minded presiding officer, but he could not prevent the House from falling into a deadlock over Kansas which lasted all spring. Finally, on the ground that two delegates from

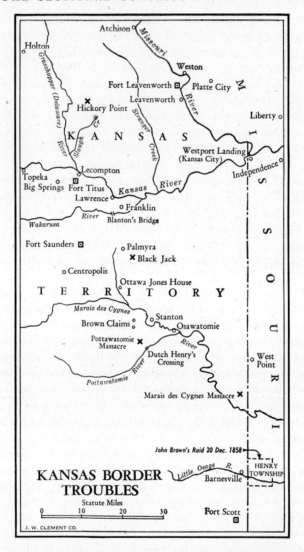

KANSAS BORDER
TROUBLES

Statute Miles

J. W. CLEMENT CO.

Kansas were asking admission, the House sent an investigating commission which held hearings in Lawrence and Leavenworth. The result was to expose the highhandedness and fraud of the proslave party as well as several killings by "border ruffians." Just as significant, however, was the disclosure of rivalries between real-estate interests and towns which found concealment under color of the struggle for and against slavery. Especially violent was the feuding among squatters, whose boundary conflicts were disclosed as land surveys were made.

But so far as the rest of the country was concerned the struggle was purely over a moral issue. Neither section was ready to listen to reason, and each boldly misrepresented the actions of the other in Kansas. A new crop of "aid societies" sprang up in the North and the South. Small companies of Southern volunteers appeared, and New England countered with shipments of fine new Sharps rifles: "Beecher's Bibles." Suddenly in the midst of the furor a grand jury in the proslave territory issued true bills for the arrest of the members of the free-state government. In May a body of at least five hundred men, trundling four brass cannon and passing themselves off as a Federal posse, invaded, wrecked, sacked, and partially burned the free-state town of Lawrence. The citizens wisely refused to resist, and only one life was lost. Nevertheless, lurid and exaggerated accounts flooded both North and South.

Sack of Lawrence, May 1856

Hard on the heels of the sack of Lawrence came vengeance. John Brown (1800–59) was a New Englander with a strain of insanity in his family, a taint which in good time he passed on to twenty children. A tanner by trade and a failure in every line to which he laid his hand, he was gaunt, prematurely old, and thoroughly despicable in his business activities. Ignorant, intolerant, and with a bigoted sense of his own destiny, he presently turned to abolitionist activities and in 1855 went to Kansas and settled on Osawatomie Creek. Probably his migration was prompted by desire for land; anyhow, he felt that he had been cheated by proslave men. Like an Old Testament prophet exacting vengeance, Brown burned to repay the five known murders of free-state men by "border ruffians." A few days after the Lawrence episode Brown, with four of his sons and two others, fell upon a proslave settlement on Pottawatomie Creek and hacked five victims to death.

John Brown and the Pottawatomie Massacre

The immediate result was war; the territory now really became "Bleeding Kansas." Guerrilla bands from both sides roamed about robbing and murdering. Osawatomie was burned, and a dozen of its inhabitants killed, and presently Brown and his sons, now officially hunted by the authorities, fled from the territory. Neutrality was impossible, and many settlers chose to leave rather than fight. The immediate response from both sections was to send hundreds of armed men to the scene of action, and when the Missouri River was closed to free-state traffic a route was marked out across Iowa. "Armies" of self-styled militia marched and countermarched, and some brushes occurred. Shannon, who had worked frantically but ineffectively to prevent bloodshed, was succeeded in September by a new governor, John W. Geary of Pennsylvania. Geary was a mountain of a man with proportionate ability, courage, and determination. Acting vigorously and impartially, he was able with the support of the United States army commander, to disperse the armed bands of both parties and restore some degree of order. But it was too late; Bleeding Kansas had become a national issue.

Bleeding Kansas

Before the news of the sack of Lawrence and of the Pottawatomie Massacre could reach the East, there occurred in Washington an event which was to have an equal effect on sectional animosities. Senator Charles

Charles Sumner: his invective on Kansas

Sumner (1811–74) of Massachusetts was a strange mixture of culture and poor taste, egotism and unselfishness, high principles and low invective—and yet despite it all an amiable man who eventually built a solid degree of popularity, partly by according the flattery of the closest and most lively attention to whatever others said. A hero to the multiplying abolitionists of New England, he was at this time the most cordially hated man in the Senate and in the South.

Sumner fancied himself as an orator, and he now (19–20 May 1856) undertook to deliver a philippic on Kansas which should rank with the great orations of history. Instead it was an overstuffed exercise in ranting invective, unsporting misrepresentations, and personal insults. Senator Andrew P. Butler of South Carolina, a courteous, mild-spoken, and silver-haired gentleman of the old school he called a Don Quixote embracing his Dulcinea, the harlot Slavery; Douglas he impaled as "the ready squire of Slavery," Sancho Panza. In the exchange which followed he described Douglas to his face as a noisome animal which could only be recognized as a skunk.

No member of Congress since John Randolph had so expertly mixed metaphors or been so directly insulting. If the matter had rested there, the public reaction against Sumner's vulgarity would sufficiently have

Brooks assaults Sumner

punished him. Unfortunately Butler's nephew, Representative Preston Brooks, resolved on direct action. After adjournment of the Senate on 22 May he approached Sumner, who was sitting at his desk on the Senate floor, and showered him with blows from a hollow gutta-percha cane. Sumner was almost stunned and blinded by the first blows and, wedged behind his desk, was unable to rise. Finally he tore the desk loose from the floor, then fell prostrate. When by-standers finally pulled Brooks away, Sumner had been so severely beaten that a series of complications, added to physical and mental shock, prevented him from resuming his duties until December 1859. Meanwhile his seat in the Senate stood empty as eloquent testimony to the strengthening resolve of the people of Massachusetts.

The effect upon North and South was deplorable. Southern editors and speakers all but unanimously gloated over Sumner's punishment, but except in South Carolina they regretted the time and the place and feared

Effects of the assault

the consequences. The House, after some altercation, censured the assailant. Brooks resigned his seat and went home to stand for re-election. After a shower of congratulatory dinners, eulogistic speeches, and gift canes, he was triumphantly returned to the House. In the North few but abolitionist extremists had excused Sumner's speech, but Brooks's assault was regarded as an outrage to civilized and democratic standards. The South Carolina reaction was confused with that of the South as a whole and went a long way to convince even Northern moderates that the code of Southern chivalry was that of naked force and that the term gentleman was merely a synonym for bully. Coming at the same time as the news of the sack of Lawrence, the effect was to convince many of those who had been hesitant. One of them was Abraham Lincoln of Illinois, who now finally left the Whig Party to join the Republicans. Just as significant was the effect abroad. The Brooks episode, together with Southern duels and hot-headedness, told against the cause of the South particularly in England, which was already ardently opposed to slavery.

The furor over Kansas and the Brooks assault was still in full control when the election campaign of 1856 opened. Pierce was a stench in the nostrils of honest believers in popular sovereignty. Douglas was hampered by his seeming lack of moral principle and his legislative violence. Indeed, his very courage and audacity were against **Campaign** him in a party which sought political availability rather than **of 1856** clean-cut decisions—and then there was Bleeding Kansas, which in the North was laid at his door. As a result the party, under the subtle guidance of a Southern senatorial clique led by John Slidell of Louisiana, tapped James Buchanan, but only succeeded because Douglas made the generous gesture of surrendering his delegates to the Pennsylvanian. Buchanan had been absent at the Court of St. James's and had not found it necessary to take a stand on fatal issues; with him was placed the name of John C. Breckinridge of Kentucky.

The Republicans, passing over Seward, struck the glamorous note of youth, nominated the dramatic Frémont and carried on with crusading fervor under the banner of "Free Soil, Free Speech, Free Men, and Frémont!" The Know-Nothings split wide open on sectional lines, and in the end the Northern wing accepted Frémont; and the Southern wing (known usually as South Americans) agreed to the "Silver Gray" Whigs' nomination of Millard Fillmore. The Whig line was to ignore the sectional crisis except for lip service to popular sovereignty.

Probably Buchanan was strengthened by threats of disunion from abolitionists and Fire-Eaters, for though the latter supported him, he was so clearly the candidate of moderation and appeasement that many old Whigs went over to him in order to defeat Frémont. In the end the Democrats won, somewhat to their own surprise. **Democrat** Frémont carried New England, New York, Ohio, Michigan, **victory** Wisconsin, and Iowa. Buchanan was saved by Pennsylvania, Indiana, and Illinois, but his margin there was narrow, and it was evident that the latter two might be lost next time if their central counties changed. All together the Republicans took eleven states and 114 votes, Fillmore carried Maryland with 8 votes, and the rest went to Buchanan with 174 votes. Comfortable Democratic majorities were won in Congress. The respective popular vote was 1,300,000; 900,000; and 1,800,000.

James Buchanan of Pennsylvania, though he had served as Senator, Secretary of State, and diplomat, was basically nothing more than a politician serving in the presidency at a time when only statesmanship of the highest caliber would have saved the nation. Even admitting his goodwill and patriotism, the conservatism of age, it was clear, had made even more pliable a man who in his prime had deserved the name Doughface for his willingness to yield to Southern demands. Weak in spirit, ill in body, and lacking in breadth of vision, Buchanan was a bad omen for the stability of the Union. His apparent resentment that it was Douglas who had given him the nomination was to play a part in his downfall.

James Buchanan (1791– 1868)

Buchanan had scarcely moved into the White House when on 6 March the Supreme Court handed down a decision in the case of *Dred Scott v. Sandford*. Dred Scott, a slave belonging to an army surgeon, had been taken to Illinois, a free state, and Minnesota Territory, then free under the terms of the Missouri Compromise. In 1846, some years after his return to Missouri, Scott brought suit in the state courts for his freedom, and eventually his plea was rejected in the state supreme court. Meanwhile Scott had by arrangement been purchased by a New York abolitionist named Sandford, and, since the suit was now between citizens of two states, the case was transferred to a Federal court whence it was passed up to the Supreme Court and there came under the guidance of Montgomery Blair.

Dred Scott case

Of the nine Justices, seven were Democrats; five of them were from slaveholding states, with Chief Justice Taney of Maryland at their head, though it should be understood that none of them held slaves, and all were more concerned with state rights than with the extension of slavery. The issue to be decided was whether a Negro was a citizen of a state, in this case Missouri, and consequently a citizen of the United States; beyond this was the question of the Constitutionality of the Missouri Compromise, though this did not necessarily have any bearing on the issue of Negro citizenship. The Court would probably have contented itself with denying jurisdiction, but the two Whig and Republican Justices signified their intention of dragging in the slavery issue. This attitude plunged the case into politics, and proslave and antislave men outside the Court thought they saw a chance to get a ruling on the Constitutional issue. Southern leaders, particularly, aided by the President-elect, brought all possible pressure to bear upon the Democratic majority.

Taney finally agreed that it was the duty of the Court to pronounce on the mooted issue. Speaking for the seven Democrats, he denied that Scott was a citizen of the United States, first because no Negro could be a citizen and second because he was a slave. Taney accepted the theory of dual citizenship (Federal and state) and asserted that, regardless of his citizenship status in Missouri, **Taney's decision** Scott could not be a Federal citizen because at the time of the adoption of the Constitution Negroes were regarded as inferior beings and were not entitled to such guarantees as the right of citizens of different states to sue in Federal courts. Anyhow, in Scott's case Missouri did not acknowledge him as a citizen, so he could not claim United States citizenship on the ground that he was a citizen of a state; moreover, Missouri asserted that he was a slave, and how could a slave be a citizen?

More than this—and here Taney laid himself open to the unjust charge that he spoke *obiter dictum*—Scott could in no case have been freed by residence in Minnesota Territory. The Missouri Compromise was unconstitutional because Congress had no right to prohibit the **Missouri Compromise unconstitutional** introduction of slave property into a territory. In a very carefully phrased statement Taney denied that Congress could exercise police power over a territory or rule it as a mere colony. It could not, therefore, "infringe upon local rights of person or rights of property," that is, could not forbid slavery. Now this was what Cass and Douglas had contended, but Taney went on to assert that it could confer no power on the territorial legislature to infringe on slave property. Actually every single Justice wrote a separate opinion, and some of them differed from Taney in important details. One of the most telling points against Taney was that at the time of the adoption of the Constitution some Negroes did exercise citizenship rights in some states, both Northern and Southern.

The elated South now saw upheld in the highest court Calhoun's old contention that the Constitution was a static instrument of government, not subject to reinterpretation in the light of changing conditions. The decision clearly knocked out free-soil doctrines, for it asserted that slavery followed the flag into all territories. At **Effect of Dred Scott Decision** the same time it just as clearly disposed of popular sovereignty; for if Congress could not exclude slavery, then how could its creation—the territorial legislature—exclude it? Republicans replied that the question before the Court had been whether Dred Scott was or was not a citizen; the matter of the Constitutionality of slavery in the territories had been dragged in by the heels. Taney had thus spoken irrelevantly and without binding effect, and his decision could and should be reversed. Even if he was legally right, he was morally wrong—all the more reason for working to reverse him. North and South had thus changed their attitudes on the Supreme Court, or was it that the Court had changed by abandoning the progressive principles of John Marshall and championing the static principles of John Calhoun? In any case, Taney's attempt to use the prestige of the Court to arrest sectional strife was a lamentable failure and actually promoted it.

Buchanan now proceeded to demonstrate his Southern bias, or, in the light of the Dred Scott Decision, his allegiance to the Constitution. Anxious to settle the problem of "Bleeding Kansas," he sent out as governor **Further** the able and fair-minded Robert J. Walker. The new gov-**rivalry** ernor called an election to choose delegates to a constitu-**in Kansas** tional convention, but the free-soilers, distrustful of Walker (and perhaps influenced by Republican politicians, who found the continuance of the Kansas struggle a political asset), boycotted the election, and it was carried by the proslave element. As a result a convention at Lecompton in October 1857 framed a proslave constitution, but instead of putting it up to the voters provided simply that the people should vote for or against the further importation of slaves; in either case the constitution would be approved. Again the free-soilers boycotted the election, and the constitution was adopted by 6000 votes with the proviso for the continuance of slave imports. In the recent election for the territorial legislature, however, the free-state men had voted; and, with Governor Walker rejecting fraudulent votes, they had won a majority. The new legislature promptly resubmitted the Lecompton constitution. This time the proslave men boycotted the election, and the document was voted down by 10,000 votes.

Kansas plainly wished to enter the Union as a free state, and the embarrassed Buchanan dismissed Walker for having let the feline out of the bag. He then (February 1858) laid the Lecompton constitution before **Kansas** Congress and recommended that Kansas be admitted as a **rejects** slave state with that constitution. This was too much for **statehood** Douglas. His popular sovereignty had been dealt a severe blow by Taney's decision, and he knew that in persisting in its defense he was sure to alienate the South. Nevertheless he sprang to defend the right of Kansas to accept or reject slavery; and though he lost in the Senate, he was upheld in the House. His allies came not only from the ranks of the Republicans but also from the old-line Whigs of the South who deplored such useless exacerbation of the slavery question.

Finally a compromise, the English Bill, submitted the Lecompton constitution to a third referendum in Kansas; if the people accepted it, they would be admitted at once as a slave state and receive a gift of public lands; if they rejected it, they would have to wait until their population reached the Congressional ratio, then 93,600, with nothing said about public lands. Kansas refused to take the bribe. The Lecompton constitution

the popular concept of the man of sorrows and compassion. In action, however, the eyes were transformed with intelligence, vivacity, and friendliness, and with them the man's entire personality; this was Lincoln the stump speaker, the courtroom partisan, and the tavern jokesmith, the Lincoln that men, women, and particularly children loved.

His uncouth manners, careless dress, and purposefully rustic speech gave him an air of oddity, an asset in frontier Illinois but of doubtful value in Washington. There were, moreover, his swift changes of mood from rollicking conviviality to deep depression, and these have given rise to explanations ranging from auto-intoxication to mental instability. Certain it is that he never took responsibility lightly, though observers often misunderstood and criticized his desire to seek in laughter (often in the form of off-color jokes) a release from the almost unbearable pressures of office.

Through a lifetime of self-discipline Lincoln attained a degree of self-control which would be sorely needed as President. Along with this went a spirit of tolerance which rose from a deep belief in democracy, and which made him slow to cast stones at the morals of his opponents. **Character** Though he never joined a church, he possessed a deep reli- **and ex-** gious sense which often found vent in prayer or in sincere **pression** expression of spiritual aspiration. In a day of florid oratory he spoke simply, clearly, and to the point. His papers and speeches are models of the clarity of the English language when used by a master, and in them are found the classical expressions of the significance of Anglo-Saxon liberties. Ideas came slowly, and in their formation they were stripped of romantic delusions and excess verbiage until they emerged concrete and unadorned. Even then there was nothing startling or even original about them, but they gave light because of their clarity and vigor. Lincoln was a superb example of that typical Anglo-Saxon leader, the "uncommon man of common opinions."

Though most of his political life was spent as a Clay Whig, Lincoln was in fundamentals a Jeffersonian liberal. Manhood suffrage, woman suffrage, the rights of labor, and the right of the Negro to freedom and a chance at self-improvement were with him but practical applications of the Declaration of Independence, in whose **Lincoln the** tenets of Natural Rights he earnestly believed. No Ameri- **politician** can, except possibly Jefferson and Jackson, was in his lifetime so close to the grass roots of the American popular will, and none more clearly received or deserved popular confidence. Nevertheless, though painfully honest in his personal life, Lincoln resembled Jefferson in his ability to cut through to basic political realities. While judging his opponents dispassionately and even admiringly, he used against them the politician's usual guileful weapons except that last and most despicable resort, scandal. It is characteristic of the man that two of his personal friends were Stephen A.

Douglas and, even more remarkable, Alexander H. Stephens, vice-president of the Confederacy, with whom he had become acquainted in Congress.

Lincoln recognized the justice of the Southern contention that free-soilism was logically the enemy of slavery in the states as well as the territories. His Peoria Speech, delivered repeatedly in 1854, made this clear even though he opened it with the statement that he wished to draw a distinction between the existing institution of slavery and the extension of it. He admitted that he had no answer to the problem of slavery and even if all earthly power were given to him he would not know what to do, but he went on to point out certain exceptions to the Southern point of view. He denied that the Missouri Compromise had been repealed by the Compromise of 1850. He denied that the slave was property as a hog was property and proved his point by the South's own antipathy toward slave traders, its consent to punish by death anyone caught engaging in the African slave trade, and by its tolerance of the residence of free Negroes in the slave states. For these reasons slave property was not on the same basis as other property in the territories. Slavery, he asserted, was undermining the rights of free labor in both the North and the South, and the territories must be preserved as a refuge for those who were undercut by slave competition or adversity, or who were just beginning life. More than this, while he did not desire equality of the races, the way must be left open for the Negro to work for himself and to better his condition.

The tragedy of the South and of America was that the South was no longer ashamed of slavery. Little by little the principles of the Declaration of Independence had been rejected, and now, with slavery as our Achilles' heel, the enemies of democracy were able to taunt us upon the tyranny of republican institutions and brand us truly as hypocrites. "No man is good enough to govern another man, without that other's consent. I say this is the leading principle—the sheet anchor of American republicanism." It was this principle that slavery and the Kansas-Nebraska Act violated. This principle must be recognized in the new territories, and its contradiction in the slave South must be confined to its present limits, otherwise American freedom was doomed. Lincoln's assertions that slavery was the affair of the nation, not solely of the states, and that slavery was a moral issue which flouted all principles of right and jeopardized the liberties of those who were already free—these were also the fundamental principles of abolitionism. Two years after Peoria, Lincoln admitted the Republican object of extinguishing slavery in his "Lost Speech": "Let us draw a cordon, so to speak, about the slave states, and the hateful institution, like a reptile poisoning itself, will perish by its own infamy."

Lincoln had been the leading Whig of Illinois, and when in 1856 he

Free-soil doctrine

went over to the Republicans he quickly became their leader. That same year he received 110 votes in the Republican national convention for the vice-presidential nomination. In 1858 he successfully sought the nomination for Senator to run against Douglas, and in his speech of acceptance delivered his justly famous House-Divided Speech. Though the Biblical phrase had been applied to the sectional controversy before, it was this use that attracted national attention. In seeking to explain the persistent agitation over slavery, Lincoln stated his belief that agitation would not cease until a crisis had been reached and passed. He then continued:

Lincoln's House-Divided Speech, 17 June 1858

> "A house divided against itself cannot stand." I believe this government cannot endure permanently half slave and half free. I do not expect the Union to be dissolved; I do not expect the house to fall; but I do expect it will cease to be divided. Either the opponents of slavery will arrest the further spread of it, and place it where the public mind shall rest in the belief that it is in the course of ultimate extinction, or its advocates will push it forward till it shall become alike lawful in all the States, old as well as new, North as well as South.

Nor would Lincoln admit that the present situation was fortuitous; Southern encroachments, culminating in the Dred Scott Decision, fitted together so neatly that they indicated a deliberate plan. What was the next step? "Another Supreme Court decision, declaring that the Constitution of the United States does not permit a state to exclude slavery from its limits." Douglas's proclaimed indifference to whether slavery was voted up or down was but contributing to this end. If he was a lion, he was "a caged and toothless one"—the prisoner of the slave interests.

Douglas had won praise for his break with Buchanan over popular sovereignty in Kansas. Even among Republicans there was a feeling that if Douglas could put across an honest enforcement of popular sovereignty, the territories would all vote for freedom, which was what Republicans wanted. Some Eastern free-soilers claimed that the coming victory of freedom in Kansas settled the whole territorial issue and ended any reason for the existence of the Republican Party. Lincoln, however, felt that the South would not be so easily counted out; moreover, there were still the burning issues of free land and internal improvements (in his mind clearly linked to democracy and the welfare of the common man) to which the South remained unreconciled. In this campaign, administration patronage was thrown against Douglas so effectively that it threatened to split the party and give the election to Lincoln. There was some pressure for Lincoln to retire in Douglas's favor, perhaps thus luring him into the Republican Party.

Republican resolution weakens

Lincoln knew Douglas well and was so certain that he was not to be trusted with the execution either of a moral program or of Western desires that he resolved to expose him. When Douglas chortled over the "radical-
The Lin- ism" of the House-Divided Speech, Lincoln challenged him
coln-Doug- to a series of debates, and it was arranged to hold seven,
las debates one in each Congressional district. Since it was the state legislature which elected Senators, the actual struggle was to win a majority of seats in the coming election. The political prominence of Douglas drew national attention to the debates; at first there was amusement at the sight of the ill-matched pair on the same platform, but as the debates continued into the autumn there was an increasing awareness of the significance of the clash.

Lincoln scored repeatedly by drawing from Douglas the admission that he had no moral scruples against slavery and did not care whether it was "voted down or voted up." This admission convinced many hesitant Re-
The Free- publicans that Douglas was not fit for their presidential
port Doc- nomination in 1860. Douglas had alienated much Southern
trine support by his rejection of the Lecompton constitution, and such as remained was cleverly spiked when at Freeport Lincoln forced from his opponent the statement which came to be called the Freeport Doctrine. "Can the people of a United States Territory," asked Lincoln, "exclude slavery from its limits prior to the formation of a state constitution?" An affirmative answer would flout the Dred Scott Decision, the darling of the South; a negative would deny popular sovereignty, the block by which Douglas had mounted to power and which he hoped would carry him higher. Nevertheless, the Little Giant boldly seized the affirmative horn of the dilemma. Actually, as he reminded Lincoln, there had never been any doubt of where he stood. "It matters not," said he, "what way the Supreme Court may hereafter decide . . . the people have the lawful means to introduce it or exclude it as they please, for the reason that slavery cannot exist a day or an hour anywhere unless it is supported by local police regulations."

The answer pleased the people of Illinois well enough to cause them to elect a legislature favorable to Douglas. Lincoln lost, but he was satisfied. Douglas had perhaps put himself in a position to carry the North-
Effect of west in 1860, but the South would have to choose between
the Free- him and the Dred Scott Decision; if it chose the first, it
port Doc- would yield all its principles for a partisan victory; if the
trine second, it would be forced to accept a sectional minority party. Southern-Rights leaders bitterly resented the way in which Douglas had kicked over the party line which they had so carefully laid around their interests in Kansas—especially his rejection of the Lecompton con-

stitution—and were determined to make him suffer even if they had to cut off their own noses. Actually none of Douglas's admissions were new; Lincoln was simply driving home again and again the lesson which he wished the country to learn. In so doing he knocked two vitally important spokes from Douglas's chariot wheels and did his share toward dooming it to crash in the race of 1860.

It is not likely that Lincoln even dreamed that he would be the successful contestant in 1860. Whether Lincoln was merely aiming at partisan advantage or was actuated by deep conviction is a question that can be answered only in the light of one's opinion of his character. **The moral** A study of his speeches, however, tends to show that he pos- **conflict** sessed the familiar Anglo-Saxon ability to take a high moral ground as an excuse for inaction, but yielding none of the practical advantages while waiting for problems to solve themselves.

Very likely Douglas had a practical solution of sectional difficulties in his scheme for obeying the letter of the Dred Scott Decision but violating its spirit by invoking the police power of the people of the territories. Actually some Southerners might have agreed with him, but the South was now so thoroughly convinced that the North was out to destroy it that it felt it was fighting for God and life. Perhaps Douglas had been short-sighted in failing to take a high moral ground as Anglo-Saxon mores demanded; perhaps it would have been asking too much, for by now North and South, each convinced of its own moral superiority, demanded a clear moral decision. At any rate, Lincoln had fastened upon the Republican Party the aura of Northern moral leadership.

The elections of 1858, as was said before, resulted in the seizure of the House by Anti-Nebraska elements. At the same time Southern displeasure with the rejection of the Lecompton constitution and with the Freeport Doctrine increased the gap between the Northern and Southern wings of the Democratic Party. The short session of 1858–59, still **Effect** technically in Democratic control, was torn by strife. Fac- **of the** tions within the Democratic Party cut each other's throats **elections** with an enthusiasm which exposed the weakness of Bu- **of 1858** chanan and foretold the coming fractionalization of 1860. Embittered Southern members rallied to the attack. Douglas was disciplined by being ousted from his chairmanship of the Committee on Territories, the Pacific railroad was spiked, and a homestead bill and a proposed raise in the tariff defeated. Some Northern states retaliated by further strengthening the Personal Liberty Laws and by openly defying the Fugitive Slave Act.

Another effect of the rising Republican tide and its absorption of the Northern Whigs was the ruination of any chance of a Whig comeback or

of obtaining the Federal spoils upon which a national party must feed.
The South- Southern Whigs, like their Northern brethren, had hoped
ern Whig that the Know-Nothing Party could serve to unite conserva-
struggle for tive interests in a national movement which could transcend
moderation the slavery issue. Southern Know-Nothings, however, had
helped to split the party by their demand that the national convention of
1856 take a proslavery stand, and the resultant defeat had shown that the
Know-Nothing Party was a will-o'-the-wisp. The old Whigs, whose solid
core was the great planters—Whigs, it was said, owned two thirds of the
slaves—feared disunion and possible war more than the Democratic small
planters because they had more to lose. More than this, the slave owners
of the Border States saw that secession would only encourage their slaves
to decamp, for it would in effect "bring Canada to the border of the slave
states."

The growth of a sectional party in the North filled them with foreboding, and in a last desperate attempt to save the nation by maintaining
a national party many of them went over to the Democrats. Unfortunately
the Fire-Eaters were strong in the Southern wing of that party, and they
welcomed secession even at the cost of war. They even proposed to reopen
the African slave trade in order to strengthen slavery by giving every
white family a slave. The old Whigs were appalled at the suggestion, for
they saw that it would turn the North into one great militant abolition
society. They pled for moderation and might have won had not one issue
after another played into the hands of the extremists. In the end the
moderates were shouted down by the small planters with the aid of the
yeomen, who feared that their precious white supremacy was in danger.
Two great compromises had been made, but the Fire-Eaters did not propose to permit the South to agree to a third, and every incident was used
to increase the emotional tension which was building up the nation to a
disastrous explosion. The small planters in their desperate struggle to become aristocrats and the non-slaveholding whites in their hatred of Negro
competition were pushing the conservative great planters into a secession
movement aimed at preserving slavery.

Unfortunately North and South found plenty of irritants close at
hand. One of these was Helper's *Impending Crisis.* Hinton Rowan Helper
was a North Carolina yeoman who had traveled largely in the West and
Helper's North and had been impressed by the superior progressive-
Impending ness of the free states. In 1857 he published in New York
Crisis his *Impending Crisis of the South,* which contrasted the two
sections and presented selected figures to prove that slavery was an economic fallacy and had impoverished the South. He therefore called upon
the yeomen of the South to overthrow the slavocracy, even at the cost of
stirring up a servile insurrection. Nonetheless Helper was a negrophobe

and, as he said in a later book, *Nojoque* (1867), would gladly write the Negro out of existence. *The Impending Crisis* was an immediate success in the North and did much to win to abolition many who had not responded to the moral appeal. The Republicans in 1859 published a compendium of the book for campaign purposes and circulated at least a hundred thousand copies. The first appearance of the book naturally roused the South to fury; numerous refutations were printed, copies were publicly burned, and those who dared to read or possess it were jailed or otherwise punished.

Suddenly in the midst of the growing sectional turmoil the half-demented John Brown flashed once more into the public view. With all the zeal of the fanatic he sought a practical way to promote abolition. Finally he evolved the plan of establishing a stronghold in the mountains of western Virginia, from which he could raid into the low country to release slaves. These would be armed, and the raids repeated until in time an independent refugee republic would be formed and the blacks in all the slave **John Brown's raid on Harpers Ferry** states would be in revolt. Brown laid his scheme of banditry and servile insurrection before certain leading abolitionists, and they actually approved and gave him financial help.

He initiated his plan by an attack on the United States Arsenal at Harpers Ferry, Virginia, up the Potomac from Washington. With twenty-one followers, white and colored, he struck on the night of 16 October 1859. The poorly guarded arsenal fell easily, but the people of the town besieged Brown in a brick fire-engine house, and soon they were joined by militia and by United States marines under Colonel Robert E. Lee. Brown and six of his men were captured; ten were killed and five escaped. Seven citizens and marines were killed in the siege. The trial for treason to the State of Virginia was begun promptly and carried out fairly. On 2 December John Brown, conducting himself with firmness and dignity, went to his death by hanging; six of his men later followed him to the scaffold.

Most Northerners were horrified by John Brown's insane action, but unfortunately the extreme abolitionists glorified the deed and counted him a martyr; Emerson bordered on sacrilege when he said that John Brown's death would "make the gallows glorious like the cross." **Reaction to Brown's raid** Some strongly abolitionist towns marked the day of execution by the solemn tolling of bells and firing of guns. With these examples before them, nothing could convince the South that the North was not all but unanimously in favor of Negro insurrection. There was perhaps a determined air about the Southern accusation, for it was too good an argument for the Fire-Eaters to permit it to be weakened by calm examination.

The echoes of John Brown's funeral guns had scarcely died away when the Congress elected in 1858 met. The overwrought state of the nation was immediately reflected. For the second time the House spent **Congressional conflict** months in selecting a Speaker. The Republican plurality supported the moderate John Sherman of Ohio, but he had endorsed *The Impending Crisis* and thereby made himself anathema to the South. A compromise Speaker was elected after two months of stubborn conflict. A year before this Buchanan had vetoed the Morrill Land-Grant Bill which would have given to the states lands for the endowment of agricultural and mechanical colleges, and now the Morrill Tariff Bill to restore the quite reasonable rates of 1846 as some measure of relief to Northern industry was buried in the Senate. Nevertheless, moderate Southern Democrats, with the coming presidential contest in mind, tried to placate the Douglas wing by assisting the passage of a homestead bill. Buchanan promptly vetoed it, probably to spite Douglas, though he marshalled against it all the arguments against cheap land from the days of Timothy Pickering on down. The Democratic Party was plainly on the verge of a split.

BIBLIOGRAPHICAL NOTE

The Northern Struggle Over Compromise

On runaway slaves see William H. Siebert, *The Underground Railroad from Slavery to Freedom* (1898); and Marion G. McDougall, *Fugitive Slaves, 1619–1865* (1891). On the problem of transcontinental railroads see Robert R. Russel, *Improvement of Communication with the Pacific Coast as an Issue in American Politics, 1783–1864* (1949). On this see also Paul N. Garber, *The Gadsden Treaty* (1923). On civil liberties see again Russell B. Nye, *Fettered Freedom* (1949).

Douglas and Nebraska

Here, as usual, see Allan Nevins, *Ordeal of the Union* as well as P. Orman Ray, *Repeal of the Missouri Compromise* (1909). On Douglas consult Allen Johnson, *Stephen A. Douglas: A Study in American Politics* (1908); and George F. Milton, *The Eve of Conflict: Stephen A. Douglas and the Needless War* (1934).

The Republicans and Kansas

GENERAL: On events from the Kansas-Nebraska Bill to the eve of the Civil War see Nevins, *Ordeal of the Union* and *The Emergence of Lincoln* (2 v., 1950); Roy F. Nichols, *Disruption of American Democracy* (1948); and Avery O. Craven, *The Coming of the Civil War* (1942).

POLITICAL: For the rise of the Republican Party see William E. Smith, *The Francis Preston Blair Family in Politics* (2 v., 1933). For the nativist movement see Humphrey J. Desmond, *The Know-Nothing Party* (1905); W. Darrell Overdyke, *The Know-Nothing Party in the South* (1950); and Ray

A. Billington, *The Protestant Crusade, 1800–1860* (1938). The *Dred Scott* case can be followed in numerous works on the Supreme Court, but see also Carl B. Swisher, *Roger B. Taney* (1935). On John Brown in Kansas see James C. Malin, *John Brown and the Legend of '56* (1942). Brown's other biographers have usually agreed with him that he had a mission; among the least objectionable is Oswald G. Villard, *John Brown* (1910).

The Emergence of Lincoln

Most books on Lincoln are hopelessly sentimental and consequently present a thoroughly distorted picture. Two reasonably reliable one-volume biographies are by Lord Charnwood and by N. W. Stephenson. The early years are best set forth by W. H. Herndon (Lincoln's law partner) and J. W. Weik in *Life of Lincoln* (see the Angle ed. of 1930); to this may be added Albert J. Beveridge, *Abraham Lincoln, 1809–1858* (2 v., 1928), and Carl Sandburg, *Abraham Lincoln* (6 v., 1929–39). On the approach to conflict see, of course, Nevins, *The Emergence of Lincoln* (2 v., 1950). The standard treatment of Lincoln as President is James G. Randall, *Lincoln, the President* (2 v., 1945), though it extends only to Gettysburg. Standard collection of speeches and writings is *Complete Works* (12 v., 1905, Nicolay and Hay, eds.). Handy collection of excerpts is Paul M. Angle, ed., *The Lincoln Reader* (1947). Edgar Lee Masters, *Lincoln the Man* (1931) should be consulted as an example of how Clio can be turned into Eris; he has made Lincoln a villain—or worse, a bumbling fool—by the simple device of allowing no good construction to be placed on anything capable of bearing a bad one.

Chapter XXV

THE HOUSE DIVIDING

1   *The Presidential Campaign of 1860*

IT WAS the custom in ante-bellum years for the parties to hold their nominating conventions in the spring so that at least six months might be devoted to the quadrennial climax of the national pastime of politick-

Charleston in the spring

ing. And what more delightful time or place could there be for a national convention than April in Charleston? This spring, however, the puckish god of chance sent unseason-able heat—perhaps to see what effect it might have in the struggle between Union and Secession. So Northern delegates sweltered in their heavy black suits, and, because hotel keepers were making hay, many of them lay in a rude dormitory above a hall and tried to snatch a few hours of sleep despite heat and snores. The result was jangled nerves and tempers that rose with the temperature. It was no help that the aristocratic hostesses of Charleston welcomed the gentlemen of the slave states to their drawing rooms but disdained to exhibit their famed Southern hospitality to North-ern boors. Tammany Hall alone remained unmoved, for its braves had brought along their own hostesses, not as aristocratic, perhaps, but even more hospitable.

Slidell and his senatorial clique were again engaged in behind-the-scenes management, but the problem was worse than it had been in 1856. The majority of the Southern delegations, whipped to a white heat of fear

Southern fears

and self-righteousness, was determined to kill compromise and place the South once for all in the saddle. The delegates' alarm was well-based. Even control in their own localities was threatened, for the Republican Party, having no organization in the

774

South, would try to build one among the nonslaveholding Jacksonian yeomanry, where the tinder for a conflagration lay ready. The politicians frantically urged a common front upon their homespun colleagues. The result of a Republican victory, they said, would be to set the classes against each other, to threaten the Southern way of leisure and good living, to impose unbearable tariffs and other taxes to benefit industry and internal improvements, and, before it was all over, to bring abolition and social chaos. The rich, ran the argument, might escape by fleeing the country, but there would be no place for the poor to hide in that day of wrath.

Northern Democrats were almost as desperate, but for other reasons. Northwesterners had seen the Republicans eating away at their political foundations and came to Charleston determined to support Douglas as the only man who could save them. They were, moreover, tired of being called Doughface helots of the Lords of the Lash **Northern** and wanted to taste the sweet savor of revenge. Northeast- **troubles** erners, for the most part, were frankly opportunistic, for they had lost most of their men of "principle"; they were willing to accept anyone who would provide loaves and fishes.

The Slidell clique was successful in having Caleb Cushing, the notorious Massachusetts Doughface, made permanent chairman, but the Douglas men tossed out the unit rule that state delegations would cast their total vote as the majority decided. The convention then **Split on** passed to the platform; at the same time the skies opened, **popular** the thermometer plunged, and the heat gave way to a damp, **sovereignty** penetrating chill. Southerners demanded a plank upholding their extreme doctrine that no power could intervene against slavery before the moment of a territory's admission as a state, and that Congress must protect slavery in the territories by positive legislation. The Clan Douglas proposed that the matter be left up to the Supreme Court, which would of course mean that the Freeport Doctrine would rule. A duel for control ensued and was carried on over the weekend, with the Douglas managers emerging victorious. On Monday a bitter exchange ensued on the floor. Yancey of Alabama cast their rascality into Northern teeth. "If you had taken the position directly that slavery was right . . . you would have triumphed and antislavery would now be dead in your midst." An Ohioan gained the floor. He thanked God that a bold and honest man from the South had spoken and revealed the full measure of Southern demands. "Gentlemen of the South," he went on, "you mistake us—you mistake us —we will not do it."

This was the moment for which Yancey, "The Prince of Fire-Eaters," had been waiting for ten years. He led the Alabama delegation from the hall and was followed by Mississippi, Louisiana, South Carolina, Florida, and Texas, and soon considerable parts of the delegations of the remaining slave states joined them. The rump convention proceeded to ballot for a candidate, but on the tenth day of the session the Douglas managers, seeing that they could not carry the two thirds necessary to put across their man, recessed the convention for six weeks (to 18 June) and set Baltimore as the place of the next meeting. Meanwhile the seceders had met in a near-by hall and awaited the peace overtures which never came. Finally they set a meeting for Richmond on 11 June and adjourned. Their bluff, if it was one, had been called; and even the compromise for which Slidell, at least, had hoped now seemed impossible. On the other hand, the Douglas managers had overreached themselves; they apparently had wanted to get rid of a few Fire-Eaters in order to carry the remaining part of the convention more easily. Now their only hope was to rally Southern Democratic fears of disunion and ask for new delegates to be sent to Baltimore.

Southern states walk out

The Douglas managers at once plunged into a desperate battle to hold their Northern position and build up Southern support. Douglas himself was ill, worried by his political fortunes and by the way in which administration officials and Southern leaders had been cutting the Douglas dinners. He began to lose his nerve under the strain and took to drink. Southern Senators, dismayed at the prospect of losing control of the only remaining national party, finally persuaded their recommissioned state delegations (except South Carolina and Florida) to return to the Baltimore convention. In some states, however, Douglas men chose contesting delegations. The bolters met as planned at Richmond but recessed while most of them went on to Baltimore.

Interconvention jockeying

In Baltimore the Douglas forces agreed to receive most of the bolters but split their votes with newly-chosen Douglas delegations. Alabama and Louisiana bolters, however, were displaced by new Douglas delegations; the intention was to exclude Yancey and Slidell, whom they blamed for the Charleston trouble. At one point in the tangle that followed Douglas would have withdrawn his candidacy in favor of Alexander Stephens of Georgia, but the Northwest refused to let him. Thereupon the non-Douglas delegations from most of the slave states (plus California and Oregon and odd Northerners) seceded again. The remainder then nominated Douglas and a vice-presidential candidate who was later replaced by Herschel V. Johnson of Georgia. Meanwhile the seceders met near by and selected as standard-bearers Vice-President John C. Breckinridge and Senator Joseph Lane of Oregon, another of Polk's political generals. A reconvened Richmond convention soon ratified the choice. Douglas, now that the dice were cast, regained his courage and energy. Though his throat was bad, he started out bravely to stump the

Rival Democratic tickets

nation, the first time any presidential candidate had done so. Breckinridge lacked a Northern organization, but Buchanan came to his rescue with such administration resources as could be mustered.

The Whig and Know-Nothing remnants had placed their ticket in the field before the Baltimore convention. At their head was Senator John Bell of Tennessee, an old Whig with a long and honorable career of public service, a slaveholder, and a strong Union man. He had stood **Constitu-** with Adams in the debate over abolition petitions, had op- **tional Un-** posed the Kansas-Nebraska Bill and the Lecompton con- **ion Party** stitution, and admitted the right of Congress to exclude slavery from the territories though he opposed using the right. Edward Everett of Massachusetts was his running mate. Their party, known as Constitutional Union or "Bell and Everett Whigs," was hastily thrown together and had no permanent organization. Its appeal was particularly to the conservative planters of the South and to the voters in the border slave states who agreed with Bell that emotionalism had led to the overstressing of the issue of slavery in the territories. The laws of climate could not be repealed, and if extremists would leave well enough alone the issue would soon be settled; certainly it was not worth the disruption of the Union. With this the Douglasites agreed, and the two parties were notably charitable to each other during the campaign.

The decisive area for the Republicans was the Northwest, and it was therefore natural to hold the nominating convention in Chicago. Seward, as the leading Republican, expected to receive the party nod, but he was handicapped by a long record of actions that verged closely **Republican** upon abolitionism; after all, the party had to collect other **ticket and** than abolition votes if it expected to win. With the conven- **platform** tion meeting in a Lincoln stronghold, with the galleries of the Wigwam filled with a Lincoln claque, and with the consciousness that the Northwest might well hold the key to victory, it was inevitable that "Honest Abe, the Rail Splitter" be nominated. Lincoln managers, after careful deals with Indiana and Pennsylvania, carried their man on the third ballot. For Vice-President they agreed on Hannibal Hamlin of Maine, a former Jacksonian Democrat. The "Chicago Platform" kowtowed to the East (especially Pennsylvania's ironmasters) by advocating a protective tariff; to the West by advocating a homestead law, internal improvements, and a Pacific railroad; and to immigrants by opposing any change in the naturalization law. Though not so radical as in 1856, the platform denied that slavery could legally exist in a territory, or that any minority had a right to rule the nation or to break up the Union if that right was denied. It was clear that the Republicans favored centralized authority and intended to use it if they won.

It is a peculiar fact that the presidential campaign was a struggle

between parties within each section rather than between the sections. Douglas and Lincoln all but monopolized attention in the North, and Breckin-

**Nature
of the
campaign**
ridge and Bell in the South. Obviously there were no champions of abolition or free-soil in the South, and in ten
Southern states Lincoln did not receive a single vote. Breckinridge was probably not a secessionist, but he was open to the charge
because the Fire-Eaters supported him. On the other hand, the Republicans were every bit as sectional and were justly charged with exacerbating
the crisis.

Republican campaign orators called Douglas a Fire-Eater and a "sub-
missionist" to the South, along with Bell and Everett; Breckinridge
orators called the Clan Douglas and the Whigs "submissionists" to the
North. All sorts of projects for co-operation among Douglas, Breckinridge,
and Bell were discussed, chiefly schemes for leaving each state to whichever man was strongest, but they all fell through. About all that fusion
could have achieved would have been to throw the election into the House;
in that case a deadlock would probably have resulted, and the safely
Democratic Senate would have elected a pro-Southern Vice-President who
would have assumed the presidency.

The election of Lincoln was rather generally being conceded by September. Republican campaigners adopted the "hurrah, boys" methods of
1840; rails split by Abe the Rail Mauler were in demand as symbols by

**Republican
campaign
methods**
marching clubs of "Wide-Awakes" for their torchlight pro-
cessions and rallies. Lincoln's appeal as a man of the people
was undoubted, but professional politicians regarded him
as merely a country lawyer of little ability and great availability who
could serve in the White House as an unsophisticated stooge to promote
their power and ambitions. The politicians knew what they wanted. With
the devil at their elbows they had gazed upon the kingdoms of the world,
and that they might the more easily win them had drawn back from the
antislavery radicalism of 1856 (as distinguished from opposition to the *expansion* of slavery). Lincoln said little; and party orators laid most stress
on issues other than slavery, though some of them could no more avoid
that subject than they could avoid scratching a mosquito bite.

Not only in its opposition to the expansion of slavery but in its championship of free farmers and of industry the Republican Party represented
new forces which were most developed in the North. The party of change

**The real
issues**
therefore had to be a sectional party. The Democrats, split
between the Jacksonian and Taylorite wings of Jeffersonianism, were unable to understand the true source of the trouble, let alone arrest it. The Jacksonian part of the West was fighting under
Douglas for a *bona fide* share in the government, but it was thinking in
outmoded terms and was reluctant to permit the centralization of power

which would enable its dreams to come true; the Republicans had no such qualms.

Even more pitiable was the dilemma of the sons of John Taylor of Caroline. If they lost, their Physiocratic way of life was gone; if they won, the battle would be to fight over. It was no wonder that they talked of secession, though thoughtful Southerners pointed out that the separation would breed in their own midst the very **Dilemma of** forces of industry, tariff, and finally abolition which they **the South** were trying to escape. The South could think of no way to meet the crisis except to insist that its property rights must be interpreted in the old way without regard to the changing standards implied in the Higher Law; in other words, it demanded that "due process of law" be given a procedural rather than a substantive interpretation. The progressing North saw its progress permanently blocked unless it managed to force unimaginative and traditional procedure to give way to a recognition of actual conditions.

Because Lincoln refused to answer questions but "stood on his record," the South feared the worst from this gaunt Black Republican; perhaps he remained silent because Southern editors vehemently announced that they would accept no olive branches from him. Presently **Republican** bold Southern spirits categorically announced that his elec- **miscalcu-** tion would be the signal for secession. In the Lower South **lations** every governor but Houston of Texas and practically all Senators and Representatives came out for secession in case Lincoln won. The South was rife with rumors of abolitionist agents poisoning wells, setting fire to towns, and plotting servile insurrections. A few of them, it was reported, were hanged by an outraged populace. However, the dissensions among Southern factions were well known in the North, and the Republican reaction to threats of secession was to call them mere Southern braggadocio. Perhaps they were on the part of many—but not of the Fire-Eaters. The result was that the Republican Party and Lincoln as well were totally unprepared for the crisis when it did develop. Perhaps they cannot be blamed in the light of the fact that even the Bell and Everett party, though it was the backbone of Southern unionism, did not take secessionism seriously enough to organize in time to resist it.

Much has been made of the fact that Lincoln was elected by a mere plurality of the popular vote. That is very true, but the same thing had happened before and was to happen again without the dire consequences that followed in 1860. Actually our peculiar electoral system gave Lincoln a decisive majority of the electoral college. Of **Lincoln** the 33 states Lincoln carried 17, and of the 303 electoral **elected** votes (152 necessary for election) he took 180. The vote stood as follows:*

---

* Edward Stanwood, *History of the Presidency from 1788 to 1897* (1913), 297. Other estimates vary slightly.

	Electoral vote	Popular vote
Lincoln	180	1,866,452
Douglas	12	1,376,957
Breckinridge	72	849,781
Bell	39	588,879
Total		4,682,069

It is noteworthy that Lincoln carried every free state except New Jersey (which he divided with Douglas 4 to 3), and not a single slave state. The vote in the slave states was so badly divided that nine out of the fifteen went to minority candidates: Douglas took Missouri; Bell took Kentucky, Tennessee, and Virginia; and Breckinridge the remainder.

It is probable that even if there had been only two tickets in the field Lincoln would have won. He ran a safe majority in thirteen states, a narrow majority in Indiana (18) and Illinois (11), and by a few hundred votes squeezed through with pluralities in California (4) and Oregon (3), where Breckinridge and Douglas each showed almost as much strength. New Jersey cast a majority for Douglas, but the electoral districts were divided: four to Lincoln and three to Douglas. Outside these five critical states Lincoln mustered 145 votes, which meant that he had to find only seven. Why did Indiana and Illinois go Republican? They were predominantly of New England origin in the North and of Upland South origin in the Ohio Valley; the break between the two occurred along the line of the National Road, where it would seem that the decisive vote was cast. It is possible that the heavy Middle States migration, which had advanced straight out the National Road, was able to tip the balances between New England and Upland South. The central counties may have been convinced by Republican orators who played down abolition, championed popular sovereignty, and claimed that their victory would assure free land and internal improvements. With Douglas the West could only look forward to continued Southern vetoes.

The critical states

Was the election of 1860 in any sense a plebiscite on Union or Secession? If either, it was probably a vote for Union. Douglas and Bell were both explicitly for Union. The Lincoln forces certainly wanted Union even though they emphasized sectional issues, the tariff in the East and free land, popular sovereignty, and internal improvements in the West. Breckinridge, without yielding Southern Rights, had pledged his loyalty to the Union, but the Fire-Eaters tried to present him as the Secession candidate. Even if the Fire-Eaters convinced Southern voters, and that is far from provable, the fact remains that the moderate candidates, Douglas and Bell, outran Breckinridge in the slave states as a whole. Only in Alabama, Arkansas, Florida, Mississippi, North Carolina, and Texas did he obtain a majority. South Carolina

Meaning of election of 1860

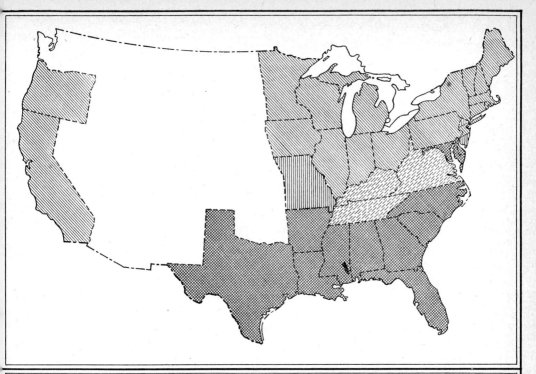

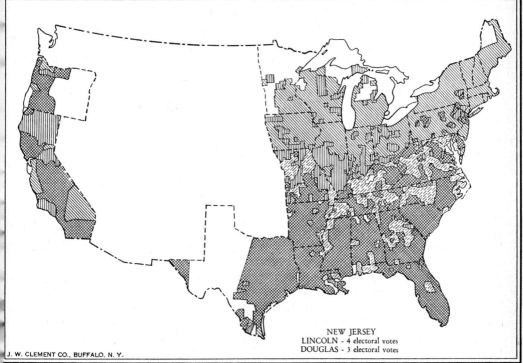

NEW JERSEY
LINCOLN - 4 electoral votes
DOUGLAS - 3 electoral votes

J. W. CLEMENT CO., BUFFALO, N. Y.

ELECTION OF 1860
BY STATES (above) AND COUNTIES (below)

 LINCOLN - Republican: 180 electoral votes   BRECKINRIDGE - Democrat: 72 electoral votes
DOUGLAS - Democrat: 12 electoral votes   BELL - Constitutional Union: 39 electoral votes
Electoral votes necessary for election: 152

might also have approved him, but there was no popular vote in that state. However, as Randall points out, the splinter votes were anti-Lincoln votes; they were convinced that Lincoln was an abolitionist and probably intended to avoid secession by defeating him. Such an antisecessionist attitude was probably in many cases "consistent with a readiness to secede in the event of Lincoln's election."

2 *The Failure of Compromise*

The disappointment of the Fire-Eaters that the election results did not pose a more obvious threat to Southern Rights must have been considerable. As it was, the Republicans fell short of the control of either house of Congress. The normal political policy would have been to wait and see what Lincoln would do, meanwhile using the Southern control of the balance of power in Congress as a threat against coercive action. But these were not normal times. Emotions had been stirred to a high pitch, especially in the Deep South, and the Fire-Eaters resolved to catch their states off balance during the hysterical reaction to the Lincoln victory and force secession. Immediate action, they constantly reminded each other, was of the essence. This time (unlike 1850) the Fire-Eaters found that most Cotton State leaders were ready to participate in a showdown, not because they wanted secession but because secession could be used as a weapon to get what they wanted in the Union. The Bell and Everett Whigs were apparently caught by surprise, despite their bitter campaign accusations, and were swept aside. The Fire-Eaters, it seems clear, were aware of the lukewarmness of the Upper South and the Border States toward secession, but they confidently expected their action to force secession upon the remainder of the slave states. Basically they depended upon an exaggerated estimate of the economic ascendance of the South over the Ohio Valley.

South Carolina as the old home of nullification was the obvious entering wedge. The state had gloried in its isolation and had never trusted even Calhoun until he renounced his nationalism. Still living under the constitution of 1790, with no elections for an area larger than the Congressional district, with the legislature choosing governor, state officials, and presidential electors, South Carolina was under the thumb of an aristocracy of rice and cotton. It had even held aloof from Democratic Party conventions until 1856, though its Congressmen had co-operated with that party. In no state was the tradition of sovereignty and independence so firmly grounded. South Carolinians gave the impression that even the great Calhoun in his palmiest days was regarded as an ambassador to Washington, and when he served as Vice-President or Secretary of State he was a diplomat on loan to help straighten out a confused neighboring country.

With nearly everyone in the state wearing the blue cockade as the badge of secession and with the enthusiastic shouts of the populace ringing in their ears, the legislators hastily called a special convention. Enthusiastic mass meetings elected an overwhelmingly secessionist **The Cotton** convention, which on 20 December unanimously declared **South se-** that "the union now subsisting between South Carolina and **cedes** other States, under the name of the 'United States of America,' is hereby dissolved." A declaration was prepared showing the grounds for secession. A Mississippi convention followed on 9 January by a vote of 84 to 15; Florida on 10 January by 62 to 7; Alabama on 11 January by 61 to 39; Georgia on 19 January by 208 to 89; Louisiana on 26 January by 113 to 17; and Texas on 1 February by 166 to 8. Most of the conventions were chosen by popular vote, but only in Texas was the secession ordinance submitted to the people. In that state Governor Sam Houston, staunchly unionist to the last, was deposed from office, and from being revered as the father of his country descended to being publicly reviled as a traitor.

The circumstances of secession were by no means simple, nor did the convention votes represent accurately either public sentiment or even a clear-cut stand by those who cast them. Few Southerners denied the right of secession, but many counseled delay. The argument which **Significance** won many to secession was that the South could "make **of secession** better terms out of the Union than in it." There was thus a rather general opinion, or at least hope, among those voting for secession that their action would force a re-formation of the Union in such a way as to give the South a permanent veto over Federal actions affecting its interests. Secession was in effect a last demand by the South for at least a negative control of the Union.

The South was fortunate in having to contend during the critical period of secession with the unfortunate Buchanan. He put his trust in conciliation; and whatever mistakes he may have made and whatever embarrassments he may have suffered, he was probably right. In his **Buchanan's** message to the old Congress which met in December before **policy** the secession of South Carolina, Buchanan castigated the North for its intolerance but denied both that secession was legal and that it was a valid remedy for the wrongs of the South. He tried to rally public opinion to a realization of the world mission of the democratic United States. He made clear, however, his belief that though secession might be illegal, it was also illegal (as well as unwise) to coerce a seceding state.

Buchanan meant his policy of conciliation to promote reunion; South

Carolina understood him to acknowledge its independence. South Carolina commissioners appeared in Washington late in December to arrange for **The South-** the severance of the last cords, among them the surrender **ern forts** by the Federal government of the three forts in Charleston Harbor. This Buchanan refused, with the support of his Southern Secretary of War. On 26 December Major Robert J. Anderson, who was in command of these forts, moved his small force of about eighty-four men into Fort Sumter at the mouth of the harbor. Fort Sumter, though still under construction, was the strongest of the three, and its guns

OUR NATIONAL BIRD AS IT APPEARED WHEN HANDED TO JAMES BUCHANAN, MARCH 4 1857 | THE IDENTICAL BIRD AS IT APPEARED A.D. 1861

American Antiquarian Society

A savage indictment of Buchanan's administration

commanded Charleston; the move was therefore taken, though mistakenly, as evidence of hostile intentions. The two evacuated forts were seized, and the surrender of Sumter peremptorily demanded.

Early in January a reorganization of the Cabinet, necessitated by the departure of Southern members and by internal squabbles, resulted in a stiffening of Buchanan's resolution. He now denied the right of a state to secede. Anderson was badly in need of reinforcements, arms, and food, and in order to avoid offense these were sent in an unarmed merchant vessel, the *Star of the West*. The ship was fired upon from the South Carolina forts (9 January), and the ship put about and returned north. From this time on the situation at Sumter became that of an open flame in a powder magazine. At the same time a somewhat similar situation at Fort Pickens, off Pensacola, added to the probabilities of explosion. Two forts near Key West remained in Federal control, but at other places in the South scores of undermanned forts and arsenals fell into local hands. The significance of Sumter and Pickens lay in the fact that they had *not* fallen but were symbols of the continuance of Federal power in the South.

As though the situation were not complicated enough, the South had no corner on secession projects. Certain politicians on the Pacific coast were weighing the advisability of a Pacific Confederacy. Clement L. Vallandigham of Ohio, handsome, self-willed, and so fanatically pro-Western that he was in his localism almost the constitutional twin of Southern Rights, was even touting a Northwestern Confederacy; it would perhaps join or be allied to the South. The merchants of New York, tied to the South and notably cool toward protective tariffs, were toying with the idea of the Free City of New York. However, most of the merchants, already harried by banking panics and facing the possibility of Southern repudiation of debts, were strongly for any compromise that would work. **Northern plans for disunion**

The people of the North, as a whole, were apparently apathetic to the crisis or at least unimpressed by its seriousness. Horace Greeley of the *New York Tribune,* who was amazingly influential in the Northwest and whose weekly edition appeared in thousands of farm homes, advised that they "let the erring sisters go in peace." The growing desire for compromise and the popular opinion that **Northern apathy** Republican legislators opposed it may have led to the series of Republican defeats which began to show up during the spring in local elections and in the belated Congressional elections held in a number of states. It is also possible to attribute some of the apparent apathy to the attitude that compromise was unnecessary because the South would yet give way, like the small boy who bravely runs away from home after lunch but returns when the terrors of night close in around him. On the other hand, during February secession was decisively voted down by the people of Arkansas, Missouri, and Tennessee; and North Carolina refused to take action. Delaware, Maryland, and Kentucky did not even consider secession officially, and the Virginia Convention was in unionist control though it declined to settle the issue and go home.

Buchanan's sane efforts to prevent an explosion were accompanied by similar efforts in the old Congress, then in session. Each house set up extraordinary committees to search for grounds of common understanding, but the Cotton States, always suspicious of the Southernism **Dilemma** of the remaining slave states, were inclined to be critical **of the re-** rather than co-operative. The remaining slave states, indeed, **maining** greatly resented the dilemma which the Cotton South had **slave states** posed. They felt with justice that the seceding states had deliberately planned to force them either (1) to protect their peaceable exit from the Union, or (2) to accept the alternative of a war fought on their soil, whether or not they joined in secession. They were particularly angered by a speech by Howell Cobb of Georgia to the effect that the Lower South need not fear battle but could plant cotton while the people of the Border

States defended them. On the other hand, so long as slave states remained in the Union the seceding states could not regard their separation as necessarily permanent nor their independence as secure. Moderate Republicans therefore devoted their first efforts to retaining the states of the Border and the Upper South.

The Senate "Committee of Thirteen" began the consideration of an extensive backlog of possible compromises. The committee was carefully chosen to represent all parties and sections and included such men as **Efforts at** Davis, Crittenden, Douglas, and Seward. Most important **compro-** suggestion before it was the Crittenden Compromise, pro- **mise** posed by Senator John J. Crittenden of Kentucky, successor of Clay and respected elder statesman. There were six Constitutional amendments aimed at guaranteeing the existing status of slavery from unilateral Federal interference and dividing at 36°30′ all territory then held or thereafter acquired. Next in importance to Crittenden's proposals was the Washington Conference Convention, called by Virginia and attended by representatives of twenty-one states, but not those of the Deep South, and presided over by ex-President John Tyler. After conferring through most of February the convention proposed the compromise line of 36°30′ with a proviso that no further territory could be acquired save by concurrent majority of free-state and slave-state Senators.

Why did these and all other efforts fail? Unfortunately the best-balanced Southern Senators, such as Davis, left late in January, but Southern extremists were still very much in evidence. On the other extreme was **Failure of** a considerable body of Republicans panting for spoils and **compromise** determined to give up neither the material nor the moral fruits of their victory and vaporing about crushing secession and reforming the Supreme Court. The Douglas and Bell remnants, between the two extremes, were demoralized and divided so effectively that they could not be relied upon to promote moderate measures. As nearly as we can judge, however, the crisis came with the consideration of the Crittenden Compromise by the Committee of Thirteen. Southerners on the committee had stipulated that no report would be presented to the Senate unless it were approved by a majority of both Republican and Democratic members.

It seems possible that three of the five Republicans were ready to approve the Crittenden proposals, but Seward waited until his friend Weed could return from a consultation with Lincoln. The President-elect was **Problem of** ready to tolerate—not "guarantee"—the continuance of **Lincoln's** slavery where it already existed and to strengthen the en- **responsi-** forcement of the Fugitive Slave Law provided the South **bility** agreed to the exclusion of slavery from then-existing territories and any territories acquired later. The restoration of the 36°30′

line he feared would only strengthen the Southern demand for Mexican and Caribbean annexations. We know, moreover, that Lincoln considered that the fundamental issue between the sections was the validity of democracy; if, said he, the minority had the right to break up the government whenever it chose, it would go far to prove that the people were incapable of governing themselves. It was a matter that had better be settled at once. The result was that the Republican committee members voted against Crittenden's proposals (24 January), and for this reason Lincoln is often accused of having blocked compromise. The failure of the Crittenden Compromise resulted in the resignation and departure of the majority of Cotton State Congressmen. Thereafter, though compromise schemes were discussed by Congress, none was found acceptable.

While Congress was bickering in Washington, representatives of the seceding states met (4 February) in Montgomery, Alabama to plan the course of secession. They proceeded at once to exceed their instructions by organizing the Confederate States of America, constituting themselves a unicameral legislature, adopting a provisional constitution, and electing Davis provisional president and Alexander Stephens provisional vice-president. **Organization of the Confederacy** The election of Davis was intended to appeal to the conservatives of the slave states still in the Union, while Stephens had been a unionist until the moment that Georgia declared for secession. Davis was inaugurated on the 18th, a cabinet was chosen, and the provisional government began to set up necessary agencies and pass necessary laws.

The Congress then turned to the formation of a permanent constitution. It has been well said that they regarded their function as that of clarifying, reforming, and perfecting the Constitution of the United States. The finished document was adopted on 11 March. Internal improvements at Confederate expense were rigidly limited, tariffs could not be protective, and states retained or exercised concurrently more rights than under the old Constitution. **Confederate States constitution** The clumsy electoral college system was repeated, but the president was to serve a single six-year term; as it turned out, the permanent government was set up on 17 February 1862, and President Davis's full term began on the 22nd. Slavery was recognized, and it was protected in the territories; rights of transit and recovery were guaranteed to slave owners; and the congress was forbidden to impair slave property in the states. In his Cornerstone Speech of 21 March at Savannah, Stephens proclaimed that the Confederacy's cornerstone rested "upon the great truth that the Negro is not equal to the white man; that slavery—subordination to the superior race—is his natural and normal condition."

Fully as significant was the silence of the Confederate constitution on those other Southern contentions: nullification and the right of seces-

sion. True, the constitution was the creation of the states. Its preamble began: "We, the people of the Confederate States, each State

**State
Rights
versus
Southern
Nation-
alism**

acting in its sovereign and independent character," but then it went on: "in order to form a permanent Federal government." At its close the Confederate constitution copied from the United States Constitution the proviso that Federal laws and treaties were the "supreme Law of the land." The fact that a state legislature could impeach Confederate officials within its borders only complicated and weakened the new government. Most amazing of all, the hated elastic clause was incorporated verbatim, but it was somewhat offset by the power of any three states to initiate amendments. Minorities were further protected by the requirement of extraordinary majorities to tax exports, to admit new states, and to appropriate money. Two ideals were plainly clashing: the old State Rights doctrine of Calhoun and the Southern Nationalism of Davis. The result was the early formation of a State Rights Party headed by Stephens, Rhett, Yancey, and Governor Joseph E. Brown of Georgia, which opposed many things Davis wanted. From the point of view of these rabid localists there was little to choose between Federal and Confederate tyranny, and they fought as hard to prevent the latter as they had the former.

Meanwhile the Republicans were riding high in the rump Congress at Washington. They passed the Morrill Tariff, which restored and in some cases increased the rates of 1846; admitted Kansas as a free state;

**Republican
actions**

and created the territories of Dakota, Colorado, and Nevada. Apparently they no longer feared slavery in the territories, for no mention of it was made in the territorial bills, and they refused to interfere with the nominal slavery then existing in New Mexico. Seward, still the most prominent Republican and confidently expecting to control the new administration, was privately negotiating with representatives of Border and Southern states. Few Republicans except Seward seemed to be greatly worried by the crisis. Even Lincoln, far from showing his legendary perspicuity, was prone to paste the label "artificial" on the bottle of poison and ignore the skull and crossbones. On the other side of the line Davis may have held a somewhat similar view that the crisis was artificial, but he nonetheless hoped to use it to scare the North into a reconstruction of the Union on new lines. Perhaps the poison was synthetic, but it was to prove none the less fatal.

Lincoln left Springfield for Washington on 11 February and made a number of speeches en route; they were masterly in their evasiveness, except on the one point that the powers of the government would be upheld.

**Lincoln's
inaugura-
tion**

Discovery of an assassination plot caused him to finish the last leg of the journey secretly, an action which naturally caused embarrassment and ridicule. Douglas, who had hope of saving the situation by a moderate coalition in Congress, called on

Lincoln, was cordially received, and was asked for advice on the inaugural address. During the inauguration ceremony Douglas sat close to Lincoln and even held his hat. The inaugural address announced a policy of forbearance and even implied an agreement to suspend Federal functions in the seceded states in order to promote negotiations for reconstruction. This was not, however, to be understood as a supine surrender to permanent disunion. The Union, he asserted, was unbreakable and still unbroken. He was determined in the end to enforce the laws, but he would do so without bloodshed or violence "unless it be forced upon the national authority."

> In your hands, my dissatisfied fellow countrymen, and not in mine, is the momentous issue of civil war. The government will not assail you. You can have no conflict without being yourselves the aggressors. You have no oath registered in heaven to destroy the government, while I have the most solemn one to preserve, protect, and defend it.

It is invidious to call Lincoln's address "double talk" and to assert that he promised "both to coerce and conciliate": to enforce Federal powers without bloodshed. As any chief of state must, he was laying the responsibility for violence upon those who resisted the regularly established laws. This was a practical, open-and-shut issue, for no government can consent to its own destruction; and such destruction would probably have followed upon the unopposed secession of one section.

As it was, almost six weeks passed before hostilities began. Lincoln, harried not only by the great crisis but by hordes of office seekers, gave a distinct impression of administrative fumbling. The Cabinet, made up largely of men who had aspired to the Republican nomination—every mother's son of whom regarded himself as the superior of the President in ability—felt that they were riding a rudderless ship and looked to Seward rather than to Lincoln for direction. Lincoln in truth was badly served. The Cabinet approved the evacuation of Fort Sumter and, still unaware that Lincoln could act for himself, assumed that the matter was settled. Of course there were leaks. Washington jumped to conclusions and supposed the evacuation a sure thing.

Lincoln's early inaction

Seward knew that Lincoln was still mulling the matter over and seeking further information in Charleston, but in his confident expectation that he could dominate Lincoln, he promised Davis through an intermediary that Fort Sumter would be abandoned; a feckless presidential emissary in Charleston, possibly prompted by Seward, gave the same impression. Actually Seward assumed too much, but a month passed before Lincoln apparently found out what he was doing and began to ride herd upon him. Meanwhile Lincoln quietly undertook to sound out Union sentiment in the South, and at the two extremes found none in South

Carolina and considerable in the mountainous area of western Virginia. It was apparent that much depended on Virginia, and Lincoln proposed to unionists in the Virginia Convention that if they would adjourn *sine die* he would evacuate Sumter. The deal proved impossible; perhaps there was doubt as to what Lincoln would do after that.

Throughout these weeks Lincoln was in a dilemma. He gave an impression of fumbling because he had to pretend that everything would turn out all right; otherwise *he* would have been accused of having started **Lincoln's dilemma** the war. The accusation was bound to be made in any case if war came, but he had to use the greatest care to see that it had no scintilla of proof. Southern opponents of a "reconstructed" Union would have welcomed an attempt at coercion on his part; it was his task to give them no excuse for action. The remaining slave states were by no means yet lost, but Lincoln could afford no positive move that would risk their protest and possible secession. On the other hand, a tame surrender would alienate many of his Northern backers.

Moreover, as General Scott pointed out, it would take twenty thousand troops to defend Sumter and to take and hold its land approaches; obviously the United States had no such trained force available, nor could it have been immediately outfitted, shipped, and supplied. Worst of all, as Lincoln learned with consternation the day after the inauguration, the Sumter bomb had a time device all set to go off, for Anderson was running out of food. The months which Lincoln had apparently planned to devote to patient negotiations were now reduced to weeks.

In the end Lincoln decided that the closest thing to preserving the existing situation would be to reprovision Fort Sumter. Though the blockade of the fort was now in Confederate charge, Lincoln informed the **Crisis at Fort Sumter** governor of South Carolina of his intention and stated that reinforcements would be landed only if the reprovisioning were interfered with. The South immediately assumed this to be "a threat, a challenge, and a breach of faith." Davis ordered General P. G. T. Beauregard, in command at Charleston, to obtain the surrender of the fort either by negotiation or by force. When Anderson was approached, he stated that he would "await the first shot" but that in any case his garrison would be starved out in a few days. When informed of this, the government at Montgomery enjoined caution.

Beauregard sent four aides out to the fort in the harbor, and finally Anderson agreed early in the morning of 12 April to surrender on the 15th unless he meanwhile received additional provisions or contrary orders from **Surrender, 13 April 1861** Washington; meantime he would not open fire "unless compelled to do so by some hostile act." Before leaving shore the aides had learned that Lincoln's relief expedition was in the offing, so upon consultation they decided that Anderson's proposal was not satisfactory. Accordingly they gave notice that bombardment would begin in one hour. After thirty-four hours of bombardment Anderson's ammunition was almost gone and the fort badly damaged, though no one had been killed. Meanwhile the rescue fleet hovered helplessly at sea, able only to carry Anderson away upon his surrender.

There is a common Southern accusation that Lincoln in deciding to reprovision Fort Sumter was deciding upon war but was with diabolical ingenuity forcing the South to take the onus of beginning it. There are even quotations to back up the accusation, such as his sup- **Problem of** posed statement to a friend: "The plan succeeded. They at- **Lincoln's** tacked Sumter—it fell, and thus, did more service than it **motives** otherwise could." There is also the thesis that he chose war rather than a peace which, whether or not the South rejoined the Union, would have meant the death of the Republican Party. Some, more tolerant, charge him simply with confusion and misunderstanding; he was "swept along, trying to hold both his party and the South, to a point where he had to take a chance at Sumter which might demonstrate his strength or produce an explosion."*

There is no good reason for accepting any of these accusations. It is possible that when Lincoln had sized up the entire situation, he saw it something like this. The country was confronted by a dilemma: either (1) let the South go, probably followed by other secessions until the Union had fallen completely apart, and admit to the world that the American democratic experiment was a failure and that the people were unable to govern themselves; or (2) fight, if that was necessary to retain the seceded states. Given the second choice, the Republican Party and its alliance of powerful interests must be preserved as the core of the national effort. More than that, if there was to be a war, the decision must be made by the South, and that under circumstances which would dramatize the issue to the people of the North by throwing the moral blame on the seceders, where in truth it already lay as a practical (not necessarily a philosophical) matter. The crisis was inevitable; and if Lincoln set the stage in order to profit by its moral value, it must be remembered that people think in moral terms and do not readily act until those values are invoked. But this is not the whole story. As Randall points out, "To say that Lincoln meant that the first shot would be fired by the other side *if a first shot was fired*, is by no means the equivalent of saying that he deliberately maneuvered to have the shot fired."

The firing on Fort Sumter resolved the situation. The North, as though suddenly springing out of a trance, rallied to the flag. Lincoln, acting

* Avery O. Craven, *The Coming of the Civil War*, 380. On the accusation that Lincoln planned to precipitate war see Charles W. Ramsdell, "Lincoln and Fort Sumter" in *Journal of Southern History*, 3: 259–88 (Aug. 1937). The similarity is readily evident to the accusation that Franklin D. Roosevelt provoked the Japanese to attack in 1941.

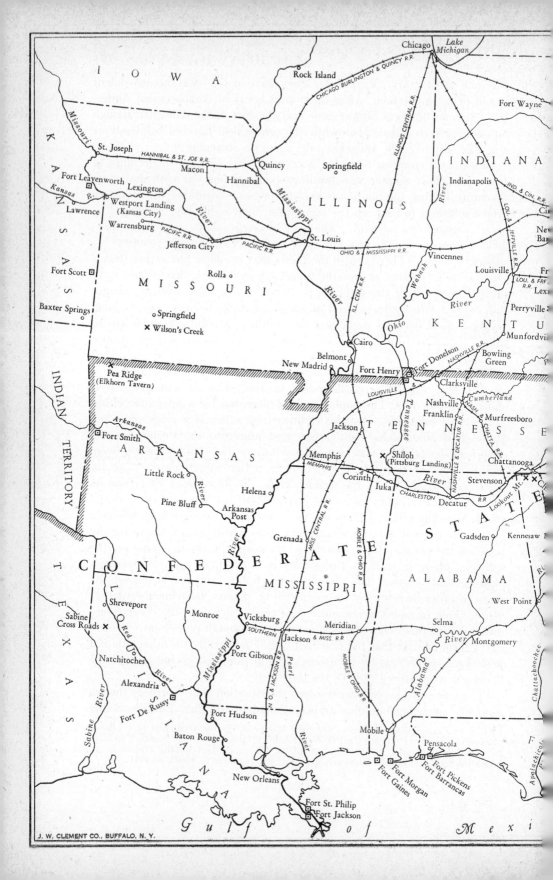

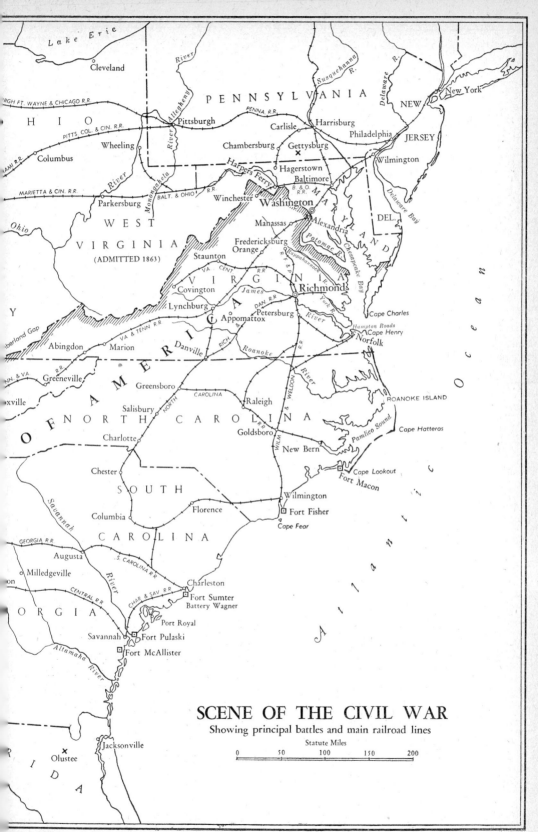

SCENE OF THE CIVIL WAR

Showing principal battles and main railroad lines

Statute Miles

0   50   100   150   200

on his executive powers, called for seventy-five thousand three-months
Lincoln's volunteers (15 April), increased the army, blockaded the
swift South, suspended the writ of habeas corpus, spent unap-
actions propriated money, and arranged with Northern governors
to raise troops, furnish supplies, and build forts and cantonments. The
Border States of Maryland and Missouri were saved to the Union by
dramatic, coercive measures; Kentucky was successfully wooed; and
when Virginia seceded, its northern and western counties were restrained.

On the other hand, the Sumter crisis and Lincoln's call for troops instantly alienated the unionists who had held the Upper South inactive.
During the next few weeks four states left the Union: Virginia on 17
Departure April by a vote of 88 to 55; Arkansas on 6 May by 65 to
of the Up- 5; Tennessee on 7 May by its legislature's ratification of a
per South league with the Confederacy; and North Carolina on 20
May by unanimous vote of the convention. The South had remained
divided upon the issue of the advisability of secession even though practically all Southerners had agreed on its legality. Now that Lincoln's call
to arms had challenged the *right* of secession, the states of the Upper
South saw no alternative but to secede; they left the Union technically
because they did not approve of Federal coercion of a state. The right of
secession existed, they said, because the states had never surrendered their
sovereignty. Perhaps they were right. The Civil War was to decide among
other things whether the United States was in fact a nation or a mere
league of sovereign independent states.

3   *The Strategic Border States*

It is a notable fact that in 1860 the main inhabited area of the United
States was largely given over to Southernism. If Mason and Dixon's line
were protracted on west to Kansas (including southern Ohio, Indiana, and
Significance Illinois), it would about make the northern boundary of the
of the bor- South; included would be about two thirds of the total in-
der region habited area and almost one half of the population of the
United States. The border region from Delaware to Missouri, though not
so large in area as the Confederate States, contained almost as many
whites. If all this vast border area had seceded or even stood together
against coercion, the North would probably have found the forcible re-
establishment of the Union impossible. The salvation of the Union lay in
the reluctance of the great border region to follow its Southernism to the
bitter end—that and prompt action on the part of pro-Union elements
in that region. It is important, therefore, to follow briefly the course of
events in this area.

Delaware, though technically a slave state, vigorously supported the

sibly decisive. Control of the vital Baltimore and Ohio Railroad route through the border region to Cincinnati and St. Louis was of inestimable advantage in the transport of troops, supplies, and coal to the battle fronts. West Virginia protected the industries and granaries of Ohio and western Pennsylvania; a Confederate line on the Ohio River would have brought the South close **Strategic significance of West Virginia** enough to the bottleneck between Lake Erie and the Ohio River to have enabled raiders to cut the remaining transport arteries of what are now the Pennsylvania and New York Central railroads.

West Virginia was a Union salient on the flank of Virginia. It not only menaced the Shenandoah and Piedmont granaries, so vital to the Confederate army in Virginia, but it also threatened the Virginia and Tennessee Railroad, which served as an important link between Richmond, Chattanooga, and Memphis, and which was to the Confederacy what the B. & O. was to the Union. Not least, the Union movement in western Virginia was a powerful deterrent to the secessionism of Baltimore, for that city came to see that its material prosperity was bound up with the B. & O., while Tidewater Virginia was notorious for its jealousy of Maryland's prosperity.

The loyalism of West Virginia may also have exercised an influence on Kentucky and have fostered the unionist sentiment, which persisted throughout the war all down the Appalachian chain as far as Alabama. Indeed, the mountain coves of the seceding states were well represented by regiments in the Union army. The sections of Tennessee had never lived happily together, for the **Southern mountain loyalists** mountainous east (like West Virginia) resented the planting section and longed to exploit its natural resources. The middle and western sections took the state South; indeed, any other course would have subjected it to Southern coercion in order to gain control of the Virginia and Tennessee Railroad. When a strong unionist movement developed in the mountains of east Tennessee, the Confederacy suppressed it with a strong hand— regardless of the concurrent rights of the minority! As it was, Tennessee fell before the Federal armies by February 1862, and Andrew Johnson was made military governor. The Richmond-Memphis Railroad was cut permanently at Corinth, Mississippi in the spring of 1862, and this action proved to be a staggering blow to the Confederacy.

Kentucky had long been a way station in the transformation of Virginia and North Carolina families to citizens of the Northwest and thus became the home of the compromisers Clay and Crittenden. The governor, though sympathetic to the South, found it expedient to refuse calls for troops from both Lincoln and Davis. Armed neutrality was officially adopted by the legis- **Kentucky's attempted neutrality** lature, and troops were raised to back it up. The policy was favored by unionists because it at least meant that the state would stay in the Union.

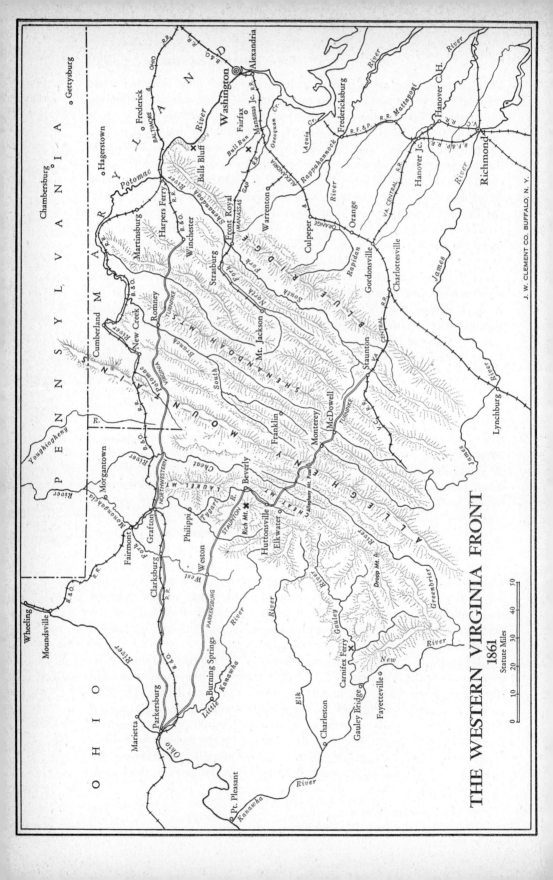

THE WESTERN VIRGINIA FRONT
1861
Statute Miles

Neutrality was not only an indication of the reluctance of Kentuckians to face the fact of war but the only practical solution (for the moment) in a state where regiments were being raised for each side, and training camps of prospective enemies were being established within cannon sound of each other. Confederate and Union units traveled on the same train and perforce observed an uneasy armistice. Lincoln protested that neutrality would in effect make Kentucky the ally of the South, but he wisely refrained from official recruiting or fortification in Kentucky.

Lincoln could afford to be patient, for there was much at stake: the secession of Kentucky would probably render the Ohio River untenable as a highway and would flank the growing Union movement in West Virginia. On the other hand, its loyalty would consolidate **Strategic** the Ohio frontier and open the Tennessee and Cumberland **significance** River routes into the heart of the Confederacy. Lincoln had **of Kentucky** his reward when in the June Congressional elections the state went unionist, and a bonus followed with the election of a unionist legislature in August. The Confederacy ended an impossible situation on 3 September by seizing and fortifying the high ground at Columbus on the Kentucky side of the Mississippi. Actually the seizure had been purposely stimulated by Federal troop movements across the river in Missouri, and as soon as it occurred U. S. Grant moved across the Ohio from Cairo, Illinois and occupied Paducah. A few days later a Confederate force passed through Cumberland Gap into Kentucky. The legislature promptly demanded the withdrawal of Confederate troops and when this was refused accepted its status as a participant in the war on the Northern side.

A pro-Southern convention attempted to take the state out of the Union, and the Confederacy recognized Kentucky as one of its member states. In truth, the people of the state were sorely divided; such families as the Clays and the Breckinridges had members on both **Kentucky's** sides—the former Vice-President became a Confederate gen- **nostalgic** eral—and two of Crittenden's sons were major generals, one **Southern-** in each army. Actually Kentucky seems to have furnished **ism** 75,000 Union troops as against 10,000 Confederates. Unfortunately the later arbitrary acts of the Lincoln government under complicated wartime conditions alienated many Kentuckians. After the war the state became more of a hotbed of Southernism than it had ever been during the war; as Randall says, Kentucky sentimentally joined the Confederacy after Appomattox, and novelists and movie directors have preserved the fiction that Kentucky was overwhelmingly "secesh" and was only held in the Union by force. Who ever heard of a Kentucky colonel—until the recent and inferior crop—who did not wear Confederate gray?

We have noted Clement L. Vallandigham's hope that the Northwest would depart from the Union. Actually he never had a chance. The pro-

duce of the Great Lakes area was now going to the East, but that of the
Southern Ohio Valley was still largely going to the South; neither part
failure to could spare either its exit route or its market, so the North-
seduce west as a whole could afford neither to split off from the East
Northwest nor to allow the South to depart. The South tried to win
Northwestern neutrality by guaranteeing the free navigation of the Mississippi, but the effect was destroyed by the clear assertion of the right
to control the conditions of passage and by the erection of forts on the
lower river. Provisions were permitted to proceed southward despite certain Northern protests, and their seizure by the Confederacy helped to
turn the merchants and people of the Ohio Valley against the South, a
fact which may have been foreseen by Lincoln. Public opinion soon forced
the cessation of the trade; only then did Lincoln (16 August) forbid trade
with the seceded states. A strong pro-Union force in the Northwest during
the critical spring of 1861 was Stephen A. Douglas, and it is probable
that the physical strain so weakened his resistance that it caused him to
fall prey to the typhoid fever which carried him away on 3 June.

Kentucky's decision was a tribute to Lincoln's wisdom and patience
and to Davis's ineptitude. On the other hand, Missouri was a monument
to Federal ineptitude—if not that of Lincoln, then certainly that of his
Missouri appointees. The Sumter crisis led to active recruiting by
saved to the both sides and the establishment of hostile camps. The
Union stanchly Republican and antislavery Germans of St. Louis
found a leader in the able and alert commandant of the Federal arsenal,
Nathaniel Lyon, who was given command of the Union troops on the
recommendation of the powerful Republican politician Frank Blair, Jr.
Lyon now (perhaps unnecessarily) precipitated hostilities by seizing the
Confederate center at Camp Jackson, just outside St. Louis, and after
severe street fighting consolidated his control of the city. When he moved
westward, however, he was met and defeated (10 August) at Wilson's
Creek by a strong Confederate and Missouri force; Lyon fell in the fighting.

The brash and radical John C. Frémont, now wearing the stars of a
major general, had recently assumed command of the Department of the
West and displayed his usual picturesque rashness, including the truly
unfortunate blunder of antagonizing Frank Blair. An attempt to emanci-
pate the slaves of secessionist Missourians was rescinded by Lincoln, and
presently Frémont was removed. It was about time, for his "man on
horseback" complex was in danger of so antagonizing both Missouri and
Kentucky as to force them into the Confederacy. The next March a
battle at Pea Ridge, Arkansas definitely placed Missouri in Federal hands.
However, a secessionist state government maintained an existence in
Arkansas and was accepted by the Confederacy. The state furnished
109,000 Union troops as against 30,000 Confederate.

Missouri was of considerable strategic value to the Union. The machine shops and repair facilities of St. Louis were of inestimable use in the "River War" which soon began, and which would have been seriously handicapped if the Confederates had successfully occupied **Strategic** the state's river front. As it was, the Mississippi remained **value of** open between the grain and lumber of the upper country **Missouri** and the scene of battle. Less important but still of use was the control of the Oregon and Santa Fe trails which began at Independence and by which specie shipments reached the East.

Union control of the Missouri-Kansas frontier was subject to interruption. Pea Ridge had ended military action in Missouri, but its place was taken by a renewal of the Border Ruffian-Jayhawker War, chiefly in the form of a plague of guerrilla robberies, murders, and raids such as scourged no other part of the country, even **Frontier** tortured east Tennessee. In the worst of the raids W. C. **wars** Quantrill gutted long-suffering Lawrence and massacred one hundred forty-two of its inhabitants. Quantrill proved to be an able tutor of such later criminal lights as the James, Dalton, and Younger gangs.

The Confederacy claimed control of the Indian Territory (Oklahoma) and was able to make sufficient show of force to persuade the sorely bewildered Civilized Nations to sign treaties. In 1862 an Indian brigade recruited in Kansas was engaged on the Union side in the battle at Pea Ridge and presently absorbed an Indian regiment which had been on the Confederate side. The Indian brigade then moved into Indian Territory, where it was active for a couple of years. On the whole, the Civil War demoralized the Indian nations of Oklahoma by ravaging their lands and undoing the real progress toward civilization which they had made.

Meanwhile a Texas invasion under General Henry Hopkins Sibley occupied Santa Fe in July 1862 and set up the Confederate territories of New Mexico and Arizona. However, in the next April Union columns from California and Colorado drove out the Confederates and cleared the overland trails. Abortive Confederate movements in Nevada and southern California were soon suppressed.

The struggle for the control of the great border region was over by the coming of the spring of 1862, and though the Federal grip was several times challenged in Maryland and Kentucky it was never loosened. It is perhaps not too much to say that the fatal strategic blunder **Decisive** of the Confederacy was its failure to realize that the rail- **importance** road had diluted the Southernism of the Ohio Valley; or **of the bor-** perhaps Southern leaders moved in 1861 because they feared **der region** that the dilution would be even worse in another decade. At any rate, the Federal government now had most of the deciding factors—strategic, industrial, and man-power—in its favor and could proceed at leisure to wear down the Confederacy.

4 *The Crystallization of Sectional Attitudes*

The causes of the Civil War, perhaps more properly called the War between the States or the War for Southern Independence, have never been stated to the satisfaction of any majority group of historians. Here are **Problem of** some of the more important theories:
the causes (1) The war was a clash between nationalisms: Ameri-
of the Civil can nationalism in the North and a growing Southern na-
War tionalism.

(2) It was a clash between social systems: basically slavery and freedom, the first represented by agrarian aristocracy and slavery at the South; and the other by industry, free labor, and small farmers at the North.

(3) It was a political conflict between sections determined to rule and/or between selfish and ambitious politicians conspiring for their own advancement. Of course, the observer can place evil on one side and good on the other to suit his prejudices.

(4) It was a clash between democracy and aristocracy: the first represented by the North, the second by the South.

(5) It was a clash between economic systems: agriculture at the South and industry at the North.

(6) It was a conflict over Constitutional interpretations, the sides in general splitting along the lines laid down by Jefferson and Hamilton in the 1790's.

(7) It was a conflict between two moralities, each created by psychological forces bent on asserting one or more of the foregoing values and points of view.

Probably each theory has some basis of truth. The seventh, it will be noted, seeks to weld them together to form a single spur to action.

It has for years been a common joke among historians that "what is needed is an impartial history of the United States written from the Southern point of view." It is quite true that until recent years most **Historians** historians were wrong in their views of the South, and most **of the South** Northern historians were not only wrong but wrongheaded in attributing all Southern problems and characteristics to slavery. It has in considerable part been historians of Southern origin who have clarified the issues and introduced some measure of impartiality into the study of the causes of the Civil War. Their facts have been painfully winnowed and honestly weighed, yet the conclusions they have drawn have sometimes been curiously ambivalent. Southerners have been confronted by one embarrassing fact: the South's support of slavery was patently against developing moral standards. The result sometimes has been a strangely illogical denial that slavery could have been the cause of the Civil War. Slavery, they say, was the *symbol* of sectional conflict; the real subjects of strife were labor, race, and agrarianism.

Actually, however, it may be held that even with Negroes present in the United States, unless they had been slaves there would have been no plantation economy with its effective American Physiocratic opposition to industrialization and to the democratic process; no block to European immigration into the South; no alleged question of white supremacy or of a Negro social menace which would have brought war, for the North would not have gone to war to enforce race equality; and finally no crucial question of the extension of slavery to the territories. But since the Negro would not have been here except as a slave, it is almost impossible to imagine his racial influence up to 1865 apart from his "slaveship." **Significance of the Negro as slave**

Slavery—not simply the Negro, but the Negro as slave—was woven into every aspect of Southern life. Southernism and the Confederacy were based, as Alexander Stephens put it, on the "great truth" that slavery was the Negro's "natural and normal condition." The *primary* basis of sectional division was between slavery and freedom, not between agriculture and industry or white and black labor, nor from any deliberate Republican intention to menace white supremacy. This basis of division was well recognized before 1860. A nonslaveholder in the Kentucky Constitutional Convention of 1849 proclaimed that "Kentucky, sir, will be ready for emancipation when she is ready to cut loose all her feelings for the South."

Slavery, then, lay at the root, but it is not our concern to place the ultimate blame in a moral or causal sense on any section. If slavery was a sin, that sin lay at the door of both North and South. Our objective is to try to understand why the democratic process broke down. We must be careful, however, to distinguish between the causes of three separate phenomena: (1) sectional controversy, (2) secession, and (3) war. They followed in order, each of the latter two growing out of its predecessor, but we must avoid the implication of inevitability. Statesmanship and restraint might have arrested or deflected the evolution, and American history might have been acted out quite differently. **Objective of our analysis**

We have been at pains to set forth the economic, social, and moral factors which met on the political plane and swayed the contestants during a generation of conflict. At the risk of oversimplification, let us note the basic contradictions between North and South. First, the North believed that slavery was the root of a menace to the democratic way of life, an attempt to override both the rights and the political majority of the free farmer and the growing industrialist. On the other hand, the South distrusted democracy because it ruled by majorities—or rather, the South defined democracy as **Clash over the democratic process** based upon the concurrent majority, which of course put the whip in the hand of the minority.

In a democracy, according to the Northern view, all subjects of dispute can be tossed into the political arena if they are not first settled otherwise. The South not only refused to yield to changing economic and moral standards but sought to prevent the submission of its "peculiar institution" and its results (such as the territorial issue) to the democratic process. The North, whether or not justly, felt that it was forced to organize a sectional political party which should bring the country up-to-date, not only on the slavery issue but in problems of governmental organization and finance, tariff, land, and education.

Second, the North saw in the Southern interpretation of democracy a further menace in its denial of civil liberties. It is perhaps only just to say that most Northerners were but little concerned with the rights of the

Southern denial of civil liberties Negro *per se,* and some Northern state laws discriminated outrageously against the free Negro. The Northern complaint, however, was that Southern actions against Negroes directly affected the civil liberties of whites. In the South the critic of slavery was driven out by riot and arson, and the spirit of free inquiry and criticism—the basis of liberty and progress—was throttled by legislative and lynch law. But not content with stifling civil liberties of whites in the South, progressive encroachments had been attempted on Northern whites. There had been the demand for the suppression of abolitionist propaganda; the Gag Rule; the activities of slave catchers in the North; and finally the demand that the North silence all criticism or even discussion of slavery.

As the North viewed the last forty years, the South had in the more purely political sphere gotten its way or at least satisfactory compromises in a long list of disputes by threats of nullification and secession; obvious

Southern blackmail illustrations were the Missouri Compromise, Indian removal, the Tariffs of 1832 and 1857, slavery in the District of Columbia, the Kansas-Nebraska Bill, and the Dred Scott Decision. Some Southern elements were now demanding expansion into the Caribbean, the right of slave transit across free states, and the re-opening of the African slave trade. In earlier years many Northerners had tried to co-operate with the South, but they began to lose support when after each point gained the South demanded more. Some observant Northerners were now convinced that the South would never be content until slavery was legalized in all the states. These interpretations were of course prejudiced, but nevertheless they reflected the solidifying Northern view that Calhoun's right of minority veto had developed into a demand for minority rule.

Northern capitalists resembled the South in seeing democracy as based upon property, but they meant industrial property rather than land or slaves. To them democracy must guarantee the freedom of industrial property to multiply itself freely. They now began to see that it was not enough to assure Federal subsidies in the form of cheap raw materials, government-financed railroads, and protective tariffs, even where and if these could be obtained. These could still be of limited use if the South and its farmer allies could interfere with the right of property to multiply itself freely. In other words, "due process of law" must be transformed from a mere guarantee of a fair trial to a substantive limitation of the power of both the states and the Federal government to interfere with the rights of property. Capital probably did not foresee the steps which it took, nor is it likely that it deliberately sought war. But when the Civil War came it saw how war could play into its hands, and presently it stumbled upon substantive due process of law as the answer to its need for freedom of property.

> **Capitalists' view of democracy**

Third, the North saw in the Southern course a growing threat to the Union. Developing nationalism and democracy had become so intertwined in the North that most people in that section could not envisage the preservation of democracy without national supremacy. Northerners saw the United States as a democratic babe in the woods with the wolves of monarchism and authoritarianism howling for its blood; the view was essentially correct. They felt also that the United States had a mission to furnish an inspiration and an example to the world by fostering and developing democracy. At any rate, many profound and well-balanced American thinkers, while recognizing the shortcomings of our democracy, felt that Southern independence would be a fatal blow to any hope of a democratic future for the world. Not only was the South evolving toward an antidemocratic goal, but its successful secession would perhaps be the signal for the breakup of the Union into its component states or sections. At best the remaining Union would be so weakened and so discredited in the eyes of the world that democracy would lose its fighting chance for survival.

> **Disunion a threat to the American mission**

These were the bases of sectional controversy, but secession did not need to follow unless politicians and statesmen failed to find solutions. Their failure lay essentially in too great a reliance on the political Federalism of the Constitution of 1787. Americans of 1787 were but vaguely aware of the tremendous currents which were to sweep the world during the next two generations and thought of their problems in relatively simple economic and political terms. Their invention of the Federal system was of tremendous importance, but the framers of the Constitution left unsettled a host of problems because they were ignorant of them, could not agree upon solutions, or did not regard them as the concern of the convention.

> **Imperfections of Federalism**

One of the most serious questions concerned the nature of sovereignty. Was it divisible, as the Constitution seemed to imply? If not, where was the location of ultimate sovereignty—in the states or the Federal government? Was the Union a permanent national sovereignty or a temporary league of sovereign and independent states? In the answer lay the final decision as to the exact character and the permanent value of the Federal system. Until 1860 the Union managed to rock along by pretending that national and state sovereignty could exist on parallel lines. Einstein was yet to come, and the geometry of Euclid ruled.

Breakdown of Federalism

In neither section, unfortunately, was there enough *effective* statesmanship to make political federation work by mapping out supplementary federations of economic, cultural, and emotional diversities. It was, unfortunately, the opportunity which extremists had long sought and which they had deliberately helped to create. Secession followed when the Fire-Eaters were joined by such men as Davis, who hoped to use secession as a weapon to force a re-formation of the Union. The parallelism of national and state sovereignties as apparently envisioned by the framers of the Constitution had broken down. The Euclidean dream was over; Abraham Lincoln, the Einstein of Federalism, announced that parallel lines do merge and that the nation was sovereign.

Effective statesmanship might still have found a way to save the Union without war and have afforded time for the slave issue to settle itself. It is readily apparent that many of the subjects of sectional conflict were mere wish-fulfillments and at their most tangible were based on prejudiced views. Thus the economic, social, moral, and political factors may have been tinder to the fires of sectional war, but war was not in any practical sense irrepressible or inevitable. None of these problems was unsolvable by reasonable men. Indeed, the world before and since has seen similar bitter differences settled without war. The spark which turned sectional differences and secession into war must then be sought in another direction, the psychological.

Psychological factor

American society wore a superficial air of broadclothed solemnity; men strutted behind an amusing variety of beard designs, spouted flowery clichés with hands smugly on hearts, leaned perilously on Latin quotations, and turned every puny public address into an impassioned oration on property, respectability, Constitutionality, and the American eagle and the British lion. And yet this owlish sedateness was easily dissolved into an emotionalism which might bring on a vulgar, belly-rending guffaw or a murderous stabbing affray between men rolling like canines in the mud. The per-capita consumption of liquor was appalling, and even some revered statesmen almost invariably advanced from a genial glow at noon to a full conflagration at midnight. Liquor and custom and a semibarbaric demand for personal

Emotionalism

dominance led to amazingly sordid personal and political vilification, justified neither by truth nor expediency and hinging upon absurdly petty causes. The mortality among editors and politicians was something to consider before choosing those careers.

Southerners especially, despite their self-bestowed reputation for good manners, their basic good-heartedness, and their loud-mouthed, backslapping good fellowship, were touchy and unpredictable. Northerners never knew just how to take them, for they were the most astute of political traders, claiming everything in sight, yielding a little to gain a lot, and often flying into a rage and proceeding to direct action when they lost an argument or perceived an obscure insult. They made their bewildered political opponents and finally the entire Northeast skittish at every proposition; the Southern version of the situation, naturally, was that the Yankees were trading and squeezing the South out of everything worth having—and beyond cavil, some of them were doing their best at it.

In those days Americans took their politics seriously, perhaps because there were fewer rivals as amusements. What with local, state, and Federal elections, there were mass meetings, resolutions, barbecues, banquets, and toasts in almost any month of the year, the more so be- **Political exacerbation** cause elections were not concentrated as they are now but were spread out so as to occur perhaps as often as twice a year. Not only was this the result of the search for the entertainment of speeches and parades, but there was an almost savage faith in annual elections as the safeguard of democracy. Politics, though pathologically prevalent, was poorly articulated: national parties were little more than state alliances, and localities and states were able to make supposed national elections the vehicles for local feuds.

Elections, as 1860 proved, thus hinged so often on local problems and animosities that they were poor indexes of popular attitudes toward national issues. The unfortunate result of all these conditions was the continual exacerbation of party feeling. There was no way in which issues could lie fallow while the electorate considered them calmly. Debates on slavery or its related problems only confirmed prejudices and rubbed salt on unhealed wounds. "Reactions," as Avery O. Craven says repeatedly, "were more important than realities." Each side stubbornly interpreted every action as an assault upon its rights, and with this attitude came unreasoning confusion, prejudice, and finally fear.

A pointed illustration, which might be multiplied on both sides, was Robert Toombs's speech in Congress in 1850. "We have the right," he taunted the North, "to call on you to give your blood to maintain the slaves of the South in bondage! Deceive not yourselves; **Provocations** you cannot deceive others. This is a proslavery government. Slavery is stamped on its heart!" Of course, he was saying that the North must help to preserve not only Southern property rights but that social order which (he presumed) could be maintained only by slavery. But he was casting the helplessness of the North into its teeth, glorying that the South held the whip hand. Of course, on the other hand, Benton offered his breast to the leveled pistol of Foote; and Thaddeus Stevens spoke iron-faced in the House, lashing the "slavocracy" with the scorpions of his scorn while Southerners surrounded his desk, cursing and snarling but fearing to break through his bodyguard, the gigantic Roscoe Conkling of New York. Such episodes as these helped to convince the self-righteous partisans of each section that their opponents were not so much fearful of losing their rights as sadistically bent on domination.

The essential immediate cause of the Civil War lay in fear, deliberately induced fear which promoted in both sides a stubborn self-righteousness which created a political hotbox. Politics became so heated that it lost its **Transfer to** ability to function in its true sphere: the compromise and **moral bases** solution of conflicts. It failed to prevent economic and social **of conflict** factors from being transposed into moral principles. For this failure we can blame the extremists of both sides. They knew perfectly well that principles cannot be compromised, so they made it their object to convince the public that they were championing eternal moral standards.

Unfortunately conditions and events played into their hands. Their activities present an instructive warning of the way in which two stubborn extremes can wear away the moderate center and precipitate an entirely **Building** unnecessary conflict. Each demanded a complete surrender **hyperten-** and refused to let the issue die with anything else. The dis- **sion** contented, whatever the source of their discontent, were convinced by specious but plausible arguments that the other extreme was to blame. Lurid novels, poems, anecdotes, and even nursery rhymes and arithmetic problems were summoned to the aid of editors and evangelical orators as propaganda of self-righteousness and fear and hatred. Worst— and most powerful argument of all—the Deity was summoned through the Bible to give witness for and against slavery, and the followers of the meek and lowly Jesus split into mutually hateful denominations on the issue. Finally as each partisan presentation failed to convince the opposition, the sense of moral outrage and sectional injury mounted and emotions spiraled until a tension was built up which was exploded by the attack on Fort Sumter.

It is an interesting and perhaps significant comment upon the "irrepressibility" of the Civil War that, even if both North and South had continued to exist as separate nations, secession would have been futile. **Futility of** Consider the threatened loss of Southern Rights in the **secession** territories. They were lost by the very act of secession. What about the Southern antipathy to tariffs and manufactures? During the 1850's Southerners were frantically striving to increase their industrial self-sufficiency, and this movement would have been strengthened by independence. With industrialists and bankers exerting a growing economic pressure on the Confederacy, what would have become of free trade? And what of that unique rural way of life of which Southerners were so proud?

Consider slavery, the taproot of secession. The Republicans did not control Congress, nor could they have controlled it before 1863 without the withdrawal of the South. Moreover, they could not have interfered with slavery in the states without a Constitutional amendment; and, regardless of Southern accusations about plans to create new states to pass such an amendment, there was no sign that it was Republican policy; with fifteen slave states such an amendment could be blocked even today. Nevertheless, thoughtful seceders in 1861 knew that, win or lose, emancipation would come, for slavery could not survive the economic stress of war. They were right. Early in 1865 Jefferson Davis offered to abolish slavery in the Confederacy in exchange for British recognition.

But suppose that by some miracle slavery had persisted? Secession would "bring Canada" to the Southern border and increase the inducements to slaves to run away; moreover, secession could not stop abolitionist propaganda, nor could it raise Southern moral stature in the eyes of the world. Slavery was already, though the Southerner of 1860 refused to admit it, a dying institution. Depletion of the soil by a one-crop system was making slavery increasingly uneconomical. The only cure was diversification of crops—but that would have made inefficient slave labor even more uneconomical. Then, besides these facts, there was the gradually growing competition of cheap free labor in Egypt and India. But suppose the South could have given itself a shot of adrenalin by expanding into the Caribbean or even into Brazil. Here nothing can be clearer than that a titanic imperial struggle would have ensued involving not only the North and the peoples of the invaded areas but jealous, abolitionist Great Britain. The six million whites of the South would have overtaxed their strength, and in the end their last state would have been worse than the first.

BIBLIOGRAPHICAL NOTE

The Presidential Campaign of 1860

Besides the general references given in previous chapters, see Ollinger Crenshaw, *Slave States in the Presidential Election of 1860* (1945); Dwight L. Dumond, *The Secession Movement, 1860–1861* (1931) and *Southern Editorials on Secession* (1931); Reinhard H. Luthin, *The First Lincoln Campaign* (1944); Henry C. Hubbart, *The Older Middle West, 1840–1880* (1936); and Joseph H. Parks, *John Bell of Tennessee* (1950).

The Failure of Compromise

In addition to authorities previously cited see the unusually careful and penetrating study by David M. Potter, *Lincoln and His Party in the Secession Crisis* (1942). See also Philip G. Auchampaugh, *James Buchanan and His Cabinet on the Eve of Secession* (1926); Mary Scrugham, *The Peaceable Americans of 1860–1861* (1921); Kenneth M. Stampp, *And the War Came: The North and the Secession Crisis, 1860–1861* (1950); Du Bose Heyward and Herbert R. Sass, *Fort Sumter, 1861–1865* (1938); Howard C. Perkins, ed., *Northern Editorials on Secession* (1942).

The Strategic Border States

THE EAST: For a lurid description of the Capital during the war see Margaret Leech, *Reveille in Washington, 1860–1865* (1941). For Richmond see Alfred H. Bill, *The Beleaguered City* (1946); T. C. DeLeon, *Belles, Beaux and Brains of the 60's* (1907); and J. B. Jones, *A Rebel War Clerk's Diary at the Confederate States Capital* (2 v., 1935). On Bull Run see Robert M. Johnston, *Bull Run: Its Strategy and Tactics* (1913).

WEST VIRGINIA: For its creation see James C. McGregor, *The Disruption of Virginia* (1922); and Charles H. Ambler, *Sectionalism in Virginia from 1776 to 1861* (1910), and *Francis H. Pierpont* (1937); Pierpoint changed the spelling of his name to Pierpont after the war.

THE OHIO VALLEY: Edward C. Smith, *The Borderland in the Civil War* (1927); Albert L. Kohlmeier, *The Old Northwest as the Keystone of the Arch of American Federal Union* (1938); James W. Patton, *Unionism and Reconstruction in Tennessee, 1860–1869* (1934); E. Merton Coulter, *William G. Brownlow, Fighting Parson of the Southern Highlands* (1937) and *The Civil War and Readjustment in Kentucky* (1926).

WESTERN FRONTIER: William E. Connelley, *Quantrill and the Border Wars* (1910); Wiley Britton, *The Civil War on the Border* (2 v., 1890–99) and *The Union Indian Brigade in the Civil War* (1922); and Annie H. Abel, *The Slaveholding Indians* (3 v., 1915–29).

The Crystallization of Sectional Attitudes

On the theories of the origin of the war see Howard K. Beale, "What Historians Have Said about the Causes of the Civil War," in Social Science Research Council, Committee on Historiography, *Theory and Practice in Historical Study* (1946), 53–102. An excellent bibliography accompanies the study. A worthy collection of interpretations is Edwin C. Rozwenc, ed., *Slavery as a Cause of the Civil War* (1949) in D. C. Heath & Co., *Problems in American Civilization*. On hypertension see Avery O. Craven, *The Coming of the Civil War,* but especially Roy F. Nichols, *The Disruption of American Democracy* (1948), Chapter 27 and Judge Campbell's analysis on pages 395–97.

Chapter XXVI

BEHIND THE ARMIES

1 *The Civilian Battle*

A PERIOD of eighty days elapsed between the firing on Fort Sumter and the convening on 4 July of the Thirty-seventh Congress by presidential call. The reason for the delay may be that Congressional elections had not yet been held in the strategic state of Kentucky, and that time was needed for Northern opinion to mature. Perhaps even more vital, Lincoln was aware of the divisions in Con- **Delay in meeting of Congress** gress and may not have been willing to risk the frustrations of the inevitable dog fight until executive policy had jelled. When Congress met, Lincoln laid before it a cogent explanation of his actions in raising troops, spending unappropriated money, and suspending the writ of habeas corpus, and his acts were ratified with relatively little complaint.

It soon became evident that Congress was divided into three main parties, with their differences shading into each other. The Copperheads (so called from the snake which, unlike the rattlesnake, strikes without warning) were extreme state-rights men who opposed coer- **Congressional divisions** cion of the South and favored letting it go if conciliation did not bring it back. Most prominent leader of this group was Vallandigham. At the other extreme were the Radicals, violently anti-Southern and advocates of extreme measures and harsh punishments, hence their common name of Vindictives. Most numerous was the party of the center, the Conservatives (or Moderates, if you prefer), made up of Republicans, Old Whigs, and Douglas Democrats; it advocated a policy of firm prosecution of the war but without closing the door upon the easy return of the seceded states. Leaders of the Conservatives in the Senate were such men as Jacob Collamer of Vermont; Orville H. Browning of

813

Illinois, close friend of Lincoln; and John Sherman of Ohio, prominent in national affairs for half a century. In the House Frank P. Blair, Jr. was a Conservative leader who oscillated between Congress and an army command and managed to perform brilliantly in both.

The common delusion that Lincoln was inept, despite the evidence of his decisive actions after the Fort Sumter crisis, made it inevitable that Congress try to continue its traditional role as mentor of the President.

Lincoln's parliamentary skill Actually there was no dependable administration party in Congress, and there was no dependable outstanding administration leader except Blair. Conservative leaders, desperately anxious for military victory and regarding Lincoln as wishy-washy, often felt justified in joining the Radical coalition against him. As a result he was driven to making use of such leaders and factions as he could rally on each issue. A lesser man would have been completely stymied, and Lincoln himself was so frequently overruled that few contemporaries understood the skill with which he was guiding the ship of state over the Congressional waves.

The Vindictives were the most dynamic and aggressive party in Congress not only in the pursuit of their own objects but in their opposition to Lincoln. The core of this element, it was to become increasingly evident, included the allies of high-tariff industry and fiscal

The Vindictives monopoly who were to wangle control of the nation out of the war and become architects of the crimes of reconstruction. More immediately apparent, however, were their hatred of Southern "aristocracy," their advocacy of confiscation of "rebel" property, their insistence upon immediate emancipation and the use of Negro troops, and their intent to give the Negroes not only freedom but civil equality—in the South. The Vindictives wanted a war long enough and hard enough to punish the South by desolating it and at the same time to stir up Northern passions to support a vengeful program. Thus they hoped to assure the continuance of the Republican Party and to rivet upon the nation their plans for centralization.

In the Senate the Radicals' leaders were such men as the scholarly, idealistic, and self-centered Sumner of Massachusetts; the furious Zachariah Chandler of Michigan, "Xantippe in pants"; and "Bluff Ben" Wade

Radical leaders of Ohio, cynical, insolent, unscrupulous, and ambitious. Strangely enough a close ally of these men was Andrew Johnson of Tennessee, later their bitter foe and their victim. In the House the chief leaders were the fierily idealistic George W. Julian, spearhead of the Indiana Radicals and son-in-law of Giddings, and his Indiana colleague Schuyler Colfax, who became Speaker in 1864; Henry Winter Davis, the Catonian Marylander; and two bitter Pennsylvanians, both industrialists: John Covode, woolen manufacturer and inveterate investigator, and Thaddeus Stevens.

Thaddeus Stevens, ironmaster and lawyer of Lancaster, was above all others master mind of the Vindictives. Like so many other American radicals, Stevens was a Vermonter by birth. He first reached prominence as a fiery champion of free public schools and soon became one of the most skillful and corrupt politicians in a state notorious for its political manipulations. As chairman of the Committee on Ways and Means he held a position of influence in the promotion of the Republicans' key policies. *Thaddeus Stevens (1792–1868)* Stevens was handicapped by a clubfoot, and this may have helped to mold his temper in its vindictive form, yet he possessed an insouciance that was oddly at variance with his grim reputation. Though he was a witty and convincing speaker, a brilliant parliamentary manager, and a courageous champion of what he regarded as right, his intolerance and vengefulness stopped him short of true statesmanship. Despite his shortcomings there was something of nobility in his provision that he be buried in an obscure cemetery which was open to Negroes, and that this choice be carved on his tombstone to illustrate in his death as in his life his belief in the "Equality of Man before his Creator."

The support of the Vindictives in the prosecution of the war was unstinted; Lincoln's chief problem was to keep them from alienating public opinion in the North, prolonging the war by adding to Southern desperation, and instituting chaos in the conquered areas. A resolution establishing the Joint Committee on the Conduct of the War was crammed through Congress in December 1861. The committee frankly aimed to control executive actions, and with Wade as chairman it was clearly dominated by the *Joint Committee on the Conduct of the War* Vindictives. It assumed that civilians knew more about war than did soldiers, joyously broadcast news of proposed military movements, tried to dictate strategy, and hounded generals who resisted its will or were unfortunate in battle. It promoted legislation which confiscated the property of Confederate citizens, including slaves of course, and continually fumed at Lincoln because of his "rose-water" moderation. Lincoln vainly protested that confiscatory legislation was really a bill of attainder, but the support of the Radicals was so necessary that in the end he signed the bills in question. Fortunately they were but slightly enforced.

The survivors among the original abolitionists were for the most part bitter critics of Lincoln's "rose-water" policies. We have frequently mentioned Horace Greeley, editor of the *New York Tribune.* One of the original galaxy of social and economic reformers who met at Pittsburgh to found the Republican Party, Greeley long served as a party oracle and by his propaganda helped to *Horace Greeley (1811–72)* promote the state of mind which brought on the Civil War. During the secession crisis he favored letting the "erring sisters go in peace"; then switched to the Radical stand on the prosecution of the war and became the proprietor of the "On to Richmond!" slogan; and finally bogged down between Radicalism and advocacy of peace at any price. After the war he tried to maintain the Radical line, but at the same time advocated a general amnesty and went bail for Jeff Davis. Finally in 1872 he became the presidential nominee of the Democrats and the Liberal Republicans, and a few weeks after his defeat died of a broken heart.

Greeley's eccentricities in dress and manner, his squeaky voice, his baby face framed in Galway slugger whiskers, his indiscriminate charities, his pithy phrases ("Go West, young man"), and his undecipherable hand-writing all stirred up more or less affectionately humorous comment and were invaluable advertisements. Greeley was the best-hearted and the most idealistic of all American newspapermen, and he spent his life as a champion of causes—usually good ones. Unfortunately his wisdom was of the old-saw variety, he was a poor judge of men and measures, and his warm sympathies led him to espouse logically contradictory policies. Nevertheless, his influence as a popular educator and moral leader was enormous. His weekly edition circulated all over the North and became the "political Bible" in hundreds of thousands of homes.

Lincoln's Cabinet was a strange cross section of factions, for no three of its members were on basically friendly terms. Seward, Secretary of State, once he had learned that he was not to be the power behind the throne, handled foreign affairs with a competence which needed only occasional checking by the President. In the end he became a sincere admirer and supporter of Lincoln. Salmon P. Chase, Secretary of the Treasury, was honestly sympathetic with the Radicals and injudiciously critical of Lincoln both as to person and policies. The Navy Department was under a former Democrat, Gideon Welles of Connecticut, though technical affairs were administered by the competent career man Gustavus Vasa Fox. Welles, a man of poise and sense, left his observations of frantic wartime Washington in a remarkable diary. Edward Bates of Missouri made a satisfactory Attorney-General; Montgomery Blair of Maryland represented the potent political influence of his family as Postmaster-General; and Caleb Smith and John P. Usher were undistinguished Secretaries of the Interior. The Cabinet was divided into two factions. Seward, Welles, Bates, and Blair agreed in general with Lincoln.

Lincoln's Cabinet

Simon Cameron of Pennsylvania was replaced in the War Department by Edwin M. Stanton of Ohio. Stanton was without doubt the greatest war minister in American history, and without his administrative vigor the war might well have been lost. Nevertheless he was devious, double-faced, and though ambitious apparently loved mischief for its own sake. He was an ally of the Radicals, a relationship which was tempered during the latter part of the war

Edwin M. Stanton (1814–69)

by his growing admiration of Lincoln. His services to the Radicals included co-operation both in concealing peculations of their friends and in ruining the reputations of selected generals. He exercised powerful influence over public opinion by his military censorship and by his ability to throw plums of carefully graded juiciness to editors and contractors.

Lincoln assumed from the first that the bulk of the war powers belonged to the President rather than to Congress, and he interpreted them as authorizing the laying aside of many Constitutional restraints in order to meet the emergency. However, in addition to the basic crisis of secession and war he was faced by a determined Democratic antiwar faction in the North (the Copperheads) **The President's war powers** and by treasonable elements in the Border States. Congress supported the executive arm against conspiracy by passing acts to meet the situation. Lincoln, however, did not enforce them rigorously, for convictions not only would have been hard to obtain but would have made martyrs of the accused. He preferred to suspend the right of habeas corpus and to resort to wholesale arrests of suspected parties. Persons guilty of disloyal practices such as communication with the enemy or obstructing enlistments were declared subject to martial law and were to be tried by courts-martial or military commissions. At least thirteen thousand arbitrary arrests were listed, and the number may have been greater. Some of those arrested were held for months and in a few cases for years without hearings or trials, though at the time of the administrative transfer of such cases to the War Department (January 1862) there was a great clearing of the prisons.

Such drastic executive actions led inevitably to conflict with the judiciary. One significant case concerned Vallandigham, who in May 1863 delivered a strong antiwar speech, though it is not clear that he proposed active resistance to Federal actions. At any rate, he was hailed before a military commission, found guilty of obstructing the war effort, and was sentenced to imprisonment for the duration of the war. Embarrassed at being thus presented with a martyr, Lincoln ordered the sentence commuted to banishment and sent Vallandigham through the Confederate **The Supreme Court and habeas corpus** lines. Meanwhile the Supreme Court refused to review the case on the ground that its authority did not cover military commissions. Soon afterward, however, L. P. Milligan and others were tried and condemned to hanging by a military commission in Indiana on the charge of plotting the release of prisoners of war in support of Confederate military action. In April 1866 the Supreme Court in the case of *Ex Parte Milligan* decided that martial law could not be exercised over civilians where the civil courts were open but must be confined to the "locality of actual war."

There was much wrangling over whether the right to suspend habeas corpus lay with the President or with Congress; and though Congress finally approved the suspension, the enactment was so muddy that the issue was not settled. Actually there were few trials of ci- **Lincoln no dictator** vilians by courts-martial outside military areas, and on the whole life remained remarkably free. Freedom of speech was seldom interfered with after the first few months, and the press remained free to spew venom against the President and the war. No attempt was ever made by the President to control or purge Congress or to suppress parties in political opposition or even to exert unfair pressure on them. Such action as he did take Lincoln defended cogently to a committee of protesters: "Must I shoot a simple-minded soldier boy who deserts, while I must not touch a hair of a wily agitator who induces him to desert?" He met the eternal democratic dilemma by asserting that he would not permit the Constitution to stand in the way of the preservation of the democracy which it had been established to preserve.

Copperheads were especially strong in the Ohio Valley, where they perhaps numbered several hundred thousand and were organized in a number of secret societies. Among these was the Knights of the Golden **Copper-heads** Circle, which had risen in the 1850's to support filibusters in Middle America. These secret societies were popularly supposed to be well armed and only waiting for the proper moment to rise in support of the Confederacy, and some government reports encouraged this belief for political purposes. Some Copperheads undoubtedly engaged in subversive activities, but the courts, though armed with special legislation, proved unable to reach them—partly because Lincoln discouraged drastic action. Vallandigham, for example, returned to Ohio by way of Canada and was permitted to operate unhindered. Actually government spies were well informed of Copperheads' activities, and there was more danger in their votes than in their bayonets.

Lincoln and the Republican Party endeavored to rally the support of the people behind the war by providing something for everybody. The financiers of the East were placated, and a market for government bonds **Republican policies: National banks** was opened by the National Bank Act of 1863 (amended in 1864). By this act associations with specified sums of capital could receive Federal charters of incorporation and could establish banks. One third of their capital was to be invested in Federal bonds, but on their security the banks could issue banknotes up to ninety per cent of their face value. A law of 1865 laid a ten-per-cent tax on state banknotes and quickly drove them out of existence, leaving the currency field to national banknotes and government-issue legal tender.

The Morrill Tariff of 1861 did a little more than restore the rates of

1846. However, as the financial demands of war drew on the Treasury, the tariff was raised again and again. High internal taxes on manufactured goods led to "compensatory duties" intended to protect them from foreign competition. By the end of the war the average rate had doubled that of 1860, and some duties stood at one hundred per cent of value.

Protective tariff

Another Northern ambition was fulfilled with the passage of the Morrill Land Grant Act in 1862 for the establishment of colleges which were to be devoted to education in agriculture, engineering, and military science. The real father of the act was Jonathan B. Turner of Illinois College, who devoted years to its promotion, using the practical nature of the proposed educational institutions as its chief selling point. By the act all states received donations of thirty thousand acres of land for each Senator or Representative. The endowment was not, of course, sufficient to develop the great Land Grant colleges and universities of today, but they initiated the institutions in many cases and stimulated the growth in all. Of course, the states were at liberty to divide their endowment among two or more institutions, so there are today sixty-six Land Grant colleges, seventeen of them for Negroes.

Land Grant colleges

The Western farmer finally was granted his demand for free land when in 1862 the Homestead Law was passed. Any citizen, or foreigner who had declared his intention to become a citizen, could register for a quarter section of land, and after five years of residence upon it would receive title. Actually most of the better agricultural land was already gone, and the operation of the Homestead Law did not become the unalloyed blessing that was anticipated. But more of this in a later chapter.

Homestead Law, 1862

The project for a Pacific railroad which had helped to precipitate the Kansas-Nebraska crisis had been shelved ever since. Now, with the Republicans in control of Congress, it was dusted off and the "northern" route (really the central) selected. Two Federal corporations were authorized; one was to advance westward from Omaha, while the other was to come east from the vicinity of Sacramento, California. These corporations were to be turned over to private enterprise as soon as feasible, and inducements were offered of thirty million acres of land and vast government loans secured by second mortgages. The building of these railroads was a postwar enterprise, but the passage of the acts showed that Congress was not thinking in terms of national defeat and frustration.

The Pacific railroad

The war was financed chiefly by loans and inflation. United States notes to the sum of about $432,000,000 were issued as legal tender at face value for all debts except—on the insistence of bankers—"duties on im-

Finances: greenbacks ports and interest on the public debt." Actually all paper currency depreciated, but these so-called greenbacks most of all. Bankers took advantage of the exceptions in the Legal Tender Act to refuse to receive them at face value. Importers therefore had to buy from bankers at a high rate in greenbacks or banknotes the gold which they paid to customs; the banker bought government bonds, paying greenbacks at face value; the government then paid the gold to the bankers at the legal valuation as interest on the bonds; and eventually the bonds were redeemed in money which the United States Treasury guaranteed to be as good as gold. At one swoop the bankers managed to get back their gold and at the same time make a thumping profit on it; thus was the government punished for infringing on their monopoly of credit. At the time of Early's dash on Washington in July 1864, it took $2.84 in greenbacks to buy one dollar in gold.

As the war progressed new taxes were laid. The tariff was an obvious and welcome source of revenue. Income taxes were laid for the first time in American history; they were graduated to run from five to ten per cent. **Taxes** Excise taxes took on an importance they had not held since the palmy days of Hamilton and have remained a permanent part of our fiscal system. Among the articles subjected to revenue were tobacco and liquors, but in fact the excise touched almost everything in one way or another and was so minute that the law took twenty thousand words to express its provisions.

The Civil War cost approximately $3,720,000,000; of this $667,000,000 was collected in taxes ($305,000,000 of it from customs), $432,000,000 was created in greenbacks, and $2,621,000,000 was borrowed. Such unprecedented borrowings were prompted by Congressmen's un- **Loans** willingness to jeopardize the war effort, the stimulus to private profits, or their own political positions by unpopular taxation. At the very outset Union reverses and international complications, added to the government's evident intention to finance the war by borrowing, frightened the skittish moneybags of Wall Street. The result was the suspension of specie payments and the collapse of government credit. In this crisis Jay Cooke and Company of Philadelphia agreed to take over the flotation of government loans. Cooke turned to the public and by a remarkable system of advertising and speeches by "minutemen" reversed the tide and won the title of Financier of the Civil War. In the end the banking community regained confidence and loaned far more than the people at large. The National Bank Act was a scantily disguised method of borrowing from the business community, and greenbacks were a form of forced loan. Cooke was well paid for his efforts, and lenders received interest ranging from 4 to 7.3 per cent.

Before 1862 was well under way war prosperity had almost swamped the country. Easy money brought a wave of unprecedented luxury and extravagance, and places of amusement were jammed with profiteers— the "shoddy aristocracy"—while even workingmen and sixteen-dollar-a-month soldiers found places of entertainment within their reach. Prosperity brought a perceptible desire in some quarters for the war to continue, and this may have had some effect upon the rather ghoulish manipulations of some of the Vindictives. Cotton sold for twenty cents in the South and almost tenfold in the North; and as a result cotton runners, some of them army officers, ran their more or less illicit investments into fortunes. Swindling and bribery in army contracts were too common under the chaotic conditions which afflicted a nation whose business was suddenly multiplied. And yet (aside from Cameron, who to say the least was remarkably loose in his administration) there is little corruption to be found among high Federal officials, though there were waste and desperate overbidding.

Unprecedented prosperity

The enormously increased demand for goods that coincided with the drop in the labor supply led to the rapid utilization of labor-saving machinery. The sewing machine revolutionized the manufacture of clothing, shoes, harness, and saddles, and these industries moved from small shops into centralized factories. The petroleum industry, begun in 1859, mushroomed as a result of the demand for lubricants, kerosene, and waterproofing materials. The arms and powder industries and the railroad-supply industries boomed. Canned milk and canned foods found some acceptance in the army and navy; Chicago began its rise to dominance in the meat-packing industry, when its capacity was doubled in a single year and the Union Stock Yards were established. The sudden drain of man power from the farms increased the already-growing demand for farm machinery. About a quarter of a million reapers came into use during the war, and with their aid and that of a series of good crop years the wheat production of the North was increased as much as a third and became a significant factor in foreign trade.

Industrial development

Farmers were prosperous during the war, and they profited by the cheap rates that resulted from competition among the various trunk-line railroads and lake and river carriers. It is likely, however, that the bulk of agricultural profits went to middlemen and speculators. It was the clerical and laboring classes that suffered most. Manufacturers, no matter what their profits, were reluctant to grant wage increases and in many cases at least yielded only to pressure or to outright strikes. While prices in the North about doubled during the war, it is not likely that wages went up more than fifty or sixty per cent. Many laborers failed to attain even this much, particularly female factory workers who included many dependents of soldiers. Labor shortages led to the hiring in factories and trades of free Negroes, and this practice

Farmers and laborers

resulted in some cities in race riots, for the Northern worker was by no means reconciled to Negro competition. At the close of the war the cancellation of contracts led to a sudden cut in wages, sometimes to a standard below even that of 1860. As usual, prices were reluctant to descend.

The war abruptly stanched at least a part of the stream of immigrants, which had in 1854 actually passed 425,000. The years 1861–63 saw only 350,000 entries. With this source of cheap labor drying up, industrialists called for government encouragement of immigration. Con-

Immigration

gress obliged by passing a contract labor law (July 1864) which may have helped. The rise to 191,000 in 1864 and 180,000 in 1865, however, was more likely due to the war-born economic opportunities which gradually became known to Europeans. Thousands of aliens, of course, entered the armies though they were not subject to draft unless they had voted or declared their intention of becoming citizens. It seems also that the Homestead Law may have had some attraction for immigrants as well as citizens. At least 2.5 million acres were homesteaded in two and a half years, and sales of state and railroad lands were brisk. The war years saw a considerable shift of population from the perilous Border States to the North, and large emigration to the mining areas of the Far West.

The North became more prosperous than ever during the war, but the lot of the South from the first was that of poverty and privation. The North became well organized for war; the South never did. True, the

Precarious situation in the South

Confederate army was a magnificent fighting machine, but it was ill supplied from the first and its victories failed to keep up civilian morale. The North could afford to make mistakes because it had strength to spare; the South could not, for it had no margin of safety. Southern banks suspended specie payments immediately after the election of 1860 and called in their loans. Southern merchants cut down their orders, perhaps in an attempt to pressure Northern business interests, but the result was that they met the war with almost empty shelves. Shortages thus existed from the first.

Of course, after the beginning of the war serious efforts were made to fill deficiencies, but circumstances almost invariably interfered. Little wool was produced in the South. Cattle were plentiful, but tanners few.

Difficulties in manufactures

The few foundries of the South were kept busy on military orders and so could produce no appreciable quantities of civilian goods or machinery. Speculators cornered such stocks as there were, and laws proved unable to touch them. Salt, necessary in the preservation of meat and in seasoning, ran from eighty cents a bushel to $30 a bushel at the end of 1862, and thereafter entered the ionosphere. When individuals found means of embarking upon the manufacture of leather and textiles, the government stepped in and took (at

its own price) most of their product for the use of the army. Home manufactures were officially approved, but the average Southern home was no
longer self-sufficient, and such equipment as cotton and wool cards was
almost impossible to obtain. One thing the South could do, however, was
reduce the production of cotton and tobacco and increase that of grain
and meat. Southern railroads were never able to meet the strain placed
upon them, and before the end of the war they broke down almost completely. Wagons and draft animals were so scarce that they could not
make up the deficiency.

One of the most discouraging factors was the depreciation of Confederate currency, though even at that prices outstripped inflation. Wages,
of course, lagged behind. The result was great suffering in the towns and
among the poorer farmers. Storekeepers themselves had to **Southern**
pay inflated prices for their goods, but they were classed **currency**
as profiteers by the resentful people; and by 1863 bread riots **inflation**
had begun. Drought and crop diseases were prevalent in 1862, and the
removal of farm animals was a hardship all through the war on the women
and children who were bravely trying to cultivate the farms. Meanwhile
government purchasing officers impressed food, horses, and goods. Obviously areas near railroads and army camps were denuded first, and some
remote sections suffered comparatively little. It is easy enough to prate
of the evils of inflation and to prove them, but no one has ever demonstrated that the Confederacy could have avoided them. George C. Eggleston tells of a saying current at the time. "Before the war, I went to
market with the money in my pocket, and brought back my purchases in
a basket; now I take the money in the basket, and bring the things home
in my pocket." The only real cure was a greater supply of consumer
goods, and there was no way to obtain it.

It must not be thought that either states or Confederacy were indifferent to civilian misery. At first, when the war was expected to be short,
private individuals took care of soldiers' families. Later on, state appropriations were given to county officials for distribution, but
scarcities and inflation reduced the value of such main- **State**
tenance. Presently states began interfering to set prices, but **rights**
they had little effect. The Confederate government hesitated to cut into
the "customary liberties" of the people, since these were the business of
the states, but in the end it had to. Its conscription of men for the army,
suspension of the writ of habeas corpus, expansion of controls over railroads and industries, impressment of private property, and collection of
taxes in kind were all stoutly resisted by state-rights champions. Nevertheless the once-conservative South seems to have favored any sort of
government controls if they would only help solve the problems of preventing starvation and winning the war. However, several states made

vigorous attempts to control their troops and arms, even while in the national service, and to retain the right to recall them for local defense. Owsley finds the basic reason for Southern defeat in this refusal of the states to submit to common direction.

The role of President Davis in the history of the Confederacy has been variously assessed. He was courteous, honest, and supremely self-controlled, but possibly too fine-edged for utility. He revealed little of himself in his speeches or writing, though he spoke and **Davis as** wrote extensively. Stubborn, controversial, and confident of **a leader** his own military judgment (it will be remembered that he was a West Pointer), he backed up his military appointees so strongly that he was often accused of favoritism. His cabinet personnel changed frequently, and seldom were any of them outstanding. Lee was one of the few top Confederate generals who got along with him; in contrast, Davis's quarrel with Joseph E. Johnston, it has been said, "shook the whole fabric of the Confederacy." Probably Davis had no desire to be a dictator or even to encroach unnecessarily on state rights, but he tried to do what he felt was needful. The result was that he earned the hatred of both localists and that "speculative" element which was opportunistically sucking the blood from the dying Confederacy. The increasingly evident failure of his measures also served to antagonize the unreflecting public and further to divide support for a cause which needed every bit of co-operation.

Lincoln made many mistakes—even blunders—but he never lost sight of the fact that the war, to be successful, must be backed by both Congressional and public opinion. Congress he handled with a finesse which **Lincoln a** at times meant that he yielded against his better judgment **tower of** to Radical demands. Not that he yielded in cases where he **strength** was convinced that to surrender would be disastrous. He knew that in the last resort the responsibility was his as the elected President. There is the well-known occasion when he laid the preliminary Emancipation Proclamation before a Cabinet meeting. "I have got you together to hear what I have written down," he said. "I do not wish your advice about the main matter—for that I have determined for myself . . . and bear the responsibility of taking the course which I feel I ought to take." Then there is the story, possibly apocryphal, of how he submitted a problem to Cabinet vote. When all seven voted "no" and he voted "aye," he calmly announced: "The aye has it."

No President save perhaps Jefferson and Jackson has equaled Lincoln in his ability to sense the thinking at the grass roots. Lincoln possessed no military or routine administrative abilities to make him great, and indeed he often showed painful ignorance of both fields. His contribution, and possibly in the end the decisive one, was to summon political support behind the material and military efforts. In this he was so successful that even before his death the Lincoln Legend had begun to bourgeon, and men in the ranks had begun to speak affectionately of him as Father Abraham. Edwin Markham, after portraying the substances from which the Norn Mother made "a man to meet the mortal need," ends on the heroic note:

> So came the Captain with the mighty heart;
> And when the judgment thunders split the house,
> Wrenching the rafters from their ancient rest,
> He held the ridgepole up, and spikt again
> The rafters of the Home. He held his place—
> Held the long purpose like a growing tree—
> Held on through blame and faltered not at praise.
> And when he fell in whirlwind, he went down
> As when a lordly cedar, green with boughs,
> Goes down with a great shout upon the hills,
> And leaves a lonesome place against the sky.*

2 *The American Question Abroad*

The ruling classes of Europe and the chancellories of the European nations had long been irritated and alarmed by the United States, and the breaking out of the Civil War gave them a thrill of hope. Wrote Montalembert: "An instinct, involuntary perhaps, all-powerful and unconquerable, has at once arrayed on the side of the pro-slavery people all the open or secret partisans of the fanaticism and absolutism of Europe." Even many of those **Ruling-class sympathy with South** who did not choose a side nursed the hope that the Americans, like the Kilkenny cats, would eat each other up. Democracy, it was thought, might well be destroyed by the war or at least fall into such disrepute that it would cease to be an inspiration to the masses. America, then, divided among two or more rival authoritarian republics, would cease to be a menace and might even become a part of the European system of balance of power.

The South took full advantage of the situation. During the first two years of the war Confederate victories gave the South the propaganda edge, and this was sharpened by the reluctance of both Lincoln and Davis to admit that slavery had anything to do with the war; the **Southern propaganda edge** former because he did not dare to alienate the border slave states and the latter because he did not dare to alienate foreign sympathy. Europeans, thus encouraged to believe that no moral principle was involved, could and did sympathize with the "aristocratic" South, which also opposed high tariffs and was conveniently in control of the cotton supply so essential to the earning of dividends in English and

* Edwin Markham, "Lincoln, the Man of the People." Reprinted by permission.

French textile manufactories. The Confederate commissioner, James M. Mason, with a cud of Virginia tobacco in his jaw, moved among the gentry of England smugly casting aspersions on the vulgarian North and wooing them with hopped-up tales of its crass materialism, so deplorably in contrast to the fine manners and aristocratic splendor of the South. In London the *Times* raged and pontificated and thundered while *Punch* consistently caricatured Lincoln as a Yankee boor, rascal, and poltroon.

Harper's Weekly printed this cartoon, "What the Tyrants of the Old World Think of Secession," in 1860. In the front row, from left to right, are Queen Victoria, Louis Napoleon, King William of Prussia, and the Emperor Alexander of Russia.

American papers replied sharply, and the Confederates rejoiced in the mounting editorial battle until they discovered that it was not likely to lead to decisive results.

On the other hand, the Civil War confronted European cabinets with a delicate dilemma. They hesitated to brave the wrath of the United States by recognizing the South lest war follow. In that case not only would their commerce fall prey to swarms of Yankee privateers, but there was always the chance that Russia might renew the struggle (the Crimean War) it had so grudgingly suspended in 1856. Russia, like the United States, was classed by Western Europe as a semibarbarian power, and it stood ready to disrupt any game to which it was not admitted on equal terms. Moreover, it did not approve of revolutions, and the South was plainly in revolt. In 1863 friction between Russia and the Western powers over Poland seemed to foreshadow the renewal of war, so the Czar ordered his fleets to foreign waters where they would be in a position to raid allied commerce. Visits of these

The risks in European intervention

roving Russian fleets to New York and San Francisco led to the popular American legend that there was a secret understanding that, in case the British and French undertook to break the blockade, Russia would intervene on behalf of the North.

The attitude of the United States was that the Civil War was a domestic affair and the Confederacy was not entitled to the privileges ordinarily extended by neutrals to belligerents. Nevertheless, the Confederacy was a *de facto* government carrying on a war of such magnitude that it was certain to affect other countries. Great Britain therefore led (13 May 1861) with a proclamation of neutrality which in effect acknowledged the belligerent status of the Confederacy. Other countries soon followed. The Confederacy, much encouraged by thus being placed on a basis of practical equality with the United States, strove to extend the recognition of belligerent status to recognition of independence and finally to convince Britain and France that they should intervene to break the blockade. The blockade, it would seem from the Southern argument, was not only illegal but hampering to commerce—and quite ineffective!

Southern belligerency recognized

The American minister to the Court of St. James's was Charles Francis Adams, son of John Quincy Adams. He served with skill and distinction and did much to prevent international friction from deteriorating into war. Though he could not keep Confederate agents out of England, he did win the promise of the foreign minister, Lord John Russell, to give them no interviews. Adams was a fortunate balance to Seward, who was much distrusted by England because he had once remarked to a visiting milord that as Secretary of State it would become his duty to insult England. Actually this was not the half of it, for during the Fort Sumter crisis he had proposed a "wrap-the-world-in-fire" policy of cementing North and South by picking a fight with Western Europe. Lincoln quietly pigeonholed the project.

Charles F. Adams (1807–86)

The year 1861 ended with the *Trent* crisis. John Slidell and James M. Mason had been sent by the Confederate government respectively to France and England. They sailed from Havana on the British mail steamer *Trent*, but on 8 November Captain Charles Wilkes of the U.S.S. *San Jacinto* forcibly removed them, then took them to Boston, where they were confined in Fort Warren. The North literally went as mad with joy as though a great victory had been gained. Great Britain promptly and rightly sent a stiff protest and a demand for redress and an apology, and even went so far as to send eight thousand troops to Canada and to put the navy in readiness. The jubilant Confederacy saw its fondest dreams about to be realized. Britishers were scarcely behind the North in their emotional response. Fortunately cooler judgment prevailed on both sides of the Atlantic. Thurlow Weed, then in

The Trent Affair

England, exhibited his lobbying wizardry as a diner-outer, and presently the death of the Prince Consort helped to sober the British. Lincoln and Seward used the excuse that Wilkes had acted without instructions from Washington and so disowned his act and released the envoys. Seward transmitted a letter which yielded the main point but saved Yankee face by carrying a few allusions to Britain's impressments and America's historic espousal of freedom of the seas. Mason and Slidell reached London late in January 1862 and presently the whole incident dropped out of public attention on both sides of the ocean.

The string of Confederate victories in Virginia during the spring and summer of 1862 brought what was doubtless the crisis in Anglo-American relations. Lord Palmerston, the prime minister, and Earl Russell were on

The crisis of 1862

the verge of proposing mediation which was intended to obtain Southern independence, and Russell was consulting on the plan with France and Russia. Suddenly in October W. E. Gladstone, chancellor of the exchequer, without consulting his cabinet colleagues let the cat out of the bag in a speech which forecast British interference and Confederate victory. A group of British liberals immediately took up the issue against Gladstone and Russell, and Palmerston hesitated. Adams, who had instructions to return home when and if Britain recognized the Confederacy, categorically refused to accept mediation and dropped a hint that he was packing. Then came the Union victory at Antietam and Lincoln's preliminary Emancipation Proclamation. By the end of October the crisis had vanished and with it the last chance that England would interfere on behalf of the Confederacy.

Nevertheless, there remained the painful episodes of the British-built and/or British-equipped Confederate commerce destroyers. Altogether there were around fifteen Confederate cruisers, of which eight were the

Confederate cruisers

most effective. Of these eight at least six were either purchased in England or built on order in British yards and were partly manned by British sailors, some of them on special leave from the British navy. Best known of these was the *Alabama*, which left Liverpool in July 1863 and after a career of destruction was sunk by the U.S.S. *Kearsarge* in combat off Cherbourg in June 1864. A picture of the *Alabama* circulated in the North, bearing the inscription: "Built of English oak, in an English yard, armed with English guns, manned by an English crew, and sunk in the English Channel."

Another raider, the *Shenandoah*, wrought havoc among Pacific whalers until August 1865, then sailed on around the world to Liverpool, where it hauled down the Confederate flag in November. Confederate cruisers are estimated to have sunk or taken as prizes three hundred vessels. One important result was to accelerate the decline of the American merchant marine and the movement of American ships to British registry.

There was no doubt that British shipping interests planned for the Confederate cruisers to do just what they did: destroy American carriers or force them into British hands. Americans of that generation were convinced that this was done with the active connivance of the British government; probably active negligence would be a more accurate phrase. Finally the building by the Laird shipyards of two powerful ram-equipped ironclads, the Laird rams, gave prospect that the Confederacy would be able to break the blockade and shell any coastal city it might choose. Seward instructed Adams (10 April 1863) to let it be known that if these rams were permitted to sail there would be serious danger of war. As a matter of fact, Russell had already shaken off his inertia and had seized an intended raider, the *Alexandria;* the seizure of the rams followed in October after the admonitions served by the Union victories at Vicksburg and Gettysburg.

The Laird rams

Napoleon III was emperor of France during the Civil War, and his desire to build up a large colonial empire caused him to regard the war as a heaven-sent opportunity. There is no doubt that he would have gladly joined England in breaking the Union blockade and ensuring Confederate independence, but he was held back not only by England's reluctance to act but by uncertainty as to whether his own people would approve. He did take advantage of the war, however, to gain an entry into Mexico. That country had been greatly weakened by the War of the Reform, fought between the Conservatives, who sought to preserve over the people the tight control which was the heritage of Spain, and the Liberals, who were determined to break the civil power of the Church, to distribute land to the peasants, and to make liberal institutional, legal, and educational reforms.

Napoleon III

The great Liberal leader, Benito Juárez, emerged victorious. What success he might have had is problematical, for Napoleon now stepped in with a consortium composed of France, England, and Spain to collect by force the debts owed to their citizens. Troops were sent to Mexico, and terms were arranged which were satisfactory to England and Spain; thereupon they withdrew. Napoleon, however, made such absurd demands that war ensued, and in June 1863 the French, aided by the resurgent Conservatives, took Mexico City. Napoleon now set up a puppet government and by flagrantly misrepresenting the situation induced Maximilian, a wool-gathering Austrian prince, to accept the title of Emperor of Mexico. Maximilian was influenced also by his beautiful and high-spirited wife, Carlotta, whose dearest ambition was to be an empress. Napoleon's schemes flourished, and the power of the new régime seemed to have a prospect of becoming permanent.

French seizure of Mexico

The United States could at the moment do nothing beyond lodging a caveat. However, at the close of the Civil War Seward made Napoleon's ears ring with protests while troops massed on the Mexican border. The

U. S. acts against the French

Mexicans were supplied by covert means. Army officers developed the careless habit of leaving munitions lying around where they could be stolen, and when the thefts were reported they received reprimanding letters written with tongue in cheek. Maximilian meant well, and he actually sought to put Juárez's reforms into effect, but his actions only drove his Conservative supporters over to Juárez in the expectation that when the French were expelled they would at least have a chance to restore their own hegemony. Juárez carried on a persistent and effective guerrilla warfare, which not only was exhausting and expensive to the invaders but made the war very unpopular with the thrifty French and perhaps made Napoleon fear for his throne.

It has been claimed that Napoleon's growing apprehension of Prussia (the Franco-Prussian War began in 1870) even more than fear of the United States caused him to withdraw his troops from Mexico. The

Maximilian's defeat and death

Juáristas, now well equipped with Americans arms, renewed the offensive. In May 1867 Maximilian was captured at Querétaro, and soon afterward he was shot. Carlotta went insane. Juárez's program of reforms, perhaps too advanced for the condition of the people, was continued after his death by his successor, but in 1876 Díaz seized the government and imposed an iron dictatorship which lasted until 1910.

Why did both Britain and France fail to intervene on behalf of the Confederacy when apparently their sympathies and presumed national interests lay with the South? Britain's historic advocacy of the blockade

Why Europe did not intervene

made her hesitate to break the Northern blockade of the South in order to obtain the cotton she needed. Certainly there was distress in the British and French textile industries, but both obtained enough cotton to enable them to limp along; besides, profits stayed up because cotton-textile prices were enhanced. Northern wheat may have meant something, especially in view of the fact that it was being exchanged for quantities of munitions which boomed the armaments industry in England and France; in England, at least, munitions manufactures actually kept total unemployment at about the normal figure.

Probably more important than these, however, was public opinion—this time not of the classes but of the masses. Peasants and workers knew the United States as the land of freedom and opportunity, and they saw the war quite simply as a struggle between freedom and slavery. *Uncle Tom's Cabin* had done its work well. Such great English liberals as W. E. Forster, John Bright, and Richard Cobden had long been in correspondence with Northern leaders and now became the spearheads of Northern propaganda both in Parliament and in public gatherings. The philanthropic ideals of the Enlightenment and of the Wesleyan Revival had deeply permeated the English masses, and while Lancashire textile operatives were getting along on part-time work or were living on the dole, they accepted the situation with a minimum of complaint. In France the heirs of the Enlightenment had begun the campaign for liberalization of institutions which was such a thorn in the flesh to Napoleon, and now they sided with the North.

The effect of Northern victory on European politics was dramatic. Mazzini, father of the democratic movement and of unification in Italy, wrote to a Northern friend: "You have done more for us in four years than fifty years of teaching, preaching, and writing from all your European brothers have been able to do." The cause of democratic reform had lagged in England under the lukewarm Palmerston, but now its champions confidently took heart. **Impact of Northern victory** There were, however, other and more sinister repercussions. More or less vague uneasiness at the growing might of the United States changed to poignant alarm. Not only were the ruling classes shaken, but merchants and industrialists were concerned by the prospective competition of America's war-born industries. Few expected the Union armies to be disbanded quietly and the navy to be laid up, and there were confident prophecies of aggression in Mexico and Canada. America, for the moment, was the world's greatest military power, and some quoted seriously a paraphrase of Shakespeare's Cassius:

> America bestrode the narrow world
> Like a colossus, and we petty men
> Walked under her huge legs, and peeped about
> To find ourselves dishonorable graves.

American public opinion, always antipathetic to Europe, was confirmed in its dislike. Northerners felt that England had played a cold and selfish part in not supporting legality and moral justice, and there was much gasconading about retaliating by seizing Canada. The South felt the injustice of England's course for its own reasons, and there were even Southerners who (now that the problem of slavery was removed) would have applauded the seizure and an- **Laxness of Canadian neutrality** nexation of Canada. British alarm at such a prospect led to a small war scare. Nor was the British conscience altogether clear, for Canada had sheltered, though not officially encouraged, Confederate plotters against the United States. In September 1864 such plotters had seized two American steamers on Lake Erie in an abortive attempt to release Confederate prisoners on Johnson's Island, near Sandusky; a month later a raid was made across the border into St. Albans, Vermont, where three banks were looted and a bystander killed. Not only were such raids permitted, but Canadian courts protected the raiders from extradition. On the other hand it should be noted that forty thousand Canadians enlisted in the Union army.

Northern reaction to the British and Canadian attitude toward the war had led to abrogation of the Rush-Bagot Agreement for partially disarming the border, though fortunately cooler judgment led to its renewal.

American retaliation The cancellation of the Elgin-Marcy Reciprocity Treaty in 1866, though it may have had the support of certain economic interests, was deliberately intended to strike at the Canadian provinces, and various petty annoyances were added. Most serious of all was America's semiofficial encouragement of the Irish Fenian movement. When the Fenians failed in Ireland, thousands of Irish-Americans plotted a Fenian invasion of Canada. In June 1866 they actually crossed the Niagara River and the Vermont border and fought several skirmishes before they retreated to the United States. Seward deliberately delayed putting the neutrality law into effect, and in the end the raiders received little more than token punishment.

Fear of American aggression and desire to strengthen Canada against the United States were among the leading motives for British encouragement of the formation of the Dominion of Canada. If the vast northern

Movement for Canadian federation stretch between Atlantic and Pacific was to be saved for the British Crown, British and Canadian statesmen felt that political and economic union must support each other. Northern victory also encouraged plans for Canadian union by its demonstration of the strength of the Federal system. Observers felt, however, that the weakness of the Constitution of 1787 and the causes of the Civil War lay in the retention by the states of all residuary powers; they proposed to improve Federalism by giving the limited powers to the provinces and vesting the residue in the Federal government. The logic was excellent, but in Canada as in the United States sectional and economic interests were in time to modify the ideal.

Though the plain people of Canada were apparently little concerned with union, the project made gradual headway by political and economic pressures and compromises. By the British North America Act of 1867

Dominion of Canada, 1867 the British Parliament set up the Dominion of Canada— with a sweetener of the guarantee of a £3,000,000 loan for a transcontinental railroad. The new dominion, with the elder statesman John A. Macdonald as premier, was composed of the four provinces of Quebec, Ontario, New Brunswick, and Nova Scotia and boasted a population of three and a half million. Manitoba entered the federation in 1870, British Columbia in 1871, and Prince Edward Island in 1873. The great Northwest was added in 1869, when the Hudson's Bay

Company surrendered its proprietary and governmental rights to the Dominion.

In the end it was British conciliation which brought about the restoration of normal relations with the United States. The British, confronted

Harper's Weekly

The Irishman, who had hoped for an Anglo-American war, is plainly disgruntled by the reconciliation of John and Jonathan —by the Treaty of Washington which was to lead to the settlement of the *Alabama* dispute.

by the possibility of the renewal of European war, saw that the *Alabama* had set a bad precedent by violating the old British conten- **The Ala-** tion that commerce raiders must be *bona fide* national war- **bama** ships. Now they envisioned the possibility of scores of **claims** *Alabamas* flying the Russian flag but issuing from American ports and working havoc to the British merchant marine. Then, of course, there was the fact that Canada stood as hostage for British behavior. Eventually Secretary of State Hamilton Fish was able to conclude the Treaty of Washington (1871). This referred American claims for recompense on account of Confederate depredations to a Tribunal of Arbitration which included appointees of Great Britain, the United States, Italy, Brazil, and the Swiss Confederation. In the treaty the British expressed regret for the escape of the *Alabama* and agreed to a set of rules which yielded all arguments and in effect made the tribunal a mere fact-finding commission. Provision was also made for the settlement of other outstanding disputes.

In the hearing before the tribunal at Geneva the American counselors were notable for their truculence, their fulminations on British guilt, and their extravagant demands for "indirect" damages because British actions **Settlements** had prolonged the war. Most of the Britishers conducted themselves somewhat better, but upon the inclusion of the demand for indirect damages they felt obliged to break off the meetings. However, C. F. Adams, the American member, with the aid of Fish made it clear that extreme demands would not be pressed, and indirect damages were ruled out. In the end the sum of $15,500,000 gold was awarded to the United States (1872). Meanwhile in Washington a joint commission allowed various British claims to the extent of $2,000,000. The German emperor, as arbitrator, awarded (1872) to the United States the San Juan Islands in the Strait of Juan de Fuca (off Vancouver Island) which had long been in dispute. Lastly a fisheries commission at Halifax, in return for extensive fishing concessions off the Maritime Provinces, awarded (1877) $5,500,000 to Great Britain.

There remains yet one more episode which was in great part an outcome of the Civil War. Russia knew very well that in Alaska it had a valuable possession rich in fish, furs, and gold. On the other hand, the **Purchase** Russian-American Fur Company had fallen on evil days, the **of Alaska,** area was an administrative headache, and there was danger **1867** that in the not unlikely case of war with England Alaska would fall to the British navy. But even beyond that was the likelihood that the American swarm would reach Alaska sooner or later and simply appropriate it. The United States had previously shown some interest in its acquisition, so why not now take advantage of current American friendliness and get cash in exchange for this "frozen asset"? Seward, who dreamed of seeing the Stars and Stripes float over all of North America, was delighted, and in his eagerness let the shrewd Russian minister, Stoeckl, run the price up to $7,200,000.

However, Congress and a considerable part of the public were either amused or indignant, and Alaska was variously dubbed "Seward's Folly" and "Seward's Icebox." The Secretary of State lobbied industriously with editors and Congressmen and disseminated to the public all the information he could gather on Alaska's resources. One of his most telling moves was to dig up and republish the comments of the newspapers of 1803 on the worthlessness of the Louisiana Purchase. In the end the treaty was pushed through with the powerful aid of Charles Sumner, who favored the purchase (he said) because it would "set a watchful Yankee on each side of John Bull." Even at that it seems likely that Stoeckl had to bribe some Congressmen before the appropriation bill was passed. Nevertheless, the American people were apparently satisfied that they had not only gotten their money's worth but made "an act of recompense to a tried friend."

3 The Sinews of War

The final line-up of states by the end of 1861 showed eleven in the Confederacy and twenty-three (not counting West Virginia) remaining with the Federal government. The North possessed a population of about twenty-two million; the South had six million whites and **Comparison** three and a half million Negroes. The latter were not avail- **of section-** able as soldiers, but they were invaluable as agricultural **al resources** workers and as members of military labor corps to relieve white men for combat duty. Even more disproportionate were the material resources of the two sections. Most of the known mineral resources of the country were located in the North, and it possessed at least ninety per cent of the industries and as much of the skilled labor. The North was an area of diversified farms, and its resources in grain, beef, pork, horses, and mules were almost inexhaustible. The tiny regular army of sixteen thousand men remained with the North except that a quarter of the officers resigned and went with their home states.

The Civil War was the first war in which railroads played a decisive role. The North possessed about two thirds of the railroad mileage of the nation: twenty-one thousand miles as against nine thousand. Not only was the North crisscrossed by a network of railroads which furnished transportation in almost any desired direction, **Northern** but its lines were soundly built and were intended as the **railroads** main reliance for freight and travel over great distances. It possessed ample cross-country facilities in the combinations of lines that now correspond to the New York Central, the Pennsylvania, and the Baltimore and Ohio. More than this, its railroads thrust toward the battle front beyond Cairo, Louisville, Cincinnati, and Washington.

Southern efforts to attain battle efficiency were doomed from the first by the inadequacy of the section's railroads. They were for the most part short because they had been chiefly built as feeders to river towns and seaports, and most cities were connected by rail only in roundabout fashion. Different lines were built with different **Southern** gauges, so it was common to have to haul goods by dray **railroads** across town, with consequent loss of time and labor. Most roads were not built for heavy traffic, some had old-fashioned rails of strap iron laid on stringers, some possessed few cars and locomotives, and some tried to get along without machine shops. Military necessity frequently caused the

impressment of rolling stock or forced the taking up of track for use elsewhere. The tremendous weight of military traffic threw the Southern railroad system into a snarl and kept it there. It is literally true that some
warehouses were filled with clothing that had mildewed and rations that
had spoiled simply because the railroads could not move them. By the
end of the war Southern railroads had all but ceased to operate.

The disparity in financial resources was fully as great as in everything
else. Not only were the gold and the banking facilities of the nation concentrated in the North, but the property was there; and the common man

Financial disparity
possessed resources which made him a prospective purchaser of government bonds. Southern property was too
largely in land and slaves, neither of them highly negotiable.
Almost from the beginning the South was forced to resort to fiat currency;
but since it did not possess the consumer goods to purchase with the
money, it was not long before runaway inflation ensued. True, the North
also suffered from inflation, but far less than the South.

Why then, in the light of these facts, was the South confident of victory almost to the point of arrogance? Part of the reason was that it believed its own propaganda. Northerners had been pictured so thoroughly

Southern confidence
as cowed and defenseless wage slaves, or as cowardly capitalists who were willing to sell out any principle for money,
that the South did not expect the North to *dare* to try to
stop secession. Even if there were such a disposition, the South expected
it to be vetoed by New York City, which depended upon the cotton trade,
and by the Ohio Valley, which sold a large part of its products to the
South and which still relied on New Orleans as an entrepôt. Even if there
was a fight, it had such a sincere contempt for the plowboys and mechanics
of the North that it confidently held that "One Southern gentleman, suh,
can whip five Yankees!" Bull Run all but made the boast good. These
opinions were closely related to the inevitable contempt of the untutored
for the complexities of civilization—in this case a blind disregard of the
material and spiritual power of a commercial and mechanical civilization.
But even beyond such strengthening illusions there lay a fundamental attitude inseparable from the violent psychological and cultural stage then
existent in the South, what Cash calls the conviction of the Southerner
"that nothing living could cross him and get away with it."

The American Physiocrat, however, far from seeing that he was de-
luded, held that it was the rest of the world that was blind, and he
triumphantly slapped down the card which he was confident gave him the

King Cotton
power of life and death over industry: cotton. The Cotton
South, though in large measure the creation of the Industrial
Revolution, had arrogated to itself the role of creator and
molder of industrial destiny, and this despite its contempt for industry.
With the slogan "Cotton is King!" the South confidently expected to

maintain its precious agrarian aloofness while it drew tribute from industry in peace and stopped its wheels in time of war. New York's patent commercial and financial control of the cotton trade was interpreted as parasitism; though the South had lost some blood to the leech, it was sure that it could pull away at will and in so doing ruin New York together with all Northern industry. Secession brought a deliberately concerted attempt to make use of this threat. The cotton crop of 1860 was kept off the market and its export prohibited; some of it was stored in warehouses, and some of it was burned. The South then confidently waited for the wheels of civilization in the North and in Europe to grind to a stop and for a great cry to go up from the nations that the North must lift its blockade and let the South go in peace.

The cry never came, nor did the wheels of industry stop altogether. Why? At the cost of some repetition, it is worth giving the reasons here. In the first place, the South underrated the availability and utility of cotton substitutes; after all, Western Civilization had known but little cotton up to less than a century before this. In the second place, the world was not as bare of cotton as the South thought. There was a fifty-per-cent oversupply in **Dethrone-ment of King Cotton** British warehouses, and Brazil, Egypt, and India could and did step up their production fourfold. Advancing Northern armies pounced on cotton warehouses, and there was a considerable trade through the lines which was winked at by both Federal and Confederate governments. Though the Northern blockade of the South had set in before the subjects of King Cotton learned their mistake, a considerable quantity was presently slipped out in swift steamers to exchange for the arms and goods which the Confederacy so badly needed.

Third, the North could appeal to factors more fundamental even than cotton. Britain's historic weapon was the blockade, and it could not afford to deny it now by breaking up the Northern blockade to obtain an unhampered flow of cotton; also Northern wheat was important to British workers, and Northern purchases important to British munitioneers. But even more significant was the growing European conviction that the North was fighting for Negro emancipation—a psychological factor which the South had cast aside in its assessment of the spiritual assets of industrial civilization.

Though the North had overwhelming man power and material superiority, its victory was not easy nor in any military sense inevitable. The Southern armies had the inside lines, chose the ground of combat, and had the psychological advantage of being engaged in defending their homes. They were made up largely of men **Southern advantages** who were used to an outdoor life and to physical exertion, did not expect to be provided with luxuries, and were already expert in the handling of weapons and horses; Southern superiority in cavalry was evident at the outset. Moreover, the South had the best commanders, for the military life was more attractive to capable Southerners than to comparable Northerners. Each of these Southern advantages was on its reverse side a Northern disadvantage, and progress through an area of decrepit railroads and notoriously bad roads was painfully slow for armies that not only had to bring supplies from distant bases but lived relatively well in the field and expended ammunition recklessly. There was also the fact that the North not only had to fight to take cities and territory but had to devote about half of its soldiers to transport, garrison, and patrol duty and to performing the physical labor done in the South by Negro labor corps. In the end the North needed all its material resources and its grim determination to preserve the Union.

For the first two years of the war the Southern armies, though inferior in supply and equipment, were the better fighters. However, once the North had accustomed its troops to military life and had brought capable commanders to the top, there was little to choose **Fighting** between the competence of the fighting men. March and **capacities** camp discipline have always been poor in American armies, but the soldiers of the South failed to improve with experience. Actually many Confederate soldiers were so poorly fed and shod that they could not keep up and were continually dropping out from sheer inability to march, or perhaps to liberate the knapsacks and shoes of Union prisoners or dead. Both armies, in fact, entered battle with considerably fewer men in the ranks than the rosters showed.

Winfield Scott, himself a Southerner, as early as February 1862 foretold the course of the conflict. Mary Boykin Chesnut,* Confederate diarist, quoted him as saying that "we have courage, woodcraft, consummate horsemanship, and endurance of pain equal to the **Why the** Indians, but that we will not submit to discipline. We will **South lost** not take care of things, or husband our resources. Where we are, there is waste and destruction. If it could all be done by one wild, desperate dash, we would do it; but he does not think we can stand the . . . waiting. . . . Now for the other side. They can wait. They can bear discipline. They can endure forever. Losses in battle are nothing to them. Their resources in men and materials of war are inexhaustible, and if they see fit they will fight to the bitter end." True enough, a couple of hundred thousand Southern heroes hung on to the end, but well before the end of 1864 Southern military and civilian morale had both collapsed.

We have mentioned the Owsley thesis that the Confederacy lost the war because it failed to articulate politically. There is also the Ramsdell thesis that the true cause of defeat was the breakdown of finance, production, and transportation in the rear areas, and the consequent loss of

* Mary Boykin Chesnut, *Diary from Dixie,* ed. by B. A. Williams (1949), 245.

civilian morale; it denies that the South lost primarily for military reasons, for the lack of foreign recognition, or even because of the strangle hold of the blockade. Perhaps here once more is a problem involving the precedency of the hen or the egg.

Beauregard* insisted that with the moral and material resources at the disposal of the Confederacy, it should have won independence. The war was lost, he said, by the failure to adopt an integrated strategy at the beginning and to apply it with boldness and decision. Only **Beauregard's opinion** thus could the Confederacy have triumphed before the North had a chance to build up the magnificent fighting machine which Grant and Sherman had at their disposal in 1864. Beauregard did not hesitate to lay the principal blame on the timidity and jealousy of Davis, where certainly some of it lay. Davis and Lincoln both thought in defensive terms, each of them placing the defense of his capital first. The North could afford to wait, but the South could not. Davis's defensiveness left the Mississippi Valley undermanned and resulted in its loss; at the same time it handicapped Lee's sporadic attempts to end the war by decisive offensive actions and helped to wear down Confederate strength to the point where the offense was no longer possible.

The Federal government could not recognize that the Confederacy had any legal status in either a domestic or an international sense without admitting that disunion had been consummated. It did not regard itself as the agent of the Northern states but as the legitimate government of *all* the states. When Great Britain recognized **Federal attitude toward the Confederacy** the Confederate States as a belligerent there was great resentment at the North, for though the fact of belligerence was plain the war was regarded as a purely domestic affair. Nevertheless, Northern threats of "death to traitors" were eminently unrealistic, and the government never contemplated the extreme penalty for Confederate officials and soldiers. In a practical sense, as the Supreme Court put it, the United States sustained toward the Confederacy the double status of "a belligerent and a sovereign, and had the rights of both." The very size of the opposition dictated that the Confederate States of America be recognized, even though only tacitly, as a belligerent, that negotiations be conducted and cartels arranged, and that prisoners be given the status of prisoners of war.

It will never be known how many men served on either side. Not only were enlistments made for periods that varied from two weeks to three years, but there are no reliable records as to how many men served more than one enlistment. It seems likely that over 2,000,000 **Numbers and losses** men wore Union blue at one time or another, and somewhat under 1,000,000 wore Confederate gray. At the close of the

* R. U. Johnson and C. C. Buel, eds., *Battles and Leaders of the Civil War,* 1: 222–24.

war there were somewhat over 900,000 Northern troops under arms, while the Confederate forces had wasted away to probably less than 200,000. The greatest mortality on both sides was from disease. It is estimated that out of 360,000 Union deaths about 110,000 were in battle, and of 258,000 Confederate dead about 94,000 fell in battle or died of wounds. It is, of course, impossible to know how many were seriously maimed, but it seems reasonable to estimate that the war killed or permanently disabled a million men. It is notable that despite Union losses there were more men available at the North at the close of the war than there had been at the beginning. The untapped "national forces" at the call of the Federal government were still double the number under arms. Basically the war was won for the North by the blockade, by unlimited matériel, and by unlimited reinforcements.

On both sides somewhat similar methods of raising troops were used. The bulk of the armies was composed of regiments of volunteers raised by the states, officered by election from the ranks or by appointment by the governor, equipped at the expense of the state or the general government, organized and trained in state cantonments, and finally mustered into Federal or Confederate service. One favorite resort was to organize regiments of men of the same occupation, such as the Fire Zouaves, or of similar national origins, chiefly German, Irish, and French. Politicians who coveted military glory found it easy to obtain commissions, and scores of them eventually obtained general's stars. Lincoln tried to be impartial and made it a point to commission deserving Democrats as well as Republicans. Unfortunately the system of offering competitive bounties to induce enlistments in various units eventually ran wild. Its effect was actually to slow down recruiting, for many waited for a higher figure to be offered; on the other hand, "bounty jumpers" enlisted and collected the bounty, then disappeared and repeated the process elsewhere. It is estimated that three quarters of a billion dollars were paid out as bounties and for substitutes.

Recruiting

The man-power crisis became acute in the Confederacy early in 1862, and during that year two bills were passed which made all men between eighteen and forty-five years of age subject to military service. The result was a clash between state and Confederate authorities, with the former in some cases releasing conscripts by judicial process. Before the war was over, the Confederacy had not only drafted into the army much of its badly needed skilled labor but had used the threat of drafting employees as a means of controlling contractors and manufacturers.

Confederate conscription

The Militia Act of 1862 as passed by the United States Congress was technically a draft since it subjected all able-bodied men between eighteen and forty-five to service, but it was not until March 1863 that the "national forces" were created of men between twenty and forty-five and forced service begun. There was riotous resistance in various places, most significantly in New York **Union conscription** City. There the strongly state-rights governor stood by passively while mobs of workingmen (who resented Negro economic competition) in a four-days riot looted, burned, and lynched. Federal troops finally took over and restored order. Less than 50,000 men were actually drafted in the North; the creaking law had been designed to accelerate the enlistment of volunteers, and it provided that draftees could escape military service by paying a commutation fee of $300 or by hiring a substitute. About 87,000 paid commutation, and 118,000 hired substitutes. The system naturally came in for severe criticism as one intended to coddle the rich. The Confederacy also had the substitute system, and objections were probably even more widespread.

Desertion was a problem of amazing proportions in both armies. The Union army reported about 200,000 deserters from its ranks; many of them were bounty jumpers, but others were affected by disgust at hardships or what they regarded as "undemocratic" treatment, **Desertion** or by cowardice or just plain ennui. The problem was never met firmly by the Federal government. Confederate deserters were largely from the poorer back country. Such areas were probably among the first to suffer from drought and inflation, and as early as 1862 their men were deserting to go home and look after their families. As conscripting officers began reaching out for them, such men had to hide during the day and work their land at night. Sometimes they took to the hills in bands and turned to robbery which they dignified with the name of guerrilla warfare; oftentimes they claimed to be Unionists and openly resisted the Confederacy.

The Confederate conscription law had exempted one white man for each twenty slaves on plantations, and this action was resented as favoritism to the rich. Then presently the Emancipation Proclamation began to make it look as though a war begun to prevent invasion were being continued to preserve the planters' Negro property. "It's a rich man's war and a poor man's fight" became a slogan quoted with approval. It is difficult to know just how to weigh all factors, but it seems true that conditions in the South were accelerating the cleavage between classes visible before the war. It is interesting to note that after the war political realism overcame the early contempt for deserters; though an honorable discharge was presumed essential to any veteran who wished to draw a pension, thousands of men in the North benefited by Congressional acts "correcting" the military record, and state acts performed a similar service in the South.

The use of Negro troops was suggested not only by the lag in recruiting but by those who felt that the Negro should have a right to fight for his own freedom. Northern public opinion, however, was race-conscious and deplored setting Negroes to fight against white men. It **Negro troops** was only the swing in sentiment that came with the Emancipation Proclamation that reversed the trend. Late in 1862 regiments recruited from both slave and free Negroes were begun. Altogether about 185,000 Negroes served. Since they were commanded by picked white officers and were all volunteers actuated by a great ideal, Negro troops performed in a highly creditable manner.

The Confederacy naturally resented Northern use of Negroes in combat and announced that captured Negro troops would be enslaved and their white officers shot as inciters of servile insurrection. Such statements were threats which so far as we can tell were not carried out, though in Tennessee at Fort Pillow (12 April 1864) three hundred men of the Negro garrison were slain under circumstances that were at the North called a "massacre." The accusation has never been proved or disproved.

In the light of Southern threats it is an interesting fact that as early as the spring of 1861 free Negroes were being enlisted as soldiers in the Confederacy, though Negro units were later disbanded. There were some Southern advocates of the enlistment of slaves (rewarding them with freedom, of course), but it was not until the last few days of the war that the Confederate Congress authorized the policy. A few Negro troops were enlisted and paraded in Richmond but never saw combat. At least it was a demonstration of the truth of the claim that, win or lose, secession had doomed slavery.

As in all armies up to this time, medical services were helter-skelter at the beginning of the war. Little improvement was made in the Confederate army, partly because of lack of medicines and equipment, but **Medical and auxiliary services** Surgeon-General William A. Hammond was responsible in the Union army for an administrative revolution which became the basis of modern military medical service. He organized field and base hospitals, set up a separate medical corps, and provided enlisted personnel for stretcher bearers, first-aid services, and hospital orderlies. Civilian hospitals and homes were opened to the wounded, the ill, and the convalescent. Directing such work was the civilian-controlled United States Sanitary Commission, financed by gifts and by money raised in a great series of "sanitary fairs." Camp recreation and special services were directed by the Christian Commission, a Young Men's Christian Association project. A notable feature of the Civil War was the part that women played as nurses in military hospitals, a custom newly-introduced in the Crimea by Florence Nightingale and now carried on in the United States by Clara Barton, who was later an organizer of the American Red Cross.

The subject of military prisons has led to long recrimination between

North and South, and this was for half a century stirred up by the publications of the memoirs of ex-prisoners whose recollections were chiefly on the bitter side. The whole controversy is a deplorable example of war psychosis and of the human tendency to refuse **Prisons** to see anything but cruelty and bad faith in the enemy. The truth seems to be that prisoners were on both sides given the same rations as soldiers in the field but were not as snugly housed as troops in winter quarters. The scant resources of the Confederacy led eventually to a steady diminution of the food and medical care of the Union prisoners in its hands, and uncounted thousands died as a result. Resentful prisoners blamed Southern sadism, and undoubtedly there was an element of that in some prison officials (and on the Union side as well), but more responsible were mismanagement and the general breakdown of Confederate transportation services. It is a notable fact that after all the Northern fulminations about vengeance on rebels only one execution was carried out, that of the commandant of Andersonville Prison—and he was a foreigner. During the first two years of the war exchange of prisoners was frequent, but by 1863 the cartel broke down due to complications rising from war resentments and charges of bad faith. Union reluctance to add to the strength of the Confederate army by releasing prisoners probably played a part in the decision to stop exchanges.

The picture of military preparations on both sides shows too much inefficiency and waste. Part of this was due to haste, but much of it, especially in the lower echelons, was due to grafting inspectors. Even in the North the Federal government had to nurse state pride, and this situation led to duplication of effort, bickering, and **Services of supply** rivalry in bidding for arms and equipment which inflated prices and yielded outrageous profits. Even at that, many purchases were of defective matériel: exploding rifles, shoddy clothing, paper shoes, and moldy rations were commonplace during the first half of the war. Secretary of War Cameron showed so little disposition to cure the evils of supply that Lincoln was forced to replace him. Stanton was autocratic, but he got results. Nevertheless, he had his blind spots: the war might have been greatly shortened but for his stubborn insistence on retaining the old muzzle-loading Springfield rifles instead of replacing them with the newer and more efficient breech-loading repeaters.

The Bull Run disaster made it clear to even the most severe contemner of military rules and discipline that the Union army had to be rebuilt from the ground up. Fortunately for the North, the Confederacy seemed willing to wait. General McClellan took command **McClellan rebuilding the Union army** of the Army of the Potomac in July 1861, and upon the retirement of Scott he became general in chief. He did a superb job of rebuilding. A staff was organized for command, inspection, and planning functions. The three-months volunteers were replaced by men enlisted for three years. Camp and leave discipline were tightened. The troops were equipped and drilled. McClellan's influence was, of course, most felt on the Potomac front, but other generals—notably U. S. Grant in the West—were with his support performing a similar task elsewhere. Disciplinary standards in the West, however, never reached those of the gentlemanly Army of the Potomac; there were occasions when the free and easy Westerners on parade greeted a cowardly or unenterprising general with bleats as he rode down the lines.

BIBLIOGRAPHICAL NOTE

The Civilian Battle

THE RADICALS: General treatments are Thomas H. Williams, *Lincoln and the Radicals* (1941); Harry J. Carman and Reinhold H. Luthin, *Lincoln and the Patronage* (1943); and William B. Hesseltine, *Lincoln and the War Governors* (1948). Best biography of Stevens, though biased, is James A. Woodburn, *Life of Thaddeus Stevens* (1913). Greeley's own *Recollections of a Busy Life* (1868) is almost naïvely frank; see also Don Seitz, *Horace Greeley* (1926), and Jeter A. Isely, *Horace Greeley and the Republican Party, 1853–1861* (1947).

THE CABINET: For a readable account see Burton J. Hendrick, *Lincoln's War Cabinet* (1946). On Welles see his *Diary* (3 v., 1911), and Richard S. West, *Gideon Welles: Lincoln's Navy Department* (1943). Works on other Cabinet members are cited elsewhere. It is amazing that there is no competent biography of Stanton.

WAR POWERS: See James G. Randall, *Constitutional Problems Under Lincoln* (1926). On Copperhead opposition see Wood Gray, *The Hidden Civil War* (1942).

THE NORTH, SOCIAL AND ECONOMIC: Emerson D. Fite, *Social and Industrial Conditions in the North During the Civil War* (1930); Arthur C. Cole, *The Irrepressible Conflict* (1934); Ellis P. Oberholtzer, *Jay Cooke, Financier of the Civil War* (2 v., 1907); Earle D. Ross, *Democracy's College: The Land-Grant Movement in the Formative Stage* (1942). See again Margaret Leech, *Reveille in Washington, 1860–1865* (1941).

THE SOUTH, SOCIAL AND ECONOMIC: See especially Charles W. Ramsdell, *Behind the Lines in the Southern Confederacy* (1944); Bell I. Wiley, *The Plain People of the Confederacy* (1948); E. Merton Coulter, *The Confederate States of America* (1950). On particular subjects see the following: Ella Lonn, *Salt as a Factor in the Confederacy* (1933); Francis B. Simkins and James W. Patton, *The Women of the Confederacy* (1936); Frank L. Owsley, *State Rights in the Confederacy* (1925); and John C. Schwab, *The Confederate States of America, 1861–1865: A Financial and Industrial History of the South During the Civil War* (1901). Works on Davis and Richmond during the war have been previously cited; however, see also Burton J. Hendrick, *Statesmen of the Lost Cause* (1939), and Clifford Dowdey, *Experiment in*

Rebellion: The Human Story of the Men Who Guided the Confederacy (1946).

The American Question Abroad

DIPLOMACY: From the point of view of the South see Frank L. Owsley, *King Cotton Diplomacy* (1931). On Seward see the life by Frederic Bancroft. Charles Francis Adams is portrayed in the biography by his son, of the same name, and in Worthington C. Ford, ed., *A Cycle of Adams Letters, 1861–1865* (2 v., 1920). On European opinion see Donaldson Jordan and Edwin J. Pratt, *Europe and the American Civil War* (1931); and for relations with Britain, Ephraim D. Adams, *Great Britain and the American Civil War* (2 v., 1925). On the Mexican imbroglio see Ralph Roeder, *Juárez and His Mexico* (2 v., 1947). On Alaska, Victor J. Farrar, *Annexation of Russian America to the United States* (1937); and Benjamin P. Thomas, *Russo-American Relations, 1815–1867* (1930). The title of this section comes from the excellent summary of the subject in James G. Randall, *The Civil War and Reconstruction* (1937).

CONFEDERATE CRUISERS: Follow Raphael Semmes and the *Sumter* in Harpur A. Gosnell, ed., *Rebel Raider* (1948); and the *Shenandoah* in the account by a crew member, Cornelius E. Hunt, *The Shenandoah* (1910). The effect of the cruisers on American carriers is seen in George W. Dalzell, *The Flight from the Flag* (1940). Best sources on the *Alabama* settlements are Allan Nevins, *Hamilton Fish* (1936) and Lester B. Shippee, *Canadian-American Relations, 1849–1874* (1939).

The Sinews of War

KING COTTON: The proposed use of cotton as a means of economic pressure found championship in David Christy, *Cotton Is King: or Slavery in the Light of Political Economy* (1855). For its actual use and effect see Frank L. Owsley, *King Cotton Diplomacy* (1931).

ENLISTMENTS AND CASUALTIES: For a discussion of statistics see James G. Randall, *The Civil War and Reconstruction* (1937), 685–87. Statistics of battle losses were notoriously inaccurate; best estimates are by Thomas L. Livermore, *Numbers and Losses in the Civil War* (1900).

MISCELLANEOUS ASPECTS: Albert B. Moore, *Conscription and Conflict in the Confederacy* (1924); Ella Lonn, *Desertion During the Civil War* (1928); George W. Williams, *History of Negro Troops in the War of the Rebellion* (1888); Emery Upton, *Military Policy of the U.S.* (1904); Fred A. Shannon, *The Organization and Administration of the Union Army, 1861–1865* (2 v., 1928); William B. Hesseltine, *Civil War Prisons: A Study in War Psychology* (1930); Richard F. Hemmerlein, *Prisons and Prisoners of the Civil War* (1934).

Chapter XXVII

THE CIVIL WAR: AMERICAN ILIAD

1 *The Strategy of the Civil War*

PROBABLY no other war in history is so fascinating in its military aspects as the Civil War. It exhibits all the traditional and professional phenomena of strategy and tactics, of siege and battle, of cavalry as eyes and protective cushions and destructive arms, of naval blockade and vast amphibious operations. One of the last great wars of movement in the old sense, it was yet the first to rely on railroads and the first to find a use for air reconnaissance. Complex as was the war, its strategy is nevertheless easily grasped and was in the main well understood at the time. One effect of this understanding was that the public followed with interest the fortunes of scores of easily distinguishable generals in a way which has been impossible in the mass-production wars of our own century. And yet it was a big war, involving perhaps three million men, and there were battles in which the number of deaths was almost as large as in all the battles of the United States before 1860.

Fascina-
tion of the
Civil War

Not only was the Civil War the apogee of traditional warfare, but it was also the travail which brought forth the modern age. With the old and the new thus meeting it was inevitable that, as soon as it passed, the war should be invested with a halo of romance. And yet it is evident that one must keep his illusions bright if he wishes to see this romance. Ordinary combatants saw little glory or romance until long after the war was over. What they experienced in the midst of the war (as that disillusioned veteran Oliver Wendell Holmes, Jr. put it) was nine tenths intense boredom and one tenth intense fear.

Romance
and reality

They saw filth, rags, and spoiled rations; the nagging discomforts and tedium of garrison life relieved by wild binges in town or by cruel marches under fifty-pound packs. They smarted under the highhandedness of officers and military courts and their cruel and unusual punishments, or, just as bad, the blows of the company bully or the outrages of organized gangs of camp ruffians. They fell before diseases that swept the tented fields: dysentery (the "Tennessee quick step"), cholera, typhus, malaria, pneumonia, and syphilis. Then after the brief half-drunkenness of battle, both numbing and exhilarating but laced with the screams of the wounded and the stench of blood and feces, came the return of boredom or of fatiguing marches—unless varied by the gangrenous stench and even greater pain or boredom of hospital or prison.

The grand strategy of the Civil War was basically a development of Scott's much ridiculed Anaconda. As a matter of fact, Lincoln declared a blockade of the Southern coast immediately after Sumter and rushed into service every old tub capable of floating a gun off a Southern seaport. Though ludicrously ineffective at first, the **Basic strategy** blockade was gradually strengthened as the navy was built up; meanwhile amphibious landings picked off the ports one by one until by the end of 1864 only Charleston and Wilmington remained to the Confederacy. The second part of Union strategy was the movement which we have seen to consolidate control of the Border States, both to deny their resources and man power to the South and to serve as springboards for the invasion of the South. The third part of Union strategy was to cut the Confederacy into segments by army and river-navy thrusts down the Mississippi, toward Atlanta, and toward Richmond; the intention was not only to separate the parts of the Confederacy but to decimate its armies and disrupt its transportation. These movements were aided by a maze of cavalry raids which destroyed communications and supplies by tearing up railroads and burning bridges, warehouses, and supply dumps. Then at the very last, as it turned out, the Eastern armies of the Union held Confederate strength immobile in Richmond while the Western armies swung around through Georgia and the Carolinas to catch the capital of the Confederacy in a vise.

The tactics of the Civil War were no less interesting than its strategy. It should be borne in mind that the United States possessed relatively few of the well-barbered fields such as those over which European armies fought. The American terrain was rough, wooded, and **Tactics of** swampy; even land once reclaimed from wilderness was **the Civil** often covered with thickets and gullied by the rains. Ar- **War** tillery and cavalry were greatly handicapped, and there were relatively few full-dress artillery duels and cavalry charges. Cavalry, indeed, was little used in direct support of the armies but served chiefly as scouts and raiders. Confederate cavalry was more efficient at first, but by 1864 Northern cavalry had become under Phil Sheridan and others a powerful Union weapon against the Confederate supply lines.

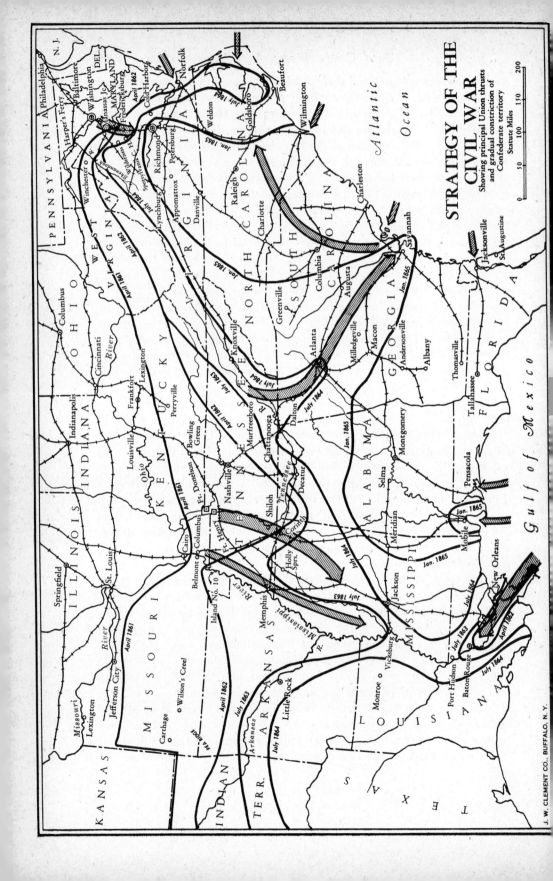

STRATEGY OF THE
CIVIL WAR

Showing principal Union thrusts
and gradual constriction of
Confederate territory

Statute Miles

0   50   100   150   200

J. W. CLEMENT CO., BUFFALO, N.Y.

The rifle displaced the musket, though due to military prejudice the magazine rifle did not come into common use until late in the war. Signaling was very well developed, and booby traps, wire entanglements (not barbed wire), and observation balloons were used. Staff planning and inspection were introduced but did not become efficient until the last year of the war, partly because American individualists in Congress and among the volunteers (both in the North and in the South) had a deep suspicion of plans and resented what they called West Point dictation. This antipathy had something to do with the Federal decision to keep younger West Pointers with their regular army units and to appoint civilians as officers of state volunteers. It is notable that such men as McClellan, Grant, and Sherman owed their rise to the fact that they were in civil life at the beginning of the war and were available for high commands with volunteer troops.

From the beginning the South approached the conflict in a chivalric spirit which showed that its sons had not only read but believed the Waverley novels. Apparently it expected the North to permit the importation of European arms for the equipment of Southern **Chivalry** armies to wage war in the best civilized tradition. Actually **versus** the North exhibited that same superior sense of realism **reality** which during the Revolution had so callously upset European rules of warfare. Total war was now waged against everything but the actual lives of civilians. The exchange of prisoners was stopped, and medicines were not permitted through the blockade. In the end the Deep South, which had so confidently expected the war to be fought in the Upper South and Border States, found itself invaded and desolated. Owen Lovejoy, brother of the murdered abolitionist, announced that "if there is no other way to quell the rebellion, we will make a solitude, and call it peace." John Hickman of Pennsylvania added that conquest would "leave the track of the chariot wheels of war so deep on the Southern soil that a century may not obliterate it." Sherman, the scourge of Georgia and South Carolina, has been called the first modern general because of his scorched-earth policy.

An overview of the character of the Civil War must stress the role of the United States navy. During the war it performed a variety of functions which, though they are less well remembered, were not a whit behind the work of the army in drama and significance. In **Work of** general these consisted of: (1) the pursuit of Confederate **the navy** commerce destroyers; (2) the blockade; and (3) co-operation with the army in a series of amphibious expeditions on Southern rivers and against Southern seaports. Confederate naval strength was greatest on the rivers and in the bays and estuaries. It never succeeded in creating a mobile sea-going fleet, but on the ocean relied on privateers and Confederate cruisers which engaged chiefly in raids on Union merchant ships. Privateers soon fell out of use because they could not take their prizes into neutral ports nor through the blockade into Confederate ports.

We have referred repeatedly to the blockade as an important weapon against the Confederacy. The South bitterly denounced the blockade as not only unfair but in effect nothing more than a "paper blockade." As a **The blockade and blockade runners** matter of fact, Davis had given some excuse for the Northern action—which would have been taken anyhow—in his announcement (17 April 1861) that he would commission privateers to prey on Union shipping. The task of patrolling three thousand miles of coast was tremendous, and at first the force available was far from adequate. As a result the beleaguered Confederacy found it possible to run the blockade with cargoes of cotton and tobacco which were exchanged at Nassau or Bermuda or Matamoros for British arms and medicines. Presently especially built small steamers, long, low, and swift, were put into the trade and won fortunes for their owners and captains. It has been estimated that in 1861 blockade runners successfully completed nine in ten voyages; in 1862 seven in eight; in 1863 three in four; in 1864 two in three; and in 1865 one in two. Actually the estimated 8250 successful voyages were chiefly made by small vessels of low cargo capacity. The blockade, while obviously far from complete, was effective in preventing the building-up of adequate supplies for the Confederate armies and was a vital factor in the eventual Union victory. It is estimated that about 1500 blockade runners were captured.

The growing effectiveness of the blockade was due not only to the increasing size and efficiency of the Union navy but to the way in which Southern seaports were picked off one by one. The Federal government **Amphibious warfare** had retained control of Fortress Monroe at the mouth of the James River and Fort Pickens in Pensacola Bay. In August 1861 the ports of northern North Carolina were crippled by the capture of the Confederate forts at Hatteras and Ocracoke inlets and were presently made useless by the occupation of Roanoke Island and of New Bern and Plymouth on the mainland. In November of 1861 Port Royal, South Carolina was seized, and the occupation was later extended southward along the sea islands. Norfolk, the principal Confederate port in Chesapeake Bay, was abandoned as the result of Union operations on the James. Before the end of 1862 Union forces had occupied practically the entire Atlantic coast of the Confederacy except Wilmington and Charleston and in addition had crippled Savannah. Savannah held out until its capture by Sherman in December 1864, and Fort Fisher at the mouth of the Cape Fear River guarded Wilmington until January 1865.

The Gulf Coast possessed fewer important seaports. Of these New Orleans fell 1 May 1862 after a fleet commanded by David G. Farragut (1801–70) ran past the protecting forts and destroyed a Confederate flotilla. Pensacola, Galveston, Corpus Christi, and Sabine Pass were taken during 1862, though the latter two were to be held again by the Confederacy. In August 1864 Farragut in one of the most dramatic of American naval ventures ran the heavily mined entrance to Mobile Bay despite the fire of the protecting forts and fleet. The bay was thus blocked, though the city did not surrender until the next spring. As rewards for his services a grateful Congress by special acts successively made Farragut the first rear admiral, vice-admiral, and full admiral on the American naval list. Farragut, the son of a Spanish immigrant, was a Tennessean by birth and a Virginian by residence. He had spent his life in the navy from his days as a midshipman aboard the *Essex* in the War of 1812. Probably the most capable and decisive of all the Union commanders on land and sea, Farragut occupied in American public estimation a place much like that of Lord Nelson in Great Britain. Certainly no American naval commander until World War II could rival him in significant accomplishments.

Farragut and the Gulf ports

2 Triumph in the West

By the spring of 1862 the Border States had been saved to the Union, and Lincoln could plan his military strategy without undue fear of alienating them. The Union forces now consisted of 600,000 men, fairly well drilled and equipped; about 200,000 of them were under McClellan's immediate command around Washington. The North, proud of its magnificent army and tired of communiques announcing "All quiet along the Potomac," was anxious for action and was again crying: "On to Richmond!" The East, however, was destined to suffer two years of stalemate while the Northern arms swept from one victory to another in the West.

Spring, 1862

It will be recalled that Frémont had been dislodged from command of the Missouri Department because of his witless political actions. His successor was Henry W. ("Old Brains") Halleck, a scholarly book warrior with a tremendous inferiority complex. While he had some ability as an organizer, the outsize reputation which he soon accumulated as a field commander was largely due to the genius and the luck of his most important subordinate, Ulysses Simpson Grant.

Henry W. Halleck (1815–72)

Grant was the son of a tight-fisted Ohio tanner. His boyhood was thoroughly unhappy and helped to make him turn from human society and toward that of animals, particularly horses—a not uncommon result of the thwarted urge for power. At the age of seventeen he went, reluctantly, to West Point. There he spent four dreary years, quite undistinguished save for his skill in mathematics and with horses. He served capably under Taylor and Scott in the Mexican War. After eleven years of otherwise colorless service he had risen to the rank of captain, but boredom, loneliness, and chronic ague had driven him to heavy drinking. This led to a warning from his commander, to which Grant reacted by presenting his resignation. Meanwhile he had married the daughter of a St. Louis slaveholder, and from 1854 to 1861 he earned a precarious living for his family by a variety of occupations, some of them involving manual labor. The war found him working in the Grant family leather store at Galena, Illinois. Despite his utter dislike of the military life he was ready to serve, but a command was slow in coming. Finally in June 1861 he became a colonel of Illinois volunteers and a couple of months later, much to his surprise, a brigadier general.

U. S. Grant (1822–85)

Grant was a difficult man to know. Physically he was short, squarely built, with snuff-colored hair and beard. To all appearances he was silent, painfully shy, sluggish in disposition, completely matter-of-fact, and obsessively stubborn in finishing what he began. With no social gifts or personal magnetism he had few friends and attracted little attention except on occasion to stir the impression that he was stupid. And yet underneath this phlegmatic exterior there was a sensitive, even prudish man, frustrated, lonesome, and forlorn, so grateful for attention that he bore a doglike devotion to those who were kind to him. He was extremely careless in his dress and neglected the niceties of etiquette, military and political. Nevertheless, he was courageous, self-controlled (except where whisky was involved), ready to take responsibility, and intelligent—or at least absorptive—enough to know good advice, and humble enough to take it. Above all, he learned by experience, and he possessed a quality of determination which was to fire the Union armies and to lead them to victory after a series of appalling defeats.

Character

It was during his days in the West that Grant gathered about him a coterie of generals who were to aid him in the march to victory. There was Sherman, fiery, voluble, profane, self-confident, and "fiercely reasonable"; Sheridan, the frantic adolescent, the congenital cheer leader; McPherson, loyal, magnetic, a born commander, and a universal favorite; and Thomas, phlegmatic, slow-moving, and indomitable—not unlike Grant himself. These were West Pointers. No less important to the fame of Grant was John A. Rawlins, a lawyer of Galena who became his chief of staff. Rawlins was keen-minded, aggressive, and coldly calculating. Outside of military affairs Grant pos-

Grant's generals

sessed no more knowledge, initiative, or competence than the law allowed, but Rawlins served as Dutch uncle in political affairs and in time developed the ambition to make Grant the head of the nation and himself the power behind the throne. As Grant's alter ego he made it his business to present ideas, not directly but in the way of informal staff discussions; no less important was his role of withholder of the bottle. There was some truth to the saying common in the Western army: "If you hit Rawlins on the head, you'll knock out Grant's brains."

Grant was the first of the great Union commanders of the Civil War, after McClellan, to rise above the ruck. We have noted how Grant, in command at Cairo, had seized Paducah in September 1861 as a countermove to the Confederate occupation of Columbus. Now in January 1862 Grant, with Halleck's consent, moved southward up the Tennessee River with 17,000 men of the Army of the Tennessee and seven gunboats. At a point just south **Fall of Forts Henry and Donelson** of the Kentucky border the Tennessee and Cumberland rivers are about eleven miles apart, and at this place the rivers were defended respectively by Confederate forts: Henry and Donelson. Fort Henry fell on 6 February, and ten days later Fort Donelson surrendered with 15,000 prisoners, more than half as many as were in Grant's augumented army. It was on the latter occasion that Grant won his popular name of "Unconditional Surrender" Grant, from the terms that he dictated to the garrison.

At this time the Confederate commander of the Army of the Mississippi was Albert Sidney Johnston, one of the best Southern leaders. Johnston's immediate command had been at Bowling Green, Kentucky, where he was being watched by Don Carlos Buell with 35,000 men of the Army of the Ohio. Grant's victory exposed Johnston's left flank, and Johnston retreated across Tennessee to Corinth, Mississippi, where he could protect the complex of railroads centered in that region which led to the principal cities of the Confederacy.

Grant and Buell moved southward slowly and confidently, planning to unite and crush Johnston. A strange interlude came when Halleck, who was insanely jealous of his commanders, placed Grant under arrest for a week, then restored him to command. Johnston was perfectly aware of Grant's and Buell's plan and did not propose to wait. Suddenly on 6 April he fell upon Grant's army, **Shiloh, 6–7 April 1862** which had been carelessly thrust out west of the Tennessee in the vicinity of Pittsburg Landing. Grant was completely surprised, and his green troops were thrown into confusion. They were driven back, and the key position, Shiloh Church, was taken. However, the death of Johnston in the battle discouraged his forces, and the next day Grant, reinforced by Buell, retook the field. In this battle the Confederate forces of 40,000 suffered 11,000 killed, wounded, and missing; and the Union army of 80,000 (not all engaged) lost 13,000.* Halleck, torn by jealousy, relegated Grant to innocuous desuetude—he did not dare to deprive him of his command—and took charge in person. As he gingerly probed southward the Confederates evacuated Corinth.

Tennessee was now in Union hands, and Andrew Johnson was appointed military governor of the state. No less important was the blow to Confederate transportation suffered by the breaking of the through railroads from Memphis southward and eastward. However, Grant came in for much criticism for his carelessness, and accusations were made that he had been surprised because he had been in an alcoholic daze. There is a story—doubtless apocryphal—that when Lincoln was informed of this he asked what brand of whisky Grant drank so that he could send a barrel of it to each of his generals. Actually the victory at Shiloh owed more to the stamina of the troops than to anybody's generalship.

Grant had begun the river war at Fort Henry and carried its eastern effort to a successful conclusion at Shiloh. By the opening of 1862 both sides had equipped themselves with steamboats which carried superstructures shaped like truncated pyramids and covered with

The river war armor or steel rails. These were presently supplemented by other types, including rams, and by mortar boats. Equipped with heavy guns and manned by rivermen and navy personnel, the Union fleet on the Western waters was in 1862 and 1863 probably the most formidable navy in the world. Captain Andrew H. Foote was the commander of this ironclad fleet.

Halleck had placed the Mississippi wing of the river war under the command of General John Pope, a man whose good qualities were sometimes clouded by bombast and poor judgment. Moving down the tortuous river, Pope took New Madrid by siege; then, to avoid the heavily fortified positions on Island No. 10, he cut a canal across a neck of land for the troop transports; the gunboats ran by the batteries on the island and joined the expedition downriver. Island No. 10, thus cut off, was forced to surrender on 7 April. The river was now open to Memphis, but operations were delayed during the advance on Corinth. In July Lincoln called Halleck to Washington to succeed McClellan as general in chief, a post to which he managed to cleave during the remainder of the war, apparently by consenting to act as Stanton's lickspittle.

While Grant lay quietly at Corinth the scene of warfare shifted to the

---

* Battle losses as stated hereafter include killed, wounded, and missing; though the greater number may have returned to duty later, they were of no immediate service. Statistics are taken from Thomas L. Livermore, *Numbers and Losses in the Civil War in America, 1861–65* (1900). Those who disagree with his statistics are invited to undertake the task of providing better ones.

center. General Braxton Bragg, in command of the Confederate Army of the Mississippi at Chattanooga, has sometimes been credited with winning for the Union the war in the center. Certainly he was **Braxton** in many ways typical of too many of the second-grade regu- **Bragg** lar army officers on both sides: honest and courageous but **(1817–76)** a humorless and disputatious martinet striving for the perfection of the European military prototype. Grant, who had known him before the war, told a striking anecdote of Bragg.

> On one occasion, when stationed at a post of several companies . . . he was himself commanding one of the companies and at the same time acting post quartermaster and commissary. . . . As commander of the company he made a requisition on the quartermaster—himself—for something he wanted. As quartermaster he declined to fill the requisition, and indorsed on the back of it his reason for so doing. As company commander he responded to this, urging that his requisition called for nothing but what he was entitled to, and that it was the duty of the quartermaster to fill it. As quartermaster he still persisted that he was right. In this condition of affairs Bragg referred the whole matter to the commanding officer of the post. The latter, when he saw the nature of the matter referred, exclaimed: "My God, Mr. Bragg, you have quarreled with every officer in the army, and now you are quarreling with yourself."

In August 1862 General Bragg with 35,000 men left Chattanooga and moved into Kentucky, hoping to rally Kentuckians to his standard and perhaps seize Louisville and Cincinnati. Buell had placed himself with his Army of the Ohio between Nashville and Chatta- **Bragg's in-** nooga but when Bragg by-passed him hastened northward. **vasion of** At Perryville, sixty-five miles southeast of Louisville, on 8 **Kentucky** October the two armies fought an indecisive action. Bragg had gained few recruits in Kentucky and saw little use in holding the state, and so he retreated to Chattanooga. Buell was ordered to follow him but refused to move beyond Nashville on the ground that he could not protect his line of supply. There was a great deal to be said for his claim. Two magnificent Confederate cavalry leaders, Generals John Hunt Morgan and salty Nathan Bedford Forrest, who summarized the art of war in the words "git thar fustest with the mostest," had long harried his communications and menaced his depots, while bushwhackers were ever present to pick up the leavings. Nevertheless, Buell's attitude gave the Radicals the opportunity they had been awaiting, for he was opposed to the great object of emancipation. Such pressure was exerted on Lincoln that he removed Buell and placed Rosecrans in command of the forces which were now called the Army of the Cumberland.

As it turned out, Rosecrans agreed with Buell and refused to leave

Nashville until December, when Bragg, whose command was now called the Army of Tennessee, moved to Murfreesboro and offered battle. The bitter three-day battle of Murfreesboro, sometimes called Stone River, was joined on 31 December. Rosecrans's right wing was driven back, but General George H. Thomas saved the day by holding the center. Bragg attacked again on 2 January but was beaten off and returned to Chattanooga. In this battle the Federals lost 13,000 of 45,000, and the Confederates 12,000 out of 38,000.

Murfrees-boro, 31 Dec. 1862– 2 Jan. 1863

Halleck's departure left Grant in command of the Army of the Tennessee. Ranged against him were two armies, that of Bragg in Tennessee and that of John C. Pemberton in Vicksburg; both were from November 1862 under the general command of Joseph E. Johnston. Johnston, after the victory at First Bull Run, had commanded the army which resisted McClellan's peninsular thrust at Richmond but had been seriously wounded and forced to give up the command. Though Johnston was one of the great names of the Civil War, the question of his capacity has always been puzzling. He was always playing in hard luck; he was wounded ten times, and disease stalked him incessantly. Several times he was thrust into crises where the stage was already set for disaster, but no sooner did he glimpse a way out—he thought—than he was wounded or, even more baffling, removed from command. Johnston himself was at no loss for an explanation. He blamed Davis, who had been his bête noire from West Point days and who now sought his disgrace by hampering orders and by withholding men and supplies. Johnston may have been more responsible than he realized. Though he possessed winning manners and was thoroughly conscientious, he was foolishly reckless in exposing his person and was dogmatic, jealous, self-defensive, and overcritical.

Joseph E. Johnston (1807–91)

New Orleans had fallen 1 May 1862. Union strategy now aimed at opening the Mississippi by taking heavily fortified Vicksburg and at cutting the Confederacy farther east by capturing Chattanooga as a base for a push through Georgia. Late in 1862 Grant moved against Vicksburg, which with Port Hudson constituted the last Confederate strongholds on the Mississippi. After a brilliant campaign through the swamps of the Vicksburg area, Grant finally in May 1863 penned up Pemberton and 30,000 men in Vicksburg. Grant had been greatly aided by Johnston's hesitations and by the conflicting orders given to Pemberton by Davis and Johnston. In the end the disgusted Johnston retired southward with his Army of the Mississippi.

Vicksburg campaign

With the aid of David D. Porter, Foote's successor as commander of the river gunboats, Grant laid siege to Vicksburg. For six weeks his mortar boats and artillery shelled the town while his trenches were advanced toward the Confederate lines. By July hunger had supple- **Fall of** mented the inexorable Federal guns, and on the 4th Pem- **Vicksburg** berton surrendered his ragged and starving men. Meanwhile **and Port** Port Hudson had been besieged by N. P. Banks's army and **Hudson,** Farragut's fleet. On 9 July it surrendered, and, as Lincoln **July 1863** put it, the Father of Waters flowed unvexed to the sea. The Confederacy had been cut in two. Thereafter General Edmund Kirby-Smith, in command of the Trans-Mississippi Department, became the ruler of this detached part of the Confederacy. Except for the abortive Red River Campaign by Banks's army in 1864, the Federal armies left Kirby-Smith pretty much to his own devices.

Rosecrans did not move again until June, probably because he was waiting for a decision at Vicksburg. When he did take the field, he forced Bragg back to Chattanooga. That city lies in a bend of the Tennessee River between the northern extremities of Lookout Moun- **Chicka-** tain and Missionary Ridge, two long ridges which rise out **mauga 19–** of the hills of Alabama and extend northeastward across the **20 Sept.** corner of Georgia and into Tennessee. East of Missionary **1863** Ridge the West Branch of Chickamauga Creek flows northward toward the Tennessee. Rosecrans now determined to move across these ridges, cut the vital railroad between Chattanooga and Atlanta, and take Bragg in the rear. Bragg was surprised by the move but, being well reinforced, he did not hesitate to give battle. During the prebattle maneuvers the armies had moved in such a way that Rosecrans now had his back to Chattanooga, and his left wing under Thomas was in front of Rossville Gap through which led the Chattanooga Road.

Battle was joined on 19 September and continued on the 20th. On the morning of the latter day Bragg struck the Federal left, but Thomas stood firm, though presently other Confederate attacks dissolved the center and right and sent the panic-stricken troops streaming through the gap into Chattanooga. Still Thomas held out against every charge until after nightfall, when he was able to retreat into the gap. Thomas's stand was all that saved the Union army from destruction, and it was this heroic action that won him acclaim as "The Rock of Chickamauga." Of 58,000 Union troops 16,000 were lost, and of the 66,000 Confederates about 18,-500 were lost. Rosecrans, besieged with his Army of the Cumberland in Chattanooga, seemed to lose all power of action and was presently superseded by Thomas. Bragg was subject to just as severe criticism for his mistakes, especially for allowing himself to be surprised and for submitting his men to such slaughter, but Davis, himself something of a martinet, backed Bragg squarely and retained him in command.

The Federal government now exerted itself to relieve the besieged army. Late in October Grant arrived with reinforcements drawn from

both the Army of the Potomac and the Army of the Tennessee, and re-
Chattanoo- opened communications with the North. Bragg's lines were
ga, 24–25 formed in a semicircle around Chattanooga with the two
Nov. 1863 wings anchored on the supposedly inaccessible heights of
Lookout Mountain and Missionary Ridge. An important factor in the
campaign hitherto had been the presence of the small Army of the Ohio at

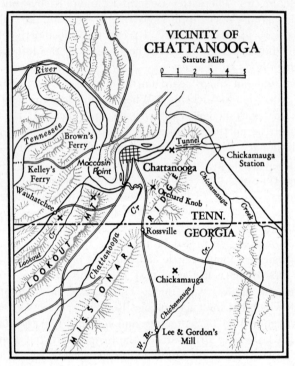

Knoxville, and Bragg, supposing that Grant would move as slowly as
usual, weakened his army by detaching several brigades to deal with this
menace.

Grant seized the opportunity and moved with dispatch. While Thomas
held the center, Hooker on the right made a feint against Lookout Mountain and finding it thinly defended went on to seize the heights in "the
battle above the clouds." The next day, 25 November, Sherman and
Sheridan proceeded to carry the Confederate rifle pits at the base of
Missionary Ridge, but the troops, galled by the fire from the heights,
swept on without orders and charged up the mountain; it was so steep
in places that the men almost had to chin themselves from tree to tree.
Despite the strategic significance of the battle, the total killed on both
sides was only about a thousand. Bragg retreated to Ringgold, Georgia.

East Tennessee, still loyal to the Union, was cleared of regular Confederate troops.

The Battle of Chattanooga was signalized by the presence of Grant, Sherman, Thomas, and Sheridan, the four great Union leaders brought to the top after two years of conflict. Grant was presently called to Washington to command all Union operations, and Sherman was **William** placed in charge of the three armies of the Cumberland, the **Tecumseh** Tennessee, and the Ohio with instructions to hew his way **Sherman** to the vital railroad center of Atlanta. William Tecumseh **(1820–91)** ("Cump") Sherman was a West Pointer from Ohio, and though his rise may have been due in part to the fact that his brother John was a Senator and his father-in-law was a politician of national caliber, it is generally agreed that he was in the end one of the two or three most competent commanders in the Union army. Though he had seen little action during the Mexican War, he was thoroughly seasoned at First Bull Run and in Grant's campaigns in Tennessee and Mississippi.

Sherman grasped and intelligently applied the lesson that Union generals were slow in learning, that calculated risks had to be taken to win victories. His famous maxim, "War is hell," was in the opinion of Southerners too conscientiously applied, but he got results. Sherman was tall and gaunt and had a military bearing; his face was bearded, lined, and severe, his eyes piercing, and his red hair was eternally tousled. Nervous and quick-thinking, Sherman bore a reputation for eccentricity; actually he was calm and farsighted. That he was almost devoid of ambition is witnessed by his lack of interest in army intrigues and by his famous declaration in 1884 when urged to seek the nomination for the presidency: "I will not accept if nominated and will not serve if elected."

Before taking up Sherman's fortunes in Georgia we must turn to the war in the East, of which his Georgia campaign was destined to become a part.

3 Stalemate in the East

The Union's armies and navies had during 1862 and 1863 successfully eaten at the coastal fringe of the Confederacy, had split it along the Mississippi River, had regained Tennessee and much of Louisiana and Mississippi, and had pierced deeply toward the vital military keystone, the State of Georgia. Meanwhile in the East, **Failure in** though the armies had surged back and forth between Rich- **the East** mond and Pennsylvania, there was little real change in the military situation. One reason was certainly the remarkable record of the Confederates under Robert E. Lee, but not far behind was the unfortunate fact that the Army of the Potomac, since it was close to Washington, was continually subject to political interference. Lincoln, who knew nothing of strategy and tactics but was under continual pressure by the public and the Radicals, was too prone to lay down conditions to his generals. There are frequent glimpses of him as a harassed and despondent commander in chief sorely puzzled by problems of command and strategy and political expedience.

No other first-rank Union commander suffered so much at the hands of the Radicals as McClellan. A Democrat in political persuasion, lukewarm toward the great Radical object of emancipation, with every button and crease of his immaculate uniform shouting of West

McClellan's problems

Point, insolently self-reliant and contemptuous of political interference, McClellan won the hatred of the Radicals almost from the first. It was only Lincoln's championship that enabled him to remain in command. At the beginning of 1862 McClellan had a magnificent army of 200,000 men to pit against Joseph E. Johnston's 50,000, but he hesitated to take the field—bluffed, his enemies said, by Johnston's batteries of wooden "Quaker guns."

McClellan was certainly more fearful than bold, though he undoubtedly regarded himself as the man of destiny who would save the republic. Yet he was quite unconscious of his megalomania and was humbly thankful that he possessed such astounding genius to place at the service of his country. The Radicals called him McNapoleon, hypocritically deplored his insolent treatment of Lincoln (which the latter bore patiently), and professed to fear that he would seize the government by *coup d'état*. Already his commanders were divided into two groups, the seniors who played along with the Radicals' Joint Committee and the juniors who (along with the rank and file) worshiped McClellan. Lincoln and the Radicals alike favored a frontal attack on Johnston in order to keep the army between Washington and the Confederates, for they were pathologically fearful for the safety of the Capital.

McClellan, however, proposed the more intelligent plan of transporting his army by boats to Fortress Monroe on the James River and attacking Richmond from the direction of the Peninsula between the York and

McClellan's plan of campaign

James rivers. In this way naval support would be available, and army and navy together might force a way through the James defenses of Richmond. Lincoln consented reluctantly but at the last moment confined McClellan's command to the Army of the Potomac and divided that army into corps, each under a senior officer who was thus effectively interposed between McClellan and his worshiping junior commanders; at the same time Lincoln insisted that the defenses of Washington must be well manned and Harpers Ferry strongly held against any Confederate flanking move on the Capital. In the end

McClellan was permitted to concentrate only about 110,000 troops for the Peninsular Campaign, while the Confederates at their peak mustered about 85,000.

It may be that Lincoln's reluctance to approve of the peninsular approach to Richmond rose in part from the presence at Norfolk of a powerful Confederate ironclad frigate. When Norfolk Navy Yard had been abandoned, the steam frigate *Merrimac* had been sunk in **Building** the river. This the Confederates proceeded to raise and to **the iron-** equip with a superstructure covered with iron, similar to **clads** those then being built in the West, and with a powerful ram in the prow. The Federal Navy Department had noted this project with anxiety and in September 1861 accepted plans drawn up by the Swedish inventor John Ericsson for a small ironclad with flush decks and two heavy guns in a revolving turret. In view of the desperate need the work was hastened, and the *Monitor*, as Ericsson's vessel was called, was completed in one hundred days.

On 8 March 1862 the *Merrimac*, now rechristened the *Virginia*, steamed across the James River to Hampton Roads, where five Federal wooden ships and a number of gunboats were at anchor. Nonchalantly ignoring the hail of shot and shell, the *Virginia* rammed the **Battle of** sloop *Cumberland* and set fire to the frigate *Congress* after **the iron-** forcing its surrender. The *Virginia*, leaving the frigate *Min-* **clads, 9** *nesota* helplessly stranded in the mud, then insolently re- **March 1862** tired for the night. That evening the *Monitor* arrived in Hampton Roads and took station behind the *Minnesota*. The next morning, when the *Virginia* appeared to complete its work of destruction, the *Monitor* steamed out from behind the *Minnesota*. This odd craft, looking like "a cheesebox on a raft," maneuvered as it pleased in shallow water and pounded the *Virginia* with its heavy guns, took little harm from its opponent's shots, and easily avoided being effectively rammed. After four hours both contestants desisted and retired, neither one fatally damaged. The action was a draw, and for various reasons the two ships never met again.

Except for the *Monitor*, it is possible that the *Virginia* could have swept the Union fleet from Chesapeake Bay and perhaps carried the war to Washington. At any rate, the battle had a profound effect on naval operation. Though several ironclads existed in Europe, they **Results of** were distrusted by old hands; but this demonstration of **the battle** their utility was incontrovertible, and all the larger countries entered a desperate race to bring their suddenly outmoded navies up to date. When in April McClellan's armies began the Peninsular Campaign the Union naval commander, worried by the threat of the *Virginia*, disposed his forces to watch it and refused to engage in army support. As a result the *Virginia* may well have helped to save Richmond. However, McClellan's advance up the Peninsula north of the James caused the Confederates to abandon the Norfolk Navy Yard and set the *Virginia* afire. The *Monitor* foundered at sea off Cape Hatteras, 31 December 1862.

McClellan's plan of campaign was good, but the Confederate counter-moves were masterly and furnished justification for McClellan's caution. Before McClellan was ready to move in the Peninsula, Stonewall Jackson

Jackson's Valley Campaign, May–June 1862 with a few thousand "foot cavalry" struck N. P. Banks's 20,000 Union troops on 23 March at Kernstown in the Shenandoah Valley. The frightened Lincoln withheld McDowell's corps from the Peninsula and placed him with 40,000 men before Washington. Four armies with a total strength of

45,000 were set to watch Jackson in the valley. Nevertheless Jackson, now reinforced to 20,000 men, moved on 8 May. Refusing to hold any certain ground or to fight long-drawn-out battles, Jackson shifted rapidly between the converging Federal armies and threw them into confusion or retreat in a series of brilliantly conducted battles. Then, with the Federal armies thoroughly demoralized and Lincoln dreading attack and refusing to reinforce McClellan, Jackson moved swiftly to join the Confederate army before Richmond.

Meanwhile McClellan had wasted a month in besieging Yorktown and then had followed the retreating Confederates and struck them an indecisive blow at Williamsburg (5 May) and received another at Fair Oaks,

Peninsular Campaign, April–June 1862 or Seven Pines (31 May–1 June). In the latter battle Johnston was severely wounded, and Robert E. Lee took command. McClellan was now astride the Chickahominy River and within sight of the steeples of Richmond, which he

prepared to besiege. All he lacked was the additional power that would have been afforded by McDowell's corps, but Lincoln, paralyzed by Jackson's maneuvers, refused to let it go. Whether McClellan could have taken Richmond at this juncture was long and bitterly debated. At any rate, Lee refused to wait and on 25 June began the Seven Days' Battle. McClellan was forced back by successive engagements at Mechanicsville (26 June); Gaines' Mill (27 June), won with the help of Jackson's newly arrived "foot cavalry"; Allen's Farm and Savage's Station (29 June); and Glendale, or Frayser's Farm (30 June). At Malvern Hill (1 July) Lee was repulsed, and McClellan's army found refuge behind the fortifications at Harrison's Landing on the James.

Though the Union army was safe, McClellan well knew that he had been defeated. As a matter of fact, he had lost 16,000 to the Confederate 20,000 and still had much the stronger of the two armies.

Recall of McClellan His ardent desire was to renew the campaign, but his resentment against Lincoln and the Radicals caused him to lose his temper and—probably with an eye on posterity—to send a telegram

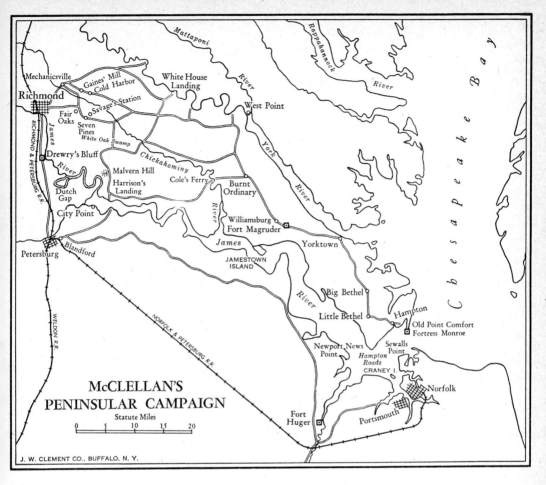

McCLELLAN'S
PENINSULAR CAMPAIGN

Statute Miles

0 5 10 15 20

J. W. CLEMENT CO., BUFFALO, N. Y.

to Stanton which read: "If I save this army now, I tell you plainly that I owe no thanks to you or to any other persons in Washington. You have done your best to sacrifice this army." The rejoicing Vindictives saw their opportunity in McClellan's arrogance and in the public disappointment at his defeat. Lincoln, who had retained McClellan without effectively reinforcing him or defending him against the Radicals, now recalled him and began to withdraw his army from the Peninsula.

Halleck, the armchair warrior who now displaced McClellan as general in chief, was supported by the Radicals in urging the bombastic Pope as commander of "The Army of Virginia" which was hastily scraped together from the defenses of Washington, northern Virginia, and the returning Peninsular veterans. Pope got off to a bad start by throwing up their defeats to his troops, boasting of his own victories, and, perhaps even worse, exciting merriment by his announcement that henceforth his headquarters would be in the saddle. Pope then vaingloriously marched southward with 75,000 men. Lee, seeing that the withdrawal of McClellan's

Pope and Second Bull Run, 29–30 Aug. 1862

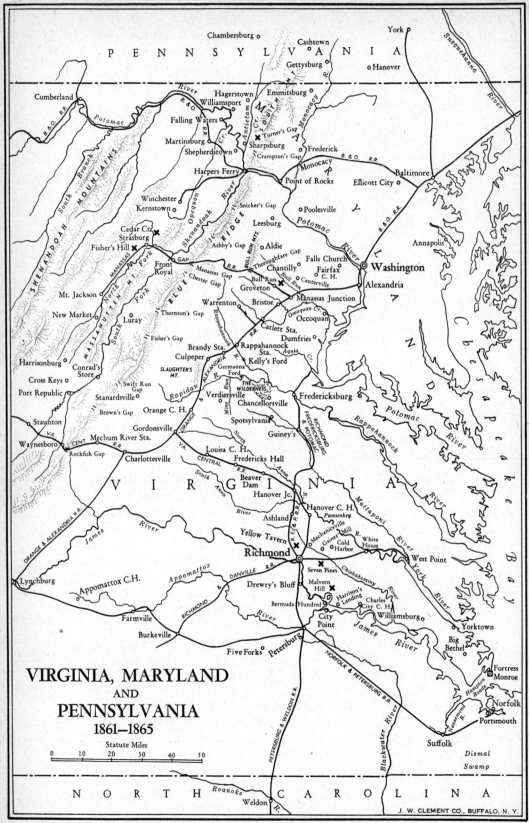

VIRGINIA, MARYLAND
AND
PENNSYLVANIA
1861–1865

Statute Miles

0   10   20   30   40   50

Adapted from *Atlas of American History*, edited by James Truslow Adams and R. V. Coleman; copyright 1943 by Charles Scribner's Sons; used by permission of the publishers.

J. W. CLEMENT CO., BUFFALO, N. Y.

army was under way, moved north with 50,000 men. As the conclusion of a series of brilliant maneuvers on the part of Lee and his lieutenants, the unwary Pope was caught and soundly beaten at the Second Battle of Bull Run, or Manassas (29–30 August), and hastily retreated to Washington. The loss was 16,000 on the part of Pope and 9000 on that of Lee. Stung by their favorite's defeat, the Vindictives deliberately laid the blame on a subordinate who had been friendly with McClellan and railroaded him out of the army.

These two resoundingly successful campaigns introduced to the world the brilliant team of Lee and Jackson and gave it a place in Confederate hearts which was not shaken even by later reverses. Thomas Jonathan Jackson, born into a poor family in Clarksburg (now West   **Stonewall** Virginia) and a West Pointer of the class of 1846—the same   **Jackson** as McClellan's—had served with distinction in Mexico but   **(1824–63)** resigned to become a professor in Virginia Military Institute. His career at VMI was neither successful nor happy, and the students, unaware that the owlish professor was a transcendent military genius, made him the butt of their jokes. Though he deplored secession and war, Jackson went with his state and at First Bull Run won recognition and the nickname "Stonewall." The Valley Campaign, one of the most brilliant in military history, established his ascendance over his "foot cavalry," who prided themselves on their incredibly long and swift marches and on serving under their invincible "Old Jack," who was not yet out of his thirties.

Jackson was not a very striking figure of a man. Grave and simple in demeanor and so shy that he was often awkward and abrupt, he was yet affectionate in his family life and unusually sensitive to the artistic. Indeed, it would seem that he was intuitive rather than intelligent. Modest though he seemed, he thirsted for military glory—perhaps the fierce passion of a backwoods boy for renown. And yet he was unquestioningly subordinate to his great leader, and on his deathbed murmured that it were "Better that ten Jacksons should fall than one Lee." He was so intensely religious (he was a Presbyterian) that he has often been called Puritan and Roundhead. His evangelical zeal, indeed, had such an effect on his troops that there were times when his camp seemed to be one vast prayer meeting. Strictly faithful to duty, he exacted like faithfulness from those under him; his iron will and demand for prompt and exact obedience remind one of the other Jackson. Ewell, his outstanding lieutenant, was firmly convinced that Jackson was insane; if so, he was in popular parlance crazy like a fox.

If Jackson represented the Roundhead zealot, his great commander represented the aristocratic Cavalier. Robert Edward Lee was born in the manor house of Stratford on the Potomac, the son of "Light-Horse

Robert E. Lee (1807–70) Harry" Lee of Revolutionary fame. Graduating with the West Point class of 1829 with a perfect record, Lee served with the engineers on army posts and on special missions all over the country. Why he remained in the army is still Lee's secret, but one may guess that he liked to build things, and, since a Southern aristocrat could not without reproach be an engineer except in the army, he chose to remain there. His marriage in 1831 to a great-granddaughter of Martha Washington brought him the estate of Arlington across the Potomac from the Capital City, now the site of a national military cemetery. In Mexico he was in effect Scott's chief of staff and was made brevet colonel. Periods followed as commandant of West Point and as head of the Department of Texas. His duty as commander of the marine assault on John Brown's citadel at Harpers Ferry came during a leave of absence from Texas. During the secession crisis Lincoln offered to Lee the command of the armies of the United States, but he turned down the offer. There was no doubt in his mind that his first loyalty lay with Virginia, though the thought of warring against the United States was none the less abhorrent; other notable Virginians including Scott, Farragut, and Thomas decided differently.

Lee's early service in the Confederate army was performed under such difficulties that his lack of success even undermined his prestige. Not least of his problems was the fact that as military assistant—whatever that meant—to the president of the Confederacy he was **As a commander** caught between two cocksure military geniuses, Jefferson Davis and Joseph E. Johnston. It was not until he became a commanding general that these conflicting pressures eased. As a matter of fact, Davis always remained a thorn in Lee's side, but Lee bore the situation with patience and tact. His position until the last few weeks of the war was simply that of commander of the Army of Northern Virginia; it is possible that with unified control of the Confederate armies in his hands he might have done more.

As it was, with forces always inferior in numbers, artillery, and equipment his accomplishments were little short of miraculous. He built an army as he fought, and with it swept back in three years no less than four major invasions by an army that was constantly being renewed in personnel and equipment. He was bold in his plans and bold in their execution; if he had any military faults, they were perhaps in his overtenacity in hopeless situations. One of his great strengths lay in his judgment of character, both of his own generals and those of the enemy. In the Civil War, it is well to remember, generals on both sides knew each other intimately—perhaps had roomed together at West Point or in post barracks —and were able to exploit each other's weaknesses.

Lee is the disproof that success is the only basis for immortality, and the proof that "human virtue should be equal to human calamity." Physically he was magnificent—tall, perfectly formed, with nobly molded head and features, and with jet-black hair that had turned almost white at the time of the Civil War. By that time his **Character** early aristocratic hauteur had mellowed to dignity and courtesy, though he never had many intimate friends. His sense of humor was restrained, rarely rollicking or obtrusive. Always deeply religious (he was an Episcopalian), he believed implicity in a ruling Providence, but one suspects that there were occasions when he used an avowal of trust in God to fob off curious inquirers into his plans. Generous to a fault, broadly tolerant, ever tactful, utterly unselfish, modest to the point of self-abnegation, there were few who were jealous of him. He maintained discipline by example, sympathy, and tact; but though his men loved him and affectionately called him "Marse Robert," they also feared him, for they knew he could and would be severe.

Legend would have it that he was oppressively perfect. Not only was he without vices large or small, but he was possessed of spotless and passionless integrity, was indifferent to praise or blame, and was lofty in his appreciation of good and in his blindness to temptation. **The Lee** Above all was his superhuman devotion to duty, which as **Legend** he said "is all the pleasure, all the comfort, all the glory we can enjoy in this world." He was the first gentleman of Virginia, which to the South meant that he surpassed the Tennysonian Sir Galahad and the Seigneur de Bayard, the *chevalier sans peur et sans reproche*.

The cloying sweetness of the Lee Legend has risen not only from the remarkable qualities of the man but from the Southern desire to personify the chivalry of ante-bellum days and the glory of the struggle for the Lost Cause. The mythus of Southern chivalry was drawn **Mythus** from the thin line of Tidewater culture which was spread **becomes** even more thinly by westward-going planters. In ante- **reality** bellum days it existed chiefly in bombast and the novels of William Gilmore Simms. But then came the paradox, when in such men as Robert E. Lee and his humble followers from the red fields of the South it attained in glorious combat its richest claim to having existed. And so in perishing the South found fulfillment. Lee's life, as Gamaliel Bradford, has said, "has the breadth, the dignity, the majesty, the round and full completeness of a Miltonic epic, none the less inspiring because it had a tragic end. It was indeed a life lived in the grand style." This verdict, though spoken of Lee, is no less the accolade of the South which he symbolized.

Lee was assisted in his campaigns by a group of commanders who fell below no other in history, not even Napoleon's marshals. Jackson, of

course, headed the list. Next to him was J. E. B. ("Jeb") Stuart, who
ranks with Nathan Bedford Forrest as a top Confederate
Lee's com-   cavalry leader, and whose organization was largely respon-
manders   sible for Lee's remarkable knowledge of Federal movements
and for his ability to harry their communications. Stuart was the picture
of the romantic warrior, with a full, sunny beard, gaudily dressed, intoxicated with recklessness, caroling snatches of song, and always accompanied by his personal banjo player. Among Lee's corps commanders
was James Longstreet, a slow, stubborn, pugnacious Dutchman from
Georgia. Though he lacked brains and speed, he was unimaginatively
self-confident, silent, cool, and practical. There was no romantic nonsense
about Longstreet; it is perhaps significant that he was one of Grant's few
close friends in the old army. Others of Lee's generals were bald, birdlike,
peg-legged Richard S. Ewell, who succeeded Jackson; Jubal A. Early, who
infested the Shenandoah like Jackson but without Jackson's success; and
A. P. Hill and D. H. Hill.

Returning now to the thread of the war after Second Bull Run, we
find Lincoln pondering the matter of command. The decision had to be
made at once, for Lee was boldly moving into Maryland in a threat against
Antietam   Baltimore and Harrisburg and probably in the expectation
17 Sept.   that Marylanders would flock to his colors. A successful
1862   campaign in Maryland, in conjunction with Bragg's advance
in Kentucky, might even bring foreign recognition and aid. The dispirited
Union soldiers were electrified by the appointment of McClellan to command of the reconstituted Army of the Potomac. With the remnants of
Pope's army and a corps from the James River, McClellan moved north
as soon as he could. At Frederick, Maryland, on 13 September he was
handed the famous "Lost Order," a dispatch from Lee to one of his generals which had been found on the road by a Union soldier and which
disclosed that Lee had divided his force by sending Jackson to seize
Harpers Ferry. Despite this vital information McClellan moved slowly,
so slowly that though he aimed to prevent Jackson's junction with Lee,
he failed. On the 17th the opposing armies met near Sharpsburg on Antietam Creek, and the Union attack was repulsed by Jackson's arrival. In
the bloodiest day of the war McClellan lost 12,000 out of 87,000 (60,000
engaged), and Lee lost 14,000 out of 52,000; about 5000 were killed. On
the 18th McClellan failed to renew the assault, and Lee retreated unhindered across the Potomac while McClellan led the army back to
Virginia and sought excuses to delay further campaigning.

During the first year of the war Lincoln steadfastly insisted that the
Union should be saved without resorting to emancipation of the slaves
against the will of the slave states, either those in the Confederacy or

those still in the Union. In part this attitude arose from the **The prob-** necessity of keeping the goodwill of the Border States, and **lem of** to keep it he even rescinded emancipation proclamations **slavery** issued by heedless generals in Missouri and Maryland. His own plan was emancipation by state action with Federal compensation, and he pled eloquently both with Congress and the Border States to adopt this course. However, Congress, which was going more radical with time, denounced Lincoln's "rose-water" policy, moved to declare the freedom of slaves belonging to "rebels," and forbade the return of fugitives. As the Federal armies advanced, increasing numbers of slaves found their way into their camps and hung upon their routes. The policy in general was to adopt the course of General Benjamin F. Butler at Fortress Monroe and treat them as "contraband," whose return to their owners would aid the Confederate cause. Attempts were made to care for the throngs of fugitives, but on the whole the problem was poorly handled. During the spring of 1862 Congress abolished slavery in the District of Columbia with compensation, and in the territories without compensation.

By the summer of 1862 Lincoln had become aware not only of the fact that the Radical demand for emancipation was growing stronger but that Europe was accusing the North of cynicism. There was real danger that Europe would throw its power on the side of the South **Emancipa-** on the plea that (since the war was not over slavery) its **tion Procla-** interest lay there. In July Lincoln definitely decided to issue **mation** an emancipation proclamation but at Seward's suggestion awaited a Northern victory so that the proclamation would not appear to be "our last shriek on the retreat." The victory at Antietam afforded the desired opportunity. On 22 September Lincoln on the strength of his war powers issued a preliminary proclamation declaring that on 1 January 1863 in all states or parts of states then in rebellion the slaves should be free.

Actually even the final Proclamation had no immediate effect upon slavery. Lincoln himself compared it to the pope's bull against the comet, and Seward remarked: "We show our sympathy with slavery by emancipating slaves where we cannot reach them and holding them in bondage where we can set them free." Nor did the Proclamation even in theory go so far as the acts of Congress already had. Nevertheless, the Proclamation was widely hailed as decisive; despite its clear limitations the North thereafter accepted emancipation as a war aim—and, even more to the point, so did Europe. The actual abolition of slavery was the work of the Thirteenth Amendment, which did not go into effect until the close of 1865.

The Congressional campaign of 1862 was waged by a Republican Party which was sadly split between Radicals and Conservatives. Radicals

resented Lincoln's promise of compensation to slave owners, and Conservatives resented his interference in the business of the states. If
Election of 1862 the Proclamation won votes for the Republicans, it also
strengthened many Democrats in their opposition. As it was,
the "War Democrats" rather reluctantly united with the Republicans
under the name of the Union Party to support Lincoln's war policy. As a
result the Union Party barely retained control of Congress, and New York,
Pennsylvania, Ohio, Indiana, and Illinois elected Democratic members

ABE LINCOLN'S LAST CARD; OR, ROUGE-ET-NOIR.

Punch, 1862

A British view of the Emancipation Proclamation

of the House; the accusation has even been made that the Lincoln majority in the House was preserved only by the use of military power in
the Border States. The regular Democrats, while not openly supporting
secession, had scored with a frustrated nation by asserting that Lincoln's
policies could never end the war and restore the Union.

No sooner were the fall elections over than Lincoln removed McClellan
for the second and last time—for which action Lee was duly grateful. As
the President expressed it to the protesting Blairs, he was through trying
Freder- to "bore with an augur too dull to take hold." At almost the
icksburg, same time he dismissed another commander who was afflicted
13 Dec. by the "slows," Don Carlos Buell. The Vindictives rejoiced
1862 at the passing of McClellan and Buell and at the accession
of Rosecrans in the West. Over the Army of the Potomac Lincoln appointed Ambrose Burnside, whose chief claim to fame is the cultivation of
Burnside whiskers. Burnside had been a McClellan man and, far from
seeking the appointment, was perfectly conscious of his unfitness. Nevertheless, he tried in his bumbling manner to win a victory. He found Lee's

army entrenched west of Fredericksburg with its left on impregnable Marye's Heights. All the day of 13 December 1862 the Union forces charged, proving their mettle but failing to take the heights. Lee, watching the gallant Blue lines charge and then melt away, uttered one of his rare emotional phrases: "It is well this is so terrible, or else we might grow fond of it." Burnside withdrew on the 15th with 12,500 lost out of 114,000, while Lee lost less than half as many.

The defeat at Fredericksburg was a profound shock to the nation. The Radicals, already angered at Burnside's appointment and by Lincoln's insistence in his annual message that slave owners should be compensated, were roused to fury. Strangely enough, Burnside escaped their wrath, for he cannily turned Radical; so they sought scapegoats in one of his generals and in Lincoln. The **Cabinet crisis** American democratic dogma, never more virile or vicious than during the Civil War, had prompted Congress as the representatives of the people to demand control of executive functions. The first step had been to set up the Joint Committee and to persecute Conservative generals.

The Senate now was able to try the second step when a number of disillusioned Conservative Senators joined with the Radicals to force Lincoln to abandon his coalition policy and to destroy the influence of Seward, the "Unseen Hand" who was supposed to be guiding him. Chase had become fearful for the fate of the nation in the hands of so slack a pilot as Lincoln, and his ambition had prompted him to do what he regarded as his patriotic duty. He began secretly tattling to the Radicals about dissension in the Cabinet and presently became their candidate for prime minister. A senatorial delegation now appeared before Lincoln, denounced Seward for his lukewarmness, and demanded that Lincoln reform his Cabinet and oust from independent command all generals who did not agree with them.

Lincoln understood very well that they were trying to force him to put himself under the control of Chase, and he met the challenge to his Constitutional authority shrewdly. He called the Senators to meet with all of his Cabinet except Seward, offered a little homily on **Lincoln's shrewd solution** the unity of the Cabinet, defended Seward, and called upon the Cabinet members for corroboration. Chase knew he could not challenge Lincoln's statements without disclosing his conspiracy with the Radicals; nor could he approve without losing their confidence. He tried hard to squirm out but had to agree that there was "a general acquiescence on public measures."

The Cabinet then retired, and Lincoln informed the Senators that Seward had offered his resignation but that he had refused it lest it lead to a complete smash-up of the administration. Chase, embarrassed and perhaps shamed, got out from under the cabal and turned in his resignation, thus destroying what might have been a Radical victory. Lincoln let the Radicals stew for a while, then kept both men in office. The Radicals were foiled: if they insisted on ousting Seward, Lincoln was in a position to send Chase packing also; not only would they lose their prime minister, but all Radical influence might be excluded from the Cabinet councils. Thereafter Chase and the Radicals viewed each other with suspicion.

Radical wounds were by no means healed when Lincoln confounded all their prophecies and put emancipation into effect on 1 January 1863. All political factions were discontented because it was too weak or too **Emancipa-** strong, and Lincoln, as usual, came in for stinging rebukes **tion put** from such editors as Horace Greeley. Strangely enough, **into effect** Wendell Phillips, Garrison's friend, was satisfied and as someone remarked sarcastically took the field on Lincoln's behalf with "a formidable army of twenty thousand adjectives." Most significant, however, was the fact that the general public both in the United States and abroad seemed to feel that a main issue of the war was clarified.

The Radicals, beaten in their attempt to seize the presidency, now turned to the problem of the reconstruction of conquered territory. Crux of the problem was Louisiana, part of which had fallen to Farragut's **B. F.** fleet in May 1862 and which was under the command of **Butler** General Benjamin Franklin Butler of Massachusetts. But- **(1818–93)** ler, a Democratic politician turned Radical, saw in the Civil War a glorious opportunity for his remarkable talents for collecting power, property, and publicity. Brilliant, epigrammatic, and joyously unscrupulous, he was bald and fat, and his wilted mustaches and the cast in his left eye gave an impression of raffish cynicism which was not in the least misleading. Unfortunately for him, he was not militarily competent, but he enjoyed the next best thing, the protective smoke screen of the Joint Committee.

Butler's administration of New Orleans, though ineffably corrupt, was conducted with a dramatic effectiveness which delighted the North and infuriated the South. Blandly ignoring orders from Washington, he **Butler** established himself as dictator, collected and expended tax **in New** money, hanged a citizen for hauling down the Stars and **Orleans** Stripes, and seized a quantity of gold bullion deposited with the French consul. One of the major problems in all occupied territory was the behavior of Southern women, who took advantage of the immunities of their sex to insult Yankee soldiers with unseemly gestures and epithets. Butler solved the problem in his Order No. 28, which directed that such women should "be regarded and held liable to be treated as a woman of the town plying her avocation." Butler rode the ensuing international storm of indignation with the insouciance of a stormy petrel. Just before the Cabinet crisis Lincoln had recalled him, and the Radicals supposed that he was to be rewarded by a higher position. They learned better when several months passed during which Butler did nothing more important than lend cachet to Washington's better barrooms. Actually Lincoln was purposely letting Butler and the Radicals dangle while his new appointee, General N. P. Banks, as we shall see, began the reconstruction of Louisiana on a conservative pattern.

After Fredericksburg the Radicals feared that the army might force the restoration of the popular McClellan, so the Joint Committee hastened to issue a slanderous report intended to kill him and all West Point influence. Actually the report was intended no less as an attack **Fighting** on Lincoln and as a deliberate attempt to arouse Northern **Joe Hooker** hatred by retailing lies about Southern ferocity. Neverthe- **(1814–79)** less, the Committee's attempt to save Burnside was in vain. Lincoln, bandied about among conflicting factions, finally appointed a Radical favorite, Joseph Hooker, a popular officer with a bold air and a weak chin. "Fighting Joe" had not hesitated to knife Burnside in the back to obtain the promotion, secure in the belief that he was the strong man destined to save the Union. Lincoln was perfectly aware of the chance he took. "I have heard," he wrote to Hooker, "in such a way as to believe it, of your recently saying that both the army and the government needed a dictator. Of course it was not for this, but in spite of it, that I have given you the command. Only those generals who gain successes can set up dictators. What I now ask of you is military success, and I will risk the dictatorship."

Though Lee had won a smashing victory at Fredericksburg, he had felt justified in not following it up and engaged in only minor activities during the winter. By the end of March Hooker's "reforms" were completed, and he announced: "My plans are perfect . . . may **Chancel-** God have mercy on General Lee, for I will have none." In **lorsville,** April he moved confidently with "the finest army on the **2–5 May** planet"—an army double the size of Lee's. Intending to **1863** catch Lee in a pincers, Hooker sent his left wing under the reliable John Sedgwick against Fredericksburg on the Rappahannock while he himself led the right across the Rappahannock and its tributary, the Rapidan, toward the village of Chancellorsville. Hooker's own right was now situated in an area of second growth and underbrush called the Wilderness, where numbers counted for little.

While Lee amused Hooker's main forces, Jackson marched around to the Wilderness and struck his right, rolling it up like a carpet. Then just at twilight (2 May) Jackson on a reconnoitering expedition ran into the fire of his own pickets and was mortally wounded. Nevertheless, battle was resumed the next day, and Hooker's troops were driven from the field; Hooker himself was dazed and confused as the result of a cannon ball striking a porch pillar against which he was leaning. On the 4th Lee turned on Sedgwick and drove him north of the Rappahannock, then the next day turned again on Hooker's own command and harried it also across the river. The Union loss during six days of contact was 17,000 out of around 105,000, while that of Lee was 12,500 out of 57,000. Most serious Confederate loss was the death of Jackson on the 10th. Well might Lee mourn the loss of his "right arm." Chancellorsville was the last great Confederate victory in the East.

Lee now moved to pluck the fruits of his victory by invading the North for the second time. Not only did his army need the food and forage available in the bursting warehouses and barns of Pennsylvania, but he **Lee's second invasion of the North** hoped to counter the impending fall of Vicksburg by the capture of a Northern city and in so doing tip the balance toward peace in the war-weary North. With an army augmented to 80,000, Lee maneuvered toward the Potomac while Hooker, mustering at the moment scarcely any more, moved on a parallel line between Lee and Washington. His desire was to let Lee go far from his base, and he actually forecast that the armies would meet at Gettysburg. Whether he could have retrieved his fortunes will never be known, for he presently quarreled with Halleck and asked to be relieved. Both public and army had lost faith in him, though the Joint Committee refused to investigate the failure of its protégé.

The old McClellan element, which had been intriguing for the succession of General George Gordon Meade, won out. On 28 June Meade assumed command. He was a candid, unpretentious, intelligent, and colorless West Pointer of Pennsylvania extraction, austere, irritable (his men called him "the old snapping turtle"), and **George Gordon Meade (1815–72)** reasonably competent except for the usual occupational disease, the "slows." Meanwhile Lee's raiders had threatened Harrisburg and forced York to pay a ransom. Meade was now concentrating his troops to offer battle, and Lee (at Chambersburg) called in his outlying forces and advanced to meet him. Unfortunately for Lee, Stuart's cavalry was absent on a prolonged raid, and so he was partially blinded as to the movements of Meade.

Contact was made between Lee's advance under A. P. Hill and a Federal delaying force west of Gettysburg on 1 July. After an action that lasted most of the day the Federal commander, General Winfield Scott **Gettysburg: First Day, 1 July** Hancock, retreated through Gettysburg and entrenched south of the town along a line which he convinced Meade was eminently suitable for battle. The Federal troops, approximately 90,000 strong, now occupied about four miles of high ground shaped like a fishhook; the eye was at the extreme south at two conical, rocky hills: Round Top and Little Round Top; the shank was Cemetery Ridge; the bend was Cemetery Hill; and the barb was Culp's Hill. Even as it was, Meade's position was made possible only because Ewell had failed to carry out Lee's order to seize Cemetery Hill before the Federals could entrench. The Confederates, about 75,000 in number, occupied lower ground. Their line on the west followed Seminary Ridge, parallel to and

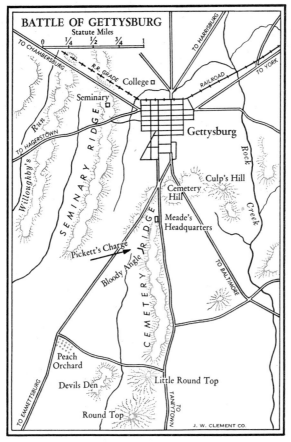

less than a mile across a shallow depression from Cemetery Ridge, swung east through the village on the flats, and then along the bed of a stream below Culp's Hill. The Confederate line was stretched to a dangerous thinness, while that of the Federals was relatively compact.

Strangely enough, Hancock had failed to occupy the Round Tops on the first day. Lee, who saw that cannon placed there, especially on the closer and more accessible Little Round Top, could rake the entire Federal line, ordered General James Longstreet to seize them. That stubborn Georgian had advised Lee to flank rather than fight, and he now took his own good time in obeying the order. By the time he was ready a Federal force had moved in. On the second day of the battle Longstreet vainly struggled for Little Round Top

Second Day, 2 July

against a Federal corps which through some error had been thrust out below the height in the area of the "Peach Orchard," the "Wheat Field," and the rocky outcropping called the "Devil's Den." Meanwhile at the northern end the Confederates under Ewell drove dangerously close to Culp's Hill and threatened to turn the Federal right. That night Meade called a council of war, and it was decided to hold the position for another day and receive the next attack, which was confidently expected in the center.

A Confederate attack on Culp's Hill at dawn failed, and the armies passed the forenoon uneventfully. At one o'clock the Confederate guns opened on the Union center, and eighty Union guns replied; the cannonade was probably the heaviest ever experienced until then on the American continent. At two-thirty the Federal fire ceased because ammunition was running low, and presently the Confederate fire slackened. Fifteen thousand Confederate infantry then stepped out along Seminary Ridge and began the charge across the valley. As they emerged from a protecting swale, the Federal guns opened, first with ball and then with canister, tearing great gaps in the advancing lines. Nevertheless the men in gray moved on until the Union infantry, which had been lying behind the guns, pushed forward and received them with volleys of rifle fire; then the two lines locked in mortal combat at the brow of Cemetery Ridge. Slowly the blue line was forced back behind its guns until a second wave of Union infantry came to the rescue. For twenty minutes the Confederates held their ground, then Hancock, badly wounded but still in action, threw fresh troops on their flank and forced them slowly and grudgingly back across the valley. This incredibly gallant action is usually known as Pickett's Charge, though Pickett's division, in the center, comprised only one third of the men charging. The farthest point attained by Pickett is still shown as "the high watermark of the Rebellion."

Third Day, 3 July

The losses at Gettysburg were 23,000 Union and 28,000 Confederate, of whom 3000 and 4000 respectively were killed. Freeman,* lamenting the loss of Jackson, recites a series of mistakes which doomed the Confederate effort, and part of which, at least, Jackson would never have made. Meade, presented with an opportunity which Grant or Sherman must have envied, failed to follow Pickett's repulse with a countercharge against the shattered enemy. On the 4th both armies lay quietly in position; during the night Lee began his retreat in the rain. Then the goddess of fortune, suddenly lavish to a Union commander, held Lee helpless north of the swollen Potomac, but the unappreciative Meade failed to improve the opportunity, though Lincoln begged him to get under way. There is some ground for supposing

Lee's retreat

* Douglas S. Freeman, *R. E. Lee* (1934–35), 3: 147–53.

that Meade was encouraged in his slothfulness by Stanton, who shared the Radical aversion to a decisive victory.

By the end of July the two armies were back on their old lines in Virginia—and the war in the East was stalemated again. Meade had his critics, of course, but the fact remained that less than a week after he assumed command he had given the Army of the Potomac **Confeder-** its first victory since Antietam and in so doing had stemmed, **acy passes** though not exactly reversed, the tide which had been running **to the** so heavily against the North. No less evident was the fact **defensive** that the Union soldier himself was now a match for his Confederate adversary. More important perhaps than the Northern victories at Gettysburg, Vicksburg, and Chattanooga was the fact that time and battle had sapped Confederate strength. In this respect Confederate victories were in the end almost as disastrous as defeats. Though many Confederates failed to recognize the fact at the time, the year 1863 saw the end of their offensive ability; thereafter only defense was possible, however superbly it might be handled.

4 *The Decisive Year*

Grant, a Conservative who had voted for Buchanan, had with Rawlins's aid seen which way the political wind was blowing. Naturally he wished to retain his command, and, moreover, he was not without ambitions, and so by early 1863 he had become an enthusiast for emancipa- **Grant in** tion and the enlistment of Negro troops. The Radicals ac- **supreme** cepted him gladly, for though his wife actually held a couple **command** of slaves, he was clearly the coming man and, moreover, was too big for them to break. In March 1864 Lincoln made the decision which was to bring the war to a close in one year. Grant was called to Washington, invested with the newly-revived rank of lieutenant general, and placed in supreme command of the Union armies.

The Radicals then handed him a list of Conservative generals who could be spared for the good of the country. To their dismay Grant balked, and such was his prestige that they could not reach him. He retained Meade in technical command of the Army of the Potomac instead of recalling the fair-haired "Fighting Joe" Hooker; Sherman was backed decisively, though he—unlike Senator John—was a Democrat and a foe of emancipation. When B. F. Butler got the Army of the James bottled up at Bermuda Hundred, Grant removed him from command as soon as the presidential election made it at all possible. Later Butler wormed his way into command of the amphibious expedition against Fort Fisher (December 1864) and proceeded to boggle it with his usual dramatic dexterity; Grant promptly lowered the boom on him and despite the anguished howls of his cronies sent him back to political life. Try as they might, the Radicals failed to touch Grant, and the country was treated to the spectacle of the bovine son of the Ohio tanner clamping his teeth doggedly on his cigar and plowing through obstacles that had stopped the wily and dexterous McClellan. Not the least element in Grant's immunity, of course, was the firm backing of Lincoln. The President had at last found the man who could win the war and did not propose to have him undermined.

When Grant took supreme command the Confederacy had received some hard blows, but the core of its strength in the crescent from Mississippi to Virginia was as yet unshattered. Grant in striking at Richmond, **The strat-** and Sherman in aiming at Atlanta, were not simply trying **egy of** to take key points. They intended to quarter across the **attrition** Confederacy in great cavalry and infantry raids which would burn the warehouses, lay waste the fields, and tear up the railroads so that there would be no more resources for war. They intended to blot out the opposing armies by the attrition of battle and starvation, even though two Union soldiers were lost to one Confederate. The industrial, agricultural, and man-power resources of the North were at last mobilized, and the leaders had been found; Scott's Anaconda was at last ready to constrict, whatever the ghastly cost. Specifically, the intention was for Grant to hold Lee before Richmond, Franz Sigel in the Shenandoah was to protect Washington, and B. F. Butler was to move up the James and threaten Richmond and its southern outwork, Petersburg. Sherman, in Georgia, was essentially operating in Lee's rear to cut off reinforcements and supplies. Farragut was to take Mobile, and E. R. S. Canby was to move northward to Sherman's support. Grant's hope was to end the war before the November election but, failing that, to provide victories which would ensure the election of the Union ticket and the prosecution of the war.

Grant moved on 3 May 1864 with 120,000 men across the Rapidan River into the Wilderness, where the leaf buds were just beginning to burst. Two days later Lee, with about 60,000 men, attacked him in the **The Wil-** jungle where Union artillery was of little help. After two **derness,** days of bloody infantry fighting in the thickets so confused **5–6 May** that it is useless to describe it, the armies appeared stalemated. On the night of the 7th Grant pulled back. The disheartened Army of the Potomac recognized the signs of the usual retreat after a battle. As the long lines reached Chancellorsville they came to a crossroads: the left turn led back to the North, the right deeper into the Wilderness and the Confederacy.

"Grant's military standing with the enlisted men," wrote one of the marching men in later days, "hung on the direction we turned. . . . At the Chancellorsville House we turned to the right. Instantly all of us

heard a sigh of relief. Our spirits rose. We marched free. The men began
to sing. The enlisted men understood the flanking movement. That night
we were happy."* The Confederates also perceived that the good old days
of Union thrust, Confederate parry, and Union retreat were over; here
was a new general who had the temerity to disregard a defeat and to insist upon trying again. Though he had not won a battle, he had driven
home to Lee the conviction that the Confederacy could no more assume
the offensive.

Grant had indeed shattered the military customs of Virginia as laid
down for Federal commanders. Instead of retreating, he moved by the
left flank to Spotsylvania. Warned by the dust, Lee was there first. Grant
hurled his corps against the "Bloody Angle," and while his   Spotsyl-
men were falling by the thousands he wrote Lincoln: "I   vania,
propose to fight it out on this line if it takes all summer."   8–21 May
The next dawn (12 May) Hancock's corps broke Ewell's center and
swarmed over the point of the "Angle." Lee rode forward on Traveler to
lead the countercharge. The retreating men turned and rallied. "General
Lee to the rear!" they cried. "We'll take it for you." A soldier took the
reins of the general's horse and led it back. Then on each face of the
breastworks the men of Hancock and Ewell fought the most desperate
action of the war, until in the evening the Confederates yielded "Bloody
Angle" and staggered back to a new line of trenches. While the battle of
Spotsylvania raged a new cavalry leader, Philip H. Sheridan, a dashing
young Irishman, rode toward Richmond to cut Lee's supplies. Jeb Stuart
by hard riding got between him and Richmond, then fell at Yellow
Tavern—a loss second only to that of Jackson, for now the right eye as
well as the right arm of Lee was gone.

By the 21st Grant had enough and sideslipped again, this time to the
North Anna River. Again Lee anticipated him, and Grant with only a
token attack moved again. On 28 May, Grant was on the Chickahominy
sixty-five miles from where he had started, on the exact   Cold
ground which McClellan had occupied two years before.   Harbor,
Anxious to carry the fortifications of Richmond before Lee   3 June
could occupy them properly and convinced that Confederate morale was
spent, Grant made a ghastly blunder in ordering a general assault at Cold
Harbor (3 June) against the well-entrenched Confederate line. Grant
seems to have been the only one who thought the operation feasible, but
the men silently pinned on their blouses scraps of paper bearing their
names and charged. It is said that in ten minutes 5000 men fell. Even
worse, Grant refused to ask for a truce to care for the wounded, and after
days of suffering they died where they lay.

* Frank Wilkeson, *Recollections of a Private Soldier* (1887), 80; this book is a good example of numerous published reminiscences and gives a graphic account of the terror and
confusion of battle. On the Southern reaction see George Cary Eggleston in *Battles and
Leaders of the Civil War,* 4: 230.

Actually the slaughter was less than in many other unsuccessful battles, but the North, with the taste of final victory in its mouth, was plunged into unfounded despair. Politicians and editors reacted savagely against "Butcher" Grant. And the cost of his campaign had been heavy, for he had lost 55,000 men, almost as many as had been in Lee's original army; the latter had probably lost over 30,000—but they were irreplaceable. Grant, usually so stolid and unimaginative, seems to have been so appalled by the apparently fruitless loss of life that for a while he again took to drink.

It was evident that the fortifications of Richmond were too strong to be carried by assault; so Grant sideslipped again in an attempt to enter by the back door. About twenty miles south of Richmond lay the tobacco-marketing city of Petersburg; the two cities were protected **Siege of** on the east by rivers, creeks, and swamps, and by im-**Petersburg** pregnable fortifications. Richmond and Petersburg were also the focus of several railroads that brought supplies from the west and south. Petersburg's fortifications had been almost abandoned during the spring in order to add its garrison to Lee's mobile army. Butler had been supposed to take advantage of this situation to move up the James from Fortress Monroe and slice the communications between the two cities, but he had failed miserably.

There was now a chance, however, that Grant could move his army over the James River and seize Petersburg before Lee could rush his mobile army into its vast fortifications. Lee was thoroughly deceived until the last moment and only got his men into the fortifications in time because Grant's subordinates dallied and in so doing ruined the whole plan. Grant did not recriminate, but in trying to storm the city threw away ten thousand men in vain. Though Grant's forces were double those of Lee, he could not yet afford to go around to the unprotected west, for such action would have cut him off from his Chesapeake supply line and given Lee the advantage. The only alternative was siege with all the paraphernalia of trenches, bomb-proof shelters, mines, mud, and rats—a siege which lasted nine months and which was varied by more or less unsuccessful flanking movements below Petersburg.

Lee's only hope was to create a diversion such as Jackson had made in the Shenandoah Valley during the Peninsular Campaign. Accordingly in July, Early with 17,000 men brushed aside the Federals in the Shenan-**Early in** doah Valley, crossed the Potomac, and descended upon **Maryland** Washington. Delayed at the Monocacy for a day by General **and the** Lew Wallace (later to become the author of *Ben Hur*), **Shen-** Early reached Washington in time to see reinforcements **andoah** from Grant's army file into the fortifications. Sheridan followed Early to the valley in September with 55,000 men and won two sharp battles at Winchester and Fisher's Hill. He then proceeded to devastate this granary of Virginia so thoroughly that, as he reported, "a crow flying over the country would need to carry his rations." When the South cried for vengeance Lee sent reinforcements he could ill afford, and Early fell on the Union army at Cedar Creek (19 October) and routed it. Sheridan, who had been at Winchester, arrived in time to rally his men and drive Early from the field. This was the end of the war in the Shenandoah Valley.

Meanwhile Sherman had sliced through the Confederate center in a smashing campaign in Georgia. Davis had reluctantly supplanted Bragg by Joseph E. Johnston, who as usual complained of shortages of troops and equipment and impossible and conflicting orders; how much Davis deliberately hampered him is a matter of interpretation. Sherman had about 100,000 men, comprising the Army of the Cumberland under Thomas; the Army of the Tennessee under James B. McPherson; and the Army of the Ohio under John M. Schofield. Sherman's tactics were much like those Grant was following in Virginia. Flanking by the left he took Dalton, Resaca, Kennesaw Mountain and by July was investing Atlanta. Johnston had been severely criticized for following the exact course which had won praise for Lee, and on 17 July Davis replaced him by John B. Hood, a gallant commander who had lost a leg at Chickamauga but had lost none of his will to fight. Sherman, greatly encouraged by the removal of his principal obstacle, repulsed Hood's impetuous attack and in six weeks of battle and maneuver took Atlanta (2 September).

Fall of Atlanta

Hood withdrew westward to threaten Sherman's base at Nashville, but Sherman refused to be drawn away. Thomas and Schofield with their armies were sent to Nashville to meet the threat. On 30 November Hood's ragged veterans were delayed by Schofield in a battle at Franklin, and in a two-days battle (15–16 December) just south of Nashville Thomas, with twice Hood's strength, destroyed the Confederate army as an effective field force. Alabama and Mississippi were now out of the war.

Battles of Franklin and Nashville

Sherman, with implicit confidence in Thomas, had already burned Atlanta and cut loose (15 November) with 60,000 men of the Army of the Tennessee. Advancing southeastward to Savannah in the famous "March through Georgia," Sherman's army cut a swath sixty miles wide, destroyed all bridges and railroads, drove off livestock, and denuded the area of food; it should be noted, however, that the screen of Confederates who were driven before him destroyed much matériel and forage to keep them out of Sherman's hands. His purpose was to split the Confederacy irrevocably in two, but his measures were unduly harsh and led to untold civilian misery and un-

Sherman in Georgia and the Carolinas

dying hatred of Sherman and the North. Nevertheless, the raid effectively
reduced the Confederacy to the Carolinas and the lower part of Virginia
and chilled Southern hearts with foreboding.

Savannah fell on 20 December, and there Sherman, now in contact
with the Union fleet, remained until February 1865. He then moved

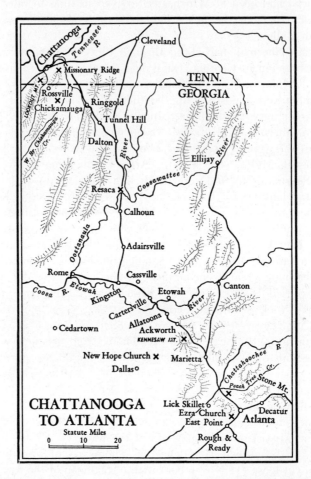

CHATTANOOGA
TO ATLANTA
Statute Miles
0   10   20

northward and wreaked vengeance on South Carolina, which was blamed
by the North for starting the war. The loosely controlled soldiers plundered as they went (though Sherman claimed that he knew of no case of
murder or rape) and in Columbia got out of hand and fired the city. Now
confronted by a hastily scraped-up army under Joseph E. Johnston (once
more recalled from disgrace), the Union army moved into North Carolina, fought a series of successful engagements, and then halted at Golds-
boro, one hundred sixty miles south of Richmond.

We must now turn back to the political scene. It was so vitally affected by the military fortunes of Grant and Sherman that it is fair to say that Lincoln would have failed in the political sphere had it not been for the support of their victories. The elections of 1863 had resulted in Republican gains, and of course Radicals and administration men alike claimed the credit. In his justly **Lincoln's Gettysburg Address** famous Gettysburg Address (19 November) at the dedication of the military cemetery at that place, Lincoln once more appealed to the country on a plane which the Radicals with their increasing economic bias were incapable of appreciating, whatever their lip service to popular government. The war, he reminded his audience, was testing whether a nation "conceived in liberty, and dedicated to the proposition that all men are created equal" could long endure. In closing he pledged himself to the task of seeing that the nation should "have a new birth of freedom; and that government of the people, by the people, for the people, shall not perish from the earth."

Lincoln may have had in mind not only the menace of the Southern armies but of the Radical program. When Congress met in December he laid before it his Ten-Per-Cent Plan of Reconstruction. Briefly, when ten per cent of the number of white citizens who had voted in **Lincoln's Ten-Per-Cent Plan** 1860 took the oath of allegiance, they might establish a civil government provided they recognized emancipation. The plan was put into effect in Louisiana under the guidance of General N. P. Banks, but the Radicals blocked this aspect of the "rose-water" policy and refused to admit Senators and Representatives until the state had approved Negro suffrage. Their purpose, of course, was to block the addition of reconstructed states to the Conservative column and to force them into the Republican Party by the aid of Negro votes. Here the matter hung, and Arkansas and Tennessee, reorganized on similar lines, were likewise refused admission.

Public support of the Ten-Per-Cent Plan was so enthusiastic that the Radicals became alarmed. In July 1864 they passed the Wade-Davis Bill, sponsored by Ben Wade and Henry Winter Davis. Among other things the bill raised the ten per cent to fifty, excluded all high "rebels" from Constitutional conventions, from legislative **Wade-Davis Bill** offices, and governorships, and demanded the prohibition of slavery and the repudiation of state war debts. Though this was less than the extreme demands of the Radicals, Lincoln killed it by a pocket veto. Davis was so enraged that he ran the risk of Republican defeat in the presidential election and issued a violent attack on Lincoln known as the Wade-Davis Manifesto.

By the autumn of 1863 the raffish Butler, the pompous Chase, and the headlong Frémont were all seeking the Republican presidential nomination for 1864. Chase had one unusual asset: his fascinating daughter,

Chase seeks the Republican nomination Kate,* who adored and ruled him and was so popular a hostess that she earned Mrs. Lincoln's cordial dislike. Chase was a poor man, but Kate remedied that by marrying William Sprague, Senator from Rhode Island, who though young and inept was possessed of multiple millions. The marriage was to end in one of the great scandals of American history. However, at this

New York Public Library

Millions of copies of Thomas Nast's "Compromise with the South" were circulated by the Republican National Committee in the presidential campaign of 1864 to drive home the "betrayal of the Republic." Note Jeff Davis's triumphant stance.

juncture the mating flight of the senatorial drone with the queen bee of capital society resulted in the financing of Chase's bid for the nomination.

Kate was not alone in her supreme confidence that she could make her father President, for she possessed unusual political talent in addition to her advantage as a woman and a reigning hostess. Then there was Jay Cooke, the "Financier of the Civil War." Chase had convinced himself that he had no *political* ambitions and that his appointments had no bearing on his political fortunes. Cooke saw to it that not only newspapers which received his advertising but the new national banks boomed the Chase candidacy, while his "minutemen" were zealous purveyors of the word. Presently there appeared the "Pomeroy Circular," which deplored

* Mary M. Phelps, *Kate Chase, Dominant Daughter* (1935).

Lincoln and puffed Chase. The latter swore to Lincoln that he knew nothing of its origin; perhaps he didn't—but Katy did!

The Radical chieftains would have preferred Chase or Frémont to Lincoln, except that it was Lincoln who gave evidence of being able to attract the votes. Lincoln believed in all humility that he was best fitted to meet the crisis, and that coolness, tolerance, and compromise were better lubricants than hatred and vengefulness. He therefore devoted himself shrewdly and successfully to ob- **Lincoln's success** taining the nomination. One by one state Republican organizations began to plump for him. Despite the desperate smiles of the incomparable Kate and the soft green rain of her bridegroom's dollars, the Chase boom collapsed in February. Soon afterward the national committee voted for Lincoln four to one, but the embittered Frémont hung on, and in June a convention of irreconcilables nominated him.

That same month the Union Party convention met in Baltimore and nominated Lincoln; Andrew Johnson, a War Democrat who was thoroughly acceptable to the Radicals, received the nomination for Vice-President. The Radicals did not bother to conceal their reluctance to accept Lincoln and sought diligently for some means of scuttling the Lincoln ship without drowning themselves. In fact, Chase's withdrawal had been a desperate measure based upon the hope that he could become the "compromise" candidate between Lincoln and Frémont, and it was supposed that the Chase cohorts had encouraged Frémont's intransigence with this in mind. Meanwhile in September Chase had quarreled with Seward, fallen into a pout, and submitted his resignation—which, to his chagrin, Lincoln accepted.

The regular Democratic convention now met in August in Chicago and adopted a platform, written by Vallandigham, which declared the war a failure and demanded its end and the restoration of peace "on the basis of the Federal Union of the States." While this ostensibly **Democrats** would have brought peace only on the condition of reunion, **nominate** it was clearly unrealistic to expect such quixotic action from **McClellan** a Confederacy which had been baptized in blood and had been powerful enough to force an armistice. McClellan received the nomination, but, embarrassed by the "peace plank" in the platform, he insisted that (though he opposed Lincoln's usurpations and denied the Radicals' fitness to rule) he favored continuation of the war. In this declaration he was supported by most party leaders. So confident was the country of Democratic victory that Lincoln laid his plans to help McClellan finish the war before the latter's inauguration would bind him to the "peace plank."

As 1864 advanced, opposition to the war (especially of the Copperhead variety) diminished. Sherman's capture of Atlanta and Sheridan's victories in the Shenandoah Valley balanced public heartsickness at the

Election of 1864

cost of Grant's victories. Vallandigham's peace plank aroused the resentment of the soldiers, who by special arrangement were casting their ballots at the front. The Radicals were sobered by the prospect that McClellan, their bête noire, might sweep into power; even Lincoln was preferable. Late in September Montgomery Blair left the Cabinet as a sacrifice to save Radical faces, and the Radicals abandoned their plans to scuttle the ship. This dropping of the Blair pilot was a clear gesture of peace to Henry Winter Davis of Maryland and John C. Frémont of Missouri. At the same time Frémont withdrew, though it is arguable whether this move was in exchange for Blair's retirement or was intended to boost McClellan. Another sop was thrown to the Radicals when upon Taney's death Lincoln made Chase the Chief Justice of the Supreme Court; nevertheless, Kate immediately began to lay wires for 1868. At any rate Lincoln won 212 to 21, with McClellan carrying only Delaware, Kentucky, and New Jersey. Out of 4,150,-000 popular votes Lincoln received a majority of 500,000. Nevada, admitted to the Union on 31 October, just got in under the wire in time to participate in the election. Congress once more went to the Republicans, this time by a majority likely to be comfortable enough if no Southern Democrats appeared. Actually there was little distinction between Lincoln and McClellan; both stood for a firm prosecution of the war and the imposition of easy peace terms.

With the fall of Wilmington in January 1865 and the closing of Richmond's last window upon the world, it was evident to unprejudiced observers that the Confederacy was doomed. A number of abortive attempts

Hampton Roads Conference

had been made to discuss peace, but Davis had stood firmly on the demand for independence while Lincoln as firmly insisted on reunion. A conference (3 February 1865) aboard an army transport at Hampton Roads, in which Lincoln, Seward, and Alexander Stephens participated, was probably motivated by Davis's desire to obtain an armistice during which Confederate strength could be recruited. Lincoln is said to have told Stephens to write the word "Union" at the top of a sheet of paper and write below it whatever he pleased. But reunion on any terms was unsatisfactory to Davis.

Lincoln's answer was to put in motion the final military measures of the war. The South's equipment had deteriorated, its two important remaining armies were reduced by desertion, and its soldiers were suffering from nakedness, starvation, and diseases of malnutrition. Transportation was disrupted, blockade runners were being picked off rapidly, and all important ports but Charleston were in Federal hands. Grant and Sherman with two large and magnificently equipped armies of veterans at their command were in a position to end the war quickly.

Lee was the first to fall. With his ranks thinned to thirty thousand starving men, he could not for long prevent Grant from breaking through to Richmond and Petersburg. On 1 April Sheridan moved out southwest of Petersburg, defeated the Confederates at Five Forks, and threatened their last railroad communications with the West. Petersburg promptly fell to an assault, and Lee evacuated Richmond and moved west in the hope of reaching a railroad by which he might join Johnston. Grant's well-fed **Lee's surrender at Appomattox, 9 April 1865** soldiers hung on his rear, and presently Sheridan's cavalry got ahead of him and blocked the retreat. When Lee prepared to attack, Sheridan's troopers moved aside and revealed a solid mass of blue infantry. That day, 9 April, Grant and Lee met in the McLean farmhouse at Appomattox Court House and arranged the terms of surrender. The Confederate soldiers were paroled; and though other public property and war matériel were to be surrendered, the officers were to retain their side arms, and all men who claimed to own a horse or mule were permitted to keep them "to work their little farms." Grant and his staff stood with bared heads while Lee rode down the lines taking leave of his men, and the victor, hearing the guns saluting the surrender, ordered them to cease firing.

The rest of the tale is soon told. Johnston's surrender to Sherman followed on 26 April, that of Richard Taylor in Mississippi and Alabama on 4 May, and that of Kirby-Smith in the Trans-Mississippi Department on 26 May. For weeks the red clay roads of the South were thronged by ragged, starving Confederate veterans returning home, gallant flotsam of the Lost Cause. Avery Craven tells the story that at Appomattox as one of Lee's veterans threw his rifle on the pile of surrendered weapons he turned and observed bitterly to a comrade, "Damn me if I ever love another country."

Davis had left Richmond late on the 3rd with a few government officials and the pitiful remains of the Confederate treasury. The next day, while Union troops were entering the city, some warehouses which had been fired by departing Confederates spread the flames and reduced the business district to ruins. Lincoln, who had been staying at Grant's headquarters at City Point, visited Rich- **Fate of Jefferson Davis** mond on the 4th and 5th and consulted with various citizens on his plans for Virginia. Meanwhile Davis, pausing here and there on his southward flight, still held the delusion that the Confederacy could be saved. The surrender of Lee and the impending surrender of Johnston destroyed his last hope, and he planned to reach Florida and find a means of leaving the country. Lincoln had been anxious to let him escape, but on 10 May some overzealous troopers arrested him in Georgia. He was imprisoned in Fortress Monroe (briefly in shackles) for two years, and then, broken in health, he was released. He was never brought to trial. The rest of his life he spent in retirement.

There is every indication that Lincoln had girded himself to force a policy of easy reconstruction upon the Radicals. His Second Inaugural ended on an affecting note of patience, tolerance, and hope:

Lincoln favors conciliation
With malice toward none; with charity for all; with firmness in the right, as God gives us to see the right, let us strive to finish the work we are in; to bind up the nation's wounds; to . . . do all which may achieve a just and lasting peace, among ourselves, and with all nations.

His last public address (11 April) was made to a serenading crowd which thronged the White House grounds while the Capital City uproariously celebrated the victory. He made a vigorous defense of his Ten-Per-Cent Plan, acknowledged that flexibility was desirable in meeting the needs of the various states, and hinted that he would soon make an announcement to the Southern states. On the next day he consulted with his Cabinet on reconstruction plans quite similar to those later announced by President Johnson. Whether his prestige, tact, and political shrewdness would have been sufficient to counteract the more bloodthirsty wing of the Radicals and the vengeful part of the public can never be known.

On the evening of 14 April the Lincolns attended a performance of *Our American Cousin* at Ford's Theatre. The fascinating and able young actor John Wilkes Booth, scion of the famous family of actors, had **Assassination of Lincoln** formed a conspiracy with other Southern sympathizers to assassinate Lincoln and perhaps also several other high officials; of the latter only Seward and his son were reached, but they suffered horrible dagger wounds. Booth himself undertook to kill Lincoln. During the performance of the play he entered the theater, where he was well known and had starred only a few weeks before, and, entering Lincoln's box, shot him through the head. Crying: *"Sic semper tyrannis! The South is avenged!"* Booth sprang down to the stage, but his spur caught in a flag, and his left leg was broken. Nevertheless, he got out of the theater, mounted his horse, and got away.* The dying Lincoln was carried across Tenth Street to a private home, and his tall frame was laid across a bed that was too short for him. There, at seven-thirty of a cold and rainy morning, he died.

Before the White House that day, shivering with grief and cold, stood hundreds of Negroes bewailing their loss. It was not theirs to know the inner story of emancipation and its connection with affairs of state. All **Emancipator and savior of the Union** they knew was that their liberator, their divinely chosen Moses was dead. But to the people of the North Lincoln was more than an emancipator. He was soon to concentrate in his own person the aura of the heroic struggle and become

* On the assassination and the trial of the conspirators see Philip V. D. Stern, *The Man Who Killed Lincoln* (1939).

the savior of the Union, the captain who had brought the ship of state
safely through four years of storm. Walt Whitman was forgiven much by
his generation because he penned the lines most expressive of this theme:

> O Captain! my Captain! our fearful trip is done,
> The ship has weather'd every rack, the prize we sought is won,
> The port is near, the bells I hear, the people all exulting,
> While follow eyes the steady keel, the vessel grim and daring;
>
>> But O heart! heart! heart!
>> O the bleeding drops of red,
>>> Where on the deck my Captain lies,
>>> Fallen cold and dead.
>
> O Captain! my Captain! rise up and hear the bells;
> Rise up—for you the flag is flung—for you the bugle trills,
> For you bouquets and ribbon'd wreaths—for you the shores a-crowding,
> For you they call, the swaying mass, their eager faces turning;
>
>> Here Captain! dear father!
>> The arm beneath your head!
>>> It is some dream that on the deck,
>>> You've fallen cold and dead.
>
> My Captain does not answer, his lips are pale and still,
> My father does not feel my arm, he has no pulse nor will,
> The ship is anchor'd safe and sound, its voyage closed and done,
> From fearful trip the victor ship comes in with object won;
>
>> Exult O shores, and ring O bells!
>> But I with mournful tread,
>>> Walk the deck my Captain lies,
>>> Fallen cold and dead.

BIBLIOGRAPHICAL NOTE

The Strategy of the Civil War

MILITARY HISTORY: This has been a favorite subject with hundreds of writers,
and only a few can be mentioned here. Most satisfactory brief account is
probably Fletcher Pratt's impressionistic *Ordeal by Fire* (1935). *Battles and
Leaders of the Civil War* (4 v., 1887) has long been a standard compilation
of accounts by eyewitnesses; similar to it is the one-volume *American Iliad*
(1947) compiled by Otto Eisenschiml and Ralph Newman; and *The Blue and
the Gray* (2 v., 1950) compiled by Henry S. Commager. Bell I. Wiley, *The
Life of Johnny Reb* (1943) is an excellent résumé of life in the Confederate
army. Best technical narrative and analysis is probably John C. Ropes and
W. R. Livermore, *Campaigns of the Civil War* (4 v., 1898–1913). Now in
process of publication is Kenneth P. Williams, *Lincoln Finds a General: A*

Military Study of the Civil War (v. 1–2, 1949). Every reader should know at least by reputation the vast *War of the Rebellion: A Compilation of the Official Records of the Union and Confederate Armies* (130 v., 1880–1901) and *Official Records of the Union and Confederate Navies in the War of the Rebellion* (30 v., 1894–1922). Of interest is Mathew B. Brady's collection of photographs published in many editions; see also William Wood and Ralph H. Gabriel, *In Defense of Liberty* (1928, v. 7 of *Pageant of America*).

NAVAL HISTORY: On the Union side see James R. Soley, *The Navy in the Civil War* (1887). On the Confederate, J. T. Scharf, *History of the Confederate States Navy* (1887); William M. Robinson, *The Confederate Privateers* (1928); Jim Dan Hill, *Sea Dogs of the Sixties* (1935); F. B. C. Bradlee, *Blockade Running During the Civil War* (1925).

Triumph in the West

GRANT: There is no definitive biography of Grant. His youth is well portrayed in Lloyd Lewis, *Captain Sam Grant* (1950); and his entire career in William E. Woodward, *Meet General Grant* (1928). On his military career see J. F. C. Fuller, *The Generalship of Ulysses S. Grant* (1929). His own *Memoirs* (2 v., 1885–86) sold 312,000 copies, an enormous number for that day.

UNION GENERALS IN THE WEST: See Gamaliel Bradford, *Union Portraits* (1916); for Thomas see the biographies by Freeman Cleaves and Richard O'Connor; for Sherman see his own *Memoirs* (1875), Lloyd Lewis, *Sherman: Fighting Prophet* (1932), and B. H. Liddell Hart, *Sherman—Soldier, Realist, American* (1929). For the river war see the readable account by Harpur A. Gosnell, *Guns on the Western Waters* (1949).

CONFEDERATE GENERALS IN THE WEST: See Gamaliel Bradford, *Confederate Portraits* (1914); Don C. Seitz, *Braxton Bragg* (1924); Andrew N. Lytle, *Bedford Forrest and His Critter Company* (1931). For Joseph E. Johnston see his *Narrative of Military Operations* (1874); for Davis's rebuttal see his *Rise and Fall of the Confederate Government* (1881).

Stalemate in the East

THE PENINSULA: *McClellan's Own Story* (1887) is amorphous and embarrassingly defensive. Much better is William S. Myers, *A Study in Personality: General George Brinton McClellan* (1934), but see the general works cited above for Section 1 of this chapter. Best account of the battle of the ironclads is James P. Baxter, *The Introduction of the Ironclad Warship* (1933).

LEE: Definitive biography is Douglas S. Freeman, *R. E. Lee* (4 v., 1934–35). More manageable is Frederick B. Maurice, *Robert E. Lee the Soldier* (1925). An unforgettable "psychographic" portrait is Gamaliel Bradford, *Lee the American* (1912). See also J. F. C. Fuller, *Grant and Lee* (1933).

LEE'S LIEUTENANTS: See Freeman's *Lee's Lieutenants* (3 v., 1942–44). For a professional analysis of Jackson's brief career see the fascinating but rather romantic biography by the Englishman George F. R. Henderson, *Stonewall Jackson and the American Civil War* (2 v., 1919). On others see John W. Thomason, *Jeb Stuart* (1930); and H. J. Eckenrode and Bryan Conrad, *James Longstreet: Lee's War Horse* (1935).

Chapter XXVIII

THE TRAGEDY OF RECONSTRUCTION

1 *Presidential Reconstruction*

WHEN Lincoln breathed his last in the humble home on Tenth Street, Stanton, who had joined the death vigil, turned to the windows and, with the words "He now belongs to the ages," darkened them to the rain-clouded rays of the ascending sun. Perhaps there was something symbolic in the action, for Booth by his witless action had cut off the hope of the South and surrendered it to the vengeance of the Radicals.

Lincoln's death a godsend to Radicals

They cared not a rap for Lincoln, but they saw a priceless opportunity to make capital out of his death. Abolition ministers intoning that God had taken him because his work was done failed to hide the note of exultation in their words. A funeral train bore the body of the martyred President from city to city for two weeks, while the Radical press stirred the nation to vows of vengeance. Millions turned out to see the funeral train pass, while at stops the cortege was met by parades, floats, triumphal arches of mourning, and by the slow toll of bells and the boom of cannon. Whatever the Radicals may have been doing, the people mourned with Walt Whitman the passing of "the sweetest, wisest soul of all my days and lands."

Stanton, however sincerely he may have regretted the passing of Lincoln, had not lost his duplicity and quickly made common cause with the smugly rejoicing Radicals. He overrode Sherman's liberal terms to Johnston (which had been prompted by Lincoln); and soon after the funeral cortege reached Springfield, Jefferson Davis was captured and loaded with chains. Booth was overtaken and shot (or shot himself) in a Virginia barn, but his confederates were rooted out and after a disgraceful trial by military tribunal four of them were hanged.

891

And yet it is a notable fact that for almost two years the Vindictives failed to visit the full weight of their vengeance on the South. This was due chiefly to their amazing strategic error in not having assessed Andrew Johnson correctly. Though he was a War Democrat, the Re-

Their hope in Johnson

publican Vindictives had jumped at the chance to add him to the ticket in 1864, and now they rejoiced at his ascendance to the presidency. At a conference held soon afterward, Wade read his own hopes into Johnson's comments and expressed the Radical state of mind when he exclaimed; "Johnson, we have faith in you. By the gods, there will be no trouble now in running the government." Johnson gave every evidence of intending to punish "treason," but the Radicals soon found to their dismay that he had his own interpretation of what the punishment should be. Moreover, the situation had changed; at the time of the interview the Union was still in peril both from Confederate armies in the field and from the dreadful possibility of protracted guerrilla warfare.

In reconstructing the South, Johnson was ready to restore to political rights all repentant Confederates, and these men, along with those who had not participated in the "rebellion," were the "loyal" Southerners upon

Johnson's actual opinions

whom he depended to occupy responsible state positions. Indeed, he was anxious to avoid permanent maladjustments by leaving the local details of reconstruction to them. Johnson believed that the aristocracy was responsible for secession. True to the principles which he had imbibed as a hoplite in the ranks during the Jacksonian era, he stood for state rights, free trade, and agrarianism. His fellow-feeling with the West followed naturally upon his east Tennessee antecedents, and he was even more truly than Morrill the father of the Homestead Act. The Radicals' developing program of economic and Federal centralization was to this Southern Democrat only less abhorrent than their program of Negro rule in the South. On the latter point he shared the Southern plebeian's antipathy for the Negro. He was determined to preserve white supremacy even at the cost of turning the South back to the hated aristocrats.

Johnson was peculiarly unfitted for the task of combating the Radical program. As a Southerner and a Democrat placed by circumstances at the head of a Northern sectional party with whose program he was inevitably at odds, he was faced with a situation which brought some

Johnson's handicaps

of his personal traits into an unfavorable light. He was a man of will, not only reserved and noncommittal but stubborn and unable to compromise. He had no close friends whom he could trust, and his perplexities were increased by the distrust among his Cabinet members: Stanton (and probably others) was in constant communication with the Radicals. Johnson himself had been brought up in the rough school of Jacksonian politics, and as a result his speeches were often extemporaneous stump harangues in which he met hecklers on a common ground that destroyed presidential dignity. The reiterated Radical assertion that he was a drunkard was based solely on an incident at his inauguration as Vice-President, when, weak from a siege of typhoid fever, he drank a little too much whisky in the hope of strengthening himself for the ordeal. His wife was an invalid, but his family life was happy except that one son was a rounder and frequently shamed his father.

The fundamental problem in reconstruction lay in the decision as to what relationship the conquered states bore to the Union. Lincoln's view, in which the North concurred until halfway through the war, was that secession was illegal and impossible. Therefore the Southern **Theories on** states had not left the Union but were incapable of normal **the status** action because their officials were in rebellion. All that was **of the** necessary to restore them to normal action was for the Presi- **Southern** dent to pardon the insurgents and for Congress to accept **states** their representatives. The South, with secession a dead issue, was ready to accept Lincoln's interpretation, whatever mental reservations it may have had about having been on a journey.

During the war the Radicals had come to see that they would be snowed under if the South were quietly restored, and so they sought means of undermining this view. Sumner asserted that the Southern states had committed suicide and were now territories; Stevens held that they were conquered provinces. In either case the South would be at the mercy of Congress. The Radicals therefore pitched upon the Forfeited Rights Theory. The Southern states were moribund, neither destroyed nor out of the Union, but deprived of some of their normal rights. Congress could decide the terms of restoration—and meanwhile accept with a straight face the Southern approval of the Thirteenth Amendment!

The Radicals had laid the groundwork for Congressional reconstruction by refusing to accept Pierpoint's rump government as truly representing the state of Virginia, but only after it had fulfilled its mission of consenting to the secession of West Virginia. Radicals re- **Radical** ceived political support from diverse elements. There were, **hates** of course, those humorless souls who looked upon secession **and fears** as a clear case of treason which should be atoned for by blood and ruin, and who insisted that the South in taking the oath of loyalty had "blistered its lips with a lie." There were those who wished to pay for the war by confiscations of Southern property. There were those who had lost relatives or property and wanted revenge. There were the old abolitionists who wished to protect Negro rights by essentially turning the South over to them; any injustice thus done to Southern whites was but visited upon them for the "sin" of slavery.

Even sensible and moderate Northerners sometimes saw red at the prospect of having Jeff Davis and Aleck Stephens and John Slidell back in Congress coolly taking up where they had left off, sneering at the Northern vulgarians, subtly dividing and dominating their opponents, and renewing by political means the struggle for Southern Rights which they had lost on the battle field. The prospect was not solely a bugaboo. Democrats and Copperheads were willing Southern allies, and the representation of Southern whites would be expanded, for of course they expected to elect the additional Congressmen who would be apportioned to them as the result of emancipation's repeal of the Three-fifths Compromise. What might happen was anybody's guess. With slavery out of the way, it might even be possible for the South to seize the Federal government and place the shoe of secession on the other foot. It might scrap the tariff, repudiate the public debt, and drive industry to such desperation that the next time it would be the North which would secede—and who could say but what the wily Jeff Davis was plotting this in his cell?

Probably the most important backers of the Radicals were the new industrial capitalists, though they seldom cared to be open about it. Most of them lived and worked in the Northeast, but their power in the North-

Industrial capitalism

west was clearly growing. In them were reborn not only Hamilton and Clay but the extreme individualism of Jefferson. It is not at all likely that capitalists deliberately planned the Civil War, but once it was under way they saw how it could be utilized for their benefit, and now that it was over they plotted to seize control of the nation. The prospective spoils were enormous: a mile-high protective tariff wall; cheap raw materials from mineral and timber lands bought at rock-bottom prices; vast profits from public lands given as subsidies for railroad construction; and, not least of all, the endless opportunities opened in financing the greatly expanded activities of government and in financing (or merely manipulating) the growing industrial machine. A war which had been fought primarily to "preserve" the Union and secondarily for the abolition of slavery was now utilized in victory to reconstruct the Union on an entirely new legal and economic base.

The purpose was to break down the power of the states, to centralize national power in the Federal government, and to place the latter—all three branches—permanently in the control of the Republican Party.

The Radical revolution

From 1867 to 1933 the goal was almost, but never quite completely attained; the states did shrink in relative importance, the Supreme Court did become an adjunct of the Republican Party, and for only sixteen years was the executive in control of the Democratic Party. Nevertheless, American democracy was too deeply ingrained to permit conservatism ever to rule unchallenged. In the long run it was able to force industry (with the aid of many industrialists as well) to contribute to the emerging pattern of national welfare.

The backers of the new program were willing to leave the actual strategy to the Radical politicians, not all of whom were themselves capitalists. These politicians had no intention of reconstructing in the sense, as Randall puts it, of "repairing the damage of war, returning to normal acting and sane thinking, undoing war-time blunders, rebuilding the nation." Northern grief and **Radical problems** outrage at Lincoln's assassination had been fed by Radical editors and politicians, but they were perfectly aware that only a minority of the public wanted extreme vengeance either for the war or for the assassination. Democrats and Conservative Republicans clearly outnumbered the Radicals, and the latter found it necessary to enter upon a long campaign of propaganda and political chicanery in order to gain undisputed control in the Congressional elections of 1866. Of course they could and did buy up and suborn elections, kick dissident Democrats out of Congress, and pressure Conservative Republicans. But more than this was necessary.

Their political strategy hinged upon the vital point of preventing the restoration of the ante-bellum alliance between Southern and Western Democrats; in other words, to hamstring agrarianism, whether of Taylor or of Jackson. Southern whites, it was apparent, would not **Radical** vote Republican; so they must be ousted from political **strategy** control of their states and the power turned over to the **and tactics** Negroes who would vote Republican, or rather to those complaisant whites who would herd the Negroes to the polls and would manipulate the state machines in favor of the Republicans. The Conservatives and Democrats of West and of East were rather a different problem, but they were vulnerable. Republican tacticians concentrated there on identifying loyalty to the Union with Republicanism, and Democracy with Copperheadism and Southernism. With the "notable ferocity of noncombatants" they "waved the bloody shirt," exhorted veterans to "vote as they shot," and summoned to their support the nostalgia of the people for the heroic days of the great crusade. In the end they were so successful that for a generation there was in North and West a perceptible stigma attached to the Democratic Party and its members.

Nevertheless, in 1865 superficial events gave promise that reconstruction of the conquered states would be relatively painless. Confederate military men went back to the arts of peace. Lee retired to the presidency of Washington College and devoted himself to setting an example of civil obedience and sectional reconciliation. **Southern attitudes** Some Confederate soldiers and civilians emigrated, chiefly to the West or to Mexico or Brazil, but the vast majority resolved to work out their problems in their old homes; this included most of the high civil officials, who after short arrests were allowed to return home.

Indeed, there were some indications in the South of a sense of relief at the return to the Union. Southerners laid aside the weapons of secession and military force and prepared to renew the ante-bellum political struggle. Their expectation that the South would resume its place in the Union as though nothing had happened was galling to the Radicals, who demanded slavish adherence to the new program of political concentration and industrial dominance. Those Southern irreconcilables who were sullen and resentful, and who sometimes boasted to hide the bitter taste of defeat, furnished the Radicals with ammunition. Even Southern moderates, who tried to save what they could by political quibbles, were no help to Johnson in his attempts to help them. A perpetual source of irritation was the continued military occupation of the South. The fact that most white men had sought their discharge at the close of the war and large numbers of Negroes had not was eagerly seized by the Radicals as a chance to station Negro soldiers among their former masters. In the eyes of Southerners such tactics only added insult to injury.

Lincoln's Emancipation Proclamation had supposedly freed all slaves within the Confederacy but left those outside untouched. During the remainder of the war Congress and the loyal states acted piecemeal, until **The Thirteenth Amendment** in 1865 slavery existed only in Delaware and Kentucky. Slavery was a matter of state jurisdiction, and there were objections to using the amending power to wipe out the remaining traces of slavery, and it was therefore not until January 1865 that Congress sent the Thirteenth Amendment on to the state legislatures. There were at this time presumed to be thirty-six states in the Union, with the consent of twenty-seven necessary to amend. Delaware and Kentucky refused to approve, four free states delayed, and eleven states were being reconstructed under a presidential mandate not approved by Congress. Nevertheless, eight of the reconstructed states approved the Thirteenth Amendment in time to enable Seward to proclaim its adoption in December 1865.

Johnson's ideas of reconstruction differed little from Lincoln's Ten-Per-Cent Plan, and he accepted Tennessee, Louisiana, Arkansas, and Virginia as fully restored to the Union. In each of the seven remaining **Johnsonian reconstruction** Confederate states Johnson appointed a local man as provisional governor with instructions to hold an election for a constitutional convention. The only orders laid on the constitutional conventions were that they must invalidate their ordinances of secession, abolish slavery, and repudiate their war debts. He advised that the best-qualified Negroes be given the vote in order to spike the guns of the Radicals; unfortunately no state took the advice. As the elections proceeded, it became evident that the states intended to lay no disqualifications on high Confederate officials, but on the contrary were electing them to state offices and to Congress. Nevertheless, by December every state but Texas and Florida had reorganized and had adopted the Thirteenth Amendment, and its Senators and Representatives had appeared before Congress for admission.

The South had been bled white by the war and was as yet in no mood for vigorous action of any kind. Homes, warehouses, and bridges had been destroyed or had decayed because there were no means to repair them, many farms had returned to wilderness, livestock was de- **Material** pleted, the labor supply was uprooted, and railroads were in **ruin of** ruin save where the Union armies had repaired them for **the South** military purposes. Steamboats were burned or sunk, wharves rotted away, and river channels choked. Highways, never adequate, had sunk once more into the mud. Broad strips of country, as in the Shenandoah Valley, Georgia, and South Carolina had been deliberately and fiendishly devastated. Rows of blackened chimneys marked the sites of a number of once-flourishing towns and cities.

Factories were destroyed, banks and insurance companies gone, specie was unobtainable, and currency was only useful to kindle fires. Farms were being knocked down for taxes at one twentieth of their value, public facilities were paralyzed, and swindlers and speculators were in their glory. War had wiped out billions of capital investment in slaves and physical plant, and there was no certain way of restoring them. Even the cotton market, once the proud monopoly of the South, was now being encroached upon by Egypt and India, and the trade of the Northwest was setting more strongly than ever toward the Atlantic coastal cities and away from the South. Even those Southerners with the energy to farm were hard-set to obtain tools and seed. In more than one part of the South mass starvation was avoided only by the distribution by the Union army of millions of rations.

The physical destruction beggars description, but the moral and psychological destruction was even more heartrending. The South was a land of broken and uprooted men and women, perhaps spoiled for peace by the long excitement of war, perhaps too disheartened to **Human** face their tasks. Law enforcement, never perfect, suffered **ruin** from the general deterioration, and thievery and outright banditry flourished in many areas. Schools and churches barely remained open. Untold thousands of men were physically handicapped and despondent, while untold thousands of widows and orphans struggled despairingly for the bare essentials of life. Society was upended and redistributed, and not alone by the passing of slavery. Confederate generals labored with section gangs or lived in their Negro huts and followed a plow drawn by a flea-bitten mule, while overseers took over plantations with their proudly pillared mansions. Among the yeomen and the poor whites there was a political restiveness which forebode change, either an alliance with the Black Republicans or a resurgence of Jacksonian democracy.

What of the Negro, for whose emancipation the war had in part been fought? To him freedom meant simply that he could go where he pleased while "Massa Linkum's sojers" would provide his living. The long lines of
Negro camp followers runaway slaves in the wake of marching Union armies were perpetual nuisances, and their near-by camps were often centers of thievery, debauchery, and disease. Union commanders never solved the problem completely, and in the end many Negroes settled in shack towns near cities or drifted back to their old homes. The end of the war, however, brought out to the highways additional thousands of slaves who were now for the first time able to taste the sweets of freedom. They thronged into occupied seaports and to army camps, changing their names to indicate their new status; joining in orgies of religious enthusiasm out of which came the various Negro church organizations; flocking into makeshift schools in their eagerness to obtain learning—even Latin and Greek; living on government rations and by theft—"spilin' the 'Gyptians"; and falling prey to unscrupulous adventurers both white and colored who purchased their stolen goods, sold them whisky and snake oil, and performed bogus marriages and granted bogus divorces. Most pathetic of all was the way in which they suffered from plague; it is claimed that in 1865 alone more Negroes died in these teeming camps than men killed in battle in the Confederate army during the entire war.

Congress had tried to meet the situation by setting up the Freedmen's Bureau in March 1865, financing it by a thumping big tax on cotton. Under the superintendence of General Oliver O. Howard, the "Christian general," the bureau was authorized to dispense relief to both
Freedmen's Bureau races and to act as guardian of the freedmen. It established schools and hospitals for Negroes, took jurisdiction of legal cases involving them, and parceled out abandoned or confiscated lands to them. The Freedmen's Bureau labored hard to do its duty, though it was handicapped by scoundrels among its agents and idealistic do-gooders with more charity than discrimination. Presently, however, as the Radicals increased in power, the Freedmen's Bureau became a flagrant weapon of the Republican machine, devoted to pressuring and bribing the Negroes and to using its legal powers to mulct the whites.

Never before had so great a mass of slaves been suddenly projected not only into freedom but also into full political rights. After generations of dependence, it is no wonder that the Negroes were utterly unprepared
The Negro and the land for freedom. They were actually incapable of grasping the legal concept of freedom and quite misunderstood its duties and responsibilities. Nevertheless, the freedmen realized

that two of the first things needful were the ability to read and write and the ownership of land.

The original intention of Congress was to confiscate the land of Confederates and turn it over to the freedmen, but this project was blocked by Johnson. Unfortunately Stevens and Sumner made statements which started the rumor in the South that the government intended by the end of 1865 to give every Negro family "forty acres and a mule" as a Christmas present. Of course this was out of all reason. Since most of the Negroes refused to work in gangs even for wages, because it was too much like slavery days, a system was presently developed of renting to each family a few acres in return for a share of the crop; but more of this "sharecropping" system later on. The undramatic truth would seem to be that the freedman's greatest aid to adjustment to freedom was his old master. Men bred to a sense of responsibility through the generations now quietly added the burden of the freedmen to their own.

Southern whites, now that the long-threatened day of Negro emancipation had arrived, sought to forfend social chaos by subjecting the freedmen to strict regulation. There is no indication that the legislators intended to use the so-called Black Codes as a means either of revenge or of exploitation. Though the details of the **The Black Codes** codes varied so greatly from state to state as to make generalization difficult, it would seem that, as the whites saw it, the principal problem was to get the Negroes to work. Vagrants (idlers as well as Negroes caught outside their own neighborhoods) were bound over to labor, a system which led to widespread peonage. Breach of contract by Negroes as well as misdemeanors were punished more harshly than similar actions by whites. Though they were not given the vote, the freedmen were granted most of the essential civil rights, such as the right to make contracts, to go to court, and to own property. They could not, however, serve on juries, testify against whites, carry arms, nor engage in all occupations.

Johnson had taken a long chance in proceeding with his own plan of reconstruction without calling Congress for consultation and, indeed, had acted over the anguished protests of the Vindictives. His hope was that by confronting Congress and the country with the accomplished fact he could rally moderate sentiment to his support. His **Johnson's hopes** intention was to make the Union Party, which had elected him, the arcanum of the center, from which the extremists of both North and South could be excluded. His course did win approval in the South, though perhaps no gratitude, for the Southerners felt that they were receiving no more than their rights. It is tragic that Johnson failed, for however galling Southern self-assurance may have been to the victorious North, it would better have been passed over than viciously punished.

Whether Lincoln could have succeeded where Johnson failed will always be an interesting question to which no conclusive answer can be made.

When Congress met in December 1865 the Radicals were seething with rage, and they proceeded at once to seize the initiative by a series of bold strokes. A Joint Committee on Reconstruction was set up with a membership of nine Representatives and six Senators under the chairmanship of the once-moderate Fessenden and the real control of Stevens. The latter was more embittered than ever by the burning of his Chambersburg iron foundry by Confederate raiders in 1864.

Joint Committee on Reconstruction

The recent Confederate states were excluded from representation in Congress on the ground that they were not legally reconstructed, though their support of the Thirteenth Amendment was accepted as legal. By an act passed over Johnson's veto, a Civil Rights Bill made the freedmen citizens of the United States, gave them all the rights of white citizens in their states, and provided harsh penalties for anyone who blocked those rights. This was clearly intended by Congress to invalidate the Black Codes, which were regarded not only as unjust but as intended to exclude the Republican Party from the South. The Freedmen's Bureau was turned into the agent of the Radicals in the South by giving it such inclusive rights over cases involving freedmen that it supplanted the authority of the states. Johnson's veto was narrowly overridden by a series of fantastically brutal maneuvers.

The Radical program

Doubt as to the Constitutionality of the Civil Rights Bill prompted the Joint Committee to introduce the Fourteenth Amendment; it was passed and sent on to the states in June 1866, but ratification was not completed until July 1868. The amendment has five parts. They respectively define citizenship and the civil rights of the citizen; aid the Negro to the suffrage and counteract emancipation's repeal of the Three-fifths Ratio by depriving the states of representation in Congress proportionate to the number of citizens to whom they deny the vote; reserve to Congress the power to pardon former public officials who have engaged in rebellion; outlaw debts incurred in support of rebellion or incurred to pay owners for emancipated slaves; and give Congress authority to enforce the foregoing. The chief significance of the amendment then and since lay in the first section.

The Fourteenth Amendment

All persons born or naturalized in the United States, and subject to the jurisdiction thereof, are citizens of the United States and of the State wherein they reside. No State shall make or enforce any law which shall abridge the privileges or immunities of citizens of the United States; nor shall any State deprive any person of life, liberty, or property, without due process of law; nor deny to any person within its jurisdiction the equal protection of the laws.

The intention of Section I was to overrule the Dred Scott Decision and guarantee to Negroes all the rights of citizenship, and it was accepted as such by the public and most Congressmen. Far more important in the long run, however, were two deductions which have become the basis for numerous enactments and judicial decisions and which have vitally changed the legal and economic structure of the United States. The Fifth Amendment had forbidden the Federal government to deprive any person "of life, liberty, or property, without due process of law." Now this prohibition was extended to the states, and the Federal government was given the right to enforce it; for the first time (outside of the vague guarantee of the republican form of government) Federal authority was specifically extended over the states as such, and not merely over citizens. This power, granted to protect the freedmen, was exercised halfheartedly before the 1930's but has now become the center of a fierce struggle over the nature and extent of civil rights and whether and how they shall be enforced.

Basis of civil rights

Even more significant—thus far, at least—has been the interpretation that "person" was intended to include "legal persons," that is, corporations. This interpretation was first made by the Supreme Court in 1886 (in *Santa Clara County v. Southern Pacific*) and opened up an entire vista down which business enterprise could jog without fear of interference by state laws. This aspect of the amendment received no public attention at the time it was before the states, but two members of the Joint Committee later asserted that in formulating the section they had in mind precisely the interpretation later made. Arguments have been offered for and against their prescience, and probably the question of deliberate intention will never be settled.

Basis of property rights

The Radicals had jammed through their program thus far by appeals to party and patriotic spirit, to Congressional self-esteem, and to the traditional ascendance of Congress over the executive. By summer, however, they had reached the end of the possibilities in these appeals. Congressmen were restive at the rising tide of public criticism and were inclined to debate over the Radical program rather than to vote on it. The former Confederate states rejected the Fourteenth Amendment, all of them except Tennessee, which was rewarded by having its Representatives admitted to Congress in July 1866. The Southern objection to the amendment was not so much the provisos for Negro citizenship and suffrage (perhaps they expected to circumvent those) but the denial of the right of their trusted leaders to hold office. The amendment was clearly doomed to defeat unless the Radicals found

Radicalism temporarily blocked

means of forcing it down the throats of the stubborn Southern states. Actually it soon became evident that the Radicals would not have admitted the South to Congress even if it had accepted the Fourteenth Amendment.

On the Congressional election of 1866 hinged the issue of Southern reconstruction. The Radicals were too smart to lay stress either on their economic program or on their hope of turning the South over to the Negroes, for they knew that most Northerners were opposed both to undue centralization and to race equality. But they did not lack for issues. They piously defended the Constitution against Johnson, the "usurper," in cynical disregard of their own notorious contempt for the document. The bloody shirt was waved from every platform, and race riots in Southern cities gave point to their warnings. Pressure was brought on government workers and on Conservative Congressmen who depended on Federal loaves and fishes for political life. The newly organized Grand Army of the Republic (G.A.R.) marshaled the enthusiastic veterans once more to the "support of the Union." Grant, now the idol of the people, kept silent when the Radicals claimed him; the presidential bug was eating at his vitals, and the realistic Rawlins was still directing his every action. Even would-be Conservative voters often found it impossible to vote their convictions, for balloting was open, and employers and strong-arm men stood by to see that they voted "right."

Campaign of 1866

Of course all this cost money, but Northeastern financiers and industrialists aided with ample funds, for the Radicals had come through handsomely in their economic legislation. The tariff was high, public lands were being given out freely to the deserving, and there was the prospect of the early reduction of income and internal taxes. All these conditions would be jeopardized if a Johnson victory brought the South back into Congress and recemented the old Southern and Western democracy. There was even a chance, ran the argument, that the war debt would be repudiated or—even worse—paid off in greenbacks.

The Conservatives handled their campaign with deadly ineptness. A great rally in Philadelphia of Northern and Southern Conservatives turned out to be no more than a pep meeting. Perhaps a new party might yet have saved the day, but Johnson was so fearful that the Conservative movement would fall into Democratic or even Copperhead hands that he stuck by the Union Party. The result was that the very thing he feared happened: Radicals seized the Republican nominations, and Conservatives voted for them rather than vote for Democrats or Copperheads. He should have disposed of the members of the Cabinet who did not agree with his policies; instead, his desire for harmony led him to retain them all, even the unscrupulous Stanton, of whose actions he would seem to have been well aware.

Conservative ineptness

When Johnson made a "swing around the circle" to defend his policies he met with disaster. The Radicals organized hostile demonstrations which shouted him down when he attempted to speak or baited him into making intemperate statements which could be used against **Personal** him. Such slips were, of course, deplorable and unfortu **abuse of** nately gave handles to those who would overturn him; but **Johnson** one marvels at the relative patience and dignity Johnson exhibited under direct physical and vocal provocations such as no President has faced before or since. He was ridiculed in cartoons and editorials, falsely accused of being drunk in public, his private life was slandered, and the old canard was revived that he had been privy to the assassination of Lincoln. His enemies even forged and circulated as his, speeches which made him out to be a fool, a knave, and a traitor so mad for power that he was ready to sell his country to get it.

Where so much mud was flung, some was bound to stick. By autumn it was evident that the tide, which at first had run in Johnson's favor, was now running strongly against him. In the tussle for control of the Union Party it had broken apart, with the Republicans largely **Radicals** going over to the Radicals, and the War Democrats return **sweep the** ing to the regular Democratic fold. The Radicals received **boards** priceless reinforcements in the election to the House of Ben Butler and General John A. Logan of Illinois, and to the Senate of Oliver P. Morton, war governor of Indiana, and Roscoe Conkling of New York. These men were the core of the Radical board of strategy. The elections had only confirmed the foregone conclusion. The Radicals returned to power with a Congressional majority so huge that they could override presidential vetoes with ease. The curtain was about to rise on the tragedy of reconstruction.

2 Congressional Reconstruction

The effect of the election was not lost upon the old Congress, which met for its lame-duck session in December 1866. It readily agreed to a Radical bill to change the opening date of Congressional sessions to 4 March instead of the first Monday in December. The **Ground** newly-elected Fortieth Congress would thus meet upon the **work of** first day of its life and would not be dependent upon a **Congres** presidential call. An army appropriation act disbanded the **sional re** militia of the Southern states and provided that all execu **constructon** tive orders to the army be issued through the general of the army (Grant), who was to be stationed in Washington and was not to be moved without the consent of the Senate. Next, the Tenure of Office Act denied to the President control over his own Cabinet. Officials in whose appointment the Senate had participated were not to be removed without the consent of the Senate during "the term of the President by whom they may have been appointed and for one month thereafter." Obviously the act permitted Johnson to remove holdovers from Lincoln's Cabinet; it may be that the clumsy wording of the act was essential to obtain the necessary two-thirds majority to pass it over Johnson's veto.

As soon as the Fortieth Congress was seated, the Radicals strengthened their control by ousting or holding up the admittance of as many as possible of the Conservatives who opposed their program. It then pro-**First Re-** ceeded to pass a series of reconstruction measures on the **construc-** assumption that the Southern states had no lawful govern-**tion Act** ments and were subject to the will of Congress. John Sherman and Stevens were the authors of the First Reconstruction Act, passed over Johnson's veto in March 1867. The ten Southern states were divided into five military districts, each under the well-nigh absolute control of a general. The states were to hold elections for constitutional conventions; Negroes were to vote in these elections, while whites disqualified under the proposed Fourteenth Amendment could not. The new constitutions must accept Negro suffrage and disfranchise Confederate leaders and must be ratified by a majority of the qualified voters. Then, if the new legislature had ratified the Fourteenth Amendment, Congress would consider the matter of admitting the state's Representatives. Until such admission the state governments were merely provisional, "subject in all respects to the paramount authority of the United States"—which meant the Radicals.

The passage of the First Reconstruction Act was a rude shock to the South, and few possessed the realism of the farmer who, when told of the act, asked drily, "Will it kill the corn?" Southerners had been confident **Southern** that if they remained firm they could essentially get their **reception** own way regardless of the outcome of the war. This was not **of the act** so much confidence in Northern fairness as an unimaginative failure to envision any course but their own. The old tradition of Northern weakness died hard. As it was, the act, perhaps intentionally, left so much to administrative (that is, Radical) decision that Southerners were honestly puzzled as to its exact meaning. The upshot was that Southerners determined to remain quiescent, to make no move toward supplanting their Johnsonian constitutions and governments.

Congress now passed the Second Reconstruction Act (also March 1867), instructing the commanders in the new military districts to set up electoral machinery and hold elections for members of the new constitu-**Three more** tional conventions. Johnson believed that the business of **Reconstruc-** the generals was to co-operate with the existing state gov-**tion Acts** ernments, not to overrule or abolish them. Congress replied with the Third Reconstruction Act (July 1867) which denied the legality

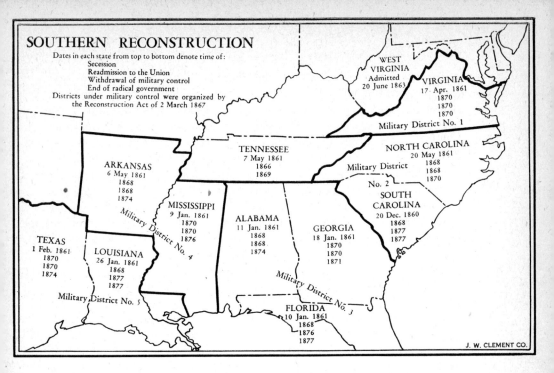

SOUTHERN RECONSTRUCTION

Dates in each state from top to bottom denote time of:
Secession
Readmission to the Union
Withdrawal of military control
End of radical government
Districts under military control were organized by
the Reconstruction Act of 2 March 1867

WEST
VIRGINIA
Admitted
20 June 1863

VIRGINIA
17 Apr. 1861
1870
1870
1870

Military District No. 1

TENNESSEE
7 May 1861
1866
1869

NORTH CAROLINA
20 May 1861
1868
1868
1870

Military District
No. 2

SOUTH
CAROLINA
20 Dec. 1860
1868
1877
1877

ARKANSAS
6 May 1861
1868
1868
1874

MISSISSIPPI
9 Jan. 1861
1870
1870
1876

ALABAMA
11 Jan. 1861
1868
1868
1874

GEORGIA
18 Jan. 1861
1870
1870
1871

Military District No. 4

TEXAS
1 Feb. 1861
1870
1870
1874

LOUISIANA
26 Jan. 1861
1868
1877
1877

Military District No. 5

Military District No. 3

FLORIDA
10 Jan. 1861
1868
1876
1877

J. W. CLEMENT CO.

of the Southern state governments, confirmed the overriding powers of the generals, and set forth a clumsy mass of detailed instructions. But even this was not enough. According to the law, ratification required the consent of a majority of the *registered* voters, and when the Alabama whites stayed away from the polls they defeated the proposed Radical constitution. Congress promptly countered (March 1868) with the Fourth Reconstruction Act, which made a majority of the votes *cast* enough to ratify a constitution. This cleared away the last "legal" obstacle to the adoption of the Radical constitutions. Henceforth the Southern states were subject to Radical rule backed by military force.

By now it was clear what the Radicals were doing. They were seeking (1) to break down the division of powers between state and Federal governments, and (2) to break down the separation of powers among the three branches of the Federal government. Ostensibly this endeavor was prompted by a determination to enforce the will of the people as expressed through Congress by instituting the system of parliamentary government, but it is certain that the Radicals felt that they could control elections and admissions to Congress more easily than they could grasp control of all three branches.

Radicals seek parliamentary government

The Joint Committee of Fifteen on Reconstruction had now in effect become the Federal executive. Its campaign was not only against the President but against the Supreme Court. It will be remembered that in

Radical subversion of the Supreme Court *Ex parte Milligan* the Supreme Court denied the jurisdiction of military courts over civilians in areas where the civil courts were open. This decision was a blow at a whole series of Radical actions during and after the war, and they had met the challenge (July 1866) by reducing the number of justices from nine to seven—thus also eliminating the danger of having any Johnson appointees. Nevertheless, the decision now threatened to overturn the whole basis of Radical control in the South; so Congress now withdrew from the Supreme Court the right to hear appeals on violations of the right of habeas corpus. The Supreme Court took the hint and refused to sit on cases involving the Reconstruction Acts, though it did in *Texas v. White* (1869) approve the Lincolnian theory that the Southern states had not ceased to be members of the Union.

The Radicals' attempt to seize the presidency began in January 1867 with a legislative inquiry into Johnson's acts with a view to impeachment. This was plainly a political move, intended to give Congress control of the

Search for grounds for impeachment presidency by establishing the precedent of impeachment and removal. However, the Constitution provided that impeachment could be undertaken only for "high crimes and misdemeanors," and the Judiciary Committee's attempt to find criminal grounds for a political impeachment was deservedly voted down by the House in December. The Tenure of Office Act afforded another entry. Cabinet personnel had changed gradually, so that by 1868 Johnson had a Cabinet in harmony with his views except for Stanton. Of course, Johnson knew that Stanton was co-operating with the Radicals and doing *sub rosa* everything he could to thwart his chief. Finally in August Johnson reached the end of his considerable store of patience and dismissed Stanton and put Grant in his place.

When Congress met, the Senate refused to concur in Stanton's removal. Johnson had expected this course of action and had planned to challenge the Tenure of Office Act in the courts, but at this juncture

Johnson impeached Grant surrendered his office to Stanton, doubtless prompted by Rawlins, who was aware that he could not afford to alienate the Radicals. Johnson again fired Stanton and this time put General Lorenzo Thomas in his place. Stanton barricaded himself in the War Department and kept control of its functions, while Thomas attended Cabinet meetings. The Radicals were overjoyed, and Covode promptly introduced a resolution of impeachment which swept through the House (February 1868). Though no articles accompanied the resolution, it was apparent that the Radicals' main accusation would be that Johnson had violated the Tenure of Office Act. A House committee now began under the guidance of Stevens to erect a ridiculous tissue of charges consisting of eleven articles artfully calculated to condemn John-

son if any one were approved. The tenure-of-office issue was presented in
every possible guise in the first eight articles, but for good measure articles
were added to the effect that the President had criticized Congress, ob-
structed its will, and had tried to exercise authority over the army!
Stevens and B. F. Butler were important among the seven "managers"
appointed by the House to handle the trial.

Meanwhile Congress had increased the number of anti-Johnson Senators by admitting Nebraska (1867) over Johnson's veto, though his veto
of Colorado's admission was upheld. According to the Constitution the
function of the Senate in a case of impeachment is to sit as **The func-**
a court. The Radicals, however, vigorously denied that the **tion of**
Senate constituted a court and insisted that it sat in judg- **the Senate**
ment as a political body. When the Senate met to hear the impeachment
charges under the presidency of Chief Justice Chase, it did not demand
the personal appearance of Johnson; however, Ben Wade, president pro
tempore of the Senate who would have succeeded to the presidency in the
event of Johnson's removal, was cynically permitted to sit in judgment.
Chase presided with dignity and impartiality, thereby antagonizing such
of his Radical friends as remained.

The trial lasted from 30 March to 11 May. Though the Senators frequently overrode Chase by refusing to admit evidence on the President's
intent, Johnson's defenders nevertheless slowly destroyed the eleven articles. William M. Evarts, a brilliant trial lawyer and public **The trial**
man of New York City, was the most effective spokesman
for the defense. He showed that Johnson was within his Constitutional
rights and that he had not even violated the Tenure of Office Act, for
Stanton had been appointed by Lincoln and so did not come under the
act. But even if Johnson had violated the act, it was with the intent of
seeking a court test, and in any case Stanton remained—and still remained—in control of the office. Evarts laid bare the political intent of
the Radicals to destroy the spirit and the letter of the Constitution. Their
denial that the Senate was sitting as a court was an admission that they
were seeking to enact a bill of attainder, that is, to convict by vote rather
than by *bona fide* trial.

Johnson's counsel had demolished the articles of impeachment, but no
one expected that action to influence the Senate's decision. A vote of 19
to 36 on one article on 16 May showed that the Radicals had one less
than the two thirds necessary to convict, so they adjourned
until the 26th. Seven Republicans had voted against the ar- **Johnson**
ticle, but one of them, Edmund G. Ross of Kansas, was the **acquitted**
victim of ruthless pressure to change his vote. Ross stood firm while
votes were taken on two more articles; then the Radicals in despair adjourned *sine die*. The attempt to use impeachment as a weapon to estab-

lish Congressional control of the presidency had collapsed, though the Tenure of Office Act was not completely repealed until 1887. Stanton resigned and was replaced by Schofield. However, the Republican Senators who had voted for Johnson's acquittal were hounded from public life.* Johnson finished out his term in quiet dignity, and on Christmas Day 1868 issued a general amnesty to all remaining Confederates whom it was within executive power to pardon.

Congress had failed to oust the President, but it still controlled the South. Arkansas, completely reconstructed to conform to Radical specifications, was readmitted in June 1868, and Florida, Alabama, Louisiana,

Completion of Congressional reconstruction and the Carolinas followed promptly. Georgia, Mississippi, Virginia, and Texas each offered special complications which delayed their rehabilitation until 1870. The Fourteenth Amendment was finally certified in July 1868 under curiously complicated circumstances which, to say the least, cast doubt upon the legality of its passage.

With Grant safely in the bag, the nomination in 1868 was no problem for the Republicans. Grant's name was the only one presented to the convention, and he was unanimously chosen on the first ballot. Schuyler

Campaign of 1868 Colfax of Indiana was selected as his running mate. Chase, who had hoped for the nomination, found that the judicial calm with which he had presided over the Johnson impeachment trial had antagonized his former allies among the Radicals. He then turned to his first love, the Democratic Party, and Kate waged a valiant campaign for her father. "Competent judges," says one biographer of Chase, "have believed that had she been able to go into the convention and make her combinations on the spot she would have secured his nomination." As it was, he was almost shut out in the vote, and the Democrats chose Horatio Seymour, the lukewarm war governor of New York, and Frank Blair, Jr. The Republican dependence for victory upon military glamor was no more evident than the Democratic hope of rallying all Conservatives to lay the mantle of charity over the war and to defend the rights of the states against the Radical Federal machine. The Republicans won 214 to 80 (3,000,000 to 2,700,000), their Southern machine delivering the vote in all the reconstructed Southern states except Louisiana. Unreconstructed Georgia through a curious slip was permitted to register a Democratic vote.

It seems certain that it was the Negro vote that gave the Republicans their popular majority, a situation that was to be duplicated again and again in presidential elections. Though the Republican platform of 1868

Fifteenth Amendment asserted that the suffrage was the business of the states, the Radicals now discovered that the election had been a mandate to enforce the Constitutional guarantee of a "republi-

* David M. Dewitt, *The Impeachment and Trial of Andrew Johnson* (1903).

can form of government" by foisting the Negro franchise upon the South. Early in 1869 the Fifteenth Amendment was sent to the states for ratification. It proposed that the "right of citizens of the United States to vote shall not be denied or abridged by the United States or by any State on account of race, color, or previous condition of servitude." The loopholes by which states later avoided giving the vote to Negroes were clear at the time, but Northern supporters of state control of the suffrage were able to prevent the adoption of a stronger measure. The Radical-controlled state governments, North as well as South, ratified the amendment with alacrity, and it became a part of the Constitution in March 1870.

Grant the President was a pitiful contrast to Grant the soldier. He was so utterly ignorant of the sciences of government and human relations that he seems actually to have regarded the presidency as a sinecure awarded to him for his share in saving the Union. His education began when in his inaugural month he sought to have the Tenure of Office Act repealed. The Radical Congressional clique led by Morton, Conkling, and Chandler quickly brought him to heel, but they permitted him to surround himself with West Pointers, with Rawlins serving as chief of staff and idea man until his death late in the summer of 1869. Unfortunately Grant had made his appointments without regard to political or geographical availability, and to make it worse those who showed ability he quickly disposed of, except for Hamilton Fish* of New York, the Secretary of State. **Grant as President**

Grant was a kindly, loyal, unimaginative man amenable to flattery and a convinced conservative, who saw nothing wrong in consulting on economic affairs with men like Jay Cooke who had been economically successful or in receiving from them as gifts the fine horses in which his heart delighted. The wave of political backstabbing and public protestation which presently penetrated his rather dim consciousness made him react with a pathetic mixture of lethargy, dignity, obstinacy, and baffled fury. In only one case did he rouse himself to fight viciously for a policy —the annexation of Santo Domingo, the pet measure of the military crowd—and then he lost because of the opposition of Senator Sumner.

The letdown in moral standards which now swept the nation may or may not have been the result of the war, but it penetrated to every state and city. The Tweed Ring, headed by Tammany's William Marcy Tweed, which mulcted New York City of untold millions of dollars, was only the most dramatic of many steals. At least it had the advantage of bringing into political prominence the reformer who broke it up and sent Tweed to jail: Samuel J. Tilden. **Scandals of the Grant era**

It would be tedious and useless to follow in detail the political scandals of the Grant era. Many of them found a focus in Grant's own secretary and former aide, Orville E. Babcock. This personable and ingenious

* Allan Nevins, *Hamilton Fish: The Inner History of the Grant Administration* (1936).

"Design for a Proposed Monumental Fountain in the City Hall Park," in *Harper's Weekly*, 1871 attacked the looting of New York's treasury by the Tweed Ring.

young man profited by the corrupt procedures connected with the much-needed rebuilding of Washington's streets and government housing; he organized a successful racket to force importers to use his customs warehouses; he was a leading light in the Whisky Ring centered in St. Louis, which milked the distillers and the government revenues for the support of the Republican Party; and he was even a party to the nefarious Black Friday attempt to corner the gold market. When the Whisky Ring was exposed and Babcock was brought to trial, Grant threw so many obstacles in the way that he was acquitted.

Not only did scandal enter the White House, but some members of Grant's own family and of his wife's were involved. The Secretary of War was impeached for selling licenses to Indian traders and resigned to escape punishment. Even as far away as London the American minister was forced to resign for allowing his name to be used in selling silver-mine stock of doubtful value. Through all these scandals the unfortunate Grant seems to have been convinced that his enemies were merely trying to get at him by besmirching his friends and relatives.

3 The South During Reconstruction

By July 1870 all the Southern states had been reconstructed according to Radical specifications, the Black Codes had been washed out, and the three reconstruction amendments to the Constitution were in effect. The Radicals' control over the South, and consequently over **Radical** the nation, seemed to be assured for as long as they could **triumph** look into the future. This control, however, had been gained **in the** only after a stubborn resistance on the part of Southern **South** whites which had not only taxed the legislative ingenuity of the Radicals but had forced them frequently to make clear their basic reliance on military force. Southern whites had lost the political struggle, but they now began to turn to forms of pressure which could not be so easily countered by Congressional legislation and Federal bayonets.

In no part of the ante-bellum United States were classes so clearly differentiated as in the South, and yet for the most part all classes of whites united in support of Southernism and the Confederacy, and po- litical democracy (on a white basis) actually made progress. **Relative** More than this, the Negroes, whatever they may have **solidarity** thought secretly, kept the peace during the war and labored **of the** not only on the farms and plantations but on fortifications **South** as well. The attempt of Negro historians to show that the Union won be- cause of a vast general strike among the slaves simply has no basis.

Reconstruction, however, brought definite signs of cleavage. The old Jacksonian clash between planters and yeomen was renewed, and a new white element appeared: the Carpetbaggers. These were technically Northern men who became Republican leaders and office holders in the South, and from them the reconstruction **Carpet-** state governments are usually known (not quite accurately) **baggers** as Carpetbagger governments. Their name arose from the Southern ac- cusation that they were destitute men who carried all their belongings in a carpetbag when they came South to suck riches from the prostrate sec- tion. Actually the South swarmed with Northerners, most of whom sought to invest their money and their energy in legitimate channels; these men had little or nothing to do with the Carpetbaggers and usually got along well with their Southern neighbors.

So far as the South was concerned, the problem of Northern capital ranked second only to the Negro problem and, indeed, the two were closely related. The South as an investment area had its resemblance to **Northern** an economic colony, and Northern corporations and some **corporate** of the smaller personal investors as well sought to protect **investments** their investments by winning political influence or control. For this endeavor the Carpetbaggers and the Republican Party offered obvious instruments. Indeed, the inception of Radical reconstruction was due not only to capitalist desire to maintain its gains in the North and West but to its desire to get control of the coal, iron, timber, and transportation of the South. At first there was a disposition among Southerners to welcome Northern corporate capital, but when its connection with Carpetbag government became clear the welcome mat was often withdrawn.

Southern whites who made common cause with the Radical Republicans were called Scalawags, from the colloquial term for anyone who was scabrous and disreputable. According to Southern tradition they were **Scalawags** self-seeking exploiters of sectional and racial hatreds. Doubtless some were, but it is difficult to include in this definition ex-Governor Joseph Brown of Georgia and Generals James Longstreet and William Mahone. Such men as these were usually Jacksonians like Andrew Johnson. They accepted the results of the war and sought to rebuild the South on a democratic and perhaps also an industrial basis; they were even willing to acknowledge the right of the Negro to legal justice and to a chance to make a living, but they definitely were not ready to accept him as an equal. It is notable that most of the so-called Scalawags were of yeoman or poor-white origin. In the end their old phobias triumphed over progressive tendencies.

The survivors of the planter class were confronted by a desperate situation. The war had cut in half the assessed values of the South, including the loss in slave property, and this hit the planters hardest. Yet, **The Con-** as owners of much of what was left they had to find ways to **servatives** pay huge taxes and at the same time restore their capital. To do this they would have to hold down and exploit labor, and the Black Codes were no less an effort to ensure a docile and reliable labor supply than an attempt to avoid social chaos. Planters were less Negrophobe than yeomen and poor whites and seem to have been little impressed by the argument that white supremacy was in danger. They knew that they could maintain their old ascendance over their former slaves and could even control their votes if necessary. They opposed the Radical program principally because it would institute prohibitive costs in wages and in what they regarded as unreasonable public investments in schools and public facilities, such as railroads.

The Negro needed time and a helping hand if he were to bridge the gap between slavery and democratic responsibilities, but the South was not greatly concerned even with the rise of its own yeomen and poor whites and was desirous of holding down the Negro. Com- **Resentment** moners' ante-bellum jealousy of the Negro now turned into **against the** hatred, and the war was scarcely over before a campaign **freedmen** of violence was under way to "keep the Negro in his place." Negroes who made themselves conspicuous either by their prosperity or by their failure to remain humble were often beaten and burned out. Before long, race riots, outrages, and even murders became fairly common on both sides, and the Freedmen's Bureau and the army of occupation both found that they were unable to guarantee order. Untold numbers of victims perished in these clashes, even before the Johnson governments were displaced by the Radicals, and indeed they gave the Radicals plausible excuses for their action.

One can find what he seeks when he examines the role of the Negroes in the reconstruction period. The extremes of good and bad were present; the inarticulate masses of Negroes sent to constitutional conventions and put into legislatures and administrative offices men of their race who were variously rascals, fools, and intelligent high- **Negro** minded men, often with education and experience. These **leaders** leaders came from among the preachers, the free Negroes, former soldiers, and even on occasion house servants or plantation drivers. Negro leaders, whether good or bad, tended to accept the white standards of the superior respectability of the property holder, and many of them fought to give their people a start by providing education and a stake in the land. By and large, after the first frenzied months of freedom the Negro masses and their leaders returned to their original trust in their old masters— with the possible exception of voting. Already pride of country was appearing. In Georgia a convention of Negroes addressed the whites: "This is your country, but it is ours too; you were born here, so were we; your fathers fought for it; but our fathers fed them."

Responsible Negro leaders persistently demanded for their race the benefits of education, land ownership, admission to labor unions, and the other aspects of political and economic (but rarely social) equality. Just how deeply the Negro masses felt these needs is open to **Failure to** argument. The Radicals had promoted Negro suffrage in **give the** the South in order to strengthen Republican support of in- **Negro land** dustrial capitalism. Sumner and Stevens went further: they wanted Negro equality not only to protect capitalism but because they were perfection-ists. They realized, after the Jeffersonian precept, that Negro political equality was futile unless it was based on economic equality. This was one cogent reason why they fought so strongly to confiscate "rebel" estates and divide them among the freedmen. Stevens died (1868) in the bitter knowledge that Northern capital had rejected the scheme lest it set a bad example to restive Northern labor. Sumner hoped that by forcing Negro political equality upon North as well as South he could give the Negroes power to gain economic equality, but he also died (1874) in the midst of defeat.

Southern planters naturally followed the struggle with intense interest. If Sumner and Stevens won even a partial victory and set the Negroes up on purchased farms, the planters would nonetheless lose all hope of recovery because their labor supply would be gone. Yeomen and poor whites were no less alarmed, but in their case it was fear of the loss of their social and economic prestige as whites and landholders. With the defeat of Sumner and Stevens the white South drew a sigh of relief; it knew now that with time and patience it could beat the Radicals on the race issue.

The Radical attempt to take over the Negro vote in the South began even before Congressional reconstruction. The feckless utopians and the hard-souled realists of army and Freedmen's Bureau alike sought to im-

The Southern Republican machines press upon the Negroes that Lincoln, freedom, Republicanism, and free rations were inseparable. During the war an organization known as the Union or Loyal League had been of significant service in the Northern and Border states and even in the South itself by keeping alive Union sentiment, aiding escaped prisoners, and sending on military information. Now that the war was over the Union League had a phenomenal growth in the South among the Negroes, though it was rather generally under the control of whites, and became in effect a sort of Republican lodge.

The work of the Republicans was done so thoroughly that Negroes were politically almost a unit. Indeed, few of them dared to vote Democratic—remember, this was before the day of the secret ballot—lest they be socially ostracized, their rations be cut off, and they be horsewhipped by the Union League. In theory at least Negroes would have stirred up less opposition if they had divided, but for some years whites gave them no chance. At any rate, Radical politicians developed remarkable dexterity in many ingenious means of fraudulent voting and counting. Their masterpiece, however, was the state board-of-election returns which ruthlessly and cynically trimmed and threw out the local returns until they met the desired standard. The time was to come when the Democrats attained like skills.

Neither Carpetbaggers nor Scalawags were anxious to have Negroes in office, and only in Louisiana and South Carolina did Negroes comprise a majority of the legislature. Sixteen Negroes were sent to Congress, and, though they were not outstanding, most of them served as capably as the rank and file of their white colleagues. The common complaint was, "History, till now, gives no account of a conqueror so cruel as to place his vanquished foes under the domination of their former slaves." Actually this was more appearance than reality, for white Republicans were definitely in control. Carpetbag rule was corrupt, but it was not Negro rule. If it was Negro votes that made some astonishing steals possible, it should be remembered that it was white men who got the bulk of the swag and that this was the generation of the grafter even in states where no Negro ever entered office.

It would be easy to multiply authentic instances of corruption in Southern legislatures—to tell of gold spittoons, champagne, and fancy ladies furnished at state expense; to retail the bogus contracts, the wild bond issues, the public lands sold at give-away prices, and **Carpet-** the bare-faced sale of votes and legislative favors. American **bagger** states had traditionally purchased or guaranteed railroad **extrava-** bonds, but the Radical governments abused the custom out- **gance and** rageously and left the states holding the bag. It is worth **corruption** noting in passing that Democrats also managed to get in on the ground floor of many a shady state-chartered enterprise. The chances for the impoverished Southern states ever to repay their bonds was so poor that Northern financiers demanded extravagant premiums and outrageous rates of interest; South Carolina sold millions of dollars worth of its bonds at twenty-five cents on the dollar. At the same time public revenues were drying up, even though tax rates were zooming; in 1870 state and local governments in the late Confederacy collected only $32,000,000 in taxes while the state of New York alone collected half as much again. Naturally millions of acres of land changed hands in forced sales. Upon the restoration of Conservative rule the public debt was either repudiated or scaled down.

While the Radicals were extravagant by the standards of the antebellum regime and of the Bourbon regime which followed, yet they were in a real sense making up for the failures of their predecessors. Not only did the ravages of war have to be repaired, but the South **Carpetbag-** had to be institutionally modernized after a generation of **ger accom-** opposition to most reforms. Among the Radical accomplish- **plishments** ments were the reform of local government and of the courts and judicial procedure, the overhauling of the tax structure, the foundation of public schools and charitable institutions, and the inception of poor relief. They brought in immigrants and established many Negro families on the land.

Indeed, Radical constitutions were so clearly fitted to the new day that most of them were continued in use for many years after the Conservative restoration.

Nevertheless, the era of Carpetbag government was one of violence. This was not solely due to the dislocations of war, for indubitably Radical leaders and organizations promoted it. The natural irresponsibility of the **Carpet-** freedmen was encouraged by the Union League's efforts to **bagger** crush Southern opposition. Radicals pandered to the lust **violence** for personal revenge and plunder by ignoring killings and incendiarism. Northern firearms factories were kept busy supplying the pistol toters of the South. Militia was organized to support the Radical régimes; in several states it was composed largely of Negroes whose principal duty it was to keep whites from the polls, burn out Conservatives, and "preserve order" whenever the whites rallied to defend their rights. Tennessee, readmitted to the Union in 1866, and now under the domination of the Radicals led by Parson Brownlow, suffered no less than the states still in process of reconstruction. Federal troops in the South, now less than twenty thousand in number, proved incapable of stopping the rule of riot, partly because they were under the thumb of the Radicals and largely composed of Negroes.

The Radical intention of building up the Republican Party among Southern whites was thwarted by their policy of promoting Negro independence. With unerring accuracy the Radicals had laid their fingers upon **Growth of** the one policy sure to wreck their program and to blast any **Southern** hope of winning the South to a sense of sin and to suitable **solidarity** repentance. The tendency to glorify the Lost Cause spread widely and penetrated deeply, as Southerners rallied to save their "civilization." Northern persecution of Jeff Davis brought the South to the defense of the once-calumniated leader. The Lee cult sprang into full flower: 26 April was set apart to decorate Confederate graves; war memorials rose in town squares and on battle fields; Confederate "Survivors" organized; historical societies sprang up; books devoted to Southern justification poured from the press, and in their wake came "the sick magnolias of the false romance."

When the North heaped abuse upon these manifestations of an unconquerable spirit, true Southerners gloried in it and drew their ranks more closely together. It is probable that the whites of the South had not been so closely knit even during the war. The antipathies of wartime were now succeeded by an intensity of hatred which braced Southern determination as thoroughly as a moral purge and reimplanted the old arrogant sense of Southern perfection. The North may have won the military conflict, but the South had a haughty sense of having won the moral conflict, and, since theologians agreed that right is might, the South—at least superficially—felt and acted as though it had won the war.

Along with this new growth of Southern solidarity came practical manifestations of the determination to save the Southern way of life. Hitherto the use of violence to "keep the Negro in his place" had been sporadic, but now a number of secret organizations began to apply direct action against Radicals, whether white or **Ku Klux** black. The movement appeared under various names in all **Klan** of the late Confederate states except perhaps Virginia and Texas, but the Ku Klux Klan, strongest in Tennessee, Alabama, and North Carolina, was the most dramatic manifestation and the one best remembered. The Klan first appeared in May 1866 in Pulaski, Tennessee, where a club of skylarking young men found that their pranks and regalia were frightening Negroes. The organization quickly spread, and in May 1868 General Nathan Bedford Forrest united the "Dens" into the "Invisible Empire." The Klan's hierarchy of Wizards, Dragons, Titans, Cyclops, Genii, Hydras, Furies, Night Hawks, and Ghouls is too well known to need repetition.

At any rate Forrest's "critter company" was now riding again, this time disguised in bedsheets and dunce caps. Illiterate but horrendous warnings to Radicals to cease their activities were nailed to doors or published by editors who invariably had found them thrust under the office door. The terrors of the unknown were reinforced by simple tricks of magic to frighten superstitious Negroes away from the polls or from meetings of the Union League. Ghostly parades of sheeted men on horseback terrorized Negro shanty towns and engaged in jail deliveries. Carpetbaggers, Scalawags, and Negro leaders were driven out, or on occasion horsewhipped, shot, drowned, or strung up.

The Ku Klux Klan accomplished its purpose in some areas, but in others it only added to the violence as militia and Union League rallied to combat it. A new wave of riots and murders swept across the South. Forrest realized in 1869 that his Klan was getting out of **The Force** hand, and in consequence he dissolved it. Though it is prob- **Acts** able that most respectable and law-abiding citizens left it, some local "Dens" remained in existence and became wilder than ever. To meet the situation Congress passed a series of Military Enforcement (or Force) Acts. The first (May 1870) was intended to enforce the Fifteenth Amendment and, among other things, it put Southern elections under Federal regulation and authorized the President to use military force. The second act (February 1871) strengthened Federal control of state elections. The third act (April 1871), often called the Ku Klux Act, was directed specifically against the Klan and followed upon an exhaustive investigation conducted with a patently Radical bias. Grant now designated nine counties in South Carolina as centers of "armed combinations" and suspended habeas corpus there and rushed in troops and Federal marshals. Less drastic action was taken elsewhere, though altogether troops were used in about two hundred cases. At any rate these measures, backed up by the threat of pouring in additional Federal troops, operated to break the back of the Ku Klux movement.

During these years Northern impatience with the Southern policies of the Radicals had been fed by their obvious corruption and ineffectiveness, and even in the Republican Party there was a growing sympathy **Schurz** with the white South. At the same time the corruption **and the** among Federal officials was well known, and Grant was **Liberal** severely criticized for defending the offenders. The result **Repub-** was a swelling revolt against "Grantism," expressed in a **licans** demand for purity in government and reconciliation with the South. Among its leaders were Greeley, Sumner, Charles Francis Adams, E. L. Godkin, editor of the once-Radical *Nation*, and George W. Julian, former Indiana Radical.

Missouri was the first to make its protest felt when in 1869 it sent Carl Schurz (1829–1906) to the Senate. Schurz had fled from Germany as a result of the failure of the Revolution of 1848 and had entered Wisconsin politics as a Republican, been admitted to the bar, and had become a major general in the Union army. During and after the war he was a prominent Radical, but his perfectionism soon turned him against his former cronies and made him the leader of the developing Liberal Republican movement. For the rest of his life he was an opponent of public corruption, the spoils system, imperialism, and economic concentration. On the positive side he favored the merit system in the civil service, justice to the Indians, conservation of natural resources, and strict national isolation from foreign rivalries.

Meanwhile there had been developing in the Democratic Party the so-called New Departure movement, named and championed by Clement L. Vallandigham. Its keynote was to lay aside the sectional and **The New** ideological antipathies of the war and to return to the **Departure** Jacksonian standard of labor and agrarian opposition to **movement** economic concentration. In its Southern phase the advocates of the New Departure demanded that the results of the war and the best of the Radical reforms be accepted, and that the section subordinate politics to economic rehabilitation; this action was not intended to destroy basic Southern values but to defend them by renewing Southern strength. Benjamin H. Hill of Georgia, the outstanding Southern leader of the movement, hoped to rally honest men, whether black or white, and make

A gibe directed against Horace Greeley for aspiring to the presidency, a cartoon by Thomas Nast which appeared under the title "Adding Insult to Injury" in *Harper's Weekly*, 25 May 1872

the South once more an economic and eventually a political power in the nation. Those Southerners who held out against the New Departure movement were soon dubbed Bourbons because they were like the French royal house whose kings never learned and never forgot.

The clear fact that Grant would again be the choice of the Radical Republicans in 1872 drove the opponents of Grantism to union. They were soon joined by an embarrassing array of professionals bent on plunder or revenge. At its best the movement was a mass of contradictory elements which all but swamped its liberal program. Then to cap the confusion the Liberal Republican **Campaign of 1872** convention made the startling nomination of Horace Greeley, and the Democratic convention took the even more amazing step of supporting him. As a presidential candidate Greeley was a bumbling figure of fun, but he took himself and his chances with deadly seriousness, until in the end pathos overbalanced the comic.

The election was never in doubt, for the Radicals were well-heeled and were able to manipulate the headlines and the colored vote. Grant was renominated, but Colfax had given offense and was replaced by the furiously Radical Henry Wilson of Massachusetts. Grant was returned to office with 3,600,000 popular votes to Greeley's 2,800,000; Greeley had carried only six states, all in the South. Exhausted by the strain of the hustings, crushed by his defeat, and grieved by the death of his wife, Greeley himself died three weeks after the election. Grantism was triumphant, but not necessarily because the North favored corruption in government and oppression of the South. Rather, it was the result of the nostalgia for the heroic days, not for Grant the politician but for Grant the leader—as Allan Nevins puts it, "the rocklike center of four years of terror and glory."

Shortly before the end of the campaign of 1872 the Crédit Mobilier scandal broke in the *New York Sun,* and during the next winter Congressional investigations uncovered an appalling mess. The owners of the **The Crédit** Union Pacific Railroad had deliberately milked the assets of **Mobilier** the enterprise through the Crédit Mobilier, their own con- **scheme** struction company to which they awarded construction bids at enormously inflated figures. Representative Oakes Ames of Massachusetts, brother of the railroad's president, had been active in its dealings with Congress and in the management of the Crédit Mobilier. A quarrel among the directors made Ames fear exposure and led him to write, "We want more friends in this Congress." He got them in what must have seemed to him the most practical manner. He set aside three hundred forty-three shares of Crédit Mobilier stock and sold one hundred sixty of them to Congressmen at par, a price about half of their accrued value. When Garfield, for instance, purchased ten shares, the only money passed was $329—from Ames to Garfield.

Crédit Mobilier crashed after the railroad was completed and the owners had taken their profit, but the scandal then broke into the open. An investigating committee solemnly decided that the Republican re- **Resultant** ceivers had not been bribed, that a Democratic receiver **scandal** had been, and that Ames was guilty of bribery. Vice-President Schuyler Colfax was politically ruined, and his successor, Henry Wilson, lived thenceforth under a shadow. Blaine, Speaker of the House, who had arranged Ames's defense, was accused of profiting by the milking of a branch railroad but managed to evade the issue. Garfield, the Ohio theologian turned politician, was perhaps innocent of wrongdoing but was tarred by the company he kept.

The Crédit Mobilier scandal was only one of the many whose effluvium was attacking the nostrils of the electorate. That the Radicals were losing ground was shown by the fact that every Border State had turned its government over to the Democrats. In 1872 Congress **North-** sought to reduce the number of martyrs by including one **ern Radi-** hundred sixty thousand persons in an amnesty, thus sweep- **cals lose** ing the record clear of all but about five hundred names. **ground** Other culprits were restored to grace gradually, until in the enthusiasm of the Spanish-American War (1898) all those remaining were pardoned by a general amnesty. In 1874 the Democrats captured the House of Representatives and confronted the Radicals with the early prospect of losing the South.

Political developments in the North and Border States were naturally encouraging to Southern Democrats and strengthened their battle for home rule. As early as 1869 the Radicals in the Southern states had begun to develop splits between factions, usually of Carpetbaggers **Southern** on one side and Scalawags on the other. The Democrats **Democratic** shrewdly threw their support to the milder faction and in **victories** this way managed to regain virtual political control of Tennessee in 1869 and of Virginia and North Carolina in the elections of 1870; in the same year Georgia was captured by the Democrats, the first state to go Democratic without Radical strings. Elections from 1873 to 1875 brought Alabama, Arkansas, Texas, and Mississippi under Democratic control. Louisiana, Florida, and South Carolina were now the only states left in the Republican column, and they only by the grace of Federal troops.

It is perhaps significant that the incoming Democratic governments made few investigations of corruption and impeached no one on that ground. Undoubtedly the considerable numbers of yeomen and poor whites who had supported the Republican Party in its successful effort to marshal the Negro vote was antagonized and alarmed by the very success of that effort and now revived their old race antipathies. Negroes themselves had begun to get disgusted with Radical exploitation, and numbers of them turned voluntarily to the Democrats. Those who did not found that with growing Conservative power employers were firing Negro Radicals and boycotting Radical business houses. The poll tax, long a prerequisite of the right to vote, had seldom been collected from Negroes by the Radicals, but now it was collected or even made cumulative.

The use of force was not abandoned, but after the failure of the Ku Klux Klan more subtle methods were adopted. Democratic rifle clubs sprang up throughout the South. Their members sometimes wore red shirts as distinguishing signs, and without breaking any laws managed to make the threat of their power felt. Os- **The Missis-** tentatiously armed members took control of Republican po- **sippi Plan** litical meetings and turned them into Democratic rallies, they "persuaded" Negroes to vote Democratic or stay away from the polls, and they stood solidly about the polling places and failed to hear Negro requests to be let through. Now and then a gun went off, quite by accident. If a club was broken up by the authorities, it soon reappeared as a dancing class or a missionary society and went on with its program. This method, best known as the Mississippi Plan, became the basis of white power in the South for a decade and attained complete success after the withdrawal of Federal troops.

Complete restoration of home rule to the South came as a result of the presidential campaign of 1876. The Democrats, confident at last of success, nominated a New York corporation lawyer, Samuel J. Tilden.

Samuel J. Tilden (1814–86) An old-time Barnburner and Free-Soiler, he yet was a Copperhead during the Civil War. Though himself blooded in a railroad scandal, Tilden became a reformer and successfully prosecuted the notorious Tweed Ring of Tammany Hall and as governor went on to further reform triumphs. The Democrats, conscious that their

The New York Historical Society

"The Tammany Tiger Loose," by Thomas Nast in 1871, was most influential in breaking up the Tweed Ring.

skirts were unstained, adopted a platform that read like an indictment for crime, and with the motto "Turn the rascals out" and under the chairmanship of the able Abram S. Hewitt of New York made their campaign a crusade.

To oppose him the Radical spoilsmen needed a war hero who was untainted by corruption; on one count or the other, this proviso excluded most of the Radical leaders, who, as one delegate gibed, had been "in-

Rutherford B. Hayes (1822–93) vincible in peace and invisible in war." Finally the convention selected the regular but relatively little-known Rutherford B. Hayes of Ohio. He had served in the army, in Congress, and as governor of his state, and though a Radical was not an extremist or a spoilsman. William A. Wheeler of New York was on the ticket with him. Hayes was a man of character and independence and as a candidate advocated civil-service reform and Southern home rule, but he was handicapped by his party's record and by its dependence upon waving the bloody shirt.

When the returns of the election came in it was evident that Tilden had a majority over Hayes of about 250,000 (about 4,284,000 against 4,033,000). Of the 185 electoral votes necessary to elect, Tilden had 184 against Hayes's 165. South Carolina (7) and Florida (4) sent in rival Republican and Democratic electoral slates. In Louisiana (8) two rival Radical factions, one supported by **Electoral stalemate** the Democrats, each claimed control of the state. One vote in Oregon was disputed. If one of these disputed votes were awarded to Tilden, he would be elected; if all twenty were awarded to Hayes, he would have exactly enough.

The four months that followed are among the most interesting in American history, for the Radicals were in effect making their last stand. "Visiting statesmen" of both parties appeared in the disputed states and exhorted their opposite numbers to hold fast. As it became **Four** evident to the Democrats that the Radicals were willing to **months** use force or fraud to win, public sentiment was aroused. **of inde-** Many professed to see the possibility of rival governments **cision** in Washington (a fate which the Radicals had imposed on several Southern states), and there was at the least a serious danger of the "Mexicanization" of American elections. There was even loose talk of civil war. Tilden, however, was not ready to go that far. Nor was he willing to accept the offer of the Louisiana reviewing board to throw their votes his way—for cash.

Actually the election in all three states had been noted for intimidation, and the returns made by both parties were tissues of fraud out of which even the best-intentioned umpires could have brought no just decision. The Oregon dispute arose from the fact that a Republican elector was constitutionally disqualified because he **Republican** was a Federal office holder, a postmaster; the Democratic **dilemma** governor accordingly sent in the official return, which threw out the Republican and put in his place the elector who had received the next highest vote, a Democrat. The Republicans were in a dilemma: if they refused to "go behind the returns" but accepted the official records, they would gain nineteen Southern votes but lose the one from Oregon—and give the election to Tilden. Their claim to the Oregon vote was fairly good, but if they insisted upon claiming it they opened up the Southern votes to minute investigation—and gave the election to Tilden. They could, of course, reject the disputed votes, but that would still elect Tilden, and the same thing would happen if they threw the election into the Democratic House of Representatives.

Finally, late in January 1877, Congress established an Electoral Commission of fifteen members: five from the Senate, five from the House, and five from the Supreme Court. It was supposed that there would be seven Republicans and seven Democrats with a neutral justice holding the balance; but at this juncture the proposed Justice was elected to the Senate, and a Republican Justice took his place. The result was that the commission awarded every disputed vote to Hayes, eight to seven. But before the Democrats agreed to cast no further obstacles (such as a filibuster) in the way, there was held a series of conferences between Southern leaders and Hayes's representatives in which the latter agreed to withdraw support from the three remaining Radical Southern governments by removing Federal troops. Hayes was thereupon declared elected, 185 to 184, on 2 March 1877. Radical rule had already fallen "of its own weight" in Florida, and with the withdrawal of troops in April Democratic régimes took over South Carolina and Louisiana.

Hayes elected

Whether or not it was a spoken agreement, the outcome of the election of 1876 was a compromise between the industrial capitalists of the North and the leaders of the South. The capitalists gave to the South a free hand over the Negroes in return for Southern local and Congressional encouragement and protection of their investments. The Southerners, moreover, received a bonus when they were permitted to count the total Negro population in reckoning their Congressional representation, even though Section 2 of the Fourteenth Amendment was shattered by refusing the franchise to Negroes.

"Peace of 1877"

The Radical politicians won the election but lost their long war to entrench their feet permanently in the gravy trough. Their industrialist backers were now sure of the South and of the great Middle West and saw no reason for keeping these Northern nemeses of the South in power, especially since their Southern extensions were such bad financial risks. The Radical either faded from public life or turned to other interests, while Southern "brigadier generals" surged through the doors of Congress. Technically the old quarrel was forgotten, but occasionally on provocation the old hatred ran through the Congressional delegations like a chilling wind. Nevertheless, the Southerners kept their bargain in so far as their unreconstructed constituencies would permit and in so doing swung the bulk of Democratic strength to the support of industry.

Perhaps, after all, the Radical program, however brutal, had not been without its astuteness. The South and the West of 1865 would probably have downed the Northeast in a great neo-Jacksonian crusade. Now the South, worn down by war and reconstruction and bought off by economic sweets and the offer of control of its Negroes, was ready to betray the Lost Cause to get peace. Hamilton had at last triumphed over Jefferson, New England over Virginia! Or had they? We shall see.

4 *The Civil War and Reconstruction in the Stream of American History*

The Civil War has been called the ridgepole and the watershed of American history. Examination of most of the currents of national life shows that they led, whether or not inevitably, to that grand climax. It is no less clear that the great problems and movements of American life in the last three generations have flowed out of the dislocations of that war and its aftermath or taken **General significance** form because of the decisions made then. On the other hand the drama of war and reconstruction has tended to obscure the fact that the same social, economic, and political reforms might have been made by peaceful methods without bringing desolation and sectional hatreds in their train. Such thoughts as these must have been in the mind of the poet when he sang his requiem over the grave of the fallen Confederacy.

> Bury the bygone South.
> Bury the minstrel with the honey-mouth,
> Bury the broadsword virtues of the clan,
> Bury the unmachined, the planters' pride,
> The courtesy and the bitter arrogance,
> The pistol-hearted horsemen who could ride
> Like jolly centaurs under the hot stars.
> Bury the whip, bury the branding-bars,
> Bury the unjust thing
> That some tamed into mercy, being wise,
> But could not starve the tiger from its eyes
> Or make it feed where beasts of mercy feed.
> Bury the fiddle-music and the dance,
> The sick magnolias of the false romance
> And all the chivalry that went to seed
> Before its ripening.

From *John Brown's Body* in *Selected Works of Stephen Vincent Benét*, published by Rinehart & Company, Inc. Copyright, 1927, 1928, by Stephen Vincent Benét.

Whatever might have been, the fact remains that there was a Civil War and there was a reconstruction period, and both were instruments of change. Most obvious result was the amendment by arms of the Constitution to the effect that the Federal government was **The Union now supreme** supreme—that a state could not secede. True, the doctrine of state rights remained an issue and still does, but there is no longer a question of where ultimate sovereignty resides. At the same time the question of allegiance was settled. The old state pride lingers here and there, but in the long run the first allegiance of the American is to the nation, not to the state.

Inalienably linked to the prosecution of the war was the tightening of Federal controls. This was inevitable, for it was the task of the Federal government to organize the nation for war and to suppress treason-

Centrali-
zation of
govern-
ment

able movements within the states; in short, to assume war powers which if they had been strictly enforced would have turned us into a dictatorship after the pattern of the Roman Republic in time of crisis. As we have seen, there was much muttering among those who valued state rights whatever the cost to the nation and feared that the very purchasing power wielded by the Federal government might lead to a control over men's souls. We have seen that the Radicals failed to break down state rights by reducing the states to super-counties and that they failed to consolidate all Federal functions in an all-powerful Congress. Nevertheless, the American nation was never to be the same again. A social, economic, and political revolution had whirled it into the stream of change, and the current was too strong for a return. Strangely enough, the South, which had seceded to avoid this revolution, found itself as a result of secession subject to the very controls which it had dreaded—and, to its own amazement, clamoring for more. War, like politics, makes strange bedfellows.

The democratic process was inevitably affected by these changes in Constitutional meaning, if not actually forms. Northerners had fought, probably above all else, to vindicate democracy and to open up to evolu-

Failure to
restore
democratic
balance

tion the road which the South had blocked. The basic tragedy of reconstruction lay in the fact that scarcely had one road block been removed than another was substituted. Industry and finance had forged in the fires of sectional strife a control that, while far from absolute, was strong enough to throw the balance of democratic conflict off center again. Thenceforth political and economic protest on the part of farmers and workers was directed toward re-establishing the balance with industry.

This imbalance requires further comment. We have noted repeatedly in this study that there were in American life contradictory urges to equality and to dominance. The first was expressed in the democratic

The free-
ing of
science

concept of a balance of social conflict, the second in the intense individualism which resulted in the rise of the industrial capitalist. The North was during the Civil War essentially an alliance of these two principles against the Southern principle of an Athenian democracy based on slavery. A slave régime always discourages practical technologists because labor is socially unacceptable.

Whether the North was consciously fighting the battle for free science may be open to argument, but it certainly was fighting for the free application of technology—and technology flows from science. The Northern victory cleared the way for the study of science and its technological application in ways which made profits for the entrepreneur, raised the American standard of living for the masses, and in time made the United States the economic giant whose world impact has shaken the foundations of civilization. And it will reinforce them against the uncertain future.

The acceleration of technology and industry by the temporary demands of the war itself may not have been so great as is sometimes supposed, for the country was undergoing tremendous economic expansion in the 1850's. Nevertheless, it is probably fair to credit the war with some of the growth in mining, heavy industry, and agriculture. Progress in mechanization was marked during **Economic effects** the war years in agriculture, in shoe making, and in the manufacturing of ready-made clothing. The petroleum industry got on its feet during the war years. Tariff protection became a permanent policy, and the income tax and the internal revenue on luxuries were added to the American scene. During reconstruction Northern industrial capital made its entry into the South and won the battle to force the South to protect it. The economic policies which the Hamiltonians had long been advocating were now triumphant.

There was nothing for the South and the West to do but act as purveyors of food and raw materials and do what they could to raise themselves to industrial equality with the East. This was an ambitious program, but there was a good chance of its fulfillment. Now the bolder members of the planter class and ambitious yeomen and poor whites found tremendous opportunities in commerce and industry and turned their energies to remak- **Industrialization of South and West** ing the South. The West had made good progress toward industrialization before the war, and it is possible to follow its further progress in the ensuing decades by the swelling wave of political and economic conservatism which moved westward and finally crossed the Mississippi in the 1890's.

The Civil War confirmed the American antipathy toward Europe and reinforced the conviction that European governments were inveterate enemies of democracy. Even the South bore a grudge against the European nations for their failure to render more positive and decisive aid. Europe's vague uneasiness at the growth of the western **Effect on Europe** democratic republic was turned to alarm lest with its overweening power and prestige it upset the uneasy political and economic balances of the world—as, of course, it eventually did. On the other hand, the strength of American Federalism was an encouragement to German federation, and the victory of American nationalism and democracy gave a fillip to the parallel movements in Europe. The triumph of the Southern slave states would have spelled disaster for the democratic movement on the European continent and might seriously have retarded it in Great Britain.

The Civil War brought the end of slavery, but the end of the period of adjustment did not bring complete freedom and equality to the Negro. The peculiar status of second-class citizenship held by the American

The race problem

Negro, especially in the South but also in great areas of the North, had its origin in precisely the same fears which had done so much to bring on the Civil War. The war and reconstruction settled certain political, Constitutional, and economic problems, but it did not change the Southern mind about the inferiority of the Negro. For two generations the South remained unshakable on this point, and such concessions as have been made recently have been reluctant. At the close of the Civil War few Negroes were able to compete economically with their white neighbors, so presently they settled into a condition that bore some resemblances to serfdom and some to peonage. Socially they made a few advances, but they were still the bottom layer of society. Civil liberties were drastically curtailed, but more by social than by legal pressures. Curiously enough, the franchise was not technically withdrawn until after 1890, though of course it was limited in its practical use.

Nevertheless, the Negro made remarkable progress, both by his own efforts and by the aid of some of his white neighbors. The present-age Negro naturally views his second-class status with impatience and resent-

The Negro and the democratic process

ment, yet it is worth pointing out that he is advancing in exactly the same way in which successive classes of whites have risen. The democratic process has never envisioned the award of democratic privileges to any class which has not earned it by showing an earnest and determined intention to measure up to standards of courage and self-restraint perhaps even higher than is required of those who have already arrived.

Closely related to the race problem is the phenomenon of the Solid South. We have seen how Southern nationalism was growing in the antebellum generation, basing itself on white supremacy, agrarianism, and

The Solid South

singularities of climate, products, and institutions. The war nipped Southern nationalism in the bud, but reconstruction accentuated the South's basic sectionalism until it pervaded every aspect of Southern life and psychology. Outside of the race problem, and that was basic, it is possible that the springs of Southern sectionalism would not have prevented the absorption of the South into the nation on much the same basis as, say, the Middle West. Reconstruction, however, welded the South together in a common psychological loyalty to the Lost Cause, and this was shored up by the growth of the Southern mythus, which in turn was made up of nostalgic memories of the time that never was.

Reconstruction, for a time at least, tended to reinforce the survivals of ante-bellum conservatism. It convinced Southerners that the Negro vote was dangerous and must be met by white solidarity. It extravagance reinforced the Jeffersonian prejudice that cheap government and good government were synonymous; moreover, the fact that there had been some progressive ideas connected with Carpetbag rule made them distrusted. The easy exploitation of the Negroes by the Carpetbag machines had convinced most Northern-

Reconstruction reinforces conservatism

THE "STRONG" GOVERNMENT 1869–1877   THE "WEAK" GOVERNMENT 1877–1881

New York Public Library

"Reconstruction" under Federal troops as contrasted with the period immediately after troop withdrawal from the South as pictured in *Puck* in 1880

ers that the Negroes were not ready for self-rule and made them sympathetic to the restoration of Southern conservatism.

The existence of the Solid South has, besides our industrialization, been the most vital factor in our history since the Civil War. It is difficult to think of any American problem, foreign or domestic, which has not been affected by the Solid South. True, the South has not ruled the nation in the same sense in which it perhaps did before the Civil War, but its nuisance value has been tremendous. There was for a long time an agreement that the North could name the Democratic presidential nominee subject to Southern veto. As the solid core of the Democratic Party, the South appoints committee

Political effect

chairmen in Congress and has strongly influenced the policies of the party when in opposition and administered them when in power. When the Democratic Party has failed to obey, the South has not hesitated to ally with the Republican Party in Congress to get its will, or at least to thwart the Northern wing. The result is that the Dixiecrats of the Solid South, while they may not always be able to rule their party, are in a strategic position to threaten it with ruin. This situation has been particularly evident whenever the problem of equal economic or political rights for Negroes has come before Congress.

The Southern alliance with capital has made it a considerable obstruction to the rise of labor, for capital has been able to take refuge in the South, where labor has historically been cheaper and more docile. On **Economic effect** the other hand, the South has prevented the full development of the American standard of living because it has been an economic sore spot and has not been able to buy its share of its own products. Of a piece with this is the Southern championship of state rights, for within this refuge economic concentration has found such free expression that it would scandalize the Founding Fathers of the Confederacy.

Southern conservatism fought against the evolutionary change of society and for this reason long pledged itself to the type of Christian orthodoxy which bases itself on a presumed knowledge of absolute truth and admits no room for adjustment. The effect on the Ameri- **Social effect** can religious picture has been marked. No less obvious have been the social effects. Southern Congressmen are ordinarily aligned with the opponents of social legislation, even though Prohibition, the most drastic example of social legislation, was largely the gift of the South. Southern Congressmen certainly have a point when they attribute this opposition to fear of the centralization of political power, but it would be more convincing if they showed a more practical fear of economic centralization.

It is at first glance a contradiction that the South should have been more hospitable to imperialism than the North, but this vanishes when one remembers Southern cotton exports, the Bourbon bargain with Northern capital, the heritage of military glamor from the Lost Cause, and the concept that the white man is destined to rule. Southerners have shaped many facets of American public and imperialist policy because they have always been numerous in the army, the navy, and in public administration. These men (with the enthusiastic aid of many Northern colleagues, let it be added) have introduced or strengthened race discrimination in the colonies, in the army and navy, and in the civil service. These things (along with the second-class citizenship of the Negro), whether or not justified by circumstances, have provided handles for the charge that American democracy is a hypocritical disguise for fascism.

Not the least of the psychological results of the Civil War was the creation of the Lincoln Legend,* for over much of the country, at least, the kindly, homespun Lincoln receives more worship than the aloof patricians Washington and Lee. It has been said that Lincoln **The** died at exactly the right moment to insure immortality, yet **Lincoln** the legend began even during its subject's life; the tragic **Legend** circumstances of Lincoln's death only caused it to mushroom more amazingly. The revulsion against the rather common portrayal of the ugly gorilla from the prairies of Illinois started the poets and other creators of folk myths upon their task, and even sneering *Punch* regretted its failure to recognize "this rail-splitter, as true-born king of men." In life Lincoln was the most complex of men, and along with his better attributes he was skeptical, brutally realistic, acute to the extent of foxiness, coarse to the extent of vulgarity, and indifferent to cultural nuances.

Now the other side came uppermost. He was the patient, tolerant, innately dignified, melancholy, yet whimsical man of the people, agonizing over the travail of his country like a modern Christ. "New birth of our new soil, the first American," he became the typification of American opportunity, the model boy who was bound to **The ideal-** rise. Born in a log cabin, he studied before a flickering fire, **ized hero** learned to write with charcoal on a slab, and walked miles to return a few cents overcharge. He split rails; lifted out hogs when they were stuck in the mire; never drank or swore; told off-color stories, but only as parables; and spent his years in the White House snatching widows' only sons from the firing squad. He loved and lost Ann Rutledge, and thereafter heard her voice in every sighing wind.

Lincoln has been portrayed as a Westerner, a Southerner, and even as a Yankee. The fact is that he is all things to all Americans. He has concentrated in himself the heroic essence of the war years as Emancipator and savior of the Union, and finally has become the exemplar of the best in democracy, the proof that the democratic **The symbol** process can stand the test. And yet there is truth in Basler's statement that "Lincoln is not so much the type of democracy as he is an abstract embodiment of the ancient and cosmic forces of genius and wisdom." His rise to fame was heralded by nature's portents; he wrestled in prayer; he foresaw the future in dreams; he walked with the spirits of the dead. Nancy Hanks became a wilderness madonna, and the log cabin in Kentucky a Bethlehem. His putative father was a carpenter, but his real

* See particularly Roy P. Basler, *The Lincoln Legend* (1935); and Lloyd Lewis, *Myths after Lincoln* (1929).

father was a Virginia aristocrat! He could save others but could not save himself—and died on Good Friday! And Judas Booth varied the legend only by shooting himself!

Each year we repeat in February the ritualistic observance of the birthday of the folk hero. No visit to Washington is complete without a pilgrimage to the classic marble structure over whose portal we read: "In this temple as in the hearts of the people for whom he saved the Union the memory of Abraham Lincoln is enshrined forever." There are his greatest speeches which the commoner reads with reverent, moving lips while a shaft of light falls upon the white statue of the pitying hero. Nothing can be clearer than that here Americans find the sanctuary and embodiment of their dreams of the sacredness of human dignity and of the American mission to point the way to a better life for the world. When in the hungry winter of 1931 the American people were beaten down by forces which seemed about to shatter the American dream and Lincoln's successor in the White House recommended a diet of faith, a minister lifted his prayer to the folk hero: "Oh, Lincoln. Arise! Stand forth that we may gaze upon thy furrowed face. Look upon us; pity us; speak to us as thou didst at Gettysburg; stretch forth thy hand; point the way of destiny and duty that America may be thy living monument down to the end of time. Oh, Lincoln, come down from thy summit of bronze and march."*

Events in the present century have thrown some doubt on the familiar claim that we learn from the study of history. Actually the origins, progress, and aftermath of the Civil War should have taught us two lessons which would have been invaluable in our generation. The

Lessons not learned

first is that democracy is not automatic, that it depends for its successful operation upon our courage and restraint. The two extremes can work havoc, if they refuse to compromise, by grinding away the moderate center as though between upper and nether millstones. It is open to question whether we can stay the march of evolution, but there is no doubt about our ability to increase confusion and to breed oppression and injustice.

The second lesson concerns our policies toward defeated nations. War destroys, but its aftermath can be even more fruitful of dislocations and hatreds. A defeated people does not automatically yield the principle (good or bad) for which it fought. Economic and territorial concessions may be enforced, but the deeper psychological values are almost impregnable. The belief that democracy can be implanted in short order in Germany or Japan is a delusion; the best that can be hoped for is the first step in the right direction. Many years will pass, perhaps many generations, before democracy becomes second nature in those countries. Let the doubter look at France, in the eighteenth century the exemplar of

---

* John Wesley Hill in "Lincoln and True Progress," *The National Republic* (February 1931), 18: 42.

absolutism, and now, after a dozen or so of revolutions, wistful of democracy but still under the shadow of the man on horseback. Only time can work a change, and this truth we should have known from the history of our own sectional controversy.

BIBLIOGRAPHICAL NOTE

Presidential Reconstruction

JOHNSON: See the biographies by Robert W. Winston and L. P. Stryker; Clifton R. Hall, *Andrew Johnson, Military Governor of Tennessee* (1916); and George F. Milton, *The Age of Hate: Andrew Johnson and the Radicals* (1930).

FOURTEENTH AMENDMENT: The literature is overwhelming, but for a starter see Horace E. Flack, *The Adoption of the Fourteenth Amendment* (1908); and Benjamin B. Kendrick, ed., *The Journal of the Joint Committee of Fifteen on Reconstruction* (1914).

FREEDMEN'S BUREAU: See Paul S. Peirce, *The Freedmen's Bureau* (1904).

ELECTION OF 1866: For an incomparable account see Howard K. Beale, *The Critical Year* (1930). For its sequel see Charles H. Coleman, *The Election of 1868* (1933).

RECONSTRUCTION: There is no complete and well-balanced history of reconstruction. Randall is concerned chiefly with Congressional actions. E. Merton Coulter, *The South During Reconstruction* (1949) is principally about the South and is defensive of the white point of view. W. E. B. DuBois, *Black Reconstruction* (1935) shows flashes of remarkable insight, but it is impregnated with Marxism, utopianism, and uncritical panegyrics of the Negroes and attacks upon whites. The Southern states are covered by monographic studies by the students and followers of William A. Dunning, but for the most part they are narrowly pro-white; see the bibliography in Randall. Admirable and impartial exceptions are James W. Garner, *Reconstruction in Mississippi* (1901); and Francis B. Simkins and Robert H. Woody, *South Carolina During Reconstruction* (1932). For sources see Walter L. Fleming, *Documentary History of Reconstruction* (2 v., 1906) and numerous Congressional reports—which use with caution. On the KKK see John C. Lester and Daniel L. Wilson, *Ku Klux Klan* (1884, 1905); and Stanley F. Horn, *Invisible Empire* (1939).

ELECTION OF 1872: See Claude M. Fuess, *Carl Schurz: Reformer* (1932); Schurz, *Reminiscences* (3 v., 1907–08); and Earle D. Ross, *The Liberal Republican Movement* (1919). On the Crédit Mobilier see Nelson Trottman, *History of the Union Pacific* (1923).

ELECTION OF 1876: See Paul L. Haworth, *The Hayes-Tilden Disputed Elections of 1876* (1906); C. R. Williams, ed., *Diary and Letters of Rutherford Birchard Hayes* (2 v., 1914); Hamilton J. Eckenrode and P. W. Wight, *Rutherford B. Hayes, Statesman of Reunion* (1930); Allan Nevins, *Abram S. Hewitt* (1935); and Alexander C. Flick, *Samuel Jones Tilden* (1939). On the "Peace of 1877" see C. Vann Woodward, *Reunion and Reaction: The Compromise of 1877 and the End of Reconstruction* (1951).

GENERAL BIBLIOGRAPHY

There is no up-to-date complete bibliography of United States history. The following selected titles are drawn from the more useful general references and collections of source and secondary materials.

GUIDES AND BIBLIOGRAPHIES

Guide to Historical Literature (Edited by a board headed by William H. Allison. New York, Macmillan, 1931). Pays little attention to U.S. history, but has great value in other fields.

Writings on American History (Grace G. Griffin, ed., from 1906 to 1940 was an annual publication issued by the American Historical Association. Renewed 1948. Hiatus remaining 1941 to 1947).

Guide to the Diplomatic History of the U.S., 1775–1921 (Samuel F. Bemis and Grace G. Griffin, eds., 1935. Government Printing Office).

Bibliography of the History of Agriculture in the U.S. (Everett E. Edwards, ed., 1930. U.S. Department of Agriculture).

Guide to the Study of American History (Edward Channing, Albert B. Hart, and Frederick J. Turner, eds. Boston, Ginn, 1912). Still useful as a guide to old collections of sources.

ATLASES

Atlas of American History (J. T. Adams and R. V. Coleman, eds. New York, Scribner's, 1943). Detail maps in black and white illustrating events; so far as it goes, the most useful atlas yet published.

Atlas of the Historical Geography of the U.S. (C. O. Paullin, ed. Washington, Carnegie Institution of Washington and American Geographical Society, 1932). Colored historical and analytical maps, with explanatory text; the most ambitious atlas yet attempted.

Harper's Atlas of American History (D. R. Fox, ed. New York, Harper, 1920). Reprint of maps and charts from the *American Nation* series. Useful but far from adequate.

Historical Atlas of the U.S. (C. L. and E. S. H. Lord, eds. New York, Holt, 1944). Largely analytical maps.

Shepherd's Historical Atlas (W. R. Shepherd, ed. New York, Holt, 1929). Chiefly world history, but useful attention to the U.S.

Goode's School Atlas (Chicago, Rand McNally, 1946). Useful for physical coverage.

DICTIONARIES, ENCYCLOPEDIAS, *etc.*

Biographical Dictionary of the American Congress, 1774–1949 (Washington, Government Printing Office, 1950).

Dictionary of American History (J. T. Adams and R. V. Coleman, eds., 6 v., 2d ed. rev. New York, Scribner's, 1942). Would that the DAH were three times as long!

Dictionary of American Biography (Allen Johnson and Dumas Malone, eds., 22 v., plus supplements. New York, Scribner's, 1928–37). The DAB is indispensable.

Dictionary of National Biography (21 v., 5 supplements. Oxford reprint, 1938). The DNB is useful for information on the many Britishers whose careers touched American history.

Encyclopedia of the Social Sciences (E. R. A. Seligman and Alvin Johnson, eds., 15 v. New York, Macmillan, 1930–35).

Encyclopedia of World History (W. L. Langer, ed. Boston, Houghton Mifflin, 1947). Successor to Ploetz's *Epitome.* Essential.

Historical Statistics of the U.S., 1789–1945 (Washington, U.S. Bureau of the Census, 1949).

Webster's Biographical Dictionary (Springfield, Mass., G. & C. Merriam, 1943). Useful for quick reference.

PERIODICALS

Nearly every state and region, and many interests and institutions, publish periodicals devoted to history. Usually they are quarterlies and are useful vehicles for news of what is going on among professional historians, for book reviews, and for the results of research projects too brief to warrant separate publication. Many of them publish also annual reports or proceedings devoted to the results of research. In addition many universities publish or have published with more or less regularity "Studies" devoted to history and the social sciences. Only a few of the periodicals can be listed here.

American Academy of Political and Social Science. *Annals,* 1890–
The American Historical Review, 1895–
American Journal of Sociology, 1895–
American Political Science Review, 1906–
Journal of Southern History, 1935–
Mississippi Valley Historical Review, 1914–
New England Quarterly, 1928–
Pacific Historical Review, 1932–
Political Science Quarterly, 1886–
Social Forces, 1922–
Sociology and Social Research, 1916–
Survey, 1897–

CO-OPERATIVE HISTORIES

These include the sets devoted to all or part of the field of U.S. history when each volume or part is written by a person presumably expert in the field.

The American Nation: A History (A. B. Hart, ed., 28 v., New York, Harper, 1904–18). Some volumes still of outstanding value. Harper promises an entirely new series within a few years.

Bemis, S. F., ed., *American Secretaries of State and Their Diplomacy* (10 v., New York, Knopf, 1927–29). The standard work on the subject.

Chronicles of America (Allen Johnson, ed., 54 v., New Haven, Yale Univ. Press, 1919–51). With certain exceptions, especially the later volumes, useful chiefly to beginners or the lazy.

Economic History of the U.S. (9 v., New York, Rinehart, 1945–   ).

History of American Life (A. M. Schlesinger, Sr. and D. R. Fox, eds., 13 v., New York, Macmillan, 1929–48). Fair accomplishment of a task impossible to be done well. Very useful bibliographies.

History of the South (W. H. Stephenson and E. M. Coulter, eds., 10 v., Baton Rouge, La., Louisiana State Univ. Press, 1947–   ). Now being issued; will supplant the old *The South in the Building of the Nation* (13 v., 1909–13).

Winsor, Justin, ed., *Narrative and Critical History of America* (8 v., Boston, Houghton Mifflin, 1884–89). This massive co-operative work summarizes the history of the Americas to about 1850 with particular attention to bibliography; richly illustrated with reproductions of original maps and drawings.

MONUMENTAL WORKS

Written by an individual and covering an extensive phase of American history.

Andrews, Charles M., *The Colonial Period of American History* (4 v., New Haven, Yale Univ. Press, 1934–38). Decidedly Tory in outlook, but most valuable of summaries of the colonial period.

Bancroft, George, *History of the U.S.* (6 v., rev. 1883–85, New York, Appleton-Century-Crofts). The pioneer work on the period down to 1789; how God's hand molded the American nation. Written in the turgid style of the period, it is heavy going for moderns.

Bancroft, Hubert Howe, *Works* (39 v., San Francisco, A. L. Bancroft, 1882–90). Extensive histories of the Pacific West. Still standard.

Beer, George L., *Commercial Policy of England toward the American Colonies* (New York, Columbia College, 1893); *Origins of the British Colonial System, 1578–1660* (New York, Macmillan, 1908); *Old Colonial System, 1660–1754* (2 v., New York, Macmillan, 1912); *British Colonial Policy, 1754–65* (New York, Peter Smith, 1933, Reprint). The first named summarizes the others. These are the classic works on the subject.

Channing, Edward, *History of the U.S.* (7 v., New York, Macmillan, 1927–32). Outstanding effort by an individual in spite of certain disproportions, and written largely from source materials. Extends to 1865.

Doyle, John A., *English Colonies in America* (5 v., New York, Holt, 1882–1907). Written by an Englishman; especially valuable for political history.

Fiske, John, *Historical Works* (11 v., Boston, Houghton Mifflin, 1888–1902). These deal with colonial history. Though there is no originality and there are many errors in fact and fairness, these volumes remain among the most readable and popular on American colonial history.

Gipson, Lawrence Henry, *The British Empire Before the American Revolution* (7 v., Caldwell, Idaho, Caxton Printers, 1936–49).

McMaster, John B., *History of the People of the U.S. from the Revolution to the Civil War* (8 v., New York, Appleton-Century-Crofts, 1883–1913); *A History of the People of the U.S. During Lincoln's Administration* (New York, Appleton-Century-Crofts, 1927). The first attempt to write the history of the *people* rather than the politicians. McMaster pioneered also in the use of newspapers as sources, so his work partakes of a newspaper's topical interest and too much of its superficiality.

Oberholtzer, Ellis P., *History of the U.S. Since the Civil War* (5 v., New York, Macmillan, 1917–37).

Osgood, Herbert L., *American Colonies in the Seventeenth Century* (3 v., New York, Macmillan, 1904–07); *American Colonies in the Eighteenth Century* (4 v., New York, Columbia Univ. Press, 1924–25). Concerned with legal, institutional, and administrative development of the British continental colonies; avoids the larger imperial problems, for which one should turn to Beer and Gipson.

Parkman, Francis, *Works* (12 v., Boston, Little, Brown, 1902–03). The subject is the French in North America. A one-volume abridgment by John Tebbel, *The Battle for North America* (1948), enhances Parkman by omitting footnotes and much of the background detail.

Rhodes, James F., *History of the U.S. from the Compromise of 1850 to the End of the Roosevelt Administration* (9 v., New York, Macmillan, 1928).

Schouler, James, *History of the U.S.A. Under the Constitution* (6 v., New York, Dodd, Mead, 1894–1904).

Von Holst, Hermann E., *Constitutional and Political History of the U.S.* (8 v., New York, Callaghan, 1900).

PICTORIAL AND CARTOON HISTORIES

Adams, James T., *Album of American History* (5 v., New York, Scribner's, 1944–49).

Bonte, George W., *America Marches Past* (New York, Appleton-Century-Crofts, 1936).

Butterfield, Roger, *The American Past* (New York, Simon and Schuster, 1947).

Collins, Alan C., *The Story of America in Pictures* (New York, Doubleday, 1935).

Davidson, Marshall B., *Life in America* (2 v., Boston, Houghton Mifflin in association with the Metropolitan Museum of Art, 1951).

Gabriel, Ralph H., ed., *The Pageant of America* (15 v., New Haven, Yale Univ. Press, 1925–29). A fascinating pictorial record. The approach is by subjects.

Kouwenhoven, John A., *Adventures of America, 1857–1900: A Pictorial Record from Harper's Weekly* (New York, Harper, 1938).

Lorant, Stefan, *The Presidency: A Pictorial History of Presidential Elections from Washington to Truman* (New York, Macmillan, 1951).

Murrell, William, *A History of American Graphic Humor* (2 v., New York, Whitney Museum of American Art, 1938).

Nevins, Allan and Weitenkampf, Frank, *A Century of Political Cartoons* (New York, Scribner's, 1944).

GENERAL COLLECTIONS OF DOCUMENTS, CRITICAL ESSAYS, AND ILLUSTRATIVE MATERIAL

Billington, Ray A., et al., eds., *The Making of American Democracy* (2 v., New York, Rinehart, 1950).

Chicago University, *The People Shall Judge* (2 v., Chicago, Univ. of Chicago Press, 1951).

Commager, Henry S., *Documents of American History* (4th ed., New York, Appleton-Century-Crofts, 1948). Well selected and soundly edited. Indispensable aid.

Earl Latham, et al., eds., *Problems in American Civilization* (Readings Selected by the Department of American Studies, Amherst College. 19 v., Boston, Heath, 1949–52).

Sheehan, Donald, *The Making of American History* (2 v., New York, Dryden, 1950).

Potter, David M. and Manning, Thomas G., *Select Problems in Historical Interpretation* (2 v., New York, Holt, 1949–50).

DOCUMENTS

This heading refers especially to collections of documents of official and semi-official nature. No attempt is made here to mention more than a few leading collections. It should be noted that every state has its collections of documents, records, and statutes.

American Archives [forming a documentary history of the North American Colonies] by Peter Force (9 v., 1837–53).

American State Papers (38 v., 1832–61). Carries legislative and executive papers up to 1838 in various categories. In 1817 issuance of *Public Documents* was begun.

Journals of the Continental Congress, 1774–89 (J. C. Fitzpatrick, R. R. Hill, W. C. Ford, and Gaillard Hunt, eds., 34 v., 1904–37).

Letters of Members of the Continental Congress (Edmund C. Burnett, ed., 8 v., 1921–36).

Territorial Papers of the U.S. (Clarence E. Carter, comp. and ed., 16 v., 1934–48. Still in process of publication).

U.S. Congress: Records first published as *Debates and Proceedings* (1789–1824) and often called *Annals of Congress;* succeeded by the *Register of Debates* (1824–37), *The Congressional Globe* (1833–73), and by the present *Congressional Record.*

U.S. Laws: *Statutes at Large of the U.S.* The first 8 volumes, issued in 1845–46, contain the acts, treaties, and executive proclamations to that date; most of the time since then the materials have been issued currently.

U.S. President: *Compilation of the Messages and Papers of the Presidents* (James D. Richardson, ed. Originally issued in 1897 in 10 v. Has been several times re-issued with continuations).

U.S. Supreme Court: *United States Reports* (1790 to present). Until 1874 decisions were cited by the name of the court reporter and the volume number. They were: Dallas, v. 1–4; Cranch, v. 5–13; Wheaton, v. 14–25; Peters, v. 26–41; Howard, v. 42–65; Black, v. 66–67; and Wallace, v. 68–90.

War of the Rebellion: A Compilation of the Official Record of the Union and Confederate Armies (130 v., 1880–1901). *Official Records of the Union and Confederate Navies* (30 v., 1894–1922).

CONTEMPORARY NARRATIVES AND COLLECTIONS

Hart, Albert B., *American History Told by Contemporaries* (5 v., New York, Macmillan, 1897–1929).

Jameson, J. Franklin, *Original Narratives of Early American History* (18 v., New York, Barnes and Noble, 1906–17).

Thwaites, Reuben G., ed., *Early Western Travels* (32 v., Cleveland, A. H. Clark, 1904–07). Incomparable collection and republication of travel accounts.

Thwaites, Reuben G., ed., *Jesuit Relations and Allied Documents: Travels and Explorations of the Jesuit Missionaries in New France, 1610, 1791* (73 v., Cleveland, Burrows Bros., 1896–1901). Condensation of the above is *The Indians of North America* (Edna Kenton, ed., 2 v., New York, Harcourt Brace, 1927).

INDEX OF AUTHORS

IN BIBLIOGRAPHICAL NOTES

Abbott, Edith, 586
Abel, Annie H., 529, 812
Abele, Rudolph von, 740
Abernethy, Thomas B., 208, 237
Adamic, Louis, 171
Adams, Abigail, 314
Adams, Brooks, 468, 469
Adams, Charles F., 314, 428, 468, 845
Adams, Charles F., Jr., 739
Adams, Ephraim D., 716, 845
Adams, Henry, 346, 370, 371, 427, 428
Adams, Herbert B., 279
Adams, James T., 47, 143, 144, 314, 345, 346
Adams, John Quincy, 370, 468
Adams, Randolph G., 208
Adams, William F., 611
Agar, Herbert, 370
Akagi, Roy K., 172
Albion, Robert G., 206, 501, 681
Alden, John R., 237, 238, 278
Alexander, De Alva S., 313, 346, 468
Allan, Herbert S., 238
Allen, Gardner W., 277, 347, 370, 428
Allen, Hervey, 611
Allen, Merritt P., 740
Alvord, Clarence W., 237
Ambler, Charles H., 237, 277, 812
Anburey, Thomas, 278
Anderson, Troyer S., 278
Andrews, Charles M., 142, 144, 206
Angle, Paul M., 773
Anthony, Irwin, 142
Anthony, Katherine, 345
Archibald, Warren S., 144
Arnold, I. N., 238
Asbury, Herbert, 279, 554
Auchampaugh, Philip G., 812

Bagley, William C., 681
Baird, Charles W., 171
Bakeless, John, 529, 554
Baker, G. E., 740
Baldwin, Alice M., 208, 279
Baldwin, Joseph G., 555
Baldwin, Leland D., 105, 346, 554
Ball, Timothy H., 428
Bancroft, Frederic, 681, 682, 740, 845

Barker, Eugene C., 716
Barker, Howard F., 171
Barnes, Gilbert H., 681, 682
Barnes, Harry E., 636
Barnes, Viola F., 144
Bartram, John, 172
Basler, Roy P., 931
Bassett, John S., 314, 346, 428, 468
Basye, Arthur H., 206
Bathe, Dorothy, 585
Bathe, Greville, 585
Baxter, James P., 144, 890
Beale, Howard K., 812, 933
Beard, Charles A., 313, 346, 347
Beazley, Charles R., 78
Becker, Carl, 237–238
Beer, George L., 142, 206
Beers, Henry A., 314
Beirne, Francis F., 427
Belcher, Wyatt W., 397
Bemis, Samuel F., 279, 346, 347, 400, 428, 468
Benét, Stephen Vincent, 925
Bennett, William B., 585
Benns, F. Lee, 501
Benton, Thomas Hart, 468
Best, Mary A., 238
Bestor, Arthur E., 637
Beveridge, Albert J., 346, 347, 468, 773
Bidwell, Percy W., 586
Bieber, Ralph P., 206
Biggar, Henry P., 80
Bill, Alfred H., 278, 716, 812
Billington, R. A., 554, 637, 773
Bining, Arthur C., 206
Binkley, William C., 716
Bishop, Cortlandt F., 207
Bishop, Morris, 80
Bittinger, Lucy F., 171
Black Hawk, 529
Blair, Walter, 554
Blegen, Theodore C., 611
Boas, Louise, 170–171
Boas, Ralph, 170–171
Bolton, Charles K., 143, 171, 277
Bolton, Herbert E., 207, 716
Bond, Beverley W., 169, 347, 400, 554
Bonsal, Stephen, 278

Bourne, E. G., 79
Bowen, Catherine Drinker, 238
Bowers, Claude G., 345, 346, 370, 468
Bowman, Allen, 277
Boyd, Julian P., 238, 345
Boyd, Thomas, 554, 585
Boykin, Edward, 345
Bradford, Gamaliel, 636, 867 890
Bradlee, F. B. C., 890
Bradley, Arthur G., 279
Bradley, Harold W., 502
Bradstreet, Howard, 144
Brady, Mathew B., 890
Brailsford, Mabel R., 144
Branch, Edward D., 593
Brant, Irving, 313, 345
Brebner, John B., 80, 501
Breed, Noel J., 529
Bridenbaugh, Carl, 170
Bridenbaugh, Jessica, 170
Britton, Wiley, 812
Brokunier, Samuel H., 144
Brooks, Philip C., 428
Brooks, Van Wyck, 610, 611, 628, 637
Brown, Everett S., 370
Brown, Ralph H., 47
Brown, Weldon A., 279
Browne, William H., 143
Bruce, Philip A., 143
Bruce, William C., 371
Bryce, James, 637
Buck, Elizabeth, 554
Buck, Solon, 554
Buel, C. C., 839
Buley, R. Carlyle, 554
Bullock, Charles J., 206, 277
Burlingame, Roger, 585
Burnaby, Andrew, 172
Burnett, Edmund C., 277
Burns, James J., 206
Burrage, Henry S., 80, 143
Burt, Alfred L., 371, 427
Burton, Katherine, 637
Byrd, William, 170, 171–172

Cahill, Holger, 502
Calder, Isabel M., 144
Calhoun, Arthur W., 170
Calhoun, John C., 468
Callahan, James M., 716
Callcott, Wilfrid H., 716
Callender, Clarence C., 313
Canby, Henry S., 611
Carman, Harry J., 844
Carpenter, Jesse T., 682, 734, 740
Carrier, Lyman, 169
Carter, Clarence E., 400
Cartwright, Peter, 554
Cash, Wilbur J., 637, 680, 682
Castañeda, Carlos E., 716
Catterall, Ralph C. H., 469
Caughey, John W., 400
Chamberlain, Nathan H., 170
Channing, Edward, 370
Chapin, Henry, 555
Chapman, Charles E., 716
Charnwood, Lord, 773
Chatterton, Edward K., 142, 143
Chesnut, Mary Boykin, 838
Chevigny, Hector, 529
Cheyney, Edward P., 105
Chidsey, Donald B., 80, 142
Chinard, Gilbert, 279, 314, 345
Chittenden, Hiram M., 528
Chitwood, Oliver P., 716

Christy, David, 845
Clark, Arthur H., 501
Clark, B. C., 468
Clark, Dora M., 237
Clark, Thomas D., 554
Clark, Victor S., 206
Clarke, Mary P., 206
Clauder, Anna C., 346
Cleaves, Freeman, 400
Cleland, Robert G., 529
Cleveland, Catherine C., 554
Coad, Oral S., 610
Coates, Robert M., 555
Cochran, Thomas C., 586
Codman, John R., 637
Cole, Arthur C., 682, 844
Cole, Arthur H., 585, 586
Cole, G. D. H., 637
Coleman, Charles H., 933
Commager, Henry S., 347, 468, 610, 611, 889
Commons, John R., 586
Connelley, William E., 812
Conrad, Bryan, 890
Conway, Moncure D., 238
Corbett, Doris S., 554
Corbett, Julian S., 79, 207
Corey, Albert B., 501
Corwin, Edwin S., 279
Coulson, Thomas, 585
Coulter, E. Merton, 682, 812, 844, 933
Cox, Isaac J., 400
Crallé, R. K., 468
Crane, Verner W., 207
Craven, Avery O., 237, 586, 740, 772, 791, 812
Craven, Wesley F., 143
Crenshaw, Ollinger, 811
Cresson, William P., 468
Crèvecœur, J. Hector St. John de, 171
Cross, Arthur L., 208
Cross, Whitney B., 637
Crouse, Nellis M., 80
Crow, Carl, 502
Cruikshank, Ernest A., 79
Cummings, Richard O., 501
Cunningham, Charles E., 314
Curti, Merle E., 170, 636, 637
Curtis, Edward E., 277–278
Cutler, Carl C., 501
Cutler, Manasseh, 370

Dalzell, George W., 845
Dana, Julian, 716
Dana, Richard H., 501
Davidson, Gordon C., 529
Davidson, Philip, 237
Davis, Andrew M., 206
Davis, Jefferson, 740, 890
Davis, Varina Howell, 740
Davis, William T., 143
De Koven, Mrs. Reginald, 277
DeLeon, T. C., 812
Demaree, Albert L., 586
Deming, Dorothy, 144
Dennett, Tyler, 501
Desmond, Humphrey J., 772
Deutsch, Albert, 636
De Voto, Bernard, 529, 637, 716
Dewitt, David M., 908
Dick, Everett, 555
Dickens, Charles, 555
Dickerson, Oliver M., 206
Dobrée, Bonamy, 144
Dodd, William E., 740
Doddridge, Joseph, 554
Donaldson, Thomas, 555

Donnan, Elizabeth, 171
Donovan, Herbert D. A., 739
Dorfman, Joseph, 585
Dorsey, Florence L., 585
Dowdey, Clifford, 844–845
Downes, Randolph C., 278–279, 400
Doyle, John A., 142
Driver, Carl S., 237
DuBois, W. E. B., 933
Du Bose, John W., 740
Duff, William A., 555
Duffus, R. L., 716
Dulles, Foster R., 501–502
Dumond, Dwight L., 681, 682, 811
Dunaway, Wayland F., 171
Dunbar, Seymour, 170, 585
Dunn, William E., 207
Dutton, Charles J., 428
Dyer, Brainerd, 716
Dyer, Gus W., 682

Earle, Alice Morse, 170
East, Robert A., 206
Eaton, Clement, 682
Eaton, Peggy, 469
Eckenrode, Hamilton J., 890, 933
Edler, Friedrich, 279
Edmundson, George, 79
Egerton, Hugh E., 207
Eggleston, George Cary, 879
Egleston, Melville, 172
Eisenschiml, Otto, 889
Ekirch, Arthur A., 610, 637
Elliott, Charles W., 716
Elliott, Walter, 622, 637
Ellis, George W., 144
Elsbree, Oliver W., 610
Ernst, Robert, 611
Ettinger, Amos A., 143, 740
Exquemelin, Alexandre, 79

Falconer, John I., 586
Farnam, Henry W., 586
Farrand, Livingston, 47
Farrand, Max, 313
Farrar, Victor J., 845
Fausset, Hugh, 611
Faust, Albert B., 171
Favour, Alpheus H., 529
Fäy, Bernard, 346
Ferguson, Russell J., 346
Fish, Carl R., 610
Fisher, Edgar J., 144
Fisher, Sydney G., 144, 170
Fite, Emerson D., 844
Fithian, Philip Vickers, 170
Fitzpatrick, John C., 277
Flack, Horace E., 933
Fleming, Walter L., 933
Fletcher, John G., 143
Flexner, James T., 585
Flick, Alexander C., 144, 279, 346, 933
Flint, Timothy, 554
Foner, Philip S., 345, 740
Forbes, Esther, 170
Ford, Henry J., 171, 314
Ford, Paul L., 170
Ford, Worthington C., 845
Foreman, Grant, 529
Fortescue, John W., 278
Fosdick, Lucien J., 171
Fox, Dixon Ryan, 346, 468, **610**
Fox, Early L., 681
Franklin, Benjamin, 170
Franklin, John H., 171

Fraser, Chelsea C., 585
Freeman, Douglas S., 207, 277, 876, 890
French, Allen, 238
Freyre, Gilberto, 79
Friedman, Leo M., 171
Frothingham, T. G., 277
Fry, William H., 144
Fuess, Claude M., 468, 502, 933
Fuller, George W., 715–716
Fuller, John D. P., 716
Fuller, J. F. C., 278, 890

Gabriel, Ralph H., 586, 601, 637, 890
Gammon, Samuel R., 469
Garber, Paul N., 772
Garner, James W., 933
Garrison, Winifred, 554
Gathorne-Hardy, Geoffrey, 79
Gay, Sydney H., 345
Ghent, William J., 529
Giddens, Paul H., 585
Gilbert, Edmund W., 528
Gilfillan, S. Colum, 585
Gipson, Lawrence H., 142, 206, 237
Glasgow, Maude, 171
Going, Charles B., 739
Goldman, E. F., 347
Goodman, W. H., 427
Goodykoontz, Colin B., 554
Gosling, William G., 80
Gosnell, Harpur A., 845, 890
Gottschalk, Louis R., 277
Grant, Elliott M., 610
Grant, U. S., 890
Grant, William L., 207
Gras, Norman S. B., 586
Gray, Lewis C., 586
Gray, Wood, 244
Grayson, Alexander, 278
Greeley, Horace, 844
Green, James A., 400
Greenbie, Sydney, 80
Greene, Evarts B., 206
Griffin, Charles C., 501
Griffis, William E., 739
Guttmacher, Manfred S., 237

Hacker, Louis M., 586, 681
Hafen, Le Roy R., 529
Hakluyt, Richard, 143
Halbert, Henry S., 428
Hall, C. C., 143
Hall, Clifton R., 933
Hamilton, Allen M., 314
Hamilton, Holman, 716, 740
Handlin, Oscar, 611
Hanna, Charles A., 171
Hannay, David, 142
Hansen, Marcus L., 171, 611
Harbison, Winfred A., 313, 681
Haring, Clarence H., 79
Harlow, Alvin F., 585
Harlow, Ralph V., 313
Harper, Lawrence A., 206
Harrington, Virginia D., 206
Hart, A. B., 740
Hart, B. H. Liddell, 890
Hart, James, 313
Haskins, Charles H., 400
Hatch, Louis C., 277
Hatcher, William B., 346
Hawk, Emory Q., 681
Haworth, Paul L., 277, 933
Hay, John M., 773
Haynes, George H., 313

Hazen, Charles D., 346
Headley, Joel T., 277
Heckewelder, John, 47
Helper, Hinton R., 682
Hemmerlein, Richard F., 845
Henderson, George F. R., 890
Hendrick, Burton J., 238, 844
Herndon, W. H., 773
Hesseltine, William B., 844, 845
Heyward, Du Bose, 812
Hibbard, Benjamin M., 548, 555
Hill, Helen D., 238
Hill, Jim Dan, 716, 890
Hill, John Wesley, 932
Hillquit, Morris, 637
Hinkhouse, Fred J., 237
Hirsh, Arthur H., 171
Hodge, Frederick W., 47, 528
Hohman, Elmo P., 501
Holdsworth, John T., 314
Hone, Philip, 468
Horn, Stanley F., 933
Hornblow, Arthur, 610
Hosmer, J. K., 143
Hotblack, Kate, 207
Howard, Leon, 611
Howe, Henry F., 143
Hubbart, Henry C., 811
Hudleston, Francis J., 278
Hughson, Shirley C., 143
Hulbert, Archer B., 585
Humphrey, Edward F., 279
Hunt, Cornelius E., 845
Hunt, Gaillard, 345, 468
Hunt, George T., 80
Hunter, Louis C., 585
Hunter, R. M. T., 468
Hutchinson, William T., 586

Innis, Harold A., 80
Irving, Washington, 529
Irwin, Ray W., 370
Isely, Jeter A., 844

Jacobs, James R., 400
James, James Alton, 279
James, Marquis, 428, 468, 716
James, William M., 277
Jameson, John F., 79, 144, 277, 279
Jane, Lionel C., 79
Jenkins, William S., 681, 682
Jennings, Walter W., 371
Jensen, Merrill, 279, 313
Jerome, Chauncey, 585
Jervey, Theodore D., 682
Johnson, Allen, 772
Johnson, Amandus, 144
Johnson, Edgar A. J., 169
Johnson, Emory R., 501
Johnson, Gerald W., 371, 467, 679, 718
Johnson, Robert C., 716
Johnson, R. U., 839
Johnson, Thomas H., 144
Johnston, Joseph E., 890
Johnston, Robert M., 812
Jones, Clarence F., 47
Jones, J. B., 812
Jordan, Donaldson, 845
Jordan, Philip D., 585
Judson, Isabella F., 585
Julian, George W., 682

Kaempffert, Waldemar, 584–585
Kalm, Pehr, 172
Keir, Robert M., 585

Kelley, Alfred H., 681
Kellogg, Louise P., 400, 529
Kelly, Alfred H., 313
Kemmerer, Donald L., 206
Kendall, Charles W., 428
Kendrick, Benjamin B., 933
Kenton, Edna, 47
Kilroe, Edwin P., 238
Kimball, Gertrude S., 170
Kimball, Marie, 345
King, George A., 347
Kirk, Russell, 371
Kirkpatrick, Frederick A., 79
Kittredge, George L., 171
Koch, Adrienne, 345
Kohlmeier, Albert L., 812
Konkle, Burton A., 314
Kraus, Michael, 170
Krout, John A., 610

Labaree, Leonard W., 170, 206
Landers, Howard L., 278
Lanning, John T., 207
Larkin, Oliver W., 610
Latourette, Kenneth S., 501, 610
Lauber, Almon W., 207
Lauer, Paul E., 469
Laut, Agnes, 585, 716
Leary, Lewis, 346
Leech, Margaret, 812, 844
Lester, John C., 933
Lester, William S., 237
Lewis, Charles L., 278, 370
Lewis, George E., 237
Lewis, Lloyd, 890
Lincoln, Charles H., 238
Link, Eugene P., 346
Lipsky, George A., 468
Livermore, Shaw, 237
Livermore, Thomas L., 845, 854
Livermore, W. R., 889
Lockwood, Francis C., 716
Lockwood, George, 637
Lodge, Henry C., 313, 314
Long, John C., 207, 237
Lonn, Ella, 844, 845
Lossing, Benson J., 278, 427
Lowell, Edward J., 278
Lucas, Charles P., 427
Lundin, Leonard, 278
Luthin, Reinhard H., 811, 844
Lynch, Denis T., 468
Lynch, William O., 467
Lyon, Elijah W., 400
Lytle, Andrew N., 890

McCain, James R., 143
McCaleb, Walter F., 400
McCarthy, Charles, 469
McClellan, George B., 890
McClellan, William S., 206
McCormac, Eugene I., 207, 716
McCormick, Fowler, 586
McDougall, Marion G., 772
McElroy, Robert, 740
McGrane, Reginald C., 469, 585
McGregor, James C., 812
McIlwain, Charles H., 208
MacInnes, Charles M., 143
McIntyre, J. W., 468
McKinley, Albert E., 207
McLaughlin, James F., 347
MacLean, John P., 171
Mabee, Carleton, 585
Macdonough, Rodney, 428

Mackenzie, Alexander S., 370
Maclay, Edgar S., 277, 427
Maclay, William, 313
Macleod, J. H., 370
Macleod, William C., 47, 528
Madariaga, Salvador de, 79, 501
Madison, Dolly, 345
Mahan, Alfred T., 277, 427
Malin, James C., 773
Malone, Dumas, 345, 682
Markham, Edwin, 825
Marshall, Helen E., 636
Martin, Edgar W., 586
Masefield, John, 79
Masters, Edgar Lee, 773
Mather, Frank J., 610
Matthews, Thomas E., 237
Matthiessen, Francis O., 611
Maurice, Frederick B., 890
Mayo, Bernard, 468
Means, Phillip A., 79
Meigs, William M., 468
Meine, Franklin J., 554
Melcher, Marguerite F., 637
Melville, Herman, 501
Mereness, Newton D., 143, 172
Merriam, Charles E., 208
Merriman, Roger B., 79
Mesick, Jane L., 610
Miller, Alfred Jacob, 529
Miller, James M., 554
Miller, John A., 585
Miller, John C., 207–208, 238, 278, 347
Miller, Perry, 144, 171
Miller, William, 586
Milton, George F., 772, 933
Mims, Stewart L., 79
Minnigerode, Meade, 346
Mittelberger, Gottlieb, 172
Monaghan, Frank, 279, 314
Montgomery, Richard G., 716
Moore, Albert B., 845
Morais, Herbert M., 610
Morgan, Joy E., 636
Morgan, Lewis H., 47
Morgan, Theodore, 502
Morison, Samuel E., 78, 79, 143, 144, 314, 428, 501
Morize, André, 610
Morris, John E., 144
Morris, Lloyd R., 611
Morse, Anson E., 314
Morse, John T., 313, 314, 468
Morton, Arthur S., 529
Mowry, Arthur M., 469
Mudge, Eugene T., 346
Mullett, Charles F., 208
Mumby, Frank A., 237
Mumford, Lewis, 611
Mussey, June B., 554
Myers, John M., 716
Myers, William S., 890

Namier, Lewis B., 237
Neely, Wayne C., 586
Nettels, Curtis P., 142, 206
Nevins, Allan, 279, 467–468, 610, 681, 716, 739, 772, 773, 845, 909, 933
Newman, Ralph, 889
Newton, Arthur P., 79
Nichols, Roy F., 740, 772, 812
Nickerson, Hoffman, 278
Nicolay, John, 773
Nissenson, Samuel G., 144
Nitobe, Inazo, 502

Nordhoff, Charles, 637
Nunn, George E., 79
Nute, Grace L., 529
Nye, Russell B., 611, 681, 772

Oberholtzer, Ellis P., 277, 844
O'Brien, Harriet E., 637
O'Connor, Richard, 890
Ogden, Adele, 529
Oliver, Frederick S., 314
Olson, J. E., 79
Opdyke, Frank A., 428
Osgood, Herbert L., 142
Oskison, John M., 400
Osterweis, Rollin G., 682
Overdyke, W. Darrell, 772
Owsley, Frank L., 844, 845

Padover, Saul, 345
Paine, Ralph D., 144, 501
Palmer, John M., 277
Paltsits, Victor H., 347
Pares, Richard, 207
Pargellis, Stanley M., 194, 207
Parker, Robert A., 637
Parkes, Henry B., 171
Parkman, Francis, 79, 80, 207, 237
Parks, George B., 142
Parks, Joseph H., 811
Parrington, Vernon L., 170, 314, 636
Parton, James, 170, 279, 346, 428
Patterson, Samuel W., 278
Patton, James W., 812, 844
Paullin, Charles O., 277, 370, 501
Peckham, Howard H., 237
Peirce, Paul S., 933
Penniman, J. H., 277
Perkins, Dexter, 501, 740
Perkins, Howard C., 812
Pettengill, R. W., 278
Phelps, Mary M., 884
Phillips, James D., 144, 170, 501
Phillips, M. O., 47
Phillips, Ulrich B., 170, 171, 681, 740
Phillips, Wilbur H., 636
Pickering, Octavius, 371
Pierson, George W., 610
Pinkerton, Robert E., 529
Pitman, Frank W., 206
Plooij, Daniel, 143
Plumer, William, 370
Poage, George R., 716
Polk, James K., 716
Pollock, Queena, 469
Pope, J. B., 681
Porter, Kenneth W., 529
Porter, Kirk H., 469
Potter, David M., 812
Pound, Arthur, 144
Powys, Llewelyn, 80
Pratt, Edwin J., 845
Pratt, Fletcher, 889
Pratt, Julius W., 427
Prestage, Edgar, 78
Proper, E. Emberson, 171
Purcell, Richard J., 314

Quillin, Frank U., 681
Quinn, David B., 80

Radin, Paul, 47
Raesly, Ellis L., 144
Ragatz, Lowell J., 206
Ramirez, José Fernando, 716
Ramsdell, Charles W., 791, 844

Randall, James G., 646, 681, 773, 844, 845, 933
Randolph, Sarah N., 345
Raper, Charles L., 143
Ravenal, Harriott H. R., 143, 170
Ray, P. Orman, 772
Riedesel, Baroness, 278
Rippy, J. Fred, 716
Ritter, H. L., 277
Robbins, Roy M., 555
Robertson, William S., 501
Robinson, William A., 346
Robinson, William M., 890
Roeder, Ralph, 845
Roosevelt, Theodore, 278, 427
Root, Winfred T., 207
Ropes, John C., 889
Rosenberry, Lois K. M., 172, 396
Rose-Troup, Frances, 143
Ross, Earle D., 844, 933
Ross, John F., 611
Ross, Mary, 207
Rothert, Otto A., 555
Rourke, Constance, 637
Rowe, Kenneth W., 586
Rowland, Eron, 428
Rowland, Kate Mason, 238
Rowlandson, Mary W., 144
Rozwenc, Edwin C., 812
Rugg, Winifred K., 144
Russel, Robert R., 740, 772
Russell, Elmer B., 206
Russell, Nelson V., 400

Sakolski, Aaron M., 555
Salley, A. S., 143
Salmon, Edward D., 79
Salt, Henry S., 610
Sandburg, Carl, 773
Sanders, Jennings B., 313
Sass, Herbert R., 812
Savelle, Max, 142, 170
Schachner, Nathan, 346
Scharf, John T., 170, 890
Schlesinger, Arthur M., Jr., 468, 469, 637
Schlesinger, Arthur M., Sr., 208
Schmitz, Joseph W., 716
Schneider, Herbert W., 144
Schoolcraft, Henry R., 47
Schouler, James, 314
Schultz, Harold S., 740
Schurz, Carl, 468, 933
Schuyler, Robert L., 313
Schwab, John C., 844
Scott, William R., 142
Scroggs, William O., 740
Scrugham, Mary, 812
Sears, Louis M., 371, 716
Seitz, Don, 844, 890
Sellers, Charles C., 238
Sellers, Leila, 206
Semple, Ellen C., 47
Shannon, Fred A., 845
Shepherd, William R., 144
Sherer, J. A. B., 585
Sherman, William T., 890
Shippee, Lester B., 501, 845
Shryock, Richard H., 740
Shuckers, J. W., 740
Shurtleff, Harold, 169
Siebert, William H., 772
Simkins, Francis B., 844, 933
Simms, Henry H., 346, 740
Simpson, Albert F., 682
Sly, John F., 144

Smith, Abbott E., 169, 345
Smith, Arthur D. H., 529
Smith, Edward C., 812
Smith, Joseph R., 47, 585
Smith, Justin H., 238, 703, 716
Smith, Margaret B., 370
Smith, Theodore C., 739
Smith, Walter B., 586
Smith, William E., 772
Smith, William R., 143
Smyth, Albert H., 170
Soley, James R., 890
Soulsby, Hugh G., 501
Spain, August O., 468
Spector, M. Marion, 206
Spiller, Robert E., 611
Squire, Belle, 636
Stacey, C. P., 501
Stampp, Kenneth M., 812
Stanwood, Edward, 347, 779
Starkey, Marion L., 529
Steiner, Bernard C., 143, 636
Stenberg, Richard R., 739
Stephenson, George M., 171, 611
Stephenson, N. W., 773
Stern, Phillip V. D., 888
Stevens, Frank E., 529
Stevens, Wayne E., 400
Stowe, Lyman Beecher, 682
Styron, Arthur, 468
Sumner, William G., 277, 314, 428
Swiggett, Howard, 278
Swisher, Carl B., 468, 773
Sydnor, Charles S., 680, 682

Tanner, Edwin P., 144
Taussig, Charles W., 206
Tawney, Richard H., 20
Taylor, George R., 206, 554, 585
Tebbel, John, 80
Tewksbury, Donald G., 636
Thomas, Alfred B., 716
Thomas, Benjamin P., 682, 845
Thomas, Charles M., 346
Thomason, John W., 890
Thompson, E. K., 586
Thompson, Robert L., 585
Thompson, Slason, 585
Thwaites, Reuben G., 47, 528, 529
Tocqueville, Alexis de, 597, 610, 633
Tolman, Frank L., 636
Treat, Payson J., 502, 555
Trent, William P., 682
Trevelyan, George, 278
Trottman, Nelson, 933
Tryon, Rolla M., 206
Tuckerman, Bayard, 144
Turnbull, Archibald D., 585
Turner, Frederick Jackson, 469, 554
Tuttle, Charles W., 144
Tyler, Alice F., 636
Tyler, Moses Coit, 207

Upham, C. W., 371
Upton, Emery, 845

Van Alstyne, Richard W., 740
Van Deusen, Glyndon G., 468, 740
Van Deusen, John G., 681
Vandiveer, Clarence A., 80, 528
Van Doren, Carl, 170, 277, 278, 279, 313
Van Doren, Mark, 610–611
Van Tyne, Claude H., 207, 278, 279
Vestal, Stanley, 529
Villard, Oswald G., 773

Wade, John D., 682
Wagner, Donald O., 636
Wagner, H. R., 529
Waldeman, Milton, 142
Wallace, Willard M., 278
Walsh, Correa M., 314
Walworth, Arthur C., 502
Wandell, S. H., 346
Warden, Robert B., 740
Ware, Caroline F., 585
Warren, Charles, 313
Washburne, George A., 206
Webster, Daniel, 468
Weeden, William B., 144
Weik, J. W., 773
Weinberg, Albert K., 347, 715
Welles, Gideon, 844
Wellington, Raynor G., 446
Werner, Morris R., 346, 637
Wertenbaker, Thomas J., 142, 143, 170, 278, 646
Wesley, Charles H., 586
West, Richard S., 844
Wheeler, Lynde P., 585
Whitaker, Arthur P., 400, 501
White, Laura A., 740
White, Leonard D., 313, 370
White, Melvin J., 740
Whitney, Janet, 681
Whitton, Frederick E., 278
Wiest, Edward, 586
Wight, P. W., 933
Wildes, Harry E., 278, 400

Wiley, Bell I., 844, 889
Wilkeson, Frank, 879
Williams, C. R., 933
Williams, Frederick W., 502
Williams, George W., 845
Williams, Kenneth P., 889–890
Williams, Mary W., 740
Williams, Samuel C., 400
Williams, Thomas H., 844
Williamson, Chilton, 313
Williamson, James A., 79
Willison, George F., 143
Wilson, Daniel L., 933
Wiltse, Charles M., 345, 468, 682
Winston, Robert W., 933
Winthrop, Robert C., 143
Wissler, Clark, 47
Wittke, Carl, 171, 610, 611
Wood, William, 890
Woodburn, James A., 844
Woodford, Frank B., 739
Woodward, C. Vann, 933
Woodward, William E., 890
Woody, Robert H., 933
Woody, Thomas G., 636
Wright, John E., 554
Wright, Louis B., 143, 370
Wright, Richardson L., 170, 636
Wrong, George M., 80, 238

Zeisberger, David, 47
Zimmerman, James F., 371
Zucker, A. E., 611

INDEX OF SUBJECTS

Abolitionists, suffer for their principles, 660–661; fight the Gag Rule, 662–663; oppose Mexican War, 706

Abolition movement, Lundy forms societies, 657; started by Tappan brothers, 658; splits into three wings, 662; effects crisis in Kansas, 753–757, 762

Adams, Charles F. (1807–86), nominated for vice-presidency, 722; as minister to England, 827, 828; in settlement of *Alabama* claims, 834; revolts against "Grantism," 918

Adams, Henry (1838–1918), quoted on nationalism, 423, 424

Adams, John (1735–1826), defends soldiers in Boston Massacre, 221–222; leader in independence movement, 224; attends First Continental Congress, 227; peace commissioner at Paris, 265–266; elected Vice-President, 300; biography, 304–305; political philosophy of, 305; wins second vice-presidency, 328; quoted on Democratic Societies, 330; elected President, 336; actions in XYZ Affair, 337–338; thwarts Hamilton's dream of expansion, 338; splits with Hamilton, 342; nominated for presidency, 342–343

Adams, John Quincy (1767–1848), peace delegate (1814), 417–418; in Florida problem, 425; as a dominant national figure, 430; biography, 431; presidential condidate, 438; elected President, 439; his greatness and failure, 440; and Tariff of Abominations, 448; in formulation of Monroe Doctrine, 476ff.; in Anglo-American struggle for West Indian trade, 481; fights for establishment of Smithsonian Institution, 592; fights Gag Rule, 663

Adams, Samuel (1722–1803), a leader in independence movement, 224; attends First Continental Congress, 227

Adams-Onís Treaty (1819), 425–426

Admiralty Courts, enforce Navigation Acts, 175; established by England in colonies, 220

Adventures of Captain Bonneville (Irving), fans Oregon fever, 687

Africa, ventures of Henry the Navigator in, 48

Agassiz, Louis (1807–73), naturalist, 592

Age of Reason, The (Paine), 234

Agrarianism, and American Physiocrats, 21

Agricultural Revolution, at home and abroad, 582ff.

Agriculture, *see* Farming

Airplane, role in geographical perspective, 23–24

Alabama, admitted as state, 393; growth in Great Migration (1815), 396; removes Creek Indians, 525; secedes from Union, 783; readmitted to Union, 908

Alabama, Confederate cruiser, 828; settlement of claims of, 833–834

Alabama Platform, demands protection of slavery in Mexican Cession, 721, 732

Alamán, Lucas (1792–1853), explains Mexico's fear of U.S., 685–686

Alamance River, defeat of Regulators at, 185

Alamo, Mexican victory at, 696

Alaska, Russian exploitation of, 514, 516; purchase of, 834

Albany, N.Y., site of early trading post, 135

Albany Plan of Union (Franklin), 199–200

Albany Regency, Van Buren's group, 432

Albemarle, *see* North Carolina

Albemarle, Earl of (1608–70), 117

Alcott, Bronson (1799–1888), transcendentalist, 599; founds Fruitlands, 625

Aleuts, in fur trade, 516

Alexander VI, Pope, sets Demarcation Line, 533

Alexandria, Va., in colonial days, 153; in War of 1812, 414

Alexandria, Russell seizes intended Confederate raider, 829

Algeria, in Barbary Wars, 352–353

Algonquin Indians, 41

Alien and Sedition Acts (1798), pushed through, 339

Alien Friends Act (1798), passed, 339

Allen, Ethan (1738–89), at Ticonderoga, 232

Allen's Farm, Civil War battle at, 863

Alvarado, Juan Bautista (1809–82), attempts California revolt from Mexico, 691

Amana Society, German pietist colony, 624

America, influence on Europe, 5–6; riches of, 24; geographical influences on, 24–38; discovery, 50

American Anti-Slavery Society, formed for abolition, 658; changes to evangelism, 661; taken over by Garrison, 663

American Ass'n for the Advancement of Science, founded, 592

American Bible Society, organized, 589

American Board of Commissioners for Foreign Missions, formed, 589

945

American Colonization Society, attempts to solve Negro problem, 657
American Fur Company, 517–519
American Home Missionary Society, 589
American Journal of Science and Arts, 592
American mission, a sense of developed in national character, 635–636; doctrine of Manifest Destiny, 683ff.; disunion a threat to, 807
American Notes (Dickens), criticizes America, 596
American Party (Know-Nothing), 620
American Peace Society, in 19th century, 619
American Philosophical Society, formed, 154
American Physiocracy, a form of agrarian laissez faire, 321; as basis of policies of Hamilton and Jefferson, 366ff.; as applied by Taylor to plantation system, 667–668
American Revolution, causes of, 200–205; psychological reasons for, 205; events and conditions leading up to, 209–236; phases of, 239; nature of, 239–251; fighting tactics in, 240–241; military leaders in, 242; division of American sentiment during, 245; finances of, 245–246; as part of world conflict, 251; military and diplomatic conflicts in, 251–269; American strategy in, 251–252; in the Old West, 253; British plan in 1776, 255; British plan in 1777, 256; in the South, 261–265; peace negotiations and terms, 267–268; social aspects of, 269–277
American System, Clay proposes his, 439
Ames, Fisher (1758–1808), as member of Essex Junto, 308; his view of Federalist mission, 320
Ames, Oakes (1804–73), and Crédit Mobilier scandal, 920
Amiens, Treaty of (1802), 356
Amundsen, Roald (1872–1928), explorer, 72
Anahuac, Tex., in Texas Revolution, 694
Anderson, Robert J. (1805–71), in action at Fort Sumter, 784; in crisis at Sumter, 790–791
Andersonville Prison, conditions in, 843
André, John, British spy, 261
Andros, Sir Edmund, appointed governor of Dominion of New England, 133; puts N.Y. under rule of Nicholson, 138
Anesthetics, come into use, 591
Anglican Church, theology of, 87–88; established church of Southern colonies, 120
Anglo-Dutch Wars, loosen Dutch hold on colonies, 174
Animism, Indian belief in, 44
Annapolis, Md., settled, 117; in colonial days, 153; site of convention for new Constitution, 290
Annexation Manifesto (1849), of Canadian merchants fails, 483–484
Anthony, Susan B. (1820–1906), 618, 619
Antietam, Civil War battle at, 868
Anti-Masonic Party, origin of, 457
Anti-Nebraska fusion, 750
"Antique Republicans," activities of, 668
Antirent Agitation, in Hudson Valley, 444
Antislavery movements, societies organized in Philadelphia, 274; roots of, 656; Gag Rule imposed against, 662–663
Anza, Juan Bautista de, founds San Francisco (1776), 689
Appalachian Mts. as a barrier, 29–30
Appomattox Court House, Lee surrenders at, 887
Argall, Samuel, attacks French settlements, 73
Aristocracy, planter, 113; colonial, 151–152; legend of Southern, 645–646

Arizona, outline history of, 688–689
Arkansas, admitted to Union, 396; votes down secession (1861), 785; secedes, 794; readmitted to Union, 908
Armies, in Revolution, 241–242; in War of 1812, 409; in Mexican War, 706; in Civil War, 839–840
Armstrong, John (1758–1843), Secretary of War in War of 1812, 413; resigns, 415
Arnold, Benedict (1741–1801), attacks at Ticonderoga, 232; invades Canada in Revolution, 232; as military leader, 242; commands fleet at Lake Champlain, 250; wins victories at Stillwater, 257; treason by, 261
Aroostook War, in the Maine boundary dispute, 485
Art, lags in early 19th century, 590
Articles of Confederation, struggle over, 269–270; nature of, 270ff.; basic defect of, 270
Asbury, Francis (1745–1816), helps organize Methodist Church, 274
Ashburton, Lord, negotiates treaty with Webster, 485
Ashley, William H. (1778?–1838), in St. Louis fur trade, 519
Asia, knowledge of in Middle Ages, 11–12
Asiento, contract for supplying slaves, 67–68
Assemblies, struggle for democratic rights in colonial, 180ff.
Astor, John Jacob (1763–1848), fur enterprises of, 517, 518–519
Astoria, Fort, a center of American fur trade, 517–518
Astoria (Irving), fans Oregon fever, 687
Astrolabe, as navigational reliance, 55
Atkin, Edmund, Supt. of Indian Affairs in the South, 212
Atlanta, Ga., Sherman captures, 881
Atlantic cable, laying of the, 574
Atlantic Ocean, effect of winds and currents in navigating the, 25
Aurora, Ore., German pietist colony at, 624
Austerlitz, Napoleon wins battle at, 358
Austin, Stephen F. (1793–1836), leader in prerevolutionary Texas, 693, 694
Austria, defeated by Napoleon, 358
Authoritarianism, method of, 95; theory of, 103–105
Avalon Peninsula, failure of colony on, 116
Axacan, Spanish settlement, 64
Axes, improvement of lumbering, 560–561
Ayllón, Vásquez de (1475?–1526), founder of settlement in S.C., 56
Azores, discovery of, 48
Aztecs, decline of, 39

Babcock, Orville E. (1835–84), and scandals in Grant administration, 909–910
Bache, Benjamin (1769–98), editor, 324; attacks Fenno, 337
Bacon, Nathaniel (1647–76), defies Berkeley, 113–114; elected to House of Burgesses, 114; forces through "Bacon's Laws," 115; Bacon's Rebellion, 115
Bacon, Roger, geographic theories of, 12
Bacon, Sir Francis, quoted, 19
Balance of power, in Europe, 18
Balboa, Vasco Núñez de (1475–1517), discovers the "South Sea," 56
Balloons, used in Civil War, 849
Ballou, Adin (1803–90), founds Hopedale Community, 625
Baltimore, Baron, *see* Calvert, George
Baltimore, Md., in colonial days, 153; British fleet repulsed at in War of 1812, 415; in Oriental trade, 488; in canal era, 570, 571; Democratic Convention at (1860), 776

Baltimore and Ohio Railroad, pioneer line, 571; extended to Wheeling, 572; important in secession crisis, 795

Bancroft, George (1800–91), a transcendentalist, 599; champions democracy, 602; becomes Sec. of the Navy, 701

Bank of the U.S., proposed by Hamilton, 311; opposition to, 311; closes its doors, 403; Second chartered, 434–435; in Panic of 1819, 438; difficulties over recharter, 456–457; Jackson renews war on, 459 ff.

Banks, Nathaniel P. (1816–94), captures Port Hudson in Civil War, 857; in Valley Campaign, 863; reconstructs New Orleans, 873

Banks, Newfoundland, 25, 27, 70–71

Baptist Church, Southern split in, 677

Baranov, Alexander (1746–1819), rules Alaska, 516

Barbary States, wars with, 352, 353

Barbé-Marbois, François de (1745–1837), negotiates Louisiana Purchase, 387

Barlow, Joel (1754–1812), land speculator, 549

Barnard, Henry (1811–1900), educator, 613

Barnburners, faction of Democratic Party, 463; tenets of, 718; support Wilmot, 719; unite with Liberty Party, 722

Barré, Isaac (1726–1802), champions American cause, 227

Barron, James (1769–1851), in *Chesapeake* and *Leopard* clash, 359–360

Basques, whalers in North Am. waters, 69, 71

Bastidas, Rodrigo de, explorer, 53

Bates, Edward (1793–1869), in Lincoln's Cabinet, 816

Baton Rouge, La., settled, 391; "revolution" against Spain, 402

Bayard, James (1767–1815), American peace delegate (1814), 417–418

Beauregard, P. G. T. (1818–93), at Fort Sumter, 790–791; heads army near Manassas, 795; on why the South lost Civil War, 839

Beccaria, Cesare, prison reforms of known to colonies, 159; introduces reforms, 588

Becknell, William (1790?–?1832), pioneer trader in Santa Fe, 692

Beecher, Lyman (1775–1863), president of Lane Seminary, 659–660

Bell, John (1797–1869), heads Constitutional Union Party (1860), 777; presidential votes for, 780

Bemis Heights, N.Y., victories at in Revolution, 257

Benezet, Anthony (1713–84), in peace movement, 619; as antislavery writer, 657

Bennington, Vt., Revolutionary victory at, 257

Benton, Thomas Hart (1782–1858), in brawl with Jackson, 421; as a national figure, 431; biography, 432–433; advocates hard money, 460; proposes solution to Western land problem, 547–548; becomes enemy of Polk, 711; opposes compromise of Omnibus Bill, 727; in campaign of 1852, 730

Bering, Vitus (1680–1741), discovers Bering Strait, 57; explores, 514

Berkeley, G. C., in *Chesapeake* and *Leopard* clash, 360

Berkeley, John, a proprietor of New Jersey, 139

Berkeley, Sir William (1606–77), appointed governor of Virginia, 111; quoted on education, 112–113; controls House of Burgesses, 113; defied by Bacon, 114–115; death, 115

Bessemer process, in steel industry, 559

Best Friend, pioneer locomotive, 571

Bethel, Mo., German pietist colony at, 624

Bible, quoted in defense of slavery, 673

Biddle, James (1783–1848), attempts to open trade with Japan, 497

Biddle, Nicholas (1786–1844), and the B. U. S., 456–457; fights Jackson in his "war" on B. U. S., 459ff.

Bidlack Treaty (1848), gives U.S. transit rights in Panama, 737

Biglow Papers (Lowell), opposes Mexican War and extension of slavery, 662

Bill of Rights, agitated for by George Mason, 222; added to the Constitution, 298–299

Birney, James G. (1792–1857), abolitionist, 660

Bissell, George H. (1821–84), introduces uses for petroleum, 560

Black Ball Line, of packet ships, 491

Black Codes, following Civil War, 899

Blackfoot Indians, 41

Black Hawk War, leads to land purchase (Iowa), 398; as protest against removal of Indians (1832), 521, 522

Black Warrior, American ship seized by Spain over Cuban question, 737

Blackwell, Elizabeth (1821–1910), physician, 618

Blaine, James G. (1830–93), and Crédit Mobilier scandal, 920

Blair, Francis Preston (1791–1876), in Jackson's Kitchen Cabinet, 452; sets up *Globe* as Jackson supporter, 456

Blair, Francis P., Jr. (1821–75), leader of Conservatives in 37th Congress, 814; nominated for vice-presidency, 908

Blair, Montgomery (1813–83), in Lincoln's Cabinet, 816; leaves Cabinet, 886

Blanchard, Thomas (1788–1864), inventor, 562

Blockade, used in Civil War, 850

"Bloody Angle" at Spotsylvania, 879

Bloomer, Amelia (1818–94), reformer, 618

Blount, William (1749–1800), in Western land speculation, 381; in conspiracy of Old Southwest, 385, 386

Board of customs commissioners, established by England in colonies, 220

Board of Trade and Plantations, administers Navigation Acts, 175; disallows laws, 182

Bolívar, Simón (1783–1830), Latin-American liberator, 471; calls hemispheric conference, 478

Bolivia, declares independence, 473

Bonhomme Richard, defeats *Serapis,* 250

Booby traps, used in Civil War, 849

Boone, Daniel (1734–1820), marks out Wilderness Road, 216; Indian fighter, 541, 544

Boonesborough, founded, 216

Booth, Edwin (1833–93), actor, 590

Booth, John Wilkes (1838–65), assassinates Lincoln, 888; death, 891

Border-Ruffian-Jayhawker War, 803

Border States, geography, 30–31; description, 399–400; strategic role in secession movement, 794ff.; early consolidation in Civil War, 847

Bordley, John Beale (1727–1804), agricultural experimenter, 582

Boston, Mass., growth as a shipping town, 132; intellectual capital of colonies, 152; cleared of smugglers, 225–226; Intolerable Acts aimed especially at, 226; beginning of siege in Revolution, 230; after Bunker Hill, 232; in Oriental trade, 488, 489; loses foreign trade to New York, 489–490

Boston Massacre, 221–222

Boston News-Letter, 154

Boston Tea Party, 226

Boudinet, Elias (1803?–39), Cherokee translator, 524

Bouquet, Henry (1719–65), develops modern principles of warfare, 196; defeats Indians in Pontiac's War, 211–212

Bourbons, in South after Civil War, 915
Bowditch, Nathaniel (1773–1838), pioneer in oceanography, 492
Bowles, William Augustus, makes expeditions against Florida, 386
Brackenridge, Hugh Henry (1748–1816), democratic leader, 325; quoted on French Revolution, 330; his commencement ode, 587
Braddock, Edward, slain at Ft. Duquesne, 194
Bragg, Braxton (1817–76), Confederate commander, invades Kentucky, 855; assumes command of Army of Tennessee, 856; in battle of Murfreesboro, 856; in battle of Chickamauga, 857; at Chattanooga, 858
Brandywine Creek, Washington opposes Howe at, 257
Brazil, known to John II, 53; turbulent history of, 62–63; declares independence, 473
Brazito, battle at during Mexican War, 710
Breckinridge, John C. (1821–75), nominated for presidency (1860), 776; votes for, 780
Breed's Hill, Revolutionary battle at, 230–231
Bridger, Jim (1804–81), mountain man, 520
Bright, John, influence during Civil War, 830
Brisbane, Albert (1809–90), sponsors Fourierism, 626
Bristol, England, slave-traffic port, 163
British, see Englishmen
Brook, Lord, gains control of session of Council for New England, 128–129
Brook Farm, socialist experiment, 625
Brooks, Preston (1819–57), assault on Sumner, 758
Brown, John (1800–59), at Pottawatomie, 757; at Harpers Ferry, 771
Brown, Joseph E. (1821–94), leader in State Rights Party, 788
Browning, Orville H., (1806–81), leader of Conservatives in 37th Congress, 813–814
Brownson, Orestes (1803–76), transcendentalist, 599; is converted to Catholicism, 620–621
Bryant, William Cullen (1794–1878), 590
Buccaneers, in the Caribbean, 66–67
Buchanan, James (1791–1868), as Secretary of State, 701; in campaign of 1852, 730; coauthor of Ostend Manifesto, 737; policy in secession movement, 783–784
Buell, Don Carlos (1818–98), opposes Johnston at Bowling Green, 853; removed from command, 855; dismissed, 870
Buena Vista, battle of in Mexican War, 709–710
Buenos Aires, a center of revolt, 471
Bull Run, First Battle of, 796–797; Second Battle of, 864–865
Bulwer, Henry Lytton, signs treaty with Clayton over isthmian canal, 737–738
Bunker Hill, battle at, 230–231
Bureau of Indian Affairs, created, 510
Burgoyne, John, in Am. Revolution, 256–257
Burke, Edmund (1729–97), champions American cause, 227–228
Burlingame, Anson (1820–70), diplomatic work in China by, 496
Burlingame Treaty, China and U.S., 496
Burnet, David G. (1788–1870), elected president of Texas, 696; treaty with Santa Anna, 697
Burnside, Ambrose (1824–81), commands Army of the Potomac at Fredericksburg, 870–871
Burnt District, forms Anti-Masonic Party, 457; swept by religious movements, 626ff.
Burr, Aaron (1756–1836), biography, 323–324; elected Senator, 324; vice-presidential candidate, 336, 342; in campaign of 1800–01, 342ff.; plots secession of New York, 354; duel with Hamilton, 354–355; in conspiracy in Old Southwest, 389; champions environmentalism, 587, 588

Burritt, Elihu (1810–79), peace advocate, 619
B. U. S., see Bank of the U.S.
Butler, Benjamin Franklin (1818–93), characteristics of, 872; administers New Orleans, 872–873; removed from command by Grant, 877–878; seeks presidential nomination, 883–884; elected to House, 903; his role in Johnson's impeachment, 907
Buzzard's Bay, whaling center, 493

Cabinet, President's, recognized, 301
Cabot, George (1752–1823), leader of Essex Junto, 308
Cabot, John (1450–98), voyages of, 70
Cabot, Sebastian (1476?–1557), explorer, 72
Calhoun, John C. (1782–1850), a leader of War Hawks, 402, 403; in Florida problem, 425; as a dominant national figure, 430; biography, 433; as Secretary of War, 433–434; candidate for vice-presidency, 439; supports Jackson in 1828, 447–448; effect of Eaton case on, 453; proposes nullification in his Exposition (1828), 453; in political struggle with Jackson, 453–454; his Maysville Road Bill vetoed, 454ff.; resigns as Vice-President, 458; rejects Verplanck tariff bill, 459; proposes Indian state, 522; political theorist of localism, 668ff.; leaves and returns to Democratic Party, 671; rejects Natural Rights theory, 672–673; his responsibility for secession, 678; his political methods, 678–679; his greatness, 679; signs treaty with Texas, 699; opposes Mexican War, 706; introduces Platform of the South, 721; lays Southern Address before Congressional caucus, 722–723; opposes Comp. of 1850, 726
California, under Spain, 59; outline history of, 689; thrown into chaos by Mexican revolt from Spain, 691; Americans push into, 691–692; occupied during Mexican War, 710; conquest of, 710–711; declared independent republic, 711; and discovery of gold, 724
Calvert, Cecilius (1605–75), inherits Maryland, 117
Calvert, George (1580?–1632), granted Maryland as proprietary colony, 116
Calvert, Leonard (1606–47), in Maryland, 117
Calvin, John (1509–64), and capitalism, 19–20; as proponent of conservatism, 36
Calvinism, and conservatism, 36; and democracy, 88–89; in the Enlightenment, 156; in the Great Awakening, 156–157; in the Old West, 169; and politics, 306–307; its relation to utopianism, 628; exemplified in American sense of mission, 635–636
Cambridge Platform, accepted in Mass., 126
Camden, S.C., Gates defeated in Rev. at, 261
Canada, geography of, 30; added to British Empire, 179–180, 197–198; invaded by Am. troops in Revolution, 232; American desire to annex, 401–402; American strategy against in War of 1812, 410; importance in Anglo-American relations, 479–480; nationalist uprisings (1837), 482–483; wins independence, 483ff.; during American Civil War, 831–832; becomes Dominion (1867), 832–833
Canadian Northwest, joins Dominion, 832
Canadian Refugee Tract, set up, 276
Canals, importance of, 568–570; rate wars with railroads, 573; Erie, 397, 535, 568, 570
Cannibals All! (Fitzhugh), defends slavery, 673
Canning, George (1770–1827), refuses Erskine Agreement, 403; proposes Anglo-American alliance regarding Latin America, 475–476; and Monroe Doctrine, 477

Canthook, invented by Peavey, 561

Cape Breton, named for Breton fishermen, 69

Capitalism, defined, 19, 21; and Calvinism, 19–20; and Physiocrats, 21; finance, 21–22; industrial, 21; state, 22; and labor in the 1850's, 574ff.; merchant, in cotton triangle, 652–653; industrial replaces merchant, 653–654; in Civil War, 807

Carbondale and Homesdale R.R., pioneer line, 571

Carey, Henry (1793–1879), proposes national planning, 576

Carey, Mathew (1760–1839), lays basis for Clay's American System, 576

Caribbean, European struggle for the, 63–69; clash (1849) in the, 737

Carleton, Sir Guy (1724–1808), attempts to invade New York, 232; sends troops against Wayne at Fallen Timbers, 377–378

Carlotta (1840–1927), Emp. of Mex., 829, 830

Carolina, grant made by Charles II, 117–118; European struggle for colonial trade in, 190

Caroline, Am. ship seized by Canadians, 482

Carpetbaggers, in South after Civil War, 911–912, 915–916

Carroll, John (1735–1815), bishop of Baltimore, 274

Carson, Kit (1809–68), mountain man, 520

Carteret, Sir George (1610?–80), a Carolina proprietor, 118; made New Jersey proprietor, 139

Cartier, Jacques (1494?–after 1552), French explorer, 72

Cass, Lewis (1782–1866), becomes Secretary of War, 456; orders Creeks removed to West, 525; proposes popular sovereignty to solve slavery question, 721–722, 727; nominated for presidency, 722; in election campaign of 1852, 730

Catawba Indians, 41

Catherine II, forms League of Armed Neutrality, 259–260

Cattle raising, as stage in settlement, 165

Cavaliers, English, 90

Cayuga, one of the Five Nations, 75

Cayuse uprising, in Oregon country, 688

Cedar Creek, Civil War battle at, 881

Central America, wins freedom, 473

Cerro Gordo, falls to Scott in Mexican War, 712

Champlain, Samuel de (1567?–1635), manages French fur company, 73, 74

Chancellorsville, Civil War battle at, 873–874

Chandler, Zachariah (1813–79), Radical leader in 37th Congress, 814

Channing, William Ellery (1818–1901), transcendentalist, 599

Chapman, John (1775?–1847), "Johnny Appleseed," 536

Chapultepec, American victory at in Mexican War, 713

Character, American, emergence of, 628ff.; attitude toward slavery before Civil War, 650; *see also* American mission

Charles I (1600–49), English king, growth of political parties under, 87; agrees to *Petition of Right,* 90; attempts to crush opposition, 90; executed, 90

Charles II (1630–85), English king, aims at absolutism, 91; restricts colonial trade, 112; pardons rebels in Bacon's Rebellion, 115; annuls Mass. charter, 133; presents New Netherland to Duke of York, 137; promotes Penn's plans in Pa., 140

Charles V (1500–58), Spanish emperor, supports Magellan, 56; rules Spain at its zenith, 60; in struggle for the Caribbean, 63

Charles River Bridge Case, Taney's decision in, 466

Charleston, S.C., settlement of, 118; in colonial days, 153; becomes a center of Indian trade, 190; British fleet repulsed at, 233; builds early railroad, 571; nominating conventions at (1860), 774ff.

Charleston and Hamburg R.R., pioneer line, 571

Chase, Justice Samuel (1741–1811), impeached, 352

Chase, Kate, political activities of, 884ff.

Chase, Salmon P. (1808–83), elected Senator (1848) by Free-Soilers, 722; Secretary of Treasury in Lincoln's Cabinet, 816; in Cabinet crisis of 1862, 871–872; seeks presidential nomination, 883–884; resigns, 885; made Chief Justice, 886; presides in Johnson's impeachment proceedings, 907; in campaign of 1868, 908

Chateau Clique, dominates Quebec, 482

Chatham, Earl of, *see* Pitt, William

Cherokee Indians, location of, 41; surrender land in Old West, 213; sell Kentucky lands, 216; in War of 1812, 420; removal of, 524–525

Cherokee Nation v. Georgia, defines Indian status, 510, 524–525

Cherokee Phoenix, Indian newspaper, 524

Cherokee Wars (1776–81), 253

Cherry Valley, N.Y., Tory attack on, 254

Chesapeake (U.S. frigate), fired upon by British (1807), 359–360; surrenders to *Shannon,* 408

Cheves, Langdon (1776–1857), a leader of War Hawks, 402; leader of "Antique Republicans," 668

Cheyenne Indians, 41

Chicago, Ill., growth of, 397, 606

"Chicago Platform," provisions of (1860), 777

Chickasaw Indians, location of, 41; confederacy, 43; attempt to assimilate white culture, 521; removal of, 524

Chihuahua, Mex., occupied by Doniphan in Mexican War, 710

Child labor, in the 1850's, 579

Chile, conquered by Pizarro, 56

China, Portugal in, 53; Boston's trade in, 488, 489; relation of American merchants in, 494–495; cedes southeast Siberia to Russia, 495; Opium War in, 495; Taiping Rebellion in, 495; clash with the West, 496

Chippawa, Can., in War of 1812, 413

Chippewa Indians, 41

Choctaw Indians, location of, 41; confederacy, 43; attempt to assimilate white culture, 521; removal of, 524

Chouteau family, buy American Fur Company, 519

Christianity, debt to Hebrew religion, 9; mission of, 10

Chronometer, as aid in navigation, 55

Church, disestablishment of, 273–274, 444; rise of missions, 589; establishes missions in Oregon country, 686–687; *see also* denominational names

Cincinnati, O., founded, 376; settled, 390; growth of, 396; German settlement in, 606

Circuit riders, in West, 539

Cities, rise of, 10; growth of, 17; colonial, 152

Civil Disobedience (Thoreau), stresses individualism, 599

Civilization, Oriental, 8–9; Western and American, 5ff.; in pre-Civil War South, 651–652

Civilized Nations, Indian, 41, 43

Civil liberties, defined, 84, 100; protected in colonial Pa., 141; colonial struggle for, 181ff.; Bill of Rights added to Constitution, 298–299; suppressed in South before Civil War, 676–677, 806

Civil rights, defined, 100; basis of, 901

Civil War, seeds of in expansionist movement, 686; summary of the causes of, 804ff.; cost of, 819–821; European attitudes toward, 825ff.; strategy of, 847ff.; tactics employed in, 847, 849; amphibious warfare in, 850–851; Union generals in 1862, 851–863; action in West, 851ff.; in East, 859ff.; and reconstruction, 925ff.; lessons not learned from, 932

Claiborne, William (1587?–?1677), leader of popular party in Va., 111; drives governor out of Md. (1644), 117

Clan, nature of Indian, 43

Clarendon, Earl of (1609–74), a Carolina proprietor, 117

Clark, George Rogers (1752–1818), saves Old West in Rev., 254; and land speculation, 376; in intrigue with Genêt, 383

Clark, William (1770–1838), in Lewis and Clark expedition, 516–517; governor of Missouri Territory, 517

Clay, Henry (1777–1852), a leader of War Hawks, 402, 403; peace delegate (1814), 417–418; in Florida problem, 425; as a dominant national figure, 430; biography, 432; supports Adams in election of 1824, 439–440; fights duel with Randolph, 439; votes in election of 1824, 439; proposes his American System, 439; and the Maysville Road veto, 454ff.; in the campaign of 1832, 457; presidential votes (1832), 458; offers compromise tariff, 459; earns title "Pacificator," 665; kills Independent Treasury, 699; in 1844 campaign, 700; opposes Mexican War, 706; introduces Omnibus Bill (1850), 724, 726

Clayton, John M. (1796–1856), signs treaty with Bulwer over isthmian canal, 737–738

Clermont, Fulton's steamboat on Hudson, 567

Clinton, De Witt (1769–1828), in politics, 323; builds Erie Canal, 568, 570

Clinton, George (1739–1812), in politics, 323; elected Vice-President, 355

Clinton, Sir Henry (1738?–95), replaces Howe in Revolution, 260; invades South, 261; in siege of Yorktown, 263ff.

Clipper ships, description of, 490–491

Clive, Robert (1725–74), saves India for England, 196–197

Clymer, George (1739–1813), agricultural experimenter, 582

Coal, development of mining, 560

Coast survey bureau, established, 591

Cobb, Howell (1815–68), Southern Unionist, 734; speech irritates border states, 785–786

Cobden, Richard (1804–65), influences Br. opinion in Civil War, 830

Cochrane, Alexander (1758–1832), in War of 1812, 414

Cohen v. Virginia, 437

Coke, Thomas (1747–1814), helps organize Methodist Church, 274

Cold Harbor, Va., Civil War battle at, 879–880

Colfax, Schuyler (1823–85), Radical leader in 37th Congress, 814; nominated for vice-presidency, 908

Coligny, Admiral (1519–72), plants Ft. Caroline, 64

Collamer, Jacob (1791–1865), leader of Conservatives in 37th Congress, 813

Colleges, spread of, 614–615

Collins, Edward Knight (1802–78), establishes transatlantic packet line, 491

Colombia, conquered by Quesada, 56; wins freedom, 471; gives U.S. transit rights, 737

Colonies, education in early, 148; types of government, 174; value of trade, 176–177; economic expansion of, 178; smuggling in, 178; farming, 179; manufactures, 179; struggle for democracy, 180–187; comparison with New France, 193; part played in French and Indian Wars, 198–200

Colonizing, companies, 107–109; pattern of Spanish, 689–690

Colt, Samuel (1814–62), perfecter of revolver, 562

Colter, John (1775?–1813), mountain man, 521

Columbia, S.C., burned in Civil War, 882

Columbia, Gray sails around world, 489

Columbian Institute, founded, 591

Columbus, Bartholomew (1445?–?1514), 53

Columbus, Christopher (1446?–1506), encouraged by Ferdinand and Isabella, 50; beliefs of, 51–52; voyages, 51–53; death of, 53

Commerce and manufactures, of New England, 131–132; in colonies, 179; limited by Eng., 201; see also Mass production, Trade

Committee of Thirteen, makes effort at compromise (1861), 768

Committees of Correspondence, organized by Sam Adams, 224–225; control colonies, 228

Committees of Safety, organized in colonies, 228

Common law, English, 84; gains ground in Mass., 126; gains ground in U.S., 436

Commons, development of English, 84–85

Common Sense (Paine), impact of, 234–235

Commonwealth v. Hunt, declares unions and strikes legal, 581

Communism, defined, 22; theory of, 103–105

Compact, as form of colonial democratic government, 185–186; Watauga Ass'n, 216; implemented by Constitutional Convention, 297

Company of New France, fur monopoly, 73

Compass, as navigational reliance, 55

Complacency, American, 631–632

Compromise, vs. force, 6–7; function of in a democracy, 98; necessity for, 100; accepted in democratic government, 292–293; commercial, 293–294; Am. method of, 598; of sectional strife fails, 786

Compromise of 1850, gives South guarantees, 671; discussion of, 717ff.; pushed through, 728; Southern struggle over, 728–729; in presidential campaign of 1852, 730–731; upheld by Georgia Constitutional Union Party, 734

Comte, Augustus (1798–1857), spreads socialist theory, 625

Concept of infinity, American, 34, 35

Concord, Mass., Revolutionary battle at, 229–230

Concrete liberties, Anglo-Saxon, 83–84; displaced by theory of Natural Rights, 93

Concurrent voice, Calhoun's theory in government, 668–669

Confederacy, formed, 787; provisions of constitution of, 787–788; uses British-built cruisers, 828–829; Federal attitude toward, 839; numbers and losses in Civil War, 839–840; conscripting troops, 840; desertions in ranks, 841; prisons in, 842–843; see also Civil War

Confederation, period of the, 285–290; partisan issues of the, 285–286; payment of debts of, 309–310; sets up Northwest Territory (1787), 376

Congregational Church, established in Mass., 126; disapproves of Anglican episcopate, 204

Congress, powers of, 294ff.; meets and sets up government under Constitution, 299–300; reconstructed after Civil War, 903ff.

Congress, surrenders to C.S.S. *Virginia,* 862

Conkling, Roscoe (1829–88), elected to Senate, 903

Connecticut, settled, 128; character of, 129; joined with New Haven, 129; joins in New England Confederation, 132; stronghold of Federalism, 307; and Western land grants, 376

Connecticut Compromise, accepted at Constitutional Convention, 292–293

Conquistadors, age of the, 55–56; character of, 58–59

Conscience, force of in Am. character, 634–635

Conscience Whigs, program of, 718–719

Conservatism, Am., 35–37; in Spanish-American culture, 60; reinforced by reconstruction, 929

Conservatives, definition of political, 102; in 37th Congress, 813ff.; in campaign of 1866, 902; in South after Civil War, 912–913

Constitution, first state, 270–271; movement for Second, 290; personnel devising, 290–291; as a step in political evolution, 292; powers under, 294; checks and balances, 295; battle over ratification, 297–298; Bill of Rights added, 298–299; Twelfth Amendment added, 344; implied powers upheld, 437

Constitution, in War of 1812, 407

Constitutional Convention, 290ff.

Constitutional Union Party, formed, 777

Constitution of Virginia, the work of George Mason, 222

Construction Construed and Constitutions Vindicated (Taylor), stresses compact theory of government, 667

Consultation, The, plays part in Texas revolt, 694; declares independence of Texas, 696

Continental Ass'n, adopted by First Continental Congress, 227

Continental Congress, First, meets, 227; Second, meets, 230

Continental currency, during Revolution, 246

Continental Line, in Revolution, 241

Continental shelf, described, 25

Continental System, Napoleon's, 358–359

Contract, government as social, 92

Contreras, Am. victory at in Mexican War, 713

Convention of 1800, a treaty with France, 339

Convention of 1818, settles fisheries problem in Northeast, 479; unsatisfactory to Americans, 487

Convicts, as early settlers, 146

"Conway Cabal," attempts to replace Washington, 247

Cook, James (1728–79), discovers Hawaii, 500; visits Pacific Northwest, 514

Cooke, Jay (1821–1905), floats loans in Civil War, 820; backs Chase for presidency, 884–885

Cooper, James Fenimore (1789–1851), exponent of romanticism, 593

Cooper, Thomas (1759–1839), leads Antique Republicans, 668; defends slavery, 672

Copley, John S. (1738–1815), painter, 590

Copperheads, in 37th Congress, 813ff.; strength of, 818; after Civil War, 894ff.

Corn, and its culture, 40–41

Corn belt, as attraction for farmers, 30; description of, 398

Corn Laws (British), affect emigration, 605

Cornwallis, Lord (1738–1805), defeats Gates at Camden in Revolution, 261; retreats from Guilford C. H., 263; fortifies Yorktown, 263; surrenders at Yorktown, 265

Coronado, Vásquez de (1510–54), discovers Zuñi pueblos, 56

Corporation, a form of mercantile organization, 577–578

Corpus Christi, Tex., falls to Union in Civil War, 851

Corterreal, Gaspar and Miguel (c. 1485), explore for Portugal, 71–72

Cortes, Hernando (1485–1547), conquers Mexico, 56

Corwin, Thomas (1794–1865), opposes Mexican War, 707

Cotton, John (1584–1652), quoted on Christian virtue, 89

Cotton, rise of Cotton Kingdom, 559; importance of crop in Old South, 643ff.; Cotton Kingdom secedes from Union, 783

Cotton Snobs, defined, 646; characteristics, 679–680

Cotton triangle, a tie between South and Northeast, 652–653

Cotton Whigs, in sympathy with South, 653

Council for New England, formed by royal patent, 108–109; a recharter of Plymouth Company, 121

Council of Virginia, colonial government under, 107–198

Counties, in Middle Colonies, 142

Country Party, in colonies, 184ff.

Coureurs de bois, roam over North America, 74; unite against La Salle, 189

Court Party, in colonies, 184ff.

Courts, battle for control of colonial, 182; Supreme held sovereign over state courts, 437

Covode, John (1808–71), Radical leader in 37th Congress, 814; introduces resolution impeaching Johnson, 906

Cowpens, N.C., Revolutionary battle at, 262

Crawford, William H. (1772–1834), a leader of War Hawks, 402; as a dominant national figure, 430; biography, 433; presidential candidate (1824), 438, 439; supports Jackson in 1828, 447; in Jackson-Calhoun controversy, 454

Crédit Mobilier scandal, 920

Creek Indians, location of, 41; confederacy, 43; in War of 1812, 420; attempt to assimilate white culture, 521; Georgia removes, 525

Creek War (1813–14), 421

Creole, ship's role in abolition campaign, 664

Crisis, The (Paine), influence of, 234

Crittenden, John J. (1787–1863), proposes compromise (1861), 786, 787

Crockett, David (1786–1836), folk hero, 543–544; killed in the Alamo, 696

Cromwell, Oliver (1599–1658), stiffens Parliamentary army, 90; restores religious toleration in Md., 117; attempts to capture New Amsterdam, 137; and Navigation Acts, 174

Crow Indians, 41

Cuba, seized by England, 197; Am. interests in, 736

Culture, spread of Spanish, 59–60; Portuguese in Brazil, 62–63; in Old West, 539; beginnings of typically Am., 589–602

Cumberland, rammed by C.S.S. *Virginia,* 862

Cumberland Island, seized (1815), 420

Cumberland Road, completed, 434

Cunard, Samuel (1787–1865), establishes Cunard Line, 491

Currency Act, Grenville extends provisions of, 217

Cushing, Caleb (1800–79), acts to open the door in China, 495; Chairman of Dem. Convention (1860), 775

Cushman, Charlotte (1816–76), actress, 590

Cutler, Rev. Manasseh (1742–1823), speculates in Western lands, 374; guarantees liberties on land grant, 376

Dahlenega, Ga., discovery of gold at, 524

Dallas, Alexander J. (1759–1817), prominent Philadelphian, 324

Dallas, George M. (1792–1864), nominated for vice-presidency (1844), 700

Dalton, Ga., falls to Sherman, 881

"Dark horse," defined, 700

Dartmouth College v. Woodward, upholds principle of private property, 437–438

Davis, Henry Winter (1817–65), supports Union in Md., 795; Radical leader in 37th Congress, 814; sponsors reconstruction bill, 883

Davis, Jefferson (1808–89), speaks in Senate on Clay's Omnibus Bill, 726; named Secretary of War (1852), 730–731; biography, 733; works for Southern Rights, 733; on Com. of Thirteen, 786; elected president of Confederacy, 787; offers to abolish slavery, 811; as president during Civil War, 824; keeps Bragg in command, 857; fate of, 887

Davis, John (1550?–1605), explorer for England, 72

Dawes, William (1745–99), warns minutemen, 229–230

Dearborn, Fort, falls to British (1812), 410

Dearborn, Henry (1751–1829), fails in Canadian invasion (1812), 410

De Bow, J. D. B. (1820–67), publishes *De Bow's Review,* 677; promotes Southern economic independence, 735

Decatur, Stephen (1779–1820), in Barbary Wars, 353

Declaration of Independence, adopted, 236

Declaration of Rights, drawn up by the First Continental Congress, 227

Declaratory Act (1766), follows repeal of Stamp Act, 220

Deere, John (1804–86), improves plow, 584

Defense of the Constitutions of the U.S.A., A (Adams), 305

Definition of Parties, A (Taylor), supports Jefferson, 327

De Grasse, Comte (1722–88), in siege of Yorktown, 263ff.

Deism, accepted in colonies, 587

Delancey family, leads Tory faction, 323

Delaware, Lord (1577–1618), governor of Virginia, 110

Delaware, supports Union in secession, 794

Delaware Indians, cheated in Walking Purchase, 37; location of, 41; on Manhattan Island, 135; in war with Dutch, 136; Penn signs treaty with, 141

Democracy, and science, 7; no cure-all, 8; evolution in England, 18; paradox of waste and, 37–38; among Am. Indians, 43; political, 93–94; its meaning and method, 94–105; makes headway in Virginia colony, 110–111; promoted by Bacon's Rebellion, 115; loses out to theocracy in Mass., 126; in New England town meeting, 130; in New Netherland, 135–136; in colonial New York, 137–139; in colonial Pa., 140–141; growth in religious, 157–158; contributions of Scotch-Irish to, 162, 163; general colonial struggle for, 180–187; Br. mercantilism threatens evolving American, 202–203; origin of the public domain, 271, 272; abolishment of primogeniture and entail, 273; disestablishment of churches, 273–274; beginning of emancipation of slaves, 274; form accepted at Constitutional Convention, 292–293; limited under Constitution, 295, 297; Bill of Rights, 298–299; impact of Fr. Revolution on Am. struggle for, 328–329; Hamilton's and Jefferson's theories, 365–370; as shown in law, 436; and sectionalism, 440ff.; effect of Jeffersonian movement, 463ff.; effect of Jacksonian movement, 463ff.; character in West, 544–545; influence of transcendentalism on, 599; in South before Civil War, 676–677; Civil War a clash over processes of, 805–806; balanced form thrown off by reconstruction period, 926; not automatic, 932

Democratic Party, and liberalism, 369; in westward movement, 395–396; changes name from Dem.-Rep. Party, 460; split by factions (1840's), 462ff.; taken over by Loco Focos, 463; approach break-up, 721; split in (1860), 775–777; after Civil War, 894ff.; New Departure movement, 908–919; gains strength in South, 921

Democratic-Republican Party, molded by Jefferson, 320ff.; in westward movement, 395; nominate Jackson and Van Buren (1832), 451–458

Democratic Societies, imitate Jacobin Clubs (1793), 329–330; stir up Whisky Insurrection, 332

De Soto, Hernando (1500?–42), explorer, 56

D'Estaing, Comte (1729–94), attacks Newport, 260; attempts recapture of Savannah, 261

De Tocqueville, Alexis (1805–59), opinions on America, 597, 633

Detroit, besieged in Pontiac's War, 211; surrenders to British (1812), 410; burned by Proctor, 412

Dew, Thomas R. (1802–46), defends slavery, 67

DeWitt Clinton, pioneer locomotive, 571

Dial, transcendental magazine, 599

Dias, Bartholomew (1450?–1500), makes African trips, 48

Diaz, Porfirio (1830–1915), seizes Mexican government (1876), 830

d'Iberville, Sieur (1661–1706), founds Biloxi, Miss., 190

Dickens, Charles, criticizes America, 596

Dickinson, John (1732–1808), influences matters of taxation, 222; leads moderates, 234; draws up Articles of Confederation, 269; attends Constitutional Convention, 291

Discourse on the Constitution (Calhoun), 668

Disquisition on Government (Calhoun), 668

Distribution Act (1836), prorates Federal surplus to states, 460; helps bring on panic, 461

Dix, Dorothea (1802–87), reformer, 616

Domestic Manners of the Americans (Trollope), criticizes America, 596

Dominion of New England, formed by James II, 133–134; rejects theocratic government, 133–134; New York added to, 138

Donelson, Fort, falls to Grant, 853

Doniphan, Alexander (1808–87), victories of in Mexican War, 710

Dorr, Thomas W. (1805–54), instigates rebellion over franchise, 443

Douglas, Stephen A. (1813–61), in election campaign of 1852, 730; Comp. of 1850, 724; Kansas-Nebraska Bill, 748; debates Lincoln, 768ff.; in campaign of 1860, 775–776, 780; on Committee of Thirteen, 786; relations with Lincoln, 788–789; as strong pro-Union force in Northwest, 802

Drake, Edwin L. (1819–80), strikes oil, 560

Drake, Sir Francis (1545?–96), in Caribbean, 64; against the Spanish, 64–65

Dramatic Line, of packet ships, 491

Dred Scott Decision, favors Southern view, 671–672, 760; effect of, 761

Dualism, Anglo-Saxon, 82–83; in Am. character, 629ff.

Duer, William (1747–99), land speculator, 375
Duke of York's Grants, 137–139
"Duke's Laws," proclaimed in N.Y., 137–138
Dunmore, Lord (1732–1809), partner in Loyal Company of Old West, 215–216; burns part of Norfolk, 233; proposes seizure of Florida, 386
Dunmore's War, in Old West, 216.
Duquesne, Fort, erected by Frenchmen, 194; English defeated at, 194; English take, 196
Dutch, primarily traders, 134–135; found New Netherland, 135; immigrants, 608
Dwight, Theodore (1764–1846), Federalist wheel horse, 307; warns against Jefferson, 343
Dwight, Timothy (1752–1817), of the Family Compact, 307; quoted on America, 635

Early, Jubal A. (1816–94), Confederate military leader, 868; in Md. and Valley campaigns, 880–881
East India Company, formation of (1600), 64, 108; crisis in, 225; monopolizes China trade, 488
East Indies, opened to trade by Salem merchants, 489
Eaton, John H. (1790–1856), in Jackson's Kitchen Cabinet, 452; resigns, 456
Eaton, Peggy O'Neale (1796–1897), 452–453
Eaton, William (1764–1811), in Barbary Wars, 353
Economics, founded as science by Physiocrats, 21; relationship to democracy, 367–368
Economy, Pa., German pietist colony at, 624
Ecuador, wins freedom, 471
Education, necessity for in a democracy, 96–98; in early colonial days, 148; effect of secularism on, 158; after Revolution, 275; westward spread of, 395; in Old West, 539–540; agricultural, 583; lags around 1800, 589; land grants for, 591; rise of free public schools, 613; growth of colleges, 614–615; for women, 615; spread through postal reform, 615; in South before Civil War, 676
Edwards, Jonathan (1703–58), revivalist, 156; president of Princeton, 158
Elections: (1796), 336; (1800–01), 342–343; (1804), 355; (1808), 362–363; (1812), 405–406; (1816), 429; (1824), 439; (1828), 447–449; (1832), 457ff.; (1836), 461; (1840), 462; (1844), 700; (1848), 722ff.; (1852), 730–731; (1860), 774ff.; (1862), 869–870; (1864), 886; (1866), 902; (1868), 908; (1872), 919–920
Elgin-Marcy Reciprocity Treaty, sets up free trade between U.S. and British provinces, 484; settles Anglo-American fishing rights, 487; canceled, 832
Elizabeth, Queen (1533–1603), builds up sea power, 64; faces religious and political problems, 86
Ellsworth, Oliver (1745–1807), attends Constitutional Convention, 291
El Paso, Spanish outpost, 688
Emancipation Proclamation, issued, 869
Embargo Act, passed and enforced, 360–362; repealed, 363; effects of defeat of, 364
Emerson, Ralph Waldo (1803–82), transcendentalist, 599; teachings of, 600, 601; issues intellectual declaration of independence, 612; quoted, 612, 613; joins antislavery forces, 662
Emmett, Daniel D. (1815–1904), author of Dixie, 590
Emotionalism, in Am. character, 634; in bringing on Civil War, 808–810
Empresarios, Texas land dealings of, 692–693
Empress of China, Am. trader in China, 489

Enclosure, under the Tudors, 86
Endicott, John (1589?–1665), Puritan leader, 122
Engineering, development of branches in, 564
England, founder of Industrial Revolution, 19; in struggle for the Caribbean, 63–69; rise of law and institutions of, 81–86; mercantilism in, 173ff.; value of colonial trade to, 176–177; war with France for North America, 187–200; leaders and army during American Revolution, 247–249; Europe allied against, 259–260; trade with during Confederation period, 287–288; seizes American seamen, 331–332; renews war with France (1803), 356; renews impressment of American sailors, 357–358; blockades continent (1805), 359; becomes rival of U.S. for Latin-American trade, 475; abandons mercantilism, 481–482; struggle with U.S. over commerce, 488; enters fur trade in Pacific Northwest, 514; in Trent Affair, 827–828; during Am. Civil War, 827, 839
English Civil War, results of, 91; puts end to Great Migration, 123
Englishmen, conscious of insularity, 81–82; racial elements of, 82; characteristics, 82; dualism of, 82–83; and concrete liberties, 83–84; immigrants, 141, 603
Enlightenment, in America, 156; in France, 159; influence in America, 587
Enquiry into the Principles and Tendencies of Certain Public Measures, An (Taylor), supports Jefferson, 327
Entail, abolishment of, 273
Environmentalism, colonial belief in, 587–588; leads to reform of institutions, 615
Ephrata Cloister, socialist colony, 623
Episcopal Church, colonial opposition to Anglican episcopate, 204
Era of Good Feeling, 429ff.
Era of Hard Feeling, 440ff.
Ericsson, John (1803–89), designs ironclads, 862
Erie Canal, importance in westward movement, 397, 535; effects of, 568, 570
Erie Railroad, connects seaboard with West, 572
Erskine Agreement, failure of, 403
Essays on Political Economy (Carey), lays basis of Clay's American System, 576
Essex (ship) case, 357
Essex, destroyed by British (1814), 493
Essex Junto, coterie in Mass., 307–308; declines in power, 416; collapses, 424–425
Europe, dynamism of, 5; expansion of, 16; attempts at unification of, 17–18; against Britain during American Revolution, 259–260; renewal of war in (1803), 356; mass immigration from, 604; fears America's rising power, 684; attitude toward America during Civil War, 825ff.; effect of Civil War on, 927–928
Evangelicalism, 156–157
Evans, Frederick W. (1808–93), Shaker leader, 624
Evans, Oliver (1755–1819), develops high-pressure engine, 558; engine makes steam locomotive possible, 570
Evarts, William M. (1818–1901), defends Johnson in impeachment proceedings, 907
Everett, Edward (1794–1865), inspires democracy in orations, 602; runs for Vice-President (1860), 777
Ewell, Richard S. (1817–72), characteristics of, 868; in battle of Gettysburg, 875; at Spotsylvania, 879
Excise taxes, on whisky, 312, 332; in Civil War, 820

Expansionism, England limits colonial, 202; as manifest destiny, 683ff.; into California, 691–692; into Texas, 692ff.; prominent leaders in, 736

Ex Parte Milligan, Supreme Court's ruling in, 817; effect of ruling, 906

Exposition (1828), Calhoun on nullification, 453

Factories, rise of, 575

Factory System, of dealing with Indians, 512

Fair Oaks, Va., Civil War battle at, 863

Fall Line, nature of the, 29

Falmouth, Me., seized by British, 232

Family Compact, of Conn., 307; of Ontario, 482

Farming and farmers, Indian, 40; in colonial South, 112; in New Eng., 131; in Middle Colonies, 142; in colonies, in general, 150–152, 179; as stage in settlement, 165–166; England limits colonial, 201–202; in colonial Piedmont, 210; in Confederation period, 285–286; in West, 536; careless use of soil, 581; growth of specialization, 582; limited improvement in, 582–583; in the Old South, 646–647; prospers during Civil War, 821

Farragut, David G. (1801–70), Civil War naval actions in Gulf, 851; takes Port Hudson, 857

Fascism, defined, 22

Federalist Party, leaders, 305–306; in New England, 306; the Essex Junto, 307–308; view of their mission, 320; denounce French Revolution, 328; decline in power, 336–345; in election of 1800, 342ff.; entrench themselves in judiciary, 344; accomplishments of, 344–345; fall of, 345; repeal the Embargo, 362–363; gain ground, 364–365; oppose War of 1812, 406; resist liberalism, 588–589; collapse as a party, 424–425; fold up, 429

"Federalists," in Confederation period, 287

Federal system of government, planned, 291–292; divisions of powers, 294ff.

Fenian movement, on Canadian border, 832

Fenno, John (1751–98), edits *The Gazette of the U.S.,* 319; attacks Bache, 337

Ferdinand II (1452–1516), Spanish king, agrees to Demarcation Line, 53

Fessenden, William P. (1806–69), heads Joint Com. on Reconstruction, 900

Field, Cyrus W. (1819–92), lays Atlantic cable, 574

Fifteenth Amendment, ratified, 909

Fillmore, Millard (1800–74), sends Perry to reopen Japan to trade, 497; nominated for Vice-Pres. (1848), 728; President, 728

Findley, William (1741–1821), dem. leader, 325

Fink, Mike, folk hero, 543, 544

Finney, Charles G. (1792–1875), conducts Great Revival, 657; joins Oberlin faculty, 660

Fire-Eaters (Immediate Secessionists), rise of, 729, 730; agitate for secession, 731; bolt Dem. Convention (1860), 775–776; force secession, 782

First Continental Congress, meets, 227–228

First Reconstruction Act, passed over Johnson's veto, 904

Fish, Hamilton (1808–93), settles *Alabama* claims in treaty, 833

Fisher, Fort, holds out in Civil War, 850

Fisher's Hill, Va., Civil War battle at, 881

Fishing and fishermen, early in North American waters, 70–71; promoted by Queen Elizabeth, 86; New Eng., 122, 131–132

Fitch, John (1743–98), builds steamboats, 565

Fitzhugh, George (1806–81), defends slavery, 673–674

Fitzpatrick, Thomas (1799?–1854), in St. Louis fur trade, 519

Five Forks, Va., Sheridan wins at, 887

Five Nations, Indians, description of, 43; decline of, 78; moved to Indian Territory, 527–528; *see also* Iroquois

Fletcher v. Peck, case involving land frauds, 385, 437

Florida, under Spain, 59, 190; seized by England, 197; falls to Spain, 259; Spanish policies in, 380–381; Jefferson tries to annex, 389–390; West Fla. joins the U.S., 390; Am. desire to annex, 401–402; Am. plans in War of 1812, 420; problems acute in (1815), 424–425; acquisition of, 425–426; secedes from Union, 783; readmitted, 908

Florida Strait, in struggle for the Caribbean, 64

Flying Cloud, noted clipper ship, 491

Foote, Andrew H. (1806–63), commands Union fleet on Western waters, 854

Foote, Henry S. (1804–80), Southern Unionist, 733

Forbes, John (1710–59), takes Ft. Duquesne, 196

Force Acts (1870–71), passed to control South, 917–918

Force *vs.* compromise, in developing democracy, 6–7, 8

Formosa, "gunboat policy" against, 499

Forrest, Edwin (1806–72), actor, 590

Forrest, Nathan Bedford (1821–77), Confederate cavalry leader, 855, 868; organizes Ku Klux Klan, 917

Forster, W. E. (1818–86), influences British opinion in Civil War, 830

Fort Christina (Wilmington), built by Swedes, 136

Fort Donelson, falls to Grant, 853

Fort Duquesne, erected by French, 194; English defeated at, 194

Fort Fisher, holds out in Civil War, 850

Fort Frontenac, falls to Bradstreet, 196

Fort Good Hope (Dutch), 135

Fort Henry, falls to Grant, 853

Fort McHenry, repulses Br. fleet in War of 1812, 415

Fort Meigs, repels attack in War of 1812, 412

Fort Mims, massacre at (1813), 421

Fortress Monroe, in Union hands, 850

Fort Nassau (Dutch), founded, 135

Fort Necessity, Washington defeated at, 194

Fort Orange (Dutch), founded at Albany, 135

Fort Pickens, difficulties at (1861), 784; in Union hands, 850

Fort Pillow, massacre of Negro troops at, 842

Fort Pitt, erected, 196; besieged in Pontiac's War, 211; in Revolution, 253

Fort Stephenson, in War of 1812, 412

Fort Sumter, action at, 784; crisis at, 790

Forty-Niners, rush to California, 724

Foster, Abigail Kelley (1810–87), reformer, 618

Foster, Stephen Collins (1826–64), composer, 600

Fourier, Charles (1772–1837), spreads socialist theory, 625; backed by Brisbane, 626

Fourteenth Amendment, ratified, 900

Fox, George (1624–91), Quaker leader, 91

Fox Indians, location of, 41; in Black Hawk War, 522

France, and liberty, 18; in struggle for the Caribbean, 63–69; exerts little cultural influence on colonies, 159; espouses war with England, 187–200; attitude during Am. Revolution, 258–259; declares war on England and Spain, 328; reaches crisis in affairs with U.S. (1797), 337, 338; sells La. to U.S., 353–354; renews war with England (1803), 356; acquires La., 384; seizes Mexico, 829–830

Francis I (1494–1547), French king, in struggle for the Caribbean, 63

Franklin, Benjamin (1706–90), biography, 154–155; as agent for colonies, 181; proposes Albany Plan of Union, 199–200; as land speculator, 215; arraigned for obtaining Hutchinson and Oliver letters, 225; as peace commissioner at Paris, 265–266; attends Constitutional Convention, 291; as scientist, 556; quoted on art, 590

Franklin, State of, proposal for, 289, 381

Franklin, Tenn., Civil War battle at, 881

Frayser's Farm, Va., Civil War battle at, 863

Fredericksburg, Va., Civil War battle at, 870–871

Fredonia, Americans attempt to set up Republic in Texas called, 693

Freedmen's Bureau, set up, 898; resentment against, 913

Freedom, in Mediterranean culture, 9; relativity of, 101–102; of worship, in colonies, 134, 141; of the press established in Zenger trial, 182; of press and speech in South before Civil War, 676–677

Freeman's Farm, victories at in Revolution, 257

Freeport Doctrine, 768

Free-Soil Party, formation of, 722

Frémont, John Charles (1813–90), explores along Oregon Trail, 687; activities in Cal. during Mexican War, 711; opposes Kearny, 711; removed from command, 802; seeks pres. nomination, 883ff.

French and Indian Wars, status of colonies in, 193–194; colonial opposition to, 198–199

French immigrants, 608

French Revolution, Am. reaction to, 328–329

Freneau, Philip (1752–1832), edits The National Gazette, 319; commencement ode, 587

Friends of Universal Reform (1840), 613

Friendship, Salem ship in Sumatra, 489

Fries Rebellion, over taxes, 338

Frobisher, Martin (1535?–94), explorer, 72

Frontenac, Comte de (1620–98), 188–189

Frontier, as distinguished from the West, 165, 531; methods of defense on the, 540–541

Frontier Hypothesis, introduced by Turner, 530–531

Fruitlands, socialist experiment, 625

Fuller, Margaret (1810–50), transcendentalist, 599; reformer, 618

Fulton, Robert (1765–1815), 567

"Fundamental Constitution of Carolina," drawn up by John Locke, 118

Fundamental Orders of Connecticut, drawn up, 129; of model of colonial democratic government, 185–186

Furs and fur trade, European demand for, 71, 74–75; in Plymouth plantation, 122; in New England, 131; in Middle Colonies, 142; as stage in settlement, 165; as factor in French-English wars, 188ff.; in Old Northwest, 377; frontiers, 513ff.; in St. Louis, 519

Gadsden Purchase, promoted by Jefferson Davis, 733

Gage, Thomas (1721–87), selects headquarters in New York, 219; made governor of Mass., 226; moves against Concord, Mass., 229

Gag Rule, imposed on antislavery petitions, 662–663; revoked, 664

Gaines' Mill, Va., Civil War battle at, 863

Gallatin, Albert (1761–1849), biography, 325; elected to Congress, 333; Sec. of Treasury, 349; establishes branches of B. U. S., 355; defeated in recharter of B. U. S., 403; Am. peace delegate (1814), 417–418

Gallaudet, Edward Miner (1837–1917), reformer, 616

Gallaudet, Thomas H. (1787–1851), reformer, 616

Gallipolis, O., settled by French, 375

Galloway, Joseph (1729?–1803), urges written Constitution, 222; attends First Cont. Congress, 227

Galveston, Tex., falls to Union, 851

Gálvez, José de (1729–87), projects settlement of California, 689

Gama, Vasco da (1469?–1524), voyager, 53

Garcés, Father Francisco, explorer, 689

Gardiner, Robert H. (1782–1864), sets up first agricultural school, 583

Garfield, James A. (1831–81), and Crédit Mobilier scandal, 920

Garrison, William Lloyd (1805–79), publishes The Liberator, 658–659; takes over Am. Anti-Slavery Society, 663

Gaspee, plundered by smugglers, 224

Gates, Horatio (1728?–1806), military leader in Revolution, 242; as alternate leader of Am. troops, 256; wins victories at Stillwater, 257; invades South, 261

Gazette of the U.S., The (Fenno), 319

General Court, of Mass., 125

Genêt, Citizen Edmond (1763–1834), sent to U.S. by Girondins, 328; career in U.S., 329–331; plans to seize Louisiana, 383

Genius of Universal Emancipation, The (Lundy), attacks slavery, 657

Gentleman's Party, in colonies, 184ff.

Geography, influences on American history, 24–38

George III (1738–1820), characteristics of, 200–201; wins control of Parliament, 222–223

George Washington, ship, commandeered by Algeria, 352–353

Georgia, settlement of, 119–120; founded as buffer colony, 192; Western claims of, 384–385; removes Cherokee, 524–525; removes Creeks, 525; secedes from Union, 783; Sherman's "March" through, 881–882; readmitted to Union, 908

Georgia Compact of 1802, concerning Creeks and Cherokee, 521–522

Georgia Constitutional Union Party, upholds Compromise of 1850, 734

Germain, Lord George (1716–85), British leader in Am. Revolution, 248

German immigrants, in Pa., 141; influx in 18th century, 160–161, 167; mass immigration, 604, 605–606; cultural contributions, 606–607, 608; socialist experiments, 624

Gerry, Elbridge (1744–1814), attends Constitutional Convention, 291; emissary to France (1797) to preserve peace, 337

Gerrymandering, explained, 450

Gettysburg, battle of, 874–876

Gettysburg Address, Lincoln delivers, 883

Ghent, peace negotiations at (War of 1812), 417–418

Gibbons v. Ogden, rules control of interstate commerce a Federal function, 438, 567

Gibbs, Willard (1839–1903), scientist, 556

Giddings, Joshua (1795–1864), abolitionist leader, 661; directs campaign, 664

Gilbert, Sir Humphrey (1539?–83), attempts colonizing, 72; death, 106

Giles, William B. (1762–1830), Jeffersonian Republican, 327

Girondins, send Genêt to the U.S., 328

Girty, Simon (1741–1818), "the great renegade," 541–542

Gladstone, William E. (1809–98), attitude during Civil War, 828

Glendale, Va., Civil War battle at, 863
Godey's Lady's Book, preaches equal rights for women, 618
Godkin, E. L. (1831–1902), revolts against "Grantism," 918
Godoy, Manuel de (1767–1851), allows La. to fall to French control, 383–384
Gold, discovered in Georgia, 524; in California, 724
Gomez, explorer for Spain, 72
Gonzales, Tex., skirmish near in Texas Revolution, 694
Goodyear, Charles (1800–60), develops process of vulcanizing rubber, 561–562
Gorges, Sir Ferdinando (1566?–1647), receives grant of Maine, 129–130
Government, in New France, 73; in a democracy, 93ff.; in Southern colonies, 120–121; under Fundamental Orders of Conn., 129; New England town, 130–131; in New Netherland, 135–136; in colonial Pa., 140–141; in Middle Colonies, 142; types of colonial, 174; colonial struggle for democratic, 180–187; Watauga Ass'n, 216; nationalist program in Confederation period, 286; "Federalist" program in Confederation period, 287; Federal system planned, 291–292; form accepted at Constitutional Convention, 292–293; characteristics of Federal, 294–295; Jefferson's theories of, 318–319; attitudes of Hamilton and Jefferson toward, 321–322; centralization wins in reconstruction period, 925–926
Grand Ohio Company, formed to operate in Old West, 215
Grant, Ulysses S. (1822–85), rebuilds Union army in West, 844; biography, 851–852; takes Forts Henry and Donelson, 853; opposes Johnston at Shiloh, 853–854; in Vicksburg campaign, 856–857; at Chattanooga, 857–858; placed in supreme command of Northern armies, 877–878; his strategy of attrition, 878; in battle of Wilderness, 878–879; at Spotsylvania, 879; at Cold Harbor, 879–880; in siege of Petersburg, 880; breaks through to Richmond, 887; nominated for presidency, 908; as President, 909; scandals of administration, 909–911; re-elected, 920
Graves, Thomas (1725?–1802), in siege of Yorktown, 263ff.
Gray, Elisha (1835–1901), and telephone patent, 557
Gray, Robert (1755–1806), sails around world, 489; rediscovers Columbia R., 514
Great American Desert, myth of, 521
Great Britain, see England
Great Colombia, composition of, 471
Great Lakes–St. Lawrence system, and transportation, 29
Great Meadows, Washington defeated at, 194
Great Migration (1620–40), to America, 123; (1815) to West, 396; (1850's) of immigrants, 608
Great Revival (1797–1805), sweeps settlements, 538; evangelistic movement of 1820's and 30's, 657
"Great Stone Fleet," sunk in Civil War, 494
Great Valley, nature of the, 29; as highway for pioneers, 166–167; immigrants in, 210
Great Western, Br. steam packet, 491, 568
Greeley, Horace (1811–72), advocates equal rights for women, 619; sponsors Fourierism, 626; attitude toward Civil War, 785; biography, 815–816; revolts against "Grantism," 918; nominated for presidency, 919
Green, Duff (1791–1875), supports Calhoun in United States Telegraph, 456

Greenbacks, in Civil War, 820
Greene, Nathanael (1742–86), military leader in Revolution, 242; retakes Carolinas, 262–263
Greenland, Norse settlement on, 69
Greenough, Horatio (1805–52), sculptor, 591
Gregg, William (1800–67), promotes Southern manufactures, 735
Grenville, George (1712–70), proposes four restrictive colonial acts, 217–219; falls from power, 219–220
Griffiths, John Willis (1809?–82), clipper-ship designer, 491
Grimké, Angelina (1805–79), reformer, 618
Grimké, Sarah (1792–1873), reformer, 618
Grundy, Felix (1777–1840), a leader of War Hawks, 402
Guilford C. H., Rev. battle at, 263
Gulf of Mexico, in Civil War, 851

Haiti, buccaneers in, 66–67; slaves rebel in, 386
Hale, Sarah Buell (1788–1879), reformer, 618
Half-Moon, Hudson's ship, 135
Hall, Basil, Eng. traveler in U.S., 597
Halleck, Henry W. (1815–72), displaces Frémont in Missouri Dept., 851; succeeds McClellan as general in chief, 854, 864
Hamburg, Ger., emigrant port, 608
Hamilton, Alexander (1757–1804), in siege of Yorktown, 265; at Constitutional Convention, 291; co-author of The Federalist, 298; in Washington's Cabinet, 301; Secretary of the Treasury, 302; biography, 302–303; political philosophy of, 303–304, 305; policies while in office, 308ff.; sets up The Gazette of the U.S., 319; relations with Jefferson, 320; leads aristocratic faction, 323; in Whisky Insurrection, 332–333; in election of 1796, 336; dreams of expansion, 338; splits with Adams, 342; in campaign of 1800, 342–343; a democrat at heart, 344; duel with Burr, and death, 354–355; and Jefferson, as protagonist and antagonist, 365–370; and the doctrine of laissez faire, 575–576
Hamilton, Andrew (d. 1703), lawyer in Zenger Case, 182
Hamlin, Hannibal (1809–91), nominated for Vice-Pres. (1860), 777
Hammond, James H. (1807–64), advances mudsill theory in defense of slavery, 673
Hammond, William A., introduces modern medical service in Union army, 842
Hampton Roads Conference, discusses peace (1865), 886
Hancock, John (1737–93), a leader in independence movement, 224; and Boston Tea Party, 226; pres. of Cont. Congress, 236
Hancock, Winfield Scott (1824–86), in battle of Gettysburg, 874–875; at Spotsylvania, 879
Harding, Chester (1792–1866), painter, 590
Harmar, Josiah (1753–1813), defeated by Indians, 377
Harmony, Pa., German pietist community, 624
Harper, John A., quoted, 401; a leader of War Hawks, 402
Harpers Ferry, raided by John Brown, 771; seized in 1861, 797
Harris, Townsend (1804–78), does diplomatic work in Japan, 498; quoted, 594
Harrison, William Henry (1773–1841), biography, 378; wins battle of Tippecanoe, 378; in War of 1812, 412; wins battle of the Thames (1813), 412; elected Pres., 462; death, 462; puts through land law, 546
Harrison's Landing, McClellan retreats to, 863
Harrodsburg, settled, 216

Hartford, Conn., Dutch establish post at, 128
Hartford Convention (1814), 416ff.
Hartford Wits, 307
Harvard College, founded, 148
Hatteras, Confederate fort captured, 850
Hawaii, Americanized, 500; annexation to U.S. refused, 500–501
Hawkins, Sir John (1532–95), in Caribbean, 64
Hawthorne, Nathaniel (1804–64),' novelist, 600
Hayes, Rutherford B. (1822–93), in electoral stalemate, 922–924; declared Pres., 924
Hayne, Robert Y. (1791–1839), debates with Webster, 670
Health and sanitation, in pioneer settlements, 537–538
Heartland, The, defined, 22–23
Hecker, Isaac (1819–88), founds Paulist Order, 621–622
Helderberg War, in Hudson Valley, 444
Henderson, Richard (1735–85), forms Transylvania Company, 216
Henry, Andrew (1775?–1833), in fur trade, 519
Henry, Fort, falls to Grant, 853
Henry, Joseph (1797–1878), and Smithsonian Institution, 592; Am. scientist, 556
Henry, Patrick (1736–99), pushes through "Virginia Resolves," 219; at First Cont. Congress, 227; attitude toward slavery, 274; refuses to attend Constitutional Convention, 291; in Western land speculation, 385
Henry the Navigator, Prince (1394–1460), 48
Henry VII (1457–1509), Eng. king, patron of John Cabot, 70
Herkimer, Nicholas (1728–77), repulses Rev. Tories at Oriskany, 254
Hessians, in Revolution, 248
Hewitt, Abram S. (1822–1903), crusades for Tilden, 922
Hill, A. P. (1825–65), Confederate leader, 868; in battle of Gettysburg, 874–876
Hill, Benjamin H. (1823–82), leads New Departure movement, 918–919
Hill, D. H. (1821–89), writes Southern text for Southern schools, 735; Conf. leader, 868
Hispanic America, see Latin America and entries by countries
Hispaniolization, of Latin America, 58–60
History of the U.S. (Bancroft), champions democracy, 602
Hoe, Richard (1812–86), develops rotary press, 562
Hoe, Robert (1784–1833), develops printing presses and processes, 562
Holland, in struggle for the Caribbean, 63–69; commercial supremacy of, 65; empire, 65–66; importance of carrying trade in, 112; founds New Netherland, 135; hostilities with Britain in Am. Revolution, 260; emigrants from, 608
Holmes, Oliver Wendell (1841–1935), quoted on democracy, 98, 99
Holmes, Oliver Wendell, Sr. (1809–94), fights for antisepsis, 591
Holston settlement, in Cherokee Wars, 253
Holy Alliance, formation of, 474
Homestead Act (1862), passes out free land, 548; provisions of, 819
Hood, John B. (1831–79), in battle for Atlanta, 881; defeated by Thomas at Nashville, 881
Hood, Samuel, (1724–1816), at time of Yorktown, 263ff.
Hooker, Joseph (1814–79), in battle of Chattanooga, 858; at Chancellorsville, 873–874
Hooker, Rev. Thomas (1586?–1647), settles Conn., 128
Hopedale Community, socialist experiment, 625
"Hopkinsians," 306–307

Hornet, in War of 1812, 407
Horseshoe Bend, Jackson defeats Creeks at, 421
House-Divided Speech, Lincoln's, 767
House of Burgesses, established (1619), 110–111; controlled by Berkeley, 113; dismissed by Berkeley, 114; passes Resolves of 1769, 221
Houston, Sam (1793–1863), biography, 695–696; orders Texan retreat, 696; in battle of San Jacinto, 697; first administration as pres. of Texas, 697; second administration, 698; as Southern Unionist, 733; deposed, 783
Howard, John (1726?–90), reformer, 588
Howard, Oliver O. (1830–1909), superintends Freedmen's Bureau, 898
Howe, Elias (1819–67), patents sewing machine, 561
Howe, Lord George (d. 1758), adapts Am. skirmishing methods, 196
Howe, Lord Richard (1726–99), invades New York in Rev., 255–256
Howe, Samuel Gridley (1801–76), in work for blind, 616
Howe, Sir William (1729–1814), in battle of Bunker Hill, 231; evacuates Boston, 232; invades New York, 255–256; strategy of (1777), 257–258; replaced by Clinton, 260
Hudson, Henry (d. 1611), explorer, 72; sails into N.Y. Harbor, 135
Hudson River School, of painting, 590
Hudson's Bay Company, war with French for control of Prince Rupert's Land, 191–192; monopolizes fur trade, 518; opens Ft. Vancouver, 686; acknowledges Am. government in Oregon country, 688; surrenders governing rights to Dominion of Canada, 832–833
Huguenots, forbidden to emigrate to New France, 73; influx of, 160
Hull, William (1753–1825), surrenders to British (1812), 410
Humor, standards of American, 628–629
Hunkers, faction of Dem. Party, 463
"Hunters' Lodges," in Can. struggle for independence, 483
Huron Indians, location of, 43; trade empire of, 75; conquest of, 76–77
Hu Shih, Chinese statesman and philosopher, 9
Hussey, Obed (1792–1860), invents mechanical reaper, 584
Hutchinson, Anne (1590?–1643), exiled to Rhode Island, 127
Hutchinson, Thomas (1711–80), Adams publishes letters of, 225

Iceland, Norse settlers in, 69
Idealism, of democracy, 97; American, and materialism, 630–631
Illini Indians, 41
Illinois, admitted as state, 393; growth in Great Migration, 396, 397
Illinois Central Railroad, first to receive land grant, 573
Illinois-Wabash Company, land speculators, 271ff.
Immediate Secessionists, see Fire-Eaters
Immigrants and immigration, significance of, 602ff.; heavy after 1815, 603–604; Great Migration (1850's), 608; physical conditions, 608–609; ignorance of America, 609; during Civil War, 822
Imperialism, agrarian, psychology of, 684ff.; Soviet, 103–105
Impressment of Am. seamen, 357–358
Income taxes, levied in Civil War, 820
Indentured servants, 146–147
Independence, Mo., jumping-off place of wagon trains, 692

Independence party, in Am. Rev., 245
Independent Treasury System, set up by Van Buren, 461–462; re-established by Polk, 701
India, saved by Clive for Eng., 196–197
Indiana, admitted as state, 393; growth in Great Migration, 396
Indiana Company, in Old West, 215; activities of, 271ff.
Indian Intercourse Act (1834), 526
Indians, North American location and description of, 38–47; linguistic stocks, 41; Pequot War in Conn. Valley, 132; Delawares on Manhattan Island, 135; relations with settlers in Old West, 211–212; story of their opinion of whites, 503–508; passing of Woods, 508ff.; Federal policies toward, 510ff.; retaliate on whites, 513; attempt to assimilate white culture, 521; permanent frontier for, 521ff.; removal policy, 522, 524; as problem of West, 531; pioneer fighters against, 541–542
Indian Service, supports research in Indian lore, 592
Indian Territory, final home of Five Civilized Nations, 527–528; in Civil War, 803
Indian treaties, in Northwest Territory, 376–377
Indian uprisings, in Va. (1622), 111; in Md. and Va. (1675), 113–114; in New Eng. (King Philip's War), 132–133; Cherokee (1760), 213; Shawnee (1774), 216; Cherokee (1776), 253; Iroquois (in Rev.), 254; in Ohio (1794), 377; Tippecanoe (1811), 379; Creek War (1813), 421; Seminole, 425, 521, 524; Tlingit (1799), 514, 516; Black Hawk War (1832), 522; Cayuse (1847), 688
Indigo, grown in S.C., 118
Individualism, mythus of American, 542–543; and transcendentalism, 599; and social control, 630
Industrial capitalism, rise of, 575; philosophical background of, 575–576; reasons for growth in U.S., 577; sources of, 653–654; backs Radicals after Civil War, 894; in "Peace of 1877," 924
Industrial Revolution, effect of, 18, 19
Industry, as stage of settlement, 166; booms during Civil War, 821; encouraged in South and West, 927
Inferiority complex, American, and complacency, 631–632
Inflation, in 1830's, 460; in South during Civil War, 823
Institutions, reforms of, 615–616
Intelligentsia, in colonies, 153–154
Interchangeable part, invention of principle of, 562
Interior, Dept. of, created, 510
Interstate commerce, Federal control of upheld, 438
Intolerable Acts, aimed especially at Mass., 226
Intolerance, American, 633
Inventions, American, 557ff.; patents, 563–564
Iowa, admitted to Union, 393; growth of, 398
Iowa Indians, 41
Irish settlers, in Pa., 141; 18th-century, 162; later, 603, 604–605
Iron and iron smelting, in colonial New Eng., 131–132; colonial production of, 559
Ironclads, in Civil War, 862–863
Iroquoian nations, composition of, 41, 43
Iroquois, control trade routes, 75; strategy of terror, 75–76; trade empire of, 77; decline of, 78; attack the Illinois, 189; sell land in Old West, 213; actions in Revolution, 254

Irving, Washington (1783–1859), sentimentalism of, 593; fans Oregon fever, 687
Isabela, founded on Hispaniola, 52
Isabella (1451–1504), backs Columbus, 50
Isolation, as factor in Am. conservatism, 36; policy of, initiated by Jefferson, 331

Jackson, Andrew (1767–1845), in Western land speculation, 381, 385; biography, 418–420; in East Fla., 420; in Gulf Campaign (War of 1812), 421; in Creek War (1813–1814), 421; seizes Pensacola and St. Marks (1818), 425; made governor of Fla., 426; as dominant national figure, 430; presidential candidate, 438; vote in election of 1824, 439; accuses Clay of double dealing, 440; coalition for, 447–448; elected Pres., 449; character of, 451–452; Calhoun opposes with nullification policy, 453; breaks with Calhoun, 454; vetoes Maysville Road Bill, 454–456; dismisses Cabinet, 456; votes for (1832), 458; renews "war" on B. U. S., 459ff.; nominates Van Buren (1836), 461; in struggle for West Indian trade, 481; refuses protection to Indians, 510–511
Jackson, James (1757–1806), Jeffersonian Republican, 327
Jackson, Thomas Jonathan (Stonewall) (1824–63), in Valley Campaign, 863; biography, 865; excellency as general, 867–868; at Antietam, 868; at Chancellorsville, 873
Jacksonian democracy, effect on Old South, 643–644
Jacksonian Movement, its effects on Am. history, 463ff.; sentimentalism of, 598
Jacobin Clubs, imitated in U.S., 329
Jalapa, falls to Scott in Mexican War, 712
James I (1566–1625), Eng. king, ends hostilities with Spain, 65; growth of political parties under, 87; charters Virginia Company, 107–108
James II (1633–1701), Eng. king, and Glorious Revolution, 91–92; forms Dominion of New England, 133–134; curbs democracy in N.Y., 138–139
Jamestown, Va., founded, 109
Janson, Eric, founds pietist community, 624
Japan, Portugal in, 53; early relations with U.S., 496ff.; isolation before 1850, 496–497; Westernization of, 498; Western "gunboat policy" against, 499
Jay, John (1745–1829), peace commissioner at Paris, 266–267; co-author of The Federalist, 298; becomes first Chief Justice of the Supreme Court, 301; biography, 306; leads aristocratic faction, 323; settles trade difficulties with Eng., 332
Jay's Treaty (1794), with England, 333–334
Jefferson, Thomas (1743–1826), quoted on democracy, 96, 99; prepares formal Declaration of Independence, 236; brought into Washington's Cabinet, 301; biography, 315–317; philosophy, 317–318; political tenets and methods, 318–319; sets up The National Gazette, 319; relations with Hamilton, 320; as a Physiocrat, 321; retires as Secretary of State, 331; pres. candidate, 336; writes Kentucky Resolutions, 342; nominated for presidency (1800), 342; his first inaugural (quoted), 348–349; fate of his program, 349; executive actions during first term, 350–351; re-elected, 355; recommends public works, 355; assailed by Quids, 356; puts through Embargo Act, 360–362; failure of administration, 364–365; and Hamilton as protagonist and antagonist, 365–370; introduces Northwest Ordinance

of 1784, 374; and Yazoo frauds, 385; tries to annex Fla., 389–390; and Monroe Doctrine, 476; sends out Lewis and Clark Expedition, 516–517; agricultural experiments of, 582

Jeffersonian democracy, championed by Emerson, 600; splits into two wings, 667

Jeffersonian Movement, compared to Jacksonian Movement, 463ff.

Jeffersonian Republicans, indulge in newspaper vilification, 336–337; in election of 1800–01, 342ff.

Jerome, Chauncey (1793–1868), clock manufacturer, 563

Jews, settle in colonial Newport, 160

Johnson, Andrew (1808–75), as Southern Unionist, 733; made governor of Tenn., 799; as Radical leader, 814; nominated for vice-presidency, 885; attitude toward South, 892; his handicaps, 892–893; in election campaign of 1866, 902–903; ideas on reconstruction, 896–897, 899–900; vetoes First Reconstruction Act, 904; impeachment of, 906–908

Johnson, Herschel V. (1812–80), nominated for vice-presidency (1860), 776

Johnson, Richard M. (1780–1850), a leader of War Hawks, 402; nominated for V.-P., 461

Johnson, Sir William (1715–74), biography, 196; made Supt. of Indian Affairs in the North, 212; as land speculator, 215

Johnston, Albert Sidney (1803–62), retreats after defeat at Fort Henry, 853; opposes Grant at Shiloh, 853–854

Johnston, Joseph E. (1807–91), heads army at Winchester, 796; in Vicksburg Campaign, 856; at Fair Oaks, 863; in battle for Atlanta, 881; surrenders to Sherman, 887

Joint Committee on Reconstruction, set up, 900; aims of, 905–906

Joint Committee on the Conduct of the War (1861), set up, 815

Joint stock companies, colonize America, 107; defined, 577

Joliet, Louis (1645–1700), explorer, 188–189

Jones, Anson (1798–1858), pres. of Texas, 698

Jones, John Paul (1747–92), naval victor, 250

Jones, Thomas ap Catesby (1790–1858), seizes Monterey, 692

Jones, Willie (1741?–1801), Jeffersonian Republican, 327

Juárez, Benito (1806–72), victor in Mexican War of Reform, 829

Judicial system, organized by First Congress, 301–302

Judiciary Act of 1801, provisions of, 344; repealed, 351

Julian, George W. (1817–99), Radical leader in 37th Congress, 814; against "Grantism," 918

Kalb, Baron de (1721–80), leader in Rev., 242

Kanawha Valley, Rosecrans in, 797–798

Kansas, slavery and freedom adherents battle for, 753–757, 762; admitted to Union, 763

Kansas-Nebraska Bill, 748ff.

Kaskaskia, falls to Clark in Revolution, 254

Kearny, Stephen W. (1794–1848), in New Mexico and California, 710; opposed by Frémont, 711; seizes Los Angeles, 711

Kearsarge, Union ship, sinks Alabama, 828

Kelley, Hall (1790–1874), inspires expeditions to Oregon country, 687

Kelly, William (1811–88), and Bessemer process, 559

Kendall, Amos (1789–1869), 452

Kennesaw Mt., falls to Sherman, 881

Kent, James (1763–1847), stops democratization of laws, 436

Kenton, Simon (1755–1836), Indian fighter, 541, 544

Kentucky, in Am. Revolution, 253; planned as state, 289; admitted as state, 381–382; growth in Great Migration, 396; attempts neutrality in Civil War, 799, 801; strategic significance of, 801

Kentucky Resolution (1799), passed, 341–342

Kernstown, Civil War battle at, 863

Key, Francis Scott (1779–1843), pens The Star-Spangled Banner, 415

Kidnapees, as early settlers, 146

Kieft, William (1597–1647), Director-general of New Netherland, 136

King, Rufus (1755–1827), attends Constitutional Convention, 291; as Federalist leader, 305; in election of 1804, 355; runs for Vice-Pres. (1808), 362; agricultural experimenter, 582

King, William R. (1786–1853), elected Vice-Pres. (1852), 730

King Cotton, 643ff.; role in Civil War, 836–837

King George's War, 192–193

King Philip's War, 132–133

King's Mt., N.C., Ferguson defeated at, 261–262

Kino, Father Eusebio (1645?–1711), explores Southwest, 689

Kipling, Rudyard, quoted, 632

Kirby-Smith, Edmund (1824–93), commands Trans-Mississippi Dept., 857; surrenders, 887

Kitchen Cabinet, Jackson's, 452

Knights of the Golden Circle, a Copperhead society, 818

Know-Nothing Party (Native-American), 620

Knox, Henry (1750–1806), military leader in Rev., 242; Sec. of War, 308

Korea, failure of Western "gunboat policy" against, 499

Kosciusko, Thaddeus (1746–1817), military leader in Rev., 242

Ku Klux Klan, formed, 917

Labadists, socialists, (1680), 623

Labor, and capital in the 1850's, 574ff.; conditions of, 578–579; wages, 579–580; during Civil War, 821–822; 10-hour day adopted, 581; organizations, 580–581

Labrador, named, 71–72

Ladd, William (1778–1841), in peace movement, 619

Lafayette, Marquis de (1757–1834), in Rev., 242

Laird rams, built in Eng. for Confederacy, 829

Laissez-faire theory, defined, 21; becomes political issue, 575–576; prevents government support of cultural activities, 591; varying interpretations of, 654

Lake Champlain, battle (1814), 413–414

Lake Erie, battle (1814), 412

Lamar, Mirabeau Buonaparte (1798–1859), as pres. of Republic of Texas, 697–698

Lancaster Pike, pioneer road, 568

Land, tenure among Indians, 43–44; concentration in plantations, 112; colonial significance of cheap, 147–148; democracy based on, 186; role in Revolution, 209–217; problems of speculation and ownership in drafting Articles of Confederation, 271–272; national surveys of, 374; inflationary speculation (1830's), 460; purchase from Indians, 511; a problem of the West, 531, 535–536; as capital stake in West, 546; agitation for free, 547; proposed solutions for the problem of, 547–548

Land grants, in Old West, 213; aid railroads, 573; for education, 591; establish colleges, 819; question of giving Negroes, 898–899, 913–914

Land laws (1800, 1820), enable pioneers to buy farms, 546

Land speculation, in Old West, 211, 213–215; in Old Northwest, 372ff.; Yazoo frauds, 384–385; in country as a whole, 549–550

Lane, Joseph (1801–81), nominated for Vice-Pres. (1860), 776

Lane Seminary, a center for reform movements, 659–660; "debate" on abolition, 660

La Salle, Robert Cavelier de (1643–87), imperial ventures of, 189–190

Latin America, as part of Spanish Empire, 59–60; revolts from Spain, 471–473; Wars of Independence in, 471–473; U.S. attitude toward, 474–475

Latter-Day Saints (Mormons), 627

Laud, Archbishop (1573–1645), tool of Charles I, 87; harries Noncomformists, 123

Laurens, Henry (1724–92), seized by British, 260; peace commissioner at Paris, 266

Laurentian Shield, mineral wealth of, 30

Law, common, 84, 126; democracy as government by, 100; lack of, on frontier, 543–544

Law, John (1671–1729), and "Mississippi Bubble," 191

Lawrence, James (1781–1813), captains Chesapeake, 408

Lawrence, Kans., sacked (1856), 757; gutted in Civil War, 803

League of Armed Neutrality, 259, 260

League of Universal Brotherhood, in mid-19th century, 619–620

Lear, Tobias (1762–1816), in Barbary Wars, 353

Learning, revival of in U.S., 587ff.; popularization of, 592

Leaves of Grass (Whitman), an affirmation of faith, 601–602

Le Conte, Joseph (1823–1901), geologist, 592

Lee, Arthur (1740–92), 247

Lee, Charles (1731–82), military leader in Rev., 242; refuses troop support in N.J., 256; at battle of Monmouth, 260

Lee, Jason (1803–45), establishes mission in Oregon country, 686–687

Lee, "Light-Horse Harry" (1756–1818), in Whisky Insurrection, 333

Lee, Mother Ann (1736–84), introduces Shakerism, 624

Lee, Richard Henry (1732–94), attends First Cont. Congress, 227; introduces freedom declaration, 236

Lee, Robert E. (1807–70), in Mexican War, 712, 713; takes Confederate command in Peninsular Campaign, 863; defeats Pope at Second Battle of Bull Run, 864–865; biography, 865–866; character of, 867; and the mythus of chivalry, 867; at Antietam, 868; defeats Burnside at Fredericksburg, 870–871; in battle of the Wilderness, 878–879; at Spotsylvania, 879; in battle at Cold Harbor, 879–880; in siege of Petersburg, 880; surrenders, 886–887; retires, 895

Lee-Adams Junto, leads radicals, 246ff.

Leif the Lucky, lands in America, 69

Leisler, Jacob (1640?–91), N.Y. rebel, 138

L'Enfant, lays out Washington, D.C., 311

Leopard (Br. frigate), searches Chesapeake (1807), 359–360

Lesser Antilles, settlement of, 66

Letters of a Pennsylvania Farmer (Dickinson), on tax matters, 222

Levellers, 90

Lewis, Andrew (1720–81), defeats Shawnee at Pt. Pleasant, 216

Lewis, Meriwether (1774–1809), in Lewis and Clark Expedition, 516–517

Lexington, Ky., settled, 390

Lexington, Mass., battle at, 229–230

Leyden, refuge of Pilgrims, 121

Liberals, definition of political, 102

Liberator, The, Garrison publishes, 658–659

Liberties, see Civil liberties, Concrete liberties

Liberty, relationship to economic equality, 367–368

Liberty Party, ensures Polk's victory (1844), 700; unites with Barnburners, 722

Library of Congress, lag in developing, 591

Lightning, noted clipper ship, 491

Lincoln, Abraham (1809–65), quoted on Declaration of Independence, 635–636; opposes Mexican War, 707; biography, 763–766; House-Divided Speech, 767; debates Douglas, 768; nominated for Pres. (1860), 777; votes for, 779, 780; responsibility in compromise solution of sectional strife, 786–787; inauguration, 788–789; early inaction in secession crisis, 789–790; his motives in action at Ft. Sumter, 791–792; as parliamentarian, 814; his Cabinet, 816; war powers, 817; strength as Pres., 824–825; his opinion of Grant, 854; confines McClellan to Army of the Potomac, 860; withholds McDowell's corps from Penin. Campaign, 863; issues Emancipation Proclamation, 869; faces Cabinet crisis (1862), 871–872; Ten-Per-Cent Plan, 883; delivers Gettysburg Address, 883; nominated for re-election, 885; in Hampton Roads Conference, 886; favors conciliation, 888; assassination and death, 888; the Lincoln Legend, 931–932

Lincoln, Benjamin (1733–1810), military leader in Rev., 242; attempts to recapture Savannah, 261; surrenders at Charleston, 261; crushes Shays's Rebellion, 289

List, Friedrich (1789–1846), 576

Literature, of 19th century, 589–590; Southern before Civil War, 677–678

Little Missouri Compromise (1821), 665

Little Turtle, Miami chief, defeats whites, 377

Livingston, Edward (1764–1836), becomes Secretary of State, 456

Livingston, Robert R. (1746–1813), and Louisiana Purchase, 387; builds steamboats, 565; backs Fulton, 567; agricultural experimenter, 582

Livingston family, leads a Whig faction, 322

Local government, in New England, 130; in Middle Colonies, 142

Localism, political theories of, 668ff.

Locke, John (1632–1704), and the Physiocrats, 21; theory of Natural Rights, 92ff.; draws up constitution for Carolina, 118

Loco Focos, take over Dem. Party, 463; influence Barnburners, 718

Locomotives, development of steam, 570–571

Logan, George (1753–1821), Quaker, 324

Logan, John A. (1826–86), 903

Log house, introduced by Swedes, 150; in West, 536

London Company, colonial government under, 107–108; grants land to Pilgrims, 121

Long, Dr. Crawford W. (1815–78), introduces use of ether, 591

Long, Stephen (1784–1864), explores West, 517

Long Parliament, 90

Long Point, burned in War of 1812, 413

Longstreet, James (1821–1904), characteristics of, 868; in battle of Gettysburg, 875–876

Lookout Mt., Hooker seizes, 858

Los Angeles, Cal., founded, 689

Louis XIV (1638–1715), Fr. king, ambitions of, 67; takes control of New France, 73–74

Louis XVI (1754–93), guillotined, 328

Louisbourg, in King William's War, 192–193; taken from French, 196

Louisiana, settled by French, 190–191; deeded to Spain, 198; Spain cedes to France, 339; Spanish policies in, 380–381; becomes part of U.S., 387; problems following purchase of, 387–388; admitted as state, 393; growth in Great Migration, 396; secedes from Union, 783; readmitted, 908

Louisiana Purchase (1803), 353–354, 387

Louisville, Ky., settled, 390

L'Ouverture, Toussaint (1743–1803), resists Fr. troops, 386

Lovejoy, Elijah (1802–37), attacked by anti-abolitionist mobs, 661

Lovejoy, Owen (1811–64), on Civil War, 849

Lowell, James Russell (1819–91), active in anti-slavery literature, 662; opposes Mexican War, 706

Lowell, Mass., condition of mills in, 579

Lowndes, William (1782–1822), a leader of War Hawks, 402

Loyalists, battle Whigs before Revolution, 229; fight Whigs in South, 233–234; expulsion of, 276; *see also* Tories

Loyal Land Company, organized, 211; in Old West, 215–216

Lumber and lumber products, in colonial New Eng., 131; in Middle Colonies, 142; technology of cutting and sawing, 560–561

Lundy, Benjamin (1789–1839), publishes abolition papers, 657

Lundy's Lane, Can., in War of 1812, 413

Lyon, Matthew (1750–1822), punished by Sedition Act (1798), 340–341

Lyon, Nathaniel (1818–61), commands Union troops in Mo., 802

McAdam, John (1756–1836), develops hard-surface road, 568

McClellan, George Brinton (1826–86), in campaign in western Va., 797; rebuilds Union army, 843–844; characteristics of, 860; plans campaign in the East, 860, 862; in Peninsular Campaign, 862–863; retreats, 863; recalled, 863–864; in battle of Antietam, 868; removed, 870; nominated for Pres., 885

McCormick, Cyrus Hall (1809–84), invents reaper, 584

McCulloch v. Maryland, upholds Federal sovereignty, 437

MacDonald, Sir John A. (1815–91), first premier of Canada, 832

Macdonough, Thomas (1783–1825), wins battle of Lake Champlain, (1814), 413–414

McDougall, Alexander (1731?–86), radical leader in colonies, 229

McDowell, Dr. Ephraim (1771–1830), pioneer in surgery, 591

McDowell, Irvin (1818–85), defends Washington, D.C., 795; in First Battle of Bull Run, 796–797

McGillivray, Alexander (1759?–93), leader of Creeks, 385

McGuffey, William Holmes (1800–73), publishes readers, 539

McHenry, Fort, repulses Brit. fleet in War of 1812, 415

McKay, Donald (1810–80), ship designer, 491

McKean, Judge Thomas (1734–1817), 324

McKee, Alexander, Br. superintendent in Old Northwest, 378

McLeod, Alexander, and *Caroline* affair, 482–483

McLeod Expedition, seizes Santa Fe, 698

McLoughlin, John (1784–1857), directs Hudson's Bay Company, 518; chief factor at Vancouver, 686; refuses aid to immigrants, 687

McPherson, James B. (1828–64), characteristics of, 852; in battle for Atlanta, 881

Machine tools, development of, 562

Mackenzie, Sir Alexander (1755?–1820), explores Pac. Northwest, 514

Mackenzie, William Lyon (1795–1861), stages uprising in Ontario, 482, 483

Mackinder, Halford (1861–1948), and Heartland theory, 22–23

Macon, Nathaniel (1758–1837), Jeffersonian Republican, 327

Macon's Bill No. 2, repeals Nonintercourse Act, 403–404

Madeiras, discovery of, 48

Madison, James (1751–1836), attends Const. Convention, 291; co-authors *The Federalist,* 298; biography, 326; writes Virginia Resolves, 342; Secretary of State, 349; elected Pres. (1808), 362; annexes West Fla., 390; ineffective in office, 403; sends war message to Congress, 406; accedes to Young Republican program, 433–434; vetoes Bonus Bill, 434; vetoes Cumberland Road Tolls Bill, 434; and Monroe Doctrine, 476

Madison, James (1749–1812), bishop of Va., 274

Magazines, in 19th century, 589–590, 677

Magellan, Ferdinand (1480?–1521), exploring voyages of, 56

Magna Charta (1215), 84

Maine, settled, 129; taken over by Mass., 130; occupied by Br. in War of 1812, 413; boundary dispute, 485; admitted as state, 393

Malden, burned in War of 1812, 412

Malvern Hill, Lee repulsed at, 863

Manassas, Lee defeats Pope at, 864–865

Mandan Indians, 41

Manhattan (N.Y.), origin of name, 135

Manifest Destiny, 683ff.

Manitoba, joins Dominion, 832

Mann, Horace (1796–1859), leader in education, 613

Manufactures and commerce, of New Eng., 131–132; in colonies, 179; limited by England, 201; *see also* Mass production, Trade

Marbury v. Madison, doctrine of judicial review, 351, 437

"March through Georgia," Sherman's, 881–882

Marcy, William L. (1787–1857), of Albany Regency, 432; becomes Secretary of War, 701; repudiates Ostend Manifesto, 737

Marietta, O., settled by land speculators, 375

Marine Corps, reorganized (1798), 338

Marquette, Jacques (1637–75), explorer, 188–189

Marshall, James (1810–85), discovers gold in Cal., 724

Marshall, John (1755–1835), Federalist leader, 305; emissary to France (1797), 337; Chief Justice, 344; decision in *Marbury v. Madison,* 351; rules in Burr conspiracy, 389; biography, 435; Constitutional principles of, 435–436; great decisions of, 437–438; ruling in interstate commerce, 567

Martha's Vineyard, as whaling center, 493

Martin, Luther (1748?–1826), attends Const. Convention, 291

Martin Chuzzlewit (Dickens), criticizes America, 596

Martin v. Hunter's Lessee, rules on power of Supreme Court, 437

Martineau, Harriet (1802–76), admires America, 597

Martling's Long Room, Tammany meets at, 324

Martyr, Peter (d. 1526), names New World, 57

Maryland, and Bacon's Rebellion, 115; first successful proprietary colony, 116ff.; rehabilitates farms, 582; remains in Union in secession crisis, 794

Maryland, My Maryland (Randall), occasion for writing, 795

Mason, George (1725–92), writes Resolves of 1769, 221; leader in fight for independence, 222; attends Const. Convention, 291

Mason, James M. (1798–1871), Confederate commissioner abroad, 826; in *Trent* Affair, 827–828

Mason, John (1586–1635), receives grant of New Hampshire, 129–130

Mason, John Y. (1799–1859), co-author of Ostend Manifesto, 737

Mason and Dixon's Line, laid out, 141

Massachusetts and Massachusetts Bay Colony, religious domination of, 124; government of, 125–126; takes over New Hampshire and Maine, 130; joins in New Eng. Confederation, 132; charter annulled by Charles II, 133; becomes royal colony, 134; Charter weakened by Intolerable Acts, 226; stand before Revolution, 229; sells land claims to speculators, 323

Massachusetts Bay Company, confirmed in land grant, 122

Mass production, groundwork laid for, 562ff.

Matamoros, Mex., occupied in Mexican War, 709

Materialism, American preoccupation with, 630–631

Mather, Cotton and Increase, colonial religious leaders, 157

Mathews, George (1739–1812), leads East Florida "revolution," 402

Maury, Matthew Fontaine (1806–73), pioneer in oceanography, 491–492; receives naval post, 591

Maximilian (1832–67), Emp. of Mexico, 829–830

Mayas, decline of, 39

Mayflower, voyage of, 121

"Mayflower Compact," signed, 121; as form of colonial democratic government, 185–186

Maysville Road Veto (1830), 454; its effects, 454–456

Mazzini, G. (1805–72), quoted on Civil War, 831

Meade, George Gordon (1815–72), in battle of Gettysburg, 874–877; remains in command of Army of the Potomac, 877

Mechanicsville, battle of, 863

Medicine, in early 19th century, 591; not permitted through blockade in Civil War, 849

Medicine men, Indian, 44

Meigs, Fort, repels attack in War of 1812, 412

Melville, Herman (1819–91), critic of the democratic dogma, 600–601

Memphis, Tenn., settled, 391

Menéndez de Avilés, Pedro (1519–74), founds St. Augustine (1565), 64

Mercantilism, defined, 20–21; in Spanish Empire, 59; in England, 173ff.; as one of the causes of Am. Revolution, 200ff.; England gradually abandons, 481–482

Mercator, Nicolaus (1620?–87), 14, 15

Mercer, John Francis (1759–1821), Jeffersonian Republican, 327

Merchant capitalism, defined, 574ff.; in cotton triangle, 652–653; falls before industrial capitalism, 653; and Southern extremists, 735–736

Merchant marine, decline of Am., 492–493

Merchants, colonial unite against Stamp Act, 219; oppose Br. policies, 223; of Confederation period, 285

Merrimac, Confederate frigate, in action with *Monitor,* 862; destroyed, 863

Methodist Church, organized, 274; Southern split in, 677; sets up mission in Oregon country, 686–687

Mexican Cession, effect of, 719

Mexican War (1846–48), events leading to, 702; Am. reasons for, 703; Mexican justification, 704; advantages on each side, 705–706; popular opposition to, 706–707; finances of, 707; campaign of 1846, 709; campaign in Valley of Mexico, 713; peace treaty signed, 714; results of, 715

Mexico, conquered by Cortes, 56; a center of Latin-American culture, 471; wins freedom, 471, 473; fears U.S. in 19th century, 685–686; reactions to Americans in pre-revolutionary Texas, 693–694; declares war on U.S. (1846), 702; Am. occupation of (1848), 715; seized by France, 829–830; Díaz imposes dictatorship, 830

Mexico, University of, founded (1551), 60

Miami Indians, location of, 41

Michigan, admitted to Union, 396; as fruit and dairy land, 398

Michigan-Ohio dispute over territory, 396–397

Michilimackinac, Fort, falls to British (1812), 410

Middle Ages, unity of, 10

Middle class, in colonies, 152

Middle Colonies, (states), settlement of, 134–142; climate and terrain, 141–142; agriculture in, 142; education in early, 158; as an economic and cultural area, 444ff.

Middle West, evolution of, 399

Mifflin, Thomas (1744–1800), political leader, 324

Migration, periods of Western, 391, 393; origins and lines of, 393–395; The Great, 396; to West, 534–535

Militia, character of service in Am. Rev., 241–242

Militia Act of 1862, drafts Union troops, 840–841

Millennial Church (Shakers), pietist socialist group, 624

Miller, William (1782–1849), preaches millennial dawn, 626

Mill towns, development of, 578–579

Milwaukee, Wis., settled, 397; Germans in, 606

Mims, Fort, massacre at (1813), 421

Mineral resources, of U.S., 32, 34

Minnesota, admitted to Union, 397; as dairy land, 398

Minnesota, in action against C.S.S. *Virginia,* 862

Minuit, Peter (1580–1638), buys Manhattan Island, 135; builds Fort Christina, 136

Minutemen, of Mass. militia, 229

Mission, the American sense of a, 635–636; doctrine of Manifest Destiny, 683ff.; disunion a threat to, 807

Missionary Ridge, Civil War battle at, 858

Missions and missionaries, French among the Iroquois, 78; Catholic work against La Salle, 189–190; in China, 494ff.; in Oregon country, 686–687; in Southwest, 688–689; in California, 689; break-up of Spanish, 691

Mississippi, admitted as state, 393; growth in Great Migration, 396; secedes from Union, 783; readmitted to Union, 908

"Mississippi Bubble," 191

Mississippi Plan, enforces white power in South, 921–922

Mississippi River, and transportation, 29; role in settling the country, 380ff.; Civil War along the, 847–854

Missouri, admitted as state, 393; growth in Great Migration, 396; remains in Union, 802, 803; votes down secession (1861), 785

Missouri Compromise (1820), provisions of, 665; effects of, 666

Mobile Bay, blocked in Civil War, 851

Moby Dick (Melville), allegory, 600–601

Mohawk, one of Five Nations, 75; attack Huronia, 76–77

Molasses, triangular trade in, 163; significance of trade in, 177–178

Molasses Act (1733), 178, 179

Molino del Rey, Am. victory at, 713

Money, England controls colonial, 202; issued to finance Revolution, 246; in Confederation period, 288; a problem of the West, 532; in Civil War, 819–821; in South during Civil War, 823

Monitor, in action with Confederate *Virginia*, 862; founders, 863

Monmouth, battle of, in Rev., 260

Monopolies, under mercantilism, 20–21; by corporations, 578

Monroe, Fortress, in Union hands, 850; Davis imprisoned in, 887

Monroe, James (1758–1831), Jeffersonian Republican, 327; minister to France, 337; mission to Eng., 360; negotiates Louisiana Purchase, 386, 387; supervises War Dept. (War of 1812), 415; inaugurated as Pres., 425; re-elected, 430; biography, 430; recognizes independence of Latin-American countries, 475; Monroe Doctrine, 476ff.

Monroe Doctrine, provisions of, 476–477; England's reception of, 477; Latin-American attitude toward, 477–478; significance of, 478–479

Montcalm, Marquis (1712–59), military leader, 193, 195; at Plains of Abraham, 197

Monterey, Calif., settled, 689

Monterrey, Mex., taken by Taylor, 709

Montesquieu (1689–1755), read in colonies, 159

Montgomery, Richard (1738–75), takes Montreal, 232

Montreal, named by Cartier, 72; trading post established at, 73; taken in Rev., 232

Moore's Creek Bridge, Regulators scattered at, 233

Morality, and man, 6; Am. striving for, 630–635

Morgan, Daniel (1736–1802), in Whisky Insurrection, 333

Morgan, John Hunt (1825–64), Confederate cavalry leader, 855

Morgan, William (1774?–?1826), and Anti-Masonic Party, 457

Mormon Church, 627

Morocco, in Barbary Wars, 352–353

Morrill Land Grant Act (1862), establishes colleges, 819

Morrill Tariff (1861), increases rates, 788; insufficiency of, 818–819

Morris, Gouverneur (1752–1816), attends Const. Convention, 291; Federalist leader, 305; land speculator, 549

Morris, Robert (1734–1806), leader of moderates in Rev., 247; attends Const. Convention, 291; in land speculation, 385

Morristown, Washington occupies heights at, 256

Morse, Jedidiah (1761–1826), geographer, 275

Morse, Samuel F. B. (1791–1872), inventor, 574; painter, 590

Morton, Oliver P. (1823–77), elected to Senate, 903

Morton, Dr. W. T. G. (1819–68), introduces use of ether in dentistry, 591

Mott, Lucretia Coffin (1793–1880), reformer, 618, 619

Mountaineers, in pre-Civil War South, 647

Mountain men, trappers in West, 520–521

Mount Desert, French settlement at, 73

Mudsill theory, used in defense of slavery, 673–674

Muhlenberg family, leads opposition to Federalists, 324

Murfreesboro, Civil War battle at, 856

Murrell, John (1804?–44), frontier outlaw, 543

Muscovy Company of London, 72

Muskhogean Indians, 41, 43

Mythus, the, defined, 7–8; of individualism, 542–543; of Southern chivalry, 867

Nagasaki, Japan, Dutch trading post at, 496

Nantucket, occupied by British in War of 1812, 413; as whaling center, 493

Napoleon (1769–1821), establishes Continental System, 358–359; sells Louisiana, 386–387; exiled to Elba, 413; effect of Grand Army on British-American relations, 417

Napoleon III (1808–73), during Civil War, 829

Nashville, Tenn., settled, 253; Civil War battle at, 881

Natchez, Miss., settled, 391

National Bank Act (1863), provisions of, 818

National Gazette, The, set up by Jefferson, 319

Nationalism, European, 17, 18–19; American, 34–35; resurgence of after War of 1812, 470ff.; doctrine of Manifest Destiny, 683ff.

"Nationalists," in Confederation period, 286

National Road, completed, 434; Federal project, 568

Native-American Party (Know-Nothing), formed, 620

Nativism, rises against Catholics, 620; in Old South, 644

Naturalization Act (1798), passed, 339

Natural Rights, Locke's theory of, 92ff.; democracy developed from theory of, 186–187; colonists apply, 203–204; as expressed in Declaration of Independence, 236; colonial belief in, 587; and the slavery problem, 657; in case of Negroes, 672–673

Nauvoo, Ill., Mormon center, 627

Navies, in Revolution, 250–251; in War of 1812, 407ff., 851; in Civil War, 849–850

Navigation, difficulties encountered in early, 55; clipper ships, 490–491; introduction of steam in, 491, 492

Navigation Acts, purpose of, 174–175

Nebraska Terr., 747ff.

Negroes, slavery introduced, 112; triangular trade in, 163; 18th-century immigrants, 163–164; free, before Civil War, 650; significance as slaves, 805; troops in Civil War, 841–842; camp followers, 898; and land ownership, 898–899; leaders after Civil War, 913, 915; race problem after Civil War, 928

Nelson, Lord (1758–1805), Trafalgar, 358

New American Practical Navigator (Bowditch), pioneer text, 492

New Amsterdam, founded by Dutch, 135; trade center for colonies, 136–137

New Bedford, Mass., as whaling center, 494

New Bern, N.C., occupied by Union troops, 850
Newbold, Charles, patents cast-iron plow, 583
New Brunswick, joins Dom. of Canada, 832
New Departure movement, in Dem. Party, 918–919
New England, poor soil of, 30; named, 121; settlement of, 121–134; education in early, 166; back country, 166; in King George's War, 192–193; a region of pre-Revolutionary protest, 209ff.; privateers of, 249; stronghold of Federalism, 306; Rebublicanism in, 322; institutions transferred to West, 395–396; defeatism during War of 1812, 406–407, 415–416; as an economic and cultural area, 444ff.; invests in railroads, 573; see also Dominion of New England
New England Confederation, purpose of, 132
New England Primer, The, 158
New England town, 130–131
Newfoundland, origin of name of, 70; failure of colony on, 116
Newfoundland Banks, description of, 25, 27, 70–71
New France, placed under control of fur monopoly (1627), 73; during French and Indian Wars, 193ff.
New Hampshire, settled, 129; taken over by Mass., 130; made royal colony, 133, 134
New Harmony, Ind., German pietist community, 624; bought by Robert Owen, 626
New Haven Colony, settled as theocracy, 129; joined with Conn., 129; growth as shipping center, 132; joins New Eng. Confederation, 132
New Jersey, placed under Andros, 133; becomes royal colony, 139; proposes plan of government at Const. Convention, 292; a Federalist state, 324
"Newlanders," immigration agents, 160
New Madrid, Mo., taken by Pope in Civil War, 854
New Mexico, outline history of, 688; occupied during Mexican War, 710
New Netherland, founded, 135; slow development of, 135; in war with Delaware Indians, 136; annexes New Sweden, 136; loses out to England, 137
New Orleans, La., becomes capital of La., 190; entrepôt of Mississippi Valley, 391; in War of 1812, 421–423; effect of canal building on, 570; effect of railroads on, 573; falls to Union fleet in Civil War, 851
New Orleans, steamboat, descends Mississippi R., 567
Newport, Christopher (d. 1617), lands colonists in Va., 109
Newport, R.I., as shipping town, 132; center of colonial Jews, 160; attacked by Fr. fleet, 260
Newspaper presses, developed, 562
Newspapers, cost of early, 589; Southern before Civil War, 677
New Sweden, short life of, 136
New World, named by Peter Martyr, 57
New York (city), placed under Andros, 133; seized from Dutch, 137; in colonial days, 153; as smuggling center, 226; Rev. campaigns around, 255–256; Br. troops withdrawn from, 256; Washington invests, 260–261; named capital, 299; in Oriental trade, 488, 489–490; growth after opening of Erie Canal, 570
New York (state), added to Dom. of New Eng., 138; frontier in Revolution, 254; in War of 1812, 412, 413; reforms prisons, 616
New York Central Railroad, consolidated, 573
Nicaragua, Walker fails in filibuster in, 738–739

Nichols, Richard (1624–72), proclaims "Duke's Laws" in New Netherland, 137
Nicholson, Francis (1655–1728), governor of New York, 138
Niles, Hezekiah (1777–1839), champions protective tariff, 576
Niña, one of Columbus's caravels, 50
Nonintercourse Act (1809), prohibits commerce with England and France, 363
Norfolk, Va., in colonial days, 153; burned, 233; abandoned by Confederates, 850
Norsemen, sail to America, 69
North, The, geography of, 30; as compared with South in resources during Civil War, 835ff.
North, Lord Frederick (1732–92), holds control of Parliament, 223; proposes Tea Act, 225; attains passage of Intolerable Acts, 226; blockades colonial commerce, 228; introduces bill to give up Am. taxation, 259; resigns, 265
North, Simeon (1765–1852), develops principle of interchangeable parts, 562
North America, physical characteristics of, 25ff.; England and France battle for, 187–200
North American Review, 589–590
North Carolina, and Bacon's Rebellion, 115; separated from South Carolina, 118; secedes from Union, 794; Sherman's army in, 882; readmitted to Union, 908
North West Company, builds up trade empire, 508–509; merges with Hudson's Bay Company, 518
Northwest Confederacy, collapse of, 412
Northwest Ordinances (1784), drawn up, 372–373; (1785, 1787), laid foundations for national land policy, 374; political in objective, 376
Northwest Passage, quest for, 69–78
Northwest Territory, set up (1787), 376
Nova Scotia, joins Dom. of Canada, 832
Noyes, John Humphrey (1811–86), founds Oneida Community, 625
Nullification, proposed by South Carolina, 453; Clay offers compromise, 459; Calhoun's theory of, 669–670; wins in tariff issue, 671
Núñez de Arce, Sp. poet quoted on Spain, 60

Oberlin College, Lane Seminary students move to, 660
Oberlin Volunteers, active in abolition movement, 660–661
Ocracoke, Confederate forts captured at, 850
Oglethorpe, James E. (1696–1785), appointed agent to Georgia, 120; invades Florida, 192
Ohio, admitted as state, 378; growth, 396
Ohio Company of Associates, speculators, 375
Ohio Company of Virginia, attempts to settle Old West, 211; bilked by Indiana Co., 215
Ohio-Michigan dispute, over territory, 396–397
Ohio Valley, French and English clash in, 193ff.; fall of Fr. power in, 196
Ojibway Indians, 41
Old Immigration, 602–603
Old Northwest, decline of agrarianism in, 655–656
Old South, as an economic and cultural area, 445ff.; composition of population in pre-Civil War days, 645–648; economic dilemma of, 652
Old West, 165–169; characteristics of settlers in, 168–169; a region of pre-Revolutionary protest, 209ff.; pressure of settlers in, 212–213; in Revolution, 253, 254; in Confederation period, 288–289; in War of 1812, 412–413; as an economic and cultural area, 445–446; effect of Jacksonian movement in, 467; lawlessness in, 543

Oliver, Andrew (1706–74), Adams publishes letters of, 225

Oliver, James (1823–1908), devises chilled-steel plow, 584

Omnibus Bill, provisions of Clay's (1850), 724, 726

Oñate, Juan de (1549?–?1624), founds New Mexico, 688

"On Conciliation with America," Burke delivers speech, 227, 228

Oneida Community, socialist experiment, 625

Oneida Indians, 75

Onondaga Indians, 75

Ontario, joins Dominion of Canada, 832

On the Constitution (Cooper), defends slavery, 672

Open Door Policy, foreshadowed by "gunboat policy," 499

Opium War, Brit. actions in, 495

Optimism, American, 633

Oratory, 19th-century craze for, 592–593

Orders in Council, blockade commerce to Europe, 359; Canning refuses to repeal, 362, 403; British repeal, 404

Oregon country, as fur traders' frontier, 514; Am. trade in, 516; Lewis and Clark Expedition to, 516–517; Am. infiltration into, 686–687; early government of, 687–688; organized as territory, 688; Polk settles problem by treaty, 701

Oregon Trail, blazed by Wyeth, 686; description of route, 687

Orient, routes to the, 12–14; Portugal in, 53; Spanish ignorance of, 55; opens trade with U.S. merchants, 488, 489; relations of Am. merchants in, 494ff.

Oriskany, Tory repulse at, 254

Osage Indians, 41

Osceola, leader of Seminole, 524

Ostend Manifesto (1853), states Am. stand on Cuba, 736–737

O'Sullivan, John Louis (1813–95), expansionist, 736

Otis, James (1725–83), leader in independence movement, 224

Ottawa Indians, 41

Owen, Robert (1771–1858), spreads socialist theory, 625; sets up community, 626

Owen, Robert Dale (1801–77), on socialist communities, 626

Pacific Confederacy, Northern plan for disunion, 785

Pacific Fur Company, enterprises of, 517

Pacific railroad, passage of act for, 819

Pacific Slope, geography of, 32

Packenham, Edward, loses to Jackson at New Orleans (1815), 421–423

Packet lines, transatlantic, established, 491

Paine, Thomas (1737–1809), comes to Philadelphia, 234; his *Common Sense* and other works, 234–235; promotes deism, 587

Painting, in early 19th century, 590

Palmer, Elihu (1764–1806), promotes deism, 587

Palmerston, Lord (1784–1865), attitude toward Civil War, 828

Palo Alto, battle at in Mexican War, 709

Panama, wins freedom as part of Great Colombia, 471

Panama Congress (1826), 478

Pan-American Conferences (1826), 478

Panics (1819), 438, 604; (1837), 461, 550–551, 570, 604, 663, 697; (1857), 763

Panton, William (1742?–1801), Br. controller of trade in Old Southwest, 385, 386

Papineau, Louis Joseph (1786–1871), stages uprising in Quebec, 482, 483

Paraguay, declares independence, 473

Paredes, Mariano (1797–1849), Pres. of Mexico, declares war on U.S., 702

Parker, Peter (1804–88), missionary to China, 499–500

Parker, Theodore (1810–60), transcendentalist, 599

Parliament, development of Br., 84–85; wins control of government, 92

Parsons, Theophilus (1750–1813), member of Essex Junto, 308

Partnerships, mercantile organization, 577

Pastorius, Rev. Daniel (1651–1720), settles Germans in Pa., 160

Patents and patent law, history of, 563–564

"Patriot War," for Canadian independence, 483

Patriots, *see* Whigs

Patroons, in Hudson Valley, 135, 137

Patterson, Robert (1792–1881), heads army at Martinsburg, 795–796

Pawtucket, R.I., Slater builds mill at, 559

Pax Britannica, 14, 17

Peace movement, in mid-19th century, 619–620

Peale, Charles Willson (1741–1827), painter, 590

Peale, Rembrandt and Raphael, painters, 590

Peavey, Joseph, invents canthook, 561

Pedro, Dom (1798–1834), emperor, declares Brazilian independence, 473

Pemberton, John C. (1814–81), in Vicksburg campaign, 856–857

Penn, Sir William (1621–70), 140

Penn, William (1644–1718), as Puritan, 91; biography, 140; acquires Pa., 140; death, 141; recruits settlers, 160

Pennamite Wars (Conn. *vs.* Pa.), 289

Penn heirs, and the Walking Purchase, 37

Pennsylvania, acquired by Penn, 140; colonial government of, 140–141; settlement of, 141; 17th-century German influx into, 160–161; Loyalists and Whigs in, 234; Pennsylvania-Dutch oppose Federalists, 324

Pennsylvania Gazette, 154

Pennsylvania Railroad, extended to Pittsburgh, 572

Pennsylvania University, established, 154

Pensacola, Fla., Jackson storms (1814), 421; seized (1818), 425; falls to Union in Civil War, 851

Pequot Indians, war in Conn. Valley, 132

Permanent Indian Frontier, in effect (1840), 526; shortcomings of, 527; failure of, 528; trade helps break down, 692

Perry, Matthew C. (1794–1858), reopens Japan to trade, 497

Perry, Oliver Hazard (1785–1819), wins battle of Lake Erie, 412

Perryville, Civil War battle at, 855

Peru, conquered by Pizarro, 56; wins freedom, 471

Pessimism, American, 633

Peters, Richard (1744–1828), agricultural experimenter, 582

Petersburg, Va., siege of, 880; falls, 887

Petroleum, strike in Pa., 560; development of drilling for, 560

Philadelphia, laid out, 141; in colonial days, 152–153; as smuggling center, 226; becomes capital city, 311; Federalist stronghold, 324; in Oriental trade, 488; in canal era, 570; leads in prison reform, 615

Philip ii (1527–98), Sp. king, Spain declines under, 60

Philippine Islands, discovered by Magellan, 56; seized by England, 197

Phillips, Wendell (1811–84), supports Garrison on abolition, 659

Phoenix, Stevens's pioneer steamboat, 566

Phratry, nature of Indian, 43

Physiocrats, and agrarianism, 21; and capitalism, 21; theories of French known in colonies, 159; French, 321; American, *see* American Physiocracy

Pickens, Fort, Fla., difficulties at (1861), 784; in Union hands, 850

Pickering, Timothy (1745–1829), member of Essex Junto, 308; plots secession of New England, 354; land speculator, 550

Pickett's Charge, in Civil War, 876

Piedmont, the, nature of, 29; the Old West, 166; rise of, 210

Pierce, Franklin (1804–69), elected Pres. (1852), 730; influenced by Northern merchant-Southern extremist coalition, 736

Pierpoint, Francis H. (1814–99), governor of West Va., 798

Pietists, communities of, 624

Pike, Zebulon (1779–1813), explores Southwest, Pikes Peak, 517

Pilgrims, 121ff.

Pinckney, Charles (1757–1824), attends Const. Convention, 291; Federalist leader, 305–306; becomes Jeffersonian Republican, 327

Pinckney, C. C. (1746–1825), attends Const. Convention, 291; Federalist leader, 306; emissary to France (1797) to preserve peace, 337; nominated for vice-presidency (1800), 342; in election of 1804, 355; runs for presidency (1808), 362

Pinckney, Thomas (1750–1828), Federalist leader, 306; makes treaty with Spain, 335; vice-pres. candidate, 336

Pinckney's Treaty (1795), 335; opens Mississippi to Am. navigation, 384

Pinkney, William (1764–1822), mission to Eng., 360

Pinta, one of Columbus's caravels, 50

Pioneers, in Old West, 168–169; in West, 534ff.; as Indian fighters, 541–542

Piracy, in the Caribbean, 67

Pitt, Fort, erected, 196; besieged in Pontiac's War, 211; in Revolution, 253; as frontier garrison, 541

Pitt, William the Elder (1708–78), reverses tide in war against French, 196; forced to resign, 197; battles for conciliation, 228

Pittsburgh, Pa., seized by French, 194; named, 196

Pizarro, Francisco (1470?–1541), conquest of Peru and Chile by, 56

Plains of Abraham, Wolfe's victory at, 197

Planned economy, under mercantilism, 20

Plantations, rise of, 112–113; life on colonial, 153; effect of depletion of soil on, 210; advantages and disadvantages of system of, 650–651

Platform of the South, 721

Plattsburg, N.Y., in War of 1812, 413–414

Plow, evolution of the, 583–584

Plymouth, Mass., Pilgrims land at, 121; settlement of, 122; joins New Eng. Confederation, 132

Plymouth, N.C., occupied by Union troops, 850

Plymouth Company, colonial government under, 107–108; rechartered as Council for New England, 121

Poe, Edgar Allan (1809–49), master of romanticism, 600, 601; editor, 677

Poinsett, Joel R. (1779–1851), as minister to Mexico, 693–694

Political compact, theory of, 92–93

Political machine, developed by Albany Regency, 432; Jackson's use of, 451–452; Tweed Ring, 909

Political opinion, divisions of, 102–104

Political parties, development of English, 87; American, *see* entries under party names

Political rights, defined, 100

Polk, James K. (1795–1849), elected Pres., 700; biography, 700–701; diplomatic moves of, 701–702; helps restore Santa Anna to power, 707, 709

Ponce de Leon, Luis (1527–91), explorer, 56

Pontiac's War, 211–212

Poor Richard's Almanack (Franklin), 154

Poor whites, in pre-Civil War South, 647–648

Pope, John (1822–92), in command of Union fleet on Mississippi, 854; defeated at Second Battle of Bull Run, 864–865

Popham Colony, near the Kennebec, 121

Popular sovereignty, Cass proposes, 721–722, 727

Population, colonial expansion of, 178, 193; in Western states, 391ff.

Portail, Chevalier de, military leader in Revolution, 242

Porter, David (1780–1843), attacks Br. cruisers (1813), 493

Porter, David D. (1813–91), in Vicksburg campaign, 856–857

Porter, Peter B. (1733–1844), a leader of War Hawks, 402

Port Hudson, falls to Union in Civil War, 857

Portland, Me., seized by British, 232

Portolá, Don Gaspar de (1723?–?84), settles California, 689

Port Royal (Acadia), Fr. settlement at, 73

Port Royal, Jamaica, buccaneer base, 67

Port Royal, S.C., seized by Union troops, 850

Portugal, overseas imperialism of, 48; in the Orient, 53; conquest by Spain, 60; in Brazil, 62–63; loses eminence in Orient, 65

Postal reform, spreads education, 615

Potato famine, in Ireland, affects emigration, 605

Pottawatomie massacre, 757

Powers, Hiram (1805–73), sculptor, 590

Pragmatism, of Eng. institutions, 83; the practical stream in history, 597

Preble, Edward (1761–1807), in Barbary Wars, 353

Predestination, Puritans accept doctrine of, 88; *see also* Calvinism

Pre-emption Act (1841), limits individual ownership of land, 547; endows new states with land, 548

Presbyterians, in West, 538; Southern split in, 677; set up mission in Oregon country, 687

President, and Br. *Little Belt,* 404

President of the U.S., duties of, 295

Press, Zenger sets precedent for freedom of the, 182

Prester John, kingdom of, 12, 48

Prevost, George (1767–1816), Br. general, invades U.S., 413–414

Price, Sterling (1809–67), in Mexican War, 710

Priests, Indian, 44; Spanish as teachers, 60

Primogeniture, abolishment of, 273

Prince Edward Island, joins Dominion of Canada, 832

Prince Rupert's Land, awarded to Hudson's Bay Company, 192

Princeton, N.J., battle at, 256

Princeton University, founded, 158

Printing press, set up in Mexico (1539), 60; improved by the Hoes, 562

Printz, Johan (1592–1663), governor of New Sweden, 136

Prisoners, exchange stopped in Civil War, 849

Prison reform, introduced, 588; movement, 615–616

Private enterprise, *see* Capitalism

Privateers, Am. Revolutionary, 249–250; in War of 1812, 408–409

Proclamation Line of 1763, 212ff.

Proctor, Henry, Br. colonel in War of 1812, 412

Progress, idea of, 94ff.

Prohibition, first movement for, 616–617

Property, Locke's theory of private, 92; basis of property rights, 901

Prophet, The, Shawnee leader, 379

Protestantism, and capitalism, 19–20

Providence Plantation, founded by Williams, 127; as smuggling center, 226

Pruyn, Robert H. (1815–82), Am. consul in Japan, 498

Public domain, origin of, 271–272; value of the, 548–549

Pulaski, Count Casimir (1748?–79), military leader in Am. Revolution, 242

Pulaski, Tenn., Ku Klux Klan in, 917

Puritans, theology of, 87–88, self-righteousness of, 89; in Mass., 122ff.; in Conn., 129; waning of power of, 151; in South, 677

Quadrant, as navigational reliance, 55

Quakers, in New Jersey, 139; in Pennsylvania, 140

Quantrill, W. C. (1837–65), guts Lawrence, Kans., 803

Quartering Act, proposed by Grenville, 219; aimed at Mass., 226

Quebec, named by Cartier, 72; trading post established at, 73; seized by British fleet, 73; besieged by Wolfe, 197; stormed by Am. troops, 232; (province) joins Dominion of Canada, 832

Quebec Act (1774), as factor in promoting Revolution, 216–217; classed with Intolerable Acts, 226

Queenstown, Can., Americans repulsed at (1812), 410

Quesada, Gonzalo Jimenez de (1500?–?79), conquers Colombia, 56

Quids, led by Randolph of Roanoke, 356

Quincy, Josiah (1772–1864), 308

Quitman, John A. (1798–1858), 736

Quitrents, described, 148

Quock Walker Case, 274

Racism, white, as shown in treatment of Indians, 512–513; toward Negroes, 644, 928

Radicals, definition of political, 102–103; (Revolution) split with moderates in Revolution, 246ff.; (Civil War) in 37th Congress, 813ff.; after Lincoln's death, 891ff.; program of, 900; blocked, 901–902; return to power, 903; aims of, 905–906; triumph in South after Civil War, 911ff.; lose ground in North, 920–921

Railroads, development of, 570–571; consolidation of, 572, 573; rate wars, 573–574; problem of financing, 573–574; economic effect on West, 573; decisive role in Civil War, 835–836

Rainbow, noted clipper ship, 491

Raisin River, Am. defeat (War of 1812), 412

Raleigh, Sir Walter (1552?–1618), opposes mercantilism, 106; fails as colonizer, 107

Randall, James R. (1839–1908), writes *Maryland, My Maryland,* 795

Randolph, Edmund (1753–1813), attends Const. Convention, 291

Randolph, John (1773–1833), Jeffersonian Republican, 327; organizes the Quids, 356; acts in Yazoo frauds, 385; against War of 1812, 405–406; fights duel with Clay, 439; leads Antique Republicans, 668

Rapp, George (1757–1847), founds pietist community, 624

Rawdon, Francis Hastings (1754–1826), defeats Gates at Camden S.C., 261

Rawlins, John A. (1831–69), becomes Grant's chief of staff, 852–853; in Grant's presidency, 909

Reactionaries, definition of political, 102

Read, Samuel, establishes normal school (1823), 613

Realism, democratic, 98

Reaper, development of farm, 584

Reciprocity Treaty of 1854, hailed as step in annexing Canada, 736

Reconstruction, after Civil War, 891ff.; significance of, 925ff.

Reconstruction Acts, 904–905

Redemptioners, in colonial America, 145–146

Reform, character of political, 369–370; stimuli to in early 19th century, 598; age of, 612ff.; of institutions, 615–616; movements for, 623ff.

Regulators, in colonial struggle for democracy, 184–185; join Watauga settlements, 216; scattered at Moore's Creek Bridge, 233

Religion, Indian, 44; liberal policy of Calverts in Md., 117; as factor in settling New Eng., 121, 123, 124; colonial tolerance of, 148, 150; growth of secularism in, 155–156; the Great Awakening, 156–157; colonial opposition to Anglican episcopate, 204; politics and, 306–307; westward spread of denominations, 395; disestablishment of churches, 444; in early West, 538–539; Southern conservatism in, 677; *see also* denominational entries

Renascence, in Europe, 10–11

Rensselaer Polytechnic Institute, first engineering school, 564

"Reply to Hayne," Webster's speech, 670–671

Report on Manufactures (Hamilton), 309, 312, 575–576

Report on the Affairs of British North America (Durham), instigates colonial reform, 483

Report on the Public Credit (Hamilton), 309

Representative government, Br. theories of, 183–184; *see also* Democracy

Republicanism (Jeffersonian), 320ff.; in New Eng., 322; in N.Y., 322–323

Republican Party, formation, 750–751; in 1856 campaign, 759; in 1860 campaign, 778–779; actions in 1861, 788; policies during Civil War, 818–819; in South after Civil War, 914; *see also* Democratic-Republicans and Jeffersonian Republicans

Resaca, falls to Sherman, 881

Resaca de la Palma, battle at in Mexican War, 709

Reservations, Indian, 511–512

Resolves of 1769, passed by House of Burgesses, 221

Revere, Paul (1735–1818), ride of, 229–230

Review of the Debate in the Virginia Legislature (Dew), defends slavery, 672

Revolution, causes of Am., 200–205; French, 328–329; technical, 557ff.; *see also* American Revolution

Rhett, Robert Barnwell (1800–76), State Rights Party leader, 731–732, 734, 788

Rhode Island, founded by Williams, 127; growth of, 127; joins New Eng. Confederation, 132

Rice, staple crop of South Carolina, 118

Rice, Thomas D. (1808–60), actor, 590

Richmond, Va., becomes Confederate capital, 796; campaigns for seizing (Civil War), 859ff.

Rifles, displace muskets in Civil War, 849

Rights, civil, defined, 100, 901; political, defined, 100; colonial struggle for, 180–187

"Rights of Englishmen," 84

Rights of Man (Paine), 234

Ripley, George (1802–80), founds Brook Farm, 625

Rittenhouse, David (1732–96), scientist, 324

River Raisin, Am. defeat at in War of 1812, 412

Roads, Wilderness, 216; Cumberland, 434; turnpikes, 568; toll, 568

Roanoke Island, failure of colony on, 107; occupied by Union troops, 850

Roberts, Issachar (1802–71), missionary to China, 495

Robertson, James (1742–1814), leader in Watauga, 216; in Western land speculation, 381

Rochambeau Comte de (1725–1807), in siege of Yorktown, 263ff.

Rocky Mountain Fur "Company," rendezvous of, 519–520

Rolfe, John (1585–1622), tobacco experiments of, 110

Roman Catholic Church, mission of, 10; established in New France, 73; in Mississippi Valley, 216–217; rise of societies against, 620; sets up missions in Oregon country, 687; in Southwest, 688–689

Romanticism, popular in 19th century, 593

Roosevelt, Nicholas J. (1767–1854), builds steamboats, 565

Root, Elisha King (1808–65), tool designer, 562

"Rope of Sand" speech of Webster, 670

Rosecrans, William S. (1819–98), in Virginia campaign, 797–798; in command of the Army of the Cumberland, 855–856; in battle of Murfreesboro, 856; at Chickamauga, 857

Ross, Edmund G. (1826–1907), votes against Johnson's impeachment, 907

Ross, Robert (1766–1814), takes Washington, D.C. in War of 1812, 414; death of, 415

Roundheads, in England, 90

Rousseau, Jean-Jacques (1712–78), Am. influence on, 159

Royall, Anne (1769–1854), reformer, 618

Rubber, process of vulcanizing developed, 561–562

Ruffin, Edmund (1794–1865), spearheads agricultural renascence, 582; works for Southern Rights, 732–733, 734

Rum, made for trade in colonial New Eng., 132; triangular trade in, 163; significance of trade in, 177–178

"Runaway scrape," in Texas revolution, 696

Rush, Benjamin (1745–1813), founder of medical college, 158; physician, 324; champions environmentalism, 588; in peace movement, 619

Rush, Richard (1780–1859), delivers Canning's proposal for alliance regarding Latin America, 475–476

Rush-Bagot Agreement, limits naval armament on Great Lakes, 479; status during Civil War, 832

Russell, Jonathan (1771–1832), peace delegate (1814), 417–418

Russell, Lord John (1792–1878), attitude toward Civil War, 827, 828, 829

Russia, defeated by Napoleon, 358; encroaches on Sakhalin (1850's), 497; acquires southeast Siberia from China, 495; exploits Alaska, 514, 516

Russian American Fur Company, in Alaska, 514, 516

Rutledge, John (1739–1800), attends Const. Convention, 291; as Federalist leader, 305

Sabine Pass, Tex., falls to Union in Civil War, 851

Sachems, functions of Indian, 43

Sacket's Harbor, repulse of Br. raid against, 412, 413

"Safety valve" theory, 391

St. Augustine, Fla., plundered by English, 65

St. Brendan's Isle (Iceland?), 69

St. Clair, Arthur (1736?–1818), military leader in Revolution, 242; defeated by Indians in Northwest Territory, 377

St. Eustatius, important in Revolution, 250

St. Johns River, site of Ft. Caroline, 64

St. Louis, settled, 391; growth, 397; entrepôt of American Fur Company, 519; Germans settle in, 606

St. Marks, Fla., Jackson seizes (1818), 425

St. Marys, Md., settled, 117

St. Marys River, seized (1815) in East Fla., 420

Saint-Simon, Comte de (1760–1825), spreads socialist theory, 625

Salem, Mass., founded by Endicott, 122; growth as shipping town, 132; in Oriental trade, 488, 489

Saluda Creek, defeat of Regulators at, 185

San Antonio, Tex., besieged in Texas revolution, 694, 696

San Diego, Cal., settled, 689

Sandys, Sir Edwin (1561–1629), of London Company, 108; procures charter, 110

San Francisco Bay, discovered by Portolá, 689

San Ildefonso, treaty between France and Spain at, 339, 384

San Jacinto, battle of in Texas revolt, 697

San Jacinto, in Trent Affair, 827–828

San Juan, Nicaragua, Br. commercial center, 737; bombarded (1854) by Americans, 738

San Juan Islands, awarded to U.S., 834

San Lorenzo, Treaty of, opens Mississippi to Am. navigation, 384

San Marco, University of, founded (Lima, 1551), 60

San Martín, José de (1778–1850), Latin-American liberator, 471

San Salvador, Columbus lands on, 50

Santa Anna, Antonio López de (1795?–1876), enters Texan scene, 694; attacks the Alamo, 696; drives Americans out of Texas, 696; captured, 697; in "Pastry War," 707; restored to power, 709; defeated at Buena Vista, 709–710; defeated by Scott, 712; returns to exile, 713

Santa Fe, N.Mex., built by missionaries, 688; trade post established at, 692; occupied by Confederate troops, 803

Santa María, one of Columbus's caravels, 50, 51

Santo Domingo, fort built by Columbus in, 52; plundered by pirates, 65

San Xavier del Bac, historic mission, 689

Saratoga, N.Y., Burgoyne surrenders at, 257

Saratoga, wins battle of Lake Champlain (1814), 414

Sauk Indians, in Black Hawk War, 522

Savage's Station, Civil War battle at, 863

Savannah, Ga., settled, 120; seized by British in Revolution, 261; holds out in Civil War, 850; falls to Sherman, 882

Savannah, early ocean steamship, 568

Say and Sele, Lord (1582–1662), and Council for New England, 128–129

Saybrook, Conn., built by Winthrop, Jr., 129

Scalawags, in South after Civil War, 912

Scandinavia, emigrants from, 603, 608

Schofield, John M. (1831–1906), in battle for Atlanta, 881; battle of Franklin, 881; replaces Stanton, 908

Schoolcraft, Henry R. (1793–1864), Indian folklorist, 592

Schools, rise of public, 613; *see also* Education

Schurz, Carl (1829–1906), German immigrant, 606; as Liberal Republican, 918

Schuyler, Philip (1733–1804), military leader in Revolution, 242, 256

Science, and democracy, 7; modern, 17, 19; applied to agriculture, 582ff.; *see also* Technology

Scioto Company, Western land speculators, 375

Scotch-Irish settlers, in Pa., 141; 18th-century immigrants, 161–162, 167, 168; oppose Federalists, 324–325

Scots, 18th-century immigrants, 162–163; profound influence of, 163

Scott, Sir Walter (1771–1832), popularity of, 593

Scott, Winfield (1786–1866), in War of 1812, 412; forces land cession from Indians, 522; heads army at Vera Cruz in Mexican War, 710, 712; in Valley of Mexico, 713; occupies Mexico (1848), 715; nominated for pres. (1852), 730; fortifies Washington, D.C., 795; urges blockade of South, 796

Scrooby, Puritan congregation leaves, 121

Sculpture, in early 19th century, 590–591

Seamen, England impresses American, 357–358; deterioration of American, 490

Sea power, role in Middle Ages, 14–15

Sears, Isaac (1730–86), radical leader in colonies, 229

Sea Witch, noted clipper ship, 491

Secession, New England plots, 354; South seizes as weapon, 672; Secessionists vie with Unionists on question of, 729–730; a decade of preparation for, 731; of Cotton South, 783; futility of, 810–811

Secessionists, prominent in the 1850's, 731–733, 734

Second Constitution, movement for, 290; personnel of convention, 290–291

Second Continental Congress, meets, 230; ineptness of, 246; accomplishments of, 247

Sectionalism, in Jacksonian Era, 444ff.; in 1850's, 717–718

Sedgwick, John (1813–64), in battle of Chancellorsville, 873–874

Sedition Act (1798), 339–341

Seigniory, established in New France, 73

Self-restraint, individual, to develop democracy, 96

Selkirk, Lord (1771–1820), receives land grant from Hudson's Bay Company, 518

Seminole Indians, location of, 41; attempt to assimilate white culture, 521; removal, 524

Seminole Wars (1816–18), 425, 521; Second (1835–42), 524

Seneca, one of Five Nations, 75; attack Huronia, 76–77

Seneca Falls Convention, sponsors woman suffrage, 619

Sentimentalism, of 19th century art, 593; in Am. character, 634; and slavery, 656–657

Separatists, democratic, 89; become Pilgrims, 121

Sequoyah, leader of the Cherokee, 524

Serapis, defeated by *Bonhomme Richard,* 250

Serra, Fray Junípero, settles Cal., 689

Servants, indentured, 146–147; Negro, 147

Settlements, extent of by 1688, 150–151; stages of early, 165–166

Settlers, early, reasons for coming, 145; redemptioners, 145–146; convicts, 146; kidnapees, 146; indentured servants, 146–147; Negro slaves, 147

Seven Days' Battle, in Civil War, 863

Seven Pines, Va., Civil War battle at, 863

Seven Years' War, *see* French and Indian Wars

Sevier, John (1745–1815), in Watauga, 216; in Western land speculation, 381; a leader of War Hawks, 402

Seward, William H. (1801–72), a leader of Anti-Masonic Party, 457; drafts Burlingame Treaty, 496; dominates Pres. Taylor, 723; and Clay's Omnibus Bill, 727; on Committee of Thirteen, 786; in secession crisis, 789; as Secretary of State, 816; distrusted by England, 827; settles *Trent* Affair, 828; purchases Alaska, 834; in Cabinet crisis of 1862, 871–872; in Hampton Roads Conference, 886

Sewing machine, development of, 561

Sextant, as aid in navigation, 55

Seymour, Horatio (1810–86), of Albany Regency, 432; nominated for presidency, 908

Shaftesbury, Earl of (1621–83), 117

Shaker Society, pietist socialist group, 624

Shamans, Indian, 44

Shannon, Brit. victory over *Chesapeake,* 408

Sharpsburg, Civil War battle near, 868

Shaw, Justice Lemuel (1781–1861), rules unions and strikes within law, 581

Shawnee Indians, 41

Shays's Rebellion, 289

Shelburne, Lord (1737–1805), sets Proclamation Line of 1763, 212

Shenandoah, Confederate raider, 828

Shenandoah Valley, nature of the, 29; Civil War in, 860ff.

Sheridan, Philip H. (1831–88), characteristics of, 852; in battle of Chattanooga, 858; cuts Lee's supplies, 879; in Md. and Shenandoah Valley, 880–881; wins at Five Forks, 887

Sheriff, in Southern colonies, 120

Sherman, John (1823–1900), leader in 37th Congress, 814; co-author of First Reconstruction Act, 904

Sherman, Roger (1721–93), attends Const. Convention, 291

Sherman, William T. (1820–91), introduces scorched-earth policy, 849; characteristics of, 852; in battle of Chattanooga, 858; biography, 859; backed by Grant, 877; takes Atlanta, 881; in Ga. and the Carolinas, 881–882; Johnston surrenders to, 887

Shiloh, Civil War battle at, 853–854

Shimonoseki, Japan, destroyed by Western naval expedition, 498

Shipbuilding, role in geographic perspective, 23; in colonial New Eng., 131; in Middle Colonies, 142; steamships, 565, 567–568

"Shirt-sleeve diplomacy," Jackson's, 481

Shreve, Henry M. (1785–1851), builds steamboat, 567

Sibley, Henry Hopkins (1816–86), invades Texas in Civil War, 803

Sibley, Hiram (1807–88), organizes Western Union, 574

Signaling, developed in Civil War, 849

Silliman, Benjamin, Jr. (1816–85), improves petroleum refining, 560

Silliman, Benjamin, Sr. (1779–1864), founds scientific magazine, 592

Silver Age, 430ff.

Simms, William Gilmore (1806–70), Southern author, 677–678

Simpson, Sir George (1792–1860), directs Hudson's Bay Company, 518

Singer, Isaac (1811–75), improves sewing machine, 561

Single-tax theory, 21

Siouan nations, 41

Sirius, Br. steam packet ship, 491
Slater, Samuel (1768–1835), builds spinning mill, 559
Slavery As It Is (Weld), effective in abolition movement, 661
Slaves and slavery, introduction of Negro, 112; in early colonies, 147; conditions of, 163–164; drawbacks to, 165; trade in, 274, 485–486, 649–650; abolished in British colonies, 485; in Old South, 648–649; and economics, 650–651; roots of movement against, 656ff.; Northern proposals for emancipation rejected, 666–667; theories in defense of, 672–674; after Mexican Cession, 719ff.; and Cotton South, 785; during Civil War, 868; Emancipation Proclamation, 869
Slidell, John (1793–1871), fails in mission to Mexico, 702; as expansionist, 736; in 1860 campaign, 774, 775; part in *Trent* Affair, 827–828
Sloat, John D. (1781–1867), takes possession of California, 711
Smith, Adam (1723–90), influence of, 21
Smith, Caleb (1808–64), Sec'y of Interior, 816
Smith, Jedediah (1798–1831), trapper, 520–521
Smith, Capt. John (1580–1631), leader in Jamestown, 109; names New England, 121
Smith, Joseph (1805–44), publishes *Book of Mormon,* 627
Smith, Sidney (1771–1845), on America, 597
Smith, Sir Thomas, leader of London Company, 108; "treasurer" of Virginia Company, 110
Smithson, James (1765–1829), bequest used to found Smithsonian Institution, 592–593
Smithsonian Institution, 591–592
Smuggling, in colonies, 178
Social conflict, changing balance of, in democracy, 95–96, 105
Social contract, theory of government by, 92
Socialism, defined, 22; popular in mid-19th century, 623; in colonies, 623; experiments in community living, 624–625; growth of theory of, 625–626
Society for the Propagation of the Gospel in Foreign Parts, 204
Society of Tammany, rise of, 324
Sociology for the South (Fitzhugh), defends slavery, 673
Sonoma, Cal., seized by Americans, 711
Sons of Liberty, organize against Stamp Act, 219; become prominent, 223–224; activities before Rev., 228
Soulé, Pierre (1801–70), expansionist, 736, 737; co-author of Ostend Manifesto, 737
South, geography of, 31; education in early, 158; merger of Old Southwest and Old South, 399; diversity of, 643–644; as a conscious minority, 664ff.; its role in national government before Civil War, 675; uses defense mechanism in stand on slavery, 680; dilemma in 1860 campaign, 779; blackmail tactics before Civil War, 806; financial situation during Civil War, 822–823; European attitude toward, 825–826; as compared with North in resources during Civil War, 835ff.; theories on the postwar status of the, 893ff.; ruin caused by war in the, 897–898; during reconstruction, 911ff.; Solid South emerges, 928–929; effects of war and reconstruction on the, 929–931
South America, *see* Latin America and entries by countries
South Carolina, separated from North Carolina, 118; nullifies the Tariff of 1832, 458; leads secession, 782–783; demands surrender of forts (1860), 784; Sherman's troops in, 882; readmitted to Union, 908

South Carolina Exposition (Calhoun), 668
Southampton, Earl of (1573–1624), 108
Southern colonies, founded, 106–121
Southern Literary Messenger, The, Southern periodical, 677
Southern Quarterly Review, The, Southern magazine, 677
Southern Rights, Platform of the South, 721; Alabama Platform, 721, 732; demand for intellectual independence, 735
Southern sectionalism, 664ff.
Southern Unionists, prominent, 733–734
Soviet Union, as heir of totalitarian force, 24; imperialism of, 103–105
Spain and Spaniards, overseas imperialism of, 48; character of, 58–59; empire in America, 59–60; industrial decline of, 60, 62; in struggle for the Caribbean, 63–69; hostilities with England during Am. Revolution, 259; policies in Louisiana and Florida, 380–381; grants La. to France, 384; Am. aggression against in the South, 402; cedes Fla. to U.S., 425–426; empire crashes, 470–471; in Pacific Northwest, 514; in Cuban problem, 736–737
Spanish Armada, defeat of the (1588), 65
Spanish Main, struggle for the, 63–69; a center of Latin-American revolt, 471
Speaker of the House, powers of, 301
Speculators, in land, 372ff.
Spice Islands, Portugal in the, 53
Spiritualism, in Burnt District, 626–627
Spoils system, developed by Albany Regency, 432; Jackson's use of, 451–452
"Spot Resolution," Lincoln's, 707
Spotsylvania, battle of, 879
Sprague, William (1830–1915), 884
Squatter sovereignty, *see* Popular sovereignty
Squatters, as early settlers, 165–166
Stamp Act, proposed by Grenville, 218; provides rallying point for resistance, 219; repeal of, 219–220; Congress, 219
Stanton, Edwin M., (1814–69), abolitionist leader, 661; Sec'y of War, 816–817; joins Radicals, 891; replaced by Thomas, 906; replaced by Schofield, 908
Stanton, Elizabeth Cady (1815–1902), reformer, 619
Stark, John (1728–1822), military leader in Rev., 242; wins victory at Bennington, 257
Star of the West, Union ship fired on, 784
Star-Spangled Banner, The, written during War of 1812, 415
"Starving Time," in Jamestown, 109
State constitutions, first, 270–271
State Department, organized, 300
State rights, doctrine of, 643; a weapon against Federal government, 667; problem in South during Civil War, 823–824
State Rights Party, formed, 788
Statism, defined, 22; *see also* Totalitarianism
Status *vs.* change, in social order, 612–613
Steamboat, invention of the, 565; ocean-going ships, 567–568
Steel, Bessemer process of making, 559
Stephens, Alexander Hamilton (1812–83), as Southern Unionist, 734; elected vice-pres. of Confederacy, 787; leader in State Rights Party, 788; in Hampton Roads Conf., 886
Stephenson, Fort, repels attack in War of 1812, 412
Stephenson, George (1781–1848), builds steam locomotive, 570
Steuben, Baron von (1730–94), drillmaster of Revolution, 242
Stevens, John (1749–1838), builds steamboats, 565–566; builds steam locomotive, 570

Stevens, Robert L. (1787–1856), prominent engineer, 566; builds steam locomotive, 570; designs T-rails, 571

Stevens, Thaddeus (1792–1868), a leader of Anti-Masonic Party, 457; leader in education, 613; lashes "slavocracy," 810; Radical in 37th Congress, 814–815; controls Joint Com. on Reconstruction, 900; co-author of First Reconstruction Act, 904; role in Johnson's impeachment, 906–907

Stillwater, Am. Revolutionary victories at, 257

Stock Exchange, development of, 578

Stockton, Robert F. (1795–1866), sets up military administration of Cal. (1846), 711

Stone, Lucy (1818–93), reformer, 619

Stone River, Civil War battle at, 856

Story, Joseph (1779–1845), halts democratization of laws, 436

Stowe, Harriet Beecher (1811–96), affected by Lane "debate," 660; *Uncle Tom's Cabin,* 830

Strikes (labor), in early America, 580; declared lawful, 581

Stuart, Gilbert (1755–1828), painter, 590

Stuart, John (1700?–79), Sup't of Indian Affairs in the South, 212

Stuart, J. E. B. (1833–64), characteristics of, 868; falls at Yellow Tavern, 879

Stuyvesant, Peter (1592–1672), annexes New Sweden, 136

Sublettes, in St. Louis fur trade, 519

Substantive due process of law, 654–655

Suffrage, in the 1820's and 30's, 442–443

Sugar Act, Grenville proposes, 217

Sugar islands, fall to Br. fleet, 197

Sugar plantations, in Lesser Antilles, 66

Sullivan, John (1740–95), military leader in Revolution, 242; burns Iroquois towns, 254

Sumner, Charles (1811–74), invective on Kansas, 758; assaulted by Brooks, 758; Radical leader in 37th Congress, 814; aids in purchase of Alaska, 834; revolts against "Grantism," 918

Sumter, Fort, action at 784; crisis at, 790

Supreme Court, provided by Constitution, 301; as a decisive instrument of government, 435ff.; ruling in *Ex Parte Milligan,* 817; Radicals campaign against, 905–906

Sutter, John Augustus (1803–80), gets land grant in Cal., 691

Sweden, founds New Sweden, 136; immigrants from, 608

Swisshelm, Jane Grey (1815–84), reformer, 618

Swiss immigrants, 608

Sycamore Shoals, Treaty of, 216

Symmes, Judge John C. (1742–1814), Western land speculator, 376

Talleyrand (1754–1838), plans empire in America, 338–339

Tallmadge, James (1778–1853), attacks Three-fifths Ratio, 665

Tammany, rise of, 324; wins N.Y. state elections (1800), 342

Tammany, St., 223–224

Taney, Roger B. (1777–1864), in war on B. U. S., 459–460; decision in *Charles River Bridge Case,* 466

Taos, Spanish trade center, 688; Am. settlement, 692

Tappan, Arthur (1786–1865), leads abolition movement, 658; endows Lane Seminary, 659; backs students in Lane "debate," 660; supports Birney and Liberty Party, 664

Tappan, Lewis (1788–1873), leads abolition movement, 658; supports Birney and Liberty Party, 664

Tariff, laid by First Congress, 301; levied in 1789, 311; protective proposed by Hamilton, 312; Nonimportation Act (1806), 360, 362; following War of 1812, 435; of Abominations (1828), 448; of 1832, nullified by S.C., 458; Clay offers compromise (1832), 459; Walker (1846), 701; reduced by Polk, 701; Morrill (1861), 788, 818–819

Taxes, excise, 312, 332; income, 820

Taylor, Richard (1826–79), in Civil War, 887

Taylor, Zachary (1784–1850), occupies territory in dispute between Mexico and U.S., 702; Mexican campaign of, 709; victory at Buena Vista, 709–710; biography, 710; nominated for Pres., 722; activities as Pres., 723–724; opposes compromise of Clay's Omnibus Bill, 727; death, 727–728

Taylor of Caroline, John (1753–1824), Am. Physiocrat, 326–327; joins Quids, 356; theory of balanced gov't, 667

Tea Act, proposed by Lord North, 225

Technology, in modern life, 23–24; development of Am., 557ff.; public attitude toward, 564–565; encouraged by Civil War and reconstruction, 925–927

Tecumseh (1768?–1813), forms Indian Northwestern Confederacy, 378–379; death, 412

Telegraph, developed, 574

Temperance movement, origins of, 616; first prohibition movement, 617

Tennessee, admitted as a state, 381; growth in Great Migration, 396; votes down secession (1861), 785; secedes, 794; mountain loyalists during Civil War, 799; readmitted to Union, 905

Ten-Per-Cent Plan of Reconstruction, 883

Tenure of Office Act, in Johnson's impeachment proceedings, 906–908; Grant attempts repeal of, 909

Texas, under Spain, 59; German settlements in, 606; outline history of, 688, 692–693; successful revolt (1833) from Mexico, 694; independence recognized by U.S., 697; invaded by Mexicans, 698; admitted to Union, 698, 700; secedes from Union, 783; in Civil War, 803; readmitted to Union, 908

Texas Com. of Safety, 694

Texas v. White, decision in, 906

Theater, slow gains in 19th century, 590

Theocracy, Puritan, 124, 125–126; rejected, 133–134

Thirteenth Amendment, adopted, 896

Thomas, George H. (1816–70), characteristics of, 852; in battle of Murfreesboro, 856; at Chickamauga, 857; at Chattanooga, 858; in battle for Atlanta, 881; defeats Hood at Nashville, 881

Thomas, Lorenzo (1804–75), replaces Stanton, 906

Thoreau, Henry D. (1817–62), quoted on education, 597; individualism of, 599

Three-fifths Ratio, accepted by Const. Convention, 293

Thrift, Am. ideal of, 35

Ticonderoga, falls to Am. troops, 232

Tidewater, of South, a region of pre-Revolutionary protest, 209ff.

Tigre Island (Cen. Am.), seized by British (1849), 737

Tilden, Samuel (1814–86), of Albany Regency, 432; nominated for presidency, 922

Tippecanoe, battle of (1811), 379

Tlingit Indians, attack Sitka, 514, 516

Tobacco, overproduction in Lesser Antilles, 66; important in colonies, 112, 113; affected by Navigation Acts, 174, 175; role in pre-Revolutionary protest, 210

"Toledo War," 397

Tolerance, in a democracy, 98; American, 633

Toleration Act of 1649, accepted in Md., 117

Tom Thumb, locomotive, 571

Tools, Indian, 44; development of farm, 583–584; see also Technology

Toombs, Robert A. (1810–85), as Southern Unionist, 734; quoted, 809

Toronto, Can., raided by Americans in War of 1812, 412

Tories, in Am. Revolution, 245; services of, 248–249

Tory Party, built up by George III, 201; struggles with Whigs for power, 222–223

Totalitarianism, method of, 95; theory of, 103–105

Total war, waged in Civil War, 849

Totem, nature of Indian, 43

Town meetings, in New England, 130

Towns, in New Eng., 130–131; in Middle Colonies, 142; an example of a Western, 551–553; mill, 578–579

Townshend, "Champagne Charlie" (1725–67), proposes colonial Duty Acts, 220–221

Trade, between Indian nations, 45; monopoly for N.Y. merchants, 137–138; value of colonial, 176–177; triangular, 177–178; struggle for colonial in the South, 190; limited by England, 201, 202; with Indians in Old West, 212; provinces control Indian, 213, 215; in Confederation period, 287–288; hostilities with England after Fr. Rev., 331–332; hampered by Continental System, 359; Jefferson's Embargo, 360–362; Nonintercourse Act (1809), 363; in Old Northwest, 377; in Mississippi Valley, 381; spread of American, 487ff.; relations with China, 494ff.; Factory system of Indian, 512; in furs, 513ff.; Southern doctrine of free, 643; in slaves, 649–650; over Santa Fe Trail, 692

Trade Acts, purpose of, 174–175

Trafalgar, battle of, 358

Trans-Appalachia, its settlement and growth, 390–406

Transcendentalism, the ideal stream in history, 597; defined and discussed, 598–599; communities of, 625

Transcontinental Treaty (1819), 425–426

Transportation, role of technology in, 23; a problem of the West, 531, 534; of Western farm products, 537; revolution in, 565ff.; of immigrants, 608–609

Transylvania Company, in Old West, 216

Trappers, customs of, 520

Treasury Department, organized, 300

Treaties: Tordesillas (1494), 53; Utrecht (1713), 192; Paris (1763), 197–198; Hard Labor (1768), 213; Paris (1783), 267; Jay-Gardoqui (1786), 380; Jay's (1794), 333–334; Greenville (1795), 378; Pinckney's (1795), 384; San Ildefonso (1800), 339; Amiens (1802), 356; Ghent (1814), 418; Adams-Onís (Transcontinental) (1819), 425–426; Webster-Ashburton (1842), 485; Wanghia (1844), 495; Cahuenga (1846), 711; Guadalupe Hidalgo (1848), 714; Bidlack (1848), 737; Clayton-Bulwer (1850), 737; Elgin-Marcy (1854), 487; Burlingame (1868); Washington (1871), 833–834

Trent Affair, in Civil War, 827–828

Trenton, Washington seizes garrison at, 256

Trevett v. Weeden, decision in, 288

Triangular trade, developed by Dutch, 65; American, 163, 177–178

Tripolitania, in Barbary Wars, 352–353

Trist, Nicholas P. (1800–74), fails in peace mission in Mexican War, 712–713; recalled, 714

Trollope, Frances (1780–1863), criticizes America, 596

Troup, George (1780–1856), War Hawk, 402

Trumbull, John (1756–1843), painter, 590

Tryon, Gov. William (1729–88), defeats Regulators, 185

Tudor, Frederic (1783–1864), ships ice to tropics, 489

Tudor, House of, 85–86

Tunisia, in Barbary Wars, 352–353

Turner, Frederick Jackson (1861–1932), distinguishes economic and cultural areas, 444; introduces Frontier Hypothesis, 530–531

Turner, Jonathan B. (1805–99), fathers Morrill Land Grant Act, 819

Turner, Nat (1800–31), leads slave revolt, 649; strengthens anti-emancipation feeling, 672

Tweed, William Marcy (1823–78), heads "Ring," 909

Two Treatises on Government (Locke), 92

Tyler, John (1790–1862), becomes Pres., 462; activities in office, 699; withdraws from 1844 race, 700; proposes compromise (1861), 787

Tyranny Unmasked (Taylor), attacks protective tariff, 667

Uncle Tom's Cabin (Stowe), effect in England, 830

Union army, victories, 797, 802, 831; numbers and losses in Civil War, 839–840; recruiting for, 840, 841; medical services in, 842; fleet on Western waters, 854

Union Party, formed, 870; nominates Lincoln for re-election, 885; breaks up, 903

Unions (labor), slow start of, 580; declared lawful, 581

Unitarianism, and politics, 306–307; introduced in New England, 588

United Empire Loyalists, in War of 1812, 410; dominate Ontario, 482

United Society of Believers (Shakers), 624

United States, as heir of democratic process, 24; description of physical assets, 25ff.

United States, ship, in War of 1812, 407

U.S. Military Academy, 564

U.S. Naval Academy, 564

United States v. Judge Peters, decision in, 437

Universalism, introduced in New Eng., 588

Uruguay, declares independence, 473

Usher, John P. (1816–89), Sec'y of Int., 816

Utopianism, American, 623ff.; significance of, 627–628

Utrecht, Treaty of, 192

Vallandigham, Clement L. (1820–71), plans Pacific Confederacy, 785; a leader of Copperheads, 813; banished, 817; returns, 818; offers peace plank, 886; champions New Departure movement, 918

Valley Forge, Washington fortifies, 257

Van Buren, Martin (1782–1862), as a dominant national figure, 430; biography, 431; organizes modern Dem. Party, 432; in Jackson's Kitchen Cabinet, 452; and Eaton case, 453; resigns from Cabinet, 456; appointed minister to Eng., 456; elected Pres. (1836), 461; sets up Independent Treasury System, 461–462; in Canadian struggle for independence, 483; opposes Mexican War, 706; nominated for Pres. (1848), 722

Vancouver, Fort, trade post, 686

Vancouver, George (1758?–98), surveys Pacific Northwest, 514

Vandalia Company, operates in Old West, 215, 271ff.

Van Rensselaers, in Hudson Valley, 135

Varkinskill, N.J., as part of New Haven, 129

Venezuela, wins freedom, 471

Vera Cruz, falls to Scott in Mexican War, 712; Am. troops evacuate (1848), 715

Vergennes (1717–87), Fr. minister, signs treaty of alliance, 259; at Paris peace, 266ff.

Vermont, sets up government, 289; admitted as state, 393

Verplanck Bill (tariff), rejected by Calhoun, 459

Verrazano, Giovanni da (1485?–?1528), explorer, 72

Vesey, Denmark (1767?–1822), plots slave insurrection, 666

Vespucci, Amerigo (1451–1512), accounts of, 57

Vicksburg, Miss., settled, 391; campaign at, 856–857; falls to Union, 857

Vincennes, Ill., falls to Clark in Revolution, 254

Vindictives, in 37th Congress, 813ff.; after Civil War, 892ff.

Virginia, failure of Raleigh's colony in, 107; economic and political growth of, 110–111; becomes royal colony, 111; made a dominion, 112; and Bacon's Rebellion, 115; occupies Ohio Valley, 216; leads in protest against Townshend Acts, 221–222; stand before Revolution, 229; proposes effective central gov't at Const. Convention, 292; leads Jeffersonian Republican faction, 325–326; and Western land speculation, 376; rehabilitates farms, 582; secedes from Union, 794; campaign in western (1861), 797–798; readmitted to Union

Virginia, in action with *Monitor*, 862; destroyed, 863

Virginia Capes, battle off, 263

Virginia Company, of London, 108–109; of Plymouth, 121

Virginia Declaration of Rights, work of Mason, 222

Virginia Resolutions (1798), passed, 341–342

Voyageurs, explorers, 74

Wade, Benjamin F. (1800–78), abolitionist, 661; Radical leader in 37th Congress, 814; sponsors reconstruction bill, 883

Waldseemüller, Martin (1470?–?1518), geographer, 57

Walker, Robert J. (1801–69), Sec'y of Treasury, 701; Gov. of Kansas Terr., 762

Walker, Thomas (1715–94), organizes Loyal Land Company, 211

Walker, William (1824–60), filibusterer, 738–739

Walking Purchase, by Penn heirs, 37

Wallace, Lew (1827–1905), delays Early at Monocacy, 880

Walpole, Sir Robert (1676–1745), and "salutary neglect," 179

Wampum, Indian medium of exchange, 45

Wanghia, Treaty of, opens China to U.S. trade, 495

Ward, Artemas (1727–1800), forces battle of Bunker Hill, 230–231

Ward, Frederick T., in Taiping Rebellion, 495

War Hawks, favor expansionism, 402; come out for War of 1812, 405ff.

War of 1812, incidents preceding, 404–405; declaration of, 406; popular attitude toward, 406–407; naval aspects of, 407ff.; strategy in the North, 409ff.; Br. actions (1814), 413; collapse of war effort, 415; New Eng. defeatism, 415–416; early peace attempts, 417; recovery of national spirit, 423–424; stalemate results of, 426; Young

Republican Program after, 433–434; banking problems following, 434; Nantucket loses most of whaling fleet, 493

War of Jenkins' Ear, 192

War of Pork and Beans, 485

Wars of Independence in Latin America, 471–473; U.S. attitude toward, 474–475

Warren, Joseph (1741–75), leader in independence movement, 224

Washington, George (1732–99), defeated at Great Meadows, 194; covers Eng. retreat at Ft. Duquesne, 194; as land speculator, 215; introduces Resolves of 1769, 221; commands troops besieging Boston, 230; biography, 242–245; withdraws troops in N.Y. campaign, 255–256; retreats across Delaware, 256; in N.J. campaign, 256; at Brandywine, 257; in battle of Monmouth, 260; invests N.Y., 260–261; in siege of Yorktown, 263ff.; at Const. Convention, 290, 291; inaugurated as Pres., 300; problems of initiating gov't, 300–301; as Federalist leader, 305; re-elected Pres., 327–328; issues Neutrality Proclamation (1793), 329–330; Farewell Address, 335–336; heads army in quasi war with France, 338; as farmer, 582

Washington, steamboat on Mississippi, 567

Washington, D.C., selected as capital city, 310–311; capital moved to, 349–350; Br. take in War of 1812, 414

Washington, Tex., Texan independence declared at, 696

Washington Conference Convention (1861), attempts compromise, 787

Washington Terr., erected, 688

Wasp, in War of 1812, 407

Watauga Association, as form of colonial democratic gov't, 185–186; compact, 216; in Cherokee Wars, 253; sets up State of Franklin, 381

Watertown, Mass., refuses to pay tax, 125

Watling Island, Columbus lands on, 50

Watson, Elkanah (1758–1842), agricultural experimenter, 582; develops fairs, 583

Watt, James (1736–1819), develops steam engine, 557

Wayne, Anthony (1745–96), military leader in Revolution, 242; wins battle at Fallen Timbers, 377–378

Wealth of Nations, The (Smith), 21

Weatherford, William (1780?–1824), Creek leader, 421

Webster, Daniel (1782–1852), a dominant national figure, 430; biography, 430–431; argues *Dartmouth College v. Woodward* case, 438; and the B. U. S., 457; negotiates treaty, 485; orations inspire democracy, 602; debates with Hayne, 670–671; opposes Mexican War, 706; delivers Seventh of March Speech, 726–727; quoted on Compromise of 1850, 728

Webster, Noah (1758–1843), 275

Webster-Ashburton Treaty, settles Maine boundary dispute, 485

Webster-Hayne debate (1830), 670

Weed, Thurlow (1797–1882), leader of Anti-Masonic Party, 457; dominates Pres. Taylor, 723; and *Trent* Affair, 827–828

Weekly Register (Niles), champions protective tariff, 576

Weld, Theodore Dwight (1803–95), biography, 657–658; leader at Lane Seminary, 659; success as crusader, 661, 664

Welles, Gideon (1802–78), Sec'y of Navy, 816

Wells, Dr. Horace (1815–48), introduces anesthetics in dentistry, 591

Welsh settlers, 141, 603
Wesley, John (1703–91), 274
West, Benjamin (1738–1820), painter, 590
West, The, as distinguished from frontier, 165, 531; role of, in Rev., 209–217; speculation in lands of, 271ff.; factors in movement toward, 372; routes to, 390–391; significance in Am. history, 530ff.; settlements in, 534ff.; importance of steamboats in settling, 567; economic effect of railroads, 573
Western Reserve, Conn. retains rights in, 376
Western World (Mackay), admires America, 597
West Florida, becomes part of U.S., 390
West Indies, *see* Caribbean
West India Company, in New Netherland, 135
Westsylvania, planned as a state, 289
West Virginia, enters Union (1863), 798; strategic importance in Civil War, 799–800
Wethersfield, Conn., trading fort at, 128
Wetzel, Lewis (1764–1808?), Indian fighter, 541, 544
Whaling, in colonial New Eng., 131; heyday of, 493–494
Wheeler, William A. (1819–87), nominated for vice-presidency, 923
Whigs, British, struggle with Tories for power, 222–223; Whigs, American, battle conservatives before Revolution, 229; fight Loyalists in South, 233–234; Whig Party, in westward movement, 395; nominate Clay for Pres. (1832), 457; constituents of the party (1830's), 460; win election of 1840, 462; Cotton, 653; enforce Gag Rule, 662–663; oppose Taylor's policies, 699; approach break-up, 721; nominate Taylor (1848), 722
Whisky Insurrection, 332–333
Whisky Ring, in Grant's administration, 910
White Star Line, first all-steam ships, 492
White supremacy, theory of, united South, 644
Whitefield, George (1714–70), 156
Whitman, Marcus (1802–47), establishes mission in Oregon country, 687
Whitman, Walt (1819–92), poet of democracy, 601–602; quoted on Lincoln, 889
Whitney, Eli (1765–1825), develops cotton gin, 558; develops principle of interchangeable parts, 562
Whittier, John Greenleaf (1807–92), 661–662
Wilderness, battle of the, 878–879
Wilderness Road, marked out, 216; as route to West, 390
Wilkes, Charles (1798–1877), in *Trent* Affair, 827–828
Wilkes, John (1727–97), champions American cause, 227
Wilkinson, David (1771–1852), tool designer, 562
Wilkinson, James (1757–1825), in intrigue with Spain, 383; conspires with Burr, 289; promotes annexation of West Fla., 390; in War of 1812, 412; sends Pike to explore Southwest, 517; activities in Texas, 692
Willamette Valley, missions set up in, 686–687
William and Mary College, founded, 148
Williams, Roger (1604?–83), demands separation of church and state, 126; founds Rhode Island, 127
Williamsburg, Va., in colonial days, 153; Civil War battle at, 863

Wilmot, David (1814–68), introduces Wilmot Proviso, 719
Wilmot Proviso (1846), limits extension of slavery, 719; effect on the South, 720–721
Wilson, Henry (1812–75), elected Vice-Pres., 920
Wilson, James (1742–98), attends Const. Convention, 291
Wilson's Creek, Mo., Union defeat, 802
Winchester, Va., Civil War battle at, 881
"Wineland the Good," 69
Winnebago Indians, 41
Winthrop, John (1588–1649), governor of Mass. Bay, 123; excellence as leader, 124; his view of "democratie," 124, 125
Winthrop, John, Jr. (1606–76), builds Saybrook, Conn., 129
Winthrop, John IV (1714–79), scientist, 154
Wirt, William (1772–1834), nominated for presidency by Anti-Masonic Party (1832), 457; votes for, 458
Wisconsin, growth of, 397; as dairyland, 398
Wise, John (1652–1725), 157
Wolcott, Oliver (1726–97), 307
Wolfe, James (1727–59), besieges Quebec, 197
Wollstonecraft, Mary (1759–97), reformer, 618
Women in the Nineteenth Century (Fuller), plea for equal rights, 618
Women's rights, movement for, 618–619
Wood, Jethro (1774–1834), devises new plow, 584
Wool, John E. (1784–1869), in Mexican War, 710
Woolman, John (1720–72), protests slavery, 657
Worcester v. Georgia, in objection to Indian removal policy, 524
Workingmen's parties, growth, 462, 580–581
World's Antislavery Convention (1840), increases interest in women's rights, 618–619
Wright, Frances (1795–1852), reformer, 618
Wright, Isaac, establishes packet line, 491
Writs of assistance, use of authorized, 220
Wyeth, Nathaniel (1802–56), blazes Oregon Trail, 686
Wyoming, Pa., Tory and Indian attack on, 254

Xenophilia, in America, 594
Xenophobia, in America, 594–595
XYZ Affair, in Adams's administration, 337–338

Yale University, founded, 158
Yamassee Indian War, 118, 191
Yancey, William Lowndes (1814–63), works for Southern Rights, 732, 734; leads Southern states out of Dem. convention (1860), 775–776; leader in State Rights Party, 788
Yazoo frauds, in Western land speculation, 383–385; reach Supreme Court, 437
Yorktown, Rev., siege and capture of, 263–265; McClellan besieges in Civil War, 863
Young, Brigham (1801–77), leads Mormons, 627
Young Republican Program, following War of 1812, 433–434

Zane, Ebenezer (1747–1812), Indian fighter, 541
Zavala, Lorenzo de, vice-president of Texas, 696
Zenger, John Peter (1697–1746), sets precedent for freedom of the press, 182
Zoar, O., pietist community at, 624